| Gross Domestic Product in 1992 Dollars (billions) | Personal Consumption Expenditures in 1992 Dollars (billions) | Government Purchases in 1992 Dollars (billions) | Gross Private Domestic Investment in 1992 Dollars (billions) | Exports in 1992 Dollars (billions) | Imports in 1992 Dollars (billions) | Treasury Bill Interest Rate | U.S. Dollar (1973 = 100) | Federal Budget Surplus (+) or Deficit (−) (billions) | Money Supply (December) (billions) M₁ | M₂ |
|---|---|---|---|---|---|---|---|---|---|---|
| 2,212.3 | 1,394.6 | 618.5 | 274.2 | 71.9 | 106.6 | 3.405 | — | 2.6 | 140.0 | 297.8 |
| 2,261.7 | 1,432.6 | 617.2 | 270.5 | 86.3 | 108.1 | 2.928 | — | 7.4 | 140.7 | 312.3 |
| 2,309.8 | 1,461.5 | 647.2 | 265.2 | 88.3 | 107.3 | 2.378 | — | 2.9 | 145.2 | 335.5 |
| 2,449.1 | 1,533.8 | 685.0 | 298.5 | 93.0 | 119.5 | 2.778 | — | 2.8 | 147.8 | 362.7 |
| 2,554.0 | 1,596.6 | 701.9 | 318.1 | 100.0 | 122.7 | 3.157 | — | 5.4 | 153.3 | 393.2 |
| 2,702.9 | 1,692.3 | 715.9 | 344.6 | 113.3 | 129.2 | 3.549 | — | 0.9 | 160.3 | 424.8 |
| 2,874.8 | 1,799.1 | 737.6 | 392.5 | 115.6 | 143.0 | 3.954 | — | 3.4 | 167.9 | 459.3 |
| 3,060.2 | 1,902.0 | 804.6 | 423.5 | 123.4 | 164.2 | 4.881 | — | 2.6 | 172.0 | 480.0 |
| 3,140.2 | 1,958.6 | 865.6 | 406.9 | 126.1 | 176.2 | 4.321 | — | −8.3 | 183.3 | 524.4 |
| 3,288.6 | 2,070.2 | 892.4 | 429.8 | 135.3 | 202.5 | 5.339 | — | −2.8 | 197.4 | 566.3 |
| 3,388.0 | 2,147.5 | 887.5 | 454.4 | 142.7 | 214.0 | 6.677 | 122.4 | 8.7 | 203.9 | 589.5 |
| 3,388.2 | 2,197.8 | 866.8 | 419.5 | 158.1 | 223.1 | 6.458 | 121.1 | −14.1 | 214.4 | 628.1 |
| 3,500.1 | 2,279.5 | 851.0 | 467.4 | 159.2 | 235.0 | 4.348 | 117.8 | −25.3 | 228.3 | 712.7 |
| 3,690.3 | 2,415.9 | 854.1 | 522.1 | 172.0 | 261.0 | 4.071 | 109.1 | −20.5 | 249.2 | 805.2 |
| 3,902.3 | 2,532.6 | 848.4 | 583.5 | 209.6 | 272.6 | 7.041 | 99.1 | −11.1 | 262.8 | 861.0 |
| 3,888.2 | 2,514.7 | 862.9 | 544.4 | 229.8 | 265.3 | 7.886 | 101.4 | −16.9 | 274.3 | 908.6 |
| 3,865.1 | 2,570.0 | 876.3 | 440.5 | 228.2 | 235.4 | 5.838 | 98.5 | −73.9 | 287.4 | 1,023.2 |
| 4,081.1 | 2,714.3 | 876.8 | 536.6 | 241.6 | 281.5 | 4.989 | 105.7 | −57.2 | 306.3 | 1,163.7 |
| 4,279.3 | 2,829.8 | 884.7 | 627.1 | 247.4 | 311.6 | 5.265 | 103.4 | −46.3 | 331.1 | 1,286.5 |
| 4,493.7 | 2,951.6 | 910.6 | 686.0 | 273.1 | 338.6 | 7.221 | 92.4 | −31.7 | 358.1 | 1,388.6 |
| 4,624.0 | 3,020.2 | 924.9 | 704.3 | 299.0 | 344.3 | 10.041 | 88.1 | −18.4 | 382.4 | 1,496.9 |
| 4,611.9 | 3,009.7 | 941.4 | 626.2 | 331.4 | 321.3 | 11.506 | 87.4 | −61.0 | 408.5 | 1,629.3 |
| 4,724.9 | 3,046.4 | 967.7 | 689.7 | 335.3 | 329.7 | 14.029 | 103.4 | −57.8 | 436.3 | 1,793.3 |
| 4,623.6 | 3,081.5 | 960.1 | 590.4 | 311.4 | 325.5 | 10.686 | 116.6 | −134.7 | 474.3 | 1,953.2 |
| 4,810.0 | 3,240.6 | 987.3 | 647.8 | 303.3 | 366.6 | 8.63 | 125.3 | −174.4 | 521.0 | 2,187.7 |
| 5,138.2 | 3,407.6 | 1,018.4 | 831.6 | 328.4 | 455.7 | 9.58 | 138.2 | −156.0 | 552.1 | 2,378.4 |
| 5,329.5 | 3,566.5 | 1,080.1 | 829.2 | 337.3 | 485.2 | 7.48 | 143.0 | −162.9 | 619.8 | 2,576.0 |
| 5,489.9 | 3,708.7 | 1,135.0 | 813.8 | 362.2 | 526.1 | 5.98 | 112.2 | −177.9 | 724.4 | 2,820.3 |
| 5,648.4 | 3,822.3 | 1,165.9 | 820.5 | 402.0 | 558.2 | 5.82 | 96.9 | −128.9 | 749.8 | 2,922.3 |
| 5,862.9 | 3,972.7 | 1,180.9 | 826.0 | 465.8 | 580.2 | 6.69 | 92.7 | −121.3 | 786.9 | 3,083.5 |
| 6,060.4 | 4,064.6 | 1,213.9 | 861.9 | 520.2 | 603.0 | 8.12 | 98.6 | −113.4 | 794.2 | 3,243.0 |
| 6,138.7 | 4,132.2 | 1,250.4 | 817.3 | 564.4 | 626.3 | 7.51 | 89.1 | −154.7 | 825.8 | 3,356.0 |
| 6,079.0 | 4,105.8 | 1,258.0 | 737.7 | 599.9 | 622.2 | 5.42 | 89.8 | −196.0 | 897.3 | 3,457.9 |
| 6,244.4 | 4,219.8 | 1,263.8 | 790.4 | 639.4 | 669.0 | 3.45 | 86.6 | −280.9 | 1,024.4 | 3,515.3 |
| 6,383.8 | 4,339.7 | 1,260.5 | 857.3 | 660.6 | 735.0 | 3.02 | 93.2 | −254.7 | 1,128.6 | 3,583.6 |
| 6,604.2 | 4,471.1 | 1,259.8 | 979.6 | 715.1 | 823.3 | 4.29 | 91.3 | −189.9 | 1,148.0 | 3,617.0 |
| 6,763.0 | 4,601.0 | 1,264.0 | 1,009.0 | 780.0 | 894.0 | 5.51 | 84.2 | −160.0 | 1,123.0 | 3,781.0 |

# PRINCIPLES OF
# ECONOMICS

# THE ADDISON-WESLEY SERIES IN ECONOMICS

**Abel/Bernanke**
Macroeconomics

**Allen**
Managerial Economics

**Berndt**
The Practice of Econometrics

**Bierman/Fernandez**
Game Theory

**Binger/Hoffman**
Microeconomics with Calculus

**Bowles/Edwards**
Understanding Capitalism

**Branson**
Macroeconomic Theory and Policy

**Brown/Hogendorn**
International Economics

**Browning/Zupan**
Microeconomic Theory and
Applications

**Burgess**
The Economics of Regulation and
Antitrust

**Byrns/Stone**
Economics

**Canterbery**
The Literate Economist

**Carlton/Perloff**
Modern Industrial Organization

**Caves/Frankel/Jones**
World Trade and Payments

**Cooter/Ulen**
Law and Economics

**Ehrenberg/Smith**
Modern Labor Economics

**Ekelund/Tollison**
Economics: Private Markets and
Public Choice

**Filer/Hamermesh/Rees**
The Economics of Work and Play

**Fusfeld**
The Age of the Economist

**Gibson**
International Finance: Exchange
Rates and Financial Flows

**Gordon**
Macroeconomics

**Gregory**
Essentials of Economics

**Gregory/Ruffin**
Basic Economics

**Gregory/Stuart**
Soviet and Post Soviet Economic
Structure and Performance

**Griffiths/Wall**
Intermediate Microeconomics

**Gros/Steinherr**
Winds of Change: Economic
Transition in Central and Eastern
Europe

**Hartwick/Olewiler**
The Economics of Natural Resource
Use

**Hogendorn**
Economic Development

**Hoy/Livernois/McKenna/
Rees/Stengos**
Mathematics For Economics

**Hubbard**
Money, the Financial System, and the
Economy

**Hughes/Cain**
American Economic History

**Husted/Melvin**
International Economics

**Invisible Hand**
Economics in Action, Interactive
Software

**Krugman/Obstfeld**
International Economics: Theory and
Policy

**Kwoka/White**
The Antitrust Revolution

**Laidler**
The Demand for Money

**Lesser/Dodds/Zerbe**
Environmental Economics and Policy

**Lipsey/Courant**
Economics

**McCarty**
Dollars and Sense

**Melvin**
International Money and Finance

**Miller**
Economics Today

**Miller/Benjamin/North**
The Economics of Public Issues

**Miller/Fishe**
Microeconomics: Price Theory in
Practice

**Miller/Van Hoose**
Essentials of Money, Banking, and
Financial Markets

**Mills/Hamilton**
Urban Economics

**Mishkin**
The Economics of Money, Banking,
and Financial Markets

**Parkin**
Economics

**Petersen**
Business and Government

**Phelps**
Health Economics

**Riddell/Shackelford/Stamos**
Economics

**Ritter/Silber/Udell**
Principles of Money, Banking, and
Financial Markets

**Rohlf**
Introduction to Economic Reasoning

**Ruffin/Gregory**
Principles of Economics

**Salvatore**
Microeconomics

**Sargent**
Rational Expectations and Inflation

**Scherer**
Industry Structure, Strategy, and
Public Policy

**Schotter**
Microeconomics: A Modern
Approach

**Sherman/Kolk**
Business Cycles and Forecasting

**Smith**
Case Studies in Economic
Development

**Studenmund**
Using Econometrics

**Su**
Economic Fluctuations and
Forecasting

**Tietenberg**
Environmental and Natural Resource
Economics

**Tietenberg**
Environmental Economics
and Policy

**Todaro**
Economic Development

**Zerbe/Dively**
Benefit-Cost Analysis

# PRINCIPLES OF ECONOMICS

## SIXTH EDITION

**ROY J. RUFFIN**

University of Houston

Research Associate,
Federal Reserve Bank of Dallas

**PAUL R. GREGORY**

University of Houston

## ADDISON-WESLEY

An imprint of Addison Wesley Longman, Inc.

Reading, Massachusetts • Menlo Park, California • New York • Harlow, England
Don Mills, Ontario • Sydney • Mexico City • Madrid • Amsterdam

*To our wives*
*Barbara Ann Ruffin and Annemarie Gregory*

Senior Editor: Bruce Kaplan
Developmental Editor: Barbara A. Conover
Supplements Editor: Julie Zasloff
Project Editor: Diane Williams
Design Manager and Cover Designer: John Callahan
Text Designer: Robin Hoffman
Art Studio: Electragraphics, Inc.
Electronic Production Manager: Su Levine
Manufacturing Manager: Willie Lane
Electronic Page Makeup: York Graphic Services
Printer and Binder: R.R. Donnelley & Sons Company
Cover Printer: The Lehigh Press, Inc.

Credits: Page 370, "How the Bottom Lines, and Everything in Between, Compare," adapted from *The New York Times*, September 3, 1995, p. F6. Copyright © 1995 by The New York Times Co. Reprinted by permission. Page 393, "The Public's Biggest Concerns" from nationwide telephone polls conducted by New York Times Co. and CBS News. Appeared in *The New York Times National*, January 23, 1996, p. A9 Copyright © 1996 by The New York Times Co. Reprinted by permission. Page 434, "Correlations Between Inflation Rates and Output Growth" from David Backus and Patrick Kehoe, "International Evidence on the Historical Properties of Business Cycles" from *American Economic Review*, Vol. 82 (Sept. 1992). Reprinted by permission of American Economic Association, Nashville, TN. Page 575, from Milton Friedman, "Monetary History, Not Dogma" from *The Wall Street Journal*, February 12, 1987, p. 22. Reprinted by permission of The Wall Street Journal, © 1987 Dow Jones & Company, Inc. All rights reserved. Page 615, from Steven J. Davis and John Haltiwanger, "Gross Job Creation, Gross Job Destruction and Employment Reallocation," in *Quarterly Journal of Economics*, Vol. 107, #3, pp. 819–863. © 1992 by the President and Fellows of Harvard College and the Massachusetts Institute of Technology.

Principles of Economics, Sixth Edition

**Library of Congress Cataloging-in-Publication Data**

Ruffin, Roy, 1938–
    Principles of economics / Roy J. Ruffin, Paul R. Gregory.—6th
  ed.
       p.    cm. — (The HarperCollins series in economics)
    Includes bibliographical references and index.
    ISBN 0-673-99488-0 (alk. paper)
    1. Economics.  I. Gregory, Paul R.  II. Title.  III. Series.
  HB171.5.R82    1996
  330—dc20
                                                                             96-16568
                                                                               CIP

ISBN 0-673-994880
**2 3 4 5 6 7 8 9 10-DOW-01 00 99 98 97**

# BRIEF CONTENTS

# DETAILED CONTENTS

## CHAPTER 12    Competition, Efficiency, and Innovation    209

## CHAPTER 13    The Game of Oligopoly    221

## CHAPTER 14    Regulation and Antitrust    235

## CHAPTER 15   The Economics of Information   251

## PART III   FACTOR MARKETS   269

## CHAPTER 16   Factor Markets   271

## CHAPTER 17   Labor: The Human Factor   283

## CHAPTER 21   Government Spending, Taxation, and the Economy   355

## CHAPTER 22   Public Choice   375

# PART V   GROWTH AND FLUCTUATION   389

## CHAPTER 23   Macroeconomics: Growth and Cycles   391

## CHAPTER 24   Measuring Output and Growth   411

## Appendix 24A   Time Series Analysis   429

## CHAPTER 25   Saving and Investment   437

## CHAPTER 30   Monetary Policy   527

## CHAPTER 31   Fiscal Policy, Debt, and Deficits   545

# PREFACE

We wrote the first edition of *Principles of Economics* in 1980, more than 15 years ago. At the time of its publication, there was agreement among economists about most aspects of microeconomics, but macroeconomics was in turmoil. The accepted model in macroeconomics was not working. The many new macroeconomic concepts that were part of the new explanatory models being developed were considered too difficult to be taught at the principles level. By integrating these concepts in an approachable way in the first edition of *Principles of Economics*, we created the first introductory text that was on the cutting edge of explanatory theory yet appropriate for the beginning student of economics.

We now approach the year 2000—the beginning of a new millenium. And, again, economic times have changed. It has been an era of too many theories, of teaching what isn't working, of focusing on differences rather than on emerging consensus. Economists are striving for a new consensus in macroeconomics with an overall framework that can command agreement. Remaining disagreements focus on the actual conditions in which this framework operates, not the framework itself. Thus, we have based the sixth edition of *Principles of Economics* not on the principle of *addition* (the new always seems fresh), but rather on the principle of *consolidation* (pruning the old leaves the fresh): a consensus of what is acceptable; new concepts as integrative; the addition of a new model—with only those parts that work—in place of those unworkable parts of the old model; and, most important, empirical evidence that supports the integrated parts. This book uses empirical evidence as its bedrock. We are not interested in discussing concepts and theories that do not conform to the empirical "facts."

Economic theories arise to explain economic events. We cannot understand today's prosperity and high productivity without understanding the *Industrial Revolution*. The *rise and collapse of socialism* have had a profound effect on the ways economies have worked and the way people have lived for the past century. We cannot comprehend macroeconomics without comprehending the *Great Depression*. However, the economic philosophy and theories of John Maynard Keynes can no longer guide us in the 1990s and beyond. We must once again move on. We live today in a global economy fired by the rapid growth of *globalization*. Throughout the text we refer to these four major events, the defining moments of economics, as they influence economics.

We focus on long-term growth, rather than short-term business cycles. Economists at last realize that too much emphasis has been given to short-run issues. A recurrence of the Great Depression is unlikely. With this realization, we emphasize what really counts: economic growth, not the relatively minor ups and downs of economies as they fluctuate around this growth trend. We allow economic growth and the new theories of growth, long regarded as an adjunct chapter in macroeconomics, to play a central role in this edition.

Thus, the sixth edition is, indeed, the most significant revision of *Principles of Economics*. In addition to offering the same spirit of freshness, the same cutting-edge philosophy of the first edition, it carefully consolidates the economic theories and policies of the past and present as we prepare for the economic changes of the future.

## NEW TO THIS EDITION

With the publication of the sixth edition of *Principles of Economics,* we remain the most modern and up-to-date text on the market. We discuss both traditional and new topics at a level accessible to the reader. New to this edition are the following:

- Microeconomic chapters now appear before macroeconomic chapters; international chapters appear at the end of the text. However, the parts remain interchangeable.
- Introduction of the defining moments of economics—the Industrial Revolution, the rise and collapse of socialism, the Great Depression, and globalization—in new Chapter 1. Reference to the four moments throughout the text creates a historical basis on which to understand the economic theories and policies of today.
- The topics of economic decision making—marginal analysis, incentives, games, and unintended consequences—are covered in new Chapter 5. This chapter introduces the roles of incentives, strategic behavior (game theory), and the unintended consequences that result from not understanding incentives and strategic behavior. The early placement of this chapter reflects the growing use of incentives and strategic behavior in macro as well as micro.
- The most up-to-date concepts in micro- and macroeconomics—such as oligopoly and game theory, intergenerational accounting, rational expectations, and endogenous growth theory—are explained in an understandable fashion.
- A new Chapter 38, The Economics of Transition, and a heavily revised Chapter 39, The Economics of Development, reflect the many changes taking place in the international economic realm. In addition, numerous international examples and comparisons with the United States appear throughout the text.
- A better organized, honed text offers 39 total chapters rather than the 43 of the fifth edition. The body of economic knowledge that students are required to master has become so large that all material must be carefully selected and presented in a clear and concise manner.

### MICROECONOMICS

- Chapters 10–13 present a clear comparison of the four market systems, including a summary comparison in Chapter 13.
- Chapter 17 now combines materials on both labor markets and labor unions.

### MACROECONOMICS

- Classical, Keynesian, new classical, and new Keynesian economic theories are taught directly by aggregate supply and aggregate demand analysis. The aggregate expenditure model and the multiplier models have been eliminated to provide a more concise approach to macroeconomics at the principles level.
- Recognizing that students are not interested in learning a large number of competing macro models, the authors focus on two general models—Keynesian and classical—and on the conditions that apply for each.
- Macroeconomic theories are judged by their empirical relevance. Each chapter teaches the empirical facts (of inflation, unemployment, or growth) that must be addressed by the theory. Theories that are not empirically relevant are not included.
- An entire chapter on the microfoundations of macro—Chapter 25, Consumption and Investment—teaches the microeconomic foundations of modern macroeconomics, specifically the theories of consumption and investment. These—rather than the aggregate expenditure model—serve as the building blocks of aggregate supply and aggregate demand.
- A clear distinction is made between short-run and long-run macroeconomics. Chapter 26, Growth, explains modern macroeconomic growth theory, emphasizing the Solow growth model and the new endogenous growth theory. The new appendix to Chapter 24, Time Series Analysis, provides the student with the concepts for analyzing aggregate data.
- Material on the Phillips curve and on rational expectations are now appropriately integrated in chapters on inflation and on business cycles. Stagflation, which was a phenomenon of the 1970s and early 1980s, plays a less significant role than in early editions.
- The closely related topics of fiscal policy and the national debt are now combined in one chapter, with detailed discussions of intergenerational accounting and social security.

**Pedagogy.** Pedagogy has been strengthened throughout the text. Each opening Chapter Insight is now a real-world anecdote alluding to a major concept of the chapter. Each chapter contains new, timely, and relevant examples for understanding the economy of the late 1990s. Among the topics are

- diminishing returns in American wine making
- using the law of demand to solve freeway congestion in Los Angeles
- electronic bulletin boards to monitor public choice economic decision making
- junk bonds, leverage, and the RJR Nabisco Company
- the dispute over credit card profitability
- the Intel monopoly: how long will it last?
- placing a value on the Grand Canyon
- are we underestimating GDP?
- the Japanese recession of the 1990s
- the collapse of the peso
- NAFTA
- is money becoming obsolete?

Simple color screens accent important terms and concepts.

**Use of Color.** The sixth edition again uses full color throughout the text. Color is used strategically in the many tables, charts, and graphs, and to highlight the various pedagogical devices designed to promote student understanding. For example, in graphs, demand curves are always green, and supply curves are always red. This use of color helps students to identify key terms and concepts and facilitates accurate interpretation of data.

# ORGANIZATION

*Principles of Economics*, Sixth Edition, is divided into six parts. Part I (Chapters 1–5) introduces the basic concepts of economics that provide a firm foundation for both microeconomics and macroeconomics. In addition to introducing the basic economic methodology, Chapter 1 describes four defining moments of economics—the Industrial Revolution, the rise and collapse of socialism, the Great Depression, and globalization—each of which has had a major influence on both economic theory and economic policy. An appendix to Chapter 1 explains how to read graphs and avoid distortion pitfalls. Chapters 2–4 contain the standard topics of

scarcity, opportunity costs, the production possibilities frontier, the law of diminishing returns, the law of comparative advantage, the workings of the price system, and the laws of demand and supply. Discussing the means and the ends to economic decision making, new Chapter 5 introduces the topics of marginal analysis, incentives, games, and unintended consequences—tools and themes that are used throughout the text. The early introduction of game theory reflects its growing use in both micro and macro. From the foundations established in Part I, the instructor can move to either microeconomics (Chapters 6–22) or macroeconomics (Chapters 23–39).

Part II begins the microeconomics core of the text, with ten chapters on product markets (Chapters 6–15). Chapter 6 covers price elasticities of demand and supply as well as income and cross-price elasticities of demand. Chapter 7 deals with demand and utility and includes an appendix on indifference curves. Business organization, corporate finance, and financial markets are discussed in Chapter 8, and short-run and long-run costs are explained in Chapter 9, which includes an appendix on the least-cost method of production. The standard market models of perfect competition, monopoly and monopolistic competition, and oligopoly are covered in Chapters 10–13; Chapter 13 now includes both a section devoted to game theory and a summary comparison of all four market models. Chapter 14 discusses antitrust law and regulation, and Chapter 15 introduces the role of information costs.

Factor markets are presented in the four-chapter Part III (Chapters 16–19). Chapter 16 gives a theoretical overview of the workings of factor markets, and Chapters 17 and 18 focus on specific factor markets of labor, and interest, rent, and profit. Chapter 19 examines the determinants of income distribution and poverty.

Microeconomic issues are the focus of Part IV (Chapters 20–22). Chapter 20 explains the economics of natural resources and of market failure (public goods and externalities). Chapter 21 focuses on the issue of taxation and Chapter 22 discusses public choice.

The development of macroeconomic theory begins in Part V with a discussion of the basic concepts of inflation, unemployment, short-term business cycles, and long-term growth (Chapter 23). Chapter 24 introduces the basic principles of income accounting, used to measure output and growth; a new appendix to Chapter 24 on time series analysis provides the student with the concepts for analyzing aggregate data. Chapter 25 emphasizes the microeconomic foundations of modern macroeconomics, specifically the theories of consumption and investment. New Chapter 26 brings in a long-term perspective, explaining modern macroeconomic growth theory while emphasizing the Solow growth model and the new endogenous growth theory.

Chapter 27 introduces aggregate supply and aggregate demand, the basic analytical tools of modern macroeconomics. The chapter shows that economists of different persuasions use the same tools for studying aggregate demand but differ on their approaches to aggregate supply. This chapter presents the two models of aggregate supply, the Keynesian and the classical models, and the long-run self-correcting mechanism. It is no longer necessary to go through the intermediate step of Keynesian aggregate expenditure and multiplier analysis to study aggregate demand.

Part VI considers the role of money in the economy. Chapter 28 discusses the relationship among money, prices, and interest rates. Chapter 29 considers the definition of money and the determination of the money supply. Chapters 30 and 31 discuss monetary and fiscal policy and the impact of the national debt.

Part VII concentrates on the economic goal of stabilization, with detailed discussion of inflation (Chapter 32), unemployment and stagflation (Chapter 33), and the impact of the short-term business cycle versus long-term growth (Chapter 34). These chapters raise the fundamental issue of how much control government authorities can or should exert to control the business cycle.

As well as throughout earlier chapters, the international aspects of economics are accented in Part VIII of the text. Chapter 35 shows how the law of comparative advantage applies on an international scale. Chapter 36 looks at the pros and cons of protection. Chapter 37 examines the international monetary mechanisms and the balance of payments. New Chapter 38 details the transition difficulties being encountered by the former socialist economies of Eastern Europe, while Chapter 39 discusses the problems being experienced by the developing economies of the world. Chapter 39 also provides a continuation of the discussion in Chapter 26 of growth theory as applied to low-income countries.

## SUGGESTIONS FOR COURSE PLANNING

This book is intended for the two-semester sequence in microeconomics and macroeconomics that is traditionally taught as a first- or second-year college course. The book is available in both a combined hardbound volume and micro/macro split softbound volumes. An instructor can also use the combined volume for an intensive one-semester course that covers both microeconomics and macroeconomics by selecting only core chapters as suggested below. Because the book was written with the micro/macro splits in mind, even the instructor who is using the combined volume can teach either micro or macro first.

### SUGGESTED OUTLINE FOR AN INTENSIVE ONE-SEMESTER COURSE (31 CHAPTERS)

INTRODUCTION
1. Economics and the World Around Us: Defining Moments
2. Unlimited Wants, Scarce Resources
3. The Price System and the Economic Problem
4. Demand and Supply
5. Making Economic Decisions: Incentives, Games, and Unintended Consequences.

MICROECONOMICS
6. Elasticity of Demand and Supply
7. Demand and Utility
8. Business Organization
9. Productivity and Costs
10. Perfect Competition
11. Monopoly and Monopolistic Competition
13. The Game of Oligopoly
14. Regulation and Antitrust
15. The Economics of Information
16. Factor Markets
17. Labor: The Human Factor
18. Interest, Rent, and Profit
19. Inequality, Income Distribution, and Poverty
20. Market Failure, the Environment, and Natural Resources

MACROECONOMICS

23. Macroeconomics: Growth and Cycles

24. Measuring Output and Growth

25. Saving and Investment

26. Economic Growth

27. Aggregate Supply and Aggregate Demand

28. Money, Interest, and Prices

29. The Banking System

30. Monetary Policy

31. Fiscal Policy, Debt, and Deficits

32. Inflation

33. Unemployment and Stagflation

34. Business Cycles

## SUGGESTED OUTLINE FOR AN INTENSIVE ONE-QUARTER COURSE (23 CHAPTERS)

### INTRODUCTION

1. Economics and the World Around Us: Defining Moments

2. Unlimited Wants, Scarce Resources

3. The Price System and the Economic Problem

4. Demand and Supply

5. Making Economic Decisions: Incentives, Games, and Unintended Consequences.

### MICROECONOMICS

6. Elasticity of Demand and Supply

7. Demand and Utility

8. Business Organization

9. Productivity and Costs

10. Perfect Competition

16. Factor Markets

17. Labor: The Human Factor

18. Interest, Rent, and Profit

### MACROECONOMICS

23. Macroeconomics: Growth and Cycles

24. Saving and Investment

26. Economic Growth

27. Aggregate Supply and Aggregate Demand

28. Money, Interest, and Prices

29. The Banking System

30. Monetary Policy

32. Inflation

33. Unemployment and Stagflation

34. Business Cycles

## SUGGESTED OUTLINE FOR AN INTENSIVE ONE-SEMESTER COURSE THAT FOCUSES ON GROWTH AND DEVELOPMENT (13 CHAPTERS)

1. Economics and the World Around Us: Defining Moments

2. Unlimited Wants, Scarce Resources

3. The Price System and the Economic Problem

4. Demand and Supply

23. Macroeconomics: Growth and Cycles

24. Measuring Output and Growth

25. Saving and Investment

26. Economic Growth

31. Fiscal Policy, Debt, and Deficits

32. Inflation

35. International Trade

38. The Economics of Transition

39. Economic Development: The "Haves" and the "Have-Nots"

## SUPPLEMENTS

This book has a complete package of supplements, which includes an *Instructor's Manual, Study Guide,* computer software, *Test Bank, Four-Color Transparencies,* computerized *Test Bank,* an *Economics Laser Disc,* and *Economics Videos.*

The *Instructor's Manual* was revised by Henry Thompson of Auburn University. It supplies the instructor with many teaching tools, including additional numerical examples and real-world illustrations not contained in the text. A chapter outline gives a brief overview of the material in the chapter to assist the instructor in preparing lecture outlines and in seeing the logical development of the chapter.

Special-approaches sections tell the instructor how this chapter is different from corresponding chapters in other textbooks and explain why a topic was treated differently in this text or why an entirely new topic not covered by other texts was introduced in this chapter. Optional-material sections give the instructor a ranking of priorities for the topics in the chapter and enable the instructor to trim the size of each chapter (if necessary). Each chapter also includes key points to learn, teaching hints, special projects, bad habits to unlearn, additional essay questions, and answers to the end-of-chapter "Questions and Problems."

The *Study Guide* was written by Jeffrey Parker of Reed College. The analytical nature of the *Study Guide* should challenge students and help them to better prepare for exams. The *Study Guide* supplements the text by providing summaries of critical concepts and by taking students step by step through a review of each key graph and equation presented in the text. It contains multiple-choice and true/false questions and, unlike other study guides, not only lists the answers but also gives *explanations for the answers*. In addition to objective questions, each chapter of the *Study Guide* also contains analytical problems and essay questions. Again, the *Study Guide* provides not only the answers to the questions, but also the step-by-step process for arriving at the answers.

The *Test Bank,* prepared by Brandt Stevens of B. K. Stevens Consulting, contains 3000 new and revised multiple-choice questions, most of which have already been class tested. For each chapter in the text, the *Test Bank* contains 4 different tests (coded A, B, C, or D). The *Test Bank* is available on perforated paper in book form and on the TestMaster computerized testing system.

*Four-Color Transparencies* are available for key figures and tables.

The *Economics Tutor Software* is comprised of twelve modules, six for macroeconomics and six for microeconomics. Each module has problems to be solved in a game-like setting. Each module is open-ended—students can play as long as they like. A grading feature helps users keep score.

The *Economics Laser Disc,* "Economics at Work," allows instructors and students to call up nearly a thousand images at the touch of a button. It provides video clips, lecture launchers, and many animated graphics (e.g., shifting demand and supply curves) to highlight economic principles.

The *Economics Videos* are 5–15 minute lecture starters arranged by economic topic. They cover the core topics in economics, from elasticity and product differentiation to a segment on John Maynard Keynes.

# TO THE STUDENT

As we approach the millenium, national and world events demonstrate daily that an understanding of economics is necessary. The recessions of the early 1990s again taught us that the economy remains subject to the ups and downs of the business cycle, while the recovery since then shows that economic growth is the normal state of affairs for the economy. Virtually every industrialized country is currently reexamining the economic role of government. Can or should we cut back on the welfare state? Can we have both economic prosperity and a large government? Answers to these questions are emerging as U.S. lawmakers grapple with balancing the budget, devising a workable welfare system, and reforming social security.

The global economy has taught us that our economic lives and fortunes are intertwined with those of people around the world. Bank failures in Japan affect the number of jobs in the United States. Corporate decisions made in board rooms in Japan, Korea, and Brazil determine which nations are on the economic rise. The success or failure of the difficult transitions of the former Communist world will decide whether we live in a stable, prosperous world or one fraught with political and economic instability.

Economics is valuable only if it explains the real world. Economics should be able to answer specific questions such as Why are there three major domestic producers of automobiles and hundreds or even thousands of producers of textiles? Why is there a positive association between the growth of the money supply and inflation? Why does the United States export computer software and corn to the rest of the world? Why do restaurants rope off space during less busy hours? If Iowa corn land is the best land for growing corn, why is corn also grown in Texas while some land stands idle in Iowa? Why do interest rates rise when people expect the inflation rate to increase? What is the impact of the well-publicized government deficit? Why does a rise in interest rates in Germany affect employment in the United States?

Economics cannot be mastered through memorization. Economics relies on economic theories to explain real-world occurrences—for instance, why people tend to buy less when prices rise or why increased government spending may reduce unemployment. An economic theory is a logical explanation of why the facts fit together in a particular way. If the theory were not logical, or if the theory failed to be confirmed by real-world facts, it would be readily discarded by economists.

What we call the modern developments of economics are simply new attempts to explain in a logical manner how the facts bind together. Modern developments have occurred because of the realization that established theories were not doing a good job of explaining the world around us. Fortunately, the major building blocks of modern theory—that people attempt to anticipate the future, that rising prices motivate wealth holders to spend less, that people and businesses gather information and make decisions in a rational manner—rely on commonsense logic.

As you finish the chapters of this text, you should be able to apply the knowledge you have gained of real-world economic behavior to explain any number of events that have already occurred or are yet to occur.

We have also included a number of carefully planned learning aids that should help you master the text.

1. The *Chapter Insight* that precedes each chapter provides an economic anecdote related to the important points to be learned in that chapter.

2. *Terms* and their *definitions* are set off in blue shading.

3. *Key Ideas*—important economic principles or conclusions—are set off in blue text.

4. *Boxed Examples* allow the student to appreciate how economic concepts apply in real-world settings without disrupting the flow of the text. They supplement the numerous examples already found in the text discussions.

5. A *Summary* of the main points of each chapter is found at the end of each chapter.

6. *Key Terms* that were defined in the chapter are listed at the end of each chapter.

7. *Questions and Problems* that test the reader's understanding of the chapter follow each chapter.

8. A *Glossary*—containing definitions of all key terms defined in blue-shaded boxes in chapters and listed in chapter "Key Terms" sections—appears at the end of the book. Each entry contains the complete economic definition as well as the number of the chapter where the term was first defined.

9. A thorough *Index* catalogs the names, concepts, terms, and topics covered in the book.

10. Statistical data on the major economic variables are found on the front and back inside covers for easy reference.

Several nontext learning aids should also provide review help. The *Study Guide* provides extensive review of key concepts and an abundance of drill questions and challenging problems. The computer software provides interactive review.

# ACKNOWLEDGMENTS

We are deeply indebted to our colleagues at the University of Houston who had to bear with us in the writing of this book. John Antel, Richard Bean, Joel Sailors, Thomas DeGregori, Gerald Dwyer, Paul Evans, Louis Stern, Thomas Mayor, Irwin Collier, Janet Kohlhase, and David Papell gave their time freely on an incredible number of pedagogical points in the teaching of elementary economics. Thanks are also extended to Daniel Y. Lee of Shippensburg University, Steven Rappaport of DeAnza College, Bill Reid of the University of Richmond, and Ed Coen (the Director of Undergraduate Studies at the University of Minnesota) for their valuable comments. To Gary Smith of Pomona College, Calvin Siebert of the University of Iowa, and Allan Meltzer of Carnegie-Mellon University, we are particularly grateful for sharing with us their vast knowledge of macroeconomic issues.

It is impossible to express the depth of our appreciation for the suggestions and contributions of numerous colleagues across the country who reviewed this heavily revised edition:

Daniel Biederman University of North Dakota; Geoffrey Black Bates College; William Brown California State University at Northridge; Dale Bumpass Sam Houston State University; M. O. Clement Dartmouth College; Barbara J. Craig Oberlin College; Michael Dowd University of Toledo; Michael Ellis Kent State University; Sharon Erenburg Michigan State University; Gisella Escoe University of Cincinnati; Charles Geiss University of Missouri; J. Robert Gillette University of Kentucky; Glen Graham State University of New York at Oswego; Richard Holway College of Notre Dame (California); William Mason San Francisco State University; Jon Miller University of Idaho; Patrick O'Neill University of North Dakota; Anthony Ostrovsky Illinois State University; C. Barry Pfitzner Randolph Macon College; Robert Rosenman Washington State University, Pullman; Mark Rush University of Florida; Dorothy Sanford College of Notre Dame (California); Ruth Shen San Francisco State University; Earl Shinn University of Montevallo (California); John Wells Auburn University; and Douglas Wills Sweet Briar College

In addition, we acknowledge the suggestions of reviewers of earlier editions. Their contribution to the ongoing evolution of the text are invaluable:

David Abel Mankato State University; Jack Adams University of Arkansas, Little Rock; Mark Aldrich Smith College; Ken Alexander Michigan Technical University; Susan Alexander College of St. Thomas; Richard G. Anderson Ohio State University; Richard K. Anderson Texas A&M University; Ian Bain University of Minnesota; King Banaian St. Cloud State University; A. K. Barakeh University of South Alabama; George Bittlingmayer University of

Michigan; Robert Borengasser St. Mary's College; Ronald Brandolini Valencia Community College; Wallace Broome Rhode Island Junior College; Pamela J. Brown California State University, Northridge; James Burnell College of Wooster; Louis Cain Loyola University of Chicago; Anthony Campolo Columbus Technical Institute; Than Van Cao Eastern Montana College; Kathleen A. Carroll University of Maryland, Baltimore County; Shirley Cassing University of Pittsburgh; Harold Christenson Centenary College of Louisiana; Robert E. Christiansen Colby College; Richard Clarke University of Wisconsin, Madison; John Conant Indiana State University; Barbara J. Craig Oberlin College; Jim Davis Golden Gate University; Larry De Brock University of Illinois, Urbana; David Denslow University of Florida; John Devereux University of Miami (Florida); Tim Deyak Louisiana State University, Baton Rouge; James Dunlevy University of Miami (of Ohio); Mary E. Edwards St. Cloud State University; Anne Eicke Illinois State University, Normal; Charles J. Ellard The University of Texas, Pan American; Herb Elliott Allan Hancock College; Randy Ellis Boston University; Andrew W. Foshee McNeese State University; Ralph Fowler Diablo Valley College; Dan Friedman University of California, Los Angeles; Joe Fuhrig Golden Gate University; Janet Furman Tulane University; Charles Gallagher Virginia Commonwealth University; Dan Gallagher St. Cloud State University; Eugene Gendel Lafayette College; Kathie Gilbert Mississippi State University; Lynn Gillette Northeast Missouri State University; Debra Glassman University of Washington; Philip Grossman Wayne State University; Ronald Gunderson Northern Arizona University; David R. Hakes University of Missouri, St. Louis; Charles E. Hegji Auburn University at Montgomery; Ann Hendricks Tufts University; David J. Hoaas Centenary College of Louisiana; Thomas K. Holmstrom Northern Michigan University; Edward Howe Siena College; Todd L. Idson University of Miami (Florida); S. Hussain Ali Jafri Tarleton State University; James Johannes Michigan State University; James Kahn State University of New York, Binghamton; Yoonbai Kim Southern Illinois University; Chris Klisz Wayne State University; Byung Lee Howard University; Daniel Y. Lee Shippensburg University;

Jim Lee Fort Hays State University; Richard Lotspeich Indiana State University; Robert Lucas University of Chicago; Ron Luchessi American River College; James F. McCarley Albion College; Jerome L. McElroy St. Mary's College; Roger Mack DeAnza College; Jim McKinsey Northeastern University; Larry T. McRae Appalachian State University; Michael Magura University of Toledo; Allan Mandelstamm Virginia Polytechnic Institute; Don Mar San Francisco State University; Jay Marchand University of Mississippi; Barbara Haney Martinez University of Alaska, Fairbanks; Ben Matta New Mexico State University; Michael Meurer Duke University; Robert Milbrath Catholic University of America; Masoud Moghaddam St. Cloud State University; W. Douglas Morgan University of California, Santa Barbara; Kathryn A. Nantz Fairfield University; Clark Nardinelli Clemson University; Norman Obst Michigan State University; John Pisciotta Baylor University; Dennis Placone Clemson University; John Pomery Purdue University; Marin Pond Purdue University; Hollis F. Price, Jr. University of Miami (Florida); Henry J. Raimondo University of Massachusetts, Boston; Betsy Rankin Centenary College of Louisiana; Stanley S. Reynolds University of Arizona; Dan Richards Tufts University; Jennifer Roback Yale University; Malcolm Robinson University of Cincinnati; Mark Rush University of Florida; Elizabeth Savoca Smith College; Robert Schmitz Indiana University; Steven Soderlind St. Olaf College; David Spencer Washington State University; Mark A. Stephens Tennessee Technological University; Brandt K. Stevens Illinois State University; Alan Stockman University of Rochester; Don Tailby University of New Mexico; Michael Tannen University of the District of Columbia; Helen Tauchen University of North Carolina; Robert Thomas Iowa State University; Roger Trenary Kansas State University; George Uhimchuk Clemson University; James M. Walker Indiana University; Richard J. Ward Southeastern Massachusetts University; M. Daniel Westbrook Georgetown University; John B. White Old Dominion University; Roberton Williams Williams College; F. Scott Wilson Canisius College; Laura Wolff Southern Illinois University, Edwardsville; Gary Young Delta State University (Mississippi).

It was a pleasure to work with Jeffrey Parker who, in addition to preparing the *Study Guide,* contributed insightful comments on the text. Dr. Willard W. Radell provided valuable help reviewing the art program.

At Addison Wesley, we are grateful for the continued support of Jack Greenman, and the encouragement and creativity of Bruce Kaplan, our sponsoring editor. It has been a great pleasure to work with these professionals.

Roy J. Ruffin
Paul R. Gregory

# PART I

# INTRODUCTION

# CHAPTER 1

# ECONOMICS AND THE WORLD AROUND US: DEFINING MOMENTS

In 1900, 11 million people worked on farms in the United States. Today, almost a hundred years later, fewer than 1 million people are employed on farms. A century ago there were no airline pilots, truck drivers, medical technicians, or radio and television announcers, and engineering was considered a new profession. Fifty years ago only 70 percent of U.S. households had indoor plumbing; now over 99 percent have this necessity of modern life. In the 1950s, only the richest families in town had air-conditioned homes; now air conditioners are so common that we have them in our automobiles. Life has changed so much that a time-traveler from a century ago would be lost in a technological wonderland.

The enormous improvement in our standard of living is the most important economic fact of this century. Indeed, many of the poor in the United States today live or could live like the middle class of just 50 years ago, as they enjoy a number of things that were unheard-of luxuries in the 1930s and 1940s.

The paradox of this progress is that it makes us insecure while raising our standards of living. Yesterday's luxuries become today's necessities. We soon take for granted such improvements in material well-being. Having seen a better side of life, we fear losing it. In fact, recent polls show that middle-class Americans have become more and more concerned about their economic future.

We worry that prosperity must come to an end, and that opportunities have been exhausted not only for ourselves but for our children and their children. These are not new thoughts, however. Some of our most prominent economists expressed similar thoughts a century and a half ago on the very eve of the birth of this progress.

In this text we shall consider how the economy actually works—how it influences the day-to-day lives of all of us. Those not formally trained in economics can have deep-rooted misconceptions about the workings of the economy. Because much economic activity cannot be seen, we treat matter-offactly the tremendously complicated economic problems we have solved as we have taken part in the vast transformations of this century. We take for granted, for example, the simple act of buying a 25¢ pencil, even though its production requires a complex combination of resources from areas so distant from one another as Washington state, Sri Lanka, and Brazil.

When we experience inflation, unemployment, rising prices, or shortages, it is easy to think that the underlying cause is something that is "seen" rather than some more fundamental factor that is "unseen." It is simpler to blame greedy intermediaries for higher grocery prices or profit-hungry oil companies for increases in gas prices than to understand more fundamental forces at work behind the scenes. We shall analyze the explanations for these forces throughout the chapters of this text, as we strive to bring the unseen into focus.

Economies work in complex and sometimes puzzling ways. To understand economics requires that you "think like an economist." This is an exciting and challenging task. Economics did not spring forth from a vacuum; it was developed over many years by economists in response to various events and ideas. This chapter is the first step on your journey to understanding the major ideas of economics—their evolution and their impact on the economic events of today.

## WHAT IS ECONOMICS?

The most fundamental fact of economics is that people must make choices. We cannot have everything we want. This simple fact applies to societies as well as to individuals. It applies to the rich and to the poor. Simply stated:

> **Economics** is the study of how people choose to use their limited resources (land, labor, and capital) to produce, exchange, and consume goods and services. It explains how these scarce resources are allocated among competing ends by the economic system.

We shall expand on this definition of economics in the next chapter when we review its components, such as resources, production, and exchange.

During the past one and a half centuries, as nations and their citizens have made economic choices, they have been influenced by one of two competing philosophies. The philosophy of *capitalism* maintains that private ownership and private decision making provide the best framework for creating growth and prosperity; that is, if people are simply left alone to pursue self-interests, good things will happen. The competing philosophy of *socialism* teaches that private ownership and self-interest lead to bad economic results—inequality, poverty, and depressions. Socialism argues that the state can better look after the interests of society at large through state ownership and central planning.

How we organize our economic affairs—the blend of capitalism and socialism that we select—depends on how we understand the events that shape our lives. Economists offer a framework for interpreting such events. Robert Heilbroner called the great economists of the past the "Worldly Philosophers" because, while they command no armies, they influence the way we run our world by determining what we believe about the economy and how it works.[1]

## DEFINING MOMENTS OF ECONOMICS

Our understanding of the economic aspects of our lives is conditioned by past events and ideas. Our material circumstances were not created overnight. We

---

[1]Robert Heilbroner, *The Worldly Philosophers,* 6th. ed. (New York: Simon and Schuster, 1986), esp. p. 13. This is an entertaining and beautifully written history of economic thought.

didn't wake up one day to discover high-technology factories, a complex legal system, an information superhighway, a transportation network, and organized financial markets. All these resources and institutions are the consequence of past events.

Change occurs sometimes gradually, sometimes rapidly. Sometimes monumental changes take place that we recognize only after the fact. There are even times when we think change has occurred when it has not—and so it is with economic change.

Over the past two centuries there have taken place a number of changes so important that they have defined the direction of economics and influenced the lives of millions of people. These "defining moments" have provided the stimulus for the great economic thinkers to provide explanations that became the great theories of economic science.

> A **Defining Moment of economics** is an event or idea, or a set of related events or ideas over time, that has changed in a fundamental way the manner in which we conduct our everyday lives and the way in which we think about the economy.

We focus on four Defining Moments of economics:

1. The Industrial Revolution
2. The Rise (and Fall) of Socialism
3. The Great Depression
4. Globalization

Each of these Defining Moments illustrates a fundamental idea of economics. In order to explain why each moment happened and what its consequences were, the Worldly Philosophers developed theories that remain powerful and influential to the present day. You will frequently encounter the ideas and concepts spawned by these Defining Moments throughout the text, for they continue to define the basic themes, concepts, problems, and puzzles not only of the past but also of contemporary economic life. The issues raised by the Defining Moments—growth, affluence, poverty, cycles, trade, ownership, economic institutions—constitute the major economic issues of the past, the present, and the future.

## 1. THE INDUSTRIAL REVOLUTION: THE BENEFITS OF VOLUNTARY EXCHANGE

In the early eighteenth century, enormous economic changes began to take place first in England, and then in Europe and North America. These changes are now known as the Industrial Revolution.

> The **Industrial Revolution** occurred as a result of extensive mechanization of production systems that shifted manufacturing from the home to large-scale factories. This combination of scientific and technological advances and the expansion of free-market institutions created, for the first time, sustained economic growth.

In 1700, England was primarily an agricultural nation of only ten million people. Most of its citizens were peasants tilling the soil with simple plows; a few were merchants and artisans; a very few were the ruling aristocracy living in large estates. Their lives were not much different from those of their ancestors a century or two earlier.

At first slowly and then more quickly, factories powered by water mills and later by steam engines sprang up. Employment in industry began to outpace employment in agriculture. People flocked from the countryside to the industrial centers of London, Birmingham, and Glasgow. Inventors and scientists sought and found better ways of making products that people wished to buy. With the development of mass production techniques, costs of production fell. Products that had previously been inaccessible to the average household became affordable. The Industrial Revolution created the conditions for those increased levels of living standards that we enjoy today.

Adam Smith (1723–1790), the founder of modern economics, explained simply and eloquently in terms of powerful economic theory the Defining Moment of the Industrial Revolution. Smith's 1776 masterpiece, *An Inquiry into the Nature and Causes of the Wealth of Nations*, combined simple theory with his prodigious learning and insights. One of the most important books ever written, *The Wealth of Nations* brought Smith lasting fame and changed forever the way we view the economy.

In his work, Smith explained the ongoing Industrial Revolution with one powerful insight. He realized through careful observation that a massive increase in production and wealth could take place spontaneously without government direction and control. Smith proposed that self-interest could be relied upon to organize our economic affairs. He wrote:

> It is not from the benevolence of the butcher, the brewer, or the baker, that we expect our dinner, but from their regard to their own interest.

Adam Smith's key insight was that two parties to a voluntary exchange will both benefit. It is not necessary to direct people to engage in transactions from which they benefit. Through the pursuit of self-interest, individuals voluntarily engage in those activities in which they themselves earn the most income. Individuals contribute to the well-being of the entire society not just through charitable impulses but by self-interest. Each person, as Adam Smith said, "intends only his own gain," but is "led by an invisible hand" to promote the general interest of society through the magic of the marketplace.

Smith argued that free enterprise solves economic problems better than did the pervasive government monopolies and intrusive regulations of his day. Individuals must be allowed to make their own decisions in the pursuit of their self-interest. If they make the right decisions, the result will be profit; wrong decisions mean losses. This insight paved the way for a hands-off approach of government that allowed England, through the benefits of the Industrial Revolution, to become the world's most prosperous nation.

Much of this book describes how we compete with one another in the marketplace. One computer manufacturer competes with another for customers by trying to offer better prices and better quality. Airlines fight for survival by learning how to provide safe service at a cost lower than that offered by their competitors. One architect competes with another by offering more original designs at a better price. In such a system, success is measured by profit; failure is measured by losses. It is this competition that guides the invisible hand.

Adam Smith's lesson of history is that economic growth and progress come from spontaneous interaction of self-interested individuals.

## 2. THE RISE (AND FALL) OF SOCIALISM

Spontaneous interactions create change. The Industrial Revolution was an event of monumental change. It increased the real wages of workers, and created a middle class. People began to live longer. Birth rates rose, death rates fell, and population grew. Farmers and villagers voluntarily left their homes to seek a better life in the city. The Industrial Revolution benefited many more people than just the rich. From 1760 to 1860, the poorest 65 percent of the British population increased their average real income by over 70 percent.[2]

Adam Smith taught that economic life consists of successes and failures. We must compete to prosper. We pursue our self-interest, while others pursue their self-interest. There will be winners and there will be losers.

The supporters of socialism, however, chose to focus on the misfortunes imposed by the Industrial Revolution. Whereas Smith saw economic progress, they saw struggle and failure. The Industrial Revolution centralized production by shifting workers from the farm or household shop to the factory.

Industrial workers in the coal mines of England, the steel mills of Germany and France, and the textile factories of New England began to question the fairness of a system in which they performed the work and only the owners appeared to reap the rewards. They saw themselves in a class struggle with the capitalists. They formed labor unions, struck factories, and formed political parties to represent the interests of workers. The ground was fertile for the advent of socialism, our second Defining Moment.

The foremost philosopher of socialism, Karl Marx (1818–1883), wrote about the unfairness of the capitalist system in his masterwork *Das Kapital*. He explained why class struggle would lead to the eventual overthrow of capitalism and its replacement by a superior economic system called *communism*. In 1848, 72 years after the publication of *The Wealth of Nations*, Marx issued his *Communist Manifesto*, calling for the workers of the world to revolt against their capitalist bosses. Marx promised that, under communism, class conflicts would disappear, people would work for pleasure, and distribution would reflect need.

After several failed attempts, socialism's next Defining Moment came with the formation of the world's first socialist government in Russia as a consequence of the Bolshevik Revolution in 1917. The

Soviet communists under Lenin and Stalin began the twentieth century's greatest social experiment—the creation of a socialist economy based on state ownership and the use of state planning to replace the market. The state actions of Marx replaced the spontaneous interactions of Smith. Instructions came from the state and from the Communist party; personal initiative and innovation were discouraged; and people were told to think of the interests of society, not of their own interests.

The Soviet experiment at first appeared to yield successes. Russia escaped the Great Depression that overwhelmed the capitalist world in the 1930s. Communism spread to one-third of the world's population, engulfing Eastern Europe, China, Vietnam, Cuba, and North Korea. By the late 1950s, the leaders of the Soviet Union promised to "bury capitalism." The reverse has happened: capitalism buried communism, not by waging war, but by providing living standards to ordinary people far above those available under communism. The Soviet Union was disbanded in 1991, and other countries from the former socialist world soon followed suit. The former socialist countries now face the difficult task of transition from socialism to capitalism.

The failure of socialism was predicted as early as the 1920s by two powerful economic thinkers. Ludwig von Mises and Friedrich Hayek, both Austrian economists, were early skeptics concerning the ability of a socialist economy to sustain itself. Like Adam Smith, von Mises and Hayek taught that we can best understand economic behavior by logically analyzing the actions of individuals. Capitalism works by making people pay for failure and benefit from success. Rewarding success and penalizing failure encourages people to work effectively. Under capitalism, the shoe manufacturer that produces at a high cost shoes no one wants will fail and disappear. Von Mises and Hayek predicted that socialism must fail because in that system, errors of judgment need not be corrected. If a shoe manufacturer loses money in a socialist state, the losses will be covered by the state. After all, it was the state that told the shoe manufacturer what to do in the first place. There is little or no incentive to keep costs low or to produce a product that people want. Unlike the capitalist shoe manufacturer, whose investment and property are at stake, under state ownership everyone and hence no one is the owner. And, thus, no one really cares. Indeed, we shall discuss the importance of incentives throughout this text.

The lesson of socialism regarding economics is that if people do not have the incentives to economize on their uses of goods and services, waste and inefficiency will result. Capitalism corrects mistakes by forcing those who make them to pay for them.

The Soviet Union was socialism's great experiment, but it was not socialism's only legacy. While Russia reacted to socialism's appeal with revolution in 1917, the rest of Europe reacted by introducing the welfare state.

The **welfare state** provides substantial benefits to the less fortunate—unemployment insurance, poverty assistance, old-age pensions—to protect them from further economic misfortune.

First in Germany and then in other parts of Europe, governments enacted social security legislation, government health insurance, progressive income taxes, worker safety laws, and unemployment insurance. This legislation was designed to make capitalism more humane—to reduce the risks of capitalism and to make the state responsible for those bearing the costs of capitalism.

The welfare state raises a fundamental question: To what extent are the enormous benefits of capitalism, as described by Adam Smith and Ludwig von Mises, jeopardized by a system that makes the state rather than individuals responsible for its risks?

## 3. THE GREAT DEPRESSION: THE COST OF PROGRESS

The Industrial Revolution in England, Western Europe, and North America created long-term economic growth. Prior civilizations (for example, the Greeks and Romans) had achieved growth but could not sustain it. The economic growth that followed the Industrial Revolution was not perfectly even, but occurred in cycles. Although newspaper headlines spoke of financial panics and depressions, each earlier downswing seemed to correct itself and upward progress continued. Throughout the nineteenth century and during the early part of the twentieth century, bad times were followed by good times in a seemingly endless cycle—until the late 1920s.

The Great Depression—our third Defining Moment—took hold first in Europe, and then in the

United States. Overnight, people saw their paper fortunes disappear. On Wall Street, bankrupt investors hurled themselves out of skyscrapers in despair. Banks closed. Ordinary citizens lost their homes. The stock market crash of 1929 was only a financial manifestation of a larger economic phenomenon. The Great Depression itself constituted a severe and sustained drop in output and jobs.

> The **Great Depression** was a sustained period of high unemployment and falling output that occurred in Europe and North America in the 1920s and 1930s.

Those who did not live through the Great Depression cannot possibly comprehend its effects on millions of lives. Some three years after the start of the Depression, output in the United States had fallen by one-third, and one of four people who wished to work did not have a job. It was not until the late 1930s that the economy recovered to the level of output before the market crash, and it was not until 1942 and the beginning of World War II that the unemployment rate recovered to its previous low.

The main effect of the Great Depression was to cause many Americans and Europeans to question whether growth and prosperity are automatic. The Depression created a sense of concern about the future. Prosperity was no longer something to be taken for granted. The government came to be viewed as an instrument of good to protect people against further economic downturns, both large and small.

The Great Depression was an unanticipated event of such magnitude that it required a great economist to develop a new theory explaining it. That economist was John Maynard Keynes (1883–1946), an English intellectual, teacher, journalist, and statesman.

Smith and his followers had argued that the free market would promote economic progress. In his 1936 *General Theory of Employment, Interest and Money,* Keynes advanced a theory that showed why capitalist economies are subject to periodic breakdowns that can be corrected only by massive doses of government spending. While Smith emphasized the incentives to produce goods and services, Keynes emphasized the incentives of people to buy goods and services.

Keynesian economics is the source of the idea that buying a car or a house is "good for the economy." The importance of spending was hard to deny

in the years following the Great Depression. Keynes argued that the Great Depression occurred because we did not spend enough. If there is not enough private spending, then government spending must make up the difference.

Keynes provided a justification for more government spending: If government spending is needed to keep the economy healthy, politicians can spend more without taxing. They can make their constituents happy without the pain of higher taxes. While households and businesses must be subject to financial discipline, the government need not be. Indeed, most of us are aware that the federal government has been running deficits year after year for the past 50 years.

> The rise in government spending and the expansion of the welfare state raise the question of the extent to which we can reap the benefits of capitalism if we protect individuals from the risks and competition of capitalism.

Another great economic thinker presented an entirely different picture of the Great Depression. The Austrian-born American economist Joseph Schumpeter (1883–1950) developed the theory that the Great Depression had roots in technological changes that were transforming the twentieth century. His main insight was that the *business cycle* is necessary for economic progress. New products always displace old products. The automobile replaced the horse-drawn carriage; the personal computer replaced the typewriter. Schumpeter considered the Great Depression to be an event in which many different forces converged at the same time. According to Schumpeter, it was no accident that the Soviet Union escaped the Great Depression, because it also escaped the opportunity for economic progress. Progress requires the freedom to develop new goods and new markets. Progress requires the competition of old and new ideas; progress requires winners and losers.

## 4. GLOBALIZATION

Archaeologists are astonished by evidence of trade in remote times. Bronze artifacts cast in the Middle East in 3500 B.C. have been found thousands of miles away in ancient French villages. Through the ages, school children have been fascinated by Marco Polo's thirteenth-century accounts of traveling from his native Venice to China in search of exotic silks and spices. Human beings have always sought out for their own use new and exotic products produced by other societies. Human beings have, as Adam Smith remarked, a "propensity to truck, barter, and exchange one thing for another." He wrote:

> Nobody ever saw a dog make a fair and deliberate exchange of one bone for another with another dog. Nobody ever saw one animal by its gestures and natural cries signify to another, this is mine, that yours; I am willing to give this for that.

Although we are naturally drawn toward trading with one another, trade has grown unevenly. Trade depends on the ease of communication and the costs of transporting goods and services long distances. Marco Polo's journey to China consumed more than half his lifetime; today, the same trip can be made in one day on a commercial jet. His letters from China to Venice took years to deliver; now, such messages can be delivered in seconds by fax or electronic mail.

Like the Industrial Revolution, the socialist revolution, and the Great Depression, the globalization of the world economy is a Defining Moment.

**Globalization** refers to the degree to which national economic markets and international businesses are integrated and interrelated into a world economy.

The participation of any economy in global markets may not take place swiftly and continuously; it may be a long-term process with stops and starts.

Globalization, like the other Defining Moments, was a response not only to inexorable events but also to a powerful economic insight—that trade benefits both parties irrespective of their strengths and weaknesses. This insight had already paved the way for the expansion of trade in Great Britain in the nineteenth century.

Adam Smith had to argue against the narrow merchant interests of his day claiming that trade with other nations could lead to national bankruptcy. However, the great English economist David Ricardo (1772–1823) demonstrated that both weak and powerful nations benefit from trade by doing those things they do relatively more efficiently than others. His discovery of the surprisingly simple yet subtle law of comparative advantage (explained in later chapters) is perhaps one of the greatest contributions economics has made to our understanding of the world about us. As we will show, this law demonstrates that every country can specialize in those goods in which it has a comparative advantage, regardless of how rich or poor the country might be or how high or low its wages.

It was Ricardo's law of comparative advantage that persuaded the English Parliament to adopt a free trade policy in the first half of the nineteenth century, with the passage of the Corn Laws. The remarkable success of England's experiment with free trade forced other countries to reduce barriers to trade imposed by narrow special interest groups.

The Industrial Revolution brought forth the first strong and sustained wave of globalization of the world economy. Coal-powered boats and railroads linked markets; the telegraph and later the telephone made long-distance communication possible. The Industrial Revolution was accompanied by strong and sustained growth in international trade. Two world wars and the Great Depression halted the globalization of the world economy. However, the major powers entered the postwar era determined to avoid the mistakes of the past and to promote the growth of trade and commerce.

Thus, in the past 50 years we have experienced an explosion of international commerce and trade. We can rightly say that we are a world economy, made possible by the revolutionary developments in transportation and communication and the conscious decisions of countries to lower their barriers to trade. In the 1990s agreements to create common markets in Europe and North America have provided new impulses for globalization.

A world economy has benefited our lives in a variety of ways. We now have a wealth of choices among cars, foodstuffs, computers—almost every product that we consider. Companies are no longer national in nature: A Japanese company located in Germany can be headed by an American president. Stocks of U.S. companies are traded in Japan as we sleep, continue to be traded in London as we begin our day, and complete their trading in New York as we finish lunch. The car you drive might be made in Korea, your neighbor might work for British Petroleum, and your business loan could be from a Canadian bank. Despite its complexities, globalization has enriched our lives not only in terms of economic opportunities and options but also in a broader philosophical sense.

International trade brings broad benefits, but it hurts special interest groups. Markets that were secure are threatened by foreign competitors. Everyone must take part in competition to win customers with superior products, lower prices, or a combination of both. For example, domestic beef producers are threatened by lower-cost foreign producers. Automobile companies and their unions warn against the threat of foreign imports.

> Although it brings broad benefits, globalization is opposed by special interest groups. Thus, the progress of globalization is not steady or guaranteed.

## ECONOMIC THEORY AND THE SCIENTIFIC METHOD

The economy is a complex mixture of many types of decision makers, each with different goals and knowledge about how things work. The U.S. economy is made up of millions of households and firms, and thousands of separate federal, state, and local governments. Each makes production and consumption decisions. Consumers want to pay low prices for the things they buy and earn high wages. Firms want to charge high prices and pay low wages. Automobile companies want low-priced steel; steel companies want high-priced steel. Gathering information about all these choices is a complex task. It is essential to abstract from the irrelevant or unimportant facts in order to gain an understanding of the way the economy works.

*not always accurate*

### ECONOMIC THEORIES AND MODELS

Smith, Marx, Keynes, Schumpeter, and Ricardo all explained events by formulating economic *theories* of how the world works. Theories can cover the workings of an entire economy or limit their scope to explain, for example, what happens to consumer spending when prices change. Simply defined:

> A **theory** is a simplified and coherent explanation of the relationship among certain facts.

The most important economic theories explain in a logical manner the Defining Moments we have just discussed. Adam Smith explained how an industrial revolution could occur using a system of free enterprise. Karl Marx explained how people might turn

to socialism. Von Mises and Hayek explained why socialism would fail. John Maynard Keynes sought to explain the Great Depression. When the industrialized countries experienced rising inflation and rising unemployment in the 1970s and 1980s, new and powerful theories were put forward to explain this unusual phenomenon.

The world is so complicated that all theories, economic or physical, must be devised by eliminating irrelevant facts and concentrating on only the most important relevant ones. For example, in explaining the demand for gasoline, the color of cars—black, white, or red—is not important and should be ignored. Other things, however, like the price of gasoline or the incomes of automobile owners, may be important and should be considered. Economic theories focus on the most important systematic factors that explain economic behavior.

For example, we might theorize that the demand for coffee depends inversely on the price of coffee and positively on the price of tea. A model illustrating this theory might show that an increase in the price of coffee by $1 would reduce worldwide sales by one million pounds. Models can be illustrated by graphs, equations, or words; they show the concrete workings of the theory.

### THE SCIENTIFIC METHOD

Economic theories are not fanciful abstract exercises; they must explain the real world to be useful. If a theory is not supported by the facts, it should be discarded in favor of one that is. How do we know that a theory is correct? A theory is a simplified explanation of the relationship between two or more facts. You observe that when the price of video cassettes rises, the number that are sold falls. To explain this observation, you come up with the following theory: "People have allocated so many dollars to the purchase of video cassettes. Thus, if the price rises, people must buy fewer units in order to keep from exceeding their budget." You check the actual facts and find that as the price of videos fell, people spent more dollars on videos. This finding would refute your theory, which requires that people spend the same amount.

> The **scientific method** is the process of formulating theories, collecting data, testing theories, and revising theories.

This simple example shows that the scientific method requires confronting theories with additional facts. The scientific method enables us to evaluate our beliefs in a way that can be tested by others. The Nobel physicist Richard Feynman put it this way:

> If you make a theory, . . . and advertise it, or put it out, then you must also put down all the facts that disagree with it, as well as those that agree with it. . . . You want to make sure, when explaining what it fits, that those things it fits are not just the things that gave you the idea for the theory; but that the finished theory makes something else come out right, in addition.[3]

The advantage of learning a theory is that you are freed from having to learn the facts of each situation covered by the theory. If the theory is correct, the facts of each situation will be consistent with it.

According to the scientific method, a theory that does not work in practice cannot be a good theory. Finding that a theory does not fit the facts leads to new theories that cover more experience. In science, this represents progress. The Italian economist Vilfredo Pareto (1848–1923) once remarked,

> Give me a fruitful error anytime, full of seeds, bursting with its own corrections. You can keep your sterile truth for yourself.

## LOGICAL FALLACIES

Logical fallacies plague all scientific thinking. The three most common to economics are the *ceteris paribus fallacy*, the *false-cause fallacy*, and the *fallacy of composition*.

Economic phenomena are complicated; they are generally caused by several factors. Consider a video cassette example in which you observe that the number of units that are sold increases when the price rises. Does this mean that price increases cause customers to buy more? In this case, we might suspect that the number of video cassettes sold depends on something other than the price. Income may be increasing, so the number of buyers may be increasing along with the prices of video cassette recorders. To understand the true relationship between the price of cassettes and units sold (which we presume to be negative), we must hold these other factors constant. To

conclude from these facts that a higher price brings about greater sales is a *ceteris paribus* fallacy.

*Ceteris paribus* is a Latin term meaning "other things being equal." Any attempt to establish the relationship between two factors must hold constant the effects of other factors to avoid confusing the relationship; otherwise, the *ceteris paribus* problem will occur.

To understand how one factor affects another, we must be able to sort out the effects of all other relevant factors. An entire branch of economics, econometrics, combines economic theory and statistics to deal with the *ceteris paribus* problem.

> The *ceteris paribus* problem occurs when the effect of one factor on another is masked by changes in other factors.

*Difficult to isolate variables*

Consider the odd fact that in 20 of the last 22 years, the stock market rose when the National Football Conference team won the Super Bowl and fell when it lost. To conclude that the one event (the NFC team wins the Super Bowl) caused the other event (a rise in stock market prices) is a false-cause fallacy. Some people even buy or sell in the stock market on the basis of which team wins the Super Bowl!

> The **false-cause fallacy** is the assumption that because two events occur together, one event has caused the other.

Economic theory tries to establish in a scientific manner whether a cause-and-effect relationship exists. Since there is no logical reason for a football game to affect the stock market, we must reject a cause-and-effect relationship. Economics, however, can offer a number of logical theories that specify cause-and-effect relationships between variables (such as the overall state of the economy, interest rates, expectations of inflation) and the stock market.

The third major fallacy involves reasoning from special cases to the general case, or the reverse. Imagine a fire in a crowded movie theater. If *one* of us runs to the exit, he or she will escape unharmed. If *all* of us run to the nearest exit, few will escape unharmed. It is a *fallacy of composition* to suppose that what is true for one is true for all.

If your employer replaces you with a robot, you would rightly complain that the robot has put you out of a job. But beware of committing a fallacy of

---

[3]Richard Feynman, *"Surely You're Joking, Mr. Feynman!" Adventures of a Curious Character* (Bantam Books: New York, 1986), pp. 311–312.

composition. If you say, "robots are destroying American jobs," you have fallen into a logical trap. For the whole economy, robots might be increasing the number of jobs of all types. It is only correct for you to say that the robot took your particular job, and now you have to find a new one!

> The **fallacy of composition** is the assumption that what is true for each part taken separately is also true for the whole or, in reverse, that what is true for the whole is true for each part considered separately.

## POSITIVE AND NORMATIVE ECONOMICS

We often hear people joke about getting "six different answers from five economists." This image of disagreement is a distortion of the truth. There is, in fact, considerable agreement among economists about what *can* be done.

Economists agree that widespread freezes in citrus-growing areas raise citrus prices, that rising gas prices reduce gas consumption, and that price controls cause shortages. Disagreements about "what is" focus primarily on complex phenomena like inflation, unemployment, and business cycles. We can use the scientific method to test the theories of positive economics.

> **Positive economics** is the study of how the economy works; it explains the economy in measurable terms.

There is, however, considerably more disagreement over what *ought to* be done. You will find economists disagreeing on whether we should have government-mandated universal health insurance; whether income taxes should be lowered for the middle class, the rich, or the poor; whether there should be job programs for the poor. These disagreements are only partly over "what is." We may agree on what will happen if program A is chosen over program B, but we may disagree sharply over the desirability of those consequences.

> **Normative economics** is the study of what ought to be in the economy; it is value-based and cannot be tested by the scientific method.

Disagreements in other sciences are less visible than in economics. Theoretical physicists still dis-

agree about the physical nature of the universe, but this controversy is understood by only a few theoretical physicists. On the other hand, economic disputes attract immediate attention. We are concerned about whether inflation will accelerate, whether we will lose our jobs, or whether interest rates will fall. We all want to know what the future holds in store.

Should economists be able to foresee the future? If they cannot correctly predict what will happen, does this mean that economics has failed? Some events can, indeed, be predicted. If gas prices rise sharply, we shall eventually buy less gas. Other events—such as stock market fluctuations, inflation, or the business cycle—are difficult if not impossible to predict. As we shall see in later chapters, economic principles themselves imply that systematically correct predictions about complex economic phenomena are not possible.

## UNANSWERED QUESTIONS

The four Defining Moments of economics we have discussed reveal the major issues of economics that will occupy our attention in this text—growth, business cycles, unemployment, inflation, competition, incentives, economic systems, and technology.

Economics is constantly evolving as events unfold. There will be new Defining Moments, and future economists must establish important theories to explain them. In fact, today there is much economists do not know or can explain only poorly.

1. They do not understand well how to dismantle socialist economic systems to return them to capitalism. This task will probably occupy us for the next quarter century.

2. They do not fully understand the business cycle—why economies are still subject to ups and downs—despite the powerful explanations of Keynes and Schumpeter.

3. They do not understand how to measure the links between technological advances, the business cycle, and the true rate of economic growth.

If we knew the answers to these and other economic questions, economics would not be the exciting field of study it is. Because we are still searching for answers, we require building blocks of knowledge to formulate explanations.

In the next chapter let us use some of the tools of the scientific method to understand how economic choices are made in a world of scarce resources. What are the costs of making choices? What arrangements are used to resolve the problem of choice? Graphical analysis makes these questions easier to answer. As an aid to using these tools, we shall review the guidelines for working with graphs in the appendix to this chapter.

## SUMMARY

1. The Defining Moments of economics are the Industrial Revolution, the rise (and fall) of socialism, the Great Depression, and the globalization of the world economy. Each Defining Moment is associated with a great economic idea. Adam Smith explained the Industrial Revolution; Karl Marx, the appeal of socialism; John Maynard Keynes and Joseph Schumpeter, the Great Depression; David Ricardo, the benefits of globalization; and Ludwig von Mises and Friedrich von Hayek, the weaknesses of socialism.

2. Theory allows us to make sense of the real world and to learn how the facts fit together. There is no conflict between good theory and good practice. Economic theories are based on the scientific method of hypothesis formulation, collection of relevant data, and testing of theories.

3. The *ceteris paribus* problem occurs when it is difficult to determine relationships between two factors because other factors have not been held constant.

4. Two other logical fallacies plague economic analysis: the false-cause fallacy (assuming that event A has caused event B because A is associated with B) and the fallacy of composition (assuming that what is true for each part taken separately is true for the whole or, conversely, assuming that what is true for the whole is also true for each part).

5. Economists tend to agree on positive economic issues (what is), whereas they tend to disagree on normative issues (what ought to be). Disagreements among economists are more visible to the public eye than disagreements in other scientific professions.

## KEY TERMS

economics
Defining Moment of
    economics
Industrial Revolution
welfare state
Great Depression
globalization
theory
scientific method
*ceteris paribus* problem
false-cause fallacy
fallacy of composition
positive economics
normative economics

## QUESTIONS AND PROBLEMS

1. In what ways has the growing globalization of the economy changed our everyday lives?
2. Explain how you would use the scientific method to determine what factors cause the grade point averages of students in your class to differ.
3. "If I stand up at the game, I will see better." Explain under what conditions this statement is true and under what conditions it is a logical fallacy. Also explain which logical fallacy is involved.
4. "The price of corn is low today because people are now watching too much TV." This statement is a potential example of which logical fallacy (or fallacies)?
5. Economists are more likely to agree on the answers to which of the following questions? Why?
    a. Should tax rates be lowered for the rich?
    b. How would lowering tax rates for the rich affect economic output?
    c. How would an increase in the price of VCRs affect purchases of VCRs?
    d. Should government defense expenditures be reduced?
    e. How would an increase in military spending affect employment?
6. "The severe heat and drought this summer substantially reduced revenue from wheat and corn crops in the Midwest. The incomes of all wheat and corn farmers therefore will fall." Which logical fallacy may be involved in this statement and why?
7. Use the data in Table A to devise some simple theories and to test them against "the facts."

| Table A | | |
| --- | --- | --- |
| | *1980* | *1990* |
| New passenger cars (millions sold) | 9.0 | 9.3 |
| New car prices (1980 = 100) | 100 | 137 |
| Personal income (billions of dollars) | 2265 | 4680 |

8. Can we say that the data in Table A "prove" the theory? Is it better to say that they "support" the theory?

9. Identify which of the following statements are theories (or hypotheses).
   a. The U.S. population rose more rapidly in the 1950s than in the 1990s.
   b. People who get severely sunburned are more likely to develop skin cancer.
   c. An increase in income causes people to buy more consumer goods.
   d. The United States and Western Europe have the highest incomes among the world's nations.
   e. Cats can see better in the dark than dogs.
   f. If people believe that a product is hazardous to their health, they will consume less of it.

10. Marx, von Mises, and Hayek had quite different views of socialism. Explain their basic differences of opinion.

11. What was the Industrial Revolution?

# APPENDIX 1A

# UNDERSTANDING GRAPHS

## APPENDIX INSIGHT

Economics makes extensive use of graphs. In Chapter 1 we discussed economic theories and models. Graphs are tools we use to illustrate economic models. A graph is a visual scheme for picturing the quantitative relationship between two variables.

This appendix reviews graph construction, positive and negative relationships, and dependent and independent variables, and it details how we calculate the areas of rectangles and triangles. It explains slopes for both linear and curvilinear relationships and shows how we can use them to find maximum and minimum values. It distinguishes between time series and cross section data. Finally, it describes three common pitfalls of using graphs.

# THE USE OF GRAPHS IN ECONOMICS

Graphs can efficiently describe quantitative relationships. As the Chinese proverb says, "a picture is worth a thousand words." A graph is easier both to understand and to remember than the several hundred or perhaps thousands of numbers that the graph represents.

## POSITIVE AND NEGATIVE RELATIONSHIPS

The first important characteristic of a graph is whether it shows a positive (direct) or a negative (inverse) relationship between the two variables.

> A **positive (direct) relationship** exists between two variables if an increase in the value of one variable is associated with an *increase* in the value of the other variable. A **negative (inverse) relationship** exists between two variables if an increase in the value of one variable is associated with a *reduction* in the value of the other variable.

Panel *(a)* of Figure A1 depicts how an increase in horsepower will increase the maximum speed of an automobile. The *vertical axis* measures the maximum speed of the car from the 0 point (called the *origin*); the *horizontal axis* measures the horsepower of the engine. When horsepower is 0 (the engine is off), the maximum speed the car can attain is obviously 0; when horsepower is 300, the maximum speed is 100 miles per hour. Intermediate values of horsepower (between 0 and 300) are graphed. When a line is drawn through these points, the resulting curved line describes the effect of horsepower on maximum speed. Since the picture is a line that goes from low to high speeds as horsepower increases, it is an *upward-sloping curve.*

Now let's consider an example of a negative (inverse) relationship. As the horsepower of the automobile increases, the gas mileage will fall. In panel *(b)* of Figure A1, gas mileage is now measured on the vertical axis. Since the graph is a curve going from high to low values of gas mileage as horsepower increases, it is an example of a *downward-sloping curve.*

## DEPENDENT AND INDEPENDENT VARIABLES

In relationships involving two variables, one variable is the dependent variable and the other is the inde-

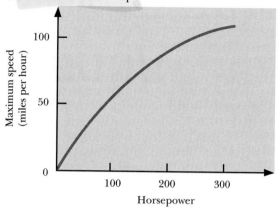

(*a*) A Positive Relationship

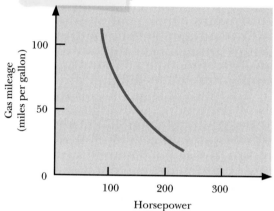

(*b*) A Negative Relationship

**FIGURE A1    Graphing Positive and Negative Relationships**

Panel *(a)* shows a positive relationship. As the horizontal variable (horsepower) increases, the value of the vertical variable (maximum speed) increases. The curve rises from left to right. Panel *(b)* shows a negative relationship. As the horizontal variable (horsepower) increases, the vertical variable (mileage) decreases. The curve falls from left to right.

pendent variable. The dependent variable—denoted by Y—changes as a result of change in the value of another variable. The independent variable—denoted by X—causes the change in the dependent variable.

In panel *(a)* of Figure A1, an increase in engine horsepower causes an *increase* in the maximum speed of the automobile. In panel *(b)*, a horsepower increase causes a *reduction* in gas mileage. In both examples, horsepower is the independent variable. The other two variables depend upon horsepower because the changes in horsepower bring about changes in speed and gas mileage.

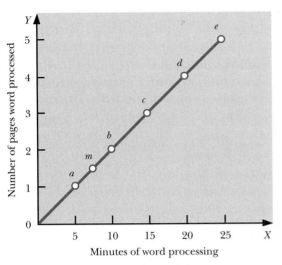

FIGURE A2   Constructing a Graph

## ADVANTAGES OF GRAPHS

We can tell from a quick glance at a graph whether a curve is positive or negative. We have to work harder to reach this conclusion if the same information is presented in a table. Table A1 details the quantitative relationship between minutes of word processing and number of pages processed. (The quantitative relationship between minutes and pages is that every 5 minutes of word processing produces 1 page of manuscript. Thus 5 minutes produce 1 page, 15 minutes produce 3 pages, and so on.) The data are graphed in Figure A2.

Points *a*, *b*, *c*, *d*, and *e* completely describe the data in Table A1. Indeed, a graph of the data acts as a substitute for the table. This is the first advantage of graphs over tables: Graphs provide an immediate visual understanding of the quantitative relationship between the two variables just by the plots of points.

| Table A1   The Relationship Between Minutes of Word Processing and Number of Pages Processed | | |
|---|---|---|
| | Minutes of Word Processing (X axis) | Number of Pages Processed (Y axis) |
| | 0 | 0 |
| *a* | 5 | 1 |
| *b* | 10 | 2 |
| *c* | 15 | 3 |
| *d* | 20 | 4 |
| *e* | 25 | 5 |

| Table A2   The Relationship Between Minutes of Word Processing and Number of Pages Processed (Data Rearranged) | | |
|---|---|---|
| | Minutes of Word Processing (X axis) | Number of Pages Processed (Y axis) |
| *b* | 10 | 2 |
| *a* | 5 | 1 |
| | 0 | 0 |
| *e* | 25 | 5 |
| *c* | 15 | 3 |
| *d* | 20 | 4 |

Since the points in this case move upward from left to right, there is a *positive relationship* between the variables.

This advantage may not seem to be great for such a simple and obvious case. However, suppose the data had been arranged as in Table A2.

After looking at the data, we should eventually see that there is a positive relationship between X and Y; however, it is not immediately obvious. A graph makes it easier for us to see the relationship.

A large table would be required to report all intermediate values in Table A1. In a graph, however, all these intermediate values can be represented simply by connecting points *a*, *b*, *c*, *d*, and *e* with a line. A second advantage is that large quantities of data can be represented more efficiently in a graph than in a table.

The data in Tables A1 and A2 reveal the relationship between minutes of word processing and number of pages processed (Figure A2). The relationship can change, however, if other factors change that affect word-processing speed. Table A1 shows minutes and pages input on a computer with limited memory. If the word processor works with a more advanced computer, a different relationship will prevail. He or she can now process 2 pages instead of 1 page every 5 minutes. Both relationships are graphed in Figure A3. Thus, if factors that affect speed of word processing (for example, the quality of the computer) change, the relationship between minutes and pages can shift. Because economists frequently work with relationships that shift, it is important to understand shifts in graphs.

> The first advantage of graphs over tables is that it is easier to see the relationship between the variables.

The second advantage of graphs over tables is that large quantities of data can be represented efficiently in a graph.

## UNDERSTANDING SLOPE

The magnitude of the reaction of a dependent variable *(Y)* to a change in an independent variable *(X)* is represented by the *slope* of the curve depicting their relationship. Many central concepts of economics require an understanding of slope.

> The **slope of a curve** reflects the response of one variable to changes in another. The **slope of a straight line** is the ratio of the rise (or fall) in Y over the run in X.

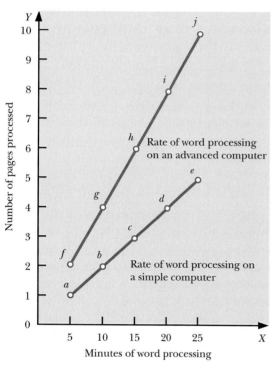

**FIGURE A3    Shifts in Relationships**

The curve *abcde* graphically illustrates the data in Table A1 that shows the relationship between minutes and pages with a limited memory computer. The new (higher) curve *fghij* shows the relationship between minutes and pages with an advanced computer. As a consequence of the upgraded computer, the relationship has shifted upward. Any given *X* is now associated with a higher *Y* value.

Consider the original computer example. Every 5 minutes of inputting on a limited memory computer produces 1 page; equivalently, every minute of inputting produces one-fifth of a page.

To understand slope more precisely, consider the straight-line relationship between the two variables *X* and *Y* in panel *(a)* of Figure A4. When $X = 5$, $Y = 3$; when $X = 7$, $Y = 6$. Suppose that variable *X* is allowed to *run* (to change horizontally) from 5 units to 7 units. Now, variable *Y* rises (increases vertically) from 3 units to 6 units.

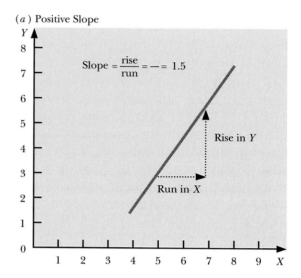

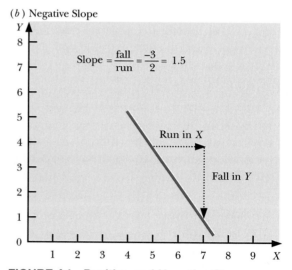

**FIGURE A4    Positive and Negative Slope**

The slope is measured by the ratio of the rise in *Y* over the run in *X*. In panel *(a)*, *Y* rises by 3 and *X* runs by 2, and the slope is 1.5. In panel *(b)*, the rise in *Y* is −3, the run in *X* is 2, and the slope is −1.5.

The slope of the line in panel *(a)* is

$$\frac{\text{Rise in } Y}{\text{Run in } X} = \frac{3}{2} = 1.5$$

A *positive value of the slope* signifies a *positive relationship* between the two variables.

This formula works for negative relationships as well. In panel *(b)* of Figure A4, when X runs from 5 to 7, Y falls from 4 units to 1 unit, or rises by $-3$ units. Thus, the slope is:

$$\frac{\text{Rise in } Y}{\text{Run in } X} = \frac{-3}{2} = -1.5$$

A *negative* value of the slope signifies a *negative relationship* between the two variables.

If $\Delta Y$ (delta Y) stands for the change in the value of Y and $\Delta X$ (delta X) stands for the change in the values of X,

$$\text{Slope} = \frac{\Delta Y}{\Delta X}$$

This formula holds for positive or negative relationships.

Let us return to the word-processing example. What slope expresses the relationship between minutes of inputting and number of pages? When minutes increase by 5 units ($\Delta X = 5$), pages increase by 1 unit ($\Delta Y = 1$). The slope is therefore $\Delta Y/\Delta X = 1/5$. In Figures A2, A3, and A4, the points are connected by straight lines. Such relationships are called *linear relationships*.

Figure A5 shows how the slope is measured when the relationship between X and Y is curvilinear. When X runs from 2 units to 4 units ($\Delta X = 2$), Y rises by 2 units ($\Delta Y = 2$); thus the slope between *a* and *b* is 2/2 = 1. Between *a* and *c*, however, X runs from 2 to 6 ($\Delta X = 4$), Y rises by 3 units ($\Delta Y = 3$), and the slope is 3/4. In the curvilinear case, the value of the slope depends on how far X runs. The slope changes as we move along a curve. In the linear case, the value of the slope will *not* depend on how far X runs, because the slope is constant and does not change as we move from point to point.

There is no single slope of a curvilinear relationship and no single method of measuring slopes. An individual slope can be measured between two points (say, between *a* and *b* or between *b* and *c*) or at a particular point (say, at point *a*). A uniform standard must be adopted to avoid confusion. This standard requires that tangents be used to determine the slope at any single point on a curve.

A **tangent** is a straight line that touches the curve at only one point.

To calculate the slope at *a*, let the run of X be "infinitesimally small" rather than a discrete number of units such as 1/2, 2, or 4. An infinitesimally small change is difficult to conceptualize, but the graphical result of such a change can be captured simply by drawing a tangent to point *a*.

If the curve is really curved at *a*, there is only one straight line that just barely touches *a* and only *a*. Any other line cuts the curve at two points or none. The tangent to *a* is drawn as a straight line in Figure A5.

The **slope of a curvilinear relationship** at a particular point is the slope of the straight-line tangent to the curve at that point.

The slope of the tangent at *a* is measured by dividing the rise by the run. Because the tangent is a straight

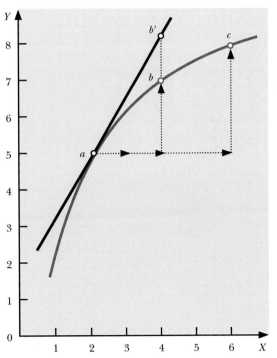

**FIGURE A5   Calculating Slopes of Curvilinear Relationships**

The ratio of the rise over the run yields a slope of 1 from *a* to *b* but a slope of 3/4 from *a* to *c*, and 1/2 from *b* to *c*. To compute the slope at point *a*, the slope of the tangent to *a* is calculated. The value of the slope of the tangent is 3/2 since between *a* and *b'*, $\Delta Y = 3$ and $\Delta X = 2$.

line, the length of the run does not matter. For a run from 2 to 4 ($\Delta X = 2$), the rise ($\Delta Y$) equals 3 (from 5 to 8). Thus the slope of the tangent is 3/2, or 1.5.

## MAXIMUM AND MINIMUM VALUES

Figure A6 shows two curvilinear relationships that have distinct high points or low points. When a curvilinear relationship has a zero slope, at the $X$ value where slope is zero the value of $Y$ reaches either a high point, or maximum, as in panel *(a)*, or a low point, or minimum, as in panel *(b)*. In panel *(a)* of Figure A6, the relationship between $X$ and $Y$ is positive for values of $X$ less than 6 units and negative for values of $X$ more than 6 units. The exact opposite holds for panel *(b)*: The relationship is negative for values of $X$ less than 6 and positive for $X$ greater than 6. Notice that at the point where the slope changes from positive to negative (or vice versa), the slope of the curve will be exactly zero; the tangent at point $X = 6$ for both curves is a horizontal straight line that neither rises nor falls as $X$ changes.

Maximum and minimum values of relationships are important in economics because business firms seek to *maximize* profits and *minimize* costs.

## SCATTER DIAGRAMS

Statisticians may have more powerful tools with which to measure relationships, but the scatter diagram is a convenient analytical tool to examine whether a positive or negative relationship exists between two variables.

> A **scatter diagram** consists of a number of separate points, each plotting the value of one variable against a value of another variable for a specific time interval.

In Figure A7, mortgage interest rates are measured along the horizontal axis, and new housing starts (the number of new homes on which construction has started) are measured along the vertical axis. Each of the dots on the scatter diagram shows the combination of mortgage rate and number of housing starts for a particular year. The pattern of dots provides visual information about the relationship between the two variables. If the dots show a pattern of low mortgage rates and high housing starts but high mortgage rates and low housing starts, the scatter diagram indicates a *negative relationship*, indicated by a generally declining pattern of dots from

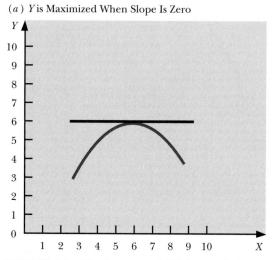

(*a*) *Y* is Maximized When Slope Is Zero

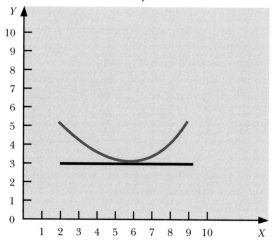

(*b*) *Y* is Minimized When Slope Is Zero

**FIGURE A6   Maximum and Minimum Points**

Some curvilinear relationships change directions. Notice that in panel *(a)*, when the curve changes direction at $X = 6$, the corresponding value of $Y$ is *maximized*. In panel *(b)*, when $X = 6$, $Y$ is *minimized*. In either case, the slope equals zero at the maximum or minimum value.

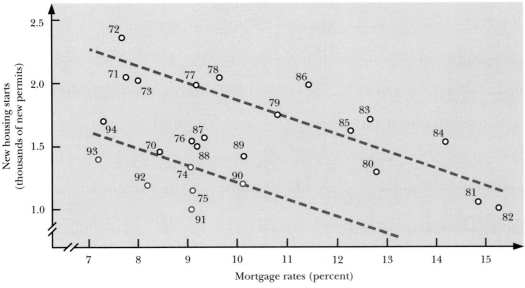

FIGURE A7   **A Scatter Diagram of Mortgage Rates and Housing Starts, 1970–1994**

The generally falling pattern of dots suggests that there is a negative relationship between these two variables. The fact that not all dots lie on a single line suggests that other factors besides the independent variable (mortgage rates) affect the dependent variable (housing starts). *Source: Economic Report of the President.*

left to right. A generally rising pattern of dots from left to right shows a *positive relationship*. If there were no relationship, the dots would be distributed randomly.

Figure A7 shows a negative relationship between mortgage rates and housing starts. The broad, negatively sloped band traces out the general pattern of declining dots. Such a pattern makes sense: The number of houses being built should drop when the cost of borrowing to buy a home rises.

## AREAS OF RECTANGLES AND OF TRIANGLES

In economics, it is important to understand how to calculate areas of rectangles and of triangles. Panel *(a)* of Figure A8 shows the area of a rectangle, and panel *(b)* shows the area of a triangle. In panel *(a)*, a firm sells 8 units of its product for a price of $10, and it costs $6 per unit to produce the product. How much profit is the firm earning? The firm's profit is the area of the rectangle *abcd*. To calculate the area

of a rectangle, we must multiply the height of the rectangle (*ad* or *bc*, or $10 − $6 = $4 per unit) by the width of the rectangle (*ab* or *dc*, 8 units). The area of the rectangle is $4 per unit times 8 units, or $32 of total profit.

Panel *(b)* of Figure A8 shows the area of triangle *efg*. Because this triangle accounts for one-half the area of the rectangle *efgh*, we must first determine the area of the rectangle (which equals 8 × 6 = 48) and multiply it by $1/2$. In this example, the area of the triangle is 0.5 × 48 = 24.

## THE PITFALLS OF GRAPHS

When used properly, graphs help us to understand complex data in a convenient and efficient manner. They may, however, be used to confuse or even misinform. Factions in political contests, advertisers of competing products, or rivals in lawsuits can take the same set of data, apply the standard rules of graph construction, and yet create graphs that support their own positions.

(*a*) The Area of a Rectangle

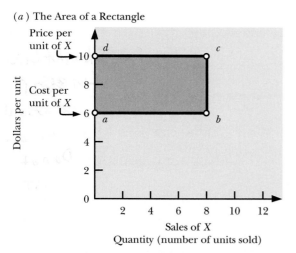

(*b*) The Area of a Triangle

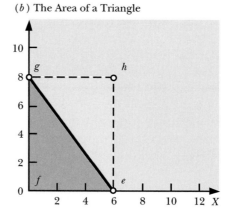

**FIGURE A8   Calculating Areas of Rectangles and Triangles**

The area of the rectangle *abcd* in panel *(a)* is calculated by multiplying its height (*ad,* or equivalently, *bc*) by its width (*ab,* or equivalently, *dc*). The height equals $4, and the width equals 8 units; therefore, the area of the rectangle equals $32. Thus, $32 is the amount of this firm's profits. The area of the triangle *efg* in panel *(b)* is one-half the area of the corresponding rectangle *efgh*. The area of the rectangle is $8 \times 6 = 48$. The area of the triangle *efg* is therefore $0.5 \times 48 = 24$.

This section warns us about three of the many pitfalls of using and interpreting graphs: (1) the ambiguity of slope, (2) growth and inflation distortion, and (3) unrepresentative data.

## THE AMBIGUITY OF SLOPE

The steepness of the rise or fall of a graphed curve can be an ambiguous guide to the strength of the relationship between the two variables. The slope is affected by the scale used to mark the axes, and the slope's numerical value depends upon the unit of measure.

In Figure A9, on pages 26 and 27, panel *(a)* provides an example of the *ambiguity of slope.* If you look carefully, you will see that both the left-hand and right-hand graphs plot exactly the same numbers: the annual sales of domestically produced cars for the years 1978 to 1986. In the left-hand graph, because each unit on the vertical axis represents 1 million cars, the decline in sales appears to be small. In the right-hand graph, because each unit now measures a half-million cars, the decline appears to be steep. The impression you would get of the magnitude of the decline in auto sales is affected by the choice of units on the vertical axis even though both graphs depict identical information.

## IMPROPER MEASUREMENT

A variable may give the appearance of measuring one thing while in reality it measures another. In economics, two common types of improper measurement are (1) inflation-distorted measures and (2) growth-distorted measures. These are encountered in *time-series graphs,* in which the horizontal *X* axis measures time (in months, quarters, years, decades, and so forth) and the vertical *Y* axis measures a second variable whose behavior is plotted over time.

Panel *(b)* of Figure A9 gives an example of the importance of inflation distortion by showing graphically the per capita national debt before and after adjustment for inflation.

> **Inflation distortion** is the measurement of the dollar value of a variable over time without adjustment for inflation over that period.

Per capita national debt (without adjustment for inflation) increased more than five times between 1950 and 1994. The orange line shows the per capita national debt *adjusted for inflation.* The rather surprising result is that, after the effects of inflation are removed, the per capita national debt actually decreased over the 30-year period from 1950 to 1980. From 1980 to 1994, per capita debt rose sharply after adjustment for inflation. If we look at the entire 44-year period, per capita debt in 1994 was only moderately above that of 1950 after adjustment for inflation.

Output, employment, and the like tend to rise over time even after adjustment for inflation. They rise because population grows, the labor force expands, the number of plants increases, and the technology of production improves. To look at the growth of one thing without taking into account this overall expansion can lead to growth distortion.

> **Growth distortion** is the measurement of changes in a variable over time that does not reflect the concurrent change in other relevant variables with which the variable should be compared, such as population size or the size of the economy.

People who want to demonstrate alarming increases in alcohol consumption or crime can point to increases in gallons of alcohol consumed or crimes reported without noting that population may be increasing at a rate that is as fast or faster. Panel (c) of Figure A9 shows the problem of growth distortion. The left-hand graph shows the inflation-adjusted output of the 100 largest manufacturing concerns. By looking at this graph, we might conclude that the dominance of American manufacturing by giant concerns has risen by a considerable amount. However, by looking at the output *share* of the 100 largest manufacturing companies (the right-hand chart), we find that the output of these companies has just been keeping up with the manufacturing output in general.

## UNREPRESENTATIVE DATA

A third pitfall of graphs is the use of *unrepresentative* or *incomplete data*. A graphed relationship may depend upon a time period or a choice of regions or countries. For example, panel (d) of Figure A9 shows how unemployment data can be manipulated. Suppose the agenda is to demonstrate that the U.S. unemployment rate was lower than the rates of other countries. The left-hand chart, comparing U.S. unemployment with that of three other industrialized countries, suggests that U.S. unemployment is lower. However, in the right-hand chart of nine industrial-

ized countries, the U.S. unemployment rate appears about in the middle.

We all use statistics. We see them in our newspaper; we hear them on news broadcasts. Because they can be abused, it is important that we know how to use them, and to interpret them, correctly.

## SUMMARY

1. Graphs are useful for presenting positive and negative relationships between two variables. A positive relationship exists between two variables if an increase in one is associated with an *increase* in the other; a negative relationship exists between two variables if an increase in one is associated with a *decrease* in the other. In a graphical relationship, one variable may be an independent variable and the other may be a dependent variable.

2. Graphs have certain advantages over tables: The relationship between the variables is easier to see, and graphs can accommodate large amounts of data more efficiently.

3. The slope of a straight-line relationship is the ratio of the rise in Y over the run in X. The slope of a curvilinear relationship at a particular point is the slope of a straight-line tangent to the curve at that point. When a curve changes slope from positive to negative as the X values increase, the value of Y reaches a *maximum* when the slope of the curve is zero; when a curve changes slope from negative to positive as the X values increase, the value of Y reaches a *minimum* when the slope of the curve is zero. Scatter diagrams are useful tools for examining data for positive or negative relationships between two variables.

4. The area of a rectangle is calculated by multiplying its height by its width. The area of a triangle is calculated by dividing the product of height times width by 2.

5. There are three pitfalls to be aware of when using graphs: (1) the choice of *units* and *scale* affects the apparent steepness or flatness of a curve, (2) the variables may be inflation-distorted or growth-distorted, and (3) omitted data or incomplete data may result in an erroneous interpretation of the relationship between two variables.

(*a*) Ambiguity of Slope: Sales of Domestically Produced Cars. 1978–1986

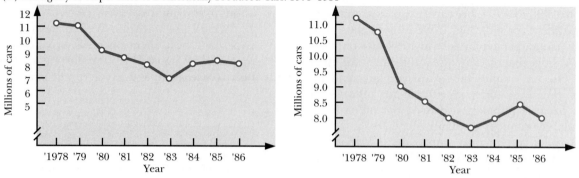

(*b*) Inflation-Distorted Measures: Per Capita Government Debt. 1950–1994

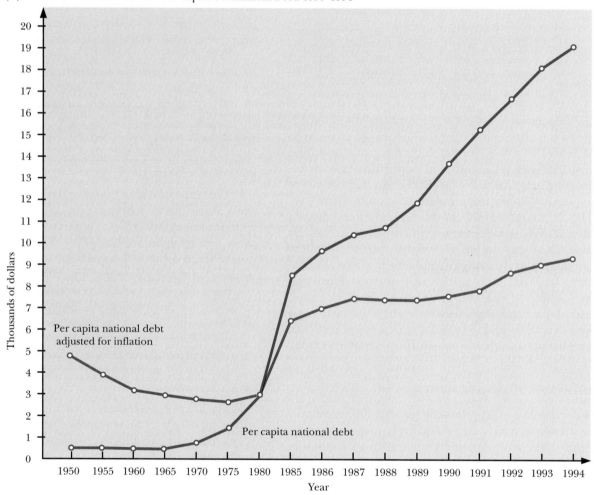

(*c*) Growth-Distorted Measures:
   Output of 100 Largest Manufacturing Companies

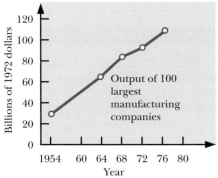

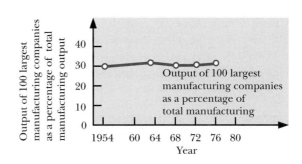

(*d*) Unrepresentative Sample:
   U.S. Employment in International Perspective in 1990

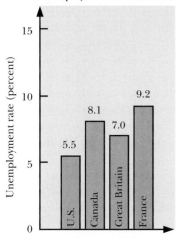

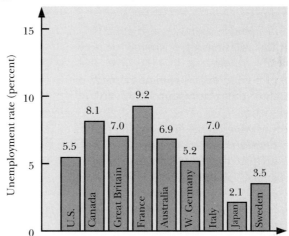

**FIGURE A9    Examples of Pitfalls in the Use of Graphs**

In panel *(a)*, the choice of units on the vertical axis determines the steepness of slope. Although both figures plot the same data, the graph on the right appears to yield a steeper decline in domestic auto sales. In panel *(b)*, the graph of per capita government debt (not adjusted for inflation) shows a steady rise in per capita debt. After the inflation distortion is removed (the orange line), we find that per capita debt actually declined over the 44-year period from 1950 to 1994. From 1980 to 1994, per capita debt rose prior to and after adjustment for inflation. In panel *(c)*, the left-hand graph shows that the output of the 100 largest manufacturing firms has been increasing since 1954 by substantial amounts. This graph, however, fails to reflect the overall growth of the economy, including the growth in total manufacturing. The right-hand graph adjusts for growth distortion and shows that the share of output of the 100 largest manufacturing firms has barely changed since 1954. In panel *(d)*, when the sample is limited to four high-unemployment countries (the left-hand graph), the U.S. unemployment rate does not appear to be high by international standards. When a broader and more representative sample is taken of nine countries (as shown in the right-hand graph), the U.S. unemployment rate appears to be average by international standards.

## KEY TERMS

positive (direct) relationship

negative (inverse) relationship

slope of a curve

slope of a straight line

tangent

slope of a curvilinear relationship

scatter diagram

inflation distortion

growth distortion

## QUESTIONS AND PROBLEMS

1. Graph the following data:

   X:   0   1   2   3
   Y:  10  20  30  40

   What is the slope?

2. As income falls, people spend less on cars. Is the graph of this relationship positively or negatively sloped?

3. As the price of a good falls, people buy more of it. Is the graph of the relationship positively or negatively sloped?

4. Answer the following questions using Figure A.
   a. What is the slope?
   b. What is area A (shaded in blue)?
   c. What is area B (shaded in pink)?

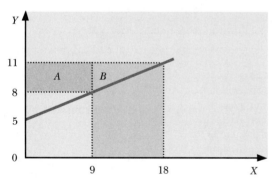

**FIGURE A**

5. The federal government spent $96 billion in 1970 and almost $1 trillion in 1995 on goods and services. What types of distortions affect this kind of comparison?

6. Prepare two scatter diagrams (A and B) from the data in Table A. In your opinion, do these diagrams reveal any positive or negative relationships?

| Table A | | | | |
|---|---|---|---|---|
| | Diagram A | | Diagram B | |
| | *Unemployment Rate* | *Inflation Rate* | *Interest Rate* | *Inflation Rate* |
| 1970 | 4.8 | 5.2 | 8.0 | 5.2 |
| 1971 | 5.8 | 4.8 | 7.4 | 4.8 |
| 1972 | 5.5 | 4.0 | 7.2 | 4.0 |
| 1973 | 4.8 | 6.0 | 7.4 | 6.0 |
| 1974 | 5.5 | 9.4 | 8.6 | 9.4 |
| 1975 | 8.3 | 9.1 | 8.8 | 9.1 |
| 1976 | 7.6 | 5.8 | 8.4 | 5.8 |
| 1977 | 6.9 | 6.3 | 8.0 | 6.3 |
| 1978 | 6.0 | 7.8 | 8.7 | 7.8 |
| 1979 | 5.8 | 9.5 | 9.6 | 9.5 |
| 1980 | 7.0 | 9.8 | 11.9 | 9.8 |
| 1981 | 7.5 | 9.3 | 14.2 | 9.3 |
| 1982 | 9.5 | 6.2 | 13.8 | 6.2 |
| 1983 | 9.5 | 4.1 | 12.0 | 4.1 |
| 1984 | 7.4 | 4.0 | 12.7 | 4.0 |
| 1985 | 7.1 | 3.6 | 11.4 | 3.6 |
| 1986 | 6.9 | 2.7 | 9.0 | 2.7 |
| 1987 | 6.1 | 3.4 | 9.4 | 3.4 |
| 1988 | 5.5 | 3.3 | 9.7 | 3.3 |
| 1989 | 5.3 | 4.1 | 9.3 | 4.1 |
| 1990 | 5.5 | 4.2 | 9.3 | 4.2 |
| 1991 | 6.7 | 2.9 | 8.8 | 2.9 |
| 1992 | 7.4 | 3.0 | 8.1 | 3.0 |
| 1993 | 6.8 | 3.0 | 7.2 | 3.0 |
| 1994 | 6.1 | 2.6 | 8.0 | 2.6 |

*Source: Economic Report of the President.*

7. During a 1996 U.S. presidential debate, suppose the incumbent faces an increase in unemployment last year of 240,000 workers, or approximately 0.1 percent. Which figure will the incumbent mention in his public statements? To which will his opponent refer?

8. Suppose thefts in a small town rise from a total of 1 to 2 cases in a given year. A sheriff running for reelection will refer to which change in her public speeches—the absolute change ("only" 1 additional break-in last year) or the percentage change (a 100 percent increase)?

# CHAPTER 2

# UNLIMITED WANTS, SCARCE RESOURCES

There is nothing more heartrending than parents appealing to the public for a heart or liver transplant for their dying child. Without such a transplant, the child has no chance of survival; yet the waiting must go on. This example starkly illustrates the fact of scarcity: More sick people need organ transplants than there are available organs. Given that there are not enough organs to go around, how should we allocate them among those who need them? Scarcity necessitates that we somehow decide who gets them and who does not. Should we sell them to the highest bidder, so that the children of the rich would get transplants while those of the poor do without? Should these decisions be made by medical boards on the basis of survival chances or some other criterion? Such a board might decide in favor of those who are more important in some sense, such as the governor of a populous state. In the United States, the first option is eliminated by the National Organ Transplant Act, which outlaws the buying and selling of vital organs. Other countries, however, do allow such buying and selling.

## THE ECONOMIC PROBLEM

Only a few of the scarce goods mean the difference between life and death, but all raise the same economic problem. There is not enough Black Sea caviar to satisfy all who want it; therefore, some system must be established to determine who will get it and who will not.

How shall we use our scarce resources? Because we cannot produce enough to meet our virtually unlimited wants, we must choose among alternatives, and we must make these hard choices in an orderly fashion. We must use our limited resources to decide *what* to produce, *how* to produce, and *for whom* to produce.

**What?**   Should we devote our limited resources to producing civilian or military goods, luxuries or necessities, goods for immediate consumption or goods that increase the wealth of society (capital goods)? Should small or large cars be produced? Should buses and subways be produced instead of cars? Should the military concentrate on strategic or conventional force?

**How?**   What combination of the factors of production will be used to produce the goods that we want? Will coal, petroleum, or nuclear power be used to produce electricity? Will bulldozers or workers with shovels build dams? Should automobile tires be made from natural or synthetic rubber? Should Diet Coke be sweetened with saccharin or another sugar substitute? Should tried-and-true methods of production be replaced by new technology?

**For Whom?**   Will society's output be divided equally or unequally? Will differences in wealth be allowed to pass from one generation to the next? What role will government play in determining allocation? Should government change the way the output is distributed?

The *for whom* question also addresses the future. How do we go about providing for the future—building the roads and power plants, and finding the technologies that will benefit future generations?

The imbalance between what people want and what they are able to acquire illustrates the most basic facts of economic life: the economic problems of *scarcity* and *choice*. The economy cannot fulfill everyone's wants; therefore, someone or something must decide which wants will be met. There will never be enough resources to meet everyone's wants.

The Defining Moment economists of Chapter 1 wrote about how we, as consumers, owners of businesses, or employees deal with scarcity and choice. As consumers, we are motivated to spend our money wisely, including saving some of it. As owners of businesses, we must combine resources wisely and produce products that customers will buy. We must do this to make a profit. As employees, we must find and keep jobs and put in a satisfactory performance. All these actions create the spontaneous interactions described by Adam Smith.

## THE DEFINITION OF ECONOMICS

As we know from Chapter 1, economics is the study of how people allocate their scarce resources among competing ends within a specific economic system, to produce, exchange, and consume goods and services. To understand this definition, however, we must also know the exact economic meanings of *scarcity, choice, resources, allocation, competing ends,* and *economic systems.*

### SCARCITY

If there were no scarcity, there would be no need to study economics. Scarcity is present wherever virtually unlimited wants are greater than available resources can supply. Scarcity does not imply that most of us are poor or that our basic needs are not being met. Scarcity exists simply because it is human nature for us to want more than we can have.

Along an Idaho highway stands an amusing sign: "Tumbleweeds are free, take one." Idaho tumbleweeds are free because the number of tumbleweeds available far exceeds the number people want. In Alaska, however, tumbleweeds may be such a rarity that the number people want exceeds the number available. Exotic orchids can be freely picked in some remote Hawaiian islands, but they command high prices elsewhere.

Congested airports like New York's LaGuardia, Washington's National, London's Heathrow, and Tokyo's Narita can handle only a limited number of takeoffs and landings per day. More planes wish to use these airports than can be accommodated. Committees allot takeoff and landing slots, and competing airlines intensely negotiate to obtain them. Landing slots are scarce at these major airports. At

## EXAMPLE 1
## THE PACIFIC YEW AND CANCER: SCARCITY, ALLOCATION, AND OPPORTUNITY COSTS

The Pacific yew, a shrublike tree native to the Pacific West Coast, was long regarded as a weed, which loggers would burn. So uninteresting was this tree that no one kept inventories on the number in existence. It was a free good . . . until recently.

Studies by the National Cancer Institute revealed that taxol, a substance that comes from the Pacific yew, is effective in treating advanced cases of ovarian and lung cancer. However, it takes six 100-year-old trees to treat a single cancer patient, and most of the mature Pacific yews have been destroyed; they can be found only in one of every 20 acres of Oregon's forests.

Until recent production of synthetic taxol, there was not enough natural taxol to treat all patients who needed it. The Pacific yew's scarcity meant that an allocation system had to be used to distribute the available taxol. The National Cancer Institute continues to determine which patients will receive the drug. However, as the production of synthetic taxol increases, its distribution will be handled by doctors' prescriptions, and payments will be made by insurance companies or by the patients themselves.

------------------------------------------------

*Source:* "Tree Yields a Cancer Treatment, but Ecological Costs May Be High," *New York Times,* May 13, 1991.

uncongested airports, on the other hand, landing slots are a free good because there are more slots than the airlines want.

> An item is a **scarce good** if the amount available is less than the amount people would want if it were given away free of charge.
>
> An item is a **free good** if the amount available is greater than the amount people want at a zero price.

These examples show that goods may be scarce even if they are free, and goods may be free at one time and place and scarce in another time and place. (See Example 1.)

## CHOICE

Choice and scarcity go together. We all face *trade-offs.* To have more of one thing, we must have less of another. An individual must choose between taking a job and pursuing a college education, between saving and consuming, between going to a movie and eating out. Businesses must decide where to purchase supplies, which products to offer on the market, how much labor to hire, and whether to build new plants. Nations must choose between spending more for defense or more for public education, they must decide whether to grant tax reductions to businesses or to individuals, and they must decide how much freedom their citizens should have to buy or sell goods in foreign countries.

## RESOURCES

> **Resources,** also known as **factors of production,** are the inputs used to produce goods and services.

Resources are divided into four categories: land, capital, labor, and entrepreneurship. They include the natural resources, the capital equipment (plants, machinery, and inventories), the human resources (workers with different skills, qualifications, and ambitions), and the skills to organize production that are used as *inputs* to produce scarce goods and services. These resources represent the economic wealth of society because they determine how much *output* the economy can produce. The limitation of resources is the fundamental source of scarcity.

**Land** is a catchall term that covers all of nature's bounty—minerals, forests, land, and water resources.

Land includes all natural resources—unimproved and unaltered—that contribute to production. Desert land that has been irrigated is not "land" by this definition because labor and capital are used to alter its natural condition. Other items such as air and water are in this category, as long as they are in their natural state.

**Capital** includes equipment, buildings, plants, and inventories created by the factors of production; that is, capital is used to produce goods both now and in the future.

When capital is used to produce output, it is not consumed immediately; it is consumed gradually in the process of time. An assembly plant can have a life of 40 years, a lathe a life of 10 years, and a computer a life of 5 years. In 1995, the total value of all U.S. capital was approximately $30 trillion.[1]

Capital means physical capital goods— computers, trucks, buildings, plants—rather than *financial capital*, which represents ownership claims to physical capital.

AT&T shareholders own financial capital, but their shares really represent ownership of AT&T's physical capital.

Economists also make a distinction between the stock of physical capital and additions to that stock. The stock of capital consists of all the capital (plants, equipment, inventories, and buildings) that exist at a given time. This stock grows when new plants come on line, new equipment is manufactured, and additions are made to inventories. Through *investment* we add to our stock of capital.

**Labor** is the combination of physical and mental talents that human beings contribute to production.

Labor resources consist of the people in the work force, with their various natural abilities, skills, education, and ambitions, who contribute to production in various ways. The loading-dock worker contributes muscle power; the computer engineer contributes mental abilities; the airline pilot contributes physical coordination and mental talents. In the United States today, the labor force consists of more than 120 million individuals.

Capital investment adds to the stock of human capital just as it adds to the stock of physical capital.

**Human capital** is the accumulation of past investments in schooling, training, and health that raise the productive capacity of people.

Investment in training and education raises the wealth of society because, like investment in physical capital, it increases production capacity.

**Entrepreneurs** organize the factors of production to produce output, seek out and exploit new business opportunities, and introduce new technologies and inventions. The entrepreneur takes the risk and bears the responsibility if the venture fails.

The Defining Moment economists all understood that the entrepreneur creates economic progress. The entrepreneur is the one who sees an opportunity that others do not see, is prepared to accept risk, raises the capital to take advantage of the opportunity, and then organizes production. Without the entrepreneur, there would have been no Industrial Revolution.

The entrepreneur accepts the vast responsibility of risk. The entrepreneur who makes a wrong decision loses money, assets, and reputation. If we do not allow appropriate rewards for the entrepreneur, such as profits from successful ventures, there is no reason for the entrepreneur to assume risk. The failure of the Soviet experiment to allow appropriate incentives for the entrepreneur contributed to its downfall. Von Mises and Hayek predicted that socialism would fail because of the lack of incentives for entrepreneurs.

## ALLOCATION

**Allocation** is the apportionment of scarce resources to specific productive uses or to particular persons or groups.

---

[1]OECD (Organization for Economic Cooperation and Development), Department of Economics and Statistics, *Flows and Stocks of Fixed Capital* (Paris: OECD, 1983), p. 9. Figures updated by the authors.

## EXAMPLE 2
## THE RUSSIAN
## MAFIA

Prior to the collapse of the Soviet Union at the end of 1991, the Soviet Union allocated resources through a strict administrative-command economy. Planners and ministers decided what, how, and for whom, and the Soviet communist party enforced discipline. The Soviet administrative-command economy collapsed before there was a new market economic system in place to allocate resources. The result, at least the first five years, has been chaos. Mafia groups determine who will be allowed to sell on street corners. Businesspersons with outstanding debts are eliminated by contract killers. More than 25 bankers have been assassinated for not supplying confidential bank records to the mafia. The Russian mafia has become so powerful that it now operates on a worldwide basis, operating drug and prostitution rings throughout the Middle East, Eastern Europe, and even the United States. Russian mafia have even been caught smuggling fuel oil in the northeastern states. It is hoped that as Russia's new market system is strengthened, order will be restored, and allocation can proceed in an orderly fashion.

*need police or military force to maintain order*

Consider what would happen without organized allocation. We would have to fight with one another for scarce resources. The timid would compete ineffectively; the elderly or weak would be left out. Such free-for-all allocation was common in ancient times, but it is rare in modern societies. It reappears when social order breaks down. Martial law must be declared and the national guards or U.N. peacekeepers must be brought in to prevent looting and violent competition for scarce goods during floods, natural disasters, and wars. With the breakdown of the Soviet Union, much resource allocation came to be handled by thugs and a "mafia." Societies cannot function unless the allocation problem is resolved in a satisfactory manner. (See Example 2.)

### COMPETING ENDS

Whatever allocation system is used, it must somehow allocate scarce resources among competing ends.

> **Competing ends** are the different purposes for which resources can be used.

Individuals compete for resources: Which families will have a greater claim on scarce resources? Who will be rich? Who will be poor? The private sector (individuals and businesses) and the government compete for resources. Even current and future consumption compete for resources: When scarce resources are invested in physical and human capital to produce more goods and services in the future, these same resources cannot be used in the present. Society must choose between competing national goals when allocating resources. What is most important: price stability, full employment, elimination of poverty, or economic growth? The Defining Moment economists disagreed about whether this competition for resources is harmful or helpful. Adam Smith believed that each person's pursuit of self-interest was good for society. Karl Marx thought that the pursuit of self-interest would lead to collapse.

### ECONOMIC SYSTEMS

Each society uses an economic system to solve allocation problems and to maintain order.

> An **economic system** is the property rights, resource-allocation arrangements, and incentives that a society uses to solve the economic problem.

Economic systems are differentiated according to the specific institutions for determining property rights and incentive systems.

The two major economic systems are capitalism and socialism, philosophies introduced in Chapter 1 as we discussed the Defining Moments in Economics. Capitalism is characterized by private ownership of the factors of production, market allocation of resources, and the use of economic incentives. Socialism is characterized by state ownership or control of the factors of production, the use of noneconomic as well as economic incentives, resource allocation by central state or government plan, and centralized decision making.

No actual economy fits exactly into one of these two molds. Economies combine private and public ownership, administrative and market allocation, economic and noneconomic incentives, and centralized and decentralized decision making. The economies of most nations reflect a mixed system that combines features of both capitalism and socialism. However, in most economies, the major traits of one particular economic system dominate. Experience has shown that capitalist countries have outperformed socialist countries in terms of living standards, innovation, and technological advances.

## PROPERTY RIGHTS

> **Property rights** are the rights of an owner to buy, sell, or use and exchange property (that is, goods, services, and assets).

In our capitalist economy, most of us take property rights for granted. We are accustomed to being able to freely buy and sell, or rent property and goods. In a socialist economy, property belongs to the state and its use and disposition are handled quite differently.

**Property Rights in a Capitalist System.** In a capitalist society, most property is owned by private individuals. Private owners of property are motivated by self-interest to obtain the best deal possible for themselves. The legal system protects private property from theft, damage, and unauthorized use, and defines who has property rights. With property rights, property owners will reap the benefits of using their property wisely and will suffer the consequences of wrong decisions concerning the use of

their property. Obviously, property owners will try to use their property for their own economic gain.

**Property Rights in a Socialist System.** In a socialist society, most property (except labor) is owned by the state, and the state has rights to use and exchange that property. Individual ownership of property has been limited to a few head of livestock, a private home in some circumstances, a private car, a TV, and so on. If state property is misused, the "state" suffers the consequences. In the former Soviet Union the saying was: "Everybody and thus nobody is the owner of property. Why should we care?"

## ALLOCATION ARRANGEMENTS

Resources can be allocated either by market or by plan. Capitalism uses market resource allocation. Socialism allocates resources by government decree.

**Market Allocation.** Market allocation allows buyers and sellers to exchange goods and services through markets. Owners of private property have the right to use the property to their best advantage and to sell the property at the best price possible. The actions of the owners of private property will be guided by markets.

> A **market** brings together buyers and sellers and in doing so determines prices.

The farmer looks at the prices of corn and soybeans to decide how much of each crop to plant; the owner of an oil refinery uses the prices of gasoline, fuel oils, and kerosene to determine how much of each petroleum product to refine. The private owner of labor (that is, the individual worker) looks at wage rates, job descriptions, and different occupations to determine where to work.

These decisions are made spontaneously and without government direction. They are guided by what Adam Smith described as the invisible hand. The invisible hand (described more fully in the next chapter) ensures that these individual actions will be coordinated.

**Allocation by Plan.** Under planned resource allocation, a central authority determines output targets and makes the basic investment decisions. Industrial ministries issue output targets to enterprises and tell them what materials to use. Although planners cannot decide exactly for whom the output is produced, they play a significant role in determining who will get the scarce automobiles, apartments, and vacations.

## INCENTIVES

Any economic system must provide incentives for people to work hard and to take economic risks.

### Incentives in a Capitalist System.
A capitalist system uses economic incentives to motivate employees. Higher salaries, bonuses, and stock options are rewards for tasks that are well done. Entrepreneurs are rewarded by having the value of their businesses grow. It is economic incentives—the opportunity to earn bonuses, profits, and higher salaries—that make us work hard and take business risks. Without economic incentives, there would be little reason for us to pursue our self-interest.

### Incentives in a Socialist System.
A socialist system relies more heavily on nonmaterial incentives, although socialist systems quickly learned that they could not rely on nonmaterial incentives alone. In socialist systems, there is greater emphasis on "working for the good of society." Medals, honorary positions, and other noneconomic incentives are used to motivate workers. However, there is in this system little to motivate the risk-takers. Under capitalism, the entrepreneur can earn substantial rewards for taking advantage of profit opportunities. Under socialism, the state must be the entrepreneur. Any rewards from successful entrepreneurship will go to the state—to everyone and hence to no one.

With the fall of socialism in the Soviet Union and Eastern Europe and the dramatic economic reforms of the Chinese economy, few countries of the world now follow the socialist ideal. The appeal of socialism, however, has been with us for almost two centuries, and even earlier. We have not seen the last of socialism. The major socialist experiment has failed. However, socialist principles still have appeal on the grounds that they can make capitalism more humane or even make capitalism work better. Whether socialism's appeal continues will depend on the solutions to the ongoing transitions of the former socialist economies.

## OPPORTUNITY COSTS

Whenever we make choices among competing ends, we must sacrifice valuable alternatives. The value of such a sacrifice is an opportunity cost.

> The **opportunity cost** of a particular action is the loss of the next-best alternative.

If you buy a new car, its opportunity cost might be a trip, an investment in the stock market, or enrollment in a university. To find the true cost of the car you must consider the cost of losing your next-best alternative. If the government increases health spending, the opportunity cost is the next-best alternative that had to be sacrificed (such as reduced spending on public education or a tax reduction).

Opportunity costs provide a shortcut method of differentiating free goods from scarce goods.

The Idaho tumbleweed had no opportunity cost. If one tumbleweed is taken, nobody has to go without a tumbleweed. A 9 A.M. landing slot at Heathrow Airport has a positive opportunity cost: If American Airlines gets it, British Airways must do without it.

The opportunity cost of an action can involve the sacrifice of time as well as goods. To gather the free tumbleweed, the traveler must sacrifice time (although the time cost may be very small). Attending a football game with a free ticket is not necessarily free. The three hours you spent at the game you could have devoted to alternative activities such as studying. If a major exam were scheduled for the next day, the opportunity cost of the game could be quite high.

Economic decisions are based on opportunity costs. In committing its resources to a particular action (such as producing cars), a business must consider the opportunities it forgoes by not using these resources for another activity (such as producing trucks). Before signing a contract to work for Ford Motors, workers must consider the other employment opportunities that they are passing up. People with savings must weigh the various alternatives before they commit their funds to a particular investment, such as certificates of deposit, stocks, or bonds.

> Every choice involved in the allocation of scarce resources has opportunity costs. Free goods have an opportunity cost of zero. Scarce goods have a positive opportunity cost.

## PRODUCTION POSSIBILITIES

Economists use the concept of the production possibilities frontier (PPF) to illustrate the function of scarcity, choice, and opportunity costs. The PPF reveals the economic choices open to society. An economy can produce any combination of outputs on or inside the PPF.

> The **production possibilities frontier (PPF)** shows the combinations of goods that can be produced when the factors of production are used to their full potential.

Suppose an economy produces only two types of goods: compact discs and wheat. Figure 1 shows the amounts of wheat and compact discs that this hypothetical economy can produce with its limited supply of factors of production and technical knowledge.

The economy has resources that can be used for either wheat or compact discs. Land may be better suited for wheat; compact discs may require more capital. If the economy chooses to be at point *a* on Figure 1, it will produce no compact discs and the maximum of 18 tons of wheat from the factors of production available. At point *f*, the economy produces no wheat and the maximum of 5000 compact discs. At point *c*, 2000 compact discs are produced; the maximum number of tons of wheat that can be produced is therefore 15. Each intermediate point on the PPF between *a* and *f* represents a different combination of wheat and compact discs that are produced using the same resources and technology.

Although this hypothetical economy is capable of producing output combinations *a* through *f*, it cannot produce output combination *g* (17 tons of wheat and 3000 compact discs) because *g* uses more resources than the economy has. It can, on the other hand, produce the output combination at point *h*, which is inside the frontier, because it requires fewer resources than the economy has.

### THE LAW OF INCREASING COSTS

When the economy is at point *a* in Figure 1, it is producing 18 tons of wheat and no compact discs. The opportunity cost of increasing the production of compact discs from zero to 1000 is the 1 ton of wheat that must be sacrificed in the move from *a* to *b*. The opportunity cost of 1000 more compact discs

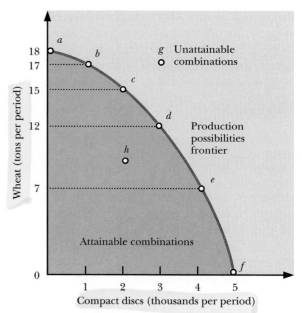

**FIGURE 1   The Production Possibilities Frontier (PPF)**

The PPF shows the combinations of outputs of two goods that can be produced from society's resources when these resources are used to their maximum potential. Point *a* shows that if 18 tons of wheat are produced, no compact disc production is possible. Point *f* shows that if no wheat is produced, a maximum of 5000 compact discs can be produced. Point *d* shows that if 3000 compact discs are produced, a maximum of 12 tons of wheat can be produced. Point *g* is beyond society's PPF. With its available resources, the economy cannot produce 17 tons of wheat and 3000 compact discs. Points like *h* inside the PPF represent an inefficient use of resources.

| Combination | Compact Discs (thousands) | Wheat (tons) | Opportunity Cost of Compact Discs (in tons of wheat) |
|---|---|---|---|
| a | 0 | 18 | 0 |
| b | 1 | 17 | 1 |
| c | 2 | 15 | 2 |
| d | 3 | 12 | 3 |
| e | 4 | 7 | 5 |
| f | 5 | 0 | 7 |

(moving from *b* to *c*) is 2 tons of wheat. The opportunity cost of the move from *e* to *f* is a much higher 7 tons of wheat. In other words, the opportunity cost of compact discs rises with the production of more compact discs. This tendency for opportunity costs to rise is the law of increasing costs.

> The **law of increasing costs** states that as more of a particular commodity is produced, its opportunity cost per unit increases.

The bowed-out shape of the PPF shows the law of increasing costs. Suppose the economy starts at *a,* producing only wheat and no compact discs. People now want compact discs, and the economy must suddenly increase its production of compact discs. Because the amount of resources available is not altered, the increased compact disc production must be at the expense of wheat production. The economy must move along its PPF in the direction of more compact disc production.

As compact disc production increases, the opportunity costs of a unit of compact disc production rises. At low levels of production, the opportunity cost of a unit of compact disc production is relatively low. Some factors of production are suited to producing both wheat and compact discs; they can be shifted from wheat to compact disc production without raising opportunity cost. As compact disc production increases further, resources suited to wheat production but ill-suited to compact disc production (experienced farmers make inexperienced workers in the disc industry) must be diverted into compact disc production. Ever-increasing amounts of these resources must be shifted from wheat production so that compact discs keep expanding at a constant rate. There will be a rise in the opportunity cost of a unit of compact disc production (the amount of wheat sacrificed), reflecting the law of increasing costs.

## THE LAW OF DIMINISHING RETURNS

Underlying the law of increasing costs is the law of diminishing returns. Wheat is produced by using land, labor, and tractors. Suppose a farm has a fixed amount of land (1000 acres) and a fixed amount of capital (10 tractors). Initially, 10 farm workers are employed. Each has 100 acres to farm and 1 tractor. If the number of farm workers increases to 20, each worker will have 50 acres to farm and 2 workers will have to share 1 tractor. If the number of farm workers increases to 1000, each worker will farm 1 acre and 100 workers will share each tractor. Obviously, workers will be less productive if each has only an

acre to farm and has to wait for 99 other workers to use the tractor. When labor is increased in equal increments, with the amount of land and tractors constant, the corresponding increases in wheat production will be smaller and smaller.

> The **law of diminishing returns** states that when the amount of one input is increased in equal increments, holding all other inputs constant, the result is ever-smaller increases in output.

The law of diminishing returns recognizes that output is produced by combinations of resources. Vegetables are produced by labor, farm machinery, and chemical fertilizers. Compact discs are produced by skilled labor, microelectronic equipment for stamping circuits, and managerial talent. The law of diminishing returns applies whenever one or more factors are fixed, and output must be expanded by an increase in the factors that can be varied. As more and more of the variable factors are used, there will eventually be too much of them relative to the fixed factors. Accordingly, the extra output produced by additional inputs of the variable factor will decline. (See Example 3.)

## EFFICIENCY

An economy operates on its production possibilities frontier only when it uses its resources with maximum efficiency.

In Figure 1, if the economy produces output combinations that lie on the PPF, the economy is efficient. When an economy is operating on its PPF, it cannot increase the production of one good without reducing the production of another good. If the economy operates at points inside the PPF, such as *h,* it is *inefficient* because more of one good could be produced without cutting back on the other good.

> **Efficiency** occurs when the economy is using its resources so well that producing more of one good results in less of other goods. No resources are being wasted.

If workers are unemployed or if machines stand idle, the economy is not operating on its PPF because available resources are not being employed. If these idle resources were used, more of one good could be

## EXAMPLE 3
## DIMINISHING RETURNS AND
## AMERICAN WINES

The finest wine-growing regions of the world are in France, Germany, Austria, and Italy. These wine-growing regions combine the right soil, temperature, and rainfall conditions to produce the grapes for vintage wines and champagne. With the exception of some parts of California, U.S. land is not as well suited to wine production as are these parts of Europe. Nevertheless, U.S. vintners produce more than 600 million gallons of wine for sale each year—some in states like Texas and Oklahoma, which are definitely not known for their wines.

The law of diminishing returns explains why not all wine is produced in Germany, France,

Austria, Italy, and California. As wine production expands in established regions, new acreage must be cultivated that is less suited to wine production. As diminishing returns set in for established wine-producing areas, the marginal acre of land devoted to wine production eventually becomes inferior to new wine-growing regions such as Texas and Oklahoma. Instead of being produced in Europe or California, new wine is produced in Texas or Oklahoma.

If our taste for wine continues to grow, eventually we will be buying wine from Kansas and Nebraska—an event explained by the law of diminishing returns.

produced without reducing the output of other goods. Misallocated resources are those that are not used to their best advantage. Except for the most unusual of circumstances—if a surgeon works as a ditch digger, if cotton is planted on Iowa corn land, or if supersonic jets are manufactured in Tahiti—resources are misallocated. If resource misallocations are removed, more of one good could be produced without sacrificing the production of other goods. How to best achieve economic efficiency is a core question of economics. Our resources are limited; we should make best use of them. Adam Smith argued that an economy will operate efficiently if people are allowed to pursue their self-interest. Von Mises argued that socialist economies cannot be efficient. In later chapters we shall consider the conditions required for economic efficiency.

## ECONOMIC GROWTH

When the fabled traveler Marco Polo reached China in 1275, he was amazed at the riches he saw. Compared to his native Venice, China was a much richer and more prosperous country. Although modern China has been growing rapidly, it is today a much poorer country than Italy. A modern Marco Polo would be surprised by China's poverty, not by its wealth.

This example shows the importance of economic growth. The economic reality is that Italy grew more rapidly than China over the long run. Italy participated in the Industrial Revolution (see the Defining Moments of Chapter 1); China did not. In fact, China may even have failed to grow for centuries after its power and prosperity had peaked. Economic growth is not synonymous with rising living standards. For living standards to rise, the output of goods and services must expand more rapidly than population.

**Economic growth** occurs when an economy expands its outputs of goods and services.

Prosperity can be achieved only if economic growth is sustained for a long period of time. Relatively few countries of the globe have experienced such growth, and prosperity remains limited to a small percentage of the world's population. Economic growth has not been steady even in the advanced industrialized countries. England, the country in which the Industrial Revolution began, experienced rapid growth in the eighteenth and nineteenth centuries but relatively slow growth in the twentieth century. Germany and Japan grew so rapidly after World War II that they were both called "economic miracles."

## ECONOMIC GROWTH AND THE PPF

Economic growth is an expansion of the PPF outward and to the right. The PPF can expand for two reasons: The capital and labor resources of the economy can expand, or the efficiency of the use of those resources can improve. The first type of growth is extensive growth; the second type is intensive growth. *Extensive economic growth* is the result of the expansion of the economy's resources. *Intensive economic growth* is the result of the more efficient use of available resources. Improvements in technology, better management techniques, and the creation of better legal and economic institutions—as first witnessed during the Industrial Revolution—are all sources of intensive economic growth.

Economic growth can be influenced by policy. Policies promote economic growth when they encourage the formation of capital, the improvement of science and technology, and the development of new business techniques. Some economic growth is not controllable. There can be periods of slow technological progress or there can be unanticipated breakthrough inventions—such as the steam engine or the computer—that change the economy forever.

**Capital Accumulation.** Deciding where to locate on the PPF represents a choice between capital goods and consumer goods. As you know, capital goods are the equipment, plants, and inventories added to society's stock of capital. These goods satisfy wants in the future. Consumer goods are food, clothing, medicine, and transportation that satisfy consumer wants in the present.

The choice between capital goods and consumer goods is shown in Figure 2. In this figure, the economy with the PPF labeled XX must choose among the combinations of consumer goods and capital goods located on XX. If b is selected over a, fewer wants are satisfied today, but additions to the stock of capital are greater. More capital today means more production in the future. The society that selects b will therefore experience a greater outward shift of the PPF and will be able to satisfy more wants in the future.

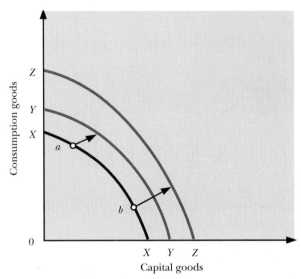

**FIGURE 2    The Effect of Increasing the Stock of Capital on the PPF**

The initial PPF is curve XX. If the economy chooses point a, allocating most resources to the production of consumption goods and few to the production of new capital goods, the PPF in the future will shift out to curve YY. But if the economy chooses point b, with comparatively little consumption and comparatively high production of new capital goods, the future PPF will shift out further to ZZ.

If a society chooses a, the PPF expands from XX now to YY in the future. If it chooses b, the PPF expands more: from XX now to ZZ in the future. The economy will be able to satisfy more wants at ZZ than at YY.

There are limits to the rule that less consumption today means more consumption tomorrow. If all resources were devoted to capital goods, the labor force would starve. If too large a share of resources is put into capital goods, worker incentives might be low and efficiency might be reduced.

**Shifts in the PPF.** Figure 2 shows extensive growth due to capital accumulation. Increases in labor or land or discoveries of natural resources also shift the PPF outward. Intensive growth occurs when society learns how to get more output from the same inputs. Technological progress also shifts the PPF outward. Technological progress and increases in land, labor, and capital have different effects on the PPF. Technical progress may affect only one industry—whereas labor, capital, and land can be used across all industries. Figure 3 illustrates a technical

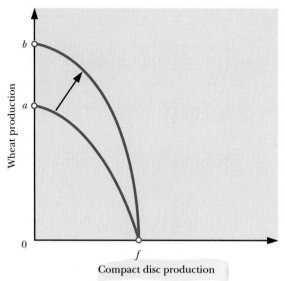

**FIGURE 3   Technical Progress in Wheat Production**

If a higher-yielding strain of wheat is discovered, a larger quantity can be produced with the same resources. Since this increase in wheat production will not influence compact disc production, the PPF will rotate from *af* to *bf*.

advance in wheat production without a corresponding change in the productivity of compact disc production. Accordingly, the PPF shifts from *af* to *bf*. Here the PPF shifts upward but not to the right.

## MICRO AND MACRO

Economics concerns scarcity, choice, allocation, economic systems, and growth. We can study these core issues from either a micro or a macro perspective.

### MICROECONOMICS

*Individuals + Firms*

Economics is divided into two main branches called *microeconomics* and *macroeconomics*. These branches deal with economic decision making from different vantage points.

> **Microeconomics** studies the economic decision making of firms and individuals in a market setting; it is the study of individual decision making and its impact on resource allocation.

Microeconomics focuses on the individual participants in the economy: the producers, workers,

employers, and consumers. In everyday economic life, things are bought and sold. People decide where and how many hours to work. Managers decide what to produce and how to organize production. These activities result in *transactions* that take place in markets where buyers and sellers come together. Individuals are motivated to do the best they can for themselves in these transactions, with the limited resources at their disposal.

Microeconomics considers how businesses operate under different competitive conditions and how the combined actions of buyers and sellers determine prices in specific markets.

Microeconomics assumes that the individual economic actors weigh the costs and benefits of their actions. Households spend their limited income to gain maximum satisfaction; they decide where to work and how much to work in the same fashion. Businesses choose the type and quantity of products and the manner of production in order to obtain maximum profits.

In effect, microeconomics studies the spontaneous interactions of Adam Smith's invisible hand—how individuals and businesses come together in markets. Because microeconomics studies the results of our weighing costs and benefits, it has expanded into areas outside the traditional realm of economics. Economists use microeconomics to deal with environmental problems, to explain how voters and public officials make their political decisions, and to analyze marriage, divorce, fertility, crime, and suicide. Even the court system uses microeconomic analysis to determine legal settlements and compensation for personal injuries.

*national economy ~~take~~ as a whole*

### MACROECONOMICS

> **Macroeconomics** is the study of the economy as a whole, rather than individual markets, consumers, and producers. It concerns the *general* price level (rather than individual prices), the national employment rate, government spending, government deficits, trade deficits, interest rates, and the nation's money supply.

Macroeconomics uses measures called *aggregates,* which add together (or aggregate) individual microeconomic components. These aggregates include gross domestic product (GDP), the consumer price index (CPI), the unemployment rate, and the government surplus and deficit. Macroeconomics studies relationships between aggregate measures, such as the relationship between inflation and interest rates, the effects of government deficits on prices and interest rates, and the relationship between money and inflation.

## THE COMING TOGETHER OF MICRO AND MACRO

When modern economics was born more than 200 years ago with the publication of Adam Smith's *Wealth of Nations,* there was no distinction between micro- and macroeconomics. Early economic thinkers believed that it was necessary only to study consumers and producers in the marketplace to understand the economy as a whole. After all, the macroeconomy is nothing more than the sum total of individual decisions. These early pioneers did not realize that generalizing from the part to the whole can lead to mistakes (the fallacy of composition we discussed in Chapter 1).

Macroeconomics was not formally born until the late 1930s, with the publication of Keynes's *General Theory.* Specifically, macroeconomics was formed to explain the Great Depression. Why should an economy suddenly produce much less output and supply many fewer jobs?

Modern economics reemphasizes the importance of understanding individual behavior as a basis for understanding the behavior of the economy as a whole. Macroeconomists study how individuals behave to explain how the economy as a whole behaves.

In the next chapter, we shall consider how the price system solves the economic problem of *what, how,* and *for whom;* how it facilitates specialization and exchange; and how it provides for the future.

zero price. The ultimate source of scarcity is the limited supply of resources. The resources that are factors of production are land, capital, labor, and entrepreneurship. Because scarcity exists, some system of allocating goods among those who want them is necessary.

4. The opportunity cost of any choice is the next-best alternative that was sacrificed to make the choice. Scarce goods have a positive opportunity cost; free goods have an opportunity cost of zero.

5. The production possibilities frontier (PPF) shows the combinations of goods that an economy is able to produce from its limited resources when these resources are used to their maximum potential and for a given state of technical knowledge. If societies are efficient, they will operate on the production possibilities frontier. If they are inefficient, they will operate inside the PPF.

6. The law of increasing costs says that as more of one commodity is produced at the expense of others, its opportunity cost will increase. According to the law of diminishing returns, when the amount of one input is increased in equal increments, if all other inputs are constant, successive increases in output become smaller.

7. Economic growth occurs because the factors of production expand (extensive growth), or because technological progress raises productivity (intensive growth). The choice of consumer goods over capital goods is a choice between meeting wants now and meeting them in the future.

8. Economics is divided into microeconomics, the study of the behavior of markets, consumers, and producers; and macroeconomics, the study of the economy as a whole.

## SUMMARY

1. Wants are unlimited; there will never be enough resources to meet unlimited wants.

2. The economic problem is what to produce, how to produce, and for whom. All economies must resolve this economic problem.

3. Economics is the study of how scarce resources are allocated among competing ends by an economic system. A good is *scarce* if the amount available is less than the amount people would want if it were given away free. A good is *free* if the amount people want is less than the amount available at

## KEY TERMS

scarce good
free good
resource
factors of production
land
capital
labor
human capital
entrepreneur
allocation
competing ends
economic system

property rights
market
opportunity cost
production possibilities frontier (PPF)
law of increasing costs
law of diminishing returns
efficiency
economic growth
microeconomics
macroeconomics

## QUESTIONS AND PROBLEMS

1. In the early nineteenth century, land in the western United States was given away free to settlers. Was this land a free good or a scarce good, according to the economic definition? Explain your answer. Explain why land in the United States is no longer given away free.

2. The town of Hatfield charges each resident $75 per year for water. The town is running out of water.
   a. What is the opportunity cost of water to the individual customer?
   b. What is the opportunity cost of water to the town?
   c. Is water scarce?
   d. How might prices be used to solve the water shortage?

3. "Desert sand will always be a free good. More is available than people could conceivably want." Evaluate this statement.

4. A local millionaire buys 1000 tickets to the Super Bowl and gives them away to 1000 Boy Scouts. Are these tickets free goods? Why or why not?

5. In the American West, irrigation has turned desert land into farmland. Does this example demonstrate that nature's free gifts are not fixed in supply?

6. Determine in which factor-of-production category each of the following items belongs—land, capital, or labor.
   a. A new office building
   b. A deposit of coal
   c. The inventory of auto supplies in an auto supply store
   d. Land reclaimed from the sea in Holland
   e. A trained mechanic
   f. An automated computer system

7. Using Figure 1 as your model, draw two production possibilities curves for compact disc production as opposed to wheat production. In the first, show what would happen if the technology of compact disc production improved while the technology of wheat production remained the same. In the second, show what would happen if the technologies of compact disc production and wheat production improved simultaneously.

8. Consider an economy that has the choice of producing either bricks or bread. There are exactly 100 workers available. Each worker can produce one brick or one loaf of bread. There is no law of diminishing returns. What is the economy's production possibilities curve?

9. By purchasing a new color TV set, I pass up the opportunity to buy a personal computer, to take a vacation trip, to paint my home, or to earn interest on the money paid for the TV. What is the opportunity cost of the color TV? How would I determine the opportunity cost?

10. How does the production possibilities curve illustrate the choices available to an economy?

11. If widgets were given away free, people would want to have 5 million per month. When would widgets be free goods and when would they be scarce goods? Under what conditions would the opportunity cost of widgets to society be positive?

12. Using the data in Table A, explain whether these data illustrate the law of diminishing returns. Show how much extra corn can be produced by different numbers of farmhands, each working an 8-hour day.

| Table A | |
|---|---|
| Number of Farmhands | Output of Corn (thousands of bushels) |
| 1 | 50 |
| 2 | 100 |
| 3 | 140 |
| 4 | 160 |
| 5 | 170 |

13. The data in Table B describe a production possibilities frontier (PPF) for a hypothetical economy.
    a. Graph the PPF.
    b. Does the PPF have the expected shape?
    c. Calculate the opportunity cost of guns in terms of butter. Calculate the opportunity cost of butter in terms of guns. Do your results illustrate the law of increasing costs?
    d. If this economy produces 700 guns and 3 tons of butter, will it solve the *how* problem efficiently?
    e. If at some later date this economy produces 700 guns and 12 tons of butter, what do you conclude has happened?

| Table B | |
| --- | --- |
| *Hundreds of Guns* | *Tons of Butter* |
| 8 | 0 |
| 7 | 4 |
| 5 | 10 |
| 3 | 14 |
| 1 | 16 |
| 0 | 16.25 |

14. Which of the following topics falls under macroeconomics? Which under microeconomics? Explain your answer in each case.
    a. The price of fish
    b. The interest rate
    c. Employment in the computer industry
    d. The general price level
    e. The national unemployment rate
    f. Unemployment in Oklahoma
    g. The number of new homes built in the United States

# CHAPTER 3

# THE PRICE SYSTEM AND THE ECONOMIC PROBLEM

In 1973, the Organization of Petroleum Exporting Countries (OPEC) discovered that it could push up the price of oil by restricting its supply to world markets. Panic set in as the price of oil rose from $2 per barrel in the early 1970s to $35 per barrel in 1981. In the United States, the price of a gallon of regular gasoline rose from 36 cents in 1972 to $1.31 in 1981. Pundits warned that the Western world might not survive this crisis. It was said that we could not do without gas to run our cars or without fuel oils to run our industry. We did indeed survive—through the workings of the price system. The dramatic rise in gas prices told us that we must economize on gas. No government pronouncement was required. Higher prices simply invited us to use less. The gas price increase caused us automatically to drive less and to buy cars with better gas mileage. In 1973, the average passenger car consumed 736 gallons per year. By 1981, this figure had dropped to 557 gallons. Despite a growing population and more cars on the road, total gas consumption by cars fell from 78 billion gallons in 1973 to 72 billion in 1981.

The price system "solved" the energy crisis. Spontaneous energy conservation on the part of consumers reduced worldwide purchases of gas and fuel oil; new oil producers, such as Mexico, entered the market in response to high prices of crude oil and increased its supply. By 1983, consumer conservation and new production forced OPEC to reduce crude oil prices for the first time. Thereafter oil prices spiraled downward to slightly over $10 per barrel in the 1990s.

Nobel laureate Friedrich Hayek (one of the Defining Moment economists of Chapter 1) described this phenomenon as follows:

> The marvel is that in a case like that of a scarcity of one raw material, without an order being issued, without more than perhaps a handful of people knowing the cause, tens of thousands of people whose identity could not be ascertained by months of investigation, are made to use the material or its products more sparingly; i.e., they move in the right direction.[1]

---

[1]Friedrich Hayek, "The Use of Knowledge in Society," *American Economic Review* 35, 4 (September 1945): 519–530.

## EXAMPLE 1
### PENCILS: THE PRICE SYSTEM AT WORK

It is remarkable that not a single person knows how to make a pencil from start to finish. If one thinks about what it takes to make a pencil—the trees that produce the wood, the saws that fell the trees, the steel that makes the saws, the engines that run the saws, the hemp that makes the ropes that are necessary to tie down the logs, the training of loggers, the mining of graphite in Sri Lanka for the lead, the mining of zinc and copper for making the bit of metal holding the eraser, and the rape seed oil from the Dutch East Indies that is used in the eraser—it is clear that no one single person knows how to make a pencil. The decisions of the thousands upon thousands of people involved are coordinated through the price system without centralized direction. That all these activities have made it possible for you to go to the bookstore and buy a pencil for, say, a mere 25 cents, boggles the mind.

------------------------------------------------

*Source:* Milton and Rose Friedman, *Free To Choose* (Orlando, FL: Harcourt, Brace, Jovanovich, 1980).

## THE PRICE SYSTEM AS A COORDINATING MECHANISM

Our economy is made up of millions of consumers, millions of resource owners, and hundreds of thousands of enterprises. Each participant makes economic decisions to promote his or her self-interest. How are the decisions of all these people and businesses coordinated? What prevents the economy from collapsing if these decisions clash? Is it necessary to have someone or something in charge? The Defining Moment economists focused on these questions.

### THE INVISIBLE HAND

Let us consider in detail how Adam Smith (whom we met in Chapter 1) answered these questions. He described how market allocation solves the economic problem efficiently without conscious direction:

> Every individual endeavors to employ his capital so that its produce may be of greatest value. He generally neither intends to promote the public interest, nor knows how much he is promoting it. He intends only his own security, only his own gain. And he is led by an *invisible hand* to promote an end which was no part of his intention. **By pursuing his own interest he frequently promotes that of society more effectively than** when he really intends to promote it. [Emphasis added.][2]

Smith's "invisible hand" works through the price system.

The **price system** coordinates economic decisions by allowing resource owners to trade freely, buying and selling at whatever relative prices emerge in the marketplace.

Our experience—which includes the rise and fall of socialism, a Defining Moment in Chapter 1—shows that the invisible hand usually works better than the "visible hand" of the state. The invisible hand works through the price system, which provides necessary information for informed decision making.

## RELATIVE PRICES AND MONEY PRICES

How do we know whether prices are high or low? A relative price indicates how one price stands in relation to other prices. It is quite different from a money price.

---

[2]Adam Smith, *The Wealth of Nations,* ed., Edwin Cannan (New York: Modern Library, 1937), p. 423.

(*a*) Money Prices

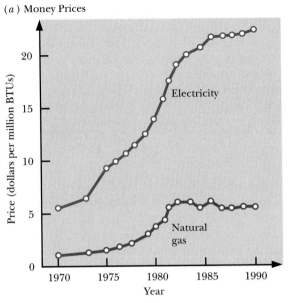

(*b*) Relative Prices

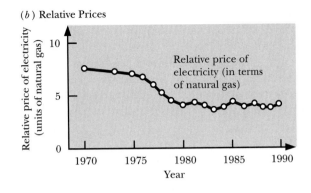

**FIGURE 1   Money Prices and Relative Prices of Natural Gas and Electricity**

The price of both electricity and natural gas rose from 1970 to 1995. Electricity prices tripled, but gas prices rose sevenfold. The price of electricity in terms of natural gas actually fell. *Source:* Department of Energy, Energy Information Administration.

A **relative price** is a price expressed in terms of other goods.

A **money price** is a price expressed in monetary units (such as dollars, francs, etc.).

If a textbook sells for 40 dollars and compact disc (CD) player for 120 dollars, three textbooks is the relative price of a CD player, or one-third of a CD player is the relative price of a textbook.

Money prices are most meaningful when they are compared to prices of *related* goods. For example, it makes sense to compare the price of electricity to that of natural gas because commercial and residential users make choices between natural gas and electricity. Should we heat and air condition our homes with electricity or natural gas? Should manufacturers use electricity or natural gas as fuel? The money prices of natural gas and electricity, shown in Figure 1a, rose substantially over the last 25 years. However, the relative price of electricity (the price of electricity divided by the price of natural gas) fell during this same period (see Figure 1b). In 1970, a BTU of electricity cost 7.37 times as much as a BTU of natural gas. By 1995, a BTU of electricity cost less than 4 times a BTU of natural gas.

The money price of a commodity can rise while its relative price falls. The money price can fall while its relative price rises. Money prices and relative prices need not move together.

Relative prices play a prominent role in resolving the economic problem of *what, how,* and *for whom* raised in the previous chapter. Money prices do not. Relative prices signal to buyers and sellers what goods are cheap or expensive. *Buying and selling decisions are based on relative prices.* If the relative price of one good rises, buyers substitute other goods whose relative prices are lower. For example, the lowering of the relative price of electricity will encourage consumers to use electricity rather than natural gas.

The emphasis on relative prices does not mean that money prices are unimportant. Money prices—or the price level—are important in macroeconomics. It is here that the concept of inflation plays an important role.

**Inflation** is a general increase in money prices.

Elections are won or lost on the basis of inflation; the living standards of people on fixed incomes can be damaged by inflation. Inflation drives up interest rates. But even in the case of inflation, money prices are not considered in isolation. Instead, the level of money prices today is compared with the level of money prices yesterday. Ultimately, this is also a form of relative price.

> In microeconomics there is greater interest in relative prices than in money prices. In macroeconomics, there is greater interest in the level of money prices than in relative prices.

## THE PRINCIPLE OF SUBSTITUTION

Virtually no good is fully protected from the competition of substitutes. Aluminum competes with steel, coal with oil, electricity with natural gas, labor with machines, movies with video rentals, one brand of toothpaste with another, and so on. The only goods for which there are no substitutes are minimal quantities of water, salt, or food and certain life-saving medications, such as insulin. Relative prices guide resource allocation through the principle of substitution.

> The **principle of substitution** states that practically no good is irreplaceable. Users are able to substitute one product for another when relative prices change.

To say that there is a substitute for every good does not mean that there is an *equally good* substitute for every good. One mouthwash may be a close substitute for another; a television show may be a good substitute for a movie; rental apartments may be good substitutes for private homes. However, carrier pigeons are a poor substitute for telephone service; public transportation is a poor substitute for the private car in sprawling cities; steel is a poor substitute for aluminum in the production of jet aircraft.

Increases in relative prices (like the increase in gas prices discussed in the Chapter Insight) provide signals for consumers to consider possible substitutes. When the relative price of coffee increases, people consume more tea. When the relative price of beef rises, people buy more poultry and fish. There is

no single recipe for producing a cake, a bushel of wheat, a car, recreation, comfort, or happiness. Increases in relative prices motivate consumers and firms to search out substitutes. Changes in relative prices signal producers to look for substitutes. When the relative price of crude oil rises, utilities switch from oil to coal. Airlines buy more fuel-efficient aircraft when the relative price of jet fuel rises.

## EQUILIBRIUM

Households and business firms make buying and selling decisions on the basis of relative prices. The family decides how to spend its income; the worker decides where and how much to work; the factory manager decides what inputs to use and what outputs to produce. Insofar as these decisions are made individually, what guarantees that there will be enough steel, bananas, foreign cars, domestic help, steel workers, copper, and lumber for homes? What ensures that there will not be too much of one good and too little of another? How will Adam Smith's invisible hand prevent shortage or surplus?

Let's consider an example: If automobile producers decide to produce more cars than buyers want to buy *at the price asked by the automobile producers*, there will be many unsold cars. Since dealers must pay their bills and earn a living, they must sell cars at lower prices. As the money price of cars falls, the relative price tends to fall, and customers begin to substitute automobiles for vacations, home computers, or remodeled kitchens. The decline in the relative price of automobiles signals automobile manufacturers to produce fewer cars. Eventually, a balance between the number of cars people are prepared to buy and the number offered for sale will be struck, and the corresponding price is called an equilibrium price.

> The **equilibrium price** is that price at which the amount of the good people are prepared to buy (demand) equals the amount offered for sale (supply).

The economy itself requires enormous information about how to produce different goods, product qualities, product prices, worker efficiencies, and so forth. The price system allows us to make decisions by knowing only the relative prices that are important to us. Each participant will specialize in information that is personally relevant. We buy more of a good that has become relatively cheap; we economize on goods that have become relatively expensive. We need not know why the good has become cheap or expensive.

Just as checks and balances in an ecological system prevent one species of plant or animal from overrunning an entire area and, in the end, extinguishing itself, relative prices provide the checks and balances in the economic system. If one product is in oversupply, its relative price will fall; more will be purchased and less will be offered for sale. If one product is in short supply, its relative price will rise; less will be purchased and more will be offered for sale.

## THE CIRCULAR FLOW OF ECONOMIC ACTIVITY

Let us consider all of the activity that must be coordinated with the invisible hand. Economic activity is circular. Consumers buy goods with the incomes

they earn by supplying land, capital, and labor to the business firms that produce the goods they buy. The circular-flow diagram shows how output and input decisions involving millions of consumers, hundreds of thousands of producers, and millions of resource owners fit together.

> The **circular-flow diagram** summarizes the flow of goods and services from producers to households and the flow of the factors of production from households to business firms.

As the circular-flow diagram in Figure 2 illustrates, the flows from households to firms and from firms to households occur in two markets: the goods market and the factors market. The *goods market* is the market in which buyers and sellers come together to buy and sell goods and services. The *factors market* is the market in which buyers and sellers come together to buy and sell land, labor, and capital.

The circular-flow diagram consists of two circles. The outer circle shows the *physical flows* of

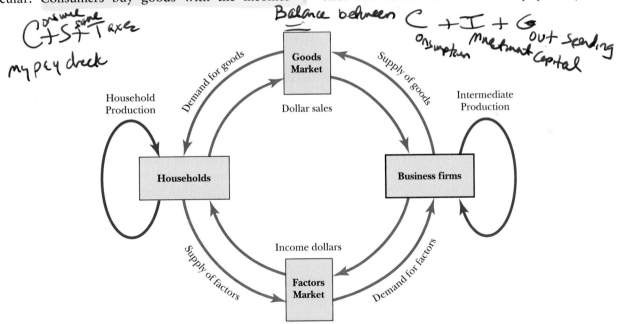

**FIGURE 2  The Circular Flow of Economic Activity**

Economic activity is circular. The outside circle describes the flow of physical goods and services and productive factors through the system: business furnishes goods to households, who furnish land, labor, and capital to business. The inside circle describes the flow of dollars: households provide dollar sales to business, whose costs become incomes to households. These two circles flow in opposite directions. The circular-flow diagram shows that flows of intermediate goods remain entirely within the business sector and do not enter the circular flow. It also shows that because household-production services are produced and consumed within the family, they do not enter the circular flow.

goods and services and productive factors. The inner circle shows the *flows of money* expenditures on goods and services and on productive factors. The physical flows and money flows go in opposite directions. When households buy goods and services, goods flow to the households, but the sales receipts flow to businesses. When workers supply labor to business firms, productive factors flow to businesses, but the wage income flows to households.

For every physical flow in the economy, there is a corresponding financial transaction. To obtain goods, the consumer must pay for them. When firms sell products, they receive sales revenues. When businesses hire labor or rent land, they must pay for it. When individuals supply labor, they receive wages.

Two types of goods and services are omitted from the circular flow diagram. *Intermediate goods* (discussed later in the chapter) are goods that businesses sell to other businesses. For example, the steel industry supplies steel to the automobile industry, which produces the automobiles that enter the circular flow. The other goods and services that are not included in the circular flow diagram are those produced and used within the household, such as the cooking, cleaning, transportation, and other services provided by one family member to another.

The amount of activity in the circular flow of economic activity is staggering. There are more than 20 million business firms in the U.S. economy, interacting with 80 million households. Business firms employ 120 million persons. The value of capital resources in the circular flow is more than $30 trillion. The annual value of goods and services that flow from business firms (including government) to households is over $8 trillion. We cannot even count the millions of distinct goods and services the economy produces. The field of economics called *national income accounting* explains how economists measure the total flow of goods and services from businesses to households and the flow of factor resources from households to businesses.

## SPECIALIZATION, PRODUCTIVITY, AND EXCHANGE

Adam Smith's invisible hand does far more than simply balance supply and demand. As the economic problem suggests, the price system needs to determine *how* we produce output and how we provide for the future. In a market economy, the price system encourages specialization, which raises efficiency and allows economies to produce ever-larger outputs from their available inputs.

> **Specialization** is the tendency of participants in the economy (people, businesses, and countries) to focus their activity on tasks to which they are particularly suited.
>
> **Exchange** complements specialization by permitting individuals to trade the goods in which they specialize for those that others produce.

Exchange is everywhere. We exchange our specialized labor services for money; then we exchange money for a huge variety of goods. The United States exchanges its wheat for video cassettes made in Japan. Within a business, different departments exchange skills in engineering, purchasing, and marketing to produce and sell the firm's output. A travel agency exchanges its ability to market group tours for discounted airline tickets. A foreign-car manufacturer agrees to supply fuel-efficient engines to an American-auto manufacturer in return for marketing and repair outlets.

## PRODUCTIVITY AND EXCHANGE

The best way to understand productivity and exchange is to consider a simple example. Suppose a sailor is stranded on an uninhabited island—a modern Robinson Crusoe. The sailor has to decide whether to make fish nets or fish hooks or whether to sleep or break coconuts. The sailor would not be specialized; he would be a jack-of-all-trades. Solving the *for whom* problem is easy—everything he produces is for himself—and the problems of *what* and *how* are solved without having to know relative prices, being concerned about ownership, or using markets.

In the modern economy, a jack-of-all-trades is rare; a specialist is commonplace. A typical household consumes thousands of articles, yet one member of the household may specialize in aligning suspension components on an automobile production line. Everyone in our economy (except hermits) is dependent on the efforts of others. We produce one or two things; we consume many things.

Specialization gives rise to exchange. If people consumed only those things that they produced, there would be no trade and there would be no need for money. Money, trade, and specialization are all characteristics of a modern economy.

Specialization raises productivity. Increased productivity was defined in Chapter 2 as the production of additional output from the same amount of resources. As Adam Smith noted in *The Wealth of Nations,* specialization is a basic source of productivity advances. Specialization raises productivity in two ways. First, specialization allows resources, which have different characteristics, to be allocated to their best use. Land, capital, and people come in different varieties. Some machines can move large quantities of earth; others can perform precision metal work. Some land is moist; other land is dry. Some people are agile seven-footers; others are small and slow. These differences offer opportunities for specialization.

Second, by concentrating certain resources in specific tasks, we can produce large amounts of output at a lower cost per unit of output. Even if all people in an automobile manufacturing plant had identical skills, it would still be better to have one person

install the engine, another bolt down the engine, and so on in an assembly line. Individuals who focus on one task can learn their jobs better and don't waste time switching from job to job. The per unit costs of production are frequently lower at large volumes of output. (See Example 2.)

David Ricardo's law of comparative advantage (mentioned in Chapter 1) shows how the invisible hand of prices promotes specialization and productivity advances.

> The **law of comparative advantage** is the principle that people should engage in those activities for which their advantages over others are the largest or their disadvantages are the smallest.

Suppose Sally is twice as good at making hats as Harry, but three times better at making shoes. Sally can make $100 a day in hats and $120 a day in shoes. Harry can make $50 a day in hats and $40 a day in shoes. Clearly, Sally will specialize in shoe production even though she has an advantage over

## EXAMPLE 2
## SPECIALIZATION AND THE PIN FACTORY

Economic science seeks to explain the facts of economic life. Perhaps the most basic question is why some people and countries are rich while others are poor. One of Adam Smith's key insights was that people and countries that effectively specialize will be wealthy.

In his classic *Wealth of Nations,* Adam Smith used the pin factory to illustrate the benefits of specialization. In his day (the late nineteenth century), pins were manufactured through a large number of separate operations. Then (and now) pin-making consisted of (1) drawing wire, (2) straightening, (3) pointing, (4) twisting, (5) cutting heads and heading the wire, (6) tinning and whitening, and (7) papering and packaging. The major advantages of specialization were achieved by separating pin production into

many operations: One set of workers would do the straightening, another the pointing, another the twisting, another the cutting of heads, and so on.

According to Adam Smith's calculations, the average specialized worker could produce 5000 pins a day (the number of pins per day divided by the number of workers in the pin factory). If each person worked alone, only a few pins would be produced by each worker. The specialized worker, in this case, could produce almost 1000 times more wealth than the unspecialized worker.

------------------------------------------------

*Source:* Clifford Pratten, "The Manufacture of Pins," *Journal of Economic Literature* 18, 1 (March 1980): 93–96.

## EXAMPLE 3
## WHY HAKEEM PLAYS BASKETBALL AND STEFFI PLAYS TENNIS

Both Hakeem Olajuwon, the National Basketball Association's Most Valuable Player in 1994, and Steffi Graf, the German tennis star, are dominant athletes in their respective sports. They are such superb athletes that they may be better athletes in other sports than any of their fellow country persons. Olajuwon may be the best soccer goalie in his native Nigeria, and Graf may be the best middle distance female runner in Germany.

Comparative advantage and opportunity costs ensure that both athletes are employed in the sports in which their comparative advantage is greatest. Olajuwon may be 10 percent better than the next-best Nigerian soccer goalie, but he is 50 times better than the next-best Nigerian basketball player. Graf may be 5 percent faster than the next-best German female middle distance runner but she is 50 percent better than the next-best German female tennis player. Accordingly, Olajuwon and Graf earn more in basketball and tennis than they do in any other activity.

Harry in hat production. Harry will specialize in hat production even though he is at a disadvantage in hat production compared to Sally. What matters is not whether you can make more or less than somebody else in some activity, but you can make more in that activity than in some other activity. Sally has a comparative advantage in shoe production because she can do better in that employment than in hats; and Harry has a comparative advantage in hats because he can make more in hats than in shoes.

Thus, a mediocre computer programmer could possibly be the best clerk in a local supermarket. The clerks in the local supermarket may not be able to stock shelves and work a cash register as well as the programmer, but they have a comparative advantage in that occupation. An attorney may be the fastest typist in town, yet the attorney is better off preparing deeds than typing them. (See Example 3.)

The law of comparative advantage applies to people as well as countries. The fact that you cannot make more than another person is irrelevant; what matters is the best that you can do. The same applies to countries. A country's resources are best committed to those activities for which its advantages are the largest or its disadvantages are the smallest. It does not matter that one country has low wages and another country high wages. What matters is how the resources are best used within a country. We will see in the chapter on international trade that every country has goods that it can profitably export—even if the country had the highest overall wage level or the lowest overall productivity level.

## MONEY AND EXCHANGE

Money is essential in an economy where people are specialized because it reduces the cost of transacting with others.

> **Money** is anything that is widely accepted in exchange for goods and services.

Money can take many forms. In simple societies, fishhooks, sharks' teeth, beads, or cows have been used as money. In modern societies, money is issued and regulated by government, and money may (gold coins) or may not (paper money) have an intrinsic value of its own.

Money enables us to trade with anyone else, unlike a barter system in which we must trade with someone who wants what we specialize in.

> **Barter** is a system of exchange where products are traded for other products rather than for money.

In barter, for example, it would be necessary for barefoot bakers to exchange goods with hungry shoemakers. A successful barter deal requires that the two (or more) traders have matching wants. Money is essential precisely because such coincidences of wants are rare.

If one form of money were abolished by law, another form would replace it. The costs of barter are so high that societies must have something to serve as money. If we did not have something that served as money, we would have to barter for everything. Barter would be so inefficient that the economy might actually not survive under such a condition.

The Industrial Revolution (a Defining Moment of Chapter 1) was accompanied by the development of banking. Banking created new forms of money called checks, which facilitated the growth of modern industry and trade. The development of international banking prompted the rapid rise of globalization after World War II. International banking made it possible for the money of one country to be electronically converted and to be instantaneously transferred to a bank or other firm in another country thousands of miles away.

## PROVISION FOR THE FUTURE

The invisible hand uses the price system to balance supply and demand and to promote specialization and exchange. But can the invisible hand provide for the future? Our high living standards today are the result of past investment in physical and human capital. What is there in the price system that encourages us to make such investments?

The stock of capital goods is one generation's legacy to the next. The interstate highway system will be enjoyed not only by the generation that built it, but by future generations. The ultimate benefits of space exploration will accrue to generations far in the future. As future chapters will show, we must save in order to invest. We are able to invest only as much as we are able to save. We save by not spending all our income. We sacrifice consumption today to save; we would not be willing to make this sacrifice unless saving allowed us to increase our consumption in the future. The sacrifice of current consumption is the cost of saving. The benefit of saving is that interest will be earned on savings.

> The **interest rate** is the price of credit that is paid to savers who supply credit.

If the interest rate is 10 percent per annum, $1000 of saving today will give us $1100 a year hence. A dollar sacrificed (saved) today yields more than a dollar tomorrow. The higher the interest rate, the greater the inducement to save.

The interest rate not only acts as an inducement to save, it also signals to businesses whether they should borrow for investment. Like any other price, the interest rate provides a *balance*—in this case, balancing the amount we are willing to save with the amount businesses want to borrow for investment. If the interest rate is low, businesses will want to invest because they find it cheap to add to their capital stock. However, at a low interest rate few are willing to save. The reverse is true at high interest rates: Few businesses will want to invest, but households will be quite willing to save.

> The interest rate balances the saving offered by households with the investment businesses wish to undertake. The price system uses interest rates to solve the problem of allocating resources between present and future consumption.

## CAN WE COMPLETELY TRUST THE INVISIBLE HAND?

More than 200 years ago, Adam Smith argued that it is better to trust the invisible hand of markets than the visible hand of government direction. This chapter showed how the price system balances the actions of millions of consumers and thousands of producers; how it encourages specialization and exchange; and how it solves the difficult problem of providing for the future. The price system has enormous strengths, but it has weaknesses as well. There is no guarantee that resource allocation through the price system will provide for the poor in a satisfying way. The price system may not handle pollution and environmental damage as well as it should. Adam Smith himself warned about the dangers of monopoly. These are some of the weaknesses that cause us at times to allow government to substitute its visible hand for the invisible hand. We shall see in later chapters (especially Chapter 5) that it is very difficult

## 54 PART I INTRODUCTION

to devise proper government policy to substitute for the invisible hand and that well-intended policies often have unintended consequences.

In this chapter we have considered how scarce resources are allocated by the price system. Equilibrium prices are like an invisible hand that coordinates the decisions of many different persons. In the next chapter we shall use the tools of supply and demand to learn more about the price system.

## SUMMARY

1. The "invisible hand" of Adam Smith describes how a capitalist system allows individuals to pursue their self-interest and yet provides an orderly, efficient economic system. If too much of a product is produced, its relative price will fall. If too little of a product is produced, its relative price will rise. The balance of supply and demand is called an equilibrium.

2. Relative prices guide the economic decisions of individuals and businesses. They signal to buyers and sellers what substitutions to make.

3. The principle of substitution states that users substitute one good for another in response to changes in relative prices.

4. The circular-flow diagram summarizes the flows of goods and services from producers to households and the flows of factors of production from households to producers. Transactions take place in goods markets and in factors markets.

5. Specialization increases productivity. It occurs because of the differences among people, land, and capital and because of the economies of large-scale production. The law of comparative advantage states that the factors of production will specialize in those activities where their advantages are greatest or their disadvantages are smallest.

6. The price system provides for the future by allowing people to compare costs now with benefits that will accrue in the future. The interest rate balances the amount of saving offered with the amount of investment businesses wish to undertake.

7. The price system may not solve in a satisfactory manner the problems of income distribution, public goods, and monopoly.

## KEY TERMS

price system
relative price
money price
inflation
interest rate
principle of substitution
equilibrium price
circular-flow diagram
specialization
exchange
law of comparative advantage
money
barter

## QUESTIONS AND PROBLEMS

1. "The principle of substitution states that virtually all goods have substitutes, but we all know that there are no substitutes for telephone service." Comment on this statement.
2. Explain why you can usually find the items you want at a grocery store without having ordered the goods in advance.
3. In 1963 an average car cost about $2000; in 1995 an average car cost about $20,000. But on the average, what cost $100 in 1963 cost about $375 in 1995. Did the relative price of a car increase or fall compared to most goods and services?
4. Not every product has a good substitute. Which of the following are good substitutes for one another? Which are poor substitutes? Explain the general principles you used in coming up with your answers.
   a. Coffee and tea
   b. Compact Chevrolets and compact Fords
   c. Cars and city buses
   d. Electricity and natural gas
   e. Telephones and express mail
5. Computer manufacturers want to sell more personal computers than customers want to buy at the current price. Explain why the equilibrium price could be higher or lower than the current price.
6. You own a one-carat diamond ring that you no longer like. In fact, you would like to have a new color television set. How would you get the television set in a barter economy? Discuss the efficiency of exchange in a barter economy versus a monetary economy.
7. "Specialization takes place only when people are different. If all people were identical, there would be no specialization." Evaluate this statement.

8. Assume that while shopping, you see long lines of people waiting to buy bread while fresh meat is spoiling in the butcher shops. What does this tell you about prevailing prices? What is your prediction about what will happen to the relative price of bread?

9. Bill can prepare 50 hamburgers per hour or wait on 25 tables per hour. Mike can prepare 20 hamburgers per hour or wait on 15 tables per hour. If Bill and Mike open a hamburger stand, who should be the cook? Who should be the waiter? Would Bill do both?

10. Why would private industry find it difficult to organize national defense? How would private industry charge each citizen for national defense?

11. In an hour's time, Jill can lay 100 tiles or can mortar 50 bricks. Tom can lay 10 tiles or mortar 20 bricks in an hour's time. Each tile laid or brick mortared pays $1. According to the law of comparative advantage, in which activity should each specialize? Explain why it is that Jill should not do both activities and let Tom rest simply because Jill is better at both activities.

12. Why in the circular-flow diagram do physical quantities move in one direction and dollar quantities move in another direction?

13. Which of the following transactions would enter the circular flow and which would not?
    a. U.S. Steel sells steel to General Motors.
    b. General Motors sells a car to Jones.
    c. Jones takes a job from General Motors and receives $100 in wages.
    d. Jones has his suit cleaned at the local dry cleaner and pays $5.
    e. Jones washes his dress shirt.

14. Explain how an increase in the interest rate alters society's provision for the future.

15. What is the opportunity cost of saving? What is the benefit?

16. Explain why, when you go to a store, there is not a surplus or a shortage of 25¢ pencils.

# CHAPTER 4

# DEMAND AND SUPPLY

Adam Smith extolled the virtues of the invisible hand of markets. Ludwig von Mises and Friedrich Hayek talked about the "miracle" of the price system—how the price system provides the right amount of information for the economy to solve incredibly complex problems.

This chapter introduces demand and supply, the most simple but powerful tools of economic analysis. In skilled hands, these tools can be used to solve subtle and complex problems.

Today's airline passengers know little of the frustration of passengers, who, until the 1980s, could be involuntarily bumped from flights for which they had valid tickets. Prior to the deregulation of the airline industry in the 1980s, airlines unceremoniously bumped passengers on overbooked flights according to the order in which they arrived at the airport.

This practice meant that passengers who urgently needed to be on that flight might have had to wait for the next flight, whereas passengers who cared little whether they were on that particular flight or the next one out might have been accommodated. Involuntary bumping caused airlines considerable grief in terms of dissatisfied customers and caused enormous inconvenience for bumped passengers.

Economists, using the tools of demand and supply, came up with a simple solution: Today, if a flight is overbooked, the airline offers bonuses—free tickets, cash, or some other inducement—to those who will voluntarily take the next flight out. First, a low bonus is offered, and, if insufficient, it is raised as the flight time approaches until the number of remaining passengers equals the number of available seats. In effect, a price is paid to reduce the number of passengers to the seating capacity of the plane. When the plane takes off, no one is dissatisfied. Those left behind have been offered enough of an inducement to cause them voluntarily to agree to stay behind.

## WHAT IS A MARKET?

To understand demand and supply, we shall focus on how a *single market* works.

> A **market** is an established arrangement that brings buyers and sellers together to exchange particular goods or services.

Markets comprise demanders (or buyers) who are motivated by different factors (or goals), and suppliers (or sellers). The prices discussed in the previous chapter are determined in markets. In each market, buyers and sellers base their decisions on price.

### TYPES OF MARKETS

Video rental stores; gas stations; farmers' markets; real estate firms; the New York Stock Exchange (where stocks are bought and sold); auctions of works of art; gold markets in London, Frankfurt, and Zurich; labor exchanges; university placement offices; and thousands of other specialized arrangements are all markets. The New York Stock Exchange uses modern telecommunications to bring together the buyers and sellers of corporate stock. The university placement office brings together university graduates and potential employers. The video rental store brings together the buyers and sellers of videos.

Some markets are local, others are national or international. Residential real estate is usually bought and sold in local markets; houses cannot be shipped from one place to another. The growing globalization of the world economy—a Defining Moment of Economics—has made more and more markets international in character. United States companies hire marketing specialists from Europe and Asia; U.S. consulting firms sell their services to companies in Latin American and Africa. The New York Stock Exchange, the various gold exchanges, and the Chicago commodity exchanges bring together buyers and sellers from around the world. (See Example 1.)

### MARKETS AND COMPETITION

In economics, we distinguish among different types of markets according to the amount of competition. Some markets comprise numerous buyers and sellers, buying and selling products that are identical or nearly identical. An example is agricultural markets, such as the markets for wheat or corn, in which there are literally hundreds of thousands of suppliers.

## EXAMPLE 1
## L.A.'S GRAND
## CENTRAL MARKET

Los Angeles's Grand Central Market lies in the geographic intersection of the four-county metropolitan area. On weekdays, an average of 20,000 customers shop in the market. On weekends, the number swells to 50,000. The Grand Central Market pulsates with activity as people look for deals and hard-to-find goods, such as pork-tongue enchiladas, skullcaps, slippery elm, 20 brands of pepper, and squaw vine. Grand Central carries parts of animals not sold at supermarkets—lambs' heads and beef lips, eyes, ears, and snouts. The booths are owned and operated by people of 17 different nationalities, many of them trading in four languages. Says one frequent customer, "If it's food and it's not here, you can't buy it anywhere."

A market is anything that brings buyers and sellers together. Los Angeles's Grand Central Market brings together in a convenient fashion buyers and sellers of exotic foods and other unusual products. The L.A. market is a living manifestation of Adam Smith's invisible hand.

------------------------------------------------

*Source:* "L.A.'s Grand Central Market," *The Christian Science Monitor*, November 23, 1990.

These markets are highly competitive. Other markets are dominated by one or several suppliers; here, buyers have fewer choices. Examples are the local natural gas or electricity company. Most markets are somewhere in between highly competitive markets and markets with little competition. There are a number of suppliers; they offer products that are differentiated from one supplier to the next.

Virtually no market is spared competition. All goods have substitutes: The question is whether the substitute is a good one or not. Natural gas substitutes for electricity, wheat for corn, and Chevrolets for Mazdas. The amount of competition determines how buyers and sellers in that market behave. Later chapters will analyze four distinct market models.

This chapter describes how buyers and sellers behave in a highly competitive market—which a later chapter will identify as a perfectly competitive market. In this market, there are a large number of buyers and sellers, buying and selling a homogeneous product, such as wheat, corn, frozen orange juice concentrate, or pork bellies.

## DEMAND

We know that we all want more than the economy can provide. But the goods and services that we *want*—those that we would take if they were given away free—are quite different from the goods and services we demand.

> The **demand** for a good or service is the amount people are prepared to buy under specific circumstances such as the product's price.

What we are actually prepared to buy depends on price and various other factors we shall discuss in this chapter.

### THE LAW OF DEMAND

The most important factor affecting the demand for a good or service is its price. We buy more if the price falls; we buy less if the price rises, holding other factors constant (*ceteris paribus*). This is a fundamental law of economics, the law of demand.

> The **law of demand** states that there is a negative (or inverse) relationship between the

*P. 18*

price of a good or service and the quantity demanded, if other factors are constant.

Demand for a good or service also depends on other factors, like the prices of related goods (for example, the demand for tea depends on the price of coffee), income, and tastes. We shall consider these other factors later. For the moment, we want to concentrate on the price of the good or service itself.

The main reason that the law of demand holds true is that we tend to substitute other, cheaper goods or services as the price of any good or service goes up. If the price of airline tickets rises, we cut back on less essential flying, and we drive rather than fly. If the price of movie tickets rises, more people will rent videos or watch TV, or movie addicts will cut back on the number of visits to the movie theater. The quantity demanded is negatively related to the price of a good or service. (See Example 2.)

> The **quantity demanded** is the amount of a good or service consumers are prepared to buy at a given price (during a specified time period), if other factors are held constant.

When a price rises enough, some of us may even stop buying altogether. As the price rises, the number of actual buyers may fall as some of us switch entirely to other goods.

As the price of a good goes up, we also buy less because we are poorer. If you buy a new car every year for $15,000 (after trade-in), and the price rises to $19,000, you would need an extra $4000 per year of income to maintain your old standard of living. The $4000 increase in the price of the car is like a cut in income of $4000.

The law of demand shows why the concept of *need* is not very useful in economics. A "need" implies that we cannot do without something. But when the price changes, the law of demand says that the quantity demanded will change. For example, "need" for a daily shower would likely disappear if it costs $50 to take one!

The negative (or inverse) relationship between quantity demanded and price is called the *demand curve* or the *demand schedule*. To avoid confusion, we shall refer to the *demand schedule* when the relationship is in tabular form and the *demand curve* when the relationship is in graphical form.

## EXAMPLE 2
## M&Ms AND THE LAW OF DEMAND

The law of demand states that the quantity demanded will increase as the price is lowered, as long as other factors that affect demand do not change. In the real world, factors that affect the demand for a particular product change frequently. Tastes change, income rises, and prices of substitutes and complements change. The makers of M&M candy conducted an experiment that illustrates the law of demand. Over a 12-month test period, the price of M&Ms was held constant in 150 selected stores, and the content weight of the candy was increased.

When the price is held constant and the weight increased, the price per ounce is lowered. In the stores where the price per ounce was dropped, sales rose by 20 to 30 percent almost overnight, according to the director of sales development for M&Ms. As predicted by the law of demand, a reduction in price causes the quantity demanded to rise, *ceteris paribus*.

------------------------------------------------

*Source:* "Why Do Hot Dogs Come in Packs of 10 and Buns in 8s and 12s?" *Wall Street Journal,* September 21, 1984.

## THE DEMAND CURVE

Figure 1 shows both a demand curve and a demand schedule for corn. Buyers in the marketplace demand 20 million bushels of corn per month at the price of $5 per bushel. At a lower price—say, $4 per bushel—the quantity demanded is higher. In this case, the quantity demanded at the lower price of $4 is 25 million bushels. By continuing to decrease the price, buyers are persuaded to purchase more and more corn. Thus, at the price of $1, quantity demanded is 50 million bushels.

Note that in graphs showing demand curves, price is placed on the vertical axis and quantity demanded on the horizontal axis. When price is $5, quantity demanded is 20 million bushels (point *a*). Point *b* corresponds to a price of $4 and a quantity of 25 million bushels. When price falls from $5 to $4, quantity demanded rises by 5 million bushels from 20 million to 25 million bushels.

The demand curve *D* drawn through points *a* through *e* shows how quantity demanded responds to changes in price. Along *D,* price and quantity are *negatively* related; that is, the curve is downward sloping.

The demand curve shows that as larger quantities of corn are put on the market, lower prices are required to clear the market (to sell that quantity). The price needed to sell 25 million bushels of corn is

$4 per bushel. To sell the larger quantity of 30 million bushels, a lower price of $3 is required.

In this book we shall encounter two types of demand curves: the demand curves of individuals (households) and the market demand curve.

> The **market demand curve** is the demand of all buyers in the market for a particular product.

The demand curve for corn in Figure 1 refers to all buyers in the corn market, an international market that brings together all buyers of corn both at home and abroad. The demand curve for Hawaiian real estate brings together all buyers of Hawaiian real estate; the demand curve for Microsoft's "Windows 95" brings together all buyers from around the globe.

## SHIFTS IN THE DEMAND CURVE

The demand curve shows what would happen to the quantity demanded if *only the good's own price* were to change. The good's own price is not the only determinant of demand; other factors can play an important role. The factors that can shift the demand curve include (1) the prices of related goods, (2) consumer income, (3) consumer preferences, (4) the number of potential buyers, and (5) expectations.

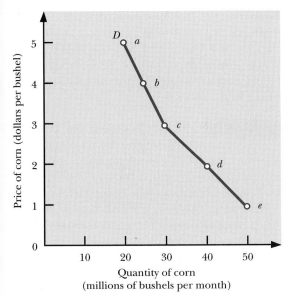

**FIGURE 1   The Demand Curve for Corn**

This figure shows how the quantity of corn demanded responds to the prices of corn, holding all other factors constant. At *a,* when the price of corn is $5 per bushel, the quantity demanded is 20 million bushels per month. At *e,* when the price of corn is $1, the quantity demanded is 50 million bushels. The downward-sloping demand curve *(D)* shows the amounts of corn consumers are willing to buy at different prices.

| Demand Schedule for Corn | |
| --- | --- |
| *Price* <br> *(dollars per bushel)* | *Quantity Demanded* <br> *(millions of bushels* <br> *per month)* |
| *a*        5 | 20 |
| *b*        4 | 25 |
| *c*        3 | 30 |
| *d*        2 | 40 |
| *e*        1 | 50 |

**The Prices of Related Goods.**   Goods can be related to each other as either substitutes or complements.

> Two goods are **substitutes** if the demand for one rises when the price of the other rises (or if the demand for one falls when the price of the other falls).

Examples of substitutes are coffee and tea, two brands of soft drinks, stocks and bonds, Macintosh

and IBM-compatible computers, pay TV and movie rentals, foreign and domestic cars, natural gas and electricity. Some goods are very close substitutes (two different brands of fluoride toothpaste), and others are very distant substitutes (cars and supersonic aircraft).

> Two goods are **complements** if the demand for one falls when the price of the other increases.

Examples of complements are automobiles and gasoline, food and drink, dress shirts and neckties, airline tickets and automobile rentals. Complements tend to be used jointly (for example, automobiles plus gasoline equals transportation). An increase in the price of one of the goods effectively increases the price of the joint product of the two goods.

**Income.**   It is easy to understand how income influences demand. As our incomes rise, we spend more on normal goods and services. But as income increases, we also spend less on inferior goods.

> A **normal good** is one for which demand increases when income increases, holding all prices constant. An **inferior good** is one for which demand falls as income increases, holding all prices constant.

For most of us, lard, day-old bread, and second-hand clothing are examples of inferior goods. For some people, inferior goods might be hamburgers, margarine, bus rides, or black-and-white TV sets. But most goods—from automobiles to water—are normal goods.

**Preferences.**   *Preferences* are what people like and dislike without regard to budgetary considerations. You may *prefer* to live in your own ten-room home but can afford only a two-bedroom apartment. You may prefer a Mercedes-Benz but can afford only a used Chevrolet. Preferences plus budgetary considerations (price and income) determine demand. As preferences change, demand changes. If we learn that oat bran muffins lower weight and cholesterol, we will increase our demand for oat bran muffins. Business firms try to influence preferences by advertising.

The goal of advertising is to shift the demand curve for the advertised product to the right.

### The Number of Potential Buyers.

If more buyers enter a market, the market demand will rise. The number of buyers in a market can increase for many reasons. Relaxed immigration laws or a baby boom may lead to a larger population. The migration of people from one region to another changes the number of buyers in each region. The relaxation of trade barriers between two countries may increase the number of foreign buyers. When Japanese restrictions on imports of U.S. rice were removed, the number of buyers of U.S. rice should have increased. Lowering the legal drinking age would increase the number of buyers of beer.

### Expectations.

If we believe that the price of coffee will rise substantially in the future, we may decide to stock up on coffee today. During periods of rising prices, we often start buying up durable goods, such as cars and refrigerators. The mere expectation of an increase in a good's price can induce us to buy more

of it. Similarly, we can postpone the purchase of things that are expected to get cheaper. During the 1990s, as personal computers have become cheaper and cheaper, some buyers have deliberately postponed their purchases on the expectation of even lower prices in the future.

### Shifting Demand.

Figure 2 shows the demand curve for dress shirts. This curve, $D$, is based on a $10 price for neckties (a complement), a $20 price for sport shirts (a substitute), a certain income, given preferences, and a fixed number of buyers.

An increase in the price of neckties (a complement for dress shirts) from $10 to $15 shifts the entire demand curve for dress shirts to the left from $D$ to $D'$ in panel (a). Dress shirts are usually worn with neckties. If neckties increase in price, consumers buy fewer of them and substitute less formal shirts for shirts that require neckties. As a result, the demand for dress shirts decreases, shifting left.

An increase in the price of sport shirts (a substitute for dress shirts) from $20 to $30 shifts the demand curve for dress shirts to the right of $D$ to $D''$ in

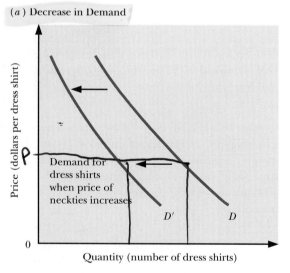

(a) Decrease in Demand

Price (dollars per dress shirt)

Demand for dress shirts when price of neckties increases

$D'$    $D$

0

Quantity (number of dress shirts)

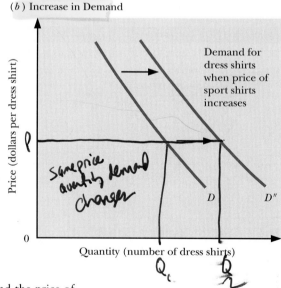

(b) Increase in Demand

Price (dollars per dress shirt)

Demand for dress shirts when price of sport shirts increases

Same price
quantity demand
changes

$D$    $D''$

0

Quantity (number of dress shirts)

$Q_1$    $Q_2$

**FIGURE 2    Shifts in the Demand Curve: Changes in Demand**

The demand curve for dress shirts depends on the price of neckties and the price of sport shirts. When the price of neckties is $10 and the price of sport shirts is $20, the demand curve for dress shirts is $D$. In panel (a), if the price of neckties rises to $15, holding the price of sport shirts at $20, then at each price for dress shirts the demand falls. The demand curve shifts to the left from $D$ to $D'$. In panel (b), keeping the price of neckties at $10 and raising the price of sport shirts to $30 will raise the demand for dress shirts. The demand curve will shift rightward to $D''$. A rightward shift depicts an increase in demand, and a leftward shift illustrates a decrease in demand.

panel *(b)*. When the price of sport shirts increases, consumers substitute dress shirts for sport shirts. As a result of this substitution, the demand for dress shirts increases, shifting right.

If consumer income increases and if dress shirts are a normal good, demand will increase (*D* will shift to the right). If preferences change and dress shirts fall out of fashion, demand will decrease (*D* will shift to the left). If buyers expect prices of dress shirts to rise substantially in the future, demand today will increase.

## SUPPLY

Supply depends on a variety of factors, just as demand depends on a number of factors. One of these factors is price.

> The **supply** of a good or service is the amount that firms are prepared to sell under specified circumstances.
>
> The **quantity supplied** of a good or service is the amount offered for sale at a given price, holding other factors constant.

Unlike demand, for which there is a *law* of demand, there is no analogous law of supply that says that firms will offer *more* of the product for sale at a *higher* price. Nevertheless, there are strong reasons why, under normal circumstances, firms *will* offer more of the product if its price rises.

Chapter 2 introduced opportunity cost and the law of diminishing returns. You will recall that opportunity costs are the value of the next-best alternative sacrificed in taking an action, and that the law of diminishing returns states that the resource cost per unit of output rises as more and more output is produced (when there are fixed factors). Both of these facts explain why, under normal circumstances, firms supply more output at a higher price.

Supply decisions are based upon a simple rule: Under normal circumstances, a product will not be supplied at a price below its opportunity cost. It doesn't make sense to sell something for $3 that has an opportunity cost of $5.

Let's use a simple example of a farm. The farmer can measure opportunity costs of producing corn in different ways. First, if the farmer has a choice of producing different types of farm products—corn, wheat, or soybeans—the opportunity cost of producing corn is the wheat or soybeans that are not produced as a consequence of growing corn. An increase in the price of corn (with the prices of the other farm products unchanged) *lowers* the opportunity cost of producing corn. The farmer is now prepared to supply more corn because of its lower opportunity cost. Second, if the farmer could produce only one product—corn—the farmer would not supply more corn unless the price of corn were to rise. The law of diminishing returns states that the cost of producing a bushel of corn rises as more corn is produced. This cost of resources used, such as tractors, fertilizers, and labor costs, is the opportunity cost of producing corn under these circumstances. Insofar as the opportunity cost of producing a bushel of corn rises as more corn is produced, the only way to get the farmer to supply more corn is to offer a higher price—to cover the farmer's higher opportunity cost of producing more corn.

> There is no law of supply, but opportunity costs and the law of diminishing returns explain why, under normal circumstances, firms are prepared to supply more output at higher prices.

### THE SUPPLY CURVE

Let's consider the normal case of a positive relationship between price and quantity supplied. Figure 3 shows a supply schedule for corn. When the price of corn is $5 per bushel, farmers are prepared to supply 40 million bushels per month (point *a*). As the price falls to $4, the quantity supplied falls to 35 million bushels (point *b*). Finally, when the price is $1, farmers are prepared to sell only 10 million bushels (point *e*).

The smooth curve drawn through points *a* through *e* is the supply curve, *S*. It shows how quantity supplied responds to price, all things being equal—in other words, how much farmers are prepared to offer for sale at each price. Along the supply curve, the price and supply of corn are positively related: A higher price is needed to induce farmers to offer a larger quantity of corn on the market.

### SHIFTS IN THE SUPPLY CURVE

Factors other than a good's own price can change the relationship between price and quantity supplied, causing the supply curve to shift. These other factors

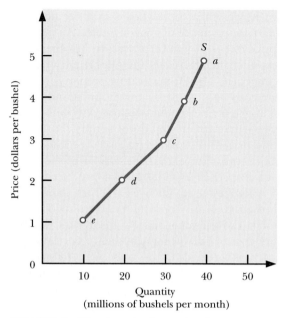

**FIGURE 3   The Supply Curve for Corn**

This figure depicts how the quantity of corn supplied responds to the price of corn. At *a,* when the price of corn is $5 per bushel, the quantity supplied by farmers is 40 million bushels per month. In the last situation, *e,* when the price is $1 per bushel, the quantity supplied is only 10 million bushels per month. The upward-sloping curve *(S)* drawn through these points is the supply curve of corn.

| Supply Schedule for Corn | | |
|---|---|---|
| | *Price* (dollars per bushel) | *Quantity Supplied* (millions of bushels per month) |
| *a* | 5 | 40 |
| *b* | 4 | 35 |
| *c* | 3 | 30 |
| *d* | 2 | 20 |
| *e* | 1 | 10 |

*Factors impact Supply*

include (1) the prices of other goods, (2) the prices of relevant resources, (3) technology, (4) the number of sellers, and (5) expectations.

**Prices of Other Goods.**   The resources used to produce any particular good can almost always be used elsewhere. Farmland can be used for corn or soybeans; engineers can work on cars or trucks; unskilled workers can pick strawberries or lettuce; trains can move coal or cars. As the price of a good rises, resources are naturally attracted away from other goods that use those resources. Thus, the supply of corn will fall if the price of soybeans rises; if the price of lettuce rises, the supply of strawberries may fall. If the price of trucks rises, the supply of cars may fall. If the price of fuel oil rises, less kerosene may be produced.

**The Prices of Relevant Resources.**   As resource prices rise, firms are no longer willing to supply the same quantities of goods produced with those resources at the same price. An increase in the price of coffee beans will increase the costs of producing coffee and decrease the amount that coffee companies are prepared to sell at each price; an increase in the price of corn land, tractors, harvesters, or irrigation will reduce the supply of corn; an increase in the price of cotton will decrease the supply of cotton dresses; an increase in the price of jet fuel will decrease the supply of airline seats at each price.

**Technology.**   *Technology* is knowledge about how different goods can be produced. If technology improves, more goods can be produced from the same resources. For example, if a new, cheaper feed allows Maine lobster farmers to lower their costs of production, the quantity of lobsters supplied at each price will increase. If an assembly line can be speeded up by rearranging the order of assembly, the supply of the good will tend to increase. Technological advances in genetic engineering can increase the supply of medicines and foods such as milk and tomatoes.

**The Number of Sellers.**   If the number of sellers of a good increases, the supply of the good will increase. For example, the lowering of trade barriers (such as licensing requirements for foreign firms) may allow foreign sellers easier entry into the market, increasing the number of sellers.

**Expectations.**   It takes a long time to produce many goods and services. When a farmer plants corn or wheat or soybeans, the prices that are expected to prevail at harvest time are actually more important than is the current price. A college student who reads that there are likely to be too few engineers four years from now may decide to major in engineering in expectation of a high income. When a company decides to establish a plant that takes five years to build, expectations of future business conditions are crucial to that investment decision.

Expectations can affect supply in different directions. If oil prices are expected to rise in the future, oil producers may produce less oil today to have more available for the future. In other cases, more investment will be undertaken if high prices are expected in the future. This greater investment will cause supply to increase.

**Shifting Supply.**   Figure 4 illustrates shifts in the supply curve for corn. The supply curve is based on a $10-per-bushel price of soybeans and a $2000 yearly rental on an acre of corn land. If the price of soybeans rises, the supply curve for corn will shift leftward in panel *(a)* because some land used for corn will be shifted to soybeans. If the rental price of an acre of corn land goes down, the supply curve will shift to the right—*S″* in panel *(b)*. The reduction in the land rental price lowers the costs of producing corn and makes the corn producer willing to supply more corn at the same price as before.

A leftward shift of the supply curve signifies that producers are prepared to sell smaller quantities of the good at each price: It indicates a *decrease in supply*. A rightward shift signifies that producers are prepared to sell larger quantities at each price: It indicates an *increase in supply*.

Table 1 summarizes the factors that cause demand and supply curves to shift.

## EQUILIBRIUM OF DEMAND AND SUPPLY

Along a given demand curve, such as the one in Figure 1, there are many price-quantity combinations from which to choose. Along a given supply curve, there are also many different price-quantity combinations. Neither the demand curve nor the supply curve is sufficient by itself to determine the *market* price-quantity combinations.

Figure 5 puts the demand curve of Figure 1 and the supply curve of Figure 3 together on the same diagram. We should remember that the demand curve

(*a*) Decrease in Supply

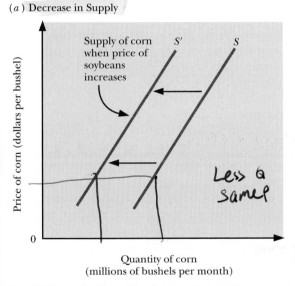

(*b*) Increase in Supply

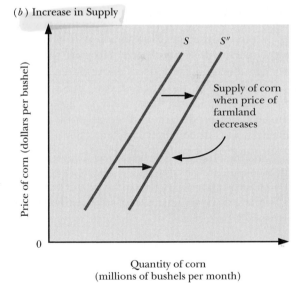

**FIGURE 4   Shifts in the Supply Curve: Changes in Supply**
The supply curve of corn depends on the price of soybeans and the price of farmland. When farmland is $2000 an acre per year and soybeans are $10 per bushel, *S* is the supply curve for corn. Panel *(a)* shows that if farmland stays at $2000 per acre per year but soybeans fetch $15 instead of $10, farmers will switch farmland from corn to soybeans and cause the supply curve for corn to shift to the left from *S* to *S′* (a decrease in supply). Panel *(b)* shows that if soybeans remain at $10 per bushel and farmland falls from $2000 to $1000 per acre, the supply curve for corn will shift to the right from *S* to *S″* (an increase in supply).

| Table 1 Factors that Cause Demand and Supply Curves to Shift | |
|---|---|
| *Factor* | *Demand Example* |
| Change in price of substitutes | Increase in price of coffee shifts demand curve for tea to right. |
| Change in price of complements | Increase in price of coffee shifts demand curve for sugar to left. |
| Change in income | Increase in income shifts demand curve for automobiles to right. |
| Change in preference | Judgment that cigarettes are hazardous to health shifts demand curve for cigarettes to left. |
| Change in number of buyers | Increase in population of City X shifts demand curve for houses in City X to right. |
| Change in expectations of future prices | Expectation that prices of canned goods will increase substantially over the next year shifts demand curve for canned goods to right. |
| *Factor* | *Supply Example* |
| Change in price of another good | Increase in price of corn shifts supply curve of wheat to left. |
| Change in price of resource | Decrease in wage rate of autoworkers shifts supply curve of autos to right. |
| Change in technology | Higher corn yields due to genetic engineering shift supply curve of corn to right. |
| Change in number of sellers | New sellers entering profitable field shift supply curve of product to right. |
| Change in expectations | Expectation of a much higher price of oil next year shifts supply curve of oil today to left; expectation of higher ball-bearing prices in future causes more investment, shifting supply curve to right. |

indicates what consumers are prepared to buy at different prices; the supply curve indicates what producers are prepared to sell at different prices. For the most part, these groups of economic decision makers are entirely different. How much will be produced? How much will be purchased? How are the decisions of consumers and producers coordinated?

Suppose that the price of corn is $2 per bushel. At a $2 price, consumers want to buy 40 million bushels and producers want to sell only 20 million bushels. This discrepancy indicates that at $2 there is a shortage of 20 million bushels.

> A **shortage** results if at the current price the quantity demanded exceeds the quantity supplied; the price is too low to equate the quantity demanded with the quantity supplied.

At a $2 price, 20 million bushels will be traded. Consumers who wish to buy 40 million will be able to buy only the 20 million bushels corn producers are willing to sell. At a price of $2 per bushel, some people who are willing to buy corn cannot find a willing seller. The demand curve shows that a number of consumers are willing to pay more than $2 per bushel. Such buyers will try to outbid one another for the available supply. As buyers compete with one another, they will bid up the price of corn as long as there is a shortage of corn.

The increase in the price of corn in response to the shortage has two main effects. On the one hand, the higher price discourages consumption. On the other hand, the higher price encourages production. Thus the increase in the price of corn, through the actions of independent buyers and sellers, leads both buyers and sellers to make decisions that will reduce the shortage of corn.

What will happen if the price is $4 per bushel? At that price, consumers want to buy 25 million bushels and producers want to sell 35 million bushels. Thus, at $4 there is a surplus of 10 million bushels on the market.

> A **surplus** results if at the current price the quantity supplied exceeds the quantity demanded: The price is too high to equate the quantity demanded with quantity supplied.

At a $4 price, 25 million bushels are traded. Although producers are willing to sell 35 million bushels, they can find buyers for only 25 million bushels. With a surplus some sellers will be disappointed as corn inventories pile up. Willing sellers of corn will not be able to find buyers. The competition among sellers will lead them to cut the price as long as there is a surplus of corn.

This fall in the price of corn will simultaneously encourage consumption and discourage production.

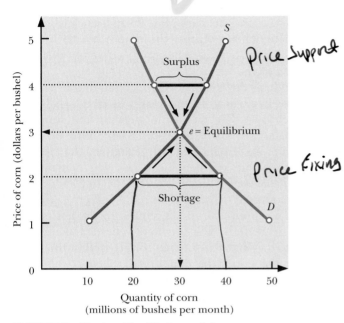

*Price Support*

*Price Fixing*

**FIGURE 5   Market Equilibrium of Corn**

This figure shows how market equilibrium is reached. The demand curve for corn is that from Figure 1 and the supply curve for corn is that from Figure 3. When the price of corn is $2, the quantity demanded is 40 million bushels, but the quantity supplied is only 20 million bushels. The result is a shortage of 20 million bushels of corn. Unsatisfied buyers will bid the price up. Raising the price will reduce the shortage. If the price of corn is raised to $4 per bushel, the quantity supplied is 35 million bushels. The result is a surplus of 10 million bushels of corn. This surplus will cause the price of corn to fall as unsatisfied sellers bid the price down. As the price falls, the surplus will diminish. The equilibrium price is $3 because the quantity demanded equals the quantity supplied at that price. The equilibrium quantity is 30 million bushels.

Through the corrective fall in the price of corn, the surplus of corn will therefore disappear.

According to the demand and supply curves portrayed in Figure 5, when the price of corn reaches $3 per bushel, the shortage (or surplus) of corn disappears completely. At this equilibrium (market-clearing) price, consumers want to buy 30 million bushels and producers want to sell 30 million bushels.

> The **equilibrium (market-clearing) price** is the price at which the quantity demanded by consumers equals the quantity supplied by producers.

There is no other price-quantity combination at which quantity demanded equals quantity supplied—any other price brings about a shortage or a surplus of corn. The arrows in Figure 5 indicate the pressures on prices above or below $3 and show how the amount of shortage or surplus—the size of the brackets—gets smaller as the price adjusts.

The equilibrium of demand and supply is stationary in the sense that once the equilibrium price is reached, it tends to remain the same as long as neither supply nor demand shifts. Movements away from the equilibrium price will be restored by the bidding of frustrated buyers or frustrated sellers in the marketplace. The equilibrium price is like a rocking chair in the rest position; after a gentle push its original position will be restored.

## WHAT THE MARKET ACCOMPLISHES

An equilibrium price does three things. First, it *rations* the scarce supply of the good among all the people who would like to have it if it were given away free. Some people must be left out if the good is scarce. The price determines who will be excluded by limiting consumption.

Second, the system of equilibrium prices *economizes on the information required to match demands and supplies.* Buyers do not have to know how to produce a good, and sellers do not need to know why people use the good. Buyers and sellers need only be concerned with small bits of information, such as price, or small portions of the technological methods of production. The market accomplishes its actions without any one participant's knowing all the details. Recall the pencil example in Chapter 3: Pencils get produced even though no single individual knows *all* the details for producing a pencil.

Third, the market coordinates the actions of a large number of independent buyers and sellers through equilibrium prices. In such a situation, every single buyer or seller is making the best possible decision.

## CHANGES IN THE EQUILIBRIUM PRICE

Sometimes prices go up, and sometimes they go down. In this section we shall investigate the reasons for price changes. Thus far we have seen that the equilibrium price is determined by the intersection of the demand and supply curves. The only way for the price to change is that the demand or supply curves themselves shift, and this occurs only if one or more of the factors that affect demand and supply *besides the good's own price* changes.

## CHANGE IN DEMAND (OR SUPPLY) VERSUS CHANGE IN QUANTITY DEMANDED (OR SUPPLIED)

We make a careful distinction between movements along a demand curve and shifts in the entire curve. A change in the good's own price—as from $p_2$ to $p_1$ in panel *(a)* of Figure 6—causes a movement along the demand curve referred to as a change in quantity demanded. When a change in a factor other than the good's price shifts the entire curve to the left or to the right, as in panel *(b)*, it is called a change in demand.

> A **change in quantity demanded** is a movement along the demand curve because of a change in the good's price. A **change in demand** is a change in the quantity demanded because of a change in a factor other than the good's price. It is depicted as a shift in the entire demand curve.

Similarly, panel *(c)* of Figure 6 shows that a rise in the price of a good (from $p_2$ to $p_1$) causes a change in quantity supplied but does not change the location of the supply curve. A change in supply, shown in panel *(d)*, occurs when a factor other than the good's own price changes, shifting the entire supply curve to the left or to the right.

> A **change in quantity supplied** is a movement along the supply curve because of a change in the good's price.
>
> A **change in supply** is a change in the quantity supplied because of a change in a factor other than the good's price. It is depicted as a shift in the entire supply curve.

## THE EFFECTS OF A CHANGE IN SUPPLY

Changes in supply or demand influence equilibrium prices and quantities in given markets.

Consider the severe flooding in the United States in the summer of 1993, a natural disaster that reduced the supply of wheat. Figure 7 on page 70 shows the demand curve, *D,* and the supply curve, *S,* before the flooding. After floods have destroyed part of their crops, farmers offer 25 million bushels at a $5 price, whereas earlier they had offered 50 million bushels at that price. The supply curve for wheat has shifted to the left, to *S'*.

When the supply curve changes for a single good—like wheat—the demand curve normally does not change. The factors influencing the supply of wheat *other than its own price* have little or no influence on demand. In our example, the flooding does not shift the demand curve. The demand and supply curves are independent in the analysis of a single market.

The supply curve has shifted to the left (supply has decreased); the demand curve remains unchanged. What will happen to the equilibrium price? After the flood, the quantity supplied at the initial price is less than the quantity demanded. At the initial price, there is a shortage of wheat. Therefore, the price of wheat will be bid up until a new and higher equilibrium price is attained, at which quantity demanded and quantity supplied are equal. As the price rises from the initial equilibrium price to the new equilibrium price, there is a movement up the new supply curve (*S'*). Even with a flood, a higher price will coax out more wheat. (See Example 3 on page 70.)

> A decrease in supply without a change in demand causes the price to rise and the quantity demanded to fall. An increase in supply without a change in demand causes the price to fall and the quantity demanded to rise.

## THE EFFECTS OF A CHANGE IN DEMAND

A change in demand for wheat is illustrated in Figure 8 on page 71. The initial equilibrium is depicted by the demand curve, *D,* and the supply curve, *S.* The equilibrium wheat price is $5, and the equilibrium quantity is 50 million bushels. *D* and *S* are the same curves as in Figure 7. Now let's imagine a change on the demand side. For example, new medical evidence shows that eating whole grain wheat will increase longevity. This news shifts the demand curve sharply to the right (from *D* to *D'*). This increase in demand for wheat would drive up the price of wheat. When the price rises, the quantity supplied rises. *There has been no increase in supply, only an increase in quantity supplied* in response to the higher price.

Notice that when the demand curve shifts as a result of a change in a demand factor other than the good's price, there need be no shift in the supply

(*a*) Change in Quantity Demanded

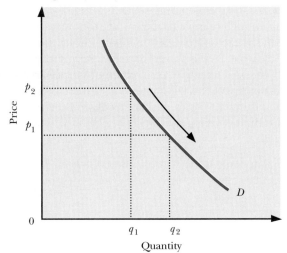

(*b*) Change in Demand

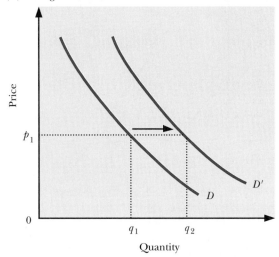

(c) Change in Quantity Supplied

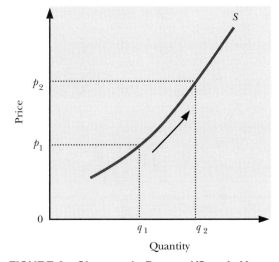

(*d*) Change in Supply

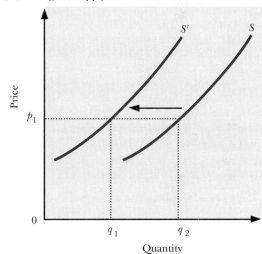

**FIGURE 6    Changes in Demand/Supply Versus Changes in Quantity Demanded/Supplied**

In panel *(a)*, the increase in quantity demanded (from $q_1$ to $q_2$) is the result of the drop in price (from $p_2$ to $p_1$). The change in price causes the movement along the demand curve *(D)*. In panel *(b)*, the increase in quantity (from $q_1$ to $q_2$) is the result of a shift in the demand curve (an increase in demand) to $D'$, holding price constant. When demand increases, the whole demand curve shifts as the result of some change that leads consumers to buy more of the product at each price.

In panel (c), the increase in quantity supplied (from $q_1$ to $q_2$) is the result of a rise in price (from $p_1$ to $p_2$). The change in price causes a movement along the supply curve *(S)*. In panel *(d)*, the decrease in supply (from $q_2$ to $q_1$) is the result of the shift in the supply curve (decrease in supply) from $S$ to $S'$, holding price constant. Firms wish to sell less at the same price.

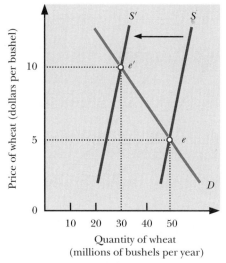

**FIGURE 7   The Effects of a Flood on the Price of Wheat**

In this figure, a flood shifts the supply curve of wheat from $S$ to $S'$. Where a price of $5 per bushel formerly brought forth 50 million bushels of wheat (on $S$), the same price now brings forth only 25 million bushels of wheat (on $S'$). This decrease in supply raises the equilibrium price from $5 to $10. The movement from $e$ to $e'$ is a movement along the demand curve. Although the demand curve does not change, quantity demanded decreases from 50 million to 30 million bushels as the price rises from $5 to $10 per bushel.

curve. As we have seen, demand and supply curves are considered independent in a single market. If a market is small enough relative to the entire economy, the link between the factors that shift demand curves (summarized in Table 1) and those that shift supply curves is weak. In our example, the change in preferences should not affect the willingness of farmers to supply wheat at different prices during any given time period. (See Example 4 on page 72.)

> An increase in demand without a change in supply causes the price to rise and the quantity supplied to rise. A decrease in demand without a change in supply causes the price to fall and the quantity supplied to fall.

## SIMULTANEOUS CHANGES IN DEMAND AND SUPPLY

Figure 9 combines the two previous cases and illustrates what happens to price and quantity if the two events (the flood and the change in preferences) occur together. The demand curve shifts to the right from $D$ to $D'$ (demand increases), and the supply curve shifts to the left from $S$ to $S'$ (supply falls).

Prior to these changes, equilibrium price was $5, and equilibrium quantity was 50 million bushels.

## EXAMPLE 3

### COFFEE PRICE HIKES: THE BRAZILIAN FREEZE AND OTHER MISHAPS

Coffee drinkers were in for a real eye-opener in June of 1994. Wholesale coffee prices had risen 125 percent since April and 50 percent between June 26 and June 30 alone. For the first time in five years, the South Street Diner in lower Manhattan raised the price it charges for coffee by 5 cents. The Au Bon Pain Restaurant near the World Trade Center raised its 16-ounce cup of coffee from $.97 to $1.05. Shoppers in grocery stores were hit with even larger price increases. Folgers raised the price for its 13-ounce packages by 40 cents.

Why the sharp increase in coffee prices? An early frost in Brazil destroyed about 25 percent of Brazil's crop. (Brazil is the world's largest coffee producer). The world's second-largest coffee producer, Colombia, was expecting a sub-par coffee harvest at 11 million bags, down from the expected 11 to 14 million bags.

The run-up in coffee prices from middle to late 1994 illustrates the effect of a reduction in supply on prices. As the coffee supply curve shifted to the left, the price of coffee shot up. This price increase encouraged coffee drinkers to drink less and to switch to substitute products like tea or soft drinks with caffeine.

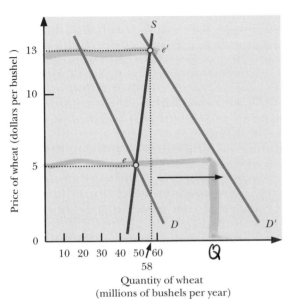

**FIGURE 8  The Effects of an Increased Preference for Whole Grain Wheat on the Price of Wheat**

If for some reason we want to eat more whole grain wheat as the result of a change in preferences, the demand curve for wheat will shift to the right. The shift in the demand curve from D to D′ depicts an increase in demand. This increase in demand drives up the equilibrium price from $5 per bushel to $13 per bushel. As price rises from $5 to $13, quantity supplied increases from 50 million to 58 million bushels resulting in movement along the supply curve, S.

The shifts in demand and supply disrupt this equilibrium. Now at a price of $5, the quantity supplied equals 25 million bushels and the quantity demanded equals 90 million bushels—a shortage. The new equilibrium occurs at a price of $18 and a quantity of 37.5 million bushels. In this example, the two shifts magnify each other's effects. As we have shown, if there had been only the supply change, price would have risen to $9. If there had been only the demand change, price would have risen to $13. The combined effects cause the price to rise to $18. In this case, the causes of the changes in demand and supply are independent.

Figure 10 summarizes the effects of all possible combinations of shifts in demand curves and supply curves. As panels *(e)*, *(f)*, *(h)*, and *(i)* demonstrate, the effects of simultaneous changes in demand and supply are sometimes indeterminate. If supply increases (shifts right) and demand decreases (shifts left), the price will fall. If supply decreases and demand increases, the price will rise. If, however, both demand

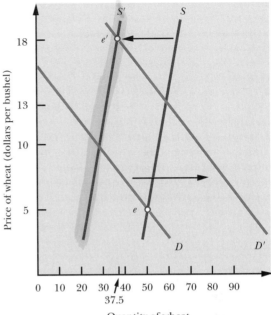

**FIGURE 9  The Effects of an Increase in Demand and a Decrease in Supply on the Price of Wheat**

This graph combines the supply change in Figure 7 and the demand change of Figure 8. The original equilibrium was at a price of $5 and a quantity of 50 million bushels. After the shift in supply (from S to S′) and the shift in demand (from D to D′), there is a shortage at the old price (quantity supplied equals 25 million bushels, and quantity demanded equals 90 million bushels). The equilibrium price rises to $18, and the equilibrium quantity falls to 37.5 million bushels.

and supply curves move in the same direction (if both increase or if both decrease), the price effect depends upon which movement dominates.

## NOVEL APPLICATIONS OF DEMAND AND SUPPLY

The concepts of demand, supply, and equilibrium price apply to a wide range of exchanges. Almost anything that admits to being priced and exchanged freely can be analyzed by the tools of this chapter. Economist and Nobel laureate Gary Becker pioneered the application of demand and supply to marriage, crime, and other economic phenomena. In some societies, marriage is a market transaction—the groom

## EXAMPLE 4
## WHEN DEMAND FALLS, EVEN LUXURY HOTELS ARE NOT IMMUNE

The city of Bangkok is famed for its grand luxury hotels. The luxurious new Grand Pacific Hotel is shaped like a boat. Its entryway is dotted with translucent plastic sculptures that give the appearance of a cruise ship nearing an iceberg. Bangkok's Oriental is cited as the best hotel in the world in surveys of a number of business travelers. Noted for its exquisite service, decor, and gourmet food, it has served as a haven for wealthy tourists and harried business travelers for decades. In the past, its rooms listed for a minimum of $252 for a single room. In recent years, however, the demand for luxury travel to Bangkok has dropped as well-heeled travelers have been frightened away by the city's grid-lock traffic and its AIDS-ravaged sex industry. This drop in demand has left luxury hotels like the Oriental half empty. When demand falls, the price should drop, if all other things remain equal. Calls to the Oriental's reservation line revealed that the hotel was routinely offering 30 percent discounts, and travel agents in Bangkok were offering even better rates. Be it wheat, stocks, or luxury hotel rooms, when demand collapses, prices fall.

--------------------------------------------

*Source:* "Bangkok's Grand Hotels, Struggling, Cut Rates," *New York Times,* June 15, 1994.

---

may pay a bride price or the bride's family might provide a dowry. The bride price or dowry equates demand and supply. If there are too many brides, the bride price will fall. In the market for crime, the price of crime is the punishment that criminals expect to receive if they break the law; they balance this punishment against the amount they expect to earn from mugging, robbing, or burglarizing. A reduction in the price of crime increases the amount of crime.

Demand and supply even apply to betting. The sports pages contain interesting "market" information every weekend during the football season. Each game has a point spread, in which one team is given an advantage over the other. The purpose of the point spread is to provide equilibrium in the market for betting so that the number of people betting on the favored team equals the number of people betting on the underdog team.[1] (See Example 5.)

In the next chapter, we shall look at incentives, strategic behavior, and unintended consequences.

---

[1]See Richard A. Zuber, John M. Gandar, and B.D. Bowers, "Beating the Spread: Testing the Efficiency of the Gambling Market for National Football League Games," *Journal of Political Economy* 93, 4 (August 1985):800–806.

## SUMMARY

1. Markets differ according to the degree of competition.

2. The law of demand states that quantity demanded falls as price goes up, if other things are equal, and vice versa; the demand curve is a graphical representation of the relationship between price and quantity demanded—again, if other things are equal. The demand curve is downward sloping.

3. As price goes up, quantity supplied usually rises; the supply curve is a graphical representation of the relationship between price and quantity supplied. The supply curve tends to be upward sloping because of the law of diminishing returns.

4. The equilibrium combination of price and quantity occurs where the demand curve intersects the supply curve or where quantity demanded equals quantity supplied. Competitive pricing rations goods and economizes on the information necessary to coordinate supply and demand decisions. A shortage results if the price is too low for equilibrium; a surplus results if the price is too high for equilibrium.

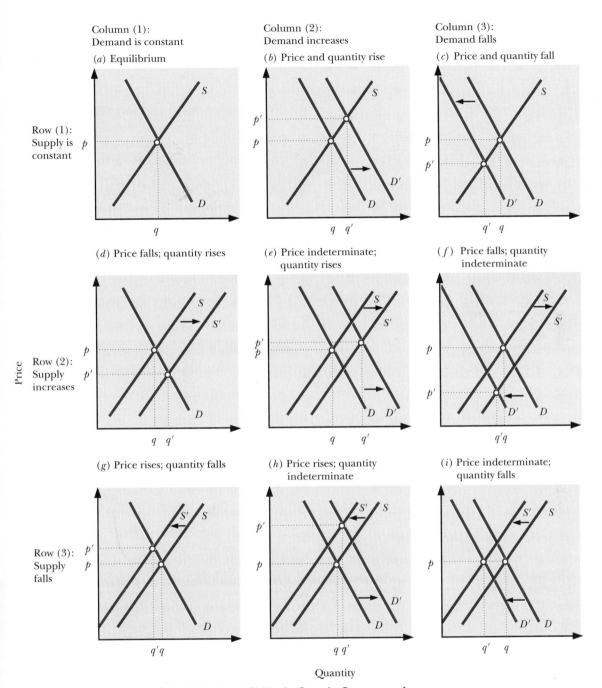

**FIGURE 10  Summary of the Effects of Shifts in Supply Curves and Demand Curves**

This figure gives the results of all possible combinations of shifts in supply curves and demand curves. To read it, match the rows and columns. For example, the figure in panel (e), at the intersection of row 2 and column 2, shows what happens when supply and demand increase simultaneously. The figure in panel (i), at the intersection of row 3 and column 3, shows what happens when both supply and demand fall.

5. A change in quantity demanded signifies a movement along a given demand curve; a change in demand signifies that the entire demand curve shifts. A change in quantity supplied is shown by a movement along a given supply curve; a change in supply, by a shift in the entire supply curve.

6. The demand curve shifts if a change occurs in the price of a related good (substitute or complement), income, preferences, the number of buyers, or the expectation of future prices.

7. The supply curve will shift if a change occurs in the price of another good, the price of a resource, technology, the number of sellers, or the expectation of future prices. A change in the equilibrium price-quantity combination requires a change in one of the factors held constant along the demand or supply curves. Demand-and-supply analysis allows one to predict what will happen to prices and quantities when demand or supply schedules shift.

8. The concepts of demand, supply, and equilibrium price can be applied to a wide range of exchanges.

## KEY TERMS

market
demand
law of demand
quantity demanded
market demand curve
substitutes
complements
normal good
inferior good
supply
quantity supplied

shortage
surplus
equilibrium (market-clearing) price
change in quantity demanded
change in demand
change in quantity supplied
change in supply

## QUESTIONS AND PROBLEMS

1. Explain the relationship between the principle of substitution discussed in the previous chapter and the law of demand.
2. "People need bread. If the price rises, people will not buy less of it." Evaluate this statement in terms of the reasons demand curves are downward sloping.
3. Plot the demand and supply schedules for jeans in Table A as demand and supply curves.
   a. What equilibrium price would this market establish?
   b. If the state were to pass a law that the price of jeans could not be more than $2, how would you describe the market response?
   c. If the state were to pass a law that the price of jeans could not be less than $8, how would you describe the market response?
   d. If preferences changed and people wanted to buy twice as much as before at each price, what will the equilibrium price be?
   e. If, in addition to the above change in preferences, there is an improvement in technology that allows firms to produce this product at lower cost than before, what will happen to the equilibrium price?

### Table A

| Price (dollars) | Quantity Demanded of Jeans (units) | Quantity Supplied of Jeans (units) |
| --- | --- | --- |
| 10 | 5 | 25 |
| 8 | 10 | 20 |
| 6 | 15 | 15 |
| 2 | 20 | 10 |
| 0 | 25 | 5 |

4. American baseball bats do not sell well in Japan because they do not meet the specifications of Japanese baseball officials. If the Japanese change their specifications to accommodate American-made bats, what will happen to the price of American bats?
5. "The poor are the ones who suffer from high gas and electricity bills. We should pass a law that gas and electricity rates cannot increase by more than 1 percent annually." Evaluate this statement in terms of demand-and-supply analysis, assuming that equilibrium prices rise faster than 1 percent annually.
6. Much of the automobile rental business in the United States is done at airports. How do you think a reduction in airfares would affect automobile rental rates?
7. If both the demand and supply for coffee increase, what would happen to coffee prices? If the demand fell and the supply increased, what would happen to coffee prices?

## EXAMPLE 5
## THE POLITICAL
## ELECTIONS MARKET

Until the political elections market, the most accurate method of predicting election outcomes was to conduct surveys of the electorate. The public looked to prestigious organizations such as Gallup and Roper to predict who the next president would be. The economists at the University of Iowa suggested that we could get even more accurate predictions of election outcomes if an "election market" were set up in which buyers and sellers could buy and sell "shares" in different candidates. That is, if you buy 100 shares of candidate X and candidate X wins, you have made money. If investors think that the chances of one candidate are on the rise, there will be an increase in demand and the price of that candidate's share would rise.

The idea was that people would spend more thought, time, and effort trying to determine the election outcome if they had their own money on the line. Respondents to the Gallop or Roper polls, on the other hand, had nothing to lose by providing vague or inaccurate information.

Indeed, the predictions of economists have been borne out. The election market has been a more accurate predictor of election results than national polling organizations.

8. Which of the following statements uses incorrect terminology? Explain.
   a. "The fare war among the major airlines in the summer of 1996 increased the demand for air travel."
   b. "The economic recovery of 1994 caused the demand for air travel to rise."
9. What factors are held constant along the demand curve? Explain how each can shift the demand curve to the right. Explain how each can shift the demand curve to the left.
10. What factors are held constant along the supply curve? Explain how each factor can shift the supply curve to the right. Explain how each factor can shift the supply curve to the left.
11. Why is the demand curve downward sloping?
12. Why is the supply curve normally upward sloping? Can you think of any exceptions?
13. What is the effect of each of the following events on the equilibrium price and quantity of hamburgers?
   a. The price of steak (a substitute for hamburgers) increases.
   b. The price of french fries (a complement) increases.
   c. The population becomes older.
   d. The government requires that all the ingredients of hamburgers be absolutely fresh (that is, nothing can be frozen).
   e. Beef becomes more expensive.
   f. More firms enter the hamburger business.
14. "As a general rule, if *both* demand and supply increase or decrease, the change in price will be indeterminate." Is this statement true or false? Illustrate with a diagram.
15. "As a general rule, if demand increases and supply decreases, or vice versa, the change in quantity will be indeterminate." Is this statement true or false? Illustrate with a diagram.
16. The number of compact discs sold in markets has more than quadrupled over the past three years. The average price of a compact disc, however, has fallen. Use demand-and-supply analysis to explain this phenomenon.

# CHAPTER 5

# MAKING ECONOMIC DECISIONS: INCENTIVES, GAMES, AND UNINTENDED CONSEQUENCES

Incentives matter because they direct our efforts where we think they will do the most good. A change in tastes, technology, new products, or government policies creates new incentives. Economics teaches that all policies must be considered with great care because they may cause unintended consequences. To choose the right economic policies, we must contemplate both the intended and the unintended consequences. As Friedrich A. Hayek, one of the Defining Moment economists, once noted: "The pursuit of our most cherished ideals . . . [can produce] results utterly different from those we expected."[1]

Hayek's quote referred to society's greatest unintended consequence: the failure of socialism. Hayek feared that once societies began to adopt well-intended socialist policies—government takeovers of private enterprises, economic planning, income redistribution—it would be difficult to turn back. They would find themselves "on the road to serfdom." Socialism, which was supposed to improve the lives of working people, would have the unintended consequence of making their lives worse. When everyone is an owner, there is no one person with an incentive to assure that plants and equipment are used efficiently. When incomes are equal, there are no incentives to work hard or to take chances.

In this chapter we shall consider how we, as consumers, employees, voters, and managers of businesses, make economic decisions. We are motivated by rewards and are deterred by opportunity costs. The games that we play in our quest to make ourselves better off determine how well or poorly the economic system works. Unless or until we understand the crucial role of incentives, we shall often follow policies that have unintended consequences.

---

[1]*The Road to Serfdom*, Chicago: University of Chicago Press, 1944, p. 11.

## MARGINAL ANALYSIS

The economy is just people making decisions about the ordinary business of earning a living. Economists study how these decisions are made and analyze their implications. The decisions of households, governments, and corporations are made by individuals trying to do the best they can, given the circumstances. Because individuals are the main actors of economics, the student of economics has an advantage over the struggling physics student, who cannot ask, "What would I do if I were a molecule?" The student is one of the "molecules" economists study.

Our individual behavior is affected by the *incentives*—the carrots and sticks—that we face in any given situation. The "carrots" are the benefits we receive from engaging in an economic activity; the "sticks" are the costs of the activity. We are guided in our economic decisions by costs and benefits.

In one of the Defining Moments of economics, as quoted in Chapter 1, Adam Smith pointed out that "it is not from the benevolence of the butcher, the brewer or the baker that we expect our dinner, but from their regard to their own self-interest." In other words, we do things if we perceive that the benefits of what we are doing will exceed their costs.

Thus, the tool most used by economists to study economic decision making is the comparison of costs and benefits, or marginal analysis. We make decisions by using marginal analysis to weigh costs and benefits. (See Example 1.)

> **Marginal analysis** examines the costs and benefits of making small changes from the current state of affairs.

### MARGINAL COSTS AND BENEFITS

Let's start with a simple example: You might use marginal analysis to decide how much studying is "enough." First, you examine the benefits of a slight (marginal) increase in your present amount of studying. If you increase your study time by, say, one hour per day, you will probably earn higher grades, the respect of your fellow students, and a better job upon graduation. Although you will not be able to measure these results exactly, you would have a general idea of the benefits of additional study. Simultaneously, you examine the costs of one more hour of studying per day. You might have to sacrifice earnings from a part-time job, or you might have to give up your gym workout, your favorite television program, or an extra hour of sleep.

Whether you are studying "enough" depends upon whether you believe that the benefits of the extra studying will outweigh the additional costs. If

### EXAMPLE 1
### THE RENT GRADIENT AND
### MARGINAL ANALYSIS

Economics teaches that people make decisions using marginal analysis, weighing costs and benefits at the margin. Consider the choices of housing locations in cities like Atlanta, Houston, or Los Angeles, where people commute to work on congested freeways. Houses and apartments located closer to the city center offer benefits in the form of shorter commuting times. Thus, the closer the location to the city center, the higher the price or the rent. In cities like Houston, for example, housing prices drop by $5000 for each additional mile from the city center.

Along with additional factors like schools and other amenities, marginal analysis says that people weigh the extra costs of more centrally located homes against the benefits of shorter commuting times. People tend to balance the marginal costs and benefits, typically choosing that location where they perceive the extra benefits of shorter commuting times to roughly equal the extra costs in the form of higher prices or rents.

they do, you will conclude that you are not studying enough, and you will study more. If the extra costs are greater than the extra benefits, you will conclude that you should not increase your study time.

Businesses make choices in a similar fashion. Consider a local fast-food restaurant. Its owners must decide if its current hours of operation (11 A.M. to midnight) are "enough." Before taking action, the restaurant's owners have to make a decision at the margin. They must estimate how much extra revenue will be gained by opening for breakfast. They also estimate the extra costs of opening earlier (the extra supplies, larger payroll, higher utility bills, more advertising dollars). If the extra benefits from opening earlier (the additional revenue) exceed the extra costs, the owners will decide to open early for breakfast. If the extra benefits are less than the extra costs, the owners will not increase their hours of operation. People and businesses make all kinds of economic decisions by comparing the extra costs with the extra benefits associated with making changes in their plans.

> To make decisions, we must consider the extra (or marginal) costs and benefits of an increase or decrease in a particular activity. If the marginal benefits outweigh the marginal costs, we should undertake the extra activity.

## MARGINAL ANALYSIS AND OPTIMAL CHOICE

Marginal analysis dictates that we should carry out any activity whose marginal benefit is greater than its marginal cost. We should cut back on any activity whose marginal cost exceeds its marginal benefit. If we combine these rules, we see that the *optimal level* of activity (how many hours to work, how many units of output to produce, how much time to devote to study, and so forth) occurs where marginal costs and marginal benefits are equal.

In the studying example, let's say that if we study one additional hour, the marginal benefit of this extra hour is greater than the marginal cost. We should study this hour. If we consider studying yet another hour, we determine that the marginal benefit still exceeds the marginal cost. If we now consider studying a third hour, the marginal cost equals the marginal benefit. The conclusion: We should continue to increase our study time until the marginal costs and marginal benefits of extra study are equal. The choice of the optimal study time—in this case, three hours—is shown in Figure 1.

MC - benefit of next unit

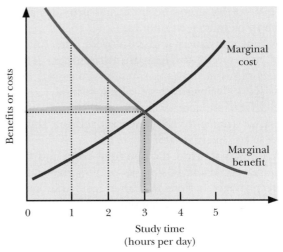

**FIGURE 1**

The optimal amount of studying is three hours per day. When less time is allocated, the marginal benefit exceeds the marginal cost; thus, it pays to study more.

In later chapters we shall apply this rule to many different types of economic choices—consumption, labor supply, unemployment, acquisition of information, and production. The rule that we carry out economic activities to the point where marginal costs and marginal benefits are equal is a powerful one that we can use to explain a wide variety of economic phenomena.

## MARGINAL ANALYSIS AND INCENTIVES

Whenever anything happens to change the marginal costs and benefits of economic actions—changes in prices, wages, incomes, regulations—we respond by changing our economic behavior. In the restaurant example, if the wages of restaurant employees rise, the marginal costs of opening early for business increase, and the restaurant is less likely to decide to open early. If the price of breakfasts rises, the marginal benefits of opening earlier are greater, and the restaurant is more likely to decide to open early. Let's suppose the city government, wishing to encourage more restaurants to open early, lowers the local taxes of restaurants that open early. This action lowers the marginal costs of being open more hours, and gives the restaurant an extra incentive to open early. Or let's suppose that the federal government mandates an increase in the minimum wage. (The fast-food restaurant hires primarily teenagers working at the minimum wage.) This mandate raises the restaurant's marginal cost of doing business and provides an incentive to be open fewer hours.

We, as consumers and employees, alter our behavior in response to changes in incentives. If government raises income tax rates, the marginal benefits of working overtime or taking second jobs are reduced. The tax increase causes us to change our behavior; we are less likely to work overtime and our spouse is less likely to work.

Actions that affect the marginal costs and benefits cause people and businesses to alter their behavior. Accordingly, actions that alter costs and benefits have both primary and secondary effects.

The secondary (or indirect) effects of an action that alters marginal costs and benefits is that people and businesses alter their economic behavior.

Secondary or indirect effects are often hard to predict and difficult to measure. The direct effect of an increase in income tax rates is to raise government tax revenues. Its secondary effect is quite different. If the tax increases cause us to work less, or to reduce taxable market activities, taxable income will tend to fall. If the government increases the minimum wage, the direct effect is to raise the income of those working at the minimum wage. The secondary effect is to reduce the employment of minimum wage workers and hence reduce their income.

Secondary effects make it difficult to predict the *net* effect of government actions, which is the sum of direct and indirect effects. The net effect of raising income tax rates on government revenue is the positive effect of higher tax rates minus the negative secondary effect of less taxable income. The net effect of raising the minimum wage on the incomes of low-skilled workers is the positive effect of higher wages of employed workers minus the loss of income of those who become unemployed as a consequence.

## THE GAMES THAT PEOPLE PLAY

We make decisions by comparing marginal costs and marginal benefits. Often, these decisions are easy to make: The marginal cost of buying a gallon of milk is its $2.25 price in the grocery store. Sometimes, however, marginal decisions are complex because they depend on how others react to our actions. If the fast-food restaurant's decision to open for breakfast does not cause other restaurants in the vicinity also to open earlier, its marginal benefits will be easy to calculate. If its decision to open for breakfast triggers competitors to do the same, then its marginal benefits will be less. As consumers, producers, and voters, we are often in situations where our actions depend on the actions and reactions of others.

When you play chess, checkers, or poker, the result depends on how well your opponent plays compared to your play. Many economic situations are similar. What we do can depend on our expectations about what others are going to do. If we expect others to cheat or harm us in some way, we will take action to minimize the cost we expect others to try to impose on us. In a word, our behavior is social: What we do depends on others.

The study of how we interact with others in our economic and social behavior is called **game theory**.

A game is simply a situation in which each player (including you) can follow different strategies (what you will do in any situation) and receives a reward or penalty depending on strategies adopted by the other players. The game's outcome depends not only on you but also on others.

In many cases, we are in complete control over the outcome, independent of the actions of others. When you go to the grocery store, whether you buy that gallon of milk or not makes no real difference to anybody else—but it does to you. If you study an extra hour and get a higher grade, you benefit and no one else is affected.

In other cases, however, your actions affect others and vice versa. If there are only two persons in your class and your instructor grades on a curve, your additional studying affects the second student's grade. Your grade now depends on how much the other student studies. Any action you take must now consider how the other student will behave. If you study more and the other student does not, your grade will improve. If you study more and the other student also studies more, your grade may be unchanged. With such interdependence, calculation of marginal costs and benefits can become complex.

The prisoner's dilemma game is used to describe many types of "games" that we must play in our economic lives. It is so called because it describes a situation in which the police are questioning two suspected bank robbers. The suspects can either cooperate with each other through silence or confess to the police. In the prisoner's dilemma game, self-interest leads people to do something that is not in their collective interest. In other words, when people are involved in a prisoner's dilemma, no one has an incentive to do what is best for all concerned.

> A **prisoner's dilemma** is a game in which all would gain by cooperating, but self-interest causes them not to cooperate.

Figure 2 shows the prisoner's dilemma. Jessie James and Billy the Kid are arrested on suspicion of robbing a bank. Billy's two possible strategies are shown by the rows; Jessie's by the columns. Each square cell shows the payoffs to Billy and Jessie for any particular combination of strategies. Billy's payoff is in the lower left corner of each cell; Jessie's payoff is in the upper right corner of each cell. If both confess, they each get 3 years in jail. The reward or payoff for each is therefore $-3$. If one confesses while the other remains silent, the one who remains silent gets 6 years while the one who confesses goes free. If both remain silent (they cooperate), they each get 1 year for carrying a concealed weapon.

What should each do? If Jessie confesses, Billy is better off confessing; otherwise, he gets 6 years. If Jessie remains silent, Billy is better off confessing because he goes free. *No matter what Jessie does, it is better for Billy to confess.* The same is true for Jessie. Thus, self-interest causes both bank robbers to confess and they each spend 3 years in jail. They would both be better off remaining silent, but self-interest leads to an outcome that is worse for both players.

The prisoner's dilemma game applies to a broad range of economic, political, and social actions. It applies to any situation in which players are driven to strategies or actions that are inferior to cooperative solutions. The prisoner's dilemma explains, among other things, why price wars take place among sellers, why governments engage in deficit financing, and why shortages cannot be solved by voluntary cooperation.

Hence, economic decision making can be studied in two contexts. In one context, your decisions do not affect others. You can decide upon your best course of action using marginal analysis without worrying how others will react. In the second context, your actions affect others and vice versa. You must consider how others will react. In effect, you are involved in a strategic game with others.

Figure 3 considers a study example in which there are two students and the instructor grades on a curve. In this case, both students must decide to study more, even though it will not raise their grade (because of the curve). They have incurred extra cost and receive no extra benefit. They would take this action because either would end up with a C if one chose to study the same amount while the other chose to study more.

## THE PRINCIPLE OF UNINTENDED CONSEQUENCES

Economics deals with real economic problems—we worry that there is too much inflation, too much poverty, too much unemployment, or inadequate medical care. When public concern grows, usually pressure grows to pass legislation that will correct the problem, but economic problems are usually not easy to solve. The principle of unintended consequences warns that because people will always try to do the best they can given the circumstances, the ultimate effects of economic policies may be different from the apparent or intended effects. Indeed, the

**FIGURE 2  The Prisoner's Dilemma**

**FIGURE 3**

## EXAMPLE 2
## BLACK MARKETS:
## TAXING FREON

Taxes reduce economic activity because they drive a wedge between what a good is worth to the seller and what it is worth to the buyer. This, however, creates an incentive for the seller and the buyer to enter the illegal or "black" market for the product. A recent example is provided by Freon, which is the brand-name of a chemical used in refrigerators and air conditioners.

Freon is a chlorofluorocarbon, or CFC, which has been claimed to contribute to the depletion of the ozone level. A group of 140 countries has agreed to ban the production of all CFCs by the end of 1995. The U.S. government, to encourage the use of alternative air conditioning chemicals, has imposed a $5.35 a pound tax on all sales of CFCs. As a consequence of these changes, the retail price of Freon has mushroomed from $1 a pound in 1989 to $15 a pound in 1995.

Big profits can be made by someone buying Freon in a foreign country (such as Russia) and selling it in the United States for about $2 a pound. After drugs, Freon is now the second-largest illegal substance imported into the United States. As long as there are 140 million cars that use Freon, the black market will simply become larger as output of the chemical drops. Incentives count.

The purpose of the ban and tax on Freon production may be noble: to save the Earth from extinction. But the consequences may actually be worse. People will still buy Freon illegally, and resources will be used up in the detection of black market activities and the evasion of taxation and production bans.

---

"cure" can sometimes be worse than the "disease." (See Example 2.)

> The **principle of unintended consequences** holds that economic policies may have ultimate or actual effects that differ from the intended or apparent effects.

The economist Robert Malthus (1766–1835) was one of the first economists to discuss how unintended consequences could change the outcome of poorly designed policies. According to Malthus, "First appearances . . . are deceitful . . . and the partial and immediate effects [of policy] . . . are often directly opposite to the general and permanent consequences."[2] In 1800, he wrote an essay on the high price of food. Malthus, who was a minister of the

Church of England, pointed out that food prices were higher in England than in Sweden because of the allowances (welfare payments) that English parishes were giving to the poor. Figure 4 illustrates Malthus's argument. The supply curve of, say, corn is shown by the vertical line $S$ at 40 units. The demand curve is $D$. The initial price of corn is $3 a bushel. Suppose now that some poor people who would like to buy more corn receive a welfare payment to do so. What will happen? The demand curve shifts to the right from $D$ to $D'$. It is still necessary to ration the supply of the scarce good; if the price stayed at $3, the quantity demanded will be 50 units. Unless some scheme such as rationing, a fight, or a lottery is used to determine who is going to get the 40 units, the price of the good must rise from $3 to $4. Payments to the poor have the unintended consequence of raising the price of food.

The same idea discussed by Malthus nearly two centuries ago applies with equal force to contemporary issues. From 1965 to 1995, the cost of medical

---

[2]*An Investigation of the Present High Price of Provisions,* London: L. Johnson, 1800.

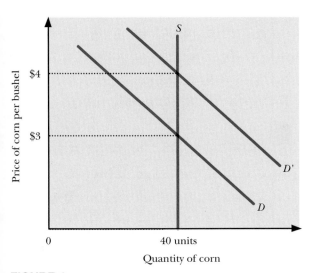

**FIGURE 4**

A subsidy to purchase the good will increase the demand from *D* to *D'*. With a perfectly inelastic supply curve, *S*, the price will have to rise to ration the scarce supply among all of those who now demand the good. All pay more.

care rose almost 10 times—twice the rate of inflation in other goods and services. One reason is higher-quality medical care. But another reason is that the government began subsidizing health-care purchases in the 1960s with Medicare and Medicaid. In the 1990s, the government finances $0.50 out of every health-care dollar. If people do not have to pay for the cost of their medical care, their demand will rise more than the supply. Again, a well-intended policy has had an unintended effect. A policy designed to make health care more attainable has raised its cost and made health care less attainable to those least able.

Consider another example: A major piece of welfare legislation in the United States is the Aid to Families with Dependent Children Program (AFDC). This program provides financial assistance to families with dependent children according to demonstrated need. If welfare authorities determine that a family with young children has "enough" income, no assistance will be provided. An unintended consequence of the AFDC program has been to encourage the breakdown of the U.S. two-parent family. Poor households qualify for more AFDC assistance if the father is absent and not contributing to the family's sustenance. Many poor families are better off if fathers desert their families to increase the amount of AFDC assistance. A program intended to stabilize

the family has had the unintended consequence of breaking it apart.

## MARGINAL ANALYSIS AND UNINTENDED CONSEQUENCES

People and businesses make decisions by weighing the marginal costs and marginal benefits of their actions. If a government policy changes marginal costs and benefits, people and businesses will respond, often in ways that defeat the original intent of the policy.

Consider the government policy of insuring bank deposits through various government deposit insurance programs. The intent is to prevent depositors from losing their hard-earned money and to create a "sound" banking system. Government deposit insurance, however, changes marginal costs and benefits and has unintended consequences: If we know that we cannot lose our bank deposits no matter what happens, the marginal benefit of spending the time to determine whether our bank is solvent or not disappears. We no longer gain advantage from keeping our funds out of poorly run banks, and deposits flow into banks that are risky and poorly managed. As these banks fail, confidence in the banking system is reduced and the policy intended to create confidence in the banking system actually serves to reduce confidence.

It may seem right for the government to protect citizens from the costs of unemployment. If people lose their jobs, through no fault of their own, it would be unfair for them to be without income. It is for this reason that most governments have unemployment insurance. Some countries have very liberal unemployment compensation; others are less generous.

Unemployment compensation changes the marginal costs and benefits of being unemployed. If an unemployed worker lives in a country that pays 75 percent or more of lost income, the marginal cost of remaining unemployed is low and that person will not search as hard to find a new job. If the unemployed worker can receive generous benefits for a very long period of time, the marginal costs of being unemployed are reduced. Accordingly, unemployment compensation—a program designed to make unemployment less onerous—can have the unintended consequence of worsening the unemployment problem.

The Social Security Act was intended to supplement the retirement incomes of older Americans. What has been the result? If the Social Security Act simply gave us back what we put into it during our working years, the result would not have been much different from that if we simply saved for our retirement years. Social security would act as a forced saving scheme designed to make people look out for their own futures. However, the Social Security Act did not just promise to repay us for our contributions: It promised to repay us more than we put in. To finance social security, future workers had to be taxed! As an unintended consequence, many Americans stopped saving. About 50 percent of all Americans save nothing toward retirement and plan to rely exclusively on social security. To finance the program, it was necessary to raise social security taxes from minuscule amounts (about 1 percent of payrolls) to the present 15 percent of payrolls. As we Americans stopped saving for our retirement, and as the U.S. population aged, the social security system is now facing a crisis: Some time in the first quarter of the twenty-first century, it will be bankrupt unless we change the system to one in which we get out of it only what we put into it.

## PRICE CONTROLS AND UNINTENDED CONSEQUENCES

We dislike high prices when we are buyers and we love high prices when we are sellers. As a consequence, there will be political pressure to rearrange prices by government control so that they are different from the prices that would prevail in a market equilibrium. The principle of unintended consequences shows that, if the government intervenes in price setting—even for a worthy cause—unintended results usually emerge, which may defeat the intent of the policy. Let us take a look at a number of controversial areas in which governmental intervention has led to unintended consequences.

We studied the rationing function of prices in the last chapter. Briefly, if a good is scarce, it is necessary to find some way of allocating the scarce supply among all of the competing claimants. Fights, favoritism, first-come-first-served, or ration booklets are possible solutions. Market prices have an enormous advantage over the other allocation mechanisms: they are more efficient.

Figure 5 distinguishes between equilibrium and disequilibrium prices. The price at which the demand and supply curve intersects is the equilibrium price.

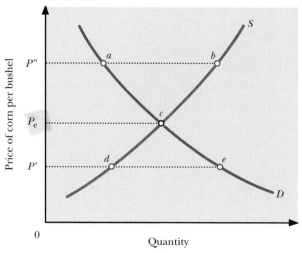

**FIGURE 5   Disequilibrium Prices**

The demand *(D)* and supply *(S)* curves intersect at *c*, which yields an equilibrium price of $P_e$, at which the quantity demanded equals the quantity supplied. At a higher price, say *P″*, there is a surplus where the quantity demanded *(a)* is less than the quantity supplied *(b)*. At a lower price, say *P′*, there is a shortage where the quantity demanded *(e)* exceeds the quantity supplied *(d)*.

> An **equilibrium price** is that price at which the quantity demanded of the product equals the quantity supplied.

Any price other than the one at which the demand and supply curves intersect is a disequilibrium price.

> A **disequilibrium price** is one at which the quantity demanded does not equal the quantity supplied.

As Figure 5 shows, if the price is above the equilibrium price, a surplus will result. When a surplus exists, buyers place a smaller marginal valuation on the good or service than sellers. If the price is not allowed to fall, then sellers will not be able to make decisions that reflect the actual demand for the good. They will want to produce more than buyers want to buy. They are experiencing the prisoner's dilemma because each seller has an incentive to sell more but cannot because the price is too high. If the price is allowed to fall, this incentive will lower the price further until the incentive vanishes.

At any price below the equilibrium price, a shortage will result. If there is a shortage, buyers want to purchase more of the good or service than is available. Buyers have a higher marginal valuation on the

## EXAMPLE 3

## INTEREST-RATE CEILINGS AND YOUR CREDIT CARD

There are more than 560 million credit cards in the United States—more than two for every man, woman, and child. We take our credit cards for granted. We get numerous offers for cards in the mail and through phone solicitations. You don't have to be rich to have a credit card. College students, the poor, and even unemployed workers have credit cards.

Credit card companies currently charge interest rates ranging from 7 to 24 percent, depending on the type of card and the state in which it was issued. Most card owners pay more than 14 percent for credit.

Various consumer groups have complained about these high interest rates. The Justice Department has subpoenaed the records of large credit card companies like Visa and Mastercard. Representatives of credit card owners call upon government regulators to place a ceiling on the maximum rates that credit card companies can charge.

Let's consider the effects of a regulation that places a 10 percent limit on credit card interest. Credit card companies are willing to give students, unemployed workers, and relatively poor families credit cards because the high interest they receive compensates them for the risk of nonpayment. Students particularly have a high default rate on credit card debt. By charging 24 percent, companies can still earn a profit after adjustment for nonpayment. An interest rate ceiling would mean that credit card companies could no longer cover the losses from defaults, and they would have to cut back on the number of credit cards in the hands of less credit-worthy people. Students would no longer be solicited for credit card business; they may have their cards cancelled.

Those people who want a limit set on credit card interest may be the very ones who find that they will have to do without a credit card, surely an unintended consequence.

good or service than sellers. If the price is not allowed to rise, each buyer faces a prisoner's dilemma. They want to buy more but cannot. Thus, each buyer acts against the collective interests of all buyers.

Adam Smith's invisible hand is based on the principle that we should allow prices to find their equilibrium levels without interference. Equilibrium prices coordinate the actions of buyers and sellers even though each is following self-interest. (See Example 3.)

### PRICE CONTROLS: THE GAS PANIC OF 1973

In October 1973, the Organization of Petroleum Exporting Countries (OPEC) placed a total ban on oil exports to the United States after the outbreak of an Arab-Israeli conflict. The United States, heavily dependent upon imported oil, faced the prospect of running short of oil.

President Nixon responded by introducing a complicated system of government allocation that set the price of gasoline far below the equilibrium price. Gasoline stations were allowed to raise their prices only to price ceilings set by the government. Violators were punished by fines and imprisonment.

The intended consequence of the gas price controls was to prevent undue hardship, especially on the poor, by limiting increases in the price of gasoline at the pump. The unintended consequence was that people had to stand in line at gas stations, often starting at 4 A.M. The government price ceiling was too low to equate quantity demanded and quantity supplied. Arguments broke out at gas stations over who was in line first, a number of people were killed in these confrontations, and many gas station attendants carried firearms. Importantly, car owners protected themselves against the shortage of gasoline by trying to keep their gas tanks as full as possible all of

Sales of locking gas caps   sales ↑

## MONOPOLY

The invisible hand may not function well when a single firm controls the supply of a particular commodity. What makes Adam Smith's invisible hand work so well is that individual buyers and sellers compete with one another; no single buyer or seller has control over the price. The problem with monopoly—a single seller with considerable control over the price—is that the monopolist can hold back the amount of goods, drive up the price, and enjoy large profits. While the monopolist would benefit from such actions, the buyer would not.

## MACROECONOMIC INSTABILITY

The invisible hand may solve the economic problem of scarcity but may provide a level of overall economic activity that is unstable. It is a historical fact that capitalist economies have been subject to fluctuations in output, employment, and prices—called business cycles—and that these fluctuations have been costly to capitalist societies. A key question is: Are they the price of progress?

In later chapters, we shall discuss in detail not only the advantages of the invisible hand but also these limits.

## SUMMARY

1. The principle of unintended consequences states that well-intended economic policies may have unintended consequences. Their ultimate effects may differ from their intended effects.

2. Marginal analysis states that people make economic decisions by weighing the consequences of making changes from the current state. People have an incentive to undertake actions as long as the marginal benefits of those actions exceed the marginal costs.

3. Game theory concerns social or economic interactions in which individuals must take into account the behavior of others before they can determine their costs or benefits. The most important game is called the prisoner's dilemma, in which everybody would gain from cooperation but nobody has an individual incentive to do so.

4. Failure to understand the incentives people have in any situation can lead to unintended consequences, such as in the cases of federal bank deposit insurance, unemployment insurance, social security, and free medical care.

5. If the price is above the equilibrium price, a surplus will exist in which the quantity supplied exceeds the quantity demanded. If the price is below the equilibrium price, the quantity demanded exceeds the quantity supplied and a shortage will prevail. Policies that cause the price to deviate from the equilibrium price have unintended consequences because society now faces a prisoner's dilemma.

6. According to the principle of unintended consequences, policymakers must be careful in their policy decisions and take into consideration both the intended and unintended effects of their policies.

7. The invisible hand may not solve the problems of income distribution, public goods, externalities, monopoly, or macroeconomic instability.

## KEY TERMS

| | |
|---|---|
| marginal analysis | equilibrium price |
| game theory | disequilibrium price |
| prisoner's dilemma | surplus |
| principle of unintended consequences | shortage |

## QUESTIONS AND PROBLEMS

1. The current welfare system has the unintended consequence of breaking up poor families. Explain why this is so and try to devise a system that avoids this unintended consequence.
2. Consider the study example of marginal analysis. Apply it to another type of activity and use it to explain the optimal level of that activity.
3. What do you think would happen to the rate of unemployment in the country of Octavia if unemployment benefits were lowered and people could qualify for such benefits for only two weeks instead of six months? Use marginal analysis to explain your answer.
4. If J.P. Billionaire declared that he would pay for everyone's medication, what effect would this have on the prices of medication? Explain your answer.
5. Bread is currently selling for $1.50 per loaf. The government now declares that all stores must

sell it for $.50 per loaf to everyone to help the poor. Consider the effects of this action and its possible unintended consequences.

6. Explain why minimum wages could hurt teenage workers. Would the amount of hurt depend upon where the minimum wage was set?

7. If you were a loan shark would you favor or oppose usury laws (legal interest rate ceilings)?

8. The equilibrium price of gas rises to $2 from $1 a gallon. A price ceiling of $1 is imposed.

If each person drives less, the benefits are $100 a year. If one person drives more, while the rest of society drives less, that person benefits by $200 a year. If all try to drive more, the benefits to each are only $50 a year because of the time wasted looking for gas. What will happen?

# PART II

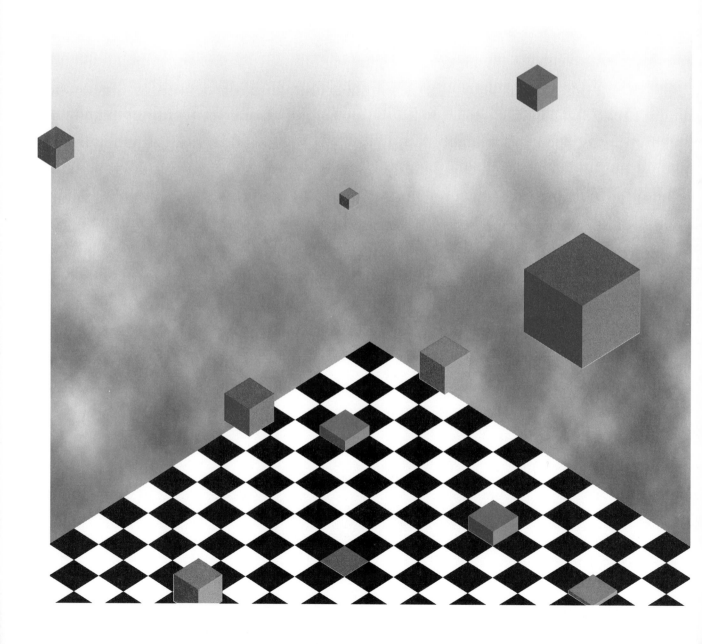

# PRODUCT MARKETS

# CHAPTER 6

# ELASTICITY OF DEMAND AND SUPPLY

The state of Texas once attempted to raise revenues with a 20 percent increase in tuition and fees at state universities and a 25 percent increase in the charge for vanity license plates. One year later, the state treasurer reported that revenues from tuition and fees from state universities were up 15 percent, while revenues from vanity license plates were down 10 percent.

This chapter uses the concept of price elasticity, which shows that the sensitivity of buyers to price increases varies from product to product, to explain why raising prices increased revenues from tuition and fees but decreased revenues from vanity license plates. The tuition raise at state universities caused only a few students (at least in the short run) to go out of state or switch to private universities, so revenues increased. However, when the price of vanity license plates was raised, many people switched to regular license plates (a perfectly good substitute), so revenues fell.

The elasticity concept applies not only to the responsiveness of quantity sold to changes in the good's own price but also to the responsiveness of demand to changes in income and in the prices of other goods. In addition, there are elasticity measures of the responsiveness of quantity supplied to changes in price.

# THE PRICE ELASTICITY OF DEMAND

Remember that the demand curve shows how quantity demanded responds to different prices, if all other things are equal, and the supply curve shows how quantity supplied responds to different prices, if all other things are equal. In panels *(a)* and *(b)* of Figure 1, the equilibrium intersection of *S* (the supply curve) and the demand curve (whether *D* or *D'*) is at point *e*, where price is $10 and quantity is 100 units. The only difference between the two diagrams is in the demand curve. *D* in panel *(a)* is much flatter than *D'* in panel *(b)*. The supply curves *(S)* are identical.

Suppose that there is a reduction in supply. The leftward shifts of the supply curve from *S* to *S'* are the same in panels *(a)* and *(b)*. When supply decreases, equilibrium price rises and equilibrium quantity falls. The equilibrium point *e* moves in panel *(a)* to *e'* and in panel *(b)* to *e"*. In panel *(a)*, the price increase (from $10 to $14) is relatively small compared to the substantial reduction in quantity demanded (from 100 units to only 20 units). In panel *(b)*, on the other hand, the price increase (from $10 to $20) is relatively large compared to the small re-

duction in quantity demanded from 100 to 80 units. The difference between the two demand curves in panels *(a)* and *(b)* is in the *responsiveness of quantity demanded to a price increase*. In panel *(a)*, quantity demanded is quite responsive to the price change; in panel *(b)*, it is less responsive. The price elasticity of demand $(E_d)$ is a measure of this responsiveness.

> The **price elasticity of demand** $(E_d)$ is the percentage change in the quantity demanded divided by the percentage change in price.

Absolute changes in price or quantity demanded are poor measures of responsiveness. If a $1 increase in the price of coal lowers quantity demanded by 1 ton, we cannot determine whether these changes are large or small unless we know the initial price and quantity. If the initial price is $2 per ton, a $1 change in price represents a 50 percent increase in price. If the initial price is $1000, a $1 change in price is minuscule. The same principle applies to quantity changes. The measure of the response of quantity demanded to change in price must therefore be the relative (or percentage) change in price or quantity demanded.

*(a)* Quality Demanded Is More Responsive to Price Change

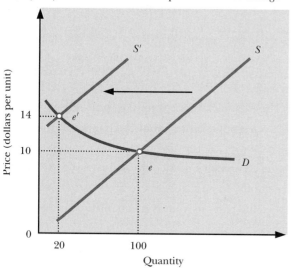

*(b)* Quality Demanded Is Less Responsive to Price Change

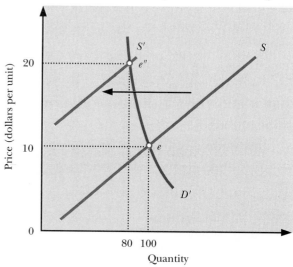

**FIGURE 1    Response to a Reduction in Supply**

In both panels *(a)* and *(b)*, *S* intersects the demand curve at the equilibrium price-quantity combination of $10–100 units. The supply conditions are exactly the same in each diagram, but the quantity demanded is less responsive to price changes in panel *(b)* than in panel *(a)*. A decrease in supply from *S* to *S'* causes a sharper increase in the equilibrium price when quantity demanded is less responsive to price. Although the price increase in *(b)* from $10 to $20 is greater than the price increase in *(a)* from $10 to $14, quantity demanded falls more in *(a)* than it does in *(b)*.

## THE COEFFICIENT OF THE PRICE ELASTICITY OF DEMAND

Because of the law of demand, the quantity demanded rises when the price falls, and the quantity demanded falls when the price rises. Thus the sign of the price elasticity of demand will be negative. It is a convention in economics that, when calculating the *coefficient* of the price elasticity of demand, you drop the negative sign and use the *absolute value* of the elasticity.

*Quiz*

The coefficient of the price elasticity of demand ($E_d$) is the absolute value of the percentage change in quantity demanded ($\%\Delta Q$) divided by the percentage change in price ($\%\Delta P$):

*PQ*

$$E_d = \left| \frac{\%\Delta Q}{\%\Delta P} \right|$$

where $\%\Delta$ stands for percentage change.

For example, if $P$ rises by 10 percent and $Q$ falls by 20 percent, $E_d$ equals 20 percent divided by 10 percent, or 2. An elasticity coefficient of 2 means that if prices were raised from the prevailing level, the percentage change in quantity demanded would be 2 times the percentage change in price. The elasticity coefficient measures the percentage change in quantity demanded for each 1 percent change in price. With an elasticity coefficient of 2, a 5 percent increase in price means a 10 percent reduction in quantity demanded.

## CALCULATING THE PRICE ELASTICITY OF DEMAND

Table 1 shows how to calculate the price elasticity of demand. The price of wheat per bushel changes from $4.50 to $5.50, and the quantity demanded responds by falling from 105 to 95 bushels. We determine the price elasticity of demand by calculating the percentage changes in quantity demanded and price. This may seem simple, but there is a trick: We must calculate the percentage change on the basis of *average* quantity and *average* price. Why? The price elasticity should be the same whether the price rises or falls. If we use the initial price or quantity, this would not be the case. When the price rises from $4.50 to $5.50, the percentage increase is ($1/$4.50) × 100 = 22 percent. When the price falls from $5.50 to $4.50, the percentage decrease is ($1/$5.50) × 100 = 18 percent. To avoid one price elasticity for rising prices and another for falling prices, we calculate the percentage change on the basis of the average price, $5 = ($4.50 + $5.50)/2. Thus, the percentage change in the price is ($1/$5) × 100 = 20 percent for both price increases and price reductions. The change in quantity demanded is 10 bushels; the average quantity demanded is 100 = (95 + 105)/2. The percentage change in quantity demanded is (10/100) × 100 = 10 percent for both quantity increases and quantity decreases. Accordingly, the price elasticity is $E_d$ = 10 percent/20 percent = 0.5.

| Table 1    How to Calculate the Price Elasticity of Demand | | |
|---|---|---|
| | *Prices (dollars per bushel)* | *Symbols* |
| Initial price | $4.50 | $P_0$ |
| Change in price | 1.00 | $\Delta P$ |
| New price | 5.50 | $P_1 = P_0 + \Delta P$ |
| Average price | 5.00 | $P = (P_0 + P_1)/2$ |
| Percentage change in price | 20% | $(\Delta P/P) \times 100$ |
| | *Quantities (bushels of wheat)* | |
| Initial quantity demanded | 105 | $Q_0$ |
| Change in quantity demanded | −10 | $\Delta Q$ |
| New quantity demanded | 95 | $Q_1 = Q_0 + \Delta Q$ |
| Average quantity demanded | 100 | $Q = (Q_0 + Q_1)/2$ |
| Percentage change in $Q$ | 10% | $(\Delta Q/Q) \times 100$ |
| Price elasticity of demand | 10%/20% = 0.5 | $(\Delta Q/Q)/(\Delta P/P)$ |

The use of the average price and average quantity to calculate the price elasticity of demand is the midpoints elasticity formula. This formula yields the same elasticity coefficient for an increase from a lower price to a higher price as for the decrease from the higher price to the lower price.[1]

> The **midpoints elasticity formula** for determining the elasticity of demand ($E_d$) for a given segment of the demand curve is
>
> $$E_d = \frac{\text{Percent change in quantity demanded}}{\text{Percent change in price}}$$
>
> $$= \frac{\dfrac{\text{Change in quantity demanded}}{\text{Average of two quantities}}}{\div\ \dfrac{\text{Change in price}}{\text{Average of two prices}}}$$

## ELASTICITY AND TOTAL REVENUE

Economists divide elasticity coefficients into three broad categories:

1. When $E_d > 1$, demand is *elastic* ($Q$ is strongly responsive to changes in $P$).
2. When $E_d < 1$, demand is *inelastic* ($Q$ responds weakly to changes in $P$).
3. When $E_d = 1$, demand is *unitary elastic* (a borderline case).

The above distinctions are made because the coefficient of the elasticity of demand shows what will happen to the total revenue (TR) of sellers when price changes along a given demand curve.

> The **total revenue (TR)** of sellers in a market is the price of the commodity times the quantity sold:
>
> $$TR = P \times Q$$

---

[1]In symbols, if $P_1$ and $P_2$ are the two prices and $Q_1$ and $Q_2$ are the two quantities, the midpoints elasticity formula can be simplified as follows:

$$E_d = -\frac{Q_2 - Q_1}{(Q_1 + Q_2)/2} \div \frac{P_2 - P_1}{(P_1 + P_2)/2}$$

$$= \frac{Q_2 - Q_1}{P_1 - P_2} \times \frac{P_1 + P_2}{Q_1 + Q_2}$$

$P\uparrow\ TR\uparrow\ \text{Inelastic}$

Along a demand curve, price and quantity demanded move in opposite directions. While a fall in price lowers total revenue, the resulting rise in quantity demanded raises total revenue. The direction of total revenue is determined by a tug-of-war between these conflicting forces. The outcome depends on the extent to which quantity demanded responds to changes in price. For example, a relatively small rise in quantity demanded will not offset the decline in revenue caused by a fall in price, but a substantial rise in quantity demanded could offset the revenue loss caused by a lower price. Thus, the response of total revenue to price changes depends on the price elasticity of demand.

**Elastic Demand.** If $E_d > 1$, the percentage rise in quantity demanded is greater than the percentage fall in price. Revenue *increases* because the increase in quantity demanded more than offsets the *decrease* in price. Price and revenue move in opposite directions.

> When $E_d > 1$, $|\%\Delta Q| > |\%\Delta P|$; thus TR will move in the opposite direction of price.

**Inelastic Demand.** If $E_d < 1$, the percentage rise in quantity demanded is less than the percentage fall in price. Revenue *falls* because the *decline* in price is not offset by the relatively small rise in quantity. Price and revenue move in the same direction.

> When $E_d < 1$, $|\%\Delta Q| < |\%\Delta P|$; thus TR will move in the same direction as price.

**Unitary Elastic Demand.** If $E_d = 1$, the percentage rise in quantity demanded equals the percentage fall in price. Revenue is unchanged because the decline in price is just offset by the rise in quantity.

> When $E_d = 1$, $|\%\Delta Q| = |\%\Delta P|$; thus TR will not change.

We can always determine whether demand is elastic, inelastic, or unitary elastic by the total revenue test, which simply checks what happens to total revenue when the price changes. Just to know that demand is inelastic or elastic is very important to the business firm. (See Example 1.)

> The **total revenue test** uses the following criteria to determine elasticity:
>
> 1. If price and total revenue move in different directions, $E_d > 1$ (demand is elastic).

$P\downarrow\ TR\uparrow\ \text{Elastic}$

# EXAMPLE 1
## THE DEMAND FOR CIGARETTES

We know more about the demand for cigarettes than we do about the demand for any other single product. States differ in the composition of their population, income, and taxes, and in consumption. Large differences in state taxes on cigarettes mean that consumers in different states with the same income and age face different prices. Thus, economists are able to determine with greater precision the effect of price on quantity demanded for cigarettes than for other products.

The results of detailed studies shows that the demand for cigarettes is price inelastic. If demand is inelastic, a higher price will raise revenue and, therefore, profit. If this is the case, why don't cigarette companies raise their prices? There are two explanations for this: First, competition between the cigarette companies keeps prices from rising too rapidly; and, second, cigarette companies keep the prices low in order to keep customers addicted to smoking.

--------------------------------------------

*Source:* Gary S. Becker, Michael Grossman, and Kevin M. Murphy, "An Empirical Analysis of Cigarette Addiction," *American Economic Review* 84 (June 1994): 396–418..

---

2. If price and total revenue move in the same direction, $E_d < 1$ (demand is inelastic).

3. If total revenue does not change when price changes, $E_d = 1$ (demand is unitary elastic).

## ELASTICITY ALONG A DEMAND CURVE

Figure 2 applies these tests for determining elasticity to the case of a linear demand schedule in which a given change in price always causes the same change in quantity demanded. In the accompanying table, column 3 shows total revenue (price times quantity) at different prices. In panel *a*, the price is reduced from $9 to $7; 15 units were sold at $9, and now 25 units are sold at $7. The blue area indicates the loss in revenue that occurred because the first 15 units had to be sold at the lower price of $7. But more units are sold at $7 than at $9. The orange area indicates the revenue gained from the sale of more units. Total revenue rises because the orange area is larger than the blue area when demand is *elastic*. The revenue lost through the lower price is more than offset by the revenue gained by the sale of substantially more units.

The midpoints formula also confirms that demand is elastic when price falls from $9 to $7. The percent change in quantity demanded (50 percent) divided by the percent change in price (25 percent) equals 2.

If price now falls from $7 to $5, as in panel *(b)*, demand is unitary elastic; in this case, revenue remains constant because the revenue lost (the blue area) equals the revenue gained (the orange area). As price falls further from $5 to $3, demand is inelastic. In panel *(c)*, the revenue lost (the blue area) exceeds the revenue gained (the orange area) from selling a few more units, so total revenue falls. The midpoint formula confirms that the coefficient of price elasticity is inelastic (0.5).

## PERFECTLY ELASTIC OR PERFECTLY INELASTIC DEMAND CURVES

The highest degree of elasticity possible—the greatest responsiveness of quantity demanded to price—is a perfectly horizontal demand curve. In Figure 3 on page 99, any amount on demand curve *D* can be sold at the indicated price ($5). Such a horizontal demand curve describes perfectly elastic demand.

A horizontal demand curve illustrates **perfectly elastic demand** ($E_d = \infty$), a condition in which quantity demanded is most responsive to price.

(a) Elastic Demand

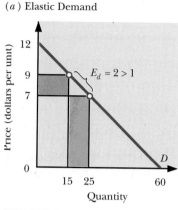

(b) Unitary Elastic Demand

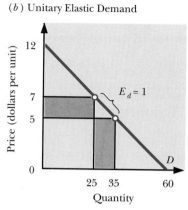

(c) Inelastic Demand

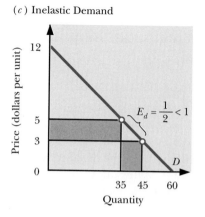

**FIGURE 2   Total Revenue and Elasticity**

The linear demand curve, D, is the same in panels (a), (b), and (c). Between the prices of $9 and $7, the elasticity of demand ($E_d$) is 2; demand is elastic. Panel (a) shows that a reduction in price raises revenue. The blue rectangle shows the revenue lost due to the lower price, and the orange rectangle shows the revenue gained due to the greater number of units sold. Because the orange rectangle has a greater area than the blue rectangle, more revenue is gained than lost. Between prices of $7 and $5, $E_d$ equals 1; panel (b) shows that the reduction in price has no impact on revenue. Finally, between the prices of $5 and $3, $E_d$ is 1/2; demand is inelastic. Panel (c) shows that the reduction in price lowers revenue because more revenue is lost (blue area) than gained (orange area). Thus, the elasticity of demand varies along a linear demand curve with constant slope. *Elasticity and slope are different.*

| | Price (dollars per unit) $P$ (1) | Quantity (units) $Q$ (2) | Total Revenue $TR = P \times Q$ (3) = (1) × (2) | Percentage Change in Quantity Demanded $\frac{\Delta Q}{(Q_1 + Q_2)/2}$ (4) | Percentage Change in Price $\frac{\Delta P}{(P_1 + P_2)/2}$ (5) | Coefficient of Price Elasticity, $E_d$ (6) = (4) ÷ (5) |
|---|---|---|---|---|---|---|
| (a) | 9 | 15 | 135 | | | |
| | 7 | 25 | 175 | $\frac{10}{20} = 50\%$ | $\frac{2}{8} = 25\%$ | $\frac{50}{25} = 2$ |
| (b) | 5 | 35 | 175 | $\frac{10}{30} = 33.3\%$ | $\frac{2}{6} = 33.3\%$ | $\frac{33.3}{33.3} = 1$ |
| (c) | 3 | 45 | 135 | $\frac{10}{40} = 25\%$ | $\frac{2}{4} = 50\%$ | $\frac{25}{50} = 0.5$ |

Columns 1 and 2 show the demand schedule graphed above. Column 3 is the total revenue of sellers. Column 4 shows the percentage change in quantity using the midpoint formula. Column 5 shows the percentage change in price using the midpoint formula. Finally, column 6 shows the elasticity of demand, $E_d$.

The elasticity formula shows that $E_d$ is infinitely large ($E_d = \infty$) when the demand curve is horizontal: The quantity demanded can be increased indefinitely without a decrease in price. As a result, the elasticity formula yields an infinitely large coefficient of price elasticity of demand.

Perfectly elastic demand curves are actually common in the real world. In competitive markets in which no single producer is large enough to influence the market price, each seller can sell all he or she wants to sell at the market price. American wheat farmers can sell all they want at the prevail-

*Do not exist*

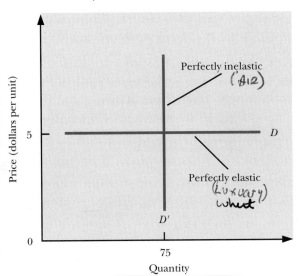

**FIGURE 3** **Perfectly Elastic and Perfectly Inelastic Demand Curves**

The demand curve *D* is perfectly elastic; it is perfectly horizontal, or parallel to the quantity axis. The demand curve *D'* is perfectly inelastic; it is perfectly vertical, or parallel to the price axis. The elasticity-of-demand coefficient of *D* is infinitely large along the entire demand schedule. The elasticity-of-demand coefficient of *D'* is zero along the entire demand curve.

ing market price and can't sell anything at a higher price. Thus each seller faces a horizontal demand curve even though the market demand curve is downward sloping.

The lowest degree of inelasticity possible—the least sensitivity of quantity demanded to price—occurs when the demand curve is perfectly vertical.

> A vertical demand curve illustrates **perfectly inelastic demand** ($E_d = 0$), a condition in which quantity demanded is least responsive to price.

In Figure 3, with the vertical demand curve *D'*, 75 units of the good will be sold regardless of the price. The coefficient of the elasticity of demand is zero because if the price were to rise above $5, the percentage change in the quantity demanded would be zero. When zero is divided by the percentage change in price, $E_d$ is zero.

With a perfectly inelastic demand curve, no matter how high the price rises, consumers will not cut back on the quantity demanded. The demand curve of insulin for the diabetic is probably as close

to perfectly inelastic as possible, but even in this case if the price rose higher and higher, diabetics would have to reduce their dosages and accept some health loss or change their behavior by eating less or exercising more.

Demand curves can be perfectly inelastic *within a range of prices*. If insulin prices rose by 10 percent, the quantity demanded would probably not change. If the price of salt rose from $0.20 to $0.22 per pound, the quantity demanded would probably stay the same. But raising these prices by 500 percent could lower quantity demanded.

## ELASTICITY VERSUS SLOPE ALONG A DEMAND CURVE

Perfectly elastic and inelastic demand curves describe very special circumstances: the extremes of infinite response and no response. A vertical demand curve shows perfect inelasticity; a horizontal demand curve shows perfect elasticity. It might be tempting to conclude, by analogy, that demand is more elastic when the demand curve is "flat" than when the demand curve is "steep." This conclusion would be wrong.

The price elasticity of demand is different from the slope of the demand curve. Although both elasticity and slope measure the response of quantity demanded to change in price, the slope of the demand curve does not indicate the size of the response. In Figure 2, each time the price falls by $2, quantity demanded rises by 10 units. The slope of the demand curve is constant because the curve is a straight line. We showed earlier that as the price falls from $9 to $7, from $7 to $5, and from $5 to $3, the price elasticity of demand falls. Why? For each successive $2 price reduction, the percentage change in price rises since *P* is falling; and for the same increases in quantity demanded, the percentage change in quantity demanded falls since *Q* is rising.

Typically, price elasticity of demand falls as prices fall: Consumers are more responsive to price changes at high prices than at low prices. When hand calculators were introduced in the 1970s, they sold for about $200. The demand for them was very price elastic: When their price started to fall, consumers eagerly increased the quantity demanded as they substituted hand calculators for slide rules. Today, the price of hand calculators is very low ($10 or less). A reduction in price would bring about a comparatively small increase in quantity demanded.

*Important section*

## DETERMINANTS OF PRICE ELASTICITY OF DEMAND

What determines the sensitivity of consumers to price? The three important determinants of the price elasticity of demand for a good are (1) the availability of substitutes, (2) the relative importance of the good in the budget, and (3) the amount of time available to adjust to the price change.

**The Availability of Substitutes.**   Every good has substitutes, but some goods have excellent substitutes and others have very poor ones. The price elasticity of demand depends upon how easily people can turn to substitutes.

Consider the price elasticity of demand for postal service. The elasticity of demand has increased substantially with the introduction of new substitutes— fax machines and electronic mail. Sending a fax is cheaper and faster than sending a letter.

The availability of substitutes depends upon how broadly a good is defined. The elasticity of demand for automobiles is lower than that for Chevrolets. The demand for energy is less elastic than the demand for natural gas. The demand for entertainment will be less elastic than the demand for movie tickets. The more narrowly defined the product (Chevrolets versus automobiles, natural gas versus energy, movie tickets versus entertainment), the greater the number of close substitutes (Plymouths for Chevrolets, natural gas for electricity, cable TV for movies) and the higher the elasticity of demand.

> The greater is the number of close substitutes for a good, the *more elastic* is its demand. The smaller is the number of close substitutes for a good, the *more inelastic* is its demand.

**The Relative Importance of the Good in a Consumer's Budget.**   Both gasoline and salt have few close substitutes. Which one should be more elastic?

An increase in the price of salt from $0.40 to $0.50 a package (a 22 percent increase by the midpoints method) would not have a substantial percentage effect on purchases of salt. The average household buys two boxes of salt per year, so a 22 percent price increase would raise the family's cost of living by only $0.20 per year. A 22 percent increase in the price of gasoline, however, translates into a price increase from $1.20 per gallon to $1.50 per gallon. The average family consumes about 1000 gallons of gas per year, so its cost of living would be increased by $300 per year. Consumers would scarcely notice the salt price increase, so their purchases would hardly be affected, but the gasoline price increase would hit their pocketbooks hard and would therefore depress gasoline purchases.

As this comparison shows, the price elasticity of demand depends upon the relative importance of the good in the consumer's budget.

> Goods that represent a small fraction of the consumer's budget (salt, pepper, drinking water, matches) are more inelastic in demand than products that constitute a large fraction of the consumer's budget (automobiles, fuel oil, mortgage payments, personal computers), other things being equal.

**Time to Adjust to Price Changes.**   Demand becomes more elastic as consumers have more time to adjust to price changes. This pattern is explained by a number of factors. Consider the response of consumers to higher electricity prices. Immediately after electric utility rates are increased, we can do little more than lower our heating thermostats in the winter and raise our air-conditioning thermostats in the summer. As time passes, additional substitutes for electricity become available. Extra insulation and more energy-efficient heating and air-conditioning equipment can be installed. If natural-gas prices have not risen as much, we can convert to natural-gas appliances when our old system needs to be replaced.

Many expenditures are determined by habits, which are often hard to break. The family may be used to setting the thermostat at 72 degrees in the winter: They may need time to adjust to cooler temperatures when energy prices rise.

> Generally speaking, demand becomes more elastic as consumers have more time in which to adjust to changes in prices.

The principles discussed in this section are illustrated by actual price elasticities, such as those described in Table 2. Two variants are presented: the *short-run* $E_d$ (where the consumer has not had more time to adjust to price changes) and the *long-run* $E_d$ (where the consumer has had more time to adjust to price changes).

The elasticities show that long-run elasticities are larger than short-run elasticities. The elasticities in

## Table 2  Short-Run and Long-Run Price Elasticities

| | $E_d$ in Short Run | $E_d$ in Long Run |
|---|---|---|
| Cigarettes | 0.44 | 0.78 |
| Jewelry | 0.41 | 0.67 |
| Toilet articles | 0.20 | 3.04 |
| Owner-occupied housing | 0.04 | 1.22 |
| China and glassware | 1.55 | 2.55 |
| Electricity | 0.13 | 1.89 |
| Water | 0.20 | 0.14 |
| Medical care and hospitalization | 0.31 | 0.92 |
| Tires | 0.86 | 1.19 |
| Auto repairs | 0.40 | 0.38 |
| Durable recreation equipment | 0.88 | 2.39 |
| Motion pictures | 0.88 | 3.69 |
| Foreign travel | 0.14 | 1.77 |
| Gasoline | 0.15 | 0.78 |

*Sources:* Hendrick S. Houthakker and Lester D. Taylor, *Consumer Demand in the United States: Analyses and Projections* (Cambridge, MA: Harvard University Press, 1970), 166–167; James L. Sweeney, "The Demand for Gasoline: A Vintage Capital Model," Working Paper, Department of Engineering Economics, Stanford University; Gary S. Becker, Michael Grossman, and Kevin M. Murphy, "An Empirical Analysis of Cigarette Addiction," *American Economic Review* 84 (June 1994): 396–418.

the table also illustrate the important role of substitutes. Medical care has fewer substitutes than most of the other products, and it has lower short-run and long-run elasticities than products such as motion pictures, recreation equipment, gasoline, and foreign travel. Electricity has no good short-run substitutes, and short-run electricity $E_d$ is low.

## OTHER ELASTICITIES OF DEMAND

We know from Chapter 4 that consumer demand depends not only on the product's own price, but also on consumer preferences, the prices of substitutes and complements, and consumer income. Although economists devote most of their attention to price elasticity of demand, the elasticity concept is also applied to the other factors affecting demand. Economists measure the responsiveness of demand to the prices of related goods (cross-price elasticity) and the responsiveness of demand to consumer income (income elasticity). The concepts of cross-price elasticity and income elasticity provide insights into the interrelationships of prices and the effects of income changes on consumer demands.

## CROSS-PRICE ELASTICITY

A change in the price of one product affects the demand schedules of related products. This responsiveness of demand to other prices is measured by the cross-price elasticity of demand ($E_{xy}$).

> The **cross-price elasticity of demand ($E_{xy}$)** is the percentage change in demand of the first product ($x$) divided by the percentage change in the price of the related product ($y$).[2]

Unlike the price elasticity of demand, which is negative, the cross-price elasticity can be either positive or negative.

A positive cross-price elasticity of demand means that an increase in the price of one product will cause an increase in the demand for the other product and vice versa. As the price of beef rises, the quantity of beef demanded falls, in part because substitutes have been purchased in place of beef. Chicken is a *substitute* for beef; therefore, the increase in the price of beef causes an increase in the demand for chicken. Generally speaking, the *closer* the substitutes, the *higher* the cross-price elasticity.

A negative cross-price elasticity means that an increase in the price of one product will cause a decrease in the demand for the other product. Airline travel and auto rentals are *complements* because a large proportion of auto rentals are made by airline travelers. If the price of airline tickets falls, auto rental companies can expect an increase in rentals from the larger number of travelers. Table 3 contains a few estimates of some actual cross-price elasticities.

> If the cross-price elasticity of demand is positive, the two products are *substitutes*. If the cross-price elasticity is negative, the two products are *complements*. If the cross-price elasticity is zero, the products are unrelated.

## INCOME ELASTICITY

A rise or fall in consumer income will affect the demands for different products. As consumer income

---

[2]The cross-price elasticity of demand is calculated by the same midpoints elasticity formula as the elasticity of demand. The only difference is that instead of the "own price" ($P_x$), the price of the related product ($P_y$) is in the denominator.

$$E_{xy} = \frac{Q_{x2} - Q_{x1}}{Q_{x1} + Q_{x2}} \div \frac{P_{y2} - P_{y1}}{P_{y1} + P_{y2}}$$

| Table 3 Selected Cross-Price Elasticities | | |
|---|---|---|
| Good No. 1 | Good No. 2 | Elasticity Coefficient |
| Butter[a] | Margarine | 0.67 |
| Natural gas[b] | Fuel oil | 0.44 |
| Beef[a] | Pork | 0.28 |
| Cheese[c] | Butter | −0.61 |

Sources: [a]H. Wold and L. Jureen, *Demand Analysis* (New York: Wiley, 1953); [b]L. Taylor and R. Halvorsen, "Energy Substitution in U.S. Manufacturing," *The Review of Economics and Statistics* (November 1977); [c]L. Philips, *Applied Consumption Analysis* (Amsterdam: North-Holland, 1974).

| Table 4 Selected Income Elasticities | |
|---|---|
| Good | Elasticity Coefficient |
| Motion-picture tickets[a] | 3.4 |
| Foreign travel[a] | 3.1 |
| Toys[a] | 2.0 |
| Automobiles and parts[b] | 1.7 |
| Clothing and shoes[b] | 1.1 |
| Furniture[b] | 0.9 |
| Beef[c] | 0.5 |
| Pork[c] | 0.3 |
| Lard[c] | −0.1 |

Sources: [a]H.S. Houthakker and L.D. Taylor, *Consumer Demand in the United States* (Cambridge, MA: Harvard University Press, 1970); [b]L. Philips, *Applied Consumption Analysis* (Amsterdam: North-Holland, 1974); [c]G.E. Brandow, "Interrelations among Demands for Farm Products and Implications for Control of Market Supply," Pennsylvania State University Agricultural Experiment Station Bulletin 680, 1961.

rises, the demand for most products increases. The responsiveness of demand to consumer income is measured by the income elasticity of demand ($E_i$).

The **income elasticity of demand ($E_i$)** is the percentage change in the demand for a product divided by the percentage change in income, holding all prices fixed.[3]

The income elasticity of demand is usually positive for most goods because higher consumer income usually means increased spending. If the income elasticity equals unity, each 1 percent increase in income will lead to a 1 percent increase in the demand for the good. Hence consumers would continue to spend the same fraction of their income on the good as before their income increased. For example, a consumer spends $10 on soft drinks out of $100 weekly income. If the income elasticity is 1, an increase in income to $110 will increase spending on soft drinks to $11; therefore, the fraction spent is still 10 percent. If the income elasticity exceeds 1, people will spend a larger fraction of their income on the good as income rises. If the income elasticity is less than 1, people will spend a smaller fraction of their income on that good as income rises. We can define the terms *necessities* and *luxuries* using the income elasticity of demand concept.

**Necessities** are those products that have an income elasticity of demand less than 1.

[3]The midpoints elasticity formula for the income elasticity of demand is

$$E_i = \frac{Q_2 - Q_1}{Q_1 + Q_2} \div \frac{I_2 - I_1}{I_1 + I_2}$$

where $I$ denotes consumer income.

**Luxuries** are those products that have an income elasticity of demand greater than 1.

Based on this criterion, goods such as food items are necessities, and recreational vehicles are luxury items. Notice, though, that the economist allows the terms *luxury* and *necessity* to be defined by the market choices people make rather than by individual perceptions about what is more "necessary" than something else. See Table 4 for some selected income elasticities ranging from movies (3.4) to lard (−0.1). (See also Example 2.)

## THE PRICE ELASTICITY OF SUPPLY

The price elasticity of demand measures the responsiveness of *consumers* to price change. The price elasticity of supply ($E_s$) measures the responsiveness of *producers* to price changes.

The **price elasticity of supply ($E_s$)** is the percentage change in the quantity supplied divided by the percentage change in price.

We calculate the elasticity of supply in the same way as the elasticity of demand, only now $Q$ refers to quantities *supplied*, not quantities demanded.

According to the midpoints formula, $E_s$ is calculated as

## EXAMPLE 2
## ENGEL'S LAW AND INCOME ELASTICITIES: WHERE HAVE ALL THE FARMERS GONE?

The income elasticity of demand is the percentage change in demand divided by the percentage change in income. If a product's income elasticity of demand is less than 1, its purchases tend to rise more slowly than income, and its share of total consumer spending falls.

The nineteenth-century German statistician Ernst Engel noted a statistical regularity in his studies of family budgets in different countries. Engel found that as family income increases, the percentage of the budget spent on food declines. Subsequent statistical studies have confirmed this finding. This statistical regularity has come to be called *Engel's law*. In terms of income elasticity, Engel's law simply means that the income elasticity of demand for food is less than 1.

The inelastic income elasticity of demand explains a trend that characterizes virtually all economies. As income grows, the share of income devoted to purchases of agricultural goods falls. A smaller share of income is spent on goods produced by agriculture, and larger shares are spent on manufacturing and services. The factors of production therefore shift in relative terms from agriculture to manufacturing and services in response to the relative change in consumer demand.

Engel's law explains (at least partially) the declining shares of the farm population in industrialized societies. At the turn of the century, U.S. families spent $0.30 of every dollar on food. In 1929, they spent $0.25 of every dollar on food; and in 1995, they spent about $0.15 of every dollar on food. At the turn of the century, one in three workers was employed in agriculture. On the eve of World War II, only one in ten workers was employed in agriculture. By 1995, only two in every hundred workers were employed in agriculture.

------------------------------------------------

*Source: Historical Statistics of the United States.*

$$E_s = \frac{Q_2 - Q_1}{(Q_1 + Q_2)/2} \div \frac{P_2 - P_1}{(P_1 + P_2)/2}$$

Like the elasticity of demand, the $E_s$ coefficients are divided into three categories: elastic ($E_s > 1$), unitary elastic ($E_s = 1$), and inelastic ($E_s < 1$). The direction of movement of total revenue along a supply curve, however, will not depend upon the value of $E_s$. The $E_s$ coefficient is positive except in rare cases because firms usually respond to a higher price by producing more.

## PERFECTLY ELASTIC AND PERFECTLY INELASTIC SUPPLY CURVES

The highest degree of elasticity possible for a supply curve is a perfectly horizontal supply curve.

A horizontal supply curve illustrates **perfectly elastic supply** ($E_s = \infty$); quantity supplied is most responsive to price.

In Figure 4, supply curve *S* illustrates a case in which, at the price of $10, producers of the good are willing to supply any amount of the good to the market at that price.

Most of the supply curves that the average consumer encounters are perfectly elastic. The grocery store is willing to sell any person all the bread, canned goods, and dairy products that person wants to buy at the prices set. Under normal circumstances, however, all buyers together (the market) must offer higher prices to induce producers to increase the quantity supplied.

The lowest degree of elasticity occurs when the supply curve is perfectly vertical, as shown in Figure 4 by supply curve *S'*.

A vertical supply curve illustrates **perfectly inelastic supply** ($E_s = 0$); quantity supplied is least responsive to price.

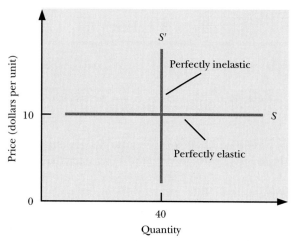

**FIGURE 4   Perfectly Elastic and Perfectly Inelastic Supply Curves**

The supply curve $S$ is perfectly elastic because at a price of $10 any quantity of output can be offered on the market by sellers. The supply curve $S'$ is perfectly inelastic because no matter how much the price rises, the quantity supplied remains the same.

The coefficient of $E_s$ in this case is zero. An increase in price has no effect on quantity supplied; therefore, the percentage change in quantity supplied is zero. A good example would be the fisher's catch of fresh fish at the end of the day. Here the supplier cannot go back out on the boat to increase that day's supply of fresh fish if the price rises.

Most market supply curves fall between the two extremes of perfect elasticity ($E_s = \infty$) and perfect inelasticity ($E_s = 0$).

## ELASTICITY OF SUPPLY IN THREE TIME PERIODS

Like elasticity of demand, elasticity of supply depends upon, among other things, the amount of time the consumer has to respond to price changes.

> In general, the elasticity of supply increases as the producer has more time to adjust to changes in prices.

When prices change, economists distinguish between three time periods during which producers adjust their supply to the new prices: the immediate run, the short run, and the long run.

The **immediate run** is a period of time so short that the quantity supplied cannot be changed at all. In the immediate run—sometimes called the *momentary period* or *market period*—supply curves are perfectly inelastic.

The **short run** is a period of time long enough for existing firms to produce more goods but not long enough for existing firms to expand their capacity or for new firms to enter the market. Thus output can be varied, but only within the limits of existing plant capacity.

The **long run** is a period of time long enough for new firms to enter the market, for old firms to disappear, and for existing plants to be expanded. In the long run, firms have more flexibility in adjusting to price changes.

The amount of calendar time required to move from the short run to the long run varies with the type of industry. The electric power industry may require a decade to expand existing power-generating facilities and bring new plants on line. On the other hand, the fast-food industry can construct and open a new outlet in a few months.

The long-run elasticity of supply is determined primarily by the specificity of the factors of production used in the production of the good or service in question. Products that use factors of production similar to those in use throughout the economy will have high elasticities of supply. In this case, it is easy to expand production of the particular product because additional supplies of the required inputs are readily available. But products that use highly specialized resources will tend to have lower elasticities of supply because additional production puts upward pressure on the prices of the required inputs. For example, Table 5 shows some estimated long-run elasticities of supply in the U.S. economy. Products like oil and natural gas have relatively low supply elasticities compared with urban housing.

## ELASTICITY AND THE TAX BURDEN

Local, state, and federal governments tax a variety of goods and services, including tobacco, alcohol, gasoline, and various foreign imports. Elasticity of demand and supply explains how the burden of such taxes falls on consumers or producers. The group with the lowest sensitivity to price pays the largest share of the tax.

## Table 5   Selected Estimates of Long-Run Supply Elasticities

| Good | Elasticity Coefficient |
|---|---|
| Wheat[a] | 0.93 |
| Corn[a] | 0.18 |
| U.S. oil[b] | 0.76 |
| Natural gas[c] | 0.20 |
| Urban housing[d] | 5.30 |

Sources: [a]M. Nerlove, "Estimates of the Elasticities of Supply of Selected Agricultural Commodities," *Journal of Farm Economics* (May 1956); [b]E.W. Ericson, S.W. Millsaps, and R.M. Spann, "Oil Supply and Tax Incentives," *Brookings Papers on Economic Activity* (1974); [c]J.D. Khazzoom, "The FPC Staff's Econometric Model of Natural Gas Supply in the United States," *The Bell Journal of Economics* (Spring 1971); [d]B.A. Smith, "The Supply of Urban Housing," *Journal of Political Economy* (1976).

## HOW THE TAX BURDEN IS SHARED

We shall consider a tax imposed only on producers because we will discover that a tax on consumers has exactly the same effects. A tax on all producers of a product will simply shift up their supply curve by the amount of the tax, because every point on the supply curve shows the lowest net price the producers are willing to accept for the corresponding quantity.

Suppose that a tax is imposed on a luxury good like perfume. Figure 5, panel (a), shows the supply curve and the demand curve for perfume before the tax is imposed. The equilibrium price is $2 per gram, and the equilibrium quantity is 8 million grams per month at point e before the tax is imposed.

For a tax of $1 per gram, sellers must now charge $3 to earn $2; they must charge $2.15 to earn $1.15. The tax will shift the supply curve *up* by exactly $1—the amount of the tax. Before the tax, suppliers were prepared to supply 5 million grams per month at a price of $2 per gram, but after the tax, suppliers will be prepared to supply the same 5 million grams per month only if the price is $3. The tax does not change the demand curve. At each price (where the price now includes the $1 tax), consumers will continue to demand the same quantities. Therefore, the new price will be higher than the original $2 price.

The new equilibrium point is e' at a price of $2.15 and a quantity of 4 million grams. Buyers pay $2.15 for perfume, and sellers receive $1.15 after paying the $1.00 tax to the government. The government gets $4 million ($1.00 × 4 million grams) in taxes. The equilibrium price *paid* by consumers goes up $0.15 (from $2.00 to $2.15), but the net price (price minus tax) received by producers goes down by $0.85 (from $2.00 to $1.15). In this particular case, the greater burden of the tax is on the sellers, who pay three-quarters of the tax. Buyers pay only one-quarter of the tax.

## ELASTICITIES DETERMINE WHO BEARS THE BURDEN

Why does the producer bear a greater part of the burden than the consumer in our perfume example? The answer is found in the elasticities of demand and supply.

The demand curve in Figure 5, panel (a), is more elastic than the supply curve in the vicinity of the equilibrium point e, as evidenced by the fact that curve S is steeper than curve D. Consumers therefore respond more to the price than do producers. Hence consumers have a greater opportunity to avoid the tax. (See Example 3.)

Had the supply curve been more elastic than the demand curve, the consumer would have borne a greater burden of the tax. If consumers have an inelastic demand, it is easier to shift the tax forward to them and harder to reduce the price paid to producers. (See Example 3.)

Panel (b) shows the case of a supply that is more elastic than demand. In this case, the consumer pays more of the tax ($0.85) than does the producer ($0.15).

Figure 6 illustrates the case of a perfectly elastic supply curve. In fact, in the long run, there are many industries with perfectly elastic supply curves. In this case, the entire burden of the tax is on the buyer or consumer. The reason is simple: If supply is perfectly elastic at a particular price, producers will not provide the good at any lower price. A tax cannot lower the net price received by producers and the entire tax must be paid by the consumer. Thus, we can see that it makes no difference whether the tax is imposed on the producer or the consumer; the final burden simply depends on the relative size of the elasticities of demand and supply.

The main reason why taxing authorities prefer to tax goods with relatively low elasticities is that they are interested in the total tax revenue. When a tax is imposed, the revenue equals the tax multiplied by the number of units sold. Every tax reduces the number of units sold. Therefore, by imposing taxes on goods with relatively low elasticities, the authorities can collect more tax revenue.

The concept of elasticity allows us to understand the extent to which changing prices and income affect demand and supply. The next chapter will look

(a) More Elastic Demand than Supply

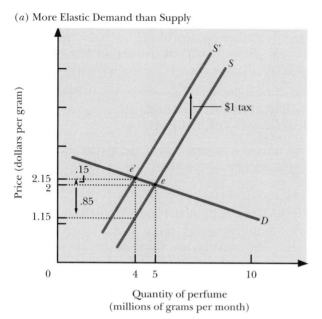

(b) More Elastic Supply than Demand

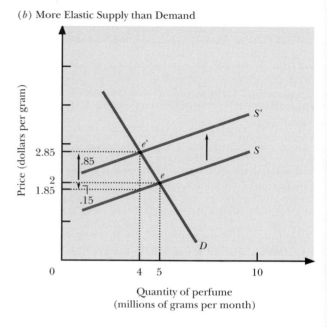

**FIGURE 5   The Burden of a Tax**

Panel (a) shows a more elastic demand than supply. A $1 tax shifts the supply curve up vertically by the amount of the tax. The price rises from $2 to $2.15. Consumers pay $0.15 of the $1 tax due to the higher price. Producers pay $0.85 because their price (after tax) falls to $1.15.
Panel (b) shows a more elastic supply than demand. The $1 tax still shifts up the supply curve by the amount of the tax, but now the price rises by $0.85. Hence consumers pay $0.85 of the tax and producers $0.15.

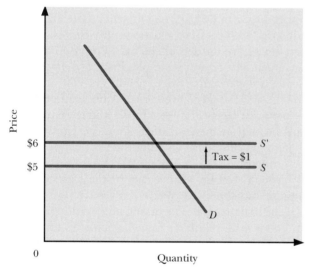

**FIGURE 6   The Effect of a Tax with Perfectly Elastic Supply**

A tax of $1 on suppliers shifts the supply curve up by $1 in order to recoup the required supply price. Market price will rise from $5 to $6 when supply is perfectly elastic. The tax on producers is shifted entirely to buyers.

behind the demand curve to explain the law of demand and consumer surplus.

## SUMMARY

1. The price elasticity of demand ($E_d$) is a measure of the responsiveness of consumers to changes in price. It is the absolute value of the percentage change in quantity demanded divided by the percentage change in price. The price elasticity of demand can be either elastic ($E_d > 1$), unitary elastic ($E_d = 1$), or inelastic ($E_d < 1$). If demand is elastic, price and total revenue move in opposite directions. If demand is inelastic, price and total revenue move in the same direction. If demand is unitary elastic, total revenue is not affected by price changes. $E_d$ can be calculated by the midpoints elasticity formula; the change in quantity is divided by the average quantity, and the change in price is divided by the average price. The price elasticity of demand is determined by the availability of substitutes (more

## EXAMPLE 3
## ELASTICITY AND THE REPEAL
## OF THE LUXURY TAX

In 1988, the federal government imposed a luxury tax on automobiles, boats, private aircraft, furs, and jewelry. The tax required buyers to pay a tax of 10 percent on the excess of the price over the following threshold amounts: automobiles: $30,000; boats: $100,000; private aircraft: $250,000; and jewelry and furs: $10,000. In 1993, this luxury tax was repealed for all categories except automobiles.

Why was the tax repealed? The demand for luxury items is highly elastic. Wealthy people can substitute travel, vacation homes, or country club memberships for an expensive boat or a new piece of jewelry. Moreover, they can buy luxury items that are priced just below the threshold value, such as a fur costing $9,999 instead of $12,000. The luxury tax on boats, jewelry, and furs caused wealthy buyers to cut back considerably on their purchases. The rich shifted the burden of the tax simply by buying less. On the other hand, the people who supply luxury boats, furs, and jewelry had to bear the major burden of the tax in the form of lower sales, lower prices, and fewer jobs.

We can explain the repeal of the tax by the fact that the luxury tax failed to raise much revenue as the rich cut back on their purchases. In addition, it imposed a substantial burden on the suppliers of these luxury goods, at whom the tax was not even aimed. As the suppliers of luxury goods and their employees protested, the tax was dropped. In other words, the *unintended consequences* of the tax led to its repeal.

---

substitutes mean higher elasticity), the amount of adjustment time (more time means higher elasticity), the importance in the consumer's budget (the more important the good, the higher the elasticity), and the status of the good as a necessity or a luxury (necessities tend to have lower elasticities).

2. Elasticities can also be used to measure the responsiveness of consumer demand to changes in income and the prices of other goods. Cross-price elasticity is the percentage change in the demand of one good divided by the percentage change in the price of the other good. If this number is positive, the two goods are substitutes; if it is negative, the two goods are complements. Income elasticity of demand is the percentage change in the demand divided by the percentage change in income. If this number is greater than 1, the good is a luxury; if it is less than 1, the good is a necessity.

3. The price elasticity of supply is the percentage change in quantity supplied divided by the percentage change in price. Supply is perfectly elastic when the supply curve is horizontal; supply is perfectly inelastic when the supply curve is vertical. The price elasticity of supply depends upon the time period of adjustment. In the immediate run, supply is fixed and the supply schedule is perfectly inelastic. In the short run, firms can produce more or fewer goods, but they do not have sufficient time to alter their capital stock or enter or leave the industry. In the long run, supply can be altered through changes in capital stock and through the entry and exit of firms. Elasticity of supply is greater in the long run than in the short run.

4. Elasticity analysis explains whether producers or consumers will bear the greater burden of a tax on a particular good. The group with the smallest price elasticity pays the largest share of the tax.

## KEY TERMS

price elasticity of demand ($E_d$)

midpoints elasticity formula

total revenue (TR)

total revenue test

perfectly elastic demand

perfectly inelastic demand

cross-price elasticity of demand ($E_{xy}$)

income elasticity of demand ($E_i$)

necessities

luxuries

price elasticity of supply ($E_s$)

perfectly elastic supply

perfectly inelastic supply

immediate run

short run

long run

## QUESTIONS AND PROBLEMS

1. Using the demand schedule in Table A, calculate the price elasticities of demand for each successive pair of rows.

### Table A

| Price (dollars) | Quantity (units) |
| --- | --- |
| 5 | 1 |
| 4 | 2 |
| 3 | 3 |
| 2 | 4 |
| 1 | 5 |

2. Suppose the price elasticity of demand for rental housing is 0.6 and the average rent increases from $500 per month to $700 per month. At $500 per month, 100,000 rental units are rented. What percentage decrease in quantity demanded would you predict from this information? Approximately how many units would be rented at $700 per month?

3. Suppose the price of gasoline falls from $1.20 per gallon to $0.60 per gallon. Why would a consumer's short-run adjustment to this price change be different from the long-run adjustment?

4. Assume that the basic monthly charge for a private telephone is $10.50 per month. If the rate were to rise to $11.00, would you expect a substantial reduction in the quantity demanded? Explain your answer. If, on the other hand, the basic monthly charge were $2.50 per month and the rate were to rise by the same percentage as the lower rate, what is your prediction for the change in quantity demanded?

5. The Chapter Insight related that the state of Texas raised the price of personalized automobile license plates from $35 to $70. The state's revenue from personalized license plates then fell. From this information, what can you say about the price elasticity of demand for personalized plates?

6. If the price of tennis balls goes up, what impact will this price increase have on the quantity demanded of tennis rackets? What sign (+ or −) will the cross-price elasticity have? What sign will the cross-price elasticity of tennis balls and golf balls have?

7. The income elasticity of demand for all services taken together is greater than 1. As the economy grows, what would you expect to happen to the share of service industries in total output?

8. During economic recessions, used car sales typically rise and new car sales decline. Explain why.

9. Assume that oranges have the following characteristics. The elasticity of demand is 0.2, and the elasticity of supply is 2. If government imposes a tax of $1 per crate of oranges, who will end up paying more of the tax (bearing the larger burden of the tax): the consumer or the producer? Why? Draw a diagram illustrating your argument.

10. Evaluate the validity of the following statement: "The elasticity of demand for oranges is 0.2; therefore, California orange growers could raise their income by restricting their output."

11. Suppose the supply curve for product X shifts to the right (supply increases). What happens to the total expenditure of consumers under each of the following conditions?
    a. The demand for X is price elastic.
    b. The demand for X is price inelastic.
    c. The demand for X is perfectly elastic.
    d. The demand for X is perfectly inelastic.

12. Suppose the supply curve for product X shifts to the left (supply decreases). What happens to the total expenditure of consumers under each of the following conditions?
    a. The demand for X is price elastic.
    b. The demand for X is price inelastic.
    c. The demand for X is perfectly elastic.
    d. The demand for X is perfectly inelastic.

13. Suppose the demand for product X increases. What happens to the total revenue of sellers under each of the following conditions?
    a. The supply of X is elastic.
    b. The supply is X is inelastic.

14. Using the determinants of the price elasticity of demand, indicate which item in each of the following pairs of goods has the highest elasticity.
    a. Wheat or grains
    b. Soft drinks or beverages
    c. Cars or clothing
    d. Toothpicks or beef
15. Double the quantities demanded at each price in Table A on page 108 (for example, when the price is $5, assume 2 units are demanded; when the price is $4, assume 4 units are demanded; and so on). What happens to the slope of the demand curve? What happens to the elasticity of demand between each successive pair of prices?

16. Who bears the burden of a tax on a good in each of the following circumstances?
    a. The supply curve is upward sloping; demand is perfectly inelastic.
    b. The supply curve is upward sloping; demand is perfectly elastic.
    c. The demand curve is downward sloping; supply is perfectly inelastic.
    d. The demand curve is downward sloping; supply is perfectly elastic.
17. Calculate the price elasticity of demand for the market demand curve $Q = 100 - 2P$ when the price changes from $P = \$42$ to $P = \$38$.

# CHAPTER 7

# DEMAND AND UTILITY

To the economist, a rational person is one who carefully weighs the costs and benefits of different actions. The theory of consumer behavior is the classic description of a rational person.

This theory would not be useful if it did not explain the facts of everyday experience. Adam Smith once observed that "nothing is more useful than water; but it will purchase scarce anything; scarce anything can be had in exchange for it. A diamond, on the contrary, has scarce any value in use; but a very great quantity of other goods may frequently be had in exchange for it."

In this chapter we shall consider a theory of consumer behavior that will not only explain Adam Smith's diamond/water paradox, but will also explain the law of demand. What motivates the theory is the idea that we try to do the best we can with what we've got. The explanation of the law of demand also directly provides a method for measuring consumer gains and losses that result from lower or higher prices.

## THE CONCEPT OF UTILITY

Economists like to make a distinction between *preferences* and *demand*. A consumer's preferences are what he or she likes; a consumer's demands are what he or she buys. You might prefer a Porsche to a Chevrolet, but you buy the cheaper car because that is what your budget will allow. You buy the Chevrolet from the list of cars you can afford. Preferences and demand are different, yet what we demand depends on our preferences. The economists' theory of demand is simply that we buy something when its price drops to the point where we prefer that alternative to others. This simple theory explains a wide range of human behavior.

Preferences indicate how we as consumers would rank different commodity bundles (combinations of goods and services) in all conceivable situations. A simple criterion for evaluating consumer preferences or satisfaction is to use the utility of various commodity bundles.

> **Utility** is a numerical ranking of a consumer's preferences among different commodity bundles.

Utility measures the rank order of different satisfactions rather than the magnitudes of those satisfactions. Utility is expressed in ordinal numbers (such as first, second, and third) because it is not possible to attach a "util-o-meter" to our arms to measure the satisfaction we get from consuming particular goods and services. In the nineteenth century, though, economists expressed utility in cardinal numbers, which indicate both rankings and magnitudes. For example, we express the concept of weight by cardinal numbers. It makes a difference whether you tell someone that last week you gained 100 pounds or 10 pounds.

The appendix to this chapter demonstrates that an absolute measure of cardinal utility is not necessary for analyzing demand. However, it is useful to quantify preferences in order to measure differences in the utility of goods. For example, if we say that my utility of consuming 51 gallons of water per week is 3010 utils (hypothetical units of utility) and my utility of consuming 50 gallons is 3000 utils, then we can quantify the marginal utility of increasing water consumption by 1 gallon as 10 utils.

> The **marginal utility** (MU) of any good or service is the increase in utility that a consumer experiences when its consumption of that good or service (and that good or service alone) is increased by 1 unit. In general,
>
> $$MU = \frac{\Delta TU}{\Delta Q}$$
>
> where TU is total utility and $Q$ is the quantity of the good.

As we shall see, however, this absolute measure of marginal utility is only a tool for comparing the relative marginal utilities for two or more goods.

## THE LAW OF DIMINISHING MARGINAL UTILITY

The more of something a person consumes, the less valuable it becomes at the margin.

> The **law of diminishing marginal utility** states that as more of a good or service is consumed during any given time period, its marginal utility eventually declines, if the consumption of everything else is held constant.

Thus, the first gallon of water we consume in a given week, for example, has an enormous marginal utility. If we have no water, we will consider 1 gallon to be very valuable. The twentieth gallon of water has a relatively small marginal utility for a person who already has 19 gallons. The *total utility* from all 20 gallons of water is the sum of the marginal utilities of all units. Why does the marginal utility of water decline so rapidly as more water is consumed? The first gallon of water is essential to sustaining life; its marginal utility is therefore astronomical. As more water becomes available, water can be applied to less urgent uses: bathing, washing clothes, feeding pets, and eventually even to watering the lawn. By the time sufficient water is available for watering the lawn, the marginal utility of the last gallon is much smaller than the marginal utility of the first gallon.

The rate at which marginal utility declines as we increase consumption varies. For food products, for example, marginal utility declines rapidly. The marginal utility of the second hamburger is much less than that of the first. The marginal utility of the third hamburger is very small or even negative. For other goods, such as collectors' items, marginal utility may decline slowly as consumption increases. (See Example 1.)

## EXAMPLE 1

## MARGINAL UTILITY, "ALL YOU CAN EAT FOR $10," AND THE DAILY NEWSPAPER

Many restaurants offer buffets where customers can eat all they want for a specified price. Such offers are possible because the marginal utility of food diminishes rapidly. Depending upon the individual's appetite, extra helpings yield smaller and smaller marginal utilities. In fact, they rather quickly yield negative marginal utility, in which the consumer's utility decreases with an extra helping. Although more food costs the consumer nothing, people will limit the amount of food they consume.

Rapidly diminishing marginal utility explains why the daily newspaper is dispensed from coin-operated boxes that permit people to take as many copies as they want. Newspaper companies know that the marginal utility of a second newspaper is zero for most people, so they don't worry about people taking more than one. Owners of coin-operated dispensers of other products (soft drinks, candies, etc.) know that they cannot give the consumer the opportunity to take more than one.

## THE DIAMOND/WATER PARADOX

In the quotation at the start of this chapter, Adam Smith poses the famous *diamond/water paradox*. The paradox questions why prices often fail to reflect the usefulness of goods. Water and salt, without which we would perish, have low relative prices, whereas goods that have little practical value, such as diamonds, gold, and high fashion, have high relative prices.

Why is it that diamonds, whose total utility is much less than that of water, have a higher relative price than water? The law of diminishing marginal utility provides the answer to this paradox. On the one hand, the consumption of water usually takes place at a low marginal utility because the supply of water is large; on the other hand, the supply of diamonds is usually so limited that consumption takes place at a relatively high marginal utility. Although water's total utility is high, its marginal utility is low. Therefore, no one will sacrifice very much for an additional gallon.

The terms of the diamond/water paradox hold under normal supply conditions, but what happens when these conditions are disrupted? At the end of World War II, people in parts of Europe gladly exchanged diamonds and precious metals for bread and potatoes. The availability of food products was so limited that food products yielded a higher marginal utility (by preventing malnutrition) than did dia-

monds and precious metals. Similarly, when the American West was being settled in the nineteenth century, range wars were fought (and people were killed) over the control of water holes, and in arid parts of the world, such as Somalia and Rwanda, armed conflicts still break out over water.

## MARGINAL UTILITY AND THE LAW OF DEMAND

The law of diminishing marginal utility explains the diamond/water paradox; relative prices reflect marginal utility rather than total utility. In this section we shall examine the exact relationship between the law of diminishing utility and the law of demand.

The theory of consumer demand is simply that we, as consumers, try to arrange our pattern of spending so that we are getting the most out of our limited budgets. To achieve maximum utility, we allocate our budgets on goods in such a way that it is impossible to obtain more utility by spending a bit more on one good and a bit less on another.

The central concept of the best allocation of the consumer's limited resources is the "bang per buck." Suppose the marginal utility of another pizza is 50 utils. If the price of a pizza is $5, then another dollar spent on pizza yields 10 (= 50/5) utils.

> The **marginal utility per dollar** for any good or service is the ratio of its marginal utility to its price (MU/P).

Note that the concept of marginal utility per dollar is a rate measure similar to miles per hour. Just as you can drive 50 miles per hour without driving a full hour, marginal utility per dollar need not involve the expenditure of exactly $1, as in the pizza example, where an extra pizza costs $5.

The best allocation of a consumer's limited budget is achieved when the last dollar spent on each good has the same marginal utility.

> A **consumer equilibrium or optimum** requires that (1) all income be spent and (2) the marginal utilities per dollar for each good purchased are equal. Thus, if goods A, B, C, . . . and so forth are being purchased, it must be that
>
> $$MU_A/P_A = MU_B/P_B = MU_C/P_C = \dots \text{ for all goods.}$$

At this point, the consumer is not inclined to change purchases unless some other factor (such as prices, income, or preferences) changes.

Why must the MU/Ps be equal? The MU/P ratio can be thought of as either the utility gained when another dollar is spent on the good, or the utility lost when spending on the good is cut by a dollar. For example, suppose one more dollar spent on pizza raises utility by 10 utils but spending one less dollar on hamburgers lowers utility by only 4 utils. Switching a dollar from hamburgers to pizza will bring about a net increase of 6 utils—the 10 util gain from more pizza and the 4 util lost from fewer hamburgers. This is why the MU/Ps of each good must be the same; if not, utility can be increased with the same total expenditure. On the other hand, when all the MU/Ps are the same, any reallocation of spending will make the consumer worse off. The reason for this is the law of diminishing marginal utility: more spent on a good lowers its MU/P; less spent on a good raises its MU/P. Starting from a situation of equality of all MU/Ps, spending more on pizza and less on hamburgers causes $MU_{pizza}$ to fall and $MU_{hamburger}$ to rise. Because $MU_{pizza}/P_{pizza} < MU_{hamburger}/P_{hamburger}$, the consumer has an incentive to substitute hamburgers for pizzas until equality is restored.

The equal MU-per-dollar rule explains the water/diamond paradox. When you note that the MU/Ps of water and diamonds are the same to the average consumer, the water/diamond paradox is explained. The marginal utility of a diamond is in the same proportion to its price as the marginal utility of water is to its price, but the total utility from water far exceeds the total utility from diamonds. Remember that total utility is the sum of the marginal utilities. The total utility of water will be enormous because of the high marginal utility of the first and second units of water.

The equal MU-per-dollar rule explains why demand curves are downward sloping. Let's say you are buying ale and bread. In equilibrium, $MU_A/P_A = MU_B/P_B$. If the price of ale falls, at that moment the ratio $MU_A/P_A$ must rise above $MU_B/P_B$. You have an incentive to buy more ale. According to the law of diminishing marginal utility, $MU_A$ must fall. In this way the equality between the MU/Ps is established once again, with a larger amount of ale purchased at the lower price. The law of demand is therefore a consequence of the law of diminishing marginal utility.

Another consequence of the equal marginal utilities rule and the law of diminishing marginal utility is that we do not spend all our money on one good or service. If we tried to spend all our money on one or two goods, we would drive down their marginal utilities. We choose instead a variety of goods and services. We sometimes eat chicken, sometimes beef, and sometimes fish. Few of us like to wear the same clothes day after day. Almost all of us spend some money on shelter, clothing, and food.

## A NUMERICAL EXAMPLE

A numerical example will reinforce how the equal MU-per-dollar rule leads to the law of demand.

Consider an individual consumer, Mr. Ruffgreg, who purchases only two goods, ale and bread. Ruffgreg's preferences for both goods are summarized in Table 1. Columns 2 and 6 show the total utility of ale ($TU_A$) and bread ($TU_B$), respectively; columns 3 and 7 show the marginal utility of ale ($MU_A$) and bread ($MU_B$), respectively. These utility schedules apply to Ruffgreg's consumption over a particular time period—say, a week. The utility of ale does not depend on the consumption of bread, or vice versa. Both ale and bread obey the law of diminishing marginal utility.

Ruffgreg's marginal utility schedule for ale is depicted in Figure 1 and is based on the data in column 3 of Table 1. The first pint of ale (per week) yields Ruffgreg a marginal utility of 40 utils; the second, 30

## Table 1   The Utility of Ale and Bread

| Quantity of Ale (pints), $Q_A$ (1) | Total Utility of Ale (utils), $TU_A$ (2) | Marginal Utility of Ale (utils), $MU_A$ (3) | Marginal Utility of Ale per Dollar (utils), $MU_A/P_A$ (4) | Quantity of Bread (loaves), $Q_B$ (5) | Total Utility of Bread (utils), $TU_B$ (6) | Marginal Utility of Bread (utils), $MU_B$ (7) | Marginal Utility of Bread per Dollar (utils), $MU_B/P_B$ (8) |
|---|---|---|---|---|---|---|---|
| 1 | 40 | 40 | 20 | 1 | 15 | 15 | 30 |
| 2 | 70 | 30 | 15 | 2 | 23 | 8 | 16 |
| 3 | 90 | 20 | 10 | 3 | 30 | 7 | 14 |
| 4 | 100 | 10 | 5 | 4 | 35 | 5 | 10 |
| 5 | 105 | 5 | 2.5 | 5 | 38 | 3 | 6 |
| 6 | 107 | 2 | 1 | 6 | 40.5 | 2.5 | 5 |

This table lists the quantities of ale and bread consumed per week by Ruffgreg, along with the utility Ruffgreg attaches to each quantity. The price of ale equals $2 per pint and the price of bread equals $0.50 per loaf. The marginal utility columns illustrate the *law of diminishing marginal utility:* the marginal utility of each product falls as the amount consumed increases.

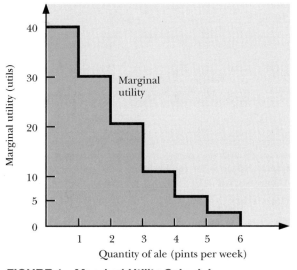

**FIGURE 1   Marginal Utility Schedule**

This figure graphs the data in columns 1 and 3 of Table 1. The width of each bar represents 1 pint of ale. The vertical height or area of each bar represents marginal utility for that extra unit of ale. Total utility up to some quantity of ale is the sum of the areas of the bars to the left of that quantity of ale. For example, the total utility of 2 pints equals 70 (= 40 + 30); the total utility of 5 pints equals 105 (= 40 + 30 + 20 + 10 + 5).

utils; the third, 20 utils; and the fourth, 10 utils. The total utility from consuming different quantities of ale is the sum of the marginal utilities up to the quantity of ale consumed. The total utility from consuming 3 pints of ale during a week, for example, is 90 (= 40 + 30 + 20).

We cannot determine Ruffgreg's demands for ale and bread from his preferences alone. As we know

from Chapter 4, demand depends not only on consumer preferences but also on consumer income and prices. Let's keep our example simple: Ruffgreg has $8 to spend on ale and bread per week. The price of ale ($P_A$) is $2 per pint, and the price of bread ($P_B$) is $0.50 per loaf. Ruffgreg can spend the entire $8 allowance on ale, buying 4 pints of ale, or he can spend all $8 on bread, obtaining 16 loaves of bread. The most likely case, however, is that Ruffgreg will spend part of the money on ale and part on bread. For instance, he can purchase 3 pints of ale per week, costing $6, and 4 loaves of bread per week, costing $2, for a total weekly expenditure of $8.

We know that consumers maximize utility by spending their budgets to equate marginal utilities per dollar. We calculate marginal utility per dollar by dividing marginal utility by the price. For each quantity of ale, priced at $2 per pint, the marginal utility per dollar in column 4 of Table 1 is half the marginal utility in column 3. For each quantity of bread, priced at $0.50 per loaf, the marginal utility per dollar in column 8 is twice the marginal utility in column 7.

Table 2 illustrates a step-by-step process through which Ruffgreg maximizes utility by making incremental expenditures for bread and ale until all of his income is allocated. At the point of the initial purchase, a loaf of bread, which costs $0.50, yields a marginal utility of 15 and a marginal utility *per dollar* of 30 (= 15/$0.50), and a pint of ale, which costs $2, yields a marginal utility of 40 but a marginal utility *per dollar* of only 20 (= 40/$2). Because bread has a higher marginal utility per dollar, Ruffgreg's first purchase is one loaf at a cost of $0.50, leaving

## Table 2   The Steps to Consumer Equilibrium

| | Available Choices | Decision | Income Remaining |
|---|---|---|---|
| 1st Purchase | 1st pint of ale: $MU_A/P_A = 20$<br>1st loaf of bread: $MU_B/P_B = 30$ | Buy 1st loaf of bread for $0.50 | $8.00 − $0.50 = $7.50 |
| 2nd Purchase | 1st pint of ale: $MU_A/P_A = 20$<br>2nd loaf of bread: $MU_B/P_B = 16$ | Buy 1st pint of ale for $2.00 | $7.50 − $2.00 = $5.50 |
| 3rd Purchase | 2nd pint of ale: $MU_A/P_A = 15$<br>2nd loaf of bread: $MU_B/P_B = 16$ | Buy 2nd loaf of bread for $0.50 | $5.50 − $0.50 = $5.00 |
| 4th Purchase | 2nd pint of ale: $MU_A/P_A = 15$<br>3rd loaf of bread: $MU_B/P_B = 14$ | Buy 2nd pint of ale for $2.00 | $5.00 − $2.00 = $3.00 |
| 5th Purchase | 3rd pint of ale: $MU_A/P_A = 10$<br>3rd loaf of bread: $MU_B/P_B = 14$ | Buy 3rd loaf of bread for $0.50 | $3.00 − $0.50 = $2.50 |
| 6th Purchase and 7th Purchase | 3rd pint of ale: $MU_A/P_A = 10$<br>4th loaf of bread: $MU_B/P_B = 10$ | Buy 3rd pint of ale for $2.00 and 4th loaf of bread for $0.50 | $2.50 − $2.00 = $0.50<br>$0.50 − $0.50 = $0 } Equilibrium |

This table shows the step-by-step process by which a consumer makes purchasing decisions to maximize satisfaction. In this example, with data taken from Table 1, the consumer has $8 to spend. At each step, the consumer chooses the commodity that has the highest marginal utility per dollar. The consumer ends up buying 3 pints of ale and 4 loaves of bread, which is the equilibrium combination because marginal utility per dollar is equal for the two goods at the last purchase, and all income is spent.

$7.50 to spend. Ruffgreg now finds that the marginal utility per dollar is higher for a pint of ale (20) than for a second loaf of bread (16), so he purchases one pint for $2, leaving $5.50 to spend. Marginal utility per dollar is higher for a second loaf of bread (16) than for a second pint of ale (15), so Ruffgreg's third purchase is a second loaf of bread. Ruffgreg continues to select the product with the higher marginal utility per dollar until his budget is exhausted.

Ruffgreg achieves consumer equilibrium when he buys 3 pints of ale and 4 loaves of bread; he has spent his entire income of $8 (3 pints at $2 each and 4 loaves at $0.50 each), and the marginal utility per dollar is 10 utils for both ale and bread. Total utility is 135 utils (90 for ale and 35 for bread). If Ruffgreg spent his $8 differently, his total utility would drop. For example, if he bought 2 more units of bread at a cost of $1 and paid for them by buying only 0.5 unit less of ale, his total utility would drop to 120.5 utils— 40.5 for 6 units of bread and 80 for 2.5 units of ale.

The law of demand can be derived from this example. When the price of ale is $2, Ruffgreg purchases (demands) 3 pints of ale, given that his income is $8 and the price of bread is $0.50. The price/quantity combination of $2 and 3 pints of ale is point *r* on Ruffgreg's demand curve (Figure 2).

We can calculate other points on the demand curve by repeating the whole process at different prices of ale, keeping income at $8 per week and the bread price at $0.50 per loaf.

If the price of ale falls from $2 to $1 per pint, the marginal utility per dollar for ale becomes greater than the marginal utility per dollar for bread at the old equilibrium of 3 pints of ale and 4 loaves of bread. Expenditures will consequently be reallocated between the two goods until the $8 is spent and marginal utilities per dollar are again equal—this time at 5 pints of ale and 6 loaves of bread. Thus, when the price of ale is $1, the quantity demanded is 5 pints. This price/quantity combination of $1 and 5 pints is

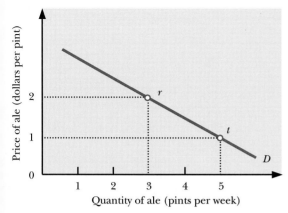

**FIGURE 2** **The Individual Demand Curve Derived from Ruffgreg's Marginal Utility Schedule**

This curve shows Ruffgreg's demand curve for ale calculated from Table 1. Say the price of bread is $0.50 per loaf and weekly income is $8. The quantity required for consumer equilibrium when the price of ale equals $2 per pint is 3 pints (point *r*). The equilibrium quantity when the price of ale equals $1 per pint is 5 pints (point *t*).

point *t* on the demand curve. As the law of demand asserts, holding all other factors constant, a decrease in the price causes an increase in the quantity demanded. (See Example 2.)

Every point on a consumer's demand curve satisfies the conditions that MU/P be the same for all goods purchased and that all income be spent. In other words, the consumer is maximizing utility at each price/quantity combination on the curve.

## INCOME AND SUBSTITUTION EFFECTS

A reduction in the price of a good has two effects. First, the savings that we gain can be used as income to purchase more goods. The part of the total increase in the quantity demanded of the reduced-price good that can be attributed to this extra income is called the income effect. Second, the cheaper good yields a higher marginal utility per dollar so consumers bent on maximizing satisfaction will substitute this now-cheaper good for other products. This part of the increase in the quantity demanded of the cheaper good is called the substitution effect.

When the price of a good falls, we buy more of it because (1) the price reduction is like an increase in income that in itself normally re-

sults in larger demands for all goods and services (the **income effect**); and (2) we tend to substitute that good for other, relatively more expensive goods (the **substitution effect**).

If we refer again to Table 2, we can see that, before the price of ale dropped from $2 to $1, Ruffgreg purchased 3 pints of ale and 4 loaves of bread for a total of $8 worth of ale and bread. At the lower price of ale, Ruffgreg can purchase the same 3 pints of ale and 4 loaves of bread for $5, leaving $3 extra. This $3 represents an increase in real income that can be spent on either ale or bread. The effect of this increase on purchases of ale constitutes the income effect.

The price reduction is also accompanied by a drop in the relative price of ale (the ratio of ale price to bread price falls from 4 to 2). As a result, Ruffgreg receives more marginal utility per dollar from ale than from bread and, therefore, switches to buying more ale. This switch from bread to ale constitutes the substitution effect.

The size of the income effect from a price change depends on the amount of the good being consumed. A change in the price of a Rolls-Royce has no income effect for the vast majority of people because that ultra-luxury car lies far outside the limits of their budgets. However, a rise in the price of gasoline affects all drivers according to the amount they use. Thus, the income effects of price changes for food, clothing, and housing can be substantial. The income effects of price changes for goods that are relatively unimportant in the consumer's budget are small or trivial.

The size of the substitution effect also depends on the ease with which other goods can be substituted for a good. A Ford has more substitutes than a Rolls-Royce, so the substitution effect of a price change for Fords is correspondingly larger.

## IS THE THEORY REALISTIC?  *NO*

Do we really behave in the mechanical fashion depicted by the theory of consumer behavior? We do not carry marginal utility schedules in our heads or calculate the marginal utility per dollar on each and every good. But we most certainly think in terms of "best buys." Advertisers often stress the fact that their product gives the consumer "more for the dollar" than the competitive products. We shop at different stores before we buy a product; and we buy magazines such as *Consumers' Report* that compare different products and even recommend "best buys."

## EXAMPLE 2

## MARGINAL UTILITY THEORY: THE USE OF HEROIN
## BY VIETNAM VETERANS

It has been estimated that about 35 percent of enlisted men in Vietnam used heroin—a highly addictive drug. The Army set up rehabilitation centers in Vietnam, but these simply led to greater use of heroin. Nevertheless, when the veterans returned home, 90 percent of those who used heroin in Vietnam stopped using the drug.

Psychiatrists might explain these facts by the influence of social control and social learning. In Vietnam, with the pressures of war, the society was more permissive than it was back at home. When the soldiers returned, they entered a different world in which heroin addiction was less acceptable.

Another explanation, however, is far simpler: The range of products available to soldiers in the field is much smaller than the range of products available at home. At home, consumers can choose from hundreds or thousands of products. In wartime Vietnam, soldiers in the field had few if any choice of products. This limitation served to raise the marginal utility of the products that were available. Moreover, the price of heroin in Vietnam was extremely low relative to other prices. Thus, even though social factors were undoubtedly present, the theory of consumer demand goes far toward explaining heroin use and misuse.

------------------------------------------------

*Source:* Norman E. Zinberg, "The Use and Misuse of Intoxicants," in R. Hamowy, ed., *Dealing with Drugs: Consequences of Government Control* (Lexington, MA: Lexington Books, 1987), p. 264.

Thus, it is not surprising that on the average we behave as predicted by the theory. We have downward-sloping demand curves. As price falls we find less valuable uses for the good. If we buy a variety of goods instead of just one or two, we must spread our spending among lots of goods in order to avoid the diminishing marginal utility or satisfaction we receive from consuming more of one particular good.

## MARKET DEMAND

The law of diminishing marginal utility implies that rational consumers will purchase less of a product, all other things being equal, if its price rises. According to the law of demand, the demand schedules of individual consumers will have negative slopes.

The individual consumer, however, is usually only a small part of the total market in which prices are established. Individual demand curves must be combined to determine the market demand curve for a particular good.

> The **market demand curve** shows the total quantities demanded by all consumers in the market at each price. It is the horizontal summation of all individual demand curves in that market.

Figure 3 shows the demand curves for ale for two consumers, Smith and White, who, for simplicity, constitute all the buyers in the market for ale. At a price of $3 per pint, Smith demands 0 pints and White demands 1 pint. We obtain the total market demand at the $3 price by adding the two individual demands (0 + 1 = 1 pint). At a price of $2 per pint, Smith demands 2 pints and White demands 3 pints. The total market demand at the $2 price is 2 + 3 = 5 pints.

The market demand curve in Figure 3 is downward sloping for the same reasons that the individual demand curves are downward sloping. Likewise, at each point along the market demand curve, just as along an individual demand curve, consumers are maximizing their satisfaction. Thus, as price decreases, more consumers might be enticed to buy a

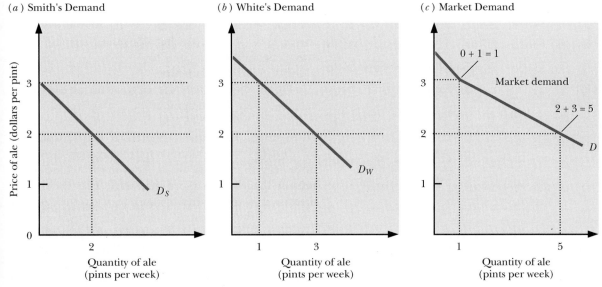

(a) Smith's Demand    (b) White's Demand    (c) Market Demand

**FIGURE 3   From Individual to Market Demand**

The market demand curve is the *horizontal* summation of all individual demand curves; it is calculated by summing the individual quantities demanded by all individuals at each price. Here, the market has only two consumers, but the principle applies to markets with any number of consumers.

product. In Figure 3, for example, when the price of ale is above $3, Smith is not in the market; at a price of $0.50, even more buyers may enter.

## CONSUMER SURPLUS

We know that a high-priced good (diamonds) has a proportionately higher marginal utility than a low-priced good (water). When we, as consumers, maximize our satisfaction, we push the consumption of each good to the point where the marginal utility per dollar ($MU/P$) is the same for all the goods consumers are buying. *The theory of consumer demand shows that price reflects marginal utility.*

> When consumers are in equilibrium, the price of a good is a *dollar measure* of the value of the *last unit* of the good (its marginal benefit).

Figure 4 pictures a market demand curve that describes a series of steps because the product is available only in whole units (such as a radio or a piano). According to the demand curve, if only 1 unit of the

product is available, some consumer is willing to pay $10 for it (point *h*). If only 2 units of the product are available, someone is willing to pay $9 for the second unit (point *i*). If 6 units are available, someone is willing to pay a price of $5 for the sixth unit. The current market price therefore reveals what consumers are willing to pay for the *last unit* of the product sold.

When the market price is $5 and the quantity demanded is 6 units (point *m*), the price paid by each consumer reflects the value of the sixth unit to the last purchaser, even though the first of those 6 units is still worth $10 to someone, the second is still worth $9 to someone else, and so on. The total value of the 6 units to consumers ($10 + $9 + $8 + $7 + $6 + $5 = $45) is greater than the total amount that consumers pay for them (6 × $5 = $30). Consumers enjoy a surplus on all the earlier units because they have a higher marginal value than later units. The surplus on each unit is the difference between the consumer's maximum willingness to pay and what the consumer must actually pay.

> **Consumer surplus** is the excess of the total consumer benefit that a good provides beyond consumer cost.

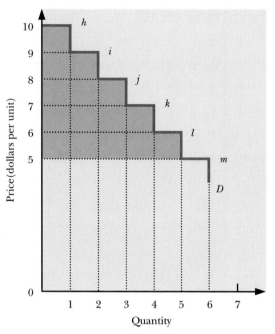

**FIGURE 4   Consumers' Surplus**

Say that the current market price is $5 and the quantity demanded is 6 units. According to the demand curve, consumers were prepared to spend $10 for the first unit, $9 for the second unit, $8 for the third unit, $7 for the fourth unit, and $6 for the fifth unit. When a total of 6 units are bought, however, consumers need pay only $5 each for all 6 units. Thus, they pay for each of the 6 units only what the sixth unit is worth to them. The difference between what each unit is worth to consumers and what the consumers actually pay is shown by the height of the orange area for each unit. Adding these surpluses for all units yields a total consumers' surplus of $5 + $4 + $3 + $2 + $1 = $15.

For example, at a price of $5 the first unit is worth $10 to someone but costs $5, so that person enjoys a surplus of $5 on the first unit. Someone enjoys a surplus of $4 on the second unit because the second unit is worth $9 to that person but costs $5. Only the last unit sold (the sixth) will yield no surplus, for its price will reflect exactly what that unit is worth to the consumer. Adding these surpluses together, one obtains a total consumer surplus of $15.

The great British economist Alfred Marshall (1842–1924) introduced the concept of consumers' surplus. This powerful tool supplies a measure of the benefits that consumers obtain from markets and from the lowering of prices in markets.

As consumers move along a demand curve, the amount of consumer surplus changes: If the price increases, consumer surplus decreases; if the price falls,

it increases. A lower price increases consumer surplus because the same benefits can be purchased at a lower cost. It follows that consumer surplus measures consumer gains and losses from price changes along a given demand curve.

Figure 5 illustrates the calculation of consumer surplus when the demand curve is a straight line. At point *f*, the price is $15 and the quantity demanded is 1000 units. Consumers, therefore, pay a total of $15,000 ($15 × 1000 units) for the product. At quantities less than 1000 units, consumers would have been willing to pay more than $15. This difference, measured by the vertical distance between the demand curve and the horizontal line at $15, constitutes the surplus for each unit. For instance, the purchaser of the 500th unit would have been willing to pay $20 instead of the $15 actually paid (point *e*). Adding all the surpluses together for quantities less than 1000 yields the consumer surplus, or the area of the orange triangle labeled *A*.[1]

What will happen to consumer surplus if the market price drops to $10? It will increase because a surplus will exist at all quantities less than 1500, whereas the surplus previously stopped at a quantity of 1000. Consumer surplus at point *g*, where price is $10, is the area of the triangle formed by the demand curve and the horizontal line at $10, or the sum of the three areas *A* + *B* + *C*. Consumer surplus at a price of $15 was area *A;* therefore, the *increase* in consumer surplus as a consequence of the drop in price is *B* + *C* = $5000 (area of *B*) + $1250 (area of *C*) = $6250.[2] (See Example 3.)

---

[1] By changing quantity demanded in very small increments, the demand schedule approximates a smooth line. Thus, instead of adding a series of rectangles together as in Figure 4, consumer surplus is measured by the smooth area of triangle *A*.

As explained in Appendix 1A, areas of *rectangles* are computed by multiplying the horizontal width of the rectangle times the vertical height of the rectangle. The width of rectangle *B* is 1000; the height is $5. Areas of triangles are calculated by multiplying the width of the triangle by its height and dividing by 2 (or multiplying by 1/2). The area of the the triangle will be 1/2 that of the rectangle formed by the height and width of the triangle.

[2] The segment of the demand curve between *f* and *g* in this example was deliberately constructed to have an elasticity of demand of unity, so that the amounts of consumer spending at both points are equal. At both prices, consumers spend $15,000, but consumer surplus is $6250 greater at the lower price than at the higher price.

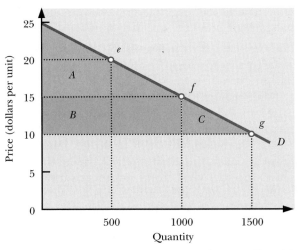

**FIGURE 5   The Gain in Consumer Surplus Resulting from a Reduction in Price**

When price is $15 and quantity demanded is 1000 units, the consumer surplus is the orange triangle *A*, the excess of what people would be willing to pay beyond the actual cost. If the price falls to $10, quantity demanded increases to 1500 units and consumer surplus is the area *A* + *B* + *C*. Consumer surplus, therefore, increases by *B* + *C*, or by $6250.

## THE ROLE OF CONSUMER SURPLUS

We can think of consumer surplus as the incentive of each person to engage in voluntary exchange. People buy many things, and each one of them yields a surplus over and above what it costs. Without this in-

centive people would not be eager to participate in the market.

In order to have a market—sellers of the goods people want—it is equally necessary to offer sellers an income that more than compensates them for the toil and trouble of providing those goods. People make an income in a capitalist society by giving others what they want and are willing to pay for. Both sides of the market are engaged in voluntary exchange. Nobody forces you to work as a lawyer, teacher, or mechanic. Nobody forces you to buy bread, milk, or personal computers. Having the means to purchase what you want in a capitalist society acts as a certificate to show that you have provided services to others.

Consumer surplus enhances our understanding of two Defining Moments in economics. The Industrial Revolution created immense consumer surpluses. The new technologies of mass production lowered costs of production and made goods that had been unheard-of luxuries accessible to the masses. Factories could now produce textiles at a fraction of the cost of home-spun garments. Textile prices dropped and consumer surplus grew. As the Industrial Revolution proceeded, science and technology created new products—electric lights, phonographs, telegraph services. Earlier consumers would have gladly purchased these products; prior to scientific advances, however, such products either could not be produced at all or entailed too high a price for consumers. New products at affordable prices, therefore, created vast sums of consumer surpluses.

### EXAMPLE 3
### CONSUMER SURPLUS AND
### YOUR TELEVISION

Consumers enjoy consumer surplus when they can buy something for less than they would have been willing to pay. We pay $20 per month for local telephone service; most of us would be willing to pay much more if we had to. We pay $75 per month for our electricity; if we had to, we would be willing to pay more.

A survey conducted by *TV Guide* asked people how much they would be willing to pay to keep their television sets. Television, after all, is

the major source of entertainment for most of us, giving instant access to news, situation comedies, and cable programming. Although respondents answered differently, some people would have been willing to pay over $100,000 to avoid being deprived of television. For the person willing to pay $100,000 for television, the $350 price of a color television set provides a consumer surplus of $99,650!

Globalization, another Defining Moment, is motivated by producers in one country being able to offer goods at higher quality and lower prices to consumers in another country. Trading goods and services according to comparative advantage creates substantial consumer surpluses and provides the gains that encourage the growth of international trade.

The consumer surpluses provided by the Industrial Revolution and by globalization constitute the vast rises in living standards that consumers have experienced over the past two centuries.

To earn an income in a capitalist society people must overcome an obstacle: costs. Goods and services are seldom free. Somebody—firms—must produce them by having the incentive—profits—to gather the required resources. It is to this story that we will turn in the next chapter.

## SUMMARY

1. *Utility* is a numerical ranking of a consumer's preferences among different commodity bundles. *Marginal utility* is the increase in total utility obtained when consumption of a good is increased by 1 unit. The *law of diminishing marginal utility* states that the marginal utility eventually declines as more of a good or service is consumed, holding the consumption of other goods constant. The fact that market prices reflect marginal utility rather than total utility explains the diamond/water paradox.

2. The law of diminishing marginal utility is consistent with the law of demand. When the rational consumer equates marginal utility per dollar on the last purchases of each commodity, the consumer is in equilibrium. If the price of one good falls, its marginal utility per dollar initially rises, and more of the commodity will be consumed. Rational consumers spend their money in a way that maximizes their satisfaction (utility). A drop in the price of a good has two effects: First, the use of the resulting increase in real income to purchase more of the good constitutes the *income effect*. Second, the increase in the amount of the good purchased that is due to the decrease in its relative price constitutes the *substitution effect*.

3. The *market demand schedule* is the horizontal summation of the demand schedules of all individuals participating in the market. The market demand schedule will have a negative slope because its individual components have negative slopes.

4. *Consumer surplus* measures the extent to which consumer benefits exceed consumer costs for a particular product. Consumer surplus follows from the law of diminishing marginal utility. Consumers pay the same market price for each unit they buy, but the market price reflects only the value of the last unit sold. The marginal benefit of earlier units, therefore, exceeds the market price. Adding these surpluses together yields total consumer surplus. The concept of consumer surplus permits the measurement of consumer losses and gains from price changes.

## KEY TERMS

utility
marginal utility (MU)
law of diminishing
   marginal utility
marginal utility per
   dollar

consumer equilibrium or
   optimum
income effect
substitution effect
market demand curve
consumer surplus

## QUESTIONS AND PROBLEMS

1. In some parts of the world, sick people seek the help of witch doctors. In the United States, most people seek medical doctors when they are ill; a few seek out faith healers. Does this variation mean that consumer preferences for medical care are basically unstable?

2. In the late 1970s and early 1980s, Americans began to buy smaller, fuel-efficient cars instead of large "gas guzzlers." In the 1990s, they switched back to buying larger cars; even Japan started exporting larger cars to the United States. Do these changes indicate that consumer preferences are unstable?

3. If the marginal utility of a good $A$ were to increase as consumption of the good increased (in opposition to the law of diminishing marginal utility), would $MU_A/P_A = MU_B/P_B$ still be the equilibrium condition?

4. Use the marginal utility information in Table 1 to calculate the demand for ale at the price of $4 per pint. What do you do when marginal utility per dollar cannot be exactly equated for two goods on the last unit sold?

5. Again using Table 1, calculate the demand for ale at the price of $2 but at a weekly income of $11. Compare this result with the answer at $8. Which is larger? Why?

6. Assume that there are 1000 identical consumers in the market, each with the same income and the same preferences. When the price of $X$ is $50 per unit, the typical consumer is prepared to purchase 20 units. When the price is $40 per unit, the typical consumer is prepared to purchase 25 units. Construct from this information the market demand curve for $X$ (assume the demand curve is a straight line). Then calculate the loss of consumer surplus when the price rises from $40 to $50 per unit.

7. A consumer is spending an entire weekly income on goods $A$ and $B$. The last penny spent on $A$ yields a marginal utility of 10; the last penny spent on $B$ yields a marginal utility of 20. Is it possible for the consumer to be in equilibrium? If so, what are the exact conditions?

8. Lisa White consumes only goods $X$ and $Y$. Column 1 of Table A shows the marginal utility she derives from various units of $X$; column 2 shows the marginal utility she derives from various units of $Y$. Her income is $20, the price of $X$ is $2 per unit, and the price of $Y$ is $4 per unit. Use Table A to answer the following questions:
   a. How much of $X$ and $Y$ will Lisa White demand?
   b. Check your answer by using the consumer equilibrium conditions. (Is all income spent? Does $MU_X/P_X = MU_Y/P_Y$?)

| Table A | | | |
|---|---|---|---|
| *(1)* | | *(2)* | |
| *Units of X* | *$MU_X$* | *Units of Y* | *$MU_Y$* |
| 1 | 20 | 1 | 2000 |
| 2 | 16 | 2 | 200 |
| 3 | 12 | 3 | 20 |
| 4 | 10 | 4 | 10 |
| 5 | 6 | 5 | 4 |

9. Can the equilibrium conditions be applied to more than two goods? How?

10. The price of ale is $10, the price of bread is $5, and the marginal utility of bread is 50 utils when the consumer is in equilibrium. Can you determine how much is spent on ale? Can you determine the marginal utility of ale?

11. The price of oranges is $0.25 each, and the price of grapefruit is $0.50 each. Assuming that all income is spent in each case, determine whether or not the consumer is in equilibrium in each of the following circumstances. If consumer equilibrium does not occur, determine which good the consumer will purchase in greater quantity and explain why.
    a. The marginal utility of oranges, $MU_O$, equals 10, and the marginal utility of grapefruit, $MU_G$, equals 15.
    b. $MU_O = 50$ and $MU_G = 100$.
    c. $MU_O$ is twice that of $MU_G$.
    d. $MU_G$ is twice that of $MU_O$.

12. *Optional Question.* Income and substitution effects can be measured. Suppose that the income elasticity of demand for housing is 1 and that the price elasticity of demand is 0.3 (these numbers are close to actual estimates). Furthermore, suppose that housing accounts for 20 percent of the average household's budget. A decrease in income of 2 percent would decrease the demand for housing by 2 percent because the income elasticity is 1. Now suppose that income is held constant and that the price of housing rises by 10 percent. Since the price elasticity is 0.3, a 10 percent increase in price will lower quantity demanded by 3 percent. What portion of this 3 percent decrease in quantity demanded is due to the income effect? What portion is due to the substitution effect? (*Hint:* A 10 percent increase in the price of housing raises the cost of living by 2 percent since there is a 10 percent increase in 20 percent of the budget. Observe also that a 2 percent increase in the cost of living has the same effect as a 2 percent reduction in income. Therefore, a 10 percent increase in the price of housing, holding income and other prices constant, is like a 2 percent reduction in real income.)

# APPENDIX 7A

# INDIFFERENCE CURVES

**APPENDIX INSIGHT**

The preceding chapter based the law of demand on the nineteenth-century conception of cardinal utility—a measure that reflects the magnitude as well as the rank of a consumer's satisfaction from different commodity bundles. Skepticism about the quantification of utility prompted economists to seek an alternative approach to understanding consumer behavior. The culmination of this search is the *indifference curve theory*. This theory assumes that consumers are able to *rank* their preferences for combinations of goods, but it does not require that utility be measured in absolute terms. A consumer who does not prefer one combination to another is said to be *indifferent*. Indifference curve theory provides a convenient graphical approach for illustrating consumer response to income and price changes, and for analyzing the breakdown of consumer behavior into substitution and income effects.

# CONSUMER PREFERENCES

The indifference curve approach is based on an analysis of the amount of one good a consumer is willing to give up in exchange for 1 unit of another good without experiencing a loss in total satisfaction. When one combination of goods yields the same satisfaction as another, the consumer is indifferent between the two combinations.

Figure A1 diagrams the preferences of a particular consumer. The horizontal axis measures the quantity of ale consumed by the individual per week. The vertical axis measures the quantity of bread consumed by the individual per week. At point *a*, 6 loaves of bread and 1 pint of ale are consumed. At point *a*, the consumer is willing to give up 3 loaves of bread for 1 more pint of ale. Making this trade would move the consumer to point *b*, where 3 loaves of bread and 2 pints of ale are consumed. At point *b*, the consumer is willing to give up only 1 loaf of bread to acquire 1 more pint of ale. Making this trade would move the consumer to point *c*, where 2 loaves of bread and 3 pints of ale are consumed per week. Finally, to acquire 1 more pint of ale, the consumer at point *c* is willing to give up only half of a

loaf of bread, which would result in the combination at point *d*. Among points *a*, *b*, *c*, and *d*, the consumer is indifferent.

A curve (U) can be drawn through points *a*, *b*, *c*, and *d* to represent all possible consumption patterns that keep the consumer at the same level of satisfaction. The consumer is indifferent among these patterns.

> An **indifference curve** shows all the alternative combinations of two goods that yield the same total satisfaction to a particular consumer and among which the consumer is indifferent.

An indifference curve is downward sloping because both goods yield satisfaction. The consumer's satisfaction will remain constant when the consumption of one good increases only if consumption of the other good decreases.

## THE LAW OF DIMINISHING MARGINAL RATE OF SUBSTITUTION

When indifference curves are used to analyze consumer preferences, the concept of marginal utility is no longer required.

> The **marginal rate of substitution (MRS)** is how much of one good a person is just willing to give up to acquire one unit of another good.

Thus, the marginal rate of substitution is simply a fancy name for an acceptable trade-off between two goods, for a person's *valuation* of an additional unit of one good in terms of another. For example, the amount of pizza a person would be willing to sacrifice for an additional hot dog indicates that person's valuation of hot dogs in terms of pizza.

An indifference curve is always convex when viewed from below (that is, the curve bulges toward the origin). This convex curvature follows from the law of diminishing marginal rate of substitution.

> The **law of diminishing marginal rate of substitution** states that as more of one good *(A)* is consumed, the amount of another good *(B)* that the consumer is willing to sacrifice for one more unit of good *A* declines.

As more ale is consumed relative to bread, the consumer is willing to give up less and less bread to

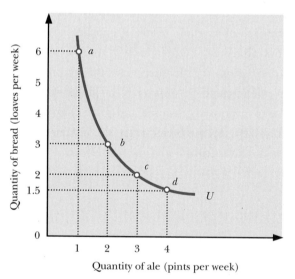

**FIGURE A1    An Indifference Curve**

When given the choice among the commodity bundles along an indifference curve, the consumer is indifferent. Consumption pattern *a* yields the same satisfaction to the consumer as *b*, *c*, or *d*. The absolute value of the slope of an indifference curve is the marginal rate of substitution and shows—in this case—how much bread the consumer is just willing to sacrifice for one more pint of ale.

acquire additional units of ale because bread is getting more valuable and ale is getting less valuable. In Figure A1, from point *a* down to point *d* and beyond, the indifference curve gets flatter and flatter because the relative valuation placed on ale is decreasing compared to that of bread.

The flatter the slope of the indifference curve, the lower the relative valuation the consumer places on *A* (compared to *B*) when *A* is on the horizontal axis. The slope of the tangent at any point on the indifference curve measures the marginal rate of substitution of good *B* for good *A*.

Indifference curves can be drawn to represent any level of satisfaction. Each consumer has an entire map of indifference curves, one for every level. Figure A2 shows three indifference curves for the same consumer. Higher indifference curves for any one consumer represent higher levels of satisfaction because more is usually better.

Indifference curves are subjective and unique to each person. Nevertheless, all indifference curves have the following five properties in common:

1. Indifference curves between two goods for which consumers derive positive benefits are downward sloping.

2. Indifference curves are bowed toward the *origin* (the point where the axes meet), reflecting the law of diminishing marginal rate of substitution.

3. The consumer is better off when he or she moves to a higher indifference curve.

4. Indifference curves cannot intersect each other because an intersection would indicate that the consumer is simultaneously worse off and better off. (Even though indifference curves cannot intersect, they need not be parallel.)

5. The entire pattern of indifference curves is independent of changes in market circumstances (income or prices), just as a map is fixed regardless of your location.

## THE BUDGET LINE

What a consumer can afford is determined by the consumer's budget. Suppose the price of ale is $2 per pint and the price of bread is $0.50 per loaf, as in the preceding chapter. Assume the consumer has $8 to spend per week on ale and bread. If the entire $8 is spent on ale, the consumer can buy 4 pints of ale (point *m* in Figure A3). If the entire $8 is spent on bread, 16 loaves can be purchased (point *n*).

> The **budget line** represents all the combinations of goods the consumer is able to buy, given a certain income and set prices. The budget line shows the consumption possibilities available to the consumer.

The budget line connecting points *m* and *n* indicates all possible combinations of ale and bread that the consumer is able to purchase by allocating the entire $8 income between the two goods.

The budget line in Figure A3 has a slope with an absolute value of $16/4 = 4$. This slope is the price of ale (the good on the horizontal axis) in terms of bread (the good on the vertical axis): $P_A/P_B = \$2/\$0.50 = 4$; it indicates that a consumer who wants to buy 1 more pint of ale must give up 4 loaves of bread.

Algebraically, point *m* in Figure A3 is income divided by the price of ale (Income/$P_A$) because it represents the maximum possible consumption of ale.

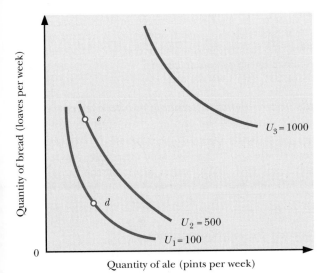

**FIGURE A2  Map of Indifference Curves**

Each consumer has an infinite number of indifference curves. Three indifference curves for a particular consumer are shown here. The higher the indifference curve is, the greater is the well-being of the consumer. The indifference map shows that commodity bundle *e* is preferred to bundle *d* because the former is on a higher indifference curve. Indifference curve $U_3$ represents a higher level of satisfaction than $U_2$, and $U_2$ represents a higher level than $U_1$. The level of satisfaction along each indifference curve is constant.

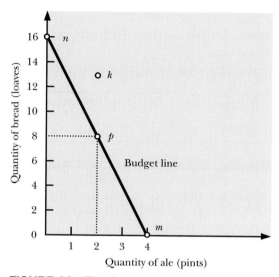

**FIGURE A3    The Budget Line**

With a budget of $8, the consumer can buy 16 loaves of bread at a price of $0.50 per loaf or 4 pints of ale at a price of $2 per pint. Spending $4 on each good would buy 8 loaves of bread and 2 pints of ale (point *p*). The budget line shows the choices open to the consumer. The consumer can afford to buy any combination of goods on the budget line. Points above the budget line, such as *k*, cannot be purchased with the consumer's income. The slope of the budget line is the ratio of the price of ale to the price of bread—here, 4.

Point *n* is income divided by the price of bread (Income/$P_B$). Then, the absolute value of the slope of the line *nm* is as follows:

$$\text{Slope} = \frac{\text{Income}}{P_B} \div \frac{\text{Income}}{P_A} = \frac{P_A}{P_B}$$

An indifference curve shows how the consumer ranks various commodity bundles; the budget line shows which bundles the consumer *is able to buy*. Combining the information represented by an indifference curve and the budget line reveals which combination the consumer *will buy*.

## CONSUMER EQUILIBRIUM

The consumer achieves equilibrium by choosing a consumption pattern that maximizes satisfaction and lies on the budget line. The consumer is *able* to locate anywhere on the budget line, but *the rational consumer will select the consumption combination that*

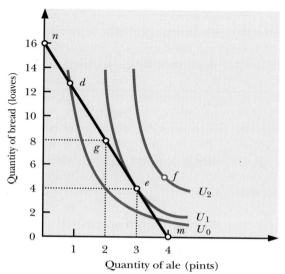

**FIGURE A4    Consumer Equilibrium**

The consumer's optimal consumption pattern is at point *e*. A point like *d* is attainable (on the budget line) but is inferior to *e* because it places the consumer on a lower indifference curve ($U_0$). Point *f* is preferable to *e* (the consumer is on a higher indifference curve, $U_2$) but is not attainable with the given set of income and prices. At *e*, the indifference curve $U_1$ is tangent to the budget line. Thus, the slope of the indifference curve equals the slope of the budget line. This tangency is equivalent to the marginal utility rule for maximizing utility ($MU_A/P_A = MU_B/P_B$) discussed in the preceding chapter.

*falls on the highest attainable indifference curve.* Figure A4 illustrates the choice of an optimal consumption pattern. By consuming 4 loaves of bread and 3 pints of ale (point *e*), the consumer can reach indifference curve $U_1$. Any other point on the budget line will fall on a *lower* indifference curve. At this optimal consumption point, the budget line is tangent to (touches the curve only at one point and has the same slope as) the indifference curve.

In equivalent terms, consumer equilibrium occurs at that point on the highest attainable indifference curve where the marginal rate of substitution equals the price ratio. At point *e*, the consumer's marginal rate of substitution is 4 because the consumer is willing to trade off 4 units of bread for 1 unit of ale. The price ratio, as we have shown, is also 4.

The consumer is in equilibrium when the budget line is just tangent to the highest attainable indifference curve. Two conditions are then satisfied: (1) The consumer is on the budget line. (2) The consumer's marginal rate of substitution of bread for ale equals the price ratio of ale to bread ($P_A/P_B$).

## INDIFFERENCE CURVES AND UTILITY

In the preceding chapter, we defined utility as a numerical ranking of a consumer's preferences among different commodity bundles. We stated that utility is an ordinal measure of consumer satisfaction, used to indicate rank-order rather than magnitude. By assigning numerical levels of utility to indifference curves, we can relate the two concepts. (We must not, however, confuse the convenient language of utility theory with the assumption that utility is measurable.) Any numbers can be assigned as long as they are increasing for higher indifference curves. Thus, in Figure A2, we assign a higher number (1000) to indifference curve $U_3$ than to $U_2$ (500) or to $U_1$ (100).

Also in the preceding chapter, the quantification of utility allowed us to define the marginal utility (MU) of a good as the increase in utility per unit change in the consumption of the good, holding the consumption of other goods constant. Marginal utility theory and indifference curve analysis are linked by the ability to use the marginal utilities of two goods to calculate the marginal rate of substitution. For example, if the marginal utility of ale ($MU_A$) is 20 and the marginal utility of bread ($MU_B$) is 5, it takes 4 extra loaves of bread to compensate the consumer for the loss of only 1 pint of ale. But if $MU_A = 10$ and $MU_B = 5$, the marginal rate of substitution of bread for ale is only 2.

We can translate the conditions for equilibrium outlined in the preceding section into the equal marginal utility-per-dollar rule for consumer equilibrium described in the preceding chapter. At point $e$ in Figure A4, the slope of the indifference curve is $MU_A/MU_B$, and the slope of the budget line is $P_A/P_B$. The indifference curve equilibrium rule is equivalent to

$$MU_A/MU_B = P_A/P_B$$

Some algebraic manipulation shows that this equation is equivalent to the marginal utility per dollar rule for equilibrium:

$$MU_A/P_A = MU_B/P_B$$

The marginal rate of substitution of bread for ale ($MRS_{B/A}$) equals the ratio of the ale's marginal utility ($MU_A$) to the bread's marginal utility ($MU_B$):

$$MRS_{B/A} = \frac{MU_A}{MU_B}$$

## THE EFFECT OF AN INCOME CHANGE

The consumer's equilibrium position is affected by changes in income, the price of ale, and the price of bread. Figure A5 shows that a reduction in the consumer's income from $8 to $4 leads to a reduction in the demand for both ale and bread. We assume the price of ale stays at $2 per pint and the price of bread remains at $0.50 per loaf. The budget line shifts downward from $nm$ to $hj$ because the consumer can purchase a maximum of only 2 pints of ale or 8 loaves of bread with an income of $4. Consumption decreases from 4 loaves of bread and 3 pints of ale to only 2 loaves of bread and 1.5 pints of ale at the new equilibrium (point $e_0$).

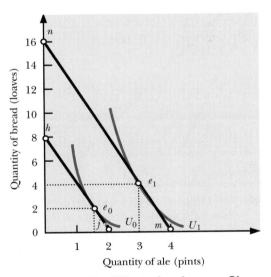

**FIGURE A5    The Effect of an Income Change**

When the price of ale is $2 per pint and the price of bread is $0.50 per loaf, a fall in income from $8 to $4 causes a parallel shift in the budget line from $nm$ to $hj$. The equilibrium point moves from $e_1$ to $e_0$, which is on a lower indifference curve ($U_0$).

Notice that because prices are held constant, the slope of the budget line, $P_A/P_B$, remains the same. Thus, all budget lines for a given set of prices are parallel, shifting downward when income falls and upward when income rises. Clearly, utility also rises and falls in concert with income.

## THE EFFECT OF A PRICE CHANGE

Now consider the effects of a change in the price of one of two goods, holding income and the other price constant. Figure A6 shows that a fall in the price of ale from $2 to $1 per pint leads to an increase in the quantity of ale demanded. The initial equilibrium situation is represented by point $e_1$, where the price of ale is $2 and the price of bread is $0.50. Reducing the price of ale to $1 allows the consumer to purchase as many as 8 pints of ale with the same income of $8. The budget line swings outward from $nm$ to $nr$.

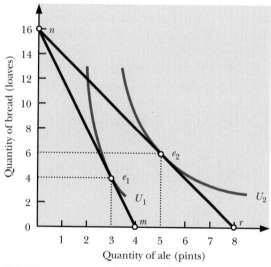

**FIGURE A6   The Effect of a Price Change on Consumer Equilibrium: The Law of Demand**

Assuming that income is $8 and the price of bread is $0.50, when the price of ale falls from $2 to $1 per pint, the budget line swings outward from $nm$ to $nr$ because the consumer is able to buy as many as 8 pints of ale. The consumer finds a new equilibrium combination, $e_2$, where indifference curve $U_2$ is tangent to the new budget line $nr$. A fall in the price of ale from $2 to $1, thus, increases the quantity of ale demanded from 3 pints at point $e_1$ to 5 pints at point $e_2$.

At the new equilibrium position, point $e_2$, the consumer buys 5 pints of ale and 6 loaves of bread. Before the price change, the consumer bought 3 pints of ale and 4 loaves of bread. The law of demand is reconfirmed: lowering the price of ale increases the quantity of ale demanded.

Moreover, the consumer is made better off (moves to a higher indifference curve) by the fall in the price of ale. The lower the price of a good bought by a consumer, holding income and other prices constant, the greater the consumer's welfare.

> When the price of one good falls, an increase in real income occurs, represented by an outward swing of the budget line.

An analysis of the effect of a price change illustrates why demand curves are downward sloping. A downward slope on a demand curve implies that as the price of a good falls, the quantity demanded rises. The preceding chapter outlined two reasons for the law of demand: the substitution effect and the income effect. When the price of a good falls, people tend to substitute that good for other goods because its relative price decreases. Thus, the substitution effect tends to increase the quantity of a good demanded when its price falls. In addition, when the price of a good falls, people have more money to spend on all goods. For a person who is accustomed to buying one $15,000 car per year, a reduction in price to $13,000 is like a $2000 increase in income. If a good is normal, increases in income raise the demand for it. Thus, the income effect of a decrease in the price of a good further increases the quantity demanded.

Figure A7 shows a consumer with an initial budget line $vw$ and an initial equilibrium at point $e$, where the consumer is purchasing $q$ units of ale. When the price of ale falls, the budget line shifts to $vz$. The quantity of ale demanded is now $q''$ at the new equilibrium point, $e''$. The consumer is better off after the drop in the ale price because curve $U''$ is higher than curve $U$. Indifference curve analysis can be used to isolate the roles of the substitution effect and the income effect on the change in the equilibrium position.

When the price of ale falls, the ratio of the price of ale to the price of bread changes. This new ratio is reflected by the budget lines $vz$ and $st$. A consumer interested only in maintaining the same level of utility achieved on curve $U$ would increase the quantity

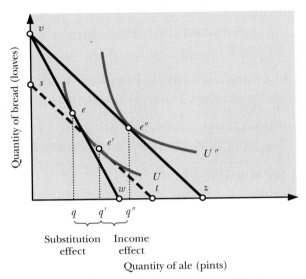

**FIGURE A7  Substitution and Income Effects**

When income is $8 per week, bread costs $0.50 per loaf, and ale costs $2 per pint, the initial equilibrium is point *e*. When the price of ale falls from $2 to $1 per pint, the budget line swings outward from *vw* to *vz*. The new equilibrium is point *e''*. The substitution effect is obtained by drawing the budget line *st* parallel to *vz* but tangent to the original indifference curve, *U*. Thus, the substitution effect is the distance *qq'* and the income effect is the distance *q'q''*. In the case of a normal good, the income effect augments the substitution effect.

of ale demanded until he or she reached point *e'*, where line *st* is tangent to *U*. At *e'*, the consumer buys more ale and less bread without changing the level of satisfaction. This change in the quantity of ale demanded, from *q* to *q'*, constitutes the substitution effect of the change in the price of ale.

At point *e'*, however, the consumer is not spending all available income. The drop in the price of ale shifts the budget line outward to *vz*, which has the same ale price/bread price ratio as *st* but enables the consumer to choose a position on a higher indifference curve. Instead of remaining at *e'*, a consumer who wishes to maximize satisfaction will choose *e''*, a point on the highest indifference curve attainable given budget line *vz*. A consumer making this choice will further increase the quantity demanded of ale from *q'* at *e'* to *q''* at *e''*. This new equilibrium, unlike *e'*, does satisfy all the conditions of consumer equilibrium. The increase in quantity demanded from *q'* to *q''* constitutes the income effect of the change in the ale price.

The importance of the distinction between the substitution and income effects is that if a good is normal, the income effect reinforces the substitution effect. In Figure A7, the price of ale falls and the substitution effect increases quantity demanded from *q* to *q'* along the convex indifference curve *U*. The move from *e'* to *e''* is like any income increase. If ale is a normal good, more ale will be consumed. In effect, a reduced price of ale gives the consumer more income to spend on both ale and bread. It follows from the above analysis that if a good is normal, the demand curve for the good must be downward sloping.

## SUMMARY

1. Indifference curve analysis requires only that consumers be able to state whether they prefer one combination of goods to another or whether they are indifferent. An indifference curve plots those combinations of goods that yield the same level of satisfaction to the consumer. In indifference curve analysis, the law of diminishing marginal rate of substitution replaces the law of diminishing marginal utility. It states that the greater the quantity of good *X* that the individual consumes relative to good *Y*, the smaller will be the quantity of good *Y* that the consumer is willing to sacrifice to obtain 1 more unit of good *X*. The budget line shows the choices of goods open to the consumer.

2. Maximizing satisfaction requires that the consumer seek out the highest indifference curve that can be attained while remaining on the budget line. This point occurs at the tangency of the indifference curve and the budget line.

3. Indifference curves can be related to marginal utilities. The marginal rate of substitution of bread for ale is the marginal utility of ale divided by the marginal utility of bread.

4. A change in income causes a parallel shift in the budget line. The budget line shifts downward if income decreases and upward if income increases. The new equilibrium is simply the point of tangency between the new budget line and an indifference curve.

5. A reduction in the price of one commodity swings the budget line outward. The new equilibrium occurs at the point of tangency between a higher indifference curve and the new budget line.

The consumer is made better off by the price reduction because the consumer is able to locate on a higher indifference curve. The effects of a price change on quantity demanded can be broken down into a substitution effect, which maintains the existing utility level, and an income effect, which results from the change in the consumer's level of utility.

## KEY TERMS

indifference curve
marginal rate of substitution (MRS)
law of diminishing marginal rate of substitution
budget line

## QUESTIONS AND PROBLEMS

1. Assume that a consumer's income is $100, the price of ale is $5 per pint, and the price of bread is $4 per loaf.
   a. Draw the consumer's budget line.
   b. How does the budget line shift if the price of bread rises to $10, holding the price of ale at $5?
   c. How does the budget line shift if the price of ale rises to $10, holding the price of bread at $10?
   d. How does the budget line shift if income doubles to $200, holding the prices of ale and bread at $5 and $10, respectively?
2. Why are indifference curves downward sloping? Why are they bowed toward the origin?
3. Why must the equilibrium position be a point of tangency between the budget line and an indifference curve?
4. Illustrate a situation in which income increases and the demand for one of two goods falls.
5. Derive the law of demand for a normal good using the distinction between substitution and income effects when the price of the good rises.
6. Assume that the marginal rate of substitution of good $X$ for good $Y$ is $MRS_{X/Y} = 6$, that the price of good $X$ is $1 per unit, and that the price of good $Y$ is $3 per unit.
   a. Illustrate the consumer's current position on the budget line relative to an indifference curve.
   b. Explain why the consumer would buy more of good $Y$.

# CHAPTER 8

# BUSINESS ORGANIZATION

This chapter emphasizes one type of business firm—the corporation—and explains how it is managed and how it raises capital. Although forms of the corporation existed in ancient Rome, the modern corporation was not created until the sixteenth century, as an innovative way to finance Europe's lucrative but risky overseas trade. The corporation offered new ways of raising large amounts of capital while protecting the fortunes of its investors.

Small merchant businesses and handicraft shops could be owned and managed by individuals or partners in the sixteenth century. To provision and operate the largest merchant ships of the day, however, required more capital than could be raised by single families or partnerships. Moreover, if a ship went down, the liabilities that had to be met could bankrupt owners. A corporation, however, could raise money by selling shares to investors. If a ship sank, investors would lose their investment, but they could not be held personally liable for the unpaid bills of the company.

The corporation developed by itself, without government direction. By the time of the Industrial Revolution, it had reached a level of maturity. It was the corporation that raised the capital and provided the management of businesses that made the Industrial Revolution possible.

# WHY BUSINESS FIRMS EXIST

> **Entrepreneurs** are risk-takers who combine the factors of production to produce output so as to realize profit opportunities.

Although it is possible for entrepreneurs to work entirely through markets without organizing business firms, such instances are rare. An entrepreneur could build a home by contracting through markets with carpenters, plumbers, electricians, and lumber and glass suppliers. Most homes are not built this way. They are built by construction firms, whose owners or managers direct employees—carpenters, electricians, and unskilled laborers—to perform particular tasks.

Almost all output is produced by business firms. Business firms have common features irrespective of their specific form of organization. They have an owner or owners. They have a manager, who may or may not be the same as the owner. Most have employees, and they have resources that can be directed by the firm's managers.

Resources are allocated within the firm by managerial coordination.

> **Managerial coordination** is the disposition of the firm's resources according to the directives of the firm's manager(s).

All business firms need a person or persons to make managerial decisions. The firm's managers allocate the capital and land owned or leased by the firm and issue directives to employees who work according to written or unwritten contracts.

> A **principal** has controlling authority and engages an agent to act subject to the principal's control and instruction.
>
> An **agent** acts for, on behalf of, or as a representative of a principal.

If the Dallas Cowboys hire Barry Switzer as head coach, he is the agent. If IBM signs a contract with American Airlines to upgrade its computer reservations, American Airlines is the principal and IBM the agent. If Jim, the owner of Jim's Motorcycle Repair, hires Bob to work as a repairman and sales clerk, Jim is the principal and Bob is the agent.

Once the principal and agent agree on terms, the principal must ensure that the agent fulfills the terms of the agreement. If the principal and agent have different goals, conflicts between the principal and agent are possible. Business firms must find effective ways of monitoring and controlling their agents.

There are four main reasons for having business firms: They can limit the costs of market transactions, take advantage of economies of scale, bear risk individuals are unwilling to bear, and provide monitoring of team production.

## COSTS OF USING MARKETS

Nobel laureate Ronald Coase[1] argued that as long as the cost of organizing an activity inside the firm is below the cost of organizing that activity using markets, the task will be carried out within the firm. Market coordination has its costs. Market-coordinated activities require contracts, paperwork, searching for the best prices, and paying legal expenses if contracts are not fulfilled. Imagine, for example, the enormous transactions costs of using market coordination to produce a modern commercial jet aircraft. Thousands of subcontracts would have to be negotiated to produce the instruments, the hydraulic control systems, the airframe, and the interior furnishings. Managerial coordination can reduce these transactions costs. Instead of negotiating thousands of market contracts, the manager simply directs employees to perform designated tasks, allocates the plant and equipment of the business enterprise, and works with fewer subcontractors. It is easier for Jim to hire Bob as a repairman/sales clerk on a year's contract than to go out and hire someone on a daily basis in the labor market.

## ECONOMIES OF SCALE

As Adam Smith pointed out more than 200 years ago, business firms can take advantage of *economies of scale.*

> **Economies of scale** are present when large output volumes can be produced at a lower cost per unit than small output volumes.

---

[1]Ronald H. Coase, "The Nature of the Firm," *Economica* 4 (1937):386–405. Reprinted in George Stilger and Kenneth Boulding, eds., *Readings in Price Theory* (Homewood, IL: Richard D. Irwin, 1952).

Economies of scale are present in many production processes (you are already acquainted with Smith's example of a pin factory). The business firm brings together workers, land, and capital: The manager directs them to specialize in different tasks; output is produced in larger production runs and at a lower cost per unit. In order for Jim to repair motorcycles at a reasonable cost, he may need a number of employees in addition to Bob to perform specialized repair tasks and handle a larger volume of business.

## BEARING THE RISK

In his classic study, Frank Knight emphasized that some individuals are more willing to bear risk than others.[2] Business ventures typically involve risk (demand can change, prices can fluctuate, and so on). The owner of the enterprise (the principal) is willing to bear the risk. The employees (the agents) are not. The employer hires workers and rents land and equipment at negotiated prices. In return for this security, employees agree to follow the owner's business directives. If the business is successful, the owner will reap the rewards; if it fails, the owner will suffer the consequences. The business firm exists because it provides a convenient way for those who are willing to bear risk—the entrepreneurs—to do so.

## MONITORING TEAM PRODUCTION

In another classic study of business organization, Armen Alchian and Harold Demsetz noted that business enterprises are formed when there are gains from team production.[3] In many cases, employees working as a team can produce more output than can employees working alone.

If team production is used, the performance of individual employees must be monitored by the owner/manager to ensure that no employees are shirking their responsibility. Because the owner of a firm is paid out of the gains of team production, the owner will be motivated to do a good job of monitoring. If Bob and Julie work together as a team to repair motorcycles, Jim, the owner, may have to

monitor their work to make sure that both members of the team are working effectively.

Team monitoring is essential when agents and principals have different goals. The principal wants to earn a maximum profit. Employees may want a lighter work load. Hired managers may value job security more than profits.

$P = R - C$

## PROFIT MAXIMIZATION

Capitalism and socialism provide different visions of the way economies should work. In Adam Smith's view of capitalism, it is healthy for business firms to pursue their self-interest in the form of profits. The profit motive causes them to pursue society's interests while pursuing their own narrow goals. In Karl Marx's view of capitalism, the selfish pursuit of profits will lead to exploitation, misery, and socialist revolution.

What is the goal of a business firm? The objective of business firms is profit maximization. (See Example 1.)

> **Profit maximization** is the search by firms for the product quality, output, and price that give the firm the highest possible profits.

Some economists have questioned whether firms do indeed maximize profits. Perhaps firms are interested in other things, like maximizing sales or growth of employment.

Natural selection theory argues that profit maximization must be the overriding objective of business firms.

> According to the **natural selection theory,** if business firms do not maximize profits, they will be unable to compete with other firms and will be driven out of the market or taken over by outsiders.

Any firm that does not seek to maximize profits may be forced to close its doors when competitors offer higher-quality products at lower cost. The natural selection argument is compelling in the case of firms that face competition. It is less compelling for businesses who are insulated from competition. Business firms that do not earn maximum profits run another risk: They can be taken over by outsiders who can earn higher profits.

Stockholders demand profits

---

[2]Frank H. Knight, *Risk, Uncertainty, and Profit* (New York: Harper Torchbooks, 1957).

[3]Armen Alchian and Harold Demsetz, "Production, Information Costs, and Economic Organization," *American Economic Review* 57, no. 5 (December 1972): 777–795.

## EXAMPLE 1
### TRASH
### TELEVISION DAYS

The evidence that firms maximize profits is all around us and, therefore, hard to see, like blades of grass or air molecules. Although some experts argue businesses are interested in maximizing revenues, a revenue maximizing strategy can lead to ruin. One major television network suffered severe losses by paying too much for the right to televise baseball. Although advertising revenues from baseball broadcasting were high, they were not enough to cover costs.

A dramatic counter example is provided by "Trash Television," in which people of questionable character, morals, and intelligence are paraded in front of viewers on a daily basis. Enough people watch the shows, they cost virtually nothing to produce, and the television networks make a healthy profit filling the market for that service. Even though pundits and politicians express outrage at such television shows, the shows continue with the support of the viewing public and the companies that advertise their products on those programs.

Businesses prosper and survive by doing things that generate more revenues than costs, not by generating revenues.

---

Our experience of the last century is that the profit motive is indeed the prime motivator for business. The industrial pioneers who initiated the Industrial Revolution were motivated by profits. The founders of the great businesses over the past century have been motivated by profits. Experience also confirms Joseph Schumpeter's insight about creative destruction, discussed in Chapter 1. No firm's profits are secure forever. All businesses must eventually face the "creative destruction" of competition.

## FORMS OF BUSINESS ORGANIZATION

Business enterprises are classified into three categories: sole proprietorships, partnerships, and corporations. The form a business enterprise takes determines who makes business decisions, how capital is raised, who bears the risk of business failures, and how principal/agent problems are resolved.

### SOLE PROPRIETORSHIPS

The sole proprietorship is the least complex form of business enterprise.

The **sole proprietorship** is owned by one individual who makes all the business decisions, receives the profits that the business earns, and bears the financial responsibility for losses.

Any individual can decide to go into business. The individual proprietor need not seek permission to enter into business unless business licenses or health permits are required. Little if any legal work is required.

The proprietor is responsible for all business decisions: how many employees to hire, what products to produce, and how to market those products. The only legal requirements the owner must meet are observing regulations and honoring contracts.

**Advantages.**    The first advantage of the sole proprietorship is that decision-making authority is clear-cut: It resides with the owner. In making business decisions, the owner need not consult anyone.

The second advantage of the sole proprietorship is that it is easy to establish—there are no agreements with other owners.

The third advantage is that the profits of the company accrue to the owner; unlike the profits of a corporation, the earnings of a sole proprietorship are taxed only once as personal income.

**Disadvantages.** The first disadvantage of the sole proprietorship is that the owner must assume unlimited liability (responsibility) for the debts of the company. The owner enjoys the profit of the business if it is successful; the owner is personally liable if the business suffers a loss. If the company borrows money, purchases materials, and incurs other bills that it cannot cover, the owner must personally cover the losses. The owner can lose personal wealth in paying off the debts of the company.

The second disadvantage of the sole proprietorship is its limited ability to raise financial capital, which explains why most proprietorships are small. Their owners raise capital by reinvesting profits; by dipping into personal wealth to invest in the company; or by borrowing from relatives, friends, and lending institutions. The firm's borrowing power is limited by the owner's earning capacity and personal wealth. Lending to an individual proprietorship can be risky. If the proprietor dies, becomes incapacitated, or declares bankruptcy, the lender must stand in line with other creditors.

The third disadvantage is that the business will often not survive the current owner. Since the firm does not have a permanent existence, it may be difficult to find reliable employees; employees prefer to work in firms that offer long-term career opportunities and provide for retirement.

## PARTNERSHIPS

A partnership is much like an individual proprietorship, but it has more than one owner.

> A **partnership** is owned by two or more people called partners, who make all the business decisions, share the profits, and bear the financial responsibility for any losses.

Partnerships are also easy to establish. Most partnerships are based upon an agreement that spells out the ownership shares and duties of each partner. The partners may contribute different amounts of financial capital to the partnership; they may divide responsibility for running the business. One partner may make all the business decisions, while the other partner (a "silent partner") may simply provide financial capital. A partnership can be a corner gas station owned by a family or a nationally known law firm or brokerage house.

**Advantages.** The advantages of partnerships are much like those of the sole proprietorship. Partnerships are usually easy to set up. The profits of the company accrue to the partners and are taxed only once as part of their personal income.

Partnerships, however, provide greater opportunity to specialize and divide managerial responsibility. The partner who is the better salesperson will be in charge of sales. The partner who is a talented mechanical engineer will be in charge of production. Each partner offers different talents. A partnership also can raise more financial capital because the wealth and borrowing power of more than one person can be mobilized. If a large number of wealthy partners can be assembled, large sums of capital can be raised.

**Disadvantages.** First, the ability of the partnership to raise financial capital is limited to what the partners can raise out of their personal wealth or from borrowing.

Second, the partners have unlimited liability for the debts of the partnership. (See Example 2.) A business debt incurred by any of the partners is the responsibility of the partnership. Each partner stands to lose personal wealth if the company is a failure. A conflict in goals can arise when one partner is more risk-averse than another. For this reason, partnerships are often made up of family members, relatives, and close personal friends.

Third, decision making can become complicated if partners disagree. Partnerships can be immobilized when partners disagree on fundamental policy. Decision making becomes more complicated as the number of partners grows.

Fourth, partnerships can be unstable. If disagreements over policy cause one partner to withdraw, the partnership may have to be reorganized. When one partner dies, the partnership agreement may have to be renegotiated.

Fifth, there may be an incentive to shirk work, especially if the partnership is large. As long as the other partners work hard, the shirking partner will earn a good income.

## CORPORATIONS

The *corporation* came into existence to overcome the disadvantages of the sole proprietorship and partnership.

## EXAMPLE 2
## PARTNERS IN PAIN:
## THE END OF THE ACCOUNTING PARTNERSHIP?

The world's six biggest accounting firms (Arthur Anderson, KPMG, Ernst & Young, Coopers & Lybrand, Deloitte Touche, and Price Waterhouse) are partnerships. They operate on the principle of unlimited liability for their own and their partners' actions. Unlimited liability has been an age-old feature of the partnership. As stated in a 1793 English common law case: "He who takes a moiety [portion] of all the profits indefinitely shall, by operation of law, be made liable for losses, if losses arise."

Clients of the Big Six accounting firms are using the principle of unlimited liability to sue accounting partnerships. Ernst & Young and Price Waterhouse face a combined claim of $11 billion over their audit of the failed Bank for Credit and Commerce. KPMG faces a claim of $2.3 billion by the State Bank of South Australia. Accounting partnerships face $30 billion in claims in the United States alone. If they lose these cases and company funds are not sufficient, the partners must ante up out of their own pockets.

The risks of unlimited liability are becoming too great for accounting firms. By the end of 1996, the Big Six accounting firms will become "limited liability partnerships." Some are even considering becoming limited liability corporations.

------------------------------------------------

*Source:* "Partners in Pain," *The Economist,* July 9, 1994, p. 61.

A **corporation** is a business enterprise that has the status of a legal person and is authorized by federal and state law to act as a single person. The corporation is owned by stockholders who possess shares of stock in the corporation. The stockholders elect a board of directors that appoints the management of the corporation.

Unlike sole proprietorships and partnerships, which can be established with minimal paperwork, a corporate charter is required to set up a corporation. The laws of each state are different, but typically, for a fee, corporations can be established (incorporated) and can become legal "persons" subject to the laws of that state. Because the corporation has the status of a legal person, officers of the corporation can act in the name of the corporation without being personally liable for its debts. If corporate officers commit criminal acts, however, they can be prosecuted.

A stockholder's share of ownership of the corporation equals the number of shares owned by that individual divided by the total number of shares outstanding (owned by stockholders). If you own 100,000 shares of AT&T stock and there are 630 million AT&T shares outstanding, then you own 0.016 percent of AT&T. Stockholders have the right to vote for the board of directors and to vote on items at meetings of the corporation.

The corporation is required by law to issue periodic reports to its shareholders on its financial results and business activities. The corporate management determines whether to reinvest profits or disburse them as dividends. The stockholder who owns 1 percent of the stock of AT&T will receive 1 percent of the dividends paid to shareholders.

Common stock, preferred stock, and convertible stock are three types of corporate stock.

**Common stock** confers voting privileges and the right to receive dividends only if they are declared by the board of directors.

**Preferred stock** does not give voting privileges, but corporations must pay dividends on preferred stock before paying those on common stock.

**Convertible stock** pays the owner fixed interest payments and gives the privilege of converting the convertible stock into common stock at a fixed rate of exchange.

Corporations can have thousands or millions of shares outstanding, owned by a large number of stockholders. Billionaire H. Ross Perot's 11 million shares of General Motors stock made him GM's largest shareholder (with 2 percent of GM stock) before he sold his shares. In closely held corporations, the number of stockholders is limited, and each stockholder owns a substantial share of the corporation's stock.

Stockholders typically do not participate directly in the running of most corporations. There are too many shareholders, and they are too involved in their own business affairs. For these reasons, there is usually a separation of ownership and management. The board of directors appoints a management team that makes decisions for the corporation. If the corporation is unsuccessful, the stockholders may vote out

the current board of directors, or the board of directors itself may decide to bring in a new management team.

Stockholders, however, can exercise substantial indirect control over management by simply selling their stock. The sale of stock by enough dissatisfied stockholders will depress the share price.

**Advantages.** The first advantage of the corporation is that its stockholders are not personally liable for its debts. If a corporation cannot meet its debts, its creditors can lay claim to its assets (bank accounts, equipment, supplies, buildings, and real estate holdings), but they cannot file claims against the stockholders. (See Example 3.) The worst case for stockholders is that their stock becomes worthless.

Limited liability contributes to a second advantage: Corporations can raise large sums of financial capital by selling corporate bonds, issuing stock, and

### EXAMPLE 3
### HOW UNLIMITED LIABILITY ALMOST RUINED LLOYD'S OF LONDON

Lloyd's of London was founded in the late seventeenth century by a group of merchants, shipowners, and insurance brokers who met regularly at the coffee house of Edward Lloyd. It grew to become the largest international provider of marine insurance and other types of risk, such as airline insurance.

Lloyd's of London made its reputation on its willingness to insure virtually anything. Lloyd's insured actress's legs, renowned jewels, and hazardous shipments. Lloyd's was one of the last great businesses that operated on the basis of unlimited liability. Various insurance packages were underwritten by "Names"—individual investors who had to make good on claims, even if they had to use all their personal assets to do so.

The Names were organized into some 300 syndicates or partnerships that would insure various activities.

The years 1991 and 1992 were disastrous for the insurance industry. The Gulf War, numerous

national disasters and airline crashes, and product liability claims caused billions of dollars of losses for Lloyd's of London insurance syndicates. Lloyd's of London Names had to sell virtually all their personal assets to cover these losses. One Name—a former heavyweight boxing champion—had to sell his championship belts. Other Names had to sell their noble titles and their estates.

As a consequence of these losses, Lloyd's of London is no longer willing to insure many high-risk activities. Policies that were previously sold by Lloyd's of London are no longer available. Lloyd's of London had to restructure its way of doing business so that its investors could underwrite insurance with limited liability. By the mid-1990s, Lloyd's had restructured itself as a corporation with limited liability for its investors.

capital movements have been reduced. International markets for goods, services, and capital are replacing national markets. Business enterprises that previously had to compete only with other domestic companies now must compete with companies from Japan, Germany, Taiwan, or Mexico.

The multinational corporation moves capital, technology, and entrepreneurial skills from areas where they are abundant to areas where they are scarce; it spreads throughout the world new ideas, new products, and new ways of organizing production. German and Swiss chemical companies introduce their products, ideas, and management skills to their affiliates in Taiwan and Brazil. Japanese automobile manufacturers introduce their manufacturing and quality control techniques to their U.S. affiliates.

Large corporations are no longer confined to the borders of their home country. They have foreign affiliates and foreign employees, and nationals from other countries are on their boards of directors. The multinational corporation has become an important instrument of change in the world economy.

## RAISING CAPITAL FOR THE CORPORATION

Corporations have an advantage in raising financial capital. Like proprietorships and partnerships, corporations can borrow and they can reinvest profits. In addition, corporations can raise capital by selling bonds or additional shares of stock.

> Corporate **bonds** are obligations to repay the principal at maturity and to make annual interest payments until the maturity date.

### SELLING BONDS

By selling bonds, corporations acquire funds to finance business expansions. Once a bond is sold, the buyer can resell it, but such sales in the bond market do not add to the corporation's financial capital.

The interest or principal payments on corporate bonds represent a legal obligation for the corporation, just as with any other debt. The purchaser of the bond has loaned the corporation money, and the corporation has promised to pay specified interest payments until maturity. Interest payments on corporate bonds have a claim on company earnings prior to dividends.

### ISSUING STOCK

A second means of raising financial capital is for the corporation to sell additional shares of stock. Suppose XYZ Corporation has 100,000 shares of stock that are already owned by stockholders. Each share of stock currently sells for $10 on the secondary market for stock. (We shall discuss financial markets in the next section of the chapter.)

The corporation decides that it needs to raise $500,000 to build a new plant and arranges with an investment bank or an underwriter to sell 50,000 new shares of stock to investors. The company prepares a prospectus to describe to potential buyers the financial condition of the company and the proposed uses for the funds.

The amount of money investors will be willing to pay for the 50,000 new shares reflects their assessment of how the proposed investment will affect the earnings of XYZ Corporation. If investors expect the new plant to raise company earnings substantially, they will offer a higher price than if they expect the investment to have a small effect.

Suppose that XYZ Corporation can sell the 50,000 new shares at the $10-per-share price. XYZ Corporation raises $500,000 through the stock issue. By contrast with corporate bonds, which legally obligate the corporation to pay fixed interest payments, stocks convey no obligation to pay dividends.

### STOCKS OR BONDS?

Corporations can raise capital by selling either stocks or bonds. What considerations determine their choice? In the example of XYZ Corporation, it raised $500,000 by selling 50,000 new shares. Prior to this sale, there were 100,000 shares outstanding; after the sale, there are 150,000. Existing shareholders have been diluted.

> **Dilution** occurs when corporations issue new stock and reduce the percentage ownership of existing shareholders.

After dilution, if the corporation declares a dividend of $150,000, each shareholder will receive a dividend of $1 per share. If there had been no dilution, the previous shareholders would have received a dividend of $1.50 per share. Dilution also dilutes the control of existing shareholders. Prior to dilution, they voted 100 percent of the stock. After dilution, they vote only two-thirds of the stock.

## EXAMPLE 4
### LEVERAGE AND CORPORATE BONDS:
### THE LESSONS OF RJR NABISCO

RJR Nabisco, the largest U.S. food products company, was formed from a merger of RJ Reynolds Tobacco and Nabisco. In 1990, the investment firm of Kohlberg, Kravis, Roberts & Company, known on Wall Street as KKR, decided to take over RJR Nabisco by offering current shareholders a premium price for their stock. After a heated bidding war (about which a movie—*Barbarians at the Gate*—was made), KKR did succeed in buying out RJR Nabisco shareholders by paying $25 billion and gaining control of the company. Such a transaction is called a "leveraged buyout" because the deal was paid for by selling "junk bonds" that paid interest rates in excess of 10 percent to the public, backed by the assets and future earnings of RJR Nabisco.

RJR Nabisco stock fell from $12 per share in 1991 to around $6 per share in 1994. Why? The leveraged buyout left RJR Nabisco with such high-interest expenses from its billions of high-interest bonds that a business downturn could place it in a position of not being able to pay shareholders dividends, or worse, not being able to meet its interest obligations. With its concentration of business in tobacco, the prospect of further business downturns appeared imminent, thereby making the stock an even more risky investment.

The main advantage of issuing new stock is that it does not obligate the corporation to make interest payments. If the corporation is doing well, it can declare a dividend for its shareholders; if it is doing poorly, shareholders must do without a dividend.

Such is not the case with bonds. Bonds obligate the corporation to make interest payments no matter what. During bad times, the corporation may not be able to afford these interest payments. The selling of bonds is thus risky for corporations. If they have large amounts of interest payments to make each year, they become very susceptible to the ups and downs of business. (See Example 4.)

## FINANCIAL MARKETS

Corporate stocks and bonds are traded in financial markets, often called capital markets. It is capital markets that provide the funds required for industrial expansion and growth. Corporate stocks are traded in stock markets, or stock exchanges; corporate bonds are traded in bond markets. The prices of stocks and bonds are determined in these markets.

A **bond market** is a market in which bonds of different types are traded. Bond markets buy and sell corporate bonds and bonds of governmental organizations.

A **stock exchange** is a market in which shares of stock of corporations are bought and sold and in which the prices of shares of stock are determined.

While there are many organized financial markets around the world, the most important stock and bond exchanges are located in New York City, London, Denver, Frankfurt, Tokyo, Zurich, and Paris. The world's largest stock exchange is located on New York City's Wall Street: the New York Stock Exchange (NYSE). The NYSE lists about 50 billion shares of stock, and most days millions of shares worth billions of dollars change hands. The shares of the largest American and multinational corporations are traded on the NYSE.

## PRESENT VALUE

Because bonds make specified payments over a specified period of time, there must be a common denominator. A $100 interest payment made today has a different value from one made ten years from now. We cannot understand bond pricing without first understanding the present value of money.

For the sake of simplicity, assume that the annual interest rate is 10 percent. If you deposit $100 in a savings account, it will earn $10 interest at the end of 1 year. At 10 percent interest, $100 today will be equal to $110 a year from now. If the interest rate is 5 percent, $100 today will be equal to $105 a year from now.

What should you be willing to pay today in order to receive $110 in 1 year? At 10 percent interest, the most you should be willing to pay is $100. Why? Investing more than $100 at 10 percent interest yields more than $110 at the end of 1 year. Thus, the present value (PV) of $110 in one year's time is $100 at 10 percent interest.

> The **present value (PV)** is the most anyone would pay today to receive the money in the future.

The price of a bond that promises to make specified payment at specified future dates will be the present value of those payments. The present value (PV) of each dollar to be paid in 1 year at the interest rate $i$ ($i$ stands for the rate of interest in decimals) is

$$PV = \frac{\$1}{1 + i}$$

If the interest rate is 10 percent, then $i = 0.10$ and $1 + i = 1.10$. The PV of each dollar equals $0.9091. If $10,000 is to be paid in 1 year, its PV today equals $9,091 ($10,000 times 0.9091).

The present-value formula becomes more complicated when the repayment period is greater than 1 year.[4] We can generalize to show that the present

---

[4]To understand this general formula, consider the following: At an interest rate of 10 percent, how much money do you have to deposit today to have $121 at the end of 2 years? If the sum PV is deposited at interest rate $i$, it will be worth $PV \times (1 + i)$ 1 year from now. At the end of the second year, it will be worth $PV \times (1 + i) \times (1 + i)$, or $PV(1 + i)^2$. Setting the sum $PV(1 + i)^2$ equal to $121 and dividing by $(1 + i)^2$ yields

$$PV = \frac{\$121}{(1 + i)^2}$$

At 10 percent interest, the present value of $121 to be received 2 years from now is $100 ($= \$121/1.1^2$).

---

value of a sum to be received in 3 years is that sum divided by $(1 + i)^3$; the present value of a dollar to be received in $n$ years is

$$PV = \frac{\$1}{(1 + i)^n}$$

At a 10 percent interest rate, $100 received 1 year from now has a present value of $90.91; $100 to be received 5 years from now has a present value of only $62.27. The longer the repayment period, the lower the present value.

> The farther in the future the money is to be paid, the lower is its present value.

## BOND PRICES

Present value falls as the interest rate rises. In the preceding example, the present value of $121 to be received in 2 years is $100 at an interest rate of 10 percent—that is, $121 ÷ 1.1^2 = $100. At an interest rate of 20 percent, the PV of $121 to be received 2 years from now falls to $84; that is, $121 ÷ 1.2^2 = $84.

> The present value of a dollar to be received in the future falls as the interest rate rises, and rises as the interest rate falls.

Bond prices fall when interest rates rise; they rise when interest rates fall. Buyers and sellers in bond markets therefore try to anticipate whether interest rates will rise or fall in the future. If bond dealers suspect that interest rates are going to rise, they sell their bond holdings and bond prices drop. It is for this reason that bond dealers and speculators expend so much effort trying to anticipate what will happen to interest rates.

Because corporate bondholders have prior claim on company earnings, bonds offer a relatively secure return. Bondholders will receive their interest and principal payments so long as the corporation does not become bankrupt.

Corporate bonds are not riskless because bond prices fluctuate in the bond market. If the bond owner sells the bond before the date of maturity, the price received for the bond may well be less than the price paid for the bond. Bond prices are the present value (PV) of interest and principal payments. However, there is an inverse relationship between interest rates and present values. As interest rates rise, investors will pay less for the stream of interest payments offered by a bond. As interest rates fall, investors will pay more for the stream of interest payments offered by the bond.

## STOCK PRICES

Stock exchanges bring together buyers and sellers of a particular stock—for example, shares of IBM. The number of shares of IBM stock outstanding is fixed (unless IBM decides to issue new shares of stock), and the current owners of these shares will be prepared to sell their shares at different prices. The supply curve of IBM shares is shown as curve *S* in Figure 2. The higher the price, the greater the number of IBM shares current owners will be prepared to sell; thus, the supply curve is positively sloped. The demand curve for IBM shares, curve *D*, is negatively sloped. The lower the share price, the greater the number of IBM shares people will be prepared to buy. The equilibrium price of IBM shares is that price at which the number of shares demanded equals the number of shares supplied. The equilibrium number of shares traded is referred to as the volume of IBM transactions.

The different assessments of the future profits of the corporation determine the supply and demand curves of Figure 2. The share owner receives dividends that the corporation pays out of profits (if any) and benefits from reinvested profits, which may increase future profits. Share prices, therefore, depend upon the present and future earnings of the corporation. Present earnings are known, but future earnings are uncertain. People have different views of the future of a particular corporation. Some see a bright future of rising profits and dividends; others, a bleak future of declining economic fortunes.

The price of a share of stock depends upon the anticipated future profits per share of outstanding stock, called earnings per share. *Earnings per share (EPS)* is the annual profit of the corporation divided by the number of shares outstanding. Suppose Jones, an optimist, expects earnings per share of XYZ Corporation to be $10 from now until eternity. Smith, a pessimist, expects earnings per share of XYZ Corporation to be $5 from now until eternity. The anticipated future profits of XYZ Corporation need to be converted by both Jones and Smith into a present value.

Take Jones's assumption that one share of XYZ Corporation will earn $10 per year forever—that is,

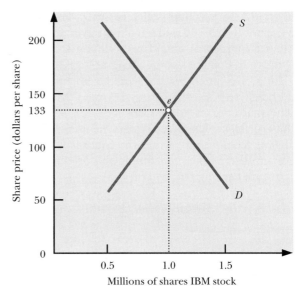

**FIGURE 2    Determination of IBM Stock Prices**
This figure diagrams the supply (*S*) and demand (*D*) curves for shares of IBM stock on September 16, 1994. The supply curve is positively sloped because owners of IBM stock offer more shares for sale at high prices than at low prices. The demand curve is negatively sloped because buyers of IBM shares are prepared to buy more at low prices than at high prices. The equilibrium price is that price at which the quantity demanded equals the quantity supplied. Share prices fluctuate daily because of shifts in demand and supply. The equilibrium price reflects the consensus present value of the future earnings per share of IBM.

it will provide a *perpetual stream* of income. How much is that $10 per year worth in present value? If the interest rate is 10 percent, $100 will earn $10 per year. This $100 is the *present value* of the $10 perpetual stream. If the interest rate fell to 5 percent, $200 will earn $10 a year in perpetuity. Hence $200 is the present value at 5 percent interest.

The general formula for calculating the present value (PV) of a perpetual stream of corporate earnings per share is:

$$PV = \frac{R}{i}$$

where *R* = the annual earnings per share. At an interest rate of 10 percent, the present value of $10 a year in perpetuity is $10 ÷ 0.10, or $100.

Applying the perpetuity formula (at a 10 percent interest rate), the present value of the anticipated earning's stream of one share of stock is $100 ($10/0.10) for Jones and $50 ($5/0.10) for Smith.

Jones would be a willing seller of XYZ stock at a price greater than $100 and a willing buyer at a price less than $100. Smith would be a willing seller at a price above $50 and a willing buyer at a price below $50. At a $75 price, Smith would sell and Jones would buy.

The share price settles at that price at which the quantity of shares demanded equals the quantity supplied. This equilibrium price is the consensus of participants in the market concerning the present value of the future earnings of the corporation.

> The price of a share of stock is the anticipated present value of the future earnings per share of the stock.

The price/earnings (P/E) ratio signals whether investors believe the profits of the company, or earnings per share, will rise or fall from current profit levels.

> The **price/earnings (P/E) ratio** is the price of a share of stock divided by the earnings per share.

If the average company has a P/E ratio of 6, companies with a P/E ratio greater than 6 are expected to have profits rising at above-average rates. Companies with a P/E ratio less than 6 are expected to have profits rising at below-average rates.

> A high P/E ratio indicates that investors believe that current profits understate the future profits of the corporation. A low P/E ratio indicates that investors believe that current profits overstate the future profits of the corporation.

## STOCK PRICES AND RESOURCE ALLOCATION

The buying and selling of stock does not have a direct effect on the corporation's financial capital. However, the price of stocks does affect the allocation of capital resources. For example, if XYZ Corporation develops a promising anticancer drug and obtains Food and Drug Administration approval to market it, investors assume that XYZ Corporation earnings will rise substantially; therefore, the price of XYZ stock will rise rapidly. Assume that prior to the development of this new drug the price of XYZ stock

was $10. The company can raise $500,000 by selling 50,000 new shares of stock. However, if the prospect of the new drug raises the stock price to $50 the issue of 50,000 new shares will raise $2.5 million instead of $500,000.

As stock prices rise, corporations find it less expensive to raise financial capital. Likewise, corporations with falling stock prices find it more expensive to raise money for expansion. In this sense, the secondary markets for corporate stocks serve as barometers that signal the direction of the allocation of financial capital. Stockholders can express their dissatisfaction by selling their shares, which drives down the price of the stock. If dissatisfaction is widespread, the falling stock price prevents the firm from raising capital by selling new shares.

This chapter considered business organization as a first step in the study of the supply of goods and services. The next chapter will examine the role of production costs.

## SUMMARY

1. Firms exist to take advantage of economies of scale, to bear risk, to limit transaction costs, and to provide for team production.

2. Business firms allocate their land, labor, and capital resources through managerial coordination. Business firms work both through market allocation in their dealings with other firms and consumers and through managerial allocation.

3. An agency relationship exists when one party—the agent—acts on behalf of another party—the principal. Principal/agent relationships are useful in describing the behavior of business firms.

4. Most economists assume that the goal of business firms is the maximization of profits. Natural selection theory says that firms that do not maximize profits cannot survive.

5. The three forms of business organization are the sole proprietorship (a business owned by one individual), the partnership (a business owned by two or more partners who share in making business decisions), and the corporation (a business enterprise owned by stockholders). Although there are more sole proprietorships in the United States than there are partnerships or corporations, corporations (due

to their larger average size) account for the bulk of business sales and profits.

6. A multinational corporation uses foreign affiliates to engage in foreign economic activities. It exercises direct control over these foreign affiliates to pursue business strategies for the world market.

7. Corporations can raise capital by selling bonds or issuing more stock. Corporate bonds are IOUs that obligate the corporation to make fixed interest payments and to repay the principal at the date of maturity. The amount of money a corporation can raise will depend upon its stock market price.

8. Prices of stocks and bonds are determined in stock exchanges and in bond markets. The price of the stock will reflect the present value of its earnings per share. Bond prices are inversely related to interest rates.

9. Stock prices affect the cost of raising capital to the corporation. Rising stock prices cause capital to be allocated in favor of the corporation with rising share prices.

## KEY TERMS

entrepreneur
managerial coordination
principal
agent
economies of scale
profit maximization
natural selection theory
sole proprietorship
partnership
corporation
common stock

preferred stock
convertible stock
multinational
    corporation
bond
dilution
bond market
stock exchange
present value (PV)
earnings per share (EPS)
price/earnings (P/E) ratio

## QUESTIONS AND PROBLEMS

1. You are deciding whether to build a home yourself or whether to hire an established building firm. What are the transaction costs of arranging to have the home built without the use of the building company? Under what circumstances would these costs be low enough for you to decide to build the home yourself?

2. Risk bearing is one function served by business firms. What risk does the owner of a new restaurant bear?

3. Generally, sole proprietorships are smaller than partnerships and partnerships are smaller than corporations. From what you know about the legal features of business organizations, explain why.

4. In limited partnerships, the liability of each partner for the debts of the company is limited. Explain why such partnerships may be more attractive than the traditional form of partnership.

5. Explain why corporations can issue bonds that mature in the next century while partnerships and proprietorships can borrow for only short periods of time.

6. Explain why a corporation would be reluctant to issue new shares of stock to raise capital when the price of the stock is at an all-time low.

7. One stock has a price/earnings ratio of 2; a second stock has a price/earnings ratio of 20. The average P/E ratio is 6. What would be the investment community's best guess as to the course of future profits for each company?

8. ZYX Corporation offers to sell bonds maturing in 20 years at an interest rate of 7 percent. If you buy a $10,000 bond from ZYX, what will be the annual interest payment? Are you more likely to buy the bond if you expect the interest rate to fall?

9. For the following transactions, explain which party is the principal and which is the agent, and why.
    a. Smith hires a remodeling company to add a room to her house.
    b. A university buys a computer from IBM.
    c. An engineer signs a contract with Aramco to work for a year in Saudi Arabia.

10. The price of one share of an airline stock is $4. The airline has not made a profit for 4 years. If share prices reflect corporate profitability, why is the price not $0?

11. Professional football teams take detailed films of each football game so that they can observe the performance of each player on each play.

Using the Alchian/Demsetz theory, explain why they are monitoring player performance.

12. Assume an aerospace corporation does not manufacture its own jet engines. Instead, it buys them on subcontracts from other manufacturers. Using Coase's arguments about why firms exist, explain why the aerospace corporation would make this decision.

# CHAPTER 9

# PRODUCTIVITY AND COSTS

There is no free lunch. The law of scarcity implies that it costs us something to produce the things we want. But the costs of basic products like television sets, wheat, cars, and personal computers are constantly changing. Ultimately, the prices we pay reflect these costs. As prices fall or rise, we buy more or less of the product.

Why do costs change? In this chapter we shall study the role of the law of diminishing returns, the scarcity of the resources used in production processes, and the impact of technological progress itself over long periods of time, such as several decades. Technological progress is the major determinant of costs. For example, in the 1930s a tire cost about $13 (in today's prices) and today a tire costs about $70. However, because modern radial tires last more than 10 times longer than the old two-ply tires of the past, the actual cost of a tire per 1000 miles driven has fallen to about half of what a tire cost in the 1930s. This calculation does not even take into consideration the opportunity cost of frequently changing tires: Flat tires were commonplace in the 1930s and are rare in the 1990s.

In this chapter we also explore the costs that firms bear in producing the goods we want. But what are costs? How are they measured? How are they related to production? The costs that we study in this chapter will become in future chapters the basis for supply and how markets work.

# PRODUCTIVITY

Once a business firm has chosen its basic organizational form (proprietorship, partnership, or corporation) it must get down to the main task—making a profit. Business activities may be complicated (for example, a corporation producing a commercial jet airliner) or simple (a teenager mowing lawns for summer earnings). To make a *profit* the business firm must earn revenues in excess of costs. The firm must understand revenues and costs to make sound business decisions.

Production costs depend upon input prices and productivity. Production costs rise as input prices rise, and they fall as productivity improves. Let us look at what happens to the costs of production as firms expand the level of output.

## THE SHORT RUN VERSUS THE LONG RUN

A business firm expands the volume of its output by using additional resources. Every good or service is produced by a combination of resources (land, labor, capital, raw materials, entrepreneurial or managerial talent). The combination of resources used depends upon three factors: (1) the productivity of the resources, (2) the prices of the resources, and (3) the time available to the firm for altering output. The first two are important because the business firm will try to keep costs as low as possible. The last is important because time is required to change the level of resource use. Some resources can be adjusted immediately. Other resources require considerable time to change.

A firm can obtain more labor resources quickly by asking each employee to work overtime. The firm might also be able to acquire additional raw materials immediately.

> The **short run** is a period of time so short that the existing plant and equipment cannot be varied; such inputs are fixed in supply.

Additional output can be produced if the variable inputs of labor and raw materials are expanded. But the installation of a new piece of capital equipment or the construction of a new plant may require a significant amount of time.

> The **long run** is a period of time long enough to vary all inputs.

The long run is not a specified amount of calendar time; it may be as short as a few months for a fast-food restaurant, a couple of years for a new automobile plant, or a decade or more for an electrical power plant. In the case of manufactured goods, engineering complexity determines whether the long run is a matter of weeks or years in actual calendar time.

## THE LAW OF DIMINISHING RETURNS

To understand the meaning of productivity, we must understand the concept of a production function.

> A **production function** summarizes the relationship among labor, capital, and land inputs and the maximum output these inputs can produce for a given state of knowledge.

A production function is a technological recipe. A simple analogy would be a cake recipe. It tells how much output can be produced from a given combination of inputs and tells by how much output will increase if one (or all) input(s) increase(s). For example, doubling the ingredients in a cake recipe will produce two cakes.

The production function for cars, computers, or wheat is more complicated than a cake recipe. The firm's production function is determined by the engineering and technical knowledge relevant to the firm's business. The firm's production function dictates the relationship between increases in inputs and increases in outputs in the short run—a relationship that follows a distinctive pattern, called the *law of diminishing returns*. As you know from Chapter 2, the law of diminishing returns states that as ever-larger amounts of a variable input are combined with fixed inputs, eventually the extra product attributable to each additional amount of the variable input must decline.

The extra product that is attributed to an additional unit of an input, if other inputs are fixed, is our most basic concept of productivity.

> The **marginal physical product (MPP)** of a factor of production is the change in output divided by the change in the quantity of the input, if all other inputs are constant.

The law of diminishing returns asserts that as more of a variable input is used in the short run, diminishing MPP must eventually be encountered by any firm. Alternatively, the law states that additional units of output require more resources when the point of diminishing returns is reached.

A shrimp boat along the Texas Gulf Coast illustrates the law of diminishing returns. The fixed inputs are the boat, nets and other fishing equipment, and the ocean. The variable inputs are the number of workers (shrimpers) employed. Table 1 shows the daily output (in bushels) as a function of the number of shrimpers. Figure 1, panel *(a)*, shows the total output curve; Figure 1, panel *(b)*, shows the marginal product curve.

If the boat is operated by only one shrimper, his or her time must be divided between piloting the boat, setting the nets, pulling in the nets, and unloading the nets. A lone shrimper catches 2 bushels per day. A second shrimper brings the total output to 12 bushels per day. The additional shrimper allows each person to specialize and save time switching from job to job. A third shrimper proves even more valuable, raising daily output to 32 bushels. The fourth shrimper raises output to 62 bushels, the fifth to 82, the sixth to 92, and so on.

| Table 1   The Law of Diminishing Returns, Shrimp Fishing | | |
|---|---|---|
| *Number of Shrimpers* | *Daily Output (in bushels)* | *Marginal Physical Product* |
| 0 | 0 | |
| | | 2 |
| 1 | 2 | |
| | | 10 |
| 2 | 12 | |
| | | 20 |
| 3 | 32 | |
| | | 30 |
| 4 | 62 | |
| | | 20 |
| 5 | 82 | |
| | | 10 |
| 6 | 92 | |
| | | 5 |
| 7 | 97 | |
| | | 3 |
| 8 | 100 | |
| | | 2 |
| 9 | 102 | |
| | | 1 |
| 10 | 103 | |

(a) Total Product

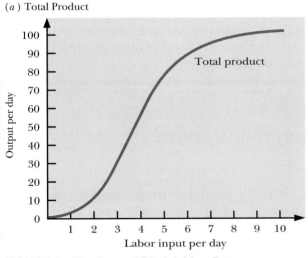

(b) Marginal Physical Product

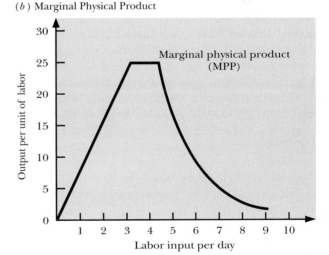

**FIGURE 1   The Law of Diminishing Returns**

Panel *(a)* shows the total daily output; panel *(b)* shows the marginal physical product. Both graphs are based on the data in Table 1. When the total daily output is increasing rapidly, the marginal physical product curve (MPP) is increasing. When the total daily output is increasing, but at a slower and slower rate, the MPP curve is declining.

The MPP is the change in output per unit change in the input. Raising the input of shrimpers from 0 to 1 raises output by 2 bushels. Adding the sixth shrimper raises output from 82 to 92 bushels for an MPP of 10 bushels. Adding the tenth shrimper raises output from 102 to 103 bushels for an MPP of 1 bushel.

As Figure 1, panel *(b)*, shows, diminishing returns set in after the fourth shrimper. Up to the fourth shrimper, each additional shrimper has a higher MPP. Starting with the fifth shrimper, each additional shrimper has a lower MPP than the previous one. As more shrimpers are added to the fixed inputs of a boat and fishing equipment, the benefits from specialization by each shrimper are exhausted. With the addition of the fifth shrimper, the variable inputs start to get in each other's way.

The law of diminishing returns applies to the production of any good or service. When some inputs are fixed, adding variable inputs causes each variable input to have less of the fixed input with which to work. When the fixed input becomes "crowded" with variable inputs, the law of diminishing returns sets in.

## OPPORTUNITY COSTS

The land, labor, and capital used by the firm are costly. But what are these costs? Costs are not always what they seem. Indeed, we shall see that it is not always what the firm paid for its inputs that counts as much as what the firm must give up in the future. In economics and commerce, as the economist William Stanley Jevons (1835–1882) put it, "bygones are forever bygones; and we are always starting clear at each moment, judging the values of things with a view of future utility."

Suppose your rich aunt gives you a brand new Miata sports car, which has a market value of $15,000. She tells you, "This car is yours. You may keep it or sell it. If you sell it, the $15,000 is yours. As long as you keep it, I'll pay for all gas, oil, maintenance, repairs, and your insurance. The car is yours—free in every way." This car is a generous gift. But the car is not free. There is a cost to *using* the car, a cost that may actually be higher than the annual cost of a small car that you would have to buy yourself.

Suppose that you could put into a savings account the $15,000 that the "free" sports car is worth. If the account earns 6 percent interest per year, $15,000 would bring you $900 per year in interest income. Suppose that your using the car for 1 year will reduce its resale value from $15,000 to $11,000—a cost to you of $4000. The total yearly *cost* of using the car is therefore $4900.

The lesson is that *costs are not necessarily what has been paid but what must be given up by taking one action rather than another.* Opportunity cost is the measure of what has been given up.

> The **opportunity cost** of an action is the value of the next best forgone alternative.

The concept of opportunity costs was embodied in the production possibilities frontier we discussed in Chapter 2. When more of one good (such as cars) is produced, a certain amount of some other good (such as wheat) must be given up.

Consider a business firm that makes personal computers. To produce the personal computers requires resources. To acquire these resources, payments must be paid to the owners of the resources because the resources have alternative uses. The minimum payments that are necessary to attract resources into personal computer production are the opportunity costs of production. Some of these payments are *explicit* (as money changes hands) and some may be *implicit*. The manager of the firm must also consider the implicit costs (the value of those resources if used elsewhere) of the resources owned by the firm.

## SHORT-RUN COSTS

### FIXED AND VARIABLE COSTS

In the short run, some factors (such as plant and equipment) are fixed in supply to the firm; even if the firm wanted to increase or reduce them, this is not possible in the short run. The firm pays these *fixed costs (FC)* even if it produces no output. In the short run, it produces greater output by using more of its *variable inputs* such as labor and raw materials. The costs of these variable factors are *variable costs (VC)*. The sum of variable and fixed costs is *total costs (TC)*.

**Fixed costs (FC)** are those costs that do not vary with output.

**Variable costs (VC)** are those costs that do vary with output.

**Total costs (TC)** are variable costs plus fixed costs:

$$TC = VC + FC$$

The short run is defined as a period of time so short that some costs must be fixed. As the time horizon expands, more and more inputs can be varied. Thus, in the long run, all costs are variable—that is, fixed costs are zero.

Fixed costs and variable costs play different short-run roles in the behavior of the firm, as you will see in the next chapter.

## MARGINAL AND AVERAGE COSTS

The behavior of costs in the short run depends on the law of diminishing returns. Indeed, productivity and costs are inversely related. The higher the productivity, the lower costs are; the lower the productivity, the higher costs are.

**Marginal Costs.**   As output increases, both total cost and variable cost increase by the same amount. Suppose, for example, that when the output of shrimp increases by 2 bushels, total (and variable) costs rise by $10. The change in costs divided by the change in output is called the marginal cost (MC) of production. ~producing one additional output~

**Marginal cost (MC)** is the change in total cost (or equivalently in variable cost) divided by the increase in output or, alternatively, the increase in costs per unit of increase in output.

$$MC = \frac{\Delta TC}{\Delta Q} = \frac{\Delta VC}{\Delta Q}$$

In this example, MC is $5 ($10 ÷ 2). In other words, MC is the increase in cost per unit of increase in output. If the increase in output is only one unit, the MC is simply the increase in costs associated with increasing output by one unit. You can determine MC for any increase in output.

**Average Costs.**   While marginal costs reflect the change in costs per unit of change in output, average costs spread total, variable, or fixed costs over the entire quantity of output.

In the short run the most important average cost is the firm's average variable cost (AVC). To obtain AVC, divide variable costs by output. Fixed cost per unit produced is called average fixed cost (AFC) and is calculated by dividing fixed costs by output. Average total cost (ATC) is total cost divided by output. Alternatively, ATC is the sum of AFC and AVC.

**Average variable cost (AVC)** is variable cost divided by output:

$$AVC = VC \div Q$$

**Average fixed cost (AFC)** is fixed cost divided by output:

$$AFC = FC \div Q$$

**Average total cost (ATC)** is total cost divided by output, or the sum of average variable cost and average fixed cost:

$$ATC = TC \div Q = AVC + AFC$$

## THE AVERAGE/MARGINAL RELATIONSHIP

The relationship between *average* values and *marginal* values is an important one. In this chapter we examine the relationship between average costs and marginal costs; in later chapters we shall discuss the relationship between average revenues and marginal revenues. There is a common arithmetical background to all average/marginal relationships. It will be useful to examine this arithmetical relationship before discussing costs.

We all know what an average is: It is the total amount of something divided by the number of instances. The margin is simply the increase in the total as the number of instances increases. Suppose you are budgeting your meals for five days. You have a food budget of $50. You can spend no more than $10 a day. If in the first 2 days you have spent $20, your daily average is $10. The third day you see a luscious dessert and spend $13 (the margin). Now you have spent $33 for an average of $11. You know at this point that the fourth and fifth days will require cutting back. On the fourth day, you spend exactly $11; your average is now $11 because your total spending is $44. You don't need a course in economics to tell you that your fifth day will be tough—you will have to give up one of your favorite drinks or snacks. Clearly, the last day you must spend much less than $11—that is, $6—to reach your goal. To raise the average, you spend more than the preceding average; to lower the average, you spend less. This rule applies to all average/marginal relationships.

> The average/marginal rule states that whenever the marginal value exceeds, equals, or falls short of the preceeding average value, the new average value rises, remains the same, or falls, respectively.

Another example: Suppose the average height of the students in your classroom is 5'8". If a new student arrives, what happens to the average? If the new (marginal) student has a height that exceeds 5'8", the average height of the class will increase; if the student

has a height that is less than 5'8", the average will fall; and if the student is exactly 5'8", the average will remain the same.

## THE COST CURVES

The average/marginal relationship can help us to understand costs. Table 2 and Figure 2 show cost and output information for the Texas Hat Company, which produces only hats. The costs shown include all opportunity costs (explicit and implicit). The firm has fixed costs of $48 per day. The fixed costs consist primarily of the interest on the Texas Hat Company's capital, lease payments, and depreciation. As more hats are produced, variable costs must rise because more inputs, such as labor and raw materials, are needed. Figure 2, panel (a), graphs total costs, variable costs, and fixed costs; Figure 2, panel (b), graphs average variable costs, average total costs, and marginal costs.

### Table 2   The Short-Run Costs of the Texas Hat Company

| Quantity of Output (units), Q (1) | Variable Cost (dollars), VC (2) | Fixed Cost (dollars), FC (3) | Total Cost (dollars), TC (4) = (2) + (3) | Marginal Cost (dollars), MC (5) | Average Variable Cost (dollars), AVC (6) = (2) ÷ (1) | Average Fixed Cost (dollars), AFC (7) = (3) ÷ (1) | Average Total Cost (dollars), ATC (8) = (4) ÷ (1) = (6) + (7) |
|---|---|---|---|---|---|---|---|
| 0 | 0 | 48 | 48 | | | ∞ | ∞ |
| | | | | 20 | | | |
| 1 | 20 | 48 | 68 | | 20 | 48 | 68 |
| | | | | 10 | | | |
| 2 | 30 | 48 | 78 | | 15 | 24 | 39 |
| | | | | 6 | | | |
| 3 | 36 | 48 | 84 | | 12 | 16 | 28 |
| | | | | 4 | | | |
| 4 | 40 | 48 | 88 | | 10 | 12 | 22 |
| | | | | 8 | | | |
| 5 | 48 | 48 | 96 | | 9.6 | 9.6 | 19.2 |
| | | | | 12 | | | |
| 6 | 60 | 48 | 108 | | 10 | 8 | 18 |
| | | | | 20 | | | |
| 7 | 80 | 48 | 128 | | 11.4 | 6.9 | 18.3 |
| | | | | 32 | | | |
| 8 | 112 | 48 | 160 | | 14 | 6 | 20 |
| | | | | 44 | | | |
| 9 | 156 | 48 | 204 | | | | |

This table shows the family of cost schedules for the Texas Hat Company operating in the short run with total fixed cost of $48. The table shows the basic data. *Variable cost* (column 2) rises with the level of output. *Total cost* (column 4) is the sum of total fixed cost and total variable cost. *Marginal cost* is shown in column 5, and *average variable, average fixed,* and *average total cost* are shown in the remaining columns.

(a) Fixed, Variable, and Total Costs

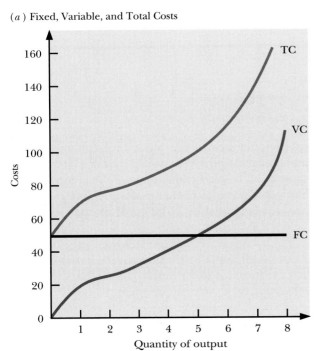

(b) Marginal and Average Costs

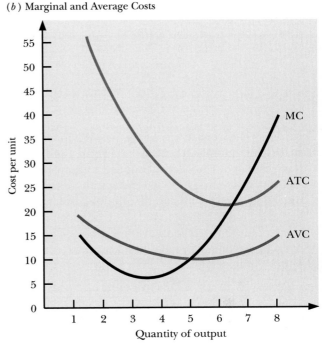

**FIGURE 2    The Short-Run Costs of the Texas Hat Company**

In panel (a), total and variable costs are graphed from data in Table 2. In panel (b), the marginal and average figures (except for average fixed cost) are graphed from the data. Average total cost is the sum of average variable cost and average fixed cost. Note that ATC approaches AVC as output grows and that MC intersects both curves at their minimum points.

In Table 2, variable and total costs are shown in columns 2 and 4. The marginal cost figures in column 5 are shown *in between* the various output levels, because they are in this case the extra cost of going from one output level to another.

In the Texas Hat Company example, MC at first falls and then rises. When MPP is rising, each additional worker produces a larger addition to output than the previous worker. If the firm pays each worker the same wage, the addition to cost (MC) will then decline. When MPP is falling, each additional worker produces a smaller addition to output; therefore, the addition to cost (MC) will rise. Thus, according to the law of diminishing returns, MC will eventually rise in the short run as output is expanded.[1] (See Example 1.)

According to the law of diminishing returns, marginal physical product will fall as output expands in the short run. But marginal cost rises when marginal physical product falls. Therefore, marginal cost will rise as output expands in the short run.

In column 6 of Table 2, variable costs are divided by output to arrive at AVC. In column 7, fixed costs are divided by output to arrive at AFC. Notice that AFC declines throughout because the same fixed cost is being spread out over more units of output. In column 8, total cost—column 4—is divided by output to obtain ATC.

Figure 2, panel (b), shows the graphical relationship between MC and AVC and between MC and ATC. Recall that when MC is below AVC (or ATC), the margin is pulling down the average. Thus, in increasing output from 3 units to 4 units, AVC falls from $12 to $10, and ATC falls from $28 to $22. The MC of $4 is below AVC and ATC and pulls

---

[1]The formula for calculating marginal cost from MPP is MC = W/MPP, where W denotes the wage rate.

## EXAMPLE 1
## WILL DIMINISHING RETURNS
## SPOIL CHRYSLER'S SUCCESS?

Chrysler is currently one of the world's most successful automakers. Near bankruptcy only a few years ago, Chrysler rebounded by implementing cost-cutting efficiencies and by introducing fast-selling models like the Grand Cherokee, the Dodge Intrepid, and the Dodge Ram truck. Chrysler makes an average gross profit of over $8000 on its Grand Cherokees and almost $6000 on its sedans.

Chrysler did not open new plants despite growing demand for its cars, trucks, and minivans. How did it keep the law of diminishing returns from driving up costs? The law of diminishing returns holds constant technology and plant size. Chrysler has kept its costs low by creating a new platform design concept, whereby an integrated team is responsible for designing and building a particular model. It has kept its capital costs low by closing plants and by refusing to build new assembly plants. The company simply added shifts so that existing plants are capable of running at 120 percent of rated capacity (100 percent assumes two 8-hour shifts per day). Thus, Chrysler has followed the policy of not building plants that may stand empty in the next business downturn.

Eventually, if success continues, Chrysler could encounter serious diminishing returns in the form of bottlenecks in its existing plants, driving up costs and cutting into profits unless new plants are built.

------------------------------------------------

*Source:* "Will Success Spoil Chrysler?" *Fortune,* January 10, 1994, pp. 88–92.

them both down. When output is 5 units, MC is slightly above AVC, and so just begins to pull AVC upward. When output is larger than 5 units, MC exceeds AVC and is pulling AVC up. When output is smaller than 5 units, MC falls short of AVC and is pushing AVC down.

Cost curves show what happens to costs of production as the level of output changes. Figure 2, panel (b), illustrates an important principle: the MC curve intersects the AVC and ATC curves at their minimum points because of the average/marginal rule. At the minimum point, the average value is neither rising nor falling; therefore, the marginal and average values must be equal.

Minimum ATC occurs after the minimum AVC because when AVC reaches its minimum point, MC is equal to AVC and is still below ATC. Thus, when AVC is minimized, the ATC curve must still be falling by the average/marginal rule. When the ATC curve reaches its minimum point, the plant is being operated at its most efficient level.

Because ATC = AVC + AFC, the distance between the AVC and ATC curves represents AFC. As a given fixed cost is spread over a larger output, AFC gets smaller. Thus, the AVC and ATC curves get closer together as output rises.

> The MC curve intersects the AVC curve and the ATC curve at their respective minimum values. AVC is at its lowest value when marginal cost equals average variable cost. ATC is at its lowest value when marginal cost equals average total cost.

## LONG-RUN COSTS

Firms have no fixed factors of production in the long run; therefore, they do not have any fixed costs. In the long run, the business enterprise is free to choose any combination of inputs to produce output. All costs are variable. However, once a business makes its long-run decisions (the company completes a new plant, the commercial-farming enterprise signs a 10-year lease for additional acreage), it again has fixed

## EXAMPLE 2
## FLIGHT MANAGEMENT SYSTEMS
## AND COST MINIMIZATION

Businesses combine resources to minimize the cost of providing a particular good or service. Finding minimum-cost combinations is one of management's most important functions.

Advanced commercial aircraft produced by Boeing and Airbus, the two major producers, have on-board computers that help airlines minimize their operating costs. The flight management system (FMS) contains several dozen microprocessors that analyze the entire flight plan.

First, the pilot types in the route, wind information, altitude, and the plane's weight. The FMS regulates the speed to achieve the most efficient fuel budget. There is even a cost index that

balances the cost of paying a flight crew against the cost of fuel. When fuel is relatively cheap, the computer increases the airspeed to reduce pilot and crew hours; when fuel is relatively expensive, the computer lowers airspeed. The FMS finds the optimal speed that minimizes the total cost of fuel and flight crew hours.

In other businesses, management uses similar procedures to minimize operating expenses. Pipeline and electrical power plants have automated systems that minimize costs.

*Source: Scientific American* (July 1991), p. 99.

factors of production and fixed costs. Long-run cost-minimizing decisions are based on the prices the firm must pay for land, labor, and capital. (See Example 2.)

## SHIFTS IN COST CURVES

The Texas Hat Company can determine the ATC curves it would face with different size plants. With a small plant and highly unspecialized machinery, Texas Hat would face the cost curve $ATC_1$ (See Figure 3), whose lowest point is at output level $q_1$. With a slightly larger plant and more specialized equipment, Texas Hat's cost curve, ATC, would be lower for sufficiently larger levels of output, such as at $q_2$. The remaining ATC curves show the average costs for even larger plants. The curve $ATC_3$ yields the most efficient plant size, because at output level $q_3$, ATC is at its lowest point. (See Example 3 on page 159.)

## THE LONG-RUN COST CURVE

For each level of fixed input such as plant size, there is a different ATC curve. If there are an infinite number of fixed input levels from which to choose, there are an infinite number of associated ATC curves. Because all costs are variable in the long run, there is no

distinction between long-run variable costs and long-run total costs.

> **Long-run average cost (LRAC)** consists of the minimum average cost for each level of output when all factor inputs are variable (and when factor prices and the state of technology are fixed).

In the long run, the enterprise is free to select the most effective combination of factor inputs because none of the inputs is fixed. The LRAC curve "envelopes" the short-run average total cost (ATC) curves, forming an LRAC curve that touches each ATC curve only at one point, as shown in Figure 4 on page 160. In the short run, the fact that some factors of production are fixed causes the ATC curve to be U-shaped. The law of diminishing returns does not apply in the long run because all inputs are variable.

## ECONOMIES AND DISECONOMIES OF SCALE

The LRAC curve will also be U-shaped, as shown in Figure 4. Long-run average costs first decline as output expands and then later increase as output expands even further. Firms experience first economies

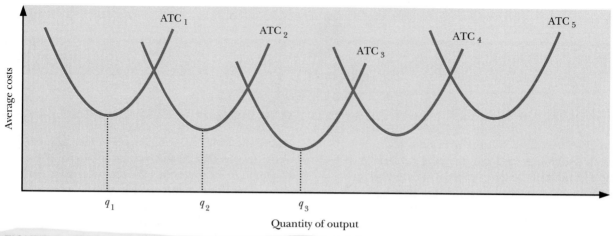

**FIGURE 3   Shifts in Cost Curves with Changing Plant Size**
Economies of scale are achieved with larger plant sizes up to the plant size $ATC_3$.
When diseconomies of scale are encountered, larger plant sizes entail larger unit
costs, as with $ATC_4$ and $ATC_5$.

of scale, then constant returns to scale, and finally diseconomies of scale as output expands.

**Economies of Scale.**   The declining portion of the LRAC curve is due to economies of scale that arise out of the indivisibility of the inputs of labor and physical capital goods or equipment.

> **Economies of scale** are present when an increase in output causes long-run average costs to fall.

The division of labor is much more specialized in a large firm than in a small firm. People are indivisible; it is difficult for an employee of a small firm to be one part mechanic, two parts supervisor, and three parts electrician and still remain as efficient as an employee who specializes in just one task. In a large firm, workers increase their productivity or dexterity through experience and save time in moving from one task to another.

The principles of specialization also apply to machines. A small firm might have to use general-purpose machine tools whereas a large firm might be able to build special equipment or machines that will substantially lower costs when large quantities are produced. Small-scale versions of certain specialized machines simply cannot be made available.

Economies of scale can occur because specialization allows for greater productivity in any of a variety of areas, including technological equipment, market-

ing, research and development, and management. The optimal rate of utilization for some types of machinery may occur at high rates of output. Some workers may not be able to perfect specialized skills until a high rate of output allows them to concentrate on specific tasks. As the output of an enterprise increases with all inputs variable, average costs will decline because of the economies of scale associated with increased specialization of labor, management, plant, and equipment.

**Constant Returns to Scale.**   Economies of scale will become exhausted at some point when expanding output can no longer take advantage of specialization. At this point constant returns to scale set in.

> **Constant returns to scale** are present when an increase in output does not change long-run average costs of production.

**Diseconomies of Scale.**   As output continues to expand after experiencing constant returns, the size of the firm becomes a problem, and long-run average costs will begin to rise. At this point diseconomies of scale set in.

> **Diseconomies of scale** are present when an increase in output causes long-run average costs to increase.

Diseconomies of scale can be caused by a series of factors. As the firm continues to expand, manage-

## EXAMPLE 3
### SHIFTS IN COST CURVES:
### THE CASE OF NUCLEAR POWER

Environmental groups oppose nuclear power on safety and environmental grounds. Government regulatory agencies have been slow to license nuclear power plants.

Although public relations and politics are usually blamed for the problems of nuclear power, the problems are more a matter of economics. When capital capacity expands, short-run cost curves shift out and the industry operates on a new cost curve suited to greater demand. In the case of electrical power, there is a substantial lag between the decision to build generating plants and their completion. Most nuclear power plants were planned during the late 1960s and early 1970s when the long-run demand for electricity was expected to expand rapidly. New plants would meet the increased demand at lower average costs. In fact, the first nuclear power plants that became operational during a period of expanding demand proved quite profitable.

The energy crisis of the mid- and late 1970s had a profound impact on electricity demand in the 1980s and 1990s. With rising energy prices, consumers cut back and the new power plants could not be operated efficiently at the lower-than-anticipated demand levels.

Figure A shows an electrical utility that expected to be generating 600 megawatts of electricity in 1996. Therefore, it built a nuclear

power plant to expand its capacity. The completion of the nuclear power plant shifted its cost curve from ATC to ATC'. ATC' yields a much lower cost for generating 600 megawatts than ATC. However, the 1996 demand for electricity was much less than expected. Only 400 megawatts were generated. The electrical utility (now located on ATC') generated this lower-than-expected output at high cost.

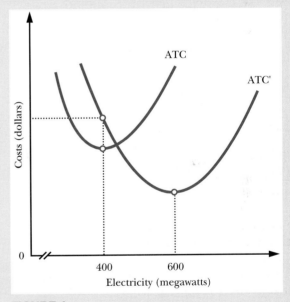

**FIGURE A**

ment skills must be spread over a larger and larger firm. Managers must assume additional responsibility, and managerial talents may eventually be spread so thin that the efficiency of management declines. The problem of maintaining communications within a large firm grows, and red tape and cumbersome bureaucracy become commonplace. Large firms may find it difficult to correct their mistakes. Employees of large firms may lose their identity and feel that their contributions to the firm are not recognized. As

the output of an enterprise continues to increase, average cost will eventually rise because of the diseconomies of scale associated with the growing problems of managerial coordination.

## MINIMUM EFFICIENT SCALE

Why are some companies more profitable than others? Why are some industries more concentrated than others? Why is a particular company doing well

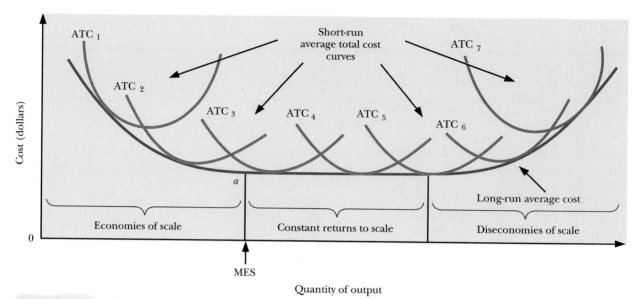

**FIGURE 4** **The Long-Run Average Cost Curve as the Envelope of the Short-Run Average Total Cost Curves**

For each level of fixed input, there is a corresponding short-run average total cost curve. The long-run average cost curve is the envelope of the short-run average total cost curves. The long-run average cost curve is U-shaped. The declining portion shows economies of scale. The rising portion shows diseconomies of scale. The horizontal portion shows constant returns to scale.

or poorly? Economies of scale can help provide answers for these questions.

The LRAC curve in Figure 4 is flat over a large range. Empirical studies for a number of industries suggest that such constant returns to scale occur over a significant range of output. The output level at which average costs are minimized (at point *a*) is called the minimum efficient scale (MES) of the firm.

> The **minimum efficient scale (MES)** is the lowest level of output at which average costs are minimized.

Economies of scale differ substantially among industries. Some industries experience economies of scale up to output levels that are a high proportion of total industry sales. These industries tend to have a small number of firms because larger firms can drive smaller firms out of business. Studies show, for example, that the electricity and automotive industries have significant economies of scale, while others, such as garments and concrete, do not. Table 3 reports the results of studies of selected industries showing that the minimum efficient firm size is as high as a 21 to 30 percent market share in the case of

diesel engines and as low as a market share of only 0.2 percent in the case of shoes.

## PRODUCTIVITY ADVANCES AND THE COST CURVES

The cost curves reflect the productivity and prices of the factors of production. A factor's *productivity* is the amount of output that can be obtained from a given level of its input. The production function shows how much output can be produced from any given set of inputs. A *productivity advance* results when *more* output can be produced with the *same* inputs. For example, when American farm productivity increased by over 50 percent from the 1960s to the 1990s, the production functions for grains, dairy products, poultry and eggs, and meat animals changed in such a way that fewer inputs were needed to obtain the same output. As a consequence, for any level of output and for given prices of the inputs, productivity advances will result in lower unit costs of production.

Figure 5 shows what happens to the LRAC curve as productivity improves, if input prices are constant. For each level of output, unit production costs fall.

| Table 3    Estimates of the Minimum Efficient Scale (MES) in Selected U.S. Industries | |
|---|---|
| *Industry* | *MES as a Percentage of U.S. Demand* |
| Diesel engines | 21–30 |
| Electronic computers | 15.0 |
| Refrigerators | 14.1 |
| Cigarettes | 6.6 |
| Beer brewing | 3.4 |
| Bicycles | 2.1 |
| Petroleum refining | 1.9 |
| Paints | 1.4 |
| Flour mills | 0.7 |
| Bread baking | 0.3 |
| Shoes (nonrubber) | 0.2 |

*Sources:* F.M. Schere, Alan Beckenstein, Erich Kaufer, and R.D. Murphy, *The Economics of Multiplant Operation* (Cambridge, MA: Harvard University Press, 1975), 80–94. Leonard W. Weiss, "Optimal Plant Size and the Extent of Suboptimal Capacity," in Robert T. Masson and P.D. Qualls, eds., *Essays on Industrial Organization in Honor of Joe S. Bain* (Cambridge, MA: Ballinger, 1975) 128–131; adapted in part from C.F. Pratten, *Economies of Scale in Manufacturing Industry* (Cambridge, U.K.: Cambridge University Press, 1971).

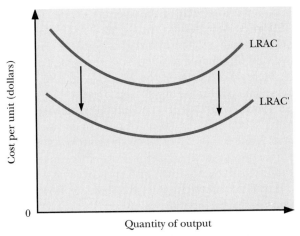

**FIGURE 5    The Effect of a Productivity Advance on the Long-Run Average Cost Curve**

An improvement in technological knowledge can cause an advance in productivity, where more output can be produced with the same inputs or where the same output can be produced with fewer inputs. The basic consequence is that the long-run average cost (LRAC) curve shifts down. Thus, productivity advances imply that unit production costs fall for each level of output, assuming that factor prices are constant.

Thus, the entire LRAC curve shifts downward. The minimum efficient scale of the firm can rise or fall, depending on the type of technological breakthrough that has taken place. To illustrate, Henry Ford's assembly-line production of the famous Model T required a larger scale of plant, but a move away from assembly-line production with the use of modern industrial robots can involve a smaller minimum efficient scale.

Because unit production costs fall for each level of output, productivity advances are different from cost reductions arising from economies of scale. The fall in costs arising from economies of scale is a movement along a given LRAC curve, while a fall in costs resulting from a productivity advance is a downward shift in the entire curve.

## DEFINING MOMENTS

It is costly to produce goods and services. As the cost of any good or service rises, it is more difficult for individuals to find mutually advantageous exchanges with people who want to use that good or service. The competition from others supplying the good makes it even harder to find mutually advantageous exchanges. If a person can find a cheaper way of doing something, either through an invention or through better use of a particular plant or economies of scale, then surviving the challenges of competition becomes easier.

We discussed in the first chapter that the Industrial Revolution switched production from the household to the factory. This change caused production costs to drop enormously. Adam Smith's pin factory is the classic example of how, through economies of scale and the division of labor, production costs can be brought down to extremely low levels. Pin-making then and now required a large number of separate operations in which each worker specialized. According to Smith's calculations, the average worker in an eighteenth-century factory could produce almost 5000 pins a day, but alone could produce only a few pins per day. Today, the average worker in a modern pin factory produces around 80,000 pins a day!

Competition keeps firms alert. Henry Ford was considered the genius of his age. He produced the famous Model-T Ford in 1912 in only one color— black. He beat out his competitors by developing mass production methods that kept the price of a

Model-T within reach of the average person—about $9300 in current dollars. In the mid-1920s General Motors offered a Chevrolet that was faster, easier to drive, and obtainable in a variety of colors. To compete, Henry Ford offered the Model-A in 1927. The process has continued up to the present. An entry-level 1995 Ford Escort can still be purchased for about $8000, which is about 14 percent cheaper than a new Model-T in 1912. The current Ford is also much better than a Model-T Ford in terms of its durability, safety, comfort, and speed.

In the next few chapters we shall see how costs are harnessed by the market.

## SUMMARY

1. In the short run, plant and equipment cannot be varied; in the long run, all inputs are variable.

2. The marginal physical product is the increase in output divided by the change in the quantity of an input, if all other inputs are constant. The law of diminishing returns states that as one input is increased (if other inputs are constant), the marginal physical product of the variable input will eventually decline.

3. The opportunity cost of an action is the value of the next best forgone alternative. The average of a series of values falls when the marginal value is below the previous average value; the average stays constant when the marginal value equals the previous average; the average rises when the marginal value exceeds the previous average.

4. Variable costs are those costs that vary with output; fixed costs do not vary with output. In the long run, all costs are variable. Marginal cost (MC) is the increase in cost divided by the increase in output. Average variable cost (AVC) is variable cost divided by output; average total cost (ATC) is total (fixed plus variable) cost divided by output. The AVC and ATC curves tend to be U-shaped with the MC intersecting AVC and ATC at their minimum values.

5. In the long run, a firm can alter the size of its plant. For each plant size, there is a particular average total cost (ATC) curve. The envelope of all such ATC curves is the long-run average cost (LRAC) curve, which gives the minimum unit cost of producing any given volume of output. Along the LRAC curve, the firm is choosing the least-cost combination of inputs.

6. Economies of scale prevail when increasing output lowers average costs of production. Constant returns to scale prevail when increasing output does not change average costs of production—in which case, the LRAC curve is horizontal. Diseconomies of scale prevail when increasing output lowers the average unit costs of production. A firm's minimum efficient scale is the lowest level of output at which average costs are minimized.

7. Advances in productivity shift the LRAC curve down (assuming input prices are constant).

## KEY TERMS

short run
long run
production function
law of diminishing returns
marginal physical product (MPP)
opportunity cost
fixed costs (FC)
variable costs (VC)
total costs (TC)
marginal cost (MC)
average variable cost (AVC)
average fixed cost (AFC)
average total cost (ATC)
long-run average cost (LRAC)
economies of scale
constant returns to scale
diseconomies of scale
minimum efficient scale (MES)

## QUESTIONS AND PROBLEMS

1. Your uncle gives you a "free" car and pays for the insurance, gas, oil, and repairs. You are told you may sell the car at any time. Assume the car is now worth $20,000 and will have an estimated value of $12,000 after 1 year. If the interest rate is 10 percent, how much does it cost you to use the car for 1 year?

2. Explain the distinction between explicit costs and opportunity costs. Why are opportunity costs a better guide to resource-allocation decisions?

3. A firm's out-of-pocket costs are $15,000 per month. In addition, the firm's implicit opportunity costs are $5000. What are the firm's total opportunity costs? How much revenue must the firm generate in sales in order to stay in business over the long run?

4. If a baseball player enters a game with a batting average of 0.250 (25 hits per 100 times at bat)

and gets 2 hits out of 4 tries on that day, what happens to his batting average? Why?

5. Contrast the average total cost (ATC) curve of a firm that has very large fixed costs relative to variable costs with the ATC curve of a firm that has very small fixed costs relative to variable costs.

6. For a given production plan, a firm's fixed costs are zero and its variable costs are $1 million. Is the plan short-run or long-run? Explain.

7. Answer the following questions using the production-function information in Table A. Assume that 1 unit of labor costs $5 and 1 unit of capital costs $10.

   a. Derive the marginal physical product (MPP) schedule. Does it obey the law of diminishing returns?

   b. Derive the short-run cost schedules.

   c. Derive the MPP and short-run cost schedules if labor productivity doubles (with 1 labor unit, for example, being used to produce an output of 10 units instead of 5 units).

   d. Explain why the short-run cost curves shift if the amount of capital input changes.

| Table A | | |
|---|---|---|
| Labor (units) | Capital (units) | Output (units) |
| 0 | 2 | 0 |
| 1 | 2 | 5 |
| 2 | 2 | 15 |
| 3 | 2 | 20 |
| 4 | 2 | 23 |
| 5 | 2 | 24 |

8. At the current output level, ATC is $25, AVC is $10, and marginal cost (MC) is $15. If output increases by 1 unit, what happens to the new ATC? To the new average variable cost (AVC)? If ATC stays at $25 and MC increases to $25, what happens to the next ATC?

9. Suppose FC = $25, VC = $Q$, and MC = $2Q$. Draw the AFC, AVC, MC, and ATC curves. At what output level does the minimum ATC occur?

10. What is the role of the law of diminishing returns in explaining the shape of the cost curves? Construct a numerical example.

11. If MC rises, what conclusion can you draw about whether ATC or AVC is rising or falling?

12. What is the opportunity cost of a worker to a firm that mistakenly pays the worker $40 an hour instead of the worker's wage of $25 an hour?

13. Industry A, with $10 million in sales, comprises three equal-sized large firms. Industry B, also having $10 million in sales, is made up of 50 equal-sized firms. From this information, make rough sketches of the long-run average-cost curve of a typical firm in each industry. Also make predictions about the minimum efficient scale as a given percentage of industry output in both cases.

14. Suppose that the MPP of the third worker is 100 units of output per week and that the MPP of the fifth worker is 50 units of output per week. If each worker is paid $25 per week and labor is the only variable input, what is the MC associated with the output of the third worker? Of the fifth worker?

15. Using Table B, plot all the short-run total-cost and average-cost curves discussed in this chapter. Do the cost curves have the expected shapes? Explain your answer.

| Table B | | |
|---|---|---|
| Output (units) | Fixed Costs (dollars) | Variable Costs (dollars) |
| 1 | 10 | 5 |
| 2 | 10 | 8 |
| 3 | 10 | 12 |
| 4 | 10 | 20 |
| 5 | 10 | 40 |

# APPENDIX 9A

# PRODUCTION ISOQUANTS

## APPENDIX INSIGHT

To choose the right combination of resources, a firm should use the *least-cost method* of production. In this appendix we shall discuss how firms determine the level of output that uses the least costly combination of resources.

## THE PRODUCTION FUNCTION

A production function shows the maximum output that can be achieved by a given combination of inputs. Figure A1 shows a hypothetical firm that employs only two factors—capital and labor—to produce its output. The horizontal edge measures the labor input from 1 to 8 workers; the vertical edge measures the capital input from 1 to 8 machines. The amount of output that can be produced from any combination of labor and capital is shown in the cells corresponding to the intersection of a row of capital input and a column of labor input. For example, 8 machines and 1 worker produce 50 units of output; 8 machines and 2 workers produce 71 units of output. Thus, the production function shown in Figure A1 gives the possible methods of producing the outputs shown at each intersection.

## MARGINAL PHYSICAL PRODUCT

The marginal physical product (MPP) of a factor is the extra output associated with increasing the input of the factor by 1 unit, if all other factors are constant. Suppose that the amount of capital is held constant at 4 machines. With 1 worker, output is 35 units; with 2 workers, output is 50 units; and so on. Clearly the marginal product of labor is 35 for the first worker and 15 for the second worker (because output rises from 35 to 50 units). We can read the MPP of labor in the figure simply by noting the difference between consecutive outputs along a given row. Using similar reasoning, we can determine the marginal product of capital by varying the machine input, if labor is constant.

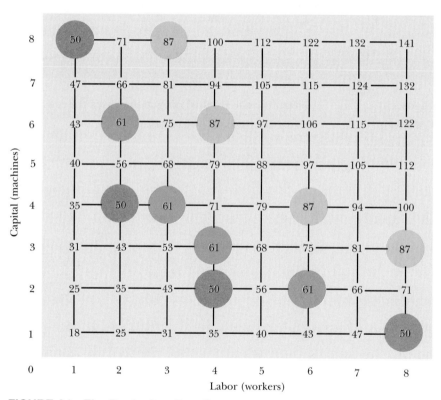

**FIGURE A1   The Production Function**

Capital inputs are measured vertically; labor inputs are measured horizontally. The number at the intersection of a row and column shows the output for that level of capital and labor input. For example, 4 machines and 2 workers produce 50 units of output. The law of diminishing returns can also be seen because, when the input of machines is held constant at 4 units, additional units of labor bring about smaller additions to output; thus, along a given row, output *increases* but at a *decreasing* rate.

## THE LAW OF DIMINISHING RETURNS

According to the law of diminishing returns, the MPP of a factor eventually declines as more of the factor is used, if all other productive inputs are constant. In Figure A1, when capital equals 4 machines, the MPP of the second worker is 15 and the MPP for the third worker is only 11.

The production function summarized in Figure A1 assumes constant returns to scale. When there are 3 units of capital and 3 units of labor, output is 53 units; when inputs double to 6 units of capital and 6 units of labor, output doubles to 106 units. When there are 3 units of capital and 3 units of labor, the fourth unit of labor has an MPP of 8 units, as output rises from 53 to 61. When there are 4 units of capital and 4 units of labor, the fifth unit of labor also has an MPP of 8 units, as output rises from 71 to 79. Thus, *the MPP of labor remains the same as long as the ratio of capital to labor remains the same.* The source of the law of diminishing returns is the increasing ratio of workers to machines.

## THE PRINCIPLE OF SUBSTITUTION

We know from Chapter 3 that there are substitutes for nearly everything. This principle of substitution is also illustrated in Figure A1, which shows that 50 units of output can be produced by four different combinations of capital and labor. These combinations are listed in columns 2 and 3 of Table A1.

From the information provided so far, there is no reason to choose the combination of 8 units of capital/1 unit of labor over the combination of 1 unit of capital/8 units of labor to produce 50 units of output. *The production function alone cannot tell us how to produce the 50 units of output.* We must also consider cost information.

## LEAST-COST PRODUCTION

The price of labor $(P_L)$ and the price of capital $(P_C)$ help us determine what combination of capital and labor the firm will use. (Think of the price of capital as the implicit or explicit rental on a machine, truck, or building.) Suppose $P_L = \$50$ per worker and $P_C = \$25$ per machine. Column 4 of Table A1 shows the costs of each combination of labor and capital that yields 50 units of output. For example, combination *a* costs $250 because 8 machines cost $200 (8 × $25) and 1 worker costs $50. From Table A1 we can determine that the minimum-cost combination is *b*. This combination calls for 4 units of capital and 2 units of labor, the total cost (TC) of which is $200. The average total cost of production is ATC = TC/Q = $200/50 = $4 per unit, which is the lowest possible cost per unit when total output is 50 units.

In moving from combination *a* to combination *b*, the firm can substitute an extra unit of labor for 4 machines without a loss of output. Labor costs $50, but 4 machines cost $100. Thus, the firm saves $100 in machine costs by substituting 1 worker for 4 machines and spends $50 on the added worker for a net gain of $50 (without a loss in output). Clearly, it pays the firm to select *b* over *a*.

## THE ISOQUANT

These principles of least-cost production can be illustrated by graphs. Figure A2 plots combinations *a,b,c,* and *d* from Table A1 and connects these points by a smooth curve. The curve *abcd* shows all the combinations of capital and labor input that produce 50 units of output; hence, it can be called the isoquant for 50 units of output. (*Iso* means same; *isoquant* means same quantity.)

> An **isoquant** shows the various combinations of two inputs (such as labor and capital) that produce the same quantity of output.

Isoquant curves are similar to the indifference curves studied in the appendix to the chapter on demand and utility. Just as the indifference curves were convex to the origin, so isoquants are convex to the origin. The ratio of the line segment *af* to *fb* is the amount of capital that can be substituted for the extra unit of labor. The slope of the curve between *a* and *b* reflects the fact that the MPP of labor is four times the MPP of capital. The vertical distance *af* is

| | Table A1 | Factor Combinations for Producing 50 Units of Output | | |
|---|---|---|---|---|
| | *Output (units),* $Q$ *(1)* | *Capital (machines),* $C$ *(2)* | *Labor (workers),* $L$ *(3)* | *Total Cost (dollars),* $TC$ *(4)* |
| *a* | 50 | 8 | 1 | 250 |
| *b* | 50 | 4 | 2 | 200 |
| *c* | 50 | 2 | 4 | 250 |
| *d* | 50 | 1 | 8 | 425 |

*Note:* The price of capital is $25 per machine; the price of labor is $50 per worker.

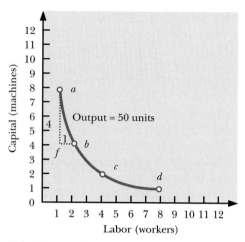

**FIGURE A2   The Isoquant**

The isoquant shows all the combinations of labor (number of workers) and capital (number of machines) that produce the same amount of output. It is bowed toward the origin because the law of diminishing returns dictates that substituting capital for labor becomes easier as the ratio of workers to machines increases.

four times the horizontal distance *fb*, which reflects the rate at which capital must be substituted for labor to keep output constant. The ratio of the marginal physical products measures the marginal rate of substitution (or the rate at which capital can be substituted for labor). This ratio equals the slope (in absolute value) of an isoquant between two points or the absolute slope of the tangent to any point of the equal-output curve.

> The marginal rate of substitution of capital for labor
>
> $$= \frac{\text{MPP of labor}}{\text{MPP of capital}}$$
>
> = The (absolute) slope of the isoquant

The isoquant is bowed toward the origin because when workers are substituted for machines, the MPP of labor falls relative to the MPP of capital; to keep output constant as labor is substituted for machines, fewer and fewer machines can be given up for each worker acquired.

## ISOCOST LINES

If we assume that the price of labor ($P_L$) is $50 per worker and the price of capital ($P_C$) is $25 per machine, the total cost (TC) of production is

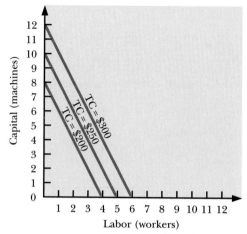

**FIGURE A3   Isocost Lines**

Isocost lines show all the combinations of labor and capital that cost the same amount. The line for TC = $300 shows all the combinations costing $300. The slope of each equal-cost line is measured by the ratio of the price of labor to the price of capital; in this case, labor is $50 per worker and capital is $25 per machine, so each equal-cost line has an absolute slope of 2.

$$\text{TC} = (P_L \times L) + (P_C \times C) = \$50L + \$25C$$

where $L$ = the number of workers and $C$ = the number of machines. In Figure A3, the line TC = $300 consists of all the combinations of labor and capital that cost $300. For example, if $C = 12$ and $L = 0$, TC = $300; if $C = 0$ and $L = 6$, TC = $300; the combination of 6 machines and 3 workers also costs $300. Thus, line TC is the isocost line for costs of $300.

> The **isocost line** shows all the combinations of labor and capital that have the same total costs.

Figure A3 gives three illustrative isocost lines, but there is one for every level of total costs. These isocost lines are parallel because each has the same slope. The absolute slope of any isocost line is simply $P_L/P_C$. In this example, the (absolute) slope is 2 since the price of 1 unit of labor is twice that of 1 unit of capital; therefore, 2 units of capital can be substituted for 1 unit of labor without increasing or decreasing total costs.

> The (absolute) slope of the isocost line is the price of labor divided by the price of capital, which represents the rate at which firms can substitute labor for capital without affecting total costs.

## THE LEAST-COST RULE

Figure A4 shows how the firm minimizes the cost of producing a given volume of output (in this case, output is 50 units). When the isoquant for 50 units of output and the isocost lines for three representative cost levels appear on the same graph, we can determine the least-cost combination by observing where the isoquant *abcd* just touches the *lowest* isocost line (at point *b*). The lowest isocost line that curve *abcd* can reach is TC = $200. All other combinations of labor and capital on *abcd* cost more than $200. Thus, point *b* is the least-cost production point; it is the best combination of labor and capital (4 machines and 2 workers) for producing 50 units of output.

In Figure A4, the slope of the isoquant is the same as the slope of the isocost line because both are tangent (they touch without crossing) at that point. Thus

$$\frac{MPP_L}{MPP_C} = \frac{P_L}{P_C} \qquad (1)$$

We can write the least-cost rule in a second way:

$$\frac{MPP_L}{P_L} = \frac{MPP_C}{P_C} \qquad (2)$$

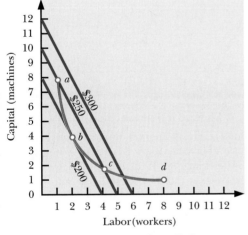

**FIGURE A4    The Least-Cost Rule**

The least-cost method of producing 50 units of output can be found at the point where the isoquant, *abcd*, touches the lowest equal-cost line, TC = $200. At point *b*, the slope of the isoquant equals the slope of the isocost line because the two curves are tangent; here the ratio of the marginal physical product of labor to that of capital equals the ratio of the price of labor to the price of capital.

In other words, the least-cost rule requires that the extra output from the last dollar spent on labor must equal the extra output from the last dollar spent on capital. A third way of writing the least-cost rule, by taking the reciprocals of equation (2), is

$$\frac{P_L}{MPP_L} = \frac{P_C}{MPP_C} \qquad (3)$$

> The **least-cost rule** is that the least-cost combination of two factors can be found at the point where a given isoquant is tangent to the lowest isocost line. In other words, the least-cost combination of two factors can be found where
>
> $$\frac{P_L}{MPP_L} = \frac{P_C}{MPP_C}$$

The price of labor divided by the MPP of labor is labor cost per additional unit of output, which is simply the marginal cost of output using labor. (Recall that marginal cost is the extra cost of producing 1 more unit of output.) Similarly, the price of capital divided by the MPP of capital is the marginal cost of production using capital. According to equation (3), least-cost production (in the long run) requires using capital and labor in such a way that the marginal cost of production is the same whether output is increased using capital or using labor. If these two were not equal, one would be substituted for the other.

When $P_L/MPP_L = P_C/MPP_C$, since all cost-lowering substitution possibilities are exhausted, the long-run marginal cost of production is equal to the common value of the two ratios.

## THE LINK BETWEEN THE SHORT RUN AND THE LONG RUN

The least-cost rule gives us the link between the short run and the long run. The long run is a period of time so long that both workers and machines can be varied. In the short run, the number of machines is fixed. It takes time to find the right machine, install it, and train workers to use it properly. Thus, fixed costs are the machine costs, and variable costs are the labor costs. In the short run, marginal cost is the ratio $P_L/MPP_L$.

As shown in Table A2, the number of machines is fixed at 4 in the short run, and the number of workers can be varied from 0 to 5. The first four columns of Table A2 are derived from Figure A1.

### Table A2   Productivity and Costs

| Capital (machines), C (1) | Labor (workers), L (2) | Output (units), Q (3) | Marginal Physical Product of Labor (units), MPP$_L$ (4) | Marginal Cost (dollars), MC (5) | Fixed Cost (dollars), FC (6) | Variable Cost (dollars), VC (7) | Total Cost (dollars), TC (8) | Average Total Cost (dollars), ATC (9) |
|---|---|---|---|---|---|---|---|---|
| 4 | 0 | 0 | | | 0 | 0 | 0 | 0 |
| | | | 35 | 1.43 | | | | |
| 4 | 1 | 35 | | | 100 | 50 | 150 | 4.29 |
| | | | 15 | 3.33 | | | | |
| 4 | 2 | 50 | | | 100 | 100 | 200 | 4.00 |
| | | | 11 | 4.54 | | | | |
| 4 | 3 | 61 | | | 100 | 150 | 250 | 4.10 |
| | | | 10 | 5.00 | | | | |
| 4 | 4 | 71 | | | 100 | 200 | 300 | 4.23 |
| | | | 8 | 6.25 | | | | |
| 4 | 5 | 79 | | | 100 | 250 | 350 | 4.43 |

*Note:* The price of labor is $50 per worker; the price of capital is $25 per machine.

Column 5 of Table A2 is the short-run marginal cost. Columns 6 through 9 show the short-run costs of production. Column 9 illustrates the average total cost (ATC) of production. Note that ATC hits its minimum at an output of 50 units where ATC = $4.00.

## APPLYING THE LEAST-COST RULE

What would the firm do if the price of capital rises from $25 per machine to $100 per machine, while the price of labor remains at $50 per worker? If the firm continues to use 4 machines and 2 workers to produce 50 units of output, the new factor prices cause total costs to be ($100 × 4) + ($50 × 2) = $500; average costs rise from $4 to $10 ($500/50). The firm, of course, would begin to substitute the now cheaper labor for the now more expensive machinery. The price of capital is now twice as great as the price of labor, so the slope of the new isocost lines is 1/2 instead of 2. Figure A5 shows what happens. The old TC line was *mn*—with the minimum-cost point *b*. The new minimum TC line is *m'n'*, which is tangent to point *c* on the isoquant. The least total cost of production is now $400 (4 units of capital now costs $400 and 8 units of labor costs $400). Because 50 units are still produced, the average cost of production is now $8 ($400/50). The firm saves $2 per unit of output by substituting labor for capi-

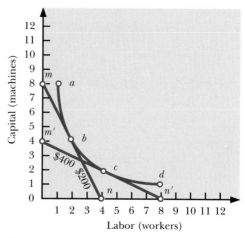

**FIGURE A5   A Change in Factor Price**

The isocost line *mn* shows the minimum cost of producing 50 units of output when capital is $25 per machine and labor is $50 per worker. (Line *mn* is the same as TC = $200.) If the price of capital rises to $100 per machine, the equal-cost line *m'n'* shows that the lowest cost of producing 50 units of output rises to $400 and the least-cost combination of capital and labor shifts from point *b* to point *c* as cheaper labor is substituted for machines.

tal. Quadrupling the price of capital causes the average cost of production to double (from $4 to $8). The optimal ratio of machines to workers is now 2 machines per 4 workers, or 1/2 machine per worker. The production process has become less capital intensive and more labor intensive.

## SUMMARY

1. An isoquant shows all the combinations of two factors that will produce a given level of output.

2. An isocost line shows all the combinations of two factors that have the same total costs.

3. The least-cost combination of two factors can be found at the point where an isoquant is tangent to the lowest isocost line.

## KEY TERMS

isoquant
isocost line
least-cost rule

## QUESTIONS AND PROBLEMS

1. Why is an isoquant convex to the origin? Why is it downward sloping?

2. What should be the cost objective of the firm?

3. Show that raising the price of capital relative to labor will lead a firm to choose more labor-intensive techniques of production.

4. Assume a firm is hiring labor and capital until $MPP_L = 3$ and $MPP_C = 15$ units. Suppose $P_C = \$4$ per unit and $P_L = \$10$ per unit.
   a. Is the firm minimizing costs?
   b. Should the firm hire more capital and less labor or more labor and less capital? Explain your reasoning.

# CHAPTER 10

# PERFECT COMPETITION

The law of scarcity invites us to try to produce what we want at the lowest possible cost. If not, we are wasting resources that might be used to feed, clothe, and shelter our population, especially the poor. It is a worthy objective. But scarcity requires competition.

Competition is often misunderstood. Social critics frequently lament the fact that our society is "competitive" rather than "cooperative." Competition, however, is unavoidable: In a world of scarcity, few of us will freely give up our claims to a share of the wealth.

The theory of perfect competition tells us how the goods that people want are produced at the lowest cost to society. Competition, thus, lightens the burden of scarcity. If a business firm does not sell at the lowest cost, it goes out of business. If firms in an industry are making positive economic profits, new firms enter the market and drive the price down to the lowest cost possible. Firms come and go in the race for the consumer dollar. In this chapter, we shall encounter the fascinating tale of how firms and consumers are forced to cooperate by following the trail of price.

## SCARCITY AND COMPETITION

Competition can take a variety of forms. A free-for-all system of catch-as-catch-can or steal-as-much-as-one-can constitutes one possible scheme. In such a system, property rights do not exist; each person takes whatever he or she can find. It is easy to see that such a system will not work well. If property rights are not protected by law, people will have little incentive to buy or produce property. Likewise, such conditions will create a demand for security guards or mafia-style protection against the bullies and thugs who might prevail. Such conditions actually exist today in the former Soviet Union.

A system that allows people to buy and sell property rights *freely,* with those rights protected by the state, will be more orderly. Firms will find it profitable to enter into market transactions with buyers, and all participants will attempt to strike the best deal for themselves. Such a system can exist under varying degrees of competition. In this chapter we shall study firms operating in the most competitive markets possible.

## COMPETITION AS A MARKET MODEL

An *industry* is a collection of firms producing a similar product or service (such as steel, aluminum, milk, wheat, haircut, or tax preparation). A crucial characteristic of each industry is the extent to which competition is present. Economists recognize four basic market models, from the most to the least competitive: *perfect competition, monopolistic competition, oligopoly,* and *monopoly.* (See Table 1.) Perfect competition is the subject of this chapter. The other three market models will be discussed in detail in the following chapters.

As a brief preview of these models, perfect competition exists when individual firms in an industry have no control over the market price and new firms are free to enter the industry. Perfect competition is

most likely found in an industry where there are many small producers of a homogeneous product. Farming and low-priced clothing are classic examples of perfect competition. Monopolistic competition prevails when there are many small producers of a differentiated product and new firms can enter freely. Local supermarkets and service stations are good examples of monopolistic competitors. When firms are large relative to the market and some impediments to the entry of new firms exist, the industry is oligopolistic. For example, there are only a handful of large automobile companies, steel companies, soap manufacturers, and cereal producers in the United States. Finally, a monopoly exists when an industry's product is supplied by only one firm. Some examples of monopolies include local telephone service or the local newspaper; only one company in each industry is able to serve a community.

Firms in an industry may be price takers or price makers.

A firm that is a **price taker** considers the market price as something over which it has no control.

In the real world, almost every seller exercises some influence over price; but the more competition the seller faces, the less control each individual seller can exercise over the prices charged. In the extreme case, the seller has absolutely no control over price.

**Perfect competition** prevails in an industry when each individual seller faces so much competition from other sellers that the market price is taken as given.

This type of behavior tends to prevail when there are many firms selling a homogeneous product to an informed public, and new firms are free to enter or old ones to leave the industry. The conditions for perfect competition are four:

| Table 1   Market Models | | | |
|---|---|---|---|
| *Type* | *Number of Firms* | *Product* | *Entry* |
| Perfect competition  Farms, low price cloth | Many | Homogeneous | Easy |
| Monopolistic competition  Grocery | Many | Heterogeneous | Easy |
| Oligopoly  GM, steel | Few | Not specified | Not easy |
| Monopoly | One - Phone, Newspaper | Irrelevant | Difficult |

1. The industry contains so many buyers and sellers that no single one can influence the price of the product.

2. Each buyer or seller is perfectly informed about prices and the quality of the product.

3. The product is homogeneous; that is, it is not possible or even worthwhile to distinguish the product of one firm from that of another in the industry.

4. No barriers obstruct entry into or exit from the market; that is, there is complete freedom of entry and exit.

As a consequence of these conditions, no firm in the industry can sell the product at a price higher than that of another firm—people will always try to buy from the firm with the lowest price. This competition will cause every firm to sell at the same price.

The difference between the perfectly competitive firm and the industry as a whole is illustrated in Figure 1. Panel (*b*) shows the industry demand curve, *D*, for the product. When the market price is $7, the quantity demanded in the industry is 10,000 units. The individual firm, shown in panel (*a*), can sell all it

wants (from a practical standpoint) at the going industry price of $7. Whether the firm sells 3 units or 10 units, the price is still the $7 market price. (See Example 1.)

> The demand curve facing the perfectly competitive firm is *horizontal* or *perfectly elastic* at the going market price.

The individual firm in a perfectly competitive industry produces very small amounts relative to the industry as a whole. Thus, an individual firm cannot change the industry price by altering the quantity of the good it offers in the marketplace. Because the individual firm faces a perfectly elastic demand schedule, the firm is a price taker. If the firm tries to sell at a price higher than the market price, it will sell nothing.

## ECONOMIC PROFITS

The theory of perfect competition, as well as other market models, rests on the assumption that firms seek to maximize profits. Therefore, in order to ana-

(*a*) The Representative Firm

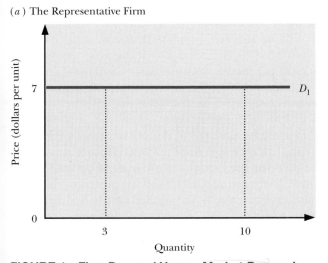

(*b*) Industry Demand

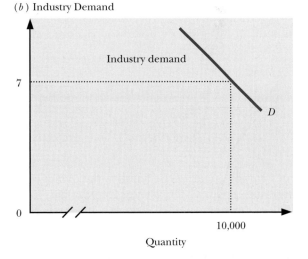

**FIGURE 1   Firm Demand Versus Market Demand**
The industry demand curve *D* in panel (*b*) shows the total industry demand for a homogeneous product being produced by many relatively small firms. The demand curve $D_1$ in panel (*a*) shows how this demand is perceived by the individual firm. Because the individual firm is so small relative to the market, it cannot significantly influence the market price. The firm is, thus, a price taker and can sell all it wants at the going price.

# EXAMPLE 1
## COMPETITION, FREEDOM OF ENTRY, AND ONE-HOUR PHOTO PROCESSING

As recently as 15 years ago, people had to wait at least overnight for film to be developed. In the early 1980s, French and Japanese manufacturers revolutionized the photo-processing industry by developing low-cost minilabs that could fit into a corner space in a pharmacy or any other small retail establishment. When introduced, these minilabs required an investment of $33,000. As technology was perfected, the price of the minilabs dropped substantially.

The one-hour photo-processing business is characterized by minimal barriers to entry. Anyone who wants to enter the business can do so by buying the necessary equipment. The first entrepreneurs to offer one-hour processing made considerable, but transitory, profits. Later investors, attracted by these profits, entered the business and competed for customers without restriction.

Economic theory states that entry into competitive businesses will cease when all participants earn normal profits. The one-hour photo-processing industry reached this level of saturation in the early 1990s, when one-hour processing was available in virtually every pharmacy, in addition to specialized outlets.

---

lyze how markets operate, we must first understand the concept of profits.

Economists do not use the general term *profits* in the way most people do, nor do they always measure profits in the same manner as accountants. Economic profits indicate whether or not resources are being directed to their best use.

> **Economic profits** represent the amount by which revenues exceed total opportunity costs.

For example, pharmacist Smith is the owner and operator of Smith's Drugstore. Smith has put $60,000 of her own money into the business. She could, however, earn $2000 per month working as a pharmacist in a chain drugstore. Moreover, Smith's capital investment in her own drugstore might earn $500 per month if invested elsewhere. This sum of $2500 (= $2000 + $500) is an *implicit* cost of doing business. (Although this $2500 is a true opportunity cost, no money changes hands.) The *explicit* (accounting) costs involved are Smith's rent payments on the building, inventory costs, business taxes, and

wage payments to clerks and other pharmacists. These add up to $37,000 per month. Smith's total monthly opportunity cost for operating her own drugstore is the sum of explicit costs ($37,000) and implicit costs ($2500), or $39,500.

Now suppose Smith's Drugstore has monthly sales of $40,000. Smith's accounting profits are $3000 per month (that is, sales = $40,000; accounting costs = $37,000). Smith's economic profit, however, is only $500 because total opportunity costs are $39,500. Accounting costs ignore the implicit costs that must be assigned to the use of Smith's entrepreneurial talents and funds. These implicit costs must be paid for the entrepreneur/owner to commit entrepreneurial resources and financial capital to the business. In this case, if accounting profits had been below $2500, Smith would not have entered the business because she would not earn a normal profit, which equals the cost of doing business.

> A **normal profit** is the return that the time and capital of an entrepreneur would earn in the best alternative employment. It also is the return that is earned when total revenues equal total opportunity costs.

# PERFECT COMPETITION IN THE SHORT RUN

Perfectly competitive firms have no control over price; they are price takers. Therefore, the major decision they face is how much output to produce. In the short run, a perfectly competitive firm makes its output decisions by varying the quantities of variable inputs (such as labor, raw material, energy) that are combined with its fixed plant and equipment. The fixed level of plant and equipment is both a burden and a blessing. It is a blessing to established firms because in the short run fixed costs prevent new firms from entering the industry. Time is needed to build more plants or install more equipment. Yet, the fixed level of plant and equipment is also a burden. In the short run, the firm is obliged—even if it shuts down temporarily—to make certain contractual payments (taxes, rent payments, contractual obligations to some employees) and to forgo interest receipts that it could earn if it could sell the plant and equipment.

In the short run, the firm must make two decisions: first, whether to temporarily shut down, and second, how much to produce if it decides not to shut down. In the long run, the firm has the additional options of building more plants and acquiring more equipment or leaving the business permanently. We shall consider the long run in a later section.

## THE TWO RULES OF PROFIT MAXIMIZATION

When calculating the appropriate level of output, firms are guided by the goal of profit maximization (or loss minimization). To maximize profit, firms must follow some simple rules.

**The Shutdown Rule.**   The first decision faced by the perfectly competitive firm is whether to shut down temporarily or produce some output. Surprisingly, it is not important whether the revenues that the firm earns cover fixed costs. In the short run, firms must live with fixed costs. Thus, fixed costs should not affect decision making in the short run because they must be paid even if the firm shuts down. Only in the long run can fixed costs be avoided. Instead, according to the shutdown rule, the decision to shut down for the short run depends on the relationship between revenues and variable costs.

The **shutdown rule** states that if a firm's revenues at all output levels are less than vari-able costs, it can minimize its losses by shutting down. If there is at least one output level at which revenues exceed variable costs, the firm should not shut down.

For example, brick manufacturer Smith has fixed costs of $1000 per week. She can sell $3000 worth of bricks per week while incurring a variable cost (VC) of $2900. Should the bricks be produced or should the plant be shut down? If no bricks are produced (the shutdown case), the fixed costs of $1000 must be paid anyway, so the manufacturer will incur a loss of $1000. By producing $3000 worth of bricks, the manufacturer can *reduce* her losses to $900 because producing bricks results in an excess of $100 of revenues ($3000) over variable costs ($2900). The reasoning behind the shutdown rule is that any excess of revenues over variable costs can be applied to cover a portion of fixed costs.

**The Profit-Maximization Rule.**   Once the firm has decided not to shut down, what rule should it follow to maximize profits or minimize losses? The decision about *how much* to produce is guided by marginal analysis, as we discussed in Chapter 5. If at any point producing another unit of output *raises the profit of the firm (or reduces its losses)*, more output should be produced. Marginal adjustments in the level of output will be made as long as each change increases profit or reduces losses.

What is the best output? As we learned in the preceding chapter, marginal cost (MC) is the increase in costs that results from increasing output by 1 unit. The marginal benefit of producing 1 more unit of output is the revenue it generates.

**Marginal revenue (MR)** is the increase in total revenue (TR) that results from each 1-unit increase in the amount of output:

$$MR = \frac{\Delta TR}{\Delta Q}$$

As long as an extra unit of output adds more to revenue than to costs, the profits of the firm increase (or its losses diminish) with greater production. If the marginal cost of an additional unit of output exceeds its marginal revenue, the firm's profits will be reduced (or its losses increased) by producing that extra unit. It follows that the profit-maximization rule

*Profit max is profit max output MR = MC*

holds that marginal revenue should equal marginal cost. This rule applies to all firms, be they perfectly competitive or monopolistic.

> The **profit-maximization rule** states that a firm will maximize profits by producing that level of output at which marginal revenue (MR) equals marginal cost (MC).

What is MR for a competitive firm? Because the competitive firm can sell all it wants without depressing the going market price, that price ($P$) is equivalent to the marginal revenue. Thus, for a competitive firm, the rule is to produce where $P = MC$.

**The Cost Curves Again.**  Consider the Texas Hat Company, described in Table 2, the same firm that you met in Table 2 of the previous chapter. The firm's average variable costs (AVC) for different levels of output are listed in column 2; average total costs (ATC) in column 3; total costs (TC) in column 4; and marginal costs (MC) in column 5. Figure 2 presents the same information in graphical form. Remember that the difference between the ATC and AVC curves measures average fixed cost (AFC) and the MC curve intersects both the AVC and ATC curves at their minimum points.

The minimum points on the AVC and ATC curves are important to keep in mind. In Table 2, the minimum average variable cost listed in column 2 is $9.60—which occurs when the output equals five units. The minimum average total cost listed in column 3 is $18—which occurs when the output equals six units.

Whether or not the firm can make a profit depends upon the price. The competitive firm can sell all it wants at the going price. When the price exceeds the minimum ATC of $18, the firm can make a profit by producing six units of the good.

## THE FIRM'S SHORT-RUN SUPPLY CURVE

In the short run, the competitive firm's objective is either to maximize profits or, if necessary, to minimize losses. The firm's supply curve indicates how much it

| | | Table 2 | The Profit-Maximizing Firm: The Texas Hat Company | | | | |
|---|---|---|---|---|---|---|---|
| Output (1) | Average Variable Cost (2) | Average Total Cost (3) | Total Cost (4) | Marginal Cost (5) | P = Marginal Revenue (6) | Revenue (7) | Profit (8) |
| 0 | — | ∞ | $48 | | $26 | $0 | −$48 |
| 1 | $20 | $68 | 68 | $20 | 26 | 26 | −42 |
| 2 | 15 | 39 | 78 | 10 | 26 | 52 | −26 |
| 3 | 12 | 28 | 84 | 6 | 26 | 78 | −6 |
| 4 | 10 | 22 | 88 | 4 | 26 | 104 | 16 |
| 5 | 9.6 | 19.2 | 96 | 8 | 26 | 130 | 34 |
| 6 | 10 | 18 | 108 | 12 | 26 | 156 | 48 |
| 7 | 11.4 | 18.3 | 128 | 20 | 26 | 182 | 54 |
| 8 | 14 | 20 | 160 | 32 | 26 | 208 | 48 |
| 9 | 17.3 | 22.7 | 204 | 44 | | | |

*(MR = MC at output 7)*

When MR = MC, profit is maximized. If $P = MR = \$26$, the firm should produce 7 units.

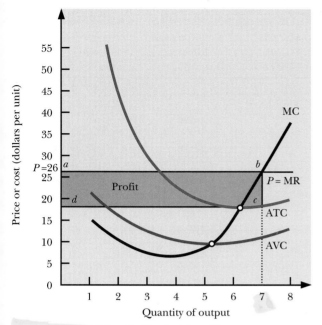

**FIGURE 2    The Profit-Maximizing Firm**

The market price is $26. The firm maximizes profit at an output level of seven units (where $P = MC$). At $P = \$26$, price exceeds ATC by the distance $bc$. Total profit is the rectangle $abcd$.

is prepared to sell at each price. Once the market price is set, the firm will find itself in one of three positions:

1. The price may be high enough that the firm can make economic profits.
2. The price may be low enough that the firm stays in business but produces at a loss.
3. The price may be so low that the firm's best option is to temporarily shut down and hope for the price to rise.

**The Profitable Firm.**    Let us start with a price of $26. Because the firm is perfectly competitive, $P = MR = \$26$. Columns 4, 7, and 8 in Table 2 show the total cost, total revenue, and profit (positive or negative) of the firm. If the firm produces six units, minimizing average total costs at $18, it can make a profit of $48. However, at this output, the MC of the seventh unit equals $20. Since MR = $26, the firm can increase its profit by producing more units; the increase in revenue will exceed the increase in costs. If output is raised to seven units, profit in-

creases to $54. This $6 increase represents the difference between the increase in revenue ($26) and the increase in costs ($20). Profit is maximized at $54 because the MC of the eighth unit is $32, which exceeds MR = $26.

The graph in Figure 2 shows us the same results. At any point along the line $P = MR$, the firm's total revenue equals the price times the quantity produced. Profit is maximized where the $P = MR$ line intersects the MC curve; when $P = \$26$, this occurs at an output level of seven units. On the graph, the MC curve is filled in for all levels of output. The vertical difference between the $P = MR$ line and the ATC curve at that point—the distance $bc$—indicates profit per unit of output. Total profit is determined by multiplying this difference by the output of seven units and is measured by the rectangle $abcd$. Profit will not be maximized at any output other than seven units because MC will not equal $P$ or MR.

**The Loss-Minimizing Firm.**    Let us turn to the second case, in which the market price is not high enough for the firm to make a profit. A market price lower than the minimum ATC of $18 will result in losses. Consider a price of $16. Table 3 and Figure 3 use the same cost figures as the previous example, but columns 6, 7, and 8 of the table now reflect the lower price. The firm cannot make a profit; instead, it must worry about minimizing its losses. If the firm produces an output of zero, column 4 shows that total costs will still be $48—the firm's fixed costs do not disappear if it shuts down. The firm's revenue will be zero, as shown in column 7, and its loss (its negative profit) will be $48.

If the firm shuts down, it loses its entire fixed costs of $48. Can it do better? If the firm's revenue exceeds its variable costs, it will be able to cover some portion of its fixed cost. If the firm can pay even a small portion of its fixed costs, it is better off staying in business than shutting down. The minimum AVC ($9.60) occurs when output is five units. By producing five units, the firm's price exceeds AVC by $6.40, revenue that can be used to cover some of the fixed costs. If the firm produces five units of output, its loss is $16, as shown in column 8, less than the $48 loss of shutting down. Yet, at an output of five units, the firm is still not minimizing its losses. The price of $16 exceeds the $12 marginal cost of the sixth unit; an additional unit of output would add

## Table 3   The Loss-Minimizing Firm: The Texas Hat Company

| Output (1) | Average Variable Cost (2) | Average Total Cost (3) | Total Cost (4) | Marginal Cost (5) | P = Marginal Revenue (6) | Revenue (7) | Profit (8) |
|---|---|---|---|---|---|---|---|
| 0 | — | ∞ | $48 | | $16 | $0 | −$48 |
| | | | | $20 | | | |
| 1 | $20 | $68 | 68 | | 16 | 16 | −52 |
| | | | | 10 | | | |
| 2 | 15 | 39 | 78 | | 16 | 32 | −46 |
| | | | | 6 | | | |
| 3 | 12 | 28 | 84 | | 16 | 48 | −36 |
| | | | | 4 | | | |
| 4 | 10 | 22 | 88 | | 16 | 64 | −24 |
| | | | | 8 | | | |
| 5 | 9.6 | 19.2 | 96 | | 16 | 80 | −16 |
| | | | | 12 | | | |
| 6 | 10 | 18 | 108 | | 16 | 96 | −12 |
| | | | | 20 | | | |
| 7 | 11.4 | 18.3 | 128 | | 16 | 112 | −16 |
| | | | | 32 | | | |
| 8 | 14 | 20 | 160 | | 16 | 128 | −32 |
| | | | | 44 | | | |
| 9 | 17.3 | 22.7 | 204 | | | | |

When $P = \$16$, losses are minimized when output is 6 units.

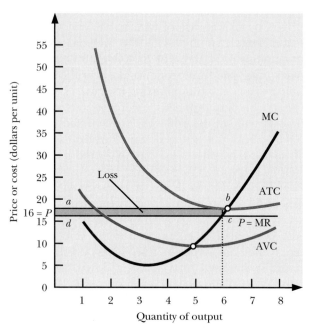

**FIGURE 3   The Loss-Minimizing Firm**
In this case, minimum ATC is $18 and $P = \$16$, so the firm loses money. But the firm minimizes its losses by adjusting output to 6 units, where $P = \text{MC}$. At this level, it is able to cover not only its variable costs but also some portion of fixed costs. By shutting down, the firm would lose its fixed costs of $48.

$16 to revenue and only $10 to costs. According to the profit-maximizing rule, the firm should increase production until $P = \text{MC}$. In Figure 3, when the MC curve is filled in or smoothed, this occurs at point $c$, where the $P = \text{MR}$ line intersects the MC curve yielding an output of six units. At this point, the firm's losses per unit of output are measured by the distance $bc$, or $P - \text{ATC} = \$16 - \$18 = -\$2$. The firm's total losses of $12 (the six units times the $2 loss per unit) are shown by the rectangle $abcd$.

> Perfectly competitive firms choose that level of output where $P = \text{MC}$—or, in graphical terms, where the $P(= \text{MR})$ line intersects the MC curve—provided price is greater than the minimum level of AVC. This rule holds whether the firm is maximizing its profit or minimizing its losses.

**The Shutdown Case.** In the previous two cases, the price of the product exceeded the minimum AVC of $9.60. If, however, the price falls short of the minimum AVC, what should the firm do? A price below the average variable cost causes the firm's revenues to fall short of variable costs, so the firm should temporarily shut down. If the firm does not shut down,

## Table 4  The Shutdown Case: The Texas Hat Company

| Output (1) | Average Variable Cost (2) | Average Total Cost (3) | Total Cost (4) | Marginal Cost (5) | $P$ = Marginal Revenue (6) | Revenue (7) | Profit (8) |
|---|---|---|---|---|---|---|---|
| 0 | — | ∞ | $48 |  | $8 | $0 | −$48 |
|  |  |  |  | $20 |  |  |  |
| 1 | $20 | $68 | 68 |  | 8 | 8 | −60 |
|  |  |  |  | 10 |  |  |  |
| 2 | 15 | 39 | 78 |  | 8 | 16 | −62 |
|  |  |  |  | 6 |  |  |  |
| 3 | 12 | 28 | 84 |  | 8 | 24 | −60 |
|  |  |  |  | 4 |  |  |  |
| 4 | 10 | 22 | 88 |  | 8 | 32 | −56 |
|  |  |  |  | 8 |  |  |  |
| 5 | 9.6 | 19.2 | 96 |  | 8 | 40 | −56 |
|  |  |  |  | 12 |  |  |  |
| 6 | 10 | 18 | 108 |  | 8 | 48 | −60 |
|  |  |  |  | 20 |  |  |  |
| 7 | 11.4 | 18.3 | 128 |  | 8 | 56 | −72 |
|  |  |  |  | 32 |  |  |  |
| 8 | 14 | 20 | 160 |  | 8 | 64 | −96 |
|  |  |  |  | 44 |  |  |  |
| 9 | 17.3 | 22.7 | 204 |  |  |  |  |

When $P$ = $8 (< AVC), losses are minimized by shutting down.

it loses not only its fixed cost, but also the portion of its variable cost that is not covered by dollar sales.

Table 4 and Figure 4 illustrate the situation of the competitive firm when the price is only $8. Column 8 in Table 4 shows that its losses are minimized when output is zero. When the firm produces nothing, its losses are limited to its fixed cost of $48. Any additional output, since the price does not cover AVC, will increase the firm's losses. By producing the first unit, for example, the firm's AVC is $20. Since the price is only $8, the firm loses $12 on the first unit. Thus, its losses increase from $48 to $60 as output rises from zero to one unit. Figure 4 demonstrates graphically the rationale for a shutdown. The $P$ = MR line is less than AVC for all outputs. Thus, for any positive level of output, the firm loses more money than by shutting down; the firm minimizes its losses by producing nothing.

## THE FIRM'S SUPPLY CURVE

The supply curve for a competitive firm shows the level of output that it is prepared to supply at each price. The three cases presented in this section illustrate that the profit-maximizing level of output increases as the price increases.

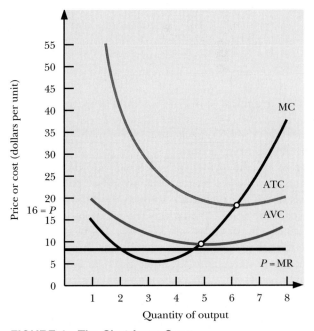

**FIGURE 4  The Shutdown Case**

In this case, $P$ = $8 and the minimum AVC is $9.60. The firm minimizes its losses by shutting down because the price is less than AVC.

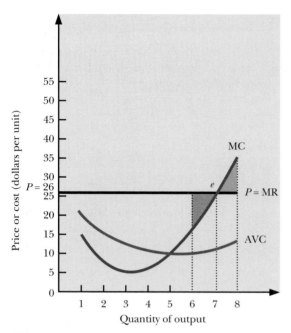

**FIGURE 5  Profit Maximization**
Profit is maximized where MR = MC. The green area is lost if output is too low, and the red area is lost if output is too high.

> The competitive firm's supply curve is that portion of the firm's MC curve that lies above the AVC curve. It indicates the profit-maximizing level of output for the firm at different price levels. Because the marginal cost curve is positively sloped, the competitive firm's supply curve is also positively sloped.

A graphical summary of the competitive firm's supply curve is shown in Figure 5. The $P = $ MR line intersects the MC curve above the minimum point on the AVC curve. If output is short of the intersection (point $e$), the firm can make the additional profit shown by the green area, which represents MR in excess of MC. If the firm pushes output above point $e$, it loses the amount shown by the red area, which represents MC in excess of MR. We know the firm is better off producing at point $e$ than shutting down because $P$ exceeds AVC. Since the firm is more than covering its variable costs, it is paying off at least some of its fixed costs.

## THE INDUSTRY'S SHORT-RUN SUPPLY CURVE

The behavior of the profit-maximizing firm explains the short-run behavior of the perfectly competitive industry of which it is a part. Recall that the short run is a period so short that old firms cannot build new plants and equipment; new firms cannot enter; old firms cannot leave. Thus, there are a fixed number of competitive firms of given sizes. Each individual firm's supply curve is its MC curve above its AVC curve. The industry supply curve is just the horizontal sum of each firm's supply curve.

> In the short run, the **industry** or **market supply curve** is the horizontal summation of the supply curves of each firm, which in turn are those portions of the firms' MC curve located above minimum AVC.

Figure 6 illustrates how the industry supply curve is derived in the case of four identical firms, but the principles are the same for any number of firms. We have considered an even simpler marginal cost curve than in the previous example. The marginal cost curve (above AVC) for a single firm is shown as $S_1 = $ MC. The firm wishes to sell zero units at a price of \$15, two units at a price of \$20, three units at a price of \$25, four units at \$35, and five units at \$50. The curve $S_4$ is the market supply curve for all four firms.

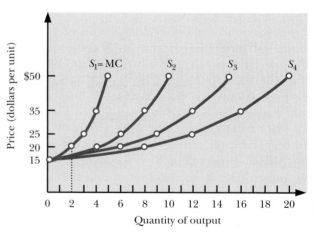

**FIGURE 6  The Industry Supply Curve**
The industry supply curve is the horizontal summation of all individual firms' supply curves. In the present case, there are four identical firms. Each firm has the MC curve $S_1$. As additional firms are added, the supply curve shifts rightward to $S_2$ (for two firms), $S_3$ (for three firms), and finally to the market supply curve $S_4$ for all four firms.

Graphically, the industry supply curve is the *horizontal* summation of each firm's supply curve. With four identical firms, no industry output is supplied at a price of $15. At a price of $20, eight units are supplied (the four firms at two units each). At a price of $50, the industry is prepared to supply 20 units (four firms at five units each). The supply curves $S_2$ and $S_3$ show what the industry supply curves would be with only two and three firms in the industry. The addition of firms simply shifts the market supply curve to the right.

## SHORT-RUN EQUILIBRIUM

The market or industry equilibrium occurs at the market price that balances the market supply with the market demand for the good. Figure 7 demonstrates how the short-run equilibrium price is determined, for the firm of Figures 2 through 4. Panel (*a*) of Figure 7 shows the individual firm, and panel (*b*) an industry consisting of 1000 such firms. The supply curve *S* in panel (*b*) is the horizontal summation of each individual firm's MC curve above AVC. For example, at a price of $26 each firm sells seven units and the industry sells 7000 units. If the market demand curve *D* intersects the market supply curve at the price of $26, then the quantity demanded also equals the quantity supplied (7000), and the $26 price becomes the individual firm's horizontal demand curve. In response to this price, the firm produces seven units, at the point where the MC curve intersects its demand curve. The profit-maximizing behavior of the individual firm is consistent with the profit-maximizing behavior of all the firms in the market.

Panel (*a*) shows a representative firm that is making an economic profit. ATC at the profit-maximizing output level of seven units is $18.30; therefore, the firm is making a per-unit profit of $7.70 (= $26 − $18.30) on each of the seven units for a total of $54 economic profit. The representative firm would experience economic losses if ATC were greater than the price. Even in such a case, however, the firm would not shut down in the short run as long as it could pay part of its fixed costs.

*Industy StD sets pria*

(*a*) The Representative Firm

(*b*) The Industry

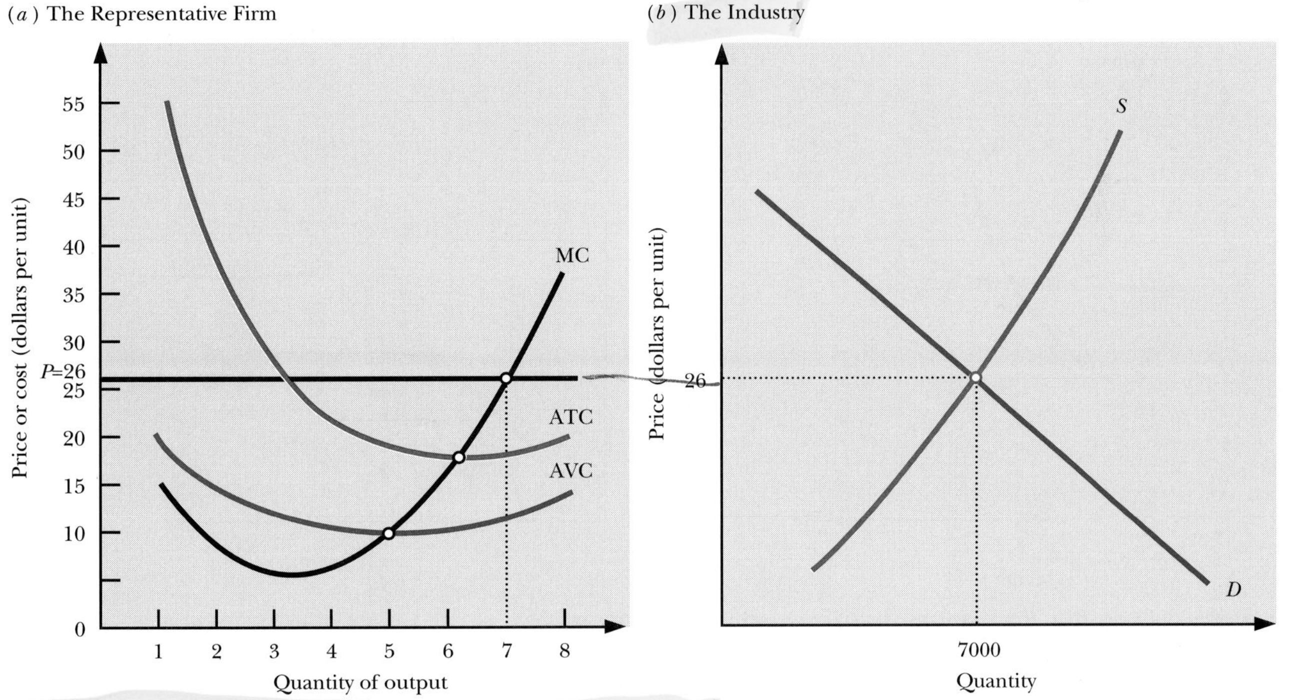

**FIGURE 7   Short-Run Equilibrium: The Firm and the Industry**

Panel (*a*) shows the representative firm; panel (*b*) shows the industry, in which there are 1000 firms. Firm demand occurs at the point where industry demand and supply are in equilibrium, in this case at a price of $26 and an output of 7000 units. The individual firm in panel (*a*) is making a short-run profit.

# PERFECT COMPETITION IN THE LONG RUN

The effect of economic profits on perfectly competitive industries occurs primarily in the long run, when new firms can enter the industry and established firms can exit. As competitive firms respond to economic profits or losses, the industry short-run supply schedule shifts, and prices change.

## LONG-RUN EQUILIBRIUM

The persistence of economic profits ($P > ATC$) or economic losses ($P < ATC$) cannot be sustained in the long run for a competitive industry. If losses continue to be sustained, in the long run, firms will leave the industry for greener pastures. If economic profits continue to be made, there will be an incentive in the long run for new firms to enter the industry to earn above-normal profits.

An industry in long-run equilibrium provides no incentive for new firms to enter or old firms to leave; the number of firms remains static. In long-run equilibrium, existing firms will operate at a level of output at which average total cost equals the price. (See Example 1.)

Figure 8 diagrams a perfectly competitive industry in long-run equilibrium. In the long run, the firm operates at an efficient scale of operation. Thus, the ATC curve for the optimal plant will have a minimum average cost equal to the minimum average cost on the long-run average cost curve (LRAC). The long-run equilibrium for the representative firm occurs at $q_0$, where $P = ATC = LRAC$.

When $P = MC$ and $P = ATC = LRAC$ at the long-run equilibrium output, and when MC intersects ATC at its *minimum point,* the perfectly competitive firm is producing at the lowest average cost in the long run.

> Long-run equilibrium occurs for the competitive industry when economic profits are zero and long-run average costs are minimized.

*Not profitable*

This finding suggests that perfectly competitive firms will operate at maximum efficiency (produce at minimum LRAC) in the long run.

*Poor stock to buy*

(a) The Representative Firm

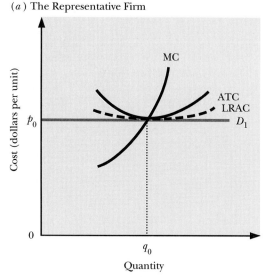

(b) The Industry

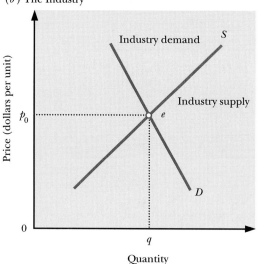

**FIGURE 8   Long-Run Equilibrium: The Firm and the Industry**

These graphs illustrate the relationship between the firm and the industry in long-run equilibrium. Notice that three conditions are satisfied: (1) quantity supplied equals quantity demanded; (2) price equals marginal cost; and (3) price equals average total cost, which equals long-run average cost. (The representative firm makes zero economic profit.) The representative firm in panel (a) produces at the point where the $D_1$ curve intersects the MC curve ($P = MC$). Its profits are zero because price just covers the minimum average total cost of production. The industry supply curve in panel (b) is based on the number of firms in existence in long-run equilibrium.

## THE MECHANISM OF ENTRY AND EXIT

A perfectly competitive industry adjusts toward a long-run equilibrium of zero economic profits through entry and exit. For the economy as a whole, entry and exit are opposite sides of the same coin. If it is profitable to enter one industry, resources must be exiting another industry. In other words, if revenue exceeds opportunity costs in some industries, it falls short of opportunity costs in others.

This is difficult to see in a large economy, such as that of the entire United States. But in a small economy it would be obvious. For example, in the state of Hawaii the success of the tourist industry crippled the pineapple industry through the effect of higher wages in the former.

**Entry.**   In the long run, the mechanism of free entry eliminates economic profits and ensures that goods are produced at minimum average cost with an efficient plant size.

Consider the perfectly competitive industry in Figure 9. Panel (*a*) graphs the ATC and MC curves of a typical firm in this industry; we assume ATC is the short-run average total cost curve for an efficient scale of plant. Panel (*b*) graphs the market supply curve derived by summing the supply curves of the 100 firms in the industry. When the market demand curve is $D$, the equilibrium price is $10. At this price, the representative firm makes zero profits (a normal return). The demand curve facing the representative firm is $D_1$; each of the 100 firms produces seven units of the product, yielding a market output of 700 units. Point $e_1$ represents both a short-run and a long-run equilibrium.

Suppose that consumers increase their demand for the product, causing the market demand curve to shift from $D$ to $D'$. The short-run equilibrium price rises to $12, and the short-run equilibrium output of the industry rises to 800 units (point *a*).[1] At this higher price, the firm's short-run equilibrium occurs at eight units of output, where price and marginal cost are equal. The typical firm now makes economic profits [$= 8 \times (\$12 - \$10.50) = \$12$]. In the short

run, which may be a few months or many years, the individual firm will enjoy above-normal returns.

In the long run, above-normal profits will attract more firms. *As these new firms enter the market, the supply curve shifts to the right* because the market supply is the sum of individual supply curves. The entry of new firms will continue as long as economic profits remain positive. But as the supply curve shifts to the right (to $S'$), the market price falls, shrinking profits. Eventually, economic profits disappear. The new long-run (and short-run) equilibrium is point $e_2$, at the old equilibrium price of $10. The individual firm again produces seven units; but the total output is now 980 units, produced by 140 firms.

> In the long run, the number of firms in a perfectly competitive industry is not fixed. If the typical firm is making economic profits, the number of firms will expand. If the typical firm is sustaining economic losses, the number of firms will contract. In other words, if $P >$ ATC, the number of firms will increase. If $P <$ ATC, the number of firms will decrease.

**Efficient Scale.**   Competition induces the perfectly competitive firm to produce at $P = $ MC; free entry causes $P = $ ATC $= $ LRAC, thereby eliminating economic profits. Both forces combined result in *efficient* production, in which the good is being produced at the minimum cost to society. The firm in a competitive industry cannot be inefficient in the long run. For example, any firm in Figure 9 that is not the best possible size for producing seven units will cease to exist in the long run.

**Exit.**   The entry of some firms into profitable industries implies a simultaneous exit of other firms from unprofitable industries. As with entry, the mechanism of exit leads to a long-run equilibrium, with the average firm producing at the minimum average cost and with price equal to marginal cost. Just as entry into profitable industries is healthy for an economy, so is exit from unprofitable ones. Indeed, to say that economic profit attracts new entrants implies that those entrants were making economic losses elsewhere. Greater profits in one industry become the opportunity costs of other industries.

> One of the most important lessons in all of economics is that entry and exit are different sides of the same economic mechanism.

---

[1]Remember that in the short run, the number of firms is fixed. As market demand increases, movement occurs along the short-run supply schedule $S$. In the long run, new firms can enter, resulting in a rightward shift of the supply curve to $S'$.

(a) The Representative Firm

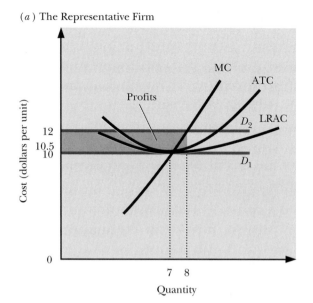

(b) The Industry

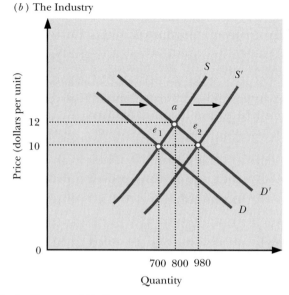

**FIGURE 9    Free Entry of Firms Drives Economic Profits to Zero and Unit Costs to a Minimum**

The initial long-run equilibrium is $e_1$, at the intersection of $D$ and $S$ in panel (b). When demand shifts to $D'$, the short-run equilibrium price rises to $12 (point $a$), creating economic profits for the individual firm facing the new demand curve $D_2$ in panel (a). In the long run, new firms enter the market until the supply curve shifts to $S'$. The long-run equilibrium is established at point $e_2$, where price again equals $10. Each firm returns to producing seven units of output, but the number of firms rises from 100 (700 ÷ 7) to 140 (980 ÷ 7).

In Figure 10, the initial demand and supply curves are $D$ and $S$ in panel (b). Point $e_1$ is both a short-run and a long-run equilibrium for an industry with 100 firms. Point $e_1$ is a short-run equilibrium because, in panel (b), the market quantity supplied equals the market quantity demanded and because, in panel (a), $P = MC$ for the representative firm. The market is in long-run equilibrium because when price is $10 (the firm demand curve is $D_1$), the representative firm makes zero profits.

Suppose now that consumers reduce their demand for the product, causing the market demand curve to shift from $D$ to $D'$ in panel (b). As a result, the short-run equilibrium shifts from point $e_1$ to point $a$, where the price is $7 and the quantity is 500 units. The representative firm produces five units. Because $7 is less than ATC, the representative firm has economic losses. In the long run, firms will begin to exit, shifting the industry supply curve to the left until economic losses are eliminated (at $S'$) and price is driven back up to the original $10. The new equilib-

rium is at point $e_2$, where total output is 336 units, and there are now only 48 firms who again produce an average of seven units each.

## CAPITALISM THE CREATOR

In Chapter 1 we discussed the Industrial Revolution as one of the Defining Moments of economics. But there are mini-industrial revolutions going on all of the time. When people demand the new products that new technologies create, their demand for old products must fall. The old industries must shrink or disappear. If resources are allocated politically rather than economically, vested interests will seek to preserve the old. But an unintended consequence of preserving old industries is the slowing down of the development of new industries. Capitalism is creative. It is an economic system that allows changes to take place in the most efficient way possible. The entry of

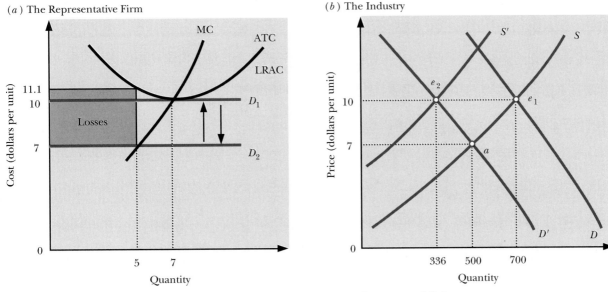

**FIGURE 10    Exit of Firms Eliminates Losses and Drives Unit Costs to a Minimum**

The initial long-run equilibrium is $e_1$, the intersection of $D$ and $S$ in panel *(b)*. Demand drops to $D'$, causing the short-run equilibrium price to fall to $7 (point *a*). The representative firm incurs losses as $D_1$ shifts downward to $D_2$. The exit of firms in the long run shifts the supply curve to $S'$, which lifts the price back to $10 and eliminates losses. Each firm returns to producing seven units of output, but the number of firms falls from 100 ($700 \div 7$) to 48 ($336 \div 7$).

new firms and the exit of old firms is the mechanism that keeps the economy up to date with the latest technologies, fashions, and fads. (See Example 2.) Socialism, as an economic system, broke down in part because it could not adapt to the incessant change that goes on in the world.

## THE GAINS FROM VOLUNTARY EXCHANGE OR TRADE

The theory of perfect competition demonstrates that both producers and consumers can gain from voluntary exchange between many independent buyers and sellers.

Figure 11 on page 189 shows an industry that is in equilibrium when price is $9 and output is 400 units. Because the industry supply curve begins at $5, the first unit can be coaxed out of some supplier by paying just $5; any price less than $5 would result in a zero output. To coax the hundredth unit out of another supplier, a price of $6 must be paid; to elicit the four hundredth unit requires a price of $9. Although

the market price is $9, some production of this good would have occurred even at a price less than $9. Those firms that would have been willing to supply the good at lower prices obtain a surplus return when the market price is $9. The supplier of the first unit receives a surplus of $4 (= $9 − $5); the supplier of the 100th unit, a surplus of $3 (= $9 − $6). The total surplus obtained by the suppliers of this good equals the area of the triangle *ceb*. Alfred Marshall, the great nineteenth-century British economist, called this area above the supply curve and below the price the producers' surplus.

> **Producers' surplus** represents the amount that producers receive in excess of the minimum value the producers would have been willing to accept.

In Figure 11, when the market price is $9, producers' surplus is the area *ceb*, which equals $800.

The concept of producers' surplus is similar to the concept of consumers' surplus discussed in an earlier chapter.

## EXAMPLE 2
## THE INVISIBLE HAND:
## THE PARADOX OF PROGRESS

As the U.S. economy entered the 1990s, Adam Smith's invisible hand brought about stunning downsizing in America's best-known companies. General Motors cut its labor force by 74,000, Sears by 83,000, IBM by 25,000, and Boeing by 27,000. Such layoffs are big news and frightening to all of us.

But the invisible hand creates as well as destroys. While Sears downsized, Wal-Mart added 260,000 jobs; while IBM cut back, Microsoft, Intel, and Dell Computer expanded. General Motors downsized, but some 29,000 Americans were employed at new jobs with Honda, Toyota, Nissan, and other new Japanese plants built in the United States.

Every day jobs are created and destroyed. In the short run, the process seems cruel. But in the long run, it is integral to economic progress. In 1900, for example, 40 out of every 100 Americans worked on farms. Today, only 3 out of 100 need be farmworkers, while the remaining 97 out of 100 workers are involved in providing new homes, computers, pharmaceuticals, appliances, movies, video games, and many other goods and services.

Joseph Schumpeter called this process "creative destruction." In 1920, there were over 2 million railroad employees; now there are but 230,000. In 1900 only 51,000 workers repaired electronic equipment; today, 711,000 people do such work on much more advanced equipment. There are hardly any blacksmiths, boilermakers, or milliners today, but there are plenty of engineers, computer programmers, and truck, bus, and taxi drivers.

The entire process is led by the invisible hand. Most people fear the process because it leads to lost jobs. Politicians sometimes want to freeze old jobs through government intervention. As pointed out by Michael Cox of the Federal Reserve Bank of Dallas:

> History demonstrates the futility of saving jobs. For instance, it's hard to miss the absurdity of a well-intentioned program that 100 years ago might have aimed to keep blacksmiths and harness makers employed. As recently as 70 years ago, the United States had 10 million registered passenger cars but 20.5 million horses. Had our ancestors been able to freeze jobs, the United States would be stuck in the horse-and-buggy era.

------------------------------------------------

*Source:* Adapted from "The Churn: The Paradox of Progress," Federal Reserve Bank of Dallas, 1992 Annual Report, and Joseph Schumpeter, *Capitalism, Socialism and Democracy,* 3d ed. New York: Harper and Brothers, 1950.

---

**Consumers' surplus** represents the consumer benefits (the dollar value of total utility) from consuming a good in excess of the dollar expenditure on the good.

In Figure 11, when the market price is $9, the consumer surplus is the area *aec*, which equals $1600.

What is the value of an industry? In Figure 11, the first unit is worth $17 to some consumer because the demand curve intersects the vertical axis at $17. The first unit can be coaxed out of some producer for $5. Thus, the first unit is worth approximately $12 to society [($17 − $9) + ($9 − $5)]. This $12 that is gained from trade is shared by the supplier who values the first unit at only $5 and the buyer who values the first unit at $17. Similarly, the hundredth unit is worth $15 to some buyer and $6 to some supplier, yielding a net gain of $9 [($15 − $9) + ($9 − $6)] at a market price of $9. The four hundredth unit squeezes out all the gains from trade.

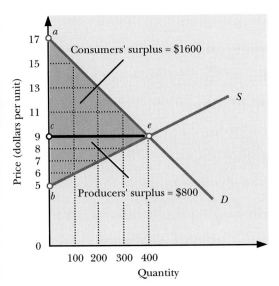

**FIGURE 11  The Gains from Trade**

When the price is $9, producers' surplus is the area *ceb*, and consumers' surplus is the area *cea*. The first unit is worth $17 to buyers and costs $5; it yields a gain of $12 to society from trade. All 400 units of output at the $9 price are worth the sum of the consumers' surplus and the producers' surplus, or area *aeb*. The total of consumers' and producers' surplus is $2400 (area of triangle *aeb* = 1/2 × base × height = 1/2 × $12 × 400 = $2400).

## PROHIBITION AND UNINTENDED CONSEQUENCES

Consumer surplus analysis suggests that prohibiting a product can have dire consequences for the welfare of consumers. But there are always unintended consequences. One of the most dramatic examples is the legal prohibition of alcohol in 1920s America. The unintended consequences were dramatic.

Prohibition was ended in the 1930s because of the obvious negative consequences. The law simply was not observed by the ordinary citizen; the demand for illegal liquor was great. The 1920s saw a rapid increase in organized crime. People who were willing to engage in "bootleg" liquor found their incomes increasing. Al Capone, the famous Chicago gangster, flourished under these conditions.

But prohibition was not without positive unintended consequences. America's love affair with Italian food began at this time. Before prohibition, Americans ate English food—such items as meat, potatoes, and corn. But prohibition sent Americans scurrying to find restaurants where they could get an alcoholic beverage with their meals. These restaurants were Italian. Today, Italian restaurants are among the most popular restaurants in America.

The value of a free market, or the benefit of trade or voluntary exchange, to the economy is measured by the sum of producers' and consumers' surplus. It is important to realize that the sum of the two surpluses is the value to society of the product net of the costs of production. Because the consumers' surplus *aec* = $1600 and the producers' surplus *ceb* = $800, society's net gain in the market illustrated in Figure 11 is $2400. The triangle area *aeb* can be interpreted as the potential loss to society if this market industry were eliminated.

In the real world, the gains from trade are enormous. Think of the cost to society of prohibiting the purchase and sale of a simple product like tomatoes, forcing about two-thirds of the population that does not now engage in gardening to grow their own tomatoes. The opportunity cost of forcing a multitude of busy electricians, lawyers, and doctors to weed, seed, and tend tomatoes, and the lost profits of those farmers with a comparative advantage in tomatoes, would amount to many billions of dollars. (See Example 3.)

## PERFECT COMPETITION IN THE REAL WORLD

### APPROXIMATING THE CONDITIONS FOR PERFECT COMPETITION

Most industries are not perfectly competitive, but the conditions of perfect competition are met in a number of markets. Most agricultural markets—fibers, grains, livestock, vegetables, fruits—are perfectly competitive. Stock markets and commodity markets are also perfectly competitive. More important than these purely competitive markets are industries that closely *approximate* the conditions of perfect competition. In such industries, the number of producers may not be large enough to make each firm a perfect price taker, but the degree of control over price may be negligible. Information on prices and product quality may not be perfect, but consumers may have a significant amount of that information at their disposal. The product may not be perfectly homogeneous, but the distinctions between products may be

## EXAMPLE 3
## GROWING YOUR OWN TOMATOES
## CAN BE COSTLY!

About 35 percent of America's 97 million households have a garden, and most of them grow tomatoes—the most popular of all vegetables. If tomatoes were made illegal to buy or sell, we would all have to have gardens. What would it cost? We cannot figure the cost unless we know what each household would have to be paid in order just to compensate it for growing its own tomatoes. However, we can make an estimate. If we were to place a mere $10 per week value (on the average) for the privilege of an individual's buying rather than growing tomatoes, the total cost to society would be over $32 billion per year ($520 times 63 million households). If we were to include the loss of producers' surplus because farmers are not selling tomatoes, the cost would be astronomical.

-------------------------------------------------

*Source:* "Increase in Home Gardening Yields Bumper Crop of Sales," *New York Times,* August 20, 1994.

inconsequential. The number of firms in the industry may not be exceptionally large, but many firms may be waiting in the wings to enter on short notice if economic profits are earned. An industry need not meet all the conditions of perfect competition for the theory of perfect competition to apply to its business behavior.

## GROWTH OF WORLD TRADE AND COMPETITION

The opening up of domestic markets to international competition is always a Defining Moment. The growth of world trade has ushered in a new era of competition. From 1970 to 1995, for example, world trade increased by more than 6 percent per year, about twice the growth rate of economic activity in general. For the most part, this high growth rate has resulted from the dismantling of barriers to international competition. Three important forces have been at work. First, explicit trade barriers such as tariffs and quotas have been relaxed by many countries. Second, international communications are now much cheaper because of the development of satellite technology, which allows telephone, television, and radio transmissions to be beamed almost anywhere in the world. Third, computer technology now makes it possible for companies to monitor developments all over the world. Consequently, firms in many countries are facing increasing competition in auto, TV, electronics, computers, and hundreds of other industries.

For example, although there are only three major automobile manufacturers in the United States, they must compete against rivals located in Japan, Germany, France, Italy, Brazil, and Korea for customers throughout the world. Likewise, restaurants in Paris and Tokyo must compete for customers with McDonalds and Burger King.

Increasing international competition in the last several decades has expanded the number of industries to which the perfectly competitive model is applicable.

## AN OVERVIEW OF PERFECT COMPETITION

The theory of perfect competition tells us that economic profits will be eliminated in the long run by the entry of new firms and that when the markets are in equilibrium, price and marginal cost will be equal. It also states that short-run behavior will differ from long-run behavior. In the short run, firms will stay in business as long as the price covers average variable cost; in the long run, if the price fails to cover average costs (remember that in the long run there are no fixed costs), firms will leave the industry. In the short run, demand increases will lead to price increases; in the long run, the price will ultimately depend upon the costs of the representative firm. Finally, the theory tells us that competition will result in rising and declining industries and that these changes are the source of progress in an economy.

Two of the most important characteristics of perfectly competitive industries are (1) that perfectly competitive firms will operate at minimum average cost in the long run and (2) that perfectly competitive firms will produce that quantity of output at which price equals marginal cost in both the short run and the long run. These characteristics are important for us to remember when we evaluate the other types of markets—monopoly, oligopoly, and monopolistic competition—that we shall consider in subsequent chapters. In the next chapter we shall examine the behavior of firms that are able to exercise some control over price. Monopolists exercise considerable control over their prices; monopolistically competitive firms have only limited control over their prices.

## SUMMARY

1. A market is perfectly competitive when it contains a large number of sellers and buyers, when buyers and sellers have perfect information, when the product is homogeneous, and when there is freedom of entry and exit. These conditions ensure that each seller will be a price taker. The price will be dictated to sellers by the market.

2. In the short run, the number of firms in an industry is constant, and the firm has fixed costs. In the long run, the number of firms can change through entry and exit, and fixed costs become variable costs. Profit-maximizing competitive enterprises face two decisions in the short run: first, whether or not to shut down: second, how much to produce, provided the enterprise does not shut down. If the market price covers average variable cost, the competitive firm will produce a positive level of output, the quantity at which price and marginal cost are equal. The firm's supply curve is its marginal cost curve above average variable cost. The industry supply schedule is the horizontal summation of all the supply schedules of individual firms in the industry. The price at which the quantity supplied equals the quantity demanded is the

market price. Each firm takes this market price as given.

3. In the long run, firms enter competitive industries where economic profits are being made and exit from industries where a below-normal profit is being earned. Economic profits must be zero for the competitive industry to be in equilibrium. In the long run, goods are produced at minimum average cost, with price equal to marginal cost for the average competitive firm.

4. Capitalism is a creative process, allowing economic systems to respond to change. The response of firms to profits and losses is what creates change and progress.

5. The sum of consumers' surplus and producers' surplus represents the gain from voluntary exchange or trade.

6. The theory of perfect competition can explain the behavior of firms in an industry even when that industry does not meet all the conditions of perfect competition.

7. The growth of world trade has ushered in a new era of international competition.

## KEY WORDS

price taker
perfect competition
economic profits
normal profit
shutdown rule
marginal revenue (MR)

profit-maximization rule
industry or market
 supply curve
producers' surplus
consumers' surplus

## QUESTIONS AND PROBLEMS

1. Explain why each firm may not be a price taker in an industry in which there is product differentiation among firms.
2. A firm that is contemplating whether to produce its tenth unit of output finds its marginal costs for the tenth unit are $50 and its marginal revenue for the tenth unit equals $30. What advice would you give this firm?
3. A firm has fixed costs of $100,000. It receives a price of $25 for each unit of output. Average variable costs are lowest (equal to $20) at 1000

units of output. What advice would you give this firm in the short run? In the long run?

4. Explain the relationships between accounting profits, normal profits, and economic profits. Will they always be different amounts?

5. The representative firm in the widget industry, which is perfectly competitive, is making a large economic profit. What predictions can you make about what will happen in this industry in the long run?

6. Evaluate the following statement: "The theory of perfect competition claims that economic profits will disappear in the long run. This assumption is incorrect because I know a family that has a farm that earns more than $1 million per year."

7. When will the long-run price be less than the current price?

8. Jones is a genius at farming, knowing exactly what to plant and when. As a result, Jones's farm consistently earns higher profits than other farms. From the economist's perspective, do these represent higher profits or something else?

9. In Table 2, fixed costs are $48. If fixed costs were raised to $100, how would the supply schedule be affected in the short run?

10. Imagine that a firm faces the cost schedule given in Table A.

a. Calculate the firm's profit or loss for each level of output when the price is $5.99, when the price is $6.01, and when the price is $10.01.

b. Calculate how many units of output the profit-maximizing or loss-minimizing firm will produce at each of those three prices.

c. Graph the firm's supply schedule.

11. You observe that the (competitive) airline industry is incurring economic losses. What do you expect to happen to ticket prices, to the quantity of airline passengers, and to the number of airline companies as time passes?

12. You observe that a highly profitable new industry is manufacturing a product of advanced technology (such as computers). What do you expect to happen to the price of the product, to profits, to the industry's output, and to the number of firms as time passes?

13. The demand and supply curves for a product are $Q = 10 - P$ for the former and $Q = P$ for the latter. What are the equilibrium values of $P$, $Q$, and the total of consumer and producer surpluses?

| Table A | | | |
|---|---|---|---|
| Quantity, $Q$ | Variable Cost, $VC$ | Fixed Cost, $FC$ | Total Cost, $TC$ |
| 0 | $0 | $5 | $5 |
| 1 | 6 | 5 | 11 |
| 2 | 14 | 5 | 19 |
| 3 | 24 | 5 | 29 |
| 4 | 36 | 5 | 41 |

# CHAPTER 11

# MONOPOLY AND MONOPOLISTIC COMPETITION

For 60 years, the production and sale of beluga caviar were controlled by a secret monopoly arrangement between the Soviet Ministry of Fisheries and the Paris-based Petrossian S.A. company. The Petrossian family split profits from foreign sales of beluga with Soviet authorities, who placed strict limits on the quantity available for export. Although the annual catch was 2000 tons of caviar, Soviet authorities allowed only 150 tons to be sold abroad. In 1990, the Petrossian Restaurant in Manhattan sold its best beluga caviar for $1000 per pound. The breakup of the Soviet Union in 1991 ended the caviar monopoly by multiplying the number of suppliers. Thus, in 1991 the official export price of beluga caviar fell 20 percent. Since then, it has fallen even more.[1]

In this chapter we shall examine monopoly and monopolistic competition. We shall consider how monopoly enterprises influence the price of goods by controlling the quantity offered to the market. Monopolies are price makers, seeking out the price/quantity combination that maximizes profit. We shall also analyze the operation of firms under monopolistic competition, in markets with a large number of competitors but with a limited control over price. The theory of monopolistic competition uses the same tools as the theory of monopoly.

[1]"Horrors! Fine Caviar Now Could Become Cheap as Fish Eggs," *Wall Street Journal,* November 18, 1991.

## CONDITIONS FOR MONOPOLY

*Monopoly* literally means "single seller." A pure monopoly has the following characteristics.

> A **pure monopoly** exists when
> 1. There is one seller in the market for some good or service that has no close substitutes.
> 2. Barriers to entry protect the seller from competition.

As with perfect competition, examples of pure monopoly are rare, but the theory of pure monopoly does shed light on the behavior of firms that approximate the conditions of pure monopoly. Monopoly power allows the seller to have some control over the price of the product; this power is possessed to some degree by many firms. For example, a certain corner at a busy intersection may be the best spot in a town for a service station, giving one firm a locational monopoly at that spot. Such a service station could charge a higher price than its competitors.

## THE SOURCES OF MONOPOLY

There are three basic theories about how monopolies can come about. Monopolies can arise because (1) one large firm may have lower costs than many smaller firms, (2) the government grants a monopoly to a single individual or corporation, or (3) a single firm controls a critical raw material.

### THE NATURAL MONOPOLY

A firm has a natural monopoly if its costs of production are less than the total costs of production of two or more separate firms producing the same total output. Large-scale production may be cheaper because of *economies of scale* or *economies of scope*.

> A **natural monopoly** prevails when industry output is cheaper to produce with one firm than two or more firms.

In the case of economies of scale, as the firm produces more its average costs fall. Economies of scale usually result from the use of costly specialized equipment. Economies of scope are similar, but they include the production of many similar products. For example, automobiles and trucks are produced by the same types of equipment and so a firm that produces a large number of trucks will have a lower cost of producing automobiles.

Throughout all levels of output, the natural monopoly's long-run average cost curve is declining. Clearly, in this case, there is room for only one firm because it will have the lowest costs.

Public utilities, such as local telephone service, electric utilities, and natural gas utilities, offer the most ready examples of possible natural monopolies. In a later chapter, we shall study the regulation of natural monopolies by the state.

### GOVERNMENT PROTECTION

Most examples of monopoly that come to mind are situations in which the government has granted a monopoly, through patents, public franchises (such as the public utilities mentioned above), and licensing. Indeed, in most cases, monopolies exist because of government involvement in one way or another.

**Patents.**   American *patent* laws allow an inventor the exclusive right to use the invention for a period of 17 years. The patent holder is thereby protected from competition during that period. The IBM Corporation's patents on tabulating equipment, Microsoft's patents on its software, and Smith Kline's patent on the drug Tagamet are examples of this type of entry barrier. The Bell System achieved a monopoly in the nineteenth century when Alexander Graham Bell obtained a patent for the telephone just hours before a rival inventor. (See Example 1.)

**Public Franchises.**   State, local, and federal governments grant to individuals or organizations exclusive *franchises* to be the sole operator in a particular business. Competitors are legally prohibited from entering the market. The U.S. Postal Service's delivery of mail is a classic example of a public franchise. Only the Post Office can use your mail box! States grant exclusive franchises to operate restaurants and service stations along tollways. Duty-free shops in airports and at international borders are also fran-

## EXAMPLE 1
## THE ORIGINAL
## BELL TELEPHONE MONOPOLY

The key characteristic of a monopoly is its ability to charge a price much higher than its average costs. The original Bell patents on the telephone provided the American Telephone and Telegraph Company (AT&T) with a monopoly from 1877 to 1894. Consequently, telephone service was extremely expensive. The cost of basic telephone service for a residential customer was about 5 percent of a typical worker's wage. Today, basic local service costs less than 1 percent of a typical worker's wage.

The effect of competition on prices is illustrated by the events that occurred when the Bell patents expired in 1894. From 1894 to 1900, almost 2000 new non-Bell telephone systems sprang up around the country. The number of telephones in the United States skyrocketed, from 240,000 in 1894 to over 6 million in 1907. In those areas where a Bell company competed with a non-Bell company, the price of basic telephone service dropped by about one-half. Bell's profits on stockholder equity plunged from around 46 percent to about 8 percent.

---------------------------------------------

*Source:* Gerald Brock, *The Telecommunications Industry* (Cambridge: Harvard University Press, 1981).

chise operations. Many public utilities operate under state or local franchises.

**Licensing.** Entry into an industry or profession may be regulated by government agencies and autonomous professional organizations. The American Medical Association licenses medical schools and allocates hospital/staff privileges to physicians. The Federal Communications Commission licenses radio and television stations and controls entry into the lucrative broadcasting industry. Most countries license airlines and, thus, limit entry into the industry. In the United States, nuclear power plants must be licensed by the federal government.

### EXCLUSIVE OWNERSHIP OF RAW MATERIALS

Established companies can be protected from the entry of new firms by their control of raw materials. The International Nickel Company of Canada once owned almost all of the world's nickel reserves. Virtually all of the world's diamond sales are under the control of the DeBeers Company of South Africa. American Metal Climax Corporation controls most of the world's supply of molybdenum (a metallic element used in strengthening and hardening steel).

## PRICE-MAKING BEHAVIOR

The most fundamental difference between monopoly and perfect competition lies in the determination of price. The perfectly competitive firm is a *price taker;* it must accept whatever price the market dictates. The monopolist, however, is a *price maker;* it has its own market demand curve along which it seeks the profit-maximizing price. Such price-making behavior is not restricted to pure monopolies. Even the local grocery store has some ability to set a price that maximizes profit.

> A **price maker** is a firm with some degree of control over the price of the good or service it sells.

Figure 1 illustrates the difference between price takers and price makers. The price taker's demand curve is perfectly elastic because the price is dictated by the market and more units can be sold without lowering the price. In contrast, the price-making firm must lower its price on all units sold in order to sell more. In other words, the demand curve facing a price maker is downward sloping.

Like price takers, price makers want to maximize profits by producing that level of output at which

*Price Setter*

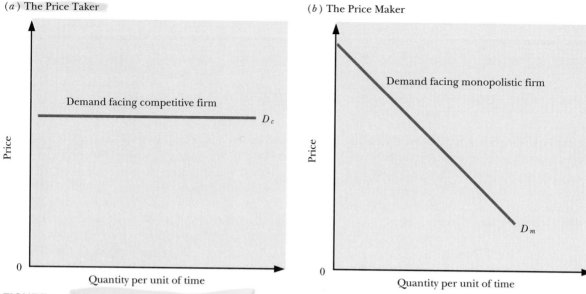

**(a) The Price Taker**

Demand facing competitive firm

$D_c$

Price

Quantity per unit of time

**(b) The Price Maker**

Demand facing monopolistic firm

$D_m$

Price

Quantity per unit of time

**FIGURE 1    A Price Maker Versus a Price Taker**

In panel *(a)*, the demand curve $D_c$ facing the competitive firm is perfectly horizontal, meaning that the firm can sell as many additional units as it wants without lowering its price. In panel *(b)*, the demand curve $D_m$ facing the monopolistic firm is downward sloping, meaning that the firm must lower its price in order to sell additional units.

marginal revenue (MR) and marginal cost (MC) are equal. For the price taker, however, price equals marginal revenue; for the price maker, price does not.

> **Marginal revenue (MR)** is the additional revenue raised per unit increase in quantity sold; that is, MR = $\Delta$TR/$\Delta$Q, where TR is total revenue.

## PRICE IN RELATION TO MARGINAL REVENUE

The perfect competitor can always sell additional output at the going market price.

For the price maker, price exceeds marginal revenue. In order to sell an additional unit of output per sales period, the price maker must lower the price on the units previously sold at a higher price. Thus, the extra revenue generated per period equals the (new) price of the extra unit sold minus the revenue lost due to the lower price for the previous units of output sold. In effect, selling one more unit "spoils the market" for the earlier units.

For a price maker, because the price for all units must decrease to sell one more unit, price is greater than marginal revenue:

$$P > \text{MR}$$

There is another way to explain why price exceeds marginal revenue for the monopolist price maker. In the chapter on productivity and costs we considered the relationship between average and marginal values. Recall that an average value falls if the marginal value is smaller than the previous average. Thus, if average revenue is falling, marginal revenue (MR) must be below it.

> **Average revenue (AR)** equals total revenue (TR) divided by output.

Average revenue and price are the same when all units are sold at the same price. In general, TR = $P \times Q$, and TR = AR $\times$ Q. To say that the price maker faces a downward-sloping demand schedule is to say that AR, or *P*, falls as output increases. In this case, marginal revenue must be below the previous average revenue, pulling it down. Thus, if AR is declining, MR must be less than AR. Since AR = *P*, *P* must be greater than MR.

We can measure marginal revenue per additional unit sold by taking the ratio of the change in revenue to the change in total units sold brought about by the change in price: that is, MR = $\Delta$TR/$\Delta$Q. It is not necessary to change the number of units by increments of only one unit, as in the forgoing examples. To illustrate, imagine that a producer of chocolates increases revenue by $400 when it sells another 100 boxes of chocolates. The change in revenue is $400 and the change in quantity sold is 100. Thus, the marginal revenue is MR = $400 ÷ 100 = $4.

A monopolist faces the demand schedule shown in columns 1 and 2 of Table 1. Column 3 lists the total revenue produced at each level of output (P × Q), and column 4 gives the marginal revenue schedule.

The values in column 4 that are positioned vertically between the rows correspond to the marginal revenue for each change in output level in Table 1. Since the first unit can be sold at a price of $19, the marginal revenue of that unit is also $19. To sell two units the monopolist must lower the price to $17. Total revenue is now $34; thus, MR = $34 − $19 = $15. Again, we see that MR is less than P for all units but the first. To sell three units requires a price of $15; total revenue rises by the MR of $11 to $45. As long as selling another unit lowers the price by $2, marginal revenue falls by $4 (twice as much).

The demand and marginal revenue schedules for the firm in Table 1 appear as demand and marginal revenue curves in Figure 2. The advantage of using an MR curve rather than a numerical schedule is that on a graph we can read MR at or between different levels of output. The negative slope of the firm's demand curve, labeled D, shows that the firm is a price maker (it must lower price to sell a greater quantity).

The location of the MR curve below the demand curve shows graphically that price is greater than marginal revenue for any quantity of output (except for the first unit sold). Whenever the demand curve is a straight line, the MR curve will be horizontally halfway between the demand curve and the vertical axis because the slope of the MR curve is twice as steep as the slope of the demand curve. In Table 1, as we noted above, when price falls by $2, marginal revenue falls by $4. Accordingly, the marginal revenue curve intersects the horizontal axis halfway between the origin and the intersection of the straight-line demand curve with the horizontal axis, as shown in panel (a) of Figure 2. This relationship between the demand and mar-

### Table 1    Monopoly Equilibrium

| Output (units), Q (1) | Price or Average Revenue, P = AR (2) | Total Revenue, TR = P × Q (3) = (1) × (2) | Marginal Revenue, MR (4) | Total Cost, TC (5) | Marginal Cost, MC (6) | Average Cost, ATC (7) | Profit = TR − TC (8) = (3) − (5) |
|---|---|---|---|---|---|---|---|
| 0 | $21 | $0 | | $12 | | | −$12 |
| | | | $19 | | $10 | | |
| 1 | 19 | 19 | | 22 | | 22 | −3 |
| | | | 15 | | 6 | | |
| 2 | 17 | 34 | | 28 | | 14 | 6 |
| | | | 11 | | 8 | | |
| 3 | 15 | 45 | | 36 | | 13 | 9 |
| | | | 7 | | 10 | | |
| 4 | 13 | 52 | | 46 | | 11.5 | 6 |
| | | | 3 | | 13 | | |
| 5 | 11 | 55 | | 58 | | 11.6 | −3 |
| | | | −1 | | 15 | | |
| 6 | 9 | 54 | | 72 | | 12 | −15 |

This table shows the demand and marginal revenue schedules of a monopolist. The demand schedule is given in the first two columns. Because all customers are charged the same price, price and average revenue are the same. Total revenue, in column 3, equals P × Q. Marginal revenue is the increase in total revenue brought about by increasing output by 1 unit. The monopolist's profit is maximized by producing 3 units of output, where profit equals $9. If the monopolist had attempted to produce 1 more unit of output, total revenue would have increased by $7 and costs would have increased by $10, so profit would have fallen by $3. If the monopolist had produced 1 less unit, total revenue would have fallen by $11 and costs would have fallen by $8, reducing profit by $3. The firm expands outputs as long as MC does not exceed MR.

(*a*) Demand and Marginal Revenue

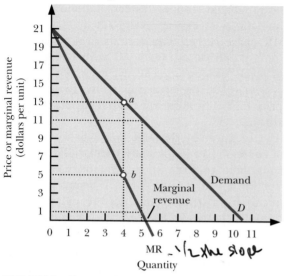

MR ~ 1/2 the slope
Quantity

(*b*) Elasticity

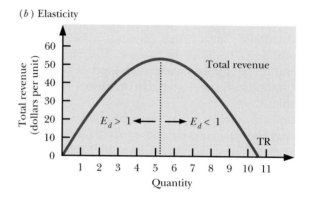

**FIGURE 2   Demand, Marginal Revenue, and Elasticity**

In panel *(a)*, the demand and marginal revenue schedules of Table 1 are plotted as *D* and MR. At an output level of 4 units, the price is $13 and the marginal revenue is $5. In other words, the value of MR for any given price is at that point on the MR curve directly below the point on the demand curve corresponding to that price. If the demand curve is a straight line, the marginal revenue curve will be located horizontally halfway between the demand curve and the vertical axis.

In panel *(b)*, the total revenue schedule of Table 1 is plotted, showing the relationship between MR and total revenue. When MR is positive, total revenue is rising; when MR is negative, total revenue is falling; when MR is zero, total revenue reaches its highest value. When the price elasticity of demand ($E_d$) is greater than 1, total revenue is rising; when it is less than 1, total revenue is falling. Thus, when demand is elastic, reductions in price raise total revenue; when demand is inelastic, reductions in price lower total revenue.

ginal revenue curves is sometimes called the half-way rule.

> The **halfway rule** states that when the demand curve can be represented by a straight line, the marginal revenue curve bisects the horizontal distance between the demand curve and the vertical axis.

## THE THEORY OF MONOPOLY

### HOW MONOPOLIES DETERMINE OUTPUT

The monopolist differs from other types of price makers in two ways. As we discussed earlier, first, the monopolist is the sole producer of a product for which there are no close substitutes. Second, the monopolist is protected by barriers to entry.

The monopolist has a profit incentive to lower price and expand output when marginal revenue exceeds marginal cost. For example, if the marginal revenue of an additional unit of output is $19 and the marginal cost of the additional unit is only $10, the firm can add $9 to profit by producing the additional unit. Thus, the monopolist will cut prices when marginal revenue exceeds marginal costs.

If the monopolist finds that marginal revenue is less than marginal cost, it pays to lower output and raise price. If MC = $10 and MR = $7, a cut in output by 1 full unit would lower costs by $10 and revenue by only $7, so profits would rise by $3 (or losses would fall by $3). Thus, the monopolist maximizes profit by choosing an output level where marginal cost (MC) equals marginal revenue (MR).

The monopolistic firm can raise profit by expanding output (by lowering price) when MR > MC. The firm can raise profit by cutting output (by raising price) when MR < MC. The monopolist—or the price maker in general—maximizes profit by producing that quantity for which MR = MC.

Table 1 gives cost schedules for the monopolistic firm that faced the demand and revenue schedules discussed in the previous section. Like the marginal revenue values in column 4, the values in column 6 that are positioned vertically *between* the rows correspond to the marginal cost for each change in output level. What level of output will the monopolist choose to produce? Remember that the monopolist will expand output as long as marginal revenue exceeds marginal cost. The first unit of output raises total revenue by $19 (MR = $19) and raises costs by only $10 (MC = $10), thus contributing $9 toward paying the monopolist's $12 fixed cost and reducing a $12 loss at zero output to a $3 loss at 1 unit of output. The second unit of output raises revenue by $15 and adds $6 to costs. The second unit, therefore, turns a $3 loss into a $6 profit. The third unit adds $11 to revenue and $8 to cost, adding $3 to profit (now $9). If the fourth unit were produced, only $7 would be added to revenue but $10 would be added to cost, decreasing profit by $3. The monopolist should, therefore, produce 3 units of output. Profit is maximized at P = 15, where profit is $9.

Once the monopolist selects an output level of 3 units, it will charge the price of $15 dictated by the demand schedule. The monopolist can set either price or quantity. Once one is chosen, the other will be determined by the market demand schedule. Monopolists maximize profits *either* by selecting the profit-maximizing output level and letting the market set its price *or* by selecting the profit-maximizing price and letting the demand curve determine the quantity of output.

Figure 3 shows a graph of the same monopoly profit maximization. The demand schedule is graphed as the demand curve D; the marginal revenue schedule is graphed as curve MR. When output is two units, marginal revenue exceeds marginal cost (point *m* is higher than point *n*), so profits rise if more than two units are produced. When output is four units, marginal revenue is less than marginal cost (point *r* is lower than point *q*), so profits rise if fewer than four units are produced.

Once again, to maximize profit the monopolist selects that output at which marginal revenue and marginal cost are equal. The MR and MC curves intersect at point *a*. We can determine the output level, price, and profit per unit of output by drawing a vertical line through *a*. That point at which the vertical line crosses the horizontal axis (at point *g*) is the monopolist's output level (three units). The price corresponding to the point where the vertical line intersects the demand curve (at point *c*) is the monopolist's price ($15). The point at which the vertical line intersects the ATC curve (at point *b*) is the average total cost of producing three units ($12). The distance between *c* and *b* ($15 − $12) represents the economic profit per unit of output ($3). Total economic profit is, therefore, profit per unit times the number of units, or the shaded area of the rectangle *cbed*. Algebraically, total economic profit = (P − ATC) × Q = 3 × 3 = 9.

## MONOPOLY PROFITS IN THE LONG RUN

When there is competition in an industry, the distinction between the short run and the long run is critical. In the short run, the number of firms in the industry is fixed; in the long run, new firms can enter or old firms can exit in response to economic profits or losses. This long-run entry and exit of firms ensures that economic profits will be squeezed out of perfectly competitive industries. In the case of the monopolist, the distinction between the short run and the long run is not as important because barriers prevent new firms from entering the industry and systematically eliminating monopoly profits.

> Unlike competitive profits, because of barriers to entry monopoly profits can persist for long periods of time.

In the real world, it is difficult to find pure monopolies because actual or potential substitutes abound and because absolute barriers to entry are rarely present. Rather, most real-world monopolies are *near monopolies,* subject to the profit squeeze in the very long run, particularly if monopoly profits are exceptionally high.

Exceptional monopoly profits have historically inspired the development of closer substitutes for the monopolist's product. The railroads' monopoly over freight transportation was eventually broken by the emergence of trucking and air freight capabilities; the

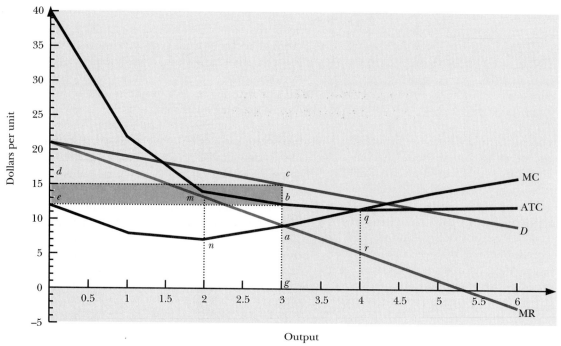

**FIGURE 3   Equilibrium of a Monopoly**

This monopolist has cost curves ATC and MC and faces demand curve *D*. However, the maximum profit occurs where MR = MC. The equilibrium price/quantity combination is found by drawing a vertical line from the demand curve through point *a*, where MR = MC, down to the horizontal axis. The output level represented by point *g*, where the vertical line hits the horizontal axis, gives the optimal output level (three units). The price corresponding to point *c*, where the vertical line hits the demand curve, is the optimal price ($15). Profits are represented by the rectangle *cbed*.

Bell System's monopoly over long-distance telephone service was broken by the advent of microwave transmission.

Although monopoly profits are not systematically driven down to the normal return, there is a tendency for high monopoly profits to inspire the development of substitutes in the very long run. (See Example 2.)

## AN OVERVIEW OF MONOPOLY

Our analysis sheds light on some basic facts concerning monopoly.

1. *Monopoly profits are persistent.* Barriers to entry protect monopoly profits, although in the very long run substitutes may be developed.

2. *Monopolists need not produce where average costs are minimized.* In the long run, perfectly com-

petitive firms will be forced to produce that quantity of output at which average costs are minimized. Monopolists, however, both in the long run and in the short run, may produce a level of output that is smaller than or larger than the level necessary to minimize average costs. In Figure 3, average total cost is minimized at an output of four units, but the monopolist produces only three units. In this sense, monopolists are less efficient than perfectly competitive firms.

3. *Monopolists charge a price higher than marginal cost.* The monopolist equates marginal revenue and marginal cost, and price is greater than marginal revenue. Thus, in the case of monopoly, *P* > MC.

4. *Monopolists produce where demand is elastic.* The profit-maximizing monopolist produces that quantity of output at which MR = MC. We have demonstrated that marginal revenue is positive only when demand is elastic. If the monopolist were to expand into the inelastic portion of the demand schedule, total revenue would decline and the firm's prof-

## EXAMPLE 2
## HOW LONG WILL THE
## INTEL MONOPOLY LAST?

Although not well known to the public, few companies have dominated their industry like Intel. After inventing the microprocessor in the early 1970s, Intel's microprocessors—the chips of silicon brain of every PC—operate 90 percent of the several hundred million PCs operating today. Intel achieved this dominance by learning how to manufacture better and smarter microprocessors at lower and lower prices. Intel's chips went into every IBM-compatible computer, and they became the industry standard.

All monopolies are meant to be broken sooner or later. For the first time, Intel faces a formidable challenge from a much-heralded new chip, the PowerPC, jointly developed by Apple, IBM, and Motorola. The PowerPC is said to operate better in a multimedia environment, which combines data processing with sound, graphics, and video.

The battle for control of the present generation of microprocessors—Intel's Pentium or the PowerPC—has cost billions of dollars of research. Only time will tell whether Intel can withstand this challenge.

----------------------------------------

*Source:* "Chipping at Intel," *Newsweek,* February 21, 1994, pp. 70–72.

---

its would fall. We can use this characteristic of monopoly pricing as a partial test for the existence of monopoly behavior. If the demand for a product is inelastic at the current price, the seller is not behaving like a profit-maximizing monopoly.

5. *There is no supply curve for monopolists.* The monopolist does not have a supply curve showing how much output will be supplied at different prices because the monopolist chooses the price. The same marginal revenue can be compatible with quite different prices, depending on the elasticity of demand.

## THE THEORY OF MONOPOLISTIC COMPETITION

In reality, few price makers are monopolies. Price makers can be anything from pure monopolies to firms that bear a close resemblance to perfect competitors. Their common characteristic is that they face a downward-sloping demand schedule for their product. In order to sell more, they must lower their price.

In the real world, there is usually some basis for distinguishing between the goods and services produced by different sellers. These distinctions may be based on the physical attributes of the product (ham-

burgers vary from restaurant to restaurant), on location (one gas station is more conveniently located than another), on the type of service offered (one dry cleaner offers 2-hour service; another offers 1-day service), and even on imagined differences (one type of aspirin is "better" than another). The point is that there are differences among products. Sellers of each product have some monopoly power over the customers who have a preference for their product. The extent of their monopoly power depends upon the strength of this preference.

The theory of monopolistic competition was developed by the American economist Edward Chamberlin and the English economist Joan Robinson in order to describe markets that produce heterogeneous products. A monopolistically competitive industry is one that blends features of monopoly and competition.

In an industry characterized by **monopolistic competition,**

1. The number of sellers is large enough to enable each seller to act independently of the others.

2. The product is differentiated from seller to seller.

Free Exit + Entrance Drives profit to zero

3. There is free entry into and exit from the industry.

4. Sellers are price makers.

When sellers are acting independently, each presumes that its output or price decisions have no discernible effect on the rest of the market. Therefore, the monopolistic competitor need not worry about the reactions of rivals.

The price-making ability follows from product differentiation; because products differ, the seller has some control over price. The degree of control may be quite limited, but it exists. The seller who raises the price will not lose all customers (as would the perfect competitor) because some will have such a strong preference that they will accept the higher price.

## PROFIT MAXIMIZATION BY THE MONOPOLISTICALLY COMPETITIVE FIRM

To maximize profits, firms produce that quantity of output at which marginal revenue equals marginal cost. The monopolistic competitor is no exception to this rule; that is, MR = MC. Like the monopolist, the monopolistic competitor faces a downward-sloping demand curve; marginal revenue is less than average revenue (price). It, therefore, selects the *quantity* at which marginal revenue equals marginal cost and charges the *price* that clears the market for its good. Analytically, in the short run the theory of monopolistic competition is the same as the theory of the monopoly. The analyses of Table 1 and Figure 3 apply equally to monopolistic competition and monopoly in the short run.

Indeed, in the short run, the main difference between monopolistic competition and monopoly is the price elasticity facing the firm. Because a monopolistic competitor faces more competition from the substitute products of other firms in the industry, its price elasticity of demand will greatly exceed that of a typical monopolist.

In the long run, however, the two types of market organization are strikingly different. *Barriers to entry* protect the monopolist from competitors. The entry of new firms will not systematically squeeze out monopoly profits. Monopolistic competition, however, shares with perfect competition the characteristic of *freedom of entry*. Thus, if a monopolistic competitor earns economic profits in the short run, new firms can (and will) enter the market, gain access to those profits, and even-

tually drive them down to zero. Long-run equilibrium requires that price be equal to average costs.

One example of a monopolistic competitor is a service station located on a busy intersection. It may earn substantial economic profits in the short run. Like a profitable monopolist, its price is greater than average total cost after equating marginal revenue and marginal cost. If the station were a monopolist (say, a gas station with an exclusive franchise along a tollroad), new firms could not gain access to these profits, and the monopoly could continue to earn them for a long period of time. This is not the case with the monopolistic competitor.

In the long run, new firms can enter the monopolistically competitive market. Attracted by high profits, a competitor can build another service station on the opposite corner of the intersection—a close but not perfect substitute. The two stations can differ in terms of access, number of gas pumps, friendliness of service, and operating hours. The entry of the second firm will have two effects on the demand schedule of the first: (1) When customers are attracted away from the first station, the demand schedule for its product will shift to the left. (2) Because buyers now have more substitutes for the product of the first station, its demand schedule will become more elastic. If both stations continue to make economic profits, even more gas stations will be built—perhaps one or two more at the same intersection. Each new entrant will reduce the demand facing other stations and increase its price elasticity. As in the case of perfect competition, this adjustment process ends when economic profits have been eliminated.

The long-run equilibrium of a typical monopolistically competitive firm is shown in Figure 4. In the long run, new firms will enter until economic profits are driven down to zero. The relevant cost curve is the long-run average cost (LRAC) curve because revenue must cover costs in the long run. Graphically, profits equal zero at a point to the left of the lowest point on the LRAC curve, where the downward-sloping demand curve is tangent to the LRAC curve. In Figure 4, point *b*—at which output is 600 units and price is $10—is the point of zero profits and, therefore, the point of long-run equilibrium. In Figure 4, 600 units is the quantity that equates marginal cost and marginal revenue, and $10 is the price that corresponds to 600 units on the demand curve. Therefore, point *b* is the point of maximum profit. To see this differently, you might notice that because the demand curve is tangent to the LRAC curve at

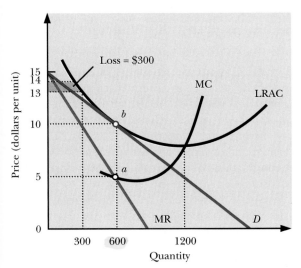

**FIGURE 4    The Long-Run Equilibrium of a Monopolistically Competitive Firm**

A firm engaged in monopolistic competition faces a downward-sloping demand curve such as $D$. In the long run, because of free entry, economic profits will be driven down to zero. Thus, the long-run equilibrium must be a point such as $b$, where $D$ is just tangent to the LRAC curve. For any price other than \$10, profits are negative. Profits, though equal to zero, are at a maximum when price is \$10 and output is 600 units, indicating that marginal revenue must equal marginal cost at 600 units. Thus, the MC and MR curves must intersect directly below point $b$.

point $b$, price is less than long-run average cost to the left or to the right of point $b$. Thus, although profit is zero at point $b$, it is negative elsewhere. For example, at an output of 300 units, price is \$13 and long-run average cost is \$14, resulting in a loss of \$1 per unit. We know that profits are always maximized where marginal cost equals marginal revenue. Accordingly, the MC and MR curves must intersect directly below the tangency of the demand curve and LRAC curve at point $b$, as Figure 4 illustrates.

The minimum unit cost output, or optimum capacity, is clearly 1200 units in Figure 4 because at that output level, MC = LRAC. In long-run equilibrium, each firm in a monopolistically competitive industry will produce an output that is smaller than the optimal capacity. This smaller-than-optimal output results because the demand curve is downward sloping and tangent to the long-run average cost curve. Thus, there is *excess capacity,* making monopolistic competition less efficient than perfect competition. This need not mean that monopolistic competition is

less socially desirable than perfect competition, since many economists regard such excess capacity as the price we must pay for variety.

## PRODUCT DIFFERENTIATION AND ADVERTISING

The threat of the entry of new firms and the loss of economic profits are facts of life for monopolistic competitors. If they can erect artificial barriers to entry (by exclusive government franchises, licensing, or zoning ordinances), they can delay the day when their economic profits are driven down to zero. Another tactic for protecting economic profits is to engage in nonprice competition. Since monopolistic competitors, by definition, produce goods and services that are somewhat different, if they can succeed in further differentiating their products from those of their competitors, they can gain loyalty. The stronger this customer loyalty, the smaller will be the loss of customers as new firms enter and the less elastic will be the demand for a product.

> **Nonprice competition** is the attempt to attract customers through improvements in product quality or service, thereby shifting the firm's demand curve to the right.

Advertising is frequently used to differentiate products in monopolistically competitive markets. In fact, nonprice competition can yield considerable short-run profits for a firm and offer potential long-run profits if new entrants cannot copy the nonprice attribute. Profits on some brand-name products, such as Bayer aspirin or Borden's condensed milk, have persisted for very long periods of time. In other cases, profits are transitory. If the gas station owner differentiates the product by staying open all night or by offering a free car wash with fill-ups, then competitors can do the same.

## APPLICATIONS

The theories of monopoly and monopolistic competition explain a variety of behavior patterns exhibited by price-making firms, including price discrimination and improvements in product durability. These two examples, in particular, are accounted for by the theory of price making, which holds that both monopolists and monopolistic competitors produce that quantity of output at which marginal revenue equals marginal cost.

## PRICE DISCRIMINATION

Thus far, this chapter has assumed that the price maker charges a single price to all buyers, but this is not always the case. Customers often pay different prices for the same product. Senior citizens typically pay less for movie tickets, airline fares, and sporting events; doctors and lawyers often charge wealthy clients more than poor clients. All of these situations are examples of price discrimination.

> **Price discrimination** exists when the same product or service is sold at different prices to different buyers.

In order for firms to engage in price discrimination,

1. The seller must exercise some control over the price (price discrimination is possible only for price makers).
2. The seller must be able to distinguish easily among different types of customers.

3. It must be impossible for one buyer to resell the product to other buyers.

If the firm is not a price maker, it cannot control its price. The seller that cannot distinguish between customers will not know to which buyers it should charge the lower price. The electric company can readily distinguish residential from industrial users; doctors and lawyers can often identify wealthy clients on the basis of appearance, home address, and stated profession. If one buyer can sell to another, then low-price buyers can sell to high-price buyers and no one will be willing to pay the high price. Thus, poor clients cannot resell legal and medical services to the wealthy, and industrial users of electricity cannot sell their electricity to households.

If the forgoing conditions are met, the seller can divide the market into various noncompeting groups. A profit-maximizing seller will then charge prices according to the price elasticity of demand of each group. The higher the price elasticity of demand, the lower will be the price charged. For example, if working adults have a less elastic demand for newspapers than do retired adults, it pays the newspaper to charge a higher price to working adults.

(*a*) The Retired Market

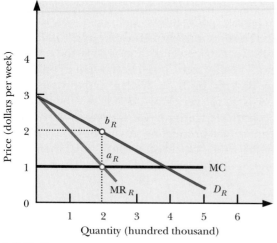

(*b*) The Workers' Market

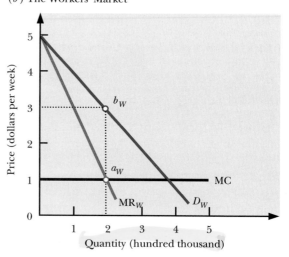

**FIGURE 5    Price Discrimination: Newspapers**

The demand and marginal revenue curves of retired customers are drawn as $D_R$ and $MR_R$ in panel *(a)*. They are more elastic than the demand and marginal revenue curves ($D_W$ and $MR_W$) of working customers in panel *(b)*. The marginal cost of providing newspapers is the same for both customers and is constant at \$1 per week. The newspaper will maximize profits in each market by equating marginal revenue and marginal cost in each market. In the workers' segment, MR = MC at a price of \$3; in the retired segment, MR = MC at a price of \$2.

Price makers see that they can achieve a substantial increase in sales by *lowering* prices in price-sensitive markets. They also see that they don't lose many sales by *raising* prices in price-insensitive markets. Hence, they will end up charging different prices in each market.

Figure 5 graphs a specific case of price discrimination. Panel (*a*) shows the demand curve of retired readers, $D_R$; panel (*b*) shows the demand curve of working readers, $D_W$. The marginal revenue curve in panel (*a*) is $M_R$ and in panel (*b*) is $MR_W$. The marginal cost (MC) of weekly newspaper service is assumed to be $1.

The newspaper equates marginal revenue and marginal cost in each market by charging $3 to working readers (whose price elasticity is 1.5) and by charging $2 to retired readers (whose price elasticity is 2). The $3 workers price corresponds to the output quantity that equates marginal cost and workers' marginal revenue; the $2 retirees' price corresponds to the output quantity that equates marginal cost and retired marginal revenue. Thus, the monopolist exploits the differences in demand elasticities by charging different prices in order to earn more profit. (See Example 3 on page 207.)

## PRODUCT DURABILITY

Tires, cars, light bulbs, television sets, and no-run pantyhose are just a few of the products whose durability—the amount of time they last—has been remarkably increased over the years. These improvements in durability are a prediction of economic theory. If there is competition, it is clear that firms will want to extend the life of their products in order to avoid losing business. What about monopoly? Many of us might assume that a monopoly would want to suppress durability because it would hurt future sales. But we know from the text that even monopolies will want to extend their product durability as far as costs permit.

As a simple example, let's consider a monopolist that discovers a costless method of doubling the life of a light bulb; that is, the monopoly learns that it can continue to produce a light bulb for the same marginal cost, but the bulb will now last twice as many hours. Will the monopolist introduce the new light bulbs? Clearly, this discovery would cut the cost of producing a *light bulb hour* in half. This monopolist could increase its profits just by doubling the price of the (improved) product and cutting the output in half because the price of a light bulb hour would remain the same. To keep the example simple, if the price of a two-hour bulb were twice the price of a one-hour bulb, people could satisfy their demand by buying half as many light bulbs each period as before. If the firm maintained the price of a light bulb hour (by doubling the price of a light bulb), the firm's profits would rise because revenue would stay the same while costs fell. As Figure 6 shows, however, the firm could do even better. Note that in Figure 6 everything is measured in terms of *light bulb hours* rather than in terms of *light bulbs*. Because the firm's marginal cost of producing light bulb hours has fallen, it would pay the firm to reduce the price per light bulb hour in order to equate marginal revenue and marginal cost. In Figure 6, the firm increases its profits by charging $5 per light bulb hour ($10 per bulb) for its improved bulb.

Business firms do not extend the durability of all goods because of the cost involved. To produce a space vehicle with virtually no chance of breaking down costs millions of dollars; the cost could be reduced dramatically if all the backup systems and safety checks were eliminated. Similarly, to produce more durable cars requires certain trade-offs: either the car must have a higher price (like the Mercedes-Benz or Rolls-Royce), or other characteristics—such as style and handling performance—must be sacrificed (as in the Chevrolet).

In this chapter we have examined the price-making behavior of monopolists and monopolistic competitors. In the chapter that follows we shall evaluate monopoly and monopolistic competition in relation to perfect competition. Characteristics that will be important in such a comparison include (1) the fact that monopolists are not pressured to produce at minimum average cost in the long run and (2) the fact that price makers do not equate marginal cost and price.

## SUMMARY

1. A pure monopoly exists when a market contains only one seller producing a product that has no close substitutes. Barriers to entry keep out competitors. The monopolist is a price maker with considerable control over price. Pure monopoly is rare in the real world because of the existence of substitutes and the absence of absolute barriers to entry,

(a) 1 Light Bulb = 1 Light Bulb Hour

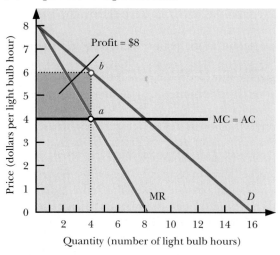

(b) 1 Light Bulb = 2 Light Bulb Hours

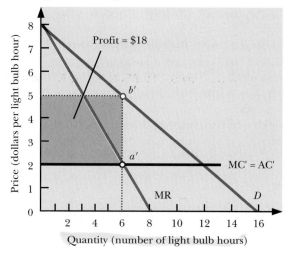

**FIGURE 6    Light Bulb Durability and Monopoly Profits**

The demand curve D shows the demand for light bulb hours (not light bulbs). Panel (a) shows a situation where 1 light bulb equals 1 light bulb hour (each light bulb burns only 1 hour). If the marginal cost of a light bulb is $4, monopoly profits are maximized where output is 4 bulbs, where marginal revenue equals $4, and where price equals $6. Monopoly profits are $8. A costless doubling of light bulb durability (to make 1 light bulb burn 2 light bulb hours) is shown in panel (b). Marginal cost per light bulb hour is now reduced to $2, but demand remains the same. The monopolist now maximizes profit at an output level of 6 light bulb hours (= 3 bulbs). The monopoly price is now $5 per light bulb hour, and monopoly profit equals $18.

especially in the long run. Sources of monopoly include economies of scale, economies of scope, patents, ownership of critical raw materials, public franchises, and licensing.

2. Price makers face downward-sloping demand curves; they must lower their price in order to sell more. For price makers, price exceeds marginal revenue. Marginal revenue is positive when demand is elastic; marginal revenue is negative when demand is inelastic.

3. Monopolists maximize profits by producing that output quantity at which marginal revenue and marginal cost are equal or by changing that price at which MR = MC.

4. Monopolists do not produce where price equals marginal cost. Monopolists need not produce in the long run where average costs are minimized. Monopolists produce where demand is elastic.

5. A monopolistically competitive industry has a large number of individual firms that are price makers selling differentiated products, with freedom of entry and exit. Monopolistic competitors, like monopolists, produce where marginal revenue equals marginal cost. In the long run, the entry of new firms will drive profits down to zero. When profits are zero and MR = MC, the firm's output will be less than the minimum efficient scale; that is, unit costs are not minimized as in perfect competition. By engaging in nonprice competition—through product differentiation and advertising—monopolistically competitive firms can delay the disappearance of economic profits.

6. Price makers can raise their profits through price discrimination. Buyers with inelastic demand will pay higher prices than those with elastic demand. Product durability will depend upon the cost of supplying durability.

KEY TERMS

pure monopoly                 economies of scope
natural monopoly              price maker

## EXAMPLE 3
## PRICE DISCRIMINATION: MANUFACTURERS' COUPONS

Grocery shoppers are familiar with manufacturers' coupons that arrive through the mail or can be clipped out of the daily newspaper. Economic theory explains why some manufacturers offer coupons and others do not. In effect, the holder of the coupon is entitled to buy the product at a lower price than others. If Nabisco places a coupon offering a 50¢ discount on one of their cereals in the daily newspaper, this means that a customer can buy the cereal at a lower price than other shoppers. Manufacturers' coupons are a form of price discrimination. The coupon issuer reasons as follows: Anyone taking the trouble to cut out the coupon has a higher elasticity of demand than other shoppers. Without the 50¢ off, many shoppers would not buy the cereal. The 50¢ reduction, therefore, brings about a substantial increase in quantity purchased from careful shoppers. Shoppers not tak-

ing the trouble to clip out the coupon have a lower price elasticity of demand. Their purchases are not strongly affected by the 50¢ price reduction. We have seen that price discrimination is possible only when the manufacturer has price-making power, when high-price elasticity customers can be identified, and when low-price buyers cannot resell the product. Manufacturers' coupons follow this pattern. Typically, manufacturers in highly concentrated markets (with only a few sellers), such as cereal or soap manufacturers, offer coupons. Such manufacturers exercise significant market power. Requiring coupons to obtain the lower price allows manufacturers to differentiate high-elasticity from low-elasticity customers. Although low-price buyers could theoretically sell to high-price buyers, the price difference usually is not great enough to yield this result.

marginal revenue (MR)
average revenue (AR)
halfway rule

monopolistic competition
nonprice competition
price discrimination

## QUESTIONS AND PROBLEMS

1. Firm A can sell all it wants at a price of $5. Firm B must lower its price from $6 to $5 to sell more output. Explain why the marginal revenue of Firm A is not the same as the marginal revenue of Firm B even though they are both charging a $5 price.
2. Evaluate the validity of the following statement: "The shutdown rule applies only to firms operating in competitive markets and does not concern monopolies."
3. Explain why a price maker can choose either its profit-maximizing output level or its profit-maximizing price. Why can it choose only one, not both?
4. A monopolist produces 100 units of output, and the price elasticity of demand at this point

on the demand curve is 0.5. What advice would you give the monopolist? From this information, what can you say about marginal revenue?
5. A price maker produces output at a constant marginal cost of $5 and has no fixed costs. The demand schedule facing the price maker is indicated in Table A.
   a. Determine the price maker's profit-maximizing output, price, and profit.
   b. What will happen to profit if the firm produces more output? Less output? Why?
   c. Explain what happens to marginal revenue when output is raised from 15 to 20 units.

| Table A | |
| --- | --- |
| Price (dollars) | Quantity Demanded (units) |
| 12 | 0 |
| 10 | 5 |
| 8 | 10 |
| 6 | 15 |
| 4 | 20 |

6. A food concession in a sports stadium makes an economic profit of $100,000 in the first year of operation. Explain what will happen to profits in subsequent years under the following conditions.
   a. The concessionaire is granted an exclusive franchise to stadium concessions.
   b. Potential competitors have the freedom to set up concession stands in the stadium.
   In the latter case, can the concessionaire do anything to protect long-run profits?

7. Prices of tickets to movies, sports events, and concerts are typically lower for children and the elderly than for working-age adults. Explain why, using the theory of price discrimination.

8. Explain why the entry of new firms into a monopolistically competitive market makes the demand curves of established firms more elastic.

9. Assume a monopoly is making an economic profit. The monopoly is sold to the highest bidder. Will the new owner make an economic profit? Why or why not?

10. Suppose the price at which a monopolist can sell its product is $P = 10 - Q$, where $Q$ is the number of units sold per period. The monopolist's MC = ATC = $4.
    a. Graph the demand curve.
    b. Graph total revenue for output levels from 0 units to 10 units.
    c. Graph the marginal revenue at each output level.
    d. Which output level maximizes profit?
    e. How much is maximum profit?

11. A monopolist is making an economic profit of $100,000 per year. Explain what will happen to the monopolist's price and output if:
    a. The government imposes a fixed tax of $90,000 per year on the monopolist.
    b. The government imposes a fixed tax of $110,000 per year on the monopolist.

12. What advice would you give to a monopolist that is setting output to maximize revenue?

13. Evaluate the validity of the following statement: "The medical care industry is not a monopoly because the price elasticity of demand for medical care is less than unity. Monopolists would charge prices higher than current ones."

14. Explain why marginal revenue is less than price for a price maker.

15. How does monopolistic competition differ from monopoly?

16. A natural water fountain is discovered in the middle of a city. The demand schedule for the drinking water is shown in Table B. There is no cost of production.
    a. Draw the demand curve.
    b. Use the halfway rule to derive the marginal revenue curve.
    c. How would the city maximize its revenues from the water fountain?

| Table B | |
| --- | --- |
| Price (cents per drink) | Quantity Demanded (drinks per day) |
| 6 | 0 |
| 5 | 10 |
| 4 | 20 |
| 3 | 30 |
| 2 | 40 |
| 1 | 50 |
| 0 | 60 |

17. Which of the following are examples of price discrimination?
    a. Discount coupons
    b. First-class airline tickets
    c. Stand-by tickets
    d. More expensive seaside rooms in a hotel

# CHAPTER 12

# COMPETITION, EFFICIENCY, AND INNOVATION

"Greed is good," said the fictional financier Gordon Gecko in the movie *Wall Street*. Greed drives competition, monopoly, new products, and new ways of doing things. Is greed good?

Historians write about the late nineteenth century as the period of the Robber Barons, when people such as John D. Rockefeller and J. Pierpont Morgan amassed unbelievable wealth. During the late 1870s and 1880s, workers complained of low wages, and farmers of low prices and high railroad tariffs. We might think that greed was causing the economy to collapse. Yet the United States came out of this period the greatest economic power the world has ever known.

Some analysts credit the economic growth and stock market boom of recent years to the "greed" of the Robber Barons of the 1980s, the junk bond dealers, the corporate takeover specialists, who raised capital and provided new management for the restructuring of U.S. industry.

In this chapter we explore the static and dynamic implications of profit maximization (greed?) in a world of competition and monopoly. We compare the efficiency of competition with that of monopoly, and we examine the logic of patents, the consequences of externalities, and, finally, the link between new products and the desire for profits.

# THE EFFICIENCY OF COMPETITION

Ever since Adam Smith argued that the invisible hand of competition would guide profit-maximizing producers and utility-maximizing consumers to an efficient allocation of society's resources, economists have been captivated by its appeal. The antitrust laws of the United States, for example, have attempted to make a competitive order the law of the land.

We know from the chapter on perfect competition that competition forces an industry to produce where the price of the product just equals the lowest unit production cost. If the price were any higher than the minimum unit cost, someone could make a profit from producing the good at that cost. Competition is efficient because it utilizes *given* resources and *given* technology in such a way that the cost of producing the desired output of the society is as low as possible. In short, all resources and all technical know-how are being used in the best possible way. Nothing is being wasted. Since the economy consists of many industries, efficiency in each industry indicates that the economy is producing the largest possible output with its given resources and technology.

> **Economic efficiency** means that the economy is producing the maximum output of useful things with its given resources and technology.

## PRICES AND ECONOMIC EFFICIENCY

**Prices Matter.**  In perfectly competitive markets, economic efficiency also results from the right balance between consumer utility and costs of production. The competitive price will reflect this balance.

Consumers buy an enormous variety of goods—milk, shirts, cars, housing, bread, and so on. As discussed in the chapter on demand and utility, well-informed, rational consumers carry out their purchases of any particular good until the ratio of its marginal utility (MU) to price is the same as that for all other goods. Individual consumers follow consumption patterns in which the prices of the goods they buy reflect the marginal utilities of those goods: low-priced goods have low MUs, and high-priced goods have high MUs. Thus, the price of a good is a dollar measure of the good's marginal utility to the individual; indeed, we can say that the marginal benefit of the good to the consumer equals its price. Because in a perfectly competitive market the price is the same for all buyers and sellers, each consumer has the same marginal benefits.

> The price of a good measures its marginal benefit to society because each utility-maximizing consumer equates the good's MU/P ratio to that of all other goods.

Now let's consider the other side of the market, the competitive firms that produce the various goods. Each producer will expand production until price and marginal cost are equal. As long as price exceeds marginal cost, the competitive producer finds profit opportunities. These are exhausted when diminishing returns drive marginal cost up to the level of price.

> In a perfectly competitive industry, every producer faces the same price and expands production to the point where marginal cost equals price. Therefore, each producer has the same marginal cost of production. The marginal cost of bread for one producer, which equals the marginal cost for other producers, is the same as the marginal cost of bread to society.

Society's cost of producing a good is minimized when each producer has the same marginal cost. If a good is produced by firms at different marginal costs, the same quantity of the total cost to society can be lowered if production is shifted from high-marginal-cost producers to low-marginal-cost producers. Market equilibrium is the state in which a good is produced at minimum cost in a quantity that yields a marginal benefit (price) equal to marginal cost. An economy at market equilibrium is efficient; $P = $ MC, markets have cleared, and opportunities to increase profits have been exhausted.

## MEASURING ECONOMIC INEFFICIENCY

It is possible to measure economic inefficiency. Let's imagine that for some reason a good is being produced at a level where $P > $ MC. The difference between price and marginal cost not only represents a profit opportunity for individual producers but also signals a social opportunity. If $P > $ MC, society will benefit from producing more of the good. Remember that marginal cost is the opportunity cost at the margin—the value of what is being given up elsewhere. To say that price exceeds marginal cost is to say that the resources used in the production of this particular good have a higher marginal benefit to society in this use than in any other.

In Figure 1, the equilibrium quantity is 8000 units of output. Suppose for some reason that output is only 5000 units. The marginal cost to society is $70 (at point *a*), and the marginal benefit to society is $120 (at point *b*). Moving from an output of 5000 units to an output of 8000 units benefits society by the green area *abc*. Point *c* is an efficient output level. Economic efficiency is achieved when resources are allocated such that no one can be made better off by reallocating resources without making someone else worse off.

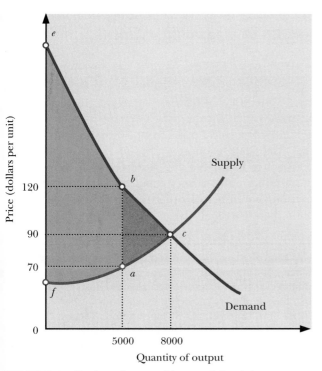

**FIGURE 1   Perfect Competition and Social Efficiency**

When output is restricted to 5000 units, the marginal cost of the 5001st unit of output is the price at point *a*, or $70; the marginal benefit is the price at point *b*, or $120. Moving to the equilibrium quantity of 8000 units results in a net gain to society of area *abc* because marginal benefits exceed marginal costs on the intervening 3000 units. Social efficiency is achieved when the price is $90 and the total of consumer and producer surplus equals area *ecf*.

If price does not equal marginal cost for all goods, there is inefficiency in the system. Resources are allocated efficiently when price equals marginal cost.

## THE ECONOMIC INEFFICIENCY OF MONOPOLY

### SOURCES OF INEFFICIENCY IN MONOPOLY

Monopoly has two sources of inefficiency. First, monopoly leads to contrived scarcities. Second, the resources used to acquire monopoly power can be better employed elsewhere in the economy.

### CONTRIVED SCARCITY

The main argument against monopoly is that monopolies maximize profit by restricting output to the scale where price exceeds marginal cost. We know that monopolies maximize profit where MR = MC, but $P > $ MR. Therefore, price will exceed marginal cost at the output that maximizes monopoly profit.

> Price measures marginal benefit to society, and marginal cost measures marginal cost to society (if externalities are not present); therefore, when $P > $ MC, there is contrived scarcity in the economy.

Contrived scarcity occurs when the economy would be more efficient—in the sense of giving more to everyone—if more of the monopolized good were produced.

> **Contrived scarcity** is the production of less than the economically efficient quantity of a good by a monopoly.

When $P > $ MC, 1 more unit of output adds more to social benefits than to social costs, so it is possible to rearrange the allocation of resources (to produce more of the monopolized good and less of other goods) to make everyone better off.

To compare monopoly with perfect competition, consider an industry in which both are possible. Figure 2 depicts an industry in which there are no economies of scale; to simplify the comparison, average costs are the same for each level of output. Therefore, average cost and marginal cost are the same:

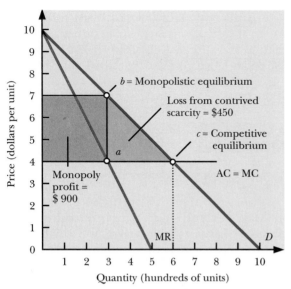

**FIGURE 2  Monopoly and Competition Compared**

This industry has constant returns to scale where AC = MC = $4 for all levels of output. If the industry were perfectly competitive, price would be $4 and output would be 600 units. If this industry were a single-firm monopoly, price would be $7 and output would be 300 units, with a monopoly profit of $900 (= $3 × 300). Monopoly profit is the green-shaded area. The monopolist creates profits through the contrived scarcity of 300 units (the monopolist produces 300 units less than the competitive industry). The loss from contrived scarcity is the red area, which equals $450, or the deadweight loss to society. Moving from monopoly to competition creates consumer surplus of $1350 (which is the sum of $900 + $450) while destroying only $900 worth of profits for the monopolist. More is gained by all parties taken together than is lost.

AC = MC. Either one large firm (a monopoly) or a large number of small firms (a perfectly competitive market) can satisfy consumer demand at the same average cost. Marginal cost (= AC) is a constant $4 per unit. The monopoly output (300 units) is at the level where MR is also $4 (point *a*); the monopoly price is $7. Monopoly profits are represented by the green-shaded area, which equals $900. Under conditions of perfect competition, meanwhile, free entry would squeeze out economic profits. The long-run competitive price would, therefore, be $4, and the competitive output would be 600 units (point *c*).

We can calculate the cost of monopoly in this case from Figure 2. If this industry is transformed from a monopoly to perfect competition, the equilibrium price/quantity combination would shift from

point *b* to point *c,* and the price would fall from $7 to $4. The increase in consumer surplus, defined in an earlier chapter, resulting from the shift is the sum of the green-shaded area (the monopolist's profit of $900) and red-shaded area ($450), equaling $1350. But the monopolist, who is also a member of society, loses monopoly profits of $900 in the process. Therefore, the net gain to society (the consumers' gain minus the monopolist's loss) is simply the red-shaded triangle, which equals $450.[1] Notice that everyone involved is better off under the move to perfect competition. Because consumers gain $1350 in consumer surplus, they can buy off the monopolist with a payment, say $901, greater than the original monopoly profit—which would make the monopolist better off by $1 and the consumers better off by $449. The $450 loss from monopoly is a deadweight loss because nothing is received in exchange for the loss. The deadweight loss of monopoly is equivalent to throwing away valuable scarce resources. (See Example 1.)

A **deadweight loss** is a loss to society of consumer or producer surplus that is not offset by anyone else's gain.

How large are losses from contrived scarcities in the American economy? Economist Arnold Harberger has estimated the deadweight loss from all monopolies to be a very small fraction of total U.S. output. A number of other researchers roughly estimate these losses at about 1 percent of GDP.[2]

---

[1]We can calculate the deadweight loss in another way. When Q = 300 and P = $7, the difference between marginal social benefits and marginal social costs is $3 ($7 − $4). Hence, it pays society to expand output beyond the 300th unit. In effect, the 301st unit adds $3 to social welfare. The 601st unit adds nothing to social welfare because from Q = 300 to Q = 600, the extra benefit per unit declines from $3 to $0. Thus, on the average, the 300 additional units between 300 (the monopolist's output) to 600 (the output under perfect competition) add $1.50 each (the average of $3 and $0), or $450.

[2]Arnold Harberger, "Monopoly and Resource Allocation," *American Economic Review* 44 (May 1954): 77–87. We can mention only a few of the economists who have contributed to this estimate: David Schwartzman, Dean Worcester, Jr., David Kamerschen, and Michael Klass.

### EXAMPLE 1
### MONOPOLY AND COMPETITION
### IN THE SKIES OVER EUROPE

In this chapter, we consider why a monopoly produces less output than a competitive industry and charges consumers higher prices. If an industry were converted from monopoly to competition, consumers would be better off because more output would be available at lower prices.

The effects of monopoly on prices can be seen when an industry changes from being monopolistic to being competitive. An example of an industry in such a transition is the European passenger airline industry. Prior to the 1990s, only the national airlines had the right to provide service between two cities in different countries. For example, only Swissair and Lufthansa were entitled to fly passengers between Frankfurt and Zurich. Moreover, prevailing rules required that each national airline provide the same number of flights and that revenues be divided equally between them. By blocking entry of competitors into these markets, this system allowed the national airlines to charge monopoly prices. Air-

fares within Europe have been more than double those in the United States, a market in which different airlines are allowed to compete for customers.

Following the American deregulation example, the European airlines have begun to phase in competition. More landing rights are being given to private airline companies, and third-country national airlines will be allowed to serve markets from which they had previously been excluded (for example, Swissair would be allowed to fly between London and Copenhagen). European airfares have begun to drop. For example, British Air has entered the German market and has driven down prices. The national airlines will lose their monopoly profits, but the public will gain millions of dollars of consumer surplus from the lower fares. As Figure 2 in the text showed, the consumers' gain outweighs the loss of monopoly profits.

## MONOPOLY RENT-SEEKING BEHAVIOR

The previously cited estimates of the deadweight losses from monopoly represent lower bounds to the true loss of society from monopoly.[3] In terms of Figure 2, if the industry were perfectly competitive, the price/quantity combination would be $4/600 units, or point c, and there would be no deadweight loss. If someone could turn this industry into a monopoly through political activities, that person could gain the potential monopoly profit of $900 (green-shaded area). People would be willing to spend real re-

sources—or engage in what we will call rent-seeking behavior—to turn the industry into a monopoly and acquire the monopoly profit. We should think of the monopoly profit as the rent received in return for expending the resources needed to turn a competitive industry into a monopoly or to maintain an existing monopoly.

> **Monopoly rent-seeking behavior** is the use of scarce resources on lobbying and influence-buying to acquire monopoly rights from government.

In the extreme case, *all* monopoly profits are spent by the persons engaging in monopoly rent-seeking behavior, thereby multiplying the deadweight loss of monopoly. Not only do consumers lose the orange-shaded area in Figure 2 (the loss of

---

[3]Anne Krueger, "The Political Economy of the Rent-Seeking Society," *American Economic Review* 64 (June 1974): 291–303; Gordon Tullock, "The Welfare Cost of Tariffs, Monopolies, and Theft," *Western Economic Journal* 5 (June 1967): 224–232.

consumer surplus) but the monopolist does *not* gain the green-shaded area (monopoly profit).

Rent-seeking behavior does not simply apply to achieving a single-firm monopoly. Any industry in which free entry is prevented by government restrictions can achieve profits that exceed competitive levels. For example, steel companies and textile unions have lobbied Congress for protection from foreign imports. It has been estimated that there are about 100,000 lobbyists in Washington, D.C. The offices they occupy, the secretarial services they employ, their advertising budgets, and their own labor could be used elsewhere in our world of economic scarcity. Instead, lobbyists use their resources to restrict competition through government charters, franchises, regulations, and either taxes on rival competitors or subsidies for themselves.

Rent-seeking behavior can lead to substantial social losses. To limit rent-seeking behavior, the government must act to substantially lessen the possibility of "buying" monopoly power. This, however, is not an easy task. (See Example 2.)

## EXTERNALITIES

A perfectly competitive allocation of resources will be economically inefficient if externalities are present.

> **Externalities** exist when an economic activity of one party results in direct economic costs or benefits for someone else who does not control that economic activity.

Externalities arise when a factory belches black smoke that raises the cost of laundry or medical care for those people living in the vicinity, when a chemical plant dumps wastes that affect fishing and agricultural production, when a pulp mill pollutes the air others must breathe, or when an airport pollutes an area with deafening noise.

When externalities are present, the total cost to society of producing a good equals the sum of its private and external costs; the total benefit to society is the sum of its private and external benefits. The total

## EXAMPLE 2
## MONOPOLY RENT-SEEKING BEHAVIOR:
## LOBBYING AND LAWYERS

Economists are just beginning to study the effect of monopoly rent-seeking behavior on the economy. Its impact is difficult to evaluate because of the complexity of calculating the value of the resources exhausted by lobbyists attempting to create monopolies. For example, in 1991 Texas began licensing "interior designers" but not "interior decorators." This distinction in the law resulted from a seven-year effort by lobbyists aiming to protect those who meet certain requirements. This story has been repeated many times in the realm of government regulations. The efforts of a vast number of researchers would be required to evaluate this wealth of information.

Stephen Magee, William Brock, and Leslie Young have attempted to estimate the effects indirectly. They argue that lawyers are the main resource employed by monopoly rent seekers. Although lawyers are generally useful, rent-seeking increases the demand for lawyers relative to other professions. Examining a group of 34 countries, the researchers discovered a strong negative correlation between national growth rates and the national ratios of lawyers to physicians. For example, income in the United States grew at a rate of 2.3 percent between 1960 and 1980, whereas the lawyer/physician ratio during the same period was over 1.25. By contrast, Japan and Hong Kong grew at nearly 7 percent per year and had lawyer/physician ratios of only about 0.1 and 0.3, respectively.

------------------------------------------------

*Source:* S. Magee, W. Brock, and L. Young, *Black Hole Tariffs and Endogenous Political Economy in General Equilibrium* (Cambridge: Cambridge University Press, 1989), chap. 8.

costs or benefits to society of producing a good are the social costs or social benefits.

> **Social costs** are private costs plus external costs.
>
> **Social benefits** are private benefits plus external benefits.

The main effect of an externality is that the *marginal private cost* (MPC) of production does not necessarily reflect the *marginal social cost* (MSC). The marginal social cost of producing steel includes not only the marginal private costs of the steel mill but also the marginal external costs imposed on others (the extra laundry costs, medical care costs, and so on). A steel mill might not take these external costs into account when making its economic decisions.

Figure 3 shows the effects of externalities in steel production. The MSC curve measures marginal social costs, and the supply curve measures only marginal private costs (MPC). At competitive equilibrium, 1 million tons are produced at a price of $100 per ton (point *a*). With a marginal social cost of $160 per ton, the equilibrium output level constitutes too much steel production from the standpoint of society. Marginal social costs ($160) do not equal marginal social benefits ($100) because externalities are present. Efficiency requires that 0.8 million tons of steel be produced (point *e*), yielding both a marginal social cost and a price of $120.

Economic activities can have external benefits as well as external costs. When one neighbor plants flowers, surrounding neighbors also benefit. The person who considers personal pleasure to be the sole benefit from growing flowers will plant flowers only to the point where marginal costs and marginal benefits are equal. The marginal cost to the person growing the flowers does not equal the marginal benefits enjoyed by society (the neighborhood) because other neighbors gain some marginal benefits as well. The situation results in economic inefficiency because too few flowers get planted.

The problems created by externalities are not limited to conditions of perfect competition. All systems of resource allocation—from monopoly to planned socialism—are plagued by externalities. Pollution is more troublesome in socialist countries than it is in capitalist ones. The presence of externalities is a problem that the invisible hand of perfect competition does not automatically solve and that different

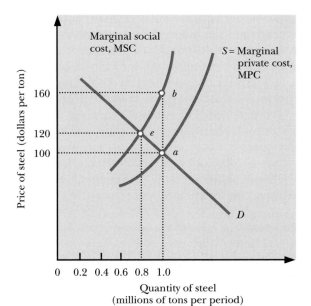

**FIGURE 3   Externalities and Competition**

The supply and demand curves of this hypothetical steel industry intersect at the price/quantity combination of $100 per ton and 1 million tons of steel (point *a*). The supply curve, *S*, reflects only marginal *private* costs. The MSC curve shows marginal *social* costs. At the equilibrium point *a*, the marginal social cost of an extra ton of steel is $160, but the marginal social benefit is only $100, as measured by the height of the demand curve. Too much steel is produced from the society's point of view.

economic systems may treat with varying degrees of success. We shall examine externalities in detail in a later chapter.

## TECHNOLOGICAL PROGRESS, PATENTS, AND COMPETITION

It is possible that competition will not be efficient in a *dynamic* (changing) situation. Perfect competition has been shown to be most efficient when resources and technology are *static* (unchanging). Some economists have argued that competition does not encourage the creation and promotion of technological change.

### PATENTS

The major rationale for *patents*—which, in the United States, give the holder a legal monopoly on a product for 17 years—is that they are necessary to spur innovation. Why should a company or individual expend time and money on an invention that can be copied by a rival firm? Thus, patents are deemed to be a price society must pay for innovation. Basically, they protect the inventors by hindering the legal development of products related to ones that have been patented. For example, consider an electronics firm that has patented a production technology that gives it a cost advantage. Its rivals will find it difficult to develop a substitute technology that does the same thing but is different enough to avoid infringement on the patent.

> A **patent** is an exclusive right granted to an inventor to make, use, or sell an invention for a term of 17 years in the United States.

Economists Edwin Mansfield, Mark Schwartz, and Samuel Wagner studied the protection a patent actually provides from competition in the real world. They concluded that patents provide surprisingly little protection from competition. In a survey of 48 product innovations, 31 of them patented, Mansfield and his associates found that patents increased the cost of legally imitating the original invention by only 11 percent. They also found that 60 percent of the patented inventions were successfully imitated within 4 years—far less than the 17-year life of the patent. They further discovered that patent protection was not essential for the development and introduction of at least 75 percent of the inventions they studied. In fact, patents have played a relatively small role in the most innovative fields of the past 25 years, electronics and bioengineering. Companies in these two fields have relied more on secrecy than on patents to protect their inventions. The major exception to this trend is the prescription-drug industry, in which patents have effectively protected inventions for long periods of time.

The research of Mansfield and his associates raises an important question: If patents do not effectively discourage imitation, are they really necessary to encourage innovation? Secrecy may be more effective. For example, companies like Coca-Cola and McDonalds have made large profits for years by keeping their recipes secret.

## NEW PRODUCTS AND MONOPOLISTIC COMPETITION

Perfect competition cannot really explain the introduction of new products because, by assumption, all firms produce the same product. Except for governmental research, such as that undertaken by the Agricultural Department, new products are introduced by individual firms. One of the virtues of both monopoly and monopolistic competition is that firms have an incentive to introduce new products. Monopolies will capture a monopoly return; monopolistic competitors will capture a return on their investment in developing new products.

Enormous variety exists in the real world. Each monopolistic competitor finds it profitable to differentiate its product from rival or competitive products. When entering a supermarket or department store we are confronted with thousands of choices. There are so many types of soft drinks, breads, shirts, suits, dresses, television sets, and so forth that few of us have tried more than a small sample of available products. There are 11,000 varieties of Seiko brand watches alone. These mind-numbing choices are the result of monopolistic competition.

To understand how monopolistic competition explains the introduction of new products, let's consider a case from the watch industry. A company decides that by putting a picture of George Foreman, the former heavyweight boxing champion, on a watch face its sales will soar from middle-aged male buyers who want a role model. George Foreman—for a price—gives the company the exclusive right to use his picture. This creates a short-term monopoly profit for the firm, as shown in Figure 4, panel (*a*). The profit is the area *abcd*. Other watch firms will see their sales dwindle to a precious few. They may then try to imitate the "Foreman watch" with the "Madonna watch." Some of the customers who would have bought a Foreman watch now decide to buy a Madonna watch. This shifts the demand curve for Foreman watches to the right, causing the firm to earn a normal return on its investment in Foreman watches. As a sufficient number of rivals enter the market, the long-run monopolistically competitive equilibrium is reached where the economic profits of the original innovator are reduced to zero (that is, a competitive return), as shown in Figure 4, panel (*b*).

This hypothetical story applies in reality to the thousands of new products that come out each year. Firms introduce new or better products in order to make a profit, and the free entry from rival firms keeps profits at a competitive level.

The proliferation of new products is actually self-reinforcing. Each new idea or invention suggests other new products that might be introduced. Sony

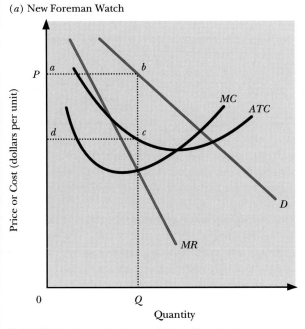

(a) New Foreman Watch

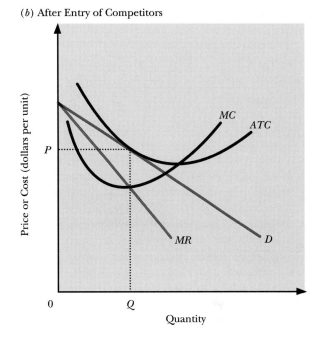

(b) After Entry of Competitors

**FIGURE 4   Introduction of New Products**

Panel (a) shows a watch company that makes profits of *abcd* after introducing a new "Foreman watch." Panel (b) shows the long-run equilibrium after competitors drive the profits from the Foreman watch to zero.

was the first to introduce the video cassette recorder (VCR); soon, other companies introduced superior VCRs using a different format. In the 1950s, television sets had poor resolution and were bulky and expensive. In the 1980s, the application of advanced electronics led to better and cheaper television sets. Communication has evolved from the telegraph and early primitive telephones to today's touch-tone direct dialing to any country, satellite transmission, answering machines, call-waiting and call-return, cordless phones, cellular phones, fax machines, fax/modems on computers, and so on, as each idea builds on a preceeding one. Thus, each new product or innovation has lowered the cost of future new products or innovations. As costs fall, profit opportunities are created for even newer products; and new products proliferate at an ever hastening pace.

Monopolistic competition is, of course, not efficient in the sense that price equals marginal cost. It is inefficient in the static sense that the given resources could be allocated more efficiently by an all-knowing and all-powerful dictator, but in the real world it is impossible to interfere with the pricing mechanism without also destroying the ability of monopolistic competition to yield a stream of new products at ever-lower costs. Thus, the static inefficiency of mo-

nopolistic competition is the price we pay for having a workable method for generating progress. (See Example 3.)

In this chapter we have examined the efficiency of competition—both perfect and monopolistic—and monopoly under the assumption that both are feasible. We have looked at the role of patents and monopolistic competition or monopoly in promoting technological progress and the introduction of new products. In the next chapter we shall examine the more complicated problems created by oligopolies.

## SUMMARY

1. Perfect competition can lead to economic efficiency. Goods are produced at lowest cost and in the right amounts. The most efficient allocation of resources occurs when $P = MC$ reflects marginal benefits and marginal costs to society at large. Interference with the $P = MC$ condition results in economic inefficiency.

2. Monopoly is inefficient because of contrived scarcity and rent-seeking behavior. Monopolists make a profit by reducing output to the point

## EXAMPLE 3
### DO YOU REMEMBER
### THE CARBURETOR?

Technological progress has been so rapid in the last 15 years that a number of products that Americans grew up with in the first three-quarters of the century are now just part of the language. We have seen the virtual disappearance of typewriters, carbon copies, rotary dial telephones, record albums, snow tires, and carburetors.

Electronic mail and faxes are rapidly displacing first-class letters and stamps. Thus it was that the typewriter was displaced by the computer, carbon copies by duplicating machines and laser printing, rotary dial phones by push-button phones, record albums by CDs, snow tires by all-season radial tires, and carburetors by electronic fuel injection. Soon, the automobile tune-up will be a thing of the past.

The change is not just in the goods we produce, but the way we produce them. The Chase Manhattan Bank of New York once had 100 data-processing centers. Powerful new computers have reduced the number of centers to only two: one in New York and one in London. Productivity has soared. When one center is overloaded, work is switched to the other.

The advanced technologies of today are the product of centuries of innovation carried out for the sake of profit.

------------------------------------------------

*Source:* "New Economy Dashes Old Notions of Growth," *New York Times,* November 27, 1994.

where $P$ exceeds MC. Rent-seeking behavior can prevent competition and can add to the social costs of monopoly power by absorbing resources in the associated lobbying.

3. Externalities exist when the decisions of one consumer or producer incidentally benefit or harm someone else who does not control the decision. In this case, perfect competition does not result in economic efficiency because $P$ and MC simply reflect private benefits and costs instead of social benefits and costs. Social efficiency requires that marginal social costs equal marginal social benefits. All market types and economic systems, however, have difficulty dealing with externalities.

4. Monopoly and monopolistic competition are more conducive to technological progress. In some cases, patents may give some firms the incentive to develop new products.

## KEY TERMS

economic efficiency
contrived scarcity
deadweight loss
externalities
social costs

social benefits
patent
economic inefficiency
monopoly rent-seeking
    behavior

## QUESTIONS AND PROBLEMS

1. Restate why $P$ = MC is the condition for economic efficiency.
2. Give examples of positive external benefits and negative external costs.
3. Why do economists claim that monopolists contrive scarcity?

4. The marginal cost of production in industry A is $8 and is equal to the average cost. The demand schedule is linear and is given in Table A. What is the deadweight loss of monopoly that results from contrived scarcity in this case? What is the maximum monopoly rent-seeking loss?

| Table A | |
|---|---|
| *Price (dollars per unit)* | *Quantity (units)* |
| 20 | 0 |
| 15 | 500 |
| 10 | 1000 |
| 5 | 1500 |
| 0 | 2000 |

5. Explain why monopolists produce too little output from the standpoint of economic efficiency.

6. Explain the resource allocation problem that would exist in a competitive market economy if the following undertakings have externalities: (a) the production of electricity by burning coal and (b) the immunization of children against communicable diseases. Draw a supply-and-demand diagram for each undertaking, indicating both the market allocation and the correct resource allocation result.

7. What does the historical evidence indicate about the relationship between the size of business firms and technological progress? Do large business enterprises hold a "monopoly" on technological innovation?

8. What is the difference between rent-seeking losses and losses that result when the monopolist produces where marginal revenue equals marginal cost?

9. Why is production at an output level where marginal cost equals marginal revenue socially inefficient for monopolies but socially efficient under perfect competition?

10. The marginal cost of production for a new drug is $2 per dozen. The demand schedule for the drug is shown in Table B.
    a. What is the monopoly price for the drug?
    b. Compare the gains that consumers would receive to the losses that the monopolist would incur if the drug were sold competitively.

| Table B | |
|---|---|
| *Price (dollars per dozen)* | *Quantity (dozens)* |
| 10 | 0 |
| 9 | 1 |
| 8 | 2 |
| 7 | 3 |
| 6 | 4 |
| 5 | 5 |
| 4 | 6 |
| 3 | 7 |

11. The Mafia obtains protection "rents" through the threat of violence, exacting payments in return for securing the physical or economic safety of one person against potential criminals or predators. Is this a form of economic rent seeking?

# CHAPTER 13

# THE GAME OF OLIGOPOLY

In 1993, cigarette companies started a price war because of the discount segment of the market. Philip Morris dropped the prices of its premium cigarettes because RJR Nabisco had lowered prices on discount brands. The price war caused the profits of Philip Morris and RJR to drop considerably. In 1994, the cigarette companies ended their price war; prices and profits both rose.

Philip Morris knows that if it lowers its prices, RJR will match them. If both companies raise prices, their individual profits are likely to increase. Why would they engage in a price war? To answer this kind of question we must understand the theory of oligopoly—the rivalry that exists between a relatively small number of large firms.

*Oligopoly* is an umbrella term that describes the market structures that fall between monopoly and monopolistic competition. The complex and varied behavior of oligopolies arises from the many different strategic situations in which the firms may find themselves. In this chapter we shall consider why some oligopolies behave more like monopolies while others behave more like competitive industries. Finally, we shall discuss how game theory—the study of rivalry—is used in the analysis of oligopoly.

## OLIGOPOLY

An oligopoly is an industry in which there are so few firms that the firms are large enough to have a significant impact on the price of the product. For example, the automobile industry in the United States is certainly an oligopoly because companies like Ford, Chrysler, and General Motors can all affect the prices of cars and trucks.

> An **oligopoly** is an industry (1) that is dominated by a few firms, (2) whose individual firms must consider the policies of their rivals in making their decisions, and (3) whose firms are price makers.

In contrast to perfect or monopolistic competition, individual oligopolists are deeply concerned with the policies of their rivals. Ford certainly not only must worry about its own pricing and product line, it also must formulate some plans about what prices and products will be offered by Toyota, Honda, Chrysler, and General Motors. The same is true for each of the others. Oligopolists think of themselves as engaging in a market game in which their profits depend on the behavior of rivals. They advertise, introduce new products, change prices, or do anything else that is acceptable in their bid to entice customers away from their rivals.

Firms like IBM, Intel, General Electric, and Ford are involved in oligopolistic industries. When we speak of "big business," it is frequently an oligopoly we have in mind. Oligopolies, however, are all around us. If a city has several newspapers, each newspaper will be principally concerned with the editorial, advertising, and pricing policies of the others in the same city. Therefore, the theory of oligopoly applies to a great many business situations involving both large and small businesses.

Mutual interdependence is the key to oligopoly behavior. In making decisions on prices, quantities, and qualities of its product, an oligopolist must consider the possible reactions of rival firms. In some cases, the pattern of reaction may be easy to anticipate for all participants. In other cases, participants must engage in strategic behavior to outguess and outmaneuver their rivals.

> **Mutual interdependence** exists when a firm recognizes that its decisions are likely to invite reactions by rivals.

Oligopolies are a diverse lot. One oligopoly will behave like a monopoly; some are far closer to perfect or monopolistic competition. Thus, there are several different ways for us to approach the study of oligopoly.

## COLLUSION

The most simple approach to oligopoly is the one suggested by Adam Smith: "People of the same trade seldom meet together, even for merriment or diversion but the conversation ends in a conspiracy against the public, or in some contrivance to raise prices." Doesn't it make sense that, say, a handful of firms that completely dominate an industry simply get together and do what's best for them?

There are several ways to conspire together on pricing and output decisions. Firms can form a cartel that assigns to each member how much output to produce or what price to charge. Alternatively, firms can sell their product at the price determined by the industry price leader.

> A **cartel** is an organization of producers whose goal is to operate the industry as a monopoly.

### CARTELS

The most notable example of a cartel in recent times is the Organization of Petroleum Exporting Countries (OPEC). OPEC had operated for many years as a loosely formed organization, but as the members noticed that their share of world output had grown to overwhelming proportions they began to act in unison. In 1973–1974, the OPEC countries quadrupled the price of oil. As this dramatic "oil shock" sent tremors through the industrial world, the profits rolled into the OPEC countries. OPEC again dramatically increased oil prices in 1979–1980. In the mid-1980s, however, turmoil in the Middle East and a falling share of world output controlled by OPEC led to a collapse of oil prices that has continued to the mid-1990s.

How does a cartel work? Each member must act on behalf of the group by restricting its output below what it would do if acting alone. When each firm restricts output, the cartel can maintain a price that is far above the marginal cost of production for each firm. Acting as perfect competitors, each firm would produce where P = MC. Acting as a cartel, each firm can make greater profits by producing at that level where the cartel's marginal revenue equals marginal cost.

To understand cartels we must make a sharp distinction between the cartel's MR and the firm's MR. The cartel's MR is the industry MR curve that is derived from the industry's demand curve. The firm's MR depends on the firm's demand curve. By cutting the price to one slightly below the cartel price, the firm can sell much more than if the cartel reduced the price slightly, because it would take business away from those firms adhering to the cartel price. Thus, the firm's MR may be only slightly less than the market price established by the cartel. If all firms but one are charging the cartel price, the cheating or deviant firm can then sell its entire output at a price slightly below the cartel price.

Figure 1 gives a simple example of a cartel: Four firms have access to a particular mineral spring. It costs $20 to produce and distribute each bottle of water. Thus, AC = MC = $20. The industry demand curve is P = 100 − Q. The industry's MR curve is MR = 100 − 2Q, since for a linear demand curve it is twice as steep. Figure 1 shows that when MR = MC = $20, the cartel produces Q = 40 at a price of P = $60. Each firm sells exactly 10 bottles. The profit per bottle is $40; thus, each firm makes a profit of $400. If three firms insist on selling at the price of $60, the remaining firm could sell as many as 45 units at a price of $55 by attracting all of the business away from the other firms. Its profit would be $35 × 45 = $1575. Thus, even if the other firms would soon follow suit, which they most certainly would, the deviant firm could make large profits for a short time. But the cartel would now break down.

The key point about the theory of cartels is that cartel members always have an incentive to cheat. This prediction of the theory of cartels is basically borne out by historical experience: Except in a few cases, cartels do not last very long. The OPEC cartel was wildly successful and lasted about 10 years. The diamond cartel lasted much longer, but it is now beginning to lose its grip. (See Example 1.) Cartels in sugar, cocoa, tin, coffee, and other commodities have failed to get a firm grip over prices.

## PRICE LEADERSHIP

Even though in the long run cartels might break down, in the short run they can be profitable for the

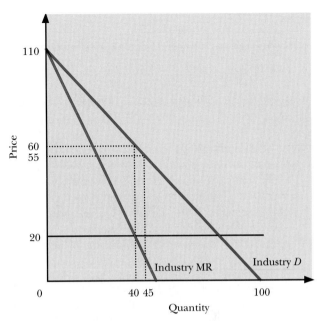

**FIGURE 1  Theory of Cartels**

Four identical firms with MC = $20 could form a cartel with common P = $60, with each making $400 of a $1600 industry profit on sales of 10 units. A cheating firm could shade price to $55, sell at most 45 units on its own, and make at most $1575.

cartel members. Cartels were made illegal in the United States in 1890 by the Sherman Antitrust Act, which we shall discuss in the next chapter. If a cartel is illegal, the members of an industry must find another way of colluding on the price of the product.

Price leadership exists when the firms in an industry set the same price as one of their number. The price leader might be expected to be the largest firm. Such a firm has the greatest interest in preventing a price war from breaking out. If it also has the lowest costs, it could certainly discipline firms that broke with its leadership by lowering price below the costs of its less efficient rivals.

One of the most notable examples were the so-called Gary dinners of the early twentieth century. Mr. Gary, president of the U.S. Steel Corporation, invited steel company executives to dinner to urge them to follow his lead in prices. Walter Adams describes the dinners:

> He exhorted them like a Methodist preacher at a camp meeting to follow the price leadership of U.S. Steel. There was no need for any formal agreements. U.S. Steel simply assumed the lead incumbent on a firm its size: its rivals followed,

## EXAMPLE 1
## GENERAL ELECTRIC, DEBEERS,
## AND INDUSTRIAL DIAMONDS

Industrial diamonds are used in everything from oil-well drilling bits to high-precision cutting tools. They are mainly produced synthetically by means of a secret technology developed by General Electric in 1954. General Electric and DeBeers of South Africa, the two largest sellers of industrial diamonds, account for 80 percent of world sales. DeBeers sells both natural raw diamonds and synthetic diamonds produced under licensed G.E. technology. The two companies have controlled the industrial diamond market as a two-member cartel since the early 1960s.

The G.E.-DeBeers duopoly is under challenge from two directions. First, the U.S. Justice Department filed a criminal complaint against De-Beers and G.E. for raising their industrial dia-mond prices together after DeBeers provided G.E. with a fax of its upcoming price increases. Second, the industrial diamond duopoly is being challenged by newcomers from Germany and South Korea, who have learned how to produce high-quality industrial diamonds. In response to this new source of competition, G.E. has begun what its general counsel describes as "trench warfare" against competitors, accusing them of acquiring G.E.'s technology illegally.

Cartels are not long lasting. They have difficulty controlling prices and they cannot keep out competition forever.

*Source:* "How G.E. Plays for Keeps in Diamonds," *New York Times,* September 18, 1994.

fully realizing the security and profitability of cooperation.[1]

A recent example is the price war (mentioned in the introduction) between Philip Morris and RJR Nabisco. Philip Morris has the best-selling cigarette: Marlboro. RJR cut prices on the discount portion of the market and a price war followed. But RJR lost more in the premium market where it competed with Marlboro and other premium brands. In 1994, after inflicting heavy damage on RJR, Philip Morris raised cigarette prices and RJR followed closely behind.

### FOCAL POINTS

Another form of collusion between firms is the use of common knowledge or *focal points.* The use of focal points leads to a *conscious parallelism* of action. Thomas Schelling has given a nice example of how people use focal points:

You are to meet someone in New York City. You have not been instructed where to meet: you have no prior understanding with the person on where to meet: and you cannot communicate with each other. . . . You are told the date but not the hour of this meeting: The two of you must guess the place and exact minute of the day for the meeting.[2]

According to Schelling, given these instructions, most people familiar with New York City would pick the information booth at Grand Central Station at noon (in the 1960s).

How do oligopolists use focal points? Oligopolistic firms are intimately acquainted with the way things work in their own industries. The focal points may be standardized business practices—such as common percentage markups, the use of round numbers, the charging of prices like $4.95, and policies like "splitting the difference" or charging high rates

[1]Walter Adams, *The Structure of American Industry,* 4th ed. (New York: Macmillan, 1971), p. 71.

[2]Thomas Schelling, *The Strategy of Conflict* (Cambridge: Harvard University Press, 1960), p. 56.

at the same time each year. As long as each oligopolist understands these standard practices, it can anticipate how rival firms will behave in given situations.

## THINKING STRATEGICALLY: GAME THEORY

We introduced game theory in Chapter 5. Game theory provides a way of thinking about strategic situations that managers, economists, generals, and politicians find useful in making decisions against an intelligent foe.

In competitive business situations, the players are not interdependent. One firm's actions do not affect another firm in the industry. In this case, equilibrium is established at the intersection of the industry supply and demand curve. At this equilibrium, firms are selling what they want to sell and buyers are buying what they want to buy. When firms are interdependent, we must use a different concept of equilibrium, the Nash equilibrium, named for its discoverer, John Nash, the 1994 Nobel Laureate in economics.

Recall from Chapter 5 that a game is really just a situation in which several players follow different possible strategies with various outcomes or payoffs.

> The **Nash equilibrium** of a game is the point at which each player is doing the best he or she can given what the other players are doing.

In other words, a Nash equilibrium is achieved when the chosen game plan or strategy of each player is his or her best response to the strategies of others. Thus, in a Nash equilibrium, each person correctly anticipates what the others will do for the simple reason that there is no incentive for anyone to change from that position.

For example, in the 1994 elections, politicians were told by their advisors that negative campaigning worked. As a consequence, most politicians engaged in negative ads about their adversary (for example, "My opponent is a liar"). But why take the low road? If all politicians were to engage in positive campaigning (such as "I promise a free lunch"), no one's reputation would be smeared. It would seem just as easy for two politicians to agree to be civilized.

The reason that many of the politicians did not take the high road is the belief that negative campaigning works. Suppose two politicians think they have an equal chance of winning an election if both campaign negatively or positively. If one campaigns negatively while the other does so positively, both believe that the negative campaigner will win. Thus, there is nothing to gain from a positive campaign by one of them because it increases the perceived chances of losing the election.

In the same way, whether oligopolists collude in a cartel or act independently, they must act strategically within their understanding of the competitive situation in which they find themselves. Many examples of oligopolistic behavior can be explained as a Nash equilibrium. Let us now consider the Cournot oligopoly game, the prisoners' dilemma game, the advertising game, and the credible threat.

### THE COURNOT OLIGOPOLY GAME

One of the most important models of oligopoly was developed by a French economist, Augustin A. Cournot (1801–1877), in 1838. A Cournot oligopoly occurs when each firm in a group producing a homogeneous product acts as though all other firms will continue to produce their current outputs. Thus a Cournot oligopolist supposes that if it increases its own output, the price of the product must fall by just enough to sell its planned increase in output since all rivals are expected to maintain their production levels. Similarly, if the firm cuts output, the price will rise by just enough to reduce market demand by the firm's planned reduction in output.

> In a **Cournot oligopoly**, (1) the product is homogeneous, (2) each firm supposes that its rivals will continue to produce their current outputs independently of that firm's choice of outputs, and (3) there is a fixed number of firms.

Consider again the example of mineral springs supplied by an underground lake. The mineral water is accessible through two springs owned by Bob and Ted. Customers are indifferent about whether they buy mineral water from Bob or Ted, so Bob and Ted must sell at the same price. Figure 2 shows Ted's output on the vertical axis and Bob's on the horizontal axis. The line $TM$ describes Bob's profit-maximizing response to Ted's output, and the line $T'M'$ describes Ted's profit-maximizing response to Bob's output. These *reaction curves* show the best response (or

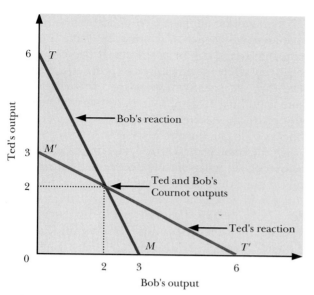

**FIGURE 2    Cournot Strategies**

$T'M'$ is Ted's reaction curve; $TM$ is Bob's reaction curve. Each person's monopoly output is 3 and each person's predatory output is 6. The Cournot solution is 2 each.

profit-maximizing response) of one firm to the other firm's output. In other words, they show the output level each firm would pick if it knew what the rival firm's output would be.

The reaction curves are easy to understand. First, they are both downward-sloping because the more Ted produces, the less of the market remains for Bob (and vice versa). Second, when the output of one is zero, the other assumes he has a monopoly and produces accordingly. In Figure 2, the monopoly output is 3 units. Third, if one firm fully saturates the market, the other will produce nothing. This is called the *predatory output* because it drives the other firm out of business. In Figure 2, the predatory output of each firm is 6 units. This exceeds monopoly output because in monopoly the price exceeds marginal cost, leaving room for the other firm to make some sales. Therefore, the reaction curves must appear as in Figure 2. The two reaction curves intersect at the point where each firm's expectations about the other firm are fulfilled; it is a Nash equilibrium because each firm is doing the best it can given the other firm's choice of output. In the figure, the Cournot equilibrium occurs where each firm produces 2 units; the market therefore consists of 4 units.

The world of Cournot is more competitive than monopoly but is not as efficient as perfect competition. However, as the number of firms increases, the

Cournot model predicts that prices will fall and output rise, just as in the competitive model.

The model also shows how unrealistic beliefs can actually result in correct predictions. Let's return to the reaction curves of Ted and Bob. When Ted is producing zero units, Bob wants to produce 3 units. If Bob produces 3 units, then Ted will *not* produce zero units because Bob's predatory output is 6 units. Therefore, when the industry is not in the Nash equilibrium, each firm's beliefs about what the other firm is going to do turn out to be incorrect. However, in the Cournot or Nash equilibrium, the unrealistic belief that the other firm will maintain its output is actually justified by what happens!

The Cournot game has been criticized for its assumption that firms suppose their rivals are passive, but experimental studies support this model. In a classic study, 16 pairs of undergraduates were given a Cournot game that would have resulted in a Cournot output of 40 (per subject). Surprisingly, the average output of each student firm, following their own rules, was approximately 40![3]

## THE PRISONERS' DILEMMA GAME

The famous prisoners' dilemma game introduced in Chapter 5 was developed by game theorists as a way to analyze a situation much like that often faced by oligopolistic producers. The game assumes that two bank robbers have been apprehended by the police; they are being interrogated in separate rooms. If both talk, both go to jail but with 3-year sentences. If one talks and the other remains quiet, the one who talks gets off with a 1-year sentence and the silent bank robber gets a 6-year jail sentence. If neither talks, both get 1 year for carrying a deadly weapon. Each prisoner has a dilemma. Each knows that if he or she keeps quiet, both can get a light sentence, provided the other remains quiet; but keeping quiet is risky, because the other prisoner might talk. Moreover, if the other prisoner remains quiet, confessing lowers the sentence from 1 year to 0 years. If the other prisoner confesses, the first must confess to avoid a 6-year sentence. A Nash equilibrium occurs if both bank robbers confess. If one believes the other will confess, his or her best strategy is also to confess. If both actually confess, each has guessed correctly

---

[3]Lawrence Fouraker and Signey Siegal, *Bargaining Behavior* (New York: McGraw-Hill, 1963).

about the other's behavior and is able to employ the best strategy for the situation in which the other confesses. If the prisoners could communicate and make a binding agreement, they would both be better off remaining quiet.

> A **prisoner's dilemma game** is a game with two players in which both players benefit from cooperating, but in which each player has an incentive to cheat on the agreement.

The prisoners' dilemma is much like an oligopolist's dilemma of deciding whether to collude or to act independently. In both cases, the consequences of one player's decision depend upon the decision of another player. Suppose Firm A and Firm B each sell a differentiated product. Suppose also that when the two products have equal prices, both firms enjoy exactly the same profit. If one charges a slightly lower price than the other, however, that firm will make large profits while the high-priced firm will make only a small profit.

Figure 3 illustrates a simple example of the oligopolist's dilemma. Each firm can choose a price of either $20 or $19. The prices Firm A might charge are shown down the left side of the figure; the prices Firm B might charge are shown along the top. The *profits* earned by each firm are the payoffs from any set of prices the *two firms together* might charge. Firm A's profit payoffs are shown in the lower left-hand corner of each box (in green). Firm B's profit payoffs are shown in the upper right-hand corner of each box (in red). When both charge $20, both earn $2500; when both charge $19, both earn $1500. When one charges $20 and the other charges $19, the low-priced firm earns $3000, and the high-priced firm earns only $1000.

The two firms reach a Nash equilibrium when both firms charge $19. If each believes the other is charging $19, the best strategy for each is to charge $19. When both actually charge $19, each has guessed correctly, and each is able to employ the best strategy for the situation in which the other charges $19.

If A and B play this game repeatedly over a fairly long period of time, it is likely that A and B will eventually learn that they are both better off charging higher prices. They might learn to cooperate and choose the strategy that maximizes joint profits. In this case, both would charge $20 and earn profits of $2500 each. (See Example 2.)

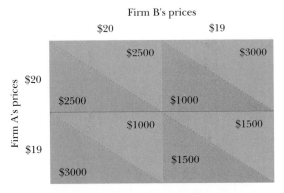

**FIGURE 3   Profit Payoffs to a Two-Firm Oligopoly**

Each square (cell) shows the profits that each firm would earn when various combinations of prices are charged by the two firms. Firm A's profits are shown in green in the lower left-hand corner of each cell, and Firm B's profits are shown in red in the upper right-hand corner of each cell. For example, if A charges $19 and B charges $20, A would earn a profit of $3000 and B would earn $1000. The Nash equilibrium solution is for both firms to choose a price of $19.

## THE ADVERTISING GAME

If a firm's rival advertises that "my product is better than all others," it is difficult for the firm to fail to respond with its own advertising message. Let's consider a rivalry between two hypothetical hamburger giants: Big Burger and Best Burger. Table 1 shows what the strategy of each hamburger company is in response to the various amounts of daily national television commercials run by its rival.

Big Burger strategists calculate that the company can maximize its profits by running 3 ads per day if Best Burger places no ads per day, by running 6 ads if Best Burger places 8 ads, and by running 9 ads if Best Burger places 16 ads. The green curve in Figure 4 graphs Big Burger's optimal strategies. On the other hand, Best Burger strategists calculate that the company can maximize its profits by running 4 ads per day if Big Burger places no ads per day, by running 8 ads if Big Burger places 6 ads, and by running 12 ads if Big Burger places 12 ads per day. The red curve graphs Best Burger's optimal strategies. The Nash equilibrium occurs where Best Burger's strategy curve intersects Big Burger's strategy curve. When Big Burger is running 6 ads a day and Best Burger is running 8 ads per day, there is a Nash equilibrium. Big Burger maximizes its profit with 6 ads when Best Burger places 8 ads; Best Burger maximizes its profit with 8 ads when Big Burger places 6

# EXAMPLE 2
## THE KINKED
## DEMAND CURVE

The concept of a prisoner's dilemma explains many facts about the real world. One of the most interesting is the inclusion of an essentially incorrect model in almost all introductory economics textbooks. This is the so-called kinked demand curve model. Economists have roundly condemned it because it cannot explain how prices are formed and falsely predicts that oligopoly prices are more stable than monopoly prices.

The model posits that firms will not change current prices because they think that rivals will match price cuts but not price increases. Under these circumstances, no firm would raise its price because it thinks that its rivals would then get all of the business; no firm would cut its price because it believes that such a move would be futile.

Why do textbooks include this model when the facts contradict it? The answer: It is part of a Nash equilibrium in the market for economics textbooks. The reason for its popularity in textbooks is that no model is easier to discuss or to criticize. In short, the model is easy and, perhaps, even fun to teach. Therefore, each textbook includes it on the grounds that some professors will find it useful while the others will ignore it. If all textbooks excluded discussion of the kinked demand curve, all textbook authors would be better off because they would have the satisfaction of telling the truth. But this is not an equilibrium because each textbook author would then have an incentive to include the kinked demand curve model!

## Table 1  Advertising Strategies

| Big Burger's Strategies (ads per day) | | Best Burger's Strategies (ads per day) | |
|---|---|---|---|
| Big Burger Optimum | Best Burger Number | Big Burger Number | Best Burger Optimum |
| 3 | 0 | 0 | 4 |
| 6 | 8 | 6 | 8 |
| 9 | 16 | 12 | 12 |

This table shows the profit-maximizing number of TV advertisements for each hamburger chain in response to its rival. The Nash equilibrium is reached when Best Burger runs 8 ads per day and Big Burger runs 6 ads per day because at this point each firm's profit-maximizing behavior is based on a correct guess about the other firm's behavior.

ads. At this point, each company is employing its best strategy for dealing with a correct assessment of how many ads the other company will place.

The advertising example is interesting because the firms advertise much more at the Nash equilibrium than they would if they reached an informal agreement to deliberately keep their advertising expenditures to a minimum.

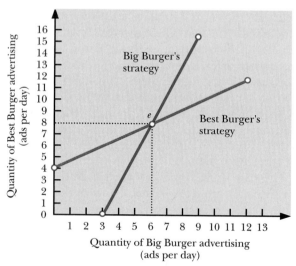

**FIGURE 4  Nash Equilibrium: Advertising**

The green line shows Big Burger's best response to Best Burger's ads. The red line shows Best Burger's best response to Big Burger's ads. Where the two curves intersect is a Nash equilibrium, where each firm's guess about the other firm's strategy is confirmed. In other words, Big Burger wants 6 ads when Best Burger places 8 ads, and Best Burger wants 8 ads when Big Burger places 6 ads.

## THE CREDIBLE THREAT

Suppose an industry contains one actual monopolist and one *potential* entrant. To discourage entry, the monopolist might let the potential rival know that there would be a costly price war (prices would be set below costs) if the potential rival were to enter the industry. The rival may not believe the monopolist's threat, however, unless the monopolist makes some commitment to make this threat credible. If the potential entrant calculates that the monopolist would also lose from the price war and would eventually have to share the market, the monopolist's threat will be ignored. But the monopolist can make an irreversible commitment. For example, the monopolist might spend $10 million to secure the services of the best advertising agency before the potential rival enters the business. Or the monopolist might accumulate large cash resources to convince the potential rival of its willingness to engage in a price war. A credible threat makes it easier for the potential en-

trant to make a correct assumption about the monopolist's behavior.

> A **credible threat** is the commitment of significant resources by existing firms to convince potential entrants to the industry that entry would result in severe losses for the entrant.

A Nash equilibrium results when the monopolist maximizes profits by making a credible threat that succeeds in keeping out the potential entrant (on the correct assumption that the potential rival would actually enter the market in the absence of the credible threat) and when the potential entrant minimizes losses by not entering the market, on the correct assumption that the monopolist would indeed start a price war. (See Example 3.)

The behavior of a wide variety of noncooperative oligopolies can be explained using the concept of a Nash equilibrium. Indeed, the Nash equilibrium

## EXAMPLE 3
## PREDATORY PRICING AND
## THE CREDIBLE THREAT

The theory of predatory pricing is quite simple. An oligopolistic firm drives out all its competitors by setting price below cost. The most famous case is the creation of the Standard Oil Company. In the nineteenth century, John D. Rockefeller supposedly lowered the price of oil, drove the small oil refineries to the brink of bankruptcy, and then bought them out at a bargain price.

The only trouble with the theory of predatory pricing is that in most cases the scenario works out differently, as two classic studies have shown. John McGee studied the historical record and found that Rockefeller's rivals were bought out on very favorable terms. Roland Koller examined 26 cases of alleged predatory pricing dating from 1890. Koller found only seven cases in which there was pricing below cost. Of these seven cases, only one resulted in the rival's disappearing without a trace.

Price predation is not likely to be a profitable strategy, because it does not represent a credible threat. If two oligopolistic firms have identical costs, how could one drive the other out by lowering price? Both firms can play the same game. Suppose firm A tells firm B, "I am going to lower the price until you go out of business." There is no reason why firm B could not do the same thing to firm A. Any damage firm A inflicts on firm B it also inflicts on itself. Unless B thinks that A might have lower costs, predation is not likely to work.

------------------------------------------------

*Sources:* John McGee, "Predatory Price Cutting," *Journal of Law and Economics* 1 (1958): 137–169; Roland Koller, "The Myth of Predatory Pricing," *Antitrust Law and Economics Review* (Summer 1971): 105–193.

concept can even be applied to many social behaviors. Game theorists are hard at work on new concepts of equilibrium that can explain even more complicated oligopolistic strategies—such as setting low prices today and high prices tomorrow.

## OLIGOPOLY: THE INDUSTRIAL ORGANIZATION APPROACH

A cartel will fail if each member believes that cheating on the agreement is profitable. In the Cournot game, each oligopolist thinks that its rivals will maintain their existing outputs; in the prisoner's dilemma, each prisoner thinks the other might confess; in the advertising game, each firm thinks the other firm will maintain its current advertising budget.

Thus, the various solutions to the oligopoly problem depend on the beliefs each oligopolist has about its rivals. In these examples, collusion is not a Nash equilibrium and, therefore, the oligopolists will tend to act independently.

### OBSTACLES TO COLLUSION

Industrial organization is the study of how industries actually behave in the real world. The industrial organization approach to understanding whether oligopolies are likely to collude is to examine the actual circumstances in which they find themselves. The chances for effective and lasting collusion decrease when there are (1) many sellers, (2) low entry barriers, (3) product heterogeneity, (4) high rates of innovation, (5) high fixed costs, (6) many opportunities for cheating, and (7) legal restrictions.

**Many Sellers.**  The more sellers there are in the industry, the more difficult it is for the sellers to join a conspiracy to raise prices. The communication network becomes much more complicated as the number of conspirators grows. When there are two sellers, there is only one communication link. When there are three sellers, there are three different information links: A must agree with B; B must agree with C; C and A must agree. When there are 10 sellers, information must flow in 45 ways! The number of information channels increases at a far greater rate than the rate at which the number of sellers increases. It becomes far more difficult to coordinate collusive actions as the number of colluders grows. [The for-

mula for the number of information flows is $n(n - 1)/2$, where $n$ is the number of sellers.]

**Low Entry Barriers.**  If it is easy for new firms to enter an industry, existing firms may not find it worthwhile to work out agreements to raise prices. Effective collusion would cause new firms to enter the industry.

High prices create profitable opportunities for new firms. For example, if an industry has constant returns to scale (no economies or diseconomies of scale), the average cost of production is the same whether there is one firm or many firms. Suppose that such an industry currently has two firms and the average cost of production—including a normal return—is $10. With complete free entry, the existing firms can not charge more than $10 in the long run. Any price above $10 will bring in new firms to capture above-normal returns. The entry of firms will eventually drive the price down to $10, where only a normal return is earned. The two existing firms will gain no lasting benefit by conspiring to raise the price above $10.

**Product Heterogeneity.**  The more heterogeneous (differentiated) the product is from firm to firm, the more difficult it is for the industry to achieve coordination or collusion. Reaching an agreement creates both costs and benefits. It is costlier to reach an agreement if the product is not homogeneous. Because steel is homogeneous, an agreement on prices and market shares between two major steel producers may be fairly easy to conclude. But an agreement between McDonnell Douglas and Boeing over the relative prices of the MD-11 and the Boeing 767 might be difficult because of the differences between the two planes. An agreement between the producers of high-quality goods and low-quality goods might break down because of differences of opinion over one good's quality relative to the other good's quality. It would be difficult for a fast-food chain like McDonald's to enter into a pricing agreement with a full-service restaurant chain like Red Lobster because of the difficulty of agreeing on the proper relative price.

**High Rates of Innovation.**  If an industry has a high rate of innovation, collusive agreements are more difficult to reach. In unstable, quickly changing markets, oligopolies have more difficulty finding the joint profit-maximizing solution. The costs of reaching an agreement are higher in relation to benefits when the industry is constantly turning out new products and developing new techniques. For example, it would be difficult for Compaq and IBM to reach an agreement because of the fast pace of technological change in the personal computer market.

**High Fixed Costs.**   As fixed costs become higher relative to total costs, collusive agreements become more likely to break down. Firms ask themselves what they can gain by cheating on the pricing agreement. If fixed costs are high, variable costs are a low percentage of total costs. As long as the price covers average variable costs, something is left over with which to pay fixed costs. By granting secret price concessions, firms may gain much in the short run if marginal costs are very low.

**Opportunities for Cheating.**   If it is easy to cheat without being detected, firms will tend to break a collusive agreement. It is easier to cheat on price agreements when actual prices charged by one party cannot be known with certainty by the other parties to the agreement. For example, when the terms of price negotiations are not revealed (as in the cases of long-term oil delivery contracts or purchases of commercial aircraft by the airlines), it is easier to cheat on pricing agreements.

**Legal Restrictions.**   In the United States, the Sherman Antitrust Act (1890) holds that combinations in restraint of trade are illegal. The Sherman act and additional acts designed to prohibit and punish collusive behavior make up the antitrust laws of the United States (which we shall discuss in the next chapter). Antitrust laws reduce collusion by increasing the costs of forming agreements.

## UNINTENDED CONSEQUENCES OF GOVERNMENT REGULATION

Government regulation of business often results in the unintended consequence of more collusive behavior on the part of oligopolists. Prohibiting cigarette advertising solved a prisoners' dilemma facing cigarette firms. Requiring all automobile firms to provide seat belts, airbags, and side-impact bags—while possibly good ideas from a social standpoint—reduces the different strategies firms might follow and, there-

fore, can lead to more collusive behavior. For example, if all firms must install passenger side airbags by a certain date, all automobile manufacturers might simply raise their prices by the cost of such airbags plus the same margin of profit. Without government guidance, firms introducing safety features on their own might be uncertain about the price they can charge. This uncertainty results in more competition. Government absolute prohibitions on smoking in domestic airlines removed an opportunity for airlines to compete among themselves by offering some smoke-free flights.

In all of the above cases, government regulations created a result that would have required collusion or cooperation to achieve.

## A DEFENSE OF OLIGOPOLY

Industrial organization economists tell us that profit rates in many oligopolies dominated by large firms tend to persist over time. This fact has prompted many economists to be critical of oligopoly. Some economists, however, defend oligopoly as an efficient form of market. Harold Demsetz, for example, cites the positive relationship between profit rates and oligopoly as an indicator of the greater efficiency of large firms.[4]

Demsetz maintains that higher profits are the result of the superior cost performance of larger firms in the industry. Even if prices are set competitively so that each firm acts more or less like a price taker (exerting no monopoly power over prices), economic profits will accrue only to those firms that have lower costs, not to all firms in the industry. There is evidence that oligopoly profits are earned only by the largest firms in oligopolistic industries, not by all firms. Demsetz therefore concludes that oligopoly profits are the result not of excessive market power but of the superior efficiency of large oligopolistic firms.

Figure 5 illustrates the Demsetz argument. It takes the case of a homogeneous product that is being produced by a large low-cost producer and by small high-cost producers. Perfect competition prevails, and each firm equates marginal costs to the

---

[4]Harold Demsetz, "Industry Structure, Market Rivalry, and Public Policy," *Journal of Law and Economics* 16 (April 1973): 1–10.

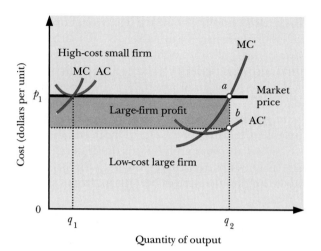

**FIGURE 5   The Demsetz Thesis**

The large, efficient firm produces an output of $q_2$ units with a per-unit profit of $ab$. The small, inefficient firm produces an output of $q_1$ units with a zero economic profit. According to Demsetz, perfect competition can be consistent with the positive association between concentration rates and economic profits.

price. When these conditions prevail, economic profits are earned only by the large low-cost producer. The small high-cost firms earn only a normal return. Higher profits are associated with large firms because they can produce at lower costs due to significant economies of scale.

One of Chapter 1's Defining Moment economists, Joseph Schumpeter, argued that large enterprises generate more technological progress, the moving force behind economic progress that temporarily establishes some firms as dominant in their industry. Through the process of "creative destruction," Schumpeter believed that new ideas and new technologies replace the old and that the monopoly power created by technological innovation will prove to be transitory.

It is clear that large enterprises can be the natural outcome of the competitive process. One firm may come to dominate an industry because it is more innovative, its management is more efficient, and it has taken more risks. If one or two firms tower over an industry because they have played the game better than others (Schumpeter's "creative destruction"), are not high profits their just reward? We cannot hope to answer the question, "Are concentrated oligopolists necessarily bad?" We shall consider this important policy issue in the chapter on antitrust policy.

## A COMPARISON OF THE FOUR MARKET FORMS

We are now finished with our study of the four market forms: perfect competition, monopoly, monopolistic competition, and oligopoly. Table 2 summarizes the key features of each.

Only perfect competition is efficient in the strict, static sense of allocating given resources with known technology. The key to efficiency is the relationship between price and marginal cost. Efficiency is achieved when price equals marginal cost. In perfect competition, $P = MC$. Monopolistic competition is mildly inefficient because $P > MC$, but nothing can or should be done about it. Oligopoly can range from a solution close to perfect competition to one close to monopoly; thus, no general conclusion is possible on static efficiency. But it is likely that $P > MC$. Monopoly is clearly inefficient because $P > MC$.

All market forms can be conducive to technological progress. We know that monopoly, monopolistic competition, and oligopoly often result in new products. But even firms engaged in perfect competition will have an incentive to discover new ways of producing their product in order to have lower operating costs than their competitors. They also have an incentive to develop new products that can be differentiated from their competitors; perfect competitors may strive to become monopolistic competitors or oligopolists.

| Table 2   Characteristics of Four Market Forms | | | | |
|---|---|---|---|---|
| *Market* | *Static Efficiency* | *Long-Run Profit* | *Equilibrium Conditions* | *Technological Progress* |
| perfect competition | efficient | zero | $P = MC$ $P = AC$ | yes |
| monopoly | inefficient | positive | $P > MR = MC$ | yes |
| monopolistic competition | mildly inefficient | zero | $P > MR = MC$ $P = AC$ | yes |
| oligopoly | varies | varies | varies | yes |

We shall see in the next chapter, however, that the portion of the U.S economy that is for all practical purposes "competitive" has been growing. Competition is far from dead as some economists have claimed. The existence of different market forms also raises policy issues. We shall also examine in the next chapter the use of government action in the forms of regulation and antitrust legislation to deal with monopoly power.

## SUMMARY

1. An oligopoly is characterized by a small number of firms, barriers to entry, mutual interdependence, and price making. The number of firms is so small that the actions of one firm have a significant effect on other firms in the industry.

2. Methods of oligopoly coordination range from formal agreements (cartels) to informal arrangements, such as price leadership or conscious parallelism. Collusive agreements, if successful, allow the participating firms to earn monopoly profits. Because there are incentives to cheat on the cartel agreement, however, collusive agreements tend to be unstable.

3. Game theory analyzes the strategies that should be followed by intelligent rivals. A *Nash equilibrium* prevails in an oligopolistic market if each firm's profit-maximizing behavior is based on a correct guess about the behavior of rivals. Four examples of business games that have a Nash equilibrium are playing the Cournot oligopoly game, playing the prisoners' dilemma game, advertising, and making a credible threat.

4. Many factors can make collusion more difficult: (1) many sellers, (2) low entry barriers, (3) product heterogeneity, (4) high rates of innovation, (5) high fixed costs, (6) many opportunities for cheating, and (7) legal restrictions. However, government prohibitions or laws can sometimes promote collusion as an unintended consequence.

5. Some industrial organization economists argue that an oligopoly is an efficient form of market structure, despite its higher profits, because of economies of scale and technological innovation.

## KEY TERMS

oligopoly
mutual interdependence

cartel
Nash equilibrium

Cournot oligopoly
prisoners' dilemma game

credible threat

## QUESTIONS AND PROBLEMS

1. What is the relationship between the small number of firms and mutual interdependence in oligopoly theory? Why was mutual interdependence not considered in the chapter on monopoly and monopolistic competition?

2. Firm ZYX is one of three equal-sized firms in the widget market. It currently charges $20 per widget and sells 1 million widgets per year. It is considering raising its price to $22 and needs some estimate of what will happen to its widget sales. Why would it be difficult to make such an estimate?

3. Firm ZYX and the two other widget manufacturers meet in secret and agree to charge a uniform price of $50 and share the market equally (each gets one-third of sales). At the price of $50, each firm's marginal cost is $10. What are the rewards for cheating on the agreement if ZYX does not get caught? What is likely to happen if all three try to cheat?

4. The prisoners' dilemma game is also used to explain how oligopolists devise advertising strategy. Try to apply the prisoners' dilemma game to advertising.

5. In an oligopolistic industry composed of three large firms and ten small firms, the large firms earn an economic profit while the small firms earn normal profits. What do you know about the sources of economic profit in this industry?

6. How does oligopoly theory explain why there are so many different types of oligopoly behavior—collusion, conscious parallelism, price leadership?

7. What is a *Nash equilibrium?*

8. Which of the following are examples of a Nash equilibrium?
   a. The prisoners' dilemma game
   b. Cartel pricing
   c. The credible threat
   d. Pricing by focal points

9. Consider an industry that consists of two equal-sized firms. Their marginal cost of production is $2 at each level of output. The industry demand schedule is given in Table A. Assume that the two firms divide the market equally.
   a. What will be the cartel price and quantity?

b. What is the incentive for each firm to cheat on the agreement?

| Table A | |
| --- | --- |
| Price (dollars per unit) | Quantity Demanded (units) |
| 18 | 0 |
| 15 | 3 |
| 12 | 6 |
| 9 | 9 |
| 6 | 12 |
| 3 | 15 |
| 0 | 18 |

10. Which industry is more likely to collude? One with
    a. low fixed costs or high fixed costs?
    b. heterogenous product or homogeneous product?
    c. large government sales or no government sales?
Why?

# CHAPTER 14

# REGULATION AND ANTITRUST

Although the 1980s have often been cited as the epitome of materialism, every era has had its own symbol of greed. In the late nineteenth and early twentieth centuries, John D. Rockefeller was the most prominent "Robber Baron." His Standard Oil had monopolized the oil industry by gaining control of the refining and transportation of oil. The public clamor against Rockefeller, fueled by the "trust busting" efforts of President Theodore Roosevelt, culminated in a series of court actions against Standard Oil under the Sherman Antitrust Act. In May 1911, a mumbling Chief Justice Edward White announced the dissolution of Standard Oil. It was to be broken up into a number of separate companies. No one at Standard Oil's New York headquarters was prepared for the devastating effect of the Supreme Court judgment. John Archibald, the chief executive of Standard Oil, walked over to the mantle and stated, "Well, gentlemen, life's just one damn thing after another."[1]

---

[1]Daniel Yergin, *The Prize* (New York: Simon and Schuster, 1991), pp. 109–110.

# GOVERNMENT AND BUSINESS

While we recognize that monopoly creates problems, we are not quite sure what to do about it. In some cases, we have to live with monopoly, but we can try to limit its damaging effects. In other cases, we do indeed have a social choice, such as the 1911 decision to break up Standard Oil, but we must decide how that choice is to be exercised.

## THE NATURAL MONOPOLY

In the 1911 case of Standard Oil, it was possible to break up a monopoly by dividing it into the "smaller" companies that went on to become Exxon, Chevron, and so on. Such an alteration of the market structure is not possible in the case of the natural monopoly, which we discussed in an earlier chapter.

In an industry that is a natural monopoly, output will be produced at a lower long-run average cost by one firm than it would if the industry were made up of more than one producer. Let's consider, for example, three electric utilities that operate in the same market with three systems of power lines and underground cables. For natural monopolies, economies of large-scale production are so dominant that there is little choice but to operate as a single-firm industry. Some examples of natural monopolies are electric utilities, natural gas utilities, and local telephone service (see Figure 1).

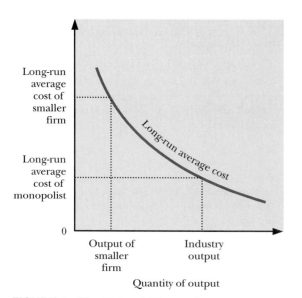

FIGURE 1   The Natural Monopoly

Like other monopolies, even natural monopolies do not last forever, but can be changed by technological progress and innovation. (See Example 1 on page 238.) In the case of natural monopoly, government must decide whether and how to control monopoly power. If a government chooses to control the monopoly, it has three options: government ownership, regulation, or antitrust legislation.

## GOVERNMENT OWNERSHIP

The government can own and operate a monopoly "in the public interest." Public ownership of business in the United States is more common at the municipal and state than at the federal level and is utilized for such services as local transportation, water, sanitation, gas, and electricity. During the 1990s, about one-quarter of all electricity was generated by government-owned enterprises.

At the federal level, government enterprises are fewer in number. They include, among others, the Tennessee Valley Authority (a giant, government-owned electrical utility), the U.S. Postal Service, government home mortgage programs (the Veterans Administration and Federal Housing Authority), various weapons arsenals, and the Government Printing Office. These activities account for about 2 percent of the output of the U.S. economy.

How should the government operate a public enterprise in the public interest? What instructions, for example, should be given to the public enterprise in Figure 2? One option is to produce that quantity of output at which price and marginal cost are equal (point $c$). Point $c$ is *efficient* because the marginal cost (of society's resources) is equated with the marginal benefit as reflected in the price. However, the $P = MC$ rule requires that the enterprise be run at a loss to be paid by taxpayers.

Alternatively, the public enterprise can be instructed by the government to break even—to produce where price equals average total cost (at point $b$). At point $b$, price is greater than marginal cost, and the efficiency rule $P = MC$ is broken. But the customer is offered a larger quantity of output ($q_b$) at a lower price ($p_b$) than if the firm were an unregulated monopoly.

The public enterprise can also be told to operate like a private, unregulated monopoly. The enterprise then chooses the quantity, $m$, that equates marginal revenue and marginal cost. Again, the basic efficiency rule is broken: Price is more than marginal

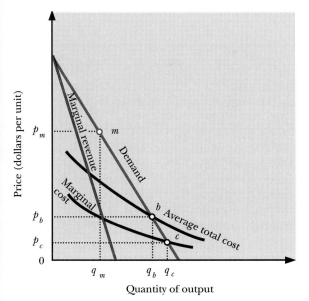

**FIGURE 2   The Dilemma of a Public Enterprise**

This figure depicts a monopoly that is owned by the public. It is not clear which rules the manager should follow to operate this enterprise "in the public interest." The manager could equate marginal cost and price (point *c*), but the enterprise would be operating at a loss. The manager could attempt to break even (point *b*) by operating where price and average total cost are equal, but the manager would have little incentive to economize on costs because higher costs would translate into higher prices and higher revenues. Finally, the manager could try to maximize profits (point *m*), but consumers would receive a relatively small quantity of output and pay relatively high prices while monopoly profits accrued to the state.

cost. The public is offered a relatively small quantity of output ($q_m$) for which it must pay a monopoly price ($p_m$).

Just how much government (public) ownership there should be is a matter of public choice. We devote an entire later chapter to this issue.

# REGULATION

Regulation of prices and services is a second means of controlling monopoly.

> **Regulation** is government control of firms, exercised by regulatory agencies through rules and regulations concerning prices and service.

With regulation, the enterprise remains in private hands, but its activities are regulated by government agencies. The goals of regulation are to ensure the availability of service, establish standards for the quality of service, and guarantee that the public will be charged "reasonable" prices.

Regulation at the state and local level is largely directed at monopolies—the electric, gas, water, and telephone companies. Localities have commissions or city councils to set water and sewer rates and local telephone and cable TV rates. Most states have public utility commissions to set long distance telephone rates within the state. At the national level, federal regulatory commissions regulate a number of industries, some of which are potentially competitive. Table 1 on page 239 lists the four major federal regulatory commissions.

A number of federal regulatory agencies stop short of setting prices and rates. The Food and Drug Administration is responsible for the safety of our food supplies and the safety of drugs. The National Transportation Safety Board monitors the safety of air travel. The Federal Trade Commission is charged with preventing unfair and deceptive trade practices. The Environmental Protection Agency regulates industrial pollution emissions.

## WHO IS REGULATED?

Gas and electric companies and local telephone service are not the only industries regulated at the state and local level. Much state and local regulation is directed at competitive industries (taxicab licensing, concession franchises in sports stadiums, licensing of barbers and beauticians) and creates more rather than less monopoly power. Likewise, federal commissions regulate potentially competitive industries such as transportation and broadcasting, often limiting competition.

> Government regulation is not consistent; some is designed to combat monopoly power, but some actually discourages competition.

The amount of supervision also varies. For example, the Food and Drug Administration is stricter in its supervision of the prescription drug industry than the Environmental Protection Agency is in its regulation of the automobile industry.

Most businesses are regulated in one way or another by licenses, safety and health regulations, or occupational safety requirements. If we use this stan-

## EXAMPLE 1
### HOW TECHNOLOGY CAN CHANGE A NATURAL MONOPOLY:
### COMPETITION FOR ELECTRICITY

For years, economists used electrical power as one of the best examples of natural monopoly. Electrical power, it was argued, could be produced only by a single producer in each particular market. The creation of national electrical energy grids and long-distance high-voltage lines has changed all of this. The regional electrical utilities have created a long-distance grid system whereby they can "import" electricity generated thousands of miles away. This national grid system has created the opportunity to have a competitive market for electrical power. In fact, in a few years, customers will be able to shop for the cheapest electricity just as they shop for the cheapest groceries or cheapest clothes.

Here's how the system works: Local electrical utilities will continue to deliver electricity from the national grid system and will charge a standard fee for this service. Customers can, however, shop around for the cheapest electricity being supplied to this grid. One month you may use electricity produced in New York; the next month, you may use electricity produced in New Mexico. This option is already available to large industrial users. Later, it is already available for household customers.

This vast change was made possible by a 1992 change in federal law that requires utilities to open their transmission lines to carry competitor's electricity. Regulators in states such as California and Texas already allow industrial customers to shop around freely for electricity.

------------------------------------------------

*Source:* "Electrical Utilities Bracing for an End to Regulation and Their Monopolies," *New York Times,* August 8, 1994.

---

dard, then all U.S. businesses are regulated and the amount of regulation is growing daily. All businesses must comply with hiring laws, workplace regulations, and reporting laws. On the other hand, if regulated industries include only those industries in which prices are controlled by government agencies (transportation, communications, utilities, banking, and insurance), less than 10 percent of output is produced by regulated firms.[2]

The deregulation that began in the late 1970s markedly reduced government regulation of prices and rates. We shall discuss deregulation—in particular, that in the airline industry—later in the chapter.

## PRINCIPLES OF RATE REGULATION

Regulatory commissions are required to set "reasonable" prices, establish standards for minimum quality of service, and guarantee customers access to the service without discrimination. Regulatory commissions are bound by the private property safeguards of the U.S. Constitution to protect the property rights of the owners of the regulated business. Rates must cover operating costs plus a "fair" rate of return on invested capital. If regulators do not allow regulated monopolies a fair rate of return, the monopoly can appeal to the courts for higher prices.

**The Pricing Formula.**   The usual formula for pricing is relatively simple.

Price of service = average operating cost + fair rate of return on invested capital.

---

[2]These figures have been updated by the authors based on earlier classic studies. Figures for 1939 and 1958 for the "government supervised" sector were from the studies of G. Warren Nutter, *The Extent of Enterprise Monopoly in the United States, 1899–1939* (Chicago: University of Chicago Press, 1951); G. Warren Nutter and Henry A. Einhorn, *Enterprise Monopoly in the United States, 1899–1958* (New York: Columbia University Press, 1969); and George Stigler, *Five Lectures on Economic Problems* (London: Longmans, Green and Company, 1949).

## Table 1   Federal Regulatory Commissions

1. The Interstate Commerce Commission (established in 1887) regulates railroads, interstate oil pipelines, and interstate motor and water carriers.
2. The Federal Power Commission (established in 1920) has jurisdiction over power projects and the interstate transmission of electricity and natural gas.
3. The Federal Communications Commission (established in 1934) regulates interstate telephone and telegraph service and broadcasting.
4. The Securities and Exchange Commission (established in 1934) regulates securities markets.

However, the formula raises a number of questions, such as how to measure operating costs and "fair" rate of return. The formula rules out marginal-cost pricing (point $c$ in Figure 2), which typically yields a loss because of declining average costs. The pricing formula, however, can encourage inefficient operating costs. The formula passes on cost increases to the consumer in the form of higher prices. Regulated firms may therefore not be motivated to minimize costs. Regulators typically do not have enough information to determine whether reported costs are legitimate, and they are reluctant to substitute their judgment for that of management.

**The Rate Base.**   The provision of a fair rate of return on invested capital may encourage the excessive use of capital. Let's suppose that regulators have determined 12 percent as a fair rate of return. The regulated firm will be allowed to earn annual profits equal to 12 percent of invested capital or the firm's rate base.

> The value of invested capital is the regulated firm's rate base.

For example, if a company has a rate base (invested capital) of $10 million and the profit rate ceiling is 12 percent, it will be allowed to earn a maximum profit of $1.2 million per year.

An unregulated company adds to its invested capital only if the present value of the resulting profits exceeds the cost of acquiring the capital. The regulated company, however, can increase its profits automatically by investing an additional $5 million, thereby expanding the rate base by $5 million, and earning a $1.8 million profit. Regulated firms have a greater incentive to acquire more capital than do unregulated firms. Because regulated firms invest at the margin in projects with rates of return lower than those realized by unregulated firms, they use capital less efficiently.[3]

## REGULATORY LAG

Price regulation reduces efficiency and discourages innovation more if regulators raise prices immediately when operating costs rise. In reality, price increases are not typically granted on a timely basis. Regulated utilities must file for rate increases, and lengthy hearings can create substantial delays. If rate increases are delayed while operating costs are rising, the regulated firm will not be able to earn its fair rate of return because of regulatory lag.

> **Regulatory lag** occurs when government regulators adjust rates some time after operating costs and the rate base have increased.

Regulatory lag may put pressure on regulated monopolies to economize on costs. If operating costs rise and if substantial time is required for the approval of higher rates, company earnings will fall in the meantime. By the time higher rates are granted, they are already outdated, and the incentive to hold down costs is still present. Regulatory lag is especially harmful to utility profits during inflationary periods, when costs are increasing faster than rates are being raised.

Regulatory lag may motivate regulated firms to use resources more efficiently, but it is only a partial and very imperfect solution to encourage efficient operation while guaranteeing a fair rate of return.

---

[3]The tendency of regulated monopolies to use too much capital was first analyzed by H. Averch and L.L. Johnson, "Behavior of the Firm Under Regulatory Constraint," *American Economic Review* 52 (December 1962).

## THE EFFECTIVENESS OF REGULATION

Regulation is carried out by officials, either elected or appointed, who make decisions on the basis of imperfect information.

Some experts believe that regulation cannot work because "regulation is acquired by the industry and is designed and operated primarily for its benefit."[4] Although regulators are charged with protecting the public interest, each of the consumers they protect may benefit a little by effective regulation. The regulated companies, on the other hand, stand to gain or lose a great deal at the hands of regulators. Regulated firms are big winners if they can use regulators to restrict entry into the business by licenses and other means: "Every industry that has enough political power . . . will seek to control entry."[5]

This view of regulation suggests that regulators will be proindustry, will favor the interests of the industry over those of the consuming public, and will be willing to use their power to restrict competition in that industry.

Other experts think that regulators, especially elected officials, will be more concerned about their ability to gather votes for the next election than about protecting the regulated industry. Regulators will therefore have to balance the interests of consumers and producers. How they act will depend upon politics, but a strong stand against the regulated industry may be a powerful vote-getter.[6]

These two views of regulation reflect the real world. We can find many cases in which regulators take the side of regulated industries, such as the practice of protecting established companies (such as taxi companies, dry cleaners, masseurs, etc.) from competition by restrictive licensing. (See Example 2.) We can find many cases where regulators take strong but politically popular antiindustry stances by opposing rate increases for telephone companies and electrical utilities.

Regulation provides ample examples of the law of unexpected consequences. The Food and Drug Administration's job is to protect the public from unsafe pharmaceutical drugs. If the FDA approves a drug that later proves to be harmful, heads will roll. The safe approach for FDA officials is to require years of testing and to delay certification of a new drug, sometimes until persons who could have benefited from its use have died in the meantime. The Occupational Safety and Health Administration (OSHA) is charged with promoting health and safety at the workplace, namely, to help the working man or woman. By raising the costs of paperwork and imposing new kinds of administrative burdens on companies, OSHA causes employers to cut back on the number of employees and to switch to part-time or contract workers—again an unexpected consequence of well-intentioned legislation.

## PRIVATIZATION

Government ownership can be reversed by privatization.

> **Privatization** refers to the sale of government-owned enterprises to private buyers to convert them from public to private ownership.

The public chooses privatization when it concludes that government ownership creates an inferior result to private ownership. Economic conditions such as increasing competition may change to favor private ownership. The public may become alarmed by bureaucratic inefficiency. State-owned enterprises may lack a profit motive. Bureaucratic managers often lack the incentive to combine resources efficiently, so public enterprises may operate at higher costs than private enterprises. The government-owned monopoly may make chronic losses that must be paid for by taxpayers. Privatization offers the chance to operate on commercial principles and to restore the company to profitability. (See Example 3 on page 242.)

The failure of the socialist experiment, a Defining Moment of economics, is attributed to government ownership. If property is owned by everyone, it is, in reality, owned by no one. The Industrial Revolution, another Defining Moment, was based on private ownership. The Industrial Revolution would not have occurred without private ownership.

[4]George Stigler, "The Theory of Economic Regulation," *Bell Journal of Economics and Management Science*, no. 2 (Spring 1971), p. 3.

[5]Ibid., p. 5.

[6]Sam Peltzman, "Towards a More General Theory of Regulation," *Journal of Law and Economics*, vol. 19 (August 1976), pp. 211–240.

## EXAMPLE 2
## LICENSING TAXICABS:
## WHO IS PROTECTING WHOM?

City councils often restrict entry into the taxicab business, either by limiting the number of cab licenses (called medallions) or by passing ordinances identifying which cab companies are entitled to pick up passengers at municipal airports or bus terminals. Such licensing and ordinances are justified on the grounds that they ensure safety and quality.

Restrictions on entry raise the price of taxicab services to consumers. By limiting business to a small number of licensed companies, city councils create a monopoly that permits taxicabs to charge prices above the competitive price. The number of licenses or taxi medallions in New York City has remained constant at 11,787 since 1937. Medallions cost more than $100,000 in 1995. Medallion restrictions limit entry into the business, but they also create incentives for new forms of competition. "Gypsy cabs" operate without a license and offer transportation at a cheaper price. Livery services offer sleek limousines for less than the price of a licensed cab, but limousines are not allowed to roam the streets for customers.

## DEREGULATION

Economists favor deregulation of industries that are potentially competitive. Deregulation allows customers a broader choice of quality and price and eliminates stifling bureaucratic rules. Where the potential for competition exists, it is better for professional managers, not government bureaucrats, to make decisions about prices and services. The public will receive better service at lower cost. As a former chairman of a federal regulatory agency put it, "I have more faith in greed than in regulation."

Prior to deregulation, the Interstate Commerce Commission (ICC) forced truckers to travel roundabout routes and to return with empty trucks from long hauls. The ICC also required that prices charged by motor carriers and railroads be the same despite substantial cost differences. The Civil Aeronautics Board (CAB) required airlines to charge the same fare per passenger mile even if the plane were habitually full on one route and habitually empty on another. Consumers paid for these inefficiencies with higher prices.

### DEREGULATION LEGISLATION

In October 1978, President Jimmy Carter signed the Airline Deregulation Act, the first of several major deregulation acts. The Airline Deregulation Act allowed the airlines, rather than the Civil Aeronautics Board, to set their own fares and select their own routes. Service to smaller communities, financed by government subsidy when necessary, was continued until 1988. The act phased out the CAB at the end of 1984.

Three major federal deregulation acts followed in 1980. The Motor Carrier Act curbed the ICC's control over interstate trucking, allowing truckers greater autonomy in setting rates and changing routes. The Staggers Rail Act gave the railroads more flexibility in setting rates and allowed railroads to drop unprofitable routes. The Depository Institutions Deregulation and Monetary Control Act eliminated interest-rate ceilings on bank savings deposits and allowed savings and loan associates to offer checking accounts, car loans, and credit cards. The 1982 Thrift Institutions Restructuring Act enabled savings and loan institutions to operate on a more equal footing with commercial banks. The Bus Deregulatory Reform Act of 1982 allowed intercity bus lines to operate in many circumstances without applying for federal licenses.

Other deregulation was introduced by the regulatory commissions themselves. The Federal Communications Commission has allowed more channels to

# EXAMPLE 3
## THE PRIVATIZATION
## WAVE

The European countries have a longer history of public ownership, from telecommunications, to electrical power, and even to manufacturing and energy production. In Germany and France, the telephone companies are state owned, and they contribute their profits each year to the state budget. In the United States, new subscribers wait only a few days for their telephone service. In Germany and France, the wait can be for several weeks. In Germany and France, the state airlines—Lufthansa and Air France—are majority owned by the state. Notably, British Air was privatized in the 1980s and was the only profitable carrier of the three in the early 1990s.

The governments of Germany and France have decided to privatize state enterprises. In the summer of 1994, the German government approved plans to sell stock in Deutsche Telekom to the public and eventually make it a private company. Lufthansa announced plans to privatize its state-owned shares in 1995. France is carrying out its own sweeping privatization plans, announcing that it would reduce its stake in Renault, the automobile company, from 79 percent to 51 percent.

What are the reasons for this interest in privatization? The increase in international competition caused European governments to question whether their state companies could compete in an international market place. The privatized British Air outcompeted Lufthansa and Air France. Foreign telecommunications companies were entering new markets, while Deutsche Telekom could scarcely satisfy its domestic market.

*Sources:* "German Privatization Plan," *New York Times,* July 11, 1994; "France's Renault Stake," *New York Times,* September 14, 1994.

---

be available to television broadcasters. The Securities and Exchange Commission made the brokerage fees charged by stockbrokers on the New York Stock Exchange freely negotiable. The Federal Communications Commission deregulated long distance telephone service in an agreement reached with AT&T in 1982. Since then, there has been a dramatic rise in competition among rival phone companies, which is now being extended to local telephone service.

## THE EFFECTS OF DEREGULATION

The early years of deregulation were not tranquil. Airline deregulation was carried out amid two costly recessions and escalating fuel bills. Many airlines went out of business. The deregulation of trucking was fought by unions and by major trucking firms. Banking deregulation was undertaken during a period of high interest rates, numerous bank failures, and an international debt crisis. Rival long distance telephone companies did not gain equal access to local telephone exchanges until the mid-1980s.

Critics of deregulation warned that without regulation, consumers would be denied an essential service. Regulation requires access to all customers, but deregulated firms serve only profitable markets. Small communities might therefore find themselves without rail or air service. Critics also warned that competition would be eliminated by the emergence of a dominant producer, which would act as a monopolist. Critics further cautioned that deregulation would cause a loss of public control of the quality of service. Public interest programming would disappear if access to the airwaves were not regulated.

Deregulation should be judged in terms of prices, costs, and quality of service. Airlines fares fell by about 30 percent below what they would have been if regulation had continued.[7] Commissions on stock transactions dropped considerably except for small transactions. An order for 100 shares cost 20 percent less but an order for 50 shares cost 12 percent more after deregulation. Deregulation gave us a choice between discount brokers and full service brokers who offer more services at higher prices. Deregulation encouraged new firms to enter into trucking, causing rates to decrease. Rates for truckload shipments fell by 25 percent (after adjustment for inflation), and rates for less-than-truckload shipments fell by 16 percent. Airline costs fell after deregulation despite rising fuel prices. Labor productivity rose by 20 percent during the first five years of deregulation. As competition among long distance services increased, long distance rates fell.

Deregulation imposed costs as well as benefits, however. Many airlines were unable to survive competitive pressures and went bankrupt. The earnings of airline and trucking employees fell as companies cut costs. Mergers were negotiated as healthy airlines acquired financially troubled ones. By the early 1990s, mergers and bankruptcies created a domestic airline industry consisting of three large carriers (United, American, and Delta) and one rapidly growing carrier (Southwest). Commercial banks and savings and loan institutions found themselves in a new highly competitive environment. Many of them failed, although it is difficult to blame deregulation itself. The three major television networks faced increased competition from Fox and other broadcasters. Stockbrokers from major brokerage firms had to face competition from no-frills brokers.

Prior to deregulation, economists estimated the price of regulation at between 0.7 percent and 1.8 percent of total national output. For the more than $7 trillion economy of the mid-1990s, a continuation of regulation would have cost about $70 billion per year—about one-third of the federal deficit.[8]

Deregulation has done exactly what economists said it would. It reintroduced competition and the positive and negative sides of competition. Firms can no longer relax knowing that no matter what their costs or service they will make a profit. The reintroduction of competition has transformed complacent industries into dynamic instruments of change. In aviation, new low-cost airlines (such as Southwest and Reno Air) entered the market and outcompeted industry giants. The deregulation of telecommunications encouraged breathtaking advances in communications, data, and fax transmissions. The U.S. deregulation experience provides a powerful example for the rest of the world, prompting a movement toward deregulation in Europe and Japan.

## ANTITRUST LAW

The major alternative to direct regulation of monopolies is legislation to control market structure and market conduct. Rather than telling monopolies what prices and services they must offer, the government sets the legal rules of the economic game.

> Antitrust law is legislation designed to control market structure and conduct.

The cornerstone of federal antitrust legislation is the Sherman Antitrust Act of 1890. The Sherman Act was passed in reaction to the public outrage against the trust movement in the railroad, steel, tobacco, and oil industries of the late nineteenth century. It was this act under which Standard Oil was broken up, as described in the Chapter Insight.

> A **trust** is a combination of firms that sets common prices, agrees to restrict output,

---

[7]William G. Sheperd and James W. Brock, "Airlines," in Walter Adams and James Brock, eds., *The Structure of American Industry* (Englewood Cliffs, NJ: Prentice-Hall, 1995), pp. 242, 272; Elizabeth E. Bailey, "Price and Productivity Change Following Deregulation: The U.S. Experience," *The Economic Journal* 96 (March 1986): 1–17.

[8]Robert Litan and William Nordhaus (eds.), *Reforming Federal Regulation* (New Haven, CT: Yale University Press, 1983). These figures are based on studies by Murray Weidenbaum and R. DeFina, T.G. Moore, Ann Friedlander, Gerald Jautscher, G.W. Douglas, James C. Miller, and W. Comanor and B. Mitchell.

and punishes member firms who fail to live up to the agreement.

## THE SHERMAN ACT OF 1890

The Sherman Act contains two sections. Section 1 provides that "every contract, combination in the form of a trust or otherwise, or conspiracy, in restraint of trade or commerce among the several states, or with foreign nations, is hereby declared to be illegal." Section 2 provides that "every person who shall monopolize, or attempt to monopolize, or combine or conspire with any other person or persons to monopolize any part of the trade or commerce among the several states, or with foreign nations, shall be guilty of a misdemeanor."

Section 1 prohibits a particular type of market conduct (conspiring to restrain trade), whereas Section 2 outlaws a particular market structure (monopoly). The vague language of Section 2 prohibits monopolization, not monopolies; although the act of creating a monopoly is clearly prohibited, the legality of existing monopolies is not resolved.

## THE CLAYTON ACT AND THE
## FEDERAL TRADE COMMISSION ACT OF 1914

The Sherman Act did not identify specific monopolistic practices that were in violation of the law, nor did it establish any agency (other than the existing Department of Justice) to enforce its provisions.

The Clayton Act of 1914 declared specific monopolistic practices to be illegal if their "effect was to substantially lessen competition or to create a monopoly."[9] The act gave private parties the right to sue—along with other penalties—for damages from injury to business or property resulting from violations of the antitrust laws.

The Federal Trade Commission Act established the Federal Trade Commission (FTC) to secure compliance with the ban on "unfair methods of competition." It was granted the authority to prosecute unfair competition and to issue cease and desist orders to violators.

The Clayton Act was revised and amended by subsequent acts. The Robinson-Patman Act—which was passed during the Great Depression in 1936, when the rate of failure for small businesses was high—protected small businesses from the competition of the growing chain stores that were receiving discounts for large purchases. The primary purpose of the Robinson-Patman Act seemed to be protection of competitors—small companies—rather than protection of competition. The Wheeler-Lea Act of 1938 extended the general ban on "unfair methods of competition" to include "unfair or deceptive" acts or practices. Under this amendment the FTC was empowered to deal with false and deceptive advertising and the sale or harmful products.

The Celler-Kefauver Act of 1950 broadened the Clayton Act's ban on corporate mergers by limiting the acquisition of one company's assets by another company, if the acquisition served to substantially lessen competition or to create a monopoly.

## INTERPRETATION OF THE SHERMAN ACT

American antitrust policy is determined in the courts as well as in Congress. The Sherman Antitrust Act, the mainstay of antitrust legislation, left a basic issue unresolved: Do antitrust laws prohibit only market conduct that leads to monopoly, or does monopoly by the mere fact of its existence constitute a violation?

## THE RULE OF REASON, 1911–1945

In early rulings, the courts interpreted the Sherman Act as outlawing specific market practices that restrained trade (mergers, price fixing, price slashing to drive out competition), not the existence of monopoly in and of itself. This interpretation became known as the rule of reason.[10]

---

[9]The illegal acts are
1. Price discrimination (charging different prices to different customers for the same product),
2. Exclusive dealing and tying contracts (requiring a buyer to agree not to purchase goods from competitors),
3. Acquisition of competing companies, and
4. Interlocking directorates, in which the directors of one company sit on the board of directors of another company in the same industry

---

[10]This discussion of court rulings is based on Frederic Sherer, *Industrial Structure and Economic Performance,* 3rd ed. (Boston: Houghton Mifflin, 1990); Oliver Williamson, *Markets and Hierarchies: Analysis and Antitrust Implications* (New York: The Free Press, 1975); and William Shepherd, *The Economics of Industrial Organization,* 3rd ed. (Englewood Cliffs, NJ: Prentice-Hall, 1990).

> The **rule of reason** stated that monopolies were in violation of the Sherman Act if they used unfair or illegal business practices. Being a monopoly in and of itself was not a violation of the Sherman Act.

The early landmark tests of the Sherman Act were the Standard Oil and American Tobacco Company cases, both tried in 1911. In both cases, the Supreme Court ruled that these companies should be broken up into smaller companies. Both companies accounted for more than 90 percent of industry output, but they were ruled in violation of the Sherman Act for engaging in unreasonable restraint of trade, not for being monopolies.

The rule of reason was upheld in a number of cases, such as the U.S. Steel case of 1920. U.S. Steel was, in effect, ruled to be a "benevolent" monopolist. In this case, the court stated that the law did not consider mere size or the existence of "unexerted power" to be an offense.

## QUESTIONING THE RULE OF REASON

The rule of reason prevailed until the Aluminum Company of America (Alcoa) case of 1945, when the courts ruled that Alcoa violated the Sherman Act because it controlled more than 90 percent of the aluminum ingot market. In a famous decision written by Judge Learned Hand, the courts ruled that size alone was a violation of the Sherman Act, thereby appearing to overturn the rule of reason.

## DEFINITION OF MARKET

The Alcoa decision raised a fundamental issue: If the existence of monopoly is itself a violation of the Sherman Act, how is the market to be defined?

In the Alcoa case, Alcoa controlled 90 percent of the aluminum ingot market, but it had to compete in the scrap ingot market and faced competition from stainless steel, lead, nickel, tin, zinc, copper, and imported aluminum. The court ruled that substitutes for aluminum should not be included in Alcoa's market; thus, Alcoa was characterized as a monopoly.

DuPont produced almost 75 percent of the cellophane sold in the United States but accounted for less than 20 percent of the sales of flexible wrapping materials. Du Pont was accused in 1956 of monopolizing the cellophane market. The Supreme Court ruled that the flexible wrapping materials market should be defined to include "reasonably interchangeable" products such as aluminum foil or waxed paper, and that Du Pont's 20 percent share of this larger market was insufficient for a monopoly.

In 1982, after more than a decade of litigation involving 66 million pages of documents, the Justice Department dropped its suit against IBM for monopolizing the "general-purpose computer and peripheral-equipment industry." By the time of the 1982 decision, IBM dominated only the mainframe computer industry (with 70 percent of the U.S. market). In its other lines of business, IBM's shares were relatively small: 20 percent of the minicomputer market, 18 percent of the word-processor market, and less than 5 percent of the telecommunications and computer services market. Based on these developments, the Justice Department decided that IBM did not monopolize the computer industry as broadly defined. In fact, in the 1990s, IBM's share of the computer market continued to slip as it failed to keep up with its more aggressive competitors.

Also in 1982, American Telephone and Telegraph agreed to give up its regional Bell affiliates, the "Baby Bells," in return for permission to enter unregulated telecommunications and computer markets. (See Example 4.) This decision opened up the telecommunications market to the intense competition—from AT&T, Sprint, cellular telephones—that we take for granted today.

## SUPERIOR INNOVATION

The Alcoa decision raised concern among businesses that it would, in the words of a former head of the Justice Department's Antitrust Division, be used "to punish innovative success."[11]

Many companies gain monopoly positions not through unfair business practices but with superior innovation. Is a company that attains a dominant position through superior foresight, good planning, proper risk taking, and aggressive technological innovation violating the Sherman Act?

In decisions beginning in the 1970s involving industrial powerhouses like Eastman Kodak and Du Pont, antitrust charges were dismissed on the

---

[11]*Wall Street Journal,* November 10, 1980.

## EXAMPLE 4
## COMPETITION FOR YOUR
## PHONE BUSINESS

Prior to 1982, local and long distance telephone service was supplied by a monopoly, the Bell System, which consisted of AT&T, the regional Bell affiliates such as Southwestern Bell and Pacific Bell, and Bell Laboratories. In 1982, the Bell System agreed to give up its monopoly (in an agreement with the Justice Department) in return for being allowed to enter into computer and telecommunications markets. Since then, we can hardly turn on the television or open the mail without being bombarded by claims that one long distance service (Sprint, MCI, AT&T) is better and offers lower prices than the others.

Such competition had been limited to long distance service. Now it appears headed for local telephone service. In September of 1994, the FCC ap-

proved the acquisition of McCaw Cellular Communications, the world's largest cellular telephone operator, by AT&T. By uniting AT&T's marketing power in long distance with McCaw's power to provide wireless local telephone service, AT&T will be able to compete with the "Baby Bells"—the former regional affiliates of the Bell System—for local service. Soon we shall be bombarded with ads to quit the local telephone company for AT&T's combination of local and long distance service, all based upon a wireless cellular service. To protect themselves the various regional Bells, such as Nynex and Bell Atlantic, have begun to merge.

*Source:* "AT&T Completes Deal to Buy McCaw Cellular," *New York Times,* August 20, 1994.

---

grounds that the company had earned certain advantages by "reaping the competitive rewards attributable to efficient size,"[12] and that

> the essence of the competitive process is to induce firms to become more efficient and to pass the benefits of the efficiency along to consumers. That process would be ill served by using antitrust to block hard, aggressive competition, even if monopoly is an inevitable result.[13]

This type of thinking was reaffirmed in 1994 with an agreement between Microsoft, founded by Bill Gates, and the Justice Department. Although Microsoft had been accused of monopolistic practices, the Justice Department did not want to take on a "man and a company who were symbols of U.S.

technological industry."[14] Gates's plans for expansion into the telecommunications industry are again attracting attention from the Justice Department, which is concerned about Microsoft's growing share of the information industry.

## MERGERS

The Clayton Act of 1914 and the Celler-Kefauver Act of 1950 prohibit the acquisition of one company by another if such action reduces competition. Mergers, in which two firms combine to form one, can be of three general types: horizontal mergers, vertical mergers, and conglomerate mergers.

> A **horizontal merger** is a merger of two firms in the same line of business (such as two in-

---

[12]This case is summarized in "FTC Dismisses Charges against Du Pont in Major Statement of Its Antitrust Policy," *Wall Street Journal,* November 10, 1980.

[13]*Wall Street Journal,* November 10, 1980.

[14]"Microsoft Will Remain Dominant Despite Pact in Antitrust Dispute," *Wall Street Journal,* July 18, 1994.

surance companies or two shoe manufacturers). A **vertical merger** is a merger of two firms that are part of the same materials, production, or distribution network (such as a personal computer manufacturer and a retail computer distributor). A **conglomerate merger** is a merger of companies in different lines of business.

The courts (especially since 1950) have adopted a virtual prohibition of horizontal mergers if both firms have substantial market shares. The Federal Trade Commission blocked Coca-Cola's acquisition of Dr. Pepper and Pepsico's acquisition of Seven-Up in 1986. If the mergers had been allowed, the combined market share of Coca-Cola and Pepsico would have been 80 percent. Exceptions are allowed when one firm takes over another firm that is on the verge of bankruptcy. The many airline mergers of the 1980s were motivated by the desire to keep in the airline business the assets of failing companies. The State of New York allowed the merger of Macy's and Federated Department Stores in 1994 to bring Macy's out of bankruptcy. With the decline in defense spending, two leading military subcontractors—Lockheed and Martin Marietta—have proposed to merge. Growing competition from European aircraft manufacturers caused merger talks to begin between Boeing and McDonnel Douglas in late 1995.

Vertical mergers are in violation of the Clayton Act if merging with a supplier enables the buyer to cut out competitors, or if the vertical merger results in a transfer of significant market power. In 1957 Du Pont (a major supplier of automotive fabrics and finishes) was required to sell its 23 percent ownership of General Motors stock, which gave it a competitive advantage over other automotive suppliers. Brown Shoe Company was not allowed in 1962 to acquire Kinney (a large retain shoe chain). However, in 1986, the ban on vertical mergers between moviemakers and movie theaters was eased because of increased competition from network TV, cable TV, and pay-per-view television.

Over the past 40 years conglomerate mergers have led to substantial increase in the share of corporate assets controlled by the largest U.S. corporations. According to FTC statistics, the 451 largest corporations controlled half of corporate assets in 1960; in the mid 1990s, they controlled almost three-quarters.

The pace of mergers has been highly uneven (see Figure 3). In part, this pattern reflects the fact that both antimerger legislation and the rigor of enforcement of such legislation have varied over the years. Republican administrations have tended to be more favorable toward mergers than have Democratic administrations.

The rapid pace of mergers of the 1980s slowed in the 1990s. An economic downturn and limited success of diversified mergers caused some companies—for example, pharmaceutical-cosmetic ventures—to rid themselves of their acquisitions. Food products companies, such as RJR Nabisco, are considering selling off their tobacco interests.

# PROPOSALS FOR IMPROVED GOVERNMENT MONOPOLY CONTROL

Proposals for improving government control of monopoly include selling monopoly franchises, requiring consumer representation in management, and repealing antitrust laws.

## SELLING MONOPOLY FRANCHISES

Some economists argue that natural monopolies would be better managed if they were not regulated at all. An unregulated monopoly would be motivated to minimize costs, limit prices to keep potential competitors out of the market, and seek out innovation.

If natural monopolies were deregulated, the government could sell monopoly franchises (licenses to operate the monopoly) to the highest bidder, thereby recapturing most of the monopoly profits. Competitive bidding would force private investors to pay the present value of future monopoly profits. The monopoly would, however, continue to produce an output less than the social optimum and charge a price higher than the optimum.

## REQUIRING CONSUMER REPRESENTATION IN MANAGEMENT

Another proposal is to place consumer representatives on the board of directors of natural monopolies or to grant consumers a voting interest in such firms. Important actions of the board of directors could be referred to consumers by means of municipal elections.

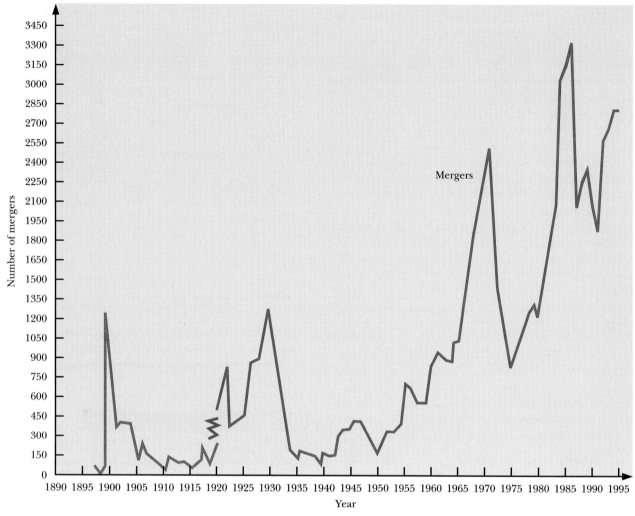

**FIGURE 3  Mergers in the United States, 1890–1995**

*Sources:* The National Bureau of Economic Research and the Federal Trade Commission, *Mergers and Acquisitions.* Updated data courtesy of Merrill Lynch, *Mergerstat Review.*

If these measures were undertaken, it is argued, management would identify more closely with the interest of consumers and would refrain from abusing monopoly power.

## REPEALING ANTITRUST LAWS

Some economists argue that the costs of applying antitrust laws outweigh the benefits to consumers. Antitrust battles force corporations to spend billions of dollars on legal expenses, and litigation can last decades. For example, before its dismissal, the IBM case lasted 13 years, costing the government more than $12 million and IBM even more. Microsoft's ongoing battles with the Justice Department in the 1990s have cost both sides millions of dollars.

The growth in international trade has largely outmoded antitrust laws, which were passed in the early part of this century. Major U.S. corporations that account for substantial shares of U.S. production must now compete with foreign companies. Moreover, modern technology facilitates the development of substitutes that pose a competitive threat to all monopolies that earn monopoly profits. Finally, monopolies may indeed be the result of superior innovation and better management. The breakup of efficient companies may actually reduce efficiency by punishing aggressive innovation.

## EVOLVING VIEWS OF ANTITRUST

Why has antitrust policy changed over the years? In 1945, at the time of the Alcoa decision, economists wanted to hold the world to strict standards of perfect competition. Today, we have come to understand that it is not so much the world that is imperfect but the theory of perfect competition. The presence of information and transaction costs precludes the existence of perfect competition in its pure form. Thus, the resulting divergence of real-world industries from perfect competition does not necessarily represent a case for antitrust action. Economists realize that the world is complex, and efficient arrangements may take many forms.

We are coming to appreciate the fact that diversity may be a good thing. We may need Microsofts, Intels, and AT&Ts for certain industries and a large number of highly competitive firms for other industries. We also know that monopoly power tends to be transitory and that the threat of competition is ever-present, if not today then tomorrow.

In this chapter we have reviewed antitrust law and regulation. In the next chapter we shall consider the role of information in the economy.

SUMMARY

1. In a natural monopoly, industry output is produced by a single producer because of economies of scale over the entire range of the industry's output.

2. It is not clear how to operate government monopolies "in the public interest." Marginal-cost pricing normally leads to losses. A break-even strategy provides little incentive to reduce costs or innovate. If the government monopoly tries to maximize profits, the consumer receives no benefit.

3. Regulation of natural monopolies is aimed at limiting monopoly profits while allowing the monopoly to operate profitably, encouraging efficient operation, and preventing predatory competition. Regulated monopolies are normally allowed to charge a price that covers operating costs plus a "fair" rate of return on invested capital. This pricing formula fosters inefficiency because higher costs can be passed on to the consumer and higher investment automatically yields higher profits. Regulatory lag provides some incentive to minimize costs.

4. Regulation of potentially competitive industries creates inefficiencies and poor service. A significant deregulation movement to free competitive industries in the United States from government supervision began in the late 1970s.

5. The goal of antitrust legislation is to control market structure and market conduct by setting legal rules for businesses to follow. The Sherman Act outlaws the restraint of trade and the act of monopolization. The Clayton Act specifies which business practices illegally restrain trade. The Federal Trade Commission Act established the Federal Trade Commission and banned unfair methods of competition. The Celler-Kefauver Act toughened the antimerger provisions of the Clayton Act.

6. The "rule of reason," which held that only unreasonable restraint of trade violated the Sherman Act, was applied by the courts in antitrust cases until 1945. The rule of reason appeared to be overturned in 1945 with the Alcoa decision, when the courts judged size alone to be a violation of the Sherman Act. In subsequent cases, however, the courts have ruled that monopolies created by superior technological achievement do not violate the Sherman Act.

7. Mergers between firms in the same industry are prohibited if both have substantial market shares. Exceptions are allowed when one firm takes over another that is on the verge of bankruptcy. Conglomerate mergers are not opposed because they do not involve competing companies.

8. Some alternative methods of controlling monopoly that have been proposed include deregulating natural monopolies and selling monopoly franchises to the highest bidder, placing consumer representative on the boards of directors of monopoly corporations, and repealing antitrust laws.

KEY TERMS

regulation     privatization
regulatory lag    trust

rule of reason
horizontal merger

vertical merger
conglomerate merger

## QUESTIONS AND PROBLEMS

1. Explain why, in the case of a natural monopoly, the industry functions most efficiently with only one producer.

2. Devise a set of rules that would, in your opinion, allow a government-owned natural monopoly to operate "in the public interest." How would these rules be different if the firm were not a natural monopoly?

3. You are the president of a regulated monopoly. You know that the regulators will allow you to set prices to cover operating costs plus a "fair" rate of return on invested capital. How would you behave? Would you behave differently if you were not regulated?

4. One explanation offered for why regulation of electric utilities has not made much difference in utility rates is that electric utilities face competition. What kind of competition can a monopoly like an electric power utility face?

5. You operate a regulated monopoly that sells in both a competitive and a monopolistic market. How would your company's price and output decisions differ in the two markets? What steps would you take to improve your position in the competitive market?

6. Deregulation of the television broadcasting industry has been opposed by the three major networks. They wanted to keep the number of channels limited to four. How would deregulation affect their profits?

7. Explain the contradiction raised by the rule of reason.

8. Why would innovative and risk-taking firms such as Boeing and Eastman Kodak fear the Alcoa decision?

9. Evaluate the proposal to auction off monopoly franchises to the highest bidder. Why would this return most of the monopoly profits to the government?

10. Evaluate the validity of the following statement: "Several ill-informed people have suggested doing away with our antitrust laws. To do so would return us to the days of the nineteenth-century robber barons."

11. Would regulatory lag tend to raise or lower economic efficiency? Why?

12. Which of the following pairs of companies would antitrust authorities be more likely to allow to merge? Why?
    a. General Motors and Chrysler
    b. Prudential Insurance and McDonald's
    c. Hyatt Hotels and American Airlines
    d. U.S. Foods and Kroger Stores
    e. U.S. Steel and Ford Motor Company
    f. B.F. Goodrich and General Motors

13. Economists who have studied the regulation of electric utilities have found that regulation has had little effect on prices. How do you explain the absence of a change in prices despite the ability of regulators to set prices?

14. Explain why the definition of the market has become a critical issue in antitrust law.

# CHAPTER 15

# THE ECONOMICS OF INFORMATION

*[handwritten note: Only if marginal cost exceeds marginal benefit (why?)]*

"Speculators," "intermediaries," and others in the "information business" are often unpopular people. Farmers complain about the speculators who buy from them when the price is low and resell later at a higher price. Consumers complain about rising grocery prices, which they attribute to greedy grocers. The family that sells its home for $100,000 complains about the $6,000 fee collected by their realtor. In the former Soviet Union buying low and selling high was considered a crime.

In this chapter we shall examine the role of information in an economy. The information pro-

vided by those in the "information business"—speculators, realtors, agents, intermediaries, stockbrokers, and others—is a valuable commodity. People and businesses voluntarily pay billions of dollars to acquire information on prices, location, and quality.

We shall also focus on why information is a valuable commodity; the role of intermediaries, speculators, and hedgers; the costs of gathering information about markets and products; and the problems of moral hazard and adverse selection.

# TRANSACTION COSTS AND INFORMATION COSTS

It is costly to bring buyers and sellers together. The costs associated with making exchange possible are transaction costs. Some examples are the cost of travel, the cost of negotiation, the cost of property-rights enforcement, and the cost of acquiring information.

> **Transaction costs** are the costs associated with bringing buyers and sellers together.

In real-world markets—even those that are highly competitive—there is considerable uncertainty about current or future prices and even about product qualities. If such information were available instantaneously at no cost of time or money, such uncertainty would evaporate. But acquiring information typically does have its costs, and information costs have a substantial effect on real-world markets.

> **Information costs** are the costs of acquiring information on prices, product qualities, and product performance.

Information costs include the costs of telephoning, shopping, checking credentials, inspecting goods, monitoring the honesty of workers or customers, placing ads, and reading ads and consumer reports in order to acquire more economic information.

Information is costly because we have a limited capacity to acquire, process, store, and retrieve facts and figures about prices, qualities, and location of products. Information is distributed over the population in bits and pieces.

Transaction costs are affected by information costs. The buyer and seller must first find each other and then agree on the price and other terms of the contract. Knowledge of the existence and location of a willing buyer is valuable information to the seller, just as knowledge of a willing seller is valuable information to the buyer. Without this information, economic transactions cannot take place.

The microprocessor—the miniature brain behind modern computers and the so-called information superhighway—has substantially brought down the cost of communicating and processing information. Despite enormous progress, though, the computer cannot read minds, predict the future, or start a fad. For example, computer software is an enormous

market, but it takes a human being to write the software and make a prediction about what people will want to buy. Bill Gates became a multibillionaire with his Microsoft Corporation. This required unique human imagination. It is information costs that makes multibillionaires possible. If information costs were zero, the billions made by Bill Gates would have been spread over millions of people.

Because information is costly, each individual accumulates information that is specific to that person's particular circumstances. For example, a farmer has detailed knowledge about local growing conditions, and consumers know a great deal about local food prices. This special information can be valuable. (See Example 1.) To quote the Nobel Prize laureate Friedrich A. Hayek:

> a little reflection will show that there is beyond question a body of very important but unorganized knowledge which cannot possibly be called scientific in the sense of knowledge of general rules: the knowledge of particular circumstances of time and place. It is with respect to this that every individual has some advantage over all others in that he possesses unique information of which beneficial use might be made.[1]

By allowing people to be paid for their scarce information, the price system economizes on information costs. The auto mechanic does not have to learn nuclear physics, and the physicist does not have to know how to repair a car.

> Information is typically a scarce and valuable commodity.

# THE ECONOMICS OF SEARCH

We know that *a perfectly competitive market* is one in which all buyers pay the same price for the same product. In many real-world markets, however, the prices of even homogeneous goods (milk, bread, gasoline, etc.) differ from store to store. In these real-world markets, it is more difficult for consumers to know the prices charged for the same items in different stores—even if consumers are aware of price dif-

---

[1]F. A. Hayek, "The Use of Knowledge in Society," *American Economic Review* 35 (1945): 510—530.

## EXAMPLE 1
## THE VALUE OF GOOD TASTE:
## A FISH STORY

Tokyo's Tsukiji fish market may well be the largest wholesale fish market in the world. Fish are everywhere—in bins and forklifts, on bidding floors and tables, on the shoulders of workers. There are live squid and octopus, huge shrimp, big crabs, tuna—about 500 varieties of fish from all over the world. The place is so clean and the fish so fresh that there is no telltale fish odor. In about 90 minutes, the Tsukiji fish market sells 3000 metric tons of fish.

Perhaps the most interesting part of this fish story is the tuna market. Even though several thousand tuna are sold on a given day, each tuna is auctioned individually. A platoon of tuna experts checks each tuna for the ratio of fat to meat. Tuna buyers use this information to bid on the individual tunas. A high-quality tuna with a high ratio of fat to meat tastes better and, therefore, might sell for as much as $36 per pound, while a tuna with very little fat might only sell for $1.80 per pound. The information regarding fat content can cause the price to vary by as much as 20 times! Without this information—in a world of ignorance—all tuna would sell for the same price. People are willing to pay for better-tasting tuna.

------------------------------------------------

*Source:* George L. Rosenblatt, "Fish Story," *Houston Chronicle,* April 21, 1991.

ferences, the transaction costs of always going to the cheapest store may outweigh the advantages of the lower price. As a consequence, the price for the same good differs from location to location. Such markets are usually imperfect because different buyers appear to pay different prices for the same product. From an economic viewpoint, however, the same good in a different location is considered a different product.

## INFORMATION GATHERING AND PRICE DISPERSION

A consumer incurs search costs while shopping, reading, or consulting experts in order to acquire pricing or quality information. Search costs explain why homogeneous products sell for different prices in different locations. A 19-inch Sony color TV set may sell for different prices in stores one block apart, the same brand of milk may sell for different prices in adjacent grocery stores, and the same brand of automobile may sell at different prices in two dealerships located in the same part of town.

If information about the prices charged by different retail outlets were free (assuming that no location is more convenient than another), the same commodity would sell for the same price, as predicted by the theory of perfect competition. But information is not free; real resources must be devoted to gathering information. Therefore, in the real world, the prices of homogeneous products sold in different locations will be dispersed.

In gathering costly information, people follow the optimal-search rule.

> The **optimal-search rule** states that people will continue to acquire economic information as long as the marginal benefits of gathering information exceed the marginal costs.

When a person decides to buy a new car, the more information that person has on the prices and on technical qualities of various automobiles, the better the eventual choice is likely to be. But it is costly to gather such information. It is costly to drive all over town to the various dealers; it is costly to take time off from work or from leisure activities to compare prices; it may be expensive in terms of time and money to acquire and master technical information contained in the various consumer-guide reports on new automobiles. To gather all the available information about new cars would take an inordinate amount of time and money; therefore, the prospective buyer must draw the line at the point where the marginal benefit from acquiring more information is equal to the marginal cost of acquiring more information.

Figure 1 illustrates the optimal-search rule. Suppose a consumer has just moved to a new town and is looking for the best place to buy a particular product. The consumer might visit several stores to collect valid price information. Thus, after some comparison shopping, the consumer will have a sample of the various prices charged. The vertical axis measures the benefits and costs of search per visit. The horizontal axis measures the lowest known price ($S$) that the consumer has collected through search. If the lowest known price is very small, the marginal benefit of search for that consumer will be low; if the lowest known price is very high, the marginal benefit of search will also be high. The upward-sloping curve in Figure 1 shows the marginal benefit of search for different values of the lowest sampled price. Since the marginal cost of search is assumed to be independent of the lowest price sampled, it will remain unchanged over the range of $S$ values. The price at which the marginal cost of search equals the marginal benefit of search (at point $e$) is the consumer's reservation price.

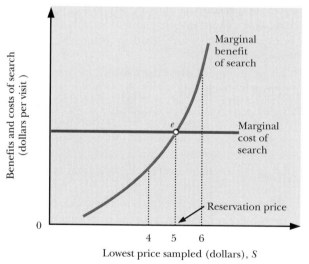

**FIGURE 1　Optimal-Search Rule**

The higher the lowest price sampled, the higher the marginal benefit of search. (The lowest price sampled is the best price quoted to the consumer.) The reservation price is the best price when the marginal benefit of search equals the marginal cost of search, or $5 in the case illustrated. If the lowest price sampled is $6, further search is required.

> The **reservation price** is the highest price at which the consumer will buy a good. Although the consumer will buy any good with a price lower than the reservation price, he or she will continue to search for a lower price only if the lowest price found exceeds the reservation price.

The reservation price in Figure 1 is $5. If the lowest price sampled is $6, the consumer should still search because the marginal benefit of search exceeds the marginal cost of search. If the lowest price is below $5—say, $4—the consumer will purchase the good because the marginal cost of search exceeds the marginal benefit of search. If the lowest price sampled is $5, the consumer is indifferent regarding continued search, because $5 is the highest price the consumer will pay for the product.

> The reservation price occurs at a sampled price at which the marginal benefit of search equals the marginal cost of search.

We can apply the theory that consumers use a search rule where marginal benefits equal marginal costs to predict the extent of price dispersion on different products. Clearly, anything that raises the marginal benefits of search relative to the marginal costs of search will increase the amount of searching. The more resources devoted to searching, the closer will be the prices of homogeneous products sold at different stores (high-priced stores will lose business to low-priced stores). The marginal benefits of search should be greater for more expensive items; therefore, the theory of search suggests that prices of more expensive items will be less widely dispersed than those of less expensive items. (See Example 2.)

There is considerable evidence to support this proposition. In a classic study, prices were found to be less widely dispersed for identical makes of automobiles than for identical brands of washing machines.[2]

An interesting paradox is that the greater the number of people who search, the less the individual needs to search. If everyone devoted considerable resources to information searching, price dispersion—and the gains to further search—would be reduced because the sellers would be aware of the search behavior.

[2]George Stigler, *The Theory of Price*, 4th ed. (New York: Macmillan, 1986), 4.

## EXAMPLE 2
## SHOPPING IN THE
## TWENTY-FIRST CENTURY

In the year 2005 shopping costs could be a fraction of what they were in 1995. Just click the remote control and a couple of buttons and the TV set lights up with a menu of shopping possibilities. Click on "Grocery Stores" and then on "Price Comparison." The computer can tell you the best prices of the products you buy and can even figure out the store where it is cheapest for you to shop.

As the printing press lowered the costs of printing by 99 percent, computerized shopping will lower the costs of shopping by 99 percent. The consequence will be that no store will be able to sell an item for a price much higher than that of its competitors. Shoppers, armed with all the prices, will buy at the store with the lowest price—especially for big-ticket items. Programs might even compare the travel costs of shopping at several stores with the savings from buying at the lowest price.

This system may not work with certain products, such as fresh fish and vegetables, where shoppers might like to pick for themselves. But for the vast majority of products, the computer could revolutionize shopping as it has revolutionized data processing and electronics.

------------------------------------------------

*Source:* "The Future of Shopping," *The Economist,* August 20, 1994, p. 6.

Information costs can be minimized for consumers by organizations such as the Consumers' Union, which tests products and sells the results in a monthly magazine. Government can also reduce information costs by establishing minimum standards and carrying out inspections to ensure that these standards are being observed. Municipal governments usually have health inspectors to inspect public dining places and public swimming pools. There are universal standards of weights and measures, and inspections to ensure that the butcher's scale is accurate. Without these governmental regulations and inspections, the costs of personal inspection and information gathering would be excessive.

## INFORMATION PROBLEMS

Economic dealings between individuals are governed by contracts. When a good is purchased, the seller explicitly or implicitly guarantees that the good will work according to an expected performance standard. An insurance contract stipulates that for a certain premium, the insurance company will pay out a certain amount of insurance if one or more specified events (a fire, a theft, or an automobile accident) occur. When information is costly, however, it can become difficult for one party in a contract to monitor the other party's performance, and it can be difficult to check the claims made by economic agents trying to secure favorable contracts.

## THE MORAL-HAZARD PROBLEM

It is not possible to buy insurance against poverty. No insurance company will sell you a policy that will pay you in the event of bankruptcy or unemployment. Such insurance does not exist because it could provide an incentive for a person to quit working or seek bankruptcy.

A **moral-hazard problem** exists when one of the parties to a contract has an incentive to alter his or her behavior after the contract is made at the expense of the second party. It arises because it is too costly for the second party to obtain information about the first party's postcontractual behavior.

Moral hazard is the reason why every fire insurance policy contains a provision that fires deliberately set by a policy owner (or agent of the owner) are not covered. Indeed, insurance companies spend millions to investigate fires to determine if there was any foul play.

The basic consequence of the moral-hazard problem is that firms can offer only those contracts that will not be flagrantly abused by their customers. The kinds of contracts offered must be limited to those that will minimize the moral-hazard problem.

As an illustration of the moral hazard problem, consider the guarantees that are offered on products. When a car is purchased, the manufacturer often gives a warranty on a car such as "the first four years or 50,000 miles, whichever comes first." The reason it does not offer a simple four-year warranty is moral hazard: there is little cost imposed on the person driving the car 200,000 miles the first year. Taxi drivers, for example, could easily take advantage of a simple four-year warranty: they would not have to worry about the car breaking down after 50,000 miles. Thus, in order for taxi drivers and the like to pay the cost of extraordinary usage, the limit of 50,000 miles is added to the basic warranty.

A second example is provided by smoking. We have known for decades that smoking cigarettes is harmful to the smoker. Some people want to make cigarette manufacturers liable for the health damage caused by smoking. However, if manufacturers are made liable for the health risks of smoking, the unintended consequence would be that the incentive to smoke would be much greater. The higher health costs would be passed from the individual to the company. This is a highly inefficient method of social engineering. If the cigarette companies had to pay some of the health costs of their customers, they would have to charge a higher price for cigarettes, whether or not they smoked one cigarette a day (presumably fairly safe) or 100 (presumably fairly unsafe). When it is known that smoking exposes the person to an additional health risk, it makes sense for society to place the cost on the individual doing the smoking.

A third example of moral hazard would be an automobile insurance policy that pays all damages if the policyholder is involved in a collision. Although it is unlikely that insured drivers would deliberately have collisions, such an insurance policy might give the driver an incentive to alter driving behavior. The driver might be less cautious in parking lots where most fender-bender accidents occur and might generally drive less defensively than normal. The insurance company cannot write into the contract that the dri-

ver must drive defensively because it is not possible to monitor the behavior of individual drivers.

The contracting parties who stand to suffer will adopt measures to minimize or prevent postcontractual opportunistic behavior. Most life insurance policies contain a clause that nullifies the contract in the case of suicide. The automobile insurer will require that drivers who have had accidents share the costs of losses by paying the first $250 or $500 to repair the damage, or by paying higher premiums in the future. If the claim is extremely large, the insurance company may even expend resources to investigate whether careless driving was involved.

In some instances, the moral-hazard problem is so severe that certain contracts cannot be written at all, at least not by private profit-maximizing companies. The poverty insurance mentioned earlier is such an example. In other cases, the moral-hazard problem is threatening enough that contracts must be limited. For example, private insurance companies find it difficult to issue general disability insurance because of opportunistic behavior. Although it is easy to establish disability in the case of lost arms or legs, it is difficult in the case of general back problems or emotional disturbances. Insurance companies expend enormous sums on information costs (maintaining a staff of physicians and investigators) to detect the opportunistic behavior that threatens their profitability.

When private markets cannot provide goods and services because of moral-hazard problems, these goods and services are sometimes provided by the state.

## THE ADVERSE-SELECTION PROBLEM

The moral-hazard problem occurs when one party to a contract engages in opportunistic behavior after the contract is made. The adverse-selection problem arises prior to the making of the contract.

> The **adverse-selection problem** occurs when a buyer or seller enters a disadvantageous contract on the basis of incomplete or inaccurate information because the cost of obtaining the relevant information makes it difficult to determine whether the deal is a good one or a bad one.

When a contracting party does not know the real intentions of the other party, the party with the superior information may be able to lure the other party into accepting an unfavorable contract. A contract is unfavorable if one of the contracting parties would not have entered into it if he or she had the same information as the other party. (See Example 3.)

The adverse-selection problem is encountered by those who set automobile insurance rates. Good drivers are less likely than bad drivers to have accidents that lead to costly claims against the insurance company. With full information, good drivers would not have to subsidize bad drivers, because insurance companies would be able to differentiate between good drivers and bad drivers.

Insurance companies face a different world: Smith and Jones are exactly alike except that Smith is a good driver who has never had an accident and Jones is a terrible driver who has been lucky never to have had an accident. Smith knows she is a good driver; Jones knows she is an accident waiting to happen. What about the insurance company? Unless insurance agents were to follow Smith and Jones around town and interview friends and neighbors, the insurance company cannot differentiate between Smith and Jones. Unable to gather such costly information, the insurance company sells automobile insurance to Smith and Jones at the same rate. Jones, who knows she is a terrible driver, will jump at the chance to buy insurance at the same rate as Smith. If the insurance company knew more about Smith and Jones, Jones would have to pay higher insurance rates to compensate for the higher probability of an accident.

In another example, business firms wish to hire high-quality workers, but it is very costly to find out in advance the true characteristics of workers. O'Neill and O'Leary are alike except that O'Neill is diligent and hardworking while O'Leary is lazy and without ambition. There is no reason for O'Leary to inform a potential employer of his laziness, and O'Neill's claims of diligence are likely to be dismissed as boasting. Because O'Leary and O'Neill appear alike to the firm, they are hired at the same wage rate. O'Leary, aware of his bad work skills, jumps at the chance. Armed with better information, the firm would not have entered into this contract.

Health insurance companies must also face the adverse-selection problem. If insurance companies had perfect information on the health of insurance applicants, they would offer health insurance to healthy 70-year-old people at rates that would reflect their likely health claims. However, it is impossible for insurance companies to gather extensive health data on individuals, so the insurance company will have to rely on available statistical data on general trends for different age groups. The healthy 70-year-old has private information about his or her plans to follow a healthy life-style, but the insurance company does not have the same information. For example, whether a person takes a daily walk and eats plenty of fresh fruits and vegetables is information that an insurance company cannot monitor. The healthy 70-year-old must therefore enter into a health insurance contract paying the same premiums as unhealthy 70-year-olds. If the insurance company had access to private information, a more favorable contract would have been written for the healthy 70-year-old.

Markets have developed responses to a variety of information problems. Every effort is made by buyers and sellers to devise contracts that will somehow reveal the true character of the parties involved. For example, to deal with adverse selection and moral hazard, insurance companies include clauses allowing them either to cancel a person's insurance or to raise the rates as experiences dictates. Adverse selection can be countered by changing the relative sizes of the basic insurance rate and the penalties, so that drivers will self-select themselves into good-risk or bad-risk categories. A low insurance rate with a high penalty for an accident will attract good drivers. A high insurance rate with a low penalty will attract bad drivers. The same principle applies to different categories of coverage. If you have *liability insurance*, the insurance company pays for the damage you cause to the other party. If you have *collision insurance*, the insurance company pays for part of the damage to your own car. Good drivers might opt for liability insurance instead of collision insurance.

## THE ROLE OF INTERMEDIARIES

Intermediaries specialize in information concerning

1. Exchange opportunities between buyers and sellers

2. The variety and qualities of different products

3. The channels of marketing distribution for produced goods

**Intermediaries** buy in order to sell again or simply bring together a buyer and a seller.

# EXAMPLE 3
## PRODUCT
## LIABILITY

In one of the Defining Moments of Chapter 1, Adam Smith stated that voluntary exchange or trade between buyers and sellers must be mutually beneficial; otherwise, the exchange would not take place. If one party is under compulsion, the law declares the contract null and void. Or, if one party misrepresents the product that is being sold, again, the law declares the contract null and void. If there is no "meeting of the minds," there is no contract.

Until recently, the Supreme Court reaffirmed the inviolability of contracts: People were presumed competent to decide for themselves whether a deal was good or not. In *Lochner* vs. *New York* (1905), for example, the Supreme Court ruled, "The general right to make a contract . . . is part of the liberty of the individuals." People just had to adhere to their agreements and not promise something they would not deliver. If nothing was promised, it did not have to be delivered. If the seller of a lawn mower said nothing, the buyer was responsible for any likely injuries from a swiftly moving blade. But if the seller said, "This lawn mower is child-proof" and a child is severely cut by the blades, the courts would hold the seller liable.

In the last several decades, the courts have reinterpreted the law of contracts to include seller liabilities that were not part of the original contracts. The courts now blame the product, not the people who use them. The following examples indicate the new direction:

1. Sears had to pay a man $1.2 million because its lawn mower rope was too hard to pull, causing the man to have a heart attack.
2. A Goodyear tire designed for a maximum speed of 85 miles per hour exploded at more than 100 miles per hour, but Goodyear was held liable because the product did not foresee consumer negligence.
3. In 1994 a woman bought a cup of coffee at a McDonald's restaurant, but burned herself when she tried to hold the cup between her legs while driving her car. She sued and McDonalds had to pay her $400 thousand in damages.

Thousands of such incidents are causing products to disappear from the market, and are causing the prices of others to rise to reflect the cost of possible lawsuits. It has been estimated that a stepladder costs 30 percent more and a childhood vaccine costs about twice as much as it might because of the cost of safety. Shortly after the McDonald's case cited above, the Wendy's restaurant chain discontinued serving hot cocoa, because the company was afraid of lawsuits by the parents of children burned from drinking it.

The price of a good or service reflects more than just the good or service: It reflects the legal obligations of the buyer and seller after the sale. If the courts continue to read into every contract social or cultural conditions, the price must rise to reflect that added liability. If restaurants must pay millions of dollars to customers who burn themselves by being served hot food, the price of hot food must rise to meet that cost. Moral hazard and adverse selection must be paid for, ultimately, by those who buy the product.

----------------------------------------

*Source:* Peter W. Huber, *Liability: The Legal Revolution and Its Consequences,* New York: Basic Books, 1988.

Real estate brokers, grocery stores, department stores, used-car dealers, auctioneers, stockbrokers, insurance agents, and travel agents are all intermediaries. All these professions "mediate" or stand between ultimate buyers and sellers in return for a profit. Today, many of these same intermediaries are facing competition from on-line computer services. For example, it is now possible to buy and sell stocks on a home computer.

Suppose an individual is willing to sell a private airplane for no less than $20 million, and a potential buyer residing in some distant country is willing to pay $25 million for such an airplane. How will they locate one another? Someone with information about the existence of the potential buyer and seller can act as an intermediary and bring the two together. It is possible for the seller to get $20 million, for the buyer to pay $25 million, and for the intermediary to charge as much as $5 million for the service of bringing the two together.

Transactions of this sort occur frequently, although most transactions are less spectacular. The buyers and sellers of residential homes are brought together by realtors who charge a fee for this service. Stockbrokers bring together buyers and sellers of a particular stock. Auction houses bring together sellers of rare works of art and potential buyers, and they charge a fee for this service. Are such intermediaries cheating innocent buyers and sellers, or are they providing a service that is worth the price?

The role of intermediaries in providing information to buyers and sellers is often misunderstood. The export/import agent who brings the airplane buyer and seller together and pockets $5 million may be regarded as criminal by people who think that this "go-between" is trading on the ignorance of others. When food prices rise, many consumers blame the intermediaries. Buyers and sellers of real estate often become upset with the high fees charged by realtors. Implicit in these complaints is the belief that the intermediaries are getting a reward for doing nothing or for doing very little.

The intermediary's share of the price varies substantially from good to good. In real estate, the broker typically receives a 5 to 10 percent fee for bringing together the buyer and seller. This fee depends upon competitive conditions in the market. In stock market transactions the fee varies from about 0.5 percent to about 2 percent of the price of the stock. Supermarkets charge an intermediary fee of perhaps 10 percent to 50 percent of the wholesale price at which they buy.

The fee that intermediaries charge for their services, like other prices, depends on the amount of competition, on the degree of freedom of entry into the business, and on the opportunity costs of bringing goods to the market. If the business is competitive, the fee will reflect a normal profit in the long run. For example, retail grocery stores are in a very competitive business; the typical supermarket earns an accounting profit of about 1 percent on its sales. The markups on supermarket products are almost entirely used for paying rent, stock clerks, checkout clerks, produce specialists, and butchers. The grocery store, for example, must hire employees to prepare produce and meat for display in quantities convenient for inspection and purchase; the store must maintain inventories of products on which it must pay carrying charges. The grocery store must select a location convenient to its customers and pay substantial rents for a good location. In return for the intermediary fee, consumers receive a convenient location, the convenience of inspecting goods before purchase, and the convenience of finding the quantity and quality of goods they want without packing, sorting, and searching for themselves.

Buyers and sellers could, in most situations, avoid paying the intermediary fee. Consumers could drive to farmers' markets and to wholesale distributors of meats and dairy products. They could even drive to canning factories. The intermediary, by specializing in bringing together buyers and sellers, is able to provide the service at a lower cost than if the individuals performed the service themselves.

Another function of intermediaries, such as department stores, is to certify the quality of goods. The consumer is confronted with a vast array of goods, some of which are so complicated that the buyer is at an enormous information disadvantage relative to the producer. In short, the consumer faces the adverse-selection problem. The number of producers is larger than the number of actual stores with which the consumer deals. In such circumstances, the intermediary performs the function of certifying the quality of the good for the buyer. The customer is prepared to pay a price for this valuable service; thus, the intermediary is able to charge a higher markup over costs.

Car dealerships are certifiers of quality. These intermediaries are better informed about the quality of cars (because they can hire skilled mechanics) than the typical car buyer, and they will take advantage of profit opportunities by buying used cars (perhaps from their new-car customers) and reselling them on

# EXAMPLE 4
## THE LEMONS PRINCIPLE: ADVERSE SELECTION

The certification of quality helps prevent market breakdown resulting from adverse selection. In the case of used cars, the seller knows the value of the product, but the buyer must guess the quality. Most buyers would probably assume that the car is of average quality. If every used-car dealer operated on a disreputable basis, the only used cars that would sell would be the lemons—those of lowest quality. If there were used cars in the market ranging from $1000 to $6000 in true value (a range known, say, to all potential buyers), but potential buyers could not tell the difference among them, would any rational consumer buy a used car priced at $5000? At a price of $5000, cars worth more than $5000 would not be offered for sale; only those worth $5000 or less would be put on the market—so that the average car offered for sale would be worth $3000. Why pay $5000 for a car that is more than likely worth much less

than $5000? At a price of $3000, only cars worth $3000 or less would be placed on the market (so the average car offered would be worth only $2000). Why pay $3000 for a car that is likely worth much less than $3000? Indeed, any price above $1000 would bring forth cars worth less than the price. What type of cars would, therefore, be sold in this fly-by-night market? Only those lemons that are worth exactly $1000 because buyers paying more could only expect to be ripped off. In these circumstances, only when established dealers serve as certifiers of quality will nonlemons be placed on the market.

--------

*Source:* Based upon George Akerlof, "The Market for 'Lemons': Quality, Uncertainty, and the Market Mechanism," *Quarterly Journal of Economics* 84 (August 1970): 488–500.

their used-car lots. They may even provide a guarantee (usually with a time limit) that the used car is not a "lemon." Customers will be willing to pay a fee (in the form of a price markup) for this certifier-of-quality service. (See Example 4.)

Manufacturers also certify quality by identifying their products with brand names. If prior to purchase and use consumers could not distinguish the product of one manufacturer from that of all other manufacturers, there would be little incentive for the manufacturer to produce products of reasonable or uniform quality. Brand names such as Sara Lee, Levi's, Maytag, Intel, and Xerox serve as certifiers of product quality.

## SPECULATION AND RISK BEARING

Although product information is important to consumers, information about changes in the market conditions for any number of goods and services is important to speculators.

> **Speculators** are those who buy or sell in the hope of profiting from market fluctuations.

The person who stocks up on peanut butter after hearing of a shortage of peanuts, the frozen-orange-juice distributor who buys oranges in response to a late frost in Florida, and the young couple that buys a house now because they fear home prices will rise beyond reach if they wait another year are all speculators. The professional speculator, however, is more maligned than any other economic agent.

Most people, however, do not associate the term *speculator* with the family that stocks up on goods whose prices are expected to increase dramatically or purchases a home as an inflation hedge. Most people associate the term *speculator* with the person who buys up agricultural land and holds it for future shopping-center development or the person who buys and sells foreign currencies or gold in the hopes of buying low and selling high. Such speculators buy or sell commodities in huge quantities hoping to profit from a frost, war scare, bumper crop, bad news, or good news.

## THE ECONOMIC ROLE OF THE SPECULATOR

Speculators do, indeed, often profit from the misfortunes of others. They buy from the hard-pressed farmer when prices are low, and they sell later at much higher prices. Has the farm family been robbed by the speculator? Not really. The farmer is not in the business of risk-bearing. Upon hearing of a frost in Florida, speculators buy oranges in large quantities, thereby driving up the prices of orange juice for the consumer. At the first sign of international trouble, speculators may buy gold and sell American dollars, thereby weakening the American dollar. The popular view of speculators is that they do only harm; however, speculators are performing a useful economic function—that is, engaging in arbitrage *through time.*

> **Arbitrage** is buying in a market where a commodity is cheap and reselling in a market where the commodity is more expensive.

The arbitrageur buys wheat in Chicago at $5 per bushel and resells it for $5.10 the next minute in Kansas City. Arbitrageurs, therefore, serve to keep the prices of wheat in Chicago and Kansas City approximately equal.

Simple arbitrage of this type is not very risky because information about prices in Chicago and Kansas City can be obtained instantly from commodity brokers. Arbitrageurs must act quickly and have fast calculators and keen minds if they are to prosper. Unlike the arbitrageur, who buys in one location and sells in another, the speculator buys goods *at one time* and resells *at another time.* Speculation is a risky business because tomorrow's prices cannot be known with certainty. The speculator is bearing risks that others do not wish to carry.

> The speculator is performing the economic function of sharing in the risky activities of producers and consumers.

## PROFITABLE SPECULATION

The objective of the speculator is to make a profit by buying low and selling high. When the speculator is making a profit—and when there are enough speculators—low prices will be driven up and high prices will be driven down. When speculators buy at low prices, they add to the demand and drive prices up. When speculators sell when prices are high, they drive prices down by adding to the supply.

> Profitable speculation (that is, speculation that succeeds in buying low and selling high) stabilizes prices and consumption over time by reducing fluctuation in prices and consumption over time.

Profitable speculation is illustrated in Figure 2. Panel (*a*) shows that the supply of wheat in the first period (say, 1996) is $S_1$, or 4 million bushels. Panel (*b*) shows that the supply of wheat in the second period (say, 1997) is $S_2$, or 2 million bushels. If there were no speculation, the price of wheat would be $3 in period 1 and $5 in period 2 (we assume that demand does not change between the two periods). Thus, without speculation, prices and consumption would vary dramatically between the two periods.

If speculators correctly anticipate that next year's wheat crop will be small, they could make handsome profits by buying at $3 and selling next year at $5. But what happens as speculators begin to buy this year's wheat? When speculators buy wheat, they withdraw it from the market and place it in storage. As a result, the supply of wheat offered on the market is reduced. This will continue until the profits of the marginal speculator are driven down to zero. When speculators buy 1 million bushels in the first period, the effective supply shifts (left) to 3 million bushels, and the price rises to $4. When speculators resell this wheat in the second period, the effective supply also shifts (right) to 3 million bushels in year 2. When speculative profits are zero, the price will remain stable at $4 and the quantity of wheat sold on the market will remain stable at 3 million bushels—despite substantial differences in the wheat harvest in the two periods. In this example, we assume that storage costs are zero. Had storage costs been positive, the price of wheat in the second period would have been higher by the cost of storage.

> Profitable speculation shifts supplies from periods when supplies are relatively abundant and prices potentially low to periods when supplies are relatively scarce and prices potentially high. In this sense, profitable speculation provides the valuable economic service of stabilizing prices and consumption over time.

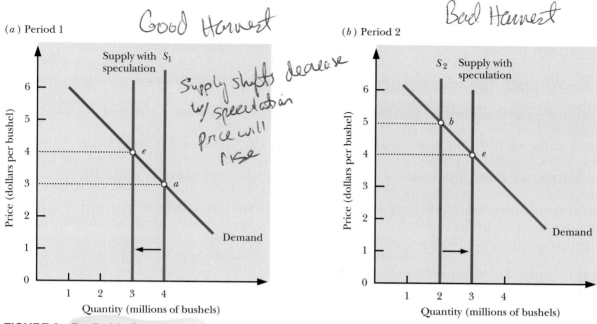

*(a)* Period 1

Good Harvest

*(b)* Period 2

Bad Harvest

Supply shifts decrease w/ speculation price will rise

**FIGURE 2    Profitable Speculation**

Period 1's wheat harvest is 4 million bushels, while period 2's wheat harvest is only 2 million bushels. If there were no speculation, the price would be $3 in period 1 and $5 in period 2. Perfect speculation will cause 1 million bushels of wheat to be purchased and stored by speculators in period 1, to be sold in period 2. As a result, the price is driven up to $4 in period 1 and driven down to $4 in period 2. Both price and consumption are stabilized by the speculation in this case.

The $4 price of wheat reflects all the available information about the future. In this sense, the market is efficient. No one can then make a profit buying wheat and reselling it because the price is the same in both periods. Profits can be made only when information available to some people is not reflected in the current market price. Those individuals can make a profit by exploiting their information advantage.

In the preceding example, speculators accurately predicted the future. Such predictions are not as difficult as one might expect. For example, spring wheat is harvested in September and winter wheat is harvested in June or July. The amount of wheat harvested in other months is negligible. This seasonal pattern of wheat supply is predictable. What if no one were to speculate in this situation? In harvest months, farmers would harvest and sell their wheat, and wheat prices would be driven down to very low levels. In the months when very little wheat is harvested, wheat prices would be astronomical. Such a situation would not be satisfactory.

Because the pattern of wheat harvesting is well known, speculators (who also include the farmers who put their grain into storage rather than sell it immediately) purchase grain at harvest time, put it into storage, and then sell it throughout the rest of the year. This activity assures that we will not lack for wheat during the remainder of the year and that consumers will not have to pay wildly fluctuating prices. Of course, speculators will make some errors in the process; for instance, they may incorrectly predict the size of the coming harvest. However, these mistakes are minor compared to the situation that would exist if there were no speculators.

## UNPROFITABLE SPECULATION

Speculation is risky. Speculators cannot always guess correctly. They may buy when they think prices are low only to find that prices sink even lower. They may sell when they think prices are at their peak only to watch the prices rise even further. In such cases, speculation destabilizes prices and consumption over time. When prices would otherwise be high, such speculators are buying and driving prices even higher; when prices would otherwise be low, such speculators are selling and driving prices even lower.

(a) Period 1

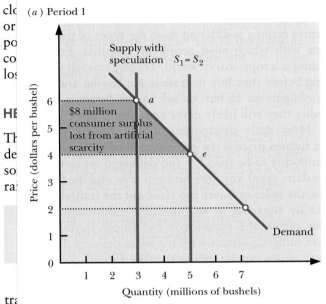

(b) Period 2

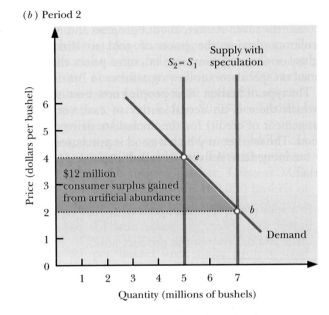

**FIGURE 3   Unprofitable Speculation**

In this example, period 1 and period 2 have the same demand and supply conditions. Without speculation, the price would be $4 in both periods. Speculators guess incorrectly that the supply of corn in period 2 will be less than in period 1. They buy 2 million bushels in period 1 and drive period 1's price up to $6. When they must resell the 2 million bushels in period 2, they drive the price down to $2. In the case of unprofitable speculation, price and consumption are seriously destabilized.

Unprofitable speculation is shown in Figure 3. The supply of corn is 5 million bushels in period 1 and will also be 5 million bushels in period 2. Because demand remains the same in the two periods, the equilibrium price of corn will be $4 in both periods without speculation. Now assume speculators incorrectly guess that the supply of corn will decrease in period 2 because of an anticipated poor harvest. Speculators buy 2 million bushels, which they place in storage for later sale, driving up the price to $6 in period 1 (point a). The speculators then wait in vain for a decline in supply that never materializes. They must then sell the 2 million bushels in period 2, and they drive the price down to $2 a bushel (point b).

Without speculation, the price and consumption of corn would have been the same in both periods (point e). With unprofitable speculation, consumption is 3 million bushels in period 1 and 7 million bushels in period 2. Period 1's price is $6 and period 2's price is $2. Unprofitable speculation is inefficient for the economy as a whole.

Unprofitable speculation is destabilizing because it creates artificial scarcities in some

periods and artificial abundance in other periods. In this sense, speculation can be costly to society.

## THE FUTURES MARKET

Speculation is so highly specialized that markets have developed that separate the business of storing the commodity being bought and sold from the actual business of speculation. The grain speculator does not have to worry about what the purchased grain looks like, where it is stored, and how much to take out of storage. Those who wish only to speculate can buy and sell in a futures market.

A **futures market** is an organized market in which a buyer and seller agree now on the price of a commodity to be delivered at some specified date in the future.

Many of us are familiar with futures markets only through sensational press reports, like those

grossly simplified; however, the future is always uncertain. Clearly, having a futures market that establishes effective future prices today is of great benefit in an uncertain world. For those who need to know future prices, a futures market provides a summary indicator of market sentiment—a single price reflects much of what people know today about tomorrow.

This chapter completes our study of product markets. The next section will turn to the bottom half of the circular-flow diagram: factor markets. In the next chapter we shall consider factor markets and how they compare to product markets. In subsequent chapters we shall examine individually the markets for the different kinds of factors—labor, land, capital, entrepreneurship.

## SUMMARY

1. Information is costly because of our limited ability to process, store, and retrieve facts and figures about the economy and because real resources are required to gather information. Individuals acquire information to the point where the marginal cost of acquiring more information equals the marginal benefit of more information.

2. Search costs explain the observed dispersion of prices. When the benefits to further search are great, price dispersion will be limited.

3. Two problems encountered by buyers and sellers because of the cost of information are the moral-hazard problem and the adverse-selection problem. The moral-hazard problem refers to postcontractual opportunistic behavior; the adverse-selection problem refers to precontractual opportunistic behavior. Both arise because one party cannot verify the claims of the other party.

4. Intermediaries bring together buyers and sellers; they often buy in order to sell again and sometimes serve as certifiers of quality.

5. Speculators buy at one time in order to sell at another time. If speculators are profitable, they stabilize prices and consumption over time. If they are unprofitable, they destabilize prices and consumption over time.

6. In a futures market, contracts are made now for payment and delivery of commodities in the future. Futures markets provide information about the uncertain future and allow hedging by those who wish to reduce risks.

## KEY TERMS

transaction costs
information costs
optimal-search rule
reservation price
moral-hazard problem
adverse-selection
    problem

intermediaries
speculators
arbitrage
futures market
spot (cash) market
hedging

## QUESTIONS AND PROBLEMS

1. Investors can purchase shares of stock through a full-service broker (who provides information and investment advice) or through a discount broker. The commission charged by the full-service broker is much higher than that charged by the discount broker. They both provide the service of buying the shares of stock ordered by the buyer. Explain why most investors use the services of the higher-priced brokers.

2. The market for wheat is highly centralized. In fact, one can say there is a world market for wheat. Why is this market centralized while other markets, such as the automobile market, are decentralized?

3. You have learned that prices of $3, $3.50, and $4 are being charged by various pharmacies for the same generic drug. The marginal benefit of further search is $0.15; marginal cost is $0.10. Should you search for a lower price?

4. You have been quoted the prices of $20, $21, $23, and $24 for a wheel alignment on your car. The marginal benefit for further search is $1, and the marginal cost is also $1. What is your reservation price? Should you search further?

5. What are the transaction costs of selling a home? What effect do real estate brokers have on these costs?

6. Explain why more is spent on the advertising of deodorants than on the advertising of farm machinery.

7. If search costs in a market are zero and the market is competitively organized, what predictions can you make about prices in this market?

8. The stock market is highly competitive, with thousands of speculators trying to buy low and sell high. Using the concepts of information and search costs, explain why we all can't get rich

with a little study and research by playing the stock market.

9. What is the moral-hazard problem? Give examples.
10. An attendance clause gives a major-league baseball player a season-end bonus if attendance exceeds a target figure. Explain how this is a result from the moral-hazard problem.
11. What is the adverse-selection problem? Give examples.
12. Assume that on January 1, July wheat is selling for $4. How could a speculator profit from the expectation that in July spot wheat will sell for $3.50? How could a speculator profit from the expectation that in July spot wheat will sell for $4.50?
13. Indicate which of the following examples is a potential moral-hazard problem or a potential adverse-selection problem.
    a. "The chair broke when I sat down," complained the customer to the furniture store.
    b. "This chair will last a lifetime," asserted the furniture salesperson.
    c. "I am a safe, married driver," claimed the student buying car insurance.
    d. "We insure all drivers," claims the ad.

# PART III

# FACTOR
# MARKETS

# CHAPTER 16

# FACTOR MARKETS

*Factor MKTS act as one* (handwritten)

As a college graduate in the late 1990s you can expect to earn about $1.5 million over your lifetime. Drop out of college and your lifetime income will fall to slightly less than $1 million. Your cousin who never finished high school will earn only $600,000 over his lifetime. What determines these incomes?

We have completed our examination of the product markets, where the prices of goods and services are determined. It is now time to consider the factor markets, where the prices of land, labor, and capital are determined.

*Winners + Losers* (handwritten)

The study of factor markets takes us into a battleground of economics. Almost all of us think we should be earning higher wages on our labor, higher interest on our money, or higher rents on land. The pay people earn often determines whether they like or don't like the economy in which they reside. It is therefore important for us to understand the general principles that govern the determination of factor prices.

*MKT power is very important in Factor MKT. However controls markets wins?* (handwritten)

## COMPETITION IN FACTOR MARKETS

A business firm participates both in the product market, where it sells the goods or services it produces, and in the factor market, where it buys the land, labor, and capital it needs to produce this output. The previous chapters discussed the four types of markets firms can face in the product market. This chapter is about the types of markets it faces in the factor market.

Factor markets differ from product markets in one important respect. They tend to be more competitive than product markets. In product markets, firms compete against other sellers of like or similar products. In many cases, there are few enough producers or their products are sufficiently differentiated that they can exercise some control over price—they are price makers.

In factor markets, all business firms tend to compete for the same factor resources. General Motors, Intel, Microsoft, grocery stores, and television stations, while producing quite different goods and services, compete for the general pool of labor, capital, and land. They all need word processing specialists, computers, trucks, drivers, and managers. It is therefore rare that one firm can exercise sufficient control over a particular factor market so as to be able to influence the price of that factor. There are indeed cases where specific firms are price makers in specific factor markets, but most firms are price takers in factor markets.

Price taking means that business firms simply must pay the going rate for the factors of production they hire. If the going wage rate for computer programmers is $10 per hour, this is what they have to pay for one more hour of programming. If retail space rents for $100 per square foot, this is what they have to pay for one more square foot of space.

In this chapter, we examine the behavior of firms that are price takers in the factor market. Price taking means that the extra (marginal) cost of hiring one more unit of the factor is simply its factor price.

## BASIC CONCEPTS OF FACTOR DEMAND

The firm's demand for a factor input depends upon the input's physical productivity and the demand for the good the factor is being used to produce. The chapter on productivity and costs defined the production function as the relationship between outputs and inputs. Recall that a factor's marginal physical product (MPP) is the increase in output divided by the increase in the amount of the factor, if all other factors are constant.

As explained earlier, all production functions exhibit the law of diminishing returns, which states that as ever-larger quantities of a variable factor are combined with fixed amounts of the firm's other factors, the marginal physical product of the variable factor will eventually decline.

## DERIVED DEMAND

A consumer buys products because they provide satisfaction. The firm buys factors of production because they produce goods and services that create revenue for the firm. The garment industry buys sewing machines because they help to produce suits, shirts, and dresses that consumers will buy. Automobile workers are hired because they help produce automobiles that people will buy. Farmland is rented because it yields wheat that people will consume. The demand for workers, the demand for farmland, and the demand for tailors are all examples of derived demand.

> The demand for a factor of production is a **derived demand** because it results (is derived) from the demand for the goods and services the factor of production helps produce.

The principle of derived demand is essential to understanding the workings of factor markets. (See Example 1.) If consumers reduce their demand for lettuce, the demand for workers employed in lettuce growing, the demand for farmland used for lettuce, and even the demand for water used in farm irrigation will also fall. When the demand for automobiles falls, there is unemployment in Detroit. When world demand for Boeing commercial aircraft is booming, employment rises in Seattle and Wichita, the cities where Boeing is located.

## JOINT DETERMINATION OF FACTOR DEMAND

The production of a good requires the cooperation of different factors of production. Farm workers can produce no corn without farmland; farmland without farm labor is useless. Both farmland and farm workers require farm implements (ranging from

**EXAMPLE 1**

**DERIVED DEMAND:**

**AIR TRAVEL AND AIRCRAFT LEASES**

We know from this chapter that the demand for factors of production is a derived demand. The demand for the factor depends on the demand for the product that the factor assists in producing. A clear case in point has been the worldwide slowdown in passenger air travel that characterized the early and mid-1990s. The U.S. recession and its spread to Europe caused a sharp cutback in the volume of air travel and exerted downward pressure on ticket prices.

Air travel is produced by combining labor (pilots, flight attendants, mechanics) and capital (aircraft). If the demand for the product (air travel) falls, there should be a comparable decline in the demand for these two factors of pro-

duction. Accordingly, the decline in wages for pilots, flight attendants, and mechanics and the decline in aircraft prices and lease rates should mirror declines in passenger air travel.

True to form, wages and salaries in commercial aviation have fallen dramatically behind wages in other industries in the early 1990s. Even more hard-hit have been the prices of new and used aircraft. A Boeing 737 that would have leased for $100,000 per month in 1990 leased for $40,000 per month in late 1992.

As air travel picked up in 1994 and 1995, the derived demand for aircraft picked up. By late 1995, airlines were hard pressed to find Boeing 737 aircraft to rent for less than $90,000 per month.

hand tools to sophisticated farm machinery) to produce corn.

> In general, the marginal physical product of any factor of production depends upon the quantity and quality of the cooperating factors of production.

The marginal physical product of the farm worker will be higher on 1 acre of farmland than on 1 square yard of land, it will be higher on 1 acre of fertile Iowa land than on 1 acre of rocky New England land, and it will be higher with the use of modern heavy farm machinery than with hand implements. The interdependence of the marginal physical products of land, labor, and capital does not make the problem of factor pricing in a market setting difficult.

## MARGINAL REVENUE PRODUCT

The demand for a factor of production—land, labor, or capital—is a derived demand. The factor is valuable because the firm sells the output on the product market. The dollar value of an extra worker, an ex-

tra unit of land, or an extra machine is that factor's marginal revenue product (MRP).

> The **marginal revenue product (MRP)** of any factor of production is the extra revenue generated per unit increase in the amount of the factor.

We can calculate a factor's marginal revenue product in two ways. Both approaches yield the same value.

**Method 1.** The first method of calculating marginal revenue product is to simply change the quantity of the factor and observe the change in revenue. According to this direct method, marginal revenue product is the change in total revenue (TR) divided by the change (increase or decrease) in the factor.

$$MRP = \frac{\Delta TR}{\Delta Factor}$$

Table 1 demonstrates this method. The different quantities of labor the firm employs are given in column 1, and the resulting output is given in column 2.

## Table 1    Marginal Revenue Product

| Labor (workers), L (1) | Output (units), Q (2) | Price, P (3) | Total Revenue, TR (4) = (2) × (3) | Marginal Revenue Product, MRP (5) = (6) × (7) = Δ(4) ÷ Δ(1) | Marginal Revenue, MR (6) = Δ(4) ÷ Δ(2) | Marginal Physical Product (units), MPP (7) = Δ(2) |
|---|---|---|---|---|---|---|
| 0 | 0 | $24 | $ 0 | | | |
| | | | | $95 | $19 | 5 |
| 1 | 5 | 19 | 95 | | | |
| | | | | 40 | 10 | 4 |
| 2 | 9 | 15 | 135 | | | |
| | | | | 9 | 3 | 3 |
| 3 | 12 | 12 | 144 | | | |

Columns 1 and 2 give the production function (the amount of output produced by 0, 1, 2, and 3 units of labor input). Columns 2 and 3 give the demand schedule facing the firm. MRP is calculated by taking the increase in total revenue associated with one-unit increases in the labor input. It can also be calculated by multiplying MR times MPP. MR in column 6 is calculated by dividing the increase in revenue in column 5 by the difference between rows in column 2. MPP in column 7 is the increase in output for every unit increase in the factor, or the difference between rows in column 2.

Columns 1 and 2, therefore, represent the production function. Column 3 shows the market prices that clear the market (equate quantity supplied and demanded) for the various output levels produced. This firm is a price maker in the product market because the price falls with higher output levels. The firm's total revenue (price times quantity of output) is given in column 4. Because marginal revenue (see column 5) is the difference between the revenues generated at consecutive levels of labor input, it is recorded between the rows corresponding to the input levels. The revenue generated when one worker is employed is $95; the revenue when two workers are employed is $135. The marginal revenue product of the second worker therefore, is $135 − $95 = $40. In other words, the firm's total revenue increases by $40 if the firm hires a second worker.

**Method 2.**   We can calculate a factor's marginal revenue product indirectly as well. The marginal physical product (MPP) is the increase in output from a one-unit increase in the factor; the marginal-revenue (MR) indicates the increase in revenue associated with this increase in output of one unit.[1] Therefore:

$$MRP = MPP \times MR$$

This formula works for the price maker (see Table 1). Because the firm increases its output from

five to nine units as a consequence of adding a second unit of labor, marginal physical product equals four units. The four extra units of output add $40 to revenue, or $10 per extra unit ($40/4); therefore, the marginal revenue is $10. The marginal revenue product equals $40($10 × 4). Thus, the indirect method of calculating marginal revenue product yields the same answer as the direct method.

> The marginal revenue product of a factor can be calculated directly, by determining the increase in revenue at different input levels, or indirectly, by multiplying marginal physical product by marginal revenue.

## PROFIT MAXIMIZATION

In the product market, the firm maximizes profit by producing that output at which marginal revenue and marginal cost are equal. The firm is also guided by profit maximization in the factor market. Profit-maximizing decisions in the factor market are basically the same as profit-maximizing decisions in the product market because deciding on the quantity of inputs determines the level of output.

To understand how firms choose the profit-maximizing level of factor inputs, consider the case of a firm deciding how much unskilled labor to hire. *The firm will hire one more unit of unskilled labor if the extra revenue (the extra benefit) the firm derives from the sale of the output produced by the extra unit exceeds the extra cost of the extra unit of unskilled labor.* If the firm is a price

---

[1]For a price taker in the product market, $P \times MPP = MR \times MPP$. For a price maker in the product market, $P \times MPP > MR \times MPP$. In intermediate textbooks, the product $P \times MPP$ is called the *value of the marginal product*.

taker, the extra cost will be the market wage. As in any other economic activity, a firm will hire inputs to the point where marginal benefits equal marginal costs.

The firm will continue to hire unskilled labor as long as their marginal revenue product exceeds the market wage. If the marginal revenue product of labor is $40 and its price (the wage) is $30, it pays the firm to hire another unit. By hiring an additional unit of the labor, the firm can increase its profit by $10.

## THE DEMAND CURVE FOR A FACTOR

Figure 1 shows the MRP curve of Factor A. The curve is downward sloping because in the short run, the greater the amount of Factor A used, the lower its marginal physical product (because of the law of diminishing returns). Also, if the firm is a price maker in the product market, higher levels of output will result in a lower marginal revenue. Thus, as the quantity of Factor A increases, both marginal physical product and marginal revenue tend to decline, so that MRP (which is MPP × MR) declines. The firm will hire Factor A until its price equals marginal revenue product.

The MRP curve is the firm's demand curve for a factor because the firm hires that factor

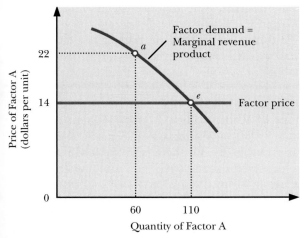

**FIGURE 1 Firm Equilibrium: The Hiring of Factor Inputs**

The firm's derived demand for Factor A is the MRP curve. The supply schedule of Factor A as seen by the firm is perfectly horizontal at the market price of $14. Equilibrium $e$ will be reached at a price of $14 and a quantity of 110 units of Factor A. At this point, MRP = factor price.

quantity until the marginal revenue product of the factor equals the price of the factor.

In Figure 1, the supply curve of Factor A to the firm is horizontal at the market price of $14. The price-taking firm in the factor market can hire all it wants at $14. If the firm hired only 60 units of Factor A (point *a*), it would not maximize its profit: at 60 units, A's MRP equals $22 and A's factor price or cost equals $14. The firm's incentive to hire additional factors continues as long as MRP exceeds $14. Thus, the firm will continue to hire to the point where MRP and the factor's price are equal, which occurs at 110 units of Factor A (point *e*). The firm will be in equilibrium (earning a maximum profit or minimizing its losses) when each factor is employed up to the point where the price of the factor equals the marginal revenue product of the factor.

In equilibrium, $MRP_A = P_A$, $MRP_B = P_B$, and so on, where $A$ and $B$ are specific factors and $P_A$ and $P_B$ are their prices.

## THE TWO SIDES OF THE FIRM

In the product market, the rule of profit maximization is MR = MC. In the factor market, the rule is MRP = the price of each factor. These rules are logically the same. Recall that marginal cost is the mirror image of marginal physical product. That is:

$$MC = \frac{W}{MPP_L} \qquad (1)$$

where $MPP_L$ is the marginal physical product of labor and $W$ is the wage rate.

The rule for profit maximization in the product market is:

$$MR = MC \qquad (2)$$

Because MC equals $W/MPP_L$ according to equation (1), equation (2) can be rewritten as:

$$MR \times MPP_L = W \qquad (3)$$

Because the wage for a factor is equal to its extra cost, and because MR × MPP = MRP, equation (3) can become:

$$MRP = W \qquad (4)$$

which is the profit-maximizing rule in the factor market.

## Table 2   Two Ways of Looking at Profit Maximization

| Labor Hours L (1) | Units of Marginal Physical Product, MPP (2) | Price Equals Marginal Revenue, P = MR (3) | Wage, W (4) | Marginal Revenue Product, MRP (5) = (2) × (3) | Marginal Cost, MC (6) = (4) ÷ (2) |
|---|---|---|---|---|---|
| 0 | | | | | |
| | 5 | $10 | $20 | $50 | $4 |
| 1 | | | | | |
| | 4 | 10 | 20 | 40 | 5 |
| 2 | | | | | |
| | 2 | 10 | 20 | 20 | 10 |
| 3 | | | | | |

This firm is a price taker on both sides of the market. Column 5 equals column 2 times column 3 because the additional revenue from 1 more unit of labor is simply the marginal product multiplied by the price (or marginal revenue). Column 6 equals column 4 divided by column 2 because marginal cost equals the wage per unit of marginal physical product. This table shows that profits are maximized at 3 units of labor where W = MRP and P = MC.

Table 2 provides a numerical example of how profit maximization in the product market is equivalent to profit maximization in the factor market. The firm is a price taker in both markets. The product price is $10 and the wage rate is $20 per day. The MPP schedule is given in columns 1 and 2 of Table 2. Column 3 shows marginal revenue (which equals price in this case), and column 4 shows the wage rate. Marginal revenue product is simply column 2 multiplied by column 3 and is shown in column 5. Marginal cost is the wage for an additional unit of labor divided by the change in output resulting from the additional unit, or W ÷ MPP (see column 6). When P = MC (both $10), it is also true that MRP = W (both $20). When one rule is satisfied, the other rule is also satisfied. (See Example 2.)

## COST MINIMIZATION

The rules of profit maximization explain the behavior of firms in the factor market. These rules predict that firms will employ that level and combination of inputs that maximizes their profit.

To maximize profit, it is necessary to minimize the cost of producing a given quantity of output. Thus far, we have explained how a firm selects the optimal level of *one* factor input. But firms produce output with cooperating factors. How will they know when they are combining *all* their inputs in a least-cost fashion? Suppose a firm has decided to

produce 200 units of output and currently uses 15 labor hours and 25 machine hours to produce this output. The wage rate (the price of labor) is $5 per hour, and the rental rate on the machinery is $20 per hour; thus, an extra hour of machine time costs *four* times as much as an extra hour of labor. The marginal physical product of capital is 30 units of output. The marginal physical product of labor is 10 units of output. Thus, an extra hour of machine time produces *three* times as much as an extra hour of labor. Is the firm using the optimal amount of labor and capital?

In this example, the firm is using too much capital and too little labor. If the firm substitutes 3 hours of labor for 1 hour of capital, total output will not change, but costs will be reduced by $5. One hour of capital (at the margin) is three times as productive as 1 hour of labor. Adding 3 units of labor increases output by 30, and subtracting 1 machine hour decreases output by 30; there is no net change in output. However, cutting back on 1 machine hour saves $20, while hiring 3 more hours of labor costs $15. Output remains the same, but costs fall by $5.

To determine whether a substitution of this sort will increase profits, the firm looks at marginal physical product *per dollar of cost*. In this example, because an extra hour of labor increases output by 10 units and increases costs by $5, an extra dollar spent on labor produces 2 units (10/$5) of output. Because an extra machine hour increases output by 30 units and increases costs by $20, an extra dollar spent on capital produces 1.5 units of output. In our example,

## EXAMPLE 2
## IS THE MARGINAL PRODUCTIVITY THEORY TRUE?

Theories are tested by what they imply about the real world. Let's consider the implications of the marginal productivity theory. Over time, we know that in most industries productivity improves because of technological innovations. Since $W = P \times MPP$, it follows that as productivity rises as a result of technological changes, the ratio of wages to prices must rise in that industry. But the wages paid in a particular industry must be competitive with wages in other industries. Thus, the wages paid in a particular industry should not change as much as productivity growth in that industry. Productivity growth in a particular industry that is in excess of productivity growth in other industries must translate into relatively lower prices. If productivity in general is growing at 2 percent, but pro-

ductivity is not growing in construction, for example, we would expect that construction prices would be rising relative to other prices. This is exactly what happens. The accompanying figure shows the average annual productivity growth in a number of industries. Productivity growth was high (3 percent) in agriculture, and the relative price of agricultural goods fell. Productivity growth in construction was virtually zero, and the construction prices rose relative to other goods. Productivity growth in mining was closer to the national average, and the prices of mining products barely changed.

------------------------------------------

*Source: The Economic Report of the President,* 1994, p. 118.

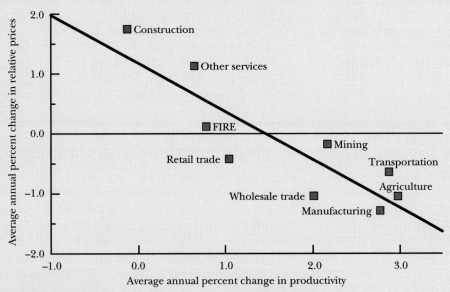

**Productivity Growth and Price Reductions, 1950–1990**

Productivity growth in an industry leads to lower relative prices.

*Note:* FIRE = finance, insurance, and real estate.
*Source:* Department of Commerce.

a dollar spent on more labor is more effective than a dollar spent on more capital.

The marginal physical product per dollar of a factor is its marginal physical product divided by its price. The price-taking firm takes both the wage rate for labor ($W$) and the rental rate on capital ($R$) as given. As the preceding example shows, if the marginal physical product per dollar of labor is greater than the marginal physical product per dollar of capital, the firm is not combining inputs in a least-cost fashion. It can produce the same output at lower cost by substituting labor for capital until:

$$\frac{\text{MPP}_L}{W} = \frac{\text{MPP}_K}{R}$$

where $\text{MPP}_K$ is the marginal physical product of capital.

> According to the least-cost rule, the price-taking firm is producing at minimum cost only if the marginal physical products per dollar of the various factors are equal to one another.

## THE MARGINAL PRODUCTIVITY THEORY OF INCOME DISTRIBUTION

Economists distinguish between the functional distribution of income and the personal distribution of income, both of which are determined in the factor market.

> The **functional distribution of income** is the distribution of income among the four broad classes of productive factors—land, labor, capital, and entrepreneurship.
>
> The **personal distribution of income** is the distribution of income among households, or how much income one family earns from the factors of production it owns relative to other families.

The profit-maximizing and least-cost rules resolve the *how* problem in economics. They show how firms go about combining inputs to produce output. These same rules also resolve the *for whom* problem. Given the prices of the factors of production, what people earn depends on the resources they own. We shall consider the details of the personal distribution of income in a later chapter.

Factors of production, unless they are highly specialized (such as 7-foot basketball players), are demanded by many firms and by many industries. For example, the market demand for truck drivers comes from a wide cross section of American industry: The steel industry, retailers, the moving industry, and the local florist all have a derived demand for truck drivers. The demand for urban land also comes from a broad cross section of American industry: Heavy industry requires land for its plant sites, motel chains require land for their motels, and home builders require land to develop subdivisions. Similarly, the demand for capital goods comes from a cross section of American industry.

How the price (wage) of truck drivers is determined is shown in Figure 2. The wage rate of truck drivers reflects two forces: the derived demand for truck drivers as represented by their marginal revenue product and the supply of truck drivers. At equilibrium (point *e*), quantity supplied and quantity demanded are equal and the wage equals the marginal revenue product. In other words, truck drivers will be paid their marginal revenue product. The same is true of the other factors of production, as the marginal productivity theory of income distribution states.

> According to the **marginal productivity theory of income distribution**, the functional distribution of income between land, labor, and capital is determined by the relative marginal revenue products of the different factors of production. The price of each factor will equal the marginal revenue product of that factor.

### MARGINAL PRODUCTIVITY AND EFFICIENCY

In the preceding chapters on product markets we examined the relative efficiency of different market structures, particularly perfect competition and monopoly. We know that monopoly is inefficient because it creates contrived scarcity by failing to expand output to the point where price (the measure of the marginal benefit to society) and marginal cost (the measure of the extra cost to society) are equal.

If a firm has monopoly power in the product market, $P > \text{MR}$. Although the monopolistic firm will pay each input its marginal revenue product, which will equal $\text{MR} \times \text{MPP}$, the factor is actually worth $P \times \text{MPP}$ to society because each unit of MPP is valued at $P$. Because $\text{MR} \times \text{MPP}$ is less than

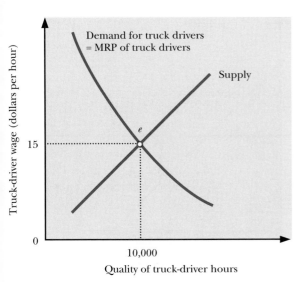

**FIGURE 2   Determination of the Market Price (Wage) of Truck Drivers in a Competitive Market**

The market supply curve of truck drivers is upward slop-ing, which indicates that truck drivers are prepared to work more hours at high wages than at low wages. The market demand curve is derived from the MRP curve of truck drivers across several industries. Equilibrium is achieved at point *e*, where the supply of truck drivers equals the quantity demanded. At the equilibrium wage of $15, there are 10,000 labor hours used in the various in-dustries using truck drivers.

$P \times$ MPP, the monopolist is paying less for factors than what they are worth to society.

Figure 3 illustrates a monopolist in the product market who is a price taker in the factor market. The curve $P \times$ MPP shows the marginal benefits to soci-ety of an additional unit of the factor. The MRP curve shows the marginal benefit to the monopolist of hiring an additional unit of the factor. When the monopolist operates at point *a* rather than at point *b*, the monopolist stops hiring workers short of their marginal worth to society (or pays them less than they are worth to society, as represented by point *c*). Society loses the green area *abc*.

If the firm is perfectly competitive in the product market, the marginal revenue product of a factor equals the marginal benefit of the factor to society. Because price equals marginal revenue in a competi-tive firm, the firm will hire factors until the point at which $P \times$ MPP equals the factor's price. Each factor adds a net marginal benefit to society equal to the factor's market price. This market price reflects its opportunity cost to society.

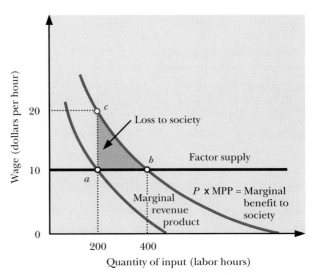

**FIGURE 3   The Monopolist Hires Too Few Inputs**

The firm is a monopolist in the product market and a price taker in the factor market. The value of the mar-ginal product to society is $P \times$ MPP (the marginal benefit to society), and the marginal benefit to the monopolist is its marginal revenue product. If the wage rate is $10, the monopolist employs 200 labor hours because at that point marginal revenue product equals the wage.

## MARGINAL PRODUCTIVITY AND FACTOR INCOMES

The marginal productivity theory of income distrib-ution suggests that a productive factor is usually paid its marginal revenue product. The marginal rev-enue product of one factor depends upon the quan-tity and quality of cooperating factors. For example, two textile workers, one in the United States and the other in India, may be equally skilled and diligent, but one works with a $50 sewing machine while the other works with a $100,000 advanced knitting ma-chine. The New England farmer may be just as skilled as the Kansas farmer but may have a low MRP because of the low quality of the land. Mar-ginal revenue product also depends upon the sup-plies of factors. The supply of residential land is lim-ited in Hawaii but abundant in Iowa. The equilibrium MRP of land is, therefore, higher in Hawaii. If women are limited to employment oppor-tunities in only a few professions, they will over-crowd these professions and drive down the MRP and, thus, wages. Finally, marginal revenue product, as stated earlier, depends upon the demand for the product being produced. If product demand falls, so will the factor's MRP.

The marginal productivity theory of income distribution states that a competitively determined factor price reflects the factor's marginal revenue product. Marginal revenue product is the result of (1) the relative supplies of the different factors, (2) the quantity and quality of cooperating factors, and (3) the market demands for the goods the factors produce.

## THE AGGREGATE PRODUCTION FUNCTION

The marginal productivity theory of income distribution has both wide and narrow applications. In its narrow form, the theory can explain why one person earns more than another or why one plot of land rents for more than another. The aggregate economy is the summation of all the participants in the economy; therefore, it is possible to talk about average wages, average land-rental rates, and average interest rates. The relationship between the total inputs used by an economy and the total amount of goods and services produced by an economy can be expressed by an aggregate production function.

> The **aggregate production function** shows the relationship between the total output produced by the economy and the total labor, capital, and land inputs used by the economy.

The aggregate production function is a simplified representation of the economy, but it is a useful tool for investigating the functional distribution of income among the broad factors of production—land, labor, and capital. (See Figure 4.)

To simplify the analysis, assume the economy produces only one product—corn—and that it is perfectly competitive in all markets. The demand curve for labor is then the marginal physical product of labor for the entire economy. If we assume that the price of a bushel of corn is $1, then the demand curve for labor measures both the marginal physical product and marginal revenue product for the entire economy. The supply of labor is assumed to be fixed at 50 million workers. The equilibrium wage rate is $w_o$, which brings about a quantity of labor demanded of 50 million workers (the quantity supplied).

The total output of the economy is the area under the demand curve in Figure 4, because each point on the curve shows the additional corn produced by

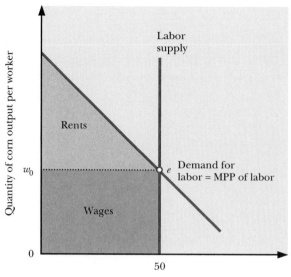

**FIGURE 4 The Aggregate Production Function and the Functional Distribution of Income**

This figure represents the aggregate production function of an entire economy. The economy produces a generalized physical output at a product price of $1. All markets are assumed to be perfectly competitive. Because the price of a unit of output is $1, the demand curve for labor is the marginal physical product of labor; it declines according to the law of diminishing returns. The vertical supply line represents the supply of labor, which is fixed at 50 million workers. The MPP curve will be the demand for labor, and the market wage will be set at $w_o$ where the quantity of labor supplied equals the quantity of labor demanded.

How much output has the economy produced and how much will go to labor? Each unit of labor adds to the economy's output. The area under the demand curve is the total output of the economy at that point. The 50 million workers will produce an output equal to the entire red area. Workers will receive their wage, $w_o$, times the number of workers. Their share of output is the dark red rectangle labeled *Wages*. The cooperating nonlabor factors (land and capital) will get what is left over, or the light red triangle labeled *Rents*.

the last worker. (The demand curve shows the MPP at each level of labor input. We add together the MPPs for each successive unit of labor to get total output. For 50 million workers, total output is the entire red area in Figure 4.) Of this total output, labor will receive the area of the dark red rectangle labeled *Wages*. The nonlabor factors, such as capital and land, will receive the area of the light red triangle labeled *Rents*. Each worker is paid the dollar value of the marginal physical product of the 50-millionth unit rather than the dollar value of earlier units that have larger MPPs (as measured by the height of the demand curve).

The marginal productivity theory states that each factor of production will be paid its marginal revenue product. If the world is sufficiently competitive, the theory suggests that each factor of production will be paid the dollar value of its marginal physical product.

In this chapter we have an overview of how factor markets work. We should note, however, that each market has its own unique features. In the labor market, the supply of labor is determined by how individuals choose among market work, work in the home, and leisure. These are choices not faced by the owners of capital and land. Moreover, the labor market is affected by the organization of workers into unions and by the effect of education and training on labor's marginal physical product. In the capital market, buyers of capital receive the benefits of capital over a long period of time; suppliers of capital must choose between consumption today and more consumption tomorrow. The market for land is characterized by the relatively fixed supply of land.

In the next three chapters we shall examine each factor market in detail, building upon the general theoretical framework established in this chapter.

## SUMMARY

1. Firms sell their output in the product market, and they buy inputs to produce output in the factor market. Because all firms compete for basically the same inputs, there is more competition in factor markets than in product markets. A price taker in the input market will usually have a marginal factor cost equal to the price of the input.

2. The firm's demand for a factor of production will depend upon the demand for the product being produced and upon the factor's productivity. The marginal physical product (MPP) of a factor of production is the increase in output that results from increasing the factor by one unit, other things being equal. The demand for a factor of production is a derived demand because it depends on the demand for the goods and services the factor helps produce. Marginal revenue product (MRP) is the increase in revenue brought about by hiring one more unit of the factor of production.

3. Profit-maximizing firms that are price takers will observe the following rule in the factor markets: Factors of production will be hired to the point where MRP = factor price.

4. The least-cost rule for firms is to hire factors of production so that MPP per dollar of one factor equals the MPP per dollar of any other factor.

5. The marginal productivity theory of income distribution helps to explain the functional distribution of income (among the three classes of production factors) and the personal distribution of income (among households).

## KEY TERMS

derived demand
marginal revenue
   product (MRP)
functional distribution
   of income
personal distribution of
   income

marginal productivity
   theory of income
   distribution
aggregate production
   function

## QUESTIONS AND PROBLEMS

1. The MPP of a 100th worker is 33 units of output. The marginal revenue of the firm for the corresponding level of output is $2, the price of the product is $3, and the wage rate is $99.
   a. Is the firm maximizing its profit?
   b. What would the wage rate have to be for 100 workers to maximize profit?

2. Explain how workers in Country X could earn $10 per hour while workers in the same industry in Country Y earn only $0.50 per hour. Do the higher wages in Country X mean that workers in this country work harder than those in Country Y?

3. The last unit of land rented by a farmer costs $100 and increases output by 1000 bushels. The last unit of capital costs $1000 to rent and increases output by 20,000 bushels. Is this farmer minimizing costs? If not, what should he or she do?

4. Evaluate the following statement: "Income distribution as explained by the marginal productivity theory is entirely fair. After all, people are simply getting back what they personally have contributed to society."

5. One type of equipment—such as specialized oil-drilling equipment—can be used only in one particular industry. Another type—such as general-purpose lathes—can be used in a wide variety of industries. How would the amount of monopsony differ for these two types of equipment?

6. Complete Table A by filling in columns 4 and 5. If the wage rate is $55, how many units of labor should the firm hire?

### Table A

| Labor (number of workers), L (1) | Units of Output, Q (2) | Price, P (3) | Units of Marginal Physical Product, MPP (4) | Marginal Revenue Product, MRP (5) |
|---|---|---|---|---|
| 0 | 0 | $8 | | |
| 1 | 10 | 8 | | |
| 2 | 17 | 8 | | |
| 3 | 23 | 8 | | |
| 4 | 28 | 8 | | |

7. Assume that the MPP of a first worker is 20 units of output, that the MPP of a second worker is 30 units, that the MPP of a third worker is 20 units, and that the MPP of a fourth worker is 15 units. If four workers are hired, how many units of output are produced?

8. A Ph.D. engineer costs a firm $100,000 a year; an engineer with a B.A. degree costs a firm only $50,000 a year. What information is required to determine the firm's optimal decision?

# CHAPTER 17

# LABOR:
# THE HUMAN FACTOR

In 1910, the 7-year-old Ford Motor Company moved into a new plant in Highland Park, Michigan, that boasted the world's first automobile assembly line. This new factory used the "work-in-motion" concept, in which individual workers repeated one or two steps over and over while rope cables towed partly assembled cars from one worker to the next. This method enabled the rate of production to increase from 15 cars per day to one car every 10 seconds. Ford's use of the assembly line spread to other industries, perpetuating the successes of the ongoing Industrial Revolution (a Defining Moment in economics) in the United States, which had become the world's leading industrial power.

On January 5, 1914, Henry Ford announced he would pay his workers the then-incredible sum of $5 per day. Just a few years earlier, auto workers had been paid only $0.15 per day. Despite paying workers the outrageous daily wage of $5, Ford was

able to sell cars to a mass market and achieve the high levels of profits that made him one of the richest men of his day.

Ford understood how the labor market worked. By encouraging higher productivity by means of higher pay, he succeeded where others had failed. Relying on increased productivity to lower the price to fit the average consumer's pocketbook, he achieved a mass market in automobiles.

In this chapter, we shall examine how wages are determined, why wages and productivity are positively related, why some people earn more than others and why some jobs pay more than others, and why some people remain out of the labor force. We shall discuss how demand, supply, and market equilibrium are determined in the labor market. We shall also consider the role of labor unions, and we shall review the history of the American labor movement and the effects of unions on wages, employment, and efficiency.

## THE DIFFERENCE BETWEEN LABOR AND OTHER FACTORS OF PRODUCTION

In the preceding chapter, we considered how factor markets work and reviewed economic principles for the use of land, labor, and capital inputs. Four special features differentiate labor from the two other factors:

1. We cannot be bought like an acre of land or a computer or office phone system; slavery is against the law. As the owners of labor, we can only rent our services. True, we can sell our labor services under short- or long-term contracts, but we cannot legally sell ourselves.
2. We have alternatives to using our time for labor. If land and machines are not put to productive use, they stand idle. When we are not engaged in the labor market, we can spend our time in domestic or leisure activities.
3. Land and capital cannot care about the use to which they are put. We, however, have preferences for particular types of work in particular locations. We care whether we work in Alaska or New York and whether we are actors or programmers.
4. Labor unions differentiate labor from the other factors of production. By joining labor unions, we can affect the conditions of work and pay.

## LABOR MARKET TRENDS

To understand the economics of labor, we must be able to explain trends and patterns in labor markets. Some of the most important of these are listed in Table 1.

1. The labor force has expanded substantially in the United States. The number of nonagricultural employees today is almost five times greater than it was 80 years ago.
2. The composition of the labor force has changed dramatically. The share of manufacturing employment has been stable since 1970, and the share of service employment has risen. The gender composition of the labor force has changed. Eighty years ago, only one in five women worked in the labor force. Today almost 60 percent of women work in the labor force.
3. The average number of hours worked per week has declined. In 1914, manufacturing workers worked an average of 49.4 hours per week. By 1995, this number had fallen to less than 40 hours per week.
4. Real wages have risen. The real (adjusted for inflation) hourly wage rate of American manufacturing workers increased almost four times between 1914 and the present. An hour of work today buys nearly four times the quantity of goods and services as did an hour of work in 1914.

### Table 1   Facts About the Labor Market, 1914 to Present

| Year | Nonagricultural Employees (millions) | Manufacturing (percent) | Services (percent) | Average Hours Worked per Week | Hourly Earnings (real dollars) | Fringe Benefits (real dollars per hour) | Female Labor Force Participation Rate (percent) |
|------|------|------|------|------|------|------|------|
| 1914 | 23.2 | 8.2  | 7.4  | 49.4 | 3.27  | —    | 22.8 |
| 1930 | 29.4 | 9.6  | 10.7 | 42.1 | 4.87  | .06  | 24.8 |
| 1940 | 32.4 | 11.0 | 15.0 | 38.1 | 6.90  | .32  | 27.4 |
| 1950 | 45.2 | 15.2 | 16.7 | 40.5 | 8.80  | .47  | 31.4 |
| 1960 | 54.2 | 16.8 | 21.5 | 39.7 | 11.22 | .96  | 34.8 |
| 1970 | 70.9 | 19.4 | 30.3 | 39.8 | 12.70 | 1.41 | 42.6 |
| 1975 | 77.0 | 18.3 | 35.1 | 39.4 | 13.16 | 1.88 | 45.9 |
| 1980 | 90.4 | 20.2 | 43.4 | 39.7 | 13.00 | 2.40 | 51.5 |
| 1995 | 111.0 | 19.0 | 60.8 | 39.0 | 12.00 | 4.81 | 57.5 |

*Sources:* Hours and real wages are from Ronald Ehrenberg and Robert Smith, *Modern Labor Economics: Theory and Public Policy* (New York: HarperCollins, 1991), Table 2.4. The data are from *Historical Statistics of the United States: Colonial Times to the Present*, series D29-41, 133; and from *Statistical Abstract of the United States*. Figures updated using the *Survey of Current Business*. The data on average hours and real hourly earnings are for manufacturing.

5. Despite their rising trend, real wages have fallen during some periods. Real wages rose by over 400 percent from 1914 to 1975, but then fell by about 9 percent from 1975 to 1995.

6. The composition of compensation has changed. Today, fringe benefits constitute more than one-quarter of compensation; the rest, wages. Eighty years ago virtually all compensation was from wages.

## THE WORKING OF THE LABOR MARKET

Markets bring together buyers and sellers of a particular good or service for the purpose of making transactions.

> A **labor market** brings together buyers and sellers of labor services to determine pay and working conditions.

Labor markets may be local, national, or even international in scope. The services of sales clerks, teenage employees, unskilled workers, and sanitation workers are bought and sold in local markets, whereas there are national and even international labor markets for engineers, academics, airline pilots, and upper-level executives, among others.

Some labor markets are informal. Job announcements are posted at the factory gate, "help wanted" ads are placed in the local newspaper, and jobs are promoted by word of mouth. Other labor markets fill positions according to a well-defined set of rules. Civil service jobs are regulated by detailed legislation and rules, and in unionized industries, rules for hiring and firing are spelled out in considerable detail.

Most labor arrangements are governed by contracts between the employer and employee. Labor contracts, which spell out conditions of work and pay, can be either *explicit* (formal) or *implicit* (informal). An explicit contract such as a union contract specifies the wage rate, the term of employment, working conditions, and the conditions under which the contract can be terminated. Other labor contracts are implicit. An informal understanding may exist that workers receive generous wages when jobs are available but will be laid off when business is slow. There may also be an understanding that laid-off workers will not seek other jobs during short layoffs in return for being rehired when business improves.

Employers can also use an internal labor market to hire the most qualified persons with a minimum of information costs.

> An **internal labor market** works by promoting or transferring workers it already employs.

Workers enter a firm's internal labor market through general entry-level positions such as management trainee, bookkeeper, or apprentice machinist. Rules and established procedures then determine who will be promoted and the manner in which vacancies are filled. Firms that use an internal labor market hire a large number of entry-level people without much testing, interviewing, or screening. A large department store hires a large number of management trainees; a factory hires a large number of general laborers. Once a person is on the job, the firm has the opportunity to observe actual job performance. The firm can learn a great deal about the person being considered for a promotion. Promoting from within is often less costly than hiring from outside. The major cost of using the internal labor market is that the firm passes up the opportunity to hire more-qualified persons from outside by restricting promotions to those it already employs.

Labor markets are differentiated by the ability of hiring firms to affect wage rates. Firms may be price takers or price makers in the labor market.

> If a firm must pay the wage rate dictated by the market regardless of how much labor it hires, the firm is a price taker. If the firm is large enough to raise the wage rate by hiring more, and lower it by hiring less, the firm is a price maker.

*Most employees price taker*

As we know from the preceding chapter, competition is more common in the labor market (and other factor markets) than it is in the product market. In this chapter we consider price-taking firms.

## HOUSEHOLD PRODUCTION AND LEISURE

Household production and leisure are alternatives to working in the labor force. These options affect the total supply of labor to the economy.

**Household production** is work in the home, including such activities as meal preparation, do-it-yourself repair, child-rearing, and cleaning. **Leisure** is time spent in any activity other than work in the labor force or work in the home.

Economists believe that we use rational economic decision making to allocate our time among work in the labor market, household production, and leisure.

The opportunity cost of leisure is the income (or household production) that must be given up. The opportunity cost of leisure rises when the price of market work rises. We would therefore expect leisure to decline as real wages rise. Why, then, have average hours worked per week declined while real wages have increased?

Figure 1 shows a labor supply curve relating wages and hours worked. The curve is backward bending; it has a section with a negative slope. Let's consider why an increase in wages first raises and then lowers the quantity of labor supplied.

An increase in wages raises the price of leisure and motivates individuals to substitute other things—

in this case, market work—for leisure, thereby discouraging leisure. But the increase in wages also raises income, making leisure more affordable.

In Figure 1, when the wage is $2 per hour and only 15 hours are worked per week, a dollar increase in the wage rate adds an additional $15 per week to income. This is not enough extra income to afford much more leisure. When wages are $4 per hour and 25 hours are worked per week, a dollar increase in wages is like an extra $25 per week; the increase in income is much larger. When wages are $10 per hour and 45 hours are worked per week, the income effect of another $1 increase in the wage rate is even stronger. In Figure 1, the effect of higher income dominates the effect of higher wages after wages reach $10 per hour. Further increases in wages cause hours worked to decline, as shown by the backward-bending section of the labor supply curve.

Some of us worry about the effects of mechanization on job opportunities. As machines become more and more efficient, will there one day be no jobs left? Mechanization raises labor productivity, which translates into higher real wages. With higher real wages, we can take more leisure and work fewer hours. The ultimate payoff of mechanization is that it gives us more leisure and higher incomes. People in various societies choose between labor and leisure in different ways. (See Example 1.)

Those who worked long hours in factories during the Industrial Revolution (a Defining Moment in economics) could hardly know that one of its results would be an eventual increase in leisure.

## WAGES AND HOUSEHOLD PRODUCTION

Most people cite social factors such as high divorce rates, one-parent families, and the enforcement of antidiscrimination legislation for the rising female labor-force participation rate reported in Table 1.

Economic theory provides another plausible explanation. Whether we work in the labor force or in household production also depends upon the value of our household production. If my work in the home (child-rearing, cleaning, food preparation) is worth $10 per hour, and my market wage is $8 per hour, I would work at home. If my market wage rises to $15 per hour, I would work at a job. The market wages of women have risen more rapidly than the value of household production, causing more and more women to enter the labor force. This principle explains the rise in the female labor force participation rate in Table 1.

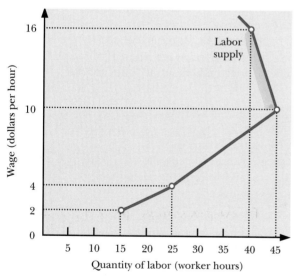

**FIGURE 1   The Backward-Bending Labor Supply Curve**

The labor supply curve is upward sloping until a wage of $10 per hour is reached. Below $10, the substitution effect of higher wages dominates the income effect of higher wages. At wage rates above $10, the quantity of labor supplied falls as the wage rate increases because the income effect dominates the substitution effect.

## EXAMPLE 1
## HAVE THE GERMANS
## BECOME LAZY?

The average American works 1798 hours per year; the average German 1554 hours. Compared with Germans, Americans are two times as likely to work on Saturdays and three times as likely to work on Sundays. Thirty percent of Americans prefer to work longer hours; only 14 percent of Germans want to work longer hours. Americans work hard "even if it interferes with the rest of their lives." Germans report working "only as hard as they have to."

The Germans have the reputation of being hard and conscientious workers. Why is it that Germans have become less work-oriented?

The economist's answer is that Germans lack the incentives to work harder. The average German production worker faces a marginal tax rate 30 percent higher than the American production worker. If the American worker gets to keep 70 cents of every extra dollar earned, the German worker gets to keep 60 cents after taxes. German workers also have what amounts to a guaranteed annual income. They get welfare transfers, health care, generous unemployment insurance, and subsidized college educations. Moreover, Germany has a highly centralized system of setting wages. There is little earnings difference between high-paid and low-paid jobs, and there are laws that make employee dismissals difficult. The rewards to hard work are simply less.

------------------------------------------------

*Source:* Linda Bell and Richard Freeman, "Why Do Americans and Germans Work Different Hours?" National Bureau of Economic Research Working Paper No. 4808, 1994.

## THE DEMAND FOR LABOR

The wage rate for a particular type of labor is determined in the market for that type of labor. The wage rate and the quantity of labor are determined by demand and supply, just as product price and quantity are determined by demand and supply.

We know, from the preceding chapter, that profit-maximizing firms hire factors up to the point where the factor price equals the marginal revenue product (MRP) of the factor. The firm will continue to hire labor as long as the marginal revenue product of the additional worker exceeds that worker's wage. The firm shown in Figure 2, panel (*a*), is perfectly competitive in the computer programmer market (it must take the market wage as given). It can hire all the labor it wants at the prevailing wage rate. Its labor supply schedule is a horizontal line (perfectly elastic) at the market wage.

Table 2 shows the outputs associated with different inputs of labor of a single grade, such as computer programmers. Columns 3 and 4 give the marginal physical product (MPP) and marginal revenue product (MRP) for each level of input. The firm's product sells for $2 per program line, and the capital input is fixed in the short run. With capital fixed, the law of diminishing returns applies to the labor input; MPP and MRP decline as labor inputs rise.

The firm is a price taker in both the product market and the labor market; therefore, its marginal revenue product equals its product price, *P,* times labor's marginal physical product (MPP). The firm will demand the quantity of labor at which $W = \text{MRP}$.

When the market wage is $28, the firm will demand that quantity of labor (2 hours) at which MRP is $28. If the wage falls to $16 per hour, the firm will hire more labor. As the firm increases its labor inputs, the law of diminishing returns causes MRP to fall. At the $16 wage, the firm will use 4 programmer hours because the MRP of the fourth hour is $16. The quantity of labor demanded varies inversely with the wage rate, which is shown by the downward-sloping shape of the demand curve in Figure 2, panel (*a*).

The individual firm's demand curve for labor is its marginal revenue product curve.

(*a*) The Firm's Demand

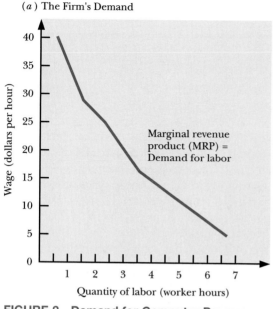

(*b*) The Market Demand

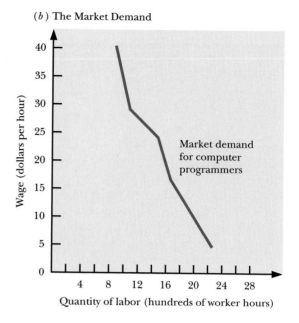

**FIGURE 2  Demand for Computer Programmers**

In panel (*a*) the price of this firm's output is $2 per line. Its capital input is fixed in the short run. Hence, MRP = MPP × $2. The labor demand curve shows the marginal revenue product of different quantities of labor hours. The firm uses 4 programmer hours when the wage rate is $16 per hour (the MRP of the fourth hour is equal to the $16 wage). If the wage rises to $28, the firm would employ only 2 programmer hours because the MRP of the second hour equals $28.

In panel (*b*), the market labor demand curve for programmers indicates the number of programmer hours that would be demanded by all firms that hire programmers at different wage rates. Because the demand curves of each firm are negatively sloped, the market labor demand curve is also negatively sloped.

The demand curve for labor is a derived demand curve, reflecting the demand for the product that that particular labor produces. If there is no demand for computer programming, the price of computer programming will be zero and MRP will equal zero. The greater the demand for the product, the higher the price and the higher the MRP. (See Example 2.)

The market demand is the sum of the demand of all firms hiring that single grade of labor.

> The market demand curve for labor shows how the total quantity of labor demanded varies as the wage changes.

The market demand curve for computer programmers is given in Figure 2, panel (*b*). This curve shows the quantities of a single grade of labor demanded by all 400 potential employers. Because the labor demand curves of individual firms are negatively sloped, the market demand curve will be negatively sloped as well. The market demand curve in

panel (*b*) is the sum of 400 firms like the one shown in panel (*a*).

## THE SUPPLY OF LABOR

If all other factors are held constant, the amount of labor of a single grade (such as computer programming) supplied depends on the wage rate. We compare the wage we can earn in one occupation with our opportunity cost—the wage we could receive in another occupation. The higher the wage offered for labor of a particular grade, the more the workers of that grade will offer their services. (The backward-bending supply curve in Figure 1 refers to the supply of all labor relative to the average wage across all occupations. It doesn't apply in this case.)

We receive a wage that is at least equal to the opportunity cost of our next-best alternative. The employer who fails to pay us our opportunity costs

## Table 2

| Labor Input (hours) (1) | Quantity of Output (lines programmed) (2) | Marginal Physical Product (lines), MPP (3) | Marginal Revenue Product, MRP = P × MPP (4) |
|---|---|---|---|
| 0 | 0 | | |
| | | 20 | $40 |
| 1 | 20 | | |
| | | 14 | 28 |
| 2 | 34 | | |
| | | 12 | 24 |
| 3 | 46 | | |
| | | 8 | 16 |
| 4 | 54 | | |
| | | 6 | 12 |
| 5 | 60 | | |
| | | 4 | 8 |
| 6 | 64 | | |
| | | 2 | 4 |
| 7 | 66 | | |

The price of this firm's output is $2 per line. Its capital input is fixed in the short run. Hence, MRP = MPP × $2. The demand schedule is the marginal revenue product schedule in column 4.

will have no workers because we will take a better alternative.

Figure 3, panel (a), shows a market supply curve indicating the number of hours computer programmers are willing to work at different wage rates. The supply curve is positively sloped because at higher wages, computer programming becomes more attractive relative to other occupations. Computer programmers will therefore shift hours from other occupations for which they are qualified (e.g., engineering, accounting, mathematics) into programming work. The market labor supply curve is the sum of the individual labor supply curves of computer programmers.

## LABOR MARKET EQUILIBRIUM

Wage rates are determined in labor markets by demand and supply. The market demand curve for labor of a single grade is negatively sloped; the market supply curve for labor of a single grade is positively sloped.

The market demand and supply curves for computer programmers are combined in Figure 3, panel (b). A $16 wage rate equates the quantity of programmer hours supplied with the quantity demanded, or 1600 hours. At any wage above $16, the

## EXAMPLE 2
## MARGINAL REVENUE PRODUCT AND
## BASEBALL PLAYERS

The proposition that a factor of production will be paid its marginal revenue product is supported by the market for star baseball players. Firms should hire factors of production so long as the extra revenue (the MRP) is not lower than the wage. The MRP of one more star player on a team with a full roster of star players is lower than it would be on a team with few star players. The MRP of the first star to be added to a roster would be very large, and the team should be willing to pay a high salary. Teams with few star players are therefore likely to win the bidding war for star players. In 1975, a National Labor Relations Board ruling allowed players for the first time to sell their services to any team as free agents. Of the first 69 free agents signed, 45 were signed by teams that had poorer records than the teams the players left. This pattern is exactly what the marginal productivity theory predicts.

Source: Ronald G. Ehrenberg and Robert S. Smith, *Modern Labor Economics* (New York: HarperCollins, 1991), pp. 69–70.

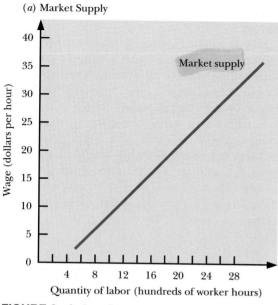

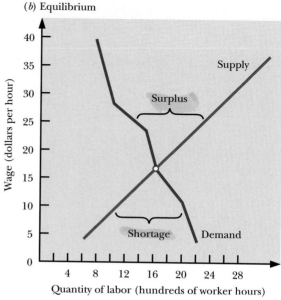

**FIGURE 3   Labor Supply, Demand, and Equilibrium Wage**

In panel (*a*), the market labor supply curve shows the number of hours programmers are willing to work at different wage rates, all other things remaining the same. The labor supply curve is positively sloped because at higher wages, programmer employment is more attractive relative to other types of employment.

In panel (*b*), the market supply of programmers, from panel (*a*), and the market demand for programmers, from Figure 2, panel (*b*), are brought together in this figure. The equilibrium wage rate is $16 per hour. At the $16 wage, the quantity demanded (1600 hours) equals the quantity supplied. At wage rates above $16, there is a surplus (quantity supplied exceeds quantity demanded); at wage rates below $16, there is a shortage of labor (quantity demanded exceeds quantity supplied).

number of hours programmers wish to work exceeds the number demanded. At any wage below $16, the number of hours firms wish programmers to work exceeds the number of hours programmers are willing to work.

> The equilibrium wage rate in a labor market is the wage rate at which the quantity of labor demanded equals the quantity of labor supplied.

If there is a *labor surplus,* some workers willing to work at the prevailing wage will be without jobs. Some will offer their services at lower wages and thus drive down the wage rate. If there is a *labor shortage,* some firms wishing to hire workers at the prevailing wage rate will go away empty-handed. Some will offer higher wages to attract employees and thus drive up wages.

When price-taking firms pay the equilibrium wage, workers are paid their marginal revenue prod-

ucts. In equilibrium, $W = MRP$. In Figure 3, panel (*b*), workers are paid $16 and their contribution to the firm's marginal revenue is also $16.

## EFFICIENCY WAGES

If a firm pays above-equilibrium wage rates, the number willing to work at those jobs will exceed the number of jobs available. Employers could still fill jobs and yet offer lower wages. It is for this reason that we expect firms to pay the equilibrium wage. The efficiency wage model explains why firms might want to pay more than the equilibrium wage rate.

> The **efficiency-wage model** states that it is rational for certain firms to pay workers a wage rate above equilibrium to improve worker performance and productivity.

Economists often cite the example of Henry Ford's 1914 policy of paying workers $5 a day (described in the Chapter Insight). By paying wages in excess of equilibrium, firms create an incentive for workers to work efficiently without careful monitoring. The costs of shirking and getting caught are high when the worker is receiving the bonus of an above-equilibrium wage.

Firms also use above-equilibrium wages to reduce turnover and create a stable work force. If all wages were finely balanced at equilibrium, workers could move from one job to another at relatively low cost. With wages above equilibrium, workers are less inclined to leave high-paying jobs. With a stable work force, training and search costs are reduced, and workers become more specialized and skilled the longer they stay on the job. Firms can use higher wages as a screening device to sort out less desirable job candidates. A higher wage attracts more able job candidates, and workers willing to work for less can be screened out as potential labor market "lemons."

## SHIFTS IN LABOR DEMAND AND SUPPLY CURVES

Four factors affect the demand curve for labor. These factors shift the demand curve for labor when they change.

1. Labor demand increases when the demand increases for the product produced by that labor. The demand increase raises the price of the product, which raises the marginal revenue product of labor and shifts the demand curve to the right.

2. Automated equipment can substitute for bank tellers, skilled labor substitutes for unskilled labor, and chemical fertilizers substitute for farm workers. If the prices of substitute factors increase, firms will increase their demand for labor.

3. Labor demand increases when the price of a factor complementary to labor decreases. Complementary factors are used in combination with labor. Materials such as steel, aluminum, and plastics are used in combination with labor to make automobiles, for example. If the prices of these materials fall, the demand for labor will rise.

4. When the MPP of labor rises, the MRP (and therefore the demand for) labor rises.

Like the labor demand curve, the labor supply curve shifts in response to changes in other factors. Three factors affect the supply of labor to a particular occupation:

1. The wages that can be earned in other occupations affect labor supply. If engineering wages increase, the supply of computer programmers should fall.

2. The nonmonetary aspects of the occupation affect labor supply. We dislike heavy, unpleasant, or dangerous work or work in harsh climates. An increase in the unpleasantness or danger associated with a particular job will decrease the supply of labor. As the number of robberies at convenience stores increases, the supply of convenience store clerks will fall. (See Example 3.)

3. Labor unions can affect labor supply through collective bargaining and strikes. We shall consider this subject later in the chapter.

We can use the tools of labor demand and supply to explain trends in real wages. Table 1 showed that real wages have increased over the long run but that they fell between the mid 1970s and the early 1990s.

The demand for labor depends on the productivity of labor. If the productivity of labor of a specific grade increases, the demand for that labor will rise. If labor productivity rises throughout the economy, the demand for labor will increase throughout the economy. The general trend for labor productivity is positive. Since the Industrial Revolution (a Defining Moment in economics), economies have experienced technological progress. We seem able to find better ways of doing things, new inventions, and new technologies. These factors cause labor productivity to rise.

The supply of labor to the economy at large depends upon labor/leisure choices. More of us are willing to work in the labor force, and work more hours, if real wages are rising. The supply of labor to the economy also depends upon demographic factors. If a large number of young people are completing their educations and entering the labor force, the supply of labor rises. If the labor force is aging and a large number of people are retiring, the supply of labor declines.

During the period 1914 to the 1970s, the number of individuals in the prime working age population (ages 25–44) fell from almost 30 percent to 24 percent of the total population. In effect, labor became more scarce. From 1970 to 1995, the prime working age population rose from 24 percent to 33 percent of the total population. The percentage increase of the 25–44 population between 1970 and 1995 (a 25-year period) was greater than its percentage increase between 1914 and 1970 (a 56-year period). It is the growth of population that feeds the labor force and its expansion.

## EXAMPLE 3
## COMPENSATING WAGES
## IN MEAT PACKING

Meat-packing is unpleasant and dangerous work, with an injury rate five times higher than the typical industry. Meat-packing plants use automated conveyor belts carrying about 4000 cattle each day. Plants are noisy and dangerous. Workers wear ear protection gear, mesh armor protection from knives, and helmets. Long chains move a carcass down the production line at a rate of 150 to 200 head an hour. The worker makes one or two cuts on a particular type of meat and repeats those motions several thousand times a day. The workers risk being injured by knives and machines and may suffer from carpal tunnel syndrome—a wrist ailment caused by performing repetitive wrist or arm movements.

Before recent technological improvements, meat-cutting was a skilled occupation. Now, meat-packing plants are staffed by unskilled workers, who regularly migrate from Texas, where they are unemployed or earn minimum wages, to Iowa or Nebraska for jobs in meat-packing plants.

The theory of compensating wage differentials suggests that workers of a given skill level will receive higher wages for working in unpleasant and dangerous jobs. The meat-packing industry bears out this theory. An entry-level meat-cutter with no experience can earn about 70 percent more than the minimum wage. Meat-packing plants must offer such a premium to attract unskilled workers.

------------------------------------------------

*Sources:* James Pinkerton, "Hispanics Brave Meatpacking Dangers in Quest of Better Life," *Houston Chronicle,* September 2, 1990, 1A; and "Industry Giant IBP Recruiting Heavily in Texas," *Houston Chronicle,* September 2, 1990, 1D.

---

The baby boom of the early post–World War II period explains the recent phenomenal growth of the 25–44 population. Born in the late 1940s and 1950s, the baby boomers came into the labor market in force after 1970. As they entered the labor force, the supply of labor exploded.

Figure 4 shows the effects of the baby boom on real wages. Panel (*a*) includes the period 1914 to 1970. The prime age population was not growing rapidly, the supply of labor was not expanding rapidly, and increases in labor productivity caused the demand for labor to outgrow the supply of labor. The result: Real wages rose. Panel (*b*) shows the 1970 to 1995 period. The exceptionally rapid expansion of the prime age population caused the supply of labor to outpace the demand for labor. The result: Real wages fell.

After 1965, birth rates in the United States dropped. Since then, there has been a baby bust instead of a baby boom. As the baby bust cohort ma-tures, employment should grow at slower rates and real wage rates should again rise. In the year 2001, the first baby busters will be in their mid-30s, and the baby boomers will be 55 years old and thinking about retirement.

As the baby busters replace the baby boomers, real wages will rise, but other things will happen as well. With the graying of America, there will be more retirees than employed workers, and we will find it difficult to pay the social security benefits of retired workers.

## RISING SERVICE EMPLOYMENT

As we grow more affluent, we spend our income differently. Instead of spending most of our money on shelter, refrigerators, and automobiles, we spend more on travel, eating out, entertainment, health care, fitness, travel, and information/communication technology. With rising incomes, we spend a rising

(a) Rising Real Wages, 1914–1970

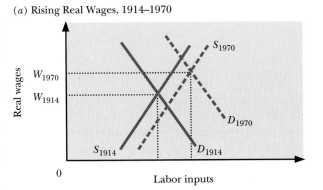

(b) Falling Real Wages, 1970–1995

*2 income family*

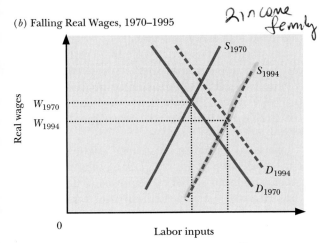

**FIGURE 4   Why Real Wages Rise or Fall**

During the period 1914 to 1970, in panel (a), the growth of the prime age labor force was slow, and the labor supply increased slowly. The increase in the demand for labor due to rising productivity was greater, and real wages rose. During the period from 1970 to 1995, in panel (b), the prime labor force grew rapidly, causing the increase in the supply of labor to outpace the increase in the demand for labor. Real wages therefore fell.

share of our income on services and less of our income on manufactured goods.

The demand for labor is a derived demand. The demands for automobile workers or for service workers depend on the demands for automobiles and services. The high rate of growth of demand for services explains the rising share of service employment. Despite contrary myths, the shift to service employment does not mean that we will all end up cooking fries at Burger King. The shift has been caused by the fact that employment and earnings opportunities in services have become better than those in manufacturing. The U.S. worker of the twenty-first century will be a software programmer, a financial analyst,

an accountant, a technician for sophisticated medical equipment, a specialist in global trading—not an assembly-line worker or a drilling rig operator.

**FRINGE BENEFITS**

Thirty years ago, virtually all compensation was in the form of money wages. Now about one-quarter of compensation is in the form of benefits.

> **Benefits** are forms of employee compensation such as employer-subsidized health insurance or employer contributions to retirement plans.

The rise in benefits as a form of compensation is explained by government mandates and by tax laws.

Obligations mandated by government regulations—including Social Security, workers' compensation, and unemployment insurance—now comprise nearly one-third of benefit costs. The rise in benefits is also explained by the rapid increase in medical costs, which raise employer contributions to employee health insurance programs.

In addition to higher medical costs and government-mandated contributions, there are several other reasons for the increase in benefits. Employees' demand for nonwage benefits is reinforced by the tax code, which gives tax benefits on retirement contributions and on the employer's portion of health and life insurance premiums. If an employee has to pay an income tax of 25 percent on every extra dollar of wages, that extra dollar is "worth" 75 cents. If the same employee receives an extra dollar of retirement or health-care benefits, which are not taxed, that dollar is worth more to the employee (see Figure 5).

**LABOR UNIONS**

Workers in the same industry or occupation may join together to form a labor union.

> A **labor union** is a collective organization of workers and employees whose objective is to improve conditions of pay and work.

Unions perform a variety of functions for employee members, the most visible of which is to engage in collective bargaining with employers. Instead

*Value set by scarcity, people are not scarce.*

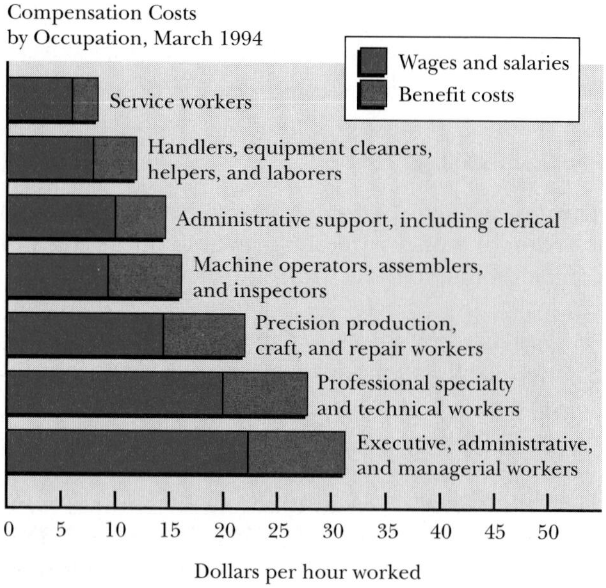
Compensation Costs
by Occupation, March 1994
Wages and salaries
Benefit costs
Service workers
Handlers, equipment cleaners,
helpers, and laborers
Administrative support, including clerical
Machine operators, assemblers,
and inspectors
Precision production,
craft, and repair workers
Professional specialty
and technical workers
Executive, administrative,
and managerial workers
0 5 10 15 20 25 30 35 40 45 50
Dollars per hour worked

**FIGURE 5 Labor Compensation: Pay Versus Benefits**

*Source:* U.S. Department of Labor, Bureau of Labor Statistics.

of individual negotiation by each employee in regard to wages, fringe benefits, job security, and work conditions, the union represents all employees in collective negotiations.

There are three general types of labor unions: craft unions, such as an electricians' union or a plumbers' union; industrial unions, such as the United Automobile Workers (a union that represents automobile workers of all types) and the United Mine Workers (a union that represents all types of workers engaged in mining); and employee associations, such as the National Education Association, the American Bar Association, the American Medical Association, and state employee associations. Historically, employee associations have primarily been concerned with maintaining professional standards. In the last few decades, however, they have become increasingly involved in the customary union function of improving the pay, benefits, and working conditions of members.

A **craft union** represents workers of a single occupation. An **industrial union** represents employees of an industry regardless of their specific occupation. An **employee association** represents employees in a particular profession in order to both maintain professional standards and improve conditions of pay and work.

## A BRIEF HISTORY OF AMERICAN UNIONISM

Unions were formed to create a more level playing field between workers and employers. Unions were not a powerful force in the American workplace until the late 1930s, even though the first national conventions of labor unions met as early as 1869. Union membership expanded rapidly after 1886, with the creation of the American Federation of Labor (AFL) under the leadership of Samuel Gompers, the father of the American labor movement.

An antiunion political climate restricted the growth of unionism until the 1930s. Antitrust laws were applied against unions; and companies used private police forces, threats, and intimidation against them. Employees had to sign "yellow dog" contracts, pledging not to join a union.

Industrial unionism blossomed in the 1930s under the leadership of John L. Lewis, who formed the Congress of Industrial Organizations (CIO) in 1936 to organize workers on an industrial rather than a craft basis. In 1955, the AFL and CIO merged to form the AFL-CIO.

Laws passed during the Great Depression promoted the growth of organized labor. The Norris-LaGuardia Act of 1932 gave workers full freedom of association, self-organization, and designation of representatives to negotiate the terms and conditions of their employment. The Norris-LaGuardia Act restricted the use of injunctions and prohibited "yellow dog" contracts. The National Labor Relations Act (the Wagner Act) of 1935 required employers to bargain in good faith with unions, and it became illegal to interfere with employees' rights to organize. The National Labor Relations Board (NLRB) was authorized to investigate unfair labor practices and conduct union elections.

The Taft-Hartley Act of 1947 permitted states to pass right-to-work laws prohibiting the requirement that union membership be a condition for employment. It also allowed major strikes to be delayed by an 80-day cooling-off period if ordered by the president. The Landrum-Griffin Act of 1959 was designed to protect the rights of union members and to increase union democracy. It included provisions for the periodic reporting of union finances and for regulating union elections.

## AMERICAN UNIONISM TODAY

Today, there are fewer than 16 million union members in the United States. Fewer than 15 of every 100 workers belong to a union, down from a peak of 25 percent in the mid-1950s.

There are a number of reasons for the decline in union membership. First, the percentage of women in the labor force has been rapidly increasing, and women have historically not joined unions. The employment share of another group that tends not to join unions, white-collar workers, has risen as well. Increased employment in the service sector (which is only 6 percent unionized) has also retarded unionization. Moreover, there has been a shift in population from the northeast and midwestern states to the southern and southwestern states, where union membership is weakest.

## UNION OBJECTIVES

Unions desire higher wages, better fringe benefits, and safer working conditions for their members. They also want to keep their members employed. Are the two objectives of higher wages and lower unemployment economically compatible?

Let's assume that two unions, A and B, collectively bargain with management to determine wages. For simplicity, we'll assume that the average worker in each union is earning the same wage ($w_c$) and that the level of employment is the same in each union (at $l_c$). The demand curve for each union's labor force is graphed in Figure 6. The demand for Union A's labor is inelastic. Thus, a large percentage increase in the wage yields a small percentage reduction in the quantity of labor demanded. The demand for Union B's labor is elastic. Thus, an increase in the wage causes a larger percentage decrease in the quantity of labor demanded than the percentage increase in the wage.

Union B is faced with a dilemma. If it pushes for higher wages, the number of union jobs will decline. Jobs will be traded for higher wages, and those who lose their jobs will be dissatisfied. This wage/employment trade-off is less acute for Union A because the same increase in wages loses fewer jobs.

> The **wage/employment trade-off** means that higher wages reduce the number of jobs; lower unemployment requires sacrificing higher wages.

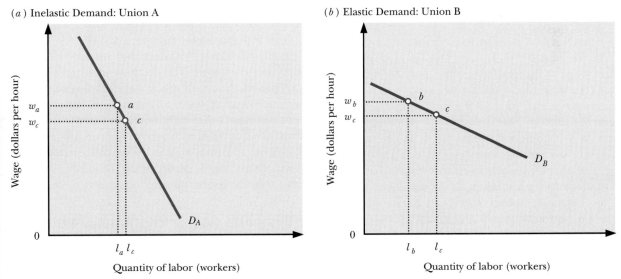

($a$) Inelastic Demand: Union A

($b$) Elastic Demand: Union B

**FIGURE 6    The Trade-off between Wages and Employment: The Competitive Case**

The demand curve for the members of Union A is relatively inelastic, whereas the demand curve for the members of Union B is relatively elastic. If both unions, in the collective bargaining process, push for the same wage increases, more jobs will be lost by workers in Union B (where demand is elastic) than by workers in Union A.

## UNION BEHAVIOR

The wage/employment trade-off explains which types of industries are most easily unionized. Unions are easier to form in industries where the demand for labor is inelastic. Indeed, skilled crafts such as carpentry, printing, glass-blowing, and shoemaking were the first occupations to be unionized.

The demand for skilled labor is relatively inelastic because of the lack of close substitutes. It is not easy to substitute unskilled for skilled labor, or a skilled printer for a skilled glassblower. The last (and presumably most difficult) occupations to organize were the unskilled occupations in which the demand for labor is highly elastic, such as wholesale and retail trade.

Unions seek not only to increase the demand for labor but also to reduce the elasticity of demand. By increasing demand, labor unions can obtain both higher wages and higher employment. By reducing the elasticity of demand, unions can raise wages with a smaller cost in lost employment.

Unions attempt to increase the demand for labor and lower its elasticity of demand in a variety of ways. They lobby for tariffs and quotas on competing foreign products, and conduct advertising campaigns telling the public to "look for the union label" or to "buy American." The AFL-CIO has opposed the relaxation of immigration laws and has spoken out against illegal immigration. Unions were strongly opposed to the North American Free Trade Agreement (NAFTA), passed in 1994. Unions support raising the minimum wage to increase wages for unskilled labor relative to the more skilled union workers.

Unions have also pushed for minimum staffing requirements called *featherbedding,* perpetuating jobs that have become redundant (such as fire stokers on diesel-powered locomotives). Unions also bargain for rules that make it difficult to substitute other grades of labor for union labor. In construction contracts, for example, unions specify in detail which jobs can be performed only by electricians or by plumbers.

## LIMITATIONS OF LABOR SUPPLY

Another strategy for raising wages is to limit the supply of union labor. Some unions control who will be allowed to work in a particular occupation by means of certification and qualification requirements. In craft unions, the number of union members can be

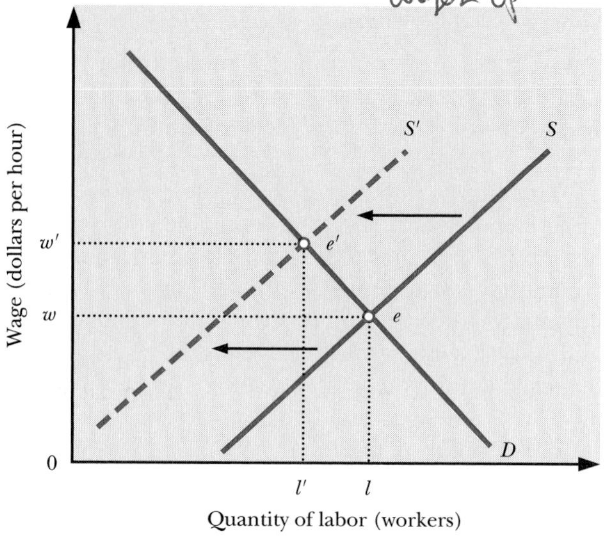

**FIGURE 7 Craft Unions and Wages: Limiting Supply**
By limiting entry into the profession, a craft union shifts the labor supply curve to the left (from S to S'), and the wage rate of union members is raised above what it would have been without the union.

restricted by long apprenticeships, difficult qualifying exams, state licensing, and ceilings on total membership. In the process of limiting labor supply, the union screens out unqualified workers, but it may also exclude some qualified people who are prepared to work in a particular occupation.

Figure 7 shows the effect that limiting the labor supply has on wages. The decrease in supply (from S to S') moves the equilibrium wage/employment combination to higher wages and fewer jobs. If unions are to control wages through limitations on the supply of union labor, it is necessary to prevent employers from substituting nonunion labor. For this reason, craft unions favor rigid certification requirements and rules prohibiting nonunion workers.

## STRIKES AND COLLECTIVE BARGAINING

Industrial unions that represent all of the workers in a particular industry cannot limit the supply of labor. Such unions wield only limited influence on overall labor supply conditions by supporting immigration restrictions, mandatory retirement, shorter work weeks, and laws against teenage employment. Unlike plumbers, electricians, and physicians, industrial unions cannot control the number of union members. Industrial unions, therefore, use collective bargaining to raise the wages of union members.

> **Collective bargaining** is the process whereby a union bargains with management as the representative of all union employees.

Collective bargaining gives workers a stronger voice than if each worker negotiated separately with management.

The threat of a **strike** is a union's most potent weapon in collective bargaining.

> A **strike** occurs when all unionized employees cease to work until management agrees to specific union demands.

The effect of the collective-bargaining process (with threat of strike) is portrayed in Figure 8. The supply curve $S$ represents the supply of labor to the industry if each individual were to bargain separately with management. When a union threatens to strike, it is, in effect, telling management that at wages less than $w_c$, no labor will be supplied; at the wage of $w_c$, management can hire as much labor as it wants up to $l_c$; as wages increase above $w_c$, management can hire increasing amounts of labor beyond $l_c$. Thus, the new labor supply curve incorporating the threat of a strike is the line $S'$ that connects $w_c$ on the vertical axis with point $c$ and then continues along the original supply curve above point $c$. Without the threat of a strike, the supply curve would be the original curve $S$, and point $e$ would be the equilibrium wage/employment combination. With the threat of a strike, the demand curve meets the new supply curve at point $a$, and the firm hires $l_a$ workers at a wage of $w_c$.

From the standpoint of union members, collective bargaining has both costs and benefits. The benefits are the higher wages that collective bargaining brings ($w_c$ is higher than $w_e$). However, if the industry is entirely unionized, some union members who are willing to work at the negotiated wage will not be employed. Although $l_c$ workers are willing to work at $w_c$, only $l_a$ workers will be hired. The unemployment effects of collective bargaining are regulated by numerous rules within the union governing the order of layoffs. Typically, union members who have senior-

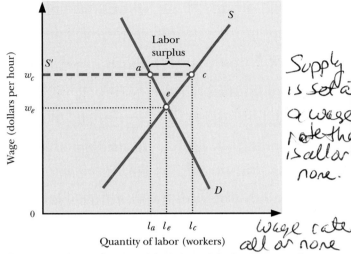

Supply is set at a wage rate that is all or none.

Wage rate all or none

**FIGURE 8   Collective Bargaining with the Threat of a Strike**

The supply curve $S$ represents the labor supply if each worker were to bargain separately with the employer. The supply curve formed by $S'$ to the left of point $c$ and $S$ above $c$ results from collective bargaining; no union labor will be supplied at a wage below $w_c$. Point $e$ is the equilibrium wage/employment combination without collective bargaining or the threat of a strike; point $a$ is the equilibrium wage/employment combination with collective bargaining.

increase demand
inelastic demand

ity (have been in the union the longest time) are laid off last. (See Example 4.)

## THE EFFECTS OF UNIONS ON WAGES AND EFFICIENCY

Workers represented by unions earn more than nonunionized workers. In the mid 1990s, the 18 percent of employed wage and salary workers represented by unions earned 29 percent more than the 82 percent not represented by unions.

The fact that unions raise the wages of their members above nonunionized workers does not prove that unionization results in generally higher wages for the economy as a whole. As discussed above, higher union wages mean less employment in unionized businesses. Those who are left without jobs due to higher union wages spill over into the nonunionized labor force. The fewer the number of union jobs, the greater the supply of labor for other jobs. Accordingly, higher union wages can depress wages elsewhere.

## EXAMPLE 4
## THE WAGE/EMPLOYMENT TRADE-OFF:
## A UNION STRIKES FOR LOWER WAGES!

One of the most unusual strikes in union history was called by the New Jersey Building and Construction Trades Council of the AFL-CIO on behalf of unionized insulation installers. The goal of the strike, which lasted two days, was to force employers to agree to pay union workers $1.60 an hour less than the employers had offered! Why would a union go on strike to gain lower wages? The union leadership interpreted management's offer as a subtle attempt to price union members out of the market. The higher wage would have provided firms with an excuse to hire more nonunion labor, causing a decline in union membership. In this case, the union members clearly understood the wage/employment trade-off. They were willing to accept lower wages for more jobs.

Most economists believe that unions have a negative effect on efficiency and labor productivity. If unions use work rules, such as prohibiting carpenters from turning a screw on an electrical fixture, business firms are prevented from combining resources in the most efficient manner. If unions use collective bargaining or control of labor supply to raise union wages above nonunion wages, labor resources will not be used efficiently. If union workers earn $20 per hour and nonunion workers $15 per hour, competitive firms will hire workers until these wage rates equal marginal revenue products. By using collective bargaining or supply restrictions, union workers have a higher productivity. More output could be produced from the same amount of labor by reallocating labor from nonunionized to unionized employment, but labor unions prevent this from happening.

Some economists argue that unions actually raise productivity by improving work conditions, giving workers a voice in the company, and by reducing turnover. Unionization could mean that firms have more experienced and dedicated workers.[1] It is unlikely, however, that these positive effects can outweigh the negative effects of unions. In fact, the share prices of companies usually fall when they are unionized. Unionization is taken as a sign that the profits of the company will suffer.[2]

## LABOR UNIONS: A BRIEF INTERNATIONAL PERSPECTIVE

There are significant differences among the labor union movements in the United States, Europe, and Asia. Although associations of journeymen existed in the form of medieval guilds, labor unions were not organized in Europe until the nineteenth century. The United Kingdom's Trade Union Act of 1871 guaranteed legal recognition for labor unions. On the Continent, unions were organized on industrial rather than craft lines, and they engaged in partisan political activity. In Germany, for example, unions were responsible for much social legislation prior to World War I. The Solidarity labor movement in Poland played a major political role in achieving Polish independence in 1989.

In Europe, labor organizations tend to be either constituted as or affiliated with political parties, usually from the left wing. In England, the labor unions joined forces with the socialists to form the Labour

---

[1]Richard B. Freeman and James L. Medoff, *What Do Unions Do?* (New York: Basic Books, 1982).

[2]Richard Ruback and Martin Zimmerman, "Unionization and Profitability: Evidence from the Capital Market," *Journal of Political Economy,* December 1984, 1134–1157.

Party in 1893. In Sweden, there is a close alliance between the two major labor unions and the Social Democratic Party. In Italy, Belgium, and the Netherlands, rival Christian and socialist trade union movements are present. The American labor movement avoided forming a political party, although it tends to support the Democratic Party.

The United States is one of the least unionized industrial economies. Ninety percent of Israel's labor force is unionized. Between 65 percent and 90 percent of workers in the Scandinavian countries are unionized. Membership in Germany, Japan, and the United Kingdom hovers around one-third. The United States resembles France, Switzerland, Hong Kong, and Taiwan, where unionization rates are 20 percent or less.

In Germany, unions are organized on an industry basis and are grouped into federations. Collective bargaining takes place at industrywide levels, and compulsory arbitration is used to settle disputes. German enterprise laws require that union representatives sit on management boards in large companies.

Sweden is dominated by a comprehensive labor movement. Virtually all blue-collar workers belong to the Confederation of Trade Unions, and white-collar workers belong to one of two other unions. As close allies of the Social Democratic Party, Swedish unions have developed profit-sharing plans and have pushed for social welfare policies to equalize the distribution of income.

In Japan each company has its own union that cuts across all craft and class boundaries. Japanese union presidents are key workers who are often promoted to the ranks of management. Japanese unions typically foster cooperation between management and workers, and commonly adopt a management perspective. The founding slogan of the Nissan Company labor union, for example, is "Those who truly love their union, love their company."

In this chapter, we have examined how labor markets work and how unions affect wages and economic efficiency. In the next chapter, we shall turn to the nonlabor factors of production: land, capital, and entrepreneurship.

## SUMMARY

1. Labor is different from the two other factors of production because workers desire leisure and have preferences concerning different jobs. Labor cannot be bought and sold. A labor market brings buyers and sellers of labor services together. The buyer who must accept the market wage as given is a price taker in the labor market.

2. When wage rates rise, the opportunity cost of leisure increases, as does income. Whether or not the aggregate labor-supply curve will be backward bending depends upon the relative strengths of the income and substitution effects. Whether people work in household production or in the market labor force depends upon the value of time in the home compared with their market wage.

3. If firms are price takers, they hire labor to the point where $W = MRP$. The firm's MRP schedule is its labor demand schedule. The labor demand curve will be negatively sloped both for firms and for the market.

4. The labor supply curve for a particular occupation will be positively sloped because workers must be paid their opportunity costs.

5. The labor demand curve will shift if the demand for the firm's final product changes, if the price of either substitute or complementary factors changes, or if the productivity of labor changes. The labor supply curve will shift if job conditions or wages in other industries change.

6. The market wage rate is typically that wage at which the quantity demanded of labor of a single grade equals the quantity supplied. A new equilibrium wage/quantity combination will result when either the market supply or market demand curve shifts. Demand and supply analysis explains the behavior of real wages and rising service employment. The post–World War II baby boom helps explain the recent decline in real wage rates. Government legislation and taxation explain the rising importance of benefits.

7. A union is a collective organization of workers and employees whose objective is to improve pay and work conditions. A craft union represents workers of a particular occupation. An industrial union represents workers of a particular industry.

8. The formation of unions in the United States was aided by prolabor legislation beginning with the Norris-LaGuardia Act of 1932, which facilitated union organizing drives. The National Labor Relations Act of 1935 made it illegal for employers to interfere with the rights of employees to organize. The Taft-Hartley Act of 1947 was a reaction against the prounion legislation of the 1930s.

9. Union membership in the United States is lower than that of most industrialized countries.
10. Unions must weigh the advantages of higher wages against the disadvantages of less employment. Unions respond to the trade-off between jobs and employment by attempting to increase the demand for union labor and reduce the elasticity of that demand. In collective bargaining, the most potent weapon of the union is the threat of a strike.
11. Unions have raised the wages of their members relative to nonunion wages. Unions can have a negative effect on nonunion wages. When unions raise wages in the union sector, the workers who lose employment spill over into the nonunion sector. This increase in the labor supply lowers nonunion wages. Most economists believe that unions adversely affect labor productivity. A more recent view argues that unions raise the labor productivity of union workers.

## KEY TERMS

labor market
internal labor market
household production
leisure
efficiency-wage model
benefits
labor union

craft union
industrial union
employee association
wage/employment trade-off
collective bargaining
strike

## QUESTIONS AND PROBLEMS

1. Why do labor's special features cause the labor market to work differently from the other factor markets?
2. What is the information cost strategy of a firm that fills all positions by promoting from within?
3. A price-taking firm in both its product and factor markets is currently employing 25 workers. The twenty-fifth worker's marginal revenue product is $300 per week, and the worker's wage is $200 per week. Is this firm maximizing its profits? If not, what would you advise the company to do?
4. There is a close positive association between labor productivity and wages. Use the theory presented in this chapter to explain this relationship.

5. State law in New Jersey requires that employees in licensed gambling casinos be residents of New Jersey for a specified period of time. What effect does this legislation have upon the demand for casino employees in New Jersey?
6. During recessions and periods of falling wages, the number of volunteers for the all-volunteer army rises. Use the theory of this chapter to explain why this supply of labor rises.
7. You are a surgeon earning $200,000 per year. When the demand for your services increases, the charge for each operation increases by 25 percent. What effect will this increase have on the number of operations you perform?
8. Rank each of the following jobs according to the difficulty of devising an incentive pay system that is compatible with the overall objectives of the firm. Explain your ranking.
   a. Janitorial work performed at night in an office building
   b. Assembly-line work in a washing-machine factory
   c. Traveling sales work
   d. The creation of hand-carved figures for a crafts company
   e. Professional basketball playing
9. Using the computer programming example in the chapter, explain what would happen to the wage of computer programmers if the number of program lines produced per hour were to double for each level of labor input. Explain what would happen if the price paid for programs fell to $1.
10. Draw hypothetical labor demand and labor supply curves for truck drivers. Shift the curves to show what happens when
   a. Truck driving becomes safer.
   b. Truck drivers become more efficient.
   c. Truck drivers must be licensed by a state agency.
   d. The earning of surgeons increases.
   e. The earning of moving-equipment operators falls.
11. Explain how the efficiency-wage model justifies paying wages that exceed marginal productivity.
12. If you were the president of a major industrial union, what would your attitude be toward free immigration? What would your attitude be toward the minimum-wage law? Explain.

13. Explain why both the automobile unions and the management of the automobile industry favor import restrictions on foreign-made cars.

14. You belong to a union of bank tellers. What would your attitude be toward automated bank tellers? Explain.

15. If unions do succeed in raising productivity, what effect would this increase have on the costs of production of unionized versus nonunionized companies?

# CHAPTER 18

# INTEREST, RENT, AND PROFIT

About 75 percent of all the income in the United States is earned from salaries and wages. While we might earn a little bit each year from interest on a savings account or dividends on shares of stock, most of us live on what we earn through the sweat of our labor. Most of us are satisfied with this arrangement—never thinking of starting a business, of saving or borrowing to buy land, or of investing our last penny in a real estate deal.

There are, however, people who live off businesses they have started, from rents they receive for renting their land to a shopping center, from interest they receive from loaning money to shopkeepers, or from profitable investments in the stock market. They do not live off a steady paycheck; they live off what they earn for themselves.

Whether these people earn a lot or a little appears to depend on several factors. Have they taken a safe or risky approach? The most successful businesspeople did not get rich by playing it safe: They took risks. Were they smarter than others? Did they see and take advantage of opportunities that others did not see? Did they have good or bad luck? Maybe others were just as talented or took as many risks, but their luck was bad.

Some of us have a tendency to look at what other people make from investments and from business startups as "unearned" or "undeserved" income. In this chapter, we shall consider the sources of nonlabor income and its relationship to risk, ingenuity, and luck.

# INTEREST

Capital goods are required for the production of consumer goods. Capital goods such as trucks, conveyors, buildings, lathes, cranes, hammers, and computers harness the mechanical, electrical, and chemical powers of nature to expand the production possibilities of society far beyond what could otherwise be accomplished by unaided human hands or minds. Productivity increases, for example, when a net is used instead of bare hands to catch fish, or when workers assemble cars on an assembly line with sophisticated equipment rather than in a small garage with hand tools.

Saving is necessary if a society is to invest in capital goods. Through saving, resources are diverted from producing consumption goods to producing capital goods. When people save, they buy stocks and bonds or deposit their funds in various bank accounts. Although some of these funds are used to finance the consumption expenditures of ordinary people, the rest are channeled directly or indirectly into investments in new buildings, plants, machinery, and inventories.

We human beings are impatient. To be convinced of the value of saving a dollar today, we must be rewarded with more than a dollar tomorrow. Because capital is productive, a dollar invested today in capital goods yields more than a dollar tomorrow. Thus, investors are willing to pay the interest that savers demand. Interest coordinates the number of dollars that businesses want to invest with the number that people want to save.

> **Interest** is the price of credit and is determined in credit markets.

## THE STOCK OF CAPITAL

Economists distinguish between *tangible capital* and *intangible capital*. Tangible capital differs from the other factors of production in that, in its concrete form (from trucks and computers to fishnets and shovels), it has already been produced. An automatic assembly line is the product of past work and effort.

Intangible capital has two forms. *Research and development (R&D) capital* consists of accumulated investments in technology, productive knowledge, and know-how; *human capital* consists of accumulated investments in human beings—in training, education, and improved health that increase the productive capacities of people. We shall consider human-capital investments, an important determinant of income distribution, in more detail in the next chapter. Human-capital theory suggests that the human capital embodied in trained labor is "produced" in the same economic sense as a truck or factory.

The stock of capital that exists in an economy at any given moment depends on (1) the accumulated savings and investment decisions that have been made in the past, and (2) the extent to which old capital goods have undergone depreciation through use or obsolescence.

> **Depreciation** is the decrease in the economic value of capital goods as they are used in the production process.

The new capital goods that are added to the stock of capital during a given period depend on how much consumers are saving and how much firms are investing. Over time, capital goods accumulate and depreciate. If the rate of accumulation exceeds the rate of depreciation, the stock of capital will grow.

> The current stock of capital is determined by past savings and investment decisions. The stock of capital grows if the rate of capital accumulation exceeds the rate of depreciation. The stock of capital declines if the rate of accumulation is less than the rate of depreciation.

## CREDIT MARKETS

Robinson Crusoe, living alone on a deserted island, did not need a special market to coordinate his saving and investment decisions. When he took three days off from fishing to weave a net, he was both *saving* (giving up some present consumption) and *investing* (increasing his future consumption). Simultaneous saving and investing were also characteristic of early agricultural societies. Farmers saved and invested in the same act of taking time off from current production to drain a swamp or to build an earthen dam in order to produce capital goods. In a modern economy, however, we use financial assets—stocks, bonds, bank credit, and trade credit—to finance the accumulation of capital goods. Investors and savers are usually separate entities, with their actions coordinated by credit, or capital markets.

Credit, or capital, markets facilitate the exchange of financial assets in a modern society.

Credit, or capital, markets are necessary because of specialization. Business firms have the ability to take advantage of profitable investment opportunities by expanding production capacities, but, unlike Robinson Crusoe, they must usually find a separate source of funds. Households, meanwhile, specialize in saving because they do not have the information to act on profitable investment opportunities. Therefore, households can trade their savings with businesses who wish to use them for investments. In credit markets, firms wishing to invest in capital goods borrow from households.

The growth of the stock of tangible capital is paralleled by the growth of the financial assets of those who accumulate savings. These financial assets, such as stocks, bonds, and various IOUs, are specific types of claims on the net productivity of real capital. The owners of such capital receive *interest* (or *dividend*) *income* from investors as payment for the use of their capital.

## THE RATE OF INTEREST

An interest rate is usually expressed as an annual percentage rate.

An **interest rate** measures the yearly cost of borrowing as a percentage of the amount loaned.

For example, if you borrow $1000 on January 1 and repay $1100 ($1000 borrowed plus $100 interest) on December 31 of that same year, the $100 interest represents a 10 percent rate of increase on an annual percentage basis. If the loan is for only 6 months and $1050 is repaid on June 30, the $50 interest still represents a 10 percent annual rate.

The rate of interest is not the "price of money." *Money* is the medium of exchange used by an economy; it is the unit of borrowing, rather than the act itself. The "price of credit" is a better description of the interest rate because the term *credit* incorporates the passage of time between borrowing and repayment.

The rate of interest shows the terms of trade between the present and future. A low interest rate means that future goods are expensive relative to present goods; a high interest rate means future goods are cheap relative to present goods. Suppose you are

planning to go to law school in four years, and you know that it will cost $50,000. If the interest rate is 10 percent, you would have set aside $34,247 now. At 5 percent interest, you would have to set aside $41,152 now. If interest rates are high, you will not have to save as much as you would with low interest rates. In other words, high interest rates make future goods and services (that is, the law degree) cheaper in terms of present sacrifices.

## DETERMINING THE RATE OF INTEREST

The interest rate is determined in credit markets just as the price of General Motors stock or the price of July wheat is determined by the forces of demand and supply—by the demand and supply for loanable funds.

**The Supply of Loanable Funds.**   Credit markets arrange for the lending and borrowing of loanable funds.

**Loanable funds** comprise the lending from all households, governments, and businesses, or the bank credit made available to borrowers in credit markets.

The supply of loanable funds comes primarily from the net savings of businesses and households. If we have savings, we have choices concerning how to invest these savings. We must decide among bank savings accounts, government bonds, stock market shares, life insurance, or even precious metals. Whether we lend our savings to borrowers or buy stocks or precious metals depends on the price we are offered. It will simplify matters if we consider the purchase of bonds. The supply curve in Figure 1 shows the quantity of loanable funds savers are willing to save and, thereby, to make available to lenders at each interest rate. This supply curve is positively sloped because a larger quantity of loanable funds will be made available to lenders at high interest rates than at low interest rates, if all other things are equal. The higher the interest rate, the more attractive are bonds and savings accounts and the less attractive are stocks and precious metals.

**The Demand for Loanable Funds.**   The demand for loanable funds is principally the demand for new investments in capital goods of businesses. Although

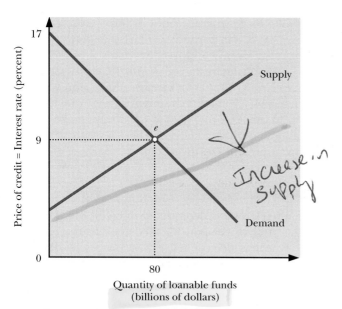

**FIGURE 1    The Market for Loanable Funds**

The supply curve shows the quantity of loanable funds offered by lenders at different interest rates; lenders will offer more at high interest rates. The demand curve shows the quantity of loanable funds demanded by borrowers at different interest rates; less will be demanded at high interest rates. The market for loanable funds is in equilibrium at an interest rate of 9 percent, where the quantity demanded equals the quantity supplied.

households also demand loanable funds for automobile loans, consumer credit, and home mortgages, here we shall concentrate on business investment.

What determines the demand for capital goods? New capital raises the output and, therefore, the revenue of the firm for a number of years because capital goods are in use for more than 1 year. A machine may be used for 8 years and a plant may be used for 35 years. Capital's *marginal revenue product* (the amount an extra unit of capital will contribute to a firm's revenues) must be estimated over each year of the capital's useful life in order to determine the rate of return of a capital good. (See Example 1.)

> The **rate of return of a capital good** is that rate for which the present value of the stream of marginal revenue products for each year of the good's life is equal to the cost of the capital good.

The law of diminishing returns applies to capital just as it applies to labor. Additional capital invest-

ment projects yield successively lower rates of return. In making their investment plans, businesses consider a variety of investment projects. By adding a new wing onto their plant, they may achieve a high rate of return. By acquiring new equipment, they may achieve a substantial but lower rate of return. Successive projects bring lower and lower rates of return due to the law of diminishing returns.

The demand curve for loanable funds in Figure 1 shows the quantity of loanable funds that investors are prepared to borrow at each interest rate. It is negatively sloped because at high interest rates there are fewer investment projects that have a rate of return equal to or greater than the interest rate. At low interest rates, there are more investment projects with rates of return equal to or greater than the interest rate. The demand curve also reflects the rate of return on capital-investment projects; business firms will be willing to add to their capital stock as long as the rate of return of investment projects exceeds the rate of interest.

The rate of return measures the marginal benefit of capital, and the interest rate measures the marginal cost of capital. Business firms will carry out those investment projects in which the rate of return exceeds the interest rate. Firms will not carry out investment projects with returns below the interest rate.

> The cost of additional capital is the interest rate that firms must pay for credit. The marginal benefit of capital is its rate of return.

> The equilibrium amount of capital for the firm will be that amount at which the rate of interest and the rate of return on the last investment project are equal.

**The Equilibrium Interest Rate.**    Like any other price, the rate of interest established by the credit market is that rate at which the quantity of loanable funds supplied equals the quantity demanded.

In Figure 1, the quantity supplied of loanable funds equals the quantity demanded at point *e*, where the interest rate is 9 percent and there are $80 billion worth of investment projects that yield a rate of return of 9 percent or above. Thus, the equilibrium rate of interest is 9 percent.

> The equilibrium interest rate equates the quantity demanded and quantity supplied

## EXAMPLE 1
## RISK, RETURN, AND CORNERING
## THE VIRGINIA LOTTERY

In the Virginia State Lottery, each $1 ticket is a combination of six numbers. To win the grand jackpot, the ticket has to have the exact combination of six numbers. If no one matches the winning combination, the jackpot continues to grow until there is a winner.

In February 1992, the jackpot had grown to $27 million. A group of investors (reputedly from Australia) decided to buy lottery tickets for all seven million possible combinations. If they were successful, the cost would be $7 million for a jackpot of $27 million. The winning ticket would be paid in 20 yearly installments of $1.3 million after an initial payment of $2.2 million in the first year.

If successful, the investment group's annual rate of return on its $7 million investment would have been 36 percent: If the group had placed its $7 million in a deposit account paying 36 percent per annum they would have been equally well off receiving $2.2 million in the first year and $1.3 million for the next 19 years. The 36 percent would be the group's annual rate of return on its investment.

Thirty-six percent is a high rate of return. Why did not more groups attempt to corner the Virginia market? The answer is that the risk of not winning was relatively high. First, if by chance someone else had a second winning ticket, the jackpot would have to be split two ways. Second, it would be difficult to buy all the possible seven million combinations. Third, there was no assurance that another investment team would not have the same idea.

Although records are cloudy, the story is that the Australian group did end up with the winning ticket after purchasing more than 90 percent of the possible combinations. The group's high rate of return can be credited to risk-taking and innovation.

for loanable funds. Only those investments yielding the equilibrium (market) interest rate or above are financed.

**Productivity and Thrift.**   The demand for loanable funds reflects the basic productivity of capital. Firms demand loanable funds for investment as long as rates of return are greater than or equal to the rate of interest. Any occurrence that makes capital more productive will shift the demand curve to the right and cause the interest rate to rise. The supply curve of loanable funds reflects the basic thriftiness of the population. Any occurrence that causes the population to be more thrifty (that is, to save more at each interest rate) will shift the supply curve to the right and cause the interest rate to fall.

If a technological breakthrough (such as new information technologies) raise the productivity of capital, the demand curve will shift to the right, driving up the interest rate, if all other things are equal,

as in panel (*a*) of Figure 2. If tax laws are changed to reward those families that save, the supply curve will shift to the right, lowering the market rate of interest, if all other things are equal, as in panel (*b*) of Figure 2.

### REAL VERSUS NOMINAL INTEREST RATE: THE IMPACT OF INFLATION

*Inflation* occurs when the money prices of goods, on the average, rise over time. Supply-and-demand analysis explains how inflation affects interest rates. Anticipated inflation affects both the demand and supply of loanable funds. Inflation causes the dollars to be repaid over the course of the loan to become cheaper. Lenders will become less eager to lend and the borrower more eager to borrow if the rate of inflation is expected to increase. Clearly, lenders will want to be compensated for the declining value of the dollars in which the loan is repaid,

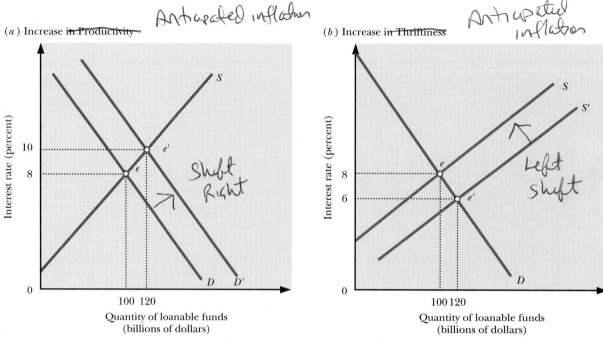

*Anticipated inflation*

*Antiupated inflation*

(a) Increase in ~~Productivity~~

(b) Increase in ~~Thriftiness~~

*Shift Right*

*Left shift*

**FIGURE 2  Interest Rates, Productivity, and Thriftiness**
Panel (a) shows that an increase in the productivity of capital raises interest rates, and panel (b) shows that an increase in the thriftiness of the population lowers interest rates.

and borrowers will be willing to pay a higher interest rate because they can repay the loan in cheaper dollars.

It is the real interest rate that matters to borrowers and lenders rather than the nominal interest rate.

> The **nominal interest rate** is the cost of borrowing expressed in terms of current dollars unadjusted for inflation.
>
> The **real interest rate** equals the nominal interest rate minus the anticipated rate of inflation.[1]

Anticipated inflation causes the demand curve for loanable funds to shift to the right and the supply curve of loanable funds to shift to the left. In Figure 3, the initial equilibrium interest rate is 4 percent when there is 0 percent inflation. If borrowers and

lenders now both anticipate a 5 percent rate of inflation, both curves shift upward by the same amount. When a 5 percent inflation is anticipated, borrowers will be willing to pay 5 percent more. Lenders will require 5 percent more to stay even with inflation.

The demand and supply curves for loanable funds at 9 percent nominal interest intersect at the same quantity of loanable funds (in constant dollars) as at 4 percent nominal interest. (See Example 2.)

## THE STRUCTURE OF INTEREST RATES: RISK, LIQUIDITY, MATURITY

The interest rate as the price of credit is not the same for all borrowers. Savings and loan associations may pay as little as 2 percent when they borrow from their depositors, whereas individuals who borrow from savings and loan associations may be charged interest rates of 9 percent for automobile and home mortgage loans. The U.S. Treasury may pay 5 percent to purchasers of its six-month Treasury bill and 7 percent on a three-year Treasury bond, whereas a near-bankrupt company may pay 21 percent on a six-month bank loan. *Different interest rates are paid on different financial assets.* Interest rates vary with

---

[1]This formula holds approximately. The actual formula is

$$r = i - p - rp$$

where $r$ is the real interest rate, $p$ is the inflation rate, and $i$ is the nominal interest rate. When $r$ and $p$ are small, $rp$ is close to zero. If $r = 0.10$ and $p = 0.05$, then $rp = 0.005$.

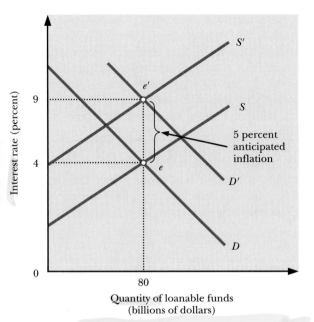

**FIGURE 3   Anticipated Inflation and Interest Rates**

The original equilibrium at a 0 percent rate of inflation is point *e*. When a 5 percent inflation rate is anticipated, borrowers will be willing to pay an interest rate 5 percent higher than before, and lenders must be paid an interest rate 5 percent higher because repayments are in cheaper dollars. Thus, both *S* and *D* shift upward by 5 percent. The new equilibrium is point *e'*, at a 9 percent nominal interest rate. The real interest rate is still 4 percent (equal to the nominal rate minus the anticipated rate of inflation).

the conditions of *risk*, *liquidity*, and *maturity* associated with a loan.

**Risk.**   Borrowers with good credit ratings pay lower interest rates than borrowers with poor credit ratings. To be competitive and earn a normal profit, lenders must be compensated for the extra risk of lending to borrowers with poor credit ratings. If one type of borrower fails to repay bank loans 1 percent of the time, banks will require that borrower to pay an interest rate at least 1 percent above the interest rate charged borrowers with a 0 percent risk of default. The extra 1 percent is called a *risk premium*. Lenders who demand 10 percent interest per month of those with poor credit histories are demanding an enormous risk premium because of the high default rate on such loans.

**Liquidity.**   A financial asset that can be turned into cash quickly or with a small penalty is said to be *liquid*. People may be willing to hold savings accounts paying 3 percent interest when six-month certificates of deposit pay 6 percent simply because the former can be turned into cash (the medium of exchange) quickly and without penalty. Interest rates usually vary inversely with liquidity.

**Maturity.**   Interest rates also vary with the term of maturity. A corporation borrowing $1000 for 1 year may pay a lower annual rate of interest than if it borrows the same $1000 for 2 years. If the credit market

*Inflation 25%*

**EXAMPLE 2**

**THE TIMELESS REAL RATE
OF INTEREST**

The real interest rate balances the thriftiness of the population with the productivity of capital.

Surprisingly, the real rate of interest has remained about the same for centuries. It is possible to trace the course of real interest rates from Roman times to the present by examining newspapers and other records. In ancient Rome, the real interest rate was 4 percent for more than a century. In the United States and the United

Kingdom, the real interest rate was around 3 percent from 1867 to 1995.

The long-term stability of real interest rates suggests that the real productivity of capital and thriftiness have been remarkably stable over time.

-------------------------------------------------

*Source:* Julian Simon, "Great and Almost Great Magnitudes in Economics," *Journal of Economic Perspectives* 4 Winter 1990: 151–152.

expects the interest rate on one-year loans to be 6 percent during one year and 12 percent during the next, the interest rate on a two-year loan covering the same period will be 9 percent—the average of the two interest rates.[2]

## RENT

The rent on land is a relatively small proportion—about 2 or 3 percent—of the total payments to factors of production. This figure includes payments for the natural fertility of the land and its locational advantages but excludes capital improvements in the land (such as irrigation). The unique feature of land and other natural resources is that they are inelastic in supply. They are nature's bounty, and the quantity supplied is not affected by the price received as a factor payment.

Relative inelasticity of supply can characterize productive factors other than land and natural resources. Because other types of factor payments resemble land rents, the study of rents for land and natural resources is much more important than the small percentages of factor payments to land suggest.

"Rents" paid for apartments, cars, tools, or moving trucks should not be confused with the *economic rents* studied in this section. "Rental payments" for the temporary use of a particular piece of property owned by someone else can be returns to land, labor, or capital. Apartment rent is a payment both to land (for the land on which the apartment building sits) and to capital (for the structure itself). Thus, the common term *rent* is simply a price or rental rate rather than a payment to a specific factor of production.

### PURE ECONOMIC RENT

The price of a fixed amount of land or some natural resource like a coal deposit or diamond mine—or

---

[2]If $1000 is invested for 1 year at 6 percent, it will yield $1060; if the $1060 is then reinvested at 12 percent it will yield $1188. Likewise, if $1000 is invested at 9 percent for 2 years, it will yield $1188. Thus, $1000 invested at 6 percent for 1 year with the proceeds invested for 1 more year at 12 percent has the same yield as investing $1000 for 2 years at 9 percent. Roughly speaking, the 2-year interest rate (expressed on an annual basis) will be an average of the 1-year interest rates that the credit market anticipates over the 2 years.

any other factor in fixed supply—is determined by its demand. The market demand curve is the demand curves of all firms in that market. The demand curve of each firm is its marginal revenue product curve. The supply curve is completely inelastic; more land is not forthcoming at higher prices. The competitive price paid to land is that price at which the fixed quantity supplied equals the quantity demanded. As such, the equilibrium price rations the fixed supply of land among its various claimants.

Pure economic rent ensures that the factors of production that are fixed in supply are put to their highest and best use.

> A **pure economic rent** is the price paid to a productive factor that is completely inelastic in supply. Land is the classic example of such a factor.

Figure 4 illustrates the concept of pure economic rent. The same quantity of land will be supplied, no matter what the price per acre (whether $0, $900, or $1400) as shown by the vertical supply curve. The quantity demanded at, say, a zero price will be very large. At that zero price, prime agricultural land might be used as a garbage dump or as a junkyard for old cars. A higher price of land will cut off the various demands for the land that have a low MRP. If the price is too high, the land will not be fully used, and there will be an excess supply. If the price is too low, the land may not be put to its best use. Prices that are below equilibrium levels can allow land to be put to uses that yield relatively low MRPs. Efficiency requires that the price be set where the quantity supplied equals the quantity demanded of land.

Suppose a piece of land is worth $1000 to you and $2000 to your friend, Jill. If both of you can rent the land for, say, $800, you would both want it, and you might get it and Jill not. If so, the land is not in its highest and best use. But if the price rises to $1001, the land will go to Jill and to its highest and best use.

> The pure economic rent that is paid to a productive factor does not increase its supply, which is perfectly inelastic. Pure economic rent in a competitive market ensures efficient resource use by rationing the available supply to the most efficient use.

If pure economic rents were not paid for beachfront properties, they might be used as used car lots

land away from other uses, the individual firm must pay the competitive price. In other words, *rents accrue to factor owners, not factor users.*

## QUASI RENTS

Naturally, productive land and land located in prime urban and manufacturing areas are inelastic in supply in the long run. No matter what is done, no matter what economic rents are paid, such land cannot be increased in supply. Payments for such land are *pure economic rents.* Because the opportunity cost of this land to society is zero in both the short and long runs, the entire factor payment is a payment of economic rent. Many factors that are fixed in supply in the short run, however, are more elastic in supply in the long run.

For example, in a booming Sun Belt city, the amount of space in office buildings is fixed in supply in the short run; when the demand for office space increases, office rental rates rise dramatically. The demand curve shifts upward (or to the right) along a vertical supply curve. In the long run, however, developers will respond to soaring office rents by constructing new office buildings. As the buildings are completed, the supply curve becomes more elastic and office rents are reduced.

The supply of professional soccer players is essentially fixed in the short run, since it takes years of training and practice for a player to attain professional caliber. If the demand for professional soccer players increases because of an increase in the popularity of the sport, the earnings of the fixed number of soccer professionals will increase. In the short run, they will be able to earn extraordinary salaries. In the long run, however, new professional-caliber players will enter the profession, attracted by the high earnings. The supply becomes more elastic, and the extraordinary earnings of soccer professionals will be bid down. (See Example 3.)

As these examples show, the owners of a resource that is fixed in supply in the short run will receive economic rent. But such a payment is a quasi rent, not a pure economic rent, because it cannot be maintained in the long run.

A **quasi rent** is a payment in excess of the short-run opportunity cost necessary to induce the owners of the resources to offer their resources for sale or rent in the short run.

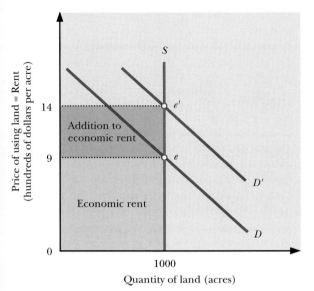

**FIGURE 4  Pure Economic Rent**

Because the supply of land is fixed at 1000 acres, the supply curve *S* is perfectly inelastic. The equilibrium price of $900 per acre at point *e* is pure economic rent, since the land has no alternative uses. The entire rental payment is a surplus over opportunity costs. In this case, opportunity costs are zero. If the demand curve for land increases from *D* to *D'*, the economic rent will rise from $900 to $1400 per acre at point *e'*. Changes in economic rents are determined by demand because supply is fixed.

or garbage dumps. If pure economic rents were not paid to the owners of underground oil deposits, they might choose to keep their land unspoiled by the sight of drilling rigs.

When something is perfectly inelastic in supply, price incentives cannot lead to an increase in its supply. This feature has made land an attractive target of taxation. The price of a good or factor that is perfectly inelastic in supply is, therefore, determined by demand. If the demand curve in Figure 4 shifts from *D* to *D'*, competitive economic rents will be bid up.

From the standpoint of the economy as a whole, rent is not a true opportunity cost to society. The land and other resources that are fixed in supply are free gifts of nature; the economy has use of the land whether it pays something or nothing. In the case of pure rent, the payment to the factor of production exceeds the payment required to keep the resource available to the economy by the entire amount of the rental payment. Thus, the opportunity cost is zero. From the standpoint of an individual firm that uses agricultural land, however, economic rent is most certainly a cost of production. In order to bid the

## EXAMPLE 3
## THE 1994 PROFESSIONAL
## BASEBALL PLAYERS' STRIKE

After unsuccessful negotiations between team owners and player representatives, professional baseball players declared a strike. Unable to resolve the strike, the acting commissioner of baseball was forced to cancel the conclusion of the 1994 season.

The theory of economic rents suggests that professional athletes can be big losers in the case of strikes. The average salary of major league professional baseball players at the time of the strike was almost $1 million. Although a few superstars could command high salaries as sports commentators or advertising spokesmen, most of the earnings of baseball players is economic rent. Their next-best job might be coaching a high school team, working as a physical fitness instructor, or selling cars or real estate. Let us say that, on average, the opportunity cost of the average baseball player outside of baseball was $50,000 per year. Therefore, the average player's economic rent was a whopping $950,000 per year.

This point was driven home by an amusing cartoon in a national newspaper—the picture of a baseball player ringing the doorbell of an unsuspecting couple and offering his services as a lawn mower for $27,000 per lawn.

---

In the long run, quasi rents will disappear as the supply curve becomes more elastic. In the long run, the supply curve will become more and more elastic until quasi rents have been dissipated. At this point, the factor of production receives no economic rents.

## ECONOMIC RENT AND OTHER FACTORS OF PRODUCTION

Pure economic rents represent an extreme case of factor payment. At the other extreme is payment to a factor that just equals its *opportunity cost* (its earnings in its next-best alternative use). A factor of production that is perfectly elastic in supply earns no economic rent because the factor is paid its opportunity cost. For example, a small farmer must compete with other farmers and potential users of the land. If the farmer does not pay what the land could earn in its next-best use, the land will be used elsewhere.

In between factors of production that are perfectly elastic in supply and those that are perfectly inelastic are numerous factors of production that earn some surplus return over their opportunity costs, or economic rent.

> **Economic rent** is the amount by which the payment to a factor exceeds its opportunity cost.

The major distinction between *economic rent* and *pure economic rent* is that a factor earning pure economic rent has an opportunity cost of zero. A factor earning economic rent has an opportunity cost that is positive but smaller than the payment to the factor.

The amount of economic rent earned by a factor depends upon the perspective from which the factor is viewed. The economic rent of John Smith as an *engineer* differs from the economic rent of John Smith as an engineer *for General Motors Corp.* Smith can earn $40,000 per year working for GM, $35,000 working for Ford, and $25,000 working in his best nonengineering job. Smith's economic rent as a GM engineer is $5,000 (his earnings in excess of his opportunity cost in the automobile industry); his economic rent as an engineer is $15,000 (his greatest potential earnings as an engineer in excess of his salary in his best nonengineering alternative).

The prices paid to a film star, a late-night talk-show host, the best pitcher in major league baseball, for Iowa farmland, and offices in New York City surprisingly have much in common: a large fraction of each factor's income is economic rent. These factors receive payments in excess of their opportunity cost (their earnings in alternative uses). The factor payment serves the function of ensuring that the factor is employed efficiently in its highest and best use. Basketball great Michael Jordan's million-dollar contracts serve the important economic function of promoting an efficient utilization of his assets; the utility of sports fans would have been reduced if he had been employed as a waiter at a local restaurant. Paying one of the world's most talented tenors $50,000 per performance ensures that he will devote himself to opera rather than working as a plumber.

Although we sometimes resent individuals with inherited talents, rare skills, or good looks who earn substantial salaries, we should recognize that oil-drilling rigs, Hawaiian real estate, Iowa corn land, and high-speed computers are earning similar rewards—namely, payments in excess of their opportunity costs. Although land is the most obvious, economic rents are paid to a wide variety of economic factors. Actors, professional athletes, musicians, surgeons, professors, television repair persons, and even nobility can earn economic rents. (See Example 4.)

## PROFITS

Many of us are suspicious of the ethics of those individuals and companies who earn high profits. (In the Middle Ages, high profits were seen as a sure sign that a pact had been made with the devil.)

Profits that are headlined on the business pages are accounting profits. Accounting profits can be misleading because they do not take into account the firm's *opportunity costs,* which include both actual payments to factors of production and the costs of the next-best alternative that the firm has sacrificed. Economists prefer to evaluate a firm's profitability on the basis of normal profits and economic profits.

**Accounting profits** are revenues minus explicit costs.

**Normal profits** are the profits required to keep resources in that particular business. Normal profits are earned when revenues equal opportunity costs.

**Economic profits** are revenues in excess of total opportunity costs (which include both actual payments and sacrificed alternatives). Economic profits are profits in excess of normal profits.

### EXAMPLE 4
### ECONOMIC RENTS AND
### "HAPPY BIRTHDAY"

There is only one "Happy Birthday" song and, believe it or not, the rights to this song are owned by the copyright holder, Birchtree, Ltd. Written by two sisters in 1893, "Happy Birthday" was copyrighted, and for it to be played at official functions, a fee must be paid to the current owners of the copyright. "Happy Birthday" currently brings in about $1 million per year. The copyright will not expire until 2010, at which time it will become part of the public domain. Birchtree, Ltd. is prepared to sell the rights to "Happy Birthday," and it expects to receive $12 million for the sale. The copyright fees earned on "Happy Birthday" are economic rents. The supply of "Happy Birthday" is fixed; it is there whether people play it or not.

*Source:* "Yes, You Did Hear It Right: "Happy Birthday Is For Sale." *New York Times,* October 20, 1988.

You may own a small business to which you devote all your time and effort. You don't pay yourself a salary. Your company's accounting profit is $40,000, but you could have earned $60,000 in a job. To make a normal profit, your company would have to earn at least $60,000—to cover your opportunity cost.

As we discussed in earlier chapters, economic profits regulate entry into and exit from an industry. When they are positive, firms will enter; when they are negative, firms will exit. If your company's accounting profits continue to fall short of your opportunity cost, eventually you would want to abandon the business.

## ENTRY BARRIERS, RISK, AND INNOVATION

There are three basic sources of economic profits. The first source is barriers to entry in an industry or business. The economic profits from barriers to entry, called *monopoly profits*, form the basis of popular misgivings about profits. The second source of profits is the dynamic and ever-changing nature of the economy, which renders the success of some activities risky or uncertain. The third source of economic profits is innovation. Economic profits that are the result of risk-taking and innovation are considered a reward for the *entrepreneurship* of individuals.

**Entry Restrictions.**   As you already know, monopolies can earn a profit rate in excess of normal profits.

Unlike the transitory profits of a competitive industry, monopoly profits can persist over a long period of time. Monopoly businesses can earn revenues that exceed the opportunity costs of the factors they employ. In this sense, monopoly profits are like economic rents, and consequently, economists often refer to monopoly profits as *monopoly rents*. Monopoly profits can also be earned in a potentially competitive industry where entry is restricted by government licensing or franchising. So long as monopoly profits cannot be eliminated by the entry of new firms, existing firms can enjoy monopoly rents. Monopoly rents are due to the ceiling placed on supply by entry restrictions.

Examples of monopoly profits due to entry restrictions are plentiful. Cable television franchises are granted by municipal authorities, protecting cable companies by law from the entry of competitors. In most cities, taxicab drivers must be licensed, and entry into the business is controlled by the high cost of the license. Monopoly profits in the prescription-drug industry are protected by patents. Economies of scale similarly limit the entry of competitors into power generation and telecommunications.

Monopoly profits are often not reflected in accounting profits because they are *capitalized* (converted to their present value) when the firm is sold to a new owner. For example, in New York City, when taxicab drivers sell their licenses (called *medallions*) to others, the market price of the license reflects the value of the cab's monopoly profits. The cab driver who purchases the license earns no economic profit because it has gone to the original owner of the license.

**Risk.**   If there were no entry restrictions, if people could predict the future perfectly, and if there were no costs for obtaining information about market opportunities, there would be no economic profits. All businesses would earn normal profits. Any opportunity to earn economic profits would be anticipated and the free entry of new firms would serve to keep profits down to a normal return.

However, no one can predict the future. Industry is unprepared for wars, new inventions, and changes in fashion, preferences, and weather. Even with free entry, at any given time some industries will earn economic profits and others will suffer losses. Unanticipated shifts in demand or costs cause economic profits to rise and fall. The majority of people wish to limit their exposure to the ups and downs of the economy; they want a steady income. Therefore, there must be rewards for those who are willing to risk the ups and downs of economic fortunes. Just as those who lend money to poor credit risks require risk premiums, so those who are willing to take risks must be rewarded with economic profits if they are successful. In his classic book, *Risk, Uncertainty, and Profit,* published in 1921, Frank Knight emphasized that uncertainty and risk-taking are the ultimate source of profit. Knight noted the presence of a large element of luck in the fortunes of different enterprises. Economic profits cannot be assured in an uncertain world; the outcome of the profit game will be, to a large extent, random. Knight's perceptions are as relevant today as they were in 1921.

Uncertainty turns the quest for profits into something resembling a game of chance in which there are winners and losers even in the long run. Entrepreneurs are the ones who bear this risk. The winners earn economic profits; the losers incur losses. As in a game of chance, profits average out to a normal return over all firms, but there is a wide range of profit outcomes. Most business firms deviate little from the average return to risk bearing. Some, though, have good luck and experience large returns; others experience large misfortunes. All is not fair in love, war, . . . and business.

**Innovation.** Luck cannot explain all economic profits, however. The economy is in a constant state of flux. Consumer tastes are changing, new technologies are being developed, new markets are being discovered, and resource availabilities are being altered. To be an innovator requires ability and foresight in order to take advantage of these changes.

Austrian-born economist Joseph Schumpeter, whom we encountered in Chapter 1, maintained that profits, primarily the return to the entrepreneur and innovator, are temporary. Economic progress requires a succession of new innovations. A successful entrepreneur will earn substantial economic profits only until another entrepreneur with a newer and better idea comes along to take customers and profits away.

Business history is replete with success stories of business geniuses—Henry Ford and the Model T, Edwin Land and the Polaroid camera, Richard Sears and Alvah Roebuck and their mass retailing, and Bill Gates and computer software. (See Example 5.) More was involved than a game of chance with an uncertain outcome; ability and entrepreneurial genius were crucial to the success of each of these companies. Yet even ability does not guarantee success. Many able people are trying to become the next Henry Ford, but few succeed.

Armen Alchian has pointed out that it is not even necessary for the entrepreneur to maximize profits:

> Realized positive profits, not *maximum* profits, are the mark of success and viability. It does not matter through what process of reasoning or motivation such success was achieved. The fact of its accomplishment is sufficient. This is the criterion by which the economic system selects

### EXAMPLE 5
### THE ENTREPRENEURSHIP
### OF FRED SMITH

Fred Smith, the founder of Federal Express, dreamed of a company that could deliver packages overnight to large and small cities. The air express business already had two giant firms, Emery Air Freight and Flying Tiger, but Smith was convinced he could offer a better product. Smith recognized opportunities that his competitors failed to see. Smith knew that nine out of ten commercial airlines were on the ground between 10:00 P.M. and 8:00 A.M., so the air lanes were wide open during these hours. Second, Smith recognized that the bulk of urgent, small package business was concentrated in the 25 largest cities. Third, Smith realized that it would be more efficient to have a single hub system

(which he eventually located in Memphis) through which all packages would flow. A package originating in Los Angeles for San Francisco would be flown to Memphis, processed, and then sent on another plane to San Francisco. Armed with these business insights, Smith risked all his own capital to starting up Federal Express. The phenomenal success of the company was due to the entrepreneurial genius of its founder. Smith created the "hub-and-spoke" system used by the largest carriers today and he created a boom in the overnight mail delivery business. Even the U.S. Postal Service was forced to copy Federal Express.

survivors: those who realize *positive profits* are survivors; those who suffer losses disappear.[3]

## SOURCES OF PROFITS

Profits arise from monopoly restrictions and barriers, uncertainty and risk, and entrepreneurial innovation. Does the factual record support these propositions? It is very difficult to test the relationship between economic profits and these three factors because it is difficult to measure economic profits. Business firms report accounting profits, not economic profits, and the theory is about economic profits. Accounting profits can sometimes be misleading. Nevertheless, empirical studies typically assume that accounting profits are indicative of economic profits.

**Barriers to Entry and Profits.** The empirical literature supports the theory that economic profits are strongly associated with monopoly barriers to entry. For example, prescription drugs protected by patents sell at 60 to 100 times average costs, and price-fixing conspiracies have been shown to create extraordinary profits. We have encountered other examples of the correlation between barriers to entry and profit rates in the chapter on oligopoly.

**Risks and Profits.** Determining the relationship between risk and profit rates is problematic because of the difficulty of measuring risk. In empirical studies, risk is typically measured by the variability of profits. If there are considerable fluctuations in profits over time or among firms in a particular industry, substantial risk is said to be present.

Figure 5 plots annual growth in employee compensation and corporate profits over time. The most striking difference between the two series is the much greater variability of profits. Unlike earnings from labor, which tend to rise smoothly from year to year, profits rise and fall—sometimes with substantial declines from one year to the next. There is much greater risk in being dependent upon profits than on wages, at least as far as the aggregate economy is concerned.

Variability of profits may not be an accurate guide to risk, however, because serious risk stems from long-run dangers from new technology and new competition that can cause a permanent decline in the profits earned by individual firms.

Economists who have studied the relationship between the rate of profit and risk (as measured by the variability of profits) find that profit rates are indeed higher in risky industries. Firms and industries that are subject to greater risk earn *risk premiums*. Entrepreneurs and stockholders who bear more risk than others are compensated in the form of higher average profits.[4]

**Innovation and Profits.** As in the case of risk, the difficulty in measuring the trends in entrepreneurial activity precludes establishing an empirical correlation with profit. Nevertheless, history provides ample examples of the relationship between innovation and profits. Huge fortunes (such as those of the Rockefeller, DuPont, Carnegie, Mellon, and Ford families) have been amassed by great entrepreneurs. It is new ideas that create profits, and it is the entrepreneur who executes this new idea who receives the profits.

In this chapter and the previous one we have surveyed how the economy determines wages, rents, interest, and profit—the payments to the productive factors of labor, land, capital, and entrepreneurship. In the next chapter, we shall turn from the functional distribution of income to the personal distribution of income, addressing such difficult questions as these: How equally or unequally is income distributed among persons? How has the personal distribution of income changed

---

[3]Armen A. Alchian, "Uncertainty, Evolution, and Economic Theory," *Journal of Political Economy* 58, 3 (June 1950): pp. 211–221; reprinted in *Economic Forces at Work* (Indianapolis: Liberty Press, 1977), pp. 15–36.

[4]Empirical studies of the relationship between risk and profitability have been conducted by I.N. Fisher and G.R. Hall, "Risk and Corporate Rates of Return," *Quarterly Journal of Economics* 83 (February 1969): pp. 79–92; and P. Cootner and D. Holland, "Rate of Return and Business Risk," *Bell Journal of Economics* 1 (Fall 1970): pp. 211–216. Both studies found a positive association between risk and corporate profit rates. A different interpretation of these findings has been suggested by Richard Caves and Basil Yamey, "Risk and Corporate Returns: Comment," *Quarterly Journal of Economics* 85 (August 1971): pp. 513–517; and by W.G. Shepherd, *The Treatment of Market Power* (New York: Columbia University Press, 1975), who argue that these higher rates of return are the result of oligopoly structure rather than greater risk.

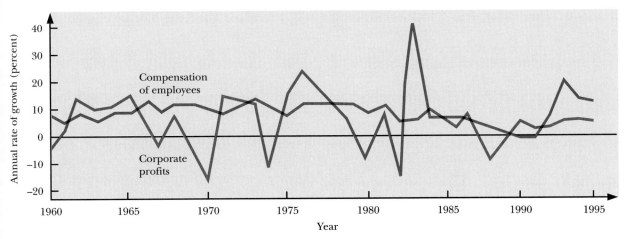

**FIGURE 5   Compensation of Employees and Corporate Profits, 1960 to Present**

This graph shows that corporate profits are characterized by greater variability than wage income over time, suggesting that it is more risky to be dependent on profits than on wage income. *Source: Survey of Current Business.*

over time? How does America's income distribution compare with that of other countries? What can be done about poverty and inequality?

entrepreneurship and innovation. Empirical evidence, though limited in the cases of risk and entrepreneurship, generally supports the correlation between profits and each of the three sources.

## SUMMARY

1. Interest is payment for the use of capital. The supply of capital is the result of past saving and investment decisions. Interest rates are determined in credit markets, which are necessitated by the specialization of savings and investment decisions in today's modern economy. Interest rates are determined in the market by the demand and supply of loanable funds. The real rate of interest is the nominal interest rate minus the anticipated rate of inflation. The structure of interest rates depends upon risk, liquidity, and maturity.

2. Pure economic rent is the payment to a factor of production that is completely inelastic in supply and for which the price is determined by demand. A quasi rent is payment to a factor of production in excess of short-run opportunity costs. In the long run, quasi rents tend to disappear. Economic rent is the amount by which the payment to a factor exceeds its opportunity cost.

3. Economic profits are revenues in excess of total opportunity costs. The sources of economic profits are restrictions to entry into an industry, risk, and

## KEY TERMS

| | |
|---|---|
| interest | nominal interest rate |
| depreciation | real interest rate |
| credit markets (capital markets) | pure economic rent |
| | quasi rent |
| interest rate | economic rent |
| loanable funds | accounting profits |
| rate of return of a capital good | normal profits |
| | economic profits |

## QUESTIONS AND PROBLEMS

1. Why is it misleading to call interest the price of money?
2. This chapter emphasized that the credit market is another example of specialization in economics. Explain how this specialization works and how it affects economic efficiency.
3. If you borrow $10,000 from the bank and repay the bank $12,000 after 1 year, what is the annual rate of interest?

4. A company is considering four investment projects that yield returns of 20 percent, 15 percent, 10 percent, and 5 percent, respectively. Explain how the company will decide which of these projects to carry out.

5. The interest rate is currently 10 percent and the inflation rate is 5 percent. If people anticipate that the inflation rate will rise to 10 percent, what will happen to interest rates?

6. Distinguish between pure economic rents and quasi rents.

7. Evaluate the validity of the following statement: "Pure economic rents play no useful role in the economy because the supply of the factor in question is fixed. The factor will be supplied no matter what rent is paid."

8. Why should the profit rate be higher for businesses that are risky? How do we measure risk?

9. What is the logic behind taxing economic rents rather than other kinds of factor incomes?

10. Identify the sources of economic profits earned by the following:
    a. Steel companies after the government imposed restrictions on competitive steel imports from foreign countries
    b. The coal industry after the Organization of Petroleum Exporting Countries quadrupled the price of oil in 1974
    c. A firm that developed a surefire method of increasing gas mileage

11. Evaluate the validity of the following statement: "High interest rates make for a better retirement."

12. The great baseball player Babe Ruth earned more than the president of the United States; yet if he had not played baseball, his income might have equaled that of a common laborer. Explain this situation in terms of the concepts of this chapter.

# CHAPTER 19

# INEQUALITY, INCOME DISTRIBUTION, AND POVERTY

## CHAPTER INSIGHT

Economics was called the "dismal science" in the nineteenth century because the great economists of that era predicted a future of poverty and overpopulation. The economics of the late twentieth century may one day incorrectly be called the "uncompassionate science." Many of today's economists argue that a society that "cares too much" about the less fortunate—that is, one that supports a strong welfare state—may be harming not only society as a whole, but the less fortunate as well.

Let us consider some facts related to the issue. In the most "compassionate" countries of Europe, such as in Scandinavia and Germany, unemployed workers indefinitely receive benefits close to their earnings while employed. True, if they work, they will earn more, but if they do not work at all, they will still be able to maintain a decent standard of living. What has happened as a result? Unemployment rates have soared in Europe.

In the United States, federal, state, and local governments pay families with children earning income below designated levels. A poverty family receives more by earning less or by making sure that the father does not live in the home. These programs pay, with few questions, unmarried teenage mothers; the greater the number of children, the larger the payment. Despite such caring programs, the incidence of poverty has not fallen. Despite the state's desire to strengthen the family, the incidence of one-parent families continues to grow.

## Table 1    Household Income in the United States (1995)

|  | National Income | Income per household | Percentage of total |
|---|---|---|---|
| Labor income | $3,602 billion | $37,520 | 63.7% |
| Proprietor's income | 465 | 4,844 | 8.2% |
| Capital income (rent, interest, dividends) | 906 | 9,438 | 16.0% |
| Net transfer payments | 680 | 7,083 | 12.1% |
| Total | $5,653 billion | $58,885 | 100.0 |

Source: Statistical Abstract of the United States.

## WHY WE DON'T ALL EARN THE SAME INCOME

We earn income from our labor and from the capital and land assets we own. Most of us earn relatively little from dividends, interest, and profits, but some earn a great deal. Some of us receive transfer payments from government programs such as Social Security or Aid to Families with Dependent Children (AFDC) programs. The most important source of income for most of us is what we earn from our labor. We all have the same amount of time—24 hours per day—but we earn different amounts of labor income because people are different and jobs are different. We also earn different amounts because some of us choose to work more hours.

Table 1 shows U.S. personal income per household—its magnitude and its sources. As a nation, we earn about 64 percent from our labor, 12 percent from transfer payments, 8 percent from businesses we own and operate, and the remainder, or 16 percent, from capital—from rental, dividend, and interest income.

Income is unevenly distributed. As Table 2 shows, about 5 percent of households earn less than $5,000 per year; while about 5 percent of households earn $100,000 per year or above. Different ethnic and racial groups have different amounts of house-

hold income. There are more upper-income whites and Asian Americans and more poor African Americans and Hispanics.

## SOURCES OF INCOME INEQUALITY

We have discussed some of the causes of income inequality in the chapters on labor and interest, rent, and profit. Here we shall consider the unequal distribution of labor income.

### NONCOMPETING GROUPS

We have different mental and physical abilities that limit our choice of occupation. Not everyone has the mental skills and dexterity to become a surgeon; few of us have the physical endowments to become professional athletes or highly paid fashion models. By contrast, many of us possess the skills to perform unskilled labor, or to serve as sales clerks and bank tellers.

Because we are different from one another, the labor market segregates us into noncompeting groups that earn different wages. Such wage differentials can persist over a long period of time. The six-figure earnings of surgeons will not cause construc-

## Table 2    How Money Is Distributed Among Households (1992)

|  | Under $5,000 | $5,000–9,999 | $10,000–14,999 | $15,000–24,999 | $25,000–34,999 | $35,000–49,999 | $50,000–74,999 | $75,000–$99,999 | $100,000 and over |
|---|---|---|---|---|---|---|---|---|---|
| All households | 4.6% | 10.0% | 9.5% | 16.9% | 14.8% | 17.1% | 16.1% | 6.1% | 4.9% |
| White | 3.6% | 8.9% | 9.1% | 16.7% | 15.1% | 17.7% | 17.0% | 6.6% | 5.3% |
| African American | 11.8% | 18.7% | 12.2% | 18.3% | 13.2% | 12.8% | 8.8% | 2.7% | 1.5% |
| Hispanic | 6.6% | 13.8% | 12.6% | 20.8% | 16.3% | 14.5% | 10.5% | 3.2% | 1.8% |
| Asian | 4.7% | 7.1% | 7.6% | 13.8% | 12.7% | 19.1% | 18.4% | 8.9% | 8.3% |

Source: Statistical Abstract of the United States.

Lowest 15 - poverty

tion workers to switch to surgery. The prospect of having to lift 100 pounds will keep many of us from seeking employment on offshore drilling rigs despite its high wage rates.

## OCCUPATIONAL DIFFERENCES

Most of us prefer to work in occupations that are safe, offer pleasant surroundings, and do not require heavy or dirty work. The supply of labor to attractive occupations and jobs is greater than that to unattractive ones. Even though garbage collectors earn more than many others with the same skills, labor does not move automatically into these higher-paying jobs to wipe out the wage differential. We demand a reward for working in unpleasant and dangerous jobs.

Figure 1 shows the effect on relative wages of the danger of the occupation. For simplicity, the demand curve for underground coal miners is assumed to be identical to the demand curve for textile workers, but the labor supply curves are quite different. The higher placement of the coal miners' supply curve reflects the fact that workers prefer less dangerous employment, if everything else is equal. To get an equivalent supply of coal miners, coal mine employers must offer higher wages than textile employers.

Compensating wage differentials explain why welders on the Alaskan pipeline have to be paid more (to compensate for the harsh climate and higher living costs) or why sanitation workers are better paid than clerical workers (to compensate for the unpleasantness and social stigma). Loggers must be paid more because of the hazardous nature of logging.

> **Compensating wage differentials** are the higher wages that must be paid to compensate workers for undesirable job characteristics.

Compensating wage differentials imply that some inequality is a matter of choice. This choice may also involve a trade-off between pay and leisure. Some of us value leisure time more than others. You may work a 60-hour week, whereas I (who earn the same hourly wage) work a 30-hour week.

Different occupations have different risks. A small business owner has a more uncertain income than a tenured university professor does. A wheat farmer, whose crops may be destroyed by blights and

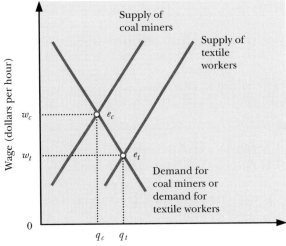

**FIGURE 1   Wages in Coal Mining and Textiles**

For simplicity, the demand curve for coal miners is assumed to be identical to the demand curve for textile workers. Wages are higher for coal miners because the quantity supplied of coal miners is less than the quantity supplied of textile workers at each wage rate.

droughts, has a more uncertain income than a union employee with seniority does. Society comprises risk seekers or risk avoiders who have different attitudes toward risk.

> **Risk seekers** are more willing to incur risks than **risk avoiders,** who are reluctant to take on risks.[1]

The more risk seekers in a society, the more unequal the distribution of income. A few risk seekers strike it rich; most risk seekers fail. The vast majority—the risk avoiders—are in the middle, earning the steadiest incomes.

## HUMAN CAPITAL INVESTMENT

Just as businesses invest in plant and equipment to increase the firm's productive capacity, so do we invest in ourselves to raise our own productivity. We

---

[1]The theory of individual choice of inequality was formulated by Milton Friedman in the article, "Choice, Chance, and the Personal Distribution of Income," *Journal of Political Economy* 61, 4 (August 1953): pp. 277–290.

invest in education, we move to areas that have better job opportunities, and we invest in medical care to improve our health or appearance.

> **Human-capital theory** teaches that we make rational choices of different lifetime earnings streams when we invest in ourselves.[2]

If human-capital investment translates into higher lifetime earnings, why doesn't everyone acquire equal levels of such investment? Although human-capital investment yields benefits, it also has its costs. Physicians must study and train an extra eight years at a cost of more than $100,000, but they are compensated by higher lifetime earnings. Confronted with the costs and benefits of human-capital investment, we make rational investment decisions. We acquire more human capital so long as the marginal benefit exceeds the marginal cost.

Because we make different human-capital choices, the distribution of income is partly the result of our own decisions. We choose between more money now (going to work after high school) and more money later (going to college with no earnings now). Those of us who place a high value on having money now are less likely to acquire human capital. When we make that choice, we will earn less lifetime income.

## DISCRIMINATION

If we are denied equal access to education and training, our career opportunities will be limited. If we are denied access to jobs in labor unions, we cannot earn higher union wages.

> **Discrimination** occurs when individuals are blocked from entering jobs and occupations or when workers with equal skills and qualifications are treated differently on the grounds of race, sex, or some other characteristic.

Different racial and gender groups earn, on average, different amounts of income. The median income of nonwhite U.S. households currently equals about 60 percent of white household income, up considerably from 50 percent in 1947. Women who work full time currently have an average income about three-quarters that of males, up from 60 percent since the late 1950s.

Are these average differences the result of discrimination? A substantial portion of ethnic and racial differences in earning reflect differences in schooling. Table 3 shows the positive correlation between schooling and earnings. More than twice the percentage of whites complete college as do African Americans or Hispanics. High school completion rates are more equal, but some 30 percent of African Americans and 47 percent of Hispanics have not completed high school. Therefore, the most effective means of reducing earning differentials by race is to provide equal access to quality education.

The female income differential does not result from a disparity in years of schooling. A higher percentage of women than men complete high school, and about the same percentage have at least some college-level education. Women work fewer hours and spend fewer years in the labor force, but these factors cannot explain more than half of the female earning gap.[3]

After completion of schooling, individuals may encounter labor market discrimination. Labor-market discrimination does not normally entail discrimination between two workers (of different race or sex) performing the same job. In fact, federal laws guarantee equal pay for equal or even "comparable" work. Affirmative action programs may even give minority job candidates an advantage in the labor market. More often, discrimination occurs when nonwhites or women are channeled into occupations

[2]The pioneering articles in human-capital theory are Gary Becker, "Investment in Human Capital: A Theoretical Analysis," *Journal of Political Economy* 70, 5 (October 1962): pp. 9–49; and Theodore W. Schultz, "Capital Formation by Education," *Journal of Political Economy* 68, 6 (December 1960): pp. 571–583.

[3]Henry Aaron and Cameron Loughy, *The Comparable Controversy* (Washington, DC: The Brookings Institution, 1986), pp. 12–13; Ronald Ehrenberg and Robert Smith, *Modern Labor Economics*, 4th ed. (New York: Harper-Collins, 1991), chap. 14; James Smith and Michael Ward, *Women's Wages and Work in the Twentieth Century*, (New York: Rand Corporation, 1984).

## Table 3   Education and Mean Monthly Earnings of Individuals (1990 and 1993)[a]

| | Not high school graduate | | High school graduate | | Bachelor's degree | |
|---|---|---|---|---|---|---|
| Age: | | | | | | |
| 25–34 | 13.1% | $859 | 35.9% | $1340 | 18.6% | $2154 |
| 35–44 | 11.4% | $947 | 34.0% | $1546 | 17.6% | $2634 |
| 45–54 | 15.3% | $1064 | 35.8% | $1790 | 14.1% | $3510 |
| 55–64 | 25.7% | $951 | 37.9% | $1393 | 10.9% | $2920 |
| Sex: | | | | | | |
| Male | 19.5% | $1166 | 33.2% | $1853 | 15.7% | $3235 |
| Female | 20.0% | $579 | 37.4% | $943 | 13.5% | $1698 |
| Race: | | | | | | |
| White | 18.5% | $909 | 35.6% | $1405 | 14.9% | $2552 |
| Black | 29.6% | $652 | 36.3% | $1009 | 8.8% | $2002 |
| Hispanic | 46.9% | $760 | 26.8% | $1092 | 6.4% | $1895 |

[a] Percentage figures from 1993; income figures from 1990.
*Source: Statistical Abstract of the United States.*

regarded as "suitable" for them. This channeling may result from an employee's own preferences (a woman may want to be a school teacher) or employer discrimination (an employer may not hire women for heavy assembly-line work). The employer may use screening rules (such as not hiring women for manual labor) that exclude women. As a consequence, "suitable" professions—say, nursing and schoolteaching for women or bus driving for African American males—become crowded, and the relative earnings of these professions are driven down. (See Example 1.)

## WEALTH AND INHERITANCE

Income from other factors of production—land, capital, and entrepreneurship—is more equally distributed than labor income. Most nonlabor income derives from the ownership of wealth (e.g., stocks, bonds, real estate).

> Personal **wealth** (or net worth) is the value of one's total assets minus one's liabilities.

In 1992 the wealthiest 20 percent of the population in the United States accounted for 84 percent of all wealth. The bottom 20 percent accounted for no wealth. In fact, their liabilities exceeded their assets. Wealth is distributed more unequally than income.[4]

We can affect the distribution of wealth through social policy.

> **Inheritance** is the passing of wealth from one generation to another.

Some societies have steep inheritance taxes, which make it difficult to pass wealth from one generation to the next. However, one incentive to accumulate wealth may be to make it easier for our children and grandchildren. If wealth is taxed away at death, there would be less reason to work hard and accumulate wealth.

## SCREENING AND INEQUALITY

Table 3 indicates that those of us who have more education earn more income. Is this because the better educated we are, the more productive we are? Although that may be true, the statistics present us with a puzzle: A person with a high school degree (and no

---

[4]These estimates are by Robert Lampman, James D. Smith, and Staunton Calvert and are cited in *Statistical Abstract of the United States.*

## EXAMPLE 1
## COMPARABLE WORTH AND
## UNINTENDED CONSEQUENCES

The Supreme Court and the federal courts have ruled that employees have a right to equal pay for "comparable" work. This is a significant extension of the law requiring equal pay for equal work. In Washington state, the courts ordered employers to adjust pay scales so that employees with comparable jobs would receive the same pay. A committee assigned points to each job on the basis of knowledge and skills, mental demands, accountability, and work conditions. Registered nurses won the highest evaluation, well above computer system analysts. Clerical supervisors won a higher rating than chemists; electricians were assigned lower points than beginning secretaries. In all these evaluations, the market had assigned different relative wages than the comparable-worth point system.

Like many policy issues in economics, the comparable-worth ruling had unintended consequences that tended to negate its noble goal. By setting the comparable-worth wages of secretaries and clerical supervisors above their market wages, surpluses of secretaries and clerical supervisors were created in the state of Washington. There were too many applicants and too few positions. A second unintended consequence of the artificial increase in wages in traditionally female-dominated professions such as secretaries and clerical supervisors was to reduce the incentive for women to break into higher-paying male professions.

---

further education) earns 60 percent more than a high school drop-out. A college graduate earns 60 percent more than someone who has attended college but has not completed college. Can it be true than an extra year or two of college makes you 60 percent more productive, or that dropping out of high school one year prior to graduation makes you 60 percent less productive? (See Example 2.)

Economists explain this puzzle by noting that completion of schooling—the act of getting a high school diploma or a college degree—signals to employers that you are likely to possess traits that they are looking for. These traits are tenacity, discipline, and endurance, all of which make you more valuable and productive. There may indeed be others who are more productive than you but lack a college or high school diploma. Employers, however, cannot take the time and expense to find them. They are content to screen out individuals who lack formal credentials because this is an inexpensive way of selecting employees.

**Screening** is the requirement that potential employees possess certain characteristics, such as a high school or college diploma, or a B+ or better average.

By using screening, employers know that they will select the right employees on average, although they know they will pass up some good employees who do not have the right credentials. This is simply a cost-effective way to select employees.

Screening indicates that more educated individuals or persons with high grades earn more not necessarily because they are more productive. They earn more because they have the credentials that qualify them for jobs that offer higher lifetime earnings.[5]

---

[5]The classic studies of screening theory are: Michael Spence, "Job Market Signaling," *Quarterly Journal of Economics* 87, 3 (August 1973): pp. 355–374; Kenneth Arrow, "Higher Education as a Filter," *Journal of Public Economics* 2, 3 (July 1973): pp. 193–216.

## EXAMPLE 2
## THINK TWICE
## BEFORE DROPPING OUT

Presumably, if you are reading this book you have graduated from high school. This was a wise move. High school graduates earn $501 per month more than high school dropouts. Cumulated over a lifetime of work, high school graduates will earn about a quarter of a million dollars more than high school dropouts. What would be the costs of not completing your undergraduate degree? Bachelor degree holders earn $944 per month more than college dropouts. Cumulated over a lifetime of work, college graduates will earn almost one-half million dollars more than college dropouts.

### Monthly Income by Highest Degree Earned

| | |
|---|---|
| Not a high school graduate | $856 |
| High school graduate | $1357 |
| Some college, no degree | $1545 |
| Bachelor's degree | $2489 |
| Master's degree | $3211 |
| Professional degree | $5554 |
| Doctorate | $4545 |

*Source: Statistical Abstract of the United States, 1994, p. 158*

## MEASURING INCOME INEQUALITY

### THE LORENZ CURVE

The most common measure of equality in the distribution of income is the Lorenz curve.

> The **Lorenz curve** shows the percentages of total income earned by households at successive income levels. The cumulative percentage of households (ranked from lowest to highest incomes) is plotted on the horizontal axis, and the cumulative share of income earned by each cumulative percentage of households is plotted on the vertical axis.

Lorenz curves are typically plotted in quintiles, or fifths. A household in the top fifth has greater earnings than at least 80 percent of all households.

A 45-degree-line Lorenz curve shows absolute equality. If income were distributed equally, the bottom 20 percent of households would receive 20 percent of all income, the bottom 40 percent of households would receive 40 percent of all income, and so on. The more the Lorenz curve bows away from the 45-degree line, or the line of perfect equality, the

more unequal is the income distribution. Figure 2 provides three U.S. Lorenz curves, for 1929, 1970, and 1993 (see also Table 4).

### THE GINI COEFFICIENT

Another measure of the inequality of income distribution is the Gini coefficient, a numerical measure of inequality.

> The **Gini coefficient** is the area between the 45-degree line and the Lorenz curve, divided by the total area under the 45-degree line.

If there is perfect equality, the Lorenz curve and the 45-degree line coincide, and the Gini coefficient is zero. If there is perfect inequality (one household gets all the income), then the difference between the Lorenz curve and the 45-degree line equals the entire area under the 45-degree line, and the Gini coefficient equals 1. In between these two extremes, the Gini coefficient can measure whether one income distribution is more or less unequal than another.

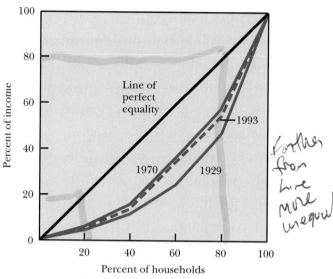

*Line of perfect equality*

*1993*

*1970    1929*

*Further from Line more unequal*

**FIGURE 2    Lorenz Curves of the U.S. Income Distribution, 1929, 1970, and 1993**

For more than 60 years, there has been a distinct trend toward more equality in the U.S. distribution of income. Since 1970, however, there has been a trend toward greater inequality. *Sources: Statistical Abstract of the United States, Historical Statistics of the United States.*

## FACTS AND FIGURES ON THE U.S. DISTRIBUTION OF INCOME

Over the past half-century, there has been a distinct trend toward greater equality. The Lorenz curve in Figure 2 gives the U.S. distributions of income in 1929, 1970, and 1993. The top 5 percent of households accounted for 30 percent of all income in 1929 but for 19.1 percent in 1993. The share of the lowest 40 percent of households rose from 12.5 percent in 1929 to 14.3 percent in 1993. The middle-class households in the third and fourth quintiles increased

their relative standing most over the past 60 years; from 33.1 percent to 39.5 percent.

Despite the long-term trend toward a more equal distribution of income, considerable inequality still exists. In 1993, the top 5 percent of U.S. households accounted for 19.1 percent of all income, whereas the bottom 20 percent accounted for only 4.2 percent. If we consider only money incomes before taxes, the U.S. income distribution became more unequal between the 1970s and 1993. In 1970, the top 5 percent earned 15.6 percent of all income. In 1993, they earned 19.1 percent.

## WHO IS AT THE TOP AND WHO IS AT THE BOTTOM?

Table 5 shows who is at the top and who is at the bottom of the income distribution. The poor—at the bottom—are likely to be African American or Hispanic, young or old, in families headed by a female, and in families with little education. The rich—those in the top 5 percent—are primarily white, married couples, between 35 and 54 years old, and with a university degree.

The fact that the young and the old are more likely to be poor tells us that we go through a life cycle of earnings in which we earn less during certain periods of life and more during other periods. In fact, the most appropriate measure of the distribution of income is the lifetime distribution of income.

The **lifetime distribution of income** measures the distribution of average income over the household's adult life.

Part of the inequality of the distribution of income occurs because it mixes households at different stages in their earnings cycle. Households in their

| | Lowest Fifth | Second Fifth | Third Fifth | Fourth Fifth | Highest Fifth | Top 5% |
|---|---|---|---|---|---|---|
| **Table 4    U.S. Income Distribution—1929, 1970, 1993** | | | | | | |
| 1929 | 3.8% | 8.7% | 13.8% | 19.3% | 54.4% | 30.0% |
| 1970 | 5.4% | 12.2% | 17.6% | 23.8% | 40.9% | 15.6% |
| 1993 | 4.2% | 10.1% | 15.9% | 23.6% | 46.2% | 19.1% |

*Sources: Statistical Abstract of the United States, Historical Statistics of the United States.*

| Table 5   Percent of Families in Various Income Groups (1993) | | | |
| --- | --- | --- | --- |
| | Lowest 20% | Highest 20% | Top 5 Percent |
| White | 16.9% | 21.4% | 5.5% |
| African American | 41.4% | 9.0% | 1.5% |
| Hispanic | 35.3% | 8.1% | 1.5% |
| Married couples | 12.7% | 24.4% | 6.2% |
| Female householder, husband absent | 49.1% | 3.9% | 0.7% |
| Age: | | | |
| 25–34 years | 25.0% | 11.5% | 2.2% |
| 35–44 years | 15.3% | 23.8% | 5.5% |
| 45–54 years | 11.3% | 34.2% | 9.4% |
| 55–64 years | 15.7% | 23.7% | 6.7% |
| 65 and over | 26.9% | 9.6% | 2.5% |
| Education: | | | |
| No high school diploma | 37.4% | 4.9% | 0.9% |
| High school graduate | 19.5% | 11.8% | 1.7% |
| Bachelor's degree or more | 4.7% | 47.4% | 15.6% |

*Source: Statistical Abstract of the United States.*

early twenties and late sixties are earning less than those in their thirties, forties, and fifties. However, if we consider only each household's average lifetime income, the differences in income are less.

## GOVERNMENT AND INCOME REDISTRIBUTION

Figure 2 shows the distribution of money income before taxes and before services provided by the government. Government can alter the distribution of income through taxes, money payments, and in-kind income.

> **In-kind income** consists of benefits—such as free public education, school lunch programs, public housing, or food stamps— for which the recipient is not required to pay.

Figure 3 and Table 6 show the substantial impact of government redistribution programs on the distribution of income. Without government money transfers, the poorest fifth of households would account for only 1 percent of money income. After such transfers, their share is raised to 5.1 percent. Income and payroll taxes do not significantly alter the distribution of income. The distribution of money incomes before and after taxes are about the same. In-kind income, such as Medicare, school lunches, and other assistance programs, significantly raises the share of the bottom fifth—from 3.8 percent to 5.1 percent of total income. Without this redistribution of income through government programs, the richest fifth would earn 50 times more than the poorest fifth. Government cash and in-kind transfers lowers this figure to 8 times.

## A BRIEF INTERNATIONAL PERSPECTIVE

Is the U.S. distribution of income like that of other countries? Does the United States have extremes of wealth and poverty unlike other countries? Figure 4 shows a mix of countries at different levels of economic development, including Hungary, a former communist state. It reveals that at a roughly equivalent level of income, the U.S. distribution of income is more unequal than that of other industrialized countries, such as Japan and Sweden. Our distribution of income is much more equal than that of developing countries, such as Brazil. In fact, there is a

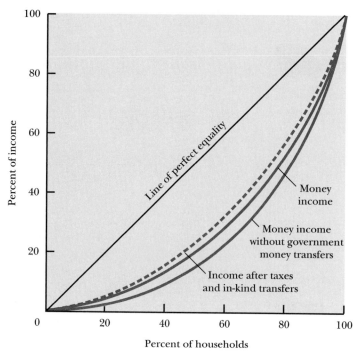

**FIGURE 3**   The Effect of Government Taxes and Transfers on the U.S. Distribution of Income (1992)

*Source: Statistical Abstract of the United States.*

| Table 6   Distribution of Income with and without Government Money Transfers and Taxes and In-kind Transfers | | | | | |
|---|---|---|---|---|---|
| | *Percent of Income* | | | | |
| | *Lowest fifth* | *2nd fifth* | *3rd fifth* | *4th fifth* | *Highest fifth* |
| Money income | 3.8 | 9.4 | 15.9 | 24.1 | 46.8 |
| Money income without government money transfers | 1.0 | 7.8 | 15.6 | 25.3 | 50.4 |
| Income after taxes and in-kind transfers | 5.1 | 11.0 | 16.7 | 23.9 | 43.3 |

strong relationship between the level of development and a country's income distribution:

> The lower the level of income in a country, the more unequal its distribution of income.

There are exceptions to the rule: Hungary is not an affluent industrialized country, but it has the equal distribution characteristics of a rich country. The United States has a more unequal distribution of income than many other highly industrialized countries because the United States remains a melting pot of different nationalities and races, unlike homogeneous countries like Hungary or Sweden. The more

heterogeneity, the more unequal the distribution of income. Also, the U.S. government plays less of a redistributive role than most of the governments in Europe. Although our welfare state appears big to us, the welfare state is more pervasive in Europe.

## WHAT IS A JUST DISTRIBUTION OF INCOME?

Philosophers have debated the ethical issue of distributive justice for centuries. Is it fair to have extremes of wealth and poverty? Economists can better

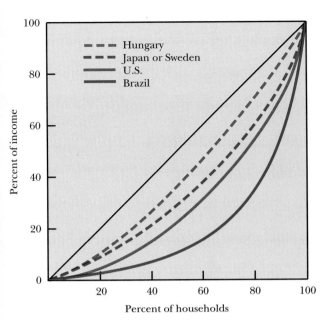

**FIGURE 4   Lorenz Curves for the Distribution of Income in the United States and Other Countries.**

*Source:* The World Bank, *World Development Report, 1991* (New York: Oxford University Press).

describe the economic consequences of different income distributions than judge whether one is better than another. Different philosophies of distributive justice have been formulated over the years.

## NATURAL LAW, MARGINAL PRODUCTIVITY, AND THE LEAKY BUCKET

According to the natural-law philosophers of the seventeenth century, we have the right to receive the fruits of our own labor.

> **Natural law** states that individuals should be rewarded according to their contribution to output.

This philosophy is consistent with the marginal productivity theory of income distribution, according to which, the owner of a factor of production receives its marginal revenue product (MRP). Under this arrangement, those who are more productive (those who have high MRPs) will receive more.

The major advantage of distributing income according to marginal productivities is that the owners of factors of production are encouraged to raise mar-

ginal productivity. Thus, we are motivated to invest in human capital and to acquire more physical capital; entrepreneurs are spurred to assume risks. If we were not paid in accordance with marginal productivity, we would reduce effort, acquire less human and physical capital, and take fewer risks—and the economy would produce less income.

There is a trade-off between equality and income. If income were redistributed away from those who possess high-priced factors of production, the efficiency of the economy would decline and less income would be produced. The equity/efficiency trade-off can be explained using the analogy of a leaky bucket.[6] Redistributing income is like transferring water from one barrel to another with a leaky bucket. In the process of making the transfer, water (income) is lost forever. If the leak is a slow one, the costs to society of the redistribution are small. If the leak is fast, the losses of total income will be substantial. We must decide whether the costs of greater equality are worth the price.

## THE UTILITARIAN CASE FOR EQUALITY

The utilitarian theory holds that a more equal income distribution will maximize the utility of society.

> **Utilitarian theory** argues for an equal distribution of income by saying that equality maximizes welfare.

The law of diminishing marginal utility supplies the rationale of the utilitarian theory. If we are basically alike (if we have the same tastes and the same satisfaction from the same amount of income), the total utility of society will be greatest when income is distributed equally because of the law of diminishing marginal utility. If your friend Jones were rich and you were poor, Jones would be getting much less utility from his last dollar than you. If income were redistributed from Jones to you, your utility would increase more than Jones's would be reduced. Therefore, the reduction in inequality would increase the total utility of society.

We are, in fact, different. Some of us care little for money and worldly goods; others care a great

---

[6]Arthur Okun, *Equality and Efficiency: The Big Trade-Off* (Washington, DC: The Brookings Institution, 1975).

deal. Therefore, it is not at all certain that the rich get less marginal utility from their last dollar. We cannot make interpersonal utility comparisons; we cannot conclude scientifically that the total utility of society is greatest when income is equally distributed. Even if it were, we would have to consider the loss of production caused if everyone earned the same amount.

## RAWLSIAN EQUALITY

In the 1970s, philosopher John Rawls proposed a new argument concerning equality.[7] Rawls maintained that inequality and injustice result from the fact that people know in advance whether they will be rich or poor. Hence, privileged people will not agree to social changes that give away their advantages through redistributive taxes. The rational self-interest of the privileged will not allow a social consensus for a more equal distribution.

According to Rawls, if everyone were operating behind a "veil of ignorance" (if people did not know in advance whether they would be rich or poor), there would be widespread social support for an equal distribution of income. We would be concerned about the poor because no one of us could be sure that we would not be poor. We would want to minimize the risk of being poor and would support social policies to redistribute income.

## POVERTY

The fact that income is distributed unequally means that there will be rich and poor. As a society, we must decide how to deal with poverty. During the Industrial Revolution (a Defining Moment), poverty was viewed as a problem for which the poor themselves were responsible. Debtors were thrown into debtors' prisons, and youths caught stealing bread were imprisoned. As the welfare state grew in Western Europe, politicians and government officials concluded that the state should do something to eliminate poverty. In the United States, the Great Depression of the 1930s (another Defining Moment)

caused federal, state, and local governments to enact poverty programs and unemployment assistance.

## DEFINITIONS OF POVERTY

Defining poverty is not an easy task. Some define poverty in terms of the income necessary to provide a family of a certain size with the minimum essentials of food, clothing, shelter, and education. This approach provides an absolute poverty standard.

An **absolute poverty standard** establishes a specific income level for a household of a given size, below which the household is judged to be living in a state of poverty.

But is an absolute measure of poverty appropriate? Poverty can, after all, be relative. If my income is 10 percent of everyone else's, I may feel poor even if my income is sufficient to purchase the minimum essentials. Similarly, our conception of poverty does not necessarily match that of other countries. The American poor might be considered wealthy in the poorest Asian or African nations. A second approach to poverty, therefore, is a measurement in relative terms. A relative poverty standard might classify a household as poor if the household's income is, say, less than 25 percent of the average household's income.

A **relative poverty standard** defines the poor in terms of their income relative to others.

The choice of a poverty definition determines the number of poor and the poverty rate. If an absolute standard is selected, increasing real living standards will push more and more families above the poverty line. According to a relative standard, poverty can be eliminated only by equalizing the distribution of income. If both the rich and the poor experience equal percentage increases in income, the poor will not have improved their relative position.

## TRENDS IN POVERTY

According to the absolute poverty standards of the U.S. government (Figure 5), the percentage of persons in poverty households declined from 22.4 percent to 12.8 percent between 1959 and 1966. Since then, progress has been uneven. During periods of rising prosperity, such as the 1960s and 1980s, the percentage of poverty households has declined. Dur-

[7]John Rawls, *A Theory of Justice* (Cambridge: Harvard University Press, 1971); and "Some Reasons for the Maximin Criterion," *American Economic Review* 64, 2 (May 1974): pp. 141–146.

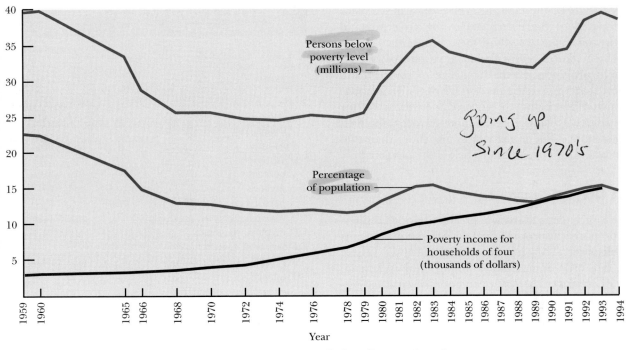

**FIGURE 5  Persons Living in Households with Incomes Below Poverty Levels, 1951–1993 (Money Income Only)**

*Sources: Economic Report of the President;* U.S. Bureau of the Census.

ing the recessions of the 1980s, 1980–1981, and 1990–1991, the rate of poverty has increased.

Figure 5 refers only to money income, which does not include in-kind services received by the poor but does include government cash transfers, such as welfare payments and unemployment insurance. The government spends $3 in noncash benefits to every $2 in cash payments for its antipoverty programs.

What effects do government antipoverty programs have on the number of persons classified as living below the poverty line? Table 7 shows that the number of persons living below poverty levels in 1992 would

have been substantially higher without government antipoverty programs. Without cash or in-kind payments, almost 23 percent of the U.S. population would have been below the poverty line. When both cash payments and in-kind benefits are included, the poverty percentage fell to 8.2 percent of the white population, 24.7 percent of the African American population, and 21.5 percent of the Hispanic population.

The percentage of elderly persons living below poverty is reduced more than that of other groups by in-kind benefits, from 15 percent to 4.5 percent. This reduction results almost entirely from government Medicare and Medicaid programs that help pay the

## Table 7  The Percentage of Persons Below Poverty Before and After Government Antipoverty Programs (1992)

|  | Before Taxes and Cash Payments | After Cash Payments | After Cash and In-Kind Payments |
|---|---|---|---|
| All households | 22.6% | 14.5% | 10.4% |
| White | 19.7% | 11.6% | 8.2% |
| African American | 41.9% | 33.3% | 24.7% |
| Hispanic | 36.6% | 29.3% | 21.5% |

*Source:* U.S. Bureau of the Census, *Current Population Reports.*

medical bills of the elderly.[8] These data make clear the concern of the elderly regarding governmental slowdowns in the growth of these programs.

These figures reveal the massive effects of government programs on the incidence of poverty and suggest that a very large percentage of the U.S. population would be below the poverty line were it not for government assistance. Even after government welfare assistance, one in ten whites and more than two in ten blacks or Hispanics live below the poverty line.

### WHO ARE THE POOR?

Table 8 provides a statistical profile of poor families. The poor are disproportionately African Americans and Hispanic. They live in large families; the family head has little education, is young, and is female. Over one-third of the American poor are children under the age of 18. The poor live in central cities and in rural areas. Contrary to popular myth, a majority are working poor. Only 64 percent of the poor receive some form of cash assistance from government antipoverty programs.

## GOVERNMENT SOLUTIONS: THE WELFARE STATE

In the United States, poverty was viewed as a problem for religious and private charitable organizations until the Great Depression. Prior to the Depression, private charity seemed sufficient to handle the job. Between 1929 and 1933, hard-working families were left without jobs, whole industries collapsed, and the banking system was in disarray. The economic suffering created by the Great Depression was clearly not the fault of the unemployed workers and was too great to be solved by private charity.

President Franklin Roosevelt and his administration enacted legislation in the 1930s—unemployment insurance, Social Security, jobs programs, and the like—that gave government the role of dealing with poverty. Subsequent administrations, particularly Lyndon Johnson's Great Society programs of

[8]U.S. Bureau of the Census, *Alternative Methods of Valuing Selected In-Kind Benefits and Measuring Their Effect on Poverty* (Washington, D.C.: U.S. Government Printing Office). Selected years.

| Table 8   Characteristics of Poverty Families (1992) | |
|---|---|
| Category | *Percentage of Families Below Poverty Levels* |
| Race | |
| White | 8.9 |
| African American | 30.9 |
| Hispanic | 26.2 |
| Size of family | |
| 2 persons | 9.4 |
| 3 persons | 11.7 |
| 4 persons | 11.0 |
| 5 persons | 16.6 |
| 7 or more persons | 34.7 |
| Education of family head | |
| No high school diploma | 24.1 |
| High school, no college | 11.0 |
| Some college, no degree | 7.2 |
| Bachelor's degree or more | 2.2 |
| Families headed by single mothers | 38.5 |
| Age of family head | |
| 15–24 years | 38.2 |
| 25–34 years | 17.9 |
| 35–44 years | 10.8 |
| 45–54 years | 6.9 |
| 55–64 years | 7.2 |
| 65 or more years | 7.8 |

*Source: Statistical Abstract of the United States.*

the mid-1960s, solidified the government's role as a provider of jobs, training, health, and education for the poorer segments of American society. Today, federal, state, and local governments oversee a vast array of welfare programs such as job-training for poor youth, Aid to Families with Dependent Children, school lunch programs, and free immunization programs.

Table 9 shows the magnitude of the U.S. welfare state: By the early 1990s, the government was spending more than $1 trillion—or almost $13,000 per U.S. household—on social welfare expenditures, and almost $300 billion of government cash and in-kind benefits directly on the poor—or almost $16,000 for every poor family. Despite this massive financial effort, the number of poor households continues to grow, and the percentage of poverty households does not fall. Why has this government effort not had a more positive impact? Has it had unintended consequences?

The U.S. welfare system is founded on the principle that public assistance should be granted pri-

| Table 9    Measures of the U.S. Welfare State (1992) | |
| --- | --- |
| 1. Social welfare expenditures under public programs, federal, state and local governments | $1,234 billion |
| 2. Total number of U.S. households | 96.4 million |
| 3. Social welfare expenditure per household | $12,800 |
| 4. Federal, state, and local government cash and noncash benefit programs for persons with limited income | |
|     Medical care         $134.0 billion | |
|     Cash aid               64.9 | |
|     Food benefits          34.1 | |
|     Housing benefits       20.5 | |
|     Education aid        16.0 | |
|     Social and child services   8.6 | |
|     Jobs training          5.5 | |
|     Total | $289.9 billion |
| 5. Number of households receiving at least one benefit | 18.4 million |
| 6. Benefits per recipient household | $15,755 |

*Source: Statistical Abstract of the United States.*

*Welfare doesn't work*

marily on the basis of need. The government has established a number of programs—such as Aid to Families with Dependent Children (AFDC), the Food Stamp Program, public housing, and Medicaid—in which the amount of public assistance is based upon family income. Welfare authorities must determine what resources the family has.

The army of welfare workers that is required to document needs and resources makes the system very costly. Dollars that could be devoted to public assistance are diverted to pay the bureaucratic costs of operating the system.

## UNINTENDED CONSEQUENCES

The intent of government welfare assistance programs is to reduce or even eliminate poverty. Like many government programs, welfare assistance programs have unintended consequences that have created long-term problems.

The granting of government assistance on the basis of demonstrated need reduces the household's incentive to earn income. A welfare mother risks losing assistance if she takes a job or if the children's father lives in the home and earns income. The welfare system, as currently structured, encourages welfare fathers to desert the home. By having assistance rise with the number of children, existing programs encourage pregnancies.

Welfare dependency is passed from one generation to another. Young women grow up in broken homes headed by their mother, who is dependent on welfare assistance. One escape from that broken home is to have children—with the father absent—and to collect welfare payments.

Despite the substantial portion of all government spending devoted to welfare, the incidence of poverty has not declined, the percentage of poverty families headed by single mothers has risen, and the incidence of illegitimate births and teenage pregnancies has increased. In 1970, 11 percent of all births were to unmarried women. In 1995, about one-third of all births were to unmarried women. In 1970, 40 percent of all births of African American children were to unmarried women; by 1995 it was 70 percent. In 1970, 9 percent of white families, 28 percent of African American families, and 15 percent of Hispanic families were headed by females. In 1995, 15 percent of white families, 48 percent of African American families, and 23 percent of Hispanic families were headed by females.

Many government programs have unintended consequences, confirming that it will be difficult to devise policies that do not have these undesired consequences. The mere recognition of unintended consequences does not necessarily explain how to devise a policy that avoids them.

These past mistakes do not suggest, however, that we should not care for the poor and less fortunate. Instead, they make clear that in establishing socioeconomic programs, we must devise policies that achieve the desired result—such as solving the problem of poverty—without perpetuating or accentuating the problem. Such economic policies must provide incentives for the poor to escape poverty, not encourage them to remain poor.

In this chapter, we have examined the causes of inequality in the distribution of income and directed attention to the role of government in the redistribution of income to the poor. In the next three chapters, we shall focus on the role of government and its impact on the environment, public finance, and public choice.

1. The sources of income inequality include different abilities, discrimination, occupational differences, different amounts of human-capital investment, and inheritance. Differences in schooling may affect earnings because employers use educational credentials to screen and select job candidates for high-paying careers. Earning differentials, both between whites and nonwhites and between males and females, have been reduced in recent years.

2. The Lorenz curve measures the degree of income inequality. It shows the cumulative percentages of all income earned by households at successive income levels. If the Lorenz curve is a 45-degree line, income distribution is perfectly equal. The more the Lorenz curve bows away from the 45-degree line, the more unequal is the distribution of income. The government may change the distribution of income through taxes and the distribution of public services. The Gini coefficient is an alternate measure of income inequality.

3. The U.S. distribution of income became more equal from 1929 to 1970. It has become less equal after 1970. It also becomes more equal after it is adjusted for taxes, in-kind services, and life-cycle effects.

4. There are different views on what constitutes distributive justice. Marginal productivity theory calls for a distribution of income according to the marginal productivity of the resources owned by households. The utilitarian school believes that an equal distribution of income maximizes total utility. John Rawls proposed a distribution of income that maximizes the utility of the least fortunate members of society.

5. Poverty can be measured in either absolute or relative terms. The absolute measure is based on a definition of the minimum income necessary to allow a household to buy the minimum essentials. The relative standard measures poverty in terms of the household's location in the income distribution. According to the absolute measures of poverty made by the U.S. government, the number of people living below the poverty line declined between 1960 and 1970 but has not had a distinct trend thereafter. Poor Americans tend to be nonwhite, poorly educated members of households headed by females, and either very young or very old.

6. Income maintenance programs provide only short-run solutions to the problem of poverty. They also have unintended consequences.

compensating wage
    differentials
risk seekers
risk avoiders
human capital theory
discrimination
wealth
inheritance
screening
Lorenz curve

Gini coefficient
in-kind income
lifetime distribution of
    income
natural law
utilitarian theory
absolute poverty
    standard
relative poverty
    standard

1. Draw a Lorenz curve for absolute equality. Draw a Lorenz curve for absolute inequality. Explain the situation illustrated by the absolute inequality Lorenz curve.

2. Evaluate the validity of the following statement: "If all people were the same, the Lorenz curve would be a 45-degree line."

3. Evaluate the validity of the following statement: "The fact that a woman earns, on average, two-thirds of what a man earns proves beyond a shadow of a doubt that there is sexual discrimination."

4. There are two views of the causes of poverty. One school says that the poor are poor through no fault of their own. The other says that the poor are poor through choice. Give arguments for each position.

5. How does screening theory explain the apparently poor correlation between ability and inequality?

6. Contrast the utilitarian view of distributive justice with the Rawlsian view.

7. Explain why measured Lorenz curves that use disposable income before and after taxes may not give an accurate picture of the distribution of real income.

8. Explain some of the unintended consequences of current poverty programs. Explain how we should devise new programs that avoid unintended consequences.

9. Assume that a society consists of eight risk avoiders and two risk seekers. Contrast that society with one that consists of five risk seekers and five risk avoiders. Which society will have a more equal distribution of income?

10. In society A, 50 percent of the adult population is between 18 and 25 or over 65. In society B, 25 percent of the adult population is between 18 and 25 or over 65. Using Lorenz curves, which society would appear to be more unequal in its distribution of income due to life-cycle effects?

11. Joe wants goods today; Bill is more willing to wait until tomorrow. Which one is more likely to invest in human capital?

12. The official U.S. poverty income standard is adjusted upward each year to account for the general increase in prices. If a family's income just keeps up with the poverty income over the years, what is happening to its relative poverty position?

13. Education is distributed among the population more equally than income. What does this tell you about the relationship between education and inequality?

14. What types of incorrect incentives are provided by the current "assistance according to demonstrated need" welfare system?

# PART IV

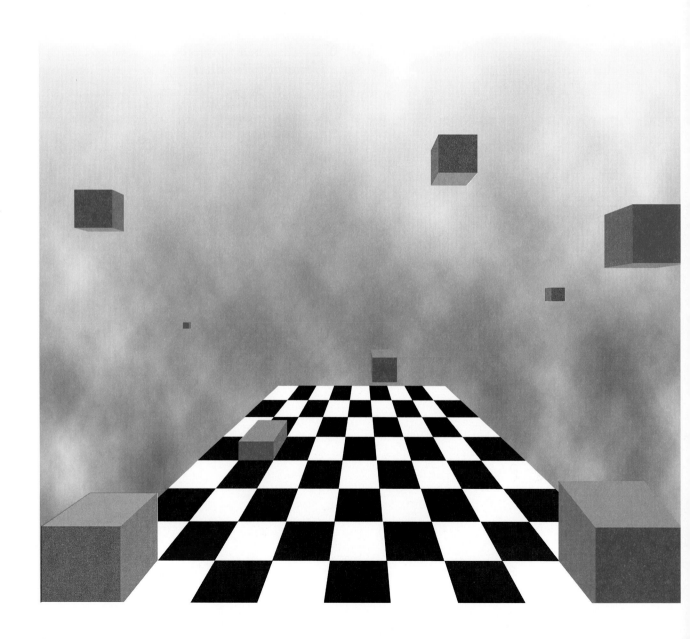

# MICROECONOMIC ISSUES

# CHAPTER 20

# MARKET FAILURE, THE ENVIRONMENT, AND NATURAL RESOURCES

## CHAPTER INSIGHT

Doomsayers warn that unless we change our ways we shall be left with a dying planet. There will be no forests, no drinkable water, no wildernesses. We shall scarcely be able to venture outdoors because of the depleted ozone layer. Global warming will cause the arctic ice caps to melt, thereby flooding much of the earth's land mass. We shall all have to move to higher land; there will not be enough land to feed us all. Even if we escape skin cancer or malnutrition, we shall face the prospect of running out of resources. We will not be able to sustain our standard of living, as we now know it; we will be forced to return to a more primitive style of life.

Optimists, on the other hand, characterize such dire predictions of doom as hogwash—as the rantings and ravings of radical ecologists, who use scare tactics to gain public support. Optimists point out that there is no firm scientific evidence of greenhouse effects, of global warming, or of other impending ecological disasters. The greatest environmental damage, they argue, has occurred in the developing countries, not in the highly industrialized world. The radical ecologists simply do not like capitalism and the high standard of living it has created. They wish to spoil the party.

Who is right? Who is wrong? That is the subject of this chapter. Does Adam Smith's invisible hand somehow protect us from pollution and resource exhaustion? Can we rely on private incentives, or must government intervene?

## WHY DOES THE MARKET FAIL?

In earlier chapters we have discussed a number of instances where the market economy may not satisfactorily solve the economic problem of *what, how,* and *for whom.* In a monopoly industry, consumers pay prices that are higher than necessary for a quantity of output that has been artificially restrained by the producer. The market economy may distribute income so unevenly among households that there is general dissatisfaction with the result. In both cases, the government can take action to correct the errors made by the market. The government might use antitrust laws to break up the monopoly; it can use progressive taxes to redistribute income from the rich to the poor.

In this chapter, we deal with market failures in which the invisible hand has not worked properly.

> **Market failure** occurs when the price system fails to yield the socially optimal quantity of a good.

Market failures can take the form of environmental pollution, in which enterprises pollute water, air, the earth's surface, and even outer space. They can also take the form of public goods—such as national defense or a legal system—that may not be produced at all or are underproduced because the decision has been left to the market. In this chapter we shall examine environmental pollution and nonrenewable resources. Can a market economy deal with pollution or with a finite resource? We shall discuss public goods in the next chapter.

Market failures have a number of causes. They occur when private costs and benefits diverge from social costs and benefits. They can occur when nonpayers for goods cannot be kept from enjoying their benefits and when your use of a good does not detract from my use.

Market failures raise the question of whether government action is required to correct the failure of the market economy.

## EXTERNALITIES: PRIVATE VERSUS SOCIAL COSTS

Externalities plague all economies. They are present whenever the actions of one agent have direct economic effects on other agents. Simple examples are the negative external effects of smoking, or noisy neighbors, or the positive effects of a neighbor's beautiful rosebushes. (See Example 1.)

### EXAMPLE 1
### NEIGHBORS
### FROM HELL

Arthur Cunningham enjoyed his Greenwich Village apartment until the Automatic Slim's Bar and Restaurant opened right below his second-floor apartment. The restaurant's venting system ends outside his window, sending a dirty grease smell into his apartment. The noise goes on until 4 or 5 o'clock in the morning. Mr. Cunningham, who has lived in the apartment for 31 years, took early retirement because he could not continue to work under these conditions. He now keeps his television set blaring until the bar closes and sleeps until 1 o'clock in the afternoon.

Mr. Cunningham's "neighbor from hell" is an example of a negative externality. The restaurant has imposed a substantial external cost that it had not internalized in the price system.

We may wonder why Mr. Cunningham simply did not move. The answer is that his apartment is rent-controlled by the City of New York, and he pays a negligible rent. If he paid a market rental rate, he would have moved long ago. The external cost of the restaurant has not been high enough to outweigh the benefits of paying such a low rent.

------------------------------------------------

*Source:* "When the Neighbors are Fuming, Literally," *New York Times,* May 24, 1995, B1.

**Externalities** exist when producers or consumers do not bear the full marginal cost or enjoy the full marginal benefit of their actions.

When externalities are present, market transactions between two parties will have harmful or beneficial effects on third parties. The effects are "external" to the price system and are not the outcome of mutual agreement between all the interested parties.

Let's take the case of a factory that pollutes the air, thereby imposing cleaning or health-care costs on the surrounding community. These external costs are paid not by the factory, but by others; external costs do not appear in the factory's cost accounting.

Externalities can be positive as well as negative. The person who pays for an education is not the only one who benefits: Society benefits when education creates a common culture, a trained work force, and scientific and technological progress.

## SOCIAL EFFICIENCY

When external costs or benefits are present, we determine social efficiency by comparing social costs and social benefits.

**Social costs** equal private costs plus external costs. **Social benefits** equal private benefits plus external benefits.

We considered private costs in earlier chapters on costs, competition, and monopoly. Private costs are the enterprise's opportunity costs. The firm's marginal private cost is its opportunity cost of increasing its output by one unit. When external costs are present, the marginal cost to society of producing one more unit of output equals this marginal private cost plus the marginal external cost. External costs create a market failure by inducing the private firm to produce too much output (see Figure 1).

External costs cause the competitive firm to produce too much output. The firm produces that level of output at which marginal private costs and marginal private benefits are equal. If a firm ignores the external costs of its actions, its marginal social costs will exceed its marginal social benefits at the profit-maximizing level of output. Society as a whole would be better off if the competitive firm reduced its output to where marginal social costs and marginal social benefits are equal. Figure 1 shows that the so-

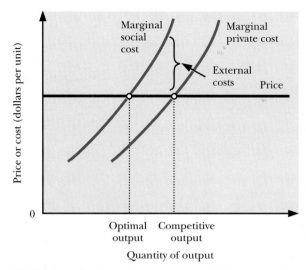

**FIGURE 1  Perfect Competition with External Costs**

When external costs are present, competitive firms produce too much output because they produce at the level where marginal private costs equal price, not where marginal social costs equal price.

cially optimal level of output is less than the competitive output when external costs are present. (See Example 2).

> Social efficiency requires that marginal social benefits and marginal social costs be equal, but private participants equate only marginal private benefits with marginal private costs.

Pollution by industry and by private cars are externalities that can impose substantial external costs on the community. Commercial fishers deplete fishing waters by not considering the external costs of overfishing. Modern reflective-glass skyscrapers raise the air-conditioning costs of neighboring buildings. A family that allows its house and lawn to deteriorate reduces the pleasure neighbors obtain from their own houses and lawns.

The failure of even competitive firms to produce the socially optimal level of output represents a market failure.

## WHAT TO DO ABOUT EXTERNALITIES

In order to eliminate an externality problem, a firm must include external costs or benefits in its calculations of private gain. The solution is to internalize, or

### EXAMPLE 2
### HOW MUCH IS
### THE GRAND CANYON WORTH?

How much would you be willing to pay to keep the Grand Canyon the way nature made it? In fact, you may be one of the 6000 Americans asked this question in a survey sponsored by the Department of Interior.

Environmentalists claim that the 31-year-old Glen Canyon Dam on the Colorado River is ruining the Grand Canyon's ecosystem. The dam's cold water and the irregular flow of water threaten natural erosion patterns and fish native to the canyon. But the dam has been a boon to 3 million Western electricity customers who benefit from its lower rates.

The survey by the Department of Interior asks Americans nationwide how much they value the Grand Canyon and what they would be willing to pay to restore its ecosystem. The resulting measure of the Grand Canyon's "non-use value" can be compared with the gains to electricity users from lower electricity rates. If people nationwide place a high non-use value, the department may decide to reduce the dam's operations. If people place a low value, the dam would continue to operate as is, despite its environmental damage.

Called a revolution in federal land-use policies, the survey approach represents a risk for environmental groups: What if people don't place a high value on protecting the environment?

--------------------------------------------

*Source:* "Survey Will Target Dollar Value of Saving Life in Grand Canyon," *Houston Chronicle*, October 8, 1994, 19A.

---

put a private price tag on, externalities. This price must be paid by those who impose costs on others.

> An externality undergoes **internalization** when private price tags are placed on external costs (or benefits) so that private and social costs (or benefits) coincide.

If we pay for the costs we impose on others or receive a payment for the benefits that others receive from our actions, we incorporate such costs and benefits into our private cost-benefit calculations. An example of internalization is the merger of two factories located on a river. Prior to the merger, the downstream factory has to pay water purification costs because the upstream factory is polluting the water. After the merger, the external costs of the downstream factory become internal costs that the merged firms consider in private cost/benefit calculations.

Internalization can be accomplished by the redefinition of property rights, by voluntary agreements, or by government action.

## REDEFINITION OF PROPERTY RIGHTS

An externality can be internalized by the redefinition of property rights.

> **Property rights** specify who owns a resource and who has the right to use it.

Poor definition of property rights is a prominent source of externalities. If we do not know who owns the property rights to the air in a domed stadium or in an airplane, to the whales in the seas, or the rights to scenic views, these resources will likely be exploited and abused. Fishing businesses will overfish ocean waters, factories will pollute the air, and scenery will be destroyed by unsightly signs.

When no one knows who the owner of a resource is, there is no one to limit its use. However, if private property rights can be clearly defined, the private owner will make sure that the resource is efficiently used. The owner of hunting land can set fees high enough to prevent game from being depleted. If the city council is somehow given ownership of the community's air, it can charge polluting factories for their use of the air. Every month, local factories would get bills from the owner of the community's air. If one country holds the property rights to the ocean's fishing grounds, it can charge fishing businesses from all countries for their use of the ocean.

These examples show that it is not easy to eliminate externalities by changing property rights. This strategy will not work when it is very costly to define or enforce property rights. Let's consider, for example, the overkilling of whales. How do we determine who owns the whales and how do we protect the owner's property rights? The ownership rights to clean air are so vague that those harmed by air pollution have difficulty suing polluters. In both cases, we have too little information to enforce property rights. If we do not know how many whales there are and how many each whaler has killed, or how much pollution each car has emitted, how can we know the real marginal cost to society of each whale killed or of the pollution from each car?

## VOLUNTARY AGREEMENTS

Voluntary agreements are a second means of internalizing externalities. The merger of the two factories on a river mentioned above is an example of such a voluntary agreement. When property rights are well defined, voluntary agreements can internalize external costs.

The proposition that voluntary agreements can solve externality problems is called the Coase theorem, after 1991 Nobel laureate Ronald H. Coase. Coase argues that external costs and benefits can be internalized by negotiations among affected parties. He uses the example of a rancher whose cattle stray onto a neighboring farm and damage the neighbor's crops. If the rancher were legally liable for the crop damage, private bargaining would result in a deal in which the farmer would be paid by the rancher for the increased cost caused by the straying cattle. These extra costs would induce the rancher either to reduce the size of the herd or to build better fences.

The same result would be achieved even if the rancher's cattle had the legal right to stray onto the farmer's land. The farmer could agree to pay the rancher to reduce the size of the herd or build a fence. Again, when a price tag is placed on the externality, it disappears. Although the social effect—the amount of crops and cattle produced—is the same, the distribution of income depends upon who has the

property rights. In the first case, the rancher transfers income to the farmer. In the second case, the farmer transfers income to the rancher.

Some externalities can indeed be resolved by voluntary agreements. Washington state apple growers actually pay beekeepers a fee for pollination. Ships pay lighthouses for their guidance during nighttime travel near the coast. Large industrial enterprises agree to buy and sell pollution rights. Like the redefinition of property rights, voluntary agreements work only in selected cases. The number of parties has to be small; the costs of bargaining must be small.

Consider the case of hayfever sufferers who would be willing to pay farmers to reduce the amount of ragweed. There are too many hayfever sufferers, dispersed over a large territory, and there are too many potential sources of ragweed. In this case, the externality cannot be internalized by voluntary agreement between hayfever sufferers and farmers.

> The Coase theorem states that if small numbers are involved and bargaining costs are small, voluntary agreements can internalize an externality. When large numbers are involved and the costs are widely dispersed, voluntary agreements will be difficult to reach.

## GOVERNMENT TAXES AND SUBSIDIES

A third way for an externality to be internalized is for the government to impose corrective taxes or subsidies. When private activities result in external costs, the volume of transactions will exceed what is efficient because private agents ignore external costs. An appropriate tax on the externality will force the business firm to take into account the costs imposed on others and will, accordingly, reduce the amount of production to the efficient level where marginal social costs equal marginal social benefits.

Figure 2 shows how taxation can be used to internalize an external cost. If a tax equal to the external cost per unit of output is imposed on the factory, the supply curve will shift automatically to the left. With the new supply curve, the firm will produce the optimal level of output at which marginal social costs and benefits are equal.

Government action to correct externalities is most appropriate when they cannot be internalized through redefinition of property rights or by voluntary agreements. Government internalization, like

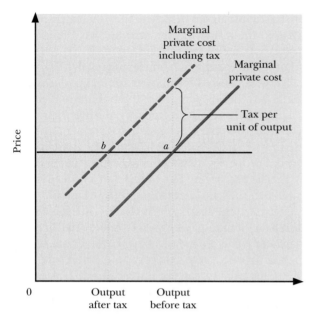

**FIGURE 2   Use of Taxes to Correct Externalities**

Competitive firms in this industry operate at point *a*, which is too much output because each unit of output creates an external cost equal to *ac*. If the government levies a tax on procedures equal to this external cost, it will be internalized and firms will produce the optimal level of output at *b*.

private solutions to externalities, requires considerable information. To levy the right tax, the government must know who is imposing external costs. The government must also be able to measure these external costs. The government must be careful not to enact measures that result in negative unintended consequences. (See Example 3.)

## POLLUTION, EXTERNALITIES, AND GOVERNMENT ACTION

Pollution illustrates the difficulties of internalizing externalities. Pollution can be the consequence of both production and consumption. Factories discharge their wastes into the atmosphere and water. Nuclear power plants must dispose of their nuclear wastes. Households produce sewage and garbage, and pollute the air with their automobiles. The polluting factory and the polluting household both create external costs. The private costs of their activities are less than the social costs.

Pollution can be local, regional, or even global. Local pollution affects the immediate surroundings of the site of emission. The damage from regional pollution is realized at a distance from its source. Global pollution occurs when pollutants are released into the earth's upper atmosphere, from which it is broadly dispersed.

Environmental pollution is an externality that often requires government intervention. Other means of internalization—redefinition of property rights and voluntary agreements—are usually not effective. It is difficult if not impossible to assign property rights to a river, a lake, air, or outer space. Even if property rights can be established, the legal costs of suing another party for violating a property right can be high. Because pollutants cross political boundaries and many parties are affected, effective action is rarely taken. It is difficult to enforce those private contracts that are negotiated when polluters are numerous or when monitoring costs are high.

Some pollutants can be returned naturally to the environment. Carbon dioxide, for example, is absorbed by plant life and by the oceans. Other pollutants, such as nonbiodegradable bottles or lead, cannot be absorbed naturally. When the emission of pollutants exceeds the environment's absorptive capacity, pollutants accumulate and cause environmental damage. Environmental waste must be disposed of, whether in the ground, in water, or in the air.

Waste disposal costs are real opportunity costs. Resources devoted to pollution prevention, such as scrubbers on smokestacks, are not available for other uses. There is an opportunity cost to you when you purchase bottled water or air filters to prevent health damage. Diseases from toxic-waste dumps represent costs to individuals and the community, be they cash outlays or less visible opportunity costs.

## OPTIMAL POLLUTION

Pollution can be reduced (abated) either by reducing the activity of the polluting agent or by paying the costs of pollution abatement. Air pollution can be reduced through cutbacks in factory production or in the use of cars that produce air pollutants, or through installation of scrubbers on smokestacks and antipollution devices on automobiles. In all these cases, the reduction of pollution has abatement costs.

What is the optimal level of pollution abatement? How much of society's resources should be devoted to pollution abatement? Optimal abatement is

## EXAMPLE 3
## UNINTENDED CONSEQUENCES:
## THE ELECTRIC CAR

The Clean Air Act set tough standards for ozone emissions from automobiles to contain urban smog. To meet the standards in the Clean Air Act, several states set the goal of having "zero emissions vehicles" constitute 10 percent of all vehicles on the road by the year 2003. The only zero emissions vehicles that are close to mass production are powered by electric lead-acid batteries.

The law of unintended consequences warns that policymakers must be careful to anticipate unforeseen secondary effects. Scientific evidence now suggests that switching from conventional gasoline engines to lead battery–powered engines would trade off one form of pollution for another. An available-technology electric car generates about 2000 milligrams of lead emissions for every mile, about six times as much as a tiny Geo Metro burning gasoline with the lead additives that were eliminated in the 1980s. Exposure to low levels of lead can cause brain damage in young children, and severe exposure can cause convulsions and death.

To devise the correct environmental policy, we must be able to measure the benefits from reducing ozone emissions versus the costs of more lead emissions. There are few if any free lunches!

-----

*Source:* "Electric Car Batteries Called a Toxic Peril," *New York Times,* May 9, 1995.

achieved at that level where the marginal social costs of further abatement equals the marginal social benefits. It may be surprising to someone who is not an economist, but the optimal level is not achieved at zero pollution. How much pollution society should tolerate is determined by weighing costs and benefits at the margin.

Figure 3 shows the marginal social costs and marginal social benefits of different amounts of pollution abatement—in this case, the number of gallons of water purified through filtration. The marginal social cost of each successive unit of abatement increases as more and more water is purified. Marginal social benefits decline as abatement intensifies because we value the first unit of abatement more highly than subsequent units.

> The **optimal level of abatement** occurs when the marginal social cost of an extra unit of abatement equals its marginal social benefit.

If abatement is undertaken beyond this optimal level, the extra benefits fall short of the extra opportunity costs. We should not aim for the total elimination of pollution. To do so, we would have to devote more and more scarce resources to abatement, until the marginal social benefits are zero. The last dollar spent on pollution abatement will yield zero benefits and will have a high marginal cost. It may cost $5 million to have the last drop of water purified, but the benefit may be worth only $5.

## POLLUTION AND
## GOVERNMENT CONSIDERATIONS

Figure 3 provides a guide to government action concerning pollution abatement. If the government can indeed calculate the marginal costs and marginal benefits of pollution abatement, it can establish either regulations or incentives to achieve the optimal level of pollution abatement.

> With the **regulatory approach,** the government requires polluting agents to limit emissions to a prescribed level.

If the government regulatory agency works efficiently, it will set the level of pollution abatement at the optimal level as described in Figure 3.

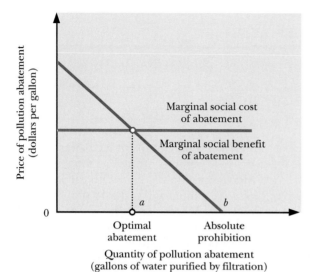

**FIGURE 3    Optimal Pollution Abatement**

This figure shows how the optimal amount of pollution abatement is determined. The marginal social benefit curve is downward sloping (people place a higher value on the first units of abatement). The marginal social cost of pollution abatement is assumed constant. The optimal amount of abatement is quantity *a* (where marginal social cost equals marginal social benefit). Point *b*, the total prohibition of pollution, is not optimal because the marginal social benefit (zero) is less than the marginal social cost.

> In the **incentive-based approach,** the government uses economic incentives or penalties (such as taxes or subsidies) to encourage polluting agents to restrict emissions.

If the regulatory agency sets its incentives properly, polluting agents themselves will be induced to select the optimal level of pollution abatement.

Figure 3 provides a standard for determining a pollution abatement strategy. However, the application of such a cost/benefit analysis presents practical problems. First, it is difficult to calculate the marginal costs and benefits of various pollution abatement activities. Some costs and benefits are apparent only over time. Pollution affects large numbers of people and different areas. Second, waste disposal involves complicated physical, biological, and chemical interactions. One abatement procedure that increases water purity may have the unintended consequence of shifting discharges to the atmosphere. Third, we must decide who should receive the benefits and who should bear the costs of pollution abatement. Should private firms pay? Should only

affected individuals pay? These decisions affect the distribution of income.

If the regulatory approach is properly applied, the government would require the polluting agent to limit emissions to the optimal level as shown in Figure 3. Each factory, for example, would have a limit on the amount of pollutants that it is allowed to discharge. Automobile manufacturers would be required to place catalytic converters on their cars and trucks; oil refiners would be required to eliminate lead from gasoline.

An incentive-based approach, on the other hand, uses economic incentives or penalties to induce polluting agents to restrict their emissions to the efficient level. Factories, for example, are charged a fee for every ton of pollutant emitted into the atmosphere. Automobile owners must pay a tax for purchasing automobiles without catalytic converters, and so on. Within the context of these incentives, we are free to make our own decisions.

## U.S. ENVIRONMENTAL POLICY

In the United States, various state, local, and federal agencies are responsible for pollution control. Since 1970, the Environmental Protection Agency (EPA), acting through the states and on its own, has been charged with regulating pollution activities. The EPA derives its legislative authority from a number of congressional acts including the Clean Air Act, the Water Pollution Control Act, the National Environmental Policy Act, and the Toxic Substances Control Act.

In enforcing federal environmental laws, the EPA has usually followed the regulatory approach. It specifies standards for waste discharge with respect to air, water, and noise pollution. It issues permits setting ceilings on the amounts of pollutants that can be discharged and requiring that the discharger meet these ceilings by a specified date using the most practical or best available technology.

It is difficult to devise regulatory controls that produce optimal abatement. The EPA usually sets discharge limits without reference to marginal costs or benefits, yet environmental policies require a balancing of costs and benefits. For this reason, the EPA has also experimented with incentive-based approaches.

Indeed, U.S. practice has demonstrated that government agencies are ineffective at devising optimal pollution abatement. The regulatory approach has been increasingly criticized for its rigidity and its high costs. Accordingly, there has been a distinct trend to-

## EXAMPLE 4
### TRADING
### POLLUTION RIGHTS

In December 1990, in an unprecedented arrangement, Metallized Paper Corporation of America bought pollution rights from USX's Clairton Works and from Papercraft Corporation in Allegheny County, Pennsylvania. Metallized Paper paid USX $75,000 for the right to emit 75 tons of pollution per year, purchased 32 tons from Papercraft, and received an additional 500-ton donation from USX. The sale of pollution rights was legal under the Federal Clean Air Act. Both USX and Papercraft Corporation possessed rights to emit a certain number of tons of pollutants into the environment up to a limit determined by the Environmental Protection Agency. By selling these rights, both agreed to cut back on their pollution emissions by the number of tons sold.

Since this initial trade in 1990, trading in pollution rights has grown into a maket managed by the Chicago Board of Trade which auctions billions of dollars of air pollution credits. Notably, the prices paid for pollution rights fell in mid 1996 to half of what they were only a year earlier. This fall in prices means that firms have learned to reduce pollution at a much lower cost. In 1996 the per ton cleanup cost was $750, down from almost $1500 a year earlier.

ward incentive-based programs, which place price tags on pollution externalities. Incentive-based programs, however, do not necessarily yield optimal abatement because of the complexity of the pollution problem and the consequent difficulty of setting appropriate price tags.

In an ideal incentive-based policy, the government controls pollutants by imposing fees—called effluent charges—that should be equal to the marginal external cost of the pollutant. Such effluent charges cause the polluting firm to consider external costs in its private economic calculations. The EPA has experimented with a number of "market solutions" to establish optimal effluent charges. Under its emissions trading program, companies are allowed to trade, or even buy and sell, pollution rights from one another. Under its bubble program, the EPA permits new pollution sources to operate if they are able to buy an equivalent reduction in pollution discharges from existing firms.

Incentive schemes reduce the costs of pollution abatement because dischargers are allowed to make their own decisions. Firms that can reduce discharges cheaply will sell their pollution rights to firms that can reduce emissions only at high costs. Even if the end result is not optimal, at least the costs of pollution control are reduced. (See Example 4.)

Incentive-based programs allow pollution reduction standards to be achieved at a lower cost of society's resources.

Although the EPA may not have been able to achieve an optimal level of pollution abatement, nevertheless achievements have been substantial. Table 1 shows that both air and water pollution have been substantially reduced since the 1970s. However, the financial resources required to achieve these reductions have been substantial. Currently, we spend more than $100 billion per annum on pollution reduction.

We do not have unlimited amounts of air and water. We need sound environmental policies to prevent their misuse. We also do not have unlimited quantities of coal, oil, and mineral resources. Do we need to worry about their exhaustion, or don't we?

## EXHAUSTIBLE RESOURCES

Externalities can cause market failure and require government action. Exhaustible resources represent another potential market failure. Government action

## Table 1    Pollution Levels in the United States

| Water Quality Pollutant | Mandated Maximum Level | Percentage of Cases Exceeding Maximum Level | |
|---|---|---|---|
| | | 1975 | 1992 |
| Fecal coliform bacteria | > 200 cells per 100 ml | 36 | 28 |
| Dissolved oxygen | < 5 mg per liter | 5 | 2 |
| Phosphorus | > 0.1 mg per liter | 47 | 2 |
| Lead | > 50 mg per liter | 42 | < 1 |
| Air Pollution Emissions | | 1970 | 1992 |
| PM-10 | 50 micrograms per cubic meter | 11.0 | 5.4 |
| Sulfur dioxide | .03 parts per million | 28.4 | 20.6 |
| Carbon monoxide | 9 parts per million | 107.7 | 79.1 |
| Lead | 1.5 micrograms per cubic meter | 199.1 | 4.7 |

Source: Statistical Abstract of the United States.

may also be necessary to prevent the exhaustion of our nonrenewable resources.

> An **exhaustible** (or **nonrenewable**) **resource** is any resource of which there is a finite amount in the long run because the stock is fixed by nature.

Examples of exhaustible resources are oil, gas, coal, titanium, gold, and other mineral resources.

## RATIONAL ALLOCATION OF EXHAUSTIBLE RESOURCES

Consider a firm that owns an exhaustible resource. It must decide how to allocate its fixed stock of the resource over time. A firm that extracts crude oil from a reservoir must decide how much to supply to the market this year, next year, 5 years from now, and 20 years from now. Will economic incentives cause it automatically to conserve on the use of this resource?

A firm extracting nonrenewable resources faces a different type of opportunity cost. In the case of renewable resources (such as trees), the decision to supply x units this year does not limit the future supply (trees can be planted). In the case of nonrenewable resources, every unit supplied this year is 1 unit not available for future years. Accordingly, suppliers of nonrenewable resources must make an *intertemporal* (across time) comparison of the costs and benefits of supplying the resource today versus supplying it tomorrow.

Let's suppose a firm can extract crude oil from a 1000-barrel reservoir at a zero marginal extraction cost (the oil simply rises by itself to the surface). For simplicity, let's also suppose that the firm must sell its entire stock of 1000 barrels within a 2-year period. The market rate of interest is 10 percent. How will this firm allocate its supply of crude oil between the 2 years? If the price of crude oil today is $20 per barrel and the price expected next year is $21.50, the firm should produce all 1000 barrels this year. By selling now, the firm gets $20 per barrel that can be invested at 10 percent interest; next year, the firm will receive $22 per barrel ($20 × 1.1), a greater return than next year's selling price of $21.50. If next year's price is more than $22, the firm should wait until next year to sell all 1000 barrels. If the price rises at the same rate as the market interest rate (in this case, by 10 percent per annum), the firm will be indifferent as to whether it sells its stock of the nonrenewable resource this year or next year. It earns the same amount of revenues.

## THE MARKET FOR EXHAUSTIBLE RESOURCES

We have looked at how a firm decides to use its exhaustible resources over time. Let's now consider a perfectly competitive market consisting of a large number of competitive firms (see Figure 4). The stock of the exhaustible resource owned by all the firms together is fixed at 30 units, and firms must sell their entire stock within a 2-year period (either in period 0 or in period 1). The market rate of interest is 10 percent.

In Figure 4, the horizontal axis is 30 units long because only 30 units of the resource are available;

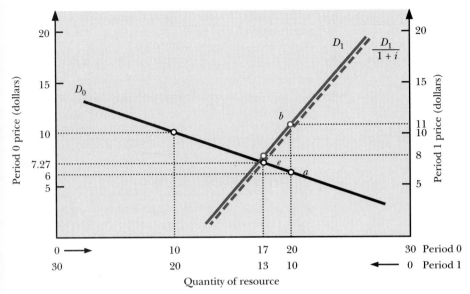

**FIGURE 4   Market Equilibrium for an Exhaustible Resource in Two Periods**

This figure represents a competitive market composed of a large number of perfectly competitive firms. The firms in the market together have a fixed supply of 30 units of the nonrenewable resource, and these 30 units must be used either in period 0 or period 1. The market demand curves are $D_0$ for period 0 and $D_1$ for period 1. (Period 1 quantity increases from right to left rather than from left to right.) Firms will contrast the price received in period 0 with the present discounted value of the price received in period 1. If the interest rate is 10 percent, $D_1 \div 1.1$ is the present discounted value of the period 1 demand curve. When the available supply is allocated between periods 0 and 1, the prices in the two periods are established. As long as the period 0 price is less than the present value of the period 1 price (as it is when the period 0 quantity is 20 and the period 1 quantity is 10), firms will reallocate supplies from period 0 to period 1. Equilibrium is attained when quantity is 17 in period 0 and 13 in period 1 and when price is $8 in period 1 and $7.27 in period 0. In equilibrium, the ratio of the price in period 1 to the price in period 0 will be 1 plus the interest rate, or 1.1.

the resource that is extracted in period 0 will not be available for period 1. The period 0 demand curve is a standard demand curve read from left to right, but the period 1 demand curve must be read from right to left. Both demand curves show what quantities are demanded in each period at various prices. Because only 30 units are available, the quantity available in period 1 is the amount left over after period 0.

The price in each period depends upon how many units are sold. If 20 units are sold in period 0 and 10 units are sold in period 1, period 0's price is $6 per unit (point *a*) and period 1's price is $11 per unit (point *b*). The individual firms will not be content with this outcome. Each unit sold in period 0 and invested at 10 percent interest is worth only $6.60 in period 1, whereas each unit sold in period 1 yields $11. Clearly, firms will want to supply fewer

than 20 units in period 0 and more than 10 units in period 1.

An equilibrium is attained when the period 0 price equals the present discounted value of the period 1 price (when the period 0 price equals the period 1 price divided by 1.1). At this point, there is no longer an incentive to switch production from one period to the other. The dashed demand curve in Figure 4 shows the period 1 prices divided by 1.1 and represents the present discounted values of the period 1 prices. The quantity where the dashed curve intersects the period 0 demand curve (at point *e*) is the equilibrium quantity. The quantity corresponding to point *e* is 17 units in period 0 and 13 units in period 1. The period 0 price for 17 units is $7.27, and the period 1 price for 13 units is $8. These prices reflect the fact that the present discounted value of $8 is

$7.27 in period 0 at a 10 percent rate of interest. At these prices, firms no longer have an incentive to shift supplies from one period to the other. Note that the price increases by 10 percent between period 0 and period 1 in this example.

> When marginal extraction costs are zero and the market is perfectly competitive, the price of an exhaustible resource will rise at the same rate as the interest rate.

## THE TECHNOLOGY OF RESOURCE EXTRACTION

Figure 4 delivers a reassuring message: Competitive markets deal automatically with the rising scarcity of exhaustible resources. The annual growth rate of the prices of exhaustible resources should equal the market rate of interest. In other words, the natural rise in the prices of nonrenewable resources should discourage their present consumption and make supplies available for the future.

We can see the long-run trend in the real price of a barrel of oil in Figure 5, which graphs the real price of oil. We cannot discern a trend in the real price of oil from the 1880s until the late 1970s, at which time the real price rose. In the 1980s and 1990s, the real price of oil fell.

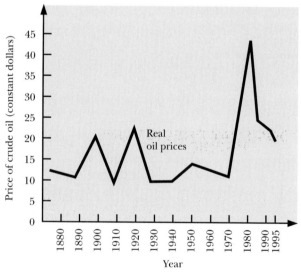

**FIGURE 5   Real U.S. Crude Oil Prices, 1880–1995**

Since 1880, overall *real* U.S. crude oil prices neither increased nor decreased significantly until the late 1970s. Since the early 1980s, the real price has been falling. *Sources:* U.S. Bureau of Mines; U.S. Bureau of Labor Statistics.

The real prices of other exhaustible resources conform even less to the theory. Since the early nineteenth century there has been a distinct *downward* trend in the real price of other exhaustible resources, such as copper, aluminum, and pig iron. Why have the real prices of exhaustible resources not risen steadily as the theory predicts? If extraction costs are falling, the price of an exhaustible resource should rise more slowly than the rate of interest.

**Technological Advances.** If technological advances allow producers of exhaustible resources to increase their recovery rates, prices would not rise at the rate of interest. In fact, if technological advances are rapid, exhaustible resource prices can even fall.

Consider a resource firm that develops a new technology enabling it to recover more of the exhaustible resource in period 1 than in period 0. For example, suppose an oil company has a total of 200 barrels underground and, with existing technology, can recover one out of every two barrels extracted in period 0. A new technology that permits the recovery of 1.5 barrels from every 2 barrels underground is scheduled to be implemented in period 1. Thus, for every barrel sold in period 0, the firm passes up the opportunity to sell 1.5 barrels (with the new technology) in period 1. The anticipation of technological advances will shift more supplies to period 1, thereby lowering the period 1 price and raising the period 0 price.

> Technological advances that are expected to take place in the future cause supplies of exhaustible resources to be shifted to the future, thereby raising current prices and lowering future prices.

**Backstop Resources.** A *backstop resource* is a close substitute for an exhaustible resource, available in virtually unlimited supply but at a higher cost. Solar energy is a backstop for conventional energy, and shale oil and tar sands are backstops for conventional crude oil.

What effect does the availability of a backstop fuel, such as shale oil, have on the allocation of crude oil and oil prices over time? Let's assume that shale oil is available in virtually unlimited supply at a price of $40 a barrel. The backstop fuel sets a price limit of $40 per barrel on conventional crude oil because consumers will switch to shale oil if the crude oil price rises above $40. With no technological advances, the price should increase by the rate of interest until the $40 backstop price is reached. After that point, the price will remain constant.

The existence of a backstop resource allows greater current consumption of the nonrenewable resource at lower current prices. Supplies of the nonrenewable resource need cover demands only up to the backstop price. As a result, more of the resource can be consumed now with the knowledge that needs in the distant future can be met by the alternative resource.

## THE PRICE SYSTEM AND EXHAUSTIBLE RESOURCES

Market forces cause nonrenewable resources to be allocated efficiently over time. As nonrenewable resources become more scarce, their price rises, and they are used more economically.

Suppliers weigh the returns from exploiting the resource now against waiting for the resource to become more scarce (and, thus, to sell for a higher price) tomorrow. Unless technological progress increases the supply of nonrenewable resources, their prices will tend to rise at the rate of interest. The fact that there is no clear trend in the relative prices of nonrenewable resources is a tribute to technological progress. As technology has improved recovery rates, we have been able to postpone the rising scarcity of nonrenewable resources.

The major threat to the rational use of nonrenewable resources is interference in the pricing of resources. If prices are controlled—for example, if price ceilings are placed on oil or natural gas—firms producing these resources will have to make resource allocation decisions on the basis of prices that do not correctly reflect scarcities today and tomorrow. In other words, price controls distort the natural balance between present and future consumption that is achieved by the price system.

## RECYCLING OF EXHAUSTIBLE RESOURCES

The price system encourages producers of exhaustible resources to sell less today in anticipation of more scarcity tomorrow. Recycling offers yet another opportunity for owners and users of exhaustible resources to be assured of a supply of the resource both now and in the future.

> **Recycling** reintroduces used exhaustible resources (such as iron, metals, and petrochemicals) into the system, providing an alternative to current production.

Recycling of exhaustible resources can occur automatically through the price system or it can be stimulated by government intervention.

Let's consider the case of mercury, an exhaustible resource in which there is an active market for recycling. Mercury is a resource that is limited in supply but is used in many products, including industrial and control instruments, batteries, and dental amalgams. It has high disposal costs because of its toxic characteristics. Currently, about 47 percent of the annual usage of industrial mercury is obtained from recycled mercury. The percentage of recycled mercury depends upon its price and disposal cost. If mercury prices rise, more mercury is recycled.

Recycling proceeds at an economically efficient level when the marginal cost of recycling equals the marginal social cost of disposal. If it costs society $200 per ton to dispose of aluminum cans and $100 per ton to recycle aluminum, too little is being recycled. Whenever the marginal private cost of disposal is less than the marginal social cost, the amount of recycling falls short of the optimum. If people do not have to bear the full marginal costs of throwing away aluminum cans, tires, used cars, or old car batteries, recycling levels will be insufficient. It is for this reason that many states and communities have passed mandatory recycling laws.

## DOOMSDAY PREDICTIONS

Can market failures, such as those discussed in this chapter, become so severe as to threaten life itself? Various doomsday models have indeed suggested that industrialization and rising living standards will one day result in worldwide disaster. We are threatened with nuclear winters, greenhouse effects, depletion of the ozone layer, and exhaustion of our natural resources.

What evidence do we have for such predictions?

First, there is no evidence that the world is running out of natural resources. (See Example 5.) Technological advances continue to improve recovery rates of exhaustible resources, and we have backstop

*Not based on Supply/Demand Economics*

## EXAMPLE 5
## DOOMSTER VERSUS BOOMSTER:
## ARE WE RUNNING OUT OF NATURAL RESOURCES?

Doomsday forecasters ("doomsters") predict that the world will run out of natural resources within the lifetime of our children or grandchildren. More optimistic economists ("boomsters") argue that markets naturally conserve exhaustible resources, as explained in the text.

In 1980, a prominent boomster, economist Julian Simon, and a prominent doomster, biologist Paul Ehrlich, entered into a $1000 bet. Simon allowed Ehrlich to select five natural resources that he thought were being exhausted. Demand-and-supply analysis suggests that if a resource is disappearing, its price will increase. Accordingly, the two decided that Ehrlich would win if the prices of the five natural resources had increased faster than inflation at the end of 10 years.

In 1990, Simon received a $1000 check from Ehrlich confirming that he had won the bet. The prices of all five natural resources declined between 1980 and 1990. More surprisingly, the prices had declined in absolute terms. Their money prices were lower in 1990 than in 1980!

resources. If the world begins to run out of a particular exhaustible resource, its relative price will rise and its consumption will be reduced.

Second, environmental pollution appears to be lessening in the advanced industrialized countries. Affluence has allowed these countries to devote scarce resources to environmental programs. In the industrialized world, air and water quality is improving, not deteriorating. (See Example 6.)

Third, scientists have little reliable data on the publicized major ecological threats to life on this earth. They cannot agree about whether the world is getting warmer or colder. They do not know whether long-term changes in the ozone layer are occurring or even whether such changes occurred before the advent of the chemical reactions (from aerosol sprays and freon, for example) that are purported to be their cause. They do not know whether radon is harmless or something to be feared.

Successful economic policy cannot be formulated without hard facts and figures. If we cannot measure costs and benefits, we are not in a position to make policy judgments.

In this chapter, we have discussed some possible arguments for government intervention. Externalities, particularly the environmental problem of waste disposal, represent legitimate cases of market failure. We also discussed how the price system handles the problem of exhaustible resources. In the next chapter, we shall examine the patterns of government spending and taxation.

## SUMMARY

1. Market failure occurs when the price system fails to produce the socially optimal quantity of a good. Externalities occur when marginal social costs (or benefits) do not equal marginal private costs (or benefits). Social efficiency requires that marginal social benefits and marginal social costs be equal, but private agents equate marginal private benefits with marginal private costs. Externalities can be internalized by redefinition of property rights, by voluntary agreements, or by government taxes or subsidies.

2. Waste disposal costs arise because modern production and consumption require disposing of residual wastes such as air pollutants, toxic chemicals, and solid wastes. Pollution problems cannot easily be solved by redefining property rights or by voluntary agreement; government intervention is typically required. In the United States, the Environmental Protection Agency (EPA) is charged with environmental protection. The EPA regulates pollution

## EXAMPLE 6
### UNDERDEVELOPMENT, NOT INDUSTRIALIZATION, CAUSES POLLUTION

Environmentalists focus on the relatively minor ecological problems of the industrialized world to show that Western materialism is the root cause of environmental evils. They emphasize the latest environmental dangers like global warming, PCBs, nuclear waste, and radon, while ignoring the more serious environmental problems of the developing world. At the Earth Summit in Rio de Janeiro in 1992, Western leaders including the United States agreed to devote billions of dollars to global warming, while ignoring the almost 8 million children who die each year from polluted air and water in underdeveloped countries.

Dangerous air and water pollution have become almost unknown in the West, but 1.3 billion people in the developing countries live in zones of dangerously unsafe air and water. Urban air pollution is much worse in Calcutta and Mexico City than in any U.S. city, including Los Angeles. The developing countries also suffer from a phenomenon unknown in the West: rural smog from burning wood, dung, and agricultural wastes. Almost 4 million children under the age of 5 have died from drinking impure water, while in the West such deaths are almost unknown. The amount of toxic water pollution in China is greater than in the whole of the Western world.

-------------------------------------------

*Source:* Gregg Easterbrook, "Forget PCB's, Radon, Alar," *New York Times Magazine*, September 11, 1994, pp. 60–64.

---

standards but in recent years, after increasing criticism of high cost, has been experimenting with incentive-based market solutions.

3. Firms that produce nonrenewable (exhaustible) resources must determine how to allocate the available fixed supply over time. When marginal extraction costs are zero, the industry is perfectly competitive, and there is no technological progress, firms will allocate the resource so that the present discounted values of the prices in each period are the same. Prices will rise at the rate of interest.

4. The prices of nonrenewable resources in general have not risen in real terms because of declining marginal extraction costs and rapid technological progress. Natural market forces should cause the efficient allocation of nonrenewable resources over time. Recycling is another means of expanding the supply of exhaustible resources.

## KEY TERMS

market failure
externalities
social costs
social benefits
internalization
property rights
optimal level of abatement
regulatory approach
incentive-based approach
exhaustible (or nonrenewable) resource
recycling

## QUESTIONS AND PROBLEMS

1. Factory A produces 1000 tons of sulfuric acid at a cost of $10,000 to produce 1000 tons. For the people in the community, the production of every 1000 tons of sulfuric acid causes an increase of $5000 in medical payments, a loss of $4000 in wages by being sick, and an increase of $1000 in dry-cleaning bills. What are the private and social costs of the 1000 tons of sulfuric acid?

2. Explain how the external costs calculated in the previous example might be internalized. Will this internalization be handled differently when there are three people harmed by the factory than when 300,000 people are harmed? In which case is government action more likely?

3. An oil producer has 100 barrels of oil that must be sold within a 2-year period. The interest rate is 10 percent, and the price of crude oil expected next year is $25 per barrel. At which prices will the oil producer sell all the oil this year? At which prices will the oil producer sell all the oil next year? What will happen if the oil producer expects an improvement in technology to increase the recovery rate (the amount of the resource that can be produced) by 10 percent next year?

4. If new cost-efficient technologies that reduce the marginal costs of pollution abatement are developed, what will happen to the optimal level of pollution abatement?

5. Does the pollution-trading concept used in recent years by the EPA solve the problem of determining the optimal level of pollution?

6. Explain why economists do not favor the total elimination of pollution.

7. It has been proposed that a worldwide tax be placed on aerosol sprays to protect the world's ozone layer. What methods would be used to determine at what rate the tax should be set?

8. In which of these three cases would it be easiest to establish property rights? First, I wish to keep stray cattle off my farm. Second, I wish to prevent the commercial jets landing at a nearby airport from disturbing my egg-laying chickens. Third, I wish to keep my neighbor from depleting the stock of fish in a lake that is shared by the two of us.

9. Many agricultural crops are harmed by beetles and other insects. These harmful insects are prey for the praying mantis, a large insect. The praying mantis is not an endangered species, but several agricultural states still impose a fine on anyone caught killing a praying mantis. Is there a good economic reason for such a fine? Explain.

10. For about 4000 years, mariners have been dumping wastes into the ocean. In many places, the ocean floor is covered with plastics, bottles, and other refuse. Explain why the market mechanism does not correct for this waste disposal problem. How might the problem be solved by internalization?

# CHAPTER 21

# GOVERNMENT SPENDING, TAXATION, AND THE ECONOMY

Is the U.S. government too big or too small? Although the Republican victory in the 1994 congressional elections may have been a reaction against "big government," this question will continue to be asked. The budget standoff between President Clinton and the Republican Congress in early 1996 was caused by differences of opinion on the size and shape of government. Liberals want more government, conservatives want less government. It is unlikely that anyone wants no government. Almost everyone agrees that there are some things that a government must do. There are some kinds of goods, called *public goods,* that private markets cannot supply. If the government must provide some goods and services, it must have the power to raise revenues through taxation.

Government affects our economic lives in a number of ways. We are particularly reminded of government on April 15 when we must file our federal income taxes. We are reminded of government when we receive our property tax statements from local government. We may be less reminded of government when we receive government services—when we drive on state or federal highways, when we enroll our children in public schools, when we see our troops in a peacekeeping mission on foreign soil, or when we file a suit in a small claims court.

We all ask: Are we getting good value out of our taxes? Does the government intrude too much on our private economic lives? Are we spending our limited public resources on the right things?

# PUBLIC GOODS

In the last chapter we considered market failures. Market failures occur when private costs and benefits diverge. The market failures described in the previous chapter were externalities, environmental pollution, and exhaustible resources. Public goods represent another and different form of market failure.

Because competitive markets undersupply or fail to supply them, public goods—such as public schools, public parks, public roads and bridges, national defense, police protection, or public health services—are generally supplied by government at no charge and are financed by taxes.

> A **public good** is a good or service whose use by one person does not reduce its use to others and whose use by nonpayers cannot be prevented.

U> Public good

The first characteristic of public goods is referred to as nonrival consumption. Their second characteristic is referred to as nonexclusion.

## NONRIVAL CONSUMPTION

If a dam is built to prevent flooding, everyone who lives in the protected flood zone benefits. Moreover, the fact that your house is protected by the dam does not reduce the protection of other homeowners. You can watch a television program without reducing the viewing of other viewers. Both are cases of nonrival consumption.

> A good is characterized by **nonrival consumption** if its consumption by one person does not reduce its consumption by others.

A classic example of nonrival consumption is national defense. If the government builds an antimissile system that reduces the likelihood of nuclear attack, everyone in the protected area benefits. The protection of one person's life and property does not reduce the protection of others.

Most goods and services are characterized by rival consumption.

> A good is characterized by **rival consumption** if its consumption by one person lowers its consumption by others.

Food and drink, cars, houses, shoes, dresses, and medical services are rival in consumption. The hamburger that you eat cannot be eaten by someone else; the house that you live in cannot be occupied by another. Some goods can be either rival or nonrival, depending on the circumstances. An uncrowded movie is nonrival; you can enjoy it without reducing any other person's consumption. A sold-out movie, however, is rival because your presence would displace another viewer. Rival goods are rationed by charging prices; only those who are willing to pay the market price can use it.

## NONEXCLUSION

The second characteristic of public goods is nonexclusion, which results when it is very costly to exclude nonpayers.

> A good is characterized by **nonexclusion** if extreme costs eliminate the possibility (or practicality) of excluding some people from using it.

Flood control illustrates nonexclusion. It is impossible to exclude nonpayers in the area protected by flood control from being protected. It would be too costly to devise a flood-control system that excludes nonpayers.

> **Exclusion costs** are the costs of preventing those who do not pay from enjoying a good.

Most goods are rival and have low exclusion costs. Goods that are rival in consumption and have low exclusion costs can be produced by private markets. Goods that are nonrival and have high exclusion costs cannot be produced by private firms. Nonpayers cannot be prevented from using the good. Figure 1 shows that goods with high exclusion costs, whether rival or nonrival, are normally provided through the government.

## FREE RIDERS VERSUS COOPERATION

A person who enjoys the benefits of a good without paying is a free rider.

> A **free rider** enjoys the benefits of a good or service without paying the cost.

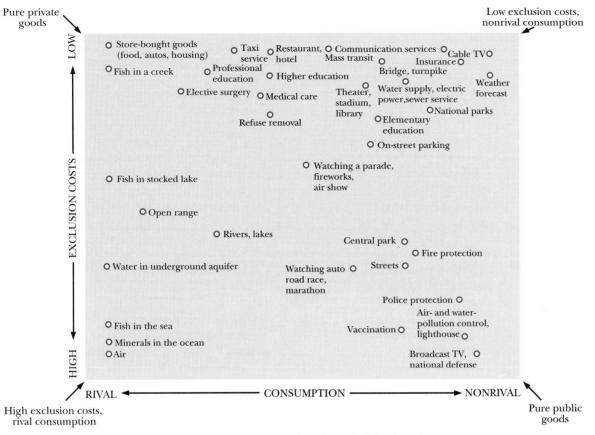

Pure private goods

Low exclusion costs, nonrival consumption

LOW

EXCLUSION COSTS

HIGH

o Store-bought goods (food, autos, housing)
o Fish in a creek
o Taxi service
o Restaurant, hotel
o Communication services
o Cable TV
o Mass transit
o Insurance
o Professional education
o Higher education
o Bridge, turnpike
o Weather forecast
o Elective surgery
o Medical care
o Theater, stadium, library
o Water supply, electric power, sewer service
o National parks
o Refuse removal
o Elementary education
o On-street parking
o Watching a parade, fireworks, air show
o Fish in stocked lake
o Open range
o Rivers, lakes
o Central park
o Fire protection
o Water in underground aquifer
o Watching auto road race, marathon
o Streets
o Police protection
o Fish in the sea
o Vaccination
o Air- and water-pollution control, lighthouse
o Minerals in the ocean
o Air
o Broadcast TV, national defense

RIVAL ←——— CONSUMPTION ———→ NONRIVAL

High exclusion costs, rival consumption

Pure public goods

**FIGURE 1   Classifying Selected Goods as Private Goods or Public Goods**

Pure private goods, in the upper left corner, are characterized by low exclusion costs (free riders can be excluded easily) and by rival consumption. Pure public goods, in the lower right corner, are characterized by high exclusion costs (free riding can't be prevented) and by nonrival consumption (one person's consumption of a good does not detract from another's consumption of it). Goods in the other two corners meet only one of the two characteristics of a public good. In the lower left corner, goods are characterized by high exclusion costs but rival consumption. In the upper right corner, goods are characterized by nonrival consumption but low exclusion costs.
*Source:* E.S. Savas, *Privatizing the Public Sector* (Chatham, NJ: Chatham House Publishers, Inc., 1982), p. 34.

Why should free riders pay for a public good if they cannot be excluded from its use? If we understand that we cannot have the good (flood control, roads, etc.) unless we cooperate, we may be able to finance the good through voluntary contributions. If there is too much free-riding, such goods will not be produced. Consider a dam that costs $2000 to build and protects a community consisting of ten people. That flood protection is worth $400 to each person. The dam is therefore worth $4000 to the 10 people, and it is worth building by charging each person $200 because its benefits ($400) are double costs ($200).

Voluntary agreement to build the dam may be difficult to reach. There is a strong temptation to be a free rider. Each person realizes that if the other nine build the dam without his or her contribution, the person can still enjoy the benefits. In this example, if six people behave as free riders, the dam will not be built by voluntary agreement; they can raise only $1600. If only four people behave as free riders, the dam will be built.

Voluntary agreements work only if the amount of free riding is not excessive.

## EXAMPLE 1
## TECHNOLOGICAL CHANGE
## AND PUBLIC GOODS

Public goods are characterized by nonexclusion. It is simply too costly to exclude free riders from enjoying the good. Technological change has made it possible to exclude free riders from enjoying a number of goods. In the old days, championship fights or special concerts were viewed in movie theaters, which were equipped to receive special cable feeds. Such events could not be carried on regular television because there was no way to exclude free riders. With the development of cable television, new scrambling technologies make it possible to exclude viewers who do not call up a special number to pay for viewing the event. Soon most households will be able to receive a television signal via their telephone line, so that viewers can au-

tomatically be charged for viewing just as they are charged for long distance phone service.

In the past, drivers on toll highways could be charged only by going through toll booths that often slowed traffic flow. Modern electronics now allows electronic scanners to charge users of toll roads by activating electronic receivers in the users' automobiles.

As technology develops, more and more goods will have low exclusion costs. One day we may all have electronic monitors on our cars, television sets, phone lines, and even on our bodies so that we can be electronically charged for the use and enjoyment of services that were previously supplied free of charge.

Despite the existence of free riding, we are able to cooperate in many cases. We make voluntary contributions to civic associations for extra police protection, most of us obey the law, and we do volunteer community work. However, if the group is large, if collective decisions are made infrequently, and if individual gains to cooperation are small, free riding will prevent cooperative behavior. If there is too much free riding, either the public good will not be produced privately or it must be produced by government.

Private markets and new technology can provide ingenious solutions for public goods. TV signals can be blocked for non-subscribers. Toll highways can charge motorists electronically through electronic sensors. (See Example 1.)

There is no simple formula for dealing with public goods. Different societies have come up with different solutions. Let's consider television. Some countries have state television monopolies, where the state provides all television programming at taxpayer expense. The rationale for this approach is that it doesn't cost us anything to add one more viewer (nonrivalry). Therefore, it is not socially optimal to exclude

non-paying viewers. But is it fair for general taxpayers who do not like television to pay for those who do. An alternative approach is pay television, made possible by technologies that allow broadcasters to block signals to nonpaying customers. With pay television, only those who watch programming pay; it excludes nonpayers even though they could watch without affecting the viewing of paying customers.

Some countries, such as the United States, have a mix of "free" network and local programming, public television, and pay television (cable, pay-per-view, and satellite dishes). Network programming is paid for by advertisers, who pay programming costs to gain access to customers. With advertising, there is no problem of forcing nonviewers to pay or excluding nonrival viewers who are not prepared to pay. Pay television excludes viewers not willing to pay even though they do not diminish the enjoyment of payers. Public television is funded largely by government to permit "quality" TV programming that does not have to attract large audiences for advertisers and because free riding limits voluntary contributions.

# GOVERNMENT SPENDING

Government spending is carried out by the 87,000 federal, state, and local governments in the United States. Government provides not only public goods but also goods that could have been provided by the private sector. Governments spend their money differently. The federal government focuses on national and international matters such as defense, international diplomacy, and a national highway system. State governments spend their funds on state universities, state highways, and the state court system. Local governments spend their funds on local schools, roads, and police protection.

Government expenditures are either exhaustive expenditures or transfer payments.

> **Exhaustive expenditures** are government purchases that divert resources from the private sector, making them no longer available for private use. **Transfer payments** transfer income from one individual or organization to another.

In 1995, the government purchased 18 percent of all goods and services. In an economy that produced $7 trillion worth of goods and services, government purchases totaled more than $1.5 trillion. Exhaustive expenditures accounted for 53 percent of total government spending (see Figure 2). The remaining 47 percent of government expenditures were transfer payments. Most transfers are made by the federal government; state and local governments make more exhaustive expenditures on goods and services than the federal government.

Transfer payments affect the distribution of income among families but do not change the amount of goods and services that are exhausted (consumed) by government. For example, the Social Security program transfers income from currently employed workers to retired or disabled workers. The federal government transfers funds to state and local governments.

*\Know Definition (SSA)*

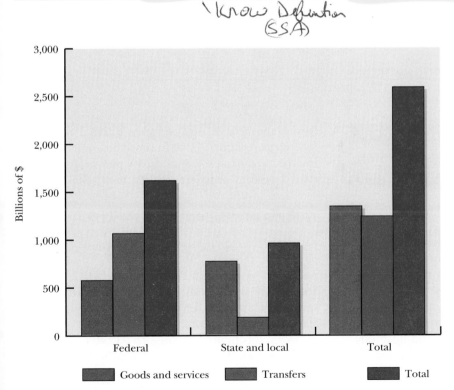

**FIGURE 2   Government Spending 1995 Exhaustive and Transfer Payments**

Government spending is for goods and services or for transfer payments.
*Source: Statistical Abstract of the United States.*

## Table 1   How the Government Spends Money
### (per capita expenditures, 1995)

| | Federal | State and Local |
|---|---|---|
| **By Function** | | |
| Defense | $1210 | 0 |
| Education | $113 | $1383 |
| Public welfare | $202 | $653 |
| Health and hospitals | $130 | $373 |
| Highways | $4 | $282 |
| Police protection | $28 | $146 |
| Fire protection | 0 | $60 |
| Corrections | $9 | $121 |
| Natural resources | $218 | $52 |
| Sewerage and sanitation | 0 | $137 |
| Housing and community development | $68 | $72 |
| Government administration | $71 | $213 |
| Parks and recreation | $8 | $67 |
| Interest on general debt | $845 | $234 |
| Insurance trust expenditure | $1925 | $382 |
| Intergovernmental | $787 | $15 |
| Utility and liquor store expenditures | 0 | $357 |
| Total | $6445 | $5781 |
| **By Character** | | |
| Current operations | $2119 | $3486 |
| Capital outlays | $394 | $570 |
| Assistance and subsidies | $409 | $140 |
| Interest on debt | $845 | $274 |
| Insurance trust expenditures | $1926 | $382 |

*Source:* Statistical Abstract of the United States.

Total government expenditures in 1995 accounted for 35 percent of the total output of the U.S. economy. The ratio of total government expenditures to total output is a common measure of the economic scope of government.

Table 1 tells us what we get from government spending. The federal government spends almost $6500 annually for every man, woman, and child. State and local governments provide most of the government services that are so important to our daily lives, like education, police, sewage and sanitation, parks and recreation, and fire protection. The federal government provides a significant portion of government spending on education, welfare, and hospitals, but its most significant spending items are for defense, interest on the national debt, and for social security. The federal government spends more on welfare assistance and subsidies than do state and local governments.

Federal, state, and local governments all spend for social infrastructure—buildings, highways, equip-ment, laboratories, and so forth. Table 2 shows that federal government expenditures on human and infrastructure capital equal $250 per capita, or less than 5 percent of federal government spending.

## TRENDS IN GOVERNMENT SPENDING

Government expenditures have increased at a rapid pace over the past 70 years. In 1929, government purchases of goods and services were $112 billion; in 1995, they were $940 billion (both figures in constant 1987 prices). In 1929, the government purchased $924 worth of goods and services per capita. By 1995, this figure had risen to $3790 per capita (in 1987 prices). Government expenditures rise with population growth and with the growth of the economy. The most relevant yardstick is the ratio of total government spending to total output (see Figure 3). In 1890, government expenditures accounted for 6.5 percent of total output, but by 1995 this ratio had risen to 35 percent. An increase in the government

| Table 2   Federal Government Human and Capital Investment, Per Capita (per capita dollars, 1995) | |
|---|---|
| **Human investments** | |
| Young children | $32 |
| Education | $37 |
| Work force investments | $26 |
| Subtotal | $95 |
| **Infrastructure** | |
| Transportation | $116 |
| Water treatment | $11 |
| Water resources | $7 |
| Subtotal | 134 |
| Total | $229 |

*Source: Statistical Abstract of the United States.*

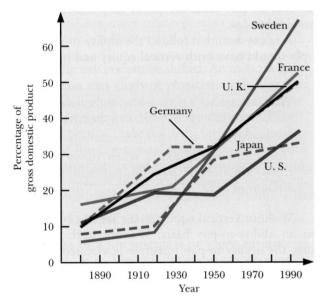

**FIGURE 3**   **Total Government Spending as a Percentage of GDP, U.S. and Other Countries, 1890–1992**

The ratio of total government expenditures to total economic activity (or GDP) is a better measure of the changing role of government than measures of government spending alone. *Source: World Development Report 1991* (Oxford: Oxford University Press, 1991), p. 139. Figures updated by authors.

share has characterized other industrialized countries, as Figure 3 shows as well.

The economic role of government, especially of the federal government, has increased because government has increasingly taken responsibility for health, education, and welfare. The Industrial Revo-

lution (a Defining Moment in economics) created a need for more government services. A modern and complex economy requires more government services than rural societies—sanitation, police protection, traffic control, water supplies, legal systems.

Government's claim on resources has also increased because government is less efficient than the private sector. It has proven easier to increase productivity in the private sector than in the public sector. Hence, price increases have been more rapid in the public sector. Since 1950, prices paid by government to purchase goods and services have increased at roughly double the rate of private goods. Whereas private businesses must earn a profit to survive, the public sector is financed by taxpayer dollars. There is therefore less incentive to provide the public service efficiently.

The growing power of special-interest groups and lobbyists also increases government spending. Special interests have made it increasingly difficult to control government spending. (See the next chapter for further discussion of special-interest groups, logrolling, and vote trading.)

## SPENDING BY FEDERAL, STATE, AND LOCAL GOVERNMENTS

Government economic activities are distributed among federal, state, and local governments. Each society must determine at what level of government public services—roads and public education, for example—should be provided. There has been intense debate over these issues since the founding of this country. The 1996 debate over balancing the federal budget and transferring authority back to the states is a continuation of this longstanding debate. Many citizens think that the federal government is too remote and too powerful and that the states and localities have too little power.

In 1995, the federal government (not including spending from grants in aid to state and local governments) accounted for 60 percent of all government expenditures, while state and local government accounted for the remainder. The dominance by federal government is a fairly new phenomenon. In 1932, state and local government accounted for almost 70 percent of government expenditures, and, as late as 1940, state and local government still accounted for one-half of all government revenues and expenditures. World War II dramatically altered the

the extra hours, economic efficiency has been reduced because fewer goods and services are being produced than without the tax.

Many tax reformers favor lowering marginal tax rates to encourage greater work effort. Lower marginal tax rates raise the output of goods and services, thereby improving economic efficiency.

## TAXES AND SOCIAL GOALS

Many people believe that the tax system should be an instrument of social policy. Because we respond to marginal tax rates, the tax system can be used to cause us to engage in desirable behavior. If we wish to promote private home ownership, we offer tax incentives to buy homes. If we wish to encourage marriage, we tax married couples at lower rates. If we wish to encourage risk taking or innovation, we give tax breaks to those who earn income through innovation and risk taking.

Taxes affect economic decision making. The challenge to politicians and tax authorities is to devise a tax system that minimizes the efficiency losses of taxes while moving society in the direction of desirable social goals.

Taxes can have many unintended consequences. Taxes intended to raise government revenues may actually lower them. Taxes intended to "soak the rich" may be paid by the poor. Taxes on employers end up being paid by employees.

## THE U.S. TAX SYSTEM

The U.S. tax system consists of a variety of federal, state, and local taxes. The federal government obtains most of its revenues from individual income taxes and Social Security contributions (see Figure 4). Corporate income taxes and sales taxes (excises, customs, and duties) account for a small percentage of the total. Over the past 40 years, the structure of federal revenues has changed substantially. The revenue share of the personal income tax has remained fairly constant, near 40 percent, but the shares of corporate income taxes and of sales taxes have dropped considerably. The share of Social Security contributions has risen considerably (from about 12 percent in 1955 to more than 40 percent today).

The financing of state and local governments has also changed over the past 40 years (see Figure 4). The share of sales taxes has declined somewhat, but there has been a notable drop in the share of property taxes and a notable rise in the share of state income taxes. Local and state governments have become more dependent upon transfers from the federal government.

## THE FEDERAL INDIVIDUAL INCOME TAX

As Figure 4 shows, the personal income tax is the single most important source of revenue for the federal government. The current federal income tax system is the result of countless changes, reforms, and revisions. (See Example 2.)

The U.S. federal income tax is administered by the Internal Revenue Service. The personal income tax is levied on taxable income according to tax rates set by Congress. In 1995, taxable income was taxed at four rates: 15 percent, 28 percent, 34 percent, and 36 percent. A fifth rate in the form of a 10 percent surcharge was applied to high-income families. (See Table 3.)

> **Taxable income** is the income that remains after all deductions and exemptions are subtracted. Taxes are levied on taxable income.

We are allowed to take itemized deductions (medical and dental expenses, state and local taxes, mortgage interest, and charitable contributions), standard deductions for each family member, and deductions for contributions to retirement accounts. Because of these various deductions, our taxable income averages only 65 percent of our gross income.

Since 1970, various tax reforms (particularly the 1986 tax reform) lowered marginal tax rates. In 1970, the marginal tax rate for a family earning $75,000 per year was 56 percent. In 1993, the marginal tax rate for that same family was 34 percent. The trend toward lower marginal rates was reversed in 1993 when marginal tax rates were raised. In 1996, Congress began serious consideration of reducing tax rates again.

The federal income tax serves as an instrument of social policy. By allowing charitable contribution deductions, the tax system encourages families to

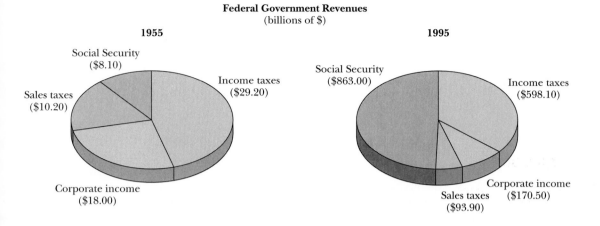

Federal Government Revenues
(billions of $)

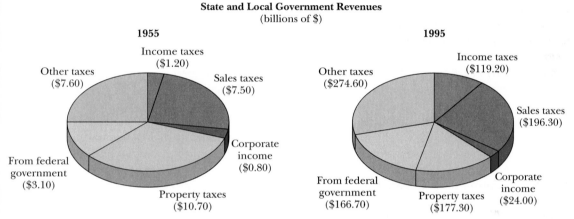

State and Local Government Revenues
(billions of $)

**FIGURE 4  Sources of Government Revenue: Federal and State and Local Governments, 1955 and 1995**

The federal government's two main sources of revenue are income taxes and contributions to Social Security. The major increase in federal government revenues since 1955 has been in Social Security contributions. State and local governments get their revenues from sales taxes, other taxes, property taxes, and from the federal government. The major change since 1955 has been the reduction in the share of property taxes and the rise in the share of federal transfers. *Source: Statistical Abstract of the United States.*

give to charities. By allowing interest deductions on home mortgages, it encourages home ownership. By allowing deductions for contributions to retirement programs, it induces workers to save for retirement.

## THE FEDERAL CORPORATE INCOME TAX

U.S. corporations are subject to a federal tax on their profits, called the federal corporate income tax. As Figure 4 shows, the share of the corporate income tax of total federal tax revenues has been declining

over the years, accounting for about 10 percent in the mid-1990s.

Critics of corporate income taxes argue that corporations pass corporate taxes forward to consumers. Although voters may think that the tax burden of corporations is rising, this opinion may be purely illusory. We are all paying in the form of higher prices.

Corporate profits that are distributed to stockholders as dividends are taxed twice: once as corporate income and again when stockholders pay taxes on their dividends. Many tax specialists have argued

## EXAMPLE 2
## THE U.S. INCOME TAX:
## A BRIEF HISTORY

In 1913, the Sixteenth Amendment to the U.S. Constitution authorized the federal government to levy a personal income tax. Prior to World War II, the personal income tax was not a major source of federal government revenue. In the 1930s, it accounted for 14 percent of federal revenues. In the 1920s and 1930s, the tax rate on an income of $100,000 (the equivalent of more than $1 million today) was 25 percent. During World War II, tax rates were raised. By 1948, the personal income tax accounted for 40 percent of all federal revenue.

The United States entered the postwar era with high personal tax rates. The tax rate on $200,000 and above was 91 percent. Tax rates of this magnitude were unacceptable; therefore, various tax reforms were passed that altered the personal income tax system in three directions. First, tax rates were reduced. By 1970, the tax rate on the lowest income bracket was 20 percent, and the tax rate on the top income bracket was 75 percent. The tax reform of 1981 lowered rates to a range of 11 to 50 percent.

The second direction of tax change established numerous deductions and exemptions from taxable income—interest earned on bonds of state and local governments (so-called *tax-exempt bonds*), contributions to retirement programs (such as Keogh accounts), taxes paid to state and local governments, medical expenditures, and charitable contributions.

The third direction of tax change was to use the personal income tax to promote economic or social goals. Tax credits for investments in equipment (the investment tax credit) were used to encourage capital formation. The deduction of certain forms of savings (such as in retirement accounts) encouraged savings. Mortgage-interest deductions encouraged home ownership.

These changes made the federal income tax extremely complex. Its critics argued it gave too many tax loopholes to the rich and that its high marginal tax rates discouraged hard work and risk taking.

In September 1986, Congress passed, and President Reagan signed, the Tax Reform Act of 1986. The number of tax rates was reduced from fourteen to three. The top tax rate was lowered from 50 percent to 34 percent. Tax rates were partially adjusted for inflation. Many low-income families were removed from the tax rolls. Deductions, exemptions, and exclusions from income were restricted to make up for the lower tax rates.

The trend toward lower tax rates was reversed with the Omnibus Reconciliation Act signed by President Clinton in 1993, which raised to 36 percent the tax rate for individuals earning $115,000 or married couples earning $140,000 or more. A fifth tax rate of 39.6 percent was placed on families earning $250,000 or more.

With the election of a Republican Congress in 1994, sentiment grew for tax reductions, more favorable treatment of capital gains, and the eventual introduction of a flat tax. As the 1996 presidential campaign began, the Republican presidential contenders favored either a flat tax or substantially lower tax rates.

against the double taxation of corporate profits, and some propose only one tax on dividends.

### SOCIAL SECURITY AND PAYROLL TAXES

Founded in 1935 during the Great Depression (a Defining Moment), the Social Security Program is fi-

nanced by a payroll tax. Unlike the individual income tax, under which families below a certain income level are not taxed, Social Security payroll taxes are paid starting with the first dollar of earnings. In 1996, the payroll tax was 19.7 percent of the first $72,600 of earnings, of which the employer paid 60 percent and the employee 40 percent. A worker earn-

| Table 3   Tax Rate Schedules, 1995 Income Taxes | | | |
| --- | --- | --- | --- |
| *If taxable income is:* | | | |
| *Over* | *But not over* | *Tax payment* | *Of the amount over** |
| $0 | $39,000 | 15% | $0* |
| $39,000 | $94,250 | $5,850 + 28% | $39,000* |
| $94,250 | $143,600 | $21,320 + 31% | $94,250* |
| $143,600 | $256,500 | $36,619 + 36% | $143,600* |
| $256,500 | — | $77,262 + 39.6% | $256,500* |

The above rates are for married couples filing jointly.
*Source:* Internal Revenue Service, 1995, 1040, p. 53.

ing $15,000 per year pays $1,182 in payroll taxes (and the employer pays $1,773). Because the tax is imposed only on the first $72,600, a person earning $500,000 pays the same tax as one earning $72,600.

Social Security payroll taxes finance the Social Security retirement, health, and disability programs. The Medicare program that subsidizes medical care for the elderly is also part of the Social Security system.

Current recipients of Social Security can look forward to receiving more in benefits than they contributed to government taxes. Young people, however, do not face such a bright prospect. With the graying of America, there will be fewer and fewer working-age people to support the retirement income of older Americans. It is for this reason that changes in the Social Security system must be made in the near future. In fact, most young Americans do not believe that they will eventually get back what they put into their Social Security taxes or get back anything at all! Although it is politically difficult to reduce Social Security benefits, experts tell us that, within a decade, payments into the system will not be sufficient to pay benefits, as they currently exist.

## STATE AND LOCAL GOVERNMENT REVENUE SOURCES

State and local governments rely on revenues different from those utilized by the federal government. They earn revenues primarily from sales taxes and property taxes. State and local governments also operate utilities, sanitation departments, and liquor stores, from which they earn fees. The major change in state and local revenues over the past 40 years has been the growing importance of state income taxes and the declining importance of property taxes. As of 1996, only seven states—Alaska, Florida, Nevada, South Dakota, Texas, Washington, and Wyoming—did not have a state income tax. The decline in the

share of property tax is explained by the tax revolt against property taxes in the 1970s and 1980s.

## IS THE U.S. TAX SYSTEM PROGRESSIVE?

The fraction of income paid by taxpayers who earn different amounts of income determines whether the tax system redistributes income. A tax can be either proportional, progressive, or regressive.

> With a **proportional tax,** each taxpayer pays the same percentage of income as taxes.
>
> With a **progressive tax,** the percentage of income paid as taxes increases as income increases.
>
> With a **regressive tax,** the percentage of income paid as taxes decreases as income increases.

The federal income tax is progressive. Families with higher incomes pay higher tax rates. Sales taxes are regressive because wealthy families spend a smaller portion of their income than do poor families. Suppose a family with $40,000 of taxable income spends $20,000 and saves the rest, while a family with $10,000 taxable income spends the full $10,000. Each pays a 5 percent sales tax; the higher-income ($40,000) family pays sales taxes of $1000, or 1/40 of its income, while the lower-income ($10,000) family pays sales taxes of $500, or 1/20 of its income. Although the poor family spends fewer dollars on sales taxes, it pays a larger percentage of its income.

When progressive income taxes are combined with regressive sales taxes, is the overall U.S. tax system regressive, proportional, or progressive? The answer depends on the measurements of the incidence of taxation. Experts have fundamental disagreement on how the burden of taxes is distributed among different income groups because, to answer this question, we must know the extent to which taxes are shifted.[1]

# PROPOSALS FOR FEDERAL TAX REFORM

Our system of federal taxation has evolved over the years through a series of tax reforms, legislative amendments, and court interpretations.

Specialists have recommended a number of reforms of the tax system to make it more efficient or equitable.

## TAX CONSUMPTION

Personal taxes are normally levied on personal income. The higher the earnings, the higher the income tax payments. Numerous distinguished economists and social thinkers have favored the taxing of consumption rather than income for two reasons. First, if we are taxed according to what we take out of production (consumption) rather than according to what we put in (saving), we would gain a larger stock of capital. We could reduce our taxes by saving more; hence, savings and capital formation would rise. Second, expenditures are a more accurate measure of a household's permanent spending power or ability to pay taxes than is current income.

Consumption taxes are typically collected as sales taxes. The value-added tax (or VAT) that is widely used in Europe is a consumption tax. Although sales taxes are regressive, consumption taxes can be made progressive. For example, taxpayers could be taxed on their income minus savings (which would equal their consumption), using progressive tax rates.

[1]For classic studies of the progressivity of the U.S. tax system see Joseph Pechman and Benjamin Okner, *Who Bears the Tax Burden?* (Washington, DC: The Brookings Institution, 1974); Joseph A. Pechman, *Who Paid the Taxes, 1966–85?* (Washington, DC: The Brookings Institution, 1985); Edgar K. Browning and William R. Johnson, *The Distribution of the Tax Burden* (Washington, DC: American Enterprise Institute, 1979); Edgar K. Browning, "Pechman's Tax Incidence Study: A Note on the Data," *American Economic Review,* 76 (December 1986): 1214–1218.

## ELIMINATE CORPORATE INCOME TAXES

The earlier chapter on business organization showed that corporations are useful devices for raising capital. Many economists argue that taxing corporate income reduces the social gains of the corporation. Currently, corporate profits are taxed twice, once as corporate income taxes and then as dividends in personal income taxes. Corporations can avoid the second tax by reinvesting their profits in the corporation. The double taxation of dividends thus dams up billions of dollars of investment funds inside corporate treasuries and encourages reinvestment in the corporation itself. Eliminating the tax on corporate dividends would allow these funds to be used for other purposes.

## IMPOSE A FLAT TAX

Advocates of a flat tax call for everyone earning above an agreed-upon poverty level to pay the same tax rate (say, 20 percent). No deductions or exemptions from income would be allowed. Wealthy taxpayers would pay the same tax rate as middle-income taxpayers, but they would lose their tax loopholes. Because we would all pay the same tax rate (which would be kept low), there would be less unproductive tax-avoidance, and we would go about the business of earning money, not avoiding taxes.

## TAX *REAL* CAPITAL GAINS

When we sell stocks, bonds, or other assets for more than their purchase price, we earn a capital gain.

> A **capital gain** occurs whenever assets such as stocks, bonds, or real estate increase in market value over the price paid to acquire the asset.

The capital gain is "realized" when the asset that has risen in value is actually sold, thereby creating the gain. Prior to the 1986 tax reform, capital gains were taxed at considerably lower rates than ordinary income to encourage risk taking and innovation. Since 1986, capital gains have been taxed at about the same rate as other forms of income.

When a capital gain is realized on the sale of an asset that has been held for a period of time, much of the gain may have been eaten up by inflation. If a stock that has been held for 10 years is sold at a price 50 percent higher than the purchase price but inflation over that same period has also been 50 percent, there is no real profit after inflation. For this reason, experts favor taxing only real capital gains—capital gains in excess of the inflation that has occurred over the period during which the asset has been held.

## INDEX FOR INFLATION

When individuals whose earnings have been raised by inflation are pushed into higher tax brackets, their real income after taxes can be reduced. Indexing prevents inflation from pushing taxpayers into higher tax brackets.

> **Indexing** is the tying of tax rates to the rate of inflation.

With indexation, tax rates are lowered with inflation to prevent the taxpayer's real income after taxes from falling. (Real income is income after adjustment for inflation.) Let's say that the Jones family pays $5,000 in income taxes on its income of $25,000 (a tax rate of 20 percent) and has $20,000 after taxes. A 10 percent inflation raises the Jones family income to $27,500. At $27,500, however, the tax rate is 22.5 percent, and the Jones family pays $6,188 in income taxes and has $21,312 after taxes. After adjustment for inflation, the Jones's $21,312 is worth less than the original $20,000. With indexation, tax rates would automatically fall to ensure that inflation does not lower after-tax income. (See Example 3.)

## GOVERNMENT SURPLUSES AND DEFICITS

Governments collect revenue primarily through taxes; they purchase goods and services and make transfer payments. Like households and businesses, governments can spend more or less than their income. The government budget surplus or deficit shows the relationship between government revenue and outlays.

> A **government budget surplus** is the excess of government revenues over government outlays.

> A **government budget deficit** is the excess of government outlays over government revenues.

Governments that run deficits typically use deficit financing.

> **Deficit financing** is government borrowing in credit markets to finance a government deficit.

If a government borrows over a number of years to finance its deficits, it accumulates a government debt.

> The **government debt** is the cumulated sum of outstanding IOUs that a government owes its creditors.

Government debt is reduced by running a surplus. If the government debt is $100 billion and government runs a $10 billion surplus, its debt would be reduced to $90 billion.

Government finances differ from household and business finances in one important respect: Governments can make up the difference between expenditures and revenues by printing money. The financing of deficits through the printing press has been used by governments to pay for wars and for costly government programs.

Figure 5 shows federal, state and local budgets, surpluses, and deficits. The total government deficit is less than the federal deficit because state and local governments tend to have surpluses. Since 1950, the federal government has run surpluses in only 5 years. In 1950, the federal debt was $257 billion—only 3 percent of today's debt. Today, the federal debt is more than $4 trillion.

## HOW BIG SHOULD GOVERNMENT BE?

Many of us think that the government is too large. How do we determine what is "too large" or "too small"? One way is to look at the government's role in our economy in international perspective. Compared to other affluent countries, is our government relatively large or small?

Figure 6 shows that the role of government in our economy is actually smaller than that in other affluent countries. Its role is particularly small when compared with the welfare states like Sweden or Germany. Our tax burden is relatively low, the percent of output we spend on government is relatively low. (See Example 4.)

How big a role government should play is a decision that must be made by democratic societies at

## EXAMPLE 3
## TAX REFORM PROPOSALS

With 1996 a presidential election year, numerous proposals for tax reform have been advanced. This example considers the effects of three such proposals on families earning $20,000, $50,000, and $200,000 per year. The three proposals are the flat tax, the Unlimited Savings Allowance (USA) tax, and the National Sales Tax. All examples are for a family with two children, with one in college. The family with $20,000 annual income does not own a home or have income from investments. Numbers in parentheses indicate a refund from the government. The popularity of the flat tax was shown by the appeal of the Steve Forbes candidacy for the Republican nomination in the winter of 1996.

### Current Income Tax

|  | | | |
|---|---:|---:|---:|
| Adjusted gross income | $20,000 | $50,000 | $300,000 |
| Personal exemptions | 9,800 | 9,800 | 0 |
| Standard or itemized deductions | 6,350 | 9,823 | 47,836 |
| Taxable income | 3,850 | 30,377 | 252,164 |
| Tax | (355) | 4,557 | 76,162 |

### Flat Tax

*Sponsored by Representative Dick Armey, R-Tex.*

| | | | |
|---|---:|---:|---:|
| Wages and salaries | $20,000 | $46,623 | $189,267 |
| Pension and retirement benefits | 0 | 0 | 0 |
| Total compensation | 20,000 | 46,623 | 189,267 |
| Less personal exemption and allowances | 29,650 | 29,650 | 29,650 |
| Taxable income | 0 | 16,973 | 159,617 |
| Tax (at 20 percent) | 0 | 2,885 | 27,135 |

### Unlimited Savings Allowance (U.S.A.) Tax

*Sponsored by Senators Pete Domenici, R-N.M., and Sam Nunn, D-Ga.*

| | | | |
|---|---:|---:|---:|
| Adjusted gross income | $20,000 | $49,463 | $295,061 |
| Less: | | | |
|   Personal exemptions | 9,600 | 9,600 | 9,600 |
|   Family allowance | 6,950 | 6,950 | 6,950 |
|   Home mortgage deduction | 0 | 4,429 | 21,582 |
|   Charitable contribution deduction | 250 | 746 | 6,532 |
|   Higher education deduction | 2,000 | 2,000 | 2,000 |
|   Net deductible savings | 0 | 1,979 | 35,407 |
| Taxable income | 1,200 | 23,759 | 212,990 |
| Tax | (2,234) | 2,584 | 77,208 |

### National Sales Tax

*Sponsored by Representatives William Archer, R-Tex., and Richard Lugar, R-Ind.*

| | | | |
|---|---:|---:|---:|
| Payroll tax | $1,530 | $3,567 | $4,636 |
| Charity | 250 | 746 | 6,532 |
| Mortgage interest | 0 | 4,429 | 21,582 |
| State and local tax | 0 | 4,648 | 19,722 |
| Savings | 0 | 1,979 | 35,407 |
| Taxable spending | 16,220 | 34,631 | 212,121 |
| Federal tax at 18 percent | 3,280 | 6,234 | 38,182 |
| Credit | 900 | 900 | 900 |
| Total tax | 2,380 | 5,334 | 37,282 |

*Source:* Adapted from the *New York Times*, September 3, 1995, p. F6.

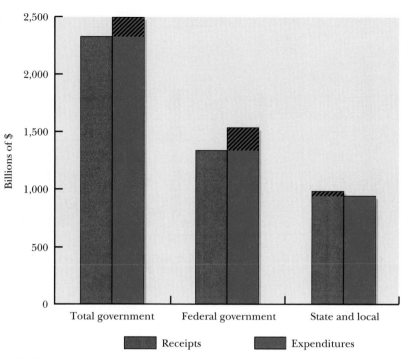

**FIGURE 5   U.S. Government Budgets, 1995**

Federal government expenditures exceeds revenues by the amount of the rectangle in hatch marks, which represents the federal deficit. The fact that state and local revenues slightly exceed expenditures shows that they ran a small surplus. The deficit of total government is therefore less than the federal deficit by the amount of the state and local surplus.

*Note:* The hatch-marked areas are government deficits and surpluses.

*Source: Statistical Abstract of the United States.*

the ballot box. Once a country decides that it has allowed government to play too large a role, voters can reverse this process. In recent elections, for example, Swedish voters reacted against the overwhelming role of government. Voters in the United Kingdom for almost 15 years have supported policies of a conservative government designed to reduce the role of government through privatization of public enterprises and reductions in tax rates. The Republican victory in the 1994 congressional elections was a reaction against "big government."

Voters decide on the scope of government. We must decide whether education, health, postal services, sanitation services, electricity, and other goods and services are to be provided by government or by private enterprise. We must decide whether our children should be educated by private or public schools, whether we should entrust government or private health providers with our health problems, or

whether prisons should be operated by private or public providers.

Irrespective of the market in which they operate, private firms are motivated to produce at minimum costs and they produce goods and services whose benefits outweigh their costs. If a company spends $20 to produce a good that buyers are willing to purchase only for $15, it cannot stay in business. It will fail the market test. Private goods must pass a market test that their benefits (as measured by the price customers are prepared to pay) exceed their costs.

Government does not have to pass this market test. In fact, in the next chapter we shall discuss why government goods are often produced at costs that outweigh benefits. This is no accident. If the federal government runs the postal service, there is no requirement that it make a profit. Losses will automatically be covered by taxpayers. Postal employees can

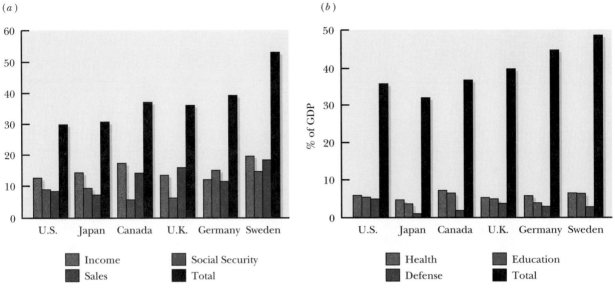

**FIGURE 6   Relative Size of Government**

Panel (*a*) shows that the relative share of taxes as a percent of GDP is smaller in the United States than in other highly industrialized countries. Panel (*b*) shows that the relative share of government expenditures as a percent of GDP in the United States is also small relative to other highly industrialized countries. Both tables show the different distributions of tax revenues and of expenditures. *Source: Statistical Abstract of the United States.*

be paid high salaries. If the city education department runs the public schools, there is no requirement that public education be provided at a reasonable cost or at an acceptable quality. In fact, the actual providers of the service (administrators and teachers) decide on standards, services, and costs. If a state health department supplies the community with medical care, it will determine how and in what form medical services are to be provided.

Government provision of goods and services is very different from private provision. With private provision, "the customer is king." The customer can simply put a company out of business by not buying the product. With public provision, such safeguards do not prevail. The parent dissatisfied with local public schools cannot put them out of business. The customer of the federal post office cannot put it out of business by not sending mail, although we can increase its deficit by using Federal Express. Only in our roles as voters can we exercise control over publicly provided goods.

The particular danger of government deficits is that they allow government to pass the costs of government programs to future generations. Balanced government budgets at least create pressure to limit spending to programs whose benefits at least equal costs. Politicians know that taxes are unpopular. Having to balance the budget would also pressure government to provide goods and services at a reasonable cost. Being able to pay for government by deficit financing allows politicians to place the burden of payment on future generations.

In the next chapter we shall assess how well we voters are able to exercise control over the goods and services provided by government.

## SUMMARY

1. Public goods have two characteristics: First, the consumption of the good by one user does not reduce its consumption by others (nonrival consumption), and second, no one can in practice be prevented from using the good (nonexclusion).

2. Government expenditures are either exhaustive expenditures or transfer payments. Exhaustive expenditures divert resources to the public sector. Transfer payments affect the distribution of income. Government spending rose from 10 percent of GDP in the late 1920s to 34 percent in the mid 1990s.

## EXAMPLE 4
### THE U.S. TAX SYSTEM
### IN INTERNATIONAL PERSPECTIVE

To what degree is the U.S. tax system typical of the tax systems of other industrialized countries? The accompanying table shows that taxes as a percentage of total output are relatively low in the United States, compared with other industrialized countries. With the exception of Japan, other industrialized countries collect more tax revenues out of each dollar of income than the United States does. Payroll tax rates for Social Security are also lower in the United States than in the other industrialized countries (except the United Kingdom and Canada).

The United States relies less on sales taxes than the other industrialized countries (with the exception of Japan) and more on income and profit taxes. The other countries rely on a combination of social security taxes and sales taxes, the most prominent of which is the VAT mentioned in the text.

### The U.S. Tax System in International Perspective

|  | Tax Revenues as a Percentage of Total Output (1) | Percentage Distribution of Tax Receipts (2) | | |
|---|---|---|---|---|
|  |  | Income Tax (a) | Social Security (b) | Sales Taxes (c) |
| United States | 29.8 | 43.1 | 29.7 | 16.9 |
| Canada | 34.0 | 46.1 | 13.2 | 30.1 |
| France | 44.0 | 17.4 | 43.3 | 29.4 |
| Italy | 37.1 | 35.7 | 33.3 | 28.0 |
| Japan | 31.3 | 47.3 | 29.0 | 12.6 |
| Netherlands | 48.2 | 27.9 | 42.5 | 25.9 |
| Sweden | 55.3 | 43.9 | 25.1 | 24.2 |
| United Kingdom | 37.3 | 37.5 | 18.5 | 31.2 |
| Germany | 37.4 | 34.2 | 37.4 | 25.2 |

*Source: Statistical Abstract of the United States, 1995, Comparative International Statistics.*

Expenditures shifted away from local government and toward state and federal government.

3. There are two competing principles of fairness in taxation. One is that taxes should be levied according to benefits. The other is that taxes should be allocated on the basis of ability to pay. If the ability-to-pay principle is used, the tax system should have both vertical and horizontal equity.

4. A neutral tax system does not influence production, consumption, and investment decisions. Neutral taxes are almost impossible to devise. Other taxes do affect economic efficiency. The challenge is how to devise a tax system that moves the economy in a socially desired direction without severe losses of efficiency. Taxpayers are presumed to base their economic behavior on marginal tax rates.

5. The U.S. tax system blends personal income taxes, corporate income taxes, sales and property taxes, and payroll taxes collected by the federal, state, and local governments. The federal tax system has changed over the years from high tax rates combined with liberal exemptions, deductions, and credits to lower tax rates for both individual and corporate income taxes. The tax reform of 1986 lowered tax rates for both persons and corporations and eliminated many tax loopholes that had previously eroded the tax base. The tax reform of 1993 raised tax rates for higher-income families. There is disagreement as to whether the overall U.S. tax system is progressive or proportional.

6. Suggestions to change the current tax system include taxing consumption instead of income, eliminating the corporate income tax, taxing real capital gains, indexing for inflation, and levying a flat tax.

7. Publicly provided goods are not subject to a market test. Deficit financing allows government to pass the burden of payment for government programs to future generations.

## KEY TERMS

| | |
|---|---|
| public goods | marginal tax rate |
| nonrival consumption | average tax rate |
| rival consumption | taxable income |
| nonexclusion | proportional tax |
| exclusion costs | progressive tax |
| free rider | regressive tax |
| exhaustive expenditures | capital gain |
| transfer payments | indexing |
| benefit principle | government budget |
| ability-to-pay principle | surplus |
| vertical equity | government budget |
| horizontal equity | deficit |
| incidence of a tax | deficit financing |
| neutral tax | government debt |

## QUESTIONS AND PROBLEMS

1. Explain why a tax on Japanese cars (to be paid by Japanese manufacturers) may end up being paid by someone else.

2. Explain the different principles of fairness in taxation. Why can't the benefit principle simply be applied to all taxes?

3. What is meant by vertical and horizontal equity in a tax system?

4. Mr. Jones has a taxable income of $25,000. He pays a tax of $5,000. Ms. Smith has a taxable income of $50,000. How much tax would Ms. Smith have to pay for the tax system to be
   a. Proportional?
   b. Progressive?
   c. Regressive?

5. Evaluate the validity of the following statement: "A tax on shoe sales that requires the dealer to pay a $2 tax on every pair of shoes sold should not be of concern to consumers because the dealer has to pay the tax."

6. Define the marginal tax rate.

7. Explain double taxation of corporations.

8. Why is there a trade-off between equity and efficiency in any tax system?

9. When Jones's taxable income increases by $1000, Jones's income tax increases by $200. What is Jones's marginal tax rate?

10. Explain why a consumption tax would likely result in a higher national saving rate rather than a higher income tax.

11. Proponents of flat taxes maintain that flat taxes are more fair than the existing tax system. How can they make this argument when both high-income and low-income taxpayers would pay the same rate under a flat tax?

12. The state of Michigan hires an assistant professor to teach at one of its state universities. The state of Michigan pays an unemployed automobile worker $500 in unemployment compensation out of state funds. Which transaction is an exhaustive expenditure? How will the two transactions differ in their effect on resource allocation?

13. Which of the following taxes satisfies the benefit principle? Which satisfies the ability-to-pay principle?
   a. A gasoline tax
   b. A progressive income tax
   c. A general sales tax
   d. A special levy on a community to build a dam

14. Is the Social Security payroll tax progressive or regressive? Explain your answer.

# CHAPTER 22

# PUBLIC CHOICE

A distinguished politician once said that democracy is a flawed system, but society has yet to invent anything better to replace it. Television and the press provide endless accounts of corruption, of costly programs that benefit narrow special interest groups, of vote trading in smoke-filled rooms. These instances lead us to question whether public choices are indeed being made in the best interest of the majority. Consider the following example:

Every year, the Commodity Credit Corporation (CCC) of the federal government buys from 5 to 10 percent of the milk produced in the United States to remove it from the market. The CCC buys enough milk to keep its price from falling below limits set by Congress. Expert testimony shows that the government's dairy price supports cost consumers an extra 50 cents a gallon plus their share of the annual quarter billion dollar cost of the program to taxpayers. Insofar as millions of dairy consumers are hurt by the program and only 200,000 dairy farmers are helped, we would expect elected representatives to vote against the dairy subsidy. In fact,

the dairy subsidy has always passed Congress with a substantial vote majority.

The congressional victories of the dairy farmers show how a small group of persons who stand to gain a great deal from a government program can muster more votes than a much larger, diverse group who each stand to lose a relatively small sum as consumers or taxpayers. The dairy cooperatives collect substantial political contributions by withholding contributions from the checks sent to farmers for selling their milk. The cooperatives then make sizable contributions to congressional candidates, including those running in big cities who have no dairy producers in their districts. One congressman from a large city had the distinction of being the fifteenth-highest recipient of dairy money. Statistical evidence shows a strong correlation between dairy money and voting for the dairy subsidy program.

In this chapter we shall discuss how elected officials make public spending decisions. We shall see that majority-rule voting can result in inefficient public choices.

375

## COST/BENEFIT ANALYSIS OF GOVERNMENT ACTIVITY

The rule that guides the private sector's economic decision making has been repeated throughout this book: *Any economic activity should be carried out as long as its marginal benefit exceeds or equals its marginal cost.* The profit-maximizing firm expands its production to the point where marginal costs and marginal revenues are equal. It carries out investment projects as long as the rate of return exceeds the interest rate. We established in an earlier chapter that such decisions are economically efficient if carried out in a competitive market with no externalities.

The efficiency rule for the public sector would be the same as that for the private sector, except that it compares the marginal benefits and marginal costs to those of *society*. A government project that yields $10 million in benefits while costing $5 million is worth undertaking. A project that yields $50 million in benefits while costing $200 million should not be undertaken.

> The optimal amount of government spending is that amount at which the marginal social costs and marginal social benefits of the last public expenditure program are equal.

Even if public officials agree to base all public expenditure decisions on such cost/benefit analysis, they would find it difficult to assess social costs and benefits. Consider a proposed dam that will benefit down-river communities with better flood control and cheaper electricity but will displace long-time residents or threaten an endangered species of fish with extinction: What cost/benefit price tags should we use? In society at large, there are substantial differences of opinion on costs and benefits.

The benefits may go to one group, and costs to another group. Unless the people who pay the costs are somehow compensated—which seldom occurs—the government program entails a redistribution of income.

In the private sector, the market provides safeguards to prevent costs from exceeding benefits. If private firms produce a product whose benefit (as reflected in its market price) is less than its cost, the firm will incur losses. In the long run, it will either go out of business or switch to products that yield a benefit equal to or greater than cost.

The market test ensures that private goods and services yield a benefit equal to or greater than their cost.

Goods provided by government are not subject to this market test. There is no guarantee that public expenditures will yield benefits equal to or greater than cost. In the rest of this chapter, we shall consider how public expenditure decisions are made. Cost/benefit analysis provides an alternative framework for evaluating the efficiency of public choices in the absence of a market test. (See Example 1.)

## UNANIMITY: THE IDEAL WORLD

In an ideal world, government would work so well that everyone would unanimously approve its actions. A perfectly working price system also achieves a type of unanimity. The price system is *efficient* when it is impossible to make anyone better off without hurting someone else. An efficient economic system makes as large a pie as possible; to give one person a larger piece is to give someone else a smaller piece. An *inefficient* economic system is one in which the pie could be made larger without hurting anyone. Unanimity characterizes a good price system. When two people engage in voluntary exchange, they are unanimous in agreeing to the deal because it makes them both better off.

A turn-of-the-century Swedish economist, Knut Wicksell, suggested that the public analogue to the private market is unanimity.

**Unanimity** is when all voters agree on or consent to a particular government action.

Under certain circumstances, government action can reflect the voluntary and unanimous actions of each individual. Let's use the example of a community where everyone knows everything about everyone else. In such a community, unanimous collective decisions are not difficult. The community is considering a flood-control project, a pure public good because it is nonrival and no community member can be excluded from its benefits. The market will fail to provide it; the community must therefore decide how much flood control to produce.

In the community, each person's demand schedule for flood control is known to everyone else. Sup-

# EXAMPLE 1
## WHY ZERO-TOLERANCE DRUG PROGRAMS DON'T WORK

The U.S. government follows "zero-tolerance" drug enforcement, which means that arrests are authorized for possession of even very small quantities of illegal drugs. Under this program, a number of boats have been seized in which a fraction of an ounce of marijuana or cocaine were found. Enforcement rules in effect prior to 1988 set minimum possession limits for arrests and impoundment of property.

Law enforcement officials complain that zero-tolerance programs are economically inefficient. Law enforcement resources are limited; they cannot be stretched to apprehend all drug abusers and dealers. Minimum possession rules encourage law enforcement officials to pursue only drug dealers or large users. The marginal social benefits to a big drug bust are much larger than those of apprehending a small consumer of illegal drugs. The marginal social costs of arresting small drug users far exceed the social benefits. Without rules setting minimum possession limits, law enforcement resources will not be efficiently allocated.

Zero-tolerance programs present yet another example of unintended consequences. The intent of zero-tolerance is a drug-free society. The reality, however, has been to divert law enforcement resources away from major suppliers.

---

pose the community consists of individuals A, B, and C. Figure 1 shows their three demand schedules. The demand curve $D_A$ shows A's marginal valuation of flood control at different amounts. (The quantity of flood control is measured by the height of a dam. A higher dam provides a larger "quantity" of flood control.) In Figure 1, the hundredth foot of a dam is worth $1 to A. Because flood control is characterized by nonrival consumption, the same amount of flood control is available to A as to B or C irrespective of the height of the dam. According to the three demand schedules, A's marginal valuation is $5, B's is $1, and C's valuation is $6 at one hundred feet. The vertical height of each person's demand curve at each quantity of flood control is his or her marginal valuation at that quantity. The community's *total* marginal valuation of the hundredth foot of a dam is thus $12 ($1 + $5 + $6). When consumption is nonrival, the total demand curve is the *vertical sum* of each of the individual demand curves.

The market demand curve for a nonrival (public) good is the *vertical* sum of each individual's demand curve. (Recall for contrast that the market demand curve for a rival good is the *horizontal* sum of all the individual demand curves.)

The optimal quantity of flood control in Figure 1 is a 100-foot dam because the $12 marginal social cost (MSC) of this quantity of flood control (which, for simplicity, we assume to be constant) equals marginal social benefits.

In this three-person community, an optimal result (unanimity) can easily be attained. The government knows the demand schedules of all three citizens and simply taxes them according to their marginal valuations. Thus A is required to pay $1 per unit of flood control; B and C pay $5 and $6 per unit, respectively. The tax paid by each exactly matches the benefits they receive. If such taxes were imposed, citizens would vote unanimously for a 100-foot dam's worth of flood control. Each is getting his or her money's worth.

In the real world, governments do not have enough information to operate on the basis of unanimity. If the individual demand schedules for a public good are not known, some voting process other than unanimity must be used. The costs of discovering the government expenditure/tax program

# EXAMPLE 2
## THE MEDIAN-VOTER RULE
## AND SCHOOL DISTRICT BUDGETS

The median-voter hypothesis states that the preferences of the median voter will dominate in single-issue elections, like public school financing referenda.

Studies of finance referenda in Michigan and New York school districts confirm that the actual level of spending per pupil is very close to that preferred by the median voter. However, a study for Oregon school districts reveals that the level of spending exceeds that desired by median voters. If Oregon voters vote against the school board proposal, spending reverts automatically to a very low level. Thus Oregon school boards can propose a high level of spending, yet the me-

dian voter will approve because of the undesirable alternative. In Michigan and New York, if the school board's proposal fails, the school budget reverts to the status quo. In this case, the median voter is free to vote against school spending programs that are higher than desired.

------------------------------------------------

*Sources:* Radu Filimon, Thomas Romer, and Howard Rosenthal, "Asymmetric Information and Agenda Control," *Journal of Public Economics* 17 (February 1982); Randall Holcombe "An Empirical Test of the Median Voter Model," *Economic Inquiry* 18 (April 1980); Robert Inman, "Testing Political Economy's *As If* Proposition: Is the Median Voter Really Decisive?" *Public Choice* 33 (1978).

or costs (−) to each farmer from building these access roads at the public expense.

Because the $6 cost is shared equally, building each road has a $2 cost per farmer. Roads built for B or C do not benefit A at all. But a road built for B gives B a net benefit of $5, as the gains from the road

are worth $7 and B's share of the cost is only $2. If a road is built for C, B and A do not benefit, but C gains a net benefit of $5.

According to majority rule, if an access road for B is proposed, farmers A and C will vote against it; similarly, an access road for C will be defeated by A and B. Majority rule without logrolling causes the defeat of such special interest legislation.

But farmers B and C will each perceive that they can gain by voting for the other's access road. If farmers B and C link their votes, both roads will be built, and farmer A will have to shell out $4 in taxes for the two roads for which he gains no benefits. Farmers B and C each receive a net gain of $3 (= $7 − $4) from building both roads.

Logrolling's effect on economic efficiency depends on the circumstances. In this example, building both roads yields a social benefit of $14 at a cost of $12, for a net social benefit of $2; each road brings benefits of $7. Without logrolling, the roads would not have been built.

But logrolling can also result in inefficiencies (see Table 2). Suppose each road yields benefits of only $5 each to farmers B and C instead of $7. If farmers B and C link their votes, each must pay out $4 ($2 for each access road). Because the benefit to B and C

| Table 1 Building Access Roads for Farmers B and C: Benefits Exceed Costs | | |
|---|---|---|
| Beneficiaries | Net Benefit (+) or Cost (−) of Access Road for B (dollars) | Net Benefit (+) or Cost (−) of Access Road for C (dollars) |
| A | −2 | −2 |
| B | +5 | −2 |
| C | −2 | +5 |
| Society | +1 | +1 |

In this example, access roads cost $6; these costs are shared equally by each farmer ($2 each). But each access road is worth $7 to the affected farmer. Building both roads is socially efficient in this case because total benefits ($14) exceed cost ($12). Under simple majority rule without logrolling, and voting on each road separately, neither road is built, because the *number* of voters benefiting does not exceed the number of voters who do not benefit. However, if farmers B and C link their votes (if both vote for both roads), then both roads can be built and society benefits.

| | Table 2 Building Access Roads for Farmers B and C: Costs Exceed Benefits | |
|---|---|---|
| Beneficiaries | Net Benefit (+) or Cost (−) of Access Road for B (dollars) | Net Benefit (+) or Cost (−) of Access Road for C (dollars) |
| A | −2 | −2 |
| B | +3 | −2 |
| C | −2 | +3 |
| Society | −1 | −1 |

In this case, access roads still cost $6 each, and cost is still shared equally by all three farmers. But each access road is worth only $5 to the affected farmer. Building the roads is socially inefficient in this case. Under simple majority rule without logrolling, neither road is built; but when farmers B and C link their votes, both roads are built even though the benefits to the two farmers do not exceed the costs to society.

($5 each) exceeds their cost ($4 each), it is still worthwhile to them to logroll. Two roads are approved for a benefit of $10 but at a cost of $12, for a net social benefit of $2.

Table 2 demonstrates that majority rule with logrolling can reduce the size of the total economic pie in that the majority shift the cost of the public good to the minority. As a voter you can get what you want and have someone else pay. Thus, it is highly likely that majority-rule voting will result in more government spending than is optimal. As Nobel laureate James Buchanan and coauthor Gordon Tullock stated,

> There is nothing inherent in the operation of [a majority voting] rule that will produce "desirable" collective decisions. . . . Instead, majority rule will result in an overinvestment in the public sector when the investment projects provide differential benefits or are financed from differential taxation.[1]

## THE PARADOX OF VOTING

Majority rule can cause policy inconsistencies. Governments pass minimum-wage laws that create unemployment, and then create job-training programs to put people to work. Governments raise the cost of

[1]James Buchanan and Gordon Tullock, *The Calculus of Consent* (Ann Arbor: University of Michigan Press, 1962), p. 169.

| Table 3 Policy Rankings | | | |
|---|---|---|---|
| Policy | Voter A | Voter B | Voter C |
| Alpha | First Choice | Third Choice | Second Choice |
| Beta | Second Choice | First Choice | Third Choice |
| Gamma | Third Choice | Second Choice | First Choice |

food to the poor through farm price supports and then give them food stamps. Governments fight inflation and then put a tax on imports that raises the prices of foreign goods.

We can better understand these inconsistencies by analyzing an example. Let's suppose that three voters (A, B, and C) must vote on three policies (Alpha, Beta, and Gamma). The Alpha policy redistributes income to voter A, Beta redistributes income to voter B, and Gamma redistributes income to voter C. Table 3 describes how voters A, B, and C rank these policies. Naturally, the first choice of each voter is the policy that benefits him or her. But each voter also has preferences for the other policies as well. Voter A, for instance, might like voter B more than voter C. Hence, the Beta policy is A's second choice, and Gamma policy is A's third choice. Table 3 shows that voter B prefers Gamma to Alpha and that voter C prefers Alpha to Beta.

Every policy in this example is one person's first choice, another's second choice, and a third persons' third choice. The table is perfectly symmetrical in this respect. Only two issues are voted on at a time. In a contest between policies Alpha and Beta, voter C determines the outcome because A and B vote for their own policies. Because voter C prefers Alpha to Beta, the Alpha policy wins.

Table 4 shows the three possible contests and outcomes. In each contest, a different policy wins. No one policy wins more than one contest. If someone witnessed only the first two contests and realized that Alpha was preferred to Beta and Beta to Gamma, logic would suggest that Alpha should be preferred to Gamma. However, the third row of Table 4 shows that Gamma is preferred to Alpha. Majority rule has resulted in an inconsistent outcome. If the second and third choices of just one of the voters are reversed, however, the paradox disappears.

> The **paradox of voting** is that majority rule can yield inconsistent social choices. Even if each voter is perfectly rational, the majority of voters can choose *a* over *b*, *b* over *c*, and then choose *c* over *a*.

| Table 4   Possible Contests and Outcomes | |
| --- | --- |
| *Contest* | *Winning Policy* |
| Alpha versus Beta | Alpha |
| Beta versus Gamma | Beta |
| Alpha versus Gamma | Gamma |

## THE POLITICAL MARKET

The political market consists of voters, politicians, political parties, special interest groups, and government bureaucracy. How does each group affect the public choices made by democratic governments?

### VOTERS

After an election, journalists and television commentators frequently bemoan the difficulty of motivating people to vote. The decline in voter turnout in the U.S. presidential elections from 1960 to the 1994 election has led observers to conclude that there is considerable voter apathy.

What motivates us to vote? Objectively, there is a marginal cost (in time and effort) of voting. The probability of any single person's vote deciding an election is close to zero. According to one study,[2] most people vote out of a sense of obligation and duty, but important determinants of voter turnout are the cost of going to the polls and the closeness of the election. If we expect a close election, the chances of our voting are larger. We make a cost/benefit calculation when we decide whether to vote. The benefit is the knowledge that we have performed our civic duty; this benefit increases with closer elections.

Do we make informed decisions when we go to the polls? Anthony Downs called the lack of information-gathering on the part of the voting public rational ignorance.[3]

> **Rational ignorance** is a decision not to acquire information because the marginal cost exceeds the marginal benefit of gathering the information.

[2]O. Ashenfelter and S. Kelly, Jr., "Determinants of Participation in Presidential Elections," *Journal of Law and Economics* 18 (December 1975): 695–733.

[3]Anthony Downs, *An Economic Theory of Democracy* (New York: Harper and Row, 1957).

In an earlier chapter on information costs we concluded that we gather information as long as the marginal benefits exceed the marginal cost. The cost of acquiring information is greater for public choices than for private choices because public programs are more complicated and the link between voting and the benefits received is very uncertain. Hence, most people know much more about private choices than public ones. This public ignorance is a rational response to the costs of information.

### SPECIAL-INTEREST GROUPS

The major implication of rational ignorance is that voters know much more about legislation that affects them than about legislation that affects someone else. Special interest groups can take advantage of rational ignorance (See Example 3.)

> **Special interest groups** are minority groups with intense, narrowly defined preferences about specific government policies.

In this type of situation, vote trading among politicians can result in special-interest legislation that is economically inefficient.

### POLITICIANS AND POLITICAL PARTIES

President John F. Kennedy was fond of quoting the mother who wanted her offspring to grow up to be president but did not want a politician in the family. We somehow expect politicians to behave on a higher or more altruistic level than we do. When politicians act just like anyone else or worse, we are disappointed in their low moral character.

The successful politician is a political entrepreneur who determines government policies by voting and logrolling. Like a private entrepreneur who stays in business by offering consumers what they want, the political entrepreneur can stay in office only by offering a record that will attract enough votes at election time. The rewards of reelection are many: popularity, power, prestige, and increased income opportunities. Politicians may be more interested in getting votes than in serving the public interest. Even if they are completely unselfish, politicians cannot serve society unless they are reelected.

Given that most voters are rationally ignorant about the complex policies a particular politician supports, a vote-maximizing politician can put to-

## EXAMPLE 3
## SPECIAL INTEREST LEGISLATION:
## ETHANOL

Archer Daniels Midland (ADM) is an agricultural conglomerate that processes and sells agricultural commodities, producing, among other products, oil, seeds, flour, biochemical animal foods, ethanol, and pasta. ADM is headed by a hard-charging chief executive officer, well known as a Washington insider and major campaign contributor to both political parties.

ADM is the major producer of ethanol, a clean-burning fuel made from corn. Under current federal regulations, automobile gasoline must contain a certain percentage of ethanol. This single regulation boosts the demand for ADM's ethanol, thereby raising its price, and allowing ADM to make monopoly-like profits from its ethanol division.

The public argument for the ethanol additive sounds convincing—to create a cleaner-burning fuel. The unstated argument for ethanol is that it is good for ethanol producers. ADM every year mounts a massive lobbying campaign to promote its interests. The result of this lobbying, the requirement for an ethanol additive in gasoline, raises gas prices to the consumer less than one cent, but it creates enormous benefits for one company.

gether a package of policies in support of special-interest legislation that benefits a minority but hurts the majority. Each member of each minority will benefit enormously while each member of the majority will be hurt only a small amount. The politician can thereby attract enough support from a coalition of minority groups to win. The politician who opposes all the special-interest legislation would probably be looking for a job after the next election.

> The central problem of public choice is that the benefits of government policies are highly concentrated while the costs are highly diffused.

Restricting Japanese car imports makes the American automobile manufacturer and automobile worker better off. The costs of import restrictions, however, are distributed over the entire population in such a subtle fashion that we cannot distinguish between the increase in the price caused by import restrictions and that caused by other factors. The French economist Frederick Bastiat referred to *what is seen* and *what is unseen*. What is seen is the fact that auto firms and workers are better off with import restrictions; what is unseen is that the price of automobiles is higher for everyone.

## BUREAUCRATS

Besides assorted lobbyists and pressure groups, another actor on the political stage is the much-maligned bureaucrat.

> A **bureaucrat** is a nonelected government official responsible for carrying out a specific, narrowly defined task.

A bureaucracy is needed to run the government programs enacted by politicians. Bureaucrats tend to be the experts (e.g., social scientists, lawyers, and accountants) who execute the programs.

Bureaucracies tend to produce budgets that are too large. In private firms, profit seeking provides the incentive to minimize costs. If the firm's resources are not allocated efficiently, profits will disappear and the firm will go out of business. In bureaucracies, there are few incentives to minimize costs; instead, bureaucrats may maximize "personal profits" in the form of plush offices, large staffs, or unnecessary "inspection" trips.

Because of their rational ignorance, taxpayers do not even know which bureaucrats run their offices efficiently. Because of *their* rational ignorance, elected politicians cannot monitor the large budgets they must approve. Legislators, who must be concerned with thousands of different programs, get their information from bureaucrats. The bureaucrat has an enormous information advantage over the typical legislator. Because bureaucrats are interested in expanding their budget, government budgets tend to be larger than necessary.

## PROPOSALS FOR GOVERNMENT REFORM

Most economists and voters believe that government has grown too large. The 1986 Nobel Prize–winner James Buchanan has argued that constitutional limits must be imposed to constrain the inherent tendency of government to overexpand;

> Modern America confronts a crisis of major proportions in the last decades of the 20th century. In the seven decades from 1900 to 1970, total government spending in real terms increased 40 times over. . . . The point of emphasis is that this growth has occurred, almost exclusively, within the predictable workings of orderly democratic procedures.[4]

We now understand those forces—special interests, vote trading, and rational ignorance—that increase the size of government. Public spending in support of particular groups or industries such as agriculture or steel is in the public interest, these groups argue.

Not everyone thinks government has grown too large. Anthony Downs has pointed out that the voter will usually underestimate the *benefits* (not just the costs) of fully justifiable government expenditures because they are remote and uncertain. In Downs's view, a fully informed voter would vote for larger budgets.

Modern public choice theory suggests that, regardless of the size of government, substantial failures exist in the way public choices are made. The preferences of everyone, from the on-line worker to the captain of industry, should be duly registered when public choices are made. Currently, however, the median voter dominates, logrolling allows the

passage of special-interest legislation, and voters are rationally ignorant about the costs and benefits of government programs. Thus, as Buchanan has argued, there is constant pressure for the government to engage in economically inefficient activities. Experts have proposed a variety of reforms to make government more responsive to individual preferences, including the following[5]:

1. Elected officials should be subject to term limits so they can devote themselves to making the right decisions rather than worrying about reelection. Term limits also motivate them to think like private citizens and not professional politicians.

2. A three-fourths majority should be required for some types of legislation (particularly obvious special-interest legislation, such as tariffs, price supports, minimum-wage laws, and loans to bankruptcy-prone firms).

3. Decisions on major spending or taxation proposals should be made by direct majority voting by the general public.

4. Whenever possible, public expenditures should be replaced by market-type allocation. Prisons, schools, library, and garbage collection should be handled by private companies that are able to provide the service more efficiently.

5. All new expenditure programs should be linked to a visible tax increase.

6. Members of Congress should be determined by a process of random selection from the general public.

7. More public expenditures should be handled locally where there is competition among communities. As economist Charles Tiebout pointed out, voters can "vote with their feet as well as the ballot box." Households, Tiebout observes, are not frozen in particular localities but can instead shop around for the bundle of public goods and taxes that most closely approximates their demands for local public goods, such as parks, police protection, roads, zoos, and schools.[6] Con-

---

[4]James M. Buchanan, *The Limits of Liberty* (Chicago: The University of Chicago Press, 1975), p. 162. Chapter 9 of Buchanan's book contains compelling reasons why governments can get too large.

[5]The proposals are given in E. Browning and J. Browning, *Public Finance and the Price System,* 3rd ed. (New York: Macmillan Publishing Co., 1987).

[6]Wallace E. Oates, "On Local Finance and the Tiebout Model," *American Economic Review* 71 (May 1981): 93–98.

## EXAMPLE 4
## ELECTRONIC BULLETIN BOARDS
## AS POLITICAL WATCHDOGS

The Republican Congressional victory in 1994 brought forward new proposals on how to control special-interest legislation. Members of the new Republican majorities have made the following proposals:

1. A system of electronic bulletin boards should be created of all pending legislation, so that the public at large could see whether a piece of legislation contained special-interest provisions.
2. Parties that stand to be injured by special-interest legislation, such as consumer groups,

dairy consumers, automobile buyers, and so forth, will automatically have the opportunity to testify against special-interest legislation.
3. Spending bills must be passed by a supermajority (three-fifths) as opposed to a simple majority.

It remains to be seen whether the Republican majority will act like politicians and succumb to special-interest groups. With personal computers linked to modems in a growing number of households, electronic bulletin boards are becoming a more realistic option.

sumers thus have some discretion over their consumption of public services. The competitive aspects of the provision of public services may stimulate local officials to try to minimize costs and respond to consumer tastes.

8. There should be increased public information on legislation including electronic bulletin boards to inform the electorate.

These reforms attempt to address the problems of rational ignorance, logrolling, and the overrepresentation of special interests.

## DEMOCRACIES AND ECONOMIC EFFICIENCY

Democracy is the best political system we have. Compared to its alternatives—dictatorships of the right or the left—majority rule looks good, despite the problems we have discussed in this chapter.

The previous section identified a number of reforms, which, if enacted, would improve public choice in democratic societies. If increased public understanding of the abuses was combined with the desire of elected officials to be reelected, public officials would shun their support of special-interest legisla-

tion. If all democratic decision making were to take place in the full light of day, elected officials would be less likely to vote for special-interest legislation. (See Example 4.)

## SUMMARY

1. Cost/benefit analysis suggests that government spending should be carried to the point where marginal social benefits and marginal social costs are equal. Cost/benefit analysis could serve as a substitute for the market test that private goods must pass.
2. The government must make resource allocations because the market fails to allocate public goods efficiently. In an ideal world, all government actions would have the unanimous support of all citizens. Unanimous collective decisions, however, require perfect information. Governments would have to price public goods according to each individual's marginal valuation of the good. Unanimity is virtually impossible in the real world.
3. The most popular alternative in democratic societies is majority rule. Under majority rule, the median voter decides on public goods. Social choices therefore do not reflect the relative intensities of preference of different voters. Majority rule does

not guarantee that the socially optimal amount of the public good will be produced.

4. Majority rule creates "paradoxes of voting" in situations involving more than one decision. By forming vote-trading coalitions, beneficiaries of public goods can create majorities that would not have been possible otherwise.

5. The political market consists of voters, politicians, political parties, special-interest groups, and the government bureaucracy. Voters use personal cost/benefit analysis in their voting decisions; they vote when the perceived costs are low and the perceived benefits are high. Voting decisions are characterized by *rational ignorance*. The costs to most voters of acquiring information on complex public issues are high, and the benefits are low. For special-interest groups, however, the benefits are high relative to the costs of acquiring information. Politicians must adopt policies that will improve their chances of re-election. The fact that voters are rationally ignorant and do not understand the effects of many government policies encourages special-interest legislation.

6. Economic analysis indicates that government undertakes many programs for which the marginal social benefits do not exceed the marginal social costs, or that government fails to undertake many programs for which the marginal social benefits exceed the marginal social costs. Suggestions to improve public choices include term limits, supermajority voting on special-interest legislation, direct voting on major issues, privatization, and a shift toward local spending and taxation.

## KEY TERMS

unanimity
majority rule
median voter
logrolling
paradox of voting
rational ignorance
special-interest groups
bureaucrat

## QUESTIONS AND PROBLEMS

1. What factors limit unanimity on political decisions?
2. In the course of political contests (for example, between the primary and the general election), some politicians switch their positions. Is this fact consistent with the theory of the role of the median voter in majority-rule elections? Why or why not?
3. If people are rational, how can public choice result in government actions with benefits that are less than the costs?
4. Explain why government bureaucrats would be less interested in cost minimization than would managers of private firms.
5. Do you think government is more or less efficient than a competitive enterprise? Is it more or less efficient than private monopoly? Explain.
6. Do you think lobbying promotes or reduces the general welfare? Explain.
7. How would you reform the political process to make majority rule work better?
8. Evaluate the validity of the following statement: "The more localized are public goods, the more likely it is that unanimity about them can be achieved in public choices."
9. A balanced-budget amendment narrowly missed being passed by Congress in 1994. How would you justify such an amendment in terms of the concepts used in this chapter?
10. How can majority rule be inefficient? Does inefficiency mean majority rule should not be used?
11. Must logrolling result in economic inefficiency? Explain.
12. Bob prefers apples over bananas and bananas over oranges. Maria prefers oranges to apples and apples to bananas. Sam prefers bananas to apples and apples to oranges. If majority rule is used to choose among these goods, does voting paradox arise?
13. Would a world with zero information costs have economic inefficiency in the provision of government services?

14. Art, Bob, and Charlie own a lake in Wisconsin that they use for recreational purposes. A proposed mosquito abatement program will benefit all. Art places a value of $1, Bob places a value of $19, and Charlie places a value of $100 on a mosquito-free environment. If approved, the program would cost each owner $35.

a. What decision would be reached under majority rule? Would the result be efficient?
b. What decision would be reached if Art, Bob, and Charlie would engage in costless negotiation? Could unanimity be achieved?

# PART V

# GROWTH AND FLUCTUATION

# CHAPTER 23

# MACROECONOMICS: GROWTH AND CYCLES

Adam Smith wrote in *The Wealth of Nations* that an invisible hand would keep economies on an even keel. By pursuing our own selfish interests, we would unwittingly work in the interests of society. For more than a century and a half after Adam Smith, economists applied the same principle to the economy as a whole—to the macroeconomy. We would not have to worry about there being too little employment or too little spending. Whatever the economy could produce from its available resources would be bought. There would be jobs for those who were willing and able to work.

Now, more than 200 years after the publication of *The Wealth of Nations,* people have been conditioned to think differently. We are warned of the constant danger of too little spending. We are told it is "good for the economy" when holiday buying is strong or that increased defense spending is necessary to prevent mass unemployment. Instead of being happy about advances in technology that increase productive capacity, we worry about there not being enough money to buy all these additional goods and services. We view increases in the working-age population or in immigration not as opportunities to produce more output but as more competition for fewer jobs.

The Great Depression shifted the focus of economics that had existed since the Industrial Revolution from production to spending—from the long run to the short run. In this chapter, we shall consider the reasons for this change in thinking and whether this change is appropriate.

## MACRO VERSUS MICRO

We know from Chapter 2 that *microeconomics* concerns the behavior of individual firms and households in the marketplace using the basic analytical tools of supply and demand. Its focus is on individual decision making. *Macroeconomics* concerns the economy "as a whole." Its basic analytical tools are aggregate demand and aggregate supply, which we shall consider in detail in later chapters. Macroeconomics explains why unemployment rises or falls, why inflation accelerates or slows down, why the total output of goods and services grows, why interest rates rise or fall, and what policies should be pursued by both government and business to reduce inflation, limit unemployment, or raise economic growth.

Families and businesses know that macroeconomic conditions affect their lives. At times, business activity is strong. Jobs are plentiful, incomes are rising, and the output of goods and services is expanding at a healthy pace. We are optimistic about the future. At other times, business activity is weak. There are many job seekers but few jobs. The output of goods and services ceases to expand or may even contract.

Macroeconomics concerns the "big issues" in economics: growth, inflation, unemployment, interest rates, and deficits. It deals with those issues that cause the public the most concern. (See Example 1.) Macroeconomics is a much younger field of economic study than microeconomics, and as such has more unanswered questions.

This is the major area of controversy: Can individuals and businesses acting in their own interest cause the economy to grow and prosper and to limit inflation and unemployment? Or, must we look to government to solve these problems for us? If we look to government to provide growth, prosperity, price stability, and full employment, how great is the danger that government will select the wrong policies? Is macroeconomics subject to unintended consequences whereby well-intentioned policies only make the problem worse?

## WHICH IS MORE IMPORTANT: GROWTH OR THE BUSINESS CYCLE?

The Industrial Revolution began the process of sustained economic growth for Great Britain, Western Europe, and the United States. For the first time in history, economic output grew in a long-run *sustained* fashion at a rate more rapid than population. The result was massive and sustained increases in prosperity and living standards throughout the industrialized world.

Growth in economic output has not been uniform. During some periods, output grew rapidly; during other periods, output grew slowly or even fell. During periods of falling output, shrill warnings were to be heard that "prosperity had come to an end" and that "our children have nothing to look forward to." Such warnings were then forgotten as the economy resumed its advance to ever-higher plateaus. For more than 100 years, each downturn was followed by an upturn that soon erased its losses. Optimism was particularly high during the expansion of the 1920s.

Then, as we discussed in Chapter 2, the Great Depression began in 1929. Almost overnight, output plummeted; jobs evaporated, prices fell, stock markets collapsed. It was not until the outbreak of World War II that the U.S. economy recovered to its level of output at the start of the Great Depression. Although the industrialized countries have experienced a series of economic downturns since World War II, none has approached the magnitude of the Great Depression. The Great Depression remains a unique experience that macroeconomics must explain.

Figure 1 places this brief economic history in perspective by plotting the total output of the U.S. economy over a century's time. From Figure 1, we can see that macroeconomics has two major themes: economic growth and the business cycle.

> **Economic growth** is the long-run expansion of the total output of goods and services produced by the economy.
>
> The **business cycle** is the pattern of short-run upward and downward movements in the output of the economy.

The business cycle focuses our attention on the short run. It shows the effects of the short-run ups and downs in the level of business activity on inflation, unemployment, interest rates, and deficits, among other matters. Economic growth focuses our attention on the long run. It shows how the productive capacity of the economy expands over the long run.

The blue line in Figure 1 traces the general growth pattern of the economy's output over the past century, ignoring the ups and downs in particular pe-

## EXAMPLE 1
## THE PUBLIC'S BIGGEST CONCERNS

Macroeconomic issues typically top the list of concerns of the American public. These concerns change as our macroeconomic problems change. As the diagram shows, at the beginning of 1996, the public was equally concerned with the economy/jobs and the deficit, which were cited as being more important than health care or crime. In 1992, when the unemployment rate was higher, the public's overwhelming concern was the economy and jobs. Few expressed concern about the deficit, health care, or crime. In the 1970s and early 1980s, when the inflation rate was high, almost 80% of the American public rated inflation as their biggest concern.

**The Public's Biggest Concerns**
What do you think is the most important problem facing the country today?

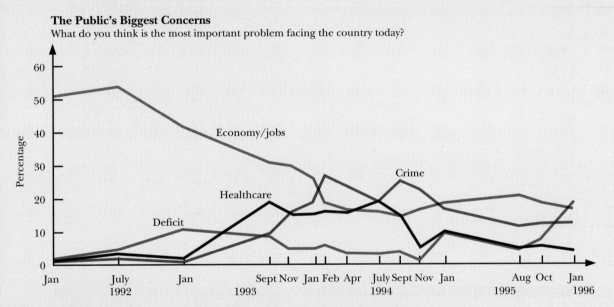

Source: Based on nationwide telephone polls conducted by *The New York Times* and CBS News. The latest was conducted Jan. 18–20, 1996, with 1,076 adults.

riods. The individual bars show the actual output of the economy in each year. Sometimes the individual bars are above the blue line; sometimes they are below. Deviations of the actual output of the economy from the long-term growth pattern of the economy depict the business cycle. When an individual bar is above the blue line, the economy was in a period of prosperity. When an individual bar is below the blue line, the economy was experiencing a period of slow growth or even an economic downturn.

Figure 1 relates an important lesson: With the exceptions of the Great Depression and the anomaly of World War II, the economic lives of Americans have been influenced much more by economic growth than by the business cycle. It is economic growth, taking place over a long period of time, that

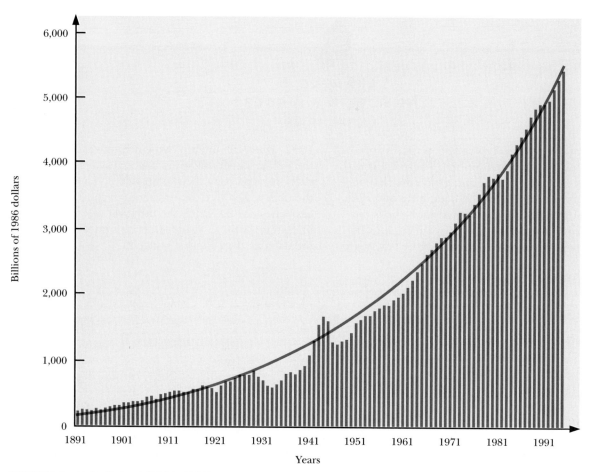

**FIGURE 1   U.S. Output (1891–1995)**

determines economic well-being. Business cycles, while seeming important at the time, have had only a temporary and transitory effect on our economic lives. A temporary economic downturn causing the economy to produce 2 percent less output in a particular year is indeed a loss of output, but this loss is transitory when growth resumes. However, if economic output is only half a percent less per annum *for a 50-year period*, this decline in growth means that the economy will be 25 percent smaller at the end of the 50-year period.

> Economic growth has lasting effects on the economy. The business cycle has transitory effects on the economy.

The two major themes of macroeconomics raise two policy issues that will occupy us in our study of macroeconomics:

1. What steps can we—individuals, businesses, and government—take to ensure that economic growth occurs?

2. What steps, if any, should we take to control or moderate the business cycle?

## BUSINESS CYCLES

As Figure 1 shows, macroeconomic activity moves in cycles, like sunspots, droughts, epidemics, and animal reproduction. Over the very long run, economies tend to increase output through the process of economic growth. Many distinguished economists have studied the fluctuations in the level of business activity around the long-run trends in output that constitute the business cycle.

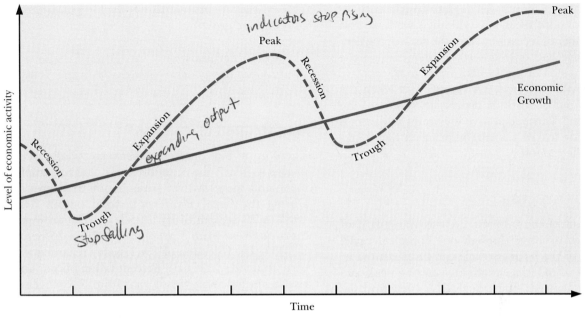

**FIGURE 2   The Phases of the U.S. Business Cycle**

This figure illustrates the four phases of the business cycle. Since 1924, the average recession has lasted 1 year, and the average recovery has lasted 4 years. Each peak in the figure is higher than the previous one because of the long-term growth of output.

## THE FOUR PHASES OF THE BUSINESS CYCLE

Business cycles are divided into phases. Figure 2 shows the four phases of the business cycle:

1. Downturn or recession (or depression if the decline in activity is prolonged and severe)
2. Trough
3. Expansion (or recovery)
4. Peak

During the *recession* phase, the level of business activity declines. The various indicators of business activity (building permits, total output, employment, new business formation, factory orders) indicate that the economy is producing a declining rate of output. The unemployment rate rises, and the number of people employed declines (or the growth of employment slows). The *trough* (or lowest point) occurs when the various indicators of business activity stop falling. The economy has reached a low point from which recovery begins.

During the *recovery* stage, the various output indicators point to expanding output. The final stage occurs when the business cycle reaches its *peak,* the

point at which the various indicators of production and employment stop rising. When the next stage—downturn—begins, the economy enters another business cycle.

## RECESSIONS AND DEPRESSIONS

The terms *recession* and *depression* are used to describe the downturn phase of the business cycle.

> As a general rule, a **recession** occurs when real output declines for a period of six months or more.
>
> A **depression** is a severe downturn in economic activity that lasts for a prolonged period. Output declines by a significant amount, and unemployment rises to very high levels.

The National Bureau of Economic Research is a nonprofit, private research organization that is accepted as an authority for deciding when a recession begins and ends. The six-month declining output rule is not ironclad. If an economic downturn is especially severe, it may be classified as a recession even if it lasts less than six months. A depression is a very severe and extended recession. Although we have had a large number of recessions since the turn of the century, we have had only one severe depression—the Great Depression of the 1930s.

As the old joke says, "A recession is when my neighbor is out of work. A depression is when I am out of work!" This perspective illustrates why a major depression leaves a lasting imprint on our thinking about the economy.

## LENGTH OF CYCLES

The duration of the business cycle is the length of time it takes to move through one complete cycle. The length of the business cycle can be measured as the number of months either between one peak and the next or between one trough of a cycle and the next trough. No two business cycles are identical. Government studies of the business cycles from 1924 to the present show that their average duration is about five years (see Table 1). The recession phase lasts, on the average, slightly less than one year. The expansion phase lasts, on the average, slightly more than four years.

Figure 2 places the peak of the second cycle above the peak of the first cycle. The trough of the second cycle is above the trough of the first cycle.

| Table 1 | American Business Cycles, 1924–1995 | |
|---|---|---|
| Trough | Peak | Length of Cycle, Peak to Peak (months) |
| July 1924 | October 1926 | 41 |
| November 1927 | August 1929 | 34 |
| March 1933 | May 1937 | 93 |
| June 1938 | February 1945 | 93 |
| October 1945 | November 1948 | 45 |
| October 1949 | July 1953 | 56 |
| May 1954 | August 1957 | 49 |
| April 1958 | April 1960 | 32 |
| February 1961 | December 1969 | 116 |
| November 1970 | November 1973 | 47 |
| March 1975 | January 1980 | 62 |
| July 1980 | July 1981 | 12 |
| November 1982 | July 1990 | 118 |
| July 1991 | — | — |

Source: U.S. Department of Commerce, *Handbook of Cyclical Indicators*, a supplement to *Business Conditions Digest*.

This upward movement shows the long-term process of economic growth.

> Business cycles show how output fluctuates around the general pattern of rising economic activity.

## MAGNITUDES OF CYCLES

There is a big difference between small cyclical swings in which the economy stays near full employment and large swings from boom to depression. During the Great Depression, total output fell in 1933 to 70 percent of its 1929 level. The unemployment rate rose from 3 percent in 1929 to 25 percent in 1933. The recession of 1982, today regarded as severe, resulted in only a 2 percent fall in output and a rise in the unemployment rate from 7.5 percent to 9.5 percent. During the milder recession of 1990–1991, real output declined 1.2 percent in the fourth quarter of 1990 and the first quarter of 1991, after which growth resumed but at a slow rate. The unemployment rate rose from 5.5 percent to slightly over 7 percent.

Business cycles affect various industries, occupations, and regions differently. Some industries, such as the auto, steel, and machine-building industries, are hit harder by economic downturns than are others. In the 1990–1991 recession, for example, automobiles and retailing were especially affected.

## UNEMPLOYMENT, INFLATION, INTEREST RATES, AND DEFICITS

The business cycle measures changes in the level of real business activity. These changes affect two key macroeconomic variables: *unemployment* and *inflation*. When real business activity expands, business firms offer more positions, employment expands, and the number of people without jobs declines. Although the relationship between employment and unemployment is complex, there is a generally negative relationship between the level of business activity and unemployment.

When business activity is expanding and employment opportunities are ample, the general level of wages and prices tends to rise. When business activity is weak and employment opportunities are scarce, there is less pressure on wages and prices, and inflationary pressures tend to moderate. However, in some periods—for example, the 1990s—expansion of business activity combined with slow increases in prices and wages. In the 1970s, falling output and rising unemployment combined with rapid increases in prices.

> The relationship between inflation and the business cycle is one of the most controversial issues in macroeconomics.

The business cycle also affects *interest rates* and *government deficits,* as we shall see in subsequent chapters. During a contraction, businesses cut back on their expansion plans; their demand for credit is weak. As a result, interest rates tend to fall during recessions. With a strong growth of business activity, credit demand surges, pushing up interest rates. In contrast, government deficits tend to rise during recessions. As business activity declines, government tax revenues fall, but government must increase its spending on unemployment insurance and welfare programs. During expansions, tax revenues increase, and fewer people require welfare assistance and unemployment benefits. The relationships among inter-

est rates, government deficits, and the business cycle are complex and require detailed explanation. However, more often than not, interest rates and government deficits are symptoms rather than causes of the business cycle.

## UNEMPLOYMENT

The U.S. government is committed by the Employment Act of 1946 to create and maintain "useful employment opportunities...for those able, willing, and seeking to work." Thus, unemployment is and continues to be an important factor in macroeconomic policy. Politicians in office know that high unemployment hurts their chances of reelection. Governments have enacted a wide range of policies to deal with unemployment, some having unintended consequences. (See Example 2.) In fact, despite efforts to reduce unemployment, the number of unemployed and rate of unemployment have increased in most countries.

**EXAMPLE 2**

**UNINTENDED CONSEQUENCES:**

**EUROPEAN UNEMPLOYMENT**

In the 1960s, Europe was noted for its low rates of unemployment. In the countries that now constitute the European Union, the average rate of unemployment was 2.5 percent in the 1960s. In the 1990s, the European Union's average rate of unemployment was 10 percent. What has caused this increase?

European countries have instituted the most liberal unemployment benefits in the world. These policies were designed to mitigate the effects of unemployment. They have had the unintended consequence of making unemployment worse.

Europe's generous welfare benefits weaken incentives to find a job. If you have generous unemployment benefits that last indefinitely, there is little incentive to find new employment. Many

European countries have high firing costs. In Germany, for example, it takes two years or more to fire an employee. Moreover, many European countries have high minimum wages; thus, unemployed workers cannot get jobs by offering to work for less.

Many European economists now argue that Europe's high unemployment must be cured by reducing the welfare state, by making it easier to fire workers, and by placing more emphasis on retraining. These are all long-term remedies to structural problems that were long in the making.

------------------------------------------------

*Source:* "Economics Focus: A Grizzly Subject," *The Economist,* September 3, 1994, p. 78.

## THE UNEMPLOYMENT RATE

Each person 16 years or older can be classified in one of three labor market categories:

1. Employed
2. Unemployed
3. Not in the labor force

A person who currently has a job is *employed*. Even persons who want to have full-time jobs but are able to find only part-time work are counted as employed. Employment is an either/or state; either you have a job or you don't.

Persons are classified as *unemployed* if they (1) did not work at all during the previous week, (2) actively looked for work during the previous four weeks, and (3) are currently available for work. Persons laid off from jobs or waiting to report to a new job within 30 days are also classified as unemployed.

Persons without jobs who do not meet the three conditions of unemployment are classified as *not in the labor force*. The labor force consists of all persons either currently working or unemployed.

> The **labor force** equals the number of persons employed plus the number unemployed.

Persons are not in the labor force either by choice (as in the case of full-time students or retired persons) or because they have concluded that they cannot find an appropriate job and have stopped looking.

The number of persons unemployed does not show the relative magnitude of unemployment. The unemployment rate relates the number of unemployed to the size of the labor force.

> The **unemployment rate** is the number of persons unemployed divided by the number in the labor force.

Although we pay a lot of attention to the number of employed or unemployed, the most frequently used measure of the state of unemployment is the unemployment rate.

## TRENDS IN UNEMPLOYMENT

Figure 3 shows long-term trends in the unemployment rate. Since 1900, the unemployment rate has varied from lows of near 1 percent to a high of 25 percent during the Great Depression of the 1930s. It is no wonder that the many Americans who experienced the Great Depression firsthand harbor a deep fear of mass unemployment.

Between 1900 and 1947, no distinct trends in the unemployment rate are apparent. However, since World War II, the unemployment rate has moved generally upward. During the period between World War II and 1960, the unemployment rate ranged from 2.5 percent to 5.5 percent. In the 1960s, the unemployment rate ranged from 3.4 percent to 6.5 percent. In the 1970s, the unemployment rate ranged from 4.8 percent to 8.3 percent. In the first half of the 1980s, the range was from 7 percent to 9.5 percent. In the 1990s, the unemployment rate moved down to between 5.5 percent and 7.5 percent.

## EMPLOYMENT AND UNEMPLOYMENT

The unemployment rate rises when unemployment increases faster than the labor force. Hence, a rising unemployment rate can be caused by rapid growth of unemployment, relatively slow growth of the labor force, or by a combination of the two.

The relationships among employment, unemployment, and the unemployment rate are complex. Panel (*a*) in Figure 4 shows trends in the number of persons employed, unemployed, and not in the labor force. Panel (*b*) graphs the unemployment rate.

Figure 4, panel (*a*), demonstrates that in the long run, both employment *and* unemployment have risen as the U.S. economy has grown. In 1950, employment was 60 million and unemployment was 3.3 million. In 1996, employment was 121 million and unemployment was 8 million.

In the short run, employment and unemployment can move together (as during the early 1970s and the early 1980s) or in opposite directions (as during most of the 1960s, the mid-1970s, and the mid-1980s). The 1960s was a period of low and declining unemployment, whereas the 1970s saw high and generally rising unemployment. Surprisingly, the rate of increase in *employment* was lower in the 1960s than in the 1970s! The higher unemployment *rates* of the 1970s were caused not by slow employment growth but by a faster rise in unemployment than in the labor force.

Figure 4, panel (*a*), also shows the effect of the business cycle on employment, unemployment, and the number of people not in the labor force. During recessions (vertical bars), unemployment rises, em-

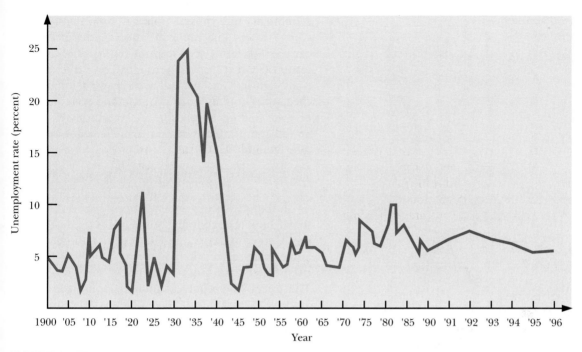

**FIGURE 3 The Unemployment Rate, 1900–1996**

The unemployment rate has been rising since the 1950s, but it is far from reaching the level experienced during the Great Depression of the 1930s. *Source: Historical Statistics of the United States; Economic Report of the President.*

ployment falls or slows its rate of increase, and the number of people not in the labor force rises. The unemployment rate rises during recessions because unemployment rises at a faster pace than the number of people leaving the labor force.

## FULL EMPLOYMENT

Full employment does not require that everyone actively looking and available for work currently have a job. If there were absolutely no unemployment, the economy would lack the movement among jobs necessary to any changing economy. Full employment occurs when the labor market is in balance. In a dynamic economy, jobs are created while other jobs disappear. Some people enter or reenter the labor force while others withdraw or retire. In some professions, there are more job applicants than jobs. In other professions, there are more jobs than applicants. In the 1970s and 1980s, there were too few accountants. In the 1990s, there were more accountants than jobs. In the 1970s, there were too few petroleum engineers; in the 1990s, there were too many petroleum engineers.

The labor market is in balance when the number of jobs being created roughly equals the number of

qualified applicants available to fill those jobs. The unemployment rate at which this balance is attained is the natural rate of unemployment.

> The **natural rate of unemployment** is that unemployment rate at which there is an approximate balance between the number of unfilled jobs and the number of qualified job seekers.

As we shall discuss in later chapters on inflation and unemployment, inflationary pressures remain the same when labor markets are in balance. When an economy is at the natural rate of unemployment, the current rate of inflation should continue at its present pace. The relationship between inflation and unemployment is one of the most important and complicated relationships of macroeconomics.

## INFLATION

Most of us fear inflation for a number of reasons—some justified, others not. Some nations have experienced runaway inflation that has paralyzed their

(*a*) The Employment Status of Workers

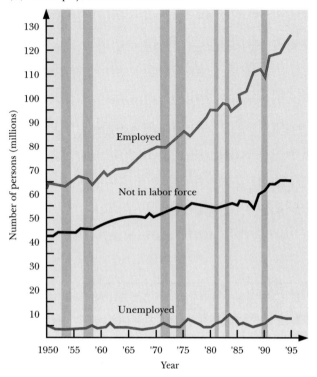

(*b*) The Unemployment Rate

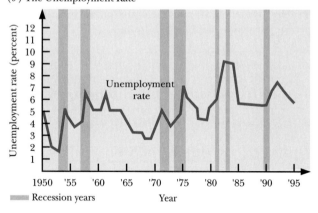

**FIGURE 4   Employment, Unemployment, and the Unemployment Rate**

Employment often increases, though its rate slows, during periods of rising unemployment. However, in the case of major recessions, as in 1975 or 1983, employment decreased.

*Source: Survey of Current Business.*

economies and caused political upheavals. In the United States, the rapid inflation of the 1970s and early 1980s left a deep imprint on many of us, similar to the Great Depression's effect on earlier generations. During this period, we regarded inflation as the nation's number one problem and even despaired of ever finding a solution. As inflation fell in the 1980s and 1990s, it ceased to be a major concern. (See Example 1.)

**Inflation** is a general increase in prices.

Inflation occurs when prices rise on average throughout the economy. Some prices rise faster than the average increase, and others rise more slowly. Some prices even fall. The price of medical care has risen faster than most other prices since the 1960s. The prices of pocket calculators, home computers, and cellular telephones have fallen consistently since the 1960s, even during periods of inflation.

Whether inflation is perceived as moderate or rapid is relative to its time and place. In the early 1960s, when prices were rising 2 percent per year or less, the "alarming" 1966 inflation rate of 3.3 percent motivated government authorities to enact strict antiinflationary measures. After several years of near double-digit inflation in the late 1970s and early 1980s, the 3 percent to 4.5 percent inflation rates of the rest of the 1980s were viewed with relief. In some Latin American countries or Russia, where prices double or quadruple (or worse) annually, the U.S. double-digit inflation rates of the late 1970s would have been the object of envy. In 1995, Russia struggled to keep its inflation rate at 10 percent *per month*—a more than 100 percent annual rate of inflation. The rate of inflation, like any other measure of prices, must be evaluated in relative terms.

The opposite of inflation, deflation, has been rare in modern times.

**Deflation** is a general decline in prices.

The U.S. economy experienced substantial deflation during the Great Depression of the 1930s. Since the mid 1930s, inflation has been the rule and deflation the exception. The last year in which a general decline in prices was recorded was 1955.

## HYPERINFLATION

There is a general agreement that it is desirable for the economy to operate at the natural rate of unemployment (full employment). There is less agreement among economists on what constitutes an optimal rate of inflation. Some economists argue that we should aim for a zero rate of inflation; others believe that we should be content with a "moderate" rate of inflation.

Everyone agrees, however, that very rapid inflation is unhealthy and that unexpected and large swings in the inflation rate can have detrimental consequences. The most extreme case is hyperinflation, when prices rise at a rapid, accelerating rate.

> **Hyperinflation** is a very rapid and accelerating rate of inflation. Prices might double every month or even double daily or hourly.

Most economies have slow to moderate inflation. A number of countries, however, have experienced hyperinflation at some time. Israel's annual inflation rate was 800 percent in the 1980s, and Brazil's annual inflation rate was 2000 percent in the first half of 1994. War-torn former Yugoslavia's inflation rate was more than 4000 percent in 1995. The American South experienced hyperinflation during the Civil War. In the 1920s Germany had the best-known historical case of hyperinflation—a con-

dition that helped bring Hitler to power. (See Example 3.) Whether the new governments of the republics of the former Soviet Union can survive the hyperinflation of the 1990s remains to be seen. Those who have witnessed the destructive power of hyperinflation know that it can cause the destruction of the established social order.

## MEASURING INFLATION: PRICE INDEXES

If all prices were to rise at the same rate—say, 3 percent per year—measuring inflation would be no problem. The inflation rate would simply be 3 percent per annum. All prices do not rise at the same rate during inflations. The different rates of price increase must be combined in a price index that measures the average increases in prices.

> A **price index** shows the cost of buying the same market basket of goods in different years as a percentage of its cost in some base year.

One type of market basket would be the combination of goods and services consumed by a representative family of four living in an urban area. Price indexes measure the changing cost of purchasing the

## EXAMPLE 3
## WHEELBARROWS OF CASH:
## THE GERMAN HYPERINFLATION

One of the best-documented cases of hyperinflation is that of Germany following World War I. The Treaty of Versailles required that the German government pay war reparations to France and Great Britain. In order to make these payments, the German government began printing money. From August 1922 to November 1923, the German government increased the supply of paper money by 314 percent per month. Within 15 months, the price level rose more than 10 billion times its starting level. Prices rose 322 percent per month.

Hyperinflation reduces economic efficiency by forcing people to devote most of their efforts to

avoiding the inflation tax. Workers paid in the morning had to be given time off to rush off and spend their wages before they became worthless. People could be seen carrying cash around in wheelbarrows. Firms paid their workers three times a day—after breakfast, lunch, and dinner. As matters worsened, people refused to accept money at all. Instead, they demanded foreign currency, precious metals, or real goods. The economic chaos created by the hyperinflation helped bring Hitler to power and explains why the Germans, even to this day, have a deep-seated fear of inflation.

same market basket of goods in different years. If the typical market basket of goods cost $200 per week in 1994, $220 per week in 1995, and $230 per week in 1996, the price index in 1994 is 100 (the base year), 110 in 1995 ($220/$200 × 100), and 115 in 1996 ($230/$200 × 100).

Economists and government officials compile different indexes to measure the general change in prices. The most widely used price index in the United States is the Consumer Price Index, or CPI.

> The **Consumer Price Index (CPI)** measures the level of consumer prices paid by households over a period of time.

Monthly reports of the CPI are closely followed by business, government officials, and the public. Many government pensions including 38 million Social Security pensions and the wages of 8.5 million

union workers and government employees, are adjusted according to changes in the CPI. Since 1985, the federal income tax has been adjusted for changes in the CPI. For these reasons, it is important that the CPI accurately gauge the rate of increase in consumer prices.

The CPI measures the prices of those goods and services that families purchase for consumption. It does not measure the prices of the other goods and services that the economy produces, such as machinery, equipment, and goods and services produced by government. In the mid-1990s, 65 percent of the total output of the economy was devoted to personal consumption. The remaining 35 percent went to business investment, government services, and exports and imports. The CPI, therefore, is not the most general measure of the rate of inflation. A more general measure is the GDP deflator.

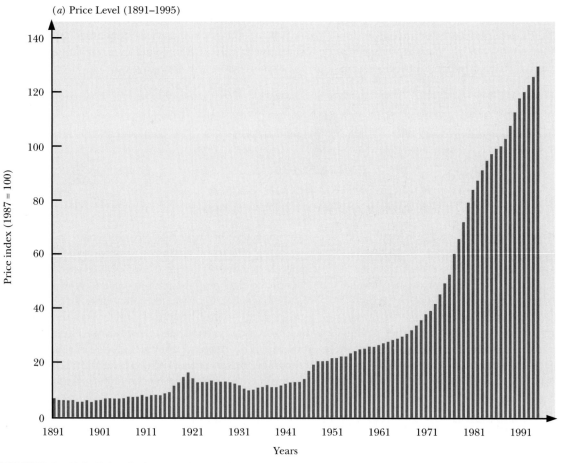

(a) Price Level (1891–1995)

**FIGURE 5   U.S. Price Indexes, 1891–1995**

The **GDP deflator** measures the level of prices of all final goods and services (consumer goods, investment goods, and government) produced by the economy.

The GDP deflator measures the change in the prices of machinery and construction, government, and exports and imports, as well as consumer prices. Because the GDP deflator is a more general measure of inflation, most of the inflation figures cited in this book are for the GDP deflator.

## INFLATION RATES VERSUS THE PRICE LEVEL

Price indexes such as the CPI or the GDP deflator show the price level in different periods of time. The rate of inflation shows the rate at which the price level is changing.

The **rate of inflation** is the rate, usually measured per annum, at which the price level, as measured by a price index, is changing.

If, for example, the CPI in 1995 is 100 and 105 in 1996, the annual rate of inflation in 1996 was 5 percent per annum.

## TRENDS IN INFLATION

Trends in the price level over the past 100 years reveal that the sustained inflation of the past 60 years is a fairly new phenomenon [see Figure 5, panels (*a*) and (*b*)]. Until 1930, prices were as likely to fall as to rise. Prior to World War II, *deflation* was just as common as *inflation*. The unusual feature of the post–World War II period has been the notable absence of deflation. Unlike earlier times, when periods

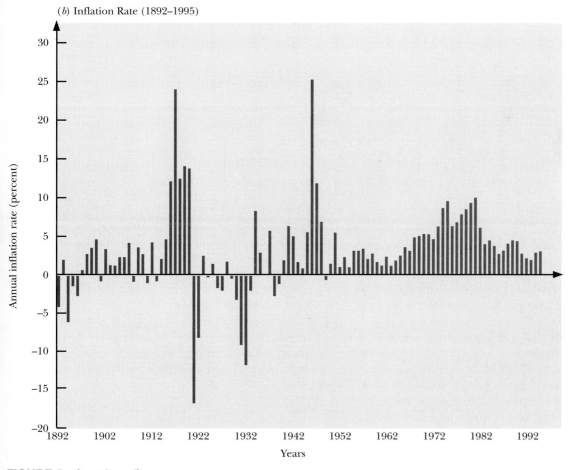

(*b*) Inflation Rate (1892–1995)

**FIGURE 5**  *(continued)*

of inflation offset periods of deflation, the postwar era has been one of continuous increases in prices, though at varying rates.

Historically speaking, inflation is not inevitable, even though it may appear so to most of us in the late 1990s. We have been conditioned to think of rising prices as one of the constants of life along with death and taxes: The CPI has fallen in only one of the last 40 years. Seventy years ago, people did not think this way because prices fell as often as they rose.

## EFFECTS OF INFLATION

Many fear that rising prices will automatically lower our standard of living. Some of us take alarming increases in housing prices, food prices, or medical bills as proof that our living standards are falling. This confusion is a classic example of the *ceteris paribus* fallacy discussed in Chapter 1. During inflations, prices of outputs and inputs, wages, rents, and interest rates all tend to rise. As the prices of things we buy rise, so do the prices of the things we sell, such as our labor.

Living standards are determined by the relationship between income and prices. If our income is rising faster than prices, our living standards are rising; if our income is rising slower than prices, our living standards are falling.

To illustrate the logical fallacy of equating rising prices with falling living standards or falling prices with rising living standards, let's consider the Great Depression. Between 1929 and 1933, prices dropped by 25 percent while personal incomes fell by 45 percent. Falling prices did not result in rising living standards because incomes declined more than prices. Similarly, the fact that coffee used to sell for one cent does not tell us that living standards were higher then. (See Example 4.)

**Inflation Redistributes Income.** Inflation can redistribute income by causing income to increase faster than prices for some of us and slower than prices for others. Contrary to popular belief, inflation does not automatically redistribute income from

### EXAMPLE 4
### A WHOLE CENT TO SPEND!
### PRICES, INCOME, AND LIVING STANDARDS

A newspaper columnist fondly recalls the year 1924, when a person could buy three candles for a penny or a box of chocolate-covered cherries for 29 cents, see a movie for a dime, or purchase the best automobile on the road for $255. This columnist, like many, yearns for the "good old days" when "you could get something for your money."

The notion that low prices mean a higher standard of living is an example of the *ceteris paribus* fallacy. This kind of thinking causes people to automatically equate rising prices (inflation) with a declining standard of living. In 1924, the average annual earnings of a full-time manufacturing employee were $1,400. Average hourly earnings were 50 cents. In 1995, average hour earnings of full-time manufacturing employees exceeded $15; average annual earnings exceeded $40,000. Between 1924 and 1995, earnings increased by more than 25 times. Consumer prices, on the other hand, increased only 8 times over this period.

Inflation does not automatically reduce living standards. Rather, living standards are determined by the relationship between what people earn (income) and what things cost (prices).

------------------------------------------------

*Source:* John Gould, "A Whole Penny to Spend!" *Christian Science Monitor,* November 23, 1990.

creditors to debtors or from the old to the young. Instead, inflation redistributes income primarily away from those who have underestimated it.

When we enter into multiyear money contracts (such as employment or loan contracts), we try to anticipate the rate of inflation over the life of the contract. If I lend you money to be repaid at some future date, we both must attempt to anticipate inflation. Errors can be costly. Suppose I lend you $10,000 for five years at an annual interest rate of 5 percent (I expect a relatively low rate of inflation), but the actual inflation rate turns out to be 10 percent per year over the five-year period. The $500 interest payment I receive each year does not compensate me for the loss in purchasing power I will suffer each year. When you repay the $10,000 principal at the end of the five years, each dollar that I receive will buy only $0.62 worth of goods and services compared with five years earlier. Clearly, inflation has redistributed income from the lender (me) to the borrower (you). If we had negotiated the loan differently (say, at a 20 percent interest rate), income would have been redistributed from the borrower (you) to the lender (me). The $2000 annual interest payment would have handsomely compensated me for the payment of interest and repayment of principal in cheaper dollars.

Similarly, wage contracts can redistribute income from employee to employer, or vice versa. If a union negotiates a three-year wage contract with annual pay increases of 5 percent, and the annual inflation rate over this period turns out to be 10 percent, income will have been redistributed from employee to employer. On the other hand, if the contract had called for a 20 percent annual pay increase, income would have been redistributed from the employer to the employee.

As these two examples show, the income redistribution effects of inflation depend upon how well we anticipate inflation. Lenders who anticipate inflation correctly will demand an interest rate that will compensate them for inflation's erosion of the value of interest and principal payments. Union negotiators generally will refuse to accept wage increases that do not compensate for inflation.

All who enter into contracts involving money payments over time try to anticipate inflation correctly. Some people succeed; others fail. For the economy as a whole, inflation can be lower or higher than generally expected. When actual inflation differs from anticipated inflation, income is redistributed.

**Inflation Creates Inefficiencies.**   When inflation is rapid and erratic, it becomes more important to predict it accurately. If we believe that the inflation rate will be 5 percent during the coming year, and the actual rate is 10 percent, we will make poor business decisions. We will agree to sell our products too cheaply, for example, or we may accept wage increases that are too low.

Rapid and erratic inflation creates three types of inefficiencies. First, businesses become more concerned with anticipating inflation than seeking out profitable business opportunities. Creative efforts are diverted from innovation and risk-taking to anticipating inflation.

Second, inflation leads to speculative practices that do not add to the economy's productive capacity. Those who expect high inflation will speculate in real estate, foreign currencies, gold, and art objects. Such speculative investments are made *in place of* productive investments in plants, equipment, and inventories.

Third, Adam Smith's invisible hand works less well during periods of high inflation. With prices changing rapidly, we no longer know what are good or bad buys. Businesses do not know what materials are cheap and what materials are expensive. The quality of decision making declines, and we make poorer consumption and production decisions. (See Example 5.)

The negative effects of inflation on economic efficiency are most pronounced during hyperinflation. Workers become reluctant to accept their wages in money (preferring to be paid in products), and whatever money is received is spent immediately. Businesses refuse to enter into fixed contracts, and difficult-to-arrange barter exchanges replace money transactions. Most efforts during hyperinflation aim at keeping up with inflation rather than at productive economic activities.

Indeed, empirical studies confirm a negative relationship between inflation and economic growth, especially for high inflation economies. High inflation also reduces the amount of productive investment.[1]

---

[1]Robert Barro, "Inflation and Economic Growth," NBER Working Paper No. 5326, October 1995.

## EXAMPLE 5
## INFLATION AND CALCULATION:
## SHOPPING IN RIO

On July 1, 1994, Brazil introduced a new currency, the *real*. Prior to its monetary reform, Brazil was the basket case of South America, having suffered through decades of high inflation and even hyperinflation. Its annual inflation rate prior to the real's introduction was over 2000 percent. The real is an integral part of an economic reform package formulated by Brazil's finance minister and endorsed by the International Monetary Fund. The Real Plan calls for balanced budgets and tight control of the money supply.

After decades of inflation, Brazil's residents were astonished at the new phenomenon of stable prices after the introduction of the real. Said one Rio resident: "Before, you would go to a store one day and the price would have gone up before you came back." Prices were rising so rapidly that people really didn't know what prices meant. Reported one shopper in her excitement over the new currency: "Prices are always the same. Before you couldn't calculate anything." Even more astonishing to her was that some prices even fell!

The Brazilian monetary reform shows that one of the costs of rapid inflation is that shoppers have great difficulty in determining what are good buys. When prices rise so rapidly, they don't provide enough information. The second lesson of Brazil's reform is that hyperinflation can be stopped in its tracks by well-designed monetary reforms.

------------------------------------------------

*Source:* "Even Rio's Poor Seem Sold on Inflation Fighter," *New York Times,* September 28, 1994.

## GLOBALIZATION OF THE BUSINESS CYCLE

Globalization is one of the Defining Moments of economics. Globalization has created a strong web of interrelationships among the economies of the world. The economic fluctuations of one economy, especially if it is large and influential, affect other economies. In an integrated international economy, U.S. business cycles are transmitted to Europe and vice versa. Higher interest rates in Europe or Asia eventually mean higher interest rates in North America. A rise in inflation at home can cause higher inflation abroad.

Business cycles do not exist in isolation. We trade goods and services with one another. Our credit markets are interrelated, with multinational firms borrowing dollars in New York, London, Zurich, Tokyo, and Hong Kong. A country that experiences rapid economic growth increases its purchases (imports) from other countries. A recession in Europe means less business for the United States and Japan. Economies are interrelated through flows of goods and services and through flows of credit. Therefore, it is not surprising that business cycles spread from country to country.

There is a saying among economists: "When the industrial economies catch cold, the developing economies of Asia, Africa, and Latin America catch pneumonia." Recessions that result in a relatively small loss of employment and output in the industrialized countries can cause severe losses of output and employment in poorer countries. True to form, the U.S. recession of 1990–1991 spread first to western Europe and then to the developing countries with increasingly strong repercussions.

Figure 6 shows that the world's economies share common periods of rapid or slow growth. Industrial countries experience similar but not identical inflation and unemployment trends. Interest rates rise and fall together. Business cycles do not move together in

(*a*) Industrial Production

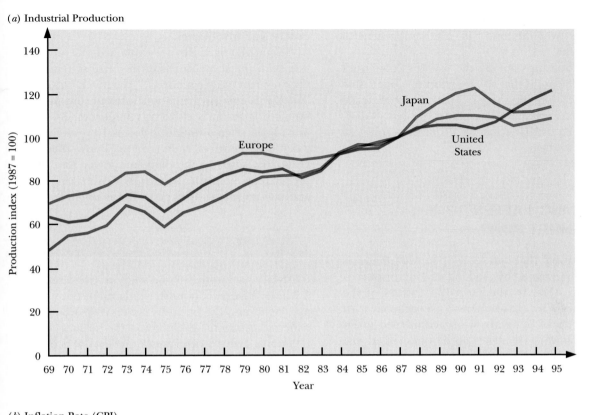

(*b*) Inflation Rate (CPI)

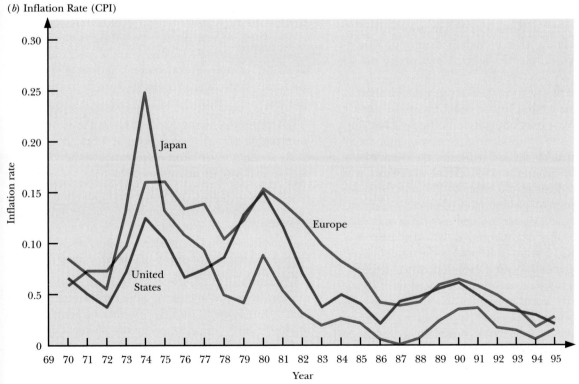

**FIGURE 6   The International Business Cycle**

*Source: Economic Report of the President.*

perfect harmony among countries. There are leads and lags, but over the long run, a common general trend is evident.

Interrelationships among the world's economies bring home the point that we are all in one boat. Just as the first picture of the earth taken from space showed us that we share our planet, so has globalization showed us that what we do in the economic sphere affects others.

## WHY SO MUCH ATTENTION TO THE SHORT RUN?

Figure 1 showed that our economic well-being is much more determined by the long-run factor of economic growth than by the short-run factors of the business cycle. Why are we then so preoccupied with the business cycle? Why are we so concerned when the unemployment rate inches up by one-half of one point? Why is each blip in the business cycle minutely studied by financial analysts?

Few of us know enough about economics to be confident that things will work out in the long run. How do we know that an uncomfortably high unemployment rate will not get progressively worse? How do we know that a current economic downturn is not signalling the end of prosperity as we know it?

We judge the performance of our elected officials on what is happening to the economy now, not on the basis of what may happen in the future. The outcome of the 1992 presidential election most likely was determined by the fact that the recovery of the U.S. economy from the 1990–1991 recession was slow and gradual at the time of the election. Although the loss of output from this recession was minimal and the increase in unemployment was relatively small, this short-term downturn was still enough to end 12 years of Republican presidents and to elect the first Democratic president since 1976.

Financial markets are also fascinated with short-run events. The world investment community spends billions of dollars on research to anticipate inflation and the business cycle. Professional investors hope that this knowledge will give them the slight edge over other investors that will allow them to earn more. The pages of the financial press are filled with the most recent indicators of the economy, such as the latest figures on housing starts, inflation, factory orders, and inventories.

John Maynard Keynes explained our preoccupation with the short run with the terse statement: "In the long run we are all dead." We live in the present. Whether we or our neighbors lose our jobs in an economic downturn is extremely important to us right now. If the current inflation rate is 10 percent, it provides little comfort right now to know that it will eventually settle back down to a lower rate. We are preoccupied with the daily routine of making a living and making our money go as far as possible.

## SUMMARY

1. Macroeconomics is the study of the economy as a whole. Macroeconomists study inflation, unemployment, and the business cycle. Macroeconomics concerns economic growth and the business cycle. Economic growth determines the level of economic prosperity in the long run. Business cycles are the fluctuations around the generally rising level of business activity.

2. The business cycle is the pattern of upward and downward movements in the level of business activity. A recession is a decline in real output that lasts six months or more. A depression is a very severe recession, lasting several years. The four phases of the business cycle are recession, trough, recovery, and peak.

3. A person is unemployed if he or she is not working, is currently available for work, and is actively seeking a job. Full employment is reached at the natural rate of unemployment.

4. Individuals are classified into three labor market categories: employed, unemployed, or not in the labor force. The labor force is the sum of the employed and unemployed. The unemployment rate is the number of unemployed divided by the labor force.

5. Since the 1950s, there has been an upward movement in the unemployment rate. Unemployment, employment, and the number of people not in the labor force are affected by the business cycle in a complex fashion.

6. Inflation is a general increase in prices. It is measured by price indexes that determine the changing cost of buying a standard market basket

of goods. The most important price indexes are the consumer price index (the CPI) and the GDP deflator. Prior to the 1930s, deflation was just as common as inflation. There has been a clear inflationary trend since the mid-1930s.

7. People fear inflation because it redistributes income, creates economic inefficiency, and makes economic calculation more difficult. Empirical studies confirm the negative association between inflation and growth and between inflation and capital investment.

8. Globalization of the world economies has made them interrelated. Business cycles spread from one country to other countries.

## KEY TERMS

economic growth
business cycle
recession
depression
labor force
unemployment rate
natural rate of
   unemployment

inflation
deflation
hyperinflation
price index
Consumer Price Index
   (CPI)
GDP deflator
rate of inflation

## QUESTIONS AND PROBLEMS

1. Explain why economic growth is more important in the long run than the business cycle.
2. How would each of the following people be classified according to the definition of unemployment?
   a. A high-school student casually looking for an after-school job
   b. A person who quits his or her job to become a full-time homemaker
   c. Laid-off auto workers waiting to be recalled to their previous job

   d. A person who has quit his or her job to search for a better job
3. Describe the relevant criteria by which government statisticians determine whether a person is "unemployed" or "not in the labor force."
4. In 1992, a typical market basket costs $500. In 1998, the same market basket costs $800. What is the price index for 1998, using 1992 as the base year?
5. Explain how inflation can redistribute wealth from lenders to borrowers.
6. Explain how and why hyperinflation reduces economic efficiency.
7. Jones lends $100 to Smith for one year. During this year, the inflation rate is 5 percent. How much interest and principal would Jones have to receive to be able to buy the same physical quantities of goods and services when the loan is repaid as when the loan was made?
8. Does the relative duration of expansions and recessions help explain the fact that long-term economic growth has been positive?
9. Do you think that an economy that is in a recession is operating at the natural rate of unemployment?
10. Evaluate the validity of the following statement: "Inflation is as inevitable as death and taxes."
11. Explain why the unemployment rate does not always rise when unemployment rises.
12. What are the apparent effects of the business cycle on employment, unemployment, and the number of individuals not in the labor force?
13. If recoveries last four times longer than recessions, what would you expect the long-term trend in real business activity to be?
14. Explain why the GDP deflator may be a better measure of inflation than the CPI.

# CHAPTER 24

# MEASURING OUTPUT AND GROWTH

Every three months, two teams meet in Washington, D.C., under the strictest of security conditions. Each team member is pledged to absolute secrecy. Guards stand at the door. Reporters are kept at bay. The two teams have deliberately been kept apart—each team works independently, so that no one has a view of the entire picture. After the teams meet for one day to reconcile their independent work, their results are announced to an anxiously waiting world.

What are we talking about? Some type of secret national intelligence meeting? An extremely sensitive congressional investigation? What is happening that requires such secrecy and stealth? Both teams comprise statisticians from the U.S. Department of Commerce. One team has been surveying businesses to determine how much output they produced in the three-month period. The other team has been examining data on households and businesses to determine what they earned during the three-month period. The result of the secretive one-day meeting is the official Department of Commerce estimate of

the gross domestic product (GDP) of the United States—that is, how much output the economy produced in the previous quarter.

Why the intense security? Gross domestic product tells the investment community how well the economy is doing. If it is increasing, the economy is expanding, and it may be a good time to buy stocks. If the economy is expanding too rapidly, it may become "overheated" and interest rates will rise. If the economy is slowing down, is a recession imminent? Investors and bankers will use this information to determine whether to invest in stocks, bonds, commodities, or foreign currencies and whether they will make these investments at home or in Europe or Hong Kong.

As we shall discuss in this chapter, measures of the total output of the economy influence far more than short-term decisions about financial investments. They trace the path of the business cycle and they measure economic growth—those two major aspects of the macro economy that we considered in the previous chapter.

# GDP INCOME ACCOUNTING

Statisticians, government officials, and private economists worked for many years to perfect a methodology to measure the total output of an economy. After World War II, they reached an agreement on the methodology that is currently in use, internationally. The United States and the other industrialized countries now have the most accurate and up-to-date statistics on economic output to guide private and public decision making.

## GROSS DOMESTIC PRODUCT: DEFINITION

The most comprehensive measure of the total output of an economy is its gross domestic product (GDP).

> **Gross domestic product (GDP)** is the market value of all final goods and services produced by the factors of production located in the country during a period of one year.

A *good* is a tangible object, such as a can of peaches or an automobile, that has economic value. A *service* is an intangible product (such as a movie or an airline trip) that has economic value.

## THE CIRCULAR FLOW

The circular-flow diagram introduced in Chapter 3 illustrates the most important principle of GDP accounting.

> The value of total output equals the value of total income.

According to this identity, if an economy produces a total output of $500 billion, a total income of $500 billion will automatically be created in the process. Let's consider why.

When output is produced, costs are incurred. Workers and capital costs must be paid, and land must be rented. The owners of businesses receive the profits that remain after all costs are met. Thus, the act of producing goods and services creates income for those supplying the factors of production. Profits or losses equate the value of output with the sum of factor payments. If $500 billion worth of output is produced and sold but only $450 billion is paid to the factors of production, the $50 billion remaining is profit income for the owners of business firms. If

$500 billion worth of output is sold but $550 billion is paid to the factors of production, the $50 billion is a loss for business owners, thereby reducing their income.

## A SIMPLE EXAMPLE OF GDP

Let's consider a simple economy consisting of five industries, whose annual sales are shown in panel (*a*) of Figure 1. These transactions are both final and intermediate. Steel is made from the intermediate goods ore and coal (in addition to land, labor, and capital), autos are made from steel, and clothing is made from the intermediate good cotton.

> **Intermediate goods** are used to produce other goods, such as cotton for making clothing.
>
> **Final goods** are goods that are purchased for final use by consumers or firms, such as cars or clothing or investment goods.

In this example, the value of final goods is the sum of the value of automobile sales and of clothing sales, or $290 billion. There are no capital goods (such as plant and equipment) produced by this simple economy.

The table in panel (*a*) of Figure 1 is divided into three parts. The first column lists intermediate goods used within the business sector; the second column shows the final goods that are produced. Intermediate goods are a means to an end. They are not produced for final sale; they are used to produce goods for final sale. Material well-being is determined by the final goods and services that the economy produces. We shall discuss the third column later.

The circular-flow diagram in panel (*b*) of Figure 1 provides an alternate way of distinguishing final goods from intermediate goods. The upper part of the circular-flow diagram includes only final goods in the flow of output from firms to households. Intermediate goods remain entirely within the business sector. They are shown in the loop to the right. Cotton is an intermediate good because it is used to produce another good, clothing. Automobiles are a final good because they are consumed by households and do not reenter the production process to produce other goods.

Gross domestic product does not include intermediate goods because, if it did, some products would be counted two times or more. In our

## Table A   (a) Annual Sales, Value Added, and GDP

| | Value of Intermediate Goods (billions of dollars of annual sales) | Value of Final Goods (billions of dollars of annual sales) | Value Added of Each Industry (billions of dollars) |
|---|---|---|---|
| Ore, coal | 20 | — | 20 |
| Steel | 100 | — | 80 |
| Autos | | 200 | 100 |
| Cotton | 50 | — | 50 |
| Clothing | | 90 | 40 |
| Total (GDP) | | 290 | 290 |

(b)

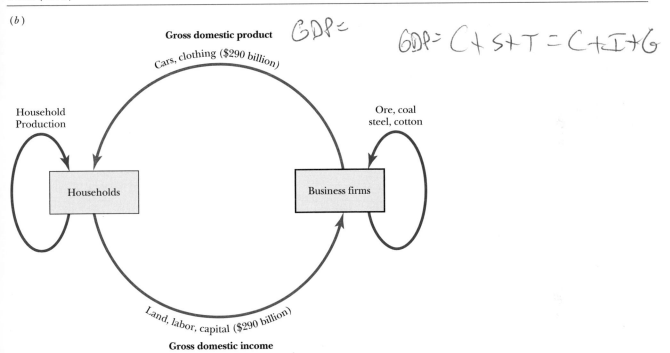

$$GDP =$$

$$GDP = C + S + T = C + I + G$$

FIGURE 1   A Simple Example of GDP

The first column of panel (a) shows the intermediate goods used to produce final goods. The arrows show the flow of intermediate goods through the production process. The second column shows the value of the final goods produced from intermediate goods and from the factors of production. GDP is the value of final goods, or $290 billion. The third column shows the value added of each industry—the value of sales minus purchases from other industries. Ore and coal and cotton are raw material industries that do not purchase materials from other industries. The value added of each industry equals its factor payments. The sum of value added ($290 billion) equals the value of final sales.

Panel (b) shows the circular flow of this economy. The upper part of the circle shows the flow of final products (automobiles and clothing) from businesses to consumers, whose personal consumption expenditures pay for the final products. The lower part of the circle shows the flow of factor services from households to businesses. Households receive payments for their factor services to equal the payments for final products in the top circle. Intermediate goods (ore and coal for making steel, cotton for making clothing) remain within the business sector and are not counted in GDP. Household production (cooking one's own meals and doing one's own laundry) remains within the household sector shown on the left.

example, ore and coal are already counted in the value of steel. Steel is already counted in the value of autos. The measure of total output should not count products more than once. The prices of final goods already include the value of intermediate goods used in their production.

> GDP includes only final goods. If intermediate goods were included, they would be counted more than once and total output would be overstated.

To produce output, firms must hire factors of production—land, labor, and capital—owned by households. The bottom part of the circular-flow diagram shows the supply of the factors of production from households to businesses and the factor payments made by businesses to households for them. The dollar flow of payments for goods and services in the upper half of the diagram exactly equals the dollar flow of factor payments in the bottom half. Goods and services produced by household members remain within the household sector.

## GROSS DOMESTIC PRODUCT: THE SUM OF OUTPUT OR INCOME

Because the total output of the economy equals the total income of the economy, GDP can be calculated either by summing the value of all final goods and services or by summing all factor incomes earned in one year. Both approaches yield the same outcome.

### GDP AS THE SUM OF FINAL EXPENDITURES

In our simplified example, only one type of final product is produced: goods for final consumption by households. In the real world, GDP is calculated by summing four types of final expenditures:

1. Personal consumption expenditures, $C$
2. Investment expenditures, $I$
3. Federal, state, and local government purchases of goods and services, $G$
4. Net exports, $X - M$

*Personal consumption expenditures* are purchases such as food, clothing, TVs, stereos, movie

tickets, plane tickets, and auto repairs. These are all expenditures on final products that are used by households rather than reused to produce other goods.

*Investments* are expenditures that add to (or replace) the economy's stock of *capital* (plants, equipment, industrial and residential structures, and inventories). Unlike intermediate goods, which are used up entirely in the process of making other goods (steel is used up to make autos, cotton is used up to make clothing), capital is only *partially* depleted in making other goods. A steel mill may have a useful life of 40 years. In producing steel during any one year, only a small portion (say, one-fortieth) of the mill is consumed. The ore and cooking coal, on the other hand, are entirely consumed in producing steel. A computer's working life may be three years before it becomes obsolete. The bank using the computer to manage its accounts uses up only a portion (say, one-third) of the computer in producing one year's banking services. The wear and tear on the machinery used during the production process causes it to depreciate. The using up of capital is called depreciation. Depreciation is a business cost, just like labor costs or material costs.

> **Depreciation** is the value of the existing capital stock that has been consumed or used up in the process of producing output.

Business investment is classified as either inventory investment or fixed investment. Both types increase the economy's productive capacity.

> **Inventory investment** is the increase (or decrease) in the value of the stocks of inventories that businesses have on hand.
>
> **Fixed investment** is investment in plant, structures, and equipment.

If business inventories are $200 billion at the beginning of the year and $250 billion at the year's end, inventory investment is $50 billion. Inventory investment can be either positive or negative. In the next chapter, on saving and investment, we shall discuss one unusual feature of inventory investment: Inventory investment can sometimes be involuntary, the result of unsold output. If an automobile producer makes more cars than it can sell, the unsold cars are counted as inventory investment, even though the producer may be very disappointed that all cars were not sold.

*Federal, state, and local government purchases of goods and services* are counted as final expenditures. Governments spend money to run the legal system, to provide for the national defense, and to run the schools. They buy disks, computers, and photocopiers from private businesses. Although some government expenditures strongly resemble intermediate expenditures—such as government regulation of business and agricultural extension services—almost all government purchases of goods and services are counted as final. Because they are typically not sold to final consumers, there is usually no market valuation for government goods and services. Unlike other services, government services are usually valued at the *cost of supplying* them. For example, the value of public education is the sum of expenditures on education; the value of national defense is the sum of expenditures on national defense. Only government *purchases of goods and services* are counted in GDP. Transfer payments are not included.

> **Transfer payments** are payments to recipients who have not earned them through the sale of their factors of production and who have not supplied current goods or services in exchange for these payments.

Transfer payments, as the name implies, are transfers of income from one person or organization to another. The largest transfer payments are handled by the Social Security Administration, which transfers incomes from those currently working to eligible retired or disabled workers. Government interest payments are also transfer payments.

Federal, state, and local governments also make expenditures on roads, bridges, sewers, septic systems, and airports. These expenditures are typically classified as investment, just like private investment, because they add to the economy's stock of capital. In the United States, however, all government expenditures are arbitrarily counted as purchases of goods and services whether they are for current or capital expenditures.

All the final expenditures by households, businesses, and government added together do not equal the total output of the economy because some of the items purchased are imported from abroad and must be subtracted. Some domestic output is exported to other countries, and must be added to total purchases. The total output of the economy is therefore the sum of final expenditures *plus* exports *minus* imports. The subtraction of imports from exports yields the *net exports* of goods and services ($X - M$).

> **Net exports of goods and services** is the difference between exports of goods and services ($X$) by a particular country and its imports of goods and services from other countries ($M$), or $X - M$.

The next chapter, on saving and investment, will also make clear that whenever a country imports from abroad more than it sells abroad, it is increasing its indebtedness to the rest of the world—it is receiving savings from the rest of the world to supplement its domestic saving. If I sell you $150 worth of goods and you sell me $200 worth of goods, this transaction results in my owing you $50. The same is true for countries. Whenever $M$ exceeds $X$, other countries have, in effect, supplied their savings to the domestic economy.

> **Foreign savings** supplied to the domestic economy are the difference between imports and exports, or $M - X$.

Unlike the simple economy of only consumer goods, real-world economies produce four categories of goods, the sum of which constitutes the total output, or GDP, of the economy.

> **GDP** is the sum of personal consumption expenditures, government purchases of goods and services, investment expenditures, and net exports.
>
> $$\text{GDP} = C + I + G + X - M \quad (+ \text{ Net Exports})$$

Table 1 gives U.S. GDP by final expenditures. It shows that the U.S. economy produced more than $7 trillion in 1995.

## GDP AS THE SUM OF INCOMES

As we noted above, the total output of the economy can be calculated either as the value of final output or as the total income created in producing that output. As we saw from the circular-flow diagram in Figure 1, the value of final goods and services produced by an economy (GDP) equals gross domestic income (GDI).

## Table 1    GDP by Final Expenditure, 1995

| Expenditure Category | Amount (billions of dollars) | Percentage of Total |
|---|---|---|
| **Personal consumption expenditures** | **4965** | 68.0 |
| Durable goods | 616 | |
| Nondurable goods | 1491 | |
| Services | 2858 | |
| **Government purchases of goods and services** | **1366** | 18.7 |
| Federal government | 517 | |
| State and local government | 848 | |
| **Gross private domestic investment** | **1067** | 14.6 |
| Nonresidential structures | 202 | |
| Equipment | 544 | |
| Residential structures | 290 | |
| Inventory investment | −31 | |
| **Net exports** | **−101** | −1.3 |
| **GDP** | **7297** | 100 |

> **Gross domestic income (GDI)** is approximately the sum of all income earned by the factors of production.

GDI equals GDP *only approximately* because GDI includes depreciation and sales and excise taxes that are not really income to the factors of production.

With GDP = GDI, GDP can be calculated either by adding up the incomes earned by the factors of production located in the country or by summing the incomes paid out by producing enterprises. Both methods yield the same total. In Figure 1, the contribution to GDP produced by any one industry—by ore and coal, by steel, by automobiles, by cotton, or by clothing—does not equal each industry's sales because of double counting. The automobile industry's share would be overstated because its sales include the value of the steel that it uses to produce cars. Instead, each industry's contribution to GDP is determined by calculating its net output, or value added.

> The **net output,** or **value added,** of an industry is the value of its output minus the value of its purchases from other industries.

The last column of panel (*a*) in Figure 1 shows that the value added of the automobile industry equals the sales of automobiles ($200 billion) minus purchases from the steel industry ($100 billion), or $100 billion. The value added of steel is the output of steel ($100 billion) minus its purchases from the ore and coal industries ($20 billion), or $80 billion.

The value added of ore and coal equals its sales ($20 billion) because, in this example, ore and coal make no purchases from other industries. The value of industry output minus the purchases from other industries equals the payments to labor, capital, land, and entrepreneurship. Panel (*a*) shows that the sum of industry value added ($290 billion) is the same as the sum of the value of final products ($290 billion).

> Gross domestic product can be calculated either as the sum of industry sales minus purchases from other industries or as the sum of incomes.

United States GDP is calculated as the sum of incomes in Table 2 and as the sum of industry value added in Table 3. They provide different information. Table 2 shows that wage income is the most important source of income. Table 3 shows that the service industry produces more output than other industries.

## OMISSIONS FROM GDP

Measuring the total output of an economy is not as easy as it looks. There are a number of areas that are difficult to define and measure. Some think we overstate GDP and its growth. Others think we understate it. (See Example 1.)

| Table 2  Gross Domestic Product by Type of Income, 1995 | | |
|---|---|---|
| Type of Income | Amount (billions of dollars) | Percentage |
| Compensation of employees | 4233 | 58.0 |
| Proprietors' income | 480 | 6.5 |
| Rental income of persons | 118 | 1.6 |
| Corporate profits | 614 | 8.4 |
| Net interest | 400 | 5.5 |
| Depreciation, indirect business taxes, net payments to rest of world, and 0000 other adjustments | 1452 | 20.0 |
| GDP = GDI | 7927 | 100 |

## NONMARKETED GOODS AND SERVICES

Vegetables can be grown in one's backyard instead of being bought at the grocery store. A leaky faucet can be repaired by the homeowner instead of the plumber. These are *nonmarketed goods and services* that have been acquired without using markets. In most cases, GDP excludes barter transactions and production within the household.

The less developed countries of Africa and Asia have a larger proportion of transactions taking place outside of organized markets. Accordingly, GDP measures tend to understate their total output. One reason people in poor African or Asian countries can get by on what appears to be a few hundred dollars a year is that many of the things they consume they make, barter, or grow themselves.

The exclusion of nonmarketed goods and services can have a substantial effect on the size of GDP.

If services performed by homemakers are purchased—if dirty clothes are always taken to the laundry or if babysitters are hired—they will be a part of GDP. If performed in the home, they are not included. The typical married couple, for example, spends one-quarter of their discretionary time on unpaid work in the home. The inclusion of the services of the more than 29 million homemakers would raise GDP as much as 20 to 50 percent.

## ILLEGAL ACTIVITIES

Gross domestic product does not include illegal goods and services—such as illegal gambling, murder for hire, prostitution, or illegal drugs—even though they are final products usually purchased in market transactions. Illicit moonlighting activities, such as an electrician working for cash after hours to avoid income taxes, are excluded also. These activities make up the underground economy.

Estimates of the size of the American underground economy vary considerably. The Internal Revenue Services thinks its volume is between 6 percent and 8 percent of GDP. These percentages suggest an underground economy in excess of $500 billion—about one-third the size of federal government spending. The American underground economy is smaller in relative terms than that of other countries, such as France and Italy, where it may reach 25 percent of GDP.

If GDP properly measures the level of economic activity, underground economic activities should be included. Official GDP could show slackening production and employment when in reality activity has

| Table 3  Gross Domestic Product by Net Output (value added), 1995 | | |
|---|---|---|
| Industry | Value Added (billions of dollars) | Percentage |
| Agriculture, forestry, fisheries | 138 | 1.9 |
| Mining | 102 | 1.4 |
| Construction | 270 | 3.7 |
| Manufacturing | 1291 | 17.7 |
| Transportation and utilities | 642 | 8.8 |
| Wholesale and retail trade | 1152 | 15.8 |
| Finance, insurance, real estate | 1342 | 18.4 |
| Services | 1437 | 19.7 |
| Government and government enterprises | 923 | 12.6 |
| GDP | 7297 | 100.0 |

*Source: Survey of Current Business.*

## EXAMPLE 1
## IS GDP TOO HIGH
## OR TOO LOW?

No other economic statistic is as important as GDP. The financial community looks at GDP as the best indicator of the health of the economy. Federal budget planners use projections of GDP to calculate what federal revenues and expenditures will be in the future. Although there is a consensus on the definition of GDP, we cannot measure it with precision. Some experts think we overestimate GDP; others think we underestimate it.

Alan Greenspan, the chairman of the Federal Reserve System, is an influential critic of GDP, arguing that we understate GDP growth because we overlook the quality improvements that new technology brings. The automobile of the late 1990s, with its many safety features and better gasoline mileage, is much better than the auto of the 1970s. Today's high-speed notebook computer is much better than the bulky low-speed computer of the early 1980s. Government statisticians cannot properly correct for these quality improvements.

The U.S. Department of Commerce, on the other hand, fears that its own estimate overestimates GDP growth because it has calculated real GDP in fixed-weight prices, such as constant 1987 prices. Any fixed-weight price will tend to overstate growth because products that have grown very fast (such as computers) will receive too much emphasis. In 1987, computers were much more expensive relative to other products than they are today. Their decline in prices is what made purchases grow so fast. When we value the fast-growing computer sector in their "high" 1987 prices, they will account for a relatively large share of GDP. If, on the other hand, we value computers at their current "low" prices, this fast-growing sector will have a smaller share of GDP. For this reason, the Department of Commerce issued a new "chain-weighted" GDP index in early 1996, which changes the GDP price weights each year. This chain-weighted index yields a slower rate of growth of GDP. (See accompanying diagram.)

Some think GDP is too high; some too low. No one can be sure.

------------------------------------------------

Source: U.S. Department of Commerce, Redefining Progress, January 1995.

---

simply shifted to the underground economy. If illegal activities are omitted, a false impression of economic activity, unemployment, and income may be obtained.

Illegal activities cannot realistically be included in GDP. First, it is impossible to obtain reliable statistics on the underground economy. Second, overtly illegal activities such as murder, according to prevailing legislation and morals, are viewed as lowering material well-being.

### THE VALUE OF LEISURE

The number of hours Americans work has declined dramatically over the past 50 years. We have chosen to produce a smaller flow of goods and services in return for more leisure. We can "afford" this extra leisure because of the great increases in productivity that have taken place since the Industrial Revolution. As we have become more efficient, our incomes have risen and more output can be produced by the same number of workers. Should GDP be adjusted upwards to reflect our voluntary choice of leisure? After all, voluntary increases in leisure raise material well-being just as increases in goods and services do.

Gross domestic product would increase dramatically if the value of leisure were included. In 1900, workers in manufacturing worked, on average, a 60-hour week. By 1996, this figure had fallen to 40 hours per week. If American workers worked the same number of hours now as they did in 1900, output would be much greater than it actually is.

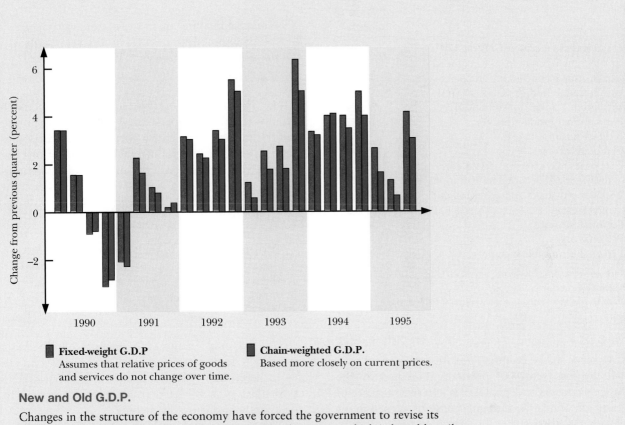

■ **Fixed-weight G.D.P**
  Assumes that relative prices of goods
  and services do not change over time.

■ **Chain-weighted G.D.P.**
  Based more closely on current prices.

**New and Old G.D.P.**

Changes in the structure of the economy have forced the government to revise its
chief gauge of output. Switching to a chain-weighted measure, which is based heavily
on current price information, eliminates upward biases.
Sources: U.S. Department of Commerce, Redefining Progress. *The New York Times*,
December 19, 1995.

## FROM GDP TO DISPOSABLE INCOME

Gross domestic product is the broadest measure of
the economy's total output. We often require less
broad measures of output and income to study the
economy, such as how much we save or spend. In addition, GDP includes items that do not represent new
production, such as depreciation, and items that do
not represent income for individuals or businesses,
such as indirect taxes and social security payroll
taxes. Gross domestic product omits transfer payments, which account for almost $1 trillion worth of
personal income in the United States.

Table 4 shows the step-by-step process for determining how much of GDP households are actually
free to spend and to save.

1. *Gross national product (GNP)*. Both GDP
and GNP measure total output, but different criteria
are used to determine which goods and services to include. Gross domestic product includes the goods
and services produced by labor and capital *located in
the United States*, whether or not suppliers are residents of the United States. By contrast, GNP includes
the goods and services produced by labor and property *supplied by U.S. residents*, whether they are located in the United States or abroad.

> **Gross national product (GNP)** measures the
> final output produced by U.S. residents
> whether located in the United States or
> abroad.

## Table 4  From GDP to Personal Disposable Income, 1995

| Item | Amount (billions of dollars) |
|---|---:|
| Gross Domestic Product (GDP) = GDI | 7297 |
| Factor income receipts from foreigners | 204 |
| Factor income payments to foreigners | −220 |
| **Gross National Product (GNP) = GNI** | 7281 |
| Depreciation (capital consumption) | −829 |
| **1. Net national product (NNP)** | 6452 |
| Indirect business taxes[a] | −607 |
| **2. National income** | 5845 |
| Corporate taxes, undistributed corporate profit, Social Security contributions | −1678 |
| Transfer payments and government interest | +1965 |
| **3. Personal income** | 6132 |
| Personal taxes | −801 |
| **4. Personal disposable income** | 5331 |

[a]Minor items, such as business payments and government subsidies, are also subtracted here.
*Source:* Department of Commerce, Bureau of Economic Analysis.

Gross domestic product measures the production taking place in the country, not the production produced by the factors of production owned by the country's citizens. Hence, GDP is a better measure of production and is the measure commonly used in international statistics.

Most U.S. labor and capital is located in the immense U.S. economy; thus, the difference between U.S. GDP and GNP is small. In some countries such as the Philippines or Turkey, where a large number of citizens work abroad, the difference is great.

2. *Net national product (NNP).* Gross national product includes depreciation. If GNP is $2500 billion and depreciation is $250 billion, then 10 percent of output simply replaces the capital that has been consumed. Net national product (NNP) measures the total value of *new* goods and services produced by the economy by excluding depreciation from GNP.

> **Net national product (NNP)** equals GNP minus depreciation.

3. *National income.* Included in NNP are sales and excise taxes, called *indirect business taxes,* that are not payments to the factors of production. Although they augment the revenues of government, sales and excise taxes do not generate income for individuals. When indirect business taxes are sub-

tracted from NNP, national income, or the total payments to the factors of production in the economy, remains.

> **National income** equals net national product minus indirect business taxes, and represents the sum of all payments made to the factors of production.

4. *Personal income.* Not all national income is actually received by persons as income. Corporate profits that are retained by corporations, corporate income taxes, and social insurance contributions are not received by persons. Personal income includes transfer payments and interest payments that individuals receive from government (which are not included in GDP).

> **Personal income** equals national income *minus* retained corporate profits, corporate income taxes, and social insurance contributions plus transfer payments and government interest payments.

5. *Personal disposable income.* Individuals must pay federal, state, and local income taxes. In order to determine potential spending power, income taxes must be subtracted from personal income to yield personal disposable income.

The various measures of output and income—GDP, NNP, personal income, and disposable income—are alternative measures of output and income. Each serves a different purpose and looks at output or income from a different perspective.

## REAL GDP

Because GDP is measured in dollar values, it can rise either because of an increase in the *quantities* of goods and services produced or because of an increase in *prices.* The concepts of nominal and real GDP serve to distinguish quantity changes from price changes.

Gross domestic product that is measured in current prices is nominal GDP, or GDP in current prices.

> **Nominal GDP,** or **GDP in current prices,** is the value of final goods and services produced in a given year in that year's prices.

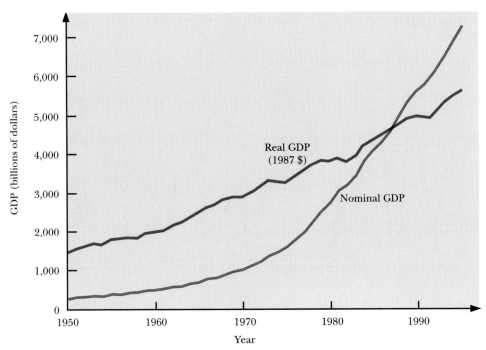

**FIGURE 2    Real Versus Nominal GDP, 1950–1995**

*Source: Economic Report of the President.*

Economists use real GDP to eliminate the effects of rising prices on the measure of output.

> **Real GDP** measures the volume of real goods and services by removing the effects of rising prices on nominal GDP.

Between 1987 and 1995, nominal GDP rose from $4.5 trillion to $7.3 trillion, while real GDP (in 1987 prices) rose from $4.5 trillion to $5.6 trillion. Nominal GDP increased by 62 percent; real GDP increased by 24 percent. The 38 percent difference was due to rising prices. (See Figure 2.)

Real GDP shows the movements in the level of real business activity we discussed in the previous chapter. Recessions occur when real GDP declines; booms occur when real GDP expands rapidly. For these reasons, economists are more interested in real GDP than in nominal GDP.

Real GDP has a number of uses: By comparing real GDP over short periods of time (quarters, years), we get a picture of the business cycle. By comparing real GDP over a long period of time (five years, or decades), we see the economic growth of the economy.

## REAL GDP AND ECONOMIC GROWTH

We measure the growth of the economy by comparing real GDP in different periods of time. Changes in real GDP measure the growth of the economy as a whole. Changes in real GDP per capita measure the growth of output per person. We calculate real GDP per capita by dividing real GDP by population.

Real GDP per capita is the best measure of living standards. If real GDP is growing faster than population, average material well-being is increasing, especially if that increase in material wealth is broadly distributed. It is the sustained rise in real per capita GDP, beginning with the Industrial Revolution, that explains the material prosperity we enjoy today in the advanced industrialized economies.

We measure economic growth, either of real GDP or of real GDP per capita, in terms of annual growth rates. Figure 3 shows the annual growth rates of U.S. real GDP and real GDP per capita for the period 1950 to the present.

## REAL GDP AND THE BUSINESS CYCLE

Real GDP is a comprehensive measure of the business cycle. We use quarterly (three-month) estimates

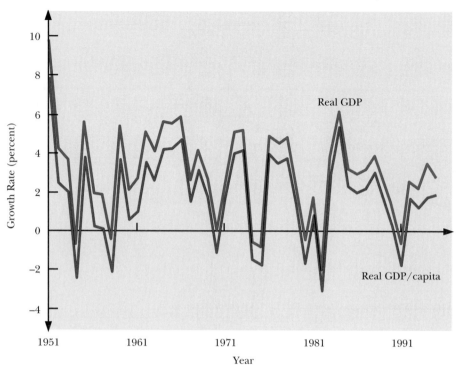

**FIGURE 3    Growth of Real GDP Versus Real GDP per Capita, 1950–1995**
*Source: Economic Report of the President.*

of real GDP for business cycle measurement. Because the business cycle is a short-run phenomenon and population does not change much over a short period, we use real GDP and not real GDP per capita to measure the business cycle. We know from the previous chapter that a recession occurs when real GDP declines for six months or more. Figure 4 uses quarterly figures to show the last recession experienced by the U.S. economy (1990 and 1991) and its ongoing recovery since then.

## REAL GDP: AN INTERNATIONAL COMPARISON

To determine the output of our economy relative to other economies, we can compare real GDP or real GDP per capita: The real GDP comparison shows the relative size of our economy relative to other economies, and the per capita comparison provides insights into the material standard of living of one country relative to other countries.

Each country's GDP is measured in its own prices. We measure U.S. GDP in dollars and Japanese GDP in yen. Therefore, to make international comparisons, we must convert these measures into a common currency, like the U.S. dollar. The simplest

way of making this conversion is to use prevailing exchange rates. If the German economy produces, say, three trillion German marks of GDP and the exchange rate is $1 = 1.5 German marks, German GDP is $2.0 trillion.

Economists do not like to use exchange rates because they often do not reflect the true purchasing power of the currency. For example, a U.S. dollar may buy more real goods and services in the United States than 1.5 German marks will buy in Germany. Therefore, for international comparisons economists usually convert GDP into a common currency using purchasing power parity.

> **Purchasing power parity (PPP)** is a rate for converting one economy's output into the prices of another country. It is the exchange rate between two currencies that equates the real buying power of both currencies.

Panel (*a*) of Figure 5 shows U.S. real GDP relative to other countries. We can see that the United States is by far the world's largest economy, more than twice as large as that of the second-largest economy, Japan. Panel (*b*) of Figure 5 shows U.S. real

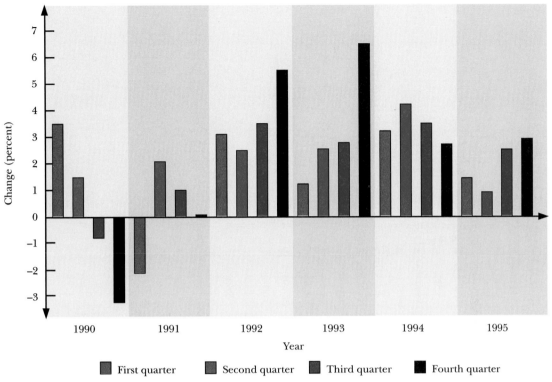

First quarter   Second quarter   Third quarter   Fourth quarter

**FIGURE 4   Real GDP by Quarter, 1990–1995**

Percent change, seasonally adjusted annual rate.

GDP per capita. Here, we see that the United States, contrary to popular opinion, still has the world's highest standard of living. (See Example 2.)

## OUTPUT, ECONOMIC ACTIVITY, AND SATISFACTION

Economists do not claim that real GDP per capita is a measure of satisfaction or happiness. It is simply a measure of the real goods and services at our disposal. Often, the more we have, the more we want, and the less time we have to enjoy our standard of living. It may be that we Americans are less happy than people who live in less rich countries and who have much less than we. (See Example 3.)

Real GDP also includes goods and services such as assault rifles, pornography, and low-quality TV programming that many believe do not improve our well-being. Real GDP also does not adjust for the external effects of production (a notion introduced in Chapter 5). If a factory that produces chemical fertilizers pollutes the environment, there is no adjustment for this negative effect on third parties.

We must recognize the specific intent in using real GDP—it measures the market output of all final goods and services. As such, real GDP is our most comprehensive yardstick of the level of economic activity, which affects how much employment and unemployment there is and how much inflation we have. Gross domestic product per capita is a better comparative measures of a country's productivity, prosperity, and wealth. We shall use real GDP as the measure of output in the chapters that follow.

1. GDP accounting measures the total output of the economy. The value of total output equals the value of total income, because the act of producing output automatically creates an equivalent amount of income. Gross domestic product (GDP) is the broadest measure of the total output of the economy. It is the dollar value of all final goods and services produced by an economy during a one-year period. Only final goods and services are included, in order to avoid the double counting of products.

(*a*) Real GDP

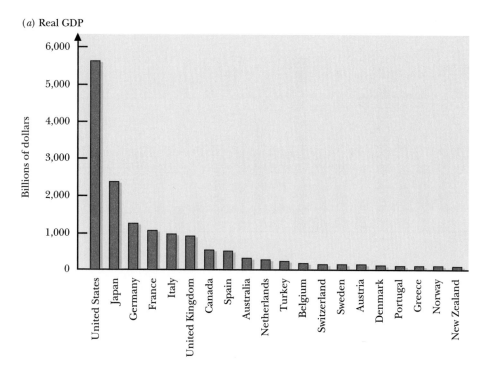

(*b*) Real GDP per capita

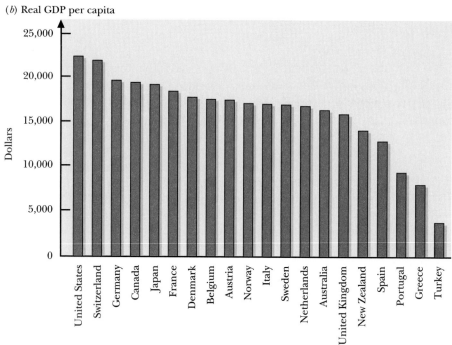

**FIGURE 5   International Comparison of GDP (1991 data)**

*Source: Statistical Abstract,* p. 864

## EXAMPLE 2
## THE UNITED STATES IS STILL
## THE WORLD'S RICHEST COUNTRY

The text described two ways of computing relative GDP. One method uses exchange rates to convert foreign GDP into U.S. dollars. The other method uses purchasing power parity rates to convert foreign GDP into U.S. dollars. The two approaches can yield quite different results when exchange rates do not reflect purchasing power. In the early 1990s, the U.S. dollar was "undervalued" in foreign exchange markets; that is, the market exchange rates at which foreign currencies exchanged for dollars were below the dollar's purchasing power. For example, $1 U.S. exchanged for 120 Japanese yen even though $1 dollar could buy much more goods and services in the United States than 120 yen could buy in Japan.

The accompanying figure shows how important it is to use proper measures. All of the countries that have higher per capita GDPs than the United States when exchange rates are used have lower values when the purchasing power parity figures are used.

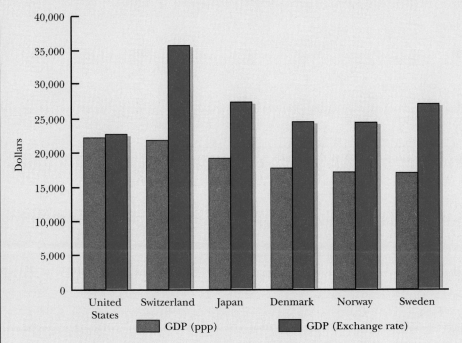

**GDP per Capita Versus Exchange Rate per Capita (1991 data)**

*Source: Statistical Abstract*, pp. 862, 864.

## EXAMPLE 3
## HAPPINESS AND
## LIVING STANDARDS

Economists do not claim a positive relationship between material well-being and happiness. Three measures that may reflect "unhappiness" are divorce, suicide, and unemployment. All should be negatively related to happiness. The accompanying figures show the lack of relation- ships between each of these "unhappiness" indicators and real GDP per capita. As these figures show, there is no significant relationship between material well-being and divorce, suicide, or un- employment. Happiness or sadness is determined by factors other than material well-being.

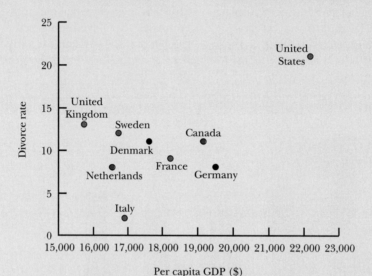

**Real GDP Versus Divorce (1991 data)**

Divorce rate per 1000 married women; data not available for Japan.

2. We can calculate GDP by measuring the total value of final products or by measuring the total value of income. We can calculate the total value of income as the sum of factor payments or as the sum of the value added by all industries. Therefore, there are three methods for computing GDP:

a. GDP = Personal consumption expenditures + Government expenditures for goods and services + Investment + Net exports.

b. GDP = Compensation of employees + Propri- etors' income + Rental income + Corporate profits + Interest + Depreciation + Indirect busi- ness taxes.

c. GDP = The sum of the value added of all indus- tries. Value added equals the value of output mi- nus purchases from other sectors. Value added also equals the sum of factor payments made by the sector.

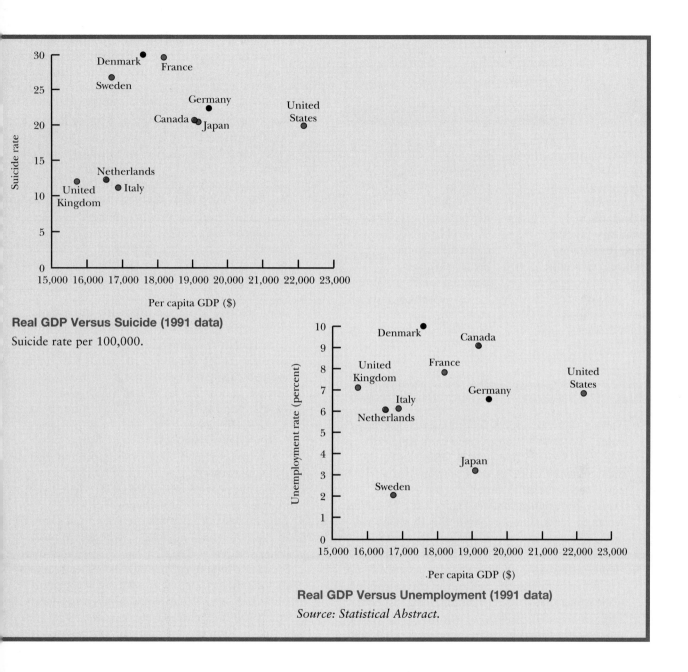

**Real GDP Versus Suicide (1991 data)**
Suicide rate per 100,000.

**Real GDP Versus Unemployment (1991 data)**
*Source: Statistical Abstract.*

3. Nominal GDP is the value of final goods and services in current market prices. Either increasing output or rising prices can cause nominal GDP to rise. Real GDP measures the volume of real output by removing the effects of changing prices.

4. Nonmarketed goods, illegal goods, and the value of leisure are not included in GDP.

5. Gross national product (GNP) measures the output produced by factors of production owned by

a country's citizens, whether these factors are used at home or abroad. Net national production (NNP) equals GNP minus depreciation. National income equals NNP minus indirect business taxes. Personal income equals national income *minus* factor payments not received by individuals and social insurance contributions *plus* transfer payments. Personal disposable income equals personal income minus personal taxes.

6. Real GDP and real GDP per capita measure long-term growth and the short-term business cycle.

7. The United States is the world's largest economy and has the world's highest per capita income.

## KEY TERMS

| | |
|---|---|
| gross domestic product (GDP) | net output, or value added |
| intermediate goods | gross national product (GNP) |
| final goods | net national product (NNP) |
| depreciation | |
| inventory investment | |
| fixed investment | national income |
| transfer payments | personal income |
| net exports of goods and services | nominal GDP, or GDP in current dollars |
| foreign savings | real GDP |
| gross domestic income (GDI) | purchasing power parity (PPP) |

## QUESTIONS AND PROBLEMS

1. The economy produces final goods and services valued at $500 billion in one year's time but sells only $450 billion worth. Does this result mean that the value of final output does not equal the value of income?

2. Discuss the implications (in Figure 1) of $5 billion worth of coal being purchased directly by households to heat their homes. Assume that nothing else in Figure 1 changes. How and why will this change affect GDP? Will it affect value added?

3. An industry spends $6 million on the factors of production that it uses (including entrepreneurship). It sells $10 million worth of output. How much value added has this industry created, and how much has this industry purchased from other industries?

4. Explain why investment is regarded as a final product even though it is used as a factor of production to produce other goods.

5. A large corporation gives a grant to a classical musician to allow her to train her skills in Europe. How will this payment enter into GDP? Into personal income? Will this payment differ from one made to an engineer employed by the corporation?

6. Which of the following investment categories can be negative: inventory investment, fixed investment, or net fixed investment (gross investment minus depreciation)? Explain your answer.

7. Explain why GDP measures may tend to overstate the GDP of rich countries relative to poor countries.

8. Personal disposable income is $100 billion, personal consumption expenditures are $80 billion, taxes are $40 billion, and government expenditures for goods and services are $50 billion. Net exports equal $0, and there is no business saving. How much total saving is there in the economy? How much is private saving?

9. In an economy, $300 billion worth of final goods and services are purchased. Explain under what conditions GDP will be more or less than $300 billion.

10. Calculate GDP, net national product, and national income from the following data: Consumption equals $100 billion; investment plus government spending equals $50 billion; net exports equal $0; depreciation equals $10 billion; indirect business taxes equal $5 billion.

11. In year 1, nominal GDP was $200 billion. In year 2, nominal GDP was $300 billion. In year 1, the GDP deflator was 100. In year 2, the GDP deflator was 125.
    a. Express year 2 GDP in the prices of year 1.
    b. Calculate the growth of real GDP.

12. What happens to measured GDP when a person marries his or her housekeeper?

13. Explain why illegal goods are not counted in GDP.

14. In Nevada gambling is legal, whereas in most other states it is illegal. If one were to measure Nevada's final output, would it be necessary to include the net income produced by the gambling industry? What would happen to measured U.S. GDP if gambling were legalized in all states?

15. A corporation earns a profit of $10 million. It distributes $4 million of this profit to its shareholders. It also sets aside in its depreciation accounts a sum of $6 million to replace depreciating capital. How much money has this corporation saved?

16. In 1995, the federal government spent more than it took in as revenues. The revenues of state and local governments, however, exceeded their expenditures. Which government units were saving and which were spending more than their income? How would total government saving or dissaving be calculated?

# APPENDIX 24A

# TIME SERIES ANALYSIS

Macroeconomics studies relationships among macroeconomic variables such as real GDP, employment, unemployment, inflation, and interest rates. Macroeconomics uses time series data to study variability, correlation, trends, and cycles.

Macroeconomists spend a great deal of their effort analyzing the behavior of economic data over time, called time series data.

> A **time series** is a measurement of some variable over a designated period of time.

Time series can be measured in months, quarters, or years. In analyzing time series, we need tools to describe their behavior and interrelationships in an efficient and convenient manner.

## STANDARD DEVIATION

The standard deviation is a measure of dispersion. It tells us where a particular value fits into the general pattern formed by the other observations. Describing a particular pattern by its standard deviation gives us a universal measure of dispersion. As we shall demonstrate, no matter what phenomenon we are discussing, a range of outcomes covering one standard deviation is large, a range covering two standard deviations is very large, and a range covering three standard deviations is gigantic.

> The **standard deviation** is a measure of the dispersion of the general pattern formed by our empirical observations of a particular variable, such as the rate of growth of real GDP or the rate of inflation.

Many patterns can be formed. Figure A1 shows the pattern formed by the normal distribution, often called the bell curve because it is shaped like a bell. The vertical height shows how often the observation takes place; the horizontal axis measures standard deviations away from the mean or average. Most observations cluster about the average (which is 0 in Figure A1) and then fan out. Very few observations occur above or below three standard deviations from the mean: thus, the height of the bell curve diminishes rapidly as we move away from the average value. About two-thirds of the observations fall within one standard deviation of the average.

The bell curve proves a good approximation in many cases, even when a pattern does not fit it exactly. For example, the average annual rate of inflation in the United States has been 4.8 percent from 1960 to 1995, with a standard deviation of about 2.4 percent. However, over 90 percent of the annual inflation rates have been within two standard deviations of 4.8 percent and, indeed, two-thirds have been within *one* standard deviation of 4.8 percent.

To say that the inflation rate in 1981 was 10 percent gives us very little information by itself. However, if we hear that the inflation rate in 1981 was two standard deviations above the mean, we know that the event was rare. If the inflation rate in 1996 is about one standard deviation below the mean, we know the difference is large but much more common than the 1981 experience.

The larger the standard deviation, the more the individual values are spread out. The smaller the standard deviation, the closer the individual values cluster about the average. Italy's inflation rate has a standard deviation that is almost twice that of the United States. Thus, the inflation rate in Italy is far more volatile than that in the United States.

The mean and standard deviation provide some insight about the future. In the case of inflation, they suggest that the probability is very low that the inflation rate in the United States will be less than zero or greater than 9.6 percent.

## HOW TO MEASURE THE STANDARD DEVIATION

It is useful to know how to calculate the standard deviation. The standard deviation is the square root of the average of the squared deviations of the individual values from their average or mean value. This is less complicated than it sounds. Suppose we observe the prices of corn and wheat in three different months—January, February, and March:

|  | *Jan.* | *Feb.* | *Mar.* |
|---|---|---|---|
| Corn | $2 | $3 | $4 |
| Wheat | $1 | $3 | $5 |

Clearly, the price of wheat varies more than the price of corn—wheat varies from $1 to $5, while corn only varies from $2 to $4. We can measure the extent to which the two prices vary just by looking at the range of prices—that is, the difference between the high and low prices. However, this measure does not always work well because it is sensitive to abnormally low or high values that are unrepresentative of the entire experience.

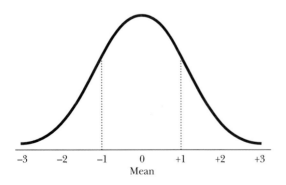

**FIGURE A1    Standard Deviations**

| | Observation | Average | Deviation | Deviation Squared (Deviation)$^2$ |
|---|---|---|---|---|
| Wheat | $2 | $3 | −$1 | $1 |
| Jan. | 1 | 3 | −$2 | $4 |
| Feb. | 3 | 3 | 0 | 0 |
| March | 5 | 3 | +2 | 4 |
| Sum | | | | 8 |

**Table A1   Calculating Standard Deviation**

Number of observations (N): 3
Standard Deviation (S.D.): $\sqrt{2.66} = 1.63$ (s) Average: 8/3 = 2.66

The definition of the standard deviation tells us first to compute the average price of both corn and wheat: It is $3 for both. The basic building block of this better measure of dispersion is the deviation of the individual observations from their average. In the case of corn, the deviations are −$1, $0, and +$1. In the case of wheat, the deviations are −$2, $0, and +$2. The standard deviation requires us next to square these deviations and take the average. The squared values of corn's deviations are $1, $0, and $1 and the average of these three values is 0.67. The square root of 0.67 is corn's standard deviation, or 0.82. Wheat's squared deviations are $4, 0, and $4. The average of the three values: ($4 + 0 + $4)/3 = $2.67. The square root of 2.67 is wheat's standard deviation of 1.63. Table A1 shows how to calculate the standard deviation in the case of wheat. Wheat's standard deviation (1.63) is more than double corn's standard deviation, showing that wheat's price is more than twice as dispersed as corn's price.

## CORRELATION

Microeconomics studies how variables are related to each other—in short, their covariation, or how they vary together. Macroeconomists are also interested in the relationship among real GDP and inflation, employment and inflation, interest rates and inflation.

No two macroeconomic time series are perfectly related. Whenever real GDP increases by $100 billion, the GDP deflator does not increase (or fall) by exactly 5 points. Sometimes, a $100 billion real GDP increase may be accompanied by a 2 point increase in the GDP deflator, next by a 4 point increase, and perhaps next by no increase or even a decrease. What we need to know is whether there is the general ten-

dency for real GDP increases to be accompanied by increases in the GDP deflator (a positive relationship) or by decreases (a negative relationship). We also need to know whether this is a strong or weak relationship.

The correlation coefficient measures how close the relationship is between two variables. The correlation coefficient ranges from +1 for a perfect positive correlation to −1 for a perfect negative correlation. The closer the correlation coefficient is to 1 or −1, the stronger the correlation; the closer the correlation coefficient is to 0, the weaker the correlation. Thus, .8 indicates a strong positive correlation and −.2 indicates a weak negative correlation.

> The **correlation coefficient** is a measure of the statistical association between two variables ranging from +1 for a perfect positive correlation to −1 for a perfect negative correlation.

Figure A2 provides graphs of several types of correlation. Panels (a) and (b) show perfect correlations of 1 and −1, respectively. The individual observations, indicated by the heavy dots, all lie on a straight line. Panel (c) shows a high positive correlation: The dots closely cluster around a straight line through the points. The straight line shows the closest possible "fit" to the set of observations. Panel (d) shows a low positive correlation: The straight line fits the points much more loosely. Panel (e) shows a zero correlation.

Correlations may be misleading. There can be a *spurious correlation* between two variables that are completely unrelated. A spurious correlation might arise because there is an indirect connection. For example, there is a positive correlation between moderate drinking and long life—perhaps because people who are sickly seldom drink alcoholic beverages, or

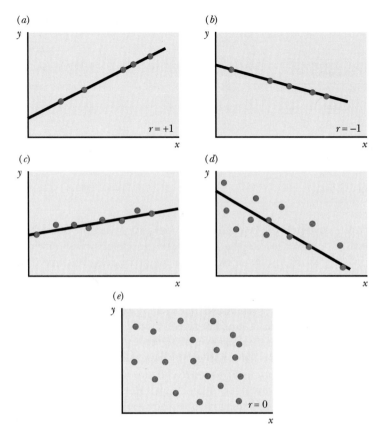

**FIGURE A2   Types of Correlation**

(*a*) Perfect positive correlation, (*b*) perfect negative correlation, (*c*) high positive correlation, (*d*) low negative correlation, and (*e*) zero correlation, variables uncorrelated.

simply because of a series of coincidences. Everything is positively or negatively correlated with *something*. We can search through data for a positive correlation or negative correlation and use it to "prove" almost any association. One purpose of scientific theories is to rule out spurious correlations. In the next section, we shall see that very subtle indirect connections can cause a spurious correlation.

## RANDOM WALKS

If we look at how the price of, say, shares of General Motors stock varies from day to day, the changes appear completely random. One day General Motors sells for $50, the next day it sells for $49, and on the third day it sells for $52. When GM's stock price is a *random walk,* the best bet is that today's price will be tomorrow's price.

> A **random walk** is a variable whose expected value in the next time period is the same as its current value.

Another way of looking at a random walk is that the value of the variable tomorrow is its value today plus some statistical "noise" that nobody can predict. What is unpredictable is the "noise," or the change in the variable. With passing time, the change in the variable will sometimes be positive, sometimes negative; over time the changes will average out to be zero. Successive changes in the variable will not be correlated.

To better understand the nature of a random walk, let us consider a game that exactly fits its definition. Suppose you flip a coin every minute. If heads appears, you take one step forward; if tails appears, you take one step backwards. Since heads and tails are equally likely, your average movement is zero.

But where will you be after ten minutes of playing the game? Where will you be after one hour of playing the game? Clearly, you will not be standing in the same spot where you started. As time passes, you will gradually move away from the starting point. After one hour and 60 flips, you will likely be further away from the starting point than after ten minutes and 10 flips.

Let us now apply the idea of a random walk to the problem of calculating correlations. If two variables are generated by a random walk, they will likely be correlated even if they are not related. The reason is simple. A variable that is a random walk moves upward or downward over time: the more time that passes, the more it moves up or down. Thus, if two variables are generated by a random walk, it is most likely that they will have a positive or negative correlation. Neither will stay in the same position. They will both move up or down together (a positive correlation) or one will move up and the other will move down (a negative correlation). Even if the two variables have no connection, our statistical measure tells us they are correlated.

The solution to the problem of a random walk is simple. Instead of looking at the behavior of the actual value of the variable, we look at the change in the variable over time. Suppose that we observe the prices of coffee and tea in the commodity markets: Each day the prices may go up or down. The changes in the prices are purely random. If we want to check the theory that as the price of coffee rises, people will shift their demand to tea and, therefore, increase the price of tea, we must be careful. We should not correlate the price of coffee with the price of tea; instead, we should check the correlation between the *change* in the price of coffee and the *change* in the price of tea. This will gives us a more valid test of the hypothesis.

> To test hypotheses that two time series are related, the *change* in one variable should be correlated with the *change* in the other to rule out the possibility that both variables are random walks.

## TRENDS AND CYCLES

Trends in economic variables cause many of the same problems as random walks.

> A **trend** is a systematic upward or downward movement in a variable over time.

Two variables that are trending upward, such as the price level and real GDP, have a positive correlation. Figure A3 compares the price level and real GDP from 1950 to 1995. The correlation between them is .96; it seems that there is an almost perfect statistical correlation. *This does not mean that there is an economic correlation*—that is, that one is causing the other. To find an economic correlation, we must remove the trend from the data.

We can remove a trend from a variable in two ways. The simpler is just to convert both series into

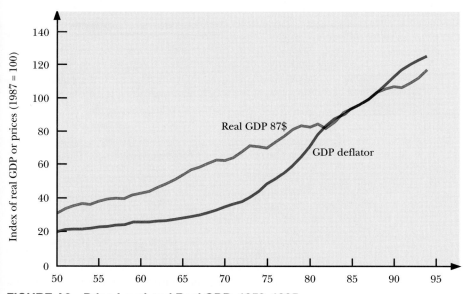

**FIGURE A3    Price Level and Real GDP, 1950–1995**

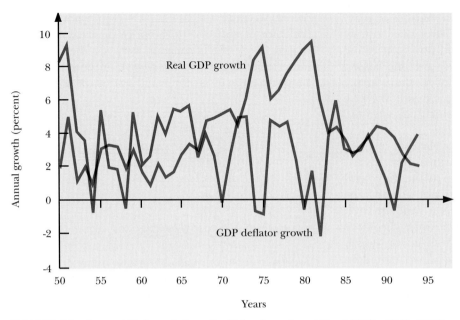

**FIGURE A4 Annual Rates of Growth, Price Level and Real GDP, 1950–1995**

percentage changes from year to year. Figure A4 shows the annual growth rates of real GDP and of the price level for the period 1950 to 1995. With the common positive trend removed, the "real" correlation, if any, between output and prices is no longer positive. Table A2 shows the same is true from a more global perspective.

The second method of removing a trend is to break a time series variable into its trend and cyclical components. The green line of Figure A5 is real GDP, while the black line is the trend of real GDP. The red line shows how actual GDP deviates from trend GDP. Again, we see that for the years 1955 to 1995, there is no trend in the cyclical component of GDP.

The cyclical component of real GDP is the difference between actual GDP and trend GDP.

When two macroeconomic variables are both subject to an upward trend, the appropriate way to test for economic correlations is to remove the trend by using growth rates or by correlating cyclical components. Once the trend is removed from two variables, we can check to see if there is a positive or negative correlation between the detrended variables.

## SUMMARY

In macroeconomics, the major variables—inflation, GDP, employment—tend to rise over time. This generally rising trend makes them all positively correlated and obscures the more subtle interrelationships among them. By removing this common trend, we can study their true correlations.

## KEY TERMS

time series                     random walk
standard deviation              trend
correlation coefficient

## QUESTIONS AND PROBLEMS

1. Here are the annual growth rates for Korea and Taiwan from past years:

| Table A2 Correlations Between Inflation Rates and Output Growth | | | |
| --- | --- | --- | --- |
| | *Prewar* | *Interwar* | *Postwar* |
| Canada | .01 | .35 | −.28 |
| Germany | .07 | .66 | −.22 |
| Italy | .06 | .34 | −.58 |
| Japan | −.48 | −.12 | −.26 |
| United Kingdom | .11 | −.28 | −.56 |
| United States | .13 | .37 | −.25 |

Prewar period is prior to World War I; interwar is between World War I and World War II; postwar is after World War II.
*Source:* David Backus and Patrick Kehoe, "International Evidence on the Historical Properties of Business Cycles," *American Economic Review,* 82 (September 1992).

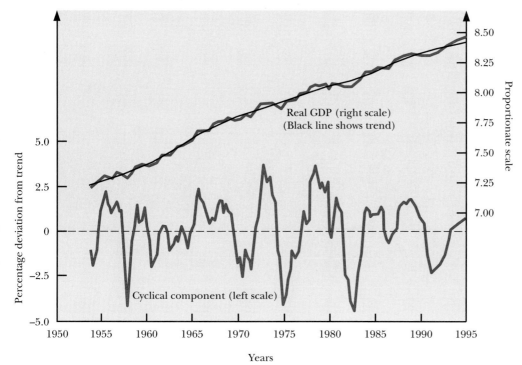

**FIGURE A5    The Breakdown of Real GDP into Trend and Cyclical Components**

The green line is real GDP, the black line is the trend, and the red line is the cyclical component, which equals the difference between real GDP and its trend.

|        | 1988 | 1989 | 1990 | 1991 | 1992 |
|--------|------|------|------|------|------|
| Korea  | 11.5 | 6.2  | 9.0  | 8.3  | 7.3  |
| Taiwan | 7.3  | 7.6  | 4.9  | 7.3  | 7.5  |

What has been the average growth rate in each country? Which country has faced the larger volatility in its rate of growth? (Korea: average = 8.46, S.D. = 1.79; Taiwan: average = 6.92, S.D. = 1.02.) If this experience continues, do you think it is more likely, less likely, or just as likely for Korea or Taiwan's growth rate to fall below 4.9 percent?

2. In the 1950–1983 period, the correlation coefficient between output growth in one year and output growth in the previous year was .03 for the United States. In the 1920–1939 period, the correlation coefficient between output growth in one year and that in the previous year was .35. On the basis of this evidence, what is the change in these correlation coefficients telling us about the behavior of the economy in the interwar period compared with the postwar period?

3. In the 1869–1914 period, the standard deviation of output growth in the United States was

5.44. In the 1950–1983 period, the standard deviation of output growth in the United States was 2.6. The average annual growth rate was 3.8 percent in the early period and 3.2 in the later period. Did U.S. fluctuations become more or less severe? Explain.

4. In the *Journal of Hypothetical Statistical Facts,* you notice that as the number of college professors of economics increases, so does the consumption of cottage cheese. The (hypothetical) correlation coefficient between the number of economics professors and pounds of cottage cheese consumed is .97. What do you conclude? How would you analyze the data?

5. During the NFL season you are in a football pool with nine other friends. Each person puts in $1 and selects the total number of points scored. Whoever is closest wins all. At the end of the third week, you have lost $3. If you play nine more weeks, can you expect to break even? Why or why not?

6. "The business cycle of nearly all industrial countries coincides with that of the United States." How would you determine the truth of this statement?

# CHAPTER 25

# SAVING AND INVESTMENT

Thrift has always been considered a virtue. As children, we were taught that if we work hard and save our nickels and dimes we should be assured a prosperous future. Benjamin Franklin wrote that "a penny saved is a penny earned." This is certainly true for the individual. But is it also true for the economy?

In fact, a contrary view of economics subscribes to the uncommon notion that saving is not particularly good for society. We have all heard the phrase, "If I buy a new car (or boat or stereo), it will be good for the economy." It is for this reason that financial experts and gurus try to peer into the minds of consumers to see if consumer spending is going to increase and, therefore, increase the overall level of output. This view that consumer spending—

which is the opposite of thrift—is good for the economy was given economic justification by John Maynard Keynes in 1936. He developed a macroeconomic model of the economy in which increased saving cut spending; reduced spending lowered output, employment, and income; and lower income resulted in lower saving. Thus, according to Keynes, there is a paradox of thrift: More is less! The more we save, the less we have to save.

On the one hand, we have the commonsense view of Benjamin Franklin that thrift is good. On the other hand, we have the view of Keynes that too much saving can be bad. In this chapter, we shall consider these two divergent views and their implications for economic policy.

## SAVING EQUALS INVESTMENT

The previous chapter showed that investment *(I)* is a component of final expenditures (GDP = C + I + G + X − M). It also showed that personal disposable income is what we have left from our income after we have paid our taxes. Here, we shall build on these concepts to understand the notion of saving and the relationship between saving and investment.

Just as individuals save by not spending all their personal disposable income, so do whole economies save by not spending all their income. Saving is necessary in order to carry out capital investment. Saving provides the funds that pay for capital investment. Sometimes savers and investors are the same; for example, GM or AT&T may build new plants or acquire new equipment paid for by their own savings. At other times, savers and investors are different. Businesses often borrow to invest in plant, equipment, and inventories. The funds they borrow come from savers.

At the economywide level, saving and investment will be equal, as will be demonstrated below. The equality of investment and saving does not mean that the amount savers *want* to save always equals the amount businesses *want* to invest. What it does mean is that actual saving and investment are *defined* to be the same.

Recall that personal disposable income is the amount of personal income that we actually have for our use after we have paid our taxes. Either we can spend it on personal consumption expenditures or we can save it.

> **Personal saving** equals personal disposable income minus personal consumption expenditures.

Personal saving is what remains of personal disposable income after personal consumption expenditures. Individuals save by refraining from consumption. Accordingly, we can determine the amount of personal saving by subtracting personal consumption from personal disposable income. When we save, we add to our assets by increasing funds in savings accounts, and by purchasing bonds, stocks, real estate, or precious metals.

> Personal saving is achieved by refraining from consumption.

Not all private saving in the economy is the personal saving of individuals. Businesses save by retaining profits that are not distributed to owners as dividends and by setting aside depreciation funds to replace capital that is depreciating. The sum of personal saving and business saving is private saving.

> **Private saving** is the sum of the personal saving of individuals and of business saving (in the form of retained profits and depreciation).

Private saving is simply what is left over from income after consumption and income taxes. By definition, therefore, the amount of gross domestic product (GDP) equals the sum of consumption *(C)*, private (business and consumer) saving *(S)*, and taxes *(T)*, or

$$\text{GDP} = C + S + T \qquad (1)$$

We saw in the previous chapter that GDP equals the sum of final expenditures, or

$$\text{GDP} = C + I + G + X - M \qquad (2)$$

where you will recall that investment *(I)* includes housing, plant and equipment, and additions to business inventories. Net exports, *X − M*, are the amount of domestic product sold to foreigners less domestic purchases from foreigners. Imports are subtracted because these are purchases by domestic residents that are included in C, I, and G, but are not produced at home.

The right-hand sides of equations (1) and (2) can be equated:

$$I + G + X - M = S + T \qquad (3)$$

Now let us rearrange equation (3) by moving *G*, *X*, and *M* to the right side. Thus, from equation (4), we can see that investment equals the sum of private saving *(S)*, the government surplus *(T − G)*, and foreign saving, *M − X*. (Remember the definition of foreign saving from the previous chapter.) In other words, investment in an economy can be financed by three sources: private domestic saving, government saving, or the savings of foreigners invested in the domestic economy:

$$I = S + (T - G) + M - X \qquad (4)$$

While equation (4) is a tautology—that is, true by definition—it alerts us to the substantial difference between the effects of government deficits and international trade deficits on investment. A govern-

| | Gross private domestic investment | Total gross private domestic savings | Total government surplus | Net foreign savings | Statistical discrepancy |
|---|---|---|---|---|---|
| **Table 1   Gross Savings and Investment (Percent of Nominal GDP)** | | | | | |
| 1990 | 14.6 | 15.5 | −2.5 | 1.4 | 0.1 |
| 1991 | 13.0 | 16.4 | −3.2 | −0.1 | 0.0 |
| 1992 | 13.1 | 16.3 | −4.3 | 0.9 | 0.1 |
| 1993 | 13.9 | 15.8 | −3.4 | 1.5 | 0.0 |
| 1994 | 15.3 | 15.6 | −2.0 | 2.1 | 0.5 |
| 1995 | 15.7 | 14.4 | −1.3 | 2.1 | 0.3 |

ment deficit means that $T - G$ is negative. A government deficit absorbs private saving, and less saving is thus available for domestic investment. A trade deficit means that $M - X$ is positive, because imports exceed exports. A trade deficit therefore allows private investment to be greater than private saving because of the influx of foreign saving.

Table 1 shows that in the 1990s, gross private domestic investment *(I)* has been around 15 percent of GDP, with the positive effect of foreign savings generally not enough to offset the negative effect of the federal government deficit. In the 1990s the average government deficit has been about 3 percent of GDP, while foreign savings has represented about 1 percent of GDP.

The reason measured saving always equals measured investment lies in the definition of investment. Remember that output and income are two sides of the same coin. Saving is simply unconsumed income. What is investment? With investment defined to include business inventories, investment is something produced that is used by a business in the future—investment is just unconsumed output. However, because output and income are the same thing, investment and saving must be the same. The key is the inclusion of business inventories in the definition of investment. A business may not want to invest in business inventories, but any products that are unsold by the end of the year are counted as business investment. Thus, actual investment must equal actual saving, whether people and businesses want it or not!

## DESIRED CONSUMPTION AND SAVING

We have established that actual or measured saving always equals actual or measured investment. However, what people *want* to save and what they *want* to invest need not be equal. Let us now look at the forces that determine the *desired amount* of saving. What

we wish to consume or save depends on how we balance our short-run desire to consume today against our long-run desire to consume more in the future.

## THE CONSUMPTION FUNCTION: THE SHORT RUN

The Keynesian theory of consumption is a short-run theory of consumption and saving. It emphasizes that what we consume today is very much dependent on today's income. For example, if you are out of a job and are not earning an income, you are not likely to consume as much as when you have a job and are earning an income. According to this view, *current consumption* depends on *current disposable income*. In fact, the average American spends $.92 of every dollar of disposable income. If we have more disposable income, we are likely to spend more. Keynes based his theory of consumption on the observation that people increase their current consumption by some portion of any increase in current income. If your weekly paycheck rises by $1000, you are likely to increase your consumption. However, for individuals as well as the economy as whole, consumption does not increase as much as income. If your weekly income rises by $1000, your consumption will rise by less than $1000—say, by $600—and saving then increases by $400, since $600 + $400 = $1000.

Table 2 shows how consumption, saving, and income are related in a hypothetical economy with no government. All variables are in real terms. The relationship between real consumption and real disposable income is called the consumption function. The effect of real disposable income on saving is called the saving function.

> The **consumption function** shows the relationship between real disposable income and real consumption.

## Table 2    The Consumption/Saving Functions

| Output =Income, Y(1) | Consumption, C(2) | Saving, S(3) |
|---|---|---|
| 100 | 125 | −25 |
| 200 | 200 | 0 |
| 300 | 275 | 25 |
| 400 | 350 | 50 |
| 500 | 425 | 75 |
| 600 | 500 | 100 |

Columns 1 and 2 show the consumption function in billions of dollars. There are no taxes, so income and disposable income are the same. The marginal propensity to consume (MPC) is 0.75; the marginal propensity to save (MPS) is 0.25. The average propensity to consume (APC) varies; it is 1 when $Y = 100$ and 0.85 when $Y = 500$. The data in the three columns are graphed in Figure 1, in which panel (a) graphs the consumption function and panel (b) graphs the saving function.

The **saving function** shows the relationship between real disposable income and real saving.

In Table 2, when income is $100 billion, consumption is $125 and saving is −$25 billion. Households must be borrowing or drawing on their financial assets (savings accounts, stocks, bonds) to be able to consume more than they earn. When income rises to $200 billion, consumption rises by $75 billion to $200 billion. Households are now breaking even. A further rise in income from $200 billion to $300 billion increases consumption to $275 billion. Households are now saving $25 billion.

The increase in consumption per dollar increase in income is called the marginal propensity to consume (MPC). The marginal propensity to save (MPS) is the increase in saving per dollar increase in income.

The **marginal propensity to consume (MPC)** is the change in desired consumption *(C)* for a $1 change in income *(Y)*:

$$MPC = \Delta C/\Delta Y$$

The **marginal propensity to save (MPS)** is the change in desired saving *(S)* for a $1 change in income *(Y)*:

$$MPS = \Delta S/\Delta Y$$

In Table 2, since consumption increases by $75 billion for every $100 billion in additional income, the MPC is .75. Since saving increases by $25 billion for every $100 billion in additional income, the MPS is .25.

In Figure 1, panel (a), real consumption (C) is measured on the vertical axis and real disposable income (Y) on the horizontal axis. The consumption function—labeled C—is upward-sloping. Where the consumption function intersects the 45-degree reference line, there is no saving. All real disposable income is spent. The vertical difference between the 45-degree line and the consumption function represents saving or dissaving (negative saving). When C is above the 45-degree line (to the left of point a), there is dissaving; when C is below the 45-degree line (to the right of point a), there is saving. For example, when income is $400 billion, consumption is $350 billion and saving is $50 billion. The slope of the consumption function is the MPC.

In Figure 1, panel (b), we measure saving on the vertical axis and, again, income on the horizontal axis. The saving function, S, is upward sloping and is the exact complement of the consumption function since $S = Y - C$. It is upward sloping because as income increases, saving also increases. The slope of the saving function is the MPS. Saving is negative (dissaving) at income levels below $200 billion and positive at income levels above $200 billion.

Since every $1 of disposable income is either saved or spent, it must be that MPS + MPC = 1. To see this in more detail, we note that

$$Y = C + S.$$

(Remember that there is no government spending or taxes in this hypothetical model.) Next, we change each variable:

$$\Delta Y = \Delta C + \Delta Y.$$

Now, divide each by $\Delta Y$ and we get:

$$1 = \Delta C/\Delta Y + \Delta S/\Delta Y = MPC + MPS.$$

## FORWARD-LOOKING CONSUMPTION: THE LONG-RUN THEORY

The Keynesian approach is really a short-run theory of consumer behavior because consumption depends on current income. Before Keynes developed his theory, the American economist Irving Fisher (1867–1947) pointed out that future as well as current income determines current consumption. This for-

Dissaving = Borrowing

(*a*) The Consumption Function

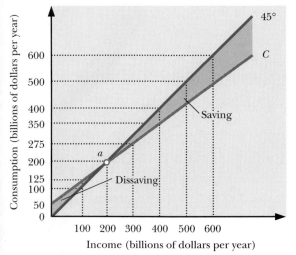

(*b*) The Saving/Income Curve

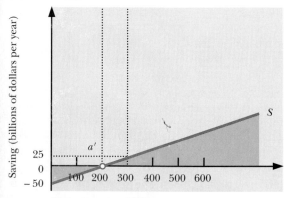

**FIGURE 1   The Consumption/Saving Function**

The consumption function, *C*, is graphed in panel (*a*) from the data in Table 2 and shows the amount of desired consumption at different levels of income. The slope of the *C* curve is the marginal propensity to consume, MPC, which in our example equals .75. In panel (*b*), the saving function, *S*, shows the amount of real saving at each level of income. Saving is positive to the right of *a'* and negative to the left of *a'*.

ward-looking view of consumption was subsequently refined by Nobel laureates Milton Friedman and Franco Modigliani.

## LIFE-CYCLE CONSUMPTION

According to Fisher's theory, people try to arrange their consumption over their lifetimes. Normally, they start out their working life with a low income and, as they gain more experience in the labor mar-

ket, their income rises. A young lawyer, for example, may start out earning $40,000 per year, but expects her annual income to rise to $200,000 within 20 years. If she simply consumes each year what she earns in that year, initially the value of consuming an extra dollar in the future would be much less than the value of consumption in the present. Even though her income is expected to rise sharply, she would have to wait patiently to buy the things she wanted until her income was high enough. Such behavior is unlikely. The young lawyer would likely want a new car and a nice house today rather than sometime in the future. Hence, she would be motivated to borrow today and repay the loan in the future. By borrowing, she would not have to wait as long to have the things she wants.

Figure 2, panel (*a*), shows the pattern of consumption of a young person who expects income to rise over time. The young person borrows rather than saves. Panel (*b*) shows the pattern for a mature person whose income is expected to fall over time; this person bolsters future consumption by saving part of today's income. Both panels show similar behavior: through buying on credit (the young person) or saving (the mature person), we can rearrange our consumption so that, over our entire lifetimes, *consumption does not vary as much as current income.*

Thus, the Fisherian theory has the simple implication that the short-run MPC will be smaller than the long-run MPC. People spend not according to their current income but according to their lifetime or permanent income. For example, if your income *temporarily* increases, you will not increase your consumption as much as if your income *permanently* increases. Clearly, a temporary increase in income will not make a consumer feel as well off as a permanent increase in income. Indeed, empirical evidence shows that the short-run MPC is about three-fourths the size of the long-run MPC.

**Real and Nominal Rates of Interest.**   A pivotal point in the Fisherian theory of consumption/saving is that interest rates are important for saving decisions. An increase in the rate of interest provides a larger reward for postponing consumption into the future, holding other factors constant.

When you put $100 in the bank this year in return for $105 next year, you are making an exchange of present consumption ($100) for future consumption ($105). If there is no inflation, next year's $105 represents a 5 percent gain in goods and services. If

(*a*) Young

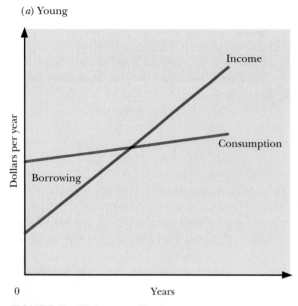

(*b*) Old

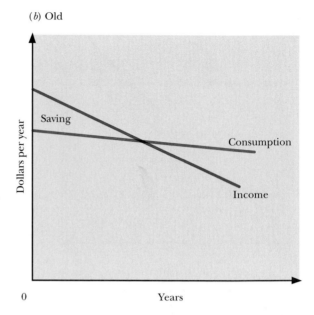

**FIGURE 2 Fisherean Theory**

Panel (*a*) shows a young person whose income is increasing over time. Panel (*b*) shows an older person who saves in his or her middle years in order to have consumption higher than income in his or her later years.

there is inflation, the $105 will not purchase 5 percent more in goods and services in a year. For example, with 2 percent inflation, the $105 will buy only about 3 percent more in goods and services in one year. The tradeoff between present and future consumption is summarized by the real rate of interest, which is the nominal or observed interest rate adjusted for the inflation rate.

> The **nominal rate of interest** is the contractual interest rate that is observed in markets.
>
> The **real rate of interest** is the nominal rate of interest over some period minus the expected rate of inflation over the same period.

The real interest rate is forward looking. At the beginning of the period, we cannot observe the real interest rate that lenders will actually earn. Lenders make their decisions based on the current nominal rate minus the expected inflation rate over the period of the loan. Actual inflation can be different from expected inflation. Except in periods of deflation, the real rate of interest is less than the nominal rate of interest. After the fact, however, we can look back and observe the actual real interest rate earned by savers by deducting the actual inflation rate from the nom-

inal rate. In the 1980s, for example, the nominal interest rate on 30-year government bonds averaged about 10.5 percent while the rate of inflation averaged about 4 percent. Thus, holders of 30-year government bonds averaged a 6 percent real rate of interest in the 1980s. During the 1990s, the real rate of interest dropped to about 4 percent. The nominal interest rate on 30-year government bonds averaged about 7.5 percent while the inflation rate averaged about 3.2 percent, yielding a real interest rate of just over 4 percent.

**Saving and Interest.** Fisher pointed out that, everything else equal, we prefer to consume today over tomorrow. To compensate for delaying consumption, a positive real rate of interest is required to encourage people to save. Changes in the real rate of interest affect the terms on which we can exchange current and future consumption. When the real rate of interest rises from 3 percent to, say, 6 percent, the real value of a dollar invested today rises from $1.03 to $1.06 next year. Thus, a higher interest rate translates into cheaper future consumption. If a dollar saved today commands more future consumption, we have an incentive to save more today. It has been estimated that an increase in the real rate of interest from, say, 4 percent to 5 percent could increase private saving by as much as 10 percent. Figure 3 shows the positive relationship between the real rate of interest and the amount of saving, where other factors, such as current income, are constant.

The Fisherian theory explains what other factors influence consumption in addition to current income, future income, and real interest rates. Also important are the stock of assets, the price level, taxation, and demographic factors. For example, a reduction in taxation, a lower price level, or a larger stock of assets shifts the entire consumption function upward, as we can see from Figure 4, and will discuss below. (See Example 1.)

**Stocks of Assets.**   Changes in the wealth of consumers can also cause shifts in the consumption function. The wealth of individuals is the net money value of the assets they own (stocks, cash balances, real estate). As the real value of these assets rises, we feel better off, and we are likely to increase our consumption expenditures, if other things are equal. When the stock market rises, for example, stock owners tend to increase their consumption spending, even though their income has not changed. When

wealth rises, we need not save as much out of current income to meet future needs.

Throughout the 1980s, Japan's stock and real estate markets boomed. Japanese consumption soared as the wealth of the typical family increased. However, the 1990s saw a reversal of fortunes. Japanese real estate and stock markets fell by about 50 percent in the first half of the 1990s. With smaller assets, Japanese consumers sharply curtailed their spending on cars, electronic equipment, and vacations.

**The Price Level.**   Financial assets, such as money, savings deposits, and money market mutual funds, are fixed in nominal value. Thus, when the price level rises, the purchasing power of nominal financial assets falls. As prices fall, their purchasing power rises. For example, if the price level doubles, the purchasing power of $100 in cash is reduced by exactly half.

> The higher the price level, the lower the purchasing power of financial assets fixed in nominal value.

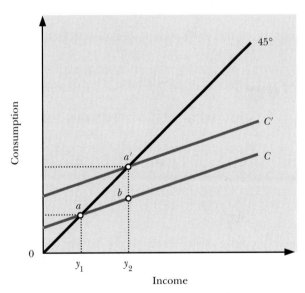

**FIGURE 4   Shifts in the Consumption Function**

The original consumption function, $C$, is drawn holding constant certain nonincome factors that affect consumption. Upward shifts in $C$ are caused by increases in financial assets, reductions in price level, reductions in taxes, a lowering of the average age of the population, a change in the distribution of income in favor of the poor, or the development of a more negative attitude toward thrift.

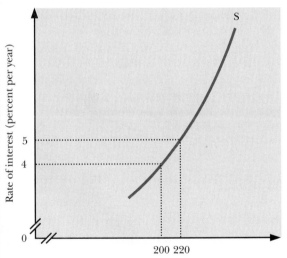

**FIGURE 3   Saving and the Rate of Interest**

When the rate of interest increases, the amount people desire to save generally increases. An increase in the rate of interest from 4 to 5 percent might increase saving from $200 billion to $220 billion.

### EXAMPLE 1
### WHY IS THE U.S. SAVING RATE
### SO LOW?

Households in America saved only about 4.5 percent of their disposable income in 1995. Household saving is down from 9.1 percent in 1981. This is of great concern because there is a strong link between saving and economic growth.

Businesses, of course, also save in the form of investment in new equipment. Including business saving, total U.S. gross saving was only about 15 percent in 1995 (as we saw in Table 1). The average gross saving rate for other advanced industrialized countries is on the order of 20 percent. Why does the United States save less?

There are four reasons:

1. The first is that the United States is the world's richest country. In rich countries households spend more on durables and educations, both of which are counted as consumption, not saving or investment. However, buying a car, acquiring a personal computer, or going to school represents investment in a future stream of benefits.

2. The baby boomers (people born soon after World War II) are now the most economically important population segment. Unfortunately, they are saving at a rate that is only one-third the rate that will give them a standard of living at retirement similar to that during their working years. Taxes are an important reason. The government triple-taxes saving. Suppose you buy a common stock—you pay taxes on any dividends the company pays, you pay taxes on any increase in the value of the stock, and if you put your money in bonds you pay taxes on the interest income you earn. Many of these returns are just a reflection of inflation.

3. Social Security also takes a bite out of private saving. Nearly every American pays Social Security taxes, but these do not pay the rate of return that private saving would pay. In other words, if a person were to move the same amount of money (about 15 percent of wages, including the employer contribution) to a private pension fund, the amount that would be earned in the private fund would be perhaps double what Social Security promises. In other words, the rate of return on Social Security saving is extremely low—an inescapable reality. This low rate of return is necessary because the Social Security people are paying now is going to pay the current generation of retirees. Thus, we are in effect taxing savers and giving the money to nonsavers. This causes people to save less.

4. Finally, from the 1980s to the 1990s, real interest rates have dropped from about 4.5 percent to about 3 percent. As we discussed in the text, people prefer present consumption to future consumption. The real interest rate compensates people for postponing their consumption to the future. If that rate falls, holding other factors constant, one would expect saving rates to fall.

*Source:* "Punishing Thrift and Investment," *Investors Business Daily,* November 17, 1994.

When the purchasing power of financial assets increases, people who hold currency and money in checking accounts feel better off and tend to increase their consumption spending even if their real income remains the same. For example, if your nominal income falls by 10 percent and prices fall by 10 percent but the amount of money in your checking account remains the same, the purchasing power of your income will remain constant while the purchasing power of your money holdings will increase by 10 percent. The rise in the real value of your money holdings makes you feel better off, and you might increase your consumption spending.

**Taxation.** As income taxes rise, personal disposable income falls, if all other things are equal. As taxes increase, we would expect less consumption spending for the same amount of personal income. As personal income taxes are cut, disposable personal income rises, holding personal income constant; thus, we would expect more consumption spending from the same income.

The consumption function should shift upward when income taxes are cut. It should shift downward when income taxes are increased.

## THE THEORY OF INVESTMENT

Let us now turn to investment. There is little disagreement among macroeconomists about the determinants of investment. The key factors appear to be the expectations of future profits and the cost of borrowing.

We can see from Figure 5 that over the years, real investment spending has fluctuated more than consumption and real GDP. Why is investment so unstable? We can answer this question by looking at the determinants of business investment.

### THE INVESTMENT DEMAND CURVE

Consider a small company that manufactures steel pipes. Because of technological changes in computers, it is now possible to install robots that will enable the

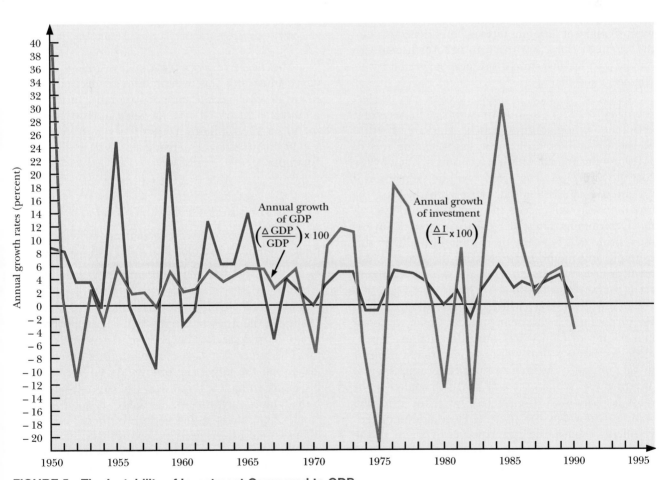

**FIGURE 5   The Instability of Investment Compared to GDP**
The data for the past 40 years show that the growth rate of investment fluctuates much more than the growth rate of GDP. *Source: Economic Report of the President.*

company to automatically produce the pipes in the desired shapes and sizes by the push of a few buttons. The firm will install the equipment because it expects to increases its profits. The steel pipe company will add to its capital stock (investment) by adhering to the same rules it follows when buying materials, renting land, or hiring labor. It compares the marginal costs and marginal benefits of acquiring more or less of the resource in question—in this case, capital.

Investment is undertaken to lower production costs or increase or maintain sales: The greater the increase in expected sales or the greater the reduction in unit costs of production, the more profitable is the new investment. But the firm also incurs immediate costs when it invests; that is, it must purchase new capital goods. The firm's immediate cost of acquiring additional capital is, basically, the prevailing cost of borrowing loanable funds, or the interest rate.

The amount of investment a typical firm will want to make at different interest rates depends upon the *rates of return* that the firm believes it can earn on the various investment projects suggested by its engineers and managers.

Suppose a $10 million investment project promises to add $1 million to profits each year for a very long (almost infinite) period. The rate of return on this $10 million investment, in this example, is 10 percent—the annual addition to profit divided by the cost of the project. The project will be carried out if the interest rate is less than 10 percent because the rate of return will exceed the cost of acquiring capital. Determining rates of return of different investment projects is typically more complicated than this example, but the principle remains the same: Investment projects are chosen when the rate of return exceeds the rate of interest.

In any given year, a firm chooses among a number of potential investment projects. Some will offer higher rates of return than others. In making investment decisions, a firm will rank investment projects by rate of return. As long as a project promises a rate of return higher than the rate at which capital funds must be borrowed (the interest rate), the firm will want to carry out the project. Since additional investments exhaust the opportunities available to the firm, eventually the rate of return will be driven down to the market interest rate.

Firms carry out additional investments as long as their rate of return *(R)* exceeds the market rate of interest *(r)*. Therefore, the last (marginal) investment project should yield a rate of return equal to the market interest rate, such that $R = r$.

The firm's investment demand curve in terms of the interest rate and the quantity of investment should be negatively sloped just as other demand curves are (see Figure 6). At high rates of interest, fewer projects offer rates of return equal to or greater than the interest rate. The lower the interest rate, the greater is the number of investments that the business will wish to undertake. In this case, what holds for individual firms also holds for the economy as a whole: At low interest rates, there is a greater quantity demanded of investments than at higher interest rates.

> The **investment demand curve** of the economy (or a firm) shows the amount of investment desired at different interest rates.

The negative slope of the investment demand curve illustrates that the amount of desired investment increases as the interest rate falls. In Figure 6, an interest rate of 10 percent yields an investment demand of $100 billion. An interest rate of 8 percent yields an investment demand of $120 billion. (See Example 2.)

## THE INSTABILITY OF INVESTMENT

Economists provide two explanations of why investment is more unstable than GDP: the accelerator principle and animal spirits.

**Accelerator Principle.** Investment is the net change in the stock of capital. In turn, the production of goods and services depends on that stock of capital: The larger the stock of capital, if all other things are equal, the larger the output. As GDP rises, it is necessary to have a larger stock of capital, which requires more investment. As GDP falls, a smaller stock of capital is required, and so many investment plans are no longer needed. Accordingly, investment can fluctuate quite rapidly in response to changes in GDP. This phenomenon is called the accelerator principle because in order for investment to increase, the output of the economy must not only increase, it must also accelerate.

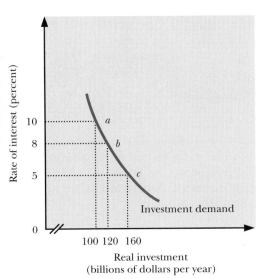

**FIGURE 6   The Investment Demand Curve for an Entire Economy**

Firms in the economy will be prepared to carry out investment projects as long as the rate of return promised by the project equals or exceeds the interest rate. There are fewer investment projects that offer rates of return of 10 percent and above than those that offer 5 percent and above. The quantity of investment demanded at an interest rate of 5 percent is greater than the quantity of investment demanded at a 10 percent rate.

The **accelerator principle** states that output must increase at an ever-increasing rate in order for investment to remain constant.

For example, if $1 worth of capital is necessary for each $1 worth of output, then an increase of output from $100 billion to $110 billion would require another $10 billion of capital or investment. If output continued to increase at a rate of $10 billion each year, annual investment will remain at $10 billion.

**Animal Spirits.**   Just as expectations can influence individuals' savings and spending behavior, so can changing expectations about the future alter business investment decisions. Insofar as rate-of-return calculations depend upon perceptions of prices, costs, and profits in the often-distant future, a shift in expectations toward a more pessimistic outlook, for example, can reduce investment demand. Consequently, since the degree of pessimism or optimism can be unstable, the investment demand function might be expected to be more unstable than the consumption function.

John Maynard Keynes wrote that business psychology played a key role in determining desired investment. Keynes, however, attributed most fluctua-

## EXAMPLE 2
## INVESTMENT IN
## THE 1990S

From 1991 to 1993, long-term real interest rates dropped from approximately 5.5 percent to approximately 4 percent from the previous year. This drop initiated an expansion in gross private domestic investment. In 1991, gross private domestic investment was only about 13 percent of GDP (see Table 1). By 1994, gross private domestic investment rose to over 15 percent of GDP. The economy grew at a rapid pace. By 1995, the rate of unemployment in the economy had fallen to its lowest level in about five years.

This was a very dynamic period in America. High-technology companies such as Compaq, Microsoft, Intel, U.S. Robotics, and IBM were producing new and better ways of controlling the flow of information through a business firm. As a result, by investment in new ways of doing things, firms of all sorts—such as General Motors and Ford—were reducing their costs and dramatically increasing their profitability. Corporate profits and the stock market all boomed in the first half of the 1990s.

tions in business investment to disturbances in the "animal spirits" of business entrepreneurs. Shifts in investment can occur even if, on objective grounds, nothing changes in the business environment. As time passes, the captains of industry accumulate much elusive information about future products, future technology, and the future attitude of government toward business. Much of this information is qualitative and subjective. Investment demand increases or decreases when the collective intuition of business entrepreneurs turns optimistic or pessimistic.

According to Keynes, spontaneous changes in "animal spirits" mean:

> not only that slumps and depressions are exaggerated in degree, but that economic prosperity is excessively dependent on the political and social atmosphere which is congenial to the average business man. . . . In estimating the prospects of investment, we must have regard, therefore, to the nerves and hysteria and even the digestions and reactions to the weather of those upon whose spontaneous activity it largely depends.[1]

In terms of Figure 6, animal spirits mean that there can be abrupt rightward or leftward shifts in the investment demand curve as business expectations change. As businesses become more optimistic, there is an increase in investment demand. As they become more pessimistic, there is a decrease in investment demand.

## COORDINATING SAVING AND INVESTMENT: INCOME OR INTEREST RATES?

Savers and investors meet in the market for capital. This market is extremely complex, because it operates through various channels. People save by making bank deposits and saving deposits, and by buying stocks and bonds; businesses borrow from banks and issue—that is, sell—stocks and bonds.

---

[1]See John Maynard Keynes, *The General Theory of Employment, Interest, and Money* (New York: Harcourt, Brace and Company, 1936), chap. 12.

## THE KEYNESIAN THEORY: THE SHORT RUN

John Maynard Keynes argued that in the short run—say, one or two years—the market for capital can fail to coordinate what people want to save with what businesses want to invest. His evidence for this hypothesis was the Great Depression. He argued, as we noted in the Chapter Insight, that when people save, they cut their consumption. This decrease in spending causes business sales to fall. Inventories rise and firm decrease production by laying off workers. As unemployment increases, incomes decrease, and consumption falls once more.

The Keynesian theory is shown in Figure 7. The horizontal axis measures GDP; the vertical axis measures saving or investment. As in our discussion of the Keynesian saving function, we assume that saving increases with GDP. Investment mostly depends on other factors: the expectations of business firms for profits and interest rates. (Note: The accelerator principle says investment depends on the growth of income, not on the level of income.) Thus, investment responds less to income than does saving to income, so that the investment function $I$ is flatter than the saving function $S$. *The level of GDP is determined at that point at which the saving function intersects the investment function.* If the saving function is $S$ and the investment function is $I$, the level of GDP that coordinates savers and investors is $Y_1$. When the saving function is $S$, any level of income above $Y_1$ will result in desired saving exceeding the amount of desired investment. This means that businesses are not spending what consumers are taking out of the economy, causing unwanted increases in business inventories. Actual investment will still equal actual saving, but business will cut back output until the level of output $Y_1$ is achieved. Similarly, when the saving function is $S$, any level of income below $Y_1$ will cause business firms to expand output because business are spending more than what consumers are taking out of the economy.

If the saving function now shifts up (people become more thrifty), from $S$ to $S'$, GDP would have to fall unless investment increases. If the investment function indeed stays the same, the increase in thrift would cause GDP to fall to $Y_2$, and saving would then actually fall from $S_1$ to $S_2$.

This result is called the *paradox of thrift*, because an increase in thriftiness results in less saving rather than more. The paradox can be cited as an example

More savings less spending — less savings — less income

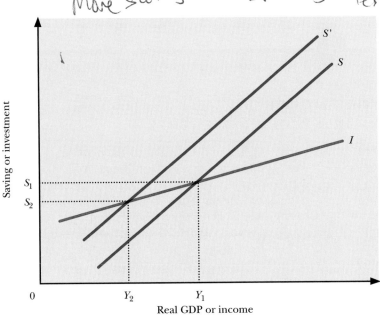

**FIGURE 7   The Keynesian Theory**

If $S$ and $I$ are the desired saving and investment schedules, saving and investment are equated at the level of GDP of $Y_1$. If the desire to save increases so the curve shifts from $S$ to $S'$, actual saving falls from $S_1$ to $S_2$.

of the fallacy of composition we encountered in Chapter 1: What is true for an individual need not be true for the economy.

> In the Keynesian model, an increase in thrift reduces income and hence can paradoxically reduce the amount of saving.

The paradox of thrift is clearly a short-run phenomenon. If it holds, it would be only during periods of recession or depression. This paradoxical result depends on a close relationship between income and saving (consumption) and on the lack of influence of increased thrift on interest rates and investment.

## THE CLASSICAL THEORY: THE LONG RUN

In the long run, as we shall see in the next few chapters, the economy's output is determined by the volume and efficiency of use of the resources at its disposal. The classical theory of interest is that the vast amount of savings and investment in the economy are fundamentally coordinated by the various rates

of interest—explicit or implicit—on all the different sources of funds. The rate of interest is explicit on externally generated funds; the rate of interest is implicit on internally generated funds. Example 3 discusses why in the modern economy external finance is far less important than in the earlier periods.

Figure 8 shows the basic classical theory of interest. On the vertical axis we measure the real rate of interest (adjusted for the rate of inflation); on the horizontal axis we measure the amount of saving or investment. Saving depends positively on the rate of interest. A higher interest rate encourages more saving as households face cheaper future consumption. Investment depends negatively on the rate of interest. The higher the rate of interest, the less businesses and others want to invest in buildings, trucks, inventories, and equipment. Clearly, there exists a rate of interest at which both functions intersect. This is the equilibrium rate of interest (5 percent in Figure 8).

The evidence that supports the classical theory is very strong. A rightward shift in the saving curve (an increase in thrift) will lower interest rates and raise investment. An increase in investment translates into

## EXAMPLE 3
## DEFINING MOMENTS:
## ARE SAVERS AND INVESTORS DIFFERENT?

The idea that saving is difficult to coordinate with investment is based on the idea that savers and investors are different groups. This may have been true in the early part of this century, when agriculture was the most important sector of the economy. Farmers must borrow from banks. But today, manufacturing, services, and high-tech firms are the dynamic sectors. About 80 percent of all nonfarm corporate investment comes from internal sources. In 1995, for example, nonfinancial corporations had about $700 billion of funds available for investment in either physical or financial assets. The vast majority of this came from the gross profits of the corporations themselves. Indeed, only about $100 bil-

lion was generated by going to the external financial markets—that is, from households placing their savings in various types of financial instruments. The majority of saving is generated by the various firms themselves, using their profits to make investments in new capital goods.

This trend does not mean that interest rates are unimportant. Interest rates are still the basic coordinating mechanism that channels the savings of noninvestors into the investment channels. What it does mean is that in modern times, the adjustment of saving to investment is probably much easier than it was in the early part of this century, when agriculture was far more important to the domestic economy.

---

increased growth of real GDP. This relationship takes place in the real world. Countries that increase their saving rates experience more investment and greater growth. In the 1980s, countries such as Taiwan, Singapore, Hong Kong, and South Korea dramatically increased their saving rates while managing to impress the entire world with their spectacular growth rates of output and income. Moreover, countries that have higher saving rates tend to lend their excess savings to other countries. The United States has had relatively low saving rates; Japan has had relatively high saving rates. As a consequence, interest rates have been lower in Japan than in the United States. Thus, the United States has borrowed from Japan, making interest rates higher in Japan and lower in the United States than they would be otherwise. This phenomenon is a direct expression of the classical theory of interest.

> In the classical (Fisherian) theory of interest, increased thrift lowers interest rates and increases investment. The larger capital stock means more income and more saving in the long run.

## SAY'S LAW

The classical theory of interest allows us to understand Say's law—that whatever GDP is produced will be demanded. As an example, let's suppose the economy produces $6 trillion worth of GDP. We know that income and output are two sides of the same coin. Actual aggregate income always equals actual aggregate expenditures. The classical economist J.B. Say (1767–1832) took this one step further. He argued that *supply creates its own demand*.

> According to **Say's law**, whatever aggregate output producers decide to supply will be demanded in the aggregate.

Let's consider the following illustration of the law. Assume an economy with no government and no net exports that produces $6 trillion worth of final goods and services (consumption and investment). This creates $6 trillion worth of income that either can be consumed or can be saved. If, say, $5 trillion is consumed, the other $1 trillion is saved. However, the classical theory of interest asserts that the $1 trillion that is saved represents $1 trillion

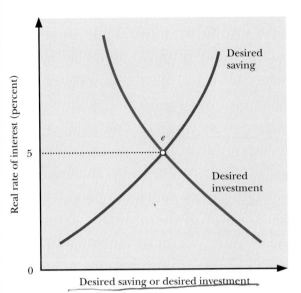

**FIGURE 8  The Interest Rate Equates Desired Saving and Desired Investment in the Classical Model**

This figure measures the (real) interest rate on the vertical axis and the amount of desired saving and desired investment on the horizontal axis. The saving curve shows the amount of desired saving at different interest rates. The investment curve shows the amount of desired investment at different interest rates. The interest rate equates the amount of desired investment and the amount of desired saving. In this example, the interest rate that equates desired saving and desired investment is 5 percent.

worth of demand for investment. Therefore, the total demand for final goods will also be $6 trillion. Investment spending injects back into the spending stream what households take out.

Say's law does not deny that an economy could produce too many quarts of milk or too many loaves of bread. If the price of milk or bread is too high, the demand will fall short of supply. The classical economists "recognized that there may be depressions, unemployment, or unsold goods."[2] Say's law asserted only that the demand for all goods and services could be counted on to purchase the supply of all goods and services.

To classical economists, Say's law proved that economic growth had no natural limit: No matter how much the economy produced, the demand for the goods would be forthcoming. In the 1990s,

[2]Thomas Sowell, *Classical Economics Reconsidered* (Princeton: Princeton University Press, 1974), p. 43.

Americans buy almost ten times as many goods and services as were purchased during the Great Depression. The increased capacity to produce output has not been restrained by insufficient spending.

## CONSUMER SPENDING AND CONSUMER SAVING: LESSONS LEARNED

The basic lesson of this chapter is that consumer spending is not what props up the economy in the long run. Most people reason that greater consumption means more sales, greater profits, and a better economy. This may be true in the short run. However, in the long run, it is consumer saving that leads to greater income and, in the end, more consumer spending. There is, indeed, a *paradox of spending*: less consumer spending eventually results in more consumption! How this happens is simple: A smaller piece of a growing pie is better than a bigger piece of a static pie. Figure 9 shows the empirical basis for this view: Higher investment results in greater economic growth. Thus, by saving and investing more today, people have more to consume in the future. The level of consumption today depends on the fact that people in the past saved and invested, giving us a higher capital stock and with it a larger volume of output.

In the next chapter, we shall consider the process of economic growth and what an economy can do about increasing its growth rate.

### SUMMARY

1. Actual measured saving and investment are always equal because the definition of investment includes business inventories so that unsold goods are part of investment. It must be the case that $I = S + (T - G) + (M - X)$; that is, investment equals private saving plus government saving plus foreign saving.

2. The consumption function shows the relationship between consumption and income. In the short run, the marginal propensity to consume (MPC) shows the change in consumption per one dollar change in current disposable income. The saving function shows the relationship between saving and

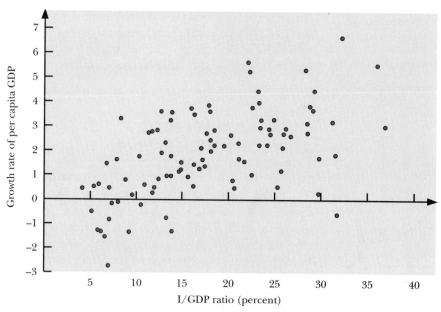

**FIGURE 9   Investment and Economic Growth in 98 Countries**

This figure shows a scatter diagram showing the rates of growth of per capita GDP and investment as a proportion of GDP in the period from 1960 to 1985 for 98 non–oil exporting countries. It shows that generally speaking, higher investment ratios correspond to higher growth rates. *Source:* Authors' calculation from data in N. Mankiw, D. Romer, and D. Weil, "A Contribution to the Empirics of Economic Growth," *Quarterly Journal of Economics,* vol. 107, 1992.

income. The marginal propensity to save (MPS) shows the change in saving for every one dollar increase in disposable income. It must be that MPC + MPS = 1.

3. In the long run people tend to save more when income is expected to fall and to save less or borrow when income is expected to rise. Moreover, when the real interest rate (the nominal or contractual rate minus the expected rate of inflation) rises, people tend to save more.

4. Firms carry out additional investment as long as their rate of return exceeds the market rate of interest. Thus, lower interest rates increase the desired amount of investment. Investment is unstable because of the accelerator principle and animal spirits.

5. According to the Keynesian theory, in the short run saving and investment are coordinated by adjustments in the level of income. According to the classical theory, in the long run saving and investment are coordinated by the rate of interest. The classical theory implies Say's law that at least in the

long run there will always be enough demand to purchase the total amount of output.

## KEY TERMS

personal saving
private saving
consumption function
saving function
marginal propensity to
   consume (MPC)
marginal propensity to
   save (MPS)

nominal rate of interest
real rate of interest
investment demand
   curve
accelerator principle
Say's law

## QUESTIONS AND PROBLEMS

1. If people do not have to save what others want to invest, why is it that in the national income accounts, saving always equals investment?

2. Using the consumption function in Table A, calculate the saving function, the MPC, and the MPS.

| Table A | |
| --- | --- |
| *Income (Y)* | *Consumption (C)* |
| 0 | 50 |
| 100 | 100 |
| 200 | 150 |
| 300 | 200 |
| 400 | 250 |

3. The equation for the consumption function in Table A is $Y = 50 + 0.5\ Y$. What is the equation for the saving function?

4. Use Figure 8 to show what would happen to an economy's saving curve if the population becomes thriftier, holding the rate of interest constant.

5. If the inflation rate is 5 percent and the nominal interest rate is 6 percent, what is the real rate of interest?

6. What is the difference between the accelerator principle and animal spirits?

7. Why does the Fisherian theory of consumption imply that the MPC out of a temporary increase in income be smaller than the MPC out of a permanent increase in income?

8. The Fisherian theory implies that the volatility of consumption should be less than the volatility of income. Economists have found this to be true if consumption excludes spending on durable goods, but not if consumption includes all spending on durable goods (such as cars, etc.). Do you think this refutes the Fisherian theory?

9. According to the investment demand curve, if the nominal interest rate rises by 3 percent while inflation is rising by 3 percent, what should happen to investment?

10. Why is investment more unstable than GDP?

11. What is the Keynesian mechanism for coordinating saving and investment? What is the short-run evidence for this theory? What is the long-run evidence?

12. Countries A and B have the same investment demand curve, but country A is thriftier than country B. Which country would have the lower real interest rate according to the classical theory? Which country would be the international lender? Draw a diagram representing this situation.

13. Define Say's law.

# CHAPTER 26

# ECONOMIC GROWTH

Movies picture life in ancient times in terms of knights in shining armor, elegantly dressed ladies, and castles. If you had lived during this time, say England in 1680, what would your life have been like? You would likely be a farmer or a peasant laborer. You would live in a two-room mud house with earthen floors, no windows, no kitchen, and, of course, no indoor plumbing. For dinner you might have bread and, with luck, coarse soup. You would sleep on an uncomfortable canvas-covered straw bed. You would have one set of clothes. The products you enjoy today—sugar, spices, chocolate, fresh vegetables, and most fruits—could be afforded only by the rich. Your trip to the next village 15 miles away would be by cart or on foot. You would probably not see a city in your lifetime.

Even more remarkable is the fact that it would not have made much difference whether you were born in 1660 or 1460. You worked in the same fields as your parents and grandparents, used the same simple tools (the pick, the shovel, and the

plow), and died at about the same advanced age of 40 years.

Indeed, for centuries prior to the Industrial Revolution, the standard of living of the average person remained about the same. Then the Industrial Revolution set off a process of sustained growth of real GDP per capita. Since then, the world has not been the same. For those of us who live in the industrialized countries, the mud hut has been replaced by a brick home or a high-rise apartment with two baths. The bread and coarse soup have been replaced by meats, vegetables, and fruits from around the world. Instead of walking by foot to the next village, we can travel to work by car or train, and to faraway places by jet airplane.

The principal feature of economic growth in the modern era has been its sustained nature. There is no simple explanation for why the industrialized world began to sustain economic growth in the eighteenth century, for the first time in human history. It is clear that the Industrial Revolution was made possible by a technological revolution. The inventions produced by eighteenth- and nineteenth-century technology, including the steam engine, the mechanized cotton spindle, and the blast furnace, raised productivity and living standards. Modern economic growth was also accompanied by the expansion of trade and the growth of free-market institutions.

This chapter is about economic growth: why it began when it did, its causes and sources, and the theories of economic growth.

## WHAT IS ECONOMIC GROWTH?

Economic growth has many manifestations: a longer life, more meaningful work, better health, more leisure time, more goods and services, and the choice of a greater variety of these goods and services. For a simple measure of economic growth, however, we can use the growth of real GDP itself, or we can divide GDP by the population to obtain the growth of real GDP per capita (per person).

These two measures provide different information about economic growth. The growth of real GDP is powered by capital accumulation, population growth, and technical progress, and it measures the degree to which an economy is growing in both scale and importance in the world. The country with the largest real GDP, the United States, is the most powerful nation economically, politically, and militarily.

> The **growth rate of real GDP** shows the extent to which the total output of the economy is increasing.

The growth rate (or rate of growth) over any number of years (a decade, a century, or longer) is expressed as the percentage change over that period. Thus, if real GDP for some country is $2500 billion in 1986 and $4000 billion in 1996, there is a 40 per cent change over the 10 years or an average annual rate of growth of 3.4 percent.

The growth rate of real per capita GDP is a measure of the growth of living standards of the average citizen. People who live in countries with high per capita GDP are, on average, better off materially. We shall see in this chapter that growth in per capita GDP is powered by improvements in technology and capital accumulation that increase the output available to each person.

> The **growth rate of real per capita GDP** shows the extent to which the economic well-being of the average person is increasing.

## THE INDUSTRIAL REVOLUTION

We have identified the Industrial Revolution as one of the Defining Moments of economic experience (Chapter 1). But what brought it about?

The Industrial Revolution was based on invention and the freedom of innovators to pursue their own interests. The fifteenth-century invention that started it all was the printing press. The printing press accomplished something that mere reading and writing could not: It allowed the quick transfer of information from one person to another. It cut the cost of copying information by over 90 per cent. For the first time in human history, scientific and technical information could be replicated and disseminated cheaply. A scientific and technical revolution soon followed with the contributions of Copernicus, Galileo, Kepler, and, of course, Isaac Newton. The Industrial Revolution applied newly acquired scientific knowledge to machinery—the cotton gin and the steam engine, among others. The traditional farm society began to disappear as the roles of peasant, landowner, and craftsman gradually gave way to new occupations such as mechanic, coal tender, mill worker, iron worker, and engineer. Between 1820 and 1850 England dominated the industrial world, producing two-thirds of the world's coal and about half its steel and cotton. In 1870, England was the most productive nation in the world; it produced about 11 percent more per hour worked than its next closest rival, the United States.

The Industrial Revolution spread from England to America and the European continent. Throughout the nineteenth century, life expectancy, population, and living standards increased to unprecedented levels. America overtook Great Britain as the world's technological leader. By 1913, the United States produced 25 percent more per hour worked than England.

Table 1 gives a detailed account of the per capita growth of the U.S. economy over 40-year periods beginning in 1800. Two facts stand out: (1) Growth rates in the late twentieth century are three times larger than growth rates in the early nineteenth century, and (2) growth rates have not increased significantly throughout this century. In short, over the past two centuries growth rates first substantially increased but now appear to have stabilized. Some economists argue that this stabilization is a statistical illusion caused by the more rapid changes taking place in today's economy; thus, it may be that the growth rate has continued to accelerate. (See Example 1.)

Modern economic growth brought about substantial changes in life-styles. The share of economic activity devoted to industry and services rose; the share of agriculture declined. These changes in the structure of the economy were accompanied by rising urbanization; the typical worker was an industrial laborer, not a farmer. With rising per capita income and rising real wages, items that had previously been available only to the rich—quality textiles, foods from other countries, automobiles, long-distance transportation—became available for mass consumption. With rising living standards, birth rates began to fall. After the initial acceleration of population growth, the rate of population growth began to decline in industrialized countries. In the late twenti-

eth century, a number of affluent countries even worry about declining population.

## PRODUCTIVITY

We know from Chapter 2 that economies grow for two reasons: because of a larger volume of labor or capital inputs, or because existing labor and capital resources are used more effectively. In other words, more output is produced from the same amount of inputs. We use *productivity* as a measure of how effectively an economy uses its available labor and capital resources.

Table 2 supplies long-term data for the U.S. economy. In the first column we see the growth rates of real GDP for different periods from 1800 to the present. In the next two columns we can compare the corresponding growth rates of labor inputs (measured in hours) and of capital inputs. In the fourth column the growth rates of labor and capital are combined. From data on real GDP growth and labor and capital growth, we can calculate productivity.

Three measures of productivity are shown in Table 2: labor productivity, capital productivity, and total factor productivity.

**Labor productivity** measures output per unit (usually per hour) of labor input.

**Capital productivity** measures output per unit of capital input.

**Total factor productivity** measures output per unit of combined labor and capital input.

These three measures of productivity are usually expressed as annual rates of growth. The growth rate of labor productivity measures the growth rate of output per unit of labor input. The growth rate of total factor productivity measures the growth rate of output per unit of combined inputs. *The growth rate of total factor productivity is approximately the growth rate of real output minus the growth rate of combined factor inputs.*

Table 2 provides some basic facts of economic growth in the United States: Labor inputs have grown more slowly than both output and capital, and the rate of growth of labor inputs has declined as population growth slowed. Real GDP has grown,

| Table 1   Per Capita Growth in the United States | |
|---|---|
| Period | Average Annual Growth Rate of Per Capita Real GDP |
| 1800–1840 | 0.58% |
| 1840–1880 | 1.44% |
| 1880–1920 | 1.78% |
| 1920–1960 | 1.68% |
| 1960–1995 | 1.85% |

*Source:* Paul Romer, "Increasing Returns and Long Run Growth," *Journal of Political Economy,* 1986, pp. 1002–1037; and *Economic Report of the President,* various issues.

## EXAMPLE 1
## ARE WE UNDERESTIMATING GDP GROWTH?

The chapter on measuring output and growth showed that real GDP growth is measured by taking the rate of growth of nominal GDP minus the rate of inflation. If the rate of inflation is overestimated, we necessarily underestimate the rate of real GDP growth.

How could such an overestimate take place? The answer is that inflation is based on price indices. The typical price index shows the change in the cost of a given bundle of goods from one period to the next. In a period of great change, when new goods are constantly being introduced and old goods are constantly being improved or replaced, we might well be "comparing apples with oranges." In the case of a quality improvement, a price index is likely to register an increase in the price level even though the price per unit of quality has remained the same or even falls.

New goods cause serious problems. Home computers, video cassette recorders, video games, digital watches, and many other goods did not exist 30 years ago. How can we calculate average prices today compared with average prices 30 years ago when, in effect, those new goods had infinite prices?

Harvard economist Zvi Griliches gives an example of how price indexes treat the same product as a different product. In the pharmaceutical industry, when a patent on a drug expires, a generic version is made available at about half the price. But the generic drug is treated as a separate commodity although it is chemically equivalent, so the price index does not register a decline unless the original drug price falls. In most cases, it does not.

Yale economist William Nordhaus has attempted to quantify the extent to which real growth rates may be underestimated. He first gives a relatively accurate estimate for the case of lighting. Nordhaus's study of the cost of light—a commodity that can be measured in a standard way—shows that technological change has lowered the cost of light astronomically. Then by extension Nordhaus derives a low-bias estimate and a high-bias estimate for the general price index. Nordhaus speculates: "In terms of living standards, the conventional growth of real wages has been a factor of 13 over the 1800–1992 period. For the low-bias case, real wages have grown by a factor of 280, while in the high-bias case real wages by a factor of 9600."

Economists are just beginning to appreciate the enormous biases that may be present in the measurement of real GDP growth. It will be interesting to see if the calculations by such economists as Griliches and Nordhaus will be accepted by future economists.

--------------------------------------------

*Sources:* Zvi Griliches, "Productivity, R&D, and the Data Constraint," *American Economic Review* (March 1994); William D. Nordhaus, "Do Real Output and Real Wage Measures Capture Reality? The History of Light Suggests Not," Yale University, February 1994.

over the long run, at between 3 and 4 percent per annum, and capital has grown at a similar rate.

Labor productivity grew more slowly in the nineteenth than in the twentieth century. In the nineteenth century, it grew at around one percent per year or less. In the twentieth century, labor productivity grew about 2 percent per year. Because output and capital grew at about the same rate, the growth rate of capital productivity has been close to zero.

## LABOR PRODUCTIVITY

Figure 1 shows the annual rate of growth of labor productivity in the United States from 1958 to the

## Table 2
### Annual Growth Rates of U.S. GDP, Factor Inputs, and Productivity, 1800–1988

| | Real GDP (1) | Labor Inputs (hr) (2) | Capital Inputs (3) | Combined Inputs (4) | Labor Productivity (5) = (1) − (2) | Capital Productivity (6) = (1) − (3) | Total Factor Productivity (7) = (1) − (4) | Proportion of Growth Explained by Inputs (8) = (4) ÷ (1) | Unexplained Residual (9) = (5) ÷ (1) |
|---|---|---|---|---|---|---|---|---|---|
| 1800–1855 | 4.2% | 3.7% | 4.3% | 3.9% | 0.5% | − 0.1% | 0.3% | 93% | 7% |
| 1855–1898 | 4.0% | 2.8% | 4.6% | 3.6% | 1.1% | − 0.6% | 0.3% | 90% | 10% |
| 1899–1919 | 3.9% | 1.8% | 3.1% | 2.2% | 2.0% | 0.7% | 1.7% | 46% | 54% |
| 1919–1948 | 3.0% | 0.6% | 1.2% | 0.8% | 2.4% | 1.6% | 2.2% | 20% | 80% |
| 1948–1988 | 3.2% | 0.9% | 3.7% | 1.5% | 2.3% | − 0.2% | 1.7% | 47% | 53% |

*Sources:* John W. Kendrick, "Survey of the Factors Contributing to the Decline in U.S. Productivity Growth," *The Decline in Productivity Growth*, Federal Reserve Bank of Boston, Conference Series No. 22, June 1980, 2; U.S. Department of Labor, Bureau of Labor Statistics, *Trends in Multifactor Productivity, 1948–81*, September 1983, 24; Edward Denison, *Trends in American Economic Growth, 1929–1982* (Washington, D.C.: Brookings Institution, 1985); *World Development Report 1991*, 43–44.

present. Labor productivity growth, as measured by the rate of growth of real GDP per hour of labor, fluctuates significantly from year to year. These fluctuations make it difficult to see the long-run trends in labor productivity shown in Table 2. The period from the late 1950s through the mid-1960s was one of high labor productivity growth. From the late 1960s to 1995, labor productivity growth was erratic, generally falling with recessions and rising with recoveries.

Figure 1 illustrates why fears of a long-term productivity decline were widespread in the 1970s and

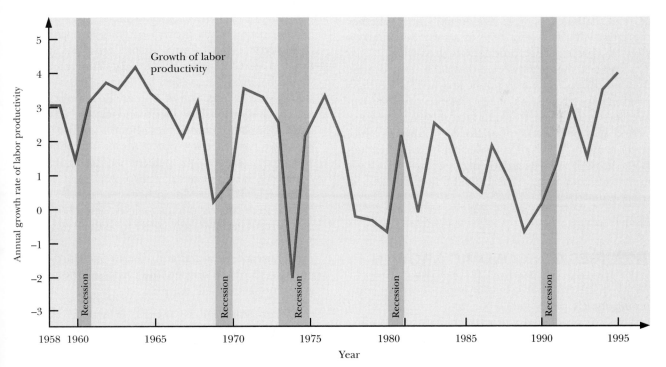

**FIGURE 1  Annual Growth Rates of U.S. Labor Productivity, 1958–1995**
The growth rate of labor productivity tends to fluctuate from year to year. Productivity growth was high from the late 1950s through the late 1960s, fell during the recessions of the 1970s and early 1980s, and rose sharply during the recovery phase of the cycle. *Note:* Figure for 1995 is estimated. *Source: Economic Report of the President.*

**Table 3  Long-Term Trends in U.S. Labor Productivity Growth**

| Period | Average Annual Growth Rate in Output per Hour |
|--------|:-----------------------------------:|
| 1900–1916 | 1.5% |
| 1916–1929 | 2.3% |
| 1929–1948 | 1.6% |
| 1948–1965 | 3.3% |
| 1965–1973 | 2.3% |
| 1973–1985 | 0.9% |
| 1985–1994 | 1.4% |

*Source:* Michael Darby, "The U.S Productivity Slowdown: A Case of Statistical Myopia," *American Economic Review* (June 1984), p. 302. Darby's figures are updated from *Economic Report of the President,* various issues.

early 1980s. From high and steady productivity growth in the 1960s, the economy experienced some years of negative productivity growth in the mid- and late 1970s. The economic recovery after 1982 and after 1990–91 generated positive and reasonably rapid labor productivity growth, underscoring the fact that labor productivity is heavily dependent upon the state of the business cycle. We do not know whether the late 1990s will be a time of steady and high or slow and erratic labor productivity growth.

Table 3 shows why fears of a long-term decline in labor productivity may not be justified. Since 1973 productivity growth has been close to the long-run average for earlier periods. In fact, the early postwar period was one of exceptionally high labor productivity growth. We shall consider below why productivity growth was exceptionally high in the 1950s and 1960s not only in the United States but also in other countries.

## THEORIES OF ECONOMIC GROWTH

As we discussed above, output is produced by combining inputs of capital, labor, and land. Technical progress or productivity growth enables an economy to produce more output with the same amount of inputs. Figure 2 tells the basic story of the growth of the U.S. economy. The top line shows that real per capita GDP has grown considerably over time. Real GDP in 1996, for example, was more than double that of 1950.

To indicate the role of capital ($K$) and labor ($L$), the middle line shows that over time the ratio of cap-

ital to labor has increased. Indeed, the 1996 capital/labor ratio was about 140 percent higher than in 1950.

Finally, Figure 2 shows capital and GDP increasing at about the same rate (as confirmed in Table 2). Thus, since 1950, the ratio of capital to GDP, called the capital-output ratio, has remained approximately constant—around 2.5 to 1. In other words, for each dollar of GDP, about $2.5 worth of plant, equipment, and inventories seem to be required.

## GROWTH ACCOUNTING

We can account for economic growth by breaking it down into its component parts. We know that output (real GDP) is produced by capital and labor. An increase in productivity—that is, technical progress—will increase output without any increase in inputs. If productivity were growing by, say, 3 percent per year, but the amount of capital and labor (population) in the economy were constant, total GDP and per capita GDP would be growing by exactly 3 percent per year. If, in addition, capital were growing by, say, 2 percent per year (% growth of $K$) and labor, say, also by 2 percent per year (% growth of $L$), you might incorrectly deduce that output would grow by an additional 4 percent per year ($2 + 2$). Your conclusion would be wrong, however, because capital and labor share in the production of output. Economists studying the importance of labor and capital have concluded that labor contributes about two-thirds to output and capital contributes about one-third. The weighted average of 2 percent capital growth and 2 percent labor growth is also 2 percent, that is, $(1/3)2 + (2/3)2 = 2$. In other words, 3 percent growth in productivity plus an average rate of growth of 2 percent in inputs will cause total GDP to grow by 5 percent.

Thus, when capital contributes one-third and labor two-thirds to output, the basic equation for the growth of total GDP is this:

$$\% \text{ growth GDP} = (1/3)\,(\% \text{ growth } K) + (2/3)\,(\% \text{ growth } L) + \% \text{ growth productivity} \tag{1}$$

The basic equation governing the growth of GDP per worker (or per capita, if the growth of workers equals the growth of population) is obtained by simply subtracting the percentage change in labor growth from both sides of equation 1. In this and the following examples, we let labor and population

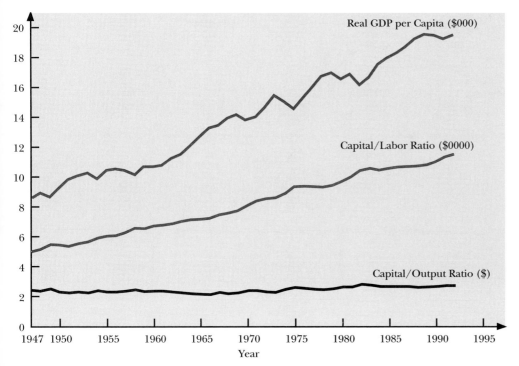

**FIGURE 2  U.S. Economic Growth (1987 dollars)**

*Sources:* Edward Denison, *Trends in American Economic Growth, 1928–1982,* (Washington D.C.: Brookings Institution, 1985). *Statistical Abstract of the United States* (Section: Gross Stock of Fixed Private Capital).

grow at the same rate. Thus, for the case in which capital contributes one-third to total output,

% growth per capita GDP =
(1/3) (% growth $K$ − % growth $L$) +
% growth productivity   (2)

As an illustration of equation 2, if both capital and labor are growing at the same rate, the entire change in per capita GDP will be due to the change in productivity. Over time, however, since capital grows faster than the labor supply or population, capital accumulation adds to the growth of per capita GDP.

## THE STATIONARY ECONOMY: A WORLD WITHOUT TECHNICAL PROGRESS

Economics was once called "the dismal science," because its prognosis for the future was a rather bleak, stationary economy in which growth in per capita output would come to an end. As we have established, this prognosis has not come true. Such classical economists as Thomas Malthus and David Ricardo did not foresee the sustained growth the world has enjoyed since the Industrial Revolution.

Let us consider why. In a world without technological progress the basic source of growth in per capita output is capital accumulation. As the equation above showed, growth of per capita output requires that capital grows faster than labor if there is no technological progress. In Figure 3 the curve PF shows the per capita production function.

> The **per capita production function** shows the relationship between real GDP per capita and the stock of capital per capita.

Capital consists of the machinery that enables workers to produce more cotton, or steel, or wheat. The position of the production function is determined by the state of technical knowledge that reflects the type of capital available to workers and their training. For a given "state of the arts," movements along the production function are governed solely by changes in the amount of capital per person.

The capital stock is increased by saving. As we discussed in the previous chapter, saving equals investment. If investment in new machinery exceeds the depreciation of old machinery, the capital stock

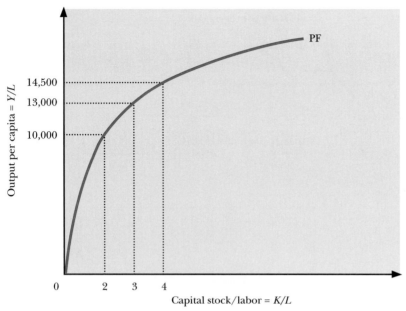

**FIGURE 3   Per Capita Production Function**

The per capita production function shows output per worker as a function of capital per worker. It shows the law of diminishing returns. As the $K/L$ ratio increases from 2 to 3 to 4, output increases by successively smaller amounts.

will increase. More capital per person means that output per capita is increasing. A key characteristic of the per capita production function shown in Figure 3 is that it exhibits the *law of diminishing returns*—that is, extra amounts of capital add smaller and smaller increments to output. Thus, the production function is concave when viewed from below. Increasing the amount of capital per person from 2 units to 3 units in Figure 3 raises output per person from $10,000 to $13,000—that is, by $3,000. Increasing the amount of capital by another unit from 3 units to 4 units raises output only by another $1,500, from $13,000 to $14,500.

Capital accumulation, however, cannot increase per capita output forever. Without technical progress, the law of diminishing returns implies that the rate of return entrepreneurs can earn from further investments in machinery will decline. Since profits are the reason for investment, reductions in the rate of return on investments will eventually cause capital accumulation to come to a halt because at some point saving is no longer rewarded. At this point, if there is no technical progress, GDP per capita will stop growing.

This was the world foreseen by such early economists as Malthus and Ricardo. They cannot be

faulted for failing to anticipate the tremendous changes in technology that were to come in the next two centuries. The experience of the world up to that point had been either no growth or extremely slow growth.

## GROWTH WITH TECHNICAL PROGRESS

How do we explain the obvious fact that people live better today than in the past? How did we overcome diminishing returns? In the face of the law of diminishing returns, technological progress explains the continuous growth of per capita GDP, as well as capital, exhibited in Figure 2.

In Figure 4 we can see the effect of technological progress on the production function. The productivity of labor increases because each worker is capable of working with more advanced machinery or knowledge. Figure 4 shows the approximate comparison between the production function for the United States in the year 2000 ($PF_{2000}$) and the production function in 1900 ($PF_{1900}$). Over 100 years, enormous technological change, as well as capital accumulation, has taken place, raising U.S. per capita GDP from $5,000 in 1900 to $28,000 in 2000 (in

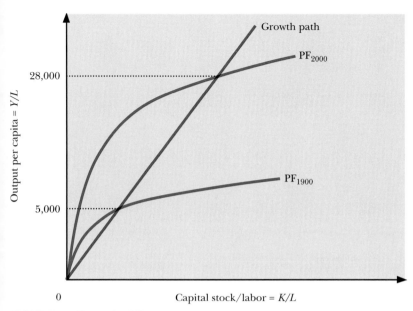

**FIGURE 4 Technical Progress**

Technical progress shifts the production function upward. The production function in the year 2000 will be much further out than the production function in the year 1900. Over time, technical progress raises both output per worker and capital per worker.

1995 dollars). By contrast with capital accumulation, there is no upper limit to the process of technological change.

## THE NEOCLASSICAL GROWTH MODEL

There are two major theories of economic growth. The first, called the neoclassical growth model, was developed principally by Robert Solow, an American Nobel laureate in economics. The neoclassical growth model explains persistent growth. The second, which may be called the endogenous growth model or the neo-Schumpeterian model (after Joseph Schumpeter), was developed principally by Paul Romer. This model predicts increasing economic growth rates.[1] We shall first discuss the neoclassical model.

> The **neoclassical growth model** explains economic growth by virtue of capital accumula-

tion, population growth, and **unexplained technological progress.**

The neoclassical growth model is depicted in Figure 5. The horizontal axis measures the capital-output ratio; the vertical axis measures the rate of growth of per capita GDP. The long-run steady rate of per capita growth is shown by the intersection of the long-run equilibrium level of the capital-output ratio and the per capita growth curve.

Let us look first at the long-run capital-output ratio. Clearly, if both capital and output are growing at the same rate, whatever that rate might be, the capital-output ratio will remain the same. Therefore it is not too surprising that in the neoclassical growth model there is a long-run equilibrium ratio of capital to output. In Figure 5 this is illustrated by the vertical line drawn at the capital-output ratio of 3 (as we noted earlier, the capital-output ratio has remained around 3 for many years). The long-run capital-output ratio itself depends on the growth rate of output and the saving rate. Since output growth raises output and saving increases the capital stock, the capital-output *ratio* is positively related to the saving rate

---

[1] See Paul Romer, "The Origins of Endogenous Growth," *Journal of Economic Perspectives* (Winter, 1994).

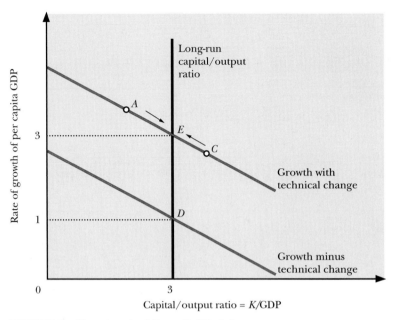

**FIGURE 5   Neoclassical Growth Model**

The growth rate of per capita GDP declines the higher the capital stock because, for given investment, the lower the rate of growth of the capital stock and, therefore, GDP. Technical progress shifts the growth curve upward. The long-run growth path is at *E* since the long-run capital-output ratio is 3. In the intermediate run (say a decade), the economy could have a capital shortage (such as point *A*) or too much capital (such as point *C*). An economy finding itself at *A* can expect a lower rate of growth of per capita GDP until it returns to *E*. An economy at *C* can expect increasing rates of growth until it returns to *E*.

and negatively related to the growth rate in output.[2] When these other factors are stable, the capital-output ratio must remain stable. If it were to increase steadily under these conditions, for example, the law of diminishing returns would depress the rate of return on capital and reduce saving.

The long-run equilibrium capital-output ratio is increased by a higher saving rate and decreased by a higher growth rate of output.

[2]The long-run capital-output ratio = $s/g$, where $s$ is the saving rate and $g$ is the growth rate of capital or output. Since the capital-output ratio is constant, the growth rate of capital and output are the same. The saving rate $s = I/Y$, where $I$ is investment and $Y$ is output. But $I/K = g$, or $I = gK$, since investment is the increase in the capital stock. Therefore, $s = gK/Y$ or $K/Y = s/g$.

If output growth and the saving rate are stable, then so will be the long-run capital-output ratio.

The second component of the neoclassical growth model is the per capita growth curve (equation 2 above). The per capital growth curve shows how the rate of growth in per capita GDP depends on the capital-output ratio, holding constant other factors.[3] The per capital GDP growth curve is downward sloping because a higher capital-output ratio implies a smaller rate of growth in the capital stock for a given amount of investment. If the economy is

[3]The per capita growth curve holds constant the saving rate, the rate of technological progress, rate of growth in the labor force (or population), and the share of capital in the production of output.

investing $100 billion, the rate of growth of the capital stock is smaller with a capital stock of $1000 billion than with a capital stock of only $500 billion. With a lower rate of growth of capital, the rate of growth of output is necessarily smaller (holding other factors constant). Thus, the higher the capital-output ratio, everything else constant, the lower the rate of growth in per capita GDP.

> The **per capita growth curve** shows the negative relationship between per capita GDP growth rate and the capital-output ratio, holding other factors constant.

Where the growth curve intersects the vertical long-run capital-output ratio illustrates the actual per capita growth rate over the long run. In Figure 5, we assume that this rate of growth is 3 percent per year.

The long run is a very long period of time—neoclassical growth theory deals in several decades rather than several years. In the intermediate run—perhaps only a decade—the economy can be just about anywhere along the growth curve. For example, in Figure 5 point A represents a situation in which the economy has a severe shortage of capital. This describes the world economy after World War II, for example. The war destroyed much of the world's capital stock in Europe and Japan, and the U.S. civilian capital stock had been reduced by wartime production. Thus, the rate of growth of the capital stock was relatively high after World War II. It is not too surprising that in the 20 years following World War II, the per capita GDP of the major industrialized countries grew at an annual rate of 4 percent or greater—far above what was sustainable over a long period of time. A similar phenomenon occurred after World War I. Over time, as capital accumulates relative to output, the rate of growth of the capital stock falls and the growth rate of per capita GDP will likewise fall until point E is reached. The smaller growth rate in the last 20 years has been in part this natural process of returning to more normal times.

Similarly, an economy can have too much capital—a capital glut—as represented by point C. This might describe the Japanese economy in the 1990s. With a very high capital stock relative to output, for a given rate of investment there is a lower rate of growth in the capital stock. With a lower rate of growth of inputs, the growth of output will be relatively low compared with historical averages. Over

time, as capital falls relative to output, the rate of growth of per capita GDP would rise until point E is reached.

Figure 6 shows how an increase in the rate of saving affects the rates of growth. Initially, the economy is at point E—per capita income grows at 3 percent per year. An increase in the rate of saving increases the rate of capital accumulation for any capital-output ratio and, therefore, increases the rate of growth of per capita output. Thus, the growth curve shifts upward. However, an increase in the saving rate will also increase the long-run equilibrium capital-output ratio. In the intermediate run (say, a decade), the increase in the saving rate will shift the growth rate up to A. At the same time, the capital-output ratio will begin to increase because investment has grown relative to the capital stock. Eventually, however, the economy moves from point A to E', as the rate of growth falls back to 3 percent per year. In the neoclassical model, the saving rate cannot influence the long-run rate of growth because it cannot influence the rate of technological progress, which is the underlying force behind per capita growth. Recall that without technological progress, the growth of both capital and output must come to a standstill because of the law of diminishing returns.[4]

## ENDOGENOUS GROWTH THEORY

The neoclassical growth model of Solow does not explain the rate of technical progress. It takes the rate of technological progress to be something that "just happens." In contrast to Solow, Joseph Schumpeter believed that insatiable human wants provide the fuel for economic growth. People always want more and better products. Therefore, research and development are carried out to make a profit on new or better products. The Schumpeterian view was supported by an economic historian, Jacob Schmookler, who found that profit was the prime motive in the historical record of important inventions in petroleum re-

---

[4]Equation 1 can be used to demonstrate that the long-run rate of growth in the economy depends only on the growth in the labor force, the rate of technological progress, and the share of capital in output. Letting $a$ = the share of capital in output, equation 1 is: $\%Y = a(\%K) + (1 - a)(\%L) + t$, where $t$ is the rate of technical progress. Since the capital output ratio is constant, $\%Y = \%K$ (the percentage change in $Y$ equals the percentage change in $K$), it follows that $\%Y = \%L + t/(1 - a)$.

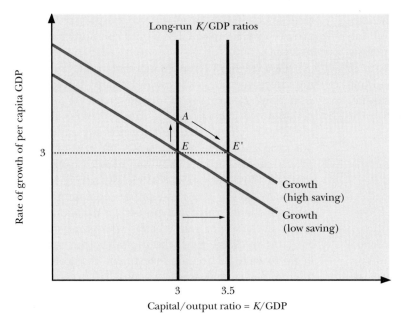

**FIGURE 6    The Effect of a Higher Saving Rate in the Neoclassical Growth Model**

The effect of an increase in the saving rate in the neoclassical model is to increase the rate of growth (from $E$ to $A$) in the intermediate run, but in the long run the capital-output ratio increases and the rate of growth falls to the previous level ($E'$). The moves from $E$ to $A$ and from $A$ to $E'$ may take one or more decades.

fining, papermaking, railroading, and farming.[5] Since neo-Schumpeterian models explain technological progress, they are also called endogenous growth models.

> **Endogenous growth** or **neo-Schumpeterian models** base their explanation of technological progress on the desire for profit.

Moreover, no one has yet discovered a law of diminishing returns in regard to technological progress, as they have for capital accumulation. Indeed, since every new product or idea adds to the stock of human knowledge, the cost of innovation falls as knowledge accumulates. When Thomas Newcomen invented the steam engine in 1712, he only added a jet stream of cold water to a boiler, a piston, and a cylinder—things that were already known. However, without, say, the piston and cylinder, all that might come from the cold water

would be a drinking fountain! The same story occurs again and again. Each idea or invention lowers the cost of having new ideas or making new inventions: The potato chip followed french fried potatoes, the hair dryer was suggested by the vacuum cleaner, and athletic shoes required vulcanized rubber.

> Every new invention lowers the cost of future inventions.

A larger stock of physical or human capital can result in more resources being devoted to the acquisition of new knowledge. However, as new knowledge becomes cheaper, greater stocks of physical and human capital lead to higher and higher rates of economic growth. It is for this reason that the endogenous growth model predicts that growth rates will increase over time. It is very difficult to determine whether economic growth has been increasing over time. To answer this question, we would have to compare today's growth statistics with those of earlier centuries. Earlier statistics were compiled differently and from different information. Moreover, there is

---

[5]Jacob Schmookler, *Invention and Economic Growth* (Cambridge: Harvard University Press, 1966), p. 199.

## EXAMPLE 2
## THE HIGH-TECH REVOLUTION

Endogenous growth theory fits neatly into the high-tech revolution that seems to going on in today's world. The computer on a chip—the microprocessor—is transforming the world economy. As a recent writer has pointed out:

> On every front, from electronics to aviation, agriculture, health care, and communications, great bursts of technological change are utterly transforming the human economy. Propelled by the computer's power to help the human brain manipulate complex information, business firms in thousands of obscure niches are participating in an awesome surge of economic speciation [that is, differentia-

tion]. In the 1990s, more new products are being introduced each year than were created during the entire nineteenth century.

The microprocessor makes possible digital watches, video games, personal computers, automatic teller machines, supermarket scanners, satellite TV, antilock brakes, cellular phones, factory robots, and thousands of other products.

The microprocessor revolution shows how wrong those experts are who argue that everything has already been invented.

*Source:* Michael Rothschild, *Bionomics: Economy as Ecosystem* (New York: Henry Holt and Company, 1992), p. 75.

the problem of the possible mismeasurement of economic growth. Proponents of endogenous growth theory argue that rapid technological change causes us to underestimate economic growth.

Is there any tendency for the process of endogenous growth to come to an end? Fortunately for our descendants, economic change is probably more pervasive today than ever before. The microprocessor—or computer on a chip—will probably rank with the printing press and the steam engine as a historically pivotal invention, by dramatically lowering the cost of storing, calculating, and communicating information. (See Example 2.)

Figure 7 describes the effect of an increase in the rate of technological progress on per capita growth rates and the capital-output ratio. The growth curve shifts up because for each capital-output ratio, a higher rate of technological progress increases the rate of growth of output for given rates of growth in inputs. The long-run capital-output ratio will fall because growth rates of output rise relative to investment. Thus, in Figure 7, the economy would shift from E to A in the intermediate run and from A to E' in the long run.

Unlike neoclassical growth theory, in endogenous growth theory a higher saving rate can cause

greater long-run growth through stimulating more invention. If, for example, companies invest in more high-powered computers, new discoveries will become cheaper and the rate of technological progress will increase.

## ECONOMIC GROWTH POLICY: FACTORS FOR SUCCESS

Endogenous growth theory suggests that since invention is pursued for profit, a society needs an economic structure that will encourage research and development. Therefore, endogenous growth theory suggests that government policy can have a substantial impact on the rate of economic growth. What policies encourage growth?

Over the past 30 or so years, economists have collected an enormous amount of information about economic growth rates in various countries. Each country has its own characteristics: the saving rate, the inflation rate, the extent of government spending, the attitude toward free markets, investment in education, political and social stability, and willingness to promote trade with other countries. This

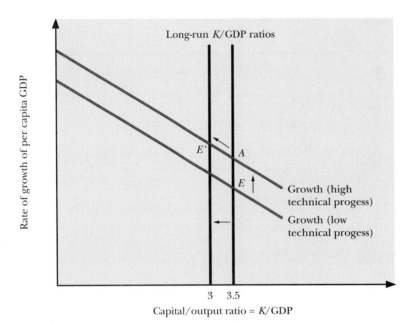

**FIGURE 7   The Effect of Greater Technological Progress on Growth**

An increase in the rate of technological progress shifts the growth curve up as well as shifting the capital-output ratio to the left (higher output growth lowers it). The growth rate will increase from $E$ to $A$ in the intermediate run and eventually to $E'$. The moves from $E$ to $A$ and from $A$ to $E'$ may take one or more decades.

body of work suggests that the following factors are important in securing economic growth.

1. *Increase human knowledge.* Educating a work force increases economic growth. Figure 8 shows the positive relationship between school enrollment—a common measure of human knowledge—and per capita growth over 25 years for 98 countries, based on the work of Robert Barro.[6] The dots represent individual countries; the straight line represents the average relationship between schooling and growth. There is a clear positive association between education and growth. The estimate controls for other factors that might affect growth, such as the level of development and political stability. Evidently, the higher human knowledge is, the greater innovation is and, hence, the larger economic growth is.

2. *Encourage saving and investment.* The most dramatic examples of growth in recent years have been in Asia. If we divide the major Asian countries into

those that have high saving rates (above 20 percent) and those that have low saving rates (20 percent or below), there is a dramatic difference in their growth rates. Table 4 shows the per capita growth rates of these Asian countries over the 1980 to 1990 period, classified into two saving groups. The high saving group had an average growth rate of per capita income of over 5.4 percent; the low saving group had a growth rate of only 1.5 percent.

3. *Discourage political instability.* Unstable governments create uncertainty about the future and, therefore, decrease the incentives to invest in future development. Measuring political instability by the number of revolutions and political assassinations, Robert Barro has also found that greater political instability lowers the rate of economic growth. This result is not surprising because political instability makes property rights more insecure. Endogenous economic growth requires that people believe that they can make profits from investing in new enterprises. Without secure property rights this expectation vanishes.

4. *Monitor government consumption.* Much government spending is necessary, such as spending for education and defense. Education represents invest-

[6]Robert Barro, "Economic Growth in a Cross-Section of Countries," *Quarterly Journal of Economics* (1991), pp. 407–443.

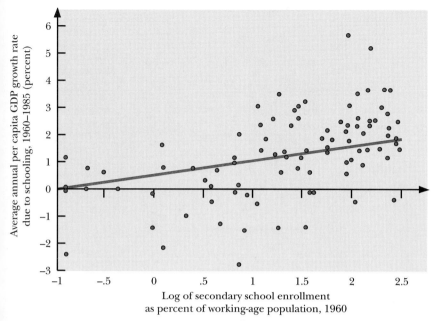

FIGURE 8   **Partial Association Between Real GDP Growth per Capita and School Enrollment Rate**

ment in the future and defense expenditures help secure property rights. What about the rest of government expenditures? Barro's study (noted above) found that the ratio of government consumption (to-

| Table 4 | Saving and Economic Growth | |
|---|---|---|
| | *Saving Rate, 1990* | *Growth Rate, 1980–1990* |
| **High saving** | | |
| Hong Kong | 33 | 5.5 |
| South Korea | 37 | 8.9 |
| Singapore | 45 | 5.7 |
| Thailand | 34 | 5.6 |
| Indonesia | 37 | 4.1 |
| Malaysia | 33 | 2.5 |
| Average | | 5.4 |
| **Low saving** | | |
| Philippines | 16 | − 1.5 |
| Nepal | 8 | 1.8 |
| Bangladesh | 2 | 1.0 |
| India | 20 | 3.2 |
| Pakistan | 12 | 2.9 |
| Sri Lanka | 15 | 2.4 |
| Average | | 1.5 |

*Source:* United Nations, *Human Development Report, 1993* (New York: Oxford University Press, 1993), pp. 186–189.

tal spending minus spending on education and defense) to GDP had a *negative* effect on economic growth. The negative relationship between per capita output growth and government consumption is shown in Figure 9, which holds other factors affecting economic growth constant.

Why should government consumption lower economic growth? Clearly, the higher government consumption is, the higher taxes are. Entrepreneurs develop new products to enjoy the profits they generate; the higher taxes are, the lower are the net profits they take home.

*5. Expand international trade.* One of the most effective ways to increase economic growth is to open up a country's markets to international competition. Expanded growth accomplishes two things: First, it allows each country to devote its resources to those goods in which it has a comparative advantage; second, the spur of greater competition induces entrepreneurs to find new and better products. The quality of American cars has improved substantially over the past decade in large part because of Japanese competition. Americans were buying Toyotas and Hondas instead of Fords and Chryslers. By the 1990s the U.S. auto industry had made a comeback.

Countries that open up their markets to foreign competition tend to grow from 1 to 2 percent per year

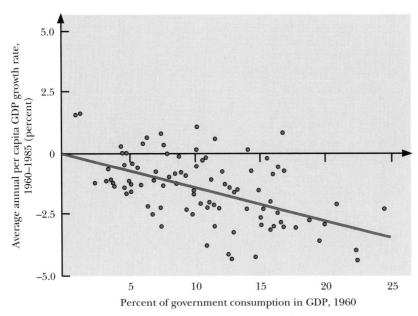

**FIGURE 9    Partial Association Between Real GDP Growth per Capita and Government Consumption in GDP**

faster than countries that protect their markets from foreign competition. The "four tigers"—South Korea, Taiwan, Singapore, and Hong Kong—served as a compelling object lesson to, for example, Mexico, India, and Chile—countries that had once practiced protectionism. Through a combination of relatively open international markets, high rates of saving, and the promotion of education, the "four tigers" lifted their living standards to about the same level as the typical industrialized country. This lesson was well learned by Mexico, India, and Chile; they have opened their markets to freer trade with the rest of the world and are enjoying the fruits of that competition. (See Example 3.)

## FUTURE DEFINING MOMENTS: WILL OUR GRANDCHILDREN BE BETTER OFF THAN WE ARE?

The most remarkable fact about economic growth is that over the past two centuries, the growth rate of real per capita GDP has not only been persistent, it may even have been increasing over time.[7] Table 5

[7]This fact has been documented by the pioneering work of Angus Maddison, *Dynamic Forces in Capitalist Development: A Long-Run Comparative View* (New York: Oxford University Press, 1991).

shows the growth rates of per capita GDP of the 14 countries for which there is more than a century of data. In the 1820–1870 period, the annual rate of per capita growth was less than 1 per cent. In the 1870–1995 period, the average per capita growth rate was 1.85 percent.

Table 5 also shows that in the 1870–1995 period, economic growth has been more than twice as high as in the 1820–1870 period. Growth rates have fallen, however, relative to the immediate postwar period, 1950–1973. This slowdown in economic growth has a straightforward explanation: the return to normalcy after World War II. The neoclassical model of growth explains this by the tremendous capital shortage after World War II.

The endogenous growth model is optimistic about our future. It predicts increasing economic growth rates provided that nothing is done to damage the machinery that produces technological progress. Our discussion indicates that government can do much to promote economic growth, but there is also much government should not do. Someone once said, "Too little government and somebody steals your strawberries; too much government and the government steals your strawberries." Government can support education, encourage saving by taxing consumption rather than income, protect intellectual property rights to new ideas, and provide a stable framework for expanding international trade.

## EXAMPLE 3
## GROWTH AND POVERTY:
## THE CASE OF SINGAPORE

In 1960 the citizens of the United Kingdom had a per capita income four times that of the average citizen of Singapore. Most Singaporeans were poor. Over the next 30 years Singapore grew enormously by following growth-oriented economic policies. By 1990 the average citizens of the two countries had about the same level of income. Most Singaporeans are now well off: They live in an advanced country. The same pattern has evolved in Taiwan, South Korea, and Hong Kong. Economic growth is the best way to lift people out of poverty. We cannot escape the law of scarcity. The only way to truly alleviate poverty is to get the economy to grow faster than the pace of the population for long periods of time. But that is the trick: How do you increase economic growth?

If we look back for over a century it becomes obvious that capitalism works well. Countries that emphasize socialism, regulations, and protectionism encounter great difficulties. Policies that redistribute rather than create wealth are doomed to failure. The countries that grow the fastest are the ones that allow private profit incentives to direct economic resources with as little interference as possible from government taxes, regulation, political instability, and other hindrances to economic growth.

| Table 5    Growth Rates of Real Per Capita GDP (Annual Average) | | |
|---|---|---|
| | 1820–1870 | 1870–1995 |
| Australia | 1.9 | 1.2 |
| Austria | 0.6 | 1.8 |
| Belgium | 1.4 | 1.5 |
| Denmark | 0.9 | 1.8 |
| Finland | 0.8 | 2.1 |
| France | 0.8 | 1.8 |
| Germany | 0.7 | 2.0 |
| Italy | 0.4 | 2.0 |
| Japan | 0.1 | 2.7 |
| Netherlands | 0.9 | 1.5 |
| Norway | 0.7 | 2.2 |
| Sweden | 0.7 | 2.0 |
| United Kingdom | 1.2 | 1.4 |
| United States | 1.5 | 1.9 |
| Average | 0.9 | 1.85 |

*Sources:* Paul Romer, "Increasing Returns and Long-Run Growth," *Journal of Political Economy,* 95 (October 1986), pp. 1002–1037; Angus Maddison, *Dynamic Forces in Capitalist Development: A Long-Run Comparative View* (New York: Oxford University Press, 1991).

However, government can also destroy economic growth.

If governments tax the rewards of innovation and entrepreneurship too highly, they discourage the engine of growth—technological progress. If they cannot maintain political stability, few will be willing to take on the risks of innovation. If they adopt pension systems that discourage, rather than encourage, saving, they reduce capital formation.

In this chapter, we have examined the long-run and intermediate-run issues facing the American economy. In the next chapter, we shall consider the shorter-run issues facing the American economy. Thus, we turn from being concerned about decades to the year-to-year behavior of the economy. We shall return in a later chapter to a discussion of fiscal policies that encourage economic growth.

1. The growth of the entire economy is measured by the growth rate of real GDP; and the growth in living standards is measured by the growth rate of real per capita GDP.

2. The Industrial Revolution applied new acquired scientific knowledge to machinery and was based on the freedom of innovators to pursue their own interests. Growth rates in the late twentieth century are three times larger than growth rates in the early nineteenth century. However, growth rates in the twentieth century appear to have stabilized. Some economists have argued that rapid technological changes in the twentieth century have caused an underestimate of the rate of growth in recent years.

3. Total factor productivity measures output per unit of combined labor and capital inputs. The growth rate of total factor productivity is approximately the growth rate of real output minus the growth rate of combined factor inputs.

4. We can account for economic growth by breaking it down into its component parts. The growth rate of GDP is a weighted average of the growth of the capital and labor inputs plus the growth in productivity of those inputs. The per capita growth in per capita GDP is the share of capital in GDP (about one-third) times the percentage growth in the capital-labor ratio plus the growth in productivity.

5. The per capita production function shows the relationship between real GDP per capita and the stock of capital per capita. Capital accumulation alone cannot increase per capita output forever because of the law of diminishing returns. Technological progress is required for persistent or increasing rates of growth in per capita income.

6. The neoclassical growth model explains persistent economic growth by simply postulating a given rate of technological progress. The neo-Schumpeterian or endogenous growth model explains technological progress as a response to profitable inventions and the ever-falling costs of innovation.

7. Empirical evidence indicates that policies that encourage economic growth are: high rates of saving, free trade, low inflation, low government spending, political stability, and investment in education.

## KEY TERMS

growth rate of real GDP
growth rate of real per
  capita GDP
labor productivity
capital productivity
total factor productivity
per capita production
  function
neoclassical growth
  model
unexplained
  technological
  progress
per capita growth curve
endogenous growth or
  neo-Schumpeterian
  models

1. Why might the growth rate of per capita or total real GDP fail to capture the growth in standards of living?
2. How do growth rates in the twentieth century compare to growth rates in the nineteenth century?
3. Suppose that capital represents one-fourth of GDP and labor represents the other three-fourths. If capital is growing at 2 percent, labor is growing at 4 percent, and productivity is growing at 1 percent, what is the growth rate of total GDP? The growth rate of per capita GDP?
4. Summarize the behavior of per capita GDP, the capital-labor ratio, and the capital-output ratio since the end of World War II.
5. In the intermediate-run, why should a higher capital-output ratio lower the rate of growth in GDP?
6. In the long-run, what will happen to the capital-output ratio in each of the following instances:
a. the saving rate increases.
b. the rate of technological progress increases.
7. What are the basic differences between neoclassical and endogenous growth theory?
8. According to endogenous growth theory, what should be the effect of an increase in the profitability of inventions on the long-run rate of growth? If saving is invested in education, what should be the impact on the long-run rate of growth?
9. If you were the advisor to the president of some country, what advice would you offer to increase that country's rate of growth?

# CHAPTER 27

# AGGREGATE SUPPLY AND AGGREGATE DEMAND

When measured on a scale of decades, a healthy economy experiences long-term growth in real wages, consumption, and per capita income. When measured on the scale of years, however, economies experience some bad years and some good ones. Interest rates rise and fall, inflation rises and falls, and real wages rise and fall. One of the major controversies in macroeconomics concerns the causes of short-run fluctuations in economic activity. These short-run fluctuations—or business cycles—are a fact of life; they have been with us for hundreds of years, and will no doubt continue to be with us for hundreds more. What causes them? Are they all caused by the same forces, or is each business cycle different?

In early 1995, the unemployment rate fell to 5.4 percent, down from 7 percent just 12 months earlier. The economy's real GDP had grown at the rapid rate of 4 percent in the previous quarter. Inflation was under 3 percent. Everything was going right, but the panic buttons began to sound. Headlines from the financial press warned that the economy was "overheating" and that high inflation was imminent. Some prominent economists, guided by one view of macroeconomics, warned that if we did not do something quickly, we would soon be inundated by inflation. Other prominent economists, guided by a different view, said that there was nothing to worry about. We can have rapid growth, low unemployment, and price stability. No wonder the public is often confused! These differences of opinion are really different views of aggregate demand and supply.

Economists do not agree on the causes of the business cycle, and this lack of agreement affects the way they approach the business cycle. If they can't agree on its causes, how can they agree on what to do about it, if anything?

In Chapter 1, we observed that a good theory must be consistent with the facts. Here, we shall apply this principle to the two different theories of the business cycle. If one view of the business cycle is not consistent with the facts, then that theory should be discarded or, at least, held with some degree of skepticism until more evidence can be collected.

# AGGREGATE SUPPLY AND AGGREGATE DEMAND IN MACROECONOMICS

Economists use supply and demand as the most important tools in microeconomics. In macroeconomics, we again use supply and demand, but now we are talking about *aggregate* supply and *aggregate* demand. We use aggregate supply and demand to explain real GDP, the price level, and the key interrelationships among macroeconomic variables. Aggregate supply and demand are not simply extensions of microeconomic supply and demand; they require separate explanation and analysis. We begin with the first building blocks of aggregate supply, the production function.

## THE SHORT-RUN PRODUCTION FUNCTION

In the previous chapter, we considered economic growth. An economy's ability to produce real output depends upon its labor, capital, and land resources and its technology. As population and labor force grow, as investments are made in plant and equipment, as we become better educated and more skilled, and as our technological and scientific knowledge improves, we are able to produce more real GDP; our productive capacity expands either because we have more inputs or because we learn how to use available inputs more effectively.

The capacity to increase real GDP normally does not expand dramatically from year to year. We know from the previous chapter that real GDP has expanded at an average annual rate of 2.5–3.0 percent over the past half century. On average, the physical capacity of the economy to produce output next year will likely be 2.5 to 3 percent greater than this year. However, each year's actual production is different: In some years, real output expands more rapidly than the average; in other years, it expands less or even contracts. These fluctuations around the average growth of real GDP are business cycles.

We know that over long periods, the average rate of expansion of real GDP is more important than are the short-run fluctuations around this average rate. At a 1 percent annual growth rate, real GDP ten years hence will be only 10 percent greater than today's. At a 4 percent annual growth rate, real GDP ten years hence will be 50 percent greater.

If we consider a relatively short period of time—say, one or two years—the capacity of the economy to produce output is more or less fixed. Both technology and the capital stock do not change much over a short period of time. If we wish to produce more output in a particular year, we can do so only by employing more labor. If, for some reason, we wish to produce less output, we can reduce employment.

Figure 1 shows how real GDP responds to changes in the quantity of labor over a short period of time when capital and technology are fixed. We simplify Figure 1 by supposing that only one type of worker produces a single good that represents the entire output of the economy. Figure 1, panel (*a*), measures the total output of this single good on the vertical axis, and employment, or the amount of labor used, *L*, on the horizontal axis. The relationship between employment and output under these circumstances is described by the short-run production function.

> The **short-run production function**—SRPF— shows how much output can be produced with a given amount of employment when capital and technology are fixed.

The short-run production function displays the law of diminishing returns that we discussed in the previous chapter. As employment increases, output increases—but by ever-smaller amounts because the capital stock is fixed. As more and more workers are employed using the same number of machines, trucks, and plants, each additional worker adds smaller and smaller amounts to total output. The SRPF curve must be concave in the downward direction.

Workers are employed by businesses that want to make a profit. Since the value of each successive worker declines as the number of workers increases, the number of workers businesses wish to hire declines as the real wage increases. The real wage shows the wage rate in terms of what workers can buy—that is, the purchasing power of labor earnings. It is measured by money wages divided by the price level (the cost of buying a bundle of consumer goods), or by *W/P*.

> **Real wages** are measured by money wages, *W*, divided by the price level, *P*—that is, *W/P*.

In panel (*b*) of Figure 1, real wages are on the vertical axis and employment is on the horizontal

(*a*) Production function

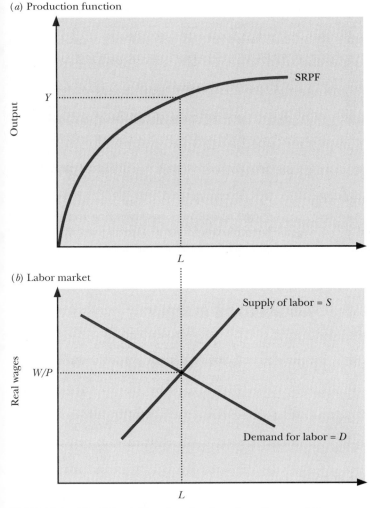

(*b*) Labor market

**FIGURE 1   The Short-Run Production Function and the Labor Market**

Panel (*a*) shows short-run production function (SRPF). Panel (*b*) shows the labor market. Demand for labor comes from SRPF; supply of labor comes from households. Real wages coordinate demand and supply.

axis. The demand for labor curve, *D*, is downward sloping, because business will not hire more workers unless real wages fall. The supply of labor curve, *S*, is upward sloping: If you want more workers, they must be offered higher real wages. The intersection of the *S* and *D* curves determines the level of real wages, employment, and output. The equilibrium real wage is *W/P*, employment is *L*, and real output is *Y*, reading up from panel (*b*) to panel (*a*). We can think of *L* as the natural or full employment amount of labor: All who want to work have a job. We can

think of *Y* as the natural (or full employment) level of output.

> The **natural** level of output (real GDP) is that level corresponding to equality in the demand for and supply of labor.

## THE NATURAL RATE OF UNEMPLOYMENT

This simple model explains an economy that produces one good. Its conclusion can be applied more broadly. Interpreted more broadly, it represents an aggregation over many types of industries and workers. In the real world, the economy is in constant flux. Some industries are expanding; others are contracting. The labor force is being shuffled from industry to industry and job to job. Spending on automobiles and other durable goods constantly rises and falls. Sometimes we spend our incomes on cars and at other times on washing machines. Technology is always on the move with new goods, new processes, and new ways of doing things. Output and employment must adjust to this constant change.

Unemployment arises naturally from the frictions inevitable in labor markets in which people are constantly looking for jobs and firms are constantly looking for workers. What can full employment mean in such a world? Even when the aggregate demand for all types of labor equals the aggregate supply of all types of labor, there will still be unemployment. How much unemployment depends on the frictions involved in matching labor demand with labor supply. The total demand for labor consists of all those working ($N$) plus available jobs or vacancies ($V$). The total supply of labor consists of all those working ($N$) plus those unemployed ($U$). The natural rate of unemployment is achieved when there is a balance between total demand and total supply, or when vacancies ($V$) equal unemployment ($U$).

> The **natural rate of unemployment** is that rate at which the labor force is in balance; that is, the number of available jobs ($V$) is equal to the number of unemployed workers qualified to fill those jobs ($U$), $V = U$, or equivalently, aggregate labor demand is equal to aggregate labor supply, $N + V = N + U$.

The level of output corresponding to the natural rate of unemployment is the natural level of real GDP discussed above. (See Example 1.)

## AGGREGATE SUPPLY

In the short run, the level of output may exceed, equal, or be below the natural level due to both aggregate demand or aggregate supply effects. The con-

### EXAMPLE 1
### WHAT IS THE NATURAL RATE
### OF UNEMPLOYMENT?

Economists are not certain about what the natural rate of unemployment is. Current estimates have ranged from 5.4 percent to 7 percent. According to Milton Friedman, who along with Edmund Phelps developed the natural rate theory, "I don't know what the natural rate is, neither do you, and neither does anyone else. I don't try to forecast short-term changes in the economy."

What this really means is that economists, investors, and policymakers should not make predictions on the basis of some precise notion of the natural rate. For example, in early 1995 the unemployment rate fell below 6 percent, which some regarded as the natural rate of unemployment. Some economists therefore predicted that the rate of inflation would increase. However, when this prediction did not pan out, their estimates of the natural rate of unemployment were reduced.

Perhaps the lesson is to think of the natural rate as a range, say, from 5 percent to 7 percent. If unemployment is less than 5 percent, real wages should rise (wages will outpace inflation), and if unemployment is larger than 7 percent, then real wages should fall (inflation will outpace wages).

------------------------------------------------

*Source:* "Inflation Calculus: Business and Academia Clash Over Economic Concept of 'Natural' Jobless Rate," *Wall Street Journal,* January 24, 1995.

cept of aggregate supply is directly related to the short-run production function discussed above. In macroeconomics, we use aggregate supply to describe the relationship between the real output that businesses in the economy are prepared to supply and the price level.

> The **aggregate supply curve** shows the amounts of real GDP firms in the economy are prepared to supply at different price levels.

You might have the impression, from the microeconomic supply curves we studied in Chapter 4, that the macroeconomic aggregate supply curve is always positively sloped—that businesses will be prepared to supply more output if they can sell their products at higher prices. In microeconomics, we can speak with confidence about the slope of the supply curve. In virtually all cases, an increase in the price of a good will cause the producer to wish to produce more of that good. If the price of wheat rises, wheat farmers will be prepared to supply more wheat to buyers. If the price of personal computers rises, manufacturers of personal computers will be prepared to supply more PCs to the market.

In macroeconomics, things are not that simple. As the circular flow showed, when prices are rising generally throughout the economy, so are wages and so are the costs of materials. In fact, during inflations there is a tendency for prices, wage rates, and material costs to rise together.

If a computer manufacturer's prices, wage rates, and material costs are all rising *at the same rate,* the increase in the price of computers will not make the company any better off. Its prices are up, say, 5 percent, but so are its costs—including its labor costs. In this situation, there is no reason for any computer manufacturer to want to supply more computers than they did previously, just because the price of computers has risen. If, however, computer prices rise faster than labor and other costs, the company is indeed better off, and it would want to produce more computers.

The same principle applies to the economy as a whole. If prices, wages, and material costs all rise at the same rate, an increase in prices should not cause businesses to wish to produce more output. The amount of output supplied should remain the same. Only if prices rise faster than wage rates and other costs would rising prices make firms willing to supply more output.

This example illustrates a fundamental principle of aggregate supply:

> An increase in prices should have no effect on the real output supplied in an economy if prices, wages, and other costs are all rising at the same rate.

When prices, wages, and material costs are rising or falling all at the same rate, the aggregate supply curve is a vertical line at the natural level of output.

This principle is illustrated in Figure 1. If wages and prices both rise at the same rate, then real wages—$W/P$—remain the same. The demand for and supply of labor will remain the same; thus, output will remain at the level $Y$—the natural level of output.

However, let's consider a situation in which wages are not as flexible as prices. In the short run, at least, wages may not be free to respond to changing economic conditions if they are fixed by contract or institutional practice. For example, a firm may hire a worker with the understanding that the worker's wage may be changed only at six-month or one-year intervals. In this case, as the price level rises, real wages—what it really costs firms to hire workers—will fall because money wages are fixed temporarily. Firms will want to hire more labor accordingly as they move up their demand curve for labor. As firms hire more labor, output increases.

Thus, the aggregate demand for labor is really just an aggregate supply of output. Figure 2 shows how fixed money wages can result in an upward-sloping aggregate supply (AS) curve. If money wages are sticky (inflexible), increases in the price level cause real wages to fall while decreases in the price level cause real wages to rise. Suppose the price level is $P = 1.0$; that is, the market basket of things consumers want costs $1. If wages were $100 a week, then the worker can buy 100 market baskets. Panel (*a*) in Figure 2 shows that if real wages are $100, firms are willing to provide employment for 180 million workers. Correspondingly, if these 180 million workers are employed, the economy will produce (according to the short-run production function) $6500 billion of real GDP, shown in panel (*b*). If the price of a market basket falls to $0.50, or $P = 0.5$, the $100 wages would now be worth $200 in real terms. Labor will cost firms twice as much. In panel (*a*), if real wages rise from $100 to $200, firms will cut employment to only 100 million workers. With a

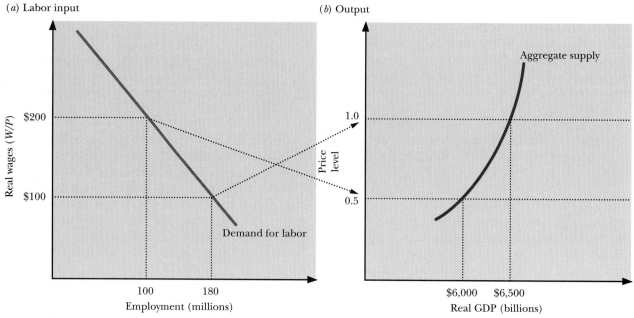

**FIGURE 2  The Demand for Labor and Aggregate Supply**

Suppose money wages are fixed at $100 a week. If price level is $P = 1$, labor demand is 180 million and the economy will try to produce $6500 billion of output. If the price level falls to $P = 0.5$, real wages double to $200 and employment and output fall to 100 million and $6000 billion.

smaller work force, as shown in panel (*b*), the economy produces only $6000 billion of real GDP. Thus, the aggregate supply curve is upward sloping; more real GDP is produced at a higher price level.

> When wages are sticky (inflexible), falling prices raise real wages and firms reduce their employment and output. The aggregate supply curve, therefore, has a positive slope.

The slope of the aggregate supply curve depends on the degree of flexibility of wages and prices. When wages and prices are free to move together, the aggregate supply curve is vertical at the natural level of output. In the case where wages are less flexible than prices, the aggregate supply curve has a positive slope. The slope of the aggregate supply curve therefore depends on price and wage flexibility. (See Example 2.)

## AGGREGATE DEMAND

As in microeconomics, we must analyze both demand and supply in macroeconomics. As explained in an earlier chapter, the GDP of an economy mea-

sures its total output. Economies produce goods and services for purchase as consumer goods, investment goods, government services, or net exports, or GDP $= C + I + G + (X - M)$. The aggregate demand curve shows the level of real GDP that we are willing to buy at different price levels. As shown by Figure 3, we must add the demands for the various components of GDP to obtain the aggregate demand curve. For example, the curves labeled $C$ and $C + I$ are, respectively, the demand for consumer goods at different price levels, and the sum of consumption plus investment at different price levels. The heavy green line in Figure 3 indicates that the aggregate demand curve is downward sloping—the lower the price level, the higher the aggregate quantity demanded.

> The **aggregate demand curve** (AD) shows the real GDP that households, businesses, government, and foreigners are prepared to buy at different price levels.

Three major factors cause the aggregate demand curve to be negatively sloped: the real-balance effect, the interest-rate effect, and the foreign-trade effect. Let's consider each of these three concepts.

## EXAMPLE 2
## HOW STICKY
## ARE PRICES?

In the Keynesian model, an increase in aggregate demand raises output and lowers unemployment because wages and prices are sticky—that is, they do not change immediately when economic conditions change. One of the most important empirical issues of modern macroeconomics is: How sticky are wages and prices in reality?

The answer is that economists still do not know the answer. There have been only three studies that make a serious attempt to document price stickiness in the postwar United States, and they are for products (news magazines, retail prices from major retail catalogs, etc.) that account for only a small portion of GDP.

Why is it we know so little? To study stickiness, we must know actual transactions prices—not list prices. We know, for example, manufacturers' suggested retail prices, but we do not know, most of the time, what the product actually sold for. Second, there are subtle ways for sellers to change prices without altering the quoted price. If demand for the product is high, sellers may not raise their price but they, instead, lengthen delivery lags or reduce the quality of auxiliary services.

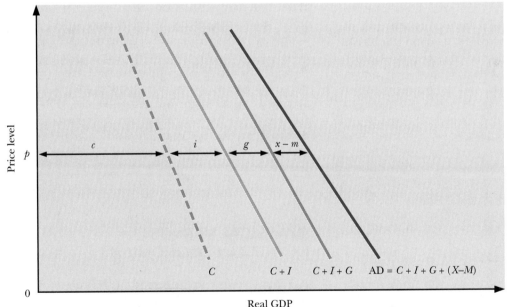

AD = GAP = NI = C + I + G

FIGURE 3   The Aggregate Demand Curve   ∝ Total Demand

The aggregate demand curve $AD = C + I + G + (X - M)$ shows that people are willing to purchase larger aggregate quantities of goods at lower prices. At the particular price level $p$, people buy the quantities $c$, $i$, $g$, and $(x - m)$ of consumption, investment, government goods, and net exports (assumed positive for illustration purposes only), respectively. The AD curve shows a larger response to a price change than any of the components because it reflects the real-balance, interest-rate, and foreign-trade effects of a lower price level.

## THE REAL-BALANCE EFFECT

We hold money assets, such as cash, savings accounts, and bonds as part of our personal wealth. The purchasing power of these money assets rises and falls with the price level. If prices are generally falling, we recognize that our money assets can buy more. Falling prices, therefore, motivate those of us with money holdings to conclude that we are better off; we tend to increase our purchases. Similarly, rising prices reduce the purchasing power of money assets. We conclude that we are worse off and we reduce our purchases. The effect of the change in the price level on real consumption spending is called the *real-balance effect.*

> The **real-balance effect** occurs when desired consumption falls as increases in the price level reduce the purchasing power of money assets.

## THE INTEREST-RATE EFFECT

Interest rates are determined by the demand and supply for credit. The higher the demand for credit, the higher are interest rates. As the price level rises, we require more credit to buy cars, plants, equipment, and inventories. This increased demand for credit raises interest rates. As interest rates rise, real investment declines. We invest less in housing, plants, equipment, and inventories, and the aggregate quantity demanded decreases. As the price level falls, interest rates fall, investment increases, and the aggregate quantity demanded increases.

> The **interest-rate effect** occurs when increases in the price level push up interest rates in credit markets, which reduces real investment.

## THE FOREIGN-TRADE EFFECT

As the domestic price level rises relative to foreign price levels, holding constant the exchange rate (the value of the dollar in terms of foreign currencies), exporters face stiffer competition and imports appear cheaper. As a consequence, exports $(X)$ fall and imports $(M)$ rise. Thus, net exports $(X - M)$ fall. For example, if the U.S. price level rises, with all other things equal, American farmers can export less of their wheat and American consumers will buy more Japanese cars and Swiss watches. If the price level

falls, the aggregate quantity demanded will increase because net exports will increase.

> The **foreign-trade effect** occurs when a rise in the domestic price level lowers the aggregate quantity demanded by pushing down net exports $(X - M)$.

## SHIFTS IN AGGREGATE DEMAND

The aggregate demand curve holds a number of factors constant. If one of these factors changes, the entire aggregate demand curve will shift. Aggregate demand is the sum of $C + I + G + X - M$ at each price level. If anything (other than a change in the price level) occurs to change any of these components, the aggregate demand curve will shift.

An increase in government spending, a reduction in tax rates, or an increase in the money supply will raise aggregate demand. If we suddenly become less thrifty and spend more or if businesses become more optimistic and invest more, aggregate demand increases.

The aggregate demand curve shifts when any of these underlying conditions changes. Panel (*a*) of Figure 4 shows the effects of an increase in the money supply or of government spending on the aggregate demand curve: The entire curve shifts to the right. In panel (*b*) of Figure 4 we illustrate the effects of an increase in tax rates or a reduction in government spending on the aggregate demand curve: The entire curve shifts to the left. When aggregate demand shifts to the right, we say that aggregate demand has increased. When it shifts to the left, aggregate demand has decreased.

# CLASSICAL VERSUS KEYNESIAN ECONOMICS

Aggregate supply and demand play a role in macroeconomics similar to the one they play in microeconomics. The intersection of microeconomic supply and demand curves determines equilibrium price and quantity. The intersection of the macroeconomic aggregate supply and aggregate demand curves determines equilibrium real GDP (how much real output the economy produces) and the economy's price level.

We have seen that the slope of the aggregate supply curve depends upon how flexible wages and

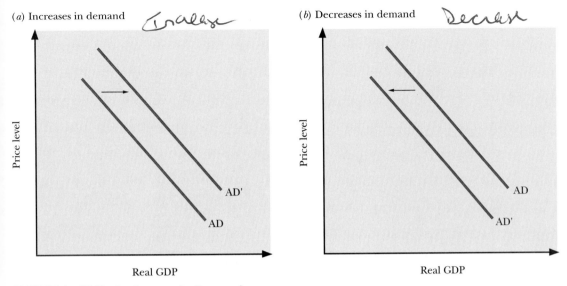

FIGURE 4   Shifts in Aggregate Demand

Panel (*a*) shows an increase in aggregate demand; the curve shifts to the right from AD to AD′. It may be due to more government spending, a larger money supply, or lower taxes. Panel (*b*) shows a decrease in aggregate demand; the curve shifts to the left.

prices are. If wages and prices move exactly together, the price level will have no effect on real output. The economy will simply produce the natural level of real GDP, and the aggregate supply curve is vertical. If wages are less flexible than prices, an increase in prices will induce business to hire more labor and to produce more output. In this case, the aggregate supply curve has a positive slope. Theories of macroeconomics differ primarily on the slope of the aggregate supply curve.

## THE CLASSICAL MODEL: FLEXIBLE WAGES AND PRICES

The Classical Model looks at aggregate supply under conditions of price and wage flexibility. If prices and wages are fully flexible, an increase in prices will be accompanied by equivalent increases in wages and material costs. Real wages remain the same; the increase in prices has made businesses neither better nor worse off, and they continue to supply the same amount of output as before. With flexible wages and prices, the economy will produce the natural level of output, no matter what the price level, as we can see in Figure 5, panel (*a*).

Let us consider the effects of supply and demand shocks in this classical case. In panel (*b*), we see the effects of a reduction in aggregate demand (a demand shock). With a vertical aggregate supply curve, the negative demand shock simply reduces the price level from *P* to *P*′ while leaving real output, employment, and unemployment unchanged. If aggregate demand increases, the price level will rise but output will not be affected.

> With flexible wages and prices, demand shocks affect only the price level. They do not affect real variables such as output, employment, or unemployment.

The effects of a supply shock are shown in Figure 5, panel (*c*). Something happens to increase aggregate supply (good weather, falling crude oil prices, or, simply, everything going right in various sectors of the economy). Throughout the economy the outputs from our farms and factories would then increase. Graphically, the positive supply shock shifts the vertical aggregate supply curve to the right from AS to AS′, thereby lowering prices and increasing output. Because such supply shocks tend to be random in nature, the effects of a favorable supply shock are likely to be wiped out by a negative supply shock (an increase in energy prices, bad weather, everything going wrong) in the next period, shifting the aggregate supply to the left from AS′ to AS (this is merely illustrative—the leftward and rightward shifts need not cancel).

(a) Equilibrium

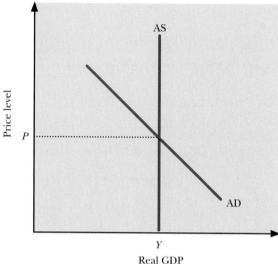

(b) Demand shocks

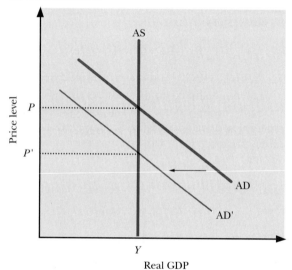

(c) Supply shocks

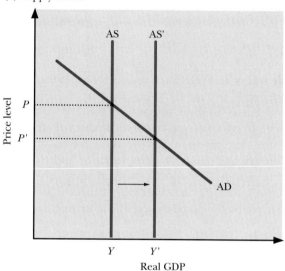

**FIGURE 5    Perfectly Flexible Wages: The Classical Model**

If wages are as flexible as prices, a demand shock will not affect output. In panel (a), aggregate demand falls from AD to AD', with only the price level falling. In panel (b), a positive supply shock from AS to AS' simply lowers the price level.

> With flexible wages and prices, adverse supply shocks raise the price level and reduce real output.

The Classical Model concludes that demand shocks affect inflation only. They do not affect real output. Fluctuations in real output are caused by supply shocks.

## THE KEYNESIAN MODEL: INFLEXIBLE WAGES

We have previewed the short-run Keynesian model in Figure 2 above. The "Keynesian" economy is in the short run where a number of prices, such as wages or material costs, are fixed by contracts, and other prices, such as the prices at which firms sell their final products, are flexible. For example, the market for automobiles might be soft, so that the automobile companies cut prices on new models while paying their workers the wages agreed upon earlier. In the long run, contracts expire so that those prices that are temporarily inflexible (in this case, wages) can adjust as much as those that are always flexible. However, we are concentrating here on the short run.

### Demand Shocks.

Figure 5 summarized the effects of a demand shock with perfectly flexible wages and prices. Let us now consider the same kind of shift in demand in the Keynesian case where wages and material costs are less flexible than prices, and thus the aggregate supply curve is positively sloped. If, beginning from an equilibrium at the natural level of output, there is a reduction in aggregate demand—as we can see in Figure 6, panel (*a*)—the effect will be a decline in the price level, a drop in real output, and a reduction in employment. Unemployment will rise above the natural rate. If the reverse had happened—an increase in aggregate demand—the effect would have been an increase in output, employment, and the price level. Unemployment would fall below the natural rate. Accordingly, the Keynesian explanation for the business cycle is demand shocks.

> In the short run, increases in aggregate demand raise output, employment (lower un-

employment), and the price level. Reductions in aggregate demand lower output, employment (raise unemployment), and the price level. Hence, fluctuations in aggregate demand can cause business cycles.

### Supply Shocks.

Figure 6, panel (*b*), describes an alternative source of business cycles. Just as the aggregate demand curve can shift in the short run, so can the aggregate supply curve. Figure 6, panel (*b*), shows an adverse supply shock (a reduction in aggregate supply). The effect is to lower output and employment and to raise the price level. A positive supply shock (an increase in aggregate supply) raises output and employment but lowers the price level.

> Supply shocks can also cause business cycles. An adverse supply shock raises the price level but lowers output and employment. A positive supply shock lowers the price level but raises output and employment.

In the Keynesian model, business cycles could be caused by demand or supply shocks. Demand shocks, however, would be a more systematic cause.

(*a*) Reductions in aggregate demand

(*b*) Reductions in aggregate supply

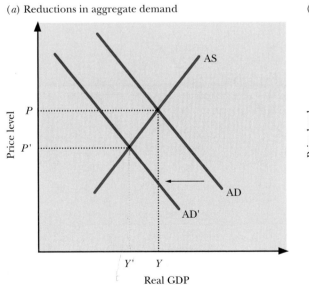
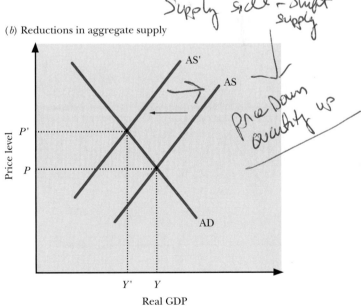

**FIGURE 6   Two Sources of the Business Cycle: The Keynesian Model**

In panel *(a)*, a reduction in aggregate demand reduces output and reduces the price level. In panel *(b)*, a reduction in aggregate supply reduces output and raises prices.

## THE LONG-RUN CASE:
## THE SELF-CORRECTING MECHANISM

Even if wages and prices are not fully flexible, the macroeconomy will produce the same results, as in Figure 5 above, given sufficient time to adjust.

Let's consider a case in which wages are set in one-year contracts. They cannot move for a period of one year even though economic conditions are changing. Prices, on the other hand, are flexible. Every time economic conditions change, they change.

We can see from Figure 7 what happens when there is a decrease in aggregate demand with prices flexible and wages inflexible. The original equilibrium is at point $e$, the intersection of AS and AD. The fall in aggregate demand from AD to AD' lowers prices and the economy moves along the fixed aggregate supply curve AS since wages are fixed for one year. Firms are made worse off; their prices are falling but their costs are not. The rise in real wages causes them to produce less output and offer less employment—they move down the short-run aggregate supply curve.

With flexible prices but inflexible wages, the short run effect of a decline in aggregate

demand is to lower prices, output, and employment.

As time passes, the effects on output and employment will be reversed by a self-correcting mechanism. In this example, after one year, employers can renegotiate wage rates with their employees. The weakness in the labor market will allow employers to achieve lower wage rates. Employees have an incentive to accept lower wage rates because they may otherwise face unemployment. Prices have already fallen, now wage rates begin to fall, and real wages begin to fall. As real wages fall (with constant prices), firms are now able to employ more workers, and increase the amount of output they are prepared to sell at each price level. The short-run aggregate supply curve shifts to the right from AS to AS' along AD' until the economy is returned to the natural level of real GDP at point $e'$. Notice that the end result of the self-correcting mechanism is the same as with flexible wages and prices.

The self-correcting mechanism achieves the same result as flexible wages and prices. A reduction in aggregate demand does not af-

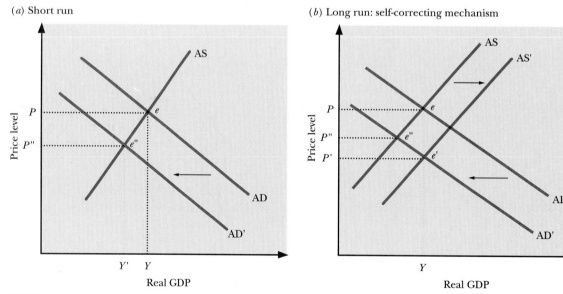

(a) Short run

(b) Long run: self-correcting mechanism

**FIGURE 7  Self-Correcting Mechanism**

In panel (a), a reduction in aggregate demand causes output and the price level to fall in the short run. The economy moves from point $e$ to $e''$. In panel (b), in the long run wages fall, causing the AS curve to shift to AS', restoring full employment.

---

**EXAMPLE 3
THE RECOVERY
FROM THE GREAT DEPRESSION**

*Invisible hand worn*

The U.S. economy recovered from the Great Depression by about 1942. In that year, unemployment was 4.2 percent, and real GDP was up 50 percent from 1929. The money supply had increased from $20 billion to $55 billion. Was the recovery due to the self-correcting mechanism or to government-induced increases in aggregate demand?

Ben Bernanke and Martin Parkinson argue that the self-correcting mechanism was robust during the recovery. In a study using quarterly data from 1924 to 1941, they estimated that at any time, about one-half of the difference between actual and natural unemployment would have been corrected within three quarters even without any stimulus from aggregate demand as measured by unexpected inflation. The growth of aggregate demand played a role, but the self-correcting mechanism was the "engine of recovery."

---

*Source:* Ben Bernanke and Martin Parkinson, "Unemployment, Inflation, and Wages in the American Depression: Are There Lessons for Europe?" *American Economic Review* (May 1989): pp. 210–214.

---

fect output or employment in the long run. It affects only the price level.

The speed of adjustment depends upon how much time is required before wages, which are temporarily inflexible, can adjust. If, in the earlier example, wages are fixed for two years, the adjustment will be even slower. If they are fixed for only a month, the adjustment is rapid. An interesting and open question is how long it would have taken for the self-correcting mechanism to complete recovery from the Great Depression. (See Example 3.)

The main evidence that a self-correcting mechanism exists comes from economic history, which shows that there was no long-term trend in the unemployment rates of the industrialized countries from the 1880s to the Great Depression. Unemployment rates fluctuated from year to year, but they returned to the natural unemployment rate.

The late nineteenth and early twentieth centuries witnessed many kinds of supply and demand shocks—wars, investment booms and busts, shifts of employment from agriculture to industry and services, stock market binges, major technological changes, and new resource discoveries. It was also a period of laissez-faire macroeconomic policy. Governments did not consciously attempt to use monetary and fiscal policy to eliminate inflation or recessions. The evidence from the nineteenth and early twentieth centuries is consistent with the theory of the long-run self-correcting mechanism.

## THE CLASSICAL VERSUS THE KEYNESIAN VIEWPOINT

Economists agree that business cycles can be caused either by demand shocks or by supply shocks. We agree, too, that in the long run, supply and demand shocks do not matter in that, over time, the economy will end up producing the natural level of real GDP at the natural rate of unemployment.

These are the areas of agreement. The areas of disagreement also focus on two issues: First, does the macroeconomy adjust quickly or slowly to demand and supply shocks? How flexible are wages and prices? (See Example 4.) And second, are supply shocks or demand shocks the cause of business cycles?

### THE CLASSICAL MODEL

The classical economists developed their theories of economic growth and the business cycle in the early

# EXAMPLE 4
## LONG-RUN
## PRICE FLEXIBILITY

The nineteenth century illustrates long-run price flexibility because it was not a period of sustained inflation. The accompanying table shows price indexes for major European countries throughout most of the nineteenth century. In France and Great Britain prices were from 10 percent to 20 percent *lower* in 1913 than in 1820. In Germany, prices were the same in 1908 as they were in 1820. As is evident, prices were flexible during that period of time, with extreme upward and downward movements in prices taking place regularly. Part of this price flexibility was due to the greater importance of agriculture in the nineteenth century. Agricultural prices tended to be more volatile than other prices in both an upward and downward direction.

------------------------------------------------

*Source:* B.R. Mitchell, *European Historical Statistics,* *1750–1970.*

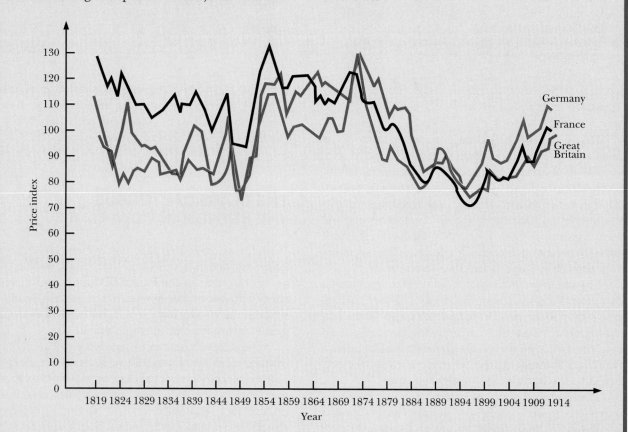

nineteenth century. They believed that an invisible hand, similar to that of Adam Smith, would work to keep economies close to the natural level of real GDP and close to the natural rate of unemployment. There would inevitably be transitory disruptions, but the economy would return to the natural level of output and to the natural rate of unemployment with little delay.

Classical economists saw no reason for there to be chronic unemployment. All who wanted to work could find jobs where they earned their pay. Labor markets, like other markets, work through voluntary exchange of mutual benefits. Employers hire workers on the basis of their contribution to profits; employees work on the principle that their pay compensates them for their opportunity costs—what they could earn elsewhere in income, benefits, or leisure.

Given that in a market economy, labor markets work on the basis of voluntary exchange, the classical economists saw no reason why economies should not operate at the natural rate of unemployment. If the number of vacancies fell short of the number of qualified job seekers, workers would compete among themselves for these jobs; they would offer their services at lower wage rates, and more of them would be hired. If, at the lower wage rate, the best opportunities for some workers would be full-time study, work in the home, or retirement, they would drop out of the labor force, and the number of qualified job seekers would decline.

Classical economists also saw no strong reason for frictions in labor markets that would prevent wages from adjusting quickly to changing economic conditions. If there was an increase in the demand for labor, wages would rise. If there was a reduction in the demand for labor, wages would fall. There was no strong reason why wages could not respond just as flexibly as prices.

The classical model of the business cycle says that the business cycle will be caused by supply shocks and not by demand shocks. Specifically, the Classical Model argues that changes in the advances of technology and productivity are the sources of supply shocks. Accordingly, it predicts specific relationships among real GDP, real wages, and inflation during the course of the business cycle.

Figure 8 illustrates what happens to real wages in the classical model when productivity increases. Productivity can increase for a number of reasons—

a new discovery, good weather, exceptional harvests, or a drop in energy prices. There may be nothing systematic about the increase in productivity; it may just happen. The economy consists of many different industries and millions of firms. Sometimes firms produce more because of random events—not as many machines break down, not as many employees report in sick, everything runs on schedule. With an increase in productivity, the short-run production function shifts up from SRPF to SRPF′, increasing the demand for labor and shifting the labor demand curve from $D$ to $D'$. Real wages increase from $W/P$ to $(W/P)'$. To summarize, with an increase in productivity, real output increases, real wages rise, and the price level falls.

Similarly, the classical model could explain a downturn in the economy with a fall in productivity. Instead of everything going right, everything goes wrong. The short-run production function shifts down, the demand for labor falls, real wages fall, output falls, and prices rise. The Classical Model therefore predicts a positive correlation between real GDP and real wages and a negative correlation between real GDP and prices.

> The Classical Model uses supply shocks to explain the business cycle. Increases in productivity cause upturns in the business cycle, which are characterized by rising real GDP, rising real wages, and falling prices. Downturns should be characterized by falling output, falling real wages, and rising prices.

The biggest shortcoming of the Classical Model is its apparent inability to explain the Great Depression—one of the Defining Moments of economics—in which unemployment rates in the United States soared to 25 percent of the labor force and stayed high for a long time. Increases or decreases in productivity can explain why output rises or falls, but cannot explain why unemployment fluctuates wildly.

## THE KEYNESIAN MODEL

The Keynesian model, developed by John Maynard Keynes to explain the events of the Great Depression,

(*a*) Production function

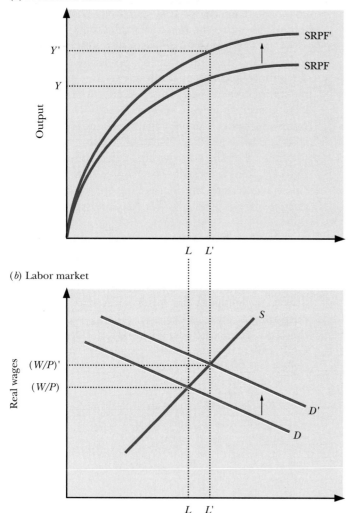

(*b*) Labor market

**FIGURE 8   The Effect of an Increase in Productivity on Real Wages**

In panel (*a*), if the production function shifts up from SRPF to SRPF′ due to an increase in productivity, the demand for labor shifts up from D to D′, causing real wages to rise from *W/P* to (*W/P*)′ in panel (*b*). Output, wages, and employment move together in response to an increase in productivity.

views the macroeconomy as behaving quite differently: The labor market is characterized by all kinds of rigidities and frictions. Wage rates are not free to move when economic conditions change. They are set by contracts for relatively long periods of time. A number of prices that affect costs of production are also set in long-term contracts and are not free to change immediately. Minimum-wage laws or other government regulations may prevent wages and costs from changing.

In his now famous remark, "In the long run, we are all dead," Keynes asserted that the speed of adjustment of the self-correcting mechanism would be very slow. Therefore, it would be too costly to wait for the self-correcting mechanism to work. The Keynesian viewpoint is expressed in Figure 6, panel (*a*), in which we can see the effect of demand shocks in a short-run context. Keynes concentrated on demand shocks because he believed it unlikely that supply shocks could explain the dramatic loss of output and employment that took place during the first four years of the Great Depression. In Keynes's view, downturns in the business cycle were caused by adverse demand shocks. Upturns were explained by positive demand shocks.

> According to Keynes, cyclical upturns are caused by positive demand shocks. Cyclical upturns should be characterized by rising real GDP, rising prices, and falling real wages. Cyclical downturns are caused by negative demand shocks and are characterized by falling real GDP, rising real wages, and falling prices.

Hence, the Keynesian model predicts a negative correlation between real GDP and real wages and a positive correlation between real GDP and prices.

## REAL WAGES, OUTPUT, AND INFLATION: THE CORRELATIONS

Any theory of short-run fluctuations in output, Classical or Keynesian, should be consistent with observed patterns. As we discussed in the chapter appendix on time-series analysis, economists measure the relationships between two variables by the correlation coefficient. The correlation coefficient ranges from +1 for a perfect positive correlation to −1 for a perfect negative correlation. The closer the correlation is to 1 or −1, the stronger the correlation; the closer the correlation is to 0, the weaker the correlation. Thus, a correlation coefficient of .8 indicates a strong positive correlation; and one of −.2 indicates a weak negative correlation.

The major theories of business fluctuations predict how output, real wages, and prices are correlated. We know that the *levels* of these variables will be positively correlated simply because they all drift upward. Real GDP is positively correlated with both real wages and the price level over time. It is more meaningful to consider correlations that are not affected by a common upward time trend (as discussed in the appendix on time-series analysis). It is for this reason that economists study the correlations between the rates of change of variables.

Figure 9 is a scatter diagram of the *annual rates of change* in real GDP versus the annual *rate of change* in real average hourly wages for the period 1959–1995. The scatter diagram shows a distinct positive relationship between real output and real wages. Indeed, the correlation coefficient is a robust .7. This positive correlation means that during economic downturns when the growth of real GDP is negative, real wages are usually falling. During periods of expansion and prosperity when real GDP is rising, real wages tend to rise as well. This correlation supports the Classical Model and disputes the Keynesian model.

Figure 10 fails to reveal a positive correlation between the growth rate of output and inflation over the same period. The scatter diagram in Figure 10, in fact, reveals that the correlation coefficient is −.4. A negative but weak coefficient suggests that, most of the time but not always, high rates of growth of output are accompanied by low rates of inflation and that low or negative rates of growth of output are accompanied by high rates of inflation. The relatively weak correlation—not as strong as the positive correlation between output and real wages—rules out a strong positive correlation between output growth and inflation.

> Macroeconomic theory must explain the positive (or direct) relationship between the growth of output and the growth of real wages, and the negative (or inverse) relationship between the growth of output and the inflation rate over the course of the business cycle.

Figures 9 and 10 reveal that the Keynesian explanation of fluctuations in output and unemployment runs into two serious empirical problems. First, the Keynesian model requires a negative association between real wages and output. As increasing aggregate demand moves the economy up the aggregate supply curve, real wages must be falling! However, there is a robust *positive* correlation between percentage changes in real wages and in real GDP. Particularly surprising is that the same positive correlation held up even during the Great Depression—a period that the Keynesian theory of aggregate demand and supply was intended to explain!

Second, the Keynesian explanation of cyclical changes requires a positive correlation between prices and output. As aggregate demand expands, prices should rise. Again, we saw in Figure 10 that there is no positive correlation between the growth of output and prices; in fact, the correlation is negative.

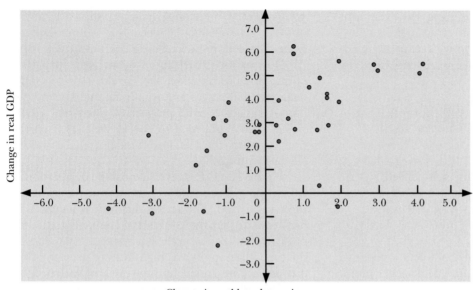

**FIGURE 9   Change in Real GDP Versus Change in Real Earnings**

*Source:* Department of Commerce (1959–1995).

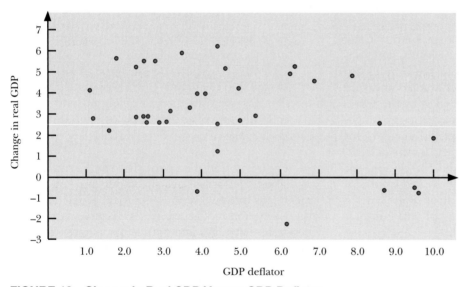

**FIGURE 10   Change in Real GDP Versus GDP Deflator**

*Source:* Department of Commerce (1959–1995).

Similar negative correlations are present in other major countries such as Germany, Italy, Japan, and the United Kingdom. However, there was a *positive* correlation between prices and output during the Great Depression in support of Keynes. Figure 11 compares monthly changes in hourly earnings with monthly changes in the CPI. The Keynesian model assumes that wages will be less flexible than prices. In fact, Keynes characterized wages as "sticky." Figure 11 shows that changes in wages and prices are highly correlated (correlation coefficient is above .9) and that the variability of wages is just as high as the vari-

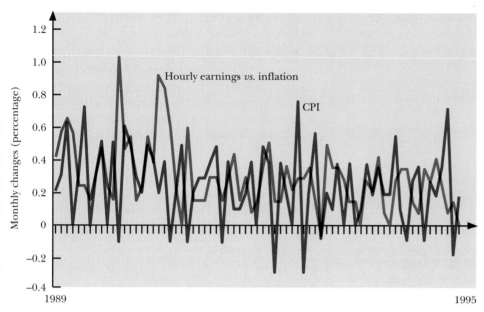

**FIGURE 11  Hourly Earnings vs. Inflation**

*Source:* Department of Commerce.

ability of prices. These correlations do not support the Keynesian view of prices being more flexible than wages.

The correlations of Figures 9 and 10 are not final and conclusive evidence. We must be on guard against the *ceteris paribus* fallacy. Strictly speaking, the Keynesian model predicts a positive correlation between prices and output after controlling for other factors. The correlation data presented in Figures 9, 10, and 11 do not control for other factors.

## MACROECONOMICS TODAY: A SYNTHESIS?

Macroeconomics in the late 1990s is in a state of flux. There is evidence in favor of both the classical and Keynesian models. Correlation analysis tends to favor classical economics; the existence of severe business contractions tends to favor Keynesian economics.

Modern Keynesian economists are attempting to shore up their theoretical models by amending them to account for the correlations explained by the classical models. In the New Keynesian models, attention is being given to the role of business competition.

Take, for example, the positive correlation between real wages and output. How can this occur? One explanation offered by some New Keynesians is that, during business expansions, the amount of competition businesses face actually increases so that markups over costs decrease. Thus, prices tend to fall relative to costs (wages) so that real wages tend to increase. In business contractions, competition becomes less stiff as more and more businesses fold, so that prices rise relative to business costs, and real wages fall.

Just as Keynesian economists are busy amending their theories to explain certain observed correlations, so are classical economists working on explanations of large increases in unemployment such as those observed in the Great Depression. Some economists are developing classical models in which technological change is the driving force behind changes in unemployment. At the start of World War II, Americans lived in an economy that was quite different from that existing on the eve of World War I. The economy had been transformed literally from dirt roads to paved roads, from iceboxes to refrigerators, from a local telegraph office to telephones, and from the isolation of the rural community to the cosmopolitan life of the city. In 1917 about 30 percent of the labor force worked in agriculture; in 1941 only 16 percent of the labor force made their living in agriculture. This was a generation in which most children could not follow in the footsteps of their parents; they had to find new occupations.

Can it be that the Great Depression was explained by technological forces? Some economists have argued that the Great Depression was caused by monetary events. In the next three chapters, we shall consider the role of money and banking in the economy.

natural rate is reached. How quickly the self-correcting mechanism works depends on the flexibility of wages and prices.

7. Classical economics explains many of the basic correlations, but it has a difficult time explaining deep depressions. Keynesian economics explains deep depressions, but it has a difficult time explaining the key facts of the business cycle.

## SUMMARY

1. The short-run production function shows the relationship between output and employment, holding constant the capital stock. In the classical model, the actual level of employment is determined in labor markets, where the real wage equates the demand for labor with the supply of labor.

2. The natural rate of unemployment is the unemployment rate at which the labor market is in balance. The natural level of real GDP is the real GDP that is produced when the economy is operating at the natural rate of unemployment.

3. The short-run aggregate supply (SRAS) curve is upward sloping, because increases in the price level relative to wages and business costs encourage firms to produce more. If prices and wages are fully flexible, the aggregate supply curve is a vertical line at the natural level of real GDP.

4. The aggregate demand curve shows the real GDP that is demanded at different price levels. It is downward sloping because of the real-balance effect, the interest-rate effect, and the foreign-trade effect.

5. The effect of changes in aggregate demand (AD) depends on the slope of the aggregate supply curve. If prices and wages are flexible, demand changes affect prices, not real output. If selling prices are more flexible than wages and material costs, changes in AD affect both real GDP and prices. If prices and wages are inflexible, a decrease in AD can create a substantial reduction in output.

6. In the long run, a self-correcting mechanism automatically brings unemployment into line with the natural rate. When unemployment exceeds the natural rate, real wages will gradually fall until the natural rate is reached; when unemployment is less than the natural rate, real wages will rise until the

## KEY TERMS

short-run production
  function (SRPF)
real wages
natural level of output
  (real GDP) $(y_n)$
natural rate of
  unemployment

aggregate supply curve
  (AS)
aggregate demand curve
  (AD)
real-balance effect
interest-rate effect
foreign-trade effect

## QUESTIONS AND PROBLEMS

1. Give three reasons why the aggregate demand curve is downward sloping.
2. Explain the interest-rate effect on aggregate quantity demanded when the price level falls.
3. What is the difference between the interest-rate effect and the real-balance effect when the price level falls? How are they similar?
4. Assume a country is engaged in foreign trade. Both the nominal money supply and the domestic price level fall by 10 percent. If foreign prices and exchange rates remain the same, describe what would likely happen to the various components of aggregate quantity demanded.
5. Why are wages and prices more inflexible in the short run than in the long run?
6. Assume that during a period when nominal wages are fixed, the price level begins to fall. What effect will this drop in prices have on real wages and on the employment decisions of firms and of workers?
7. Can actual unemployment be less than the natural rate of unemployment? How?
8. How is an increase in the expected wage rate reflected in aggregate supply?
9. Explain why the RAS curve is upward sloping.

10. What would happen to the slope of the RAS curve if the workers in the economy were covered by fewer long-term wage contracts?
11. How is the RAS curve affected by each of the following events?
    a. An increase in the anticipated price level.
    b. An improvement in technology.
12. Explain how the self-correcting mechanism drives unemployment to the natural level. Will the self-correcting mechanism work faster when wages and prices are inflexible? Why?

13. In 1933, the GDP price deflator was 11.2 (1982 = 100) and real GDP was $499 billion. In 1942, the price level was 14.7 and real GDP was $1080. Draw the AD and RAS curves.
14. Explain how shifts in the aggregate demand curve might be used in place of the self-correcting mechanism to eliminate a deflationary gap.

# PART VI

# MONEY
# AND
# DEBT

# CHAPTER 28

# MONEY, INTEREST, AND PRICES

Money is your ticket to the market for goods and services. In the long sweep of human history many different things—gold, silver, cattle, and paper currency—have been used as money. Today, we need only carry a bank card that will access the currency in any country we live in or visit. The ATM (automatic teller machine) will issue you dollars in America, or the corresponding amount of Japanese yen in Japan or British pounds in England. A credit card enables you to eliminate the use of physical currency because you can buy almost anything with it.

At the end of your billing period, you must send a check to your credit card company. Today, the newly developed debit card even eliminates the need for you to write a check to your credit card company because it directly debits your bank account for your purchase.

In this chapter we explore the nature of money. We shall consider three key questions: What is money? What is the link between money and interest? What accounts for increases or decreases in the level of prices?

# WHAT IS MONEY?

Money is not wealth; the wealth of a nation consists of its physical and human capital. A country can grow in proportion to its rate of capital accumulation and productivity growth. A rich country has a high per capita income based on such wealth. To an individual, wealth can be measured in money terms. When we say, "Bill Gates is worth $10 billion," we simply mean that Bill Gates can purchase $10 billion worth of goods and services. But place Bill Gates on a desert island and his $10 billion is worth nothing to him. Clearly, money itself is not wealth to a community. As Adam Smith said, "If a nation could be separated from all the world, it would be of no consequence how much, or how little money circulated in it."

What is money? Money facilitates trade and commerce in economies that are characterized by specialization and exchange. In such economies, money performs four functions, serving as

1. A medium of exchange
2. A unit of value
3. A standard of deferred payment
4. A store of value

## MONEY AS A MEDIUM OF EXCHANGE

The most important function of money is its use as a medium of exchange. In a modern economic system, money enters almost all market transactions. The existence of a common object acceptable to all sellers eliminates the need for the double coincidence of wants that is necessary for barter transactions. In a barter economy, in which goods are traded directly for other goods, a seller of wheat who wants to buy sugar must find a seller of sugar who wants to buy wheat. Because such a double coincidence of wants is rare, in a pure barter economy a series of transactions would be required to obtain what one wants. The seller of wheat who seeks sugar might first have to settle for potatoes, trade the potatoes for an ax, and finally trade the ax for sugar. The efficiency of the economy suffers as the efforts of the wheat grower who wants sugar are diverted from wheat cultivation into a long string of barter transactions.

 Money's most important function is to serve as a generally acceptable means of payment (for buying things and paying debts).

Money eliminates the need for costly intermediate exchanges. Because intermediate exchanges are so difficult, customs and laws designate something to serve as the medium of exchange, or money. Thus, the wheat farmer can sell wheat for money and use the money to buy sugar. Converting money into sugar is easy, and the wheat farmer is free to concentrate on growing wheat. Likewise, the sugar grower is left free to concentrate on sugar cultivation.

Money allows people to specialize according to their comparative advantage and to exchange goods and services with others. Money allows people to earn higher incomes and, hence, to consume more goods and services than they otherwise could. In the language of Chapter 2, the use of money shifts the production possibilities curve outward. The medium-of-exchange function of money increases the efficiency of the economy.

Money is a social contrivance. The object that society uses as money or the medium of exchange can be almost anything. The list of things that have been used as money staggers the imagination. American Indians used wampum (a string of shells); early American colonists used buckskins, cattle, corn, tobacco, and whiskey. Gopher tails were used as money in North Dakota in the 1880s. Cigarettes have served as money in prisoner-of-war camps. Farther from home, more exotic items have been used as money: whale teeth in Fiji, sandalwood in Hawaii, fish hooks on the Gilbert Islands, reindeer in parts of Russia, red parrot feathers on the Santa Cruz Islands (as late as 1961), silk in China, rum in Australia. Money can walk, talk, fly, be grown, be eaten, or be drunk. Our modern paper money is boring by comparison. (See Example 1.)

## MONEY AS A UNIT OF VALUE

The value of a good or service equals that for which it can be exchanged in the market. In a barter economy, a cow might sell for two pigs, for an acre of land, for 50 bushels of corn, for a motorcycle, or for dozens of other things. Of course, it is inconvenient to keep track of the value of a cow, or anything else, in terms of every other thing for which it would trade. Barter is also impractical when the units cannot be divided, as in a case where a pig is worth half a cow. Choosing a common unit of value—money—saves much time and energy in keeping track of the relative price or values of different things, and solves the problem of converting units.

## EXAMPLE 1
## THE STONE MONEY
## OF THE ISLAND OF YAP

Anything accepted by the population as a medium of exchange can serve as money. The island of Yap is a tiny U.S. trust territory in the South Pacific, 500 miles from Guam. For money, the Yapese—10,000 strong—use stone wheels from 1 foot to 12 feet in diameter, made from stones found only on distant islands. Most of the stones are 2 to 5 feet in diameter. Each stone has a hole in the middle so it can be carried on a tree trunk. A private citizen could produce money only by making what was often a treacherous sea journey. Thus, Yap money could be called a commodity money (to be discussed later). Interestingly enough, the value of the stones is related to their size as well as their scarcity and the difficulty of acquiring them.

Each stone has its own history. A stone brought over during the days of the Yap empire is the most valuable. Next in line are stones fashioned in the 1870s by David Dean O'Keffe, a shipwrecked American sailor. Last in value are those few mechanically chiseled by German traders around 1900.

Physical possession is not necessary for ownership. A particular large stone may be owned by many residents, each of whom has received some part of the stone in exchange for some product or service. Larger stones, thus, stay put, with legal ownership being transferred from person to person. How the Yapese keep their book-keeping straight is not known. On at least one occasion, a family was considered wealthy because an ancestor was known to have discovered an extremely large and valuable stone that a storm sent to the bottom of the sea!

The Yapese have several mediums of exchange in addition to stone money: U.S. dollars, necklaces of stone beads, and large sea shells. The sea shells and stone beads are used as small change in traditional transactions, but U.S. dollars must be used to make deposits in banks or to buy goods in one of the few retail stores. Will the stone money last? Probably not. The informational requirements of stone money are too great (each stone has a history) for a complicated world. As retailing and banking displace traditional person-to-person exchange, stone money will doubtless become extinct.

As this example illustrates, money can be without intrinsic value, but it must be scarce. What works as money in one society need not work in another. However, as societies become more complex and impersonal, money must become more standardized.

------------------------------------------------

*Sources:* William Furness, III, *The Island of Stone Money* (New York: J.B. Lippincott Company, 1910), pp. 92–100; "Fixed Assets, Or: Why a Loan in Yap is Hard to Roll Over," *Wall Street Journal,* March 29, 1984.

When we know the money prices of common objects, it is easy to appraise the relative price of any item just from its money price. If an apple costs $0.50, an orange costs $0.25, and a banana costs $0.10, we know immediately that an apple is twice as expensive as an orange and five times as expensive as a banana, and that an orange is 2.5 times as expensive as a banana. By reducing different economic entities to their dollar value, we can add apples and oranges, firms can subtract expenses from revenue to obtain profit, and accountants can subtract liabilities from assets.

Money serves as the common denominator in which the value of all goods and services is expressed.

## MONEY AS A STANDARD OF DEFERRED PAYMENT

When something is used as the medium of exchange, it is almost inevitable that it will also be used as the standard of deferred payment on contracts extending over a period of time. Numerous contracts extend into the future: home mortgages, car loans, all sorts of bonds and promissory notes, charges on credit cards, salaries, home rents. What serves as money will also serve for payments deferred into the future. If in the Santa Cruz Islands, red parrot feathers are money, an agreement to pay for a cart one year in the future might call for payment of 4 pounds of red parrot feathers in one year. If dollars are money, contracts to pay for some good in the future will call for payment in dollars. When a home is purchased on credit, the mortgage calls for interest and principal payments in dollars over the loan period.

> Money is a standard of deferred payment on exchange agreements extending into the future.

Inflation complicates money's role as the standard of deferred payment. When inflation occurs, deferred payments will be made in "cheaper" dollars because a unit of money buys fewer goods and services than it did before. The impact depends on the extent to which inflation is anticipated.

Unanticipated inflation will benefit debtors and harm creditors who have not had the foresight to demand a higher interest rate to compensate them for the effects of inflation. Unforeseen inflation tends to redistribute wealth from those who receive deferred payments to those who make them.

If they foresee inflation, parties entering into deferred-payment contracts can build in safeguards. The parties may agree that the deferred payment will be adjusted upward at the same rate as inflation (a cost-of-living adjustment). Interest rates, rental payments, or even salary payments may include a premium to compensate the recipient of deferred payments for the anticipated rate of inflation. When inflation is foreseen, there are ways to protect money's role as a standard of deferred payment. We shall discuss the impact of inflation in greater detail in a later chapter.

## MONEY AS A STORE OF VALUE

We do not consume all our income. When we consume less than our income, we save—in other words, we accumulate wealth. We can accumulate wealth in virtually any form that is not perishable—paintings, gold, silver, stocks, bonds, land, buildings, apartments, and money. A desirable characteristic of any asset (any possession that has value) is that it should maintain or increase its value over time. During periods of rising prices, the value of money is eroded because the amount of goods and services a unit of money will purchase falls. Paper currency or coins that have a face value greater than the value of the substance of which they are made are particularly vulnerable to this erosion. Nevertheless, money, like other assets, serves as a store of value. If we accumulate wealth in the form of money, we can use this money at some future date to purchase goods and services. The effectiveness of money as a store of value depends upon the rate of inflation. The higher the rate of inflation, the less value money will retain.

> Because money is a medium of exchange, it can also be used as a means of storing wealth.

## THE BASIC TYPES OF MONEY

Money is anything that performs the four functions of money. As we have seen, different objects and substances have served as money at different times and in different parts of the world. Historically, money ranges from things that have no intrinsic value (such as a dollar bill) or little intrinsic value (such as a dime) to things that have considerable intrinsic value (such as gold coins). Money comes in three basic varieties: commodity money, fiat money, and bank money.

### COMMODITY MONEY

Historically, the most important commodity money has been gold and silver.

> **Commodity money** is money whose value as a commodity is as great as its value as money.

Although gold and silver have nonmonetary uses in jewelry and industry, they can be easily coined, weighed, and used for large and small transactions. In early history, governments started minting gold and silver coins to avoid costly weighings each time a transaction occurred. When gold or silver serve as commodity money, private citizens can produce money simply by taking mined gold to the government mint.

A commodity money system is formally established when the commodity content of a unit of money is set at a fixed rate—say, $100 equals 1 ounce of gold. If the amount of gold mined increases (because of new discoveries), there is likely to be more money in circulation, prices of goods and services are bid up, and a unit of money buys less. In this case, gold's value as money has fallen. If the nonmonetary demand for the commodity increases (for example, if the demand for gold fillings increases), there is less money in circulation, prices fall, and a unit of money buys more. In this case, gold's value as money has risen. In this way, the value of gold as a commodity and as money are kept equal. People can never place a value on commodity money that is higher than its monetary value; dentists would never be willing to pay $400 for an ounce of gold when its monetary value is $350 per ounce because gold would be shifted to commodity use whenever its commodity price threatened to exceed its value as money.

We know that, historically (and in some primitive societies today), agriculture products such as rice, cattle, wheat, or sugar have served as money. Whatever the commodity—gold, silver, rice, sugar, or cattle—the commodity value of money will be the same as its money value.

Commodity money suffers from an inherent problem, known as Gresham's law.

> **Gresham's law** states that bad money drives out good. When depreciated, mutilated, or debased currency is circulated along with money of high value, the good money will either disappear from circulation or circulate at a premium.[1]

When people start to shave or mutilate gold and silver coins, the bad currency will circulate along with the good currency. The lesser-valued coins will be the ones spent while the more valuable coins will be hoarded. The use of tobacco money in colonial Virginia illustrates Gresham's law. Initially, both good and poor quality tobacco circulated as money. As predicted by Gresham's law, people hoarded the good tobacco and used only the worst tobacco as money. Eventually, the tobacco used as money in colonial Virginia was the scruffiest and foulest tobacco in the entire state. This opportunism tends to raise the cost of using commodity money as a medium of exchange because sellers of goods become suspicious of the money in use.

The costs associated with Gresham's law can be avoided by issuing paper currency that represents a certain amount of, say, gold. Under such a gold standard, the paper could be exchanged for gold at a fixed rate and, therefore, would be "as good as gold."

However, even a substitute paper currency cannot eliminate the most basic cost of using a commodity money: Society must devote real resources to producing the commodity money. Gold and silver mines must be discovered and operated to produce gold or silver commodity money. This gold and silver must then be set aside as backing for the currency so that it will not find its way into use as jewelry or dental fillings.

### FIAT MONEY

It is but a short step from a paper currency based on gold to a paper currency based only on the reputation of the government. If society uses something as money that costs little or nothing of society's resources (such as pieces of engraved paper), resources can be devoted to other activities. For this reason, governments create fiat money with little intrinsic value.

> **Fiat money** is a government-created money whose value or cost as a commodity is much less than its value as money.

Governments must have a monopoly over the issue of fiat money for a simple reason: If everyone were allowed to produce fiat money, so much fiat money would be issued that its value as money would fall to its production cost. If anyone could go

---

[1]Gresham's law is named after Sir Thomas Gresham (1519–1579). A successful banker and merchant, he accumulated a great fortune and endowed Gresham's College in London. Gresham's methods of making money were described as more effective than ethical. It may be that Gresham formulated his law on the basis of firsthand observation.

to private engravers and order paper currency that could be exchanged for goods and services, the consequent flood of paper money would saturate the economy and push up prices. The rush to print money would cease only when the purchasing power of a unit of money equaled the bill's commodity value, or the cost of producing the unit of paper money (which is very low). When the amount of fiat money in circulation is determined by government, however, fiat money exchanges for more than its cost of production. People require money for transactions, but the government monopoly limits the supply of money. Because money is useful, people are willing to exchange goods and services for money in excess of its commodity value.

The two basic forms of fiat money are coins and paper currency. United States coins are issued by the U.S. Treasury, and the value of the metal plus the cost of minting is less than the value of the coins used as money. Sometimes such coins are called token money. The most important example of fiat money in the United States is paper currency, called Federal Reserve Notes because they are issued by the Federal Reserve System rather than by the U.S. Treasury.

An advantage of fiat money is that it uses up little of society's resources. Critics of fiat money argue that it has one major flaw: Because fiat money is so cheap and easy to produce, governments, which have a monopoly over printing fiat money, are constantly tempted to produce more fiat money to pay their bills. However, as more fiat money floods the market, prices will be bid up throughout the economy, and the value of a unit of fiat money will fall.

> One criticism of a fiat money system is that the absence of constraints on the government to issue more paper currency increases the chances of inflation.

### BANK MONEY

We now consider the most important type of money: bank money. Most transactions in the United States, by dollar value, are carried out by the writing of a check. In the 1990s, checkwriting started to become electronic: We can now use our home computer, make a simple telephone call, or use a debit card. (See Example 2.) Legally, a check is simply a directive to the check writer's bank to pay lawful money to some other person or institution. You may think that bank money merely represents some other type of money

that you deposited in your bank. We shall see in the next chapter, however, that bank money exists in addition to these other types of money.

It is easy to understand why bank money is popular. Payments can be made more safely by check than by cash. Checks are a good record of transactions, and money is more secure from theft if it is in a checking account than in someone's wallet. A checking account at a local bank is money, simply because it is a generally acceptable medium of exchange.

A customer's deposit at a bank can be either a demand deposit (a checking account) or a time deposit (a savings account).

> A **demand deposit** is a deposit of funds that can be withdrawn ("demanded") from a depository institution (such as a bank) at any time without restrictions. The funds are usually withdrawn by writing a check.
>
> A **time deposit** is a deposit of funds upon which a depository institution (such as a bank) can legally require 30 days notice of withdrawal and on which the financial institution pays interest to the depositor.

We shall see in the next chapter that bank money is created in the same way as any other type of money: through substituting one thing that is not money for something that is money. In a gold standard, gold is exchanged for coin or pieces of paper that are backed by gold. In the case of bank money, we exchange our IOUs (for example, a car loan) for a bank account.

### THE MONEY SUPPLY

Because the United States has no commodity money, the U.S. money supply is the sum of fiat money and bank money. Note that the fiat money *held by banks* is not considered a part of the money supply. When someone cashes a check, the bank money that the person holds in a checking account is converted to fiat money. Thus, the supply of fiat money in circulation has increased by the same amount as the supply of bank money has decreased. The fiat money that the bank holds as cash is not counted in the money supply until it is held by someone outside the bank.

We hold our assets in many forms: as currency, as a deposit in a checking account or a savings ac-

## EXAMPLE 2
## IS MONEY OBSOLETE?

As technology improves, it is growing more and more likely that money as we know it will disappear. The earlier example of the stone money of Yap indicates that what really drives money is its acceptability. In a small close-knit community, the stones worked. In a more complicated society, we need physical currency or a check.

As computers grow in importance, plastic money and electronic checking will become dominant. Currency and coin may completely disappear in the future: All money will simply be a debit on the books of some bank. No one will carry money; no one will see it. Indeed, we have already reached this point for many purchases. We can buy groceries and pay all of our bills

without ever using any cash—just by using a debit card and the telephone or home computer. Soon, we shall be able to use our home computers to pay merchants and friends. Currently, many companies are seeking fraud-free methods for making electronic payments over the Internet.

These developments do not signal a fundamental change in the nature of money—only its form. Money is an evolving institution; but it is still just a medium of exchange, unit of value, a store of value, and a standard of deferred payment.

---

*Source:* "Electronic Check-Payment Plan For the Internet to be Developed," *Wall Street Journal*, August 23, 1995, p. B6.

---

count, as stocks or bonds, as real estate, and so on. These assets vary according to their liquidity.

> **Liquidity** is the ease and speed with which an asset can be converted into a medium of exchange without risk of loss.

The most basic characteristic of money is that it is perfectly liquid—it is already a medium of exchange. All of us are prepared to accept money as a means of payment. Thus, currency and demand deposits are perfectly liquid. They are a medium of exchange, a store of value, and a unit of value. They should certainly be included in the money supply. However, other types of assets can be converted to cash with varying degrees of ease. Money-market funds and savings deposits on which checks may be written can be converted into cash quickly. Time deposits with a fixed maturity date can be converted to cash with penalties. Government and corporate bonds can also be converted into cash quickly, but only when the banks are open or when the bond market is open. In addition, when these bonds fall in value, they have to be sold at a loss. Even assets such as land or old paintings can be converted into cash, though a substantial loss may be incurred if the seller

cannot wait for the right buyer to come along. Where do we draw the line between money and nonmoney?

Because it is difficult to draw a fine line dividing money and nonmoney, U.S. financial authorities use different definitions of the U.S. money supply for different purposes.

Table 1 shows the two definitions of the U.S. money supply that are most frequently used by financial authorities: M1 and M2.

> **M1** is the sum of currency (paper money and coins), demand deposits at commercial banks held by the nonbanking public, travelers' checks, and other checkable deposits, such as NOW (negotiable order of withdrawal) accounts and ATS (automatic transfer services) accounts. **M2** equals M1 plus savings and small time deposits, money-market mutual-fund shares, and other highly liquid assets.[2]

---

[2]The Federal Reserve defines even broader categories. For example, M3 includes M1, M2, and such items as time deposits in excess of $100,000 and dollar-dominated deposits of U.S. citizens in English and Canadian banks as well as foreign branches of U.S. banks worldwide.

## Table 1 The U.S. Money Supply, M1 and M2, October 1995

| Component | Amount (billions of dollars) |
|---|---|
| **M1** | |
| Currency and coin | 370 |
| Demand deposits[a] | 390 |
| Travelers' checks | 10 |
| Other checkable deposits[b] | 360 |
| | **1130** |
| **M2** | |
| Savings deposits at all depository institutions | 1110 |
| Small time deposits at all depository institutions[c] | 930 |
| Other | 460 |
| | **3630** |

[a]Demand deposits at all commercial banks other than those due to other banks, the U.S. government, and foreign official institutions.
[b]Other checkable deposits include NOW and ATS accounts, credit union share-draft balances, and demand deposits at mutual-savings banks. NOW (negotiated order of withdrawal) accounts pay interest and are otherwise like demand deposits. ATS (automatic transfer services) accounts transfer funds from savings accounts to checking accounts automatically when a check is written.
[c]A small time deposit is one issued in a denomination less than $100,000.
*Source:The Federal Reserve Bulletin.*

M1 is most closely associated with the function of money as a medium of exchange. Checkable deposits consist of ordinary noninterest-bearing demand deposits and other checkable deposits that do pay interest. The latter include NOW accounts, which are simply checkable deposits that pay interest, and ATS accounts, which allow automatic transfers out of savings into special checking accounts. They represent about 40 percent of the nation's money supply.

M2 includes M1 plus items that are most closely associated with the store-of-value function of money. Included in M2 are assets such as savings and other time deposits that earn more interest than the items in M1. Bank customers can convert savings accounts into currency or checking account money simply by going to the bank and withdrawing cash or by depositing the cash in a checking account. Banks typically allow depositors to withdraw small time deposits with little or no penalty. People may likewise convert money-market funds quickly into cash. Because such funds are close substitutes for M1, people

have a tendency to shift assets back and forth between M1 and M2. Therefore, M1 may change while M2 does not change at all.

In the United States during the 1990s, M2 was more than three times as large as M1 and just over one-half the size of annual GDP. Thus, for a GDP of $7 trillion in 1996, M2 is nearly $4 trillion while M1 is nearly $1.3 trillion.

## BOND PRICES AND INTEREST RATES

The money supply is intimately connected with interest rates. In this section, we shall consider how interest rates are related to bond prices and then examine how changes in the money supply affect interest rates.

The financial pages of the daily newspaper describe the relationship between interest rates and bond prices in the following way: "Bond prices drifted lower yesterday as interest rates moved up for the second day in a row. Last week, bond prices were higher and interest rates lower." As such statements indicate, there is an inverse relationship between bond prices and interest rates.

A bond is a promise to pay future dollars. The issuer of the bond promises to pay a prescribed number of dollars at specified dates in the future. Bonds promise a stream of future returns. For example, the simplest bond is the three-month Treasury bill (called a T-bill). In the case of a three-month T-bill, the U.S. Treasury promises to pay the face amount of the bill—$1000—in three months. The price of the T-bill will be some discount from $1000; otherwise, the buyer would earn no interest. If the price of the bill were $980, the buyer would earn $20 ÷ $980 = 2 percent interest over three months, or 8 percent per year (4 three-month periods for the year). If the annual interest rate increases to 12 percent, the buyer will pay only $970 for the T-bill ($30 ÷ $970 = 3 percent; 4 × 3 percent = 12 percent). Clearly, the interest rate on a T-bill rises if the price of the T-bill falls, and vice versa.

The same relationship between the bond prices and interest rate holds for any bond, but the calculations are more complex if bonds pay interest periodically over several years.

Because bonds promise fixed dollar payments in the future, the lower the current price of the bonds, the higher is the interest rate yielded. Similarly, the higher the current price of bonds, the lower is the interest rate.

In a bond-market rally (in which bond prices rise rapidly), interest rates are falling. When the newspaper describes a bond market as bearish (in which bond prices are falling), we know that interest rates are rising.

## THE DEMAND FOR MONEY

If an increase in the supply of money results in a larger demand for bonds so that bond prices rise, the rate of interest should fall. This scenario requires that a smaller rate of interest should increase the quantity of money demanded. To understand the link between money and interest, we must examine the demand for money.

### MOTIVES FOR HOLDING MONEY

The main motive for holding money is that money is required for transaction purposes. Money is a perfectly liquid asset. We know that liquidity is defined by the ease and speed with which an asset can be converted into a medium of exchange without the risk of loss. We can measure the liquidity of an asset by the speed of its conversion to money or the ease of its acceptance as money. The holder of money does not have to go through the time and expense of selling a less liquid asset (like a stock certificate or a bond) in order to get money. Assets such as land, apartment buildings, and paintings may serve as good stores of value, especially during inflationary periods, but they are not liquid because some time or expense is involved in converting them to cash. Because people have to carry out regular transactions, they must hold part of their wealth in the form of money.

John Maynard Keynes discussed two other motives for holding money: the precautionary and the speculative. People hold money as a precaution against unforeseen emergencies, although credit cards have nearly eliminated this motive. People have a speculative motive when they hold money to take advantage of opportunities to profit from market fluctuations. Today, the speculative motive is not important in the demand for M1 because speculative

funds can be kept in highly liquid Treasury bills or money-market funds.

### LIQUIDITY PREFERENCES AND INTEREST RATES

Although there are many benefits to holding money, there is also an opportunity cost. The basic opportunity cost of our holding ("demanding") money is that we are passing up the opportunity to accumulate other forms of wealth that promise higher returns. For example, if you hold $10,000 in cash or in a non-interest-bearing checking account, you sacrifice the opportunity to buy goods now or to put that money into stocks, bonds, or real estate that may escalate in value.

The opportunity cost of holding money is the nominal interest rate on perfectly safe securities. We discussed in the chapter on saving and investment that the real interest rate measures the opportunity cost of spending versus saving; it represents the difference between what we give up tomorrow and what we give up today by spending $1 now. The nominal interest rate measures the opportunity cost of holding assets in the form of money as opposed to holding interest-bearing assets. Inflation affects equally the real value of money and nominal interest-bearing assets. For example, a 3 percent inflation rate erodes $300 from both a $10,000 bond and $10,000 in cash. Thus, the difference between the bond and cash is the nominal interest rate.

The nominal interest rate is really the price of holding assets in the form of money. Almost two-thirds of M1 does not earn interest. According to the law of demand, quantity demanded falls when prices rise. This rule holds for the demand for money just as it holds for the demand for other commodities. People would be expected to hold (demand) more money at low interest rates (a low opportunity cost) than at high interest rates, if all other things are equal. Panel (a) of Figure 1 shows the demand curve for money. Since money is the most liquid component of one's assets, the demand curve is often called the liquidity preference (LP) curve.

The **liquidity preference (LP) curve** shows the demand for money as the nominal interest rate changes, holding other factors constant.

The liquidity preference curve holds other factors constant, such as income and the price level.

(*a*) Liquidity Preference Curve

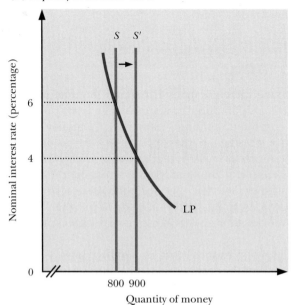

(*b*) Increase in Demand

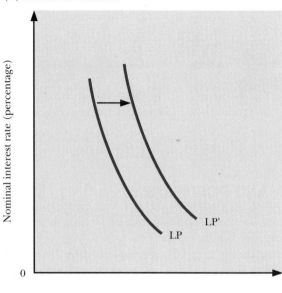

**FIGURE 1   The Demand for Money: Liquidity Preference**

Panel (*a*) shows a typical liquidity preference (LP) curve, which graphs the demand for money. Panel (*b*) shows the impact on the LP curve of an increase in real GDP or the price level. The demand for money rises with GDP and *P*, and falls with the nominal interest rate.

When the nominal interest rate is 6 percent, the quantity of money demanded is $800 billion; when the nominal interest rate is 4 percent, the quantity of money demanded is $900 billion.

> The nominal interest rate is the opportunity cost (price) of holding money. Therefore, the quantity of money demanded would be expected to vary inversely with the nominal interest rate.

Figure 1, panel (*a*), also demonstrates how changes in the money supply affect the rate of interest for a given liquidity preference or demand curve for money. The money supply (*S*) is a vertical line because at any given time the rate of interest has a negligible effect on how much money is in the economy. The negative relationship between the nominal interest rate and the quantity of money demanded indicates that a higher money supply will lower the rate of interest. When the money supply increases from $800 billion to $900 billion, the nominal interest rate must fall from 6 percent to 4 percent in order to induce people to hold the higher supply of money.

## OTHER FACTORS AFFECTING THE DEMAND FOR MONEY

The demand for money depends not only on nominal interest rates but also on real GDP and the price level. If either real GDP or the price level increases, the total value of all transactions will increase. If people spend more dollars to pay higher grocery or clothing bills, the demand for money will increase so that they can carry out those transactions.

Panel (*b*) of Figure 1 shows an increase in the demand for money. The liquidity preference curve shifts from LP to LP′ as real GDP or the price level increases. At each interest rate, there is a greater quantity of money demanded.

## MONEY AND PRICES

The relationship between the supply of money and nominal interest rates focuses on money as a store of value: People can hold money or other assets that pay interest (or more interest). As a medium of exchange, however, the supply of money affects the prices of the things we buy. We can study the relationship between money and prices by using a simple but powerful tool called the quantity theory.

## THE QUANTITY THEORY

**The Value of Money.**   The quantity theory uses common sense to argue that there will be a positive relationship between money and prices. The value of money is determined by its command over goods and services. If $1 buys a lot of goods and services, it will be valuable. If it buys few goods and services, it will not be valuable. Thus, according to the logic of supply and demand, if there is a lot of money in circulation (with a constant supply of goods), the supply of money is great and should therefore be less valuable. "Less valuable" indicates that prices should be high. If there is little money in circulation, money should be valuable.

> "Valuable" means that prices should be low.

> The *value of money* is the reciprocal of the price level, or $1/P$.

**The Equation of Exchange.**   The quantity theory uses the equation of exchange to explain the relationship between money and prices. This equation emerges from a consideration of the velocity with which money circulates through the economy. If GDP is $7 trillion during a particular year while the average money supply during that year is $1 trillion, each dollar must be spent exactly seven times. The equation of exchange is:

$$MV = PQ$$

where $M$ is the supply of money, $V$ is the velocity of its circulation, $P$ is the price level, and $Q$ is the quantity of real output or real GDP. The equation of exchange is nothing more than a definition of velocity. By dividing both sides of the equation of exchange by $V$, we obtain    *Demand of Money*

$$M = \frac{PQ}{V}$$

The term $PQ/V$ represents the demand for money; all the above factors we have discussed that operate on the demand for money must work through $P$, $Q$, or $V$. The term on the left-hand side is the supply of money.

How might an increase in the money supply increase the price level? Once new money is injected into the economy, it is impossible in the aggregate for households and businesses to get rid of their money balances (unless we bury it, burn it, or give it back to the central bank). When one person purchases a good with money, the seller's cash balance rises as the buyer's balance falls. Money is simply passed from one person to another without changing the economy's supply of money. Individuals can spend their money in order to get rid of excess cash balances, but the entire economy cannot. As each person tries to get rid of an excess supply of money, prices are driven up because there are more dollars chasing the same number of goods. As prices rise, the economy as a whole requires more money for its transactions. Thus, rising prices increase the demand for money until the excess supply of money disappears. Equilibrium is restored when the supply of money equals the quantity of money people want to hold, and prices stop rising.

The key idea of the quantity theory is that the value of money depends on its quantity, not the quality of the material (paper, gold, silver, lead) of which it is composed. What determines the value of money is simply the law of supply and demand. As the supply of anything rises relative to the demand, its value falls to maintain equality of quantity supplied and quantity demanded. (See Example 3.)

## MONEY AND PRICES: THE CLASSICAL THEORY

If we now look at $MV = PQ$, we realize that the effects of an increase in $M$ on $P$ depend upon what happens to $V$ and $Q$. If $V$ goes down and $Q$ goes up, it would even be possible that $M$ increases and $P$ decreases.

The equation of exchange itself is not a theory; it is a definition of velocity. The classical economists turned $MV = PQ$ into a theory of inflation with a couple of assumptions about the way the world works: They believed that velocity ($V$) would be stable because it is determined by the payment habits of the population. The rate at which we turn over money, they asserted, is determined by custom and payments practices that change only slowly over time. For all practical purposes $V$ is fixed. The classical economists believed that real GDP ($Q$) also is fixed over short periods because economies tend to produce the natural level of output. Of course, $Q$

## EXAMPLE 3
## THE INCONVENIENCE
## OF HYPERINFLATION

One of the worst inflations ever to befall the world occurred in Germany after its World War I defeat. Prices doubled every few weeks. The following anecdote from a contemporary describes it well:

> At eleven o'clock in the morning a siren sounded and everybody gathered in the factory forecourt where a five-ton lorry was drawn up loaded brimful with paper money. The chief cashier and his assistants climbed up on top. They read out names and just threw out bundles of notes. As soon as you caught one you made a dash for the nearest shop and bought just anything that was going.

This story illustrates two points. First, the value of money is largely determined by its quantity. Second, even in a hyperinflation a medium of exchange is useful, for virtually worthless money still buys goods. However, one of the costs of hyperinflation is that people have to make a lot more shopping trips! Indeed, hyperinflation robs money of its role in lowering the costs of engaging in economic exchange.

----------

*Source:* William Guttman and Patricia Meehan, *The Great Inflation, Germany 1919–1923* (Famborough, England: Saxon House, 1975), pp. 57–58.

would grow over time with economic growth, but in the short-run $Q$ is basically fixed.

With these two assumptions—that $V$ and $Q$ are fixed in the short run—the classical economists turned the equation of exchange into a theory of inflation that stated that money and prices would grow at the same rate over that period of time in which $Q$ and $V$ are fixed. With $V$ and $Q$ fixed, a 5 percent increase in $M$ yields a 5 percent increase in $P$. A 3 percent reduction in $M$ yields a 3 percent reduction in $P$.

As $Q$ grows over time, the classical theory (which still maintains a constant velocity) says that the growth rate of $P$ will equal the growth rate of $M$ minus the growth rate of $Q$. Why? When real output grows, there are more goods to absorb the supply of money. If real output grows, say, 3 percent and $M$ also grows 3 percent, there will be no inflation. The supply of money is just keeping pace with the real supply of goods.

The classical theory assumes that velocity is fixed. If (1) $M$ increases while $Q$ stays the same, $M$ and $P$ grow at the same rate. If (2) $M$ and $Q$ both increase, the rate of inflation equals the growth rate of $M$ minus the growth rate of $Q$.

In the next chapter, we shall examine how the money supply is actually determined in a modern economy and what role the banking system plays.

## SUMMARY

1. Money is the medium of exchange used in market transactions. In addition, money serves as a unit of value, a standard of deferred payment, and a store of value. People may be able to safeguard against inflation when they use money as a standard of deferred payment.

2. Commodity money's value as a commodity is as great as its value as money. Fiat money's value as a commodity is less than its value as money. Bank money consists primarily of checking deposits. In terms of money supply, M1 is the narrow measure, excluding such items as savings deposits and other highly liquid assets; M2 is a broader measure of the money supply.

3. Bond prices are inversely related to interest rates.

4. The major factors affecting the demand for money are nominal interest rates, real GDP, and the

price level. The liquidity preference curve shows
how a higher nominal interest rate lowers the quantity of money demanded, holding real GDP and the
price level constant. A higher level of prices or real
GDP increases the demand for money by shifting
the liquidity preference curve to the right.

3. The quantity theory of money maintains that it
is the quantity of money, not the quality, that determines its value. The rate of inflation basically reflects the rate of growth in the money supply minus
the rate of growth in output.

## KEY TERMS

| | |
|---|---|
| commodity money | liquidity |
| Gresham's law | M1 |
| fiat money | M2 |
| demand deposit | liquidity preference (LP) |
| time deposit | curve |

## QUESTIONS AND PROBLEMS

1. Evaluate the validity of the following statement:
"Anything that is legally declared by the government to be money, is money."
2. During hyperinflations, money loses its value as
a medium of exchange, as a store of value, and
as a standard of deferred payment. What would
you expect to happen to the overall efficiency of
the economy with this decline in value?
3. Evaluate the validity of the following statement:
"It is foolish to talk about the demand for
money. People want all the money they can get
their hands on."

4. Explain why the value of fiat money is determined by its relative abundance. What is the
lower limit to which the value of fiat money
can fall?
5. Discuss the social costs of having a commodity
money system. What are the benefits? How
does Gresham's law enter into this issue?
6. How does M1 differ from M2?
7. Explain why houses are not money.
8. Assume that in a prisoner-of-war camp cigarettes are used as money. What will happen
to the price level if a health scare motivates
people to reduce their commodity demand for
cigarettes?
9. Economy A uses gold as money, and Economy
B uses paper money without any commodity
backing. Economy A's money supply is growing
at a rate of 10 percent per year; Economy B's
money supply is growing at a rate of 5 percent
per year. Use quantity theory to predict which
economy will have the larger rate of inflation.
Explain your reasoning.
10. How might a fiat money system result in more
inflation over the long run than, say, a commodity money system?
11. If a bond pays, in perpetuity, $100 a year in
coupon payments and if the interest rate is 20
percent, what should be the price of the bond?
12. Polls show that only 40 percent of the public
understands the relationship between bond
prices and interest rates. How would you explain it?
13. If the newspaper reports, "The bond market is
in the doldrums; it has been depressed all
week," what is happening to interest rates?

# CHAPTER 29

# THE BANKING SYSTEM

How would you like to have to watch every word you spoke in public? The chairman of the Federal Reserve System—in the 1990s, Alan Greenspan—is widely regarded as the most powerful person in the country. He is important for two reasons: When he speaks, people listen; and when the Federal Reserve System, known simply as the Fed, acts, people have more or less money and pay lower or higher interest rates. Thus, Greenspan can literally move markets by simply stating his opinion about the economy. If he says the economy is strong, people often think that he will try to persuade the Fed to raise interest rates. This usually causes the immediate fall of bond prices as well as stock prices. If he says the economy is weak, the opposite is likely to happen. Is this power justified? In this chapter, we shall discuss the mechanisms through which the Fed exercises its influence.

Banks are also subject to many regulations about their deposits, loans, and investments. Should banks be regulated? If so, what is the proper amount of regulation? Should bank deposits be guaranteed by the government? These are some of the questions we consider at the end of the chapter.

# FINANCIAL INTERMEDIARIES

Most of us have had some experience with banks: A commercial bank cashes our checks, a savings and loan association handles our savings accounts, and the credit union at our places of work may give us loans. What services do these banks perform for us? How do they earn profits?

A savings and loan association, an insurance company, a commercial bank, a mutual savings bank, a credit union, a retirement fund, and a mutual fund are all examples of financial intermediaries, or financial institutions that mediate between borrowers and lenders.

> **Financial intermediaries** borrow funds from one group of economic agents (people or firms with savings) and lend to other agents.

Financial intermediaries serve a useful purpose in our economy. With financial intermediation, borrowers and lenders do not have to seek each other out. The lender does not have to accept the borrower's IOU, investigate the borrower's creditworthiness, or pass judgment on the wisdom of the borrower's spending plans. The commercial bank, for example, accepts a deposit with the promise to pay the depositor a specified interest rate and then lends these funds to a borrower at a higher interest rate. Borrowers and lenders thus pay a price for using the services of a financial intermediary. If they had sought each other out, the lender would have received less and the borrower would have paid more after each had paid the costs of finding each other.

The different types of financial intermediaries compete with each other for borrowers and lenders. Savings and loan associations, mutual savings banks, and credit unions offer checkable accounts that compete with commercial banks. Financial intermediaries compete among themselves to make loans to qualified borrowers. Profit rates in banking are comparable to the returns earned, for example, in retailing or the aerospace industry.

## COMMERCIAL BANKS

Commercial banks are the most important of financial intermediaries. In 1995, commercial banks held more assets than all the other financial intermediaries combined.

> **Commercial banks** are banks that have been chartered either by a state agency or by the U.S. Treasury's Comptroller of the Currency to make loans and receive deposits.

Thrift institutions, such as savings and loan associations, mutual savings banks, and credit unions, cater to noncommercial customers. In the past, thrift institutions could not offer checking account services; they could offer only various types of savings accounts—hence, the name thrift institution. However, thrift institutions are now able to offer checking accounts to both families and commercial firms. Legislation passed in the early 1980s also enables the thrift institutions to make limited commercial loans and to make direct investments in real estate.

Many economists expected that narrowing the legal difference between banks and other financial institutions would reduce the importance of banks. But habits die hard. At the beginning of 1995, commercial banks still held virtually all the checkable deposits, although most thrift institutions also offered such accounts.

Commercial banks make profits by borrowing from customers in the form of demand deposits and time deposits, and then relending these funds in the form of automobile loans, real estate loans, business loans, and student loans. Commercial banks earn profits by borrowing money at low interest rates and lending money at higher interest rates. The difference between the rate at which banks borrow and the rate at which they lend is called the interest-rate spread. (See Example 1.)

## BALANCE SHEETS

The concept of a balance sheet is essential to an understanding of how banks operate.

> A **balance sheet** summarizes the current financial position of a firm by comparing the firm's assets and liabilities.

The assets of a firm can be buildings, equipment, inventories of goods, money, or even IOUs. A balance sheet lists the claims to these assets. The liabilities of a company include unpaid bills, tax obligations, and outstanding debt.

# EXAMPLE 1
## THE NATIONAL
## COOPERATIVE BANK

The business of banking is to make a profit on having better information about creditworthy borrowers than the bank's depositors. As an intermediary, the bank is a specialist in loaning to various categories of borrowers. Even the requirement that the bank make loans to particular categories will not prevent profitability as long as the bank can exercise discretion.

A good example is the National Cooperative Bank (NCB), created by Congress in 1978. The NCB was intended to make loans to low-income communities. But the subsidies provided by the government led to careless investments by the NCB. The bank performed so poorly that 25 percent of its assets yielded no return.

In 1982, Congress withdrew its explicit federal subsidies. Completely privatized, except for the requirement that the NCB set aside about one-third of its loans to benefit low-income persons, the bank is now just as profitable as a typical bank. All banks work under federal regulations. These regulations serve in large part to direct banks to work in a particular niche of the loan market. Since many low-income borrowers are creditworthy, a bank that specializes in low-income loans can make a tidy profit. Since low-income borrowers have small assets, the bank's main criterion for evaluating loans is the cash flow generated by the investments made by their low-income borrowers.

------------------------------------------------

*Source:* "Co-op Banker Charles Snyder: Earning Profits in a Private Entity with a Public Mission," *Investor's Business Daily,* January 13, 1995.

---

**Assets** are anything of value that is owned.
**Liabilities** are anything owed to other economic agents.

The value (or net worth) of a company is measured as the excess of assets over liabilities. If a company owns assets worth $1 million and has liabilities of $900,000, the net worth of the company is $100,000.

Net worth = Assets − Liabilities

A bank's assets consist primarily of IOUs of one kind or another—the loans it has made to individuals and firms, the government bonds it has purchased, and the deposits it has with other banks. Its liabilities consist principally of the various deposits that its customers have made—demand deposits, savings deposits, and time deposits.

The combined balance sheet of America's commercial banks as of October 1995 is shown in Table 1. At that time transaction-account liabilities accounted for about 20 percent of liabilities, and sav-

| Table 1 Consolidated Balance Sheet of All Commercial Banks, October 1995 | | | |
|---|---|---|---|
| *Assets (billions of dollars)* | | *Liabilities plus Net Worth (billions of dollars)* | |
| Cash assets | 220 | Transaction deposits | 780 |
| Reserves | 57 | Non-transaction deposits | 1860 |
| Loans and investments | 3700 | Other borrowings | 1150 |
| Other assets | 230 | Net worth | 360 |
| Total | 4150 | Total | 4150 |

*Source: Federal Reserve Bulletin.*

ings and time deposits (non-transaction deposits) accounted for about 45 percent.

A large fraction of a bank's liabilities are demand liabilities, or obligations that can be called in by depositors. The fact that commercial bank transaction-account liabilities are less than their savings and time-deposit liabilities is a recent development attributable to the increased use of credit cards and the rise of money-market mutual funds and NOW accounts. Historically, demand-deposit liabilities exceeded time deposits. In other words, commercial banks have become more like thrift institutions.

The asset side of the balance sheet shows how commercial banks serve as financial intermediaries. Commercial bank deposits are loaned to individuals and businesses and are used to purchase securities. The asset statement shows that commercial banks are primarily in the business of making loans.

Any customer who withdraws a deposit is paid out of the bank's reserves. Bank reserves consist of two components: vault cash, which is simply currency and coin in the vaults of the bank, and the bank's balances with the Federal Reserve System, which we shall consider below.

**Reserves** are the funds that the bank uses to satisfy the cash demands of its customers.

The combined balance sheet in Table 1 shows that cash assets are much less than the liabilities of the banking system. In October 1995, cash assets were about $220 billion, or less than 10 percent of the deposit liabilities to the nonbanking public. Cash assets include bank reserves and various other items. Reserves themselves amount to less than $60 billion compared to $780 billion in transaction deposits.

Why are depositors and the banks not alarmed by the imbalance between bank reserves and transaction-deposit or savings-deposit liabilities? On an ordinary business day, some customers deposit money in their checking accounts. Others withdraw money from their accounts by writing checks or withdrawing cash through ATMs. If deposits come in at the same pace as withdrawals, bank reserves do not change. Reserves rise when deposits exceed withdrawals; they fall when withdrawals exceed deposits. The normal course of banking is that withdrawals and deposits proceed at roughly the same rate.

Is it not reckless for bank reserves to be such a small fraction of deposits? What would happen if suddenly there were no deposits—only withdrawals? The reason people have demand deposits is that for many transactions, checking account money is safer and more convenient than currency and coin. As long as depositors know that they can get their money from the bank, they will want to leave it on deposit. The moment they believe they cannot get their money, they will want to withdraw it. Thus, people want their money if they can't get it and don't want their money if they can!

This paradox of banking has made commercial banks subject at times to bank panics. The history of banking is filled with episodes when large numbers of depositors lose confidence in the banks and demand their cash; when the banks cannot pay, a rash of bank failures occurs. In the Great Depression, bank failures reached unprecedented levels. The government's Federal Deposit Insurance Corporation (FDIC) was established in 1933 to deal with this problem. Currently, in banks and thrift institutions that are members of the FDIC, each deposit account is insured up to $100,000. However, bank failures in the late 1980s revealed weaknesses in the system. We shall consider the issue of bank reform later in this chapter.

## THE FEDERAL RESERVE SYSTEM

Banks have their own bank—the central bank—in which they keep their reserves and from which they can borrow. In the United States, the central bank is the Federal Reserve System. All industrialized countries have a central bank. The first was the Bank of Sweden. The Bank of England, the Banque de France, the Deutsche Bundesbank, and the Bank of Japan are prominent in world financial circles.

The United States did not have a central bank throughout most of the nineteenth century and into the second decade of the twentieth century. During this period, the United States became the most important industrial nation in the world. A number of financial panics, culminating in the financial panic of 1907, convinced Congress that a central bank was needed to supervise and control private banks. The Federal Reserve System became a reality in 1913 when President Woodrow Wilson signed the Federal Reserve Act.

### FUNCTIONS OF THE FED

The Fed performs two primary functions, as do other central banks throughout the world:

1. It controls the nation's money supply.
2. It is responsible for the orderly working of the nation's banking system. It supervises private banks, serves as the bankers' bank, clears checks, fills the currency needs of private banks, and acts as a lender of last resort to banks needing to borrow reserves.

The Fed's most important function is to control the money supply. Because the supply of money is believed to have an important effect on prices, output, employment, and interest rates, the Fed wields great economic influence. Therefore, the control of the money supply places the Fed in a position to influence inflation, output, unemployment, and interest rates.

## THE STRUCTURE OF THE FEDERAL RESERVE SYSTEM

The 1913 Federal Reserve Act divided the country into 12 districts, each with its own Federal Reserve bank. These banks are located in Boston, New York, Philadelphia, Cleveland, Richmond, Atlanta, Chicago, St. Louis, Minneapolis, Kansas City, Dallas, and San Francisco. Each Federal Reserve bank issues currency for its district, administers bank examinations, clears checks, and acts as the banker to depository institutions in the district.

The Federal Reserve System is controlled and coordinated by a seven-member board of governors (formerly known as the Federal Reserve Board) located in Washington, D.C. This powerful group is appointed by the president of the United States. Each member of the board serves a 14-year term. Terms are staggered so that the appointees of a single U.S. president cannot dominate the board. The president appoints the chair of the board, who is the most powerful member and serves for four years. The Federal Reserve System has much more independence than other government agencies. Independence is ensured in part because of the long terms of the board members and because the Fed is self-financing.

## RESERVE REQUIREMENTS

A prudent banker knows that sufficient reserves must be on hand to meet the cash demands of customers. Private profit-maximizing banks would choose voluntarily to hold a portion of their assets in reserves. The Bank of England did not impose legal reserve requirements on private banks for several centuries, yet British banks held prudent levels of reserves, and England developed an excellent reputation for its banking services. In the United States, however, the Fed imposes uniform reserve requirements on all commercial banks, savings and loan associations, mutual savings banks, and credit unions. United States banks are required by law to hold reserve levels that meet a standard required-reserve ratio.

> **Reserve requirements** are rules that state the amount of reserves that a bank must keep on hand to back bank deposits. A **required-reserve ratio** is the amount of reserves required for each dollar of deposits.

A required-reserve ratio of 0.1 (10 percent) means that the bank must hold $0.10 in reserves for each dollar of deposits. Transaction accounts, such as checking accounts, have required-reserve ratios ranging from 3 percent to 12 percent, depending on the size of the bank. The reserve requirements on time and savings accounts range from 0 percent to 3 percent, depending on the size of the account and its maturity. The Fed has the power to raise or lower these required-reserve ratios and to impose supplemental requirements.

## BORROWING FROM THE FED

Any depository institution holding reserves with the Fed is entitled to borrow funds from the Fed. A bank that is allowed to borrow from the Fed, in the jargon of banking, has access to the discount window. The rate of interest the Fed charges banks at the discount window is called the *discount rate*.

In the United States, banks always have an incentive to borrow from the Fed. For example, in December 1995, the discount rate was 5.25 percent while the prime rate (the base rate charged by major banks to large corporations) was 8.75 percent. Accordingly, banks do not have unlimited access to the discount window. They must have exhausted all reasonable alternative sources of funds before coming to the Fed. The discount window is available for temporary and immediate cash needs of the banks.

The Fed sets the discount rate and can encourage or discourage bank borrowing by raising or lowering the discount rate. If the spread between the rate at which the banks themselves borrow (the discount rate) and the rates at which they lend is small, the bank's incentive to use the discount window is reduced.

## THE FEDERAL OPEN MARKET COMMITTEE

The control of the money supply is the responsibility of the Federal Open Market Committee (FOMC). The FOMC meets monthly and holds telephone conferences between meetings. It consists of the seven members of the Board of Governors and presidents of five of the regional Federal Reserve banks. The president of the New York Federal Reserve Bank is always one of these five; the presidents of the other regional Federal Reserve banks rotate in the four remaining slots.

## THE MONETARY BASE

The Fed can do something that other institutions cannot do: It can print money, a power delegated to it by Congress. Because the Fed can print money, whenever the Fed buys something, it puts money into the economy; whenever the Fed sells something, it takes money out of the economy. Imagine, for the moment, that you can print money; whenever you buy something with the money you print, everyone else (in the aggregate) will have more money; whenever you sell something, you will get some of your money back and everyone else (taken together) will have less money. Similarly, Fed purchases inject money into the economy; Fed sales withdraw money.

As we shall discuss in the chapter on monetary policy, the Fed normally buys and sells government securities. It is simpler, however, to consider a more elementary case. For example, suppose the Fed hires you as a computer programmer and pays you with a check for $5000. You deposit the check in your commercial bank—the First National Bank of Clear Lake. The Fed's check is different from other checks. When the First National Bank of Clear Lake sends the check to the Fed for collection, its balance sheet changes in two ways. On the asset side, the Bank of Clear Lake's "reserves with the Fed" increase by $5000; on the liability side, the Bank of Clear Lake's "demand deposits due (Your name)" increase by $5000, as shown in Table 2, part (a). The balance sheets in this table show only the change in bank assets and liabilities that result from the transaction under discussion.

At this point, the money supply has increased by $5000. Your bank account has increased by $5000. Everyone else's bank account has remained the same, and the currency in circulation (outside banks) is still the same. (Remember that the money supply is the quantity of checkable deposits plus the currency in circulation held by the nonbanking public.)

Had anyone but the Fed hired you for $5000, the money supply would have remained the same, your bank account would have increased by $5000, and the purchaser's account would have fallen by $5000. The two transactions would have canceled each other.

Suppose the Bank of Clear Lake does not wish to hold its new reserves as deposits at the Fed. Instead, the bank decides that it needs $5000 more in vault cash. The bank wires the Fed to send the $5000 in cash. The Fed prints $5000 in Federal Reserve Notes and issues this $5000 to the Bank of Clear Lake. At this point, the Fed lowers the Bank of Clear Lake's deposit balance by $5000. This conversion of reserve balances with the Fed into vault cash (another Fed liability), shown in part (b) of Table 2, has no impact on the money supply because neither total demand deposits nor the currency outside of banks has changed.

### Table 2    Sample Balance Sheets for the First National Bank of Clear Lake: Results of $5000 Purchase by the Fed

|  | Changes in Assets | | Changes in Liabilities | |
| --- | --- | --- | --- | --- |
| (a) You deposit the Fed's $5000 check. | Reserves at the Fed | +$5000 | Demand deposits due you | +$5000 |
| (b) The bank converts $5000 of Fed reserves into $5000 in vault cash. | Vault cash | +$5000 | No change | |
|  | Reserves at the Fed | −$5000 | | |
| (c) You withdraw $5000 cash. | Vault cash | −$5000 | Demand deposits due you | −$5000 |

These accounts show that when the Fed buys something (in this case, something for which it pays $5000), three things can happen: First, the receiving bank's reserves at the Fed can increase (a); second, the bank's vault cash can increase (b); or third, cash in circulation can increase (c).

Finally, suppose that you go to the bank and cash a check for $5000 on your account. Again, nothing happens to the money supply. Your demand-deposit account with the Bank of Clear Lake has fallen by $5000, and the Bank of Clear Lake's vault cash has fallen by $5000. Because there is $5000 more in currency in circulation and $5000 less in checkable deposits, the money supply is unchanged, as shown in part (c) of Table 2.

Of these three transactions, the only one that changes the money supply is the one in which you deposited the Fed's check for $5000 in your bank. The same effect would have occurred if the Fed had simply printed $5000 and issued the $5000 to you in cash.

In hiring you, the Fed is purchasing something and is injecting money into the economy. When the Fed sells something, it withdraws money from the economy. If your friend Joe buys a $5000 used car from the Fed's fleet of cars, the money supply will immediately fall by $5000. Joe's bank account will fall by $5000, and the bank's reserves at the Fed will be reduced by that amount. The $5000 that the Fed receives for the used car will be in the form of reduced liabilities (reserves at the Fed). If Joe paid in cash, then the Fed will receive some of the currency it has already issued and currency in circulation will fall by $5000. Whatever the case, the Fed's sale of an asset reduces the money supply.

Purchases by the Fed (1) raise reserves at the Fed, (2) increase vault cash, or (3) increase currency in circulation.

Sales by the Fed (1) reduce reserves at the Fed, (2) reduce vault cash, or (3) reduce currency in circulation.

Our simple example shows that the Fed can inject money into the economy by purchasing something; it can withdraw money from the economy by selling something. Fed purchases and sales alter the monetary base.

The **monetary base** is the sum of reserves on deposit at the Fed, all vault cash, and the currency in circulation.

Only by calculating the monetary base can we gauge the Fed injections or withdrawals of funds from the economy. The Fed can control the monetary base by varying the amounts of things it buys or sells (whether these things are goods and services or government bonds).

How does the monetary base compare with the money supply (M1)? The money supply is far greater than the monetary base. In 1996, for example, the money supply M1 was about $1200 billion, and the monetary base was about $500 billion. Where did the $700 billion difference between M1 and the monetary base come from? To answer this question, we must consider how banks create money.

## HOW BANKS CREATE BANK MONEY

Banks can create bank demand deposits (money) by lending out the money that people and firms have deposited. Each bank is simply trying to make a profit. By examining how banks create bank money, we can understand why the money supply exceeds the monetary base.

### THE GOLDSMITH: AN ECONOMIC PARABLE

We can easily understand the creation of money by considering an historical parable about how banking first got started. Imagine an ancient goldsmith in the business of shaping gold into fine products used by kings, lords, princes, and wealthy merchants. The goldsmith must keep inventories of gold on hand and, therefore, must have safe storage facilities to prevent theft. Because the goldsmith has such facilities, people find it useful to store gold with the goldsmith. In return, the goldsmith might charge a fee to defray storage costs. When people deposit their gold with the goldsmith, they want a receipt, and the goldsmith returns the gold only when a receipt is presented.

Assume that the gold is in the form of uniform bars. People do not care whether the goldsmith returns those same gold bars that they deposited. By not having to keep track of who owns which bar, the goldsmith can hold down storage costs.

The goldsmith soon discovers that only a small amount of gold is needed to accommodate the gold withdrawals on any given day. Each day customers bring in more gold to exchange for storage receipts; each day customers bring in storage receipts to exchange for their gold. The goldsmith can keep most of the gold in the back room under lock and key, and needs to maintain only a small inventory to service his customers. As long as they receive the correct amount of gold upon presentation of a storage receipt, they are content.

As the custom of storing gold with the goldsmith becomes more and more widespread, people find it convenient to use the storage receipts themselves, rather than the bulky gold, for transactions. Although storage receipts are mere pieces of paper, because they are accepted as a medium of exchange, like the circulating gold they serve as money. As long as the goldsmith keeps the gold in the back room, the money supply in such a world is the gold in circulation (outside the goldsmith's back room) plus the storage receipts issued by the goldsmith. However, the storage receipts add up only to the amount of gold stored in the back room.

Now imagine that one day the goldsmith discovers a method of making additional profit. A friend of the goldsmith says, "Because all the gold is just sitting in the back room collecting dust, why not lend me some of it?" Although the goldsmith at first objects that this gold is somebody else's, a sufficiently high interest rate convinces him to lend out some of the gold left to him for safekeeping. The friend gives the goldsmith an IOU; the goldsmith gives the friend some gold. The moment this transaction occurs, the money supply increases by the amount of the loan. The money supply now consists of the storage receipts, the gold previously in circulation, and the gold loaned out by the goldsmith. The goldsmith has monetized the debt by giving out gold in exchange for an IOU.

To make a long story a bit shorter, the friend is even willing to take a storage receipt instead of gold. Why? The storage receipt circulates as money. Indeed, what is to prevent the goldsmith from issuing many times his gold reserve in storage receipts as long as he knows that very few storage receipts are going to be presented for gold? The goldsmith bank can create money provided that (1) the storage receipts circulate as money and (2) the goldsmith makes loans. If either condition is not satisfied, it is impossible for the goldsmith to create money.

## MODERN BANKING

Modern banks do not issue storage receipts for gold; they accept demand deposits and allow customers to write checks (or use automatic teller machines) on those deposits. Checking account money does not circulate like the storage receipts of the goldsmith. Indeed, the only time checking account money has any real existence is that moment when a check is being written. Most checking account money is simply an entry on the books of some bank.

Consider what happens when you deposit $100 in currency in Bank A. (Suppose you have been keeping the cash in an old shoe.) Prior to the deposit, the bank was in equilibrium: It was neither making new loans nor calling in old loans. The moment you make the $100 cash deposit, Bank A's balance sheet changes, as shown in part (a) of Table 3. Both vault cash and demand deposits have gone up by $100.

### Table 3 The Effects of a $100 Cash Deposit and a $90 Loan

| | Change in Assets | | Change in Liabilities | |
|---|---|---|---|---|
| **Bank A** | | | | |
| (a) After $100 cash deposit: | Cash in vault | +$100 | Demand deposits | +$100 |
| (b) After $90 loan but before funds are spent: | Reserves | +$100 | Demand deposits | +$190 |
| | Loans | +$ 90 | | |
| (c) After $90 loan proceeds are deposited in Bank B: | Reserves | +$ 10 | Demand deposits | $+100 |
| | Loans | +$ 90 | | |
| **Bank B** | | | | |
| (d) After the $90 deposit but before the new loans are made: | Reserves | +$ 90 | Demand deposits | +$ 90 |

The cash deposit in part (a) does not create money because cash in the vault is not part of the money supply. The $90 loan and corresponding $90 demand deposit in part (b) creates $90 worth of new money because demand deposits have increased and currency in circulation has remained the same. When the $90 loan is deposited in Bank B in parts (c) and (d), no new money is created until Bank B makes a loan.

Nothing happens to the money supply as long as Bank A remains in this position. Currency in circulation has fallen by the amount that demand deposits have increased; the total money supply outside banks remains the same.

It is likely that Bank A will not be content to stay in this position. Banks have learned through experience that only a small fraction of deposits must be kept as reserves; the rest can be loaned out. The bank is not making any profit from the $100 cash in its vault. Because the bank is interested in making profits, the $100 deposit will allow Bank A to expand its loans. What fraction of the new deposit will Bank A keep? In the United States, banks must maintain the required-reserve ratio of reserves to demand deposits. If the required-reserve ratio is 10 percent, banks must keep $10 as reserves for each $100 of demand deposits.

Reserve requirements have typically been more conservative than the reserve ratio a profit-minded banker would consider safe and prudent. Hence, reserves above required reserves would likely be considered excess reserves. Excess reserves will usually be loaned out. Banks that have no excess reserves are said to be "loaned up."

> **Excess reserves** are reserves in excess of required reserves. Excess reserves equal total reserves minus required reserves.

Suppose that prior to your $100 cash deposit, the required reserves of Bank A equaled actual reserves (Bank A was loaned up). Assume the required-reserve ratio is 10 percent. Because the new $100 deposit would require a $10 increase in required reserves, the bank would have $90 in excess reserves after the deposit. Therefore, the bank makes $90 worth of new loans to eliminate the $90 of excess reserves. The moment the $90 loan is made, the borrower's demand-deposit account is credited with $90. Before the borrower spends this $90, Bank A's balance sheet changes as shown in part (b) of Table 3.

Notice also in part (b) that the money supply has increased by exactly $90. Bank A has created money! The bank exchanged the borrower's IOU for a demand deposit. The borrower's IOU is not money, but the bank's IOU—the $90 demand deposit—is money. The bank has created money by monetizing debt. If demand deposits were not used as money, or if the banks made no loans, banks could not create money.

Banks can create money when (1) demand deposits are used as money, and (2) banks make loans out of excess reserves.

Part (c) of Table 3 takes this process a step further. When the loan recipient spends the $90, Bank A loses $90 of its reserves. The department store, grocery store, or plumber who is paid the borrowed $90 will either cash the $90 check or deposit the $90 check in some other bank.

Whether the $90 ends up in cash that remains in circulation or in a checking account in another bank, the money supply has still increased by $90 as a result of the loan. If the check is cashed, the amount of cash in circulation goes up by $90 and Bank A's deposit liabilities go down by $90. If the check is deposited in another bank, the increase in the depositor's account equals the decrease in the check writer's account. Most transactions (in terms of dollar value) are in checks, and the $90 will likely end up as a checking account deposit in another bank.

## MULTIPLE-DEPOSIT CREATION

The expansion of the money supply does not end with the $90 increase in the money supply as long as transactions continue to be in the form of checks (as long as people do not increase their cash). In the example, we assume that when Bank A loses the $90 in reserves, some other bank—Bank B—gains the entire amount in new deposits. The example assumes that there is no cash leakage from the banking system to the public.

> A **cash leakage** occurs when a check is cashed and not deposited in a checking account. This cash remains in circulation outside of the banking system.

Because Bank B receives $90 in new deposits, its balance sheet changes, as shown in part (d) of Table 3. The transfer of $90 from Bank A to Bank B has no immediate impact on the money supply. The amount of demand-deposit liabilities remains the same, and no additional money is created.

If Bank B were originally in equilibrium with no excess reserves, it would now have excess reserves of $81. Because deposits increased by $90, required reserves increased by $9 with a 10 percent reserve requirement. As Bank A did, Bank B will loan out its excess reserves of $81. When the recipient of Bank B's loan spends this $81 (with zero leakages of cash), Bank C will receive a new deposit of $81.

The moment Bank B made the loan of $81, the money supply increased by that amount. Bank C will keep 10 percent of the $81 deposit as reserves and lend out the rest—$72.90—which again increases the money supply. When the borrower of $72.90 spends the funds, Bank D receives a new deposit of that amount (again assuming zero leakages of cash).

The $100 increase in reserves has set into motion a pattern of multiple expansion of the money supply. If there are no leakages of cash out of the banking system, the original $100 cash deposit in Bank A leads to demand deposits of $90, $81, $72.90, and so on; each succeeding figure is 90 percent of the previous deposit. If we sum $100 + $90 + $81 + $72.90 and so on down to the smallest amount, we obtain the total of $1000.

Table 4 shows what happens to each bank as a consequence of a $100 cash deposit in Bank A. The original $100 cash deposit has led to the creation of $900 in additional deposits, or a multiple expansion of deposits.

> A **multiple expansion of deposits** of the money supply occurs when an increase in reserves causes an expansion of the money supply that is greater than the reserve increase.

*Notice that one bank out of many cannot create a multiple expansion of bank deposits.* Each single bank can lend out only a fraction of its new deposits. In this example, each bank can create new money at a rate equal to only 90 percent of any fresh deposit; that is, each bank can loan out only its excess reserves. However, when there is no leakage of cash out of the system, an original cash deposit of $100 will lead to a multiple expansion of deposits. As long as the extra cash reserves are in the banking system, they provide the required reserves against deposits. If the reserve requirement is 10 percent, a $100 reserve increase will support $1000 worth of additional deposits. When each bank lends out its excess reserves, it loses those reserves to other banks; these reserves become the basis for further expansion of the money supply by other banks. The $100 initial cash deposit continues to be passed through the banking system until $900 in new money is created for a total of $1000 in deposits.

## Table 4   The Multiple Expansion of Bank Deposits

| Bank | New Deposits | New Loans or Investments | Required Reserves |
|------|------|------|------|
| Bank A | $ 100.00 | $ 90.00 | $ 10.00 |
| Bank B | $ 90.00 | $ 81.00 | $ 9.00 |
| Bank C | $ 81.00 | $ 72.90 | $ 8.10 |
| Bank D | $ 72.90 | $ 65.61 | $ 7.29 |
| Bank E | $ 65.61 | $ 59.05 | $ 6.56 |
| Sum A–E | $ 409.51 | $368.56 | $ 40.95 |
| Sum of remaining banks | $ 590.49 | $531.44 | $ 59.05 |
| Total for whole banking system | $1000.00 | $900.00 | $100.00 |

The banking system as a whole can create a multiple expansion of bank deposits; a single bank can create only as much money as it has excess reserves. If the reserve requirement is 0.10 (10 percent), a fresh deposit of $100 will lead to $1000 in total deposits and $900 in new money, provided there are no cash leakages and no bank keeps excess reserves. The original deposit of $100 in Bank A leads to a $90 deposit in Bank B (because of Bank A's new loans), and so on. Thus, $10 is manufactured out of $1, or $9 is created by the multiple expansion of bank deposits.

> One bank can lend out only its excess reserves. However, the banking system as a whole can lend out a multiple of any excess reserves.

Thus, what is true of all banks taken together is not true of any single bank.

## THE DEPOSIT MULTIPLIER

Table 4 showed how the banking system was able to turn a $100 increase in reserves into $900 of new money, for a total increase in demand deposits of $1000. The factor by which demand deposits expand is the deposit multiplier.

> The **deposit multiplier** is the ratio of the change in total deposits to the change in reserves.

A deposit multiplier of 10 indicates that for every $1 increase in reserves, demand deposits will increase by $10. We have already calculated the deposit multiplier when the required-reserve ratio is 10 percent (and when there are no cash leakages).

If the required-reserve ratio had been 20 percent in our example, the $1 increase in reserves would still add $1 to deposits in Bank A, but it would now add $0.80 in Bank B, $0.64 in Bank C, and so on, for a total increase of $5 in deposits. With a required-reserve ratio of 20 percent, the deposit multiplier is 5. These two examples suggest a formula for the deposit multiplier.

The deposit multiplier is the reciprocal of the reserve ratio (r) maintained by the banking system:

$$\text{Deposit multiplier} = 1/r$$

When the reserve ratio is 10 percent, $r = 0.1$, and the deposit multiplier is 10. If the reserve ratio is 5 percent, $r = 0.05$, and the deposit multiplier is 20. As the formula suggests, the deposit multiplier varies inversely with the reserve ratio.

## EXPANSION OF THE MONEY SUPPLY IN THE REAL WORLD

Our discussion of the multiple expansion of bank deposits has assumed that no cash ever leaks out of the banking system and that banks keep excess reserves at zero. Neither assumption is strictly true.

**Cash Leakages.** The public does not hold all of its money balances in demand deposits. When banks begin to create new demand deposits, it is likely that the public will also want to hold more currency. Thus, there will be leakages of cash into hand-to-hand circulation as the multiple creation of bank deposits takes place.

Cash leakages reduce the deposit multiplier. Returning to our numerical example, when you deposit $100 in Bank A and $90 is lent out, the next generation of banks—Bank B—might receive only $80 in new deposits rather than $90. Thus, Bank B can create only $72 in new deposits rather than $81. This erosion will occur all along the line in Table 4, and will reduce the deposit multiplier accordingly.

If we know the total cash leakage that will take place, we can apply the deposit multiplier ($1/r$) to the amount of the new reserves that are left with the banking system. Suppose that out of the $100 origi-

nally deposited with Bank A, $20 will eventually leak into hand-to-hand circulation. Because $80 of new reserves would remain in the banking system, $800 of deposits must result from the $100 deposit. Thus, the 10-to-1 multiplier applies to the quantity of reserves permanently left with the banking system. (See Example 2.)

**Excess Reserves.** If $r$ in the deposit multiplier formula is interpreted as the required-reserve ratio, the formula applies only when there are no excess reserves. However, since banks hold excess reserves, the $r$ in the formula must be interpreted as the desired-reserve ratio of banks. The desired-reserve ratio will depend on the required-reserve ratio and on the profitability of making loans.

Excess reserves are only about 2 percent of total reserves. Excess reserves are small for two reasons. First, to meet any reserve deficiency, banks can usually borrow from the Federal Reserve System at the official discount rate. Second, banks can always borrow reserves from other banks. In the next chapter we study the market (called the federal funds market) in which any bank with excess reserves can lend its reserves to banks with deficient reserves.

## BANK REGULATION AND REFORM

We now understand how banks help determine the supply of money and deposits. The money supply depends on the public's desire for currency relative to deposits, the banking system's desire for reserves relative to deposits, and the monetary base (currency outstanding plus bank reserves). The stability of the money supply depends on the stability of these three fundamental factors. Therefore, the confidence of the public in the banking system, as well as the reliability of bank lending practices, plays a major role in the monetary system.

These concerns bring us to our final topic of the chapter: Bank regulation and reform. The stability of the supply of money and credit depends in part on the way in which banks are regulated.

### BANK REGULATION

It is useful to examine the key developments in bank regulation in the United States in order to understand the current system.

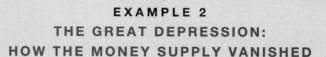

# EXAMPLE 2
## THE GREAT DEPRESSION:
## HOW THE MONEY SUPPLY VANISHED

From 1929 to 1933 more than one-quarter of the U.S. money supply vanished. If you had talked to people who lived during the Great Depression, they would have told you that "there was no money." If you asked them where it was, they might have told you that "Rockefeller had most of it."

How did the money supply vanish? Some statistics are useful. In October 1929, U.S. banks had reserves of $3.5 billion. The public held $3.8 billion in currency and $22.6 billion in demand deposits. Thus, M1 was $26.4 billion in October 1929. Only six months later, in April 1933, the money supply had fallen to $19 billion—$7.4 billion had vanished! What happened?

Bank reserves fell from $3.5 billion to $2.9 billion; thus, only $0.6 billion of bank reserves vanished. Currency held by the public increased from $3.8 billion to $5.2 billion—a $1.4 billion increase. Thus, the monetary base actually increased from about $7.3 billion to about $8 billion.

During the Depression, as banks failed people became leery of banks, and banks were afraid to make loans. Two things happened: First, the public withdrew cash from the banking system, which caused a multiple contraction of deposits, and second, banks increased their ratio of reserves to demand deposits from 14.3 percent to 21 percent, to cause a further contraction of the money supply.

Some economists argue that the Fed was inept during this period. In the 1920s, the Fed met recessions with vigorous open market operations. After the stock market crash of 1929, the Fed was timid. Why? According to Milton Friedman and Anna Schwartz, as well as Irving Fisher, who studied this period in great detail, the fault lay in the lack of experience of those in control of the Fed. The Fed had only 15 years of experience, compared with centuries for, say, the Bank of England. During the early and mid-1920s, Benjamin Strong, who was the powerful Governor of the New York Fed, provided the proper understanding of central banking. But Strong died in late 1928, and with him the required experience disappeared.

It is because of the experience of the 1930s that many economists think that another Great Depression is unlikely. The level of understanding is so great today that the Fed would never allow the money supply to fall dramatically, as we shall see in Example 1 of the next chapter.

------------------------------------------------

*Source:* Milton Friedman and Anna Schwartz, *The Monetary History of the United States, 1867–1960* (Princeton: Princeton University Press, 1963), pp. 407–419, 712–714, 739–740.

**Restriction of Interest Payments on Deposits.** The Banking Acts of 1933 and 1935 imposed limits on the interest rates banks can pay on demand, savings, and time deposits. These acts prohibited interest payments on checking accounts and provided for the Fed to adjust the other rates periodically. The United States began to phase out these interest-rate ceilings in the early 1980s.

**Deposit Insurance.** In the Great Depression, government-guaranteed deposit insurance was insti-

tuted for both commercial banks and savings and loans associations. The FDIC (Federal Deposit Insurance Corporation) insured bank deposits, and the FSLIC (Federal Savings and Loan Insurance Corporation) insured savings and loan deposits. In 1989, the two were merged under the FDIC.

**Restrictions on Permissible Activities.** Until the early 1980s, savings and loan associations were restricted to making mortgage loans. Commercial banks were free to make consumer loans, commercial loans, and mortgage loans to buy government securities. The Glass-Steagall Act of 1933 separated the activities of commercial banks from the securities industry. Commercial banks were prohibited from selling corporate securities. Investment banks (who could deal in corporate securities) were prohibited from engaging in commercial banking. Thus, the distinction between savings and loan associations, commercial banks, and investment banks is a legal one.

**Capital Requirements.**   All depository institutions must meet certain minimum capital requirements. There are two ways to finance the acquisition of assets: using the owner's equity or capital, and borrowing. Historically, there have been diverse capital requirements, depending on the size and location of the bank. Since 1983, the Fed and the Comptroller of the Currency have established the minimum capital requirement of 6 percent of a bank's assets. In other words, 6 percent of a bank's assets should be financed by the owners of the bank. This practice presumably makes the bank safer in case the bank enters a period of negative profits. Federal bank regulators have some discretion in enforcing the requirement for individual banks.

**Inspection and Control of Riskiness.**   The government has the power to examine depository institutions to determine the riskiness of their assets and liabilities.

**Entry Restrictions.**   To create a new bank, a new branch of an old bank, or a new savings and loan association, it is necessary to obtain permission from federal and state regulators.

## BANK DEREGULATION

The United States experienced high inflation rates in the late 1970s and early 1980s. During 1980, the rate of inflation—about 13 percent—put a squeeze on savings and loan associations. Interest rates on home mortgages rose, but savings and loans associations had difficulty attracting deposits because of government regulation of interest paid on deposits. The savings and loans had loaned out substantial sums on residential real estate in the 1970s, but at relatively low, fixed interest rates. Industry losses mounted to about $6 billion in 1980. From 1970 to 1982, the number of savings and loan associations dropped by about one-third.

In the early 1980s Congress deregulated banking, in the hope of solving the savings and loan crisis

and making the banking system more efficient. Both commercial banks and thrifts were deregulated. The Depository Institutions and Monetary Control Act of 1980 and the Garn–St. Germain Act of 1982 jointly reduced the legal distinction between banks and thrifts, and removed many restrictions on their investment activities and the interest rates paid on deposit accounts. For example, competitive interest rates could be paid on checking accounts, and banks could lend real estate developers in excess of 100 percent of their construction costs.

## BANKING CRISES

The combination of deregulation and deposit insurance proved disastrous, and severe unintended consequences followed. The FDIC method of insuring deposits creates an incentive problem. Banks or thrifts pay a fixed fee as a percent of their deposits. Even though there is a $100,000 nominal limit on an insured deposit, any amount can be insured through the use of deposit brokers, who spread $100,000 accounts over many banks. With such deposit insurance there is no incentive for banks to provide, nor for consumers to demand, information on how well the bank is doing. Deposits are as safe in a poorly run bank as in the most well-run bank. You can get an insured deposit from a failed or failing bank, as though you were to buy fire insurance while your house is burning or after it has burned down. Thus, banks and thrifts could and did invest in wild schemes without imposing any costs on depositors or even on themselves. Who monitors the banks and thrifts? Since depositors have no incentive to monitor banks or thrifts, that role falls on the shoulders of bank regulators. But deregulation effectively meant that "nobody was watching the store."

Banks lent money to real estate developers without carefully examining the creditworthiness of their projects. In one example among many, banks lent the entrepreneur Donald Trump about $2 billion without auditing him! Why? The competition for loans became fierce as thousands of thrifts began to make loans to real estate developers with cheap, government-insured funds. When these investments failed, so did banks and thrifts. Bank failure rates in the late 1980s and early 1990s increased tenfold over the bank failure rates in the 30 years from 1950 to 1980. (See Example 3.)

Government-insured deposits severed the link between a bank's performance and the

## EXAMPLE 3
## BANKING AND THE BUSINESS CYCLE:
## THE SCHUMPETERIAN VIEW

When banks find that they have bad loans, they have to become more careful about making new loans. Such care can unfortunately lead to serious problems for the economy at large. In Joseph Schumpeter's vision of the economy, discussed in Chapter 1, the economy is constantly undergoing renewal: New products and industries always replace old products and industries. New industries find it difficult to borrow from banks because they do not have a track record or enough assets to pledge in support of a loan. Accordingly, when old industries such as farming dry up, banks will be reluctant to lend to new industries. If it happens that banks have more bad loans than usual, banks will want to sharply curtail their loans, especially to new

firms and industries. Accordingly, bad loans can lead to a contraction of the money supply and a direct contraction of the economy.

This contraction of the money supply occurred during the Great Depression in the United States. Japan has faced the problem throughout much of the 1990s. In Japan through the 1980s, banks made many loans based on real estate. However, a collapse of the real estate market led to an enormous volume of bad loans on the books of banks. As a consequence, in the mid-1990s Japan was in a prolonged recession. It is significant that such a recession can occur even if there are no bank failures.

ability of a bank to attract deposits. Bank performance deteriorated in the 1980s because of a combination of deposit insurance and deregulation.

During the 1990s the problem of bank failure subsided. Prosperity helps banking. The return on bank equity increased from less than 3 percent in 1987 to about 15 percent in 1993–1994. Banks were also required to meet higher capital requirements; that is, the banks themselves must own assets that are not pledged against liabilities. From 1987 to 1994, the percentage of assets owned by the banks rose from about 6 percent to 8 percent.

## BANKING REFORM

Problem banks in the 1980s stimulated several plans for reforming the banking system. What would be some possible reforms that would forestall or minimize future problems?

**The Free Market Plan.**   The simplest plan calls for the elimination of deposit insurance. If banks are not

unique and must compete with other financial institutions, why should the government subsidize the banking industry through deposit insurance? Deposits are to a bank what labor and capital are to a firm. Thus, it is argued, banks should not be subsidized more than other firms in the economy.

History provides several examples of banking without much regulation or deposit insurance. The experience that is most relevant for the United States today occurred from 1863 to 1913, during the National Banking Era. This was the period between the National Bank Act of 1863 and the Federal Reserve Act of 1913. Nationally chartered banks were subject to reserve requirements, and banks were restricted in their investments. But deposits were not insured and there was no central bank.

How well did the National Banking Era work?[1] Contrary to popular views, banks failed less than

---

[1]The following discussion of the National Banking Era is based on "The Banking Industry: Withering Under the Umbrella of Protection," *Federal Reserve Bank of Cleveland Annual Report,* 1990.

nonbanks in that period. In the worst banking panic of the period (in 1873), 1.3 percent of banks failed, and the depositors of those banks lost only 2.1 cents of every dollar of deposits. If a bank were in trouble, it might stop converting notes and deposits into gold. But the bank would not usually close; it would continue to make and service loans.

Because there was no deposit insurance, banks held larger reserves, invested a larger fraction of their assets in safe securities, and maintained more capital to meet contingencies. These factors reduced the impact of a financial panic. Financial panics seemed to affect the insolvent banks, but when the public realized that a particular bank was safe, that bank was not pulled down by the panic.

**The Tobin Plan.** James Tobin, a Nobel laureate in economics, proposed a plan that has much in common with the free market plan. Tobin's plan is a minimal government plan, involving both insured and uninsured deposits.

First, Tobin's plan backs insured deposits by safe assets, such as Treasury securities, that are specifically dedicated to the redemption of those deposits. Second, the plan lets banks and savings and loan associations give depositors the option of keeping their money in uninsured deposits. Uninsured deposits would offer higher yields and be subject to the usual regulations of the banking authorities. Third, the plan would not bail out insolvent institutions, no matter how big, or pay off uninsured depositors. In this two-tiered scheme, there is no required limit on deposit insurance. If a charity wanted to keep $2 million in an insured account, the entire amount could be redeemed if the bank went bankrupt because the $2 million would be backed by Treasury securities.

If this plan were adopted, a private industry could potentially develop to insure federally uninsured deposits. Although it is difficult for individuals to monitor single banks, insurance companies could grade the banks according to risk and sell consumers private insurance policies to cover federally uninsured deposits.

**Government Plans.** The U.S. Treasury and Congress have considered plans that would reform the current system. Needless to say, these plans involve a large amount of government intervention. Such plans are usually devised to support those who already have a vested interest in regulation. It is the view of

the authors that either the free market plan or the Tobin plan would cost the economy far less.

Government-backed plans still give the FDIC the power to distinguish between big banks and small banks. Many economists believe that this distinction is inefficient because it favors the establishment of larger banks and does not promote competition. Usually, political rather than economic concerns drive regulators to favor large banks over small ones.

In this chapter we have considered the relationship between the Federal Reserve System and the money supply. We have also studied the role of bank regulation and possible plans for reform of the banking system. In the next chapter, we shall examine the role of monetary policy in the broader context of controlling aggregate demand.

## SUMMARY

1. Banks are financial intermediaries. Financial intermediaries borrow money from ultimate lenders and lend this money to ultimate borrowers. Most lending in the United States is done by financial intermediaries.

2. Commercial banks are chartered by state banking authorities or by the U.S. Treasury. Commercial banks offer their customers checking account services and savings accounts. They earn money by loaning out funds they have borrowed or by investing these funds in government securities. Banks make profits by borrowing at a lower rate of interest than that at which they lend or invest. Bank balance sheets summarize the claims on the assets of a bank. Banks must maintain reserves to meet the cash needs of their depositors. Reserves are held in two forms: cash in the vault and reserve balances at the Fed. Reserves are typically much less than the demand-deposit liabilities of the bank. The FDIC insures deposits and gives depositors the necessary sense of security.

3. The Federal Reserve System, established in 1913, is the central bank of the United States. The Fed imposes reserve requirements on banks and thrift institutions. Depository institutions can borrow from the Fed to meet their temporary cash needs, and the interest rate at which they borrow is called the discount rate. By buying and selling things, the Fed injects money into the banking system and takes money out of the banking system.

The monetary base equals reserve balances with the Fed, vault cash, and currency in circulation. The monetary base is smaller than the money supply.

4. Banks create money by monetizing debt. Banks can use reserves to make loans, and in the process of making loans, they create money. Private banks have the ability to create money because demand deposits are money and because banks make loans out of new deposits. An increase in reserves leads to a multiple expansion of deposits. Although any one bank can lend out only its excess reserves, the banking system as a whole can lend out a multiple of an increase in reserves. The deposit multiplier is the ratio of the change in deposits to the change in reserves. The deposit multiplier is the inverse of the actual reserve ratio.

5. The Depository Institutions and Monetary Control Act of 1980 and the Garn–St. Germain Act of 1982 reduced the legal distinction between banks and thrifts, removed restrictions on investment activities, and allowed competitive interest rates on deposit accounts. Bank deregulation combined with the system of deposit insurance precipitated bank and thrift failures in the 1980s and 1990s. In response, several plans for bank reform have been offered.

## KEY TERMS

financial intermediaries
commercial banks
balance sheet
assets
liabilities
reserves
reserve requirements
required-reserve ratio
monetary base
excess reserves
cash leakage
multiple expansion of deposits
deposit multiplier

## QUESTIONS AND PROBLEMS

1. Evaluate the validity of the following statement: "Banks get away with murder. They pay you no or little interest on your checking accounts, and then they turn around and lend your money to some poor borrower at 18 percent."
2. Commercial banks hold only about 10 percent of their transaction deposits in reserves. Explain how banks can get by with so few reserves.
3. Explain why bankers would maintain reserves even without required-reserve ratios.
4. Assume that the Fed sells all its old office furniture to XYZ Corporation for $10 million. What effect will this sale have on the money supply? What will happen if the Fed sells XYZ Corporation $10 million worth of its holdings of government securities?
5. Explain why banks can create money only if bank deposits are accepted as money and only if banks are willing to make loans. Explain what is meant by the monetization of debt.
6. Assume that the required-reserve ratio is 0.4 (40 percent) and that there are no cash leakages. The Fed buys a government security from Jones for $1000. Explain, using balance sheets, what will happen to the money supply. Answer the same question assuming only that Jones (and only Jones) takes payment from the Fed as follows: $500 cash (which he puts under his mattress) and a $500 check. There are no more cash leakages.
7. Rework Table 3 on the assumption that $r = 0.2$. In this case, the deposit multiplier is 5, so that the $100 fresh deposit in Bank A will ultimately lead to $500 in total deposits, or $400 in new money.
8. What will happen to the money supply if the Fed sells a large fleet of used cars to a car dealership?
9. What do you predict would happen to commercial bank borrowing from the Fed if the Fed were to raise the required-reserve ratio?
10. Assume that between year 1 and year 2, the amount of currency in circulation increases while the amount of vault cash and reserves at the Fed remains the same. Is the Fed purchasing or selling securities?
11. During the Christmas season, the public tends to withdraw large sums of cash from checking accounts. What effect do these withdrawals have upon the nation's money supply?
12. How were the savings and loan associations hurt by the inflation of the 1970s?
13. Evaluate the validity of the following statement: "Central banking is only as good as the people who run it."
14. What effect did the deregulation of the 1980s, combined with federal deposit insurance, have on banking in the United States?
15. Evaluate the various plans for reforming the banking system.

# CHAPTER 30

# MONETARY POLICY

In 1995 the U.S. economy was in a period of slow growth. Some economists believed this to be "caused" by the Fed's interest rate hikes in 1994. During 1995 and early 1996, the Fed lowered interest rates. In early 1996, it appeared that the economy was going to avoid a serious recession and enter another period of robust economic growth. The question uppermost in the business editorial pages was whether the Fed had seemingly done the impossible: to engineer a "soft landing" rather than the "hard landing" of a deep recession.

Fed policy sometimes tries to cut inflation, sometimes tries to reduce unemployment, and always tries to steer a path between the twin evils of inflation and unemployment. Too much monetary growth may stimulate inflation; too little may cause too much unemployment. Some economists charge that the Fed is actually responsible for recessions and depressions.

In this chapter, and the several that follow, we shall consider the conduct of economic policies dealing with a broad range of issues involving inflation, unemployment, growth, and the business cycles. In the next chapter we shall examine fiscal policy. We shall then turn to the policies aimed at stabilizing the business cycle itself.

*handwritten: leverage by creation of money by banks*

# FEDERAL RESERVE POLICY

The most important function of the Federal Reserve is to control monetary policy.

> **Monetary policy** is the deliberate control of the money supply and, in some cases, credit conditions for the purpose of achieving macroeconomic goals such as a certain level of unemployment or inflation.

Congress set the goals of the Fed in the Full Employment Act of 1946 and the Full Employment and Balanced Growth Act of 1978. Congress instructed the Fed to "maintain long-run growth of the monetary and credit aggregates commensurate with the economy's long-run potential to increase production, so as to promote effectively the goals of maximum employment, stable prices, and moderate long-term interest rates."

The quantity of money can affect prices, output, and employment; therefore, the Fed controls—to some degree—the pulse rate of the economy. By expanding the money supply, the Fed can speed up the pulse rate; by contracting the money supply (or by slowing down its rate of growth), the Fed can slow down the pulse rate.

The Fed controls money and credit by

1. Controlling the monetary base through open-market operations
2. Adjusting reserve requirements
3. Setting the discount rate
4. Targeting the Federal funds rate
5. Applying moral suasion
6. Imposing selective credit controls

## OPEN-MARKET OPERATIONS

We already know that the Fed can inject or withdraw money from the economy by buying or selling. An injection of money leads to a multiple expansion of deposits; a withdrawal of money leads to a multiple contraction of deposits. The Fed controls bank reserves by buying and selling federal government securities on the open market as directed by the Federal Open Market Committee.

A substantial portion of the Fed's open-market operations are purely defensive. The Fed responds to changes in the currency-holding habits of the public. For example, a large seasonal influx of cash from the public into the banking system tends to automatically increase bank reserves. When people deposit cash in their checking accounts, bank reserves rise and excess reserves are created. If the Fed does not take countermeasures, banks begin to loan out excess reserves. Likewise, spontaneous cash drains from the banking system cause a contraction of the supply of money in the absence of offsetting action by the Fed. When depositors write checks to obtain cash, bank reserves fall, and banks can be left with insufficient reserves.

The mechanics of Fed open-market transactions are the same whether the Fed is simply offsetting actions in the private economy to hold money supply steady or whether it is embarking on a course of monetary expansion or contraction.

*handwritten: you buy bonds / M1 goes down     Fed sell M1 ↓*

**Open-Market Sales.** Let's suppose the Fed sells you $10,000 worth of government securities (by means of some intermediary). You send a personal check written on a commercial bank to the Fed (although exactly the same effect is achieved if you pay cash). Panel (a) of Table 1 shows what happens to the balance sheets of the buyer (you), the commercial bank, and the Fed. Your total assets remain the same: Your bonds increase by $10,000, while your demand deposits decrease by $10,000. The commercial bank finds that its demand-deposit liabilities fall by $10,000. Its reserves with the Fed also fall by $10,000 because when the Fed receives the check drawn on the commercial bank, it reduces the bank's account by that amount. The Fed's stock of government securities falls by $10,000, and its reserve-balance liability to the commercial bank falls by $10,000.

As a consequence of the Fed sale, the money supply falls by $10,000 because demand deposits fall by that amount. In addition, the monetary base falls by $10,000; by selling $10,000 in securities, the Fed extinguishes $10,000 in reserves. Writing a check to the Fed, in contrast to writing one to someone else, destroys money instead of transferring it.

The extinction of $10,000 in reserves (monetary base) will cause a multiple contraction of deposits. In the last chapter we learned that every dollar of reserves can support several dollars of deposits. With a deposit multiplier of 10, deposits will fall by $100,000 (assuming no cash leakages).

## Table 1   Two Open-Market Transactions

| | Changes in Assets | | | Changes in Liabilities | |
|---|---|---|---|---|---|
| **(a) Effects of an Open-Market Sale of $10,000 in Government Securities** | | | | | |
| (1) Individual or household | Securities | +$10,000 | | No change | |
| | Demand deposits | −$10,000 | | | |
| (2) Commercial bank | Reserves at Fed | −$10,000 | | Demand deposits | −$10,000 |
| (3) The Fed | Government securities | −$10,000 | | Reserve balances of banks | −$10,000 |
| **(b) Effects of an Open-Market Purchase of $10,000 in Government Securities** | | | | | |
| (1) Individual or household | Securities | −$10,000 | | No change | |
| | Demand deposits | +$10,000 | | | |
| (2) Commercial bank | Reserves at Fed | +$10,000 | | Demand deposits | +$10,000 |
| (3) The Fed | Government securities | +$10,000 | | Reserve balances of banks | +$10,000 |

Panel (a) of this table shows the effect of an open-market sale by the Fed. Rows (2) and (3) of panel (a) show that commercial bank reserves fall by the amount of the sale. Thus, Fed sales of government securities lower commercial bank reserves. Panel (b) shows the effect of an open-market purchase by the Fed. Rows (2) and (3) show that commercial bank reserves rise by the amount of the purchase. Thus, Fed purchases of government securities raise commercial bank reserves.

**Open-Market Purchases.** Now let's suppose that the Fed purchases $10,000 worth of securities from you (by means of some intermediary). You receive a check from the Fed and deposit it in your bank. Panel (b) of Table 1 shows what happens to the balance sheets for you, the commercial bank, and the Fed. Your total assets remain the same: Demand deposits increase by $10,000, and government bonds decrease by $10,000. The commercial bank finds that its demand deposits rise by $10,000, as do its reserves with the Fed. Finally, the Fed's government securities and reserve balances of commercial banks both rise by $10,000. The monetary base rises by the amount of the purchase. This expansion of bank reserves sets into motion a multiple expansion of deposits.

As we can see by comparing panels (a) and (b) of Table 1, open-market purchases have the effects opposite to those of open-market sales.

**Advantages of Open-Market Operations.** The chief advantages of open-market operations as a tool of monetary policy are

1. Open-market operations give the Fed more precise control over the monetary base. By purchasing or selling a given dollar amount of government securities, the Fed adds or subtracts exactly that amount to or from the monetary base.

2. Flexible monetary control is possible through open-market operations because the Fed can buy or sell securities each day. The Fed can reverse itself if new information becomes available.

Thus, it is hardly surprising that the Fed relies more heavily on open-market operations than on any other tool of monetary control.

Open-market purchases increase the monetary base; open-market sales lower the monetary base. Open-market operations are flexible because they can be transacted quickly and in almost any desired amount. Open-market operations are powerful because they have a magnified impact on the money supply as banks create new money from new reserves.

## CHANGES IN RESERVE REQUIREMENTS

The Fed's power to change reserve requirements within broad limits is another of its tools for controlling the money supply. For example, increasing reserve requirements from 10 percent to 12.5 percent would force banks to contract demand deposits by 20 percent. Recall that the deposit multiplier is $1/r$. When $r = 0.10$, $40,000 in reserves will support $400,000 in demand deposits. If reserve requirements are raised to $r = 0.125$, $40,000 in reserves would support only $320,000 in demand deposits; demand deposits will have to contract by $80,000. Conversely, lowering reserve requirements can result in a massive increase in the money supply.

A bank meets its reserve requirements by keeping its loans and investments in the proper relationship with its total deposits. The smaller the reserve requirement, the greater its loans and investments and,

*[handwritten margin notes: Sell Bonds to lower M; Buy to raise M; Fed uses Discount Rate Consistent w/ open MKT Operations]*

therefore, bank profits. Thus, banks prefer smaller reserve requirements.

Traditionally, the Fed has been reluctant to use this tool of monetary policy. One argument against reserve-requirement changes is that they are too blunt an instrument. An open-market operation, for example, can be carried out to offset a seasonal currency drain without any fanfare or comment from the press. However, a reduction in reserve requirements that is used to offset a seasonal currency drain might be interpreted by the financial press as a fundamental change in monetary policy. In April 1992 the Fed did lower reserve requirements against checking account deposits, from 12 percent to 10 percent. The Fed made it clear that the purpose was to increase bank profits, not to increase the supply of money and credit.

> Increases in reserve requirements reduce the money supply; reductions in reserve requirements increase the money supply. Changes in reserve requirements, however, are a seldom-used instrument of monetary policy.

## THE SETTING OF THE DISCOUNT RATE

We noted in the last chapter that depository institutions, such as commercial banks and savings and loan associations, can borrow from the Fed at the discount rate. The amount that banks borrow from the Fed directly affects the monetary base. As depository institutions borrow more or less from the Fed, the monetary base increases or decreases. A key feature of the discount rate is that it is lower than bank lending rates. For example, in February 1996, banks on the average charged their best customers about 8.25 percent per year, while they could borrow from the Fed at a discount rate of 5 percent. Thus, banks normally have an economic incentive to borrow from the Fed and then lend those funds at a higher rate.

The Fed, of course, does not want depository institutions to make opportunistic use of their borrowing privileges. By administrative action, the amount banks can borrow at the discount window is limited to their seasonal borrowing needs, except for banks in financial trouble. The Fed takes a close look at depository institutions that borrow too frequently, and it can refuse to make loans. Nevertheless, the higher

market interest rates are relative to the discount rate, the greater is the incentive of depository institutions to borrow from the Fed.

To limit the incentive of depository institutions to use the discount window, the Fed attempts to keep the discount rate in line with market interest rates. Therefore, as market interest rates rise or fall, it lowers or raises the discount rate.

Some economists have suggested that the discount rate can be used to indicate the Fed's future monetary policy. Increases in the discount rate are said to be indicative of tight monetary policy, and decreases are said to suggest an easy monetary policy. Thus, changes in the discount rate can have an announcement effect. Economists are usually suspicious of this argument, however, because as yet no one has shown that changes in the discount rate can be used to predict the future monetary base or money supply.

The Fed's use of the discount rate as a tool of monetary policy has been criticized by many economists. First, the ability to borrow from the Fed reduces the Fed's control over the monetary base. If banks borrow when the Fed is interested in lowering the monetary base, the Fed must sell government bonds to offset such borrowing. Second, allowing banks to borrow at an interest rate that is lower than the market interest rate amounts to a subsidy to those depository institutions. Generally speaking, the banks that avail themselves of the discount window are usually in financial trouble. Critics argue that imprudently run banks should not be subsidized.

*[handwritten margin note: Discount rate ↑ M↓]*

## TARGETING THE FEDERAL FUNDS RATE

Banks that are short of reserves need not borrow from the Fed—they can borrow from banks with excess reserves. The market for these excess reserves is called the Federal funds market. The interest rate on those funds is called the Fed funds rate. The Fed funds market is typically an overnight one: A bank borrows enough from other banks at the end of the day to meet its reserve requirements for that day. The next day, from incoming deposits, the bank can repay the loan.

> The **Federal funds rate** is the interest rate on overnight loans among financial institutions.

Monetary policy is conducted by the Fed as it sets targets on the Fed funds rate. It sets these targets indirectly through open-market operations: an open-market purchase adds reserves and thus puts downward pressure on the Fed funds rate because banks are less likely to need reserves at the end of the day.

By focusing on the Fed funds rate, the Fed can get a good idea of the demand for reserves on the part of banks. If the Fed thinks banks are creating too much money through their loans and investments, they might signal this change in policy by raising their target for the Fed funds rate. Thus, by engaging in open-market sales, the Fed will absorb reserves and force more banks to borrow from the Federal funds market. With a higher Fed funds rate, banks will have to be more careful about meeting their reserve requirements and thus may raise their loan interest rates.

## OTHER INSTRUMENTS OF CONTROL

In addition to the four major instruments we have just considered, the Fed uses three minor tools to control money supply: moral suasion, selective credit controls, and margin credit.

**Moral Suasion.**   The chairperson of the Fed has been known at times to urge banks to expand their loans or to adopt more restrictive credit policies. What is known as moral suasion is the process by which the Fed tries to persuade banks voluntarily to follow a particular policy.

**Selective Credit Controls.**   The Fed can use selective credit controls to affect the distribution of loans rather than the overall volume of loans. The Fed can dictate terms and conditions of installment credit and requirements for consumer credit cards. Until 1986, the Fed could set interest-rate ceilings on deposits at commercial banks, and these ceilings could affect bank deposits.

**Margin Credit.**   When investors buy stocks, they are permitted to buy a portion on credit (this practice is called buying on margin). This credit, supplied by stockbrokers, is called margin credit. The Fed sets margin requirements. Current margin requirements allow purchasers of stock to finance 50 percent of the purchase with margin credit. In the speculative stock market boom of the 1920s, speculators could purchase stocks with as little as 10 percent down; the rest was financed with margin loans. Studies show margin requirements to be relatively ineffective as a tool of monetary policy because stocks can always be purchased with money borrowed from alternative sources.

## PROBLEMS OF MONETARY CONTROL

When the monetary base increases, banks have a larger base on which to make loans. As loans increase, the money supply increases. We know from the last chapter that if there is no drain of reserves into circulating currency and if the ratio of reserves to deposits is 10 percent, a \$1 increase in the monetary base will increase the money supply by \$10. The deposit multiplier equals $1/r$, where $r$ is the reserve/deposit ratio.

In reality, increasing the monetary base by \$1 will not raise the money supply by \$10. People hold their money balances in both checking accounts and currency. As the quantity of checking accounts expands, currency in circulation will also increase. Thus, as banks make loans out of additional reserves, some of those reserves will leak out into currency in circulation. If Bank A receives \$1 in extra reserves as a result of a Fed open-market purchase, the money supply will rise by \$1. When Bank A then increases its loans by \$0.90, the money supply increases again, this time by \$0.90 (as explained before). If the proceeds of this loan end up entirely as currency in circulation, the process of money expansion stops. In this case, the money supply increases by a total of \$1.90 and \$10, depending on the cash leakage from the system. Historically, an increase in the monetary base of \$1 increases the money supply (M1) by between \$2.75 and \$3.00.

A given increase in the monetary base will increase the money supply by more, the smaller the amount of currency people hold per dollar of deposit and the smaller the reserve/deposit ratio. If people hold less currency, the banking system will gain more new reserves from any given increase in the monetary base; the smaller the reserve/deposit ratio, the larger the deposit multiplier for any given increase in reserves.[1]

The ratio of currency to deposits can vary unpredictably from month to month. Thus, even if the Fed has precise control over the monetary base, it does not have precise control over the money supply. In one month, a 1 percent increase in the monetary base may be accompanied by a 5 percent decrease in the money supply; in another month, a 5 percent increase in the monetary base may coincide with a 1 percent increase in the money supply. In the short run, the Fed can never be sure how the money supply will respond to a change in the monetary base. In the long run, the Fed has much more control over the money supply because the ratio of currency to deposits is not as unpredictable.

> The Fed does not have direct control over the money supply. It can control only the monetary base. The money supply itself will depend on (1) the reserve/deposit ratio that banks hold, which depends in part on the reserve requirements imposed by the Fed as well as on the excess reserves desired by depository institutions, and (2) the public's desired currency/deposit ratio. The Fed's short-run control is less effective than its long-run control.

---

[1]The money supply formula, for interested readers, is derived as follows: Assume banks wish to hold the ratio $r$ of Fed and vault reserves ($R$) to deposits ($D$). Thus, $R = rD$. Assume the public wishes to hold the ratio $k$ of currency ($C$) to deposits ($D$). Thus $k = C/D$ and $r = R/D$. The monetary base ($H$) = $R + C$. The money supply ($M$) = $C + D$. Thus,

$$\frac{M}{H} = \frac{D + C}{R + C} \qquad (1)$$

Nothing is changed by dividing $D$ into the numerator and denominator:

$$\frac{M}{H} = \frac{(1 + k)}{r + k} \qquad (2)$$

For example, if one assumes that the currency/deposit ratio ($k$) is 0.4 and the reserve/deposit ratio is 0.1, the result is a money multiplier (the money/base ratio) of $M/H = (1 + 0.4)/(0.1 + 0.4) = 2.8$. If the currency deposit ratio fell by exactly one-half, the money multiplier would increase from 2.8 to 4 [$= (1 + 0.2)/(0.1 + 0.2)$]. But if $k$ remained at 0.4 while the reserve-deposit ratio ($r$) fell by one-half, to $r = 0.05$, the money multiplier would increase from 2.8 to only 3.11 [$= (1 + 0.4)/(.05 + 0.4)$].

## MONETARY POLICY

The classical economists believed that the supply of money affected the level of money expenditures directly. With velocity ($V$) constant and the economy tending to operate automatically at full employment, the equation of exchange ($MV = PQ$) showed that aggregate expenditures rise at the same rate as the money supply ($M$). However, classical quantity theorists did not believe that the quantity of money had any effect on real GDP or employment because of the natural tendency for economies to operate at full employment. Rather, they argued that increases in money supply translated into proportionate increases in the price level.

Modern monetary economists believe that the link between monetary policy and the economy is much less direct. Instead, the main focus is on interest rates. The Fed raises or lowers interest rates through open-market sales or purchases. By affecting real investment and perhaps even real consumption expenditures, changes in the interest rate would have an indirect effect on real output.

> Monetary policy affects output indirectly through interest rates.

In the following sections, we shall trace these indirect linkages between money and output, starting with the relationship between money and interest rates.

### FROM INTEREST RATES TO AGGREGATE DEMAND

Fed open-market operations have a direct impact on interest rates. When the Fed purchases government securities, the increased demand for those bonds will drive up their prices and thus lower interest rates. When the Fed sells government securities, the increased supply of those bonds will drive down their prices and thus raise interest rates. A similar phenomenon occurs if banks purchase or sell government securities. If banks expand the money supply by buying government securities, bond prices will rise and interest rates will fall. If banks contract the money supply by selling government securities that they own, bond prices will fall and interest rates will rise.

The exact impact that changes in the money supply have on interest rates depends on the responsiveness of the quantity of money demanded to the rate of interest. According to liquidity preference theory, monetary authorities can control interest rates by controlling the supply of money. By increasing the money supply, monetary authorities can drive down the rate of interest. By reducing the supply of money, monetary authorities can raise the rate of interest.

In Figure 1, the money demand curve is shown by the liquidity preference curve, LP. The intersection of the money demand curve with the money supply curve determines the current interest rate, $r$ in Figure 1. The reason is that at, say, a lower interest rate (than at the intersection), the demand for money will exceed the supply. Interest rates will rise because people will sell bonds in order to satisfy their demand for money. Remember, lower bond prices raise interest rates. Similarly, an interest rate higher than the intersection point will cause people to buy more bonds and thus send interest rates lower as bond prices rise. If the Fed increases the money supply from $M$ to $M'$, the interest rate falls from $r$ to $r'$ when all other things are equal. A greater supply of money induces lending institutions (banks, savings and loan associations, insurance companies) to make more loans or buy more bonds, an action that drives down market rates of interest. The extent to which the typical interest rate falls depends on the responsiveness of the money demand to the rate of interest. If the LP curve is very flat, so that the quantity of money demanded is highly responsive to the interest rate, a very small change in the rate of interest is enough to induce people to hold a larger stock of money. If the LP curve is very steep, so that the quantity of money demanded is relatively insensitive to the interest rate, a very large change in the rate of interest is needed to induce people to hold a larger stock of money.

An increase in the supply of money drives down interest rates as long as the money demand—or liquidity preference—curve is constant.

Figure 2 shows that at higher interest rates, less investment is demanded, and that at lower interest rates, more investment is demanded. Figure 3 shows how the interaction between money and investment markets depicted in Figures 1 and 2 can affect the economy's level of output.

If the Fed increases the money supply, the rate of interest falls and the quantity of investment demanded increases. This increased investment shifts

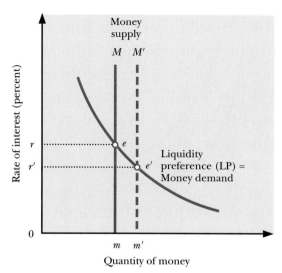

**FIGURE 1    The Demand and Supply of Money and the Interest Rate**

The money demand curve, or liquidity preference curve, has a negative slope. The amount of money demanded by the economy is greater at low rates of interest than at high rates of interest because the interest rate is the opportunity cost of holding money. The supply of money is determined by monetary authorities. The market interest rate ($r$) will be the equilibrium rate at which the quantity of money demanded ($m$) equals the quantity of money supplied. As monetary authorities increase the supply of money from $m$ to $m'$, the interest rate falls from $r$ to $r'$, if all other things are equal.

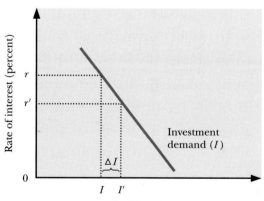

**FIGURE 2    The Effect of Interest Rate Changes on Investment**

More real investment takes place at lower rates of interest than at higher rates of interest, *ceteris paribus*. Any monetary policy that lowers the interest rate will stimulate investment, *ceteris paribus*.

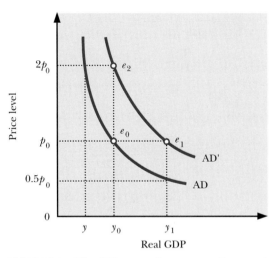

**FIGURE 3   The Effect on Aggregate Demand of Doubling the Money Supply**

When the money supply increases, the interest rate falls, increasing investment and causing a rightward shift in the AD curve. The vertical shift in the AD curve is in the same proportion as the increase in the money supply. If the money supply doubles, AD′ will be exactly twice as high as AD.

the aggregate demand (AD) curve to the right. Figure 3 shows what happens when the money supply doubles if the initial price is $p_0$. As the AD curve shifts horizontally, the economy moves from point $e_0$ to $e_1$, thereby increasing aggregate demand at the initial price level $p_0$ from $y_0$ to $y_1$. The AD curve will shift to the right for any increase in the money supply as long as a decline in interest rates occurs and is accompanied by increasing investment. The horizontal shift will be larger, the larger the marginal propensity to consume, the greater the fall in interest rates and the greater the sensitivity of investment to interest rates.[2] Example 1 shows that in the recession from 1990 to 1992, the Fed acted vigorously to increase the supply of money and credit.

---

[2]Figure 3 shows that a doubling of prices would allow the economy to stay at $y_0$ when the money supply doubles. Even though money balances have doubled, the doubling of prices leaves real money balances (the supply of money adjusted for inflation) the same as before. People who now hold twice as much money as before may recognize that there has been no real change.

*Increase monetary base = recession*

## EXAMPLE 1
## THE 1990–1992 RECESSION

The period of recession from 1990 to 1992 followed an eight-year period of expansion. Industrial production fell about 5 percent and the unemployment rate rose from about 5.5 percent to about 7.3 percent, making it a mild recession. Figure 6 shows that during 1989, the supply of money grew by only 1 percent; during 1990, it grew by only 4 percent. Some economists might even conjecture that the slow rate of growth in 1989 contributed to the recession.

The Fed's response was very dramatic. The official report of the Fed's open-market meeting of November 13, 1990, stated that "the information reviews at this meeting suggested that economic activity was weakening in the fourth quarter." Without revealing its hand, the report suggested a completely ambiguous policy:

"slightly greater reserve restraint might or somewhat lesser reserve restraint would be acceptable." The Fed then began to increase the monetary base at a very rapid pace. In January 1991 the monetary base grew at an annual rate of over 20 percent! A few months later the rate of monetary growth increased substantially. Over the year from January 1991 to January 1992, the monetary base increased by about 7.4 percent, a larger than average increase. As a consequence, M1 increased by almost 9 percent.

Subsequently, the economy enjoyed robust economic growth with relatively little inflation.

*Caused recession in 1992*

- - - - - - - - - - - - - - - - - - - - - - - - - - - -

*Source: Federal Reserve Bulletin,* February 1991, pp. 102–103.

When the money supply increases, the horizontal shift in the AD curve depends on the sensitivity of interest rates and investment to the money supply and on the marginal propensity to consume. The vertical shift will be in proportion to the change in the money supply.

## IRONING OUT THE BUSINESS CYCLE

In Figure 4, the economy finds itself with deflationary pressures resulting from a rate of unemployment above the natural rate. The aggregate demand (AD) curve intersects the aggregate supply (AS) curve to the left of the natural level of GDP. The self-correcting mechanism will eventually move the economy (through rightward shifts in the AS curve as prices fall) from point $e_0$ at price level $p_0$ to point $e_1$ at the lower price level $p_1$, restoring the economy to full-employment output, $y_n$.

John Maynard Keynes believed that waiting for deflation to solve the problem wasted far too many economic resources. Instead of letting the self-correcting mechanism use deflation to return the economy to the natural level of output (which could be slow and painful), Keynes thought the money supply should be increased immediately. As shown in Figure 4, an appropriate increase in the money supply could shift AD to AD', such that the economy will move along the AS curve to $e_2$. Output would increase from $y_0$ to $y_n$ and the price level would rise from $p_0$ to $p_2$.

In Figure 5, the economy finds itself with inflationary pressures with unemployment falling short of the natural rate. The AD curve intersects the AS curve to the right of the natural level of GDP at point $e_0$. Without monetary policy action, the economy will experience inflation; the self-correcting mechanism will move the economy along the AD curve to point $e_2$ at price level $p_2$. However, if the money supply is simply lowered sufficiently, aggregate demand will fall (the aggregate demand curve will shift to the left, from AD to AD').

A key question in macroeconomics is whether the self-correcting mechanism will remove inflationary pressures (unemployment less than full employment levels) faster than the self-correcting mechanism will remove deflationary pressures (unemployment less than full employment levels). Many

Keynesians (like Keynes himself) believe that the self-correcting mechanism will remove inflationary pressures more quickly than excessive unemployment. The argument is simple: Prices and wages rise more readily than they fall. Hence, Keynesians tend to be more activist with respect to expansionary monetary policy than with respect to contractionary monetary policy.

An important characteristic of such a Keynesian monetary policy is its potential inflationary bias. If money supply increases are used to reduce unemployment and if the self-correcting mechanism is used to reduce inflationary pressures, the money supply will increase in the long run. In this sense, Keynesian monetary policy is said to have an inflationary bias. This characteristic helps explain the strong inflationary nature of the world economy in this century.

## CREDIT RATIONING

In this analysis, monetary policy works primarily through interest rates. When the Fed reduces the money supply, interest rates rise to choke off some investment. However, credit rationing can be used as a subsidiary instrument of monetary policy.

> **Credit rationing** occurs when the demand for loans exceeds the supply of loans. In this situation, some rationing device other than interest rates must be used to ration the scarce supply of credit or loans.

Credit rationing limits investment by making investment funds unavailable to some firms that are prepared to invest at prevailing interest rates. Although credit rationing and a decrease in the money supply generally work in the same direction, there is an important difference. A decrease in the money supply raises the interest rate, and as the interest rate rises, less investment is demanded. Credit rationing operates differently; controls on interest rates prevent them from rising to a new equilibrium when the supply of money is reduced. Firms are discouraged from investing not because of a reduced demand for investment, but because of a reduced availability of

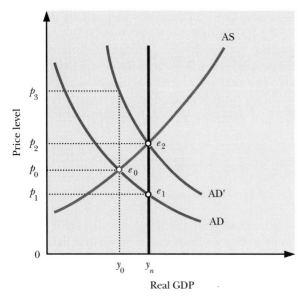

**FIGURE 4  Lowering Unemployment**

The economy is originally in short-run equilibrium at $e_0$, where the AD curve intersects the AS curve. A deflationary gap exists because $y_0$ is less than the natural level of output $y_n$. The self-correcting mechanism would require deflation until the economy reaches $e_1$ on the AD curve. Increasing the money supply sufficiently, however, could shift the AD curve to AD', thereby reducing unemployment to the natural rate.

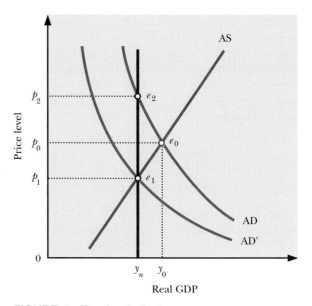

**FIGURE 5  Taming Inflation**

The economy is originally in short-run equilibrium at $e_n$, where the AD curve intersects the AS curve. An inflationary gap exists because $y_0$ exceeds the natural level of output, $y_n$. The self-correcting mechanism would require inflation until the economy reaches $e_2$ on the original AD curve. A sufficient decrease in the money supply, however, can shift the AD curve to AD', thereby reducing inflationary pressures.

loans. Moreover, credit rationing typically tends to be less evenhanded than a decrease in the money supply. Rules as to which customers will be granted credit are often set by the Fed or by the lending institutions themselves.

## THE FED'S MONETARY POLICY: TARGETS AND GOALS

### COUNTERCYCLICAL VERSUS PROCYCLICAL MONETARY POLICY

According to Keynesians, countercyclical monetary policy is preferable to procyclical monetary policy.

A **countercyclical monetary policy** increases aggregate demand when output is falling too much (or when its rate of growth is declining) and reduces aggregate demand when output is rising too rapidly. A **procyclical monetary policy** decreases aggregate demand when output is falling and increases aggregate demand when output is rising.

The countercyclical prescription is clear: If there is a recession, increase the money supply; if there is a boom, reduce the money supply. In an economy where, over time, the resource base and the natural level of real GDP grow, these policy rules translate into changes in the rates of monetary growth. In recessions, the Fed should raise the rate of monetary growth; in booms, the Fed should lower the rate of monetary growth.

Has Fed monetary policy been countercyclical in actuality? Figure 6 shows the yearly rates of growth in the money supply (measured from December of the previous year to December of the indicated year) from 1960 to 1994. We can see from the graph that until recently, the Fed did not pursue a countercyclical monetary policy. The rate of monetary growth passed through various peaks and troughs. If monetary policy were countercyclical, the peaks of monetary growth should correspond to recessions and the troughs of monetary growth should correspond to

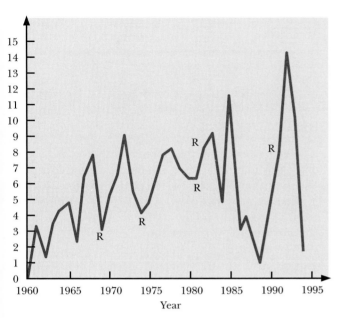

**FIGURE 6    Yearly Growth Rates in M1: 1960–1994**

Yearly growth rates in the money supply (from December of the preceding year to December of the given year) from 1960 to 1984 fluctuated between highs (peaks) and lows (troughs). With the exceptions of 1982 and 1991, years of recession (marked with an R) were accompanied by troughs in the rate of monetary growth. In later years, policy apparently became countercyclical. In 1984, monetary growth was relatively low, yet the economy was booming. *Sources: Economic Report of the President; Federal Reserve Bulletin.*

inflationary gaps. In general, the opposite holds: Monetary policy has been procyclical—troughs of monetary growth correspond to recessions, and peaks of monetary growth correspond to booms.

Each recession (a period in which growth rates in real GDP were either negative or significantly less than average) is marked by an R on the curve. Generally, the recessions occur at the troughs of monetary expansion. Instead of rapid monetary growth that pulls the economy out of a recession, the historical record shows that monetary growth has been slow during the recession stage of the business cycle. The latest recession (1991) shows that the Fed now appears to be following a countercyclical policy.

> Until recently the Fed has followed policies that are procyclical; that is, growth rates of the money supply have decreased in recessions or increased in booms. Recent Fed behavior has been countercyclical.

# THE EFFECTIVENESS OF MONETARY POLICY

## THE LIMITATIONS OF MONETARY POLICY

The old saying, "You can lead a horse to water but you can't make him drink" has been applied to monetary policy. Basically, all the Fed can do to expand the money supply is to make additional monetary reserves available to the banking system. It cannot force banks to lend out these reserves and expand the money supply, nor can it force businesses to increase their investment borrowing when interest rates drop. The use of monetary policy to induce the economy to increase investment can be compared to your pushing on a string. If banks do not loan out additional reserves or if business firms do not invest more when interest rates drop, the monetary authorities are pushing on a string. Monetary authorities may be more effective when they pull on a string. When they wish to contract the money supply, authorities can withdraw reserves and force a contraction of the money supply. If firms do not respond to higher interest rates by investing less, the monetary authorities can always use credit rationing to restrict investment. Example 2 describes the difficulties of the Japanese central bank in the 1990s when interest rates were extremely low, bank lending was weak, and the economy was in a prolonged recession.

The links in the chain connecting the money supply and aggregate demand can be very fragile. A link can break at any point in the chain. If increases in the money supply fail to lower interest rates or if changes in interest rates fail to elicit changes in investment, changes in the money supply will exert no pressure on desired aggregate demand. Moreover, even if the chain is not broken, the effects may be very weak or take some time to occur. Interest rates may respond only weakly to changes in the money supply; investment demand may be very insensitive to changes in interest rates.

## THE PROBLEM OF LAGS

If the monetary authorities can recognize inflationary or deflationary pressures, and if the effects of the change in the money supply take place before the self-correcting mechanism solves the problem, discretionary monetary policy can stabilize the economy. One possible problem with discretionary monetary policy is the recognition lag and the effectiveness lag

## EXAMPLE 2
## THE JAPANESE ECONOMY:
## HOW LOW CAN INTEREST RATES GO?

In 1995, the Japanese economy was still mired in a prolonged recession. Their banks had made bad loans in real estate and were very reluctant to lend new money to businesses. Loan demand was also weak amid pessimistic expectations about the future. The Bank of Japan faced a major hurdle: Interest rates were already at record lows. In August, the discount rate of the Bank of Japan was only 1 percent; the Fed's discount rate was, in comparison, a whopping 5.25 percent. Yet, in September, the Bank of Japan cut its discount rate to only 1/2 of 1 percent. This was the ninth cut in the discount rate since 1991 and the "last monetary card" the Bank of Japan could play to help jumpstart the economy. Corporate borrowers faced a minuscule 1.8 percent prime rate (compared to the U.S. prime rate of 8.75 percent).

Keynes once said that monetary policy was like "pushing on a string." You can lower interest rates, but you can't force people to borrow to finance new investments. When interest rates approach zero, it might appear that they cannot go any lower.

Yet, a cut from 1 percent to 1/2 of 1 percent is a massive cut. It cuts banks' costs of borrowing from the central bank by 50 percent. Whether monetary policy can always be relied upon to pull an economy out of a deep recession is under a severe test in Japan. We shall likely not know the answer until the end of the 1990s.

*Source:* "Japan's Discount-Rate Cut Comes as Mood Darkens," *Wall Street Journal*, September 11, 1995.

---

between a monetary-policy action and its desired effect.

> A **recognition lag** is the time it takes the Fed to decide to change the supply of money in response to a change in economic conditions. An **effectiveness lag** is the time it takes the change in the money supply to affect the economy.

Modern economists, even with extensive data-gathering facilities, can never be sure of current economic conditions. They do not have an accurate estimate of GDP until several months after the fact. Unemployment, industrial production, and inflation data are available more quickly, but they are still a couple of months old, and newly released data are frequently revised after a few more months. Thus, nobody knows for sure what is happening at the current moment. The recognition lag may be about 4 months (as estimated by Robert Gordon). In other words, the Fed may need 4 months to identify excessive inflation or unemployment and to initiate the appropriate technical procedures to expand or contract the money supply.

Estimates of the effectiveness lag vary widely. Robert Gordon estimates the effectiveness lag as short—from 5 to 10 months. Milton Friedman estimates the effectiveness lag as long and variable—from 6 months to 2 years.

The total lag (the sum of the recognition and effectiveness lags), according to Gordon, varies from 9 to 14 months; according to Friedman, the total lag varies from 10 months to more than 2 years. Gordon's estimates are based on recent business-cycle experience; Friedman's estimates are based on averages over nearly a century. It is possible that, as a result of improvements in communication and information, the lags have become shorter in recent years. Time will tell whether the lags are short but variable or long but variable.

If lags are short, an argument for activist monetary policy can be made. With short lags, the monetary authorities have a better chance of adopting the correct countercyclical policy. If a recession develops,

## EXAMPLE 3
## FED POLICY IN THE 1990s:
## SUCCESSFUL FINE TUNING?

Some economists might be inclined to cite Fed policy in 1993–1994 as an example of fine-tuning that worked. Briefly, the U.S. economy was expanding at an annual rate of 4 percent in 1994. The Fed raised interest rates several times during 1994 on the grounds that the economy might overheat, with rising inflation. In 1995, both economic growth and inflation slowed, but unemployment remained low. The fears that the Fed's interest rate hikes would send the economy into a recession were never realized; it appeared by late 1995 that the Fed had success-fully brought about a "soft landing," avoiding both inflation and a deep recession.

It is very difficult to say whether the Fed policy actually worked or was just lucky. As we know from Chapter 1, the fact that two events occur together does not prove that one caused the other. The business cycle is extremely complicated, and Fed policy is only one small component of business fluctuations. Economists will no doubt study the 1990s with the aid of complex computer models in order to determine the role of other factors.

*LMIS CURVE*

a 5-month effectiveness lag means that an expansionary monetary policy will affect the economy 5 months after recognition of the problem. A 2-year lag means that the effects of the policy will occur 2 years after recognition of the problem. By that time, the economy may be in a boom that requires a contraction in the money supply.

Even if lags are short but variable, monetary policy should not try to smooth out every small fluctuation in unemployment. In such a case, the self-correcting mechanism may do its work before the effects of monetary policy can take place. Thus, many economists now believe that policymakers should not try to fine-tune the economy but, rather, should aim at correcting only significant changes in unemployment. Example 3 discusses whether the Fed has been successful at fine-tuning the economy during the 1990s.

## MONETARISM

If lags are long but variable, what monetary policy should be followed? Milton Friedman has argued that the Fed should follow a constant-money-growth rule: The money supply should grow at a fixed percentage (Friedman has usually said 3 percent) per year.

> The **constant-money-growth rule** states that the money supply should increase at a fixed percentage each year.

The justification for the constant-growth-rule is that if the monetary lag varies between 10 months and 28 months, by the time the effects of any monetary policy occur, the original reasons for the policy may have disappeared through the self-correcting mechanism. More likely than not, by the time the policy affects the economy, it may be that the exact opposite of the policy is required. The choice of a constant growth rate (whether it be 2, 3, or 4 percent) depends on the long-term growth of real GDP (which, historically, has averaged about 3 percent per year). Friedman argues that if we knew more about the economy (for example, if we knew the length of the effectiveness lag), we could possibly control the business cycle better, but given present knowledge and the lags involved, an activist monetary policy (and also fiscal policy) may be destabilizing. The nonactivist policy of Milton Friedman and economists such as Karl Brunner and Allan Meltzer is known as monetarism.

> **Monetarism** is the doctrine that monetary policy should follow a constant-money-growth rule.

A monetarist policy must decide which measure of the money supply should be used. The two most frequently discussed alternatives are the monetary

*Equal to real GDP growth*

base (currency plus reserves) and M2 (the broad definition of money). If the Fed tries to control M2, an increase in the demand for M2 will cause the Fed to reduce the monetary base in order to prevent the supply of M2 from increasing too rapidly. This proves difficult in practice because at least in the short-run, the link between the monetary base and M2 is not very tight (as we discussed earlier). As a consequence, under an M2 rule, the monetary base and interest rates will fluctuate with the demand for money. Movements in the monetary base would tend to be countercyclical: In booms, the Fed would reduce the rate of growth of the monetary base, and in recessions, when the demand for money is low, the Fed would increase the rate of growth of the monetary base. Accordingly, an M2 rule will tend to exacerbate fluctuations in the rate of interest.

The authors tend to favor targeting the monetary base. Under this rule, above-normal or below-normal increases in the demand for money will cause the growth rate of M2 to increase or decrease. However, this is an advantage of the rule. M2 includes many items (savings deposits and money market funds) that reflect the public's taste for certain types of monetary assets. If people want to switch from M2 to M1 or vice versa, the Fed does not have to change its policy: The supplies of those types of money will change to accommodate public tastes.

In previous chapters we have documented a fairly close relationship between the supply of money and the price level. The advantage of a monetarist policy is that when the growth of the money supply, however defined, is constrained to, say, the approximate growth of real output, prices should remain relatively stable. (See Example 4.)

How stable should the price level be? Some economists think that the appropriate standard should be zero inflation. The reasons for this objective would be that (1) unemployment tends to the natural rate in even a zero inflation world, and (2) inflation makes comparison shopping more difficult for buyers and sellers. The first point follows from the analysis of the self-adjusting mechanism. The second follows from the fact that inflation complicates the problem of calculating relative prices. For example, outdated information may cause a shopper to think that one store charges more for a given product than another store. According to Mills and Wood:

---

## EXAMPLE 4
## THE LAST OUTPOST OF MONETARISM:
## THE BUNDESBANK

Although other leading industrial countries have dropped monetary targeting, the German central bank, the Deutsche Bundesbank, continues to conduct monetary policy by setting targets for monetary growth. The Bundesbank insists that the growth of the money supply is the most reliable indicator of inflation. The Bundesbank's unrelenting monetarism has been credited for the strength of the German mark—a bastion of stability in financial markets.

The German experience, however, reveals some of the dangers of monetary targeting. The year 1994 saw the Bundesbank unable to control the growth of the money supply due to special factors. Throughout much of the year, the German money supply grew at rates more than double the targeted rate, compounding suspicions that the Bundesbank did not really know what was happening to the money supply.

German banking authorities blame the shock of German reunification, tax changes, and currency market fluctuations for their inability to control the money supply. With German reunification virtually complete, the Bundesbank again will be able to tightly control the growth of the money supply.

------------------------------------------------

*Source:* "If Not Vindicated, Certainly a Little Wiser," *Financial Times,* July 21, 1994.

The step from a barter economy to a monetary one is enormous. Anything which makes money a less efficient conveyor of information about relative prices imposes great efficiency losses. Hence we should seek to stabilize the value of money. That is the only desirable objective of monetary policy.[3]

## NOMINAL INCOME TARGETING

Modern Keynesian economists tend to focus on nominal GDP as the appropriate target of monetary policy. Thus, the Fed should decide on a desired rate of nominal GDP growth—say, 5 percent—and then follow the appropriate policies whenever nominal GDP growth falls short of or exceeds the target. In 1994, nominal GDP growth was 6.7 percent. The Fed, perhaps following this rule, then increased interest rates and reduced the rate of growth of the monetary base.

The advantage of a nominal income target over M2 is that it allows the Fed to adjust its policy to changes in the velocity. An M2 target will correspond to a lower nominal GDP if velocity falls. Therefore, a nominal income target may lend more stability to both output and prices than, say, an M2 target.

Keynesian economists sharply disagree with the objective of zero inflation. They believe that zero inflation may increase unemployment for the sake of an objective that does not seem that important. Keynesians do not think that a mild inflation of several percentage points is anything to worry about. After all, inflation just means higher prices of goods, services, and labor. Higher unemployment, by contrast, usually signifies that average living standards are falling.

## THE INDEPENDENCE OF THE FED

Monetary policy is the responsibility of the Fed. The Fed's power to set money-supply and interest-rate targets is independent of Congress and the executive

branch of the government. Recall from the previous chapter that the Fed does not require financing from Congress; it is self-supporting. Moreover, members of the board of governors have 14-year, nonrenewable terms. The Fed can make decisions that the secretary of the Treasury, the president of the United States, and congressional leaders all oppose. The authors of the 1913 Federal Reserve Act believed that the Fed should be independent of political pressures. Opponents of an independent Fed disagree.

### THE CASE FOR FED INDEPENDENCE

The basic case for independence rests on three observations. First, if the Fed were under the direct control of politicians, it would exhibit a stronger inflationary bias because, it is argued, politicians like to spend money but do not like to tax. With a cooperating Fed, government deficits could be easily financed by money expansion, and inflation would be encouraged. Many countries with high rates of inflation have a central bank that is not independent. Nonelected, relatively anonymous central bankers can more easily adopt antiinflationary policies than can elected officials.

Second, proponents of independence argue that the Fed can carry out long-term plans, whereas politicians can see no further than the next election. There are fears of a so-called "political business cycle" (discussed in a following chapter on the business cycle): Politicians may try to engineer Fed policy to help them get reelected.

Third, supporters of Fed independence argue that the Fed will never go too strongly against the wishes of the electorate because the real independence of the Fed is somewhat constrained by political reality. If the Fed were to get out of hand, Congress would pass legislation reducing the Fed's independence.

### THE CASE AGAINST FED INDEPENDENCE

Critics of Fed independence cite two important arguments. First, independence means that what may be the most important flexible policy tool available to the government lies outside of the hands of the electorate. Even if the public does not like Alan Greenspan (the Fed chairperson appointed by President Reagan in 1987 and reappointed by Presidents Clinton and Bush) or other members of the board

---

[3]Terence Mills and Geoffrey Wood, "Interest Rates and the Conduct of Monetary Policy," in W. Eltis and P. Sinclair, *Keynes and Economic Policy* (London: Macmillan Press, 1988), pp. 246–267.

of governors, it can do nothing. The Fed cannot be thrown out of office like an unpopular, and, perhaps, incompetent politician. Many believe that in a democracy, policy should be sensitive to the wishes of the public.

Second, critics point out that monetary policy and fiscal policy should be coordinated. Under the current system, it is possible for monetary and fiscal policy to work at cross-purposes. For example, let's imagine that there is a large government deficit. The U.S. Treasury may want the Fed to expand the money supply rapidly to stimulate economic growth and thus reduce the deficit through increased tax revenues. If the Fed maintains a low rate of growth of the money supply, the government deficit is likely to increase.

The authors believe, however, that the weight of the evidence suggests that countries with independent central banks have greater stability and lower rates of inflation. Therefore, the United States should be careful before changing the current structure of the Fed.

In the next chapter, we shall examine how fiscal policy and monetary policy can be used to control inflation.

## SUMMARY

1. The Fed has an arsenal of weapons to control the money supply: open-market operations, control of the discount rate, control of the required-reserve ratio, and selective credit controls. By buying government securities, the Fed injects reserves into the system and expands the money supply. By selling government securities, the Fed withdraws reserves, and the money supply contracts. Changing reserve requirements can have a large impact on the money supply because it creates excess reserves when requirements are lowered, and reserve deficiencies when requirements are raised. This tool, however, is seldom used. Changes in the discount rate have a modest effect on bank reserves.

2. The money supply depends on the monetary base, the currency/deposit ratio, and the reserve/deposit ratio. The Fed's short-run control over the money supply is subject to unpredictable changes in the behavior of the public and banks. In the long run, the Fed can take into account changes in these factors.

3. Monetary policy is based on the indirect link between money supply and real GDP. Because bond prices and interest rates move inversely, increases in the money supply (in the short run) lower interest rates. The quantity of investment demanded rises when interest rates fall. In principle, business cycles can be smoothed by changes in the money supply.

4. Keynesians believe that monetary policy should be used actively to remove major deflationary and inflationary gaps. Monetarists believe that lags in the effectiveness of monetary policy imply that a constant-money-growth rule should be used and that activist monetary policy can destabilize the economy. It is believed by some monetarists that this rule could achieve long-run price stability. Keynesian policy normally works through targeting nominal GDP growth.

5. To maintain the efficiency of a monetary economy in conveying relative price information, some monetarists believe that the central bank should simply try to stabilize the price level, an objective that seems to be within the power of the central bank.

6. Defenders of Fed independence stress that being independent reduces the inflationary bias of government policy and allows the Fed to have a longer time horizon than politicians have. An independent Fed can follow politically tough policies. Critics of Fed independence worry about the Fed being irresponsible to the electorate and working at cross-purposes with fiscal policy.

## KEY TERMS

monetary policy
federal funds rate
credit rationing
countercyclical
    monetary policy
procyclical monetary
    policy

recognition lag
effectiveness lag
constant-money-growth
    rule
monetarism

## QUESTIONS AND PROBLEMS

1. Describe briefly how the Fed uses its three major instruments of monetary control.
2. What is the most important instrument of monetary policy and why?

3. Evaluate the validity of the following statement: "The Fed controls the monetary base precisely, but not the money supply."

4. Explain what happens to interest rates if the Fed engages in open-market purchases of government securities.

5. If the newspaper reports, "The bond market is in the doldrums; it has been depressed all week," what is happening to interest rates?

6. Compare the impact on interest rates of a change in the money supply when
   a. The quantity of money demanded is highly responsive to interest rates.
   b. The quantity of money demanded is relatively insensitive to interest rates.

7. How does a change in the money supply increase real GDP?

8. What problems could arise to reduce the impact of a change in the money supply on real GDP?

9. True or false: Monetarists believe inflation can be ignored.

10. Discuss why monetarists might not accept the Keynesian policy of targeting nominal GDP growth.

11. How do lags in the effectiveness of monetary policy affect the design of a good monetary policy?

12. What are the arguments for targeting the price level as the only reasonable objective of monetary policy?

13. How can Fed independence reduce inflation?

14. How can Fed independence result in poor monetary policies?

# CHAPTER 31

# FISCAL POLICY, DEBT, AND DEFICITS

We have identified the Great Depression as one of the Defining Moments of economics (Chapter 1); it imposed a sense of foreboding on several generations, who have feared that it could happen again. The Great Depression had an enormous impact on government economic policy. It promoted the idea of John Maynard Keynes that the government must protect us against depressions, and it caused a vast shift in policymaking and public opinion about government deficits.

Although there is debate as to exactly when policymakers changed their view of deficits, some scholars date this event to 1938.[1] In 1936, Franklin D. Roosevelt won a landslide reelection. Although the economy had begun a slow recovery from depression lows in 1933, Roosevelt was shocked by a recession that began in the fall of 1937. Was this to be a repeat of the Great Depression?

Roosevelt was barraged by conflicting advice from all sides as he considered what to do about the recession. His sober-minded secretary of the Treasury advised that he should balance the budget to restore business confidence. The chairman of the Fed and Roosevelt's closest advisor, Harry Hopkins, argued for deficit spending not just for relief assistance but for the deliberate purpose of macroeconomic stimulus that he believed the private sector could not provide.

The deficit spenders carried the day: In 1938 Roosevelt submitted a budget that, for the first time, consciously embraced a deficit for the purpose of macroeconomic stimulation. Deficit spending to stimulate an ailing economy was the recipe in Keynes's 1936 *General Theory*. Americans have had deficit spending since.

The notion that deficit spending was required to keep the economy out of recession became even

---

[1]Alan Brinkley, *The End of Reform: New Deal Liberalism in Recession and War* (New York: Alfred A. Knopf, 1995).

more deeply entrenched after World War II—so entrenched that it came to be called the Keynesian Revolution. The actions of Roosevelt's New Dealers in 1938 and the impact of Keynes's writings of 1936 established the notion that government spending is "good"—that we have to worry that private spending may not be enough. Americans have been taught that if defense spending is cut or if the federal budget is balanced, the economy may go into a tailspin that can only be corrected by increased government spending.

This type of thinking was evident in the 1996 debate concerning the balanced budget amendment in Congress. Critics of the amendment warned of the potential catastrophes associated with reduced government spending. Proponents argued that continued deficits could ruin the economy.

## FISCAL POLICY, BUDGETS, AND DEFICITS

The government is a major player in the economy whether we like it or not. It accounts for a substantial portion of all spending for goods and services. By collecting taxes, it affects the way individuals and businesses behave; by deciding what types of goods to supply and how to distribute transfer payments, it affects the way income is distributed. By borrowing in credit markets, the government can affect interest rates and the terms for credit throughout the world economy. Government carries out all these activities through fiscal policy.

> **Fiscal policy** is the way in which the government provides for and carries out government expenditures.

Through its fiscal-policy decisions concerning taxation and government spending, the government can use fiscal policy to affect economic performance measures such as output, employment, unemployment, and inflation.

Governments engage in two types of spending activity: purchases of goods and services, and government transfer payments.

> The **government budget** (B) is the sum of government spending on goods and services, and government transfers including interest payments on government debt.

In order to purchase goods and services, make transfer payments, and pay interest payments, the government must raise funds. Governments have three options for raising funds for their spending programs. First, the government can collect taxes from households and businesses. If the government cannot raise sufficient funds through taxation (T), it can borrow funds from others (DEF) or it can print money. Governments typically borrow funds by selling bonds, on which they must pay interest and repay the principal.

Private citizens and businesses can also borrow money, but unlike the government they cannot print money. At little or no cost, the government can pay its bills by printing money. With the printed money, it can acquire valuable goods and services and make transfer payments. In doing so, however, governments run the risk of printing too much money and creating too much inflation.

In this chapter, we shall discuss primarily the first two options for raising funds for the government budget—taxation and the selling of bonds. In this case, the government budget equals the sum of taxes plus the amount of government debt sold:

$$B = T + DEF$$

The term DEF stands for government deficit because that amount of the government budget not covered by taxation equals the deficit, which is financed by the selling of government debt.

Figure 1 summarizes the 1996 budget of the United States. It shows that the government raises most of its funds from income taxes and social security contributions. Most of its expenditures constitute transfer payments, including interest on its debt.

## MEASURING THE DEFICIT

The difference between the total revenues and total outlays of a government unit is either a *government deficit* or a *government surplus.*

> A **government deficit** is an excess of total government spending over total revenues.
>
> A **government surplus** is an excess of total government revenues over total spending.

If government revenues from taxes and fees equal government expenditures, the government has a balanced budget.

Although the measurement of government deficits appears straightforward, in fact, many ambiguities are involved.

The government of the United States consists of agencies and departments that make and execute government policy, such as the Department of Justice, the Environmental Protection Agency, and the State Department. They earn no revenues; they are not run as businesses. Other government agencies do act like businesses; they make investments in other countries (the Overseas Private Investment Corporation, or OPIC), manage the nation's banking system (the Federal Reserve), insure deposits in banks (the Federal Deposit Insurance Corporation, or FDIC), and manage the revenues and expenditures of the Social Security System (the Social Security Administration, or SSA).

The expenditures of the Department of Justice, the State Department, and so on clearly belong in the federal budget. The expenditures of the other type of agency, such as OPIC, FDIC, and SSA, can be placed *off-budget*—or removed from the federal budget—on the grounds that they generate their own revenues and have their own expenses and that they are able to generate a profit or at least cover their costs in the same way that private businesses can. Often, such agencies contribute part or all of their profits to the federal budget. Their losses (if they make losses) are typically covered by government borrowing.

Therefore, the size of the federal deficit depends on which agencies are reported in the budget "on-budget" and which agencies are "off-budget." If an agency that is suffering substantial losses is kept off-budget, as the FDIC was in the 1980s and early 1990s, the actual budget deficit may be understated insofar as the federal government is ultimately responsible for these losses. (See Example 1.) The calculated federal deficit very much depends upon which government activities are included in the budget and which activities are kept off-budget.

If the federal government were a private business, its accountants would distinguish between current expenditures and capital expenditures.

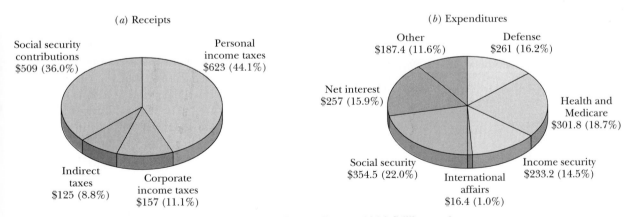

**FIGURE 1  Federal Government Receipts and Expenditures 1996 (billions of dollars)**

Panel (*a*) shows that federal government receipts are dominated by personal income taxes and contributions to social security. Panel (*b*) shows that federal government expenditures are dominated by expenditures on social security, income security, and health and medicare. Defense and interest on the national debt both equal about 16 percent of the total.

## EXAMPLE 1
## SMOKE AND MIRRORS:
## THE S&L BAILOUT COVERUP

Politicians can reduce the federal deficit by cutting spending, raising taxes, or by using "smoke and mirrors" to make the deficit appear smaller. Consider the government bailout of the Federal Savings and Loan Insurance Corporation (FSLIC) in the late 1980s. A federally insured insurance fund, FSLIC was intended to cover savings and loan failures; the fund was fed by contributions of member S&Ls. If the fund was not sufficient to bail out failing S&Ls, the federal government would have to make up the difference.

As more and more S&Ls failed in the 1970s and 1980s, the FSLIC fund could not cover the losses of depositors, and the federal government had to make up the difference. Originally, FSLIC losses were projected at $25 billion; Congress wished to keep this loss off the federal deficit even though the federal government had to pay the $25 billion.

Rather than admit that the S&L rescue operation was costing the taxpayers $25 billion, Congress used "smoke and mirrors" to put FSLIC losses "off-budget." A quasi-private corporation,

FICO, was created and borrowed what FSLIC needed to meet its obligations. In theory, FICO was to be run as a private company and pay back its borrowings like any other business. As FSLIC losses rose well above the $25 billion that FICO had borrowed, the federal government created yet another entity, the Resolution Trust Corporation, which borrowed an even greater amount to cover FSLIC losses.

By the time the FSLIC rescue operation was completed, the government had spent more than $200 billion, most of which had been kept off-budget.

If you do not understand this scheme, you are not alone. In fact, the whole scheme was designed to confuse the public as to the actual size of the deficit—a classic use of smoke and mirrors.

--------------------------------------------

*Source:* Laurence Kotlikoff, *Generational Accounting: Knowing Who Pays, and When, for What We Spend* (New York: The Free Press, 1993), pp. 14–16.

---

**Current expenditures** of government are expenditures for payrolls, materials, transportation, interest, and other current outlays.

**Capital expenditures** of government are expenditures for buildings, roads, ports, and other government capital outlays.

Private businesses depreciate capital expenditures over the life of the capital item. If a new $40 million plant is expected to last 20 years, the private business might depreciate its capital expenditure over a 20-year period at $2 million per year. The private business's deficit—its loss—would therefore be measured as revenues minus the sum of current expenditures and annual depreciation, not as revenues minus the sum of current expenditures and capital expenditures.

The federal government's accounts are handled differently from the accounts of a private enterprise. The federal deficit is calculated as federal revenues minus the sum of current expenditures and capital expenditures. If the federal government's accounts were handled like those of a private company, its deficit would be much smaller, or perhaps would even be a surplus.

### GENERATIONAL ACCOUNTING

Some economists argue that budget deficits cannot be accurately measured. The deficit depends upon what items are placed off-budget, and there is uncertainty about how to handle capital expenditures by government. Critics argue in favor of a different budget concept, called generational accounting.

**Generational accounting** shows government deficits in terms of each generation's net lifetime tax payments or the difference between that generation's expected tax payments and its expected lifetime benefits from government, such as social security benefits.

Generational accounts offer three advantages over conventional deficit accounting. First, as explained earlier, conventional deficit accounting can be arbitrary; its results can be arbitrarily changed by using "smoke and mirrors" to conceal the size of the deficit. For example, the size of the deficit depends materially on whether social security or the costs of the S&L bailout are on-budget or off-budget items.

Second, conventional deficit accounting does not provide us, as consumers and taxpayers, the information we need to make informed decisions. We need to know how much taxes we can expect to pay in the future and how much we can expect to receive from the government in return for these taxes. If we knew, for example, that each of us will have to pay $200,000 more in taxes over our lifetimes than we will receive in benefits, we might well make spending and saving decisions different from those we make in ignorance of such information.

Third, conventional deficit accounting does not tell us the generational consequences of government spending and taxation decisions. We do not know who will pay the taxes and when, and who will receive government benefits and when. We do not know whether different generations will have different tax burdens as a result of current government spending and taxation decisions.

Example 2 shows a generational account based upon each generation's age in 1989. These calculations use tax rates, social security rules, and entitlement rules in effect for that year. The bottom-line figure in a generational account is the *net tax payment* of each age group.

The **net tax payment** in a generational account is the difference between the present value of the cumulative lifetime tax payments and the cumulative value of benefits to be received from the government for each age group.

The net tax payment of 30-year-old males is $195,000, which indicates that the typical 30-year-old male will pay approximately $200,000 more in

taxes than he will receive in benefits. The 30-year-old female will pay almost $90,000 more in taxes than she will receive in benefits.

Older Americans (men over 65 and women over 60) are net beneficiaries of the present tax system. They will receive more from government than they will pay to government over their remaining lifetimes. Seventy-year-old males will receive $43,000 more in benefits than they have paid in taxes. Younger Americans, on the other hand, will pay much more to government than they can expect to receive over their remaining lifetimes.

> Generational accounts show that our current system of taxation and transfers results in an intergenerational transfer of resources from younger to older generations.

Generational accounting allows policymakers to make informed decisions. Do we wish to make these large transfers among generations or are they unacceptable? These issues are among the most important social issues of the last few years of the twentieth century.

## DEBT AND DEFICITS

Debt and deficits are intimately related. The $4 trillion federal debt of the United States is the consequence of over 40 years of deficits.

### LIMITS ON DEFICITS

Government debt is a consequence of past deficits and surpluses.

The **federal debt** is the cumulated sum of past deficits and surplus of the federal government.

If we let DEBT stand for the federal debt, then the deficit (DEF) in year $t$ equals the debt in year $t$ minus the debt in year $t - 1$, or

$$\text{DEF}(t) = \text{DEBT}(t) - \text{DEBT}(t - 1) \qquad (1)$$

The deficit in year $t$ equals government spending for items other than interest on the debt (B') plus interest payments on the debt that equal $r \times \text{DEBT}(t - 1)$ (where $r$ stands for the interest rate on government debt), minus government revenues (T). Therefore, from (1), we get:

$$\text{DEBT}(t) = (\text{B}' - \text{T}) + (1 + r)\,\text{DEBT}(t - 1)$$
$$(2)$$

# EXAMPLE 2
## GENERATIONAL ACCOUNTS
## AND THE FEDERAL BUDGET

The Congressional Budget Office has developed "generational accounts" including federal, state, and local government debt, which give the average net-payment burden on members of all future generations if the government debt is eventually to be paid off.

The accompanying chart depicts these amounts for selected generations as of 1989. Note that older generations are expected to be net recipients, since they pay low taxes but receive substantial Social Security and Medicare benefits. Younger generations will likely pay more than they receive because of their greater income, payroll, and sales taxes. Men aged 30 in

1989 can expect to pay out almost $200,000 more in taxes than they receive in benefits.

------------------------------------------------

*Source:* Federal Reserve Bank of Cleveland, *Economic Trends,* January 1992; Congressional Budget Office, *Budget of the United States Government,* fiscal year 1992.

*Explanation:* The net payment is the present value of the difference between lifetime tax payments and lifetime benefits. A negative number shows that lifetime benefits exceed lifetime tax payments. The net payments of males exceed those of females because of different patterns of lifetime earnings and the longer lifespans of women.

*Source:* Laurence Kotlikoff, *Generational Accounting: Knowing Who Pays and When, for What We Spend* (New York: The Free Press, 1993), pp. 116–119.

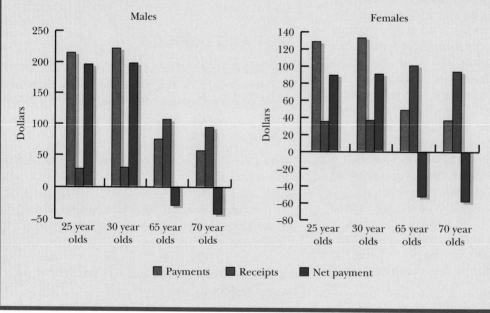

This equation indicates that even if the government balances its primary deficit, denoted above as B′ − T, its debt will grow at a growth rate equal to the interest rate.

The **primary deficit** is the government deficit not including interest payments on the government debt.

If the government incurs primary deficits, the debt will grow at a rate higher than the interest rate.

It is easy to see that government cannot continue to run deficits indefinitely if the interest rate exceeds the growth rate of GDP. If, for example, the interest rate were 6 percent and the debt grew at this rate, and real GDP grew at 3 percent per annum, eventually the interest payments on the debt would exceed

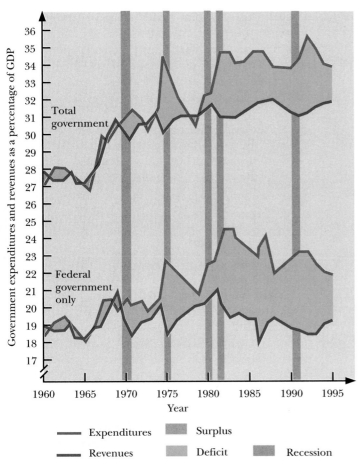

FIGURE 2    Government Expenditures, Revenues, and
Deficits as a Percentage of GDP

This figure shows that, since 1960, deficits tend to be associated
with recessions. During recessions, government revenues fall while
expenditures rise. The late 1960s (the Vietnam years) were an exception to this rule. *Source: Economic Report of the President.*

GDP—an impossible situation. If the government
were running a primary deficit, the debt would grow
even faster relative to real GDP.

The federal debt as a percentage of GDP declined
from 129 percent in 1946 to lows of around 40 percent in the 1970s. Thereafter, the debt began to grow
as a percentage of GDP. The high debt to GDP ratios
were the result of wartime borrowing from World
War II.

This experience shows that we can reduce the
federal debt as a percentage of GDP within a brief
period of time without economic calamity. Debt as a
percentage of GDP fell from 129 percent in 1946 to
70 percent in 1953. This occurred because the debt
remained about the same over this period while nom-

inal GDP increased by 75 percent, and real GDP increased by 33 percent.

Figure 2 shows that deficits as a percentage of
GDP have risen gradually from less than 1 percent in
the 1960s to about 3 percent in the 1970s, 3.5 percent in the 1980s, and 4 percent in the 1990s.
Deficits are therefore not limited to a particular political party or administration.

The deficits of the earlier years (1946 to 1965)
were accompanied by low interest rates (1 percent to
4 percent). The deficits of later years (1965 to present) were accompanied by higher interest rates (5
percent to 12 percent). If, as the formula suggests, the
debt will grow at the rate of interest in the absence of
primary deficits, the growth of debt would be lower

when interest rates were low. The combination of high interest rates and large primary deficits after 1965 made the debt grow faster, explaining the rising share of deficits and debt over the past 20 years as shown in figure 2.

## RICARDO EQUIVALENCE

The U.S. government cannot run primary deficits forever. If it did, interest on the debt would become too large a share of GDP. At some point the government would have to run primary surpluses large enough to keep the growth of the debt less than the growth of GDP. Primary surpluses, of course, mean that government spending for items other than interest payments would have to be less than tax revenues. If the government must eventually run surpluses, what effect would this knowledge have upon our behavior as consumers?

A theorem initially formulated by David Ricardo (one of the Defining Moment economists of Chapter 1), argues that people are not stupid with respect to government deficits. We can put 2 and 2 together, and we understand that higher deficits today mean more taxes tomorrow. More taxes tomorrow mean that we must have more savings tomorrow in order to pay our taxes.

The conclusion of the Ricardo equivalence theorem, therefore, is that deficits today will depress consumption today and encourage current savings to prepare for the higher taxes of the future. Accordingly, the higher deficit spending of government may be offset by lower consumption. The Ricardo theorem is contrary to the deficit spending notion that higher deficits mean more total spending for the economy; with Ricardo equivalence lower private spending can offset higher government spending.

## AUTOMATIC STABILIZERS AND DISCRETIONARY FISCAL POLICY

Government deficits and surpluses are determined by how our government conducts fiscal policy. If government spends more than its revenues, it adds to the debt. If it spends less than its revenues, it lowers the debt.

Keynes taught that we should use fiscal policy to achieve macroeconomic goals, like full employment or price stability. He argued that at times we need to deliberately spend more than our revenues to combat

a declining economy and rising unemployment. Whether the result is intended or not, government spending and taxation affect macroeconomic outcomes. Two types of government spending and tax policies contribute to this effect: automatic stabilizers and discretionary fiscal policies.

> **Automatic stabilizers** are government spending or taxation actions that take place without any deliberate government policy decisions. They automatically dampen the business cycle.
>
> **Discretionary fiscal policies** are government spending and taxation actions that have been deliberately chosen to achieve macroeconomic goals.

Many actions mandated by fiscal policy take place automatically and require no policy decisions on the part of government—as in the case of an entitlement program, such as Social Security or unemployment compensation payments.

> An **entitlement program** requires the government to pay benefits to anyone who meets eligibility requirements.

To receive entitlement payments, recipients need only demonstrate that they qualify. Once the rules are set, the government does not set the magnitude of such payments: They depend on general economic conditions. Currently, 75 percent of all federal outlays are those for relatively uncontrollable items like entitlements, permanent appropriations, and interest on the national debt. Similarly, once income tax rates and rules are set, tax revenues also depend on economic conditions.

## AUTOMATIC STABILIZERS

The income tax system and unemployment compensation and welfare programs automatically move taxes and spending *against* the current of the business cycle. These automatic stabilizers depend upon prevailing economic conditions and require no discretionary action by policymakers.

**Income Taxes as Automatic Stabilizers.**    The income taxes a government collects are the product of the average tax rate times the economy's taxable income. If an economy has an average tax rate of 20 percent and a taxable income of $100 billion, the government collects $20 billion in income taxes. If taxable income rises to $150 billion, the government collects $30 billion. Income taxes automatically rise and fall with income.

If the economy goes into a recession, personal incomes fall and tax receipts fall. Let's take as an example a family with a taxable income of $100,000, paying a tax rate of 34 percent. After paying $34,000 in taxes, it has $66,000 of income to spend. If its income falls by $20,000 as a result of the general decline in business activity, its tax bill falls to $27,200, and it has $52,800 to spend after taxes. Its after-tax income has fallen by $13,200, not by the full $20,000 reduction in income. If as a result of the drop in income the family moves into a lower tax bracket (say, 30 percent), the decline in after-tax income will be even less. Because the income tax dampens after-tax changes in income, it is considered an automatic stabilizer.

### Unemployment Compensation and Welfare Payments.
When an economy moves into recession, more people are unemployed and eligible for unemployment entitlement benefits. More families become eligible for welfare assistance. Unemployment compensation and increased welfare payments limit the decline in consumption expenditures by replacing some of the income lost.

Government spending tends to rise automatically during recessions as more people become eligible for entitlement programs. Taxes fall during recessions as income falls.

## DISCRETIONARY FISCAL POLICY

Despite the preponderance of relatively uncontrollable items, the government can raise or lower revenues and outlays through deliberate, discretionary decision making—for example, by changing the rules of eligibility for entitlement programs, raising or lowering income tax rates, or initiating major new defense expenditures or public-works programs.

Proponents of policy activism believe that discretionary actions should be taken to eliminate or soften the effects of the business cycle.

**Policy activism** is the deliberate use of discretionary fiscal or monetary policy to achieve macroeconomic goals.

The proponents of activist (discretionary) fiscal policies believe that macroeconomic policy should go beyond automatic stabilizers. They believe that better macroeconomic results can be achieved if policymakers use fiscal policy to eliminate inflationary and deflationary gaps.

Figure 3 illustrates how fiscal policy could be used to close inflationary or deflationary gaps. Panel (*a*) shows an economy in a deflationary gap; the intersection of the aggregate demand (AD) and short-run aggregate supply (AS) curves occurs below the natural level of output. If government spending and taxes could be changed to raise aggregate demand, the deflationary gap would disappear. The increase in aggregate demand raises both output and prices. A fiscal policy that increases aggregate demand is called an expansionary fiscal policy.

An **expansionary fiscal policy** increases aggregate demand by raising government spending and/or by lowering tax rates.

Panel (*b*) illustrates the use of contractionary fiscal policy to eliminate an inflationary gap. In this case, fiscal policy aims to lower aggregate demand sufficiently to achieve a lower equilibrium output.

A **contractionary fiscal policy** lowers aggregate demand by lowering government spending or by raising tax rates.

According to policy activists, if an inflationary gap is present, government should cut government spending or raise tax rates. If a deflationary gap is present, the government should raise spending or cut tax rates to raise output. If government spending and tax-rate actions are properly timed and of the correct magnitude, activist policies will cause inflationary or deflationary gaps to disappear.

Fiscal policymakers have a number of instruments: In the case of a deflationary gap, the government could raise its expenditures above the increases dictated by the automatic stabilizers (such as unemployment compensation and welfare programs). Additional funds could be spent on dams, national defense, public parks, or increased police protection;

(a) Expansionary Fiscal Policy for a Deflationary Gap

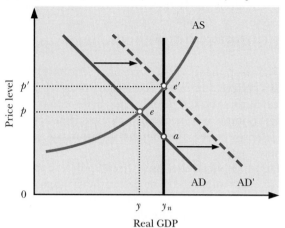

(b) Contractionary Fiscal Policy for an Inflationary Gap

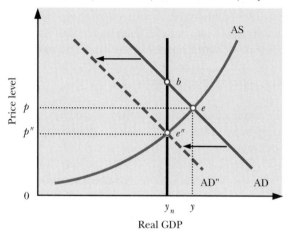

**FIGURE 3    Fiscal Policy with Deflationary and Inflationary Gaps**

Panel (a) shows how expansionary fiscal policy could be used to eliminate a deflationary gap. By an increase in autonomous government spending or an autonomous reduction in taxes, the aggregate demand curve could be shifted to the right (from AD to AD'), restoring the economy to the natural rate of output, $y_n$. Panel (b) shows how contractionary fiscal policy could be used to eliminate an inflationary gap. By a reduction in autonomous government spending or an autonomous increase in taxes, the aggregate demand curve could be shifted to the left (from AD to AD") to restore the economy to the natural rate of output.

unemployment compensation rules could be liberalized and eligibility requirements for welfare lowered.

> Activist fiscal policy operates through **autonomous changes** in tax rates and government spending that are independent of changes in income.

# THE EFFECTIVENESS OF FISCAL POLICY

The aim of discretionary fiscal policy is to eliminate inflationary or deflationary gaps quickly. Critics of discretionary fiscal policy believe that (1) fiscal policy is too slow-moving, cumbersome, and often counter-productive; (2) the effects of fiscal policies (especially tax policies) on aggregate demand are uncertain and in some cases negligible; (3) increased government spending may crowd out private investment.

## LAGS IN FISCAL POLICY

Changes in taxation and government spending must be approved by Congress and supported by the president; they often take several years or more from inception to enactment. Public-works programs must be approved by Congress and are often handled on a case-by-case basis. Lacking line-item veto authority until 1996, the president had to either accept or veto budgets forwarded by Congress.

The lags that impede fiscal policy fall into three categories. First, Congress and the president may be slow to recognize the need for a change in fiscal policy. Reliable statistics on real GDP become available only six months after the fact. No one is certain whether a downturn is transitory or the start of a serious recession. It is therefore difficult to recognize when a change in fiscal policy is required. This *recognition lag* makes fiscal policy difficult to initiate on a timely basis.

Second, fiscal policy is subject to an *implementation lag*—by the time the program goes through Congress and is implemented, the policy may no longer be the correct one. By the time a tax cut has been passed, a tax increase might be more appropriate. (See Figure 4 on the budget process.)

Third, the *effectiveness lag* is the amount of time it takes between implementation of a fiscal policy action and an actual change in economic conditions. Statistical evidence on the length of the effectiveness lag is mixed, but it appears to be long. Critics of activist fiscal policy question whether we can carry out effective activist fiscal policy when substantial time lags and political delays are involved.

## PERMANENT INCOME

The effects of discretionary tax policy can be reduced by permanent-income effects. Economists such as

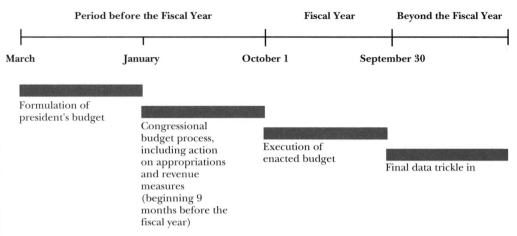

FIGURE 4    The Federal Budget Process

A minimum lead time of 20 months is required between the planning and execution of the federal budget. This lag makes it difficult to conduct discretionary fiscal policy. Final data trickle in throughout the following year; that is, final GDP data are in 9 months after the year ends.

Nobel laureates Franco Modigliani and Milton Friedman argue that we tend to base our consumption decisions on permanent income, not on transitory changes in current income.

> **Permanent income** is an average of the income that an individual anticipates earning over the long run.

A transitory change in this year's income—for instance, resulting from a temporary tax increase—will have a minimal effect on current consumption. The impact of the tax on long-run income is so small that few people will change their current consumption.

When we base our spending on permanent income, the relationship between this year's income and this year's consumption can be quite unstable. With its effects on private spending unknown, discretionary tax policy is therefore difficult to pursue.

## CROWDING OUT

An increase in government spending may crowd out private investment by pushing up interest rates. Because the amount of crowding out is hard to anticipate, the exact effects of a fiscal stimulus are difficult to predict.

Government spending can crowd out private spending. For example, increased government expenditures on health care, education, police protection, roads, and parks could directly reduce some private expenditure. Thus, when the government purchases and provides goods at a low cost as substitutes for private goods, some private expenditures will be crowded out.

> **Direct crowding out** occurs when an increase in government spending substitutes for private spending by providing similar goods.

If direct crowding out is complete, there is no increase in aggregate expenditures when government spending increases. With complete crowding out, the increase in government spending causes an equal decrease in private spending.

Figure 5 illustrates the effects of crowding out. It shows an increase in aggregate demand caused by an increase in government spending that crowds out private spending.

Can fiscal policy be used to control the business cycle? There is now widespread agreement that fiscal policy is too slow-moving and too unpredictable to be used effectively against the business cycle. Instead, economists now believe that fiscal policy should be used to create a climate for economic growth. Policymakers should focus on tax laws to ensure that they encourage capital formation, private saving, risk-taking, and business formation.

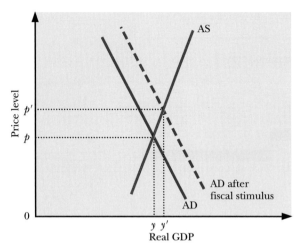

**FIGURE 5   Fiscal Policy and Crowding Out**

In response to fiscal stimulus (more government spending or lower taxes), aggregate demand increases; with a steep-sloped short-run aggregate supply curve, the price level is pushed up, and interest rates may rise. These changes reduce consumer spending and business investment, and thereby limit the increase in real GDP. If increased government spending *directly* causes less consumer spending, the initial shift in AD will be even less and real GDP will increase even less.

## DEFICITS AND THE BUSINESS CYCLE

During periods of declining real GDP, the government deficit tends to grow. As income falls, tax revenues fall, but government obligations—in the form of unemployment compensation payments and welfare transfers—rise.

> Rising expenditures and falling taxes automatically push the government budget in the direction of higher deficits during recessions.

Federal government deficits are shown by the red line in Figure 6. During recessionary periods, the deficit widens; it narrows during the recovery period. Prosperity brings rising tax revenues and declining transfer payments. Recessions bring falling tax payments and rising transfer payments. Because the deficit is partially induced by the business cycle, it is useful to distinguish between the cyclical deficit and the structural deficit.

> The **cyclical deficit** is the part of the deficit caused by movements in the business cycle.

> The **structural deficit** is the deficit that would occur even if the economy were operating continuously at the natural level of real GDP.

The effects of the business cycle can be separated from structural factors by comparing the actual deficit with the structural deficit, illustrated by the green line in Figure 6.

To understand how the cyclical and structural deficits are calculated, let's assume that the natural rate of unemployment is 5.5 percent and the economy has 8 percent unemployment. Because the economy is 2.5 percent below full employment, the government must make more payments for welfare and unemployment compensation, and it collects fewer tax dollars than it would at full employment. The actual budget deficit (actual revenues minus actual expenditures) is $40 billion; however, at full employment, revenues would have been $15 billion more and expenditures would have been $10 billion less. The structural deficit is therefore $15 billion (= $40 − $15 − $10)—considerably less than the actual deficit.

Because the effects of the cyclical deficit have been removed, the structural budget reveals the direction of activist (discretionary) fiscal policy. When the deficit is calculated as if the economy were steadily operating at the natural rate, changes in that deficit are caused by discretionary changes in government spending, eligibility requirements for entitlements, and tax rates. Fiscal policy is more expansionary when the structural deficit is rising.

## COMPETING BUDGET POLICIES

Economists are divided on budget policy. Some view budget deficits as necessary to prevent recessions. Others view the inability to control deficit spending with great alarm.

### KEYNESIAN BUDGET POLICY

The proponents of activist fiscal policy maintain that government expenditures and taxes should be chosen to induce the economy to produce at full employment. If budget deficits are required to raise output to full employment, this is a small price to be paid for full employment. The size of the government deficit

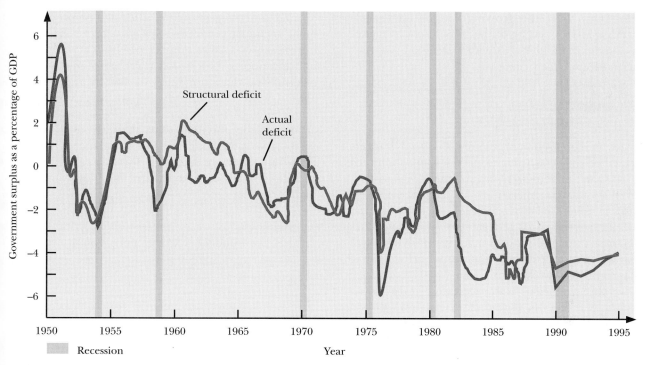

**FIGURE 6   The Actual Budget Versus the Structural Budget of the United States**

The red line shows the actual federal government surplus or deficit for the period 1950 to 1995. The green line gives the structural surplus or deficit for the same years. The structural budget should reveal changes in discretionary fiscal policy over this period. The shaded bars are periods of recession. *Source:* Robert J. Gordon, *Macroeconomics,* 6th ed. (New York: HarperCollins, 1990), Appendix A. Updated by authors.

is not critical in any one year. The budget deficit should not be allowed to stand in the way of more important macroeconomic goals, such as full employment.

According to this Keynesian budgetary philosophy, it would be very unwise to adopt the goal of a balanced federal budget. If the economy is experiencing a cyclical downturn that reduces output below full employment, tax revenues decline along with output. Therefore, to balance the budget, government expenditures must be reduced by the amount of the fall in tax collections. To pursue a balanced budget during a cyclical downturn would only make matters worse.

In the early 1960s, economists and public officials almost unanimously embraced the Keynesian budgetary philosophy. Balanced budgets per se were no longer regarded as desirable. The decline in popularity of the balanced-budget philosophy signaled an important triumph for the Keynesian revolution.

In 1964, taxes were cut, and the deficit was deliberately increased to reduce unemployment.

Keynes did not advocate sustained deficits. Instead he advocated a cyclically balanced budget.

> A **cyclically balanced budget** is one in which deficits during downturns are offset by surpluses during cyclical upturns.

According to the Keynesian budget philosophy, periods of excessive unemployment required budget deficits, but budget surpluses were required during inflationary upswings. Therefore, although there was no rule that the budget should be balanced each year, Keynes expected that budget surpluses and deficits would even out in the long run—especially because cyclical upturns last longer than cyclical downturns.

As Figure 6 shows, cyclically balanced budgets have not materialized. Since 1960, the federal budget has had only one year of surplus. In recent years, public alarm over the growing size of the federal deficit has grown, setting off bitter political struggles, especially in the mid 1990s with a Democratic president and Republican Congress.

## THE CLASSICAL CASE
## FOR A BALANCED BUDGET

The Keynesian argument against balanced budgets represented a departure from the philosophy of the classical economists. If, as they maintained, economies tend to operate at full employment, increases in government expenditures do not raise real GDP. Rather, increased government spending pushes up interest rates and reduces investment. Every extra dollar of government spending would crowd out a dollar in private investment.

In the classical view, increased government spending will occur at the expense of investment and long-run economic growth. Lower rates of investment mean lower rates of economic growth. Higher government deficits mean lower standards of living. In the Keynesian model, deficits can raise output and living standards when applied to an economy with considerable unemployed resources. The classical economists, therefore, would argue that deficits provide no benefits in terms of reduced unemployment. They are costly in that they reduce private capital formation.

> The classical case against budget deficits is that government spending crowds out investment spending and hence, lowers economic growth.

## THE PUBLIC CHOICE CASE
## FOR A BALANCED BUDGET

Nobel laureates James Buchanan and Milton Friedman advocate a balanced budget. Balanced-budget advocates support an amendment to the U.S. Constitution requiring a balanced budget. Such a proposal was narrowly defeated in Congress in 1995, falling a few votes short of the two-thirds vote required for passage. Modern advocates of a balanced budget share the fear that government deficits will crowd out private investment, but they are primarily concerned that elected politicians will not be able to limit government spending to socially necessary programs. Rational politicians know that spending programs that aid special-interest groups bring in votes. The

average voter is generally ill-informed about government spending programs. Special-interest legislation hurts each of a large number of voters in only a minor and poorly understood way; logrolling and vote trading are therefore facts of life in the political arena. With the bias toward spending, balanced-budget advocates fear that borrowing to pay for government programs will offer the easy way out for politicians. If the budget had to be balanced, the public would be more likely to want less government spending because of their unwillingness to accept higher taxes.

> Public-choice economists argue that a balanced-budget requirement would limit government spending to socially necessary programs.

This is called the public-choice approach because it studies the way politicians and bureaucrats make decisions on how to raise and spend public funds.

We know from Chapter 5 that in many economic, social, or political situations the players face a prisoners' dilemma. Recall that a prisoners' dilemma is a situation in which cooperation has benefits, but each player can gain more by being noncooperative. The same principle applies to the government deficit. If all politicians could agree to cut spending, they would be better off because the public would be happy with a balanced budget, increasing the chances of the average politician's being reelected. However—and this is the prisoners' dilemma—each politician can increase his or her chance of being reelected by voting for more spending for his or her own constituents. Thus, spending cuts are unlikely, although they would be supported by the vast majority of politicians if they could agree to cooperate.

## THE DEBT MONSTER:
## REALITY AND MYTHS

We Americans fear the deficit for real and imagined reasons. Public opinion polls reveal that we are as worried about deficits and debt as about crime and education. This concern was a major issue in the congressional elections of 1994, which installed the first Republican Congress in 40 years. Support has swollen for a balanced-budget amendment to the

U.S. Constitution, and the states may be faced with the ratification of such an amendment in the future.

## INTERNAL VS. EXTERNAL DEBT

Some of the fears concerning deficits and debt are irrational. The federal government does not face the risk of national bankruptcy. The national debt is primarily an internal debt and it is denominated in U.S. dollars.

> An **internal debt** is debt in which the residents of that country own the national debt.
>
> An **external debt** is debt that is owned by residents of other countries.

Currently, foreigners own 20 percent of the national debt. The other 80 percent is owned by U.S. banks, private citizens, government trust funds, and the Federal Reserve. Moreover, the national debt is denominated in U.S. dollars. The interest and principal must be repaid in U.S. dollars. Thus, as a last resort, the federal government could create more dollars to pay the debt. The countries in Latin America and elsewhere that have declared "national bankruptcy" are those who borrowed dollars or other currencies abroad and could not repay.

> The U.S. national debt is primarily an internal debt and is denominated in U.S. dollars. Hence, there is no danger of national bankruptcy.

Although national bankruptcy is not a concern, there are legitimate reasons for fearing that government cannot meet its other obligations.

## UNFUNDED LIABILITIES AND SOCIAL SECURITY

Governments, like private persons, enter into arrangements that create spending obligations. Sometimes these obligations are secured by formal contracts (such as a contract to pay a defense contractor to develop a new weapons system). Sometimes they are informal, but they exist nevertheless. An example of the latter is the expectation that, when we make our contributions to Social Security, we will actually receive a retirement pension, even though we have no formal contract that we will receive a certain level of benefits during our retirement years. If the government were unable to meet its

obligations, we would believe that we have been cheated and there would be a serious loss of faith in government.

Let us consider the example of the Social Security Administration, which administers the federal government's retirement program for workers, their spouses, and dependents. The government's implicit agreement with working adults is that they will receive their benefits when it comes time for them to retire. To meet this expectation, the government must have sufficient funds to meet its liabilities to future retirees. These obligations cannot be calculated with precision; they depend on how long we live, what our real wages are, population growth, how many adults chose to work, and so on. However, the Social Security Administration can project ranges of outcomes.

The Social Security Administration has an unfunded liability when it cannot meet its future obligations to retirees, given the existing system of benefits and tax rates.

> The **unfunded liability** of the Social Security Administration is the sum that must be deposited in an interest-bearing account to meet obligations to retirees in future years given existing benefits, tax rates, and interest rates.

The accompanying example (Example 3) shows that as much as $2.4 trillion would have to be put into an interest-bearing account to allow the Social Security Administration to provide the current level of benefits to future retirees (with existing tax rates) for the next 50 years. To meet its obligations for the next 75 years, we would have to put aside as much as $5.7 trillion.[2]

What these large sums of unfunded liabilities show is not that the government will have to declare bankruptcy when it is unable to meet its obligations to Social Security recipients. Rather it will either have to raise payroll tax rates of workers or it will have to reduce the benefits of retirees below levels that they thought they had been promised. If benefits are reduced, retirees will feel they have been betrayed by government. If taxes of current workers are raised, and raised substantially because of the large unfunded liabilities, their incentive to work may disap-

---

[2]Budget Baselines, Historical Data, and Alternatives for the Future, January 1993, Washington, D.C.: U.S. Government Printing Office.

## EXAMPLE 3
## WHY SOCIAL SECURITY
## IS IN A MESS

All working adults must contribute to social security. We make these contributions assuming that when we retire we will receive the retirement benefits we believe that we have paid for. The Social Security Administration funds social security primarily through the funds collected from current payroll taxes. In recent years, the Social Security Administration has been paying out less than it collects to accumulate funds in a social security trust fund.

If we take population and economic projections, we can calculate how many retirees and how many working people there will be in future years. If we then calculate the cost of supplying current benefits to those retirees, how much tax revenue will be collected from work-

ing adults, and how much income the trust fund will earn, we have a measure of the fiscal health of social security.

All indicators tells us that Social Security has an enormous unfunded liability. In 1990, we had 3.3 active workers for every social security beneficiary. Because of the aging of the population, we will have less than two active workers for each retiree by 2040. Whereas we had the payroll taxes of 3.3 workers to support each retiree in 1990; we will have less than 2 workers to support each retiree 50 years from now. These workers (and their employers) will have to pay ever higher tax rates or we'll have to reduce social security benefits.

pear, and economic growth and progress would deteriorate. In either case, the result will be unpleasant. Retirees represent a powerful political force in U.S. political life, so it would be difficult to deny them their benefits. If younger workers, however, are taxed too high, they may reduce their effort and earnings, making the unfunded liability even worse.

## DEFICITS AND INFLATION

Budget deficits could be inflationary for two reasons. First, larger deficits caused by increased government spending could raise aggregate demand and cause inflation. Second, larger deficits can cause the money supply to increase, thereby driving up prices.

The link between deficits and inflation is as follows: With a larger deficit, the government must sell more of its debt in credit markets. If government demand for credit rises substantially, interest rates may be pushed up—an action that may contradict Fed policy. To prevent interest rates from rising, the Fed could itself buy enough of the debt so that interest rates do not rise. When the Fed, rather than others, buys government bonds, it increases the supply of credit to the economy and raises the money supply.

Although there is no apparent short-run correlation between deficits and inflation, there is a positive long-term correlation. The lack of a short-term correlation is explained by the fact that budget deficits tend to rise during recessions, when inflationary pressures are weak. Deficits fall during recoveries, when inflationary pressures are rising. Hence, over the course of the business cycle, we would not expect a strong relationship between deficits and inflation. If we look beyond the short-run business cycle, we do find a positive correlation due to the temptation of the Fed to buy government bonds when interest rates threaten to rise.

## DEFICITS AND CAPITAL

Deficits can be harmful in their effects on capital formation. If the deficit is caused by increased government spending, it may crowd out private investment. The result would be an economy that is top-heavy in government spending and government capital but weak in private capital formation. The less private capital we have, the lower the rate of economic growth. This concern is basically the classical argument for balanced budgets.

## DEFICITS AND INCOME DISTRIBUTION

As evidenced by the generational accounts discussed above, under deficit spending, older generations can shift the burden of taxes to younger generations, while they enjoy the benefits of government programs. According to the present system, younger-generation Americans can look forward to paying much more in taxes than they receive in benefits.

This shifting of the burden to younger and to even unborn generations can have adverse effects on incentives. If younger people have to work half a year, for example, just to pay for the benefits of the older-generation, will they be willing to work and to take risks? If we can shift the burden to unborn generations, will there not be a great temptation to spend too much now at the expense of someone in the distant future? (See Example 4).

## DEFICITS AND BIG GOVERNMENT

Deficit spending creates a bias for big government. Deficits make it possible for us to have our favorite government programs now and pay for them later. With the problems of special-interest legislation, logrolling, vote trading, and rational voter igno-

rance, the scales are tipped in favor of too much rather than too little government spending.

If we had a pay-as-you-go system, more could not be spent on a government program without more being paid in taxes. The unpopularity of higher taxes would serve as a counterweight against special-interest legislation.

Public-choice economists argue that we must have a system that allows us to choose the right level of government spending. An "enjoy now" and "pay later" system will not create that optimal amount of government spending.

## KEYNES AND THE FORBIDDEN FRUIT

We began this chapter with the story of how the United States came to accept the notion of deficit spending as something that is "good" for us. If the government spends more, we can have more jobs, more services, and more benefits. If the government spends less, we shall have unemployment, lost jobs, and lost output. The appeal of deficit spending, therefore, is hard to resist.

## EXAMPLE 4
### IS INTERGENERATIONAL CLASS WARFARE BEGINNING?

PAC20/20 bills itself as the first political action committee dedicated to protecting the stake of young Americans in social security. PAC20/20 charges $3 to college students for membership fees that are collected in fund raisers that feature generic grunge bands.

PAC20/20 literature warns college students that they will either never collect a dime from social security when they retire (because it will be bankrupt) or that they will have to pay astronomical taxes during their working years to keep the system afloat. PAC20/20 makes it clear that the young are going to have to pay through the nose so that the older generation can collect their promised social security benefits.

On the other side is the American Association of Retired People (AARP), with more than 30 million members, the largest organization in America next to the Catholic Church.

Sometime in the near future, PAC20/20 intends to make its first campaign contribution to a candidate who will speak out on behalf of young people. PAC20/20 is not much of a match against the AARP with its 30 million votes and millions to spend on lobbying.

------------------------------------------------

*Source:* Elizabeth Kolbert, "Who Will Face the Music?" *New York Times Magazine,* August 27, 1995, pp. 56–59.

Prior to Keynes, economists believed that deficit spending was bad. If the government spent more, the private economy had to spend less. If the government spent more, there would be less investment and less economic growth.

What Keynes failed to foresee was that once policymakers had bitten into the forbidden fruit of deficit spending, it would be impossible to resist further bites. Keynes failed to understand that special-interest legislation would not allow the government to run budget surpluses even during periods of prosperity, that we would come to think of growth in government spending as automatic, and that decreases in the *rate of growth* of government spending would come to be interpreted as "cuts" in government spending.

A growing number of economists, voters, and elected officials have concluded that we can eliminate the allure of the forbidden fruit only by locking it away forever in the form of a balanced-budget amendment to the U.S. Constitution.

## SUMMARY

1. Keynesian budget philosophy opened the way for deficit spending.

2. Fiscal policy is the way government provides for and carries out government expenditures. The government budget is the sum of spending on goods and services, transfers, and interest on debt. Governments pay for expenditures through imposing taxes, selling debt, and printing money.

3. The deficit is difficult to measure because of off-budget items and government capital. Generational accounts show the net tax payments of different generations.

4. The government debt is the total of past deficits and surpluses. It will grow at the rate of interest if the primary deficit is zero. If we are running primary deficits, debt will grow faster than the interest rate.

5. Ricardo equivalence says that people reduce their spending in the case of deficits because they know they must pay higher taxes in the future.

6. A portion of government spending and tax collection depends upon income. Tax collections fall as income falls; welfare payments and unemployment compensation rise as income falls. Such automatic stabilizers soften the business cycle, but they cannot

eliminate it. Cyclical disturbances can be fully counteracted only by discretionary policies. The objective of discretionary fiscal policy is to eliminate inflationary and deflationary gaps. Fiscal policy is the deliberate control of government spending and taxation to achieve macroeconomic goals.

7. Critics question the effectiveness of fiscal policy because of lags, permanent-income effects, and the crowding out of private investment.

8. Economists use the structural deficit as a yardstick to measure changes in discretionary fiscal policy. The structural deficit is the deficit that would have prevailed had the economy been producing full-employment output.

9. Keynesian economists argue that deficits should be accepted if they are necessary to achieve full employment. Classical economists oppose deficits because they harm private capital formation. Public-choice economists argue for a balanced-budget amendment.

10. The national debt is the sum of outstanding federal government IOUs. People fear the national debt because they believe it may cause inflation, big government, national bankruptcy, and an unfair tax burden on future generations. Deficit reduction is difficult because most federal spending is relatively uncontrollable in the short run. In the long run, deficit reduction requires unpopular spending cuts and unpopular tax increases.

## KEY TERMS

fiscal policy
government budget
government deficit
government surplus
current expenditures
capital expenditures
generational accounting
net tax payment
federal debt
primary deficit
automatic stabilizers
discretionary fiscal
　policies
entitlement program
policy activism

expansionary fiscal
　policy
contractionary fiscal
　policy
autonomous changes
permanent income
direct crowding out
cyclical deficit
structural deficit
cyclically balanced
　budget
internal debt
external debt
unfunded liability

## QUESTIONS AND PROBLEMS

1. Private saving is $500 billion. Expenditures of the federal government are $700 billion, and its revenues are $650 billion. The combined revenues of state and local government are $300 billion, and their combined revenues are $350 billion. There is no foreign saving. What is the total amount of saving in the economy?

2. When an economy goes into a recession, tax collections fall. What would you expect to happen to government spending?

3. If actual government expenditures are $200 billion and actual government revenues are $100 billion, and if the economy is at less than full employment, would the structural budget show a larger or smaller deficit than the actual budget? Explain.

4. Contrast the Keynesian position on balanced budgets with that of the classical economists.

5. Explain why the U.S. government can afford to carry a heavier debt burden than private individuals.

6. In 1997, the actual deficit in Economy X is $100 billion, and the structural deficit is $80 billion. In 1988, the actual deficit is $200 billion, and the structural deficit is $80 billion. From these figures, speculate about what has happened to Economy X during this time.

7. If deficits are highest during recessions, explain why the link between large deficits and inflation may be weak.

8. Explain why supporters of activist fiscal policies would oppose a balanced-budget amendment to the Constitution.

9. Consider the reasons people fear deficits. Which of these fears appears to be most justified?

10. Explain why different age groups have different interests with respect to government budgets.

11. Explain the concept of an unfunded liability as it relates to Social Security.

# PART VII

# STABILIZATION

# CHAPTER 32

# INFLATION

Suppose you are the only person in the country with the right to print money—$1, $5, and $100 notes. The money that you have already printed is the money that is now circulating to buy goods and services. Whenever you need to buy something or you want to give a loyal employee or family friend a bonus or gift, you simply run your printing press. In this manner, new money enters into circulation and the money supply expands.

Your temptation to print more and more money would be strong. Printing money costs you hardly anything, but the more you print, the more things you can buy and the more friends and associates you can make happy. But what happens if you overdo it? As you print ever-larger quantities of money, more and more dollars in the economy chase the goods and services produced by the economy. Your printing money doesn't increase real GDP, but it does increase the demand for real GDP. Something has to give, and the result is inflation.

Inflation is not popular. You would not particularly want people to know that your printing press is

responsible; they might decide to take your printing press away. To protect yourself, you might try to blame others. You might claim that "greedy intermediaries" are driving up prices. You might even want laws that make it illegal to raise prices. These actions would allow you to point the blame at others.

After years of dispute, economists agree that inflation is a monetary phenomenon. The inflation we have experienced for more than a half century is the consequence of the growth of the money supply. The printing press story explains why these inflationary pressures exist: There is constant temptation, from both private and public sources, to expand the money supply. As consumers and owners of businesses, we wish to borrow. As public officials, we are under pressure to spend more and tax less.

If we all understood that inflation is caused by too much money, the blame for inflation would be easy to place—namely, on those who control the money supply. Luckily for politicians, relatively few voters understand this point, although you should understand it better after completing this chapter.

# THE FACTS OF INFLATION

Let's begin our discussion of inflation with five basic facts:

1. Prior to the 1930s there was no inflationary trend; the price level was as likely to fall as to rise.

2. Since the Great Depression of the 1930s, there has been a persistent inflationary trend. The price level has risen virtually every year.

3. Inflation since the Great Depression has been variable, with periods of both rapid and slow inflation.

4. Money and prices are positively associated—a relationship supporting the proposition that monetary growth causes inflation.

5. Inflation and interest rates are positively associated. Nominal interest rates are high when inflation is high.

## THE INFLATIONARY TREND

Figure 1 panel (a), which shows the U.S. price level from 1820 to the present, demonstrates that, over the very long run, inflation is not inevitable. Prices did not rise during the Industrial Revolution. The enormous increase in living standards and the transformation from an agricultural to an industrial/service economy was accomplished without setting off an inflationary trend. Prices in 1943 were about the same as prices in 1800! Until the Great Depression, there was no definitive upward trend in prices. Rather, as shown in Figure 1 panel (b), periods of inflation were followed by periods of deflation, and the two tended to cancel each other out. Throughout the nineteenth century, the price level went up and down again and again. In the mid-1930s, when the U.S. economy began its recovery from the Great Depression, prices began to rise. Since then, there have been few years of falling prices. Instead, the concern has been whether prices are rising slowly or rapidly.

## THE VARIABILITY OF INFLATION

The rate of inflation has been variable since the inflationary trend began in the 1930s. Figure 2 shows the annual rate of inflation since 1951. The average inflation rate was 2.3 percent in the 1950s, 2.5 percent in the 1960s, 7.0 percent in the 1970s, 5.4 percent in the 1980s, and 3.3 percent in the first half of the 1990s. The 1970s and early 1980s were periods of rising inflation: Inflation rates ranged from 7.9 percent to 10 percent during the period 1978 to 1981. This period, therefore, deserves our special attention. Why was inflation so rapid then?

(a) U.S. Price Level, 1820–1995

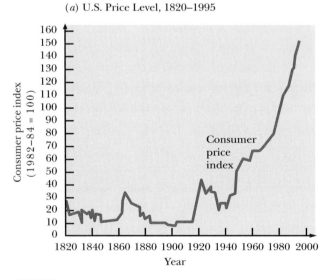

(b) Inflation Rates, 1820–1995

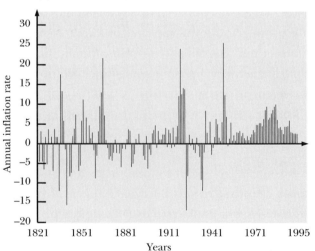

**FIGURE 1**

The price level has continuously risen since the 1930s, deviating from the pattern of the preceding 130 years. Prior to the 1930s, there were as many years of deflation as inflation. Since the 1930s, we have had mostly inflation. *Sources: Historical Statistics of the United States; Economic Report of the President.*

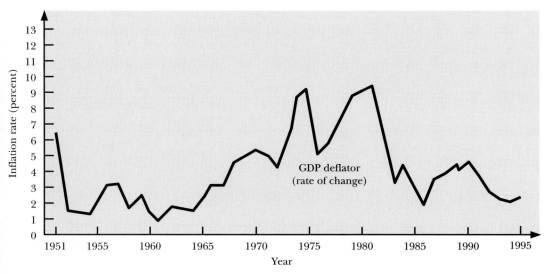

**FIGURE 2   Inflation Trends, 1951–1995**

The rate of inflation accelerated sharply from the early 1960s to 1981. After 1981, the inflation rate slowed down. *Sources: Statistical Abstract of the United States; Economic Report of the President.*

## THE POSITIVE ASSOCIATION BETWEEN MONEY AND PRICES

Figure 3 shows the clear positive correlation between the rate of growth of the money supply and the rate of growth of prices. Money and prices do not grow at the same rate. If they did, the scatter-diagram dots in Figure 3 would fall on a 45-degree line. However, as most dots fall below the 45 degree line, *money growth usually exceeds the growth of prices*. In fact, if we consider a very long period of time, 1915 to the present, the money supply has multiplied more than 70 times while the price level has multiplied about 15 times.

Figure 3 also reveals some exceptions. There were years (the mid to late 1970s) in which prices grew more rapidly than money.

An explanation of inflation must account for these usual and unusual years.

## THE POSITIVE ASSOCIATION OF INFLATION AND INTEREST RATES

The scatter diagram of Figure 4 shows a positive relationship between inflation rates and nominal interest rates: Periods of rapid inflation tend to be periods of high nominal interest rates, and vice versa. For example, in 1980 and 1981, when the inflation rate was about 9 percent, the nominal interest rate was between 12 and 14 percent. In 1971 and 1972, when

the inflation rate was between 4 and 5 percent, the nominal interest rate was less than 5 percent. In 1995, the inflation rate was 3 percent and the interest rate was 5.5 percent. Figure 4 demonstrates that the relationship between inflation and interest rates is not simple. That the dots do not lie on a straight line indicates that factors other than the current rate of inflation affect interest rates.

## THE CAUSES OF INFLATION

Any good theory of inflation should account for the five facts of inflation listed earlier. In previous chapters we used aggregate supply and aggregate demand to understand how real output, employment, and the price level are determined. Aggregate supply-and-demand analysis also shows that there are two general types of inflation: demand-side inflation and supply-side inflation.

> **Demand-side inflation** occurs when aggregate demand increases and pulls prices up.
>
> **Supply-side inflation** occurs when aggregate supply declines and pushes prices up.

Using the tools of aggregate supply and aggregate demand, Figure 5 illustrates both types of inflation. Its two diagrams indicate short-run effects only;

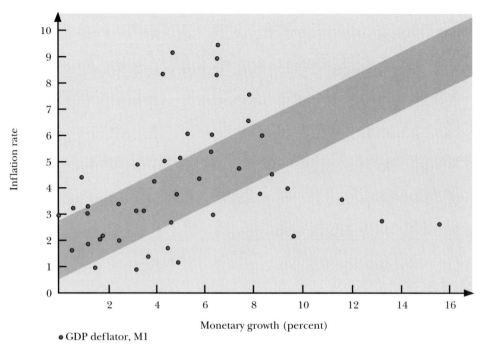

**FIGURE 3  The Growth of the Money Supply and the Price Level**

The scatter diagram shows the generally positive relationship between monetary growth and inflation. *Sources: Historical Statistics of the United States, 1970,* pp. 210–211, 992; *Economic Report of the President.*

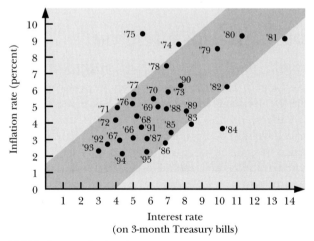

**FIGURE 4  Inflation Rates and Interest Rates, 1966–1995**

This scatter diagram reveals a strong positive relationship between inflation and interest rates. *Sources: Economic Report of the President; Federal Reserve Bulletin.*

they do not show what happens to prices, output, and employment as the self-correcting mechanism does its work.

## DEMAND-SIDE INFLATION

In panel (*a*) of Figure 5, the economy is initially operating at point *e*, where output is *y* and the price level is *p*. The short-run aggregate supply curve, AS, is positively sloped when wages and prices are not fully flexible; that is, the economy will produce more output only at a higher price level. If aggregate demand increases for some reason, the aggregate demand curve, AD, will shift to the right. At the new equilibrium, more output is produced (and unemployment falls). The increase in demand has caused the equilibrium price level to rise. In panel (*a*), the inflation caused by the increase in aggregate demand is demand-side inflation.

(a) Demand-Side Inflation

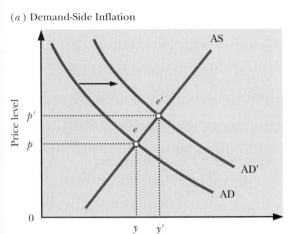

(b) Supply-Side Inflation

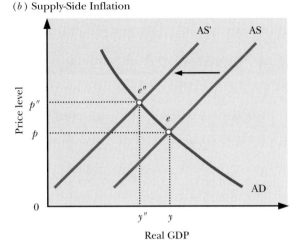

**FIGURE 5    Demand-Side versus Supply-Side Inflation**

Panel (a) illustrates demand-side inflation. The economy is initially in equilibrium at point e. Aggregate demand increases from AD to AD′ and raises the price level from p to p′ as the economy moves up along the short-run aggregate supply curve, AS, to point e′. In the short run, output increases from y to y′. The increase in aggregate demand has pulled prices up.

Panel (b) illustrates supply-side inflation. The economy is initially in equilibrium at point e. A reduction in short-run aggregate supply from AS to AS′ causes a movement back along the aggregate demand curve, from point e to point e″. Prices rise from p to p″; output declines from y to y″; unemployment increases. The reduction in short-run aggregate supply has pushed prices up.

## SUPPLY-SIDE INFLATION

Supply-side inflation occurs when there is a reduction in aggregate supply that moves the economy to a lower level of output and to a higher price level. Any factor that decreases aggregate supply can cause supply-side inflation. Reductions in labor productivity, autonomous increases in raw-material prices, crop failures, changes in the way labor and product markets work, or just bad luck can all reduce aggregate supply.

As the costs of production rise spontaneously, the economy experiences an *adverse* supply shock. Firms, on average, supply fewer goods and services than before. As the aggregate supply curve shifts to the left, the price level is pushed upward.

We have supply shocks during and after wars as a consequence of destruction of much of a country's capital stock. The most dramatic nonwar-related case of supply-side inflation was the 1475 percent rise in the price of imported oil between 1973 and 1980. When the Organization of Petroleum Exporting Countries (OPEC) started raising crude oil prices in 1973, the oil-importing countries of the world

were hit with a large adverse supply shock. Table 1 supplies data on the price of oil and the average inflation rate of seven major countries during this period.

Price shocks can also emanate from agriculture. Poor weather and bad harvests can raise wheat or coffee prices, and because agricultural goods are inputs to the world economy, agricultural price increases can shift the aggregate supply curve. The year 1973 brought with it not only the oil shock but also an increase in the price of wheat from $70 per ton to $140 per ton as a result of a poor harvest in the United States and crop disasters in the former Soviet Union. The 1990s saw soaring coffee prices.

Favorable supply shocks lower the rate of inflation. For example, inflation abated in the 1980s and 1990s as oil prices stabilized or dropped.

Panel (b) of Figure 5 shows the economy initially operating at point e, where output is y and price is p. A reduction in aggregate supply shifts the aggregate supply curve to the left, from AS to AS′. The drop in aggregate supply disrupts the initial equilibrium of output and prices. As prices rise, the economy moves

## Table 1    OPEC Crude Oil Prices and Average Inflation Rates in the Big Seven Countries (United States, Germany, Japan, France, Canada, Italy, and the United Kingdom)

| Year | Oil Price (dollars per barrel) | Average Inflation Rate (percent) |
|------|-------------------------------|----------------------------------|
| 1971–73 | 2.13 | 6.4 |
| 1974 | 10.77 | 14.5 |
| 1975 | 10.72 | 13.0 |
| 1976 | 11.51 | 10.0 |
| 1977 | 13.12 | 10.1 |
| 1978 | 12.93 | 7.6 |
| 1979 | 18.67 | 9.7 |
| 1980 | 30.87 | 9.1 |
| 1981 | 34.50 | 10.1 |
| 1982 | 33.63 | 8.4 |
| 1983 | 29.31 | 6.0 |
| 1984 | 28.70 | 5.4 |
| 1985 | 28.14 | 3.2 |
| 1986 | 15.35 | 2.5 |
| 1987 | 17.70 | 3.8 |
| 1988 | 19.00 | 3.3 |
| 1989 | 19.63 | 4.7 |
| 1990 | 20.47 | 5.0 |
| 1991 | 21.42 | 4.5 |
| 1992 | 20.50 | 3.5 |
| 1993 | 18.50 | 2.4 |
| 1994 | 17.10 | 2.2 |
| 1995 | 18.40 | 2.3 |

Sources: Handbook of Economic Statistics, 1984, p. 53: James Griffin and Henry Steele, Energy Economics and Policy (New York: Academic Press, 1980), p. 18; Economic Report of the President; Handbook of International Economic Statistics.

back up the aggregate demand curve; output falls, and the unemployment rate rises. The reduction in aggregate supply has raised both the price level and unemployment. In panel (b), the inflation caused by the reduction in aggregate supply is supply-side inflation.

### CONFUSING DEMAND-SIDE AND SUPPLY-SIDE INFLATION

Demand-side and supply-side inflation are often confused when inflation is moderate. Take the case of an increase in aggregate demand. As the various sectors of the economy seek to meet the increase in demand, prices and wages rise. Individual businesses do not see the increase in aggregate demand; they see only

their wage costs, material costs, and interest charges rising, and they raise prices as best they can in response to higher costs. On an individual level, demand-side inflation looks like supply-side inflation.

> To individuals and firms, moderate demand-side inflation looks like supply-side inflation. To determine whether inflation is demand-side or supply-side, we must know the source of rising wages and prices.

Because demand-side and supply-side inflation look the same, it is easy to place the blame elsewhere. Even though inflation may be the result of increasing aggregate demand, it is easy to blame greedy workers, intermediaries, or evil monopolists.

When inflation is rapid, there is less chance that observers will think the demand-side inflation is really supply-side inflation. In hyperinflations, people intuitively understand that the runaway inflation is caused by increasing aggregate demand associated with too much money or with runaway government spending (we shall consider the relationship between the two later in this chapter). At a macro level, demand-side inflations look different from supply-side inflations.

> At a macro level, demand-side inflation is associated with rising output and falling unemployment. Supply-side inflation is associated with falling output and rising unemployment.

### PRICE STABILITY DURING THE INDUSTRIAL REVOLUTION

As we noted in the chapter on economic growth, increases in productivity cause aggregate supply to increase. As technology advances and capital accumulation occurs, more real GDP is supplied at the same price level as before. The increase in aggregate supply is antiinflationary—it acts to push down prices throughout the economy.

The Industrial Revolution and its aftermath saw enormous technological progress, which should cause the aggregate supply curve to shift to the right. If aggregate demand did not increase simultaneously, the Industrial Revolution and its aftermath would have been characterized by falling prices, which was not the case.

As we saw in Figure 1, the century that preceded the Great Depression was one of fluctuating prices: Periods of inflation were cancelled out by periods of deflation. The substantial fluctuation in inflation rates demonstrates that there were all kinds of demand and supply shocks, but they tended to even out. The fact that there was no inflationary trend for more than a century suggests that, over the long run, increases in aggregate demand matched increases in aggregate supply—as predicted by Say's Law.

## SUSTAINED INFLATION SINCE THE 1930s

The second empirical fact that needs explanation is why an inflationary trend began in the 1930s. Why is it that today we have inflation and no deflation?

We know from Figure 5 that there are two fundamental sources of inflation—supply-side inflation and demand-side inflation. We can rule out supply-side inflation as the cause of sustained inflation. In order for the sustained inflation of the past 60 years to have been caused by supply-side effects, the economy would have to have experienced an incredible string of bad luck: bad weather, drops in productiv-

ity, increases in energy prices—many things going wrong for an extended period of time. Although things do go wrong, they do not go wrong consistently for 60 years.

In fact, over the past 60 years, the economy has profited from enormous improvements in technology, innovation, management techniques, and so on. We have evidence of only a few significant adverse supply shocks, such as the energy crises of the middle and late 1970s. It would be difficult to believe that any sustained inflation over more than half a century is the product of adverse supply shocks.

Thus, we are left with demand shocks. Aggregate demand has had to increase more rapidly than aggregate supply. With the Keynesian Revolution, economists came to believe that the crux of our macroeconomic problem is deficient aggregate demand. The government had to enact policies that stimulated private and public spending. The government should run deficits to keep up aggregate demand. Such thinking, both public and private, played a major role in the sustained inflation after 1933. We have experienced substantial growth of the money supply, and government spending has outpaced the growth of the economy. In fact, some people and groups "win" from inflation and thus actively support inflationary policies. (See Example 1.)

**EXAMPLE 1**

**AN INFLATION LOBBY?**

We have been taught that inflation is bad. It is less well understood that inflation actually benefits some people. The double-digit inflation of the 1970s provided a good inflation scare, but as memory of the 1970s dims, more and more people argue that a little more inflation may be good for us.

An increasingly vocal constituency of manufacturers, retailers, and labor unions argues against money tightening by the Fed to dampen inflationary pressures. The National Retail Federation warns that antiinflationary measures damage consumer confidence and spending. The

National Association of Manufacturers argues that tight money slows the economy just when goods are selling briskly. The AFL-CIO union argues that efforts to slow inflation reduce hiring of permanent, full-time employees.

Politicians are caught in the middle. Neither Republican nor Democrat would like to run on an antiinflation platform if it could be argued that this would cost economic growth and jobs.

*Source:* "Who's For More Inflation and Who Isn't," *New York Times*, October 2, 1994.

## VARIABILITY OF INFLATION

As we saw in Figure 2, the rate of inflation has not been even over the years. The 1950s and early 1960s were periods of low inflation. The 1970s and early 1980s were periods of high inflation. The 1990s have seen a moderation of the inflation rate.

The theories of supply-side and demand-side inflation readily explain variability in the rate of inflation. The world is full of short-run supply shocks and demand shocks. The 1970s saw two energy price shocks and run-ups in agricultural prices. The 1980s and 1990s saw generally falling energy prices. Consumer spending has fluctuated, as has the rate of private saving. In some periods, exports have been strong; in other periods they have been weak. When we mix supply shocks and demand shocks, we would expect a variable rate of inflation. In fact, it would be a surprise to see a steady rate of inflation in light of all the things that can and do happen.

## MONEY AND PRICES

We know from previous chapters that aggregate demand consists of four components—C, I, G, and net exports (X–M). Net exports make up such a small component of aggregate demand that they could hardly be the cause of sustained inflation. We also know that consumer spending, while accounting for the major portion of aggregate demand, itself depends upon the level of income and interest rates. It is endogenous except for possible shifts in consumer spending habits away from thrift and toward spending.

Can increased government spending or investment spending be the culprits? Together, real government spending and investment spending multiplied 13 times between 1933 and 1995, at a slightly more rapid pace than real GDP (9 times). Prices also multiplied 13 times. The growth of government and investment therefore was not sufficiently rapid to set off a sustained inflation, although it could have been a contributory factor.

Money and prices move together, but prices typically rise more slowly than does money supply (see Figure 3). The money supply increased 60-fold between 1933 and 1996, compared with the 13-fold increase in prices. It is this rapid and sustained increase in the money supply that has caused economists to agree that the inflationary trend is primarily a monetary phenomenon. The only variable that has grown with sufficient speed to cause a sustained inflation is the money supply. (See Example 2.)

> The rapid growth of the money supply, well in excess of the growth of real output, has caused most economists to conclude that sustained inflation is a monetary phenomenon.

This conclusion concerns the more than 60-year-old inflationary trend—it does not deny our having experienced *episodes* of supply-side inflation and of demand-side inflation caused by shifts in consumer spending, exports, or investment spending. Here we are referring to the forest—long-term inflation—and not the trees—individual episodes of inflation.

Let's now consider the relationship between money and prices using the equation of exchange to explore the role of velocity.

### MONEY AND PRICES WITH VELOCITY NOT FIXED

The chapter on money, interest, and prices introduced the quantity theory equation of exchange: $MV = PQ$, where $M$ is the money supply, $V$ is velocity, $P$ is the price level, and $Q$ is real output (real GDP). In this earlier discussion, we considered the relationship between money and prices when $V$ and $Q$ are fixed, and found them to be proportional. If $M$ increases 10 percent, so does $P$. Velocity is not fixed in the real world. Figure 6 shows that velocity has changed over the past 40 years. Velocity does not change randomly. In fact, we shall consider several theories to explain velocity later in this chapter. Let's concentrate here on the relationship between money and prices when velocity itself is subject to change.

With *fixed velocity*, money grows faster than prices as long as there is growth of real GDP. If there is no growth of real GDP, money and prices should grow at the same rate. Now, let's consider what happens when velocity rises. A growing $V$ accelerates growth of $MV$ and causes prices to rise even faster. If velocity grows sufficiently, it can cause $P$ to rise more rapidly than $M$.

> Rising velocity causes $P$ to rise faster and alters the relationship between the growth of $M$ and the growth of $P$. If $V$ is growing rapidly, it can lead to the result of P growing faster than $M$.

Growth = Technology / exploit MKTS

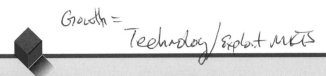

# EXAMPLE 2
## MILTON FRIEDMAN'S 100-YEAR EVIDENCE
## FOR MONETARISM

Monetarists, led by Nobel laureate Milton Friedman, maintain that the best way to control inflation is for the Fed to increase the money supply at a constant rate equal to the real growth of GDP. The accompanying diagram summarizes 100 years of empirical evidence for this position. The money supply figure measures excess monetary growth. When the figure is positive, money is growing more rapidly than real GDP; when it is negative, money is growing more slowly than real GDP.

Friedman's diagram shows that, over the past century, inflation and excess monetary growth have generally moved together. Periods of high excess monetary growth have been generally associated with rapid inflation. However, the relationship is by no means perfect over a short-run period. At times, the two series move closely together; at other times, excess monetary growth accelerates well before inflation. Friedman argues that because the exact timing of the relationship between excess monetary growth and inflation is variable and unpredictable, discretionary monetary policy is unpredictable and potentially dangerous. In his view, it is better to pursue a steady course of constant monetary growth. As Friedman writes, "The quantity of money is not a magic tool. On the contrary, the attempt to use it as such has added to the economy's instability rather than reduced it."

------------------------------------------------

*Source:* Milton Friedman, "Monetary History, Not Dogma," *Wall Street Journal,* February 12, 1987, p. 22.

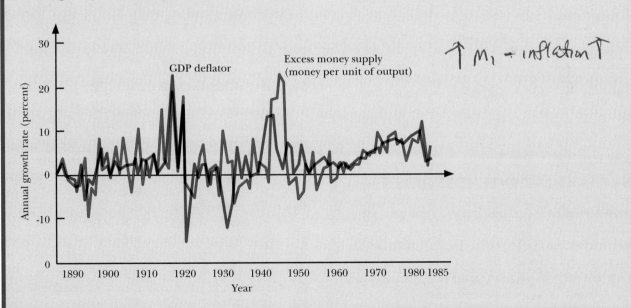

↑ M₁ → inflation ↑

M1
Ratio

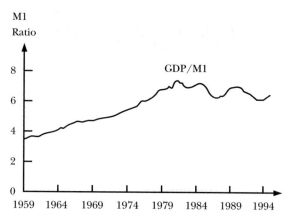

**FIGURE 6    Velocity**

*Explanation:* Velocity is calculated by dividing M1 by nominal GDP. The diagram shows that velocity rose in the 1970s and 1980s and fell in the late 1980s and early 1990s.

Understanding velocity allows us to explain the periods (already shown in Figure 3) when the growth of prices exceeded the growth of *M,* such as during the inflationary 1970s and early 1980s, periods of rising velocity.

Rising velocity is associated with periods of rising inflation.

Thus, if we are to have a complete theory of inflation, we must understand the factors that cause velocity to rise or fall.

## INFLATION AND INTEREST RATES

The fifth empirical fact of inflation is the positive association between inflation and interest rates. This positive association is explained by the simple fact that lenders require a positive reward for lending to others, an act that requires them to postpone consumption to a later date. If you lend your friend $1,000 for two years, you must postpone the use of that $1,000 for two years. Why would you be willing to do this if you did not receive some kind of reward or incentive? The incentive would have to be that, by postponing consumption now, you can consume more in the future.

Recall the simple formula for nominal and real interest rates from the chapter on saving and invest-

ment: The nominal interest rate equals the real interest rate plus the anticipated rate of inflation.

Experience shows that lenders require between 2 and 4 percent real interest in order to be induced to postpone their consumption. If we consider, say, a loan with a three-year maturity for which lenders require a 3 percent real interest rate, the nominal interest rate will equal 3 percent plus the average anticipated rate of inflation over the three-year period of the loan. If we expect 2 percent inflation, the nominal interest rate will be 5 percent. If we expect a 7 percent inflation rate, the nominal interest rate will be 10 percent.

Real interest rates are not expected to change much over time because our preferences for consumption today versus consumption tomorrow are fairly steady. Thus, most fluctuations in the nominal interest rate are due to changes in inflationary expectations. If interest rates rise or fall sharply over a short period of time, the most likely explanation is a change in inflationary expectations.

Changes in nominal interest rates are primarily determined by changes in inflationary expectations.

## SHORT-TERM VERSUS LONG-TERM RATES

The interest-rate formula indicates that the nominal interest rate equals the real interest rate plus the average anticipated rate of inflation over the period of the loan. If the lending period is 15 days, little inflation will be expected in such a short period, and the nominal rate will not be significantly affected by inflationary expectations.

If the lending period is long—say, 10 years—the average anticipated inflation rate will be a significant determinant of the nominal interest rate. Trying to anticipate inflation over a long period of time is a difficult business; 10-year inflationary expectations will obviously be more variable than 15-day inflationary expectations.

Short-term interest rates are less affected by inflationary expectations because the lending period is short. Long-term interest rates are significantly affected by inflationary expectations.

## INFLATIONARY EXPECTATIONS

To understand interest rates, especially long-term rates, we must understand inflationary expectations. Like it or not, we are all in the game of trying to anticipate inflation. As consumers, we must decide whether to speed up our purchases or to refinance our home mortgages in anticipation of inflation. Businesses must decide whether the costs of borrowing will be higher today or tomorrow. Labor leaders must try to anticipate future inflation before agreeing to multiyear labor contracts.

Two different hypotheses explain inflationary expectations. They represent two polar views. The reality is that probably both contain seeds of truth and that actual inflationary expectations are formed by using a combination of the two approaches.

**Adaptive Expectations.**    We may use adaptive expectations to form inflationary expectations.

> **Adaptive expectations** are expectations that we form from past experience and modify only gradually as experience unfolds.

For example, if the annual inflation rate has been 5 percent each year for the past 10 years, we will probably expect the inflation rate to remain at 5 percent. If the inflation rate then jumps to a steady 10 percent, following adaptive expectations, we won't immediately adjust our expectations up to 10 percent. In the first year, we might raise our expectations to 6 or 7 percent. As the rate of inflation continues at 10 percent, we will adjust upward until we finally reach a 10 percent expected inflation rate.

The main implication of adaptive expectations is that it takes us time to adjust to a new rate of inflation. As the adjustment is taking place, there will be a difference between the actual and the anticipated rate of inflation. If the rate of inflation rises, the anticipated rate of inflation will rise by less than the actual increase. If the rate of inflation falls, the anticipated rate of inflation will fall by less than the actual decrease. Only gradually will we bring our anticipated rate of inflation in line with the actual rate of inflation.

**Rational Expectations.**    Rational expectations assume that we can change our expectations more quickly by using more information to form our expectations.

> **Rational expectations** are expectations that we form by using all available information, relying not only on past experience but also on the effects of present and future policy actions.

A major difference between adaptive and rational expectations is the speed of adjustment of expectations. With rational expectations, anticipations can change simply on the basis of a policy pronouncement from monetary or fiscal authorities. If we believe a change in policy will raise a 5 percent inflation rate to a 10 percent rate, we will immediately raise our inflation projection to 10 percent.

Many people and businesses do indeed study the latest economic projections, money supply growth statistics, and fiscal policy changes. Banks, investment firms, labor unions, and small investors gather information that they hope will allow them to anticipate the future. Thus, it is to be expected that many people form expectations according to rational expectations.

## VELOCITY AND INTEREST RATES

Whether we use rational or adaptive expectations, a rise in actual inflation will raise inflationary expectations. If we use adaptive expectations, the rise in inflationary expectations will be lower than if we use rational expectations. In either case, nominal interest rates will rise more rapidly if rational expectations are used.

We know from the chapter on money, interest, and prices that the interest rate is the opportunity cost of holding money. The higher the opportunity cost of money, the lower the quantity of money balances people wish to hold. Higher interest rates cause us to reduce our money balances, which we do by increasing our spending. As we try to reduce our money balances, money turns over faster. *Higher interest rates, therefore, raise velocity.*

Figure 7 shows the effects of nominal interest rates on velocity. Panel (*a*) shows the positive relationship between anticipated inflation and nominal interest rates. Panel (*b*) shows the positive relationship between interest rates and velocity. At high nominal interest rates, velocity is high because the opportunity cost of holding money is high.

In reviewing the facts of inflation, we noted the difference between the 1970s (a period of high inflation) and the 1980s and 1990s (a period of declining or stable inflation). In the latter half of the 1970s, prices rose more rapidly than the money supply. In the 1980s and 1990s, the money supply rose faster

(*a*) The Relationship Between Anticipated
Inflation and Interest Rate 1966–1995

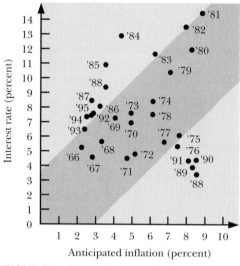

(*b*) The Relationship Between the Interest
Rate and Velocity 1966–1995

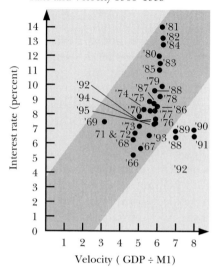

**FIGURE 7  Velocity and Inflation**

In panel (*a*), the anticipated inflation rate is measured as the average inflation rate over the last three years. The interest rate in both panels is the interest rate on 10-year U.S. government bonds. The positive slope of the scatter diagram in panel (*a*) reveals a positive relationship between anticipated inflation and the interest rate. In panel (*b*), velocity is the ratio of GDP to M1. This scatter diagram clearly shows a positive relationship between interest rates and velocity. The results of panels (*a*) and (*b*) together show that velocity tends to increase as anticipated inflation rises.

than prices. Why? As inflation rose during the 1970s, inflationary expectations pushed up nominal interest rates and velocity rose. With rising velocity, a given increase in the money supply yields a larger increase in prices. The normal relationship between monetary growth and inflation (prices rising slower than money supply rises) was disrupted by rising inflationary expectations.

The sharp reduction in inflation starting in the mid-1980s caused inflationary expectations to fall. As nominal interest rates dropped, velocity fell. With declining velocity, a given increase in the money supply yielded a smaller increase in prices. The normal situation—in which money grows faster than prices—was restored.

## MONETARY GROWTH AND INTEREST RATES

The Federal Reserve controls the money supply. In controlling the money supply, can the Fed also control interest rates? If so, what type of interest rate can the Fed control?

Let's consider what happens when the Fed initiates a one-time increase in the money supply in a situation in which no inflation is anticipated. This action has a short-run and then a long-run effect on interest rates.

## THE EFFECTS ON INTEREST RATES OF A ONE-SHOT INCREASE IN THE MONEY SUPPLY

Inflation is not likely to be anticipated if it is caused by a one-shot or once-and-for-all increase in aggregate demand. Let's use as an example an economy that has had stable prices for a number of years.

In Figure 8, a one-shot increase in the money supply causes a one-shot increase in aggregate demand. Because prices have been stable for years, we expect prices to remain stable. We do not know of the impending increase in the money supply that will cause prices to rise. The increase in aggregate demand will have both short-run and long-run effects.

**The Short-Run Effect.** In panel (*a*) of Figure 8, the economy, initially operating at point *a*, produces the natural level of output, $y_n$, at a price level of 100. In panel (*b*), the increase in money supply (from *M* to

(*a*) Aggregate Supply and Aggregate Demand

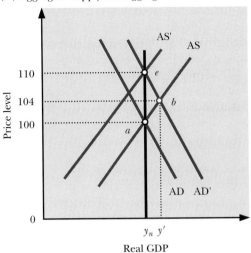

(*b*) The Money Market

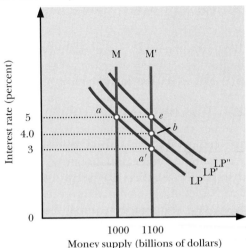

**FIGURE 8   The Effects of Increases in Money Supply on Interest Rates, Output, and Prices**

In both panels, the economy is initially at point *a,* producing an output of $y_n$ with an interest rate of 5 percent. As a result of an unanticipated move by the Fed, money supply increases, and the interest rate drops to 3 percent. At the lower interest rate, aggregate demand increases from AD to AD′. As aggregate demand shifts up along AS, both prices and output rise. As prices start to rise, the demand for money increases (the liquidity preference curve starts to shift to the right). As the price level rises initially from 100 to 104, the money demand curve shifts from LP to LP′ to establish a higher interest rate (4 percent). The interest rate has risen from 3 percent to 4 percent but is still below its original rate of 5 percent. However, the economy is operating above the natural level of output at point *b;* therefore, the price level continues to rise. As the price level continues to rise, people expect a higher price level. The economy is restored to producing $y_n$ when the short-run aggregate supply curve shifts all the way to AS′. The movement of the price level to 110 affects the credit market by continuing to increase the demand for money. Eventually, the liquidity preference curve shifts all the way to LP″. At the intersection of LP″ and M′ (at point *e*), the interest rate is restored to the original 5 percent rate. Long-run equilibrium occurs at point *e* in both graphs.

M′) adds reserves to the banking system. The increase in the supply of credit brings down the interest rate.

**The Long-Run Effect.** In the short run, an increase in aggregate demand can raise output above the natural level. In the long run, however, both output and unemployment return to the natural rate through the self-correcting mechanism. Is there an equivalent rule for interest rates?

At point *b* in panel (*a*), output is above the natural level, and the price level begins to rise toward point *e,* where output equals the natural rate ($y_n$). However, as prices rise, we need more money to carry out our transactions; the demand for money increases as LP′ shifts toward LP″. The interest rate

rises as long as prices are rising. In panel (*b*), when the price level reaches 110 (at point *e*), prices no longer rise (the inflation rate goes back to zero), and output is restored to $y_n$. The interest rate is also restored to its original rate at point *e* in panel (*b*). The economy is operating with the same real income, the same interest rate, and the same rate of inflation (zero) as it did before the increase in money supply. The only change is that the price level has risen. *Increases in money supply drive down interest rates only in the short run.*

An increase in the money supply can initially lower interest rates, but the resulting increase in prices and output pushes interest rates back up in the long run.

## THE EFFECTS ON INTEREST RATES OF CONTINUOUS MONETARY GROWTH

An economy that is experiencing continuous monetary growth (as opposed to a one-shot increase in the money supply) experiences a similar result. If there is a permanent acceleration in monetary growth that *unexpectedly* raises the inflation rate, interest rates should drop in the short run.

Remember that the nominal interest rate is the real rate plus anticipated inflation. If we fail to see the higher inflation coming, inflationary expectations are constant. However, there is now more money and credit in the economy, so nominal interest rates drop. In effect, we are temporarily earning less than the real rate of interest we expected to earn. This effect will be temporary because our inflationary expectations rise in the long run until we return to earning the real rate of interest required to induce us to lend.

In the long run, an increase in monetary growth raises the nominal interest rate but not the real interest rate.

If the higher inflation from the faster monetary growth had been anticipated, the real interest rate would not have fallen at all. In this case, lenders and borrowers anticipate higher inflation; lenders will be more reluctant to lend money at prevailing rates, and borrowers will be more eager to borrow at prevailing rates. These actions cause the nominal interest rate to rise. (See Example 3.)

## THE FED'S DILEMMA

Monetary authorities face a dilemma during periods of high inflation. With high inflation, nominal interest rates will also be high. There will be a public outcry against high interest rates, and pressure will build on the Fed to lower interest rates. The only way to lower nominal interest rates is to lower inflationary expectations. However, we usually lower our inflationary expectations only after we see inflation actually dropping. Thus, the Fed must lower actual inflation to reduce inflationary expectations. To lower inflation, the Fed must reduce the growth of the money supply. The demand for money remains

### EXAMPLE 3
### WHY THE FED CAN'T CONTROL
### LONG-TERM INTEREST RATES

In February 1995, the chairman of the Board of Governors of the Federal Reserve System, Alan Greenspan, told an angry convention of homebuilders that the "Fed does not control long-term interest rates." In fact, said Greenspan to builders upset over the rise in home mortgage rates, long-term rates might have been higher now if the Fed had not taken action to raise short-term rates.

In February 1994, the Fed became concerned that inflation might accelerate. As a consequence, the Fed restricted the growth of the money supply and raised short-term interest rates a total of seven times between February 1994 and February 1995. Long-term rates, such as 30-year home mortgages, rose from around 6.5 percent to above 8 percent.

How could Greenspan argue that the Fed was not responsible for the rise in long-term mortgage rates? The 30-year mortgage rate equals the real rate of interest (say 3 percent) plus the anticipated rate of inflation over a 30-year period. Although the Fed can control short-term interest rates, it cannot control inflationary expectations, which are the prime determinant of long-term rates. An 8 percent 30-year mortgage rate means that people are expecting an average 5 percent inflation rate over the 30-year period.

Thus, with his remark, Greenspan asserted that if the Fed had not taken action against inflation, inflationary expectations might have risen. If the Fed does not move effectively to combat inflationary pressures, long-term interest rates would rise even more.

strong because, with high inflation, we require more money to carry out our transactions. The resulting imbalance between money growth and money demand growth pushes up interest rates.

> To lower interest rates during an inflation requires that interest rates rise even further in the short run. Only when inflation actually slows will inflationary expectations fall, and only then will interest rates also fall.

The U.S. experience with rising interest rates in 1979 and 1980 illustrates the dilemma faced by monetary authorities. The Fed decided in October 1979 to reduce money growth rates in order to combat inflation. Table 2 shows that from 1978 to 1980, the rate of monetary growth was reduced from 8.2 percent per year to 6.4 percent per year. During the same period, the rate of interest (on three-month Treasury bills) rose from 9.1 percent in December 1978 to 15.7 percent in December 1980. As we might expect, interest rates rose when monetary growth was reduced in the presence of high inflationary expectations. However, as the antiinflation policy began to take hold in 1982 and 1983, interest rates started to fall. As inflation fell, inflationary ex-

pectations were reduced and interest rates began to fall. Interest rates in late 1984 (8.2 percent) were about the same as when the Fed's antiinflation action began.

## THE SPREAD OF SUPPLY-SIDE INFLATION

We have established that unless supported by an incredible string of bad luck, adverse supply shocks do not by themselves create sustained inflation. As positive supply shocks follow adverse supply shocks, the earlier effects on the price level should, in fact, be reversed. We know from Figure 5 that supply-side inflation reduces output and hence, increases unemployment. The combination of rising prices and rising unemployment characteristic of supply-side inflation puts pressure on the government to "do something" about rising unemployment. Unfortunately, government responses to this pressure can turn a supply-side inflation into a sustained inflation.

In Figure 9, the economy is initially producing an output of $y_1$ at a price level of $p_1$ (at point $e_1$). The

| | Year-to-Year Growth Rate in M1 (percent) | Inflation Rate: GDP Deflator (percent) | Yearly Average Unemployment (percent) | Year-end Rate for 3-Month T-Bill (percent) |
|---|---|---|---|---|
| 1978 | 8.2 | 7.3 | 6.1 | 9.1 |
| 1979 | 7.7 | 8.9 | 5.8 | 12.1 |
| 1980 | 6.4 | 9.0 | 7.1 | 15.7 |
| 1981 | 7.0 | 10.0 | 7.6 | 10.9 |
| 1982 | 6.6 | 6.2 | 9.7 | 8.0 |
| 1983 | 11.1 | 4.8 | 9.6 | 9.0 |
| 1984 | 6.6 | 4.4 | 7.4 | 8.2 |
| 1985 | 12.0 | 3.7 | 7.2 | 7.5 |
| 1986 | 17.0 | 2.6 | 7.0 | 5.2 |
| 1987 | 3.5 | 3.2 | 6.2 | 5.8 |
| 1988 | 4.8 | 3.9 | 5.4 | 8.2 |
| 1989 | 1.2 | 4.3 | 5.2 | 7.5 |
| 1990 | 3.9 | 4.2 | 5.4 | 6.8 |
| 1991 | 6.0 | 2.7 | 6.7 | 5.4 |
| 1992 | 12.4 | 2.2 | 7.4 | 3.5 |
| 1993 | 11.6 | 2.1 | 6.8 | 3.0 |
| 1994 | 1.7 | 3.0 | 6.1 | 4.3 |
| 1995 | −2.2 | 2.8 | 5.6 | 5.5 |

**Table 2    Money Growth, Inflation, Unemployment, and Interest Rates 1978–1995**

*Sources: Economic Report of the President; Federal Reserve Bulletin.*

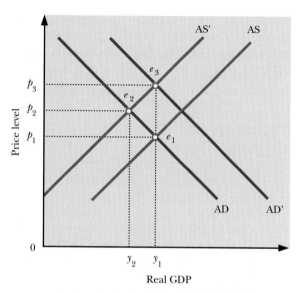

**FIGURE 9 The Ratification of Supply Shocks**

The economy is initially operating at point $e_1$, producing an output of $y_1$ at price level $p_1$. When short-run aggregate supply falls from AS to AS', the price level rises to $p_2$ and output falls to $y_2$ (unemployment rises). The government ratifies the supply-side inflation by increasing aggregate demand from AD to AD'. The price level rises to $p_3$, and output (and unemployment) returns to its original level.

economy now suffers an adverse supply shock; the aggregate supply curve shifts to the left (from AS to AS'). The economy produces less output at higher prices and the unemployment rate also rises.

If the Fed succumbs to pressure to combat rising unemployment, it raises the money supply, thereby increasing aggregate demand. As a result, the price level rises even further, and the economy returns to its original output and unemployment. The process of responding to adverse supply shocks by increasing monetary growth is known as the ratification of supply-side inflation.

> The **ratification of supply-side inflation** results when the government increases the money supply to prevent adverse supply-side shocks from raising unemployment.

As a consequence of ratification, unemployment is reduced, but the price level is driven up even further. If nothing else happens, the price increase stops. If ratification continues, a wage/price spiral can result.

## THE WAGE/PRICE SPIRAL: UNINTENDED CONSEQUENCES

When inflation continues for some time, it no longer catches workers and firms off guard. Workers who anticipate higher inflation will negotiate contracts that protect them from rising inflation. During an inflation, firms can pass wage increases along in the form of higher prices. Sellers factor the anticipated rate of inflation into their sales contracts.

When everyone anticipates higher inflation, the economy gets caught in a wage/price spiral.

> The **wage/price spiral** occurs when higher prices push wages higher and then higher wages push prices higher, or vice versa. This spiral is sustained by the monetary authorities' ratifying the resulting supply-side inflation by increasing the money supply.

Workers anticipate inflation and demand higher wages. Higher wages raise production costs and shift the aggregate supply curve in Figure 9 to the left. To prevent unemployment from increasing, monetary authorities ratify the supply-side inflation and drive prices even higher. Workers now anticipate higher prices; they demand higher wages, aggregate supply falls again, and the whole process repeats itself.

The wage/price spiral has *unintended consequences* for both government and private businesses. The Fed expands the money supply to reduce unemployment, but in doing so sets into motion forces that increase unemployment at an even higher inflation rate. Employers and employees seek higher prices and wages to protect themselves against inflation, but in doing so create even more inflation.

If everyone were to agree to stop, everyone would be better off. If businesses and firms agreed not to seek higher wages and prices, the wage/price spiral would stop. If the Fed stopped ratifying supply shocks, the wage/price spiral would stop. Instead of cooperating, all parties are caught in a chicken-versus-the-egg controversy over what and who has caused the wage/price spiral.

## MONETIZATION OF DEBT: MONEY AND DEFICITS

We began this chapter by asking you to consider what it would be like if you could print your own money. In reality, only counterfeiters do so, and they are thrown in jail when they are caught. In all industrialized societies, money is printed by government authorities, and the supply of bank money is controlled by a central bank, such as the Fed in the United States.

The relationship among money supply, government deficits, and inflation is most easily understood by considering a country that has relatively little bank money, such as modern-day Russia. Virtually all the money in circulation is currency printed by the government of Russia.

In effect, the government of Russia is like the individual who owns the only printing press. It must pay the military, school teachers, police personnel, judges, and retirees. It must buy military equipment, build schools, and so on. As the only one with a printing press, the government of Russia is able to spend more than it takes in in taxes. If it wants to spend 25 trillion rubles but has collected only 20 trillion, it can make up the difference by printing 5 trillion rubles of new currency to pay its bills. The new currency that it prints represents a growth of the country's money supply.

In the case of Russia, the relationship between government deficits and the increase in the money supply is obvious. The larger the deficit, the more new money the government prints, and the more rapidly the money supply expands. The more rapidly the money supply expands, the higher the rate of inflation. In 1995, the government of Russia printed so much money that its inflation rate was in excess of 10 percent per month.

In the more highly industrialized economies, government deficits are handled differently. The U.S. money supply is controlled by the Fed through the sale and purchases of government securities. If the Fed buys securities in the open market, commercial bank reserves rise and the money supply expands. In order for a link to exist between the federal debt and the money supply, an increase in the debt would have to result in increased purchases of government securities by the Fed. This indeed happens in certain cases.

The U.S. government finances its deficit (government spending being greater than government revenues) by selling treasury bonds (IOUs) to the public. These Treasury bonds compete with private bonds for buyers. If the U.S. government has a large deficit and has to sell a large amount of bonds, this action increases the demand for credit, and it may push up interest rates.

Let's suppose that the Fed does not want interest rates to rise, but it notes that the Treasury is selling large quantities of its bonds in credit markets. To prevent interest rates from rising, the Fed could itself buy these extra government bonds. However, by doing so, it has injected new reserves into the banking system and has increased the money supply.

> Monetization of debt occurs when the government prints money to pay its bills or the central bank buys government debt securities on the open market, thereby increasing the money supply.

There is no one-to-one relationship between the size of the federal deficit and the growth of the money supply. There is no requirement that the Fed buy the securities being issued by the Treasury to finance the deficit. During some periods, the Fed does not buy the securities being issued by the Treasury. Either it does not mind interest rates rising or it believes that sales to the public will not drive up interest rates. During other periods, the Fed does monetize the debt by buying the newly issued securities. When it does, the money supply expands.

Figure 10 shows that there is a long-run positive relationship between the federal deficits and inflation. The scatter diagram shows a tendency of inflation to be higher where the deficit rises as a percent of GDP. Short-run effects are removed by using five-year averages. The period of the late 1980s and early 1990s, however, was an exception that combined high deficits with relatively low inflation. As the federal deficit grows, pressure and temptation grow for the Fed to monetize the debt.

## INFLATION POLICY

Let's consider again the sources of the inflationary bias since the Great Depression. One source was the Keynesian view that aggregate demand must increase to provide full employment. Keynesians feared that slow monetary growth could restrain aggregate demand and cause recessions or worse; the restraining of government spending could be bad for the economy. The emphasis has been on spending, both private and public, and not on saving, either private or public. The Keynesian budget philosophy called for government deficits to stabilize the economy. These deficits, if monetized, would lead to inflationary increases of the money supply.

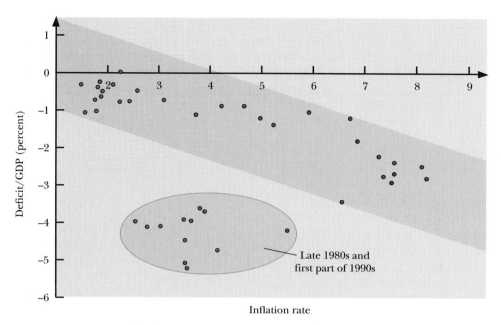

**FIGURE 10    Federal Deficit vs. Inflation, 1950–1995 (5-year averages)**

The scatter diagram shows that as the federal deficit (as a percent of GDP) rises, inflation rates become higher. The late 1980s and early 1990s appear to be an exception.

Government deficits have also been fostered by democratic political processes. Raising taxes is unpopular; spending, especially for a politician's favorite projects, is popular and a way to get reelected. Antiinflationary forces lack a powerful lobby in the political process.

Given this inflationary bias, economists must first set inflation goals, and then determine how to implement them.

## INFLATION GOALS: ZERO INFLATION?

All economists agree that very rapid inflation should be avoided. There is less agreement on whether we should accept relatively low inflation or push for zero inflation. Advocates of aiming for low inflation argue that economies tolerate low rates of inflation quite well.

Advocates of zero inflation make the following arguments: First, even moderate inflation causes us to engage in economically unproductive activities, such as investing in land or precious metals, instead of making more productive investments in plant and equipment. These unproductive activities reduce economic efficiency and growth.

Second, through the tax system, moderate inflation reduces long-term gains on invested capital. An investment that has earned 20 percent over a five-year period earns virtually nothing after adjustment for moderate inflation, especially after investment earnings have been taxed.

Third, moderate inflation causes price system distortions. When prices are generally rising, information on relative prices becomes obscured. We do not know what the cheapest input combinations are or what the best buys are. When the price level is stable, however, we are well informed about relative prices and make "good" economic decisions.

Advocates of zero inflation also point to the empirical finding that inflation tends to be negatively related to economic growth. Countries with high inflation grow more slowly than those with low inflation. Proponents cite this finding as evidence that countries should aim for a zero rate of inflation.

## MONETARISM: MONETARY RULES

Nobel laureate Milton Friedman, the major proponent of monetarism, argues that because "inflation is always and everywhere a monetary phenomenon," it cannot persist unless it is supported by monetary growth.

If inflation is "always and everywhere" caused by excess monetary growth, Friedman's solution is strict limitation of the growth of the money supply. Insofar as real GDP over the long run has grown at about 3 percent per year, Friedman would limit the rate of growth of the money supply to about 3 percent per year.

Friedman's 3 percent rule is that the Fed should increase the money supply by 3 percent every year, give or take some small margin of error. Under these circumstances, the Fed's decision-making power would be reduced to mere technical matters. The Fed's sole job would be to expand the money supply at the designated rate.

With a constant low growth rate of $M$, we could look forward to low or nonexistent rates of inflation over the long run. The major cause of inflation—excessive monetary growth—has been eliminated. We may even have less cyclical instability because the Fed is no longer raising or lowering monetary growth. We will still have supply-shock or demand-shock inflations, but their effects would be transitory.

> **Monetarism** is the prescription that the money supply must expand at a constant rate roughly equal to the long-run growth of real GDP.

Modern Keynesians oppose the 3 percent rule on the grounds that we need flexibility to deal with inflation and unemployment. If we are in a period of high inflation, perhaps we need very slow monetary growth. If we have high unemployment, perhaps we need rapid monetary growth.

## GROWTH-ORIENTED PROGRAMS

The higher the growth of output, the lower is inflation, if all things are equal. Economists agree that inflation can be moderated by increasing the growth of real output. The appeal of this proposition is enormous because it removes the need for pain and suffering (in the form of high unemployment or high interest rates) while curing inflation. If inflation can be eliminated by expanding real output, unemployment will fall along with inflation.

We cannot create economic growth instantaneously, but we can create long-run conditions that are favorable to economic growth. Economists agree on policies that promote growth: We should increase educational levels, expand trade, promote competition, and promote invention and innovation. These growth-promoting policies were discussed in the chapter on economic growth.

Supply-side economists, who were particularly influential during the Reagan administration, believe in tax reform to increase growth. Progressive taxes discourage people from working and business firms from investing in plants and equipment. Lowering tax rates therefore raises real output because of improved economic incentives. The increase in real output increases the supply of goods and services, and the increase in tax collections from higher income moderates the budget deficit.

## KEYNESIAN PROGRAMS

Modern Keynesians argue that we need to limit government spending, raise interest rates, and lower monetary growth to cure inflation. We know that there are economic costs to stopping an ongoing inflation in this fashion. It may take a while for inflationary expectations to drop; until they do, output will fall, unemployment will rise, and interest rates will rise.

Thus, modern Keynesians suggest that an incomes policy might be combined with aggregate demand restraint to moderate these costs.

> An **incomes policy** is a set of government rules, guidelines, or laws that regulate wage and price increases.

Wage and price controls can vary from loose rules to wage and price freezes, such as the 90-day freeze imposed by President Nixon in August of 1971. The principal argument for wage and price controls is that they might be able to break inflationary expectations.

Rigid wage and price controls damage productive efficiency. If wages and prices cannot adjust, the price system cannot do its job.

Rigid wage and price controls cannot be used for long because of their negative effect on efficiency. People are aware that controls will be of limited duration, and they will consider what will happen when the controls are lifted. If people generally expect a price explosion when the program ends, they will not reduce their inflationary expectations. Indeed, the

## EXAMPLE 4
## THE BEST INFLATION FIGHTER:
## THE GUILLOTINE

After the French Revolution overthrew the French monarchy, the new revolutionary government issued a new currency called the *Assignat.* The assignat was a fiat currency that was supposedly backed by the lands that the revolutionary government had confiscated from the church. As time passed, the government issued far more *assignats* than they had land, sparking an inflation. Inflationary pressures became so bad that French citizens began refusing to accept the *assignat,* preferring instead other currencies or barter transactions.

The revolutionary government issued a new law (the Law of the Maxim) that introduced extensive price controls and made it a criminal offense for citizens to refuse to accept *assignats* as a means of payment or to raise prices. Severe

penalties were established: Offenders could be beheaded.

The Law of the Maxim is another example of unintended consequences. Its purpose was to ensure a stable currency and to keep prices low for the common people. But the inflationary pressures caused by the increasing amount of money in circulation created widespread shortages. There was nothing to buy at the prices set by the government. Although the common people had money in their pockets, they had no goods to buy! Normally, under these circumstances, merchants and manufacturers will start raising their prices in response to the intense inflationary pressures, and goods will appear on the market at higher prices. A few hardy merchants did, and some were sent to the guillotine as an example to others.

failure of the Nixon wage and price controls in the period 1971 to 1973 revealed the unintended consequences of incomes policies. Inflation was higher after the Nixon controls were lifted. For the unintended consequences of a more bizarre incomes policy, see Example 4.

In this chapter we have explored the facts, causes, and possible cures of inflation. In the next chapter we shall analyze unemployment.

### SUMMARY

1. The five facts of inflation are the lack of an inflationary trend prior to the 1930s, the inflationary trend since the 1930s, the variability of that trend, the historical relationship between money and prices, and the correlation between inflation and nominal interest rates.

2. Demand-side inflation is caused by increases in aggregate demand. Supply-side inflation is caused

by decreases in aggregate supply. Demand-side and supply-side inflation can be confused during periods of moderate inflation. Sustained inflation is explained by demand-side inflation, specifically by monetary growth. Price stability during the Industrial Revolution is explained by technological progress offsetting increases in aggregate demand.

3. The growth of the price level will equal the growth of money supply minus the growth of output with constant velocity. The quantity theory uses the equation of exchange to explain the relationship between money and prices. When velocity is variable, an increase in velocity intensifies the inflationary effects of monetary growth.

4. Interest rates are determined by the following formula: Nominal interest rates equal real interest rates plus the anticipated rate of inflation. Long-term interest rates vary with anticipated inflation.

5. Inflationary expectations can be formed either by adaptive or rational expectations. If formed adaptively, inflationary expectations will be slow to

change. As inflationary expectations rise, so does velocity.

6. The effects of an increase of the money supply on interest rates depends on its effect on inflationary expectations. With rising inflationary expectations, the Fed can lower inflation only by raising interest rates.

7. Ratification of supply-side inflation occurs when aggregate demand is raised to prevent unemployment from rising as a consequence of a supply shock.

8. The wage/price spiral is caused by anticipated inflation and the ratification of supply-side inflation by monetary authorities. The wage/price spiral is an example of unintended consequences.

9. Monetization of debt occurs when government deficits result directly in an increase in the money supply.

10. Economists agree that inflation is a monetary phenomenon and that policies designed to raise aggregate supply are effective antiinflation measures. Incomes policies can have the unintended consequence of worsening inflation.

## KEY TERMS

demand-side inflation
supply-side inflation
adaptive expectations
rational expectations
ratification of supply-side inflation

wage/price spiral
monetarism
incomes policy

## QUESTIONS AND PROBLEMS

1. The owner of the apartment you are renting complains: "Wages, utilities, and other costs are rising too rapidly. I have no choice but to raise your rent." Is this increase in price a case of supply-side inflation?

2. Economists classify inflation as either supply-side inflation or demand-side inflation. Using aggregate supply-and-demand analysis, explain the differences between these two types of inflation. Is it possible to distinguish between the two types of inflation from observed information on output, employment, and prices?

3. In the country of Friedmania, the money supply has been growing at 8 percent per annum and output has been growing at 3 percent per annum. If velocity is constant, what is the rate of inflation? If velocity is declining at a rate of 2 percent per year, what is the rate of inflation?

4. Explain why increases in money supply that are unanticipated are likely to lower the interest rate. Why might the drop in the interest rate be short-lived? If the increase in money supply is fully anticipated, what will happen to interest rates?

5. Using the adaptive expectations hypothesis, what do you think the expected rate of inflation would be in 1998 if past inflation rates were 6 percent in 1997, 4 percent in 1996, and 1 percent in 1995?

6. If the Fed reduces monetary growth during a period of rapid inflation, would adaptive expectations or rational expectations be expected to cause a more rapid drop in inflation?

7. What should happen to velocity as inflationary expectations increase? What is the actual relationship between velocity and anticipated inflation?

8. Using aggregate supply-and-demand analysis, explain why adverse supply shocks combine the worst of two worlds: more inflation and higher unemployment. Also explain why governments tend to ratify supply-side inflation.

9. The wage/price spiral is blamed both on friction between unions and management and on expansionary economic policy. Explain why it is difficult to assign the blame for the wage/price spiral.

10. Evaluate the validity of the following statement: "Both the Keynesians and monetarists believe that inflation is caused primarily by demand-side factors. Therefore, there really is no difference between the two schools' approaches to the inflation problem."

11. What are some arguments for and against wage and price controls?

12. If you believe in the monetarist approach, do you see in Table 1 any evidence that inflation will increase in the late-1990s?

13. Critically evaluate the following statement: "Inflation is caused by too much money chasing too few goods. We can't reduce our 10 percent inflation rate by monetary policy, because that would increase unemployment. But we can reduce the inflation rate to perhaps 3 or 4 percent by increasing the supply of goods through supply-side tax and work incentives."

# CHAPTER 33

# UNEMPLOYMENT AND STAGFLATION

Economists and policymakers continue to disagree on the relationship between inflation and unemployment and on its consequences. One group believes that low unemployment means high inflation. In fact, we may have to deliberately raise the unemployment rate at times to keep inflation in check. This group looks back to the 1930s and the 1960s to support their view of the inverse inflation/unemployment relationship. During the Great Depression of the 1930s, unemployment *rose* from 3 percent to 25 percent and prices *fell* by 25 percent. In the 1960s, unemployment *fell* from 5.5 percent in 1960 to 3.5 percent in 1969, while the inflation rate *rose* from 1.6 percent per year to 5.0 percent.

Other economists argue that there is no simple (positive or negative) relationship between inflation and unemployment. They cite the fact that the unemployment rate rose from 4.9 percent in 1970 to 7.6 percent in 1981, while the inflation rate *also* *rose* from 5.4 percent to 10.0 percent; both inflation and unemployment fell from 1991 to 1995.

The United States experienced its last recession from mid-1990 to mid-1991. Initially, the recovery from the recession was slow, so slow that political analysts believe it cost President Bush his reelection in 1992. Unemployment rates scarcely dropped in 1992 and 1993. The year 1994 began with an unemployment rate of 6.7 percent and ended with a rate of 5.1.

With falling unemployment, Washington and Wall Street began to buzz with questions: Would such a precipitous drop in the unemployment rate set off a new round of inflation? Could we engineer a "soft landing"—that is, could we recover from the recession without setting off a new bout of inflation?

Those who believed that low unemployment is incompatible with price stability won the debate. The Fed, under the chairmanship of Alan Greenspan, decided to slow the economy and, starting in March 1994, engineered seven consecutive interest rate increases. These economists argued that this slowing of the economy was a small price to pay for avoiding inflation. Opponents of the Fed move retorted that the economy could continue to expand its output and employment without fear of inflation. The Fed was sacrificing the economy to fight an enemy that wasn't even there.

This fight affects nominations to the Fed. In early 1996, opposition from the Republican Congress caused the withdrawal of President Clinton's nominee for the vice chairmanship of the Fed on the grounds that he belonged to the school that believed the economy could absorb greater, monetary growth. Such a nominee, it was argued, would make a poor central banker.

## THE LABOR MARKET: MATCHING PEOPLE TO JOBS

Currently, about 125 million Americans have jobs. They work as manual workers, sales reps, computer programmers, assemblers, auto mechanics, physicians, professional baseball players, office managers, school teachers, and so forth. They work in agriculture, manufacturing, retail sales, health care, financial services, and many other fields.

Figure 1 shows that labor markets do not stand still: They grow in size and they change their composition. In 1959, the U.S. economy employed 59 million people. In 1995, it employed 125 million people. In 1959, the largest employment sector was manufacturing; in 1995, the largest employment sector was services. Declining shares of employment should not be confused with absolute declines. Despite all the publicity that U.S. manufacturing jobs have disappeared, there are more manufacturing jobs today than in 1959.

Figure 1 illustrates the Schumpeterian notion of "creative destruction" discussed in the chapter on growth. Economies do not stand still; they are in constant flux. Jobs are created in one industry while they are disappearing in other industries. The labor market must match people to jobs in this ever-changing environment.

Figure 2 shows that a growing economy and a growing population result in an increasing number of jobs, a growing number of people not in the labor force, and more people unemployed. In 1950, we had 59 million employed, 3.3 million unemployed, and 43 million people not in the labor force. In 1995, we had 125 million employed, 66 million not in the labor force, and 7 million unemployed. "A rising tide lifts all boats."

Figure 2 shows that the business cycle affects employment, unemployment, and not being in the labor force. During recession years (shown in shaded areas), employment growth slows down (ceases or be-

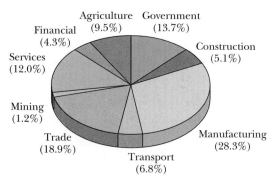

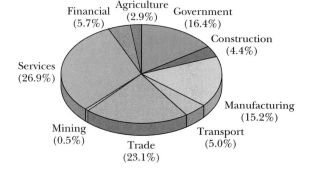

**FIGURE 1   U.S. Employment**

These figures show the relative shifts away from manufacturing and construction and towards services, trade, and government over the past quarter century.

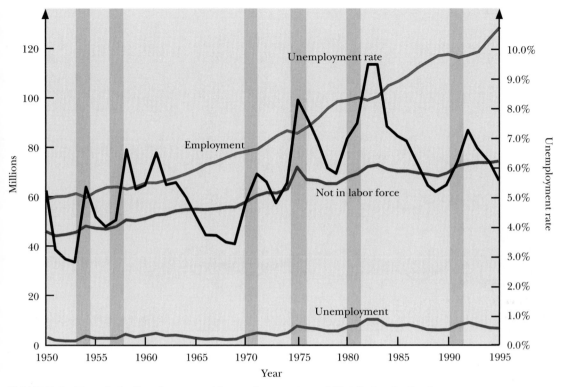

**FIGURE 2   Trends in Employment, Unemployment, and Not Being in the Labor Force**

Economic growth and rising population have increased employment, unemployment, and the numbers of people who are not in the labor force. The unemployment rate has tended to rise over the long term. These measures are all affected by the business cycle as illustrated by the recession years. Note: shaded areas are recession years.

comes negative), more people are "not in the labor force," the number unemployed rises, and the unemployment rate increases.

Figure 3 shows that we become unemployed not only by firings or layoffs. In 1995, less than half those unemployed became unemployed due to a firing or a layoff. The majority either left their job or failed to find a job upon entering or reentering the labor force. In the recession year of 1991, more than half (55 percent) lost their jobs due to firings or layoffs. How we become unemployed also depends upon the business cycle.

Many workers are said to be marginally attached to the labor force. (See Example 1.) They tend to disappear into the ranks of "not in the labor force" during cyclical downturns.

As you will recall from an earlier definition of unemployment, to be unemployed you must be with-

out a job, actively looking for work, and currently available for work. Thus, all unemployed workers, with the exception of those laid off and waiting to be recalled, are searching for jobs.

Employers are also looking for employees, in both bad times and good times. In good times, they look for more new employees; in bad times, they look for fewer new employees. Currently, there are more than five million job openings in an average month.

## MATCHING JOBS AND QUALIFICATIONS

We seek jobs that are consistent with our education, skills, qualifications, and work experience. The unemployed ditchdigger does not seek work as a certified public accountant. The unemployed aeronautical

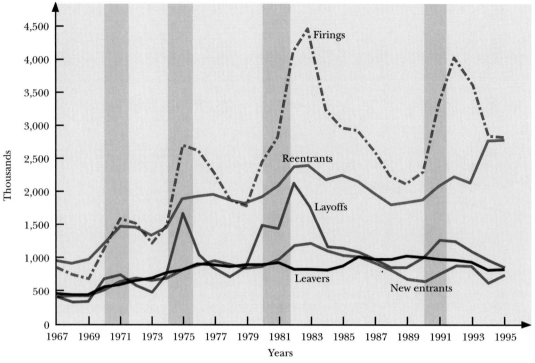

**FIGURE 3    Sources of Unemployment**

People become unemployed not only through firings and layoffs, but also through failure to find jobs upon entry or reentry into the labor force. Firings and layoffs are more important during recession years as shown in shaded areas.

## EXAMPLE 1
## MARGINALLY ATTACHED
## WORKERS

The Commission of Labor Statistics uses a new term, *marginally attached workers,* for the nearly two million unemployed people (at the end of 1994) who searched for jobs sometime during the year, but who did not search during the survey month. (The first year for which data on this category of unemployed workers was collected was 1994.)

More than one-quarter of marginally attached workers are discouraged workers—people who say they want jobs but have given up looking because they think further searching is futile. The remaining three-quarters are not searching for jobs because of difficulties with child care or arranging transportation.

Marginally attached workers show just how difficult it is to get a true measure of unemployment. If marginally attached workers just could afford a car that runs, they would look for a job. If they had a reliable babysitter for their kids, they would enter the job market. If they just felt that they could find a suitable job, they would start looking. Personal decisions such as these can raise or lower the number of unemployed by two million.

------------------------------------------------

*Source:* "Unemployment Rate in U.S. Is at its Lowest in 4 Years," *New York Times,* October 8, 1994, p. 27.

engineer would like to find employment in aeronautical engineering—and may choose to remain unemployed until a matching position becomes available. Whether we accept or reject a job that is not consistent with our background and abilities depends upon the magnitude of the mismatch (the job of janitor is a greater mismatch for the automotive design engineer than the job of automotive assembly engineer) and upon personal preferences. The problem of matching available jobs with worker qualifications again underscores the difficult distinction between voluntary and involuntary unemployment. The matching problem also explains why unemployment exists even in an economy with a large number of unfilled positions.

**Labor Market Search.**   When we become unemployed, we do not automatically step into our next job. If we did, there would be little unemployment. Instead, when we are unemployed, we begin a job search—which can be short or long. We must search because we cannot possibly know about all the possible jobs for which we are qualified. We find out about these jobs by telephoning, hiring professional placement counselors, networking, going to factory gates, and so on. We must determine which prospective employers are prepared to offer us jobs and the conditions of that job. We must decide whether to take a job that is below our expectations or to search further for a better job. Whatever the case, our job search depends on our reservation wage.

A **reservation wage** is the minimum wage offer that a job searcher will accept.

Workers who are searching for jobs enter the job market with a preconceived reservation wage. The reservation wage is a real wage, for we base our employment decisions on real, not nominal, wages. (Remember that the real wage is the nominal wage, adjusted for inflation.) We will accept the first job that offers a wage greater than or equal to our reservation wage. The higher our reservation wage, the longer the search (the period of unemployment) will last.

How do we go about determining our reservation wage? We have some idea of the distribution of wages in the occupations we are searching (the highest possible wage, the lowest possible wage, the average wage), but we do not know which firms are offering which wages. To obtain this information, we must search the job market to obtain job offers. (The bell curve in the appendix on time series analysis describes a possible distribution of wages.)

We use our common sense in making these decisions. If we turn down a job, we don't earn the income from that job. Continuing the search has opportunity costs. We continue to search as long as we expect to gain more from searching than it costs.

Shorter searches result in lower unemployment rates for the economy. Longer searches translate into higher unemployment rates. When "discouraged workers" decide to quit searching altogether and withdraw from the labor force, there is less unemployment because they are no longer in the labor force. To explain unemployment, we must understand the factors that affect search costs and benefits. Anything that happens to raise costs shortens search time and lowers the amount of unemployment.

The duration of unemployment depends upon search time. For the economy as a whole, shorter search time means lower unemployment.

Figure 4 shows the close positive relationship between the duration of unemployment and the unemployment rate. It shows that if we can explain those factors that determine duration of unemployment, we can explain the unemployment rate.

## UNEMPLOYMENT WITH FLEXIBLE WAGES AND PRICES: THE CLASSICAL MODEL

The classical model of macroeconomics considers what happens in an economy in which wages and prices are perfectly flexible. As we noted in earlier chapters, the classical model states that the amount of real GDP that the economy produces will be determined, in the long run, by the economy's capital and labor resources and by its technology. In the short run, with capital and technology fixed, the amount of real GDP will be determined by the quantity of labor inputs.

Let's consider the short-run situation. Given the classical assumption of perfectly flexible wages and prices, the amount of actual employment will be the equilibrium amount that equates the quantity of labor demanded with the quantity of labor supplied. The real wages (with perfectly flexible wages and prices) will adjust to equate the number of available jobs, or vacancies ($V$), with the number of qualified job applicants, or the number of unemployed persons ($U$).

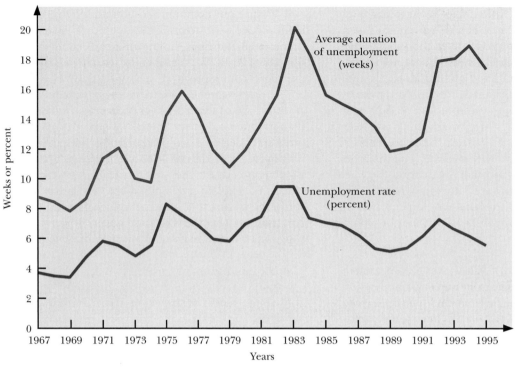

**FIGURE 4   Unemployment Rates and the Duration of Unemployment**

The average weekly duration of unemployment is strongly and positively correlated with the unemployment rate.

Why? If the number of job vacancies exceeds the number of qualified job applicants ($V > U$), some employers will be left without workers and the real wage will rise as they bid for employees. If the number of applicants exceeds the number of jobs ($U > V$), willing workers will be without jobs and the real wage will fall as they compete with each other to get a job.

## FRICTIONAL UNEMPLOYMENT

At the equilibrium real wage, there will be *frictional unemployment*. Business conditions change constantly. Employment opportunities are created in one business, locality, or industry at the same time that they are lost elsewhere. This is what Schumpeter called "creative destruction," discussed in the chapter on economic growth. Employed workers are usually on the lookout for better jobs; employers are usually on the lookout for better workers. Each worker possesses incomplete information about job opportunities, and each employer possesses incomplete information about prospective employees. It therefore takes time for people to match themselves

and to be matched to jobs. Figure 5 illustrates the task of matching people to jobs.

Because we are constantly entering and leaving the labor force, the labor market is like a revolving door. At any given time, some workers will be changing jobs. Some will be entering the labor force for the first time or reentering after an absence; others will be leaving the labor force. The result of this flux is frictional unemployment.

> **Frictional unemployment** is the unemployment associated with the changing of jobs in a dynamic economy.

In the case of frictional unemployment, there is no imbalance between the number of qualified job seekers ($U$) and the number of unfilled jobs ($V$) because $U = V$. Frictional unemployment will always be with us. It would disappear only if we were frozen in our current jobs by the lack of opportunity for job advancement or if we never left jobs until we had already found new ones. Although frictional unemployment is always present in a dynamic economy, there are ways to limit it. Measures that increase in-

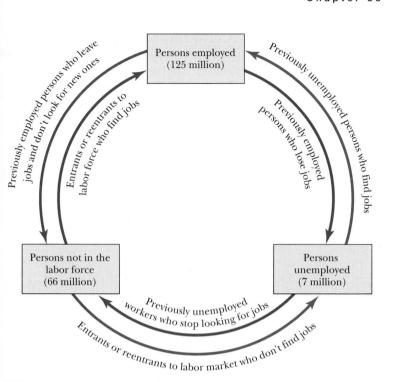

**FIGURE 5    Flows Into and Out of the Labor Force**

Persons can enter the ranks of the unemployed either by moving from the ranks of the employed or by not finding a job upon entering the labor force. People can drop out of the labor force either by departing from jobs or by giving up the job search once unemployed. *Source: Employment and Earnings.* The data are for January 1995.

formation about job opportunities or that speed up the search for jobs reduce frictional unemployment.

Figure 6 shows frictional unemployment. As we noted in the chapter on aggregate supply and demand, the labor market is in equilibrium at that real wage at which the quantity of labor demanded equals the quantity of labor supplied. In Figure 6, equilibrium occurs at the employment rate of $L_0$ at the real wage $W_0$.

At the employment rate $L_0$, there is a match between the number of jobs ($N + V$) and qualified workers ($N + U$) to fill those jobs. The economy is at full employment. "Full employment," however, does not mean that there will be no unemployment. We know that a number of people will be between jobs, entering or reentering the labor force, or dropping out of the labor force; hence, there will be frictional unemployment.

## UNEMPLOYMENT AND INFLATION

We began this chapter with the inflation/unemployment relationship. In the classical model, unem-

ployment and inflation are determined independently. Employment and unemployment rates are determined in the labor market, as we can see from Figure 6. The price level (or the rate of change in the price level) is determined separately by the level of aggregate demand. An increase in aggregate demand—say, due to an increase in the money supply—will raise the price level but will not affect the amount of unemployment.

The prediction of the classical model is that with perfectly flexible wages and prices, unemployment and inflation will be unrelated.

## EMPLOYMENT AND UNEMPLOYMENT: THE LONG RUN

In the long run, employment and unemployment depend upon factors that affect the long-run supply and long-run demand for labor. On the supply side, the rates of employment and unemployment are affected by changes in the demographic characteristics of the population, in their education and training, and in their preferences toward work in the labor force or

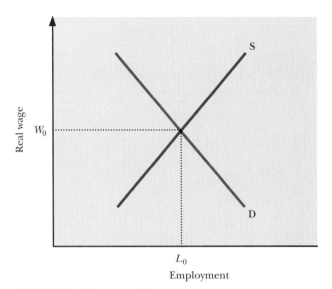

**FIGURE 6  Frictional Unemployment**

The aggregate labor demand curve (D) shows the number of jobs businesses are prepared to offer at each real wage. The aggregate labor supply curve shows the number of jobs qualified job seekers wish to have at each real wage. At real wage $W_0$, there is a balance. However, because a number of workers are in the process of changing jobs, there will be frictional unemployment at this balance.

household, as well as changes in the costs of being unemployed. On the demand side, shifts in the geographic distribution of jobs, the sectoral distribution of jobs, and the amount of union employment all affect the demand for labor.

In fact, as we can see from Figure 1, there have been substantial changes in the U.S. labor market.

On the supply side, a dramatic change in the demographic composition of the labor force has taken place. Whereas in the 1950s only one in four workers was a woman, in the 1990s half of the labor force is female. Women are more likely than men to be unemployed, and they are less likely to work in unionized jobs. There has also been a dramatic increase in unemployment benefits. Whereas in the early 1960s, only 70 percent of workers were covered by unemployment compensation, now more than 95 percent of workers are covered by unemployment benefits. The rise in multiple-earner households has also affected unemployment. Now, most families have two or more earners. The multiple wage–earner family cushions the loss of income when one family member is unemployed.

On the demand side, substantial changes in the labor market itself have taken place. There has been

a decline in the share of production-line employment and a rise in the share of service employment. There has been a decline in the share of union employment. Now, fewer than one in five workers belongs to a union. Employment has shifted from the East Coast and Midwest to the Sun Belt states and to the western states.

Figure 2 showed that since 1950 there has been a general upward trend in the unemployment rate. The three factors that have been most prominent in the long-term rise in the unemployment rate are the increasing share of women in the labor force, the rise of multiple-earner households, and the increase in unemployment benefits. The increase in unemployment benefits lowers the costs of being unemployed and makes it easier for unemployed workers to carry out longer searches for new jobs.

## THE KEYNESIAN MODEL OF CYCLICAL UNEMPLOYMENT

The Keynesian model analyzes the behavior of labor markets in which wages and prices are not flexible, but are rather characterized by a number of frictions. These frictions include "sticky" inflexible wages and "sticky" inflexible prices. In the Keynesian model, wages are presumed to be more inflexible than are prices. The Keynesian model also considers situations where the workers themselves are unable to respond to changing labor market conditions because of their inability to move or to retrain.

### SOURCES OF INFLEXIBLE WAGES: IMPLICIT CONTRACTS

In the Keynesian model, there can be numerous sources of wage inflexibilities. Unions have collective-bargaining power. They are willing to trade off some unemployment of union members in order to raise wages or to keep them steady in the face of declining demand. Governments pass minimum wage laws that prevent wages from falling to equilibrium rates for unskilled workers. Wage contracts that cover a year or more may prevent wages from adjusting quickly to changing conditions in the labor market.

The use of implicit contracting represents another source of inflexibility in the labor market. In certain industries—typically, unionized industries such as automobiles and steel—workers have an implicit contract with their employers that motivates them not to search for jobs when they have been laid off.

> An **implicit contract** is an agreement between employer and employees concerning conditions of pay, employment, and unemployment that is unwritten but understood by both parties.

Industries that use implicit contracting are subject to the ups and downs of the business cycle. During business expansions, more jobs are available; during downturns, fewer jobs are available. The employers need a long-term labor force of experienced workers who have gained skills specific to that industry. When business is bad, they do not want to lose their skilled workers permanently. Workers, on the other hand, have acquired skills that are more valuable to that particular firm than to outside firms. They know that they will earn their highest wages in that industry.

To cope with this situation, workers and employers strike an implicit bargain. Employers agree to pay workers a higher wage than they could earn elsewhere as long as they are employed. In return, workers agree to wait to be recalled when laid off during bad times, and the employer agrees that laid-off workers will be the first to be recalled when business conditions improve. The employer will not necessarily reduce the wages of those who remain employed during business downturns. Rather, wages are held steady throughout the cycle. Improvements in business conditions—not lower wages—cause jobs to reappear.

Implicit labor contracts explain the tendency of wages to remain stable during periods of high unemployment. If a large proportion of the labor force operates according to such implicit contracts, laid-off workers do not enter the job market. The presence of laid-off workers therefore need not drive down wages in the industry from which they have been laid off.

Implicit contracting explains how wages can remain steady during periods of high unemployment.

## STRUCTURAL UNEMPLOYMENT

Inflexibilities in the labor force itself provide another source of friction in the Keynesian model. In a dynamic economy, some industries, companies, and regions experience rising economic fortunes at the same time that others experience a long-term decline. In declining industries, particularly those concentrated in specific regions of the country, employees suffer structural unemployment. This ebb and flow of rising and declining industries is again Schumpeter's process of creative destruction. (See Example 2.)

> **Structural unemployment** results from the long-run decline of certain industries in response to rising costs, changes in consumer preferences, or technological change.

In the case of structural unemployment, the task of matching people and jobs is more difficult than it is for frictional unemployment because workers must move from a declining industry to an expanding industry to find jobs. People are not perfectly adaptable. If they have worked in one industry for many years, it is difficult for them to begin again in another industry. If they have lived in one part of the country and jobs disappear there, it is very hard to move.

Long-term structural unemployment is especially prominent when it is concentrated in a specific region of the country. The declining defense spending of the 1990s caused structural unemployment in California, Texas, and Massachusetts. Not only must aerospace workers find jobs in different industries, they must move to new job locations. Other examples are the high unemployment in the oil industry in the mid-1980s and massive unemployment in the steel and automobile industries of the mid-west in the 1970s. People hit hardest by structural unemployment are those who find it most difficult to relocate. Workers over 50 years old with many years of employment in the defense or oil industry would find it difficult (and perhaps not economically worthwhile) to move to another industry in another region.

## CYCLICAL UNEMPLOYMENT AND INFLATION

The Keynesian model emphasizes cyclical unemployment as a source of unemployment.

During cyclical downturns, fewer goods and services are purchased, employers cut back on jobs, and people find themselves without jobs. Many workers in basic industrial employment (steel, auto, and farm equipment manufacturing) will be unemployed until the economy improves.

## EXAMPLE 2
## WHERE WILL THE JOBS BE
## IN 2005?

Figure 1 of this chapter shows the dramatic shifts in the composition of employment that have taken place over the past quarter century. For those who are preparing for jobs in the twenty-first century, there are government projections of where the jobs are going to be. As the accompanying chart shows, the big increases in jobs will be in health services, business services, and financial services such as real estate and insurance. The typical twenty-first-century worker will be in advertising, computer and data processing, hospital employment, sales, or government service. The dominant worker will no longer be in goods-producing jobs like manufacturing or construction.

   This shift in jobs is not the result of failure or inefficiency of goods-producing industries. It is more the result of the fact that affluent societies spend their money on the above services rather than on automobiles or machine tools.

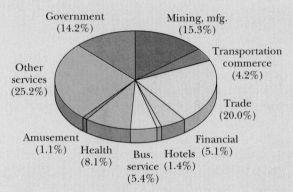

**Where the Jobs will be in 2005**

------------------------------------------------

*Source:* Statistical Abstract of the United States, section: Employment by selected industry with projections.

---

**Cyclical unemployment** is unemployment associated with general downturns in the economy.

In the case of cyclical unemployment, general declines in business activity reduce the number of unfilled positions, making it more difficult for jobs seekers to locate jobs. With cyclical unemployment, there is a mismatch between the number of unfilled jobs and qualified job seekers. As business worsens, workers are unemployed for longer periods: Family incomes fall, marriages break apart, and even the suicide rate rises during periods of cyclical unemployment. We become worried about our jobs and often express our dissatisfaction at the ballot box by voting against incumbents.

   Although jobs affected by cyclical unemployment often pay higher wages than other jobs, cyclical unemployment offers few or no benefits to the un-

employed or to society. That otherwise productive workers are sitting on the sidelines without jobs reduces the efficiency of resource utilization and causes the economy to produce less output than it is capable of producing.

   Figure 7 shows cyclical unemployment. A business downturn causes a reduction in the demand for labor (from D to D'). For reasons we shall discuss below, the reduction in labor demand does not cause real wages to fall. The real wage remains at $W_0$ and now the number of jobs ($V$) is less than the number of qualified job seekers ($N$). The difference between the number of jobs and qualified job seekers caused by a business downsizing is cyclical unemployment.

## UNEMPLOYMENT AND INFLATION
## IN THE KEYNESIAN MODEL

When wages and prices are not flexible, we would expect an inverse relationship between the unem-

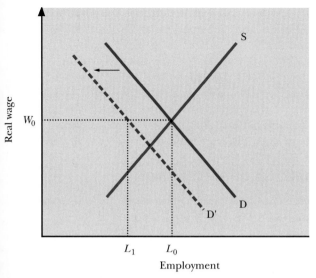

**FIGURE 7   Cyclical Unemployment**

We begin with the labor supply and demand curves S and D and a real wage of $W_0$ and employment of $L_0$. The economy is at the natural rate of unemployment with only frictional unemployment. The demand for labor falls (to D'), but real wages do not adjust. At $W_0$, there are $L_1$ jobs and $L_0$ job seekers. The resulting unemployment ($L_0 - L_1$) is cyclical unemployment.

ployment rate and the inflation rate. In Figure 7, the decrease in aggregate demand raises the unemployment rate and reduces prices. If we had increased rather than reduced aggregate demand with inflexible wages and prices, the unemployment rate would have been reduced and prices would have increased.

Recall that all the "frictions" of the Keynesian model disappear in the long run. The self-correcting mechanism will restore the economy to full employment (after a spell of unemployment), but at a lower level of wages and prices. The long-run Keynesian result is therefore the same as the classical model: The amount of employment (unemployment) is independent of the level of inflation.

## STAGFLATION AND THE PHILLIPS CURVE

In 1958, an Australian economist teaching in England published what was later termed "one of the most influential articles in economics." The economist was A.W. Phillips, and his research on inflation

and unemployment in England showed that for a very long period, the relationship between inflation and unemployment had been negative.

Phillips's study was followed by studies in the 1960s for the United States, which showed that there was also a trade-off between inflation and unemployment in the U.S. economy.

Although nothing in the theory suggests that there is an ironclad negative relationship between inflation and unemployment, many economists, journalists, and policymakers concluded that economies are indeed characterized by a Phillips curve.

> The **Phillips curve** shows a negative relationship between the unemployment rate and the inflation rate.

Widespread belief in the Phillips curve once again turned economics into a dismal science that appeared to preach a mandate of either low inflation and high unemployment or low unemployment and high inflation. That is, we cannot have both low inflation and low unemployment.

On the more positive side, the Phillips curve seemed to suggest that at least we would be spared the combination of high (or rising) unemployment and high (or rising) inflation: If inflation is rising, at least the unemployment rate should fall. If unemployment is rising, at least the inflation should drop.

## STAGFLATION AND THE PHILLIPS CURVE

Many economists, policymakers, and journalists were surprised when both inflation and unemployment rose in the 1970s, not only in the United States but also in Europe. They continued to be surprised in the 1980s and 1990s when European unemployment rates continued to rise without an apparent reduction in inflation.

The combination of high unemployment and high inflation in the 1970s and early 1980s shattered belief in an inevitable trade-off between inflation and unemployment, and prompted a search for new understanding of the relationship between inflation and unemployment.

> **Stagflation** is the combination of high unemployment and high inflation.

Virtually all industrialized countries experienced both rising inflation and rising unemployment during the 1970s and thereafter (Figure 8). Stagflation presents a serious policy dilemma. If we have both unemployment and inflation, what should we do? If we fight high unemployment, we worsen inflation; if we fight inflation, we worsen unemployment.

## UNEMPLOYMENT AND INFLATION DATA

Data on U.S. inflation and unemployment show why stagflation was a surprise in the early 1970s [Figure 9 Panel(*a*)]. In the 1950s and 1960s, high unemployment had been accompanied by low inflation. The combination of inflation and unemployment rates for the 1960s are connected by a green line in Figure 9, panel (*a*). The 1960s dots show that unemployment fell from 5–7 percent in the early 1960s to 3–4 percent in the late 1960s, while inflation rose from 1–2 percent in the early 1960s to 4–5 percent in the late 1960s.

The line connecting the 1960s dots traces out a negatively sloped Phillips curve. The combination of high unemployment and low inflation appeared logical. At low rates of unemployment, labor markets become "overheated" and push up wage inflation. Conversely, at high rates of unemployment, labor markets are "loose," and wages tend to fall.

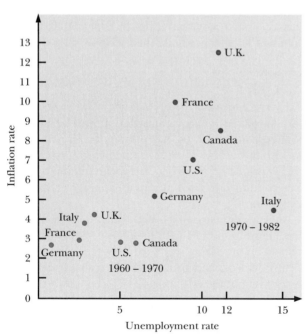

**FIGURE 8   World Stagflation: Unemployment and Inflation in the 1960s and 1970s**

*Source: Economic Report of the President,* selected years.

As we can see from Figure 9, the combinations of inflation and unemployment for the 1970s, 1980s, and 1990s do not show a clear trade-off between higher inflation and lower unemployment. The red line connects the years 1969 to 1995. Instead of the neat negative relationship of the 1960s line, the red line of the 1970s, 1980s, and 1990s dissolves into a swirling pattern. For the 1970s and the early 1980s, both unemployment and inflation rose together.

## ORIGINS OF STAGFLATION

No one can know with certainty the causes of stagflation in the United States and Europe, beginning in the 1970s. There is probably no single cause, but a combination of factors. Let's consider two.

**Full Employment Policies.**   The previous chapter on inflation demonstrated that supply-side inflations are not self-perpetuating unless they are "ratified" on the demand side. With the U.S. and European governments committed to full employment, an adverse supply shock, such as the two energy shocks of the early and late 1970s, would have increased both inflation and unemployment. If monetary and fiscal authorities respond by increasing aggregate demand to fight inflation, supply-side inflation is ratified, inflation is pushed even higher, and a wage/price spiral begins.

> One explanation of stagflation is that the pursuit of full-employment goals during a period of adverse supply shocks sets off a wage/price spiral.

**Unemployment Compensation.**   Another reaction to rising unemployment was the increasing liberalization of unemployment benefits in the United States and Europe, particularly in Western Europe. As unemployment benefits became more generous, the costs of being unemployed fell and the unemployment rate rose. In another case of unintended consequences, a policy designed to alleviate the problems of unemployment only made it worse.

## THE "NEW" SHORT-RUN PHILLIPS CURVE

Why is there a trade-off between inflation and unemployment in one period and stagflation in another period? The explanation provided by Nobel laureate Milton Friedman and Edmund S. Phelps is that a

(*a*) Inflation/Unemployment Combinations

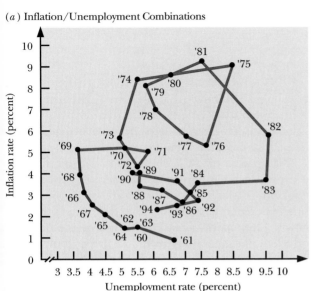

(*b*) Shifts in Short-Run Phillips Curves

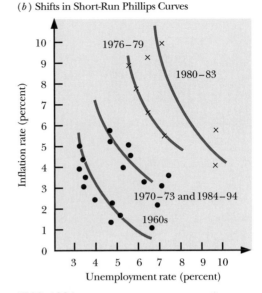

**FIGURE 9   Inflation and Unemployment in the United States, 1960–1994**

Panel (*a*) plots the inflation/unemployment combinations for the period 1960–1991. The 1960s are connected with a green line that shows a negatively sloped Phillips curve. The red line connecting the 1970s and 1980s reveals a swirling pattern, rather than the expected trade-off between inflation and unemployment. In panel (*b*), free-hand curves are drawn through the dots for the 1960s, early 1970s, late 1970s, and early 1980s, and late 1980s. These curves show shifts in the short-run Phillips curves as inflationary expectations change.

trade-off exists when inflationary expectations are constant, and stagflation will occur when inflationary expectations are rising. With stable inflationary expectations, a line connecting inflation-unemployment dots will look like the pattern of the 1960s. With rising inflationary expectations, there will be a rising pattern of both inflation and unemployment.

Figure 10 shows how the relationship between inflation and unemployment depends on inflationary expectations. We start with inflationary expectations constant. The lower curve, labeled $PC_0$, shows the relationship between inflation and unemployment for an anticipated inflation rate of 0 percent.

In Figure 10, inflation rises unexpectedly to 5 percent, although we are expecting zero inflation. Inflation causes wage offers to rise. Now more job offers exceed reservation wages. Unexpected inflation shortens job searches and the unemployment rate falls. Firms raise their production, hire more workers, and unemployment falls. With rising wages, unemployment benefits are less attractive. All these factors cause unemployment to fall.

Figure 10 shows that unexpected inflation moves the economy from point *c* (zero inflation and 5 percent unemployment) to point *a* (5 percent inflation and 3 percent unemployment).

The relationship between inflation and unemployment when inflationary expectations are constant is called the short-run Phillips curve.

The **short-run Phillips curve** shows a negative relationship between inflation and unemployment when inflationary expectations are constant.

In Figure 10, $PC_5$ is the short-run Phillips curve when we expect an inflation rate of 5 percent. It is drawn above the short-run Phillips curve for an anticipated inflation of 0 percent, $PC_0$. If we expect an inflation rate of 5 percent and the actual inflation rate is greater than 5 percent, output expands and unemployment falls for the same reasons that these occur in the $PC_0$ curve.

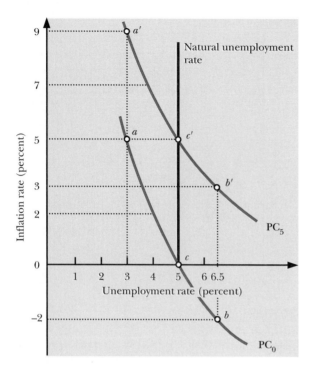

**FIGURE 10   The New Phillips Curve**

The economy is initially operating at the natural rate (assumed to be 5 percent) at point *c* on the Phillips curve $PC_0$. The actual and anticipated inflation rates are 0 percent. An increase in aggregate demand raises the inflation rate to 5 percent, and the unanticipated inflation moves the economy to point *a*, where the unemployment rate is 3 percent. If the economy had instead been at point *c'* with an anticipated inflation rate of 5 percent, the Phillips curve would be $PC_5$. On $PC_5$, a 9 percent inflation rate is required to move the economy to point *a'*, where the unemployment rate is again 3 percent.

> There is a different short-run Phillips curve for different expected inflation rates.

Why is $PC_5$ above $PC_0$? An increase in the anticipated inflation rate causes short-run Phillips curves to shift up. As this shift occurs, both unemployment and inflation rise—the phenomenon of stagflation. Let us consider why this happens.

The natural rate of unemployment is the point at which the number of qualified job seekers ($U$) and the number of vacant jobs ($V$) balance. Inflationary pressures are constant. Whether the actual inflation rate is − 10 percent, 0 percent, or + 10 percent, as long as actual and anticipated inflation are the same there will be no change in output, employment, and unemployment.

Workers and firms do not change employment or output decisions if there are no changes in real wages or in the ratio of business costs to selling prices.

Figure 10 shows that short-run Phillips curves shift up *when anticipated inflation increases*. There is an entire family of short-run Phillips curves—one for each anticipated rate of inflation.

At point *c* on $PC_0$, the economy is at the natural rate of unemployment and people expect zero inflation. An actual inflation rate of 5 percent is thus 5 percentage points above the anticipated inflation rate. In response to the unexpected rise in inflation, the unemployment rate falls from 5 percent to 3 percent (the movement from point *c* to point *a*).

> Unexpected inflation pushes the actual unemployment rate below the natural rate.

As inflation continues at 5 percent, we eventually come to anticipate this rate. Eventually, new wage and supply contracts are based on the higher (correctly anticipated) inflation rate of 5 percent. Firms that had been encouraged by the unexpected inflation to provide more employment now find that their wages and production costs are rising at the same rate as their selling prices. They accordingly reduce their output, and unemployment rises. As inflationary expectations rise from 0 to 5 percent, the short-run Phillips curve shifts up from $PC_0$ to $PC_5$.

> An increase in inflationary expectations causes the short-run Phillips curve to shift up.

We are now in a position to make more sense of the confusing swirls of Figure 9. We superimpose five freehand curves over the dots in Figure 9, panel (*a*): one each through the dots of the 1960s, the early 1970s, the late 1970s, the early 1980s, the late 1980s, and the 1990s. The result, shown in panel (*b*), is four short-run Phillips curves (the late 1980s curve coincides with the early 1970s curve), each with a negative slope. These free-hand representations show how the short-run Phillips curve shifted upward as inflationary expectations rose from the 1960s to the early 1980s and then shifted back down in the mid-1980s and 1990s as inflationary expectations fell.

## STAGFLATION POLICY CHOICES

In the 1970s and early 1980s we faced high inflation and high unemployment (stagflation). When we chose to fight back against high inflation at the end of the 1970s, the result was the most severe recession of the postwar period. If we again have a stagflation, how can we fight inflation without raising unemployment or lower unemployment without causing more inflation?

Unless the public can somehow be convinced to lower its inflationary expectations immediately, an antiinflationary program will raise unemployment and interest rates. Any program that raises both unemployment and interest rates will likely face political opposition.

Figure 11 illustrates this problem. The economy is initially operating at the natural rate of unemployment (5 percent), with an inflation rate of 10 percent. Actual and anticipated inflation are equal. How can the economy move from a high rate of inflation to a zero rate of inflation without raising unemployment (how can it move from point $c'$ to point $c$)?

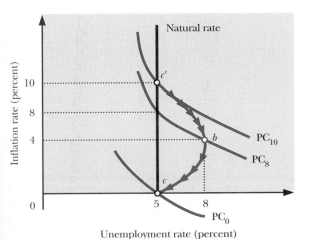

**FIGURE 11   The Unemployment Costs of Reducing Inflation**

The economy is initially operating at point $c'$—at the natural rate of 5 percent unemployment with an anticipated inflation rate of 10 percent (which equals the actual inflation rate). Monetary authorities reduce the growth of the money supply, and the rate of inflation begins to slow. The economy begins to move along the curve $c'bc$. Point $b$ is a representative intermediate point where the inflation rate is 4 percent, but the anticipated inflation rate is 8 percent; unemployment is 8 percent. Until the expected rate of inflation falls to 0 percent, the economy will continue to experience unemployment above the natural rate.

According to the new Phillips-curve analysis, moving from point $c'$ to point $c$ is very difficult because inflationary expectations must be brought down to 0 percent! If inflationary expectations drop slowly, unemployment will initially rise.

A simplified picture of the path of the economy might look something like the curve $c'bc$. The economy starts at point $c'$ with inflation at 10 percent, unemployment at 5 percent, and the anticipated inflation rate at 10 percent. When contractionary policies are applied, the economy moves to point $b$. At this intermediate point, the unemployment rate has risen to 8 percent and the inflation rate has dropped to 4 percent, but the anticipated inflation rate is 8 percent. Unemployment above the natural rate has been caused by an anticipated rate of inflation higher than actual inflation. The hardships of unemployment at point $b$ may be considerable. As the inflation rate continues to drop toward 0 percent, inflationary expectations will continue to drop. Once the economy reaches point $c$, the natural rate of unemployment is restored, and the actual and anticipated rates of inflation are both 0 percent. In the meantime, however, the economy has experienced high unemployment.

### GRADUALISM

To move from point $c'$ to point $c$ in Figure 11 requires a reduction in the rate of growth of the money supply. Even if this is accomplished all at once—say, the rate of growth of money supply is cut from 13 percent to a permanent 3 percent—the economy may require three to five years to move along $c'bc$ to $c$. During these years, the economy would have to endure considerable unemployment. A gradualist policy might reduce the impact on unemployment.

> A **gradualist policy** calls for steady reductions in monetary growth spread over a period of years to combat accelerating inflation.

Instead of reducing the growth of the money supply from 13 percent to 3 percent all at once, monetary authorities might do it gradually over a period of, say, five years. Moreover, in order to persuade the public to lower its expectations about inflation, monetary authorities would announce in advance the scheduled reductions in the rate of monetary growth. If our expectations are rational—when we believe the government policy announcements—we immediately lower the anticipated rate of inflation. If we do not believe the government's monetary-growth plans will be carried out, the anticipated inflation rate will drop only when we see the actual inflation rate dropping.

Sometimes governments can persuade the public that it will follow a policy of slow monetary growth. In response, the public lowers its anticipated inflation rate. The most famous example of this approach occurred during the German hyperinflation after World War I. To lower inflation without substantially raising unemployment, Germany announced a monetary reform (changing the monetary unit and balancing the government budget) that convinced the public that it was serious—the monetary reform ended the hyperinflation without sending the econ-

omy into a deep recession. Although the United States appears to have cured stagflation in the early 1980s, Western Europe still suffers from the combination of high unemployment and high inflation. (See Example 3.)

The next chapter addresses the most widely debated issue in macroeconomics—the business cycle.

## SUMMARY

1. The labor market matches people to jobs. Unemployed workers use labor market search to find jobs by weighing costs and benefits. They take the first job that pays their reservation wage.

### EXAMPLE 3
### EUROPE'S CENTRAL BANKERS DECLARE
### THE PHILLIPS CURVE DEAD

After years of indecision, Europe's central bankers have concluded that the Phillips curve is dead. Central banks cannot reduce unemployment by creating more inflation! The accompanying diagram for the European Union of countries shows why they have reached this conclusion. There is no apparent long-term relationship between inflation and unemployment.

Past attempts to use monetary policy to create jobs may have had some effect in the short run, but in the long run, countries have ended up with both higher inflation and higher unemployment.

- - - - - - - - - - - - - - - - - - - - - - - - - - -

*Source:* "A Grizzly Subject: Not All Central Bankers Want to Turn a Blind Eye to Unemployment," *The Economist*, September 3, 1994, p. 78.

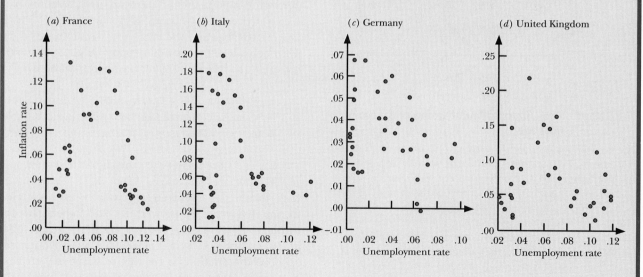

**Inflation vs Unemployment, 1962 to present**

2. The classical model with flexible wages and prices states that economies tends to operate at full employment with only frictional employment and without a trade-off between inflation and unemployment.

3. The rise in the long-term unemployment rate has likely been affected by rising unemployment benefits, the increase in the percentage of families with more than one income earner, and minimum-wage laws.

4. The Keynesian model considers reductions in aggregate demand when wages and prices are inflexible. Cyclical unemployment occurs when the economy operates above the natural rate of unemployment. In the long run, the economy should return to the natural rate of unemployment.

5. Along with structural unemployment, implicit contracts are a source of employment friction. When employers and employees in a certain industry strike implicit bargains that laid-off workers will be recalled to high-wage jobs in return for not seeking jobs elsewhere, wages in that industry tend to remain steady during periods of high unemployment.

6. Stagflation is the combination of high unemployment and high inflation. The original Phillips curve showed a stable negative relationship between unemployment and inflation. It predicted that to reduce inflation, a higher unemployment rate had to be accepted and that to reduce unemployment, a higher inflation rate had to be endured. The Phillips-curve relationship held for the 1960s but not for the 1970s and later, when increasing inflation was accompanied by increasing unemployment.

7. The short-run Phillips curve shifts up with the anticipated rate of inflation. Only if inflationary expectations are constant will there be a trade-off between inflation and unemployment.

8. Unanticipated reductions in the rate of inflation increase unemployment. Reducing unemployment without increasing inflation is difficult. It may be possible to lower the anticipated rate of inflation by using price and wage controls or a preannounced policy of monetary restraint, but such policies are difficult to implement. Inflation can be reduced by permanently lowering the rate of growth of the money supply, but until inflationary expectations fall, the unemployment rate will rise. The unemployment costs of fighting inflation can extend over a period of years. Gradualism provides one solution

to the problem of fighting inflation without creating too much unemployment.

## KEY TERMS

reservation wage
frictional unemployment
implicit contract
structural
    unemployment

cyclical unemployment
Phillips curve
stagflation
short-run Phillips curve
gradualist policy

## QUESTIONS AND PROBLEMS

1. To what extent can the different types of unemployment—cyclical, structural, and frictional—be considered voluntary or involuntary?
2. Brown is prepared to take a job that pays $50,000 per year with a two-week paid vacation in the first year, but Brown cannot find such a job. Would Brown be classified as unemployed?
3. Explain why it is unlikely for cyclical unemployment to account for the long-run rise in unemployment in the United States.
4. "Economists are on the wrong track when they say that unemployment decisions are based upon cost/benefit analysis. Cost/benefit analysis applies to most economic decision making, but not to unemployment. Able-bodied people want to work." Evaluate this statement.
5. Using cost/benefit analysis, explain why rising coverage for unemployment benefits may affect the unemployment rate.
6. Assume that tax rates are substantially reduced. In which direction would you expect the natural unemployment rate to change?
7. Explain, using job-search theory, why the duration of unemployment is lower for teenagers than for adult workers.
8. What happens to the number of people not in the labor force during recessions? Give some reasons for this pattern.
9. Draw a diagram showing the relationship between the marginal costs and marginal benefits of job search for a laid-off worker who decides not to search for a new job in order to be available for recall.
10. Assuming that the Bureau of Labor Statistics could detect all underground employment and thus exclude underground workers from the of-

ficially unemployed, which of the following cases would be considered an example of unemployment?

   a. A full-time student is detected working on an unreported basis as a waiter.
   b. An electrician is caught installing wiring after hours on an unreported basis.
   c. A woman who gives her occupation as a homemaker is found to be conducting an unreported cosmetics business from her house.

11. Explain how the unemployment rate can fall when unemployment is rising.

12. How should each of the following affect search time?

   a. The amount of time an unemployed worker can draw unemployment benefits is lowered from 6 months to 3 months.
   b. The spouse of an unemployed worker loses his or her job.
   c. State employment offices increase the amount of information they make available on job vacancies.
   d. Wages fall generally in the economy, and many people perceive them to be decreasing more rapidly than prices.

# CHAPTER 34

# BUSINESS CYCLES

The Defining Moments of economics—the Industrial Revolution, globalization, the collapse of socialism—relate the truly great events of economics. They tell us why we have achieved unprecedented levels of affluence, why we now live and work in a world economy, and why the Soviet Union collapsed. We have gained economic insight even from the devastating unemployment of the Great Depression.

Recall the old joke of the husband and wife, in which the wife says: "I'll let you decide all the big issues, and I'll take care of all the small problems. You decide how to achieve world peace; I'll decide how we'll spend our money, where we live, and whether or not to buy a house."

Macroeconomics is much like this time-worn joke. We all recognize the importance of long-term growth, the economic system we live under, and the existence of a world economy. However, we live in the present. We are concerned with all the issues of daily living; although many of the daily issues will

even out in the long run, they are terribly important to us now.

Breathless newscasters recite the latest economic statistics on unemployment, inflation, Dow Jones indexes, job loss, job creation, and plant closings. They don't talk about growth over the last decade—or the next. Pundits warn that bad times are on the horizon. The dire warnings of impending collapse and disaster are expressed by innumerable doomsters in best-selling books.

If the economy were to grow steadily and smoothly with little or no inflation, we would not be so short-sighted. We would know that tomorrow will be very much like today, only better. We could confidently make our plans for work, investment, and leisure. The economy doesn't behave in this fashion, however. Its ups and downs require us to be ever-alert to prevent personal financial harm.

Keynes spoke to an attentive world when, in 1936, he appeared to explain what caused the biggest "down" of all—the Great Depression. Even more soothing to his audience was his appearance of knowing what to do to prevent further economic downturns.

In this chapter we shall confront the causes of the business cycle and what to do about it, if any-thing. The chapter raises the most important policy issue that divides economists: Do economists know enough and do they have the tools to control or moderate the business cycle?

## BUSINESS CYCLE EXPERIENCE

We were introduced to the business cycle and its characteristics in the opening chapter on macroeconomics. Recall that business cycles last for several years (an average of five years in the United States), long enough to allow cumulative upward and downward movements in real GDP. Given the long-term trend of positive economic growth, the downturn phase of the business cycle is shorter than its expansion phase. Business cycles are different from other fluctuations in economic outputs—such as a reduction in wheat production or of automobile output—because they are larger, longer, and more diffuse.

### PERSISTENCE OF THE BUSINESS CYCLE

Economists and government officials have kept historical records of the business cycle. They occurred just as readily in Colonial America, in tsarist Russia, and in Bismark's Germany as in modern times. According to U.S. official statistics, we had seven business cycles (including the Great Depression) between 1919 and 1945 and nine business cycles between 1945 and the present.

No region of the world appears to be spared the business cycle, although Soviet Russia used to boast that its planned socialist economy made it immune to the business cycle. The industrialized countries experience business cycles; the developing countries also have business cycles. In fact, we know that business cycles are often transmitted from one country or region to another—a consequence of the growing globalization of the world economy.

### COSTS

Business cycles affect our personal finances, our jobs, interest rates, and the prices we pay. During cyclical downturns (or in anticipation of downturns), the value of our stocks may fall; our jobs may become less secure or we may even lose them. During expansions and periods of prosperity, our jobs are more secure, prices and interest rates are more likely to rise, and our stock portfolios tend to rise in value. These are all private costs and benefits that result from business cycles.

What are the costs and benefits of business cycles for the economy as a whole? The cost of business downturns, emphasized by Keynes and his later followers, is the lost opportunity to produce output. In a recession, the economy produces below the natural level of output, and the lost output is lost forever. If the economy could operate constantly at full employment—if the business cycle could be avoided—it would end up producing more cumulative output, and our standard of living would be higher.

The loss of output is measured by the GDP gap.

> The **GDP gap** is the difference between current real GDP and the natural level of real GDP.

When the GDP gap is cumulated over a period of time, it is a measure of the cumulated cost of business cycles.

Some economists argue that business cycles are not all bad. Cyclical downturns have, in fact, a cleansing effect. If the economy were to grow steadily without interruption, businesses would be under less pressure to economize on costs, to innovate, and to keep their operations lean. During recessions, businesses must learn to make do with fewer workers, hold down costs, and become more competitive in the world economy.

For example, the recession of the early 1990s and the slow recovery from that recession forced

U.S. firms to become leaner and more competitive. It was during this period that U.S. automobile manufacturers overtook Japanese manufacturers in efficiency of production (as measured by output per worker) and regained their international competitiveness.

Although few economists would argue that we should deliberately have a recession every five years or so, in view of the cost of lost output, the positive effects of downturns on the efficiency of firms cannot be overlooked.

## CAUSES OF BUSINESS CYCLES

In the chapters on aggregate supply and demand and on unemployment and inflation, we explored the causes of business cycles. However, we focused on only the classical and Keynesian explanations. We shall review these two models here, but they are not the sole competing explanations of the business cycle.

Over the last century at least two dozen explanations of the business cycle have been advanced. These explanations include monetary theories, overinvestment theories, underconsumption theories, and psychological theories. In an influential article, 1995 Nobel laureate Robert Lucas pointed out, after surveying the facts of the business cycle, that "business cycles are all alike. To theoretically inclined economists, this . . . suggests the possibility of a unified explanation of business cycles, grounded in the general laws governing market economies."[1]

What kinds of unified explanations have been offered? In this chapter, we shall consider four theories of the business cycle: the Keynesian theory, the rational expectation approach, the Schumpeterian sector-shift hypothesis, and real business cycle theory.

### KEYNESIAN THEORY: INFLEXIBLE WAGES AND PRICES

The Keynesian theory states that business cycles are demand driven. With sticky wages, increases (or

decreases) in aggregate demand raise (or lower) real GDP and employment. As we already noted in the chapter on saving and investment, investment demand is highly unstable because the accelerator and animal spirits can propel investors in unpredictable directions. Unstable investment spending causes shocks to aggregate demand. An upsurge in investment raises aggregate demand. A swing to business pessimism causes a negative shock to aggregate demand.

Figure 1 shows a cyclical contraction caused by a reduction in aggregate demand. With a positively sloped aggregate supply curve due to inflexible wages, a reduction in aggregate demand *reduces real GDP and employment* and *lowers the price level* or the rate of inflation. Expansions are caused by increases in aggregate demand, which increase real GDP and employment and raise the price level or the rate of inflation.

The Keynesian theory of business cycles has enjoyed considerable popularity. It appears to account for such factors as optimism, cumulative expansions and contractions, monetary factors, and psychology. We have only to accept the proposition that aggregate demand is unstable in order to explain business cycles. From a policy perspective, the Keynesian theory offers the hope that the business cycle can be controlled by monetary or fiscal policies. If we can use monetary or fiscal policy to stabilize aggregate demand, we could control the business cycle.

Acceptance of the Keynesian explanation of the business cycle was virtually complete by the mid-1960s. Only a few mavericks questioned the Keynesian view that business cycles are caused by fluctuations in aggregate demand. However, evidence and experience accumulated since the 1970s have caused many economists to question the Keynesian interpretation of events:

1. Industrialized countries around the world have experienced rising unemployment and inflation—or stagflation—since the late 1960s. In the 1950s, the sum of the unemployment rate and the inflation rate was in the 3–6 percent range for most industrialized countries. Starting in the mid 1970s, both unemployment and inflation began to rise together. Although inflation moderated in the 1980s and 1990s, the sum of the unemployment rate and the inflation rate remains at double-digit levels in most highly industrialized economies. Economists Robert Lucas and Thomas Sargent refer to this as "failure on a grand

---

[1]Robert Lucas, "Understanding Business Cycles," in Karl Brunner and Allen Meltzer, eds., *Stabilization of the Domestic and International Economy*, Carnegie-Rochester Conference, vol. 5 (Amsterdam: North-Holland, 1977).

(a)

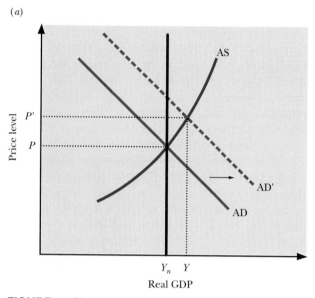

(b)

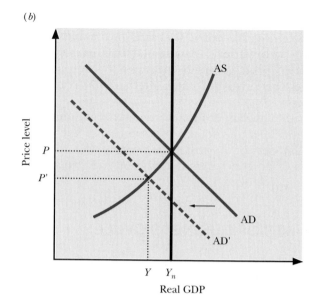

**FIGURE 1   The Keynesian Business Cycle**

Panel (a) shows an increase in aggregate demand (AD) with inflexible wages. The increase in aggregate demand raises output above the natural level of output (and lowers unemployment below the natural rate). Panel (b) shows a reduction in aggregate demand with inflexible wages. The decrease in aggregate demand reduces output below the natural level of output (and raises unemployment above the natural rate). Fluctuations in aggregate demand explain fluctuations in output and employment.

scale." According to Keynesian economics, such rising unemployment should be caused by reductions in aggregate demand. But lower aggregate demand should cause lower prices, not higher prices. The Keynesian business-cycle model does not explain stagflation.

2. After World War II, Keynesians predicted that the U.S. economy would fall into a deep depression if government spending were sharply reduced. Ignoring the warnings of Keynesians, President Harry Truman and Congress cut government spending by about 60 percent in a single year (from 1945 to 1946). In fact, this massive cut in government spending did not result in a corresponding increase in unemployment. In the years immediately following World War II, unemployment was mild despite massive declines in government spending.

3. Keynesian economics requires a negative correlation between real wages and output. We know from the chapter on aggregate supply and demand that the actual correlation is positive. Real wages behave procyclically in actual business cycles. They rise during expansions and fall during contractions, contradict-

ing the Keynesian demand-driven theory, which says that during expansions, firms should hire more workers because of lower real wages. Recall that in the upward-sloping aggregate supply schedule (Figure 1), the price level rises relative to fixed money wages and real wages fall in the expansion phase. The Keynesian theory of business cycles predicts that real wages should behave countercyclically: The higher the real GDP, the lower are real wages. This is not true, in fact.

## THE NEW CLASSICAL ECONOMICS: RATIONAL EXPECTATIONS WITH FLEXIBLE PRICES AND WAGES

Contradictions such as the ones listed above, especially stagflation, led economists to revive their interest in classical economic theory. Their thinking, called the new classical economics or rational expectations, uses the classical working hypothesis that wages and prices respond flexibly to market pressures. Unemployment, instead of being "involuntary," is the result of labor-market equilibrium determined by the costs and benefits of unemployment.

The new classical economics was pioneered by 1995 Nobel laureate Robert Lucas. Lucas maintains that business cycles can occur even with perfectly flexible wages and prices because we cannot possibly know everything that is happening around us.

Rational expectations assumes that we—as consumers, business owners, and workers—try to be as "rational" as possible in our pursuit of information about the future. It is important for us to know as much as possible about future inflation, wages, and interest rates. We don't just sit back and wait to be caught off guard by the next inflation.

We form our expectations of future prices, wages, interest rates, and the like using all the relevant information at our disposal. Not only do we look at the past, we also try to anticipate the effects of current and future policies. In effect, we use rational expectations to anticipate the future. (Recall the discussion of rational expectations from the chapter on inflation.)

*what people think will happen*

> **Rational expectations** are expectations of future inflation, wages, interest rates, and other macroeconomic variables that we form not only from past experience but also from our understanding of the effects of current policies on these variables.

When expectations are formed rationally, they can change dramatically when we perceive policies as changing. If, for example, we conclude that there has been a fundamental change in Fed policy, we might immediately change our expectation of future inflation. If residents of Russia conclude that the Russian government is serious about stopping rapid inflation and will stop running budget deficits, they will immediately change their expectation of inflation.

It is extremely important to understand that rational expectations says that we *do our best* to anticipate the future. Sometimes we succeed; many times we fail. Rational expectations does not mean that we are always right about the future.

How the economy responds to demand shocks depends upon whether we anticipate inflation correctly or incorrectly. If we make a mistake we suffer a price surprise.

> **Price surprises** occur when the actual price level is different from the anticipated price level (or when the actual rate of inflation is different from the anticipated rate).

**Anticipating Incorrectly: Price-Level Surprises.**
Let's take the case of an economy that is at the natural level of output at price level $P$ (as shown in Figure 2). Something now happens to increase aggregate demand—it does not matter what; it could be an increase in business optimism or that the Fed increases the money supply. Will this increase in demand shock cause more output to be produced, as it does in the Keynesian model? Let's consider the "classical" case where the economy has no "frictions." Wages and prices are perfectly flexible.

Whether the increase in demand causes firms to produce more output and to increase employment depends on whether we correctly anticipate the demand shock and its effect on prices. Take the case where we are caught off guard in spite of our efforts to anticipate the future. We mistakenly expect the current price level to continue as is.

As prices start to rise, as they must with an increase in aggregate demand, we become confused. We experience a price surprise. Businesses see that they can raise their prices. Workers see that they can earn higher wages. Business firms, as we know from the chapter on aggregate supply and demand, will increase their output only if their prices have risen more than their costs. Employees will want to work harder and more hours only if their real wages have risen. In this example, prices and wages are perfectly flexible, but the unexpected inflation (price surprise) has caused both firms and employees to be fooled. Firms are confused into thinking that their prices are rising faster than their costs. Employees are fooled into thinking that their real wages are rising.

How can this be? Rational expectations says that business firms and employees can easily be fooled into such a conclusion. We all specialize in the information that is most relevant to us. We cannot know everything. Businesses know very well the prices of the things they sell, but they know less well their costs. They sell one or two products but they buy hundreds or even thousands of inputs, including labor inputs. Workers know very well their money wages, but they know less well the prices of the hun-

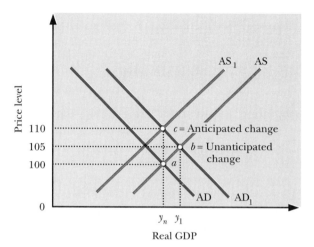

**FIGURE 2    The Rational Expectations Explanation of the Business Cycle**

The initial equilibrium of aggregate supply and aggregate demand occurs at point $a$, where the AD curve intersects the AS curve. The AD curve shifts upward to $AD_1$ as a result of monetary or demand-side fiscal policy. If the increase in aggregate demand is not anticipated, people and firms are caught off guard by inflation, and the economy moves along the AS curve from point $a$ to point $b$. If the policy is anticipated, the rational expectations hypothesis implies that the short-run aggregate supply curve shifts up at the same time to $AS_1$. The new equilibrium is then at point $c$, with the same GDP but a higher price level. When policy is anticipated, the economy adjusts directly from point $a$ to point $c$.

dreds of things they buy. In both cases, an unexpected inflation will cause them to think that a higher price or wage has made them better off in real terms, whereas it has not.

> An unanticipated inflation will cause firms to think their prices are rising faster than their costs and employees to think their real wages are rising.

With the misimpression that prices are rising faster than costs, business firms throughout the economy will produce more output. They will try to "make hay while the sun shines." Similarly, workers will be prepared to work more hours and harder because of their false impression that their real wages have risen.

In Figure 2, these two "mistakes" cause the economy to move up a positively sloped short run aggregate supply curve (from point $a$ to point $b$) to a position where more is being produced at the higher price

level. This is the Keynesian result, but the reason is quite different: In the Keynesian model, more is supplied because prices rose more rapidly than "sticky" wages. In the rational expectations model, more is produced even though prices and wages are perfectly flexible and rising at the same rate.

We can't be fooled forever. As we come to realize that both prices and wages are rising at the same rate, firms start to produce less output and workers work fewer hours and less hard (the short-run aggregate supply curve shifts to the left). As these adjustments take place, the economy returns to its original level of output but at an even higher level of prices.

This return to the original level of output, but at a higher price level, is the same result as the long-run self-correcting mechanism in the Keynesian model. The difference is that, in the Keynesian model, this return takes place after inflexible wages have time to adjust. In the rational expectations model, the return takes place when people realize they were fooled by the unanticipated inflation. Thus, it can happen quickly if people are fooled only a short while.

**Anticipating Correctly: No Price Surprises.** If the increase in aggregate demand (and of the price level) in Figure 2 is fully anticipated, there are no price surprises. Firms recognize that their prices are not rising more rapidly than costs. Workers do not mistake nominal wage increases for real wage increases. Because everyone recognizes that real wages and prices are not changing, there is no change in output or employment. The economy continues to produce the natural level of output even though prices are rising. In Figure 2, there is no movement up an aggregate supply curve (from point $a$ to point $b$). Instead, the aggregate supply curve shifts immediately to the left (from AS to $AS_1$) to offset the increase in aggregate demand, and prices rise immediately to the new long-run equilibrium at point $c$. *There is no short-run effect on output and unemployment.* An anticipated demand shock raises the price level without raising real GDP.

> Rational expectations states that anticipated demand shocks do not affect output and employment; hence, they cannot cause business cycles.

When we correctly anticipate price-level changes, the self-correcting mechanism works instantaneously. Firms and workers anticipate the full magnitude of the price increase, and the aggregate supply curve shifts immediately from AS to $AS_1$.

**Rational Expectations Evidence.** It is difficult to test the rational expectations model against real-world data. Its basic conclusion is that only *unanticipated* policy affects output and employment. In order to test this proposition, we must know (1) to what extent a policy has been anticipated, and (2) if the policy has been anticipated, whether people properly understand how the policy will affect the economy.

Rational expectations, therefore, concludes that the effects of monetary or fiscal policies depend on whether they are anticipated or not. If, for example, the Fed increases the money supply so as to lower unemployment, this action may or may not yield the desired result. If the resulting increase in aggregate demand is unanticipated, it creates a price surprise, and the economy moves from point *a* to point *b* in Figure 2. Output has increased and unemployment has fallen. If the move is anticipated, the economy moves from point *a* to point *c* in Figure 2. The Fed has not reduced unemployment; it has only created more inflation.

The arguments in support of rational expectation are many:

1. The most direct evidence in support of rational expectations is provided by the dramatic endings to the hyperinflations that have plagued the world. Following World War I, Austria, Germany, Hungary, and Poland experienced hyperinflations. For example, in Germany prices were doubling or tripling each month. Each hyperinflation stopped suddenly without causing deep recessions. In each case, the governments took concrete and widely announced steps to end government deficits and runaway monetary growth. By changing the monetary unit and by radically reconstructing the monetary and fiscal rules of the game, inflation was brought to an abrupt halt. This reversal could have happened only if people correctly anticipated these policy changes.

2. Evidence that only unanticipated monetary policy affects real GDP and employment has been compiled by Robert Barro, who correlated unanticipated increases in the rate of monetary growth with the rate of unemployment. Figure 3 shows that when money growth is higher than anticipated, the unemployment rate falls—a finding that supports the view that only unanticipated monetary policy affects real GDP and employment.

3. Experience with post–World War II fiscal policy is generally consistent with the rational expectations hypothesis. The U.S. 1964 tax cut was the first use of discretionary tax policy. Since people would have had great difficulty anticipating its effect, it raised output and employment. Subsequent tax changes, however, did not affect output and employment as much—a result consistent with rational expectations. The impact of subsequent tax changes would be easier to predict and, hence, would be offset. Once people understand how tax cuts work, tax cuts will affect only inflation.

4. The new Phillips curve, which we analyzed in the chapter on unemployment and stagflation, is consistent with rational expectations. Rational expectations would say that *unanticipated* expansionary policies raise output and lower unemployment while creating inflation. Thus, unanticipated policy would cause a movement along the short-run Phillips curve. *Anticipated* policy, however, raises only inflation; it does not affect output and unemployment. Anticipated policy therefore results in shifts in the short-run Phillips curve, as happened after 1970.

The rational expectations model does not account well for large-scale unemployment. Rational expectations requires that workers and firms be fooled into confusing nominal wage and price increases for real increases. Business firms should not be fooled for long or take major steps as a consequence. It is difficult to believe that people are unemployed because of price surprises at the macro level. Information about inflation is circulated extremely rapidly compared with the length of time some recessions last. The CPI is calculated and reported each month. If a recession is caused because prices are lower than expected, it should be very short. There is simply too much public information on prices for people to be mistaken for long.

## THE SECTOR SHIFT: BUSINESS CYCLES

Joseph Schumpeter, one of the Defining Moment economists, explained the business cycle as a re-

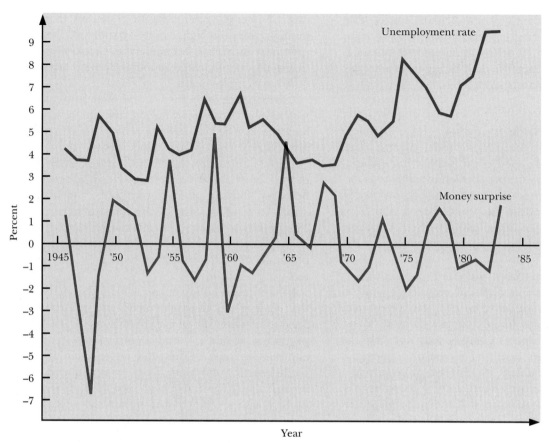

**FIGURE 3   The Relationship Between Unanticipated Growth in the Money Supply and Unemployment**

Robert Barro's estimates of the money surprise are based on the unanticipated rate of growth of the money supply (measured as the actual money growth rate minus the anticipated money growth rate). These estimates assume that people believe the rate of growth of the money supply depends on past rates of growth, the unemployment rate, and the federal fiscal deficit. The unemployment rate tends to fall when there is unanticipated growth of the money supply. *Sources:* Based on Robert Barro, "Unanticipated Money, Output, and the Price Level in its Natural State," *Journal of Political Economy* 86 (August 1978). Updated by Mark Rush, "On the Policy Ineffectiveness Proposition and a Keynesian Alternative," unpublished paper, University of Florida.

sponse to creative destruction. By *creative destruction,* Schumpeter referred to the constant struggle among business firms and industries in the face of rapidly changing technology, which "creates" new businesses while it "destroys" old businesses. In transportation, railroads were once dominant, but then lost out to trucking; trucking then lost out to air freight. The typewriter lost out to the personal computer. Each industry and each firm's time of success is transitory. Eventually a better product or a better competitor will triumph. We innovate to make a profit. In the process of innovation, over the long run, standards of living incessantly rise. In the short run, however, the economy is subject to all sorts of fluctuations as demands and supplies constantly shift in favor of one industry or firm, necessitating the constant reshuffling of the labor force. Schumpeter argued that innovation "is at the center of practically all the phenomena, difficulties, and problems of economic life in a capitalist society."

| Table 1 Job Creation and Destruction: 1973–1986 | | |
|---|---|---|
| Industry | Job Creation Rate (percent) | Job Destruction Rate (percent) |
| Food | 8.9 | 10.4 |
| Tobacco | 5.8 | 8.2 |
| Textile | 7.4 | 11.0 |
| Apparel | 11.6 | 15.6 |
| Lumber | 12.9 | 15.0 |
| Furniture | 10.1 | 12.1 |
| Chemicals | 6.8 | 8.0 |
| Petroleum | 6.6 | 9.1 |
| Machinery | 9.6 | 11.5 |
| Transportation | 9.4 | 9.9 |

*Source:* Steven J. Davis and John Haltiwanger, "Gross Job Creation, Gross Job Destruction, and Employment Reallocation," *Quarterly Journal of Economics,* August 1992.

If we combine rational expectations with Schumpeter's creative destruction, we can identify another source of business cycles, called the sector-shift hypothesis.

The **sector-shift hypothesis** states that price surprises at the micro level can cumulate to cause business cycles.

An enormous amount of simultaneous job creation and destruction takes place in the U.S. economy—in fact, in any industrial economy. In 1973, for example, manufacturing employment in the United States expanded by 7 percent. However, this expansion consisted of two components: a 13 percent increase due to the creation of new jobs and a 6 percent decrease due to the destruction of old jobs. In 1975, when the economy was suffering a deep recession, manufacturing employment dropped 10 percent while the rate of new job creation was 7 percent.[2]

---

[2]Steven J. Davis and John Haltiwanger, "Gross Job Creation, Gross Job Destruction, and Employment Reallocation," *Quarterly Journal of Economics,* August 1992. For a concise statement on the importance of churning to the U.S. economy, see "Churning: The Paradox of Progress," in the *Annual Report of the Federal Reserve Bank of Dallas,* 1992, written by Michael Cox and Richard Alms.

Simultaneous job creation and destruction take place within industries. Table 1 shows the job creation and job destruction rates for ten major manufacturing industries in the 1970s and 1980s, the latest period for which there are data.

The **job creation rate** refers to the employment gains in expanding or new companies; the **job destruction rate** refers to the employment losses in shrinking or failing business firms.

In the apparel industry, 15.6 percent of the jobs were lost in shrinking or failing firms, while 11.6 percent of the jobs were created in expanding or new firms in the same industry. Even an industry as homogeneous as lumber experienced simultaneous creation and destruction: 15 percent of the jobs were lost in shrinking or failing firms, while about 13 percent of the jobs were gained in expanding or new firms.

Figure 4 depicts a production possibilities frontier (PPF) in a hypothetical economy that produces only automobiles and personal computers. Let's suppose the economy is at point *a* at full employment (on the PPF). If there is a shift in demand from automobiles to personal computers, the economy will move from point *a* to point c *in the long run.* However, in the short run, the economy moves to a point such as *b* along the path shown by the dotted line. Why? As the demand for cars drops, people lose their jobs in the car industry and do not immediately find a job in the personal computer industry. As a consequence, unemployment rises above the natural rate. In the language of rational expectations, there has been a negative price surprise in the automobile industry and a positive price surprise in the personal computer industry. In the short run, this shift results in unemployment because firms cannot expand employment as rapidly as they contract employment.

The sector-shift hypothesis is consistent with some, but by no means all, evidence on the business cycle.

1. Studies have found that high rates of job creation and destruction cause higher unemployment. About 70 percent of unemployment in Britain during the

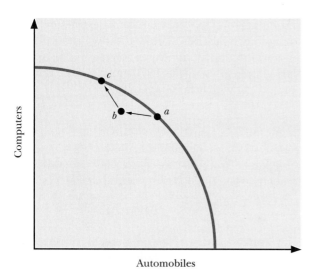

**FIGURE 4   The Sector-Shift Hypothesis and Business Cycles**

This hypothetical economy produces only computers and automobiles. Initially it is located at point *a* on the production possibilities frontier. There is a shift in demand from automobiles to computers. Employment falls in automobiles and rises in computers. Because these adjustments take time, the economy will shift to point *b* inside the PPF until there is sufficient time for employment to increase in computers, at which time the economy moves to point *c* on the PPF.

1920s and 1930s was due to structural shifts in the economy. Indeed, the amount of job creation and destruction was double its postwar average in Britain in the 1920s, as well as in Britain and the United States in the 1930s.[3]

2. Employment fluctuations are due more to fluctuations in job destruction than to fluctuations in job creation. The variance over time in the rate of job creation is significantly smaller than that of the rate of job destruction. If jobs disappear mainly when demand is falling and are created mainly when demand is rising, we would expect job creation and destruction to have similar, but opposite, patterns. The business cycle appears to correspond much more to fluctuations in the contracting sectors than to the fluctuations in the expanding sectors.

The evidence against the sector-shift hypothesis is also not definitive: If demand were shifting from automobiles to computers, we would expect unemployment to rise in one sector and job vacancies to rise in the other sector; that is, unemployment and vacancies should be positively correlated. They are, however, negatively correlated.[4]

In the long run, the past century has seen the disappearance of work for over 10 million farm workers; nearly 2 million railroad employees; 200,000 switchboard operators; 200,000 blacksmiths; and many other jobs. In their place are engineers, computer programmers and operators, medical technicians, electricians and electronic repairers, auto mechanics, and many more. Fifty years from now, there will be a new set of jobs to replace those of today. It is realistic to conclude that these massive realignments affect the cyclical movement of unemployment.

## REAL BUSINESS CYCLE THEORY

The theory of real business cycles was inspired by the work of Robert Lucas, Finn Kydland, Edwin Prescott, John Long, and Charles Plosser, who showed how business cycles could be caused by random supply shocks. The model is called real business cycle theory because it abstracts from *all* monetary phenomena, such as the banking system, money, and inflexible prices and wages, which other theories say are important factors in the business cycle.

> **Real business cycle theory** supposes that cyclical fluctuations arise from large random shocks to the rate of technological progress.

[3]See Prakash Loungani, "Structural Unemployment and Public Policy in Interwar Britain," *Journal of Monetary Economics* (August 1991), pp.149–159; R. Layard, S. Nickell, and R. Jackman, *Unemployment: Macroeconomic Performance and the Labour Market* (Oxford: Oxford University Press, 1991), p. 329.

[4]It is possible that this negative correlation results because associated with large changes is the uncertainty facing different industries. Unemployment increases when businesses facing an uncertain future reduce their vacancies. In other words, the increased uncertainty facing business firms increases unemployment while reducing vacancies as part of the same retrenchment of activity. This argument is suggested by Arthur J. Hosios, "Unemployment and Vacancies with Sector Shifts," *American Economic Review* (March 1994), pp.124–144.

Real business cycle theory accounts for the essential features of business cycles, focusing just on profit-maximizing consumers and producers in a pure market setting. In this framework, the business cycle becomes a natural response of the equilibrium levels of consumption, investment, production, productivity, and wages to the inevitable shocks that any economy faces.

### A Robinson Crusoe Economy.

To understand the real business cycle, imagine a Robinson Crusoe isolated on a desert island, producing only fish. How many fish he catches depends on luck, weather, or his discovery of a new and better way of fishing. These are the sources of "shocks" in Crusoe's world. Sometimes he catches many fish; sometimes he catches only a few. Although his consumption of fish varies, he can stabilize his consumption by storing fish caught when times are good so that he will have food when times are bad. His fish consumption is more stable than his fish production. Crusoe's investment in fishnets will fluctuate more than his consumption of fish. When he catches many fish, he can spend much more time making fishnets; when the fishing is not so good, he does not make as many fishnets.

When the fish are biting, Robinson will work more than when the fish are not biting. Crusoe's investment and hours of work will fluctuate more than his consumption.

### Technological Shocks.

Our economy can be like that of Robinson Crusoe. At times, production is booming because of new innovations, good natural conditions, or simply good luck. During these times, business investment will be high; we will all be working hard. Other times, production will be low or declining, investment will fall, and we will not work as hard. In both cases, we will stabilize our consumption by using for bad times the savings we accumulated during good times.

Figure 5 illustrates the real business cycle. As positive technology shocks occur, the aggregate supply curve shifts to the right, raising real GDP and employment and reducing prices. As negative supply shocks occur, real GDP falls, employment falls, and prices rise. Thus business cycles are explained by shocks from the supply side.

We can draw three conclusions from real business cycle theory: (1) The business cycle is caused by

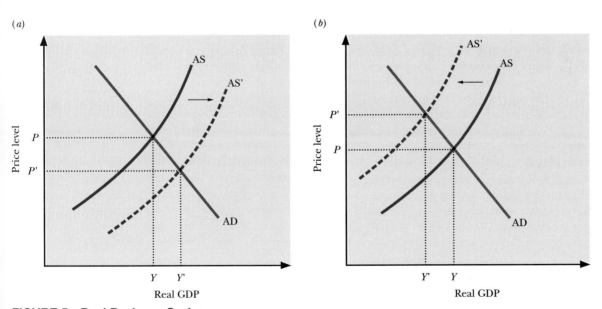

(a)

(b)

**FIGURE 5  Real Business Cycles**

Real business cycle theory says that business cycles are caused by supply shocks, primarily shocks to the rate of innovation. In panel (a), there is a positive supply shock, which increases aggregate supply, raises output, and lowers prices. In panel (b), there is an adverse supply shock, which lowers aggregate supply, reduces output, and raises prices.

random shocks to the rate of technological innovation, (2) observed changes in employment are simply the result of people choosing to work more or less in response to changing opportunities, and (3) financial factors are not crucial in explaining the business cycle.

**Evidence for the Real Business Cycle Model.**
Real business cycle theorists have used their theory to replicate many of the features of actual business cycles by experimenting with different "shocks" to their simple models of the economy. One interesting implication of the real business cycle model is that labor productivity and real wages rise in booms and fall in recessions. We know from the chapter on aggregate supply and demand that real wages indeed rise during booms and fall during recessions. Positive supply shocks raise real wages.

Support of the real business cycle view of the economy has been collected by Christina Romer, who finds that cyclical instability has remained fairly constant over the very long run. Romer challenges the historical data (as discussed below) showing that, whether measured by unemployment rates or rates of growth in real GDP, cyclical volatility was greater before 1929 than after 1947. According to Romer, this conclusion is based on a simple fallacy: As we go back in time, the quality of economic data deteriorates. Unless we are very careful with the data, the lesser volatility is simply the result of improvement in the quality of data.[5] Romer shows that if unemployment rates of the last quarter century are calculated with the same crude types of data and methods used before 1930, they are just as volatile as the long-run historical rates.

Romer's evidence supports real business cycle theory because it suggests that the business cycle is not caused by fluctuations in aggregate demand. As we shall discuss below, many economists believe that monetary instability was greater before 1930 than after 1947, causing greater cyclical volatility prior to 1930. However, if the stability of the business cycle has remained constant throughout the twentieth century, money does not affect real GDP.

In spite of its strengths, real business cycle theory has weaknesses. Critics argue that its most serious weakness is the theory's view of the economy as a single, homogeneous industry driven by supply shocks. In the actual economy, however, the ebb and flow of technological improvements have a negative impact on the productivity of only a few products at any given time. Moreover, new production techniques increase the output of other goods at any given time. Thus, supply shocks to a few sectors average out over the entire economy to be relatively insignificant.[6] It would be difficult to account for significant economic downturns in terms of negative supply shocks.

## SORTING OUT THE VARIOUS THEORIES

Economists have been fascinated by the business cycle for more than a century. There are probably more theories of the business cycle than of any other economic phenomenon. We have considered the main business cycle theories in this chapter, but not the many other business cycle theories—some credible, some bizarre.

We need a realistic explanation of the business cycle because it is a real economic phenomenon. We can categorize the business cycle theories that we have discussed in this chapter into two basic groups (see Table 2):

One group—the Keynesian model and the rational expectations model—states that business cycles are caused by demand shocks. This viewpoint appears credible because we can identify many possible sources of demand shocks, far more than we have discussed in this text: animal spirits, shifts in consumer attitudes, foreign trade shocks, exchange rate shocks, monetary growth shocks, and changes in government spending and taxation. Demand shocks, combined with inflexible wages and prices (the Keynesian model) or with price surprises (rational expectations), can cause significant increases or decreases in output, employment, and unemployment—that is, business cycles.

This group does not rule out supply shocks as a cause of cyclical disturbances. It does believe, how-

---

[5]Christina Romer, "Spurious Volatility in Historical Unemployment Data," *Journal of Political Economy* 94 (February 1986): pp.1–37.

[6]See Bennett McCallum, "The Role of Demand Management in the Maintenance of Full Employment," in W. Etis and P. Sinclair, eds., *Keynes and Economic Policy* (London: The Macmillan Press, 1988), p. 30.

## Table 2  Business Cycle Theories: A Summary

| Theory | Cause |
|---|---|
| Keynes | Demand shocks combined with inflexible wages and prices |
| Rational expectations | Demand shocks combined with unanticipated changes in prices; consistent with perfectly flexible wages and prices |
| Schumpeterian sector shifts | Technological change, which causes the "creation" of new firms and the "destruction" of old firms |
| Real business cycles | Technological shocks; other factors such as money supply or wage and price flexibility unimportant |

ever, that they will be random and of a smaller magnitude (with the exception of occasional large supply shocks, such as the energy shocks of the 1970s) than demand shocks.

The major difference between the Keynesian theory and rational expectations is that the effects of demand shocks are highly unpredictable under rational expectations. Whether the demand shock will cause business cycles or not depends upon whether people have correctly anticipated the shock.

The second group of theories—real business cycles and Schumpeterian sector shifts—focus primarily on the supply side as the source of business cycles. Real business cycle theory argues that business cycles are caused by substantial variations in technological progress. The Schumpeterian theory states, instead, that changing technology causes the creative destruction of old industries and firms, and the birth of new industries and firms. When the balance favors "creation," expansion and prosperity take place; when the balance favors "destruction," downturns and recessions occur.

After reviewing the available empirical evidence, we are unable to say conclusively that one explanation dominates all others. One theory may be better able to explain a Great Depression; another theory may better explain the stagflation of the 1970s. The inability to find one all-encompassing theory probably indicates either that real-world business cycles have a multiplicity of causes or that not enough evidence has been accumulated to distinguish one theory from the rest.

## STABILIZATION POLICY

Economists do not agree on whether we should attempt to stabilize the business cycle using activist

(discretionary) monetary and fiscal policies. We have discussed the tools and goals of monetary and fiscal policy in earlier chapters. Once again, economists divide into two distinct camps on this issue. The *activist* camp argues that we should actively employ the tools of monetary and/or fiscal policy to control or moderate the business cycle. The *nonactivist* camp argues that we do not know how to control the business cycle and that attempts to do so may make matters worse. Instead, we should impose fixed rules on decision makers, which they must obey irrespective of economic conditions.

## ACTIVISM

Activist policy deliberately manipulates fiscal and monetary policies to iron out fluctuations in the business cycle.

> An **activist policy** selects monetary and fiscal policy on the basis of the economic conditions. Activist policy changes as economic conditions change.

Activism is favored by Keynesian economists, who believe that business cycles are caused by fluctuations in aggregate demand. They argue that tools are available to moderate the ups and downs of economic activity. They believe that governments and their economists are wise enough to use these tools to manage aggregate demand in such a way as to eliminate or moderate the business cycle.

Activists argue that it is too costly to sit on the sidelines and wait for the economy to cure itself through the self-correcting mechanism. Different economic situations call for different policies. If policymaking is an art rather than a science, it is better to let the country's best economic experts decide what monetary and fiscal policies are appropriate. They can analyze a number of indicators of the state of the economy—inflation, unemployment, interest rates, trade balances, and political factors—to select the appropriate monetary and fiscal policies.

How active should activist policies be? Should we respond only to major disturbances or also to small changes in the business cycle? Some economists favor fine-tuning.

> **Fine-tuning** is the frequent use of discretionary monetary and fiscal policy to counteract even small movements in business activity.

Most activists believe that the policy dials should be adjusted only in response to major movements in real GDP and inflation. Much depends on the level of confidence of policymakers. In the 1960s, government officials thought they knew enough to fine-tune. In the 1990s, the Fed has changed monetary policy frequently in response to changes in economic conditions, so often that we can say it has attempted fine-tuning.

## THE CASE FOR ACTIVISM

Three arguments have been advanced to support activist countercyclical policies.

1. Although the business cycle has not been eliminated, it has become less severe since activist policies came into use. Figure 6 plots the annual rates of growth of real GDP and unemployment rates from 1890 to present. Since World War II, episodes of negative real growth have still occurred, but depressions have been avoided. The 1930s may have been the period of greatest cyclical instability, but the period before 1930 had more unstable growth and unemployment than the period after World War II. According to activists, the experience of the last 60 years provides important evidence that activist policy has reduced the amplitude of economic fluctuations. Earlier, we considered Romer's challenge to this conclusion.

2. Discretionary tax cuts have been applied successfully to stimulate employment and economic growth. Keynesian tax policy was given its first successful test under President Lyndon Johnson when the Revenue Act of 1964 cut personal taxes by 20 percent and corporate taxes by 8 percent. President Ronald Reagan cut taxes again in 1982. In both cases, these tax cuts were followed by extended periods of economic growth and prosperity.

3. The known is better than the unknown. The United States has had 50 years of activism without major economic catastrophes such as a deep depression or a hyperinflation. If we can't use activist policies, we might not be able to respond to major economic emergencies with a suitable policy.

No activist argues that activism has been perfect. Mistakes have been made and they will continue to be made. However, like democracy, activism—although it may have many flaws and defects—is better than any known alternative.

## NONACTIVISM

The major spokesperson for nonactivism, Nobel laureate Milton Friedman, argues for stable monetary and fiscal rules that must be followed independent of current economic conditions. In the view of nonactivists, attempts to deliberately manage monetary and fiscal policy are ineffective and even harmful. They believe that nonactivist policy will yield macroeconomic results that are superior to those of activism.

> **Nonactivist policy** consists of fixed rules independent of prevailing economic conditions that are held steady even when economic conditions change.

## THE CASE FOR NONACTIVISM

The alternative to activism is *fixed rules*. Monetary and fiscal authorities should follow fixed rules of conduct irrespective of current economic conditions.

Nonactivists fall into two related groups: monetarists on the one hand, and rational expectations economists and real business cycle theorists on the other. Monetarists want fixed monetary growth; the other nonactivists hold that monetary or fiscal policy has unpredictable effects on the economy and is incapable of controlling the business cycle.

(*a*) The Annual Rate of Growth of Real GDP

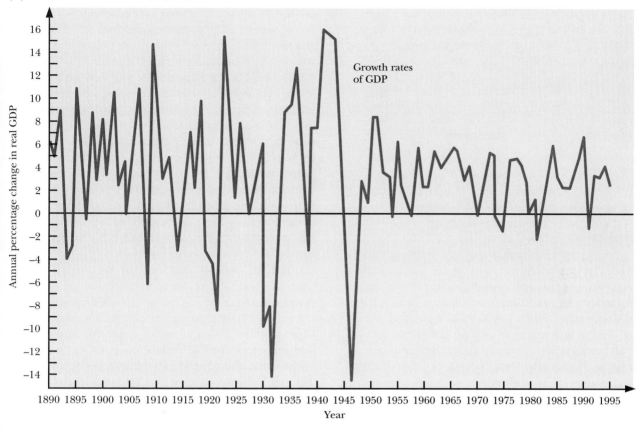

(*b*) The Unemployment Rate

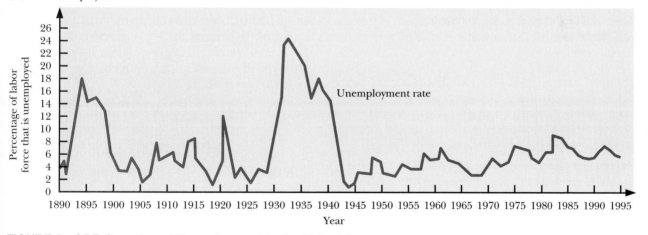

**FIGURE 6   GDP Growth and Unemployment in the United States**

Both the GDP growth rate data in panel (*a*) and the unemployment data in panel (*b*)
show less cyclical volatility after 1948. *Sources: Historical Statistics of the United
States; Economic Report of the President.*

*Monetarists* advocate the fixed rules of constant growth of the money supply every year at around the long-term growth rate of real GDP and a cyclically balanced budget.

*Rational expectations economists* maintain that anticipated monetary and fiscal policies cannot stabilize the economy; hence, activist policy should not be attempted.

*Real business cycle theorists* argue that the business cycle is caused by random shocks and cannot be controlled by factors other than the self-correcting mechanism.

For all, activism either doesn't matter or, if it matters, its application could make the situation worse. They believe in letting natural corrective forces work and in setting fixed rules, such as a fixed growth of money and a balanced budget, that would allow the corrective forces to work smoothly.

The monetarists maintain that activist policies either fail to improve the business cycle or actually make the cycle worse. The rational expectations school, led by Robert Lucas, maintains that activist policies affect only inflation, not unemployment. Activist policies can make inflation better or worse but have no lasting effect on reducing real GDP fluctuations. Real business cycle theorists believe that activist policies attack variables that are not the real causes of the business cycle.

## THE DIFFICULTY OF DEVISING ACTIVIST POLICY

Let's consider the reasons why activism may have the *unintended consequence* of making matters worse:

1. There are long and variable lags in the effect of money on the economy. If monetary authorities decide to combat unemployment by increasing the growth of the money supply, the effect on real output and unemployment will not be immediate. Milton Friedman's own research shows a variable lag of six months to two years before GDP is affected. Thus, monetary authorities can never be sure when the change in money supply will begin to affect real output and employment. If the lag is, by chance, short, the chances are less that the selected monetary policy will be inappropriate; however, if the lag is, by chance, long (say, two years), the policy may be the wrong one when the effects take place.

2. Because of the lagged effects of activist policy, it is important to be able to anticipate changes in the business cycle. If, for example, we knew six months in advance that a recession was coming, it would be easy to devise countercyclical policy. But recessions vary in length and in predictability. Through computer models of the economy and various early-warning measures, policymakers can attempt to anticipate recessions, but there are no accurate guides to the future. When activist policies are carried out at the wrong time, they destabilize the economy. (See Example 1 for sources of lags.)

3. Activist policies can aim for the wrong target. Consider the natural rate of unemployment as an appropriate target of activist policy. If the economy is operating above the natural rate of unemployment, expansionary policies could lower unemployment without accelerating inflation—but we may not know what the natural rate is at any point in time. The natural rate varies with changes in the composition of the labor force, raw material prices, and labor-force behavior. Because the natural rate itself fluctuates, it is difficult to achieve with deliberate policy actions. In the mid-1990s, for example, economists had to lower their estimate of the natural rate from over 6 percent to 5–5½ percent. During the 1970s, policymakers kept aiming for a 4 percent unemployment rate when long-term changes had raised the natural rate above 5 percent.

## UNINTENDED CONSEQUENCES: LESSONS OF THE GREAT DEPRESSION

The monetarists and other nonactivists do not share the view that activism has made things better. They believe that activist policy blunders caused the Great Depression. The Great Depression would not have occurred had a policy of fixed rules been followed by monetary and fiscal authorities.

What were the policy blunders of the 1930s? These blunders resulted in what may be one of the greatest *unintended consequences* of economic history.

## EXAMPLE 1
## NEW ZEALAND'S
## NEW RULES

Different countries have tried different approaches to economic stabilization. These different experiences, some successful, some failures, allow other countries to learn what works and what doesn't. In 1989, New Zealand adopted a unique monetary constitution. The Central bank, under this agreement, had to enter into a contract with the government to deliver over a three-year period an inflation rate that fell within a target set by the government. Under the bank's current contract, it must keep New Zealand's inflation rate between 0 percent and 2 percent. The Central bank can take whatever steps it deems necessary, free of government interference, to achieve this inflation target. The enforcement mechanism? If the

Central bank does not meet its inflation target, the governor of the Central bank is fired.

On the fiscal side, New Zealand's government budget must be prepared by following generally accepted accounting principles as used by private businesses. The use of business accounting practices prevents politicians from using "smoke and mirrors" tricks to make the deficit appear smaller. Since changing its rules, New Zealand has had low inflation, a significant decline in its public debt, and appreciating currency, and rising foreign investment.

------------------------------------------------

*Source*: Steve Hancke, "A Revolution that Paid Off," *Forbes*, May 20, 1996, p. 121.

---

1. From 1929 to 1933, the nominal supply of money (M1) fell 25 percent. The price level also fell nearly 25 percent. Therefore, there was no change in the real money supply, but an increase in the real money supply was required to get the economy moving again. If the money supply had been stable in the early 1930s, falling prices would have caused the real money supply to increase; the economy would not have fallen into the Great Depression.

2. Various government actions taken by Roosevelt's New Deal program caused wages and prices to rise after 1933 even though there was massive unemployment (remember that the self-correcting mechanism requires falling wages and prices). The New Deal increased the power of labor unions, gave more monopoly power to business firms, and encouraged them to raise prices. In short, from 1933 to 1936 a supply-side inflation in the middle of a deep depression retarded the move toward full employment.

3. In 1937, in an incredible act of self-destruction, the Federal Reserve System doubled reserve requirements. The increase in the reserve requirement

brought the needed money growth to a halt and sent the economy into another recession within the Great Depression.

4. Large tax increases were passed in 1932 and 1937 during periods of massive unemployment.

While Keynesians maintain that activist counter-cyclical policy is responsible for reducing business fluctuations after World War II, monetarists argue that greater cyclical stability is a consequence not of countercyclical policies but of a more stable money-supply growth. The evidence supporting the monetarist view is presented in Figure 7, which shows the annual growth rate of the money supply since 1885. The reduced range of GDP fluctuations coincides with the reduced range of money-supply growth. The greater relative stability over the past 40 years may be the result not of activist policy but of the increased stability of the growth of the money supply. Earlier we discussed Christina Romer's conclusion that cyclical instability has remained constant.

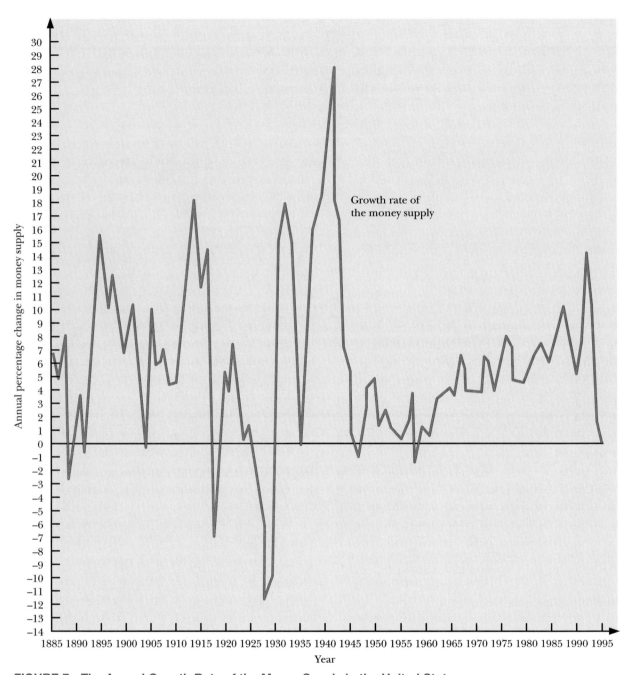

**FIGURE 7   The Annual Growth Rate of the Money Supply in the United States**

A comparison of this figure with panel (*a*) of Figure 6 shows that the reduction in the amplitude of GDP fluctuations coincides with the reduction in fluctuations in the growth rate of money supply in the past 40 years. *Sources: Historical Statistics of the United States; Economic Report of the President; Survey of Current Business; Federal Reserve Bulletin.* The percentage growth rate in money supply is based on M1 for the years from 1915 to 1981 and includes times deposits (formerly M2) for the years from 1890 to 1915.

## ACTIVISM AS THE CHOICE OF U.S. POLICYMAKERS

U.S. policymakers have chosen the activist-policy approach. Monetary-growth rates continue to fluctuate according to the dictates of the Fed. (See Example 2.) There is an important distinction between following monetary-growth targets (which can be changed as economic conditions change) and a fixed-monetary-growth rule. The current chairman of the Fed, Alan Greenspan, has advocated frequent changes in monetary policy and is known to study current macrodata for signs that monetary policy should be changed again.

Policymakers in the United States have made use of activist tax policy since the 1964 tax cut. In the post–World War II era, five tax revisions have been passed largely for activist-policy reasons. Although these tax revisions have had different degrees of success, it is clear that U.S. policymakers regard tax revision as a major instrument of activist fiscal policy. Policymakers have not, however, followed the balanced-budget rule advocated by the nonactivists. In fact, they appear unable to balance the budget over the cycle, despite their declared intentions. President Clinton's 1993 tax increase represents a move away

from earlier tax reforms, which lowered tax rates to stimulate the economy.

The 1996 presidential campaign will focus attention again on tax cuts and balanced budgets, which enjoy popularity among swing voters.

## SUMMARY

1. The Keynesian theory of the business cycle states that fluctuations in aggregate demand explain the business cycle. This theory has appeal because the theory of aggregate demand gives a number of reasons for fluctuations in aggregate demand. Keynesian theory also argues that it is possible to control the business cycle by controlling aggregate demand.

2. Rational expectations theory states that business cycles can be caused by price surprises even with perfectly flexible prices and wages. When people are caught off guard by price increases, they believe real wages and real prices have increased. They therefore work more and produce more. If aggregate demand increases and the resulting price increases are fully anticipated, there will be no effect

### EXAMPLE 2
### WILL ONE PERSON DETERMINE THE 1996 PRESIDENTIAL ELECTION?

Academic studies show that the outcomes of past presidential elections have been determined not by foreign policy or domestic issues but by the state of the economy on the eve of the election. The most significant determinants of the presidential election outcome are the rate of inflation, the rate of economic growth, and whether the growth rate of the economy has been above 4 percent. Models that use these three variables correctly predict the outcomes of virtually all presidential elections since 1916.

These models suggest that the Fed is able to determine the outcome of the 1996 presidential

election. In early 1996, there were growing signs of a "weakening" of the U.S. economy. If the Fed, under its chairman, Alan Greenspan, were to decide to put the brakes on monetary growth and to raise interest rates, the economy could find itself in a recession on the eve of election day in November of 1996. If it were, the model would predict a republican victory. If the economy remains healthy, President Clinton would be reelected.

*Source:* "Sideshows Aside, Economy Is Still Key to Election," *New York Times,* January 2, 1996, C3.

on output or employment. Accordingly, only unexpected policies will affect output and employment.

3. The Schumpeterian sector-shift hypothesis states that price surprises at the micro level can cause business cycles. When demand shifts away from a declining sector toward a rising sector as technology advances, adjustments will not take place immediately. Employment falls in the declining sector prior to increasing in the rising sector. During this adjustment period, the economy operates below its production possibilities frontier.

4. Real business cycle theory says that business cycles are caused by supply shocks. These supply shocks occur primarily through the rate of technological innovation. Real business cycle theory is consistent with many empirical phenomena, such as the procyclical behavior of real wages and the apparent unimportance of money in explaining business cycles.

5. Economists propose two opposing policies toward business cycles. Activists argue that discretionary monetary and fiscal policy should be used to control the business cycle. Monetarists, rational expectations theorists, and real business cycle theorists favor nonactivism. Activist policy uses discretionary policy. Nonactivism uses rules, such as Friedman's constant-monetary-growth rule and balanced-budget rule.

6. The arguments for activism are that the business cycle has moderated since the use of activism, that activism is required to combat the effects of supply shocks, that tax cuts have been used successfully, and that the known is better than the unknown. The arguments for nonactivism are that activism is ineffective and can even make the cycle worse through policy blunders, that activist policy is too difficult to devise, and that activist policies can aim for the wrong targets. Nonactivists argue that activism created an enormous unintended consequence—the Great Depression—as a result of wrong choices of monetary and fiscal policy.

## KEY TERMS

GDP gap  
rational expectations  
price surprises  
sector-shift hypothesis  
job creation rate  
job destruction rate  

real business cycle  
   theory  
activist policy  
fine tuning  
nonactivist policy  

## QUESTIONS AND PROBLEMS

1. The 1990–1992 recession was preceded by a dip in the growth rate of the money supply to a scant 1 percent from 1988 to 1989 (down from nearly 5 percent from 1987 to 1988). Was this a typical pattern?

2. List some of the features of business cycles.

3. What are the main points of real business cycle theory?

4. A typical feature of business cycles is that real wages rise in booms and fall in recessions. How does this fact fit into real business cycle theory? Keynesian theory?

5. Evaluate the validity of the following statement: "Real business cycle theory assumes that fluctuations in employment reflect changes in the amount people want to work."

6. If, as most economists believe, there is a self-correcting mechanism that automatically moves the economy toward full employment, how can anyone advocate discretionary policy? Will the economy not take care of itself?

7. This chapter pointed out that the advocates of nonactivism must demonstrate that activist policies tend to worsen the business cycle. What evidence is there that activism actually makes matters worse?

8. How could we have had the Great Depression of the 1930s if there is a self-correcting mechanism at work in the economy?

9. The rational expectations argument states that expectations can defeat activist policy. Assume that Congress decides to pass a tax cut to stimulate the economy. How could rational expectations defeat the purpose of the tax cut?

10. Explain the difference between monetary targets and monetarism. Is it correct to call the Fed's October 1979 decision to follow monetary growth targets a victory for monetarism?

11. This chapter showed that the conditions required for conducting ideal activist policy cannot be met in the real world. What is the activist policy's defense, given the fact that conditions are imperfect?

12. Both activists and nonactivists cite the greater stability of the economy after World War II to support their positions. Explain how both sides can use the same data to support entirely different positions.

13. This chapter explained how the economic policies of the mid-1930s forced up wages and prices, even though the unemployment rate was high. Use aggregate supply and aggregate demand curves to show the effect of these policies on real output.

14. Suppose that, to combat inflation, Congress passes a tax increase. Will the expected effect be greater if the bill calls for a permanent increase in tax rates or for a 1-year increase in tax rates?

15. Explain why both activists and nonactivists appear to agree that monetary policy is the most important policy instrument.

16. Earlier chapters explained that unanticipated inflation raises output and employment. Explain how the rational expectations school uses this argument to support its view that activist policy may have no real effect on output and employment.

17. Discuss the notion of sector shifts and explain why they can cause fluctuations in employment and unemployment.

18. Explain why proponents of real business cycles would not be in favor of activism.

# PART VIII

# THE WORLD ECONOMY

# CHAPTER 35

# INTERNATIONAL TRADE

One of the Defining Moments in the evolution of an economy is its realization that faster economic growth requires full participation in the world economy. This awareness occurs at different times for different countries. It occurred in Great Britain during the 1840s, the United States during the Great Depression, Asia during the 1970s, and in Latin America during the 1980s.

International trade has always changed the way people live. Traders throughout history have helped transmit knowledge and inventions. Today, foreign products from Sony, BMW, Mitsubishi, and Chanel are as familiar to us as U.S. products from General Electric, Chevrolet, and IBM. We continue to debate, however, whether or not trade is beneficial. In the early 1990s, a television newscast showed an angry American worker destroying a Japanese car

with a sledgehammer because of the fear that imports were taking away American jobs. Recently, some politicians have sought office by appealing to sentiments favoring protectionism—the artificial restriction of imports.

It is easy to fall prey to the fallacy that imports eliminate domestic jobs. People often fail to realize that in the long run exports pay for imports. Indeed, it was conventional wisdom in the sixteenth and seventeenth centuries that a country should encourage exports and discourage imports. In 1817, however, David Ricardo developed the law of comparative advantage, which demonstrates the benefits of international trade. In this chapter, we shall explain the workings of the law of comparative advantage and how it applies to the United States and the world economy.

## THE GLOBAL ECONOMY

The production of goods and services throughout the world has become truly global. Many Japanese cars are built in America. Nike running shoes—an American product—are produced in Malaysia. International production has obscured the dividing line between "American" goods and "foreign" goods. Electronic components are shipped to Asian countries and return as completed computers or calculators. American companies form alliances with foreign companies: Chrysler has an alliance with Mitsubishi, General Motors with Toyota, and International Business Machines (IBM) with Toshiba. Almost all large companies have foreign branches. For example, the Ford Escort is produced in Europe, and Ford owns Jaguar.

Since the end of World War II, world trade has increased faster than world output, because of low trade barriers, smaller transportation costs, and dramatic reductions in the costs of international communication achieved through the use of space satellites.

How extensive is world trade? About one-seventh of world GDP is made up of exports (or imports) from one country to the next. In the 1990s, world trade was larger than the German and Japanese economies combined.

### MERCANTILISM

Understanding the nature of international trade was one of the first accomplishments of economics as a science. In the sixteenth and seventeenth centuries, journalists and politicians promoted a set of policies called *mercantilism*. These writers held that a nation was like a business. To make a profit, a country had to sell more than it bought from foreign countries. Thus, according to mercantilist writers, the best policies would promote exports to the rest of the world and discourage imports from foreign competitors.

According to the mercantilists, domestic producers must be protected from foreign competition through various kinds of subsidies. These would increase exports and lower imports. It was the mercantilists who coined the phrase "favorable trade balance," still in use today. A favorable trade balance is one in which exports exceed imports.

What can be wrong with this philosophy? The answer: The mercantilists confused what is good for particular industries with what is good for the economy as a whole. In other words, they committed the fallacy of composition, which we discussed in Chapter 1: What is true for a part is not necessarily true for the whole. If a country subsidizes one industry, it can actually hurt other "unseen" industries, because the subsidy will cause resources to shift from relatively efficient industries (those competing without the subsidy) to those that are relatively inefficient.

From the standpoint of the whole economy, the total supply of goods and services that are available within the country equals domestic production *plus* imports *minus* exports. When the United States imports Japanese cars, we have more cars; when the United States exports wheat, we have less wheat. The import of cars brings about a reduction in the car industry; the export of wheat brings about an expansion of the wheat industry. However, by exporting wheat and importing cars, the country can actually have more of both! To understand this we must once again consider the law of comparative advantage.

## REASONS FOR INTERNATIONAL TRADE

A major tenet of market economics is that people benefit from specialization. People increase their incomes by specializing in those tasks for which they are particularly suited. Different jobs have different intellectual, physical, and personality requirements. Because people are different from one another and because each person has the capacity to learn, it pays to specialize. As Adam Smith stated, "It is the maxim of every prudent master of a family never to attempt to make at home what it will cost him more to make than to buy." People trade with each other primarily because each individual is endowed with a mix of traits that are different from those of most other people. Some of these traits are an inherent part of the individual that cannot be shared with other individuals.

Trade between individuals has much in common with international trade between countries. Each country is endowed with certain characteristics: a particular climate, a certain amount of fertile farmland, a certain amount of desert, a given number of lakes and rivers, and the kinds of people that compose its population. Over the years, some countries have accumulated large quantities of physical and human capital, whereas other countries are poor in capital. In short, each country is defined in part by the endowments of productive factors (land, labor, and capital) inside its borders. Just as one person cannot transfer intelligence, strength, personality, or health to another person, one country cannot transfer its land and other natural resources to another country. Similarly, the labor force that resides within a country is not easily moved; people have friends and family in their native land and share a common language and culture. Even if they wish to leave, immigration laws may render the labor force internationally immobile.

It is easier to transfer to another country the goods and services produced by land, labor, and capital than to transfer the land, labor, and capital themselves. Thus, to some degree various countries possess land, labor, and capital in different proportions. A country like Australia has very little labor compared with land and, hence, devotes itself to land-intensive products, such as sheep farming and wheat production. A country like Great Britain tends to produce goods that use comparatively little land but much labor and capital. Therefore, each country specializes in those goods for which its mix of resources are most suited; international trade in goods and services substitutes for movements of the various productive factors.

> The fundamental fact upon which international trade rests is that goods and services are much more mobile internationally than are the resources used in their production. Each country will tend to export those goods and services for which its resource base is most suited.

International trade allows a country to specialize in the goods and services that it can produce at a relatively low cost, and to export those goods in return for imports whose domestic production is relatively costly. Through international trade, as John Stuart Mill (1806–1873) said, "A country obtains things which it either could not have produced at all, or which it must have produced at a greater expense of capital and labor than the cost of the things which it exports to pay for them." As a consequence of obtaining goods more cheaply, international trade enables a country—and the world—to consume and produce more than would be possible without trade. We shall later see that a country can benefit from trade even when it is more efficient (uses fewer resources) in the production of *all* goods than any other country.

Trade has intangible benefits in addition to the tangible benefits of providing the potential for greater totals of all the goods and services the world consumes. The major tangible benefit is the diversity that trade offers to the way people live and work. The advantages of particular climates and lands are shared by the rest of the world. The United States imports oil from the hot desert of Saudi Arabia so that Americans can drive cars in cool comfort. We can enjoy coffee, bananas, and spices without living in the tropics. We can take advantage of the economy and durability of Japanese cars without driving in hectic Tokyo. Thus, international (and interregional) trade enables us to enjoy a more diverse menu of goods and services than we could without trade. World trade also encourages the diffusion of knowledge and culture because trade serves as a point of contact between people of different lands.

## THE LAW OF COMPARATIVE ADVANTAGE

In Chapter 3 we used the law of comparative advantage to explain the benefits people enjoy from specialization. Individuals are made better off by specializing and engaging in trade with other people. The law of comparative advantage can also help explain the gains from international specialization. In 1817, David Ricardo proved that international specialization pays if each country devotes its resources to those activities in which it has a comparative advantage.

> The **law of comparative advantage** states that people or countries specialize in those activities in which they have the greatest advantage or the least disadvantage compared with other people or countries.

Profound truths are sometimes difficult to discover; the real world is so complex that it can hide the working of these truths. Ricardo's genius was that he was able to provide a simplified model of trade without the thousands of irrelevant details that would cloud our vision. He considered a hypothetical world with only two countries and only two goods. The two "countries" could be America and

Europe; the two goods could be food and clothing. For the sake of simplicity, let us also assume the following.

1. Labor is the only productive factor, and there is only one type of labor.

2. Labor cannot move between the two countries (this assumption reflects the relative international immobility of productive factors compared with goods).

3. The output from a unit of labor is constant (in other words, productivity is constant no matter how many units of output are produced).

4. Laborers are indifferent about whether they work in the food or clothing industries, provided that wages are the same.

Table 1 shows the hypothetical output of food or clothing from 1 unit of labor in each of the two countries. America can produce 6 units of food with 1 unit of labor, and 2 units of clothing with 1 unit of labor. Europe can produce either 1 unit of food or 1 unit of clothing with 1 unit of labor. America is 6 times more efficient than Europe in food production (it produces 6 times as much with the same labor); America is only twice as efficient in clothing production (it produces twice as much with the same labor).

We have deliberately constructed a case in which America has an absolute advantage over Europe in all lines of production.

| Table 1    Hypothetical Food and Clothing Output from 1 Unit of Labor | | |
|---|---|---|
| Country | Units of Food Output from 1 Unit of Labor | Units of Clothing Output from 1 Unit of Labor |
| America | 6 | 2 |
| Europe | 1 | 1 |

Trade patterns depend on comparative advantages, not on absolute advantages. In our hypothetical example, America is 6 times more efficient than Europe in food production and twice as efficient in clothing production. America has an absolute advantage in both food and clothing but has a comparative advantage only in food production. Europe has an absolute disadvantage in the production of both goods but has a comparative advantage in clothing-production. Europe will export clothing to America in return for food, and both will gain by this pattern of trade. Each country exports the good in which it has the greatest efficiency advantage (in the case of America) or the smallest inefficiency disadvantage (in the case of Europe).

A country has an **absolute advantage** in the production of a good if it uses fewer resources to produce a unit of the good than any other country.

Even under these circumstances, however, both countries stand to benefit from specialization and trade according to comparative advantage, as we shall see.

## THE CASE OF SELF-SUFFICIENCY

Let's suppose that each country in our hypothetical world is initially self-sufficient and must consume only what it produces at home.

**America.**    A self-sufficient America must produce both food and clothing. American workers can produce 6 units of food or 2 units of clothing from 1 unit of labor (see Table 1). Since money is just a unit of account, to understand the benefits of international trade it is best that we concentrate on what goods are worth in terms of each other. Under conditions of self-sufficiency, the American price of a unit of clothing will be 3 times the price of a unit of food. Why? In the marketplace, 6 units of food will have the same value as 2 units of clothing, or, to simplify, 3 units of food ($F$) will have the same value as 1 unit of clothing ($C$) because they use the same amount of labor. To produce more clothing, food must be sacrificed because labor must be moved out of food production. Thus, America's opportunity cost of 1 unit of clothing is 3 units of food:

$$3F = 1C$$

These same facts are shown in panel (*a*) of Figure 1, which graphs America's production possibilities frontier (PPF). Labor is the only factor of production, and we assume for simplicity that a total of 15 units of labor are available to the American economy. America's PPF is a straight line because opportunity costs are constant in our example. If everyone works in clothing production, 30 (= 15 × 2) units of clothing can be produced. If everyone works in food production, 90 (= 15 × 6) units of food can be produced. The economy will likely produce a mix of food and clothing to meet domestic consumption. Such a combination might be point *a*, where 45 units of food and 15 units of clothing are produced and consumed. Thus, we can say that without trade,

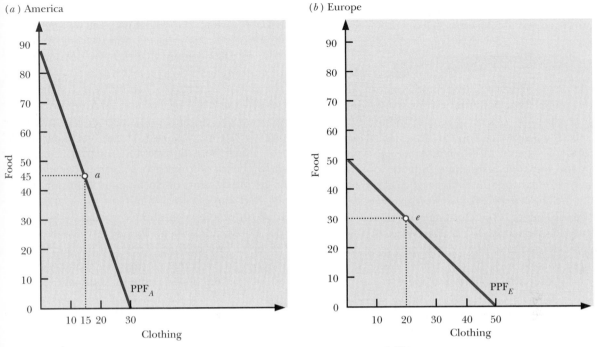

**FIGURE 1   Hypothetical American and European Production Possibilities Frontiers**

Panel (*a*) shows a hypothetical production possibilities frontier for America. Based on the labor productivity rates in Table 1, if 15 units of labor are available and labor is the only factor of production, America could produce either 30 units of clothing, 90 units of food, or some mixture of the two—such as the combination represented by point *a*, where 45 units of food and 15 units of clothing are produced. Panel (*b*) shows a hypothetical PPF for Europe, where 50 units of labor are available. Again, based on the labor productivity rates in Table 1, Europe could produce 50 units of clothing, 50 units of food, or a combination—such as that represented by point *e*, where 30 units of food and 20 units of clothing are produced.

America consumes 45*F* and 15*C*, the combination that reflects America's preferences in this case.

**Europe.**   In a self-sufficient Europe, workers can produce 1 unit of food or 1 unit of clothing with 1 unit of labor (see Table 1). A unit of clothing and a unit of food have the same costs, and hence, the same price. In other words, Europeans must give up 1 unit of food to get 1 unit of clothing. Thus, Europe's opportunity cost of 1 unit of clothing is 1 unit of food.

$$1F = 1C$$

Panel (*b*) of Figure 1 shows Europe's PPF. In our example, we assume Europe is more populous than the United States; it has 50 units of labor available. Europe also has a straight-line production possibilities frontier, and it can produce either 50 units of

food, 50 units of clothing, or some combination of the two. A likely situation is that Europe produces and consumes at a point such as *e*, where it produces 30 units of food and 20 units of clothing. Thus, we can say that without trade, Europe consumes 30*F* and 20*C*, the combination that reflects Europe's preferences in this case.

Without trade, each country must consume on its PPF. To produce (and consume) more requires either a larger labor force or an increase in the efficiency of labor.

**The World.**   If both Europe and America are self-sufficient, the total amount of food and clothing produced will be the amount produced by America (45*F* and 15*C*) plus the amount produced by Europe (30*F* and 20*C*). Thus, the total amount of food produced will be 75 units ($45F + 30F$), and the total amount of clothing produced will be 35 units ($15C + 20C$).

## THE CASE OF INTERNATIONAL TRADE

Before trade opens between Europe and America (as described in Table 1), a potential trader would find that 1 unit of clothing sells for 1 unit of food in Europe but sells for 3 units of food in America. If the trader then applies 1 unit of labor in American food production and ships the resulting 6 units of food to Europe, he or she can obtain 6 units of clothing instead of the 2 obtained by producing it in America! It makes no difference that clothing production is half as efficient in Europe. What matters is that in Europe, a unit of food and a unit of clothing have the same market value; thus, before trade, food and clothing sell for the same price in Europe.

As Americans discover that clothing can be bought more cheaply in Europe than at home, the law of supply and demand will then do its work. Americans will stop producing clothing in order to concentrate on food production, and they will begin to demand European clothing. This increased demand will drive up the price of European clothing. Europe will shift from food production to clothing production, and eventually the pressure of American demand will lead Europe to produce only clothing. In the long run, Americans will get clothing more cheaply (at less than $3F$ for $1C$) than before trade, and Europeans will receive a higher price for their clothing (at more than $1F$ for $1C$).

In making decisions about trading, people in each country need to know the prices of goods on the international market. The prices of food and clothing in this example will determine the terms of trade, or how much clothing is worth in terms of food. For example, if food is $2 and clothing is $4, 2 units of food will exchange for 1 unit of clothing.

> The **terms of trade** are the rate at which two products can be exchanged for each other between countries.

The terms of trade between Europe and America will settle at some point between America's and Europe's opportunity costs, although the final equilibrium terms of trade cannot be determined without knowing each country's preferences. If America's opportunity cost of 1 unit of clothing is 3 units of food and Europe's opportunity cost of 1 unit of clothing is

1 unit of food, the final terms of trade will settle between $1C = 3F$ and $1C = 1F$. Europe is willing to sell 1 unit of clothing for at least 1 unit of food; America is willing to pay no more than 3 units of food for 1 unit of clothing.

The cheap imports of clothing from Europe will drive down the price of clothing in America. When Europe exports clothing to America, the price of clothing in Europe will rise. If the world terms of trade at which both Europe and America can trade are set by the market at $2F = 1C$, Americans will no longer get only 2 units of clothing for 1 unit of labor; instead, they can produce 6 units of food, and trade that food for 3 units of clothing (because $2F = 1C$) in Europe. Europeans will no longer have to work so hard to get 1 unit of food. They can produce 1 unit of clothing and trade that clothing for 2 units of food instead of getting only 1 unit of food per unit of clothing.

When the terms of trade in the world are $2F = 1C$, Americans will devote all their labor to food production and Europeans will devote all their labor to clothing production. (If increasing, rather than constant, opportunity costs had been assumed, the two countries need not have been driven to such complete specialization.)

## THE GAINS FROM TRADE

When American workers specialize in food production, and European workers specialize in clothing production, the gains to each can be measured by comparing their sacrifices before and after trade. Americans, before trade, sacrificed 3 units of food for 1 unit of clothing. After trade, Americans need sacrifice only 2 units of food for 1 unit of clothing (with terms of trade at $2F = 1C$). Europeans, before trade, sacrificed 1 unit of clothing for 1 unit of food. After trade, Europeans need sacrifice only half a unit of clothing per unit of food (because clothing sells for twice as much as food after trade).

The gains from trade are shown dramatically in Figure 2. Before trade, America is at point $a$ in panel (a), and Europe is at point $e$ in panel (b). When trade opens at the terms of trade $2F = 1C$, America moves its production to point $x_A$ (specialization in food production), as the arrow shows. Thus, America increases its food production from 45 units to 90 units. America can now trade each unit of food for half a

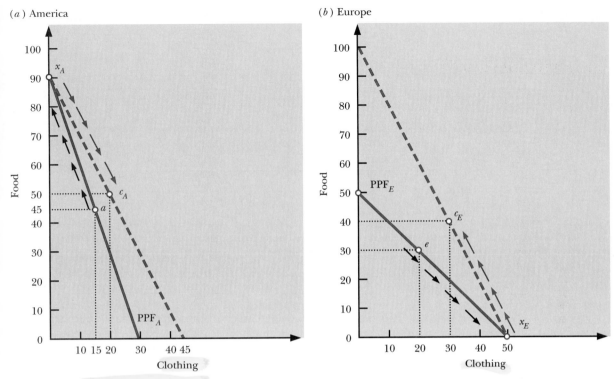

(a) America

(b) Europe

**FIGURE 2  The Effects of Trade**

As shown in panel (a), before trade, America produces and consumes at point a. When trade opens at the terms of $2F = 1C$ (where $F$ = units of food and $C$ = units of clothing), America produces at $x_A$, specializing in food production, and trades 40 units of food for 20 units of clothing. America, therefore, consumes at point $c_A$, where it consumes 50 units of food and 20 units of clothing. Trade shifts American consumption from a to $c_A$. As shown in panel (b), before trade, Europe produces and consumes at point e. When trade opens, Europe shifts production to $x_E$, specializing in clothing production, and trades 20 units of clothing for 40 units of food. Europe, therefore, shifts consumption from e to point $c_E$, where 30 units of clothing and 40 units of food are consumed. In both panels, the black arrows show the effects of trade on domestic production, and the red arrows show the effects of trade on domestic consumption. Both countries consume somewhere on the dashed line above their original production possibilities frontiers.

*By trading Both have more*

unit of clothing. If America trades 40 units of food for 20 units of clothing, America can consume at point $c_A$, with consumption at 50 units of food and 20 units of clothing. Trade enables America to consume above its production possibilities frontier. In this example, trade shifts consumption from a to $c_A$. The dotted line shows the consumption possibilities available to Americans when $2F = 1C$ in the work market.

As column 1 of Table 2 shows, America produces $45F$ and $15C$ before trade. The opening of trade shifts American labor entirely out of clothing production. As column 2 shows, America produces

only food ($90F$) after trade opens. Columns 3 and 4 describe America's trade; America keeps $50F$ for domestic consumption and sells $40F$ for $20C$. Column 5 shows consumption after trade, and column 6 shows America's benefits from trade. As a result of trade, America increases its consumption of each product by 5 units.

Europe's story is told in panel (b) of Figure 2. Europe shifts production from e, where $30F$ and $20C$ are produced, to point $x_E$, where 50 units of clothing are produced. With the terms of trade being $2F = 1C$, Europe can trade 20 units of clothing for 40 units of food. Europe's consumption shifts from e to

| | Consumption and Production Before Trade (1) | Production After Trade (2) | Exports (3) | Imports (4) | Consumption After Trade (5) | Gains (6) |
|---|---|---|---|---|---|---|
| *(a)* | 45F | 90F | 40F | 0F | 50F | 5F |
| America | 15C | 0C | 0C | 20C | 20C | 5C |
| *(b)* | 30F | 0F | 0F | 40F | 40F | 10F |
| Europe | 20C | 50C | 20C | 0C | 30C | 10C |
| *(c)* | 75F | 90F | — | — | 90F | 15F |
| World | 35C | 50C | — | — | 50C | 15C |

**Table 2   The Effects of International Trade**

F = units of food
C = units of clothing

$c_E$, which is above the original production possibilities frontier. Like America, Europe is better off with trade. Row *(b)* of Table 2 tells the same story in simple arithmetic. Columns 3 and 4 show that Europe's trade is consistent with America's. For example, America exports 40F and Europe imports 40F. The dotted line in Figure 2 shows the consumption possibilities available to Europeans when $2F = 1C$ in the world market.

In this simple world, the benefits of trade are dramatic. America consumes 5 units more of both food and clothing; Europe consumes 10 units more of both food and clothing. Row *(c)* of Table 2 shows that the world increases its production of food by 15 units, or by 20 percent (from 75 to 90 units), and increases its production of clothing by 15 units, or by 43 percent (from 35 to 50 units). Everybody is made better off; nobody is hurt by trade in this case. Trade has the same effect on consumption as an increase in national resources or an improvement in efficiency of resource use. As a consequence of trade, countries are able to consume beyond their original production possibilities frontiers. (See Example 1.)

The advantages of international trade are sometimes obvious and sometimes subtle. They are obvious when trade enables a country to acquire some good that it cannot produce (such as tin or nickel or manganese in the United States) or that would have an exorbitant production cost (such as bananas, coffee, or tea in the United States). As Adam Smith pointed out, "By means of glasses, hotbeds, and hotwalls, very good grapes can be raised in Scotland, and very good wine can be made of them at about thirty times the expense for which at least equally good can be bought from foreign countries."

The advantages of trade are subtle when a country imports goods that can be produced at home with, perhaps, the use of fewer resources than the resources used abroad for the same goods, as would be the case for the production of textiles, television sets, and videocassette recorders in the United States. It can produce these things, but (to paraphrase John Stuart Mill) at a greater expense of capital and labor than the cost of the goods and services it exports to pay for them.

In the real world, imports of goods from abroad displace the domestic production of competing goods, and in the process, some people may find that their income falls. Because the Ricardian model assumes only one factor of production, the model simply cannot account for changes in the distribution of income. The model does demonstrate that in a world with many factors and shifts in distribution of income, trade increases average real income. Since trade makes the average person better off, the people who are made better off could compensate those who are made worse off.

## LOW-WAGE AND HIGH-WAGE COUNTRIES

Hourly wages in the United States are about seven times higher than Mexican hourly wages. Japanese hourly wages are more than three times higher than Korean hourly wages. Yet the United States and Japan are two of the world's largest exporting countries; Korea and Mexico are comparatively small exporting countries. The law of comparative advantage explains how high-wage countries can compete with low-wage countries.

## EXAMPLE 1
## DOES FREE TRADE
## PAY?

Does free trade really pay? As evidenced by the unilateral adoption of free or freer trade by countries throughout the world, there is a widespread belief that free trade pays. Since 1817, the theory of comparative advantage has suggested that this is the case. Mercantilism, the sixteenth- and seventeenth-century doctrine that exports were good and imports were bad, suggested that home merchants must be protected from foreign competition. Economists did not really have extensive evidence for the benefits of free trade compared with protectionism until the half-century following World War II, by which time they had collected enough data on the growth rates of a large number of countries experiencing different degrees of protectionism.

The following table gives some evidence for the proposition that free trade pays. It shows the per capita rates of growth of countries that have the highest amounts of protection versus those with the lowest amounts of protection. The measures are based on a combination of different measures. The growth rates are measured over about three decades. The countries that had the lowest amount of protection grew at the average rate of 3.8 percent per year while those with the highest protection grew at the rate of only 1.3 percent per year. This evidence has constituted the thrust behind the worldwide movement toward freer trade.

| Highest Protection | | Lowest Protection | |
|---|---|---|---|
| *Country* | *Growth* | *Country* | *Growth* |
| Angola | −2.7 | South Africa | 1.6 |
| Zambia | −1.4 | New Zealand | 1.8 |
| Ghana | −0.5 | United States | 1.9 |
| Senegal | −0.2 | United Kingdom | 2.2 |
| Uganda | −0.2 | Luxembourg | 2.3 |
| Sudan | 0.1 | Ireland | 2.7 |
| Zaire | 0.2 | Ecuador | 2.8 |
| Somalia | 0.2 | Denmark | 2.9 |
| Guinea | 0.5 | Belgium | 2.9 |
| Nigeria | 0.7 | Netherlands | 3.0 |
| India | 0.8 | France | 3.4 |
| Ethiopia | 0.8 | Finland | 3.6 |
| Bolivia | 1.0 | Spain | 3.6 |
| Chile | 1.0 | Italy | 4.0 |
| Argentina | 1.1 | Portugal | 4.5 |
| Ivory Coast | 1.3 | Malta | 5.4 |
| Zimbabwe | 1.6 | Korea | 5.6 |
| Burundi | 1.7 | Taiwan | 6.0 |
| Pakistan | 1.9 | Hong Kong | 6.1 |
| Rwanda | 2.0 | Japan | 6.1 |
| Tanzania | 2.3 | Singapore | 6.6 |
| Burma | 2.6 | | |
| Gambia | 2.9 | | |
| Iran | 3.1 | | |
| Panama | 3.5 | | |
| Cameroon | 3.6 | | |
| Egypt | 4.3 | | |
| Gabon | 5.2 | | |
| Average | 1.3 | Average | 3.8 |

*Source:* Research Department, Federal Reserve Bank of Dallas.

Table 1 assumed that America is six times as productive in food and two times as productive in clothing production as Europe. Since wages reflect productivity, American wages should be between six and two times as high as European wages. When the world terms of trade are $2F = 1C$, the price of clothing is twice that of food. In our example, the price of food can be $3 per unit and the price of clothing can be $6 per unit. If Americans specialize in food production, food is $3 per unit, and 1 unit of labor produces 6 units of food, wages must be $18 (= $3 × 6 units) per unit of labor in America.

Europeans specialize in clothing production. Because the price of clothing is $6 per unit and 1 unit of European labor produces 1 unit of clothing, wages must be $6 (= $6 × 1 unit) per unit of labor in Europe. (Prices are measured in dollars to avoid currency differences.) Thus, with the given terms of trade, American wages are three times European wages.

Assertions that high-wage countries like the United States cannot possibly compete with low-wage countries like Taiwan or Korea are economically unsound. Wages are higher in the United States because productivity is higher. Claims that people who live in low-wage countries cannot compete with high-productivity countries like the United States are also unsound. When comparative advantage directs the allocation of resources, both high-wage and low-wage countries share in the benefits of trade. The high-productivity country's wage rate will not be high enough to completely wipe out the productivity advantage nor be low enough to undercut the low-productivity country's comparative advantage. Likewise, the low-productivity country's wage will not be high enough to make it impossible to sell goods to the rich country nor low enough to undercut the rich country's comparative advantage. (See Example 2.)

Given the hypothetical case in Table 1, American wages will be somewhere between six and two times as high as European wages (depending on the terms of trade). If American money wages are seven times higher than European money wages, American money prices will be higher than European money prices for both food and clothing because America's

## EXAMPLE 2

## NORTH AMERICAN FREE TRADE AGREEMENT (NAFTA)

On January 1, 1994, the North American Free Trade Agreement (NAFTA) among the United States, Canada, and Mexico went into force. Prior to NAFTA, Mexico had trade barriers that were 2.5 times higher than those in the United States. The United States had a preexisting agreement with Canada. This is what NAFTA achieved:

1. A phaseout of most tariffs and nontariff barriers over 10 years on industrial products and over 15 years on agricultural products.
2. Investment rules ensuring national treatment of U.S. investors in Mexico and Canada as well as reduced barriers to investment in Mexican petrochemicals and financial services.
3. Protection of intellectual property rights (patents, copyrights, and trademarks).
4. Funds for environmental cleanup and community adjustment along the border between the United States and Mexico.

Domestic opponents of NAFTA argued that terrible things would happen if it was adopted.

Ross Perot, the main opponent of NAFTA, argued that there would be a "giant sucking sound," as jobs in America would be lost to Mexico. He argued that America could not compete with Mexican workers because their daily wages were less than American hourly wages.

These fears, of course, were not realized. The fact of the matter is that advanced countries can compete with poorer countries because of the law of comparative advantage. They can because workers in each country compete with other workers in the same country, not with workers in other countries. An American company must pay wages competitive with wages elsewhere in the U.S. economy, not in Mexico. The same is true in Mexico. Thus, the successful companies in the United States are those whose productivity is relatively higher than the average productivity (wages) in the United States. These are the industries in which the United States had a comparative advantage.

labor-productivity advantage cannot offset such a high wage disadvantage. This situation cannot persist. The demand for American labor will dry up, while the demand for European labor will rise. With American wages seven times European wages, forces will be set into operation to reduce American wages and raise European wages until the ratio of American to European wages returns to a level between six and two. With market-determined wages, all countries can compete successfully.

## INTRAINDUSTRY TRADE

Differences in comparative advantage constitute one reason for international trade. Another reason is decreasing costs, or economies of scale, which explain the simultaneous export and import of goods in the same industry.

Our discussion example thus far assumes that food and clothing are produced under constant returns to scale. If America and Europe can produce food and clothing with the same labor costs but with decreasing costs as production increases (economies of scale), advantages of large-scale specialization will be gained if each product is produced by only one country.

> **Decreasing costs** are present when the cost of production per unit decreases as the number of units produced increases.

Decreasing costs play a vital role in what is called *intraindustry trade*. Many products—such as cars, television sets, clothing, watches, and furniture—come in different varieties. Germany exports ultraluxury sports cars, whereas Japan has traditionally exported economy cars (but Japan is successfully invading Germany's territory). The same generic products, such as cars or furniture, can be both exported and imported. There is two-way trade. This intraindustry trade often involves decreasing costs: When many varieties of a good are produced, an increase in the production of any one variety spreads fixed overhead costs (such as rent, machinery, and administration) over more units. As a result, each country can specialize in a particular variety of some generic production.

## TRADING BLOCS AND FREE TRADE

### THE EUROPEAN UNION

The best example of free trade within a group of nations, called a trading bloc or a common market, is the European Union (EU). The EU formally began as the European Communities (EC), with the 1957 Treaty of Rome among six nations—Belgium, West Germany, France, Italy, Luxembourg, and the Netherlands. The purpose of the EC was to create a region of free trade. By 1968 all tariffs among the member states were eliminated. From 1958 to 1972 the EC's total real GDP grew at about 5 percent per year while intra-European trade expanded at about 13 percent per year. The success of the EC attracted more nations. Between 1972 and 1985 six more countries joined—Denmark, Ireland, Britain, Greece, Spain, and Portugal.

But from 1972 to 1985, the member states did not do nearly as well as the original six. The oil price shocks in the 1970s, a slowdown in European economic growth, and rising European unemployment reversed the trend toward integration. Member states began to impose new barriers to trade with the outside world as well as with other EC countries. The growth rate in real GDP fell by about one-half.

### EUROPE 1992

Europeans became convinced that rising trade barriers were partially responsible for their economic ills. Thus, in 1986, the 12 nations of the European Communities signed the Single European Act. In 1992, the EC member countries became the European Union, and a single market for goods, financial services, capital, and labor movements. This new, unified market is called Europe 1992.

Europe 1992 eliminates many types of barriers to trade. First, countries must share the same set of standards for safety and consumer protection. Second, the large differences in tax rates must be reduced. For example, in 1987 Spain had a 12 percent value-added tax, whereas Denmark had a 22 percent value-added tax. Spain must increase its rate to at least 14 percent, and Denmark must lower its rate to 20 percent at most. Third, border controls must be minimized. For example, in the past truck drivers had to show border officials up to 100 documents—invoices, forms for import statistics, and tax reports. Now truck drivers can go through customs showing only a single document.

In addition to eliminating these barriers, Europe 1992 creates a single market for financial services. For example, a bank established in one EU country can operate a branch in another EU country, and EU firms in one country can borrow in another. European Union citizens can keep bank accounts in any member nation. Thus, capital will flow freely throughout the bloc.

## NORTH AMERICAN FREE-TRADE BLOC

The United States has responded to the EU by forming its own trading bloc. (See Example 2 once again.) The United States signed a free-trade agreement with Canada in 1989 and signed an agreement with Mexico in 1994. The Canada-United States agreement generated little debate in the United States, but much in Canada. The free-trade agreement among Mexico, the United States, and Canada was opposed by some labor and farm groups.

Labor groups have expressed the fear that a pact with Mexico will lower U.S. wages because Mexican wages are only about one-seventh as high. Yet, even though more international trade can lower some wages, the principle of comparative advantage tells us that average U.S. wages will rise. As a country specializes in the goods in which it has a comparative advantage, its average real income—and wages—will rise, not fall. In fact, the United States is more productive than Mexico. Only lower wages enable Mexico to compete in spite of the absolute advantages of the United States. Moreover, much of the impact of freer trade with Mexico has already taken place. Beginning in 1986 Mexico unilaterally opened its markets to foreign goods. Since that time American exports to Mexico have doubled.

## THE U.S. COMPARATIVE ADVANTAGE

According to Bertil Ohlin, a country tends to export those goods that intensively use the abundant productive factors with which that country is blessed. The Ohlin theory is based on the relative abundance of different productive factors. For instance, if a country has a large quantity of labor relative to land or capital, its wages will tend to be lower than wages in countries with abundant land or capital. Even if technical know-how were the same across countries, countries with cheap labor would have a comparative advantage in the production of labor-intensive goods. Whereas the Ricardian theory assumes only one factor and takes technology differences as given, the Ohlin theory explains comparative advantage as the consequence of differences in the relative abundance of different factors.

Compared with other countries, the United States is rich in agricultural land. This abundance lowers the cost of agricultural goods compared with other countries. Despite protection abroad, the United States exports large quantities of goods such as wheat, soybeans, corn, cotton, and tobacco.

The United States also has an abundance of highly skilled, technical labor. The United States tends to export goods that use highly skilled labor. Thus, the United States has a comparative advantage in manufactured goods that require intensive investment in research and development (R&D); industries with relatively high R&D expenditures contribute most to American export sales. Computers, semiconductors, software, chemicals, nonelectrical and electrical machinery, aircraft, and professional and scientific instruments are the major R&D-intensive industries. These industries generate a trade surplus, with exports exceeding imports. The manufacturing industries that are not in this category—such as textiles, paper products, and food manufactures—generate a trade deficit (a surplus of imports over exports).

The products of R&D industries tend to be new products, which are nonstandardized and not well suited to simple, repetitive, mass-production techniques. As time passes, the production processes for these products, such as personal computers, become more standardized. The longer a given product has been on the market, the easier it is for the good to become standardized and the lesser the need for highly trained workers. When new goods become old goods, other countries can gain a comparative advantage over the United States in these goods. In order to fulfill its comparative advantage, the United States then moves on to the next new product generated by its giant research establishment and abundant supply of engineers, scientists, and skilled labor. The U.S. comparative advantage in manufacturing is in new products and processes.

In this chapter, we have considered the global economy, the law of comparative advantage, the gains from trade, how high-wage countries compete with low-wage countries, regional trading blocs, and the pattern of U.S. trade.

5. The United States is rich in agricultural land and highly skilled, technical labor. This advantage gives the United States a comparative advantage in agricultural goods and high-technology research and development products.

## SUMMARY

1. Just as trade and specialization can increase the economic well-being of individuals, so specialization and trade between countries can increase the economic well-being of the residents of the trading countries. The basic reason for trade is that countries cannot readily transfer their endowments of productive factors to other countries. Trade in goods and services acts as a substitute for the transfer of productive resources among countries. The Swedish economist Bertil Ohlin has demonstrated that a country specializes in those goods for which its factors of production are most suited. In 1817, David Ricardo formulated the law of comparative advantage, which demonstrates that countries export according to comparative—not absolute—advantage.

2. In a simple two-country, two-good world, even if one country has an absolute advantage in both goods, both countries can still gain from specialization and trade. If the two countries were denied the opportunity to trade, they would have to use domestic production to meet domestic consumption. With trade, specialization allows each to consume beyond its domestic production possibilities frontier by producing at home and then trading the product in which it has a comparative advantage. Countries will specialize in those products whose domestic opportunity costs are low relative to their opportunity costs in the other countries. Through trade, countries are able to exchange goods at more favorable terms than those dictated by domestic opportunity costs.

3. Money wages are set to reflect the average productivity of labor in each country. Higher average labor productivity is reflected in higher wages. Money wages are not set in such a manner as to undercut each country's comparative advantage. Economies of scale help account for intraindustry trade among countries.

4. Regional trading blocs abolish trade barriers among member nations. The most important blocs are the European Union and the North American free-trade pact among Canada, Mexico, and the United States.

## KEY TERMS

law of comparative advantage
absolute advantage
terms of trade
decreasing costs

## QUESTIONS AND PROBLEMS

1. Adam Smith noted: "What is prudence in the conduct of every private family can scarce be folly in that of a great kingdom. If a foreign country can supply us with a commodity cheaper than we ourselves can make it, better buy it from them with some part of the produce of our own industry." Strictly speaking, a fallacy of composition is involved in Smith's famous remark. But when applied to international trade, what is true of the family is also true of the kingdom. Why is it true that the fallacy of composition does not apply?

2. Suppose that 1 unit of labor in Asia can be used to produce 10 units of food or 5 units of clothing. Also suppose that 1 unit of labor in South America can be used to produce 4 units of food or 1 unit of clothing.
   a. Which country has an absolute advantage in food? In clothing?
   b. What is the relative cost of producing food in Asia? In South America?
   c. Which country will export food? Clothing?
   d. Draw the production possibilities frontier for each country if Asia has 10 units of labor and South America has 20 units of labor.
   e. What is the range for the final terms of trade between the two countries?
   f. If the final terms of trade are 3 units of food for 1 unit of clothing, compute the wage in Asia and the wage in South America, assuming that a unit of food

costs $40 and a unit of clothing costs $120.

3. What happens to the answers to parts *a, b,* and *c* of question 2 when the South American productivity figures are changed so that 1 unit of labor is used to produce either 40 units of food or 10 units of clothing?

4. In congressional hearings, American producers of such goods as gloves and shoes claim that they are the most efficient in the world but have been injured by domestic wages that are too high compared to foreign wages. Without disputing the facts of their case, how would you evaluate their plight?

# CHAPTER 36

# PROTECTION AND FREE TRADE

The book that you are reading has copyright protection in the United States. According to U.S. law, in order to earn protection, the book must be printed in the United States. This law benefits American printers. Similarly, the American dairy industry contends that imported cheese and ice cream are bad for its business. Americans love cheese and ice cream, but the government loves the dairy industry even more. It therefore limits the imports per American to a pound of dairy cheese and a spoonful of ice cream each year. The same restrictions apply to other products in other industries. For example, American peanut farmers have prevailed upon the government to limit imports to just a handful of peanuts per year per American. These are examples of trade barriers.

When a country specializes and trades according to comparative advantage, it can consume more than would be possible if it had to produce everything itself. As we know from the previous chapter, in the absence of trade barriers or with free trade, a country can consume above its production possibilities frontier.

Is it to a country's advantage to adopt completely free trade, or should a country impose some trade barriers between itself and the rest of the world? In this chapter, we discuss the nature of trade barriers, the case against protection, the case for trade barriers, and American trade policies.

# TRADE BARRIERS

Trade barriers consist of tariffs, quotas, and various technical standards and practices.

## TARIFFS

A **tariff** is a tax levied on imports.

An import tariff raises the price paid by domestic consumers as well as the price received by domestic producers of similar or identical products. For example, a tariff on clothing from Taiwan will raise the prices paid by American consumers of clothing imports and the prices received by American clothing producers.

Let's suppose a country levies a $5 tariff on imported shoes that cost $40 in the foreign market. If domestic and foreign shoes are the same, both imported and domestically produced shoes will sell for $45 in the home market. Because consumers will pay more for shoes, the tariff discourages shoe consumption. Because the domestic producer of shoes will be able to charge more for shoes, the $5 tariff encourages domestic production and discourages shoe imports and foreign shoe production.

The same result (discouraging shoe consumption and encouraging domestic production) can be accomplished by taxing domestic consumption of shoes by $5 and giving every domestic firm a $5 subsidy per pair of shoes produced.

## IMPORT QUOTAS

An **import quota** is a quantitative limitation on the amount of imports of a specific product during a given period.

For example, U.S. import quotas on steel might specify the number of tons of a particular grade that can be imported into the United States in a given year.

Generally speaking, importers of products that fall under quota restrictions must obtain a license to import the good. When the number of licenses issued is limited to the number specified by the quota, the quantity of imports cannot exceed the maximum quota limit.

Import licenses can be distributed in a variety of ways. One option is that import licenses are auctioned off by the government in a free and fair market. If import licenses are scarce (more importers want licenses than are available), they will sell for a price that reflects their scarcity. In such a case, an import license is similar to a tariff: It restricts imports and raises revenue for the government.

Import licenses may also be handed out on a first-come-first-served basis, on the basis of favoritism, or according to the amount of past imports by the importer. When import quotas are not auctioned off, the potential revenue that the government could collect goes to the lucky few importers who get the scarce import licenses. For this reason, some importers, especially those who are likely to obtain import licenses, prefer import quotas to tariffs. The government does not collect the revenue; instead, the importers can cash in on the scarcity value of the import licenses. The license permits them to buy a product cheaply in the world market and then to sell it at a handsome profit in the home market. For example, the U.S. sugar quota keeps domestic sugar prices at almost twice the level of world sugar prices. The importers collect the difference! American consumers pay higher prices, and the government gains no revenues.

## VOLUNTARY RESTRAINTS

A **voluntary export restraint** is an agreement between two governments in which the exporting country voluntarily limits the export of a certain product to the importing country.

The U.S. government has negotiated a number of voluntary export restraints with foreign governments that limit the foreign country's volume of commodity exports to the U.S. market. Unlike tariffs or import quotas, voluntary export restraints generate no revenue for the importing country or its government. Instead, the foreign exporter or the foreign government collects the scarcity value of the right to export to the huge U.S. market. For example, from 1981 to 1985, under the U.S. threat of an import quota, the Japanese government ordered its auto companies to voluntarily limit exports to the United States to about 1.8 million units a year.[1] A Brookings Institution study

---

[1] Keith Maskus, "Rising Protectionism and U.S. International Trade Policy," Federal Reserve Bank of Kansas City, *Economic Review* (July/August 1984): p. 9.

concluded that the Japanese-American curb boosted the average car prices by about $2500.

Over the last decade, animal feeds, brooms, color TV sets, cattle, cotton, crude petroleum, dairy products, fish, meat, peanuts, potatoes, sugar, candy, textiles, stainless-steel flatware, steel, wheat and wheat flour, and automobiles have been subjected to import quotas or voluntary export quotas.

Like import tariffs, import quotas and voluntary export restraints limit the quantity of foreign goods available in the domestic market. Such nontariff barriers raise the price paid by domestic consumers and the price that can be charged by domestic producers on their import-competing products. Domestic producers benefit from quotas by being able to charge higher prices. The gains go to the importer who receives a license to buy cheap imports, or, if licenses are auctioned, the gains go to the government in the form of revenue. The loser is the consumer, who pays higher prices because such quotas exist.

A new international agreement through the World Trade Organization forbids voluntary export restraints and requires countries to gradually substitute tariffs for import restraints. The elimination of quantity restraints on international trade is a step toward liberalization.

## OTHER NONTARIFF BARRIERS

The importance of nontariff barriers in world trade has grown in the last decade. It has been estimated that nearly 50 percent of world trade has been conducted under some sort of nontariff barrier. Import and voluntary export quotas are not the only nontariff barriers. Although eliminating them is a step in the right direction, three other major impediments to trade remain: government procurement practices, technical standards, and domestic content rules. Governments tend to give preferential treatment to domestic producers when purchasing goods and services. Furthermore, the free flow of products can be impeded by technical standards that imported practices must meet. For example, imported cars must pass American pollution control and safety standards. European countries ban American beef treated with growth-inducing hormones.

Tariffs and nontariff barriers raise costs to consumers and protect the domestic producers of import-competing products. The following discussion of the economics of protection focuses on tariffs, but it also applies to quotas and nontariff barriers.

## THE CASE AGAINST PROTECTION

According to one study, 94 percent of economists agree that tariffs and quotas lower real income. Probably no other issue in economics commands so much support among economists, whose enthusiasm for free trade has remained steadfast for more than 210 years.[2]

### EXPORTS PAY FOR IMPORTS

One of the strongest correlations in all of economics is that between exports and imports. The reason is basic: A country must export in order to import. As we shall see in the next chapter, although a country can import more in one period than it exports, it must later export more than it imports in order to pay for the difference. In short, exports now or later pay for imports now or later. Exports of all things must be subtracted from domestic consumption (present or future); imports of all things must be added to domestic consumption (present or future). The gain from trade consists of the gain realized from importing goods that can be imported more cheaply than they can be produced at home. Example 1 describes the fallacy that U.S. trade deficits with a particular country measure its trade losses with that country.

In the preceding chapter we considered a simple, hypothetical world where America trades only with Europe and simply ships food in return for clothing. In this case, American exports of food are paying for clothing imports from Europe. The more food America exports, the more clothing imports are brought in, and vice versa. The reason exports of goods and services must pay for imports of goods and services is that, in the long run, countries want each other's goods, not each other's money. In the next chapter, we shall consider how a surplus of imports over exports must be financed by foreign investments in domestic industries.

If the United States, or any country, restricts imports, it necessarily restricts exports.

In other words, subsidizing import-competing industries by means of tariff or nontariff barriers penalizes

---

[2]Richard Alston, Michael B. Vaughn, and J.R. Kearl, "Is There a Consensus Among Economists in the 1990s?" *American Economic Review* 82 (May 1992).

## EXAMPLE 1
## COUNTRY-BASHING AND
## BILATERAL TRADE DEFICITS

The United States typically imports more from Japan than it exports. For example, in 1994 the United States imported about $70 billion more in merchandise from Japan than it exported. In the previous year, the U.S. merchandise trade deficit was $60 billion. The trade deficit with particular countries often leads to government action to do something about it. For example, in spring 1995 the United States threatened 100 percent duties on Japanese luxury cars unless Japan opened up its automobile market to U.S. cars. After Japan agreed (although without specific targets) to import more cars and parts, the United States backed down.

In a multilateral world, trade deficits with particular countries are offset by trade surpluses with other countries. Moreover, even if they are not offset by merchandise trade surpluses, they will be offset by surpluses elsewhere. For example, in 1994, the United States had a $16 billion export surplus with Japan in services and the Japanese invested (net) about $40 billion in the United States. In addition, over $20 billion of goods, services, and assets sold to the Japanese were not accounted for in the official statistics. In the balance of payments this is called the "statistical discrepancy"!

Targeting particular countries on a hit list because they provide us with more imports than we export to them seems highly misguided. It ignores the multilateral nature of international trade and the fact that we benefit, rather than lose, from imports.

a host of unseen export industries. Imports can be more visible than exports.[3]

## THE COST OF PROTECTION

According to the law of comparative advantage, specialization benefits the country as a whole, while tariffs or quotas eliminate or reduce those gains from specialization. The argument for free trade presented thus far has rested on the rather simple Ricardian model of the last chapter, which, for simplicity, ruled out the existence of different types of land, labor, and capital. In the real world, when trade opens, some

people are hurt. The import of Japanese cars keeps domestic car prices lower and car buyers happy, but it certainly hurts domestic auto producers, their suppliers, and auto workers. The export of American wheat keeps domestic prices of bread higher but makes wheat farmers happy. The law of comparative advantage, however, guarantees that the *net* advantages are on the side of trade rather than protection.

It is clear that protection hurts the consumers of the product being protected and helps the producers of the domestic product. We can demonstrate that consumers are hurt *more* than producers are benefited.

Figure 1 shows how much consumers benefit from lower prices. If the price of a video game is $36, the demand curve in Figure 1 shows that 6,000 games are demanded. If the price of the game were to fall to $24, about 9,000 games would be demanded. The gain to consumers of the lower price is the area $G + H$. The people who would have bought 6,000 units at $36 have to pay only $24 and therefore save $12 per unit. Their gain is $12 × 6,000, or $72,000 (area $G$). When the price is $24, new customers come

---

[3]One of the authors was once on a flight to Europe to sell his services to a foreign university for a short time (exporting). Sitting next to him was an engineer off to Europe to sell his engineering talents. Even the Boeing 747 was an export to the foreign airline. The engineer fretted that the United States "can't export anything and imports too much." The author decided it was better to have a pleasant trip than win a debating point!

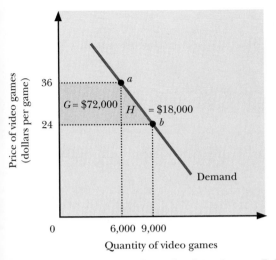

**FIGURE 1    Consumer Benefits from Lower Prices**

When the price falls from $36 to $24 per video game, consumers benefit by the area G + H. Those who would buy 6,000 units at $36 each (point a) benefit by area G because they save $12 per unit. Those new customers who buy the 3,000 additional units when the price is $24 (point b) benefit by area H.

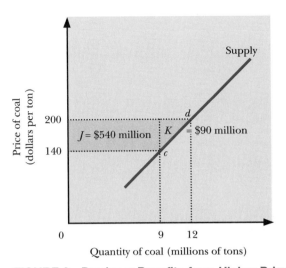

**FIGURE 2    Producer Benefits from Higher Prices**

When the price rises from $140 to $200 per ton of coal, producers benefit by the area J + K. Those who would sell 9 million tons at $140 per ton (point c) benefit by area J. Those new suppliers who sell 3 million additional tons when the price is $200 per ton (point d) benefit by area K.

---

into the market and buy 3,000 additional video games. The average new customer would have been willing to pay $30 (the average of $36 and $24). Since new customers are paying only $24 per game, their average gain is $6 × 3,000 or $18,000 (area H). Thus, if the price falls from $36 to $24 per game, consumers gain G + H. Conversely, if the price rises above $24 to $36, consumers lose G + H.

Whereas the demand curve in Figure 1 showed how consumers benefit from lower prices, the supply curve in Figure 2 shows how producers benefit from higher prices. If the price of a ton of coal is $140, 9 million tons of coal will be supplied. If the price of coal is $200, 12 million tons will be supplied. The gain to producers from raising the price from $140 to $200 is the area J + K. Coal producers who would have supplied 9 million tons at a price of $140 receive $200 per ton (a $60 gain on each of the 9 million tons). Their gain is $60 × 9 million, or $540 million (area J). When the price rises to $200 per ton, 3 million additional tons are produced. The average producer of this new coal would have been willing to receive $170 (the average of $200 and $140) for a ton of coal. Because the new suppliers are in fact receiving $200, their gain is $30 × 3 million, or $90 million (area K). Thus, if the price of a ton of coal rises from $140 to $200, producers gain J + K. Con-

versely, if the price falls from $200 to $140, producers lose J + K.

**A Prohibitive Tariff.**    We are now in a position to see that protection hurts other people more than it benefits those who are involved in the production of the protected good. The costs of protection are easiest to understand by examining the effects of a prohibitive tariff (as opposed to a nonprohibitive tariff).

> A **prohibitive tariff** is a tariff that is high enough to cut off all imports of the product.
>
> A **nonprohibitive tariff** is a tariff that does not wipe out all imports of the product.

Panel (a) of Figure 3 shows the hypothetical demand-and-supply situation in the United States for shirts; panel (b) shows the hypothetical demand-and-supply situation in Europe for shirts. For each "country," the supply curve shows the quantity of shirts supplied by domestic producers at each price, and the demand curve shows the quantity demanded by domestic consumers at each price. For simplicity, we will assume that U.S. and European shirts are the same. For simplicity, we will also assume that Europe and the United States are the only countries in the world economy.

Using these simple assumptions, we can determine the gains from trade in shirts. With free trade,

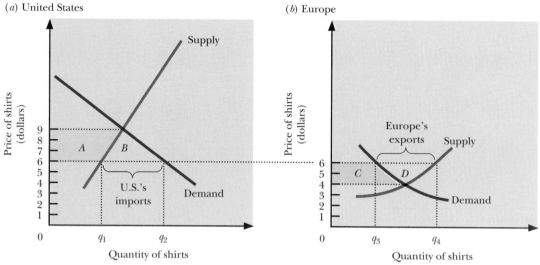

(*a*) United States    (*b*) Europe

**FIGURE 3    The Costs of a Prohibitive Tariff**

With a prohibitive tariff, the prices paid in each country are determined by the supply and demand curves in each country. If there were no tariff, prices would be the same in the two countries. The prohibitive tariff in the United States raises the price there from $6 to $9. Consumers lose area *A* + *B*, but producers gain area *A*. The net loss to the United States is area *B*. In Europe, prices fall from $6 to $4, and producers lose area *C* + *D*, while consumers gain area *C*. The gain to consumers is less than the loss to producers. The net loss to Europe is area *D*.

the price of shirts will be the same in the United States and Europe. If prices are different, importers will buy in the cheap market and sell in the expensive market until prices equalize. In our example, the price in the United States under free-trade conditions will be $6. The United States will be importing shirts from Europe. The U.S. excess of consumption over production (imports) will just match Europe's excess of production over consumption (exports).

Suppose the United States imposes a prohibitive tariff high enough to cut off all shirt imports. With no trade, the prices in the two countries will diverge; they will be determined exclusively by domestic supply-and-demand conditions. Europe's price of shirts will be $4, and the U.S. price will be $9.

Without trade, the difference between U.S. and European shirt prices is $5. Thus, if the United States imposes a tariff exceeding $5, the incentive to trade will be wiped out because imported shirts will cost more than the domestic price ($4 plus the tariff of more than $5).

As demonstrated earlier, the increase in price from $6 (with trade) to $9 (with a prohibitive tariff) will result in a consumer loss of the shaded areas *A*

+ *B*. U.S. shirt consumers lose but U.S. producers gain as a consequence of higher prices. The producers of shirts in the United States would gain area *A*. In panel (*a*) of Figure 3, the cost of tariff protection to consumers (*A* + *B*) exceeds the gains to producers (*A*). The net cost of tariff protection to the whole U.S. economy is area *B*.

Europe also loses from a prohibitive tariff, as shown in panel (*b*). With free trade, Europe's price of shirts is $6. A prohibitive tariff eliminates exports, and the European price must equate domestic supply with domestic demand. If Europe cannot export shirts, the price of its shirts must be $4. The prohibitive U.S. tariff hurts European shirt producers by the area *C* + *D* but benefits European shirt consumers by area *C*. The gain to consumers (*C*) is less than the loss to producers (*C* + *D*). Thus, Europe suffers a net loss of area *D*.

**A Nonprohibitive Tariff.**    Unlike prohibitive tariffs, nonprohibitive tariffs do not eliminate imports entirely. Figure 4 shows the supply-and-demand conditions in a country whose imports of a particular good are so small relative to the world supply that the world price ($p_w$) is taken as given. The amount imported by this country will not affect the world price.[4]

With a zero tariff, consumers can purchase all they want at the prevailing world price, $p_w$. According to Figure 4, the quantity represented by the distance between $q_1$ and $q_4$ will be imported because it constitutes the difference between the quantity demanded at $p_w$ and the quantity supplied by domestic producers.

When a tariff ($t$) is imposed, the price rises to $p_w + t$; the new domestic price equals the world price plus the tariff rate. The country now imports only that quantity represented by the distance between $q_2$ and $q_3$.

The tariff benefits domestic producers by the area $N$. The government (or public) benefits by area $T$, which equals the revenue from the tariff (the tariff rate times the quantity of imports). The loss to consumers from the increase in price is the sum of areas $N + R + T + V$. If the gains (area $N + T$) are subtracted from the losses (area $N + R + T + V$), the tariff imposes a net loss to the country of area $R + V$.

The bottom line is that protection imposes costs on society that are greater than the benefits received by the individual industries being protected. Trade barriers raise prices and lead to economic inefficiency (shifting resources from efficient to less efficient industries). For example, tariffs and hundreds of voluntary export restraints have restricted imports of textiles and clothing into the United States. It has been estimated that the costs imposed on consumers run about three times as high as the benefits bestowed on American textile producers. Moreover, the burden of these costs fall most heavily on the poor because protection is often applied to the cheapest goods.

The total costs of all U.S. tariffs and quotas to consumers has been estimated to be about $70 billion per year (1994). While protection saves jobs in some industries, it does so at the expense of other jobs. The costs per job saved, therefore, run very high. The annual costs to consumers per job protected has been estimated to be about six times

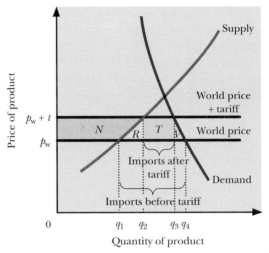

**FIGURE 4    The Effects of a Nonprohibitive Tariff**

Before the nonprohibitive tariff, the price of the product is $p_w$. The tariff raises the price to $p_w + t$—that is, the world price plus the amount of the duty. Consumers lose area $N + R + T + V$. Producers gain area $N$. The government gains the tariff revenue of area $T$, which equals the tariff per unit times the quantity of imports. The net loss is area $R + V$. The tariff lowers imports from ($q_4 - q_1$) to ($q_3 - q_2$).

the earnings of the average U.S. worker (about $170,000).

Such losses may be an underestimate, according to economists Gordon Tullock and Anne Krueger. Tullock and Krueger argue that because producers have an incentive to expend resources to get the tariff passed, the import-competing industry may form a committee, lobby Congress, or advertise the plight of its industry. When the color TV industry was hurt by imports, the industry formed COMPACT (the Committee to Preserve American Color Television). Such expenditures reduce gains to protected producers and thus further increase the costs of protection.

## THE POLITICAL ECONOMY OF TARIFFS

If tariffs impose a cost on the community, why do they exist? Why would a representative democracy, which is supposed to represent consumer interests, establish trade barriers?

The main explanation for tariffs is that the costs imposed by a tariff are highly diffused among millions of people, while the (smaller) benefits are concentrated among specific sectors of the economy associated with the protected industry. The costs

---

[4]Note that this assumption is not satisfied in Figure 3: There are only two countries, and the number of shirts imported by the United States affects the world price of shirts.

imposed on the community are large in total but so small per person that it is not worth the trouble to any one person to join a committee to fight tariffs on each imported good, while the benefits to protected sectors are well worth the costs of lobbying. For example, assume people devote about 0.5 percent of all consumptions to sugar (in all its forms). A trade barrier that raises the price of sugar by 50 percent helps domestic sugar producers enormously, but it raises the cost of living by only 0.25 percent (50 percent of 0.5 percent). To the consumer, this cost is too small to worry about. The costs of assembling a fighting coalition against each request for protection are prohibitive.

The people with an incentive to lobby heavily Congress would be the foreign competitors of the domestic import-competing industry that seek protection. However, these foreign competitors have comparatively little political clout in the United States.

## PROTECTIONIST ARGUMENTS

### PREVENTING UNFAIR FOREIGN COMPETITION

The economy gains from foreign trade because it can obtain goods more cheaply from abroad than from domestic sources. The domestic producers of goods that are close or perfect substitutes for these imports try to convince their governments, and others, that such competition is unfair. This argument takes many forms and is probably the most widely used protectionist argument.

**Low Foreign Wages.**   According to the theory of comparative advantage, high-wage countries can export to or compete effectively against low-wage countries in those industries in which their productivity advantage more than offsets their wage disadvantage. Likewise, low-wage countries can export to or compete effectively against high-productivity countries in those industries in which their wage advantage more than offsets their productivity disadvantage. Industries in each country must pay wages that are competitive for that country. In other words, the textile industry in the United States competes with other industries in the United States for labor and, therefore, must pay U.S. wages. U.S. wages tend to reflect the high average level of U.S. productivity. Hence, those industries (such as textiles) with below-average productivity find it difficult to survive with-

out protection. Since every country has industries with above-average and below-average productivities, it must be that every country has some industries in which it has a comparative advantage and others in which it has a comparative disadvantage.

In the industrialized countries, the industries that cannot compete complain that they are subjected to unfair competition because of the low wages abroad. To some business managers and politicians, it seems unfair to be more efficient in productivity yet unable to compete because wages are too high. If this view were sound, it would be necessary to erect trade barriers so that all the industries in which the United States had a comparative disadvantage could supply the home market. The erection of such barriers, however, would destroy U.S. export trade and severely lower the real income of the American people. We might argue that it is unfair to erect trade barriers that would raise the incomes of those hurt by import competition but would lower the incomes of the rest of the community even more. This trade-off is a key element of the theory of comparative advantage. The reason that we continue to import goods (such as textiles) for which we have an absolute advantage compared with the rest of the world is that such industries cannot pay the wages in those industries in which labor is *more* productively applied.

**Dumping.**   Another version of the complaint that foreign competition is unfair alleges that foreign goods are "dumped" on the home market at less than the foreign cost.

The dumping complaint is even enshrined in law. The U.S. Tariff Act of 1930, as amended by the Trade Agreements Act of 1979, provides for special antidumping duties to be imposed when foreign goods are sold in the home market for less than the price they would fetch in the foreign market. The original Anti-Dumping Law was passed in 1921.

> **Dumping** occurs when a country sells a good in another country for less than the price charged in the home country.

Public attitudes toward dumping are peculiar. As Charles P. Kindleberger has pointed out, most people appear to have a subconscious producer's bias, which leads them to applaud antidumping actions. When dumping occurs, however, domestic consumers are buying goods more cheaply than foreign consumers. The beneficiaries are the domestic consumers, and the losers are the domestic firms competing with the dumped products. The theory of comparative advantage points out that the advantage of foreign trade is that a country (as a whole) is made better off if it can obtain goods more cheaply abroad than at home: The cheaper the foreign goods, the greater the consumer benefit.

International-trade economists are suspicious of antidumping laws. The case against these laws has been made by Charles Kindleberger:

> Countervailing measures against alleged dumping are obnoxious because they reduce the flexibility and elasticity of international markets and reduce the potential gain from trade. From 1846 to 1913, when Britain followed a free-trade policy, distress goods in any part of the world could be disposed of in London . . . to the benefit of the British consumer and the overseas producer. With antidumping tariffs everywhere, adjustment after miscalculations which result in overproduction is much less readily effected.[5]

The only time antidumping duties might be appropriate is in the case of predatory dumping, where the foreign firm monopolizes the domestic market by temporarily lowering prices and then raising them to an even higher level after the domestic competitors have been driven out of business. However, predatory dumping may be difficult to prove. The costs of screening the valid claims from the frivolous ones may exceed any potential gains.

**Foreign-Export Subsidies.**   One of the most important arguments for protection in today's world is similar to the dumping complaint, but the "dumping" is caused by the actions of a foreign government rather than the actions of a foreign firm. Business managers who must compete against foreign imports argue that if a foreign government provides export subsidies to their exporters, domestic firms face unfair competition. This argument, like the dumping argument, is supported by the U.S. countervailing duty.

> A **countervailing duty** is a duty imposed on imports subsidized by the governments of the exporting country.

When a foreign government subsidizes exports to, say, the United States, the ultimate beneficiaries are the American people. The losers are the residents of the foreign country and the special interests in the United States that produce domestic import substitutes. Textiles from Argentina, radial tires from Canada, sugar from the European Community, molasses from France, tomato products from Greece, refrigerators from Italy, and chains from Spain are examples of goods exported to the United States that have received government subsidies. Even the United States, which has a solid comparative advantage in commercial aircraft, subsidizes the export of aircraft through below-market loans to the Boeing Company and McDonnell Douglass Corporation.

Those who desire protection from subsidized foreign exports have a powerful political argument, but there is no economic argument for countervailing duties. The benefit of foreign trade is imports; the opportunity cost of foreign trade is exports. Protectionists reason that exports are good and imports are bad. This reasoning is true for the businesses that must compete with foreign imports but not for the economy as a whole. Foreign-export subsidies are a gift to the American people. To offset this gift by imposing countervailing duties is a perverse policy—like the proverbial dog that bites the hand that feeds it.

## PROTECTING INFANT INDUSTRIES: INDUSTRIAL POLICY

Alexander Hamilton, the first U.S. Secretary of the Treasury, argued that the "infant" or new industries of newly developing economies need protection in their initial stages. This Hamiltonian argument is repeated today by many economists and politicians interested in accelerating the economic development of nonindustrialized countries. There are two versions of the infant-industry argument: One version is difficult to defend in terms of economic theory; the other makes more sense.

The more common infant-industry argument amounts to a disguised brand of simple protectionism. It is argued that in many industries, economies of scale are present and that an initial stage of learning by doing is necessary to make the plant competitive on an international basis. A small, new plant must face costs higher than those of its foreign rivals, who are larger and have been in the business for a long time. Hence, some economists argue that it is

[5]Charles P. Kindleberger, *International Economics*, 5th ed. (Homewood, IL: Richard D. Irwin, 1973), p. 156.

necessary to protect new industries until they can stand on their own feet.

This argument ignores the fact that in virtually every business enterprise, the first few years of activity are characterized by losses. Until businesses become known externally, until a competent staff is acquired, and until early production difficulties are overcome, it is difficult to make a profit. Most successful businesses are characterized by losses in the first few years and profits thereafter. It is not unusual to wait five or ten years or even more for a business venture to pay off. Capital markets allow business firms to borrow the funds from lenders or venture capitalists to finance their investments. If these investments paid profits from the beginning, it would not be necessary to borrow.

To argue that the government must protect an industry from foreign competition implies that the private market has failed to see the profit opportunities in the infant industry. Given the way information is distributed in this world, the argument is highly improbable. Information is costly to acquire. Those who are most likely to have information are those who would benefit the most from it. Thus, it is very unlikely that a government bureaucracy or a House committee would have more valuable information about the future course of profits in an industry than would potential investors.

Economists Leland Yeager and David Tuerck have found that, historically, new industries do not need protection:

> Manufacture of iron, hats, and other goods got a foothold in Colonial America despite British attempts at suppression. Manufacture of textiles, shoes, steel, machine tools, airplanes, and countless other goods has arisen and flourished in the American West and South despite competition under internal free trade with the established industries of the Northeast.[6]

A modern example is provided by Netscape, the company that provides software for browsing the Internet—the communications network linking computers. When the company's stock was offered to the public in the summer of 1995, even though profits were years into the future, the stock was sold at two or three times the price that the company expected! The investing public simply formed the expectation that profits would soon follow. There was no necessity for Netscape to ask for a government subsidy.

Another version of the infant-industry argument is that a particular industry may yield external benefits to the rest of the community for a certain period of time. These benefits cannot be captured by the initial investors and thus will not be included in private profitability calculations. A new firm might have to adapt from foreign to local conditions. The knowledge it acquires about new technology would not be patentable, and later users could take full advantage of their experience. The knowledge acquired by the one firm could be used by all; hence, public action in the form of protection may be called for to promote this activity. However, government action to support particular industries has failed in the vast majority of cases. (See Example 2.)

Robert Baldwin of the University of Wisconsin has pointed out that even the external benefit case for supporting an industry does not justify import duties. Baldwin argues that even if such benefits are present, a tariff does not guarantee that the most desirable type of knowledge-acquisition expenditures will be made. It may be better to subsidize firms that make the initial contacts or first acquire the knowledge to use new technology.

Tariffs are also a poor device for subsidizing an industry because they raise costs to consumers. Hence, if it is desirable to stimulate some industries, a direct subsidy that can be easily measured and does not lead to higher costs to consumers would be preferable.

## KEEPING MONEY IN THE COUNTRY

Some protectionist arguments are grossly false. The first is attributed (perhaps incorrectly) to Abraham Lincoln: "I don't know much about the tariff. But I do know that when I buy a coat from England, I have the coat and England has the money. But when I buy a coat from America, I have the coat and America has the money."

While this argument may be appealing at first glance, it contains an error in logic. It supposes that money is somehow more valuable than goods. This *mercantilist fallacy* was committed by the mercantilist writers of the seventeenth and eighteenth cen-

---

[6]Leland B. Yeager and David G. Tuerck, *Trade Policy and the Price System* (Scranton, PA: International Trade Textbook Company, 1966). This excellent book contains almost all the arguments for and against free trade, but it is strongly opposed to protection.

## EXAMPLE 2
## INDUSTRIAL
## POLICY

Industrial policy is the targeting of specific high-technology industries with the goal that the externalities generated will increase a country's rate of economic growth. In principle, there is a case for supporting such industries. In practice, however, it is necessary to choose the right industries. The most important example of such industrial targeting is that of Japan.

The government's track record has been almost uniformly poor. The Japanese Ministry of International Trade and Industry (MITI) has not targeted Japan's success stories: automobiles, stereos, VCRs, and televisions. Its decisions on the production of automobiles and trucks were consistently wrong. What we consider today as the very successful Japanese automobile and truck industry was completely missed by MITI. If MITI had had its way, Honda would have been known only for its manufacture of motorcycles—rather than being one of the world's most popular car makers. Any successes? MITI did finance semiconductors; however, the amount was small and after the mid-1970s there were no tariffs and quotas to protect home production. Although high-definition television (HDTV) was supported by both the European and Japanese governments, the technology they developed was made obsolete by U.S. firms working on their own!

turies who feared that unrestricted trade would lead to the loss of gold. Writers such as David Hume and Adam Smith pointed out that this argument confuses ends with means. The end of the economic activity is consumption: Money is only a means to that end. When England sells an American a coat, the money is eventually used to buy, say, American wheat. The cost is the wheat, not the money.[7]

## SAVING DOMESTIC JOBS

Another false protectionist argument is that imports deprive Americans of jobs: "The American market is the greatest in the world, and necessarily it should be reserved for American producers," we can read from a 1952 Senate speech. A U.S. senator once explained the mysterious mechanism by which foreign imports cause unemployment:

> The importation of . . . foreign beef is not a stimulant to our economy. For foreign producers do not employ American labor; they do not buy our feed grain and fertilizers; they do not use our slaughterhouses; they do not use our truckers; they do not invest in or borrow from our banks; they do not buy our insurance; they do very little to stimulate the national economy.[8]

As already demonstrated, if each country specializes according to its comparative advantage, every country has more real GDP. The presumption the senator makes is that when a job is lost through import competition, a job is lost forever to the economy—and this is simply untrue.

In the long run, a country must export in order to import. Even in the short run, the exports of

---

[7]Under the existing international monetary system, trade imbalances do not even lead to the loss of money (currency) to other countries. The "prices" of foreign currencies are set in foreign-exchange markets, where the supply and demand for each currency are equated. A foreign currency is demanded to pay for goods purchased from the foreign country. No actual money crosses foreign borders. Transactions in each country must be carried out in that country's currency, not in the currency of another country.

---

[8]The quotations in this section are from Yeager and Tuerck, *Trade Policy and the Price System.*

goods, services, and securities must equal the imports of goods, services, and securities. Jobs destroyed by competition from imports are eventually restored by increased exports or increased investments. Foreign trade increases economic efficiency. In the long run, import barriers simply make it costlier to purchase the goods and services. The enormous efficiency changes over the last century did not result in permanent unemployment but rather in a higher standard of living for all. Trade, according to comparative advantage, raises economic efficiency. A country would not benefit by forgoing long-term efficiency gains for short-term reductions in unemployment. Even if there is a trade deficit (imports greater than exports), greater unemployment is not the result.

To clinch the argument that imports do not cause unemployment, we need only look at the correlation between unemployment and imports in various countries. If imports clearly cause unemployment, we would expect that the higher the imports, the larger is unemployment. But the fact is that in some countries the correlation is positive while in other countries the correlation is negative. On average, there is no correlation whatsoever. The data lead us to conclude that the correlation observed in a particular country between imports and unemployment is purely accidental. Indeed, the only generalization that holds is that, whatever the correlation between imports and unemployment, just about the same correlation exists between exports and unemployment. The reason is simple: Exports and imports are highly correlated and the international trade accounts cannot be used to systematically explain unemployment.

## NONPROTECTIONIST ARGUMENTS FOR TARIFFS

Protectionists argue that tariffs should be used to benefit certain special interests (at the public expense). Four arguments for tariffs are not protectionist in nature.

### THE NATIONAL DEFENSE ARGUMENT

One nonprotectionist argument for tariffs states that an industry essential to the national defense should be subsidized to encourage it to produce at a prudent level for the public safety. Although this argument does make some sense, it is not entirely applicable to the United States. A look at the comparative advantage of the United States reveals that the manufacturing industries in which this country excels—chemicals, machinery, transportation equipment, and aircraft—are the same ones that would be important in times of war. Significant exceptions to this dominance, perhaps, are shipbuilding (which the United States does subsidize), semiconductors, and steel.

In some cases, protection even appears contrary to defense interests. Let's consider oil imports. The United States protected domestic oil by a tariff from the 1950s to the early 1970s. We might argue that it would be better to import foreign oil, save domestic oil reserves, and follow a policy of stockpiling imported oil in the case of war. The U.S. policy, instead, used up American oil.

Many industries that have little to do with national defense have used the national defense argument as a rationale for protection. These industries are, to name but a few, gloves, pens, poetry, peanuts, paper, candles, thumbtacks, pencils, lacemaking, tuna fishing, and even clothespins.

If an industry is deemed essential for the national defense, a domestic-production subsidy would be a better way to obtain more peacetime production by that industry. Such subsidies could be handed out by the Department of Defense, where the experts on defense presumably reside. As we have noted, a tariff has the same effect as the combination of a production subsidy and a consumption tax. A direct subsidy is almost always better than a tariff because the tariff also raises the cost of living for consumers.

### THE FOREIGNER-WILL-PAY ARGUMENT

International economists have long recognized that it is sometimes possible for a country to raise tariffs and thus shift the terms of trade to raise the country's real income. If a country imports widgets under free trade at a price of $10 a widget, and this country is a major importer of widgets, the less the country imports, the lower is the world price. In an extreme case, a $1 tariff might drive down the world price of widgets from $10 to $9. The country's consumers will still pay a $10 price for widgets, but the country can now import them for $9 and fill the national treasury with the tariff revenues, benefiting the entire country.

A famous turn-of-the-century British economist, Francis Edgeworth, warned that the foreigner-will-pay argument is like a bottle of poison that is useful in small doses: One should always label it *Danger*. The argument presupposes that the rest of the world cannot retaliate. Very special circumstances would have to be present for one country to be able to beat down everybody else's terms of trade by tariffs while the rest of the world could not respond. Once the possibility of retaliation is present, countries that try to use this policy could start a tariff war that would leave everybody worse off.

## THE DIVERSIFICATION ARGUMENT

An argument closely related to the infant-industry argument is that free trade may lead an economy to specialize too much and expose it to the risks of putting all its eggs in one basket. When an economy is highly dependent on only one export good—as is Bolivia on tin or Colombia on coffee—the fortunes of the country wax and wane with the price of the main export good. Such cyclical fluctuations in raw-material prices allegedly impose hardships on the specialized economy.

We seldom hear this argument in fair weather, only in foul. No one questioned the wisdom of the oil-exporting countries' specialization in oil. Kuwait is heavily dependent on oil exports and is one of the richest countries in the world (on a per capita basis) because of this specialization. When prices are going up, the diversification theorists remain strangely quiet. Private investors find it profitable to invest in the goods that promise the highest return. In nondiversified economies, investors have concluded that only a few goods are worthy of their attention. To conclude that diversification should be forced by government policy is sound only if the policymaker has more information about the future of an economy than do private investors. It is difficult to determine which industries will be profitable in the future. If one industry is much riskier than another, private investors will demand a risk premium in the risky industry—such as copper in Chile or cocoa in Ghana. A case can be made for deliberate diversification only if governments can make better decisions than investors about future comparative advantage.

Raul Prebisch, a well-known Latin American economist, once argued that if such countries impose tariffs to protect their domestic industry, this protection would permit them to diversify their industrial base. A greater range of goods produced would reduce the risk imposed on the economy by price changes. When Prebisch noticed that protectionism lowered growth rates in Latin America, he changed his recommendation.

## THE TARIFFS-FOR-REVENUE ARGUMENT

Tariffs provide protection and raise government revenue. The two goals are partly in conflict. A perfect protectionist tariff would eliminate trade entirely and thus eliminate tariff revenue!

A nonprohibitive tariff does raise government revenue. Tariffs are not an important source of revenue in the United States (slightly more than 1 percent of the federal government's revenue); however, in some countries, tariff revenue is significant. Indeed, the United States in the nineteenth century relied heavily on tariff revenues.

A revenue tariff has special justification if it is difficult for a country to raise revenues in other ways. In a poor country where tax avoidance and nonmarket transactions restrict the amount of revenue yielded by income taxes, the government may be forced to collect its revenues by imposing taxes on traded goods. Customs officers located in airports and ports may be able to collect tax revenue to pay for roads, education, and other public goods. A tariff probably has greater justification under these circumstances than in any other case.

# U.S. TRADE POLICIES

The tariff history of the United States is depicted in Figure 5, which shows that tariffs have fluctuated with the ebb and flow of protectionism in the U.S. Congress. In modern times, tariffs hit their peak with the infamous Smoot-Hawley tariff of 1930. Economists were so appalled by the prospect of this tariff bill that in a rare show of agreement, 1028 of them signed a petition asking President Hoover to veto the bill. Because politics tends to override economics in tariff legislation, the bill was signed.

## THE TRADE-AGREEMENTS PROGRAM AND THE WTO

The Smoot-Hawley tariff, like most of the preceding 18 tariff acts stretching back to 1779, was the result of political *logrolling* in the U.S. Congress. Logrolling occurs when some politicians trade their own

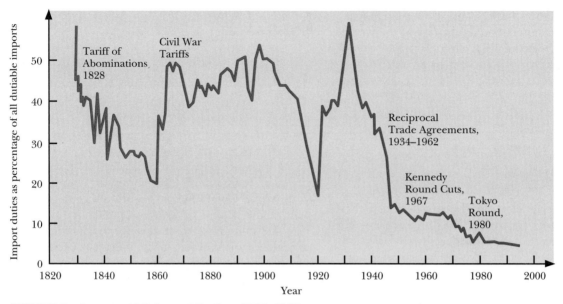

**FIGURE 5   Average U.S. Import Duties, 1820–1996**

As attitudes toward free trade and protectionism have fluctuated in the United States, average tariff rates have also fluctuated but have shown a distinct downward trend.
*Sources: Historical Statistics of the United States; Statistical Abstract of the United States.*

votes on issues of minor concern to their constituents in return for other politicians' votes on issues of greater concern to their constituents. Tariffs, historically, present the best example of sacrificing general interests for special interests.

Having established the highest tariff rates in U.S. history, the Smoot-Hawley Act triggered angry reactions overseas, as predicted by economists. As one nation after another erected trade barriers, the volume of world trade declined more than it would have in response to the Great Depression alone. The export markets of the United States shrank at the time of a very deep domestic depression.

In order to secure a large market for U.S. exports, Congress amended the Tariff Act of 1930 with the Reciprocal Trade Agreements Act of 1934. The president was authorized to negotiate reciprocal agreements that promised to lower U.S. trade barriers or tariffs in return for similar concessions abroad. The fact that Congress did not have to approve the tariff cuts marked a significant change in the power of special interests to influence U.S. tariff policy.

The trade agreements program has been broadened under successive extensions and modifications. The Trade Expansion Act of 1962 gave the president the power to reduce tariffs by up to 50 percent and to remove duties of less than 5 percent. Under the au-

thority of this act, the United States engaged in multilateral negotiations, known as the Kennedy Round, which resulted in an average reduction of 35 percent on industrial tariff rates. The Trade Reform Act of 1974 allowed the president to reduce tariffs by up to 60 percent and to eliminate duties of less than 5 percent. This act resulted in the Tokyo Round (1980) of multilateral reductions, in which the United States agreed to cut tariffs on industrial goods by 31 percent, the European Community agreed to cut tariffs by 27 percent, and Japan agreed to cut tariffs by 28 percent. The Trade and Tariff Act of 1984 authorized the president to enter into a new round of multilateral reductions in trade barriers, called the Uruguay Round.

Clearly, the trade agreements program has been an enormous success. In 1932, the average tariff rate was about 59 percent; today, the average tariff rate is about 5 percent. The trade agreement obligations of the United States and other countries are carried out under the General Agreement on Tariffs and Trade (GATT), established in 1948. The World Trade Organization (WTO) replaced GATT in 1995. The WTO spells out rules on the conduct of trade and procedures to settle trade disputes. It is also the forum in which international tariff negotiations now take place.

The new WTO marks the end of the Uruguay Round (1986–1993) of international negotiations. It provides the following:

*Tariffs:* Lowers tariffs on industrial products by an average of 34 percent

*Agriculture:* For the first time, brings agriculture under international trade rules

*Textiles and clothing:* Eliminates, over a ten-year period, quotas on textiles and clothing

*Services:* Establishes nondiscrimination by country of origin

*Voluntary export restraints:* Forbids these restraints.

Three of the many important implications for the United States, as a member of the WTO, are: First, the removing of tariffs and impediments on agricultural goods and industrial products should increase the world's demand for U.S. exports, making our imports relatively cheaper. Second, the elimination of voluntary export restraints and quotas will reduce the costs of the trade barriers the United States has in place by substituting revenue-generating tariffs for barriers that generate no revenues. Third, as the country with the strong comparative advantage in high technology goods, the United States can only be helped by increased protection of intellectual property.

International agreements such as the WTO tend to place roadblocks in the way of protectionists. However, as Example 3 indicates, protectionists now must use other forums—such as the antidumping laws—to pursue their goals.

In this chapter, we have examined the nature and consequences of trade barriers. Imports are bought with money; exports are sold for money. In the next chapter, we shall consider how monetary relationships fit into the international exchange of goods and services.

## SUMMARY

1. The major trade barriers are tariffs, import quotas, voluntary export restraints, and other nontariff barriers. A tariff is a tax levied on imports. It raises both the price paid by the domestic consumer and the price received by the domestic producer of the import-competing product. Import quotas limit the amount of imports of specified products. They raise the prices paid by domestic consumers and the prices received by domestic producers of import-competing products. Quotas are normally regulated by import licenses. If import licenses are sold to importers, the government receives their scarcity value. If they are not sold, private importers benefit from their scarcity value. Voluntary export restraints direct governments to restrict their exports to another country.

2. The basic argument against protection is that its costs outweigh its benefits. The loss to consumers from a tariff is greater than the gain to the protected producers. Additional losses include the costs of lobbying for tariff or quota protection.

3. Politics explain why tariffs are passed. Although the costs of tariffs are large in total, these costs are small per person. Special-interest groups therefore lobby and spend funds to obtain tariff protection.

4. The major economic arguments for protection are that it is necessary to avoid unfair foreign competition (low foreign wages, dumping, foreign-export subsidies), to protect infant industries, to keep money in the country, and to save domestic jobs.

5. The nonprotectionist arguments for tariffs are the national defense argument, the foreigner-will-pay argument, the diversification argument, and the tariffs-for-revenue argument. The national defense argument is potentially valid but tends to be misused and be applied to industries of little importance to national defense. The foreigner-will-pay argument normally works only if the nation's trading partners fail to retaliate against protective tariffs.

6. United States trade policies have changed over the years. The Smoot-Hawley tariff of 1930 caused a further restriction of trade during the Great Depression by setting very high tariff rates. Since then, legislation has been passed that allows the U.S. president to negotiate tariff reductions. The U.S. antidumping laws appear to have become more protectionist in recent years. The World Trade Organization settles trade disputes between nations.

## KEY TERMS

tariff
import quota
voluntary export
    restraint

prohibitive tariff
nonprohibitive tariff
dumping
countervailing duty

## EXAMPLE 3
## DUMPING AND
## PROTECTIONISM

Antidumping laws make little sense because they ignore the consumer and simply protect certain producers from foreign competition.

While the United States has pursued free-trade agreements with Mexico and Canada and encouraged lower tariffs around the world, the laws against dumping have been strictly enforced and expanded by Congress and the Commerce Department. Other nations and the WTO have been pressing to eliminate or trim antidumping laws. No other government has imposed as many antidumping duties than the United States on low-priced imports.

Economists studying the practices of the Commerce Department have been alarmed at the arbitrary nature of their determining whether a foreign firm should be subject to antidumping duties. Some examples:

1. The Commerce Department regarded lower-grade raspberries sold in the United States to make juice the same as higher-grade raspberries sold in Canada to make jam.
2. Fresh flowers sold in Amsterdam were regarded as the foreign price while wilted flowers in New York City were regarded as equivalent, even though at the end of the day flower mongers must reduce flower prices in order to clear out their stock.
3. New forklift trucks sold in Japan were compared to three-year old forklift trucks in the United States.

In addition to these examples, the information demanded by the Commerce Department can be burdensome on foreign firms and does not meet the test of fairness. Submissions of information can involve several tons of paperwork just to comply with the requests. For example, a Swedish bearings manufacturer (SKF) had about one week to supply information on more than 100 million separate sales. The result was a 180 percent dumping duty on SKF bearings. For fear of being hit by antidumping duties, some foreigners decide not to try entering the American market.

Antidumping laws are difficult to apply in a world of global production of goods and services. The same company that initiates an antidumping investigation at one time may itself be subject to an antidumping duty a few years later.

More than half of all antidumping cases have been in the iron and steel industry and the chemical industry. The target countries were Japan, West Germany, Taiwan, Korea, Italy, Canada, and Brazil (in order of importance). The antidumping laws and countervailing duty laws now provide the favorite vehicles for protectionist demands.

*Source:* Robert W. McGee, "The Case to Repeal the Antidumping Laws," *Northwestern Journal of International Law and Business* (1993), pp. 491–562.

## QUESTIONS AND PROBLEMS

1. What are the differences between an import duty and an import quota? What are the similarities?
2. What is the difference between an import quota and a voluntary export restraint?
3. Economists agree that tariffs hurt the countries that impose them. Yet nearly all countries impose tariffs. Is something wrong with the economists' argument?
4. Assume that a country can export all the wheat it wants at the world price of $5 per bushel. Using an analysis parallel to the discussion of Figure 4 in the text, show the impact of imposing a $1-per-bushel export tariff on every bushel exported. Does the benefit to consumers and gov-

ernment exceed the cost to producers of wheat? (*Hint:* An export tariff means that if a foreigner purchases wheat, he or she must pay the domestic price plus the $1 export duty.)

5. What are the best arguments that can be made for tariffs? What are the worst arguments that can be made for tariffs?

6. Frederic Bastiat, a nineteenth-century French economist and journalist, called tariffs "negative railroads." In what respects are tariffs negative railroads? In what respects is the analogy faulty?

7. Evaluate the validity of the following statement: "If we ignore political considerations, importing from China may not benefit the United States because under communism, prices need not correspond to the true Chinese comparative advantage."

# CHAPTER 37

# THE INTERNATIONAL MONETARY SYSTEM

Americans like Japanese cars and trucks. We enjoy them and other Japanese goods so much that U.S. exports to Japan were some $60 billion less than U.S. imports from Japan in 1994. The trade deficit with Japan makes headlines, and politicians often can increase their popularity by urging us to "stand up tough" to the Japanese. On the back pages of the newspapers, however, are other stories that tell about all the things we sell to Japan that pay for the trade deficit. For example, in the late 1980s Japanese investors bought the famed Pebble Beach golf course in California. The investment went bad and Americans bought it back for a fraction of what the Japanese paid. We got a good deal: We got to drive Japanese Toyotas. Japan got a good deal: They held out the hope of making a profit on U.S. real estate. The fact that the real estate was unprofitable does not say it was a bad deal for Japan at the time (hindsight is always perfect!).

Perhaps nothing in economics is more misunderstood than the subject of international money flows. What we perceive to be "bad" is often quite good and vice-versa. The most important message of this chapter is this: A country's exports of *all* things must equal its imports of *all* things. If exports of goods fall short of imports of goods, it must be that the export of other things—such as services, assets, and IOUs—will exceed the imports of those other things. To worry about imbalances in our exports and imports of *some* things is like drinking half a glass of water and then lamenting the fact that it is now half empty.

In this chapter, we shall examine the monetary mechanism behind the international exchange of goods and services. What causes trade deficits? How does the foreign-exchange market work? What happens when a currency depreciates? Why are exchange rates between the currencies of different countries allowed to fluctuate? What are the advantages and disadvantages of the present international monetary system?

# INTERNATIONAL MONETARY MECHANISMS

Money is the medium of exchange for domestic transactions because it is accepted by all sellers in exchange for their goods and services. Each seller generally wants the national currency of his or her own country. Thus, Americans want U.S. dollars, the English want pounds sterling, the Japanese want yen, Germans want marks, and the French want francs.

## THE FOREIGN-EXCHANGE MARKET

When an international transaction takes place, buyers and sellers reside in different countries. An American farmer sells wheat to a British miller, or a British firm sells a bicycle to an American cyclist. To make the purchase, the buyer needs the currency of the seller's place of residence. The currency needed for international transactions is called foreign exchange.

> **Foreign exchange** is the national currency of another country that is needed to carry out international transactions.

Normally, foreign exchange consists of bank deposits denominated in the foreign currency, but it may sometimes consist of foreign paper money when foreign travel is involved.

The buyer of international goods and services obtains his or her currency requirements from the foreign-exchange market. This market is highly dispersed around the world. Exchange between different currencies takes place between large banks and brokers. For example, an American importer of a British bicycle priced in pounds sterling pays in sterling that is deposited in a British bank. The money is transferred by a check, draft, or cable that is purchased with dollars from the importer's American bank that holds a sterling deposit in a British bank. Where does the American bank get these sterling deposits? They come from British importers of American goods who want dollars and supply pounds.[1]

America's demand for foreign exchange comes from its demand for the things that residents of the United States want to buy abroad: America's supply of foreign exchange comes from the demand by foreign residents for the things that they want to buy in the United States.

The price of one currency in terms of another is the *foreign-exchange rate*. These rates change from day to day and from hour to hour. Foreign-exchange rates are needed to convert foreign prices into American prices. When the exchange rate is expressed in terms of dollars per unit of foreign currency, the rate can be multiplied by the foreign price to obtain the American price. For example, if a British bicycle costs 90 pounds (£), the American importer pays $144 when the pound is worth $1.60 (because $144 = $1.60 × 90). When the exchange rate is expressed in terms of foreign currency per dollar, the foreign price can be divided by the rate to obtain the American price. For example, a Japanese car costing 1,500,000 yen costs $15,000 when 100 yen equals $1.

## FLOATING EXCHANGE RATES

How the exchange rate is determined depends upon whether it is a fixed exchange rate or a floating exchange rate.

> A **fixed exchange rate** is set by government decree or intervention within a small range of variation.
>
> A **floating exchange rate** is freely determined by the interaction of supply and demand.

The real world is a blend of these two polar cases. The floating system is easier to understand and roughly corresponds to the present method adopted by the United States, Great Britain, Canada, Japan, and other nations. Many small countries maintain fixed exchange rates against the dollar, the English pound, the French franc, or some basket of currencies. Eight European countries (including France, Germany, and Italy) have formed a European Monetary System and maintain fixed exchange rates relative to each other, but not relative to the United States. However, the three most important currencies—the Japanese yen, the German mark, and the U.S. dollar—float relative to one another.

Americans demand foreign exchange to buy imported commodities; to use foreign transportation

---

[1]For a clear discussion of the foreign-exchange market, see Peter H. Lindert and Charles P. Kindleberger, *International Economics*, 7th ed. (Homewood, IL: Richard D. Irwin, 1982), pp. 243–262.

services and insurance; to travel abroad; to make payments to U.S. troops stationed abroad; to remit dividends, interest, and profits to the foreign owners of American stocks, bonds, and business firms; to grant foreign aid; and to make short-term and long-term investments in foreign assets.

America's supply of foreign exchange is generated by foreigners' demand for American dollars to buy American exports; to travel in America; to pay American owners of stock, bonds, and businesses; and to invest in American assets.

To simplify the explanation of the foreign exchange market, let's again imagine that the world consists of two countries: the United States and England. The U.S. demand for foreign exchange is thus a demand for British pound sterling. Let's also assume that exports and imports of goods and services are the only things traded internationally.

Figure 1 shows the demand curve for foreign exchange by Americans. The dollar price of pounds is measured on the vertical axis; the flow of pounds into the foreign-exchange market during the relevant period of time is measured on the horizontal axis. The demand curve is downward sloping because as the price of pounds in dollars rises, if all other things are equal, the cost of British goods to U.S. importers rises as well. For example, if a British bicycle costs 90 pounds and the British pound rises from $1.60 to $2.00, the bike's price rises from $144 to $180 for the U.S. importer. This price increase will induce Americans to buy fewer bikes or switch to a U.S.-made brand. Thus, as the price of pounds rises, the quantity of foreign exchange demanded by Americans decreases.

The U.S. supply curve of foreign exchange depends on British importers of U.S. goods. When the English buy U.S. wheat, they supply pounds to the foreign-exchange market (because pounds must be exchanged to buy U.S. goods). The supply curve is upward sloping because when the dollar price of pounds rises—or when the dollar falls in value—U.S. goods are cheaper to foreigners. As a result, they will buy more U.S. goods, thereby tending to increase the quantity of pounds supplied to Americans in the foreign-exchange market.[2] For example, if a bushel

---

[2]This statement assumes that the demand for U.S. exports is elastic to the prices foreigners face. This is likely true since the U.S. faces competition from other countries for its exports.

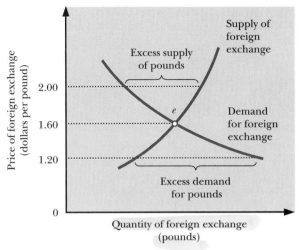

**FIGURE 1   The Foreign-Exchange Market**

The dollar price of a British pound is measured on the vertical axis; the flow of pounds on the foreign-exchange market per unit of time is measured on the horizontal axis. The equilibrium exchange rate is $1.60 = £1. If the exchange rate is $2.00 = £1, the excess supply of pounds on the market will drive down the price. At a price of $1.20 per pound, there will be an excess demand for pounds on the market and the price will be bid up.

of U.S. wheat costs $3.60, a fall in the value of the dollar from £1 = $1.20 to £1 = $1.60 will lower the cost of a bushel of wheat to foreigners from £3 to £2.25. The English will then shift their demand for wheat from English to U.S. wheat and increase wheat consumption, stimulating U.S. exports.

When the price of pounds is $2, Figure 1 shows that there is an excess supply of pounds on the foreign-exchange market. At the $2 exchange rate, desired U.S. exports exceed U.S. imports. With a floating exchange rate, the dollar price of a pound cannot be high enough to cause an excess supply. An excess supply of pounds bids the price of pounds down, as in any competitive market. Similarly, at a price per pound of $1.20, there will be an excess demand for pounds, and the price of pounds will be bid up. The equilibrium price of $1.60 per pound in Figure 1 not only equates the supply and demand for foreign exchange but also maintains an equilibrium between U.S. exports and imports. Equilibrium between imports and exports is achieved because they are the mirror image of the demand and supply for foreign exchange.

Exports and imports will be equal only if there are no factors other than exports or imports

*Impacts Price levels Exports*

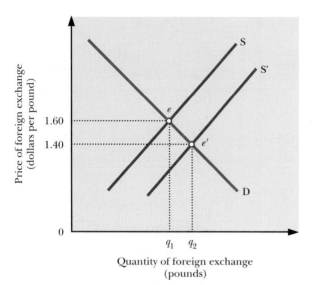

**FIGURE 2   The Effect of an Increase in Foreign Investment in America**

If foreigners decide to invest more in America, the supply curve for foreign-exchange will shift from S to S'. The equilibrium price of pounds will fall to $1.40 and will allow a surplus of imports over exports.

(tourism, paying dividends, foreign investments) entering the foreign-exchange market. Let's suppose, in addition to exporting and importing, some foreigners wish to invest in U.S. securities. The demand curve (D) in Figure 2 reflects America's foreign-exchange requirements for imports of goods. The desire to make new investments in America shifts the supply curve of foreign exchange outward to S'. The dollar price of pounds falls—the dollar rises in value—so that U.S. goods will be more expensive to the British. This brings about the required excess of imports over exports needed to accommodate the inflow of foreign capital to the United States.[3]

A currency is said to *depreciate* if it falls in value on the foreign-exchange market (if it buys less foreign exchange) and to *appreciate* if it rises in value on the foreign-exchange market (if it buys more foreign exchange). In our example, the appreciation of the

---

[3]An alternative approach to explaining the foreign-exchange market is the *monetary approach to the balance of payments*. This approach focuses on the total demand and supply for each national money. The exchange rates must induce people to hold the various national stocks of money. An excellent introduction can be found in Lindert and Kindleberger, *International Economics*, pp. 319–335.

dollar is the same as the depreciation of the pound because the dollar/pound exchange rate reflects the relative values of the two currencies: When one goes up, the other must go down.

## PURCHASING-POWER PARITY

Inflation rates in different countries play an important role in determining floating exchange rates. Countries that have enormous rates of inflation can still trade with the rest of the world because the exchange rate reflects the relative purchasing power of the two currencies in the respective countries.

This theory, popularized by Sweden's Gustav Cassel around 1917, works well when the inflation rates between two countries are quite different. When differentials are small, exchange-rate movements are dominated by other developments, such as fluctuations in the business cycle, capital movements, and changes in comparative advantage.

Suppose England and the United States were in equilibrium with an exchange rate of $1.20 = £1. If England doubles its supply of money while America maintains a constant money supply, there will be a tendency for the price of all English goods to double. If the price of the pound falls to a mere $0.60 (if the pound price falls to one-half its previous exchange rate), English prices appear exactly the same to Americans. The British bike that used to cost £60 rises to £120, but since the pound falls from $1.20 to $0.60, the bike still costs Americans $72. The exchange rate has maintained its purchasing-power parity (PPP). A dollar still buys the same goods in England as before the inflation.

> **Purchasing-power parity (PPP)** is the exchange rate between the currencies of two countries that is necessary in order for those countries to have the same prices of traded goods.

Figure 3 traces the Japanese yen value of the U.S. dollar from 1980 to 1995. Beginning in 1985, the dollar began to depreciate. The dollar fell from 55 percent from 226 yen to about 100 yen over this 15-year period. Part of the reason for this depreciation was that U.S. inflation was higher than Japan's—a 4 percent annual rate versus a 1.7 percent annual rate over this period. Over 15 years, American prices rose about 40 percent more than Japanese prices. Accordingly, to maintain some semblance of purchasing-power parity, the dollar depreciated.

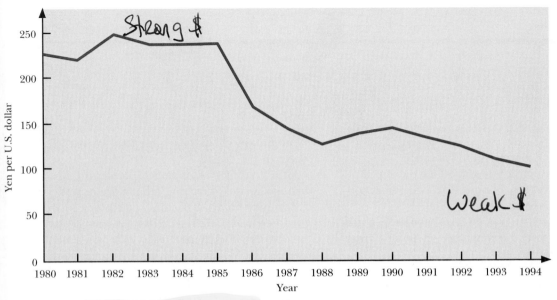

**FIGURE 3    The Value of the U.S. Dollar, 1980–1995**

*Source:* Federal Reserve Bank of Cleveland.

## FIXED EXCHANGE RATES AND THE GOLD STANDARD

The gold standard is the prototype of the fixed exchange-rate system. The classical gold standard was in its heyday before World War I, from about the 1870s to 1914. The United Kingdom used the gold standard as long ago as the 1820s and used both gold and silver during the eighteenth century—the century in which David Hume and Adam Smith lived.

A fixed exchange-rate system does not have to use gold, silver, or any commodity, but *each country must adopt monetary rules that correspond to those of the classical gold standard.* Today, numerous countries use currency boards, which are simply fixed exchange-rate systems based on the currencies of strong trading partners instead of gold. For example, Argentina and Hong Kong fix their currencies in terms of the dollar. (See Example 1.)

The blueprint for an international gold standard, brilliantly outlined by David Hume in 1752, showed how a fixed exchange-rate system can work to maintain equilibrium in the market for foreign exchange of any country.

The gold standard or modern currency boards can be explained with our hypothetical two-country world. If the United States defined the dollar as equal to 1/20 of an ounce of gold, and England defined the pound as equal to 1/4 of an ounce of gold, an English pound would contain 5 times as much

gold as a U.S. dollar. England would convert gold into pounds (and vice versa) at the established rate of £1 = 1/4 of an ounce of gold; the United States would convert gold into dollars at the rate of $1 = 1/20 of an ounce of gold. Under these circumstances, the exchange rate would be $5 = £1. No rational person would pay more than $5 for an English pound, because $5 would buy 1/4 of an ounce of gold from the U.S. Treasury and that amount of gold would buy a one pound note from the British Treasury.[4]

The next key ingredient of the gold standard is that England and the United States let their money supplies depend on how much gold is in their national treasuries. If, in our hypothetical world, the United States had a surplus of exports over imports, gold would be shipped from England to the United States to pay for the surplus of exports over imports. This gold shipment would raise the money supply in the United States and reduce the money supply in England. As a result, inflation of costs and prices

---

[4]Because shipping gold back and forth between the United States and England is costly (in transportation and insurance), the dollar price of pounds might range between $5.02 and $4.98, if it costs 2 cents to ship 1/4 ounce of gold between the countries. These upper and lower limits of exchange rate are called the *gold points.*

## EXAMPLE 1
## THE FALL OF
## THE PESO

Miss Prism:   Cecily, you will read your Political Economy in my absence. The chapter on the fall of the rupee you may omit. It is somewhat too sensational.

Oscar Wilde,
*The Importance of Being Earnest*

From December 1994 to April 1995 the Mexican peso fell by one-half, from about $0.30 to $0.15. Why did it happen? What can be done about it?

It happened because the rate of inflation in Mexico has far exceeded that of the United States while, at the same time, it was maintaining a fixed price of the peso in terms of the dollar. This cannot happen indefinitely. Purchasing-power parity eventually catches up with a currency.

There are only two ways of dealing with the value of a country's currency. One way is to insist on an independent monetary policy while allowing the exchange rate to float freely against other currencies. In the case of Mexico, this would allow the peso's value to float with respect to the dollar.

If a floating peso is unacceptable, the Mexican authorities have one other option: to set up a currency board. Basically, a currency board is just a central bank that creates money only when foreign exchange reserves increase, and decreases the money supply when foreign exchange reserves decrease. In effect, a currency board replaces the gold standard with a dollar, pound, mark, or yen standard, depending on the exchange rate that is targeted. In this manner, the Mexican peso could be fixed relative to the dollar but the central bank could no longer follow a monetary policy substantially different than that of the United States.

Currency boards have been used for over 150 years, especially among colonies of the British empire. They worked. In the past decade, they have also been successfully used in Hong Kong, Argentina, and Estonia.

-------------------------------------------

*Source:* "How to End Mexico's Meltdown," *Wall Street Journal*, January 19, 1995.

would occur in the United States, and a deflation of costs and prices would occur in England. Thus, America's exports would become less competitive, and England's exports would become more competitive. As America's exports decreased and England's exports increased, America's surplus of exports over imports would disappear—as long as the rules of the gold-standard games were followed.

When Spain conquered the New World, it brought back enormous amounts of gold. As the quantity theory predicts, a major consequence of the inflow of gold into Spain was inflation of wages and production costs. This inflation made it more difficult for Spain to compete with other European countries in world markets. Thus, Spain developed an excess of imports over exports and shipped gold to pay for the difference. Eventually, this gold caused infla-

tion elsewhere, and Spain's exports and imports were brought into approximate balance.

The equilibrating mechanism of the international gold standard is the *relationship between the domestic money supplies and the supply of monetary gold or other reserve assets that are designated to back the currency*. It is not actually necessary for gold or silver to be involved. In the case of Argentina's or Hong Kong's dollar standard, they must allow their money supplies to fall or rise as their dollar reserves fall or rise. If the country with a payments deficit (that is, its reserve assets are falling) allows its money supply to fall while the country with a payments surplus (that is, its reserve assets are rising) allows its money supply to rise, automatic adjustment mechanisms will tend to restore equilibrium.

In the country with a payments surplus, the expansion of the money supply will (1) lower exports because of higher prices and costs, (2) raise imports because prices and costs are now cheaper abroad, and (3) raise imports because real GDP may be increased because of the expansion in the money supply. In the deficit country, the contraction of the money supply will (1) raise exports because prices and costs are lower, (2) lower imports because prices and costs are now higher abroad, and (3) lower imports because real GDP may be lower because of the contraction of the money supply.

The central objection to the equilibrating mechanism of a fixed exchange-rate system is that international payments surpluses and deficits may produce unwanted inflationary or deflationary pressures. During the Great Depression, with its enormous unemployment, countries could no longer afford to allow a deficit to produce further deflation and unemployment. Hence, country after country left the gold standard during the 1930s.

Gold is not necessary to establish a fixed exchange-rate system that works like the gold standard. Fixed exchange rates can be established by official decree reinforced by central-bank intervention in the foreign-exchange market. For example, in Figure 4, we assume that the United States maintains its currency at a $2 exchange rate against the English pound, but the equilibrium exchange rate is $1.75. Thus, at the official rate, there is an excess supply of foreign exchange, because the pound is overvalued (or the dollar is undervalued). To maintain the $2 price of pounds, America's central bank must purchase the excess supply of pounds coming onto the foreign-exchange market. While the United States is experiencing this excess supply of pounds, the U.S. central bank is adding to its inventory of pounds. It can use this inventory later as international reserves to defend the value of the dollar when a deficit appears—when the supply and demand curves intersect above the $2 official price.

The surplus of exports over imports in this hypothetical example will not persist if the United States and England follow the rules of the gold-standard game. If the United States lets its money supply rise and England allows its money supply to fall, mechanisms will be set in motion that will shift the demand curve to the right and the supply curve to the left. When the United States suffers inflation relative to England, the United States exports less (decreasing supply) and imports more (increasing demand). These changes will cause the demand and

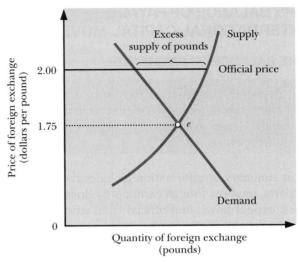

FIGURE 4   American Balance of Payments

If the exchange rate is $1.75 = £1, America's balance of payments will be in equilibrium. If the dollar price of pounds is fixed at $2.00 = £1, however, the dollar will be undervalued (the pound will be overvalued), and America's balance of payments will be in surplus by the excess of supply of pounds on the foreign-exchange market. These pounds will have to be purchased by the central banks of either the United States or England.

supply curves for foreign exchange in Figure 4 to shift until they again intersect at the official $2 price.

The term *devaluation* refers to official changes in the exchange rate in a fixed exchange-rate system. Under the old gold standard, a devaluation of the dollar occurred when the price of gold rose. Today, a country with a fixed exchange rate devalues its currency simply by lowering the official price of its currency. The country announces that it will no longer defend the old price and sets a new price to maintain by official intervention.

In Figure 4, the United States has a surplus and England has a deficit at the original price of $2 per pound. This price can be maintained if the U.S. central bank buys pounds or if the English central bank sells dollars (or if both actions take place). To avoid this inflation in the United States and deflation in England, the British might, with U.S. agreement, decide simply to devalue their currency! In Figure 4, lowering the price of pounds to $1.75 will (temporarily, at least) solve England's deficit and America's surplus. When the official value of a currency is raised, a *revaluation* is said to occur. Thus, in this case, England *devalues* its currency, and America *revalues* its currency.

## EXAMPLE 2
## TRADE DEFICITS AND
## UNEMPLOYMENT

In 1994, the United States had a merchandise trade deficit of about $163 billion. Does this deficit mean that the United States was losing jobs to workers in other countries? To the individual factory worker whose plant was closed down because of competition from imports, it must seem that the trade deficit does cause unemployment. However, what is true of the individual is not necessarily true for the economy!

The trade deficit should have nothing to do with long-run employment opportunities. In the long run, as we discussed in the chapter on aggregate supply and aggregate demand, the economy tends toward the natural rate of unemployment. Long-run employment growth is the result of a great many factors—growth in the labor force, trends in the labor-force participation rate, and structural determinants of the natural

rise of unemployment. The foreign-trade deficit, however, is not one of these factors.

The trade deficit of any country must be matched by borrowing from other countries. In fact, one reason for the U.S. trade deficit is that foreigners have invested heavily in the United States. The influx of foreign capital has financed the trade deficit. Indeed, the belief that foreign capital provides domestic jobs has muted protectionist sentiment in Congress. It is difficult for a member of Congress to take a strong position on imposing trade barriers when there are foreign-owned manufacturing and assembly plants in his or her state.

------------------------------------------------

*Source:* "Influx of Foreign Capital Mutes Debate on Trade," *New York Times,* February 8, 1987.

debit item. This statistical discrepancy arose from the fact that when all the observable credits and debits were recorded, the credits outweighed the debit items by this amount. Thus, unrecorded debits—such as spending by American tourists in France, immigrant gifts to relatives abroad, and illegal purchases of drugs—must have occurred.

As we can see in item 7, the total of all of the above credits and deficits must be zero: The balance of payments must balance.

**Official Reserve Assets.** Government agencies engage in buying and selling assets and foreign exchange. When official agencies like the central bank or the Treasury take such an action, there is a presumption that the agency is demanding or supplying foreign exchange for the purpose of stabilizing the exchange rate. The $5 billion decrease in U.S. official assets indicates that the United States sold foreign exchange, such as Japanese yen, in the hope of supporting the value of the dollar. The $39 billion increase in foreign official assets in the United States

(item 9) indicates that foreigners were buying dollar assets, thus increasing the value of the U.S. dollar.

## INTERNATIONAL CAPITAL MOVEMENTS

International capital movements considerably complicate what is happening to a country's balance of payments. Without such capital movements, exports of goods and services would equal imports of goods and services, and there would be less public confusion about the balance of payments.

Capital movements enable capital-importing nations to raise their physical capital stocks—dams, buildings, and roads—above what such stocks would be in the absence of international capital flows. When a country exports capital, it is furnishing residents of another country with funds for financing investments in plants and equipment. Thus, capital exports divert one country's saving into investments in another country. Saving still equals investments in the world as a whole, but when international trade is involved, this equality need not hold for any individual country.

We know that GDP = consumption (C) + government spending (G) + investment (I) + [exports (X) − imports (M)]. Because GDP equals income, GDP = consumption (C) + saving (S) + taxes (T). If government spending and taxes are assumed to be zero (for simplicity),

$$C + S = C + I + (X - M)$$

or

$$S = I + (X - M)$$

or

$$S - I = X - M$$

The equation shows that the excess of saving over investment in a country is reflected in the excess of exports over imports. The excess of saving over investment is the net export of capital to other countries. Thus, the export of capital is transferred into physical goods through the current account surplus. Similarly, an excess of investment over saving will match the excess of imports over exports. This excess investment corresponds to the import of capital that describes the U.S. position in the 1980s and early 1990s.

Capital movements take place for two reasons: Investors wish to take advantage of earning a higher interest rate on their capital, or investors wish to gain some measure of security. Capital seeks higher returns and lower risks.

The capital account of any country's balance of payments contains both capital inflows and outflows because investors are seeking to diversify their portfolios of investment and securities. A fundamental principle of sound investment strategy is not to put all our eggs in one basket. By holding a portfolio of international securities—for example, investments in German companies, Japanese companies, and American companies—an investor can reduce the risk of achieving a given expected rate of return.

Net capital movement is governed by the desire for higher interest rates. For example, in a simple world with no risks, investors would place their capital in the country that paid the highest interest rate (the highest rate of return on investments). This process of capital exportation would raise interest rates in low-interest-rate regions and lower interest rates in high-interest-rate regions. This allocation of capital gives rise to greater production everywhere in the world and thus a more efficient utilization of the world's scarce stock of capital.

**Stages of the Balance of Payments.** When a country first begins to export capital, its earnings on previous foreign investments are small or zero. To finance this export of capital, it is essential to generate a current account surplus of exports over imports. The current account surplus of such an immature creditor country enables the world to use the scarce capital stock efficiently. As time goes on, the country begins to collect on its investments. As it becomes a mature creditor country, it is able to import more than it exports. The United States was a mature creditor country until 1984, and it has had a merchandise trade deficit year in and year out.

When a country first begins to import capital, its payments on past indebtedness are small or zero. Thus, an immature debtor country will be able to finance an excess of imports over exports (a trade deficit). As the debtor country matures, its interest obligations will grow relative to its net borrowing until it must generate an export surplus to pay for its borrowings. As we discussed earlier, the United States recently became an immature debtor country. It has a trade deficit for two powerful reasons. First, it borrows more from foreigners than it lends to them; second, its income from foreign investments is about the same as its interest obligations to foreigners.

Why has the United States become a net capital importer? Several factors have played a role. First, fueled by a surge in productivity, and, perhaps, a large government deficit, high interest rates in the United States relative to the rest of the world led to inflows of capital. Second, many foreign investors believe that the United States is a safe haven for their investments. Third, it has become easier for foreign residents to invest in the United States because of changes in the laws abroad. Whether or not the United States remains a capital importer depends on the fundamental factors determining U.S. real interest rates—productivity and thrift. Higher productivity and lower thriftiness increase real interest rates. (See Example 3.)

**Foreign Investment and Nationalism.** When capital is exported from the United States, labor unions and workers themselves complain that the United States is giving employment to foreigners and depressing home wages. When capital is imported, capitalists complain that their rate of return is depressed. When a foreign country takes over a particular business firm, many people will regard this

## EXAMPLE 3
## WILL THE MERCHANDISE TRADE DEFICIT LAST?

The merchandise balance of trade is the difference between merchandise exports and imports. There is a "surplus" if exports exceed imports and a "deficit" if imports exceed exports. Every single year from 1900 to 1970, the United States had a surplus in its balance of trade. Since 1971 (except for 1973), the United States had a deficit in its balance of merchandise trade with the rest of the world.

This change from a surplus to a deficit on the merchandise accounts is neither surprising nor undesirable. That a country begins to have a surplus on its merchandise accounts indicates that the country must be investing in foreign countries. These investments result in net investment income from foreign countries. Since 1945, for example, the United States has enjoyed net investment income every year except 1994 and 1995. As the trade surplus slowly disappeared from 1946 to 1971, net investment income skyrocketed from $560 million to $7.3 billion,

which was three times as large as the trade deficit of $2.3 billion in 1971.

The current account deficit is the sum of the balance of trade in merchandise, services, and net investment income. The current account has been in deficit every year since 1982. Thus, the United States is borrowing from other countries or, expressed more positively, other countries are investing in U.S. stocks, bonds, and property. In 1995 we were paying out more in interest, dividends, and profit than we were receiving: Our net investment income was −$20 billion (approximately) on an annual basis. This deficit growth is an indication of the future shape of the American balance of payments. As our investment income deficit grows relative to the inflow of new capital coming into the United States, it is inevitable that the merchandise trade deficit will become the merchandise trade surplus of a mature debtor nation.

takeover as bad for the country. In recent years, for example, the Japanese have bought up some American banks, trading companies, hotels, and office buildings. Is it somehow to the disadvantage of the United States to allow foreigners to take over U.S. businesses?

When foreign investment takes the form of actual control of a domestic firm, another issue is at stake: trade in entrepreneurial services.[5] As with trade in all goods and services, if the Japanese can operate American business more efficiently than the

former management, the American people will benefit—just as they benefit from buying cheaper foreign imports of personal computers or cars.

## THE EVOLUTION OF THE INTERNATIONAL MONETARY SYSTEM

In 1870, the West was not on an international gold standard; by 1900, the world had moved to an international gold standard. The gold standard was dead in 1945 and was replaced by a system of fixed but adjustable exchange rates. The postwar system was dead by 1973, and today the world is on a system of floating exchange rates with active exchange-rate stabilization policies by the major central banks. To understand the current system, it is useful to take a backward look at this evolution.

---

[5]Indeed, there is no reason why the taking over of a domestic firm by a foreign firm should be associated with foreign investment, because a Japanese firm can take over an American firm by borrowing in the American capital market.

## THE BRETTON WOODS SYSTEM

The International Monetary Fund (IMF) was established in 1947 after an international 1944 conference in Bretton Woods, New Hampshire. The international monetary arrangements set up at this conference are now called either the "old IMF" system or the "Bretton Woods" system. It was set up to avoid the unstable exchange rates of the 1930s.[6] The IMF consisted of a pool of gold, dollars, and all other major currencies that could be used to lend assistance to any other member country having balance-of-payment difficulties.

The Bretton Woods system was set up on the theory that balance-of-payments *deficits* and *surpluses*—reductions or increases in international reserves—were usually temporary in a fixed exchange-rate system. Thus, the discipline of the Hume reserve-flow mechanism—deflation for deficit countries and inflation for surplus countries—could in many cases be avoided. The international reserves of each country could be used to maintain the exchange rate of its currency within 1 percent of the established fixed rate. Should a deficit develop, the country could rely on its international reserves to help it weather the storm until a surplus of the balance of payments developed. In the meantime, the country would not have to go through the adjustment of a domestic deflation.

If the deficit did not reverse itself, the country was considered to be facing a "fundamental disequilibrium" and was then allowed to adjust its exchange rate. A country in fundamental deficit could devalue its currency; a country in fundamental surplus could revalue its currency.

## THE FALL OF BRETTON WOODS

The problem with the Bretton Woods mechanism is that it is fundamentally illogical. It does not meet the requirements of either a fixed exchange rate or a floating rate system. Trying to compromise between them does not work.

If a country had a fundamental deficit and needed to devalue its currency, speculators more than anyone else would recognize this weakness. The chances that the country would revalue or raise the

value of its currency would be virtually zero. The speculators would be in a no-loss situation if they sold weak currencies with a vengeance and bought strong currencies. For example, the British pound was often weak and the German deutschmark (DM) was often strong. Accordingly, speculators would sell pounds and buy DMs. Their actions exacerbated the deficit in the United Kingdom and the surplus in Germany.

During the 1960s the United States was defending the value of its currency by selling gold to foreigners at the rate of $35 an ounce. As the U.S. stock of gold dwindled, it did not take speculators long to figure out that a devaluation might be imminent. In 1971, speculation against the U.S. dollar began. That August, President Nixon changed the fundamental character of the IMF system by severing the dollar's link with gold. No longer could countries convert dollars into gold at $35 an ounce; the dollar was essentially free to fluctuate. After a few attempts to fix up the system, by March 1973, all major currencies of the world were on a managed floating system, and the Bretton Woods system was shattered.

# THE CURRENT INTERNATIONAL MONETARY SYSTEM

### THE JAMAICA AGREEMENT

At a conference in Kingston, Jamaica, in early 1976, the original IMF charter was amended to legalize the widespread managed floating that replaced the Bretton Woods par-value system.

According to the new agreements, each country could adopt whatever exchange-rate system it preferred (fixed or floating). Countries were asked to "avoid manipulating exchange rates . . . in order to prevent effective balance-of-payments adjustment or to gain an unfair competitive advantage over other members." The IMF was directed to "oversee the compliance of each member with its obligations" in order to "exercise firm surveillance of the exchange rate policies of its members." Monetary authorities of a country could buy and sell foreign exchange in order to "prevent or moderate sharp and disruptive fluctuations from day to day and from week to week," but it was considered unacceptable to suppress or reverse a long-run exchange-rate movement.

---

[6]See Leland B. Yeager, *International Monetary Relations: Theory, History, and Policy*, 2nd ed. (New York: Harper & Row, 1976), chap. 18.

The key fact about the current international monetary system is, however, that the three major currencies—the dollar, the German mark, and the Japanese yen—all float relative to one another. In principle, the current exchange-rate system is a managed float because the various central banks can intervene, and have done so, to affect day-to-day exchange rates. But official U.S. intervention in the foreign exchange markets has been sporadic and infrequent. In mid-1995, the United States and Japan joined in an effort to increase the value of the dollar. We saw in Figure 3 the tremendous drop in the value of the dollar in terms of the yen. The Japanese believed that the increase in the value of the yen would hurt their exports, and with the economy in the doldrums an increase in exports was considered beneficial. Americans believed that a reduction in the value of the dollar would fan the fires of inflation. Thus, it was a match made in heaven: Both countries sold Japanese yen and bought dollars. The effects, however, proved elusive. The transactions were carried out in August while many foreign exchange traders were on vacation. In September 1995, when they returned, the dollar fell. Official attempts to maintain currency values usually fail because private foreign-exchange trading is on the order of $1 trillion a *day!*

## ADVANTAGES OF THE FLOATING RATE SYSTEM

The advantages of a floating rate system are (1) monetary autonomy and (2) ease of balance-of-payments adjustments.

When exchange rates are flexible, one country's monetary policy does not have to be dictated by the monetary policies of other countries. If everybody else wants to inflate, a country (for example, Switzerland) can maintain stable prices simply by following a long-run monetary policy of tight money (low monetary growth) and allowing its exchange rate to appreciate relative to the countries that choose to follow inflationary policies. Likewise, flexible exchange rates enable a country to follow highly inflationary policies by simply allowing its rate of exchange to depreciate.

Under a fixed exchange-rate regime, a deficit can be solved by internal deflation or unemployment. If this solution is not in the best interest of the country, a flexible exchange rate allows a country to depreciate its currency rather than undergo the discipline of Hume's reserve-flow mechanism. It is much easier to lower the value of a country's currency than to lower every internal commodity price and wage rate!

The most dramatic achievement of the current system occurred when the OPEC countries quadrupled the price of oil in 1973–1974. The resulting shock to the world economy was absorbed by floating exchange rates. The enormous deficits that developed in the oil-importing countries and the necessity of the oil-exporting countries to invest their oil revenues meant that the foreign-exchange markets had a lot of recycling oil revenues to process. The previous Bretton Woods system could not have accomplished this recycling. Indeed, the Bretton Woods system could not take much small pressures. While exchange rates fluctuated dramatically after the oil shock, the current system worked. It did not break down or cause crises like those that the world witnessed in the late 1960s and early 1970s.

## DISADVANTAGES OF THE FLOATING RATE SYSTEM

Some economists argue that floating exchange rates are inflationary. Under a fixed exchange rate, a country is constrained from following an inflationary policy because balance-of-payments deficits (that is, reserve assets are depleted) are produced. A floating exchange rate removes this constraint on domestic monetary policy. Hence, as a practical political matter, we should expect greater inflation with floating rates than with fixed rates. Some economists and politicians are now suggesting that the United States should return to the gold standard in order to prevent inflation.

Another criticism of the present system is that the only way to enjoy the full benefits of a monetary economy is that every country adopt the same currency. In other words, the current system is just a long detour away from the most efficient monetary arrangement. Presumably, in a world without nationalism and with free trade, the adoption of a truly international currency unit would come almost automatically. A single European currency is scheduled for the late 1990s. An international currency, however, requires the sacrifice of national monetary autonomy, and the European Union faces significant nationalistic obstacles.

## SUMMARY

1. Foreign exchange is the national currency of another country that is needed to carry out international transactions. America's demand for foreign exchange increases when U.S. residents demand more foreign goods and services. America's supply

of foreign exchange increases when residents of foreign countries demand more U.S. goods and services.

2. The demand curve for foreign exchange is downward sloping because as the dollar price of foreign currency rises, there is a corresponding rise in the cost of foreign goods to U.S. importers. The supply curve of foreign exchange tends to be upward sloping because as the dollar price of foreign currency rises, U.S. goods are cheaper to foreigners. Under a floating exchange-rate system, the exchange rate is allowed to float to the point where the demand for foreign exchange equals the supply.

3. When the exchange rate reflects the relative purchasing power of the currencies of two different countries, purchasing-power parity prevails between the two currencies. Under a fixed exchange-rate system, equilibrium in the demand for and supply of foreign exchange is brought about by Hume's gold-flow mechanism.

4. A country's balance of payments provides a summary record of its economic transactions with foreign residents over a period of one year. It is a two-sided (credit/debit) summary that must always be in accounting balance. If exports of goods fall short of imports of goods, the export of other things such as services, IOUs, and assets must make up the difference. International capital movements shift capital from where it has a low return to where it has a high return.

5. Today, the world operates on a system of floating exchange rates with active exchange-rate stabilization by the major central banks. The Bretton Woods system set up after World War II broke down because a currency-adjustment system is fundamentally in conflict with free international capital movements. Speculation destroyed the old Bretton Woods system. The new international monetary system involves a mixture of floating and fixed exchange rates. Since 1973, the U.S. dollar has floated with respect to all the major currencies of the world.

## KEY TERMS

| | |
|---|---|
| foreign exchange | balance of payments |
| fixed exchange rate | merchandise trade |
| floating exchange rate | balance |
| purchasing-power parity (PPP) | current account balance |

## QUESTIONS AND PROBLEMS

1. Suppose the German deutschmark is worth $0.55 (in U.S. dollars) and $1 is worth 150 Japanese yen. How much would a Mercedes-Benz cost in U.S. dollars if the German price were 30,000 deutschmarks (DM)? How much would a Toyota cost in U.S. dollars if the Japanese price were 1,200,000 yen?

2. Table A shows part of an actual newspaper report on the foreign-exchange market. Did the British pound rise or fall from Thursday to Friday? Did the Japanese yen rise or fall from Thursday to Friday? What happened to the U.S. dollar in terms of the pound? What happened to the U.S. dollar in terms of the yen?

| Table A | | | | |
|---|---|---|---|---|
| | Foreign Currency in Dollars | | Dollars in Foreign Currency | |
| | Friday | Thursday | Friday | Thursday |
| British pound | 1.5575 | 1.5505 | 0.6421 | 0.6450 |
| Japanese yen | 0.01026 | 0.01027 | 97.47 | 97.34 |

3. If there were a floating exchange rate between Japan and the United States, which of the following events would cause the Japanese yen to appreciate? Which would cause the yen to depreciate? Explain your answers.

   a. The government of Japan orders its automobile companies to limit exports to the United States.

   b. The United States places a quota on Japanese automobiles.

   c. The United States increases its money supply relative to Japan's money supply.

   d. Interest rates in the United States rise relative to Japanese interest rates.

   e. More Japanese people decide to visit the United States.

   f. Japanese productivity growth rises relative to U.S. productivity growth.

4. Indicate whether each of the following transactions represents a debit (a supply of U.S. dollars) or a credit (a demand for U.S. dollars) in the U.S. balance of payments.

a. A U.S. commercial airline buys the European-made Airbus (an airplane competing with the Boeing 747).

b. A European airline buys a U.S. Boeing 747.

c. An American makes a trip around the world.

d. A French company pays dividends to an American owning its stock.

e. An American buys stock in a French company.

f. A U.S. company borrows from a European investor.

g. A Canadian oil company exports oil to Japan on a U.S. tanker.

h. A U.S. banker makes a loan to a European manufacturer.

5. Explain the mechanism under which U.S. restrictions on its imports will lead to fewer U.S. exports under a floating exchange-rate system.

6. What would happen if Mexico and the United States had a fixed exchange rate but for 20 years Mexico had higher inflation than the United States?

7. What are some arguments for floating exchange rates?

8. What are some arguments against floating exchange rates?

9. Why is it difficult for monetary authorities to influence exchange rates by purchasing or selling billions of dollars of foreign exchange in a floating system?

10. In 1995, the Japanese central bank purchased billions of U.S. dollars to help improve the value of the dollar. What effect would this have on the Japanese money supply? Would that be consistent with Japan's objective of bouncing back from a recession? Explain.

# CHAPTER 38

# THE ECONOMICS OF TRANSITION

The world in which we live today is so different from that of just a few years ago that we can hardly remember the way things were then. A Rip Van Winkle, waking up from a quarter-century sleep, would be hard pressed to recognize the world he had last seen in the 1970s. At the beginning of his sleep, Rip Van Winkle's world was more simple: About one-third of the world's population lived under Soviet-style or Chinese-style socialism dictated by the Communist Party leadership. Although these economies were definitely not prospering, they were muddling along without any imminent threat of demise. The countries of Eastern Europe were caught in the embrace of the Soviet Union. Although there had been some reform of their Soviet-type economies, change had been modest and unsuccessful.

In the 1970s, the Western world was recovering from energy shocks, recessions, and stagflation. How well we would deal with these issues remained unknown. The rest of the world, with the exception of Japan, appeared to be stuck at a low level of eco-nomic development. Latin America, South America, Africa, and Asia did not seem to be progressing toward long-term economic development.

Imagine Rip Van Winkle's shock upon waking. The Soviet empire had disintegrated; Germany is reunited; the Communist Party no longer exists as a centralized, controlling organization. China is experiencing phenomenal growth. The "developing markets" of Asia and Latin America are attracting large sums of capital. Even small investors are betting on emerging market funds for Latin America and Asia.

This world of just a few decades ago was a product of the world's greatest social experiment—the attempt to create a socialist command economy that operated fairly and efficiently for its citizens. Socialism, as had been preached by Karl Marx, would do away with injustice and exploitation and would create an economic system superior to that of capitalism.

We now know that the great socialist experiment was the greatest unintended consequence of economics. Rather than making economic life better and fairer, it made life worse and more unfair. Rather than creating a superior, more efficient economy, it created an inferior, inefficient economy.

In this chapter, we shall consider the end of the socialist experiment and the efforts by former supporters to reverse its damages through transition from socialism to capitalism.

## THE ADMINISTRATIVE COMMAND ECONOMY

The rise of socialism began in the Soviet Union after the Bolshevik Revolution of 1917 under the leadership first of Vladimir I. Lenin and then Joseph Stalin. It took the Soviet leadership about a decade to find the formula for organizing and operating an administrative command economy.

> The **administrative command economy** is an economic system directed by a communist party and a state planning apparatus that determine the use of resources through national economic plans. Capital and land are owned by the state, and managerial rewards are based upon fulfillment of plan targets.

As its name implies, the administrative command economy allocates resources essentially without the use of markets or prices. A national economic plan dictates what is to be produced, planners tell state enterprises how they are to produce these outputs and give them allotments of materials, and production is distributed to enterprises and consumers by a state distribution network.

Although it soon became apparent that this system of resource allocation had deep flaws, it spread from the Soviet Union to Eastern Europe, to Asia, and to Cuba after World War II. In the 1950s and 1960s, it appeared as if the communist economic ideology would win over many of the poor countries of Asia, Africa, and Latin America. The Cold War was at its peak, and U.S. fear of the Soviet system was intense.

### THE FLAWS

As we know from Chapter 1, Ludwig von Mises and Friedrich von Hayek, early critics of socialism, argued even in the 1920s that socialism could not work. Hayek and von Mises thought that the administrative command economy could not gather and process enough information, that managers would be without guidance if they did not know relative prices, and that no one could be motivated to do what is best for society. Succinctly, they thought that such an economy could not function without Adam Smith's invisible hand. (See Example 1.)

Indeed, the administrative command economies did suffer from the very flaws predicted by von Mises and Hayek. For an economy to operate on its production possibilities frontier, its participants must be properly motivated and informed. If they lack motivation or information, they will be unable to use their resources to best advantage.

**The Incentive of Property.** In a capitalist economy, the private owners of capital seek out the best profit opportunities for their capital and want to economize on their use of resources. If they need to hire professional managers, owners can devise a reward system that encourages efficient use of resources. In an administrative command economy, capital is owned by the state—by everyone and hence by no one. If no one owns the capital resources, there is no incentive for the enterprise manager to innovate or increase productivity.

**Managerial Rewards.** In administrative command economies, managers must be rewarded on the basis of how well they meet the enterprise plan. Because the plan is made up of a large number of tasks—how much to produce, what assortments, what costs, what new equipment, and so on—planners must focus on one or two measurable targets

## EXAMPLE 1
## THE AUSTRIAN CRITICS
## OF SOCIALISM

Ludwig von Mises and Frederick Hayek, a Nobel laureate, founded a school of economic thought now called the Austrian School. Both economists praised the efficiency with which market economies process and utilize information on relative prices. Hayek wrote that the principal problem of economics is "how to secure the best use of resources known to any member of society, for ends whose relative importance only these individuals know."

How is the economy to utilize knowledge about product prices, qualities, and location that is not available to any one person or institution in its entirety? These economists believed that the specialization in information about the price system enables each individual to participate effectively in the economy, acquiring knowledge only about those things that he or she needs to know. Hayek writes of the "marvel" of the price system:

The marvel is that in a case like that of a scarcity of one raw material, without an order being issued, without more than perhaps a handful of people knowing the

cause, tens of thousands of people whose identity could not be ascertained by months of investigation, are made to use the material or its products more sparingly; i.e., they move in the right direction.

Von Mises was an early critic of socialism. In his classic article "Economic Calculation in the Socialist Commonwealth," published in 1922, von Mises anticipated most of the modern-day problems of the socialist economies, arguing that socialist economies would lack market exchange and would hence lack the vital information provided by the price system. Without relative prices, socialist managers would lack the information to make rational economic decisions. Moreover, lacking property rights, socialist managers would not behave in an economically rational manner, but would overdemand and waste scarce resources.

*Source:* Frederick A. Hayek, "The Price System as a Mechanism for Using Knowledge," *American Economic Review* 35, no. 4 (September 1945): pp. 519–528.

that are more important to the planners themselves, such as the volume of output. Thus, enterprise managers are rewarded on the basis of how close they come to fulfilling the state's output targets.

Basing managerial rewards on output leads to two troublesome incentive problems. First, managers can more easily fulfill output targets by sacrificing quality or assortment. The shoe manufacturer will mass-produce only one type of shoe style because the enterprise has been told to produce 10,000 pairs of shoes per month. The construction firm will rely on gravity in place of mortar, thereby producing apartments that collapse during earthquakes. The drilling company, instructed to drill ten wells per month, will select easy drilling terrain even though it will yield no oil.

Second, enterprise managers will be tempted to conceal capacity from their superiors. The managers' lives are easy when their output targets can be fulfilled using 60 percent of the enterprise's capacity. Hence, a manager will try to persuade superiors that the enterprise can produce a maximum of only 10,000 pairs of shoes per month rather than the 15,000 pairs it can realistically produce. The manager knows that if the enterprise overfulfills the plan (and reveals its true capacity), although it may gain temporary bonuses it will be subject to more ambitious plan targets in the future.

**Information Problems.** The price system provides invaluable information on opportunity costs. In market economies, opportunity costs are the basis for resource allocation decisions. When the price system shows that a previously used material has become more expensive than new materials, the manufacturer will seek out substitutes. A shoe manufacturer will switch from one shoe fashion to another when the old brand can be sold only at a substantial discount.

The administrative command economy does not use the price system to make allocation decisions. If there is "too little" of one resource, its relative price does not rise. Rather, an administration official calls users of the resource to order them to use less.

Without markets to determine relative prices, no one knows what things are worth. If the manager does not know whether aluminum, composite plastics, or ceramics are "cheap," that manager cannot make a rational decision on what material to use. If the manager does not know what goods buyers want (as reflected in a high price), the manager does not know to produce those goods in high demand.

Moreover, planners do not have as much information about local production conditions as managers do. The enterprise managers may even gain by concealing information from their superiors or by providing them with false information. Therefore, the administrative command economy often operates on the basis of inadequate or even false information. The planned economy requires enormous amounts of information, but the information it gets is limited and flawed.

**Inherent Shortages.** Administrative command economies are plagued with shortages; people stand in line for goods; enterprise managers cannot find the materials they need. Although it may appear that such shortages are a result of incorrect ordering by planners, they may be inherent in these economies.

The Hungarian economist Janos Kornai has argued that the administrative command economy automatically generates shortages because enterprises lack the incentive to use resources economically. Enterprises are judged on their ability to produce output, not on their ability to make a profit. Planners, reluctant to let their enterprises fail even when they are losing money, do not hesitate to use subsidies to bail them out. This lack of budget discipline, which Kornai calls the "soft budget constraint," leaves enterprises unrestrained in their demands for resources. This drive to stockpile resources causes all goods to

be in short supply. Everyone is chasing resources, but few succeed in getting what they want.

## THE COLLAPSE

The end of the socialist experiment came with unexpected suddenness in the late 1980s. In 1985, the Soviet Communist Party appointed the reform-minded Mikhail Gorbachev as its general secretary. Gorbachev was deeply troubled by the Soviet Union's lagging economic performance and was determined to introduce what he called "radical" economic reform in contrast to the half-hearted reforms of his predecessors (see Figure 1). Gorbachev set into motion the process of *perestroika*, with ultimate consequences more far-reaching than he had intended.

*Perestroika* was a process of economic, political, and social reform begun in the Soviet Union in 1985. It encompassed reform of the administrative command economy, political democratization, and increased freedom of expression.

In effect, Gorbachev began dismantling the rigid political and economic dictatorship put in place by Lenin and Stalin. He did so with the hope that he could create an improved form of socialism, but the *unintended consequence* was the end of the socialist system.

At home, Gorbachev dismantled the strict system of administrative allocation of resources. The planners and ministers lost their power and authority. He unsuccessfully tried to mix markets and plan. Abroad, he showed that the Soviet army was no longer going to be used to prop up unpopular communist regimes in Eastern Europe. The Berlin Wall fell in November 1989 and Germany was reunited. In the other communist-bloc countries of Eastern Europe, communist regimes were toppled by mostly bloodless revolutions. Although China remained under the control of the Chinese Communist Party, it also embarked on a program of radical capitalist reform.

In August 1991, an abortive coup of hard-line opponents of reform was put down. Gorbachev resigned as head of the Communist Party, and the Soviet Union broke up into 15 newly independent nations, with Russia being the largest.

*Perestroika* was intended to reform and improve the socialist economic and political

(a) Growth of GDP

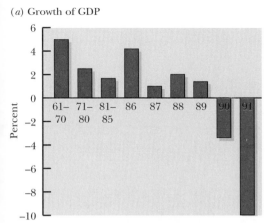

(b) Productivity Growth

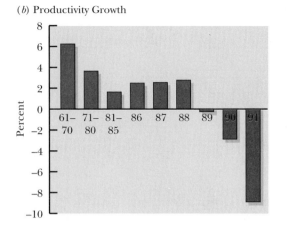

(c) Consumption Growth

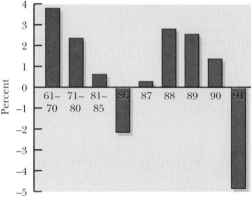

**FIGURE 1   Soviet Economic Performance**

These figures show the worsening performance of the Soviet economy from the 1960s through *perestroika*. Panel (a) shows the declining growth rate of GDP, which became negative in the 1990s. Panel (b) shows the declining growth of productivity, which became negative in 1989. Panel (c) shows the pattern of declining growth rates of per capita consumption.
*Source: Handbook of Economic Statistics,* section: Soviet Economic Performance.

system. It had the *unintended consequence* of ending the socialist experiment.

*Perestroika* ended the socialist experiment because it created a chaotic mix of capitalism and socialism. *Perestroika* destroyed the authority of the administrative command system without creating an alternative system of resource allocation. *Perestroika* resulted in the worst of all worlds—economies without any organized means of resource allocation. Figure 2 shows the resulting collapses of production and

acceleration of inflation that took place during the *perestroika* period. One by one the former administrative command economies concluded that the old system had to be abandoned.

## TRANSITION

When Gorbachev began *perestroika*, he hoped that he could solve the Soviet Union's and Eastern Europe's economic problems by reform, not by transition.

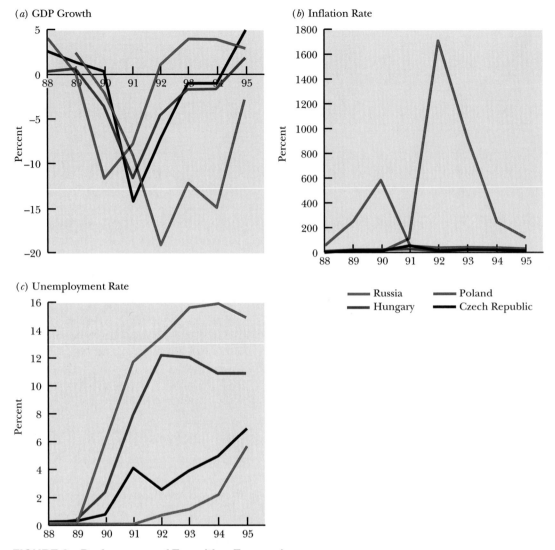

(a) GDP Growth

(b) Inflation Rate

(c) Unemployment Rate

Russia — Poland
Hungary — Czech Republic

**FIGURE 2    Performance of Transition Economies**

These figures show the pattern of economic performance of countries that are undergoing transition. Panel (a) shows that transition is accompanied by a period of declining real GDP, often of two to three years' duration before positive growth resumes. Panel (b) shows that the initial transition period is often, but not always, accompanied by very high rates of inflation, which then decline. Panel (c) shows that the transition economies begin the transition process with virtually no unemployment. Unemployment then rises during the transition.

*Sources: Economics of Transition,* vol. 2 (March 1994), Tables 3, 4, 5; "Projections for 1994 and 1995 from OECD," Developments in Selected Non-OECD Countries, *Economic Outlook,* pp. 115–117.

> **Reform** is an attempt to improve an existing economic system, such as the administrative command economy.
>
> **Transition** is the process of transforming one economic system into another, such as from the administrative command economy into a market economy.

*Perestroika* showed that the problems of the administrative command economy could not be solved by reform. Rather than working to improve the existing system, the leadership of the newly independent states realized that transition was necessary.

## THE PROBLEMS OF TRANSITION

The transition from socialism to capitalism presents the greatest economic challenge of the second half of the twentieth century. No one knows the formula for dismantling an administrative command economy. The process is not an easy one, for the following reasons:

1. The socialist administrative command economy is based on public (state) ownership of land and capital resources. In the administrative command economy, the slogan was, "Property belongs to everyone and hence to no one." A market economy cannot operate under this arrangement. There must be redistribution of property rights—an extremely difficult economic and political task. A good portion of publicly owned resources must be transferred to private hands through the process of privatization.

> **Privatization** is the conversion of publicly owned assets—such as land, buildings, companies—to private ownership.

Privatization cannot be accomplished overnight. How it is done determines how wealth will be distributed among the members of society. Privatization determines who will be rich and who will be poor. For this reason, we would expect societies in transition to take a long time to resolve the issue of privatization.

2. The transition from socialism to capitalism involves substantial economic and political costs. The administrative command economies operated on the basis of plans, not on the basis of market prices and profits. They lived isolated from a larger world economy, trying to be as self-sufficient as possible. Transition necessitates that enterprises must be able to earn profits and survive in a global market economy.

Immense economic and political problems must be solved. The administrative command economy created large enterprises and whole industries that operated inefficiently and produced products that no one wanted. These enterprises cannot survive in a market environment, yet a large proportion of the work force is employed in such industries. Enterprises that produce, for example, low-quality reinforced concrete or shoddy television sets cannot survive in a market economy; however, the bankruptcy of such enterprises would mean the loss of many jobs.

3. Market economies developed their economic laws, customs, and institutions over centuries. The administrative command economies operated for over 60 years without laws and institutions that are supportive of market allocation. To make the transition, new laws must be put in place and modern economic institutions, such as a modern banking system, must be established.

Adam Smith's invisible hand works because market economies are backed by a strong legal system, experience with business contracts, constitutions, and so on. The former administrative command economies must put all these institutions in place quickly, they must establish budgeting procedures, and they must learn how to control the money supply to prevent runaway inflation. None of these directives is easy to accomplish.

4. Transition must be politically feasible. Except in China, democracy replaced the totalitarian control of the Communist Party as the transition was beginning. In mature capitalist economies, elected politicians must worry about the economic consequences of their political actions. In the United States, for example, elected officials were barely willing to support the North American Free Trade Act (NAFTA) in 1994 for fear of political backlash from those who thought they would suffer economically. The political problems of transition dwarf those of NAFTA. A successful transition requires massive redistribution of property during the course of privatization. Not everyone can be satisfied, and there will be massive dissatisfaction from those who believe they have been cheated by the process. Unprofitable enterprises, accustomed to being propped up by state subsidies, must be shut down or downsized. State budgets must be balanced to prevent runaway inflation, so public employee salaries must be cut and pensions must be reduced.

Mature democratic societies would find it difficult to weather such shocks to the political system. Transition requires that young democracies be able to take the tough steps required for transition.

## THE TRANSITION PROCESS

Economists agree on the steps that must take place in the process of transition. They express less agreement on the sequencing of these steps and on the speed of the process. There are five concrete steps:

**Macroeconomic Stabilization.**  Capitalist economies stabilize their economies through the self-correcting mechanism or through activist monetary and fiscal policies. Economies in transition must develop methods and institutions for providing macroeconomic stabilization for their economies.

> **Macroeconomic stabilization** is the achievement of a reasonable degree of price stability, small budget deficits, acceptable rates of unemployment, and currency stability.

Macroeconomic stability is hard to achieve during the transition, for the following reasons:

During the early phase of transition, budget revenue from state-owned enterprises declines or disappears because of the economic collapse. Budget discipline declines as states and localities declare their independence. New taxes must be introduced. However, demands on the budget increase. Major sectors of the economy appeal for subsidies, while, at the same time, other new demands emerge, such as safety net provisions in a shrinking economy. The government handles the resulting imbalance between revenues and expenditures by printing money. The result is rapid inflation with severe consequences for the distribution of income, and a declining faith in the national currency. Citizens turn to parallel currencies, such as dollars, as they lose faith in their own depreciating currency. There is need for a new tax system and control of expenditure; industrial enterprises are forced to sink or swim.

Equally important to changes in the fiscal side of the economy is the development of a banking system appropriate for a market economy. The administrative command economy had a single monopoly bank. Hence, it is necessary to develop new banks to serve the needs of an emerging market economy. Here, too,

there are several major problems. First, in the initial stages of transition, banks must be created from scratch. Second, as new banks emerge, they are frequently owned by enterprises, they are small (there were over 2000 banks in Russia in 1996), and their reserves are typically inadequate. Third, steps must be taken to handle the large volume of existing enterprise debt. Under the old system, enterprises paid one another through the monopoly bank with credits provided by planners. Now, new means of payment must be found. Finally, infrastructure regulations and policies must be developed so that banks operate as banks: They must behave in a market environment—for example, extending credit based upon economic rather than political and other considerations.

**The Social Safety Net.**  Social safety net issues are especially important during transition, since the collapse of the old order and the initial absence of a new order increase the demands upon social safety net programs. While many capitalist countries are reexamining the manner in which they provide social benefits, these issues are critical in the transition economies.

> The **social safety net** includes a wide variety of programs such as unemployment benefits, pensions, job-retraining, and disability programs designed to cushion the costs of transition.

Although the actual benefits of the old socialist safety net may have been overstated, they nevertheless were broad and came to be accepted by many as a basic feature of the social contract. As these countries began to move toward market arrangements, the social contract was changed dramatically, but the extreme costs of transition required some measure of social support.

Safety net programs must meet budgetary constraints. Obviously, the extreme coverage of the old socialist safety net cannot be maintained, and new arrangements must be implemented with reasonable and stable sources of funding. Programs must be identified, participation and benefits defined, and record-keeping procedures developed.

The problem of creating a social safety net illustrates the complexity of transition. Transition imposes great costs on a population accustomed to a comprehensive safety net, *including* job security. Yet safety net expenditures must come out of the state budget, which, if imbalanced, will cause inflation.

**Privatization.**   In the administrative command economy, the state owned practically all property; in a capitalist economy, private individuals own practically all property. The transition from state to private ownership through privatization is one of the most complex tasks of transition for the following reasons:

1. It must be decided what property will be privatized and what property will be retained by the state. Even in mature capitalist economies, this is a difficult decision. In the former administrative command economies, this is an even more monumental task because virtually all property must be considered.

2. Once it is decided what property is to be privatized, privatization procedures that are efficient and equitable must be established. For the distribution to be efficient, property must be transferred to those who will use it effectively in a market economy. For the distribution to be equitable, property must be divided among citizens in a manner that is regarded as fair. The issues of efficiency and equity raise a number of questions: Should property go to workers and managers? To residents of the community? To the general population? Who will best use the property and who really deserves to get the property?

3. State property can be privatized either by selling it to the highest bidder and letting the market determine its value or by making an administrative decision concerning who will get the property. In the former administrative command economies, selling to the highest bidder meant that either foreign companies or a small domestic elite (possibly black-marketeers) ended up owning everything. Accordingly, most former administrative command economies have opted for a combination of administrative allocation (for example, assuring current workers and employees ownership shares of their enterprises) and market allocation (giving all citizens ownership vouchers that they can use to bid for state properties). Only after property has been divided among the citizens can foreigners start buying property.

4. Privatization must deal with the problem of state enterprises that have no prospects of future profitability. If a state enterprise cannot earn profits, no one will want to buy it and it cannot be privatized. Efforts can be made to restructure such enterprises to make them profitable or to make parts of them profitable. If they cannot be restructured, the state must decide whether to continue to subsidize them or to let them go out of business. In many cases, the largest state enterprises, employing thousands of people, fall in this category and present the most difficult of privatization issues.

**Price Liberalization.**   The administrative command economy did not use relative prices to allocate resources among business enterprises. These matters were handled by planners and ministries who simply issued administrative orders. Relative prices did play a role in allocating consumer goods, although many goods were priced so low that the public could get them only by standing in line or by knowing the right people.

Successful transition requires that prices start playing an allocative function—that businesses and consumers make their decisions based upon what the market tells them is cheap and what is expensive. For prices to play this type of role, they must reflect opportunity costs; they must be freely determined by the forces of supply and demand.

> **Price liberalization** is the freeing of prices during the course of transition to let them be determined by supply and demand.

Letting prices be determined by supply and demand imposes shocks on the economy undergoing transition. If energy prices had been kept artificially low under the old system, industrial enterprises would have treated energy as a "cheap" commodity; their capital stock would require too much energy. Consumers, accustomed to paying very low prices for government-subsidized milk, medicine, and housing, would be shocked by suddenly having to pay high market prices for these items.

One unusual feature of the administrative command system was its use of prices as instruments of social policy. Planners dealt with the problem of poverty not by redistributing income to the poor but by making sure that the prices of essential commodities were low and affordable by everyone.

Price liberalization, therefore, requires a substantial upward adjustment of prices that have been held artificially low by planners, such as energy, food, medicine, and housing. This upward adjustment would likely be politically unpopular and would be hard on those segments of the economy, such as heavy industry, that had become reliant on low material prices.

**Integration into the World Economy.**   The administrative command economy used a foreign trade monopoly to manage its dealings with the rest of the world. Buyers and sellers could not deal directly with foreign companies; everything was handled by a state foreign trade monopoly. Trade agreements were reached by negotiation, and the flows of goods and services to other countries were determined not by markets but by administrative orders. Currency exchange rates were set administratively by planners, and there were severe restrictions on the use of foreign currencies within the country; in fact, such use was usually a criminal offense.

Transition requires that the former administrative command economies become integrated into the world economy. Thus, business enterprises should be allowed to trade directly with foreign buyers and sellers, domestic citizens and businesses must be able to freely acquire and use foreign currencies, and the domestic currency must be convertible into foreign currencies. Integration into the world economy requires that the foreign trade monopoly be abolished and that buying and selling decisions in foreign markets be made by individuals and firms, not by the government.

One of the many benefits of integration into the world economy is that the former administrative command economies gain information on what things are worth in world markets. If crude oil is selling for $5 per barrel at home and the world market price is $15 per barrel, domestic producers and users of crude oil know that they are not buying and selling at oil's opportunity cost. Presumably, knowledge of world market prices would serve as a useful guide to businesses and consumers.

## SPEED OF TRANSITION: SHOCK THERAPY OR GRADUALISM?

Once the decision is made that the economy should make the transition from socialism to capitalism, there is no great disagreement about the steps that are required. These steps have been listed above. Experts disagree over the sequencing and speed of transition. All agree that a costless transition is not possible. In virtually all transition economies, transition has been accompanied by declining real GDP and by rapid inflation. Unemployment rates have risen from virtually nothing to rates that equal or exceed those of the industrialized countries. (See Figure 2.)

> The **sequencing** of transition is the order in which the transition steps—privatization, price liberalization, macroeconomic stabilization, and so forth—should take place.

Economic experts still disagree on whether there is an optimal sequencing, such as aiming first for macroeconomic stabilization, then for price liberalization, and, then for privatization. They also disagree on whether there is even the option of sequencing. Perhaps, all these steps must be carried out simultaneously in order for transition to work.

Experts and politicians have identified two approaches to the questions of sequencing and speed. One approach—shock therapy—argues that the transition steps must be carried out simultaneously and swiftly.

> **Shock therapy** is the policy of carrying out all the phases of transition at one time as quickly as possible.

For example, a country that is following the shock therapy approach would free all prices at once, would allow exchange rates to be set freely in foreign exchange markets, would strictly limit the growth of the money supply and government spending, and would allow firms that cannot survive in a market economy to go bankrupt. These steps would be carried out quickly and without reservations.

The philosophy behind shock therapy is that partial reforms are self-defeating. Macroeconomic stabilization without privatization and price liberalization will not improve the economy. Half-hearted reforms would create confusion and public resentment against reform. Some experts liken partial reform to a foolish country that decides to change its traffic laws—such as changing from driving on the left-hand side to the right-hand side—on a gradual basis. If the traffic authorities say that drivers with odd-numbered license plates should begin driving on the right as a "gradual" measure, the result would be unbelievable chaos.

Critics of gradualism suggest that a gradual and phased approach to transition would resemble a gradual change in traffic rules. Proponents of gradualism argue that a go-slow approach reduces the costs of transition and makes it more palatable.

## THE RESULTS OF TRANSITION

The former administrative command economies began their transitions in the late 1980s and early 1990s. The verdict is still undecided: The process is still too young, but we are able to make some generalizations about the experiences so far. What are these results?

1. *Shock therapy has worked better than gradualism.* Figure 3 shows that those countries that have used shock therapy have outperformed those that have used gradualism. The shock-therapy countries, such as Poland, the Czech Republic, and Hungary, experienced smaller production declines and started achieving positive growth of real GDP earlier. They had much lower rates of inflation, but they experi-

enced higher rates of unemployment. Thus, the main argument for gradualism—that the costs to society are less under a gradualist approach—has not been borne out.

2. *There is no standard model of transition.* Each transition process is different. Russia, which adopted a more gradualist approach, was able to privatize socialized enterprises at a rate as fast or faster than countries undergoing shock therapy. Some countries have undergone transition with relatively low unemployment rates, such as Russia and the Czech Republic, whereas other transition countries have had high unemployment rates, such as Poland and Hungary.

3. *Transition has imposed high political costs.* Even in those countries whose transitions have been successful, the political fallout has been great. Poland,

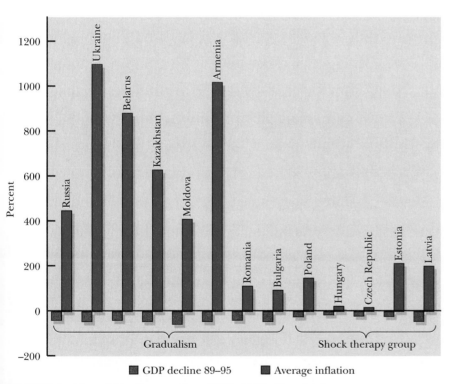

**FIGURE 3    Transition Economies, 1989–1995, Shock Therapy vs. Gradualism**

This figure shows the real GDP declines and average inflation rates for the period 1989 to 1995 for two groups of countries—countries pursuing a gradualist approach and countries using a shock therapy approach. The figure shows that gradualist countries experienced higher inflation and larger real GDP declines than the shock therapy countries. *Source:* PlanEcon, *Review and Outlook for the Former Soviet Republics; Review and Outlook for Eastern Europe.*

for example, was a pioneer in the successful application of shock therapy, yet Polish voters responded by electing an antireform communist majority to the Polish parliament. In Russia, the reformers won a narrow victory over a resurgent communist party under Gennady Zyuganov with the narrow re-election of Boris Yeltsin to a second term as president of Russia in July of 1996. In 1995, reformers were voted out of office in Estonia, a country with one of the most successful transitions.

4. *The transition process is irreversible.* Although different countries have taken different approaches to transition, the process of transition appears to be irreversible. The reason is that, once the old administrative command system was destroyed, it was necessary to replace it with a new system. Resurrecting the old system would require resurrecting a dictatorial communist party, the brutal use of political terror, taking away freedom of the press, and returning to administered allocation and administered prices. Once the reform genie is let out of the bottle, it cannot be returned.

## THE FUTURE

The world economy consists of a broad array of economic systems. Some have strong property laws, financial and budgetary discipline, a strong work ethic, and limited government intervention. They are relatively honest and obey prevailing commercial and property law. Other countries have weak laws, strong government intervention, massive corruption, and little financial or budgetary discipline. It would be foolish to think that the former administrative command economies of the former Soviet Union and Eastern Europe will end up looking and acting like the industrialized countries of the West, such as the United States, Germany, or Japan. More likely, most will resemble the economies of the Middle East, Turkey, Latin America, or Africa. Compared with the inefficiencies of the administrative command economies, this type of development will represent a major step forward.

A major issue is whether the transition economies will choose a democratic or a dictatorial path. Example 2 indicates that China has combined

### EXAMPLE 2
### CHINA'S MARKET LENINISM

The leader of the Chinese Communists, Deng Xiaoping, declared that "to get rich is glorious." In 1980, he unleashed an economic reform that made China among the fastest-growing countries of the world. Unlike the transitions taking place in the former Soviet Union, China's transition has been directed by the strong arm of the Chinese Communist Party, which has not allowed democracy or political dissent. China's reform has been dubbed "market Leninism" because it has combined strong state control with market reforms and foreign investment. This reform has allowed some to become quite rich through their industrial activity and trading, while the vast masses remain poor.

Since China began its reform in 1980, it has more than doubled its GDP, which is expected to be $6 trillion (roughly the size of the U.S. economy today) by the year 2020. The growing Chinese market is attracting foreign investment at rapid rates—almost $84 billion in 1994. The Chinese population of over one billion people represents one of the last untapped consumer markets of the world. If just one percent of the Chinese population could buy an automobile, the Chinese automobile market would be as large as that of Europe. China's economic growth, if it continues, will make it one of the world's leading economic powers in the 21st century.

*Source:* "The 21st Century Starts Here. China Booms. The World Holds Its Breath," The New York Times Magazine, February 18, 1996.

market reforms with continued dictatorial control by the Chinese Communist Party. (See Example 2.)

## SUMMARY

1. The administrative command economy had internal flaws and contradictions that led to its downfall. These flaws were problems with public ownership, lack of managerial incentives, lack of price information, and inherent shortages.

2. *Perestroika* was the attempt to reform the administrative command economy. Its unintended consequence was the collapse of the socialist economic system.

3. Transition is the process of movement from one economic system to another. Reform is the change of an existing economic system. Transition from socialism to capitalism is complicated by problems of privatization, political resistance, time required to develop economic institutions, and political feasibility.

4. There is agreement on the necessary steps of transition. They are the creation of macroeconomic stability, a social safety net, privatization, and price and foreign trade liberalization. There is disagreement on the speed and sequencing of transition. Shock therapy involves the simultaneous implementation of the various phases of transition at a rapid pace. Gradualism is the slower and phased implementation of transition.

5. Those countries that have chosen shock therapy have fared better than those that have chosen gradualism, although each transition process has been difficult.

## KEY TERMS

administrative command economy
*perestroika*
reform
transition
privatization
macroeconomic stabilization
social safety net
price liberalization
sequencing
shock therapy

## QUESTIONS AND PROBLEMS

1. Describe how the absence of price information could negatively affect the way an administrative command economy works.
2. Explain why privatization may be the transition step that requires the longest amount of time to complete.
3. Summarize the arguments made by von Mises and Hayek as to why the socialist planned economy would eventually fail. How accurate were their predictions?
4. Use the information in Figures 1 and 2 to explain the following questions:
   a. Why was *perestroika* introduced?
   b. What were the immediate economic consequences of *perestroika*?
5. Explain the slogan: "Under socialism, property belongs to everyone and hence to no one." What does this say about the efficiency of property use under such a system?
6. Distinguish between reform and transition.
7. All economic reform programs must meet the criterion of political feasibility. Why is this criterion particularly difficult to meet in the case of transition from socialism to capitalism?
8. Summarize the evidence in favor of shock therapy. What arguments can be made in favor of gradualism?
9. This chapter has referred to the unintended consequence of *perestroika*: What was this unintended consequence?
10. Summarize the notion of inherent shortage. Why does it characterize the administrative command economy?

# CHAPTER 39

# ECONOMIC DEVELOPMENT: THE "HAVES" AND THE "HAVE-NOTS"

Consider how different your life would be if you lived in a developing country. Instead of expecting to live until your late seventies, you would be lucky to live until your fifties. If you are a woman, your chances of getting a formal education would be less than 50 percent. Instead of working hard to buy a new car or large-screen television, you would work hard to buy a bicycle or a radio.

In Chapter 1 we discussed the Defining Moment of the Industrial Revolution, which began in the United Kingdom and spread to the European continent, North America, and Australia. Then it mysteriously stopped. It failed to move to most countries of Latin America, Asia, and Africa. From the time of the initial industrial revolutions in the eighteenth and nineteenth centuries, only a few countries have successfully made the transition from poverty to affluence. The most prominent example is Japan, which became an industrialized country in the early part of the twentieth century. The most recent examples are Taiwan, Singapore, South Korea, and Hong Kong, the Newly Industrialized Economies. In this chapter we shall examine the mystery of economic development. Why have sustained economic growth and prosperity been confined to such a small percentage of the world's population?

## ECONOMIC GROWTH

In an earlier chapter, we defined economic growth in terms of an increase in real GDP from one period to the next, or as an increase in real GDP per capita (that is, real GDP divided by the country's population) from one period to the next.

Long-term economic growth is the long-term trend in real output, ignoring short-run deviations around this trend caused by the business cycle. Economic growth is the expansion of the natural level of real GDP.

The two measures of economic growth provide different information about economic performance. The growth of real GDP measures the rate at which total output is expanding. Thus, it measures the degree to which an economy is growing in both scale and importance. For instance, Japan's phenomenal growth after World War II raised Japan from a relatively small economy to the world's second largest today. The growth of real GDP per capita measures the growth of average living standards. On average, people who live in countries with high per capita GDP are better off materially. If the current rapid per capita growth of countries such as Taiwan and South Korea continues, they too will soon be advanced industrialized countries.

## THE HAVES AND THE HAVE-NOTS

The modern world is divided into "have" and "have-not" nations, according to the level of economic development.

> The **level of economic development** is measured by per capita GDP, industrial structure, population dynamics, and the health and education of the population.

Although there is no single indicator of the level of economic development, per capita GDP is its most comprehensive measure. However, a country can have a high GDP per capita and yet lack the other characteristics of economic development, such as a highly educated population or an industrial structure geared to industry and services.

The industrialized countries of North America, Europe, Australia, and Japan have attained a high level of economic development. These are the Have countries. The Have-Nots—the developing countries (DCs)—have not achieved a high level of development.

> A **developing country** (DC) is a country with a per capita income well below that of a typical advanced country.

The Have-Not countries are concentrated in Africa, Asia, and Latin America. It is difficult to classify the former communist countries that are currently attempting the transition from socialism to capitalism we discussed in the previous chapter; they are located somewhere between the Have and Have-Not countries.

Figure 1 shows that approximately three out of every four persons lives in a DC. Only 15 percent of the world's population lives in the highly developed countries of the United States, Canada, Australia, Japan, and Western Europe, and 10 percent of the world's population lives in the former communist countries of the former U.S.S.R. and Eastern Europe. The DCs' share of world population has been rising since 1900 and is projected to rise throughout the twenty-first century.

A comparison of the distribution of world population with the distribution of world income dramatizes how unequally income is distributed among the different countries of the globe. As Figure 1 shows, the developed countries, which account for only 25 percent of the world's population, account for 83 percent of the world's GDP. The DCs account for 75 percent of world population but only 17 percent of world GDP. World output is concentrated in the United States, Western Europe, and Japan. The unequal distribution of income among countries also leads to an unequal consumption of natural resources between the rich and poor countries. The industrialized capitalist countries, for example, consume 71 percent of the world's oil production. Only 9 percent of the world's oil production is consumed by the DCs.

The DC share of world production has been falling as its share of world population has been rising. In 1800, the DCs accounted for 44 percent of world production. By 1900, the DC share of world production had fallen to 19 percent. The declining DC share of world production has been the result of rapid growth in the developed countries combined with slow or stagnant growth in the DCs after 1800.

As the Chapter Insight described, life in a low-income DC is very different from life in the United States. Only 1 of 5 people in a low-income DC lives in an urban area (as opposed to 78 percent in the in-

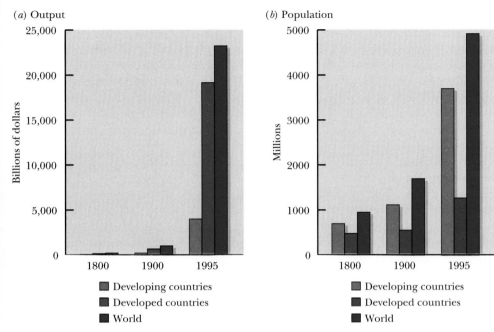

(a) Output

(b) Population

- ■ Developing countries
- ■ Developed countries
- ■ World

**FIGURE 1  The Share of Developing and Developed Countries in Population and Production, 1800–1995**

This figure shows that the developing countries' share of the world's population far exceeds their share of income. It also shows the decline in their share of world output since 1800. *Sources:* Adapted from World Bank, *World Development Report 1984*, p. 6, and from *Handbook of Economic Statistics*.

dustrial market economies). One of every 7 children dies before the age of 4, compared with 1 out of every 200 in the industrial market economies. In a community of 6000 people, there is 1 physician, compared with 11 in the industrial market economies. Life expectancy is 58 years in a typical low-income DC versus 75 years in a typical industrialized economy. In a DC, only 1 out of every 2 adults can read or write, and only 1 out of 4 school-age children attends secondary school. Only 2 out of every 100 persons own their own radios, and a private automobile is usually an unheard-of luxury. Residents of DCs come from large families and plan on having a large number of children, many of whom will not survive their infancy.

## WHY THE DEVELOPING COUNTRIES ARE POOR

The sustained productivity growth that began with the Industrial Revolution explains why the developed countries are affluent. What explains why the DCs

are poor? The "stationary state" of the classical economists provides a first explanation.

## THE CLASSICAL GROWTH MODEL

Economists first became interested in economic growth in the late eighteenth and early nineteenth centuries. The classical economists, particularly David Ricardo and Thomas Malthus, sought to explain why predominantly agricultural economies reach an upper limit to economic growth, which they called a *stationary state*. From the perspective of the classical economists writing at the very beginning of the Industrial Revolution, the stationary state of zero growth seemed to be the norm; there was very little growth of output or of population prior to 1750, the approximate starting point of the Industrial Revolution in Great Britain.

**Diminishing Returns.**  The classical economists were interested in explaining the growth of a traditional agrarian economy. In such an economy, modern science and technology had yet to be applied to agriculture, and capital equipment (such as hoes or plows) was a relatively minor input. Output was produced primarily by combining land and labor, and agricultural land was essentially fixed in supply.

The *law of diminishing returns* applies to situations in which more and more units of a variable factor (labor) are being added to a fixed factor of production (land). According to the law of diminishing returns, at low levels of labor input, increases in labor initially yield fairly substantial increases in output, but as more and more labor is combined with a fixed amount of land, additional inputs of labor create smaller and smaller additions to output. The average product of labor, after first rising, falls as diminishing returns set in.

Panel (*a*) of Figure 2 shows the aggregate output of an economy in which more and more units of a variable input (labor) are combined with a fixed input. Initially, output rises at an increasing rate, but the increase in output tapers off as more units of labor are added. Panel (*b*) shows how the average product of labor first rises but then declines.

The law of diminishing returns suggests that large labor inputs in an agricultural economy with a fixed amount of land drive down labor productivity. An economy whose population and labor force are too large would have low real wages. (See Example 1.)

**Malthusian Population Laws.**    The writings of Thomas R. Malthus, whose *Essay on the Principle of Population* was published in 1798, caused classical economics to be called the "dismal science." Malthus believed that there would be a long-term disproportion between the rate of growth of population and the rate of growth of food production. Population, Malthus argued, tends to increase at *geometric* rates (in which the *ratio* between each number and its predecessor is constant) because the "passion between the sexes" and factors such as disease and war remain constant throughout human history. On the other hand, food production tends to increase at *arithmetic* rates (in which the *difference* between each number and its predecessor is constant), following the law of diminishing returns. Because a geometric series, such as 1, 2, 4, 8, 16, . . . , grows at a faster rate and will inevitably overtake an arithmetic series, such as 10, 11, 12, 13, . . . , Malthus believed that humanity would eventually find itself on the verge of starvation, living at subsistence wages.

The crux of the Malthusian population problem is that wages can never rise above the subsistence level for long periods of time because when they do, reproduction tends to increase. Thus, if wages rise above subsistence, population will expand geometrically, and the resulting increase in the supply of labor will drive wages back down to the subsistence level. If wages fall below subsistence, famine and higher mortality rates will reduce the population and allow wages to rise back to the subsistence level.

**The Stationary State.**    The classical economists came to the pessimistic conclusion that there are distinct limits to growth. In the long run, economies would end up in a stationary state characterized by (1) a zero growth rate of output, population, and per capita output; and (2) subsistence wages.

In panel (*c*) of Figure 2, the downward-sloping labor demand curve shows the economy's demand for labor at different wage rates, and the upward-sloping labor supply curve shows the amounts of labor supplied at different wage rates. The subsistence wage ($w_s$) is drawn as a horizontal line.

The supply of labor is determined by the size of the population and by the proportion of the adult population that works, both of which change slowly over time. In the short run, the forces of supply and demand can raise wages above subsistence; then, the birth rate will rise and death rates will fall as a result of better nutrition and health. The increase in population will increase labor supply, thereby driving down the equilibrium wage rate. Population growth will not cease until the labor supply curve shifts to $S'$. At this point, wages stabilize at the subsistence level.

If a severe famine or war reduces the number of workers, wages will temporarily rise above the subsistence level, the population will begin to reproduce, and wages will be driven back to the subsistence level. During the Black Death plague of the Middle Ages, which destroyed one-third of Europe's population, real wages rose substantially but declined thereafter as population growth accelerated.

## THE SOURCES OF DEVELOPING COUNTRY POVERTY

The classical growth model has relevance to today's DCs, which are characterized by a reliance on agricultural output, limited arable land, a rapidly growing population, and limited technological improvements. Thus, DCs have the basic ingredients of a

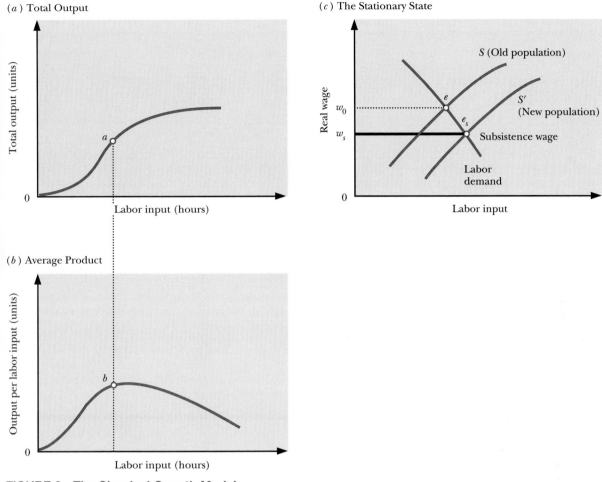

**FIGURE 2   The Classical Growth Model**

In this economy, the amount of agricultural land is fixed. As the variable factor—labor—is combined with the fixed factor, output initially rises at an increasing rate. Panel (*a*) shows that as more and more units of the variable factor are added beyond point *a*, the rate of increase in output slows. Panel (*b*) shows that the average product of labor first increases and then decreases. Panel (*c*) shows that in the short run, the market wage rate will be $w_0$—the equilibrium wage rate. The horizontal line shows the subsistence wage rate, $w_s$. If the market wage is above the subsistence level, as it is in this case, population will expand, and the labor supply curve will shift to the right (supply will increase). As long as the market wage remains above the subsistence level, population will continue to expand, thereby driving wages down even further. Population growth will cease when the market wage is driven down to the subsistence level. At this point, the economy is in a stationary state. The growth of output ceases, and wages are stuck at the subsistence level.

stationary state. Population pressure forces DCs to operate with diminishing returns. Wages are kept near subsistence, and population growth is regulated by rising and falling mortality. Good harvests cause lower mortality but increase population pressure. Poor harvests cause higher mortality but relieve population pressure.

The classical model suggests the measures that should be taken to release the DCs from the stationary state.

1. If the rate of population growth were to decline, the pressures of diminishing returns would be abated.

## EXAMPLE 1
## RWANDA:
## LITTLE LAND, MANY PEOPLE, DIMINISHING RETURNS

The world was shocked by the slaughter of over a half million Rwandans in 1994. Millions of horrified Rwandans fled to disease-infested refugee camps across the border, where they perished by the thousands.

Rwanda, an African nation the size of Maryland, has a population of 8 million people, or nearly 800 people per square mile. At its current rate of population growth, Rwanda's population would grow to 26 million by 2030, creating a density of 2600 people per square mile.

The crowding of people on scarce land has made Rwandan land among the most intensively cultivated in Africa. There are more than 2.5 people for every acre of cultivated land. The land bears stark witness to diminishing returns: virtually all land has been cleared of trees, and terraced fields clambor to the tops of hills. Given this intensity of cultivation, it is not possible to get more agricultural production by adding more labor. In fact, more output would probably be produced if there were fewer people.

The imbalance between land and population has made Rwandans more susceptible to hate campaigns. Said an aid official, "I think constant crowding, constant fighting for scarce resources, made them more desperate." Much of the killing was not for tribal reasons but to settle land disputes.

------------------------------------------------

*Source:* "Rwandan Population War: Little Land, Many People," *Houston Chronicle,* September 8, 1994, p. 20A.

---

2. If capital formation could be accelerated, labor productivity could be raised.

3. If technological progress could be achieved, diminishing returns could be avoided.

**Population Pressures.**   The rate of growth of per capita GDP equals the rate of growth of GDP minus the rate of growth of population. Thus, per capita growth can be accelerated either by increasing the growth of GDP or by decreasing the growth of population. This simple arithmetic explains why many analysts of DCs regard population growth as an enemy of economic development.

Why is population growth more rapid in the DCs than in the developed countries? Demographers have long studied a "law" of population growth called the demographic transition.

> The **demographic transition** is the process by which countries change from rapid population growth to slow population growth as they modernize.

In a country's premodern era, there is little or no population growth because birth and death rates are roughly equal. However, as modernization begins, population growth accelerates. Modernization brings with it better health care and nutrition, and the death rate, especially the infant mortality rate, declines. In addition, rising incomes may cause birth rates to rise. The first phase of modernization is, therefore, characterized by accelerating population growth.

As modernization proceeds, further reductions in the death rate become harder to achieve. Mortality from infectious diseases has already declined, and medical science is left with harder-to-combat chronic diseases, such as heart disease and cancer. Modernization eventually causes the birth rate to decline. As married couples become more educated, they use contraception to regulate the number of births. The desired number of children decreases. In industrialized societies, children are no longer the ticket to old-age security. The reduction of infant mortality eliminates the need to have many children to ensure that some will survive to adulthood. Employment opportunities for women improve, and the opportunity costs of having children increase. All of these factors combine to reduce the birth rate.

These forces cause a demographic transition from high rates of population growth to low rates. The Malthusian specter of overpopulation is removed, and advanced societies must even worry about underpopulation, or negative population growth.

The DCs have failed to experience the demographic transition for a number of reasons.

1. By contrast with the industrialized countries, declines in death rates in the DCs were not coordinated with rising modernization and prosperity. Instead, public-health improvements (such as typhoid and cholera immunizations) were introduced by the colonial powers prior to significant economic development. Improved health care and sanitization caused significant declines in mortality prior to modernization.

2. In many DCs, which remain rural societies without old-age security programs, children still provide the only guarantee that one will be looked after in one's old age. Parents who have many children stand a better chance of health and income security in their old age.

3. In many DCs, century-old traditions favor large families. The proof of manhood may be the number of children fathered. Having many children, grandchildren, and great-grandchildren may be regarded as an assurance of immortality.

4. As long as a country remains underdeveloped and employment opportunities are primarily in agriculture, the opportunity costs to women of having additional children are low. In many DCs, having a baby means the loss of only a few days or weeks in the fields. At an early age, children become productive in the fields and help their parents.

The DCs are caught in a vicious circle: Rapid population growth inhibits increases in per capita income; without substantial increases in per capita income (and the modernization that accompanies rising incomes), it is difficult to bring about substantial reductions in birth rates. There is no simple relationship, however, between per capita income growth and population growth. Some countries have both rapid population growth and rising affluence, whereas others have low population growth and economic stagnation.

**Capital Formation Problems.** The DCs encounter another vicious circle in the area of capital formation. The major portion of a nation's saving is carried out by the affluent; the poor save little or nothing. Therefore, if a whole country is poor, with most of its population living near a subsistence level of income, its saving rate will be low. Moreover, the wealthy invest their savings in nonproductive areas such as land speculation, precious metals, and foreign bank accounts. The wealthy are simply reacting to the realities of DC life: the uncertain political climate and the apparently poor development prospects of their own countries.

The Industrial Revolution began in what are now the developed countries after centuries of preparation. Canals, schools, roads, and cathedrals were built in the centuries that preceded the Industrial Revolution. By the time of the Industrial Revolution, the developed countries had accumulated an impressive stock of *social overhead capital*. The DCs have not had the luxury of centuries of steady accumulation of social overhead capital that, in effect, may be required before sustained economic development can take place.

**Technological Lag.** On the surface, it would appear that the DCs should simply borrow the modern technology already developed by the industrialized countries. However, the technology of the industrialized countries reflects the factors present in these countries. Relative to the DCs, capital is abundant in the developed countries; labor is scarce, but the quality of each worker (in training, health, and education) is high. Because of these factor endowments, the industrialized countries have created technologies that emphasize labor saving and require highly skilled labor and capital.

The modern production techniques of the developed countries are, therefore, not well suited to the DCs. The DCs require technologies that take advantage of unskilled labor and do not place heavy burdens on their more limited resources—skilled labor and capital. Although a wealth of sophisticated technology is on hand in the industrialized countries, the DCs remain in the ironic position of having to develop their own technologies.

# THE NEWLY INDUSTRIALIZED ECONOMIES

As Figure 1 showed, the fruits of the Industrial Revolution were shared by a limited number of countries in Europe, North America, Australia/New Zealand, and Japan. Japan was the next-to-last newcomer to

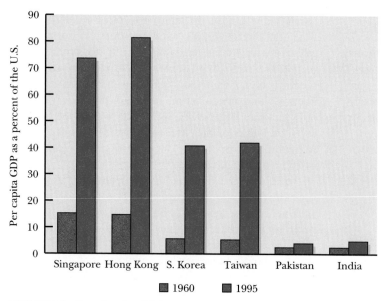

**FIGURE 3    Per Capita GDPs of Newly Industrialized Economies (NIEs) and Other Developing Countries**

The per capita GDPs of the Newly Industrialized Economies of Singapore, Hong Kong, South Korea, and Taiwan have increased remarkably as a percent of U.S. GDP (the world's richest economy). The per capita GDPs of poor countries such as India and Pakistan have scarcely increased as a percent of the United States. *Sources: Statistical Abstract of the United States; Handbook of International Economic Statistics;* Roy J. Ruffin, "The Role of Foreign Investment in the Economic Growth of the Asian and Pacific Region," *Asian Development Review,* 11(1993). The GDPs are expressed in purchasing power parities and do not use market exchange rates.

the club of affluent nations in the early part of the twentieth century.

The Newly Industrialized Economies (NIEs) of Taiwan, South Korea, Singapore, and Hong Kong broke the long dry spell in the 1970s and 1980s and now belong to the list of affluent industrialized countries.

Figure 3 shows the rapid rise of these four countries, often called the "Four Tigers." In 1960, the more affluent of them, Singapore and Hong Kong, had per capita incomes 15 percent as large as the United States. The less affluent, Taiwan and South Korea, had per capita incomes about 5 percent of the U.S. level. Since then they have grown so rapidly that Singapore and Hong Kong have passed the three quarters level relative to U.S. per capita income, and have per capita incomes about as large as Japan or England. South Korea and Taiwan are both approaching per capita income levels equal to one half the United States, the world's richest country.

What made this rise in affluence possible? The simple answer is that the NIEs grew at rapid rates for a long period of time. The more complex answer requires an understanding of the sources of this rapid growth.

Figure 3 shows the difference between the good performance of the rapidly growing NIEs and stagnant performance of developing countries such as India and Pakistan that have not been able to achieve rapid growth of per capita income. Pakistan's and India's per capita incomes in 1995 were 2 to 3 percent of the United States both in 1960 and in 1995. They have, at best, just maintained their relative position.

Why have the NIEs done so well? Can the policies that created rapid growth for the NIEs be used by other developing countries? The various NIEs are different, although they are all Asian countries. Two are small city-states (Hong Kong and Singapore) with little or no natural resources. Two are medium-sized countries both in terms of population and land mass. None of them are particularly rich in natural resources. What is their magic formula?

## TRADE POLICIES

England began the Industrial Revolution with a conscious focus on international trade. Using David Ricardo's theory of Comparative Advantage (a Defining Moment economist), England embarked upon a program of free trade to harness the power of specialization to raise its national income. Like today's NIEs, England, on the eve of the Industrial Revolution, was not particularly rich in natural resources.

Like England on the eve of its Industrial Revolution, the developing countries have a choice of trade policies. They can follow policies that protect their own industries and own markets from foreign competition. Traditionally, countries like India and Pakistan have attempted to follow the inward-looking policy of import substitution. They have tried to grow by denying the benefits of specialization and have copied the industrialized countries. Each wants its own automobile and steel industries even though it is cheaper to purchase cars and steel indirectly by producing goods for which the economy's resource base is suited (e.g., textiles and natural resources). Countries such as Argentina and Pakistan have attempted to follow the inward-looking policy of import substitution.

> **Import substitution** occurs when a country substitutes domestic production for imports by subsidizing domestic production through tariffs, quotas, and other devices.

Import substitution policies have not generated growth, primarily because the products manufactured with the assistance of tariffs and other forms of protection are not competitive.

The NIEs pursued an alternative course; namely, an outward-looking policy of export promotion—encouraging exports through various types of incentive schemes. (See Example 2.)

> **Export promotion** occurs when a country encourages exports by subsidizing the production of goods for export.

In general, those developing countries that have followed export-promotion policies have done better than those that followed import-substitution policies. The major development success stories are those countries that have become fully integrated into the world economy, competing successfully with more affluent countries in the area of manufacturing.

The successes of the export-promotion policies of the NIEs are seen in the fact that they are now among the leading producers of patents (Taiwan ranks sixth and Korea eighth worldwide) and eight of the world's largest corporations are located in the NIEs.

## CAPITAL FORMATION

For decades, the developing countries argued that they could not create capital on their own. They were too poor; their economies were too dependent upon single crops or single products. They had no tradition of saving or of capital formation. They even used arguments that the industrialized countries had exploited the developing countries and owed them a debt.

Such arguments were made most forcefully in the 1950s and 1960s. The developing-country bloc in the United Nations, for example, argued that the industrialized countries should donate approximately one percent of their GDPs annually to the developing countries in the form of development assistance. Moreover, the industrialized countries should support a new international economic order, which would stabilize the export earnings of the developing countries who relied on exports of agricultural products and raw materials.

The NIEs have been successful in creating capital formation both through domestic saving and through private direct investment. The chapter on saving and investment showed that domestic capital formation ($I$) could be financed through domestic saving ($S$) or foreign saving ($M - X$), or:

$$I = S + (M - X) \tag{1}$$

Where $S$ includes both private domestic saving and government saving or dissaving.

Figure 4 compares capital formation rates in the NIEs with those of developing countries and industrialized countries. It shows that in the early phases of industrialization the NIEs created capital both through domestic saving and through foreign investment. The NIEs were able to attract foreign investment to supplement their domestic supply of saving. By the end of the period, the NIEs were even saving

## EXAMPLE 2
## THE EMERGING STOCK MARKETS
## OF ASIA

Figure 4 shows that the "emerging markets" of Asia succeeded in attracting significant inflows of foreign capital. This inflow of foreign savings can be in the form of direct investment, loans, or purchases of shares of stock of local corporations. Typically, investors will seek out what they perceive to be "emerging markets" where they can earn higher returns than in more established stock markets. When foreign investors think that they can earn higher returns in foreign markets, they direct capital into these markets, which fund capital formation in local corporations.

The indexes reported in the accompanying figure show what $100 invested on December 31, 1991, in the various stock exchanges throughout the world was worth at the end of February 1996. The figure shows that higher returns were earned in the emerging-market stock exchanges and that some of the highest rates of return were earned in newly emerging countries like Indonesia and Thailand.

------------------------------------------------

*Source:* Dow Jones World Stock Index by Country, *Wall Street Journal,* February 27, 1996. These figures are based on share prices denominated in U.S. dollars.

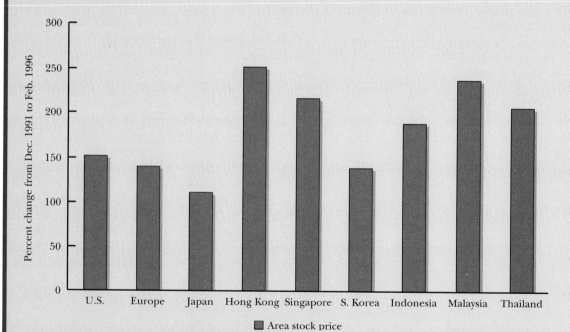

**World Stock Indexes: Industrialized Countries vs. NIEs**

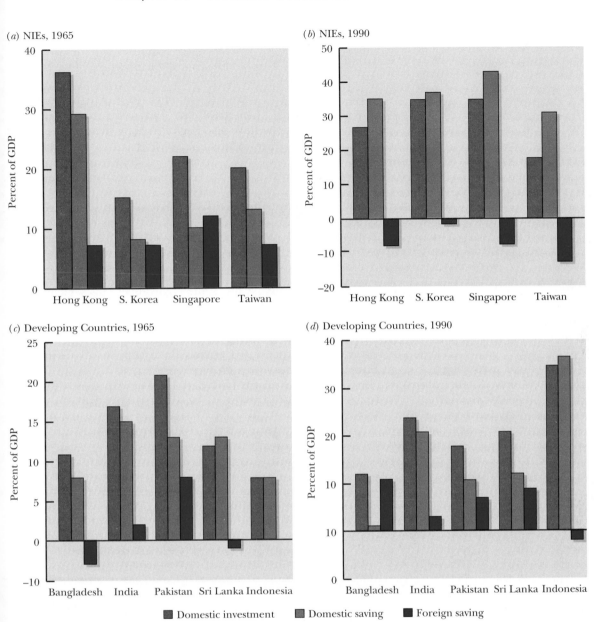

**FIGURE 4   Sources of Capital Formation: The NIEs and Other Developing Economies**

Panel (*a*) shows that the NIEs were able to attract significant amounts of foreign capital to supplement their domestic savings in the mid 1960s. Panel (*b*) shows that by 1990 the NIEs were exporting savings (capital) to other countries. (The negative figures represent an outflow of saving to other countries.) Panel (*c*) shows that poor developing countries, for the most part, did not attract foreign savings to support domestic capital formation in the mid 1960s. In fact, some even exported saving because of the poor investment opportunities in these countries. Panel (*d*) shows that by 1990 most of the poorer developing economies had begun to attract foreign saving as investors in the industrialized countries became interested in the emerging markets of Asia. *Source:* Roy J. Ruffin, "The Role of Foreign Investment in the Economic Growth of the Asian and Pacific Region," *Asian Development Review,* 11(1993), p. 5.

more than they were investing at home; thus, they began to invest their savings in other countries, such as other developing Asian economies.

Other developing economies were less successful in attracting foreign investment in the 1960s. They became more successful in the 1990s as the industrialized countries began to invest more heavily in the emerging markets of Asia.

The experience of the NIEs shows that economies that have a solid development strategy can indeed attract private capital from other countries. Those countries that have had to rely on foreign aid for capital formation have not been able to generate sufficient capital formation from this source for rapid economic growth.

## INSTITUTIONS AND ECONOMIC GROWTH

The chapter on economic growth pointed out that countries can adopt policies that promote economic growth. If the tax system penalizes saving or entrepreneurship, there will be less saving and fewer businesses formed. If a country cannot control its inflation through its banking institutions, economic development will probably not occur. If the country does not promote education, it will lack the labor resources necessary for economic development.

The choice of the economic system—market capitalism or socialism—affects prospects for economic growth. The failure of the socialist model in the former Soviet Union and Eastern Europe suggests that an economy based on public ownership and government planning and regulations cannot succeed. The experiences of the European welfare states also show that excessive government ownership, regulation, and income redistribution hurt a country's chance for continued economic growth.

The NIEs chose the market capitalist model as their economic system. Compared to the industrialized market economies, the NIEs have less government regulation, lower taxes, less income redistribution, and fewer restrictions on trade.

## OTHER NIEs?

The developing countries have profited from the experiences of the NIEs. Countries that have traditionally followed import substitution policies, like India and China, have opened their economies to trade and foreign investment. They have sought to reduce government regulation, state ownership, and other forms of government intervention. It is too early to determine whether other countries will join the ranks of the Newly Industrialized Economies. Since the mid 1990s, India has embarked upon free market policies that have caused the Indian economy to accelerate its growth. Countries like Indonesia, Thailand, and Malaysia have also begun to copy the policies of the NIEs. (See Example 2.)

## DOOMSDAY FORECASTS

The sustained growth of GDP per capita over a long period of time has provided the average citizen of the United States with a comfortable standard of living. In recent years, some environmentalists have questioned the wisdom of growth. They argue that economic growth increases environmental problems (more factories create more pollution) that threaten to exhaust the globe's finite supplies of natural resources, clean air, and pure water.

Modern doomsday forecasts are reminiscent of the predictions of the classical stationary state: Rather than using agricultural land as the limiting factor of production, doomsday forecasters see natural resources (arable land, minerals, air, and water) in this role. Some predict that economic growth will put such a severe strain on resources and on the environment that GDP per capita will begin to decline in the twenty-first century. The basic policy conclusion of this doomsday prediction is that we should adopt social policies to stop the growth of GDP and population in order to avoid catastrophe.

Most economists discount the dire predictions of the doomsday philosophers. First, doomsday models are based upon the assumption that we will continue to use resources at the same rates as we used them in the past. If past petroleum usage grew at the same rate as real GDP, the doomsday prophets assume that this relationship will continue in the future. Most economists, however, argue that when a natural resource becomes short in supply, its relative price will rise, thereby reducing its quantity demanded. A freely functioning price system will automatically retard the depletion of scarce natural resources.

Second, the doomsday models, like the models of Malthus and Ricardo, assume static technology. In the twenty-first century, the world economy will develop new energy-saving technologies or discover good substitutes for natural resources that are rising in relative price. If the world supply of petroleum and natural gas threatens to run out, scientists will develop new energy sources that will be economically feasible.

Only the future will show whether the predictions of the doomsday philosophers will prove true or whether technological progress will continue to create economic growth and rising living standards. Most economists believe that a correctly functioning price system will economize on finite resources and will create incentives to develop new technologies to replace depleted resources. Experience with rising energy prices suggests how market economies will deal with future shortages of natural resources. Rising relative prices forced our economies to combine economic growth with declining usage of petroleum inputs. In this case, economic growth was proven to be compatible with declining usage of a scarce natural resource.

## SUMMARY

1. Most of the world's population still lives in developing countries (DCs) that have failed to achieve a satisfactory level of economic development.

2. Classical economists David Ricardo and Thomas Malthus predicted that economies would reach a stationary state of zero growth and subsistence living standards. The stationary state would be caused by the law of diminishing returns and by the tendency of the population to expand whenever wages rose above the subsistence level.

3. The classical stationary state model provides a first explanation of DC poverty. The combination of rapid population growth and limited technological progress has caused diminishing returns to be a serious problem in DCs. Possible solutions to the diminishing-returns problem are reduced population growth, increased capital formation, and more rapid technological progress. The demographic transition is the process by which countries change from rapid to slow population growth during the course of modernization. The DCs as a group have yet to experience the demographic transition. The DCs suffer from inadequate capital formation. The advanced technology of the developed countries is generally not well suited to the factor endowments of the DCs.

4. The Newly Industrialized Economies chose export promotion over import substitution. They have created capital through domestic and foreign saving. They have adopted free market policies that have promoted economic growth.

5. Doomsday forecasts predict that economic growth cannot be sustained because the exhaustion of scarce natural resources and the increase of pollution will cause a new stationary state to be reached. Doomsday predictions, however, are based upon the unsupported assumption that scarce resources will continue to be used at the same rate as in the past.

## KEY TERMS

level of economic development
developing country
demographic transition
import substitution
export promotion

## QUESTIONS AND PROBLEMS

1. The amount of land in the world is fixed. The law of diminishing returns indicates that, with a fixed input, the marginal productivity of variable inputs will ultimately decline. Will we not ultimately reach Ricardo's stationary state?
2. Malthus maintained that whenever wages rise above the subsistence level, the population will grow. Has this prediction proven to be true in the industrialized countries? Why not?
3. Using the classical growth model, explain what would happen to real wages under each of the following conditions:
    a. War breaks out with a severe loss of human life.
    b. The subsistence wage level drops.
    c. There is a substantial increase in fertility.
4. Economists criticize the doomsday models on the grounds that they don't take into account the effects of relative prices. Why should prices matter if the supply of natural resources is fixed?
5. Describe the characteristics of the classical stationary state.
6. Using the information in this chapter, describe the wisdom of relying on foreign assistance versus private capital formation?

7. Explain why GDP or GDP per capita can be an imperfect measure of the level of economic development in a country.

8. Evaluate the validity of the following statement: "The stationary state of Ricardo and Malthus is not an accurate description of the situation in industrialized countries. On the other hand, it does appear to describe accurately conditions in the DCs."

9. Describe the demographic transition. Why has the demographic transition not occurred in many of the DCs?

10. Contrast the different trade policies that a DC might pursue in trying to promote its economic development.

11. Evaluate the validity of the following statement: "The DCs should not have any problem with technology. All they have to do is adopt the technologies that have been developed in the industrialized world."

12. Using the data presented in this chapter, indicate in which area—economic growth or social indicators—the DCs have made the most progress relative to the industrialized world.

# GLOSSARY

**ability-to-pay principle** states that those better able to pay should bear the greater burden of taxes, whether or not they benefit more. (**21**)

**absolute advantage** in the production of a good exists for a country if it uses fewer resources to produce a unit of the good than any other country. (**35**)

**absolute poverty standard** establishes a specific income level for a household of a given size, below which the household is judged to be living in a state of poverty. (**19**)

**accelerator principle** states that output must increase at an ever-increasing rate in order for investment to remain constant. (**25**)

**accounting profits** are revenues minus explicit costs. (**18**)

**activist policy** selects monetary and fiscal policy on the basis of the economic conditions. Activist policy changes as economic conditions change. (**34**)

**adaptive expectations** are expectations that we form from past experience and modify only gradually as experience unfolds. (**32**)

**administrative command economy** is an economic system directed by a communist party and a state planning apparatus that determine the use of resources through national economic plans. Capital and land are owned by the state, and managerial rewards are based upon fulfillment of plan targets. (**38**)

**adverse-selection problem** occurs when a buyer or seller enters a disadvantageous contract on the basis of incomplete or inaccurate information because the cost of obtaining the relevant information makes it difficult to determine whether the deal is a good one or a bad one. (**15**)

**agent** is a party that acts for, on behalf of, or as a representative of a principal. (**8**)

**aggregate demand curve (AD)** shows the real GDP that households, businesses, government, and foreigners are prepared to buy at different price levels. (**27**)

**aggregate production function** shows the relationship between the total output produced by the economy and the total labor, capital, and land inputs used by the economy. (**16**)

**aggregate supply curve** shows the amounts of real GDP firms in the economy are prepared to supply at different price levels. (**27**)

**allocation** is the apportionment of scarce resources to specific productive uses or to particular persons or groups. (**2**)

**arbitrage** is buying in a market where a commodity is cheap and reselling in a market where the commodity is more expensive. (**15**)

**assets** are anything of value that is owned. (**29**)

**automatic stabilizers** are government spending or taxation actions that take place without any deliberate government policy decisions. They automatically dampen the business cycle. (**31**)

**autonomous changes** in tax rates and government spending are independent of changes in income. (**31**)

**average fixed cost (AFC)** is fixed cost divided by output:

$$AFC = FC \div IQI \qquad (9)$$

**average revenue (AR)** equals total revenue (TR) divided by output. (**11**)

**average tax rate** is the ratio of the tax payment to taxable income. (**21**)

**average total cost (ATC)** is total cost divided by output, or the sum of average variable cost and average fixed cost:

$$ATC = TC \div IQI = AVC + AFC \qquad (9)$$

**average variable cost (AVC)** is variable cost divided by output:

$$AVC = VC \div IQI \qquad (9)$$

**balance of payments**  is a summary record of its economic transactions with foreign residents over a year or any other period. (37)

**balance sheet**  summarizes the current financial position of a firm by comparing the firm's assets and liabilities. (29)

**barter**  is a system of exchange where products are traded for other products rather than for money. (3)

**benefit principle**  of taxation states that those who benefit from a public expenditure should pay the tax that finances it. (21)

**benefits**  are forms of employee compensation such as employer-subsidized health insurance or employer contributions to retirement plans. (17)

**bond market**  is a market in which bonds of different types are traded. Bond markets buy and sell corporate bonds and bonds of governmental organizations. (8)

**bonds**  are obligations to repay the principal at maturity and to make annual interest payments until the maturity date. (8)

**budget line**  represents all the combinations of goods the consumer is able to buy, given a certain income and set prices. The budget line shows the consumption possibilities available to the consumer. (7A)

**bureaucrat**  is a nonelected government official responsible for carrying out a specific, narrowly defined task. (22)

**business cycle**  is the pattern of short-run upward and downward movements in the output of the economy. (23)

**capital**  includes equipment, buildings, plants, and inventories created by the factors of production; that is, capital is used to produce goods both now and in the future. (2)

**capital expenditures**  of government are expenditures for buildings, roads, ports, and other government capital outlays. (31)

**capital gain**  occurs whenever assets such as stocks, bonds, or real estate increase in market value over the price paid to acquire the asset. (21)

**capital productivity**  measures output per unit of capital input. (26)

**cartel**  is an organization of producers whose goal is to operate the industry as a monopoly. (13)

**cash leakage**  occurs when a check is cashed and not deposited in a checking account. This cash remains in circulation outside of the banking system. (29)

*ceteris paribus* **problem**  occurs when the effect of one factor on another is masked by changes in other factors. (1)

**change in demand**  is a change in the quantity demanded because of a change in a factor other than the good's price. It is depicted as a shift in the entire demand curve. (4)

**change in quantity demanded**  is a movement along the demand curve because of a change in the good's price. (4)

**change in quantity supplied**  is a movement along the supply curve because of a change in the good's price. (4)

**change in supply**  is a change in the quantity supplied because of a change in a factor other than the good's price. It is depicted as a shift in the entire supply curve. (4)

**circular-flow diagram**  summarizes the flows of goods and services from producers to households and the flow of the factors of production from households to business firms. (3)

**collective bargaining**  is the process whereby a union bargains with management as the representative of all union employees. (17)

**commercial banks**  are banks that have been chartered either by a state agency or by the U.S. Treasury's Comptroller of the Currency to make loans and receive deposits. (29)

**commodity money**  is money whose value as a commodity is as great as its value as money. (28)

**common stock**  confers voting privileges and the right to receive dividends only if they are declared by the board of directors. (8)

**compensating wage differentials**  are the higher wages that must be paid to compensate workers for undesirable job characteristics. (19)

**competing ends**  are the different purposes for which resources can be used. (2)

**complements**  are two goods related such that the demand for one falls when the price of the other increases. (4)

**conglomerate merger**  is a merger of companies in different lines of business. (14)

**constant returns to scale**  are present when an increase in output does not change long-run average costs of production. (9)

**constant-money-growth rule**  states that the money supply should increase at a fixed percentage each year. (30)

**consumer equilibrium** or **optimum**  requires that (1) all income be spent and (2) the marginal utilities per dollar for each good purchased are equal. Thus, if goods A, B, C, . . . and so forth are being purchased, it must be that

$$MU_A/P_A = MU_B/P_B = MU_C/P_C = \ldots \text{ for all goods.} \quad (7)$$

**consumer price index (CPI)** measures the level of consumer prices paid by households over a period of time. (23)

**consumers' surplus** represents the consumer benefits (the dollar value of total utility) from consuming a good in excess of the dollar expenditure on the good. (7, 10)

**consumption function** shows the relationship between real disposable income and real consumption. (25)

**contractionary fiscal policy** lowers aggregate demand by lowering government spending or by raising tax rates. (31)

**contrived scarcity** is the production of less than the economically efficient quantity of a good by a monopoly. (12)

**convertible stock** pays the owner fixed interest payments and gives the privilege of converting the convertible stock into common stock at a fixed rate of exchange. (8)

**corporation** is a business enterprise that has the status of a legal person and is authorized by federal and state law to act as a single person. The corporation is owned by stockholders who possess shares of stock in the corporation. The stockholders elect a board of directors that appoints the management of the corporation. (8)

**correlation coefficient** is a measure of the statistical association between two variables ranging from +1 for a perfect positive correlation to -1 for a perfect negative correlation. (24A)

**countercyclical monetary policy** increases aggregate demand when output is falling too much (or when its rate of growth is declining) and reduces aggregate demand when output is rising too rapidly. (30)

**countervailing duty** is a duty imposed on imports subsidized by the governments of the exporting country. (36)

**Cournot oligopoly** exists when (1) the product is homogeneous, (2) each firm supposes that its rivals will continue to produce their current outputs independently of that firm's choice of outputs, and (3) there is a fixed number of firms. (13)

**craft union** represents workers of a single occupation. (17)

**credible threat** is the commitment of significant resources by existing firms to convince potential entrants to the industry that entry would result in severe losses for the entrant. (13)

**credit, or capital, markets** facilitate the exchange of financial assets in a modern society. (18)

**credit rationing** occurs when the demand for loans exceeds the supply of loans. In this situation, some rationing device other than interest rates must be used to ration the scarce supply of credit or loans. (30)

**cross-price elasticity of demand** ($E_{xy}$) is the percentage change in demand of the first product ($x$) divided by the percentage change in the price of the related product ($y$). (6)

**current account balance** equals exports of goods (merchandise) and services minus imports of goods (merchandise) and services minus net unilateral transfers abroad. (37)

**current expenditures** of government are expenditures for payrolls, materials, transportation, interest, and other current outlays. (31)

**cyclical deficit** is the part of the deficit caused by movements in the business cycle. (31)

**cyclical unemployment** is unemployment associated with general downturns in the economy. (33)

**cyclically balanced budget** is one in which deficits during downturns are offset by surpluses during cyclical upturns. (31)

**deadweight loss** is a loss to society of consumer or producer surplus that is not offset by anyone else's gain. (12)

**decreasing costs** are present when the cost of production per unit decreases as the number of units produced increases. (35)

**deficit financing** is government borrowing in credit markets to finance a government deficit. (21)

**Defining Moment of economics** is an event or idea, or a set of related events or ideas over time, that has changed in a fundamental way the manner in which we conduct our everyday lives and the way in which we think about the economy. (1)

**deflation** is a general decline in prices. (23)

**demand** for a good or service is the amount people are prepared to buy under specific circumstances such as the products price. (4)

**demand deposit** is a deposit of funds that can be withdrawn ("demanded") from a depository institution (such as a bank) at any time without restrictions. The funds are usually withdrawn by writing a check. (28)

**demand-side inflation** occurs when aggregate demand increases and pulls prices up. (32)

**demographic transition** is the process by which countries change from rapid population growth to slow population growth as they modernize. (39)

**deposit multiplier** is the ratio of the change in total deposits to the change in reserves. (29)

**depreciation** is the decrease in the economic value of capital goods as they are used in the production process. (18); is the value of the existing capital stock that has been consumed or used up in the process of producing output. (24)

**depression** is a severe downturn in economic activity that lasts for a prolonged period. Output declines by a significant amount, and unemployment rises to very high levels. (23)

**derived demand** is the demand for a factor of production that results (is derived) from the demand for the goods and services the factor of production helps produce. (16)

**developing country (DC)** is a country with a per capita income below that of a typical advanced country. (39)

**dilution** occurs when corporations issue new stock and reduce the percentage ownership of existing shareholders. (8)

**direct crowding out** occurs when an increase in government spending substitutes for private spending by providing similar goods. (31)

**discretionary fiscal policies** are government spending and taxation actions that have been deliberately chosen to achieve macroeconomic goals. (31)

**discrimination** occurs when individuals are blocked from entering jobs and occupations or when workers with equal skills and qualifications are treated differently on the grounds of race, sex, or some other characteristic. (19)

**diseconomies of scale** are present when an increase in output causes long-run average costs to increase. (9)

**disequilibrium price** is one at which the quantity demanded does not equal the quantity supplied. (5)

**dumping** occurs when a country sells a good in another country for less than the price charged in the home country. (36)

**economic efficiency** means that the economy is producing the maximum output of useful things with its given resources and technology. (12)

**economic growth** occurs when an economy expands its outputs of goods and services. (2); is the long-run expansion of the total output of goods and services produced by the economy. (23)

**economic profits** represent the amount by which revenues exceed total opportunity cost (10); are revenues in excess of total opportunity costs (which include both actual payments and sacrificed alternatives). Economic profits are profits in excess of normal profits. (18)

**economic rent** is the amount by which the payment to a factor exceeds its opportunity cost. (18)

**economic system** is the property rights, resource allocation arrangements, and incentives that a society uses to solve the economic problem. (2)

**economics** is the study of how people choose to use their limited resources (land, labor, and capital) to produce, exchange, and consume goods and services. It explains how these scarce resources are allocated among competing ends by the economic system. (1)

**economies of scale** are present when large output volumes can be produced at a lower cost per unit than small output volumes. (8); are present when an increase in output causes long-run average costs to fall. (9)

**effectiveness lag** is the time it takes the change in the money supply to affect the economy. (30)

**efficiency** occurs when an economy is using its resources so well that producing more of one good results in less of other goods. No resources are being wasted. (2)

**efficiency-wage model** states that it is rational for certain firms to pay workers a wage rate above equilibrium to improve worker performance and productivity. (17)

**employee association** represents employees in a particular profession in order to both maintain professional standards and improve conditions of pay and work. (17)

**endogenous growth** or **neo-Schumpeterian models** base their explanation of technological progress on the desire for profit. (26)

**entitlement program** requires the government to pay benefits to anyone who meets eligibility requirements. (31)

**entrepreneurs** organize the factors of production to produce output, seek out and exploit new business opportunities, and introduce new technologies and inventions. The entrepreneur takes the risk and bears the responsibility if the venture fails. (2, 8)

**equilibrium (market-clearing) price** is the price at which the quantity demanded by consumers equals the quantity supplied by producers. (4)

**equilibrium price** of a good or service is that price at which the amount of the good people are prepared to buy (demand) equals the amount offered for sale (supply). (3, 5)

**excess reserves** are reserves in excess of required reserves. Excess reserves equal total reserves minus required reserves. (29)

**exchange** complements specialization by permitting individuals to trade the goods in which they specialize for those that others produce. (3)

**exclusion costs** are the costs of preventing those who do not pay from enjoying a good. (21)

**exhaustible** (or **nonrenewable**) **resource** is any resource of which there is a finite amount in the long run because the stock is fixed by nature. (20)

**exhaustive expenditures** are government purchases that divert resources from the private sector, making them no longer available for private use. (21)

**expansionary fiscal policy** increases aggregate demand by raising government spending and/or by lowering tax rates. (**31**)

**export promotion** occurs when a country encourages exports by subsidizing the production of goods for export. (**39**)

**external debt** is debt which is owned by residents of other countries. (**31**)

**externalities** exist when an economic activity of one party results in direct economic costs or benefits for someone else who does not control that economic activity. (**12**); exist when producers or consumers do not bear the full marginal cost or enjoy the full marginal benefit of their actions. (**20**)

**factors of production** or **resources** are the inputs used to produce goods and services. (**2**)

**fallacy of composition** is the assumption that what is true for each part taken separately is also true for the whole or, in reverse, that what is true for the whole is true for each part considered separately. (**1**)

**false-cause fallacy** is the assumption that because two events occur together, or one event precedes the other, one event has caused the other. (**1**)

**federal debt** is the cumulated sum of past deficits and surplus of the federal government. (**31**)

**federal funds rate** is the interest rate on overnight loans among financial institutions. (**30**)

**fiat money** is a government-created money whose value or cost as a commodity is much less than its value as money. (**28**)

**final goods** are goods that are purchased for final use by consumers or firms, such as cars or clothing or investment goods. (**24**)

**financial intermediaries** borrow funds from one group of economic agents (people or firms with savings) and lend to other agents. (**29**)

**fine-tuning** is the frequent use of discretionary monetary and fiscal policy to counteract even small movements in business activity. (**34**)

**fiscal policy** is the way in which the government provides for and carries out government expenditures. (**31**)

**fixed costs (FC)** are those costs that do not vary with output. (**9**)

**fixed exchange rate** is a rate set by government decree or intervention within a small range of variation. (**37**)

**fixed investment** is investment in plant, structures, and equipment. (**24**)

**floating exchange rate** is freely determined by the interaction of supply and demand. (**37**)

**foreign exchange** is the national currency of another country that is needed to carry out international transactions. (**37**)

**foreign savings** supplied to the domestic economy are the difference between imports and exports, or $M - X$. (**24**)

**foreign-trade effect** occurs when a rise in the domestic price level lowers the aggregate quantity demanded by pushing down net exports $(X - M)$. (**27**)

**free good** is an item for which there exists an amount available that is greater than the amount people would want at a zero price. (**2**)

**free rider** enjoys the benefits of a good or service without paying the cost. (**21**)

**frictional unemployment** is the unemployment associated with the changing of jobs in a dynamic economy. (**33**)

**functional distribution of income** is the distribution of income among the four broad classes of productive factors—land, labor, capital, and entrepreneurship. (**16**)

**futures market** is an organized market in which a buyer and seller agree now on the price of a commodity to be delivered at some specified date in the future. (**15**)

**GDP** is the sum of personal consumption expenditures, government purchases of goods and services, investment expenditures, and net exports. (**24**)

**GDP deflator** measures the level of prices of all final goods and services (consumer goods, investment goods, and government) produced by the economy. (**23**)

**GDP gap** is the difference between current real GDP and the natural level of real GDP. (**34**)

**game theory** is the study of how we interact with others in our economic and social behavior. (**5**)

**generational accounting** shows government deficits in terms of each generation's net lifetime tax payments or the difference between that generation's expected tax payments and its expected lifetime benefits from government, such as social security benefits. (**31**)

**Gini coefficient** is the area between the 45-degree line and the Lorenz curve, divided by the total area under the 45-degree line. (**19**)

**globalization** refers to the degree to which national economic markets and international businesses are integrated and interrelated into a world economy. (**1**)

**government budget** is the sum of government spending on goods and services, and government transfers including interest payments on government debt. (**31**)

**government budget deficit** is the excess of government outlays over government revenues. (**21**)

**government budget surplus** is the excess of government revenues over government outlays. (**21**)

**government debt** is the cumulated sum of outstanding IOUs that a government owes its creditors. (**21**)

**government deficit** is an excess of total government spending over total revenues. (**31**)

**government surplus** is an excess of total government revenues over total spending. (**31**)

**gradualist policy** calls for steady reductions in monetary growth spread over a period of years to combat accelerating inflation. (**33**)

**Great Depression** was a sustained period of high unemployment and falling output that occurred in Europe and North America in the 1920s and 1930s. (**1**)

**Gresham's law** states that bad money drives out good. When depreciated, mutilated, or debased currency is circulated along with money of high value, the good money will either disappear from circulation or circulate at a premium. (**28**)

**gross domestic income (GDI)** is approximately the sum of all income earned by the factors of production. (**24**)

**gross domestic product (GDP)** is the market value of all final goods and services produced by the factors of production located in the country during a period of one year. (**24**)

**gross national product (GNP)** measures the final output produced by U.S. residents whether located in the United States or abroad. (**24**)

**growth distortion** is the measurement of changes in a variable over time that does not reflect the concurrent change in other relevant variables with which the variable should be compared, such as population size or the size of the economy. (**1A**)

**growth rate of real GDP** shows the extent to which the total output of the economy is increasing. (**26**)

**growth rate of real per capita GDP** shows the extent to which the economic well-being of the average person is increasing. (**26**)

**halfway rule** states that when the demand curve can be represented by a straight line, the marginal revenue curve bisects the horizontal distance between the demand curve and the vertical axis. (**11**)

**hedging** is the temporary substitution of a futures market transaction for an intended spot transaction. (**15**)

**horizontal equity** exists when those with equal abilities to pay do pay the same amount of tax. (**21**)

**horizontal merger** is a merger of two firms in the same line of business (such as two insurance companies or two shoe manufacturers). (**14**)

**household production** is work in the home, including such activities as meal preparation, do-it-yourself repair, child-rearing, and cleaning. (**17**)

**human capital** is the accumulation of past investments in schooling, training, and health that raise the productive capacity of people. (**2**); theory teaches that we make rational choices of different lifetime earnings streams when we invest in ourselves. (**19**)

**hyperinflation** is a very rapid and accelerating rate of inflation. Prices might double every month or even double daily or hourly. (**23**)

**immediate run** is a period of time so short that the quantity supplied cannot be changed at all. In the immediate run—sometimes called the *momentary period* or *market period*—supply curves are perfectly inelastic. (**6**)

**implicit contract** is an agreement between employer and employees concerning conditions of pay, employment, and unemployment that is unwritten but understood by both parties. (**33**)

**import quota** is a quantitative limitation on the amount of imports of a specific product during a given period. (**36**)

**import substitution** occurs when a country substitutes domestic production for imports by subsidizing domestic production through tariffs, quotas, and other devices. (**39**)

**incentive-based approach** is when the government uses economic incentives or penalties (such as taxes or subsidies) to encourage polluting agents to restrict emissions. (**20**)

**incidence of a tax** is the actual distribution of the burden of tax payments. (**21**)

**income effect** is when the price of a good falls, we buy more of it because (1) the price reduction is like an increase in income than in itself normally results in larger demands for all goods and services; and (2) we tend to substitute that good for other, relatively more expensive goods (the **substitution effect**). (**7**)

**income elasticity of demand** ($E_i$) is the percentage change in the demand for a product divided by the percentage change in income, holding all prices fixed. (**6**)

**incomes policy** is a set of government rules, guidelines, or laws that regulate wage and price increases. (**32**)

**indexing** is the tying of tax rates to the rate of inflation. (**21**)

**indifference curve** shows all the alternative combinations of two goods that yield the same total satisfaction to a particular consumer and among which the consumer is indifferent. (**7A**)

**industrial revolution** occurred as a result of extensive mechanization of production systems that shifted manufacturing from the home to large-scale factories. This combination of scientific and technological advances and the expansion of free-market institutions created, for the first time, unsustained economic growth. (**1**)

**industrial union** represents employees of an industry regardless of their specific occupation. (**17**)

**industry** or **market supply curve** is, in the short run, horizontal summation of the supply curves of each firm, which in turn are those portions of the firms' MC curve located above minimum AVC. (**10**)

**inferior good** is one for which demand falls as income increases, holding all prices constant. (**4**)

**inflation** is a general increase in money prices. (**3, 23**)

**inflation distortion** is the measurement of the dollar value of a variable over time without adjustment for inflation over that period. (**1A**)

**information costs** are the costs of acquiring information on prices, product qualities, and product performance. (**15**)

**inheritance** is the passing of wealth from one generation to another. (**19**)

**in-kind income** consists of benefits—such as free public education, school lunch programs, public housing, or food stamps—for which the recipient is not required to pay. (**19**)

**interest** is the price of credit and is determined in credit markets. (**18**)

**interest rate** is the price of credit that is paid to savers who supply credit. (**3**); measures the yearly cost of borrowing as a percentage of the amount loaned. (**18**)

**interest-rate effect** occurs when increases in the price level push up interest rates in credit markets which reduce real investment. (**27**)

**intermediaries** buy in order to sell again or simply bring together a buyer and a seller. (**15**)

**intermediate goods** are used to produce other goods, such as cotton for making clothing. (**24**)

**internal debt** is debt in which the residents of that country own the national debt. (**31**)

**internal labor market** works by promoting or transferring workers it already employs. (**17**)

**internalization** of an externality involves placing private price tags on external costs (or benefits) so that private and social costs (or benefits) coincide. (**20**)

**inventory investment** is the increase (or decrease) in the value of the stocks of inventories that businesses have on hand. (**24**)

**investment demand curve** of the economy (or a firm) shows the amount of investment desired at different interest rates. (**25**)

**isocost line** shows all the combinations of labor and capital that have the same total costs. (**9A**)

**isoquant** shows the various combinations of two inputs (such as labor and capital) that produce the same quantity of output. (**9A**)

**job creation rate** refers to the employment gains in expanding or new companies; the **job destruction rate** refers to the employment losses in shrinking or failing business firms. (**34**)

**labor** is the combination of physical and mental talents that human beings contribute to production. (**2**)

**labor force** equals the number of persons employed plus the number unemployed. (**23**)

**labor market** is an arrangement that brings together buyers and sellers of labor services to determine pay and working conditions. (**17**)

**labor productivity** measures output per unit (usually per hour) of labor input. (**26**)

**labor union** is a collective organization of workers and employees whose objective is to improve conditions of pay and work. (**17**)

**land** is a catchall term that covers all of nature's bounty—minerals, forests, land, and water resources. (**2**)

**law of comparative advantage** is the principle that people should engage in those activities for which their advantages over others are the largest or their disadvantages are the smallest. (**3**); states that people or countries specialize in those activities in which they have the greatest advantage or the least disadvantage compared with other people or countries. (**35**)

**law of demand** states that there is a negative (or inverse) relationship between the price of a good or service and the quantity demanded, if other factors are constant. (**4**)

**law of diminishing marginal rate of substitution** states that as more of one good *(A)* is consumed, the amount of another good *(B)* that the consumer is willing to sacrifice for one more unit of good *A* declines. (**7A**)

**law of diminishing marginal utility** states that as more of a good or service is consumed during any given time period, its marginal utility eventually declines, if the consumption of everything else is held constant. (**7**)

**law of diminishing returns** states that when the amount of one input is increased in equal increments, holding all other inputs constant, the result is ever-smaller increases in output. (**2**)

**law of increasing costs** states that as more of a particular commodity is produced, its opportunity cost per unit increases. (**2**)

**least-cost rule** is that the least-cost combination of two factors can be found at the point where a given isoquant is tangent to the lowest isocost line. In other words, the least-cost combination of two factors can be found where

$$\frac{P_L}{\text{MPP}_L} = \frac{P_C}{\text{MPP}_C} \qquad \textbf{(9A)}$$

**leisure**   is time spent in any activity other than work in the labor force or work in the home. (17)

**level of economic development**   is measured by per capita GDP, industrial structure, population dynamics, and the health and education of the population. (39)

**liabilities**   are anything owed to other economic agents. (29)

**lifetime distribution of income**   measures the distribution of average income over the household's adult life. (19)

**liquidity**   is the ease and speed with which an asset can be converted into a medium of exchange without risk of loss. (28)

**liquidity preference (LP) curve**   shows the demand for money as the nominal interest rate changes, holding other factors constant. (28)

**loanable funds**   comprise the lending from all households, governments, and businesses, or the bank credit made available to borrowers in credit markets. (18)

**logrolling**   is the trading of votes to secure a favorable outcome on decisions of more intense interest to that voter. (22)

**long run**   is a period of time long enough for new firms to enter the market, for old firms to disappear, and for existing plants to be expanded. In the long run, firms have more flexibility in adjusting to price changes. (6); is a period of time long enough to vary all inputs. (9)

**long-run average cost (LRAC)**   consists of the minimum average cost for each level of output when all factor inputs are variable (and when factor prices and the state of technology are fixed). (9)

**Lorenz curve**   shows the percentages of total income earned by households at successive income levels. The cumulative percentage of households (ranked from lowest to highest incomes) is plotted on the horizontal axis, and the cumulative share of income earned by each cumulative percentage of households is plotted on the vertical axis. (19)

**luxuries**   are those products that have an income elasticity of demand greater than 1. (6)

**M1**   is the sum of currency (paper money and coins), demand deposits at commercial banks held by the non-banking public, travelers' checks, and other checkable deposits, such as NOW (negotiable order of withdrawal) accounts and ATS (automatic transfer services) accounts. (28)

**M2**   equals M1 plus savings and small time deposits, money-market mutual-fund shares, and other highly liquid assets. (28)

**macroeconomic stabilization**   is the achievement of a reasonable degree of price stability, small budget deficits, acceptable rates of unemployment, and currency stability. (38)

**macroeconomics**   is the study of the economy as a whole, rather than individual markets, consumers, and producers. It concerns the *general* price level (rather than individual prices), the national employment rate, government spending, government deficits, trade deficits, interest rates, and the nation's money supply. (2)

**majority rule**   is a system of voting in which a government decision is approved if more than 50 percent of the voters approve. (22)

**managerial coordination**   is the disposition of the firm's resources according to the directives of the firm's manager(s). (8)

**marginal analysis**   examines the costs and benefits of making small changes from the current state of affairs. (5)

**marginal cost (MC)**   is the change in total cost (or equivalently in variable cost) divided by the increase in output or, alternatively, the increase in costs per unit of increase in output.

$$MC = \frac{\Delta TC}{\Delta Q} = \frac{\Delta VC}{\Delta Q} \qquad (9)$$

**marginal physical product (MPP)**   of a factor of production is the change in output divided by the change in the quantity of the input, if all other inputs are constant. (9)

**marginal productivity theory of income distribution**   states that the functional distribution of income between land, labor, and capital is determined by the relative marginal revenue products of the different factors of production. The price of each factor will equal the marginal revenue product of that factor. (16)

**marginal propensity to consume (MPC)**   is the change in desired consumption *(C)* for a $1 change in income *(Y)*:

$$MPC = \frac{\Delta C}{\Delta Y} \qquad (25)$$

**marginal propensity to save (MPS)**   is the change in desired saving *(S)* for a $1 change in income *(Y)*:

$$MPS = \frac{\Delta S}{\Delta Y} \qquad (25)$$

**marginal rate of substitution (MRS)**   is how much of one good a person is just willing to give up to acquire one unit of another good. (7A)

**marginal revenue (MR)**   is the additional revenue raised per unit increase in quantity sold; that is, MR = $\Delta TR/\Delta Q$, where TR is total revenue. (11); is the increase in total revenue (TR) that results from each 1-unit increase in the amount of output:

$$MR = \frac{\Delta TR}{\Delta Q} \qquad (10)$$

**marginal revenue product (MRP)**   of any factor of production is the extra revenue generated per unit increase in the amount of the factor. (16)

**marginal tax rate**   is the increase in tax payments divided by the increase in income. The marginal tax rate shows how much extra taxes must be paid per dollar of extra earnings. (**21**)

**marginal utility (MU)**   of any good or service is the increase in utility that a consumer experiences when its consumption of that good or service (and that good or service alone) is increased by 1 unit. In general,

$$MU = \frac{\Delta TU}{\Delta Q}$$

where TU is total utility and $Q$ is the quantity of the good. (**7**)

**marginal utility per dollar**   for any good or service is the ratio of its marginal utility to its price (MU/*P*). (**7**)

**market**   is an established arrangement that brings buyers and sellers together to exchange particular goods or services. (**2, 4**)

**market demand curve**   is the demand of all buyers in the market for a particular product. (**4**); shows the total quantities demanded by all consumers in the market at each price. It is the horizontal summation of all individual demand curves in that market. (**7**)

**market failure**   occurs when the price system fails to yield the socially optimal quantity of a good. (**20**)

**median voter**   on a public expenditure program wants more expenditure than half the remaining voters and less expenditure than the other half. (**22**)

**merchandise trade balance**   equals exports of merchandise minus imports of merchandise. If positive, it is the *merchandise trade surplus*. If negative, it is the *merchandise trade deficit*. (**37**)

**microeconomics**   studies the economic decision making of firms and individuals in a market setting; it is the study of individual decision making and its impact on resource allocation. (**2**)

**midpoints elasticity formula**   for determining the elasticity of demand ($E_d$) for a given segment of the demand curve is

$$E_d = \frac{\text{Percent change in quantity demanded}}{\text{Percent change in price}}$$

$$= \frac{\text{Change in quantity demanded}}{\text{Average of two quantities}}$$

$$\div \frac{\text{Change in price}}{\text{Average of two prices}} \quad (6)$$

**minimum efficient scale (MES)**   is the lowest level of output at which average costs are minimized. (**9**)

**monetarism**   is the doctrine that monetary policy should follow a constant-money-growth rule. (**30**); is the prescription that the money supply must expand at a constant rate roughly equal to the long-run growth of real GDP. (**32**)

**monetary base**   is the sum of reserves on deposit at the Fed, all vault cash, and the currency in circulation. (**29**)

**monetary policy**   is the deliberate control of the money supply and, in some cases, credit conditions for the purpose of achieving macroeconomic goals such as a certain level of unemployment or inflation. (**30**)

**money**   is anything that is widely accepted in exchange for goods and services. (**3**)

**money price**   is a price expressed in monetary units (such as dollars, francs, etc.). (**3**)

**monopolistic competition**   has four essential characteristics: (1) the number of sellers is large enough to enable each seller to act independently of the others; (2) the product is differentiated from seller to seller; (3) there is free entry into and exit from the industry; (4) sellers are price makers. (**11**)

**monopoly rent-seeking behavior**   is the use of scarce resources on lobbying and influence—buying to acquire monopoly rights from government. (**12**)

**moral-hazard problem**   exists when one of the parties to a contract has an incentive to alter his or her behavior after the contract is made at the expense of the second party. It arises because it is too costly for the second party to obtain information about the first party's postcontractual behavior. (**15**)

**multinational corporation**   engages in foreign markets through its own affiliates located abroad, and pursues business strategies that transcend national boundaries. (**8**)

**multiple expansion of deposits**   of the money supply occurs when an increase in reserves causes an expansion of the money supply that is greater than the reserve increase. (**29**)

**mutual interdependence**   exists when a firm recognizes that its decisions are likely to invite reactions by rivals. (**13**)

**Nash equlibrium**   of a game is the point at which each player is doing the best he or she can given what the other players are doing. (**13**)

**national income**   equals net national product minus indirect business taxes, and represents the sum of all payments made to the factors of production. (**24**)

**natural law**   states that individuals should be rewarded according to their contribution to output. (**19**)

**natural level of output (real GDP)**   is that level corresponding to equality in the demand for and supply of labor. (**27**)

**natural monopoly**   prevails when industry output is cheaper to produce with one firm than two or more firms. (**11**)

**natural rate of unemployment** is that rate at which the labor force is in balance; that is, the number of available jobs *(V)* is equal to the number of unemployed workers qualified to fill those jobs *(U)*, $V = U$, or equivalently, aggregate labor demand is equal to aggregate labor supply, $N + V = N + U$. (27); that unemployment rate at which there is an approximate balance between the number of unfilled jobs and the number of qualified job seekers. (23)

**natural selection theory** states that if business firms do not maximize profits, they will be unable to compete with other firms and will be driven out of the market or taken over by outsiders. (8)

**necessities** are those products that have an income elasticity of demand less than 1. (6)

**negative (inverse) relationship** exists between two variables if an increase in the value of one variable is associated with a *reduction* in the value of the other variable. (1A)

**neoclassical growth model** explains economic growth by virtue of capital accumulation, population growth, and unexplained technological progress. (26)

**net exports of goods and services** is the difference between exports of goods and services (X) by a particular country and its imports of goods and services from other countries *(M)*, or *XM*. (24)

**net national product** (NNP) equals GNP minus depreciation. (24)

**net output** or **value added** of an industry is the value of its output minus the value of its purchases from other industries. (24)

**net tax payment** in a generational account is the difference between the present value of the cumulative lifetime tax payments and the cumulative value of benefits to be received from the government for each age group. (31)

**neutral tax** cannot be altered by a change in private production, consumption, or investment decisions. (21)

**nominal GDP** or **GDP in current prices** is the value of final goods and services produced in a given year in that year's prices. (24)

**nominal interest rate** is the cost of borrowing expressed in terms of current dollars unadjusted for inflation. (18)

**nominal rate of interest** is the contractual interest rate that is observed in markets. (25)

**nonactivist policy** consists of fixed rules independent of prevailing economic conditions that are held steady even when economic conditions change. (34)

**nonexclusion** characterises a good if extreme costs eliminate the possibility (or practicality) of excluding some people from using it. (21)

**nonprice competition** is the attempt to attract customers through improvements in product quality or service, thereby shifting the firm's demand curve to the right. (11)

**nonprohibitive tariff** is a tariff that does not wipe out all imports of the product. (36)

**nonrival consumption** characterises a good if its consumption by one person does not reduce its consumption by others. (21)

**normal good** is one for which demand increases when income increases, holding all prices constant. (4)

**normal profit** is the return that the time and capital of an entrepreneur would earn in the best alternative employment. It also is the return that is earned when total revenues equal total opportunity costs. (10); are the profits required to keep resources in that particular business. Normal profits are earned when revenues equal opportunity costs. (18)

**normative economics** is the study of what ought to be in the economy; it is value-based and cannot be tested by the scientific method. (1)

**oligopoly** is an industry (1) that is dominated by a few firms, (2) whose individual firms must consider the policies of their rivals in making their decisions, and (3) whose firms are price makers. (13)

**opportunity cost** of a particular action is the loss of the next-best alternative. (2, 9)

**optimal level of abatement** occurs when the marginal social cost of an extra unit of abatement equals its marginal social benefit. (20)

**optimal-search rule** states that people will continue to acquire economic information as long as the marginal benefits of gathering information exceed the marginal costs. (15)

**paradox of voting** is that majority rule can yield inconsistent social choices. Even if each voter is perfectly rational, the majority of voters can choose *a* over *b*, *b* over *c*, and then choose *c* over *a*. (22)

**partnership** is owned by two or more people called partners, who make all the business decisions, share the profits, and bear the financial responsibility for any losses. (8)

**patent** is an exclusive right granted to an inventor to make, use, or sell an invention for a term of 17 years in the United States. (12)

**per capita growth curve** shows the negative relationship between per capita GDP growth rate and the capital-output ratio, holding other factors constant. (26)

**per capita production function** shows the relationship between real GDP per capita and the stock of capital per capita. (26)

*Perestroika* was a process of economic, political, and social reform begun in the Soviet Union in 1985. It encompassed reform of the administrative command economy, political democratization, and increased freedom of expression. (38)

**perfect competition** prevails in an industry when each individual seller faces so much competition from other sellers that the market price is taken as given. (10)

**perfectly elastic demand** $(E_d = \infty)$ is illustrated by a horizontal demand curve; quantity demanded is most responsive to price. (6)

**perfectly elastic supply** $(E_s = \infty)$ is illustrated by a horizontal supply curve; quantity supplied is most responsive to price. (6)

**perfectly inelastic demand** $(E_d = 0)$ is illustrated by a vertical demand curve; quantity demanded is least responsive to price. (6)

**perfectly inelastic supply** $(E_s = 0)$ is illustrated by a vertical supply curve; quantity supplied is least responsive to price. (6)

**permanent income** is an average of the income that an individual anticipates earning over the long run. (31)

**personal distribution of income** is the distribution of income among households, or how much income one family earns from the factors of production it owns relative to other families. (16)

**personal income** equals national income *minus* retained corporate profits, corporate income taxes, and social insurance contributions plus transfer payments and government interest payments. (24)

**personal saving** equals personal disposable income minus personal consumption expenditures. (25)

**Phillips curve** shows a negative relationship between the unemployment rate and the inflation rate. (33)

**policy activism** is the deliberate use of discretionary fiscal or monetary policy to achieve macroeconomic goals. (31)

**positive (direct) relationship** exists between two variables if an increase in the value of one variable is associated with an *increase* in the value of the other variable. (1A)

**positive economics** is the study of how the economy works; it explains the economy in measurable terms. (1)

**preferred stock** does not give voting privileges, but corporations must pay dividends on preferred stock before paying those on common stock. (8)

**present value (PV)** is the most anyone would pay today to receive the money in the future. (8)

**price discrimination** exists when the same product or service is sold at different prices to different buyers. (11)

**price/earnings (P/E)** is the price of a share of stock divided by the earnings share. (8)

**price elasticity of demand** $(E_d)$ is the percentage change in the quantity demanded divided by the percentage change in price. (6)

**price elasticity of supply** $(E_s)$ is the percentage change in the quantity supplied divided by the percentage change in price. (6)

**price index** shows the cost of buying the same market basket of goods in different years as a percentage of its cost in some base year. (23)

**price liberalization** is the freeing of prices during the course of transition to let them be determined by supply and demand. (38)

**price maker** is a firm with some degree of control over the price of the good or service it sells. (11)

**price surprises** occur when the actual price level is different from the anticipated price level (or when the actual rate of inflation is different from the anticipated rate). (34)

**price system** coordinates economic decisions by allowing resource owners to trade freely, buying and selling at whatever relative prices emerge in the marketplace. (3)

**price taker** is when a firm considers the market price as something over which it has no control. (10)

**primary deficit** is the government deficit not including interest payments on the government debt. (31)

**principal** is a party that has controlling authority and engages an agent to act subject to the principal's control and instruction. (8)

**principle of substitution** states that practically no good is irreplaceable. Users are able to substitute one product for another when relative prices change. (3)

**principle of unintended consequences** holds that economic policies may have ultimate or actual effects that differ from the intended or apparent effects. (5)

**prisoner's dilemma** is a game with two players in which both players benefit from co-operating, but in which each player has an incentive to cheat on the agreement. (5, 13)

**private saving** is the sum of the personal saving of individuals and of business saving (in the form of retained profits and depreciation). (25)

**privatization** is the conversion of publicly owned assets—such as land, buildings, companies—to private ownership. (14, 38)

**procyclical monetary policy** decreases aggregate demand when output is falling and increases aggregate demand when output is rising. (30)

**producers' surplus** represents the amount that producers receive in excess of the minimum value the producers would have been willing to accept. (10)

**production function** summarizes the relationship between labor, capital, and land inputs and the maximum output these inputs can produce for a given state of knowledge. (9)

**production possibilities frontier (PPF)** shows the combinations of goods that can be produced when the factors of production are used to their full potential. (2)

**profit maximization** is the search by firms for the product quality, output, and price that give the firm the highest possible profits. (8)

**profit-maximization rule** states that a firm will maximize profits by producing that level of output at which marginal revenue (MR) equals marginal cost (MC). (10)

**progressive tax** is one where the percentage of income paid as taxes increases as income increases. (21)

**prohibitive tariff** is a tariff that is high enough to cut off all imports of the product. (36)

**property rights** are the rights of an owner to buy, sell, or use and exchange property (that is goods, services, and assets). (2); specify who owns a resource and who has the right to use it. (20)

**proportional tax** is one where each taxpayer pays the same percentage of income as taxes. (21)

**public good** is a good or service whose use by one person does not reduce its use to others and whose use by non-payers cannot be prevented. (21)

**purchasing power parity (PPP)** is a rate for converting one economy's output into the prices of another country. It is the exchange rate between two currencies that equates the real buying power of both currencies. (24, 37)

**pure economic rent** is the price paid to a productive factor that is completely inelastic in supply. Land is the classic example of such a factor. (18)

**pure monopoly** exists when (1) there is one seller in the market for some good or service that has no close substitutes; (2) barriers to entry protect the seller from competition. (11)

**quantity demanded** is the amount of a good or service consumers are prepared to buy at a given price (during a specified time period), if other factors are held constant. (4)

**quantity supplied** of a good or service is the amount offered for sale at a given price, holding other factors constant. (4)

**quasi rent** is a payment in excess of the short-run opportunity cost necessary to induce the owners of the resources to offer their resources for sale or rent in the short run. (18)

**random walk** is a variable whose expected value in the next time period is the same as its current value. (24A)

**rate of inflation** is the rate, usually measured per annum, at which the price level, as measured by a price index, is changing. (23)

**rate of return of a capital good** is that rate for which the present value of the stream of marginal revenue products for each year of the good's life is equal to the cost of the capital good. (18)

**ratification of supply-side inflation** results when the government increases the money supply to prevent adverse supply-side shocks from raising unemployment. (32)

**rational expectations** are expectations that we form by using all available information, relying not only on past experience but also on the effects of present and future policy actions. (32); are expectations of future inflation, wages, interest rates, and other macroeconomic variables that we form not only from past experience but also from our understanding of the effects of current policies on these variables. (34)

**rational ignorance** is a decision not to acquire information because the marginal cost exceeds the marginal benefit of gathering the information. (22)

**real-balance effect** occurs when desired consumption falls as increases in the price level reduce the purchasing power of money assets. (27)

**real business cycle theory** supposes that cyclical fluctuations arise from large random shocks to the rate of technological progress. (34)

**real GDP** measures the volume of real goods and services by removing the effects of rising prices on nominal GDP. (24)

**real rate of interest** is the nominal rate of interest over some period minus the expected rate of inflation over the same period. (18, 25)

**real wages** are measured by money wages, $W$, divided by the price level, $P$—that is, $W/P$. (27)

**recession** occurs when real output declines for a period of six months or more. (23)

**recognition lag** is the time it takes the Fed to decide to change the supply of money in response to a change in economic conditions. (30)

**recycling** reintroduces used exhaustible resources (such as iron, metals, and petrochemicals) into the system, providing an alternative to current production. (20)

**reform** is an attempt to improve an existing economic system, such as the administrative command economy. **(38)**

**regressive tax** is one where the percentage of income paid as taxes decreases as income increases. **(21)**

**regulation** is government control of firms, exercised by regulatory agencies through rules and regulations concerning prices and service. **(14)**

**regulatory approach** is when the government requires polluting agents to limit emissions to a prescribed level. **(20)**

**regulatory lag** occurs when government regulators adjust rates some time after operating costs and the rate base have increased. **(14)**

**relative poverty standard** defines the poor in terms of their income relative to others. **(19)**

**relative price** is a price expressed in terms of other goods. **(3)**

**required-reserve ratio** is the amount of reserves required for each dollar of deposits. **(29)**

**reservation price** is the highest price at which the consumer will buy a good. Although the consumer will buy any good with a price lower than the reservation price, he or she will continue to search for a lower price only if the lowest price found exceeds the reservation price. **(15)**

**reservation wage** is the minimum wage offer that a job searcher will accept. **(33)**

**reserve requirements** are rules that state the amount of reserves that a bank must keep on hand to back bank deposits. **(29)**

**reserves** are the funds that the bank uses to satisfy the cash demands of its customers. **(29)**

**resources** See factors of production.

**risk seekers** are more willing to incur risks than **risk avoiders,** who are reluctant to take on risks. **(19)**

**rival consumption** characterises a good if its consumption by one person lowers its consumption by others. **(21)**

**rule of reason** stated that monopolies were in violation of the Sherman Act if they used unfair or illegal business practices. Being a monopoly in and of itself was not a violation of the Sherman Act. **(14)**

**saving function** shows the relationship between real disposable income and real saving. **(25)**

**Say's law** states that whatever aggregate output producers decide to supply will be demanded in the aggregate. **(25)**

**scarce good** is when the amount available is less than the amount people would want if it were given away free of charge. **(2)**

**scatter diagram** consists of a number of separate points, each plotting the value of one variable against a value of another variable for a specific time interval. **(1A)**

**scientific method** is the process of formulating theories, collecting data, testing theories, and revising theories. **(1)**

**screening** is the requirement that potential employees possess certain characteristics, such as a high school or college diploma, or a B+ or better average. **(19)**

**sector-shift hypothesis** states that price surprises at the micro level can cumulate to cause business cycles. **(34)**

**sequencing** of transition is the order in which the transition steps—privatization, price liberalization, macroeconomic stabilization, and so forth—should take place. **(38)**

**shock therapy** is the policy of carrying out all the phases of transition at one time as quickly as possible. **(38)**

**short run** is a period of time long enough for existing firms to produce more goods but not long enough for existing firms to expand their capacity or for new firms to enter the market. Thus output can be varied, but only within the limits of existing plant capacity. **(6)**; is a period of time so short that the existing plant and equipment cannot be varied; such inputs are fixed in supply. **(9)**

**short-run Phillips curve** shows a negative relationship between inflation and unemployment when inflationary expectations are constant. **(33)**

**short-run production function** (SRPF) shows how much output can be produced with a given amount of employment when capital and technology are fixed. **(27)**

**shortage** results if at the current price the quantity demanded exceeds the quantity supplied; the price is too low to equate the quantity demanded with the quantity supplied. **(4)**

**shutdown rule** states that if a firm's revenues at all output levels are less than variable costs, it can minimize its losses by shutting down. If there is at least one output level at which revenues exceed variable costs, the firm should not shut down. **(10)**

**slope of a curve** reflects the response of one variable to changes in another. **(1A)**

**slope of a curvilinear relationship** at a particular point is the slope of the straight-line tangent to the curve at that point. **(1A)**

**slope of a straight line** is the ratio of the rise (or fall) in $Y$ over the run in $X$. **(1A)**

**social benefits** are private benefits plus external benefits. **(12)**

**social costs**   equal private costs plus external costs. Social benefits equal private benefits plus external benefits. **(12, 20)**

**social safety net**   includes a wide variety of programs such as unemployment benefits, pensions, job-retraining, and disability programs designed to cushion the costs of transition. **(38)**

**sole proprietorship**   is owned by one individual who makes all the business decisions, receives the profits that the business earns, and bears the financial responsibility for losses. **(8)**

**special interest groups**   are minority groups with intense, narrowly defined preferences about specific government policies. **(22)**

**specialization**   is the tendency of participants in the economy (people, businesses, and countries) to focus their activity on tasks to which they are particularly suited. **(3)**

**speculators**   are those who buy or sell in the hope of profiting from market fluctuations. **(15)**

**spot (cash) market**   is a market where agreements between buyers and sellers are made now for payment and delivery of the product now. **(15)**

**stagflation**   is the combination of high unemployment and high inflation. **(33)**

**standard deviation**   is a measure of the dispersion of the general pattern formed by our empirical observations of a particular variable, such as the rate of growth of real GDP or the rate of inflation. **(24A)**

**stock exchange**   is a market in which shares of stock of corporations are bought and sold and in which the prices of shares of stock are determined. **(8)**

**strike**   occurs when all unionized employees cease to work until management agrees to specific union demands. **(17)**

**structural deficit**   is the deficit that would occur even if the economy were operating continuously at the natural level of real GDP. **(31)**

**structural unemployment**   results from the long-run decline of certain industries in response to rising costs, changes in consumer preferences, or technological change. **(33)**

**substitutes**   are two goods related such that the demand for one rises when the price of the other rises (or if the demand for one falls when the price of the other falls). **(4)**

**supply**   of a good or service is the amount that firms are prepared to sell under specified circumstances. **(4)**

**supply-side inflation**   occurs when aggregate supply declines and pushes prices up. **(32)**

**surplus**   results if at the current price the quantity supplied exceeds the quantity demanded: The price is too high to equate the quantity demanded with quantity supplied. **(4)**

**tangent**   is a straight line that touches the curve at only one point. **(1A)**

**tariff**   is a tax levied on imports. **(36)**

**taxable income**   is the income that remains after all deductions and exemptions are subtracted. Taxes are levied on taxable income. **(21)**

**terms of trade**   are the rate at which two products can be exchanged for each other between countries. **(35)**

**theory**   is a simplified and coherent explanation of the relationship among certain facts. **(1)**

**time deposit**   is a deposit of funds upon which a depository institution (such as a bank) can legally require 30 days notice of withdrawal and on which the financial institution pays interest to the depositor. **(28)**

**time series**   is a measurement of some variable over a designated period of time. **(24)**

**total costs (TC)**   are variable costs plus fixed costs:
$$TC = VC + FC \qquad (9)$$

**total factor productivity**   measures output per unit of combined labor and capital input. **(26)**

**total revenue (TR)**   of sellers in a market is the price of the commodity times the quantity sold:
$$TR = P \times Q \qquad (6)$$

**total revenue test**   uses the following criteria to determine elasticity:

1. If price and total revenue move in different directions, $E_d > 1$ (demand is elastic).
2. If price and total revenue move in the same direction, $E_d < 1$ (demand is inelastic).
3. If total revenue does not change when price changes, $E_d = 1$ (demand is unitary elastic). **(6)**

**transaction costs**   are the costs associated with bringing buyers and sellers together. **(15)**

**transfer payments**   are payments to recipients who have not earned them through the sale of their factors of production and who have not supplied current goods or services in exchange for these payments. **(24)**; transfer income from one individual or organization to another. **(21)**

**transition**   is the process of transforming one economic system into another, such as from the administrative command economy into a market economy. **(38)**

**trend**   is a systematic upward or downward movement in a variable over time. **(24A)**

**trust**   is a combination of firms that sets common prices, agrees to restrict output, and punishes member firms who fail to live up to the agreement. **(14)**

**unanimity**   is when all voters agree on or consent to a particular government action. (**22**)

**unemployment rate**   is the number of persons unemployed divided by the number in the labor force. (**23**)

**unfunded liability**   of the Social Security Administration is the sum that must be deposited in an interest-bearing account to meet obligations to retirees in future years given existing benefits, tax rates, and interest rates. (**31**)

**utilitarian theory**   argues for an equal distribution of income by saying that equality maximizes welfare. (**19**)

**utility**   is a numerical ranking of a consumer's preferences among different commodity bundles. (**7**)

**value of money**   is the reciprocal of the price level, or $1/P$. (**28**)

**variable costs (VC)**   are those costs that do vary with output. (**9**)

**vertical equity**   exists when those with a greater ability to pay bear a heavier tax burden. (**21**)

**vertical merger**   is a merger of two firms that are part of the same materials, production, or distribution network (such as a personal computer manufacturer and a retail computer distributor). (**14**)

**voluntary export restraint**   is an agreement between two governments in which the exporting country voluntarily limits the export of a certain product to the importing country. (**36**)

**wage/employment trade-off**   means that higher wages reduce the number of jobs; lower unemployment requires sacrificing higher wages. (**17**)

**wage/price spiral**   occurs when higher prices push wages higher and then higher wages push prices higher, or vice versa. This spiral is sustained by the monetary authorities' ratifying the resulting supply-side inflation by increasing the money supply. (**32**)

**wealth**   (or net worth) is the value of one's total assets minus one's liabilities. (**19**)

**welfare state**   provides substantial benefits to the less fortunate—unemployment insurance, poverty assistance, old-age pensions—to protect them from further economic misfortune. (**1**)

# NAME INDEX

# SUBJECT INDEX